Charles Scott Sherrington (1857–1952)

A rainbow every morning who would pause to look at? The wonderful which comes often or is plentifully about us is soon taken for granted. That is practical enough. It allows us to get on with life. But it may stultify if it cannot on occasion be thrown off. To recapture now and then childhood's wonder, is to secure a driving force for occasional grown-up thoughts.

Eric R. Kandel

The questions posed by higher cognitive processes such as learning and memory are formidable, and we have only begun to explore them. Although elementary aspects of simple forms of learning have been accessible to molecular analysis in invertebrates, we are only now beginning to know a bit about the genes and proteins involved in more complex, hippocampus based, learning processes of mammals.

Carla J. Shatz

The functioning of the brain depends upon the precision and patterns of its neural circuits. How is this amazing computational machine assembled and wired during development? The biological answer is so much more wonderful than anticipated! The adult precision is sculpted from an early imprecise pattern by a process in which connections are verified by the functioning of the neurons themselves. Thus, the developing brain is not simply a miniature version of the adult. Moreover, the brain works to wire itself, rather than assembling itself first and then flipping a switch, as might happen in the assembly of a computer. This kind of surprise in scientific discovery opens up new vistas of understanding and possibility and makes the process of doing science infinitely exciting and fascinating.

Frank A. Beach (1911–1988)

Grant money comes from taxes; taxes come from a lot of folks who don't have much money. Spend that money wisely.

To what degree should my choice of research work be governed by human needs, by social imperatives, and how am I going to justify spending all of my energies on any research that does not bear directly on pressing human problems? . . . The solution, or rationalization, that I have finally come up with is that it is a perfectly worthwhile way of spending one's life to do your level best to increase human knowledge, and it is not necessary nor is it always even desirable to be constrained by possible applicability of what you find to immediate problems. This may sound very peculiar to some young people, but it is a value judgement which I myself have made and which I can live with.

Duane Rumbaugh and Sue Savage-Rumbaugh with chimpanzee Austin

Chimpanzees and bonobos are outstanding teachers of psychology. They never presume that we, as their students, know a damn thing about who they are. And, they certainly aren't impressed with our degrees. Consequently, they are able to teach all manner of important things about what it means to be human and to be ape—that is, if we as students are quiet, listen carefully, and let them tell us as only they can.

Seventh Edition

Biological Psychology

James W. Kalat
North Carolina State University

WADSWORTH

™
THOMSON LEARNING

Australia • Canada • Mexico • Singapore • Spain • United Kingdom • United States

WADSWORTH ™
THOMSON LEARNING

Psychology Publisher: *Vicki Knight*
Development Editor: *Jim Strandberg*
Assistant Editor: *Jennifer Wilkinson*
Editorial Assistant: *Traci St. Pierre*
Marketing Manager: *Marc Linsenman*
Marketing Assistant: *Colleen Delgado*
Print Buyer: *Karen Hunt*
Permissions Editor: *Bob Kauser*
Production Service: *New Leaf Publishing Services*
Text Designer: *Rob Hugel, Little Hill Design*

Art Editor: *Kathy Joneson*
Photo Researcher: *Sue C. Howard*
Copy Editor: *Frank Hubert*
Indexer: *James Minkin*
Illustrator: *Precision Graphics*
Cover Designer: *Rob Hugel, Little Hill Design*
Cover Image: © *Alfred Pasieka, Science Source/Photo Researchers*
Compositor: *GTS Graphics, Inc.*
Printer: *Transcontinental Printing/Interglobe*

Wadsworth/Thomson Learning
10 Davis Drive
Belmont, CA 94002–3098
USA

For more information about our products, contact us:
Thomson Learning Academic Resource Center
1–800–423–0563
http://www.wadsworth.com

International Headquarters
Thomson Learning
International Division
290 Harbor Drive, 2nd Floor
Stamford, CT 06902–7477
USA

UK/Europe/Middle East/South Africa
Thomson Learning
Berkshire House
168–173 High Holborn
London WC1V 7AA
United Kingdom

Asia/Thomson Learning
60 Albert Street, #15–01
Albert Complex
Singapore 189969

Canada
Nelson Thomson Learning
1120 Birchmount Road
Toronto, Ontario M1K 5G4
Canada

Library of Congress Cataloging-in-Publication Data

Kalat, James W.
    Biological psychology / James W. Kalat. — 7th ed.
        p.   cm.
    Includes bibliographical references and index.
    ISBN 0-534-51400-6 (alk. paper)   0534 514 09X
    1. Neuropsychology. 2. Psychobiology.   I. Title.

QP360.K33 2000
612.8—dc21   00–039883

About the Author

James W. Kalat (rhymes with ballot) is Professor of Psychology at North Carolina State University, where he teaches courses in introduction to psychology and biological psychology. Born in 1946, he received an AB degree summa cum laude from Duke University in 1968 and a PhD in psychology from the University of Pennsylvania in 1971. He is also the author of *Introduction to Psychology* (5th ed.) (Belmont, CA: Wadsworth, 1999). In addition to textbooks, he has written journal articles on taste-aversion learning, the teaching of psychology, and other topics. A remarried widower, he has three children, two stepchildren, and an amazingly wonderful granddaughter.

Cover Image: Brain scan

Colored magnetic resonance imaging (MRI) scan through a human head, showing a healthy brain in side view. The face is seen in profile at left. Tissues of the mouth, nasal cavity, and central nervous system are visible. The folded cerebrum of the brain (at top) makes up the larger part of the brain; intelligent thought processes, memory, and conscious movement are processed in the cerebrum. At center (yellow) is the elongated brain stem, which controls involuntary reflexes like breathing and eye reflexes; it connects with the spinal cord in the neck. To the right of the brain stem is the cerebellum (blue), important for processes requiring precise timing.

To . . .

David, Julie, Ann

Robin, Brent, Sheila, Sam

Josh

Bill and Amelia

Brief Contents

Contents

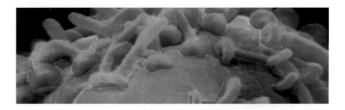

Chapter 4
Anatomy of the Nervous System 87

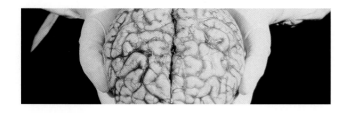

Chapter 5
Development and Plasticity
of the Brain   115

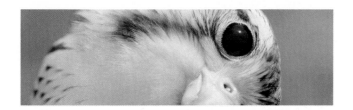

Chapter 10
The Regulation of Internal Body
States   281

Chapter 11
Reproductive Behaviors   311

Chapter 14
Lateralization and Language 393

Preface

In the first edition of this text, published 20 years ago, I remarked, "I almost wish I could get parts of this text . . . printed in disappearing ink, programmed to fade within ten years of publication, so that I will not be embarrassed by statements that will look primitive from some future perspective." Biological psychology progresses rapidly, and many statements become out of date in fewer than 10 years. Perhaps I could get this book stamped, like grocery items, "Best if used by this date . . . " The alternative is to publish frequent new editions.

The most challenging aspect of writing a text is selecting what to include and what to omit. My primary goal in writing this text has been to engage readers' interest. I have focused on the biological mechanisms relevant to key issues in psychology, such as language, learning, sexual behavior, anxiety, aggression, abnormal behavior, and the mind-body problem. I hope that by the end of the book readers will clearly see what the study of the brain has to do with "real psychology" and that they will be interested in learning more.

Each chapter is divided into modules; each module begins with its own introduction and finishes with its own summary and questions. This organization makes it easy for instructors to assign part of a chapter per day instead of a whole chapter per week. Parts of chapters can also be covered in a different order. (Indeed, of course, whole chapters can be taken in different orders. I know one instructor who likes to start with Chapter 14.)

I assume that the reader has a basic background in psychology and biology and understands such basic terms as classical conditioning, reinforcement, vertebrate, mammal, gene, chromosome, cell, and mitochondrion. Naturally, the stronger the background, the better. I also assume a high-school chemistry course. Those whose memories of chemistry have faded may consult Appendix A for a review.

Changes in This Edition

The changes in this text are my attempt to keep pace with the rapid progress in biological psychology. There are about 500 new references from 1997 through 2000 and countless major and minor changes, including new

or improved illustrations and a redesigned layout. Here are some highlights:

General

- Definitions of key terms are highlighted in blue ink. (They also appear in the combined glossary/index at the back of the text.)
- Previous editions had Review Questions at the end of each module, without answers. This edition has Stop and Check Questions at certain points within the text, with answers at the end of the module.
- Key Terms and Suggestions for Further Reading are now at the end of the chapter instead of the end of the module.
- Web Sites to Explore also are listed at the end of the chapter. A reader can go to the publisher's Web site for this text and click on these other suggested Web sites, which will be updated periodically.
- The module on methods was deleted from Chapter 4. Each method is presented in a new Methods heading where it first becomes relevant.

Chapter 1

- The new first module presents an overview of the goals and methods of biological psychology and then concentrates on the mind-brain issue (which was the Epilogue to the 6th edition).

Chapter 2

- New information indicates the ability of the adult CNS to generate additional neurons in some areas.

Chapter 3

- The module on drugs has many updates and a reorganized order of presentation.
- Material about alcohol abuse was moved to Chapter 15 (disorders).
- A new module on hormones was added here, replacing the section at the start of Chapter 11.

Chapter 4

- The module on research methods was deleted. Each method is now presented at the time it first becomes relevant in the text.
- The section on contralateral neglect after right parietal lobe damage was significantly updated.
- A substantial new section was added on how the various brain areas work together, including the binding problem, which has emerged as a major new research area closely related to the mind-body problem.

Chapter 5

- The Evolution module was deleted; sections of it were moved to Chapters 1, 4, 5, and 14.
- Most of previous Chapter 15 ("Recovery from Brain Damage") was moved to become the second module of this chapter.
- Accordingly, the chapter title was changed from "Development and Evolution of the Brain" to "Development and Plasticity of the Brain."
- The section on pathfinding by axons was shortened and simplified.
- A digression on attention-deficit disorder was substituted for the one on Rett syndrome.
- In the Development of the Brain module, note the added section, Proportional Growth of Brain Areas, taken mostly from the Evolution module of the 6th edition.
- The phantom limb discussion was moved from Chapter 7 (nonvisual senses) to here, with ties to the reorganization of the brain.

Chapter 6

- The material from Digression 6.1 (blind spot and blindsight) was removed from the digression and put into two sections of the main text.
- The section on lateral inhibition was rewritten and reillustrated.
- The description of receptive fields was revised.
- The section on building receptive fields was deleted.
- New sections were added on visual attention and visual consciousness.

Chapter 7

- Additions include a new comment on tinnitus as a probable analogue to phantom pain, a digression on tickle sensation, a short section on pain representation in the brain, a short section on individual differences in taste, and sections about supertasters

and about the effects of losing sensation from part of the tongue.
- New Try-It-Yourself demonstrations illustrate taste adaptation and olfactory adaptation.
- The digression on pheromones was moved into the text proper in combination with the vomeronasal organ.

Chapter 8

- The discussion of myasthenia gravis was moved from the third module to just after the mention of nerve-muscle junction in the first module.
- The second module was reorganized to put the motor mechanisms of the cerebral cortex before the cerebellum and the basal ganglia.
- The Role of the Spinal Cord was consolidated into the discussion of the cerebral cortex.
- The section on Movement Coding in the Primary Motor Cortex was deleted.
- Note the new information on heritability of early-onset but not late-onset Parkinson's disease.
- The discussion on neural transplantation for relief of Parkinson's disease was updated.
- Also note the new information on the ability of a presymptomatic test to predict the age of onset of Huntington's disease.

Chapter 9

- The discussion of brain mechanisms and sleep abnormalities was moved to the second module. The discussion of functions of sleep was moved from the first to the third module and theories of dreaming to the third module. Now the second module is mechanisms of wakefulness and sleep; the third module is theories of why we sleep, have REM sleep, and dream.
- A new section, How Light Resets the SCN, is now separate from evidence that the SCN controls circadian rhythms.
- Theories of REM include an increased emphasis on the role of REM in memory and mention of a new theory that REM's purpose is just to increase oxygen supply to the corneas.
- Information was added on the role of adenosine and prostaglandins.
- A new theory was added on the biology of dreaming.

Chapter 10

- The explanation was expanded concerning why we evolved the body temperature we did.

- Note the new digression on poikilothermic animals that survive temperatures near −40°.
- The discussion of leptin was updated, as was the role of culture in anorexia nervosa.
- A simple list and explanation were substituted for the overcomplicated Table 10.3.

Chapter 11

- The discussion of hormones in general, previously at the start of this chapter, was moved to Chapter 3, where it is now a new module.
- A new digression was added on premenstrual syndrome.
- The various updates include failure to replicate a link between male homosexuality and the X chromosome.
- The discussion of intersexes was updated.

Chapter 12

- The first module was split into two: one on the nature and functions of emotions; the other on stress and health. Each module was expanded.
- Note the new introduction to the chapter and to the first module, highlighting the relationship between emotions and consciousness.
- The discussions were expanded concerning the function of the emotions and the theories of emotion, such as the James-Lange theory.
- The section Where Is Emotion in the Brain? was deleted.
- The discussion of ulcers (present in editions 1–5 but not in 6) was restored with new information.
- The treatment of stress was expanded and updated. Note especially the expanded discussion of cytokines.
- A new section was added on posttraumatic stress disorder.
- The treatment of genetics and aggressive behavior was modified; the influence attributed to genetics could be from either genetics or prenatal environment.
- Two new Try-It-Yourself demonstrations were added: one on facial expressions and emotion; one on anxiety and the startle reflex.

Chapter 13

- The discussion of emotions and the consolidation of memory was updated.
- A new Try-It-Yourself demonstration was added for working memory.

- The first module was reorganized to put all the material about the hippocampus together.
- Several updates were added about Alzheimer's disease, including possible strategies for treatment or prevention.
- The LTP section has many changes, including new, simpler figures.

Chapter 14

- Phrenology was moved from Chapter 4 to a digression in this chapter.
- The section on evolution of language was reorganized, now addressing two questions: What language-type capacities do nonhumans show? Why/how did humans develop language abilities that other species lack? Two hypotheses are discussed: language as a by-product of overall intelligence and language as a special module. (Neither is fully satisfactory.) The material previously titled Genetic Abnormalities of Language and Intellect is now integrated into this discussion; so is some material previously in Chapter 5's Evolution module.
- A new section was added, Is There a Critical Period for Language Learning?
- A new Try-It-Yourself exercise illustrates the inconsistent spelling rules of English, in contrast to Italian. That difference is relevant to brain scan measures of activity during reading.

Chapter 15

- Because previous Chapter 15, "Recovery from Brain Damage," was consolidated into Chapter 5, the final chapter on psychological abnormalities is now Chapter 15 instead of 16.
- A new short module was added on alcoholism, drawn partly from material previously in Chapter 1.
- An update notes that Borna virus predisposes to psychiatric disorders in general, not necessarily to depression.
- The discussion of depression has a new order of presentation, with genetics first.
- A new Try-It-Yourself demonstration illustrates lateralization and depression.
- New data solidify the argument that treatments for bipolar disorder act by blocking certain second-messenger systems.
- In the module on schizophrenia, new data weaken the conclusion that schizophrenia depends on a strong genetic influence. Much of what we have been attributing to genetics could be due to prenatal or early postnatal environment.

Also, new data have accumulated that pose problems for the dopamine hypothesis of schizophrenia and suggest an alternative glutamate hypothesis.

The Epilogue of the 6th edition became part of Chapter 1 in this edition, so this edition has no Epilogue.

Supplements

Instructors who adopt the book may also obtain from the publisher a copy of the Instructor's Manual, written by Cynthia Crawford. The manual contains chapter outlines, class demonstrations and projects, a list of video resources, additional Web sites InfoTrac key terms, and the author's answers to the Thought Questions. The Instructor's Manual also includes a conversion guide prepared by Linda Lockwood. A separate book lists multiple-choice items written and assembled by Maria Lavooy. Note the special file of questions for a comprehensive final exam. The test items are available on disks for IBM and Macintosh computers. The Study Guide, written by Elaine Hull of SUNY, Buffalo, may be purchased by students. Also available are the multimedia products: BioPsychLink and Active Learner Link.

I am grateful for the excellent work of Crawford, Hull, Lavooy, and Lockwood.

Acknowledgments

Let me tell you something about researchers in this field: As a rule, they are amazingly cooperative with textbook authors. A number of my colleagues have sent me comments, ideas, and published materials; others supplied me with photos. I thank especially the following:

Joel Adkins, UIS

Nancy Andreasen, University of Iowa

Danny Benbassat, Slippery Rock University

Stephen Black, Bishop's University, Lennoxville, Quebec

Liv Bode, Robert Koch-Institut

William J. Clemens, UCCB, Sydney, Nova Scotia

William Domhoff, University of California, Santa Cruz

Martin Elton, University of Amsterdam

Charles Evans, LaGrange College

Elaine Hull, State University of New York, Buffalo

Jerre Levy, University of Chicago

Una D. McCann, National Institute of Mental Health

Donald Mershon, North Carolina State University

William Moorcroft, Luther College

I. S. Penton-Voak, University of St. Andrews

Edward Pollak, West Chester University

Jeffry Ricker, Scottsdale Community College

Eugenio Rodriguez, Hùpital de la Salpètrière, Paris

Allen Salo, University of Maine at Presque Isle

Mike Schaub, University of Akron

Larry Squire, Veterans' Administration Medical Center, San Diego

Paul Stanton, Indiana University, South Bend

Anthony Wagner, Harvard and Stanford Universities

Sandra Witelson, McMaster University

I have received an enormous number of letters and e-mail messages from students. Many included helpful suggestions; some managed to catch errors or inconsistencies that everyone else had overlooked. I thank especially the following:

Ian de Terte, Massey University, Palmerston North, New Zealand

Timothy Gorrill, State University of New York, Buffalo

Travis Mashburn, North Carolina State University

Esther Nobbe and Iris Schino, Catholic University of Tilburg, Netherlands

Pete Roma, West Chester University

Joe Schmerler, University of Central Florida

Lisa Solberg, Santa Monica College

Ulmo "Duke" Stanton, Charlottesville, VA

Eddie Strommen, Washington State University

I appreciate the helpful comments provided by the following reviewers:

Susan Anderson, University of South Alabama

Barry Anton, University of Puget Sound

Michael Babcock, Montana State University

Carol Batt, Sacred Heart University

Darragh P. Devine, University of Florida

Gary Dunbar, Central Michigan University

Tami Eggleston, McKendree College

Bruce Friedman, Virginia Tech University

Perry Fuchs, University of Texas at Arlington

Liisa Galea, University of British Columbia

Jill Kalat, University of Michigan

Sam Kalat, University of North Carolina at Chapel Hill

Corey Lafferty, University of North Carolina at Greensboro

Frederick Newton, California State University–San Bernadino

Steve Madigan, University of Southern California

Joseph Porter, Virginia Commonwealth University

Michael Selby, California State Polytechnic University–San Luis Opispo

Victor Shamas, University of Arizona

Aurora Torres, University of Alabama

Nancy Woolf, University of California, Los Angeles

Beth Wee, Tulane University

David Yager, University of Maryland

In preparing this text I have been most fortunate to work with Vicki Knight, a wise, patient, and very supportive acquisitions editor. She was especially helpful in setting priorities and planning the major thrust of this text. Jim Strandberg, my developmental editor, has guided every step from the review stage to the final draft. I have benefited from both his professional skills and his sense of humor. Nancy Shammas supervised the production, a major task for a book like this one. As art editor, Kathy Joneson's considerable artistic abilities helped to compensate for my complete lack. Sue Howard had charge of permissions and photos, another major task. I hope you enjoy the new photos in this text as much as I do. Jennifer Wilkinson oversaw the development of supplements, such as the Instructor's Manual and test item file. Nancy DelFavero and Hal Humphrey guided the production of the text. I thank Precision Graphics for their artistic skills and patience. I thank Stephen Rapley and Rob Hugel for the text and cover design, Frank Hubert for the copyediting, and James Minkin for the indexes. All of these people have been splendid colleagues.

I also thank my wife, Jo Ellen, for keeping my spirits high, and my department head, David Martin, for his support and encouragement.

I welcome correspondence from both students and faculty. Write: James W. Kalat, Department of Psychology, Box 7801, North Carolina State University, Raleigh, NC 27695–7801, USA. E-mail: james_kalat@ ncsu.edu

James W. Kalat

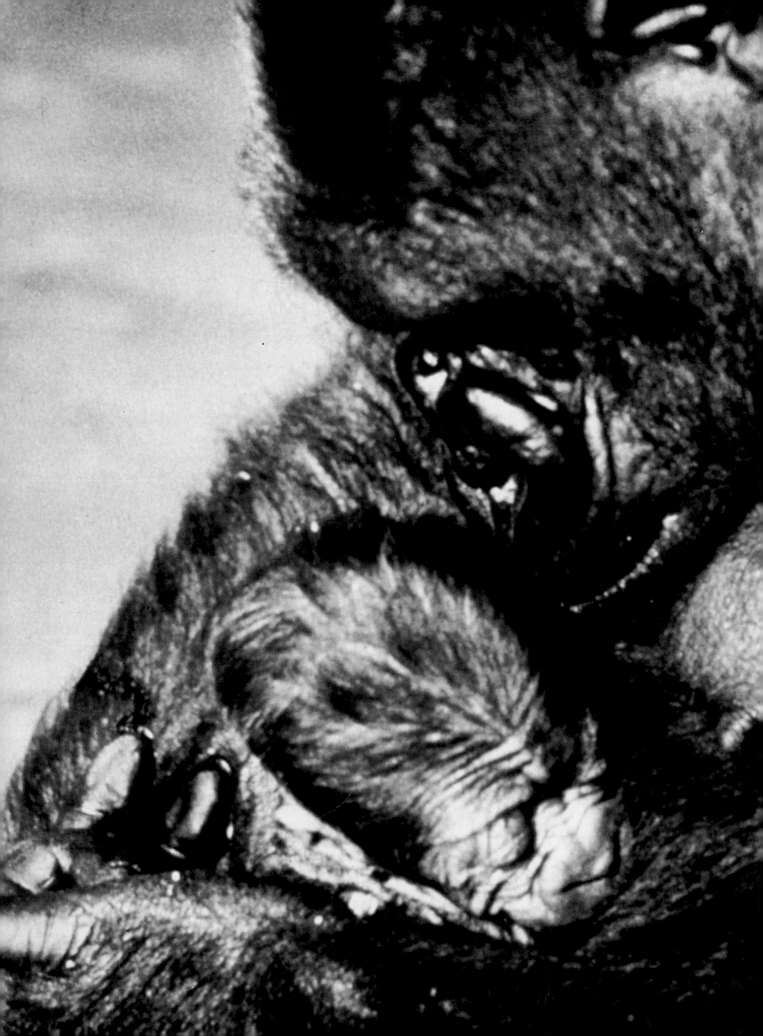

Chapter 1

The Major Issues

Opposite:
A biological psychologist tries to explain any behavior, such as the behavior of this mother gorilla toward her baby, not in terms of subjective experiences such as "love," but in terms of its physiology, its development, its evolution, and its function. *(Photo courtesy of the Cincinnati Zoo)*

Main Ideas

1. Biological explanations of behavior fall into several categories, including physiology, development, evolution, and function.

2. Nearly all philosophers and neuroscientists reject the idea that the mind exists independently of the physical brain. Still, the question remains as to how and why brain activity is connected to consciousness.

3. The expression of a given gene depends on the environment and on interactions with other genes.

4. Research with nonhuman animals can produce important information, but it sometimes inflicts distress or pain on the animals. Whether to proceed with a given experiment can be a difficult ethical issue.

It is often said that Man is unique among animals. It is worth looking at this term "unique" before we discuss our subject proper. The word may in this context have two slightly different meanings. It may mean: Man is strikingly different—he is not identical with any animal. This is of course true. It is true also of all other animals: Each species, even each individual is unique in this sense. But the term is also often used in a more absolute sense: Man is so different, so "essentially different" (whatever that means) that the gap between him and animals cannot possibly be bridged—he is something altogether new. Used in this absolute sense the term is scientifically meaningless. Its use also reveals and may reinforce conceit, and it leads to complacency and defeatism because it assumes that it will be futile even to search for animal roots. It is prejudging the issue.

Niko Tinbergen (1973, p. 161)

Biological psychology studies the "animal roots" of behavior, relating actions and experiences to genetics and physiology. In this chapter, we consider three major issues and themes: the relationship between mind and brain, the roles of nature and nurture, and the ethics of research. We also briefly consider prospects for further study.

The Mind-Brain Relationship

Biological psychology is the study of the physiological, evolutionary, and developmental mechanisms of behavior and experience. Much of it is devoted to studying brain functions. Figure 1.1 offers a view of the human brain from the top (what neuroscientists call a *dorsal* view) and from the bottom (a *ventral* view). The labels point to a few important areas, which will become more familiar as you proceed through this text. As we inspect each brain area, we find that it has recognizable subareas and sub-subareas. When we get down to the microscopic level, we find two kinds of cells: the *neurons* (see Figure 1.2) and their support cells, the *glia.* Neurons, which convey messages to one another and to muscles and glands, vary enormously in size, shape, and functions. Neurons' activities and communications *somehow* produce an enormous wealth of behavior and experience. This book is about researchers' attempts to elaborate on that word "somehow."

Biological psychology is the most interesting topic in the world. . . . No doubt every professor and every textbook author feels that way about his or her field. But they are wrong because biological psychology really is the most interesting topic. When I make this statement to a group of students, I always get a laugh.

But when I say it to a group of biological psychologists or neuroscientists, they generally nod their heads in agreement, and I do in fact mean it seriously. I do *not* mean that memorizing the names and functions of brain parts and chemicals is unusually interesting. I do mean that biological psychology deals with deep theoretical questions that almost anyone should find exciting.

Actually, I shall back off a bit and assert that biological psychology is just about tied with cosmology as the most interesting topic. Cosmologists ask why the universe exists at all: Why is there *something* instead of *nothing*? And if there is to be something, why this particular kind of universe instead of some other? Biological psychologists ask: Given the existence of a universe composed of matter and energy, why is there such a thing as consciousness? How does the physical brain give rise to vision, hunger, sexual desire, anger, fear, and other experiences? They also ask more practical questions such as: What genes, prenatal environment, or other factors predispose some people to schizophrenia? Is there any hope for recovery after brain damage? And what enables humans—and only humans—to learn language so easily?

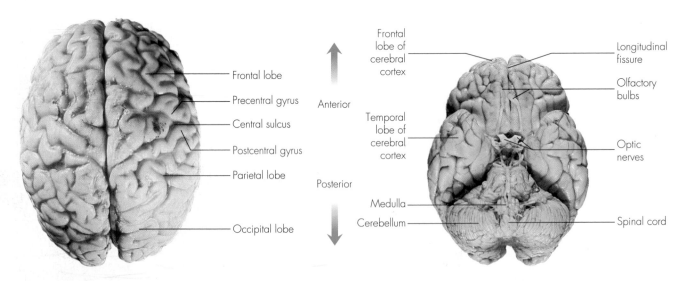

Frontal lobe

Precentral gyrus

Central sulcus

Postcentral gyrus

Parietal lobe

Occipital lobe

Anterior

Posterior

Frontal lobe of cerebral cortex

Temporal lobe of cerebral cortex

Medulla

Cerebellum

Longitudinal fissure

Olfactory bulbs

Optic nerves

Spinal cord

Figure 1.1   A dorsal view (from above) and a ventral view (from below) of the human brain
The brain has an enormous number of divisions and subareas; the labels point to a few of the main ones that are visible from outside.

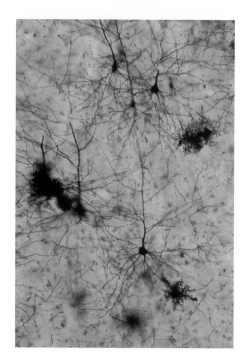

Figure 1.2 Neurons, magnified
The brain is composed of individual cells called neurons and glia.

Unlike all other birds, doves and pigeons can drink with their heads down. (Others fill their mouths and then raise their heads.) A physiological explanation would describe these birds' unusual pattern of nerves and throat muscles. An evolutionary explanation states that all doves and pigeons share this behavioral capacity because they inherited their genes from a common ancestor.

Biological Explanations of Behavior

Commonsense explanations of behavior often refer to intentional goals such as, "He did this because he was trying to . . ." or "She did that because she wanted to . . ." But for much of behavior, we have no reason to assume any intentions. A 4-month-old bird migrating south in fall probably does not know why; the next spring, when she lays an egg, sits on it, and defends it from predators, again she probably doesn't know why. Even humans don't always know the reasons for their own behaviors. (Yawning is one example.)

In contrast to commonsense explanations, biological explanations of behavior fall into four categories: physiological, ontogenetic, evolutionary, and functional (Tinbergen, 1951). A **physiological explanation** relates a behavior to the activity of the brain and other organs. It deals with the machinery of the body—for example, the chemical reactions that enable hormones to influence brain activity and the routes by which brain activity ultimately controls the contractions of muscles.

The term *ontogenetic* comes from Greek roots meaning "to be" and "origin" (or genesis). Thus, an **ontogenetic explanation** describes the development of a structure or a behavior. It traces the influences of genes, nutrition, experiences, and the interactions among these influences in producing behavioral tendencies.

An **evolutionary explanation** examines a structure or a behavior in terms of evolutionary history. For example, when people become frightened, they sometimes get "goose bumps"—erections of the hairs, especially on the arms and shoulders. Goose bumps are useless in humans because our shoulder and arm hairs are so

Researchers continue to debate exactly what good yawning does. Yawning is a behavior that even people do without knowing its purpose.

short. In hairier animals, however, erection of the hairs makes a frightened animal look larger and more intimidating (Figure 1.3). Thus, an evolutionary explanation of human goose bumps is that the behavior evolved in our distant hairier ancestors and that we still have the mechanism for producing goose bumps even though they are no longer useful for us.

A **functional explanation** describes why a structure or behavior evolved as it did. Within a small population, such as an isolated community, a gene can spread by accident through a process called *genetic drift.* (For example, sometimes one dominant male has an enormous number of offspring and thereby spreads all of his genes, including some that had nothing to do with his success.) However, the larger the population, the less powerful is genetic drift, and a gene that spreads in a large population presumably provides some advantage. A functional explanation identifies the advantage. For example, certain species can change color to match their background (Figure 1.4). A functional explanation is that such a change makes the animal inconspicuous to predators.

To illustrate the four types of biological explanation, consider how they all apply to one example, birdsong (Catchpole & Slater, 1995):

Physiological explanation: A particular area of a songbird brain grows under the influence of testosterone; hence, it is larger in breeding males than in females or immature birds. That brain area enables a mature male to sing.

Ontogenetic explanation: In certain species, a young male bird learns its song by listening to adult males. Development of the song requires both the genes that prepare him to learn the song and the opportu-

Figure 1.3 A frightened cat with erect hairs
When a frightened mammal erects its hairs, it looks larger and more intimidating. (Consider, for example, the "Halloween cat.") Frightened humans sometimes also erect their body hairs, forming "goose bumps." An evolutionary explanation for goose bumps is that we inherited the tendency from ancestors who had enough hair for the behavior to be useful.

nity to hear the appropriate song during a sensitive period early in life.

Evolutionary explanation: In certain cases, one species of bird has a song that closely resembles that of a different species. For example, dunlins and Baird's sandpipers, two kinds of shorebird, give their calls in distinct pulses, unlike other shorebirds. This similarity suggests that the two species evolved from a single ancestor.

Functional explanation: In most bird species, only the male sings, and he sings only during the repro-

Figure 1.4 A chameleon changes its appearance to match its background
A functional explanation addresses why a behavior has evolved or what function it serves. In this case, the function is that an animal that matches its background becomes inconspicuous so that potential predators overlook it.

ductive season and only in his territory. The functions of the song are to attract females and to warn other males that he is defending his territory. As a rule, a bird sings only loud enough to be heard in the territory he can defend. In short, birds have evolved tendencies to sing in ways that improve their chances for mating.

We improve our understanding of behavior when we can combine as many of these approaches as possible. That is, ideally, we should understand the body mechanisms that produce the behavior, how it develops within the individual, how it evolved, and what function it serves.

Stop & Check

1. What is the difference between an evolutionary explanation and a functional explanation?

Check your answer on page 8.

The Brain and Conscious Experience

Biological psychology is an ambitious field. We are setting out to explain as much as we can of psychology in strictly biological, physical terms. The explanations are still incomplete, littered with "maybe," "probably," and "this part to be filled in later." Nevertheless, researchers are making steady progress and are increasingly optimistic about developing more complete explanations.

If we explain the singing of a male bird in terms of hormones, brain activity, and evolutionary selection, few people worry about the philosophical consequences. But how would you feel about a completely physical explanation of your own actions and experiences? Suppose you say, "I became frightened because I saw a man with a gun," but a neuroscientist says, "You became frightened because of increased electrochemical activity in the central amygdala of your brain." Is one explanation right and the other wrong? Or if they are both right, what is the connection between them?

Many philosophers have addressed the **mind-body** or **mind-brain problem:** What is the relationship between the mind and the brain? The most widespread view among nonscientists is, no doubt, dualism, the belief that mind and body are different kinds of substance (thought substance and physical substance) that exist independently but somehow interact. The French philosopher René Descartes defended du-

alism but recognized the vexing issue of how an immaterial mind could influence a physical brain. He proposed that mind and brain interact at a single point in space, which he suggested was the pineal gland, the smallest unpaired structure he could find in the brain (see Figure 1.5).

Although Descartes gets credit for the first explicit defense of dualism, he hardly originated the idea. Nearly everyone begins as a dualist (except for the part about the pineal gland). We all grow up convinced that our thoughts control our actions, and when we are told that the brain controls behavior, we react, "Well, okay, then the brain communicates with the mind, and the mind controls the brain."

However, nearly all philosophers and neuroscientists reject dualism. The primary objection is that it conflicts with the law of conservation of matter and energy in physics: The only way to accelerate matter or transform energy, including the matter and energy in your body, is to act upon it with other matter or energy. Therefore, if your mind is going to influence the matter or energy of your brain or any other part of your body, your mind must itself be composed of matter or energy.

If we discard dualism, the alternative is monism, the belief that the universe consists of only one kind of existence. Various forms of monism are possible, most of which fit the following categories:

- **materialism:** the view that everything that exists is material, or physical. According to one version of this view ("eliminative materialism"), mental events don't exist at all, and the common folk psychology based on beliefs and experiences is fundamentally mistaken. A less drastic version is that all psychological experiences can eventually be explained in purely physical terms.

- **mentalism:** the view that only the mind really exists and that the physical world exists only in our imagination, or perhaps only in the mind of God. This is not an easy position to disprove—go ahead and

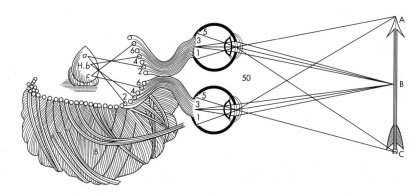

Figure 1.5 René Descartes' conception of brain and mind
Descartes understood how light from an object reached the retinas at the back of the eyes. From there, he assumed the information was all channeled back to the pineal gland, a small unpaired organ in the brain.

try!—but few philosophers or scientists take it seriously.

- **identity position:** the view that mental processes are the same thing as certain kinds of brain processes, but described in different terms. For example, one could describe the Mona Lisa as a beautiful painting by an extraordinarily skillful artist, or one could list the exact color and brightness of each point on the painting. Although the two descriptions appear very different, they refer to the same object. According to the identity position, every experience *is* a brain activity, even though descriptions of our thoughts sound very different from descriptions of brain activities. For example, the fright you feel when you see a man with a gun *is the same thing as* a certain pattern of activity in your brain.

Has monism, or any version of it, been proved correct? No. In fact, most scientists avoid the word *proved,* except in mathematics. However, the arguments against dualism seem compelling and the monist position leads to fruitful research. For example, as you will find throughout this text, stimulation of any brain area provokes changes in behavior and experience, and changes in experience evoke particular patterns of brain activity. Experiences and brain activities appear to be inseparable. Neuroscientists are free to use the terms *mind* and *mental activity* if they make it clear that they understand these terms to be just another way of describing brain activity. However, if you lapse into using *mind* to mean a ghostlike something that is neither matter nor energy, don't underestimate the scientific and philosophical arguments that can be marshaled against you (Dennett, 1991).

(Does a belief in monism mean that we are lowering our evaluation of minds? Maybe not. Maybe we are elevating our concept of the material world.)

If we accept some version of the monist position, such as the identity position, have we then solved the mind-brain problem? Hardly. Stating that mind and brain are the same thing does not resolve the mystery; it merely restates it. The questions remain: *Why* is there any such thing as consciousness? And what kind of physical structure is necessary to produce consciousness?

David Chalmers (1995) has proposed that in discussions of consciousness we distinguish the easy problems from the hard problem. The **easy problems** pertain to many phenomena to which we apply the term *consciousness,* such as the difference between wakefulness and sleep and the mechanisms that enable us to focus our attention. These problems are not really "easy" to solve, but they raise no special philosophical issues.

On the other hand, the **hard problem** is the question of why and how any kind of brain activity is associated with consciousness. Even if researchers determine which parts of the brain or which kinds of brain activity are necessary for conscious experience, most people agree that we still do not understand why or how the conscious experience occurs. As Chalmers (1995) put it, "Why doesn't all this information-processing go on 'in the dark,' free of any inner feel?" (p. 203).

Chalmers' suggested answer is that consciousness is a fundamental property of matter—fundamental in the sense that it cannot be reduced to anything else. That is, we cannot explain it; it just *is.* For example, mass and charge are fundamental properties; we cannot explain *why* matter has mass; it just does. Perhaps in the same way, consciousness might be an unexplainable fundamental. If so, conscious experience may be a widespread phenomenon in the universe, found wherever matter or energy is arranged in information-rich ways.

And then again, maybe not. Noted philosopher Daniel Dennett (1991, 1996) argues that the hard problem really consists of an enormous number of easy problems. Once we fully answer all the easy problems, the hard problem will go away. By analogy, in the 1800s many people doubted that it would be possible to explain life in physical terms. And then, step by step, biologists found convincing physical explanations for metabolism, reproduction, embryological development, and all the other phenomena of life . . . well, all except for consciousness. Today, many researchers are trying to understand the physiology of consciousness, and perhaps they will succeed.

Patricia Churchland (1996), another noted philosopher, also argues that research may explain consciousness, although she seems less insistent than Dennett. She submits that it is simply far too soon to give up on a conventional physical explanation for consciousness; it is just too soon to know which problems are really the "hardest."

Do not expect an agreement on this issue soon. The problem in doing research on mind-body relationships is that consciousness is not observable. In contrast, mass and charge—properties that we agree are fundamental—cannot be explained, but at least they can be observed and measured. But consciousness is different. Although I am directly aware of my own conscious mind, as you are of yours, we can only infer each other's. Indeed, how do you even know that other people are conscious? You don't, really. Maybe they are just very convincing robots.

Solipsism (SOL-ip-sizm, based on the Latin words *solus* and *ipse,* meaning "alone" and "self") is the philosophical position that I alone exist, or I alone am conscious. (There probably aren't many solipsists in the world, but there might be more than we know about. Solipsists don't have any reason to form an organization because each is convinced that all the other solipsists are wrong!) Although most people do not take solipsism seriously, it is hard to imagine evidence that refutes it. The difficulty of knowing whether other people (or animals) have conscious experiences is known as the **problem of other minds.**

Nonsolipsists readily assume that other people are conscious, reasoning by analogy: "Other people look much like me and act much like me, so they probably have internal experiences much like mine." How about chimpanzees? Not everyone agrees, but I would say, "Sure. They look and act less like me, but close enough that I'll infer they have conscious experiences." How about dogs? Rats? Fish? Insects? Amoeba? Trees? Rocks? At some point, most people hesitate; for example, "I'm really not sure about insects. They probably don't have experiences much like mine, but possibly they have some sort of experience. I'm not sure, and I don't know how to decide."

Even if we concede that an animal does have conscious experience, we may be unable to understand that experience. As Thomas Nagel (1974) has argued, most of us assume that other mammals have experiences, but we don't really know what it would feel like to be, say, a bat. We believe it would feel like *something,* but we don't know what. Because of our inability to observe others' subjective experiences, it is difficult even to imagine a physiological explanation.

What about computers or robots? Every year, they get more sophisticated and complicated. What if someone builds a robot that can walk, talk, carry on an intelligent conversation, laugh at jokes, and so forth? At what point, if any, would we agree that the robot is conscious?

Some people immediately respond, "Never. The robot is just a machine, and it's programmed to do what it does." True, but the human brain is also a machine, although of a very different kind. (A machine is anything that converts one kind of energy into another.) And we, too, are programmed—by our genes and our past experiences. (We did not create ourselves.) It may be that no robot can be conscious; maybe only systems based on carbon chemistry can be (Searle, 1992). (After all, we don't know the conditions necessary for producing consciousness.) But how would we know? Can you imagine any conceivable evidence that would persuade you that a robot is conscious? If you couldn't be persuaded by *any* evidence, then you're simply holding a prejudice. Try to think of some kind of evidence that could convince you of machine consciousness. If you are curious about the author's answer, check page 8. But try to think of your own answer first.

Many researchers originally became attracted to neuroscience because they were fascinated with the mind-brain problem and hoped to contribute at least slightly to its solution. As you will see throughout this text, losing various parts of the brain means losing parts of the mind, and stimulating certain brain activities can evoke experiences or behavioral tendencies. *Why* there is such a close relationship between brain and experience may still elude us, but at least we continue to explore and document the connection. If Dennett is right

that answering the easy problems does answer the hard problem, then great. If not, research findings have important applications on their own and should at least improve our philosophical musings.

Stop & Check

2. What are the three major versions of monism?

3. What is meant by "the hard problem"?

Check your answers on page 8.

In Closing: The Biology of Experience

Biological psychology is a very ambitious field. The goal is to explain as much as possible of psychology in strictly biological, physical terms. The guiding assumption is that the pattern of activity that occurs in your brain when you see a rabbit *is* your perception of a rabbit; the pattern that occurs when you feel fear *is* your fear. And so forth. This is not to say that "your brain physiology controls you," any more than one should say that "you control your brain." Rather, your brain *is* you! The rest of this book explores how far we can go with this guiding assumption.

Summary

1. The brain is composed of many identifiable areas and subareas, each composed of neurons and glia. Later chapters explore these topics in detail. (p. 2)

2. Biological psychologists try to answer four types of questions about any given behavior: How does it relate to the physiology of the brain and other organs? How does it develop within the individual? How did the capacity for the behavior evolve? And why did the capacity for this behavior evolve? (That is, what function does it serve?) (p. 3)

3. Biological explanations of behavior do not necessarily assume that the individual understands the purpose or function of the behavior. (p. 3)

4. Philosophers and scientists continue to address the mind-brain or mind-body relationship. Dualism, the popular view that the mind exists separately from the brain, is opposed by the principle that the matter and energy of the brain can be influenced only by other matter and energy. (p. 5)

5. Nearly all philosophers and scientists who have addressed the mind-brain problem favor some version of monism, the belief that the universe consists

of only one kind of substance. That substance could be either material (materialism), mental (mentalism), or a combination of both (identity position). Still, the hard problem remains: Why is there such a thing as conscious experience at all and why does it emerge from certain kinds of brain activity? (p. 5)

Answers to *Stop and Check* Questions

1. An evolutionary explanation states what evolved from what. For example, humans evolved from earlier primates and therefore have certain features that we inherited from those ancestors, even if the features are not useful to us today. A functional explanation states why something was advantageous and therefore evolutionarily selected. (p. 5)

2. The three major versions of monism are materialism (everything can be explained in physical terms), mentalism (only minds exist), and identity (the mind and the brain are the same thing). (p. 7)

3. The "hard problem" is why minds exist at all in a physical world, why there is such a thing as consciousness, and how it relates to brain activity. (p. 7)

Thought Questions[1]

1. What would you say or do to try to convince a solipsist that you are conscious?

2. Now suppose a robot just said and did the same things you did in question 1. Will you be convinced that it is conscious?

Author's Answer About Machine Consciousness (p. 7)

Here is a possibility similar to a proposal by J. R. Searle (1992): Suppose someone suffers damage to part of the visual cortex of the brain and becomes blind to part of the visual field. Now, engineers design artificial brain circuits to replace the damaged cells. Impulses from the eyes are attached to this device, which processes the information and sends electrical impulses to healthy portions of the brain that ordinarily would get input from the damaged brain area. After this device is installed, the person can see the field that used to be blind, remarking, "Ah! Now I can see that area again! I see shapes, colors, movement—the whole thing, just as I used to!" Evidently, the machine has enabled conscious perception of vision. Then, the person receives still more brain damage, and engineers replace the rest of the visual cortex with artificial circuits. Once again, the person assures us that vision looks the same as before. Next, damage occurs in the auditory cortex, someone replaces it with a machine, and the person reports normal auditory experience. One by one, additional brain areas are damaged and replaced by machines; in each case, the behavior returns to normal and the person reports having normal experience, the same as before the damage. Even brain areas storing memories are replaced. Eventually, the entire brain is replaced. At that point I would say that the machine itself is conscious.

Note that all this discussion assumes that these artificial brain circuits and transplants are possible. I don't know whether they ever will be. My point is merely to show what kind of evidence might convince us of a conscious machine.

[1] Thought questions are intended to spark thought and discussion. The text does not directly answer any of them, although it may imply or suggest an answer in some cases. In other cases, there may be several possible answers.

Nature and Nurture

Everything you are and everything you do depend on both your genes and your environment. Without your genes or without an adequate environment, there would be no *you*. So far, no problem. The controversies arise when we discuss why one person differs from another. Why do people differ in their learning and memory, eating and weight, sexual orientation, use of alcohol and other drugs, mood, and so forth? Do we differ because of our genes or because we grew up in different environments? If both, then to what extent is it one or the other?

In later chapters, we consider the evidence for genetic influences on many specific behaviors. Here we deal with the general principles of heredity and environment, nature and nurture. This module certainly does not resolve the controversies, but it should at least enable you to distinguish between reasonable questions and meaningless ones, between plausible answers and nonsense.

The Genetics of Behavior

We begin with a review of elementary genetics. Readers already familiar with the concepts may skim quickly over the next 3 pages and start with the section on heritability.

Mendelian Genetics

Prior to the work of Gregor Mendel, a late-nineteenth-century monk, scientists thought that inheritance was a blending process in which the properties of the sperm and the egg simply mixed, much as one might mix red paint and yellow paint.

Mendel demonstrated that inheritance occurs through **genes,** units of heredity that maintain their structural identity from one generation to another. As a rule, genes come in pairs because they are aligned along **chromosomes** (strands of genes), which also come in pairs. (The sex chromosomes, an exception to this rule, are unpaired.) A gene is a portion of a chromosome, which is composed of the double-stranded chemical **deoxyribonucleic acid,** or **DNA.** A strand of DNA serves as a template (model) for the synthesis of **ribonucleic acid (RNA)** molecules. RNA is a single-strand chemical; one type of RNA molecules serves as a template for the synthesis of protein molecules. Figure 1.6 summarizes the main steps in translating information from DNA through RNA into proteins, which then determine the development and properties of the organism. Some proteins form part of the structure of the body; others serve as **enzymes,** biological catalysts that regulate chemical reactions in the body.

An individual who has an identical pair of genes on the two chromosomes is said to be **homozygous** for that gene. An individual with an unmatched pair of genes is said to be **heterozygous** for that gene. For example, a gene for blue eyes might be on one chromosome and a gene for brown eyes on the other.

Certain genes can be identified as dominant or recessive. A **dominant** gene shows a strong effect in either the homozygous or heterozygous condition; a **recessive** gene shows its effects only in the homozygous condition. For example, someone with a gene for brown eyes (dominant) and one for blue eyes (recessive) will have brown eyes, although he or she is a "carrier" for the blue-eye gene and can transmit it to a child. For a behavioral example, the gene for ability to taste moderate concentrations of phenylthiocarbamide (PTC) is dominant; the gene for ability to taste it only in high concentrations is recessive. Only someone with two recessive genes has trouble tasting the substance. Figure 1.7 illustrates the possible results of a mating between two parents who are both heterozygous for the PTC-tasting gene. Because each of them has one taster (T)[2] gene, each can taste PTC. However, each parent can transmit either a taster gene (T) or a nontaster gene (t) to a given child with equal probability. Therefore, a child in this family has a 25% chance of being a homozygous (TT) taster, a 50% chance of being a heterozygous (Tt) taster, and a 25% chance of being a homozygous (tt) nontaster.

Chromosomes and Crossing Over In certain cases, the inheritance of one gene is linked to the inheritance of another gene. Each chromosome participates in reproduction independently of the others, and each species has a certain number of chromosomes—for example, 23 pairs in humans, 4 pairs in fruit flies. For example, if an

---

[2] Among geneticists, it is customary to use a capital letter to indicate the dominant gene and a lowercase letter to indicate the recessive gene.

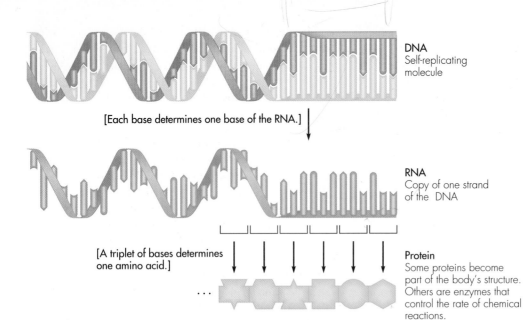

DNA
Self-replicating molecule

[Each base determines one base of the RNA.]

RNA
Copy of one strand of the DNA

[A triplet of bases determines one amino acid.]

Protein
Some proteins become part of the body's structure. Others are enzymes that control the rate of chemical reactions.

Figure 1.6   How DNA controls development of the organism
The sequence of bases along a strand of DNA determines the order of bases along a strand of RNA; RNA in turn controls the sequence of amino acids in a protein molecule.

individual has a *BbCc* genotype, and if the *B* and *C* genes are on different chromosomes, its contribution of a *B* or *b* gene has nothing to do with whether it contributes *C* or *c*. But suppose they are on the same chromosome. If one chromosome has the *BC* combination and the other has *bc,* then an individual who contributes a *B* gene probably also contributes *C*.

The exception to this statement comes about during reproduction as a result of **crossing over:** A pair of chromosomes may break apart and reconnect such that part of one chromosome attaches to the other part of the second chromosome. If one chromosome has the *BC* combination and the other chromosome has the *bc* combination, crossing over between the *B* locus and the *C* locus leaves new chromosomes with the combinations *Bc* and *bC*. The closer the *B* locus is to the *C* locus, the less often crossing over occurs between them.

Sex-Linked and Sex-Limited Genes   All but one pair of mammalian chromosomes are known as **autosomal chromosomes;** genes located on these chromosomes are referred to as **autosomal genes.** The genes located on the sex chromosomes are known as **sex-linked genes.**

In mammals, the two sex chromosomes are designated **X** and **Y**: A female mammal has two X chromosomes; a male has an X and a Y. (Unlike the symbols *B* and *C* that I introduced to illustrate gene pairs, X and Y are standard symbols for sex chromosomes used by all geneticists.) During reproduction, the female necessarily contributes an X chromosome, and the male contributes either an X or a Y. If he contributes an X, the offspring is female; if he contributes a Y, the offspring is male.

The Y chromosome is small and carries few genes other than the gene that causes the individual to de-

velop as a male. The X chromosome, however, carries many genes. Thus, when biologists speak of sex-linked genes, they usually mean X-linked genes.

A characteristic that is controlled by a sex-linked recessive gene—for example, red-green color vision deficiency—produces its effects only in the absence of the dominant gene. Any man who has the recessive gene necessarily has red-green color vision deficiency, because he has no other X chromosome that could overrule the recessive gene. A woman, however, is color-deficient only if she has that recessive gene on both of her X chromosomes. So, for example, if 8% of human X chromosomes contain the gene for color vision deficiency, then 8% of all men will be color-deficient, but fewer than 1% of women will be (.08 × .08).

Distinct from sex-linked genes are the **sex-limited genes.** A sex-limited gene is present in both sexes but

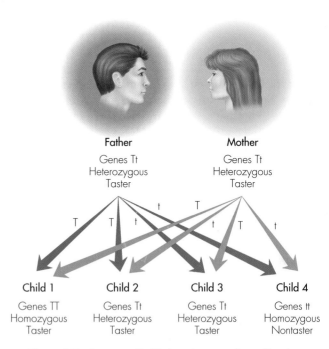

Father
Genes Tt
Heterozygous
Taster

Mother
Genes Tt
Heterozygous
Taster

Child 1
Genes TT
Homozygous
Taster

Child 2
Genes Tt
Heterozygous
Taster

Child 3
Genes Tt
Heterozygous
Taster

Child 4
Genes tt
Homozygous
Nontaster

Figure 1.7   Four equally likely outcomes of a mating between parents who are heterozygous for a given gene (Tt)
A child in this family has a 25% chance of being homozygous for the dominant gene (TT), a 25% chance of being homozygous for the recessive gene (tt), and a 50% chance of being heterozygous (Tt).

has an effect in one sex only, or at least it has a much stronger effect in one sex than in the other. For instance, genes control the amount of chest hair in men, breast size in women, the amount of crowing in roosters, and the rate of egg production in hens. Such genes need not be on the sex chromosomes; both sexes have the genes, but the genes exert their effects only after activation by the sex hormones.

Stop & Check

1. Suppose you can taste PTC. If your mother can also taste it, what (if anything) can you predict about your father's ability to taste it? If your mother cannot taste it, what (if anything) can you predict about your father's ability to taste it?

2. How does a sex-linked gene differ from a sex-limited gene?

Check your answers on page 17.

Sources of Variation If reproduction always produced offspring that were exact copies of the parents, evolution would be impossible. One source of variation is **recombination**, a new combination of genes, some from one parent and some from the other, that yields characteristics not found in either parent.

Another source of variation is a **mutation**, or change in a single gene. For instance, a gene for brown eyes might mutate into a gene for blue eyes. Mutation of a given gene is a rare, random event; that is, the needs of the organism do not guide it. A mutation is analogous to having an untrained person add, remove, or distort something on the blueprints for your new house. Only rarely would the random change be an improvement.

Most mutations produce recessive genes, however. Thus, if you or one of your recent ancestors had a harmful mutation on one gene, your children do not show the effects unless you happened to mate with someone who had the same harmful gene. Your mate is unlikely to have the same mutant genes as you, unless you both received that gene from the same ancestor. For this reason, it is unwise for people to marry their close relatives.

Heritability

Unlike PTC sensitivity and color vision deficiency, most variations in behavior depend on the combined influence of many genes and many environmental influences. You may occasionally hear someone ask about a behavior, "Which is more important, heredity or environment?" That question, as stated, is meaningless. No behavior can develop without both heredity and environment.

Consider, however, a more meaningful question: Do the observed *differences* among individuals depend more on differences in heredity or differences in environment?

For example, if you sing better than I do, the reason could be that you inherited genes that produced better vocal cords, or you have practiced more, or of course, both.

In measuring the relative contribution of heredity to variations in outcome, researchers use the concept of **heritability,** an estimate of how much of the variance in some characteristic within some population is due to heredity. Heritability ranges from 0 to 1. If the heritability of a given characteristic is 0, then hereditary differences account for none of the observed variations in that characteristic within the tested population. A heritability of 1 indicates that hereditary differences account for all of the observed differences. Naturally, an intermediate value, such as .5, indicates an intermediate role for heredity.

How do researchers determine the heritability of some human trait? We omit the mathematics here and consider only the logic. First, researchers compare the resemblances between monozygotic (identical) twins and dizygotic (fraternal) twins. A stronger resemblance between monozygotic twins indicates high heritability; equal resemblance in both kinds of twins indicates low or zero heritability. Second, they examine adopted children and their biological and adoptive parents. Resemblance to the biological parents indicates high heritability; resemblance to the adoptive parents indicates low heritability.

Heritability is difficult to measure precisely, especially with humans. Our estimates of human heritabilities depend on questionable assumptions about the extent to which people choose mates who are genetically similar to themselves and the extent to which they choose mates from similar environments (Reynolds, Baker, & Pedersen, 1996). Furthermore, most monozygotic twins share a single placenta and therefore a single blood supply during prenatal life, whereas dizygotic twins develop in separate placentas (Figure 1.8). In addition, adopted children can resemble their biological parents because of the biological mother's health, nutrition, and smoking and drinking habits during pregnancy. In short, our methods sometimes overestimate human heritabilities and underestimate the role of prenatal environment.

Heritability can vary from one population to another. For example, in a community in which everyone is closely related to everyone else, the heritability of most behaviors will be low. (Differences in heredity cannot account for much if people have almost no differences in heredity!) Conversely, if all the people in some other community have equally good environments, the heritability of most behaviors will be high in that community. (Environmental differences cannot account for much, so the remaining variability must be largely hereditary.) In short, any estimate of heritability is necessarily imprecise and may or may not apply to people at a different time and place.

Even if a trait has high heritability, it is still possible

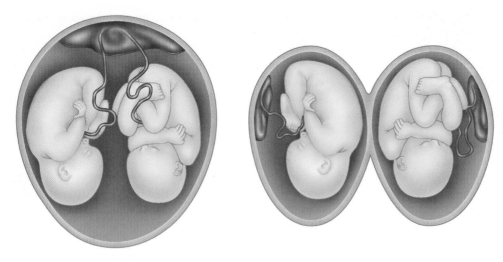

Figure 1.8 Prenatal development of monozygotic and dizygotic twins
In most cases, monozygotic (identical) twins develop in a single placenta and have the same blood supply. Dizygotic (fraternal) twins develop in separate placentas. Therefore, monozygotic twins have more similar prenatal environments as well as more similar heredities.

for environmental interventions to influence that trait. (A measure of heritability applies to a population in a specific environment; it cannot tell us about the possible effects of a different environment.) For example, different genetic strains of mice behave differently in the *elevated plus maze* (Figure 1.9). Some stay almost entirely in the walled arms, like the mouse shown in the figure; others (more adventuresome? less nervous?) venture onto the open arms. But even when different laboratories use the same genetic strains, and as far as possible the exact same procedures, some strains that are adventuresome in one laboratory become less active or more nervous in another (Crabbe, Wahlsten, & Dudek, 1999). Evidently, the effects of the genes vary depending on subtle differences in procedure, such as how the investigators handle the mice, or maybe even the investigators' odors. (Most behaviors do not show this much variability; the elevated plus maze appears to be an extreme example.)

For a human example, **phenylketonuria** (FEE-nil-KEET-uhn-YOOR-ee-uh), or **PKU,** is a form of mental retardation caused by a genetic inability to metabolize the amino acid phenylalanine. One to two percent of Europeans and Asians carry a recessive gene for PKU; few if any Africans have the gene (T. Wang et al., 1989). Because of the PKU gene, phenylalanine accumulates to toxic levels, impairing brain development and leaving children mentally retarded, restless, irritable, and sometimes prone to temper tantrums. For children on an ordinary diet, the heritability of PKU is virtually 1.

However, in many countries, physicians routinely measure the level of phenylalanine or its metabolites in the blood or urine of every baby. If the results are abnormal, they advise the parents to put the baby on a strict low-phenylalanine diet to minimize brain damage (Waisbren, Brown, de Sonneville, & Levy, 1994). Our ability

to prevent PKU provides particularly strong evidence that *heritable* or *genetic* does not mean *unmodifiable.*

A couple of notes about PKU: First, someone with the condition can relax the strict diet by about age 12–15, when the brain is mostly mature, although a woman with PKU should return to the diet during pregnancy and nursing. Even a genetically normal baby cannot handle the enormous amounts of phenylalanine that an affected mother might pass through the placenta. Second, you may have noticed that beverages containing the artificial sweetener aspartame (NutraSweet) carry this advisory: "Phenylketonurics: Contains Phenylalanine." Aspartame is a compound of phenylalanine and another amino acid. Anyone with PKU must be certain to avoid aspartame, and even genetically normal women should beware of excessive use during pregnancy.

Stop & Check

3. Suppose researchers measure the heritability of intelligence in two populations: one in which everyone shares a good, supportive environment and one in which certain individuals have a much better environment than others do. Which population will show the higher heritability? Why?

4. What example illustrates the point that even if some characteristic is highly heritable, a change in the environment may be able to change it?

Check your answers on page 17.

How Genes Affect Behavior

A biologist who speaks of a "gene for brown eyes" does not mean that the gene directly produces brown eyes. Rather, the gene produces a protein that, under ordinary circumstances, combines with other body products and environmental conditions to make the eyes brown instead of another color. Similarly, if we speak of a "gene for depression," or for any other psychological condition, we should not imagine that the gene itself produces depression. Rather, the gene produces a protein that, under certain circumstances, increases the probability of depression.

Exactly how a gene increases the probability of a

Figure 1.9   An elevated plus maze
Different genetic strains of mice behave differently in this apparatus, presumably displaying different levels of anxiety. But the results vary from lab to lab and may depend on minor, unintentional variations in procedure.

given behavior is a complex issue. In later chapters, we encounter a few examples of genes that control brain chemicals. However, genes also can affect behavior indirectly by changing other body characteristics. For example, a gene that increases a person's height increases the probability of playing basketball (if he or she lives where people play basketball). Because time spent on a basketball court is time not spent doing something else, the increased-height gene probably decreases the time that the person spends playing the violin, talking on the telephone, and so forth.

Consequently, we should not be amazed by reports that almost every human behavior has some heritability. Research on monozygotic twins and adopted children indicates significant heritability of even such culturally specific behaviors as television watching (Plomin, Corley, DeFries, & Fulker, 1990), religious devoutness (Waller, Kojetin, Bouchard, Lykken, & Tellegen, 1990), social attitudes (S. F. Posner, Baker, Heath, & Martin, 1996), and interests and hobbies (Lykken, McGue, Tellegen, & Bouchard, 1992). I do not know what gene or combination of genes might increase the probability of watching television, but we can imagine many possibilities. (Genes for low physical activity, perhaps?) The point is that genes that affect the body in any way also affect behavior, and a gene that affects one behavior also influences other behaviors. We should not assume "one gene, one behavior" or "one gene, one disorder" (Plomin, Owen, & McGuffin, 1994).

The Evolution of Behavior

Every gene that influences behavior is subject to evolution by natural selection. **Evolution** is a change over generations in the frequencies of various genes in a population. Note that, by this definition, evolution includes *any* change in gene frequencies, regardless of whether it is helpful or harmful to the species in the long run.

We must distinguish two questions about evolution: How *did* species evolve, and how *do* species evolve? To ask how species did evolve is to ask what evolved from what, and answers are inferences based on fossils and comparisons of living species. For example, biologists find that humans are more similar to chimpanzees than to other species. These similarities point to the probability of a common ancestor from which both humans and chimpanzees inherited most of their genes. Similarly, humans and chimpanzees together have some striking resemblances to monkeys and presumably shared a common ancestor with monkeys in the remoter past. Using similar reasoning, evolutionary biologists have constructed an "evolutionary tree" that shows the relationships among various species (see Figure 1.10). However, as new evidence becomes available, biologists occasionally change their opinions of what evolved from what; thus, any evolutionary tree is tentative.

Nevertheless, the question of how species *do* evolve is a question of how the process works, and that process is, in its basic outlines, a logical necessity. That is, any species that reproduces more or less the way we do *must* evolve. The study of genetics has demonstrated that offspring generally resemble their parents, but mutations and recombinations of genes occasionally introduce new heritable variations. Some individuals survive longer and reproduce more abundantly than others; the individuals who reproduce the most pass on the greatest number of genes to the next generation, which in turn resembles the older individuals who reproduced most successfully. Any new gene or gene combination that is consistently associated with reproductive success will become more and more prevalent in later generations.

This principle has long been known by plant and animal breeders, who choose individuals with a desired trait and make them the parents of the next generation. This process is called **artificial selection,** and over many generations it has produced exceptional race horses, hundreds of breeds of dogs, chickens that lay huge numbers of eggs, and so forth. Darwin's (1859) insight was that nature also selects. If certain individuals are more successful than others in finding food, escaping enemies, attracting mates, or protecting their offspring, then their genes will become more prevalent in later generations.

Common Misunderstandings About Evolution

Let us clarify the principles of evolution by addressing a few misconceptions.

- *Does the use or disuse of some structure or behavior cause an evolutionary increase or decrease in that feature?* You have probably heard someone say

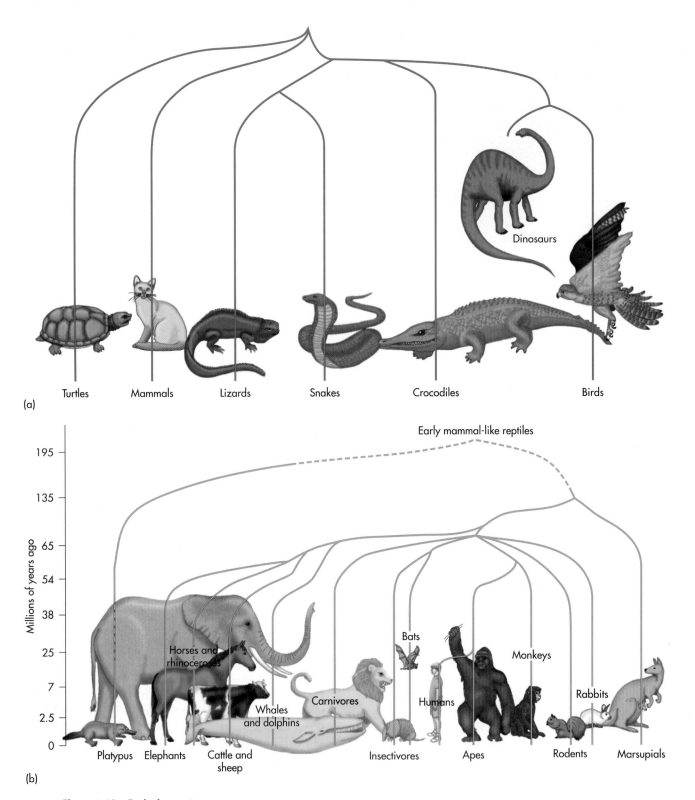

(a)

Turtles   Mammals   Lizards   Snakes   Crocodiles   Birds

(b)

Early mammal-like reptiles

Millions of years ago

195
135
65
54
38
25
7
2.5
0

Horses and rhinoceroses   Bats   Monkeys

Whales and dolphins   Carnivores   Humans   Rabbits

Platypus   Elephants   Cattle and sheep   Insectivores   Apes   Rodents   Marsupials

Figure 1.10   Evolutionary trees
(**a**) Evolutionary relationships among mammals, birds, and several kinds of reptiles. (**b**) Evolutionary relationships among various species of mammals.

something like, "Because we hardly ever use our little toes, they will get smaller and smaller in each succeeding generation." That idea is a carryover of the biologist Jean Lamarck's theory of evolution through the inheritance of acquired characteristics,

known as **Lamarckian evolution.** According to this idea, if giraffes stretch their necks as far out as possible, their offspring will be born with longer necks. Similarly, if you exercise your arm muscles, your children will be born with bigger arm muscles, and if you fail to use your little toes, your children's little toes will be smaller than yours. However, biologists have found no mechanism for Lamarckian evolution to occur and no evidence that it does. Using or failing to use some part of the body does not change the genes that one can transmit to the next generation.

(It is possible that people's little toes might shrink in future evolution if people with even smaller little toes have an advantage over other people. But we would have to wait for a mutation that decreases little toe size—without causing some other problem—and then we would have to wait for people with this mutation to outreproduce people with other genes.)

- *Have humans stopped evolving?* Because modern medicine can keep almost anyone alive, and because welfare programs in prosperous countries provide the necessities of life for almost everyone, some people assert that humans are no longer subject to the principle of "survival of the fittest." Therefore, the argument goes, human evolution has stopped or at least slowed down a great deal.

   The flaw in this argument is that evolution depends not on survival but on reproduction. One must survive at least a minimum period of time in order to reproduce, but what counts in evolution is how many healthy children (and nieces and nephews etc.) one has. Thus, keeping everyone alive doesn't stop human evolution. If some people have more children than others do, their genes will spread in the population.

- *Does "evolution" mean "improvement"?* It depends on what you mean by "improvement." Evolution necessarily improves the **fitness** of the population, which is operationally defined as *the number of copies of one's genes that endure in later generations.* However, genes that increase fitness at one

It is possible to slow the rate of evolution, but not just by keeping everyone alive. China has enacted a policy that attempts to limit each family to one child. If the government managed to enforce the policy, human evolution would indeed reach a near standstill in China.

Sometimes a sexual display, such as the spread of tail feathers of a peacock, leads to great reproductive success and therefore to the spread of the associated genes. In a slightly changed environment, this "successful" gene could prove to be extremely harmful. For example, if an aggressive predator with good color vision enters the range of the peacock, the bird's slow movement and colorful feathers could spell its doom.

time and place might be disadvantageous after a change in the environment. Consider, for example, the colorful tail feathers of the male peacock, which enable it to attract females. If the environment changes by the introduction of a new predator that responds to bright colors, the previously advantageous display may become a handicap.

- *Does evolution act to benefit the individual or the species?* Neither: It acts for the benefit of the genes! In a very real sense, you do not carry your genes around as a way of reproducing yourself; your genes carry *you* around as a way of reproducing *themselves* (Dawkins, 1989). A gene spreads through a population if—and only if—the individuals bearing that gene reproduce more than do the individuals bearing other genes. So, for example, imagine a gene that causes you to risk your own life to protect your children. That gene will spread through the population (if it really does benefit your children), even though it endangers you personally. Imagine a gene that causes you to attack other members of the species in order to provide more food for your children. If the others do not retaliate against you or your children, your aggressiveness will benefit your children's reproductive potential and your "uncooperative" genes will spread—even if they are harmful to the species.

   Given that a gene spreads only if the individuals who bear it reproduce more than others, how can we explain the (admittedly rare) phenomenon of altruistic behavior in animals? **Altruistic behavior** benefits someone other than the individual doing the behavior. Altruism is common in humans: We contribute to charities, we try to help people in distress, a student may explain something to a classmate who is competing for a good grade in a course. It is hard to know whether any genes contribute to altruistic behavior. Such behavior is rare in nonhumans, except by parents toward their young (see Figure 1.11). Even in humans, altruism is rare in early childhood, and by the time it emerges, we cannot assume that it reflects a strong genetic basis.

Still, for the sake of illustration, suppose there exists a gene that increases altruistic behavior. Could it spread through the population, and if so, how? One common reply is that the altruistic behavior costs someone very little. True, but being almost harmless is not good enough; a gene spreads only if the individuals with it reproduce more than those without it. Another common reply is that the altruistic behavior benefits the species. True again, but the rebuttal is the same. A gene that benefits the species but fails to help the individual dies out with that individual.

Figure 1.11 Sentinel behavior: altruistic or not?
As in many other prey species, meerkats (a kind of mongoose) sometimes show sentinel behavior in which one of them stands, looks for danger, and if it finds any, utters an alarm call that warns the others. Although the behavior appears to be altruistic, researchers found that the meerkat doing sentinel duty is the one that escapes from danger most quickly and most surely (Clutton-Brock et al., 1999). Many examples of apparently altruistic behavior in nonhumans turn out to have selfish motives.

A suggestion that sounds good at first is *group selection.* According to this idea, some groups are altruistic and some are not; the altruistic groups survive and the uncooperative groups do not (D. S. Wilson & Sober, 1994). However, even if cooperative groups survive better than uncooperative groups, what will happen when a mutation favoring uncooperative behavior occurs within a cooperative group? If the uncooperative individual has a reproductive advantage within its group, its genes will spread until the group as a whole is no longer cooperative.

One acceptable explanation for the spread of altruistic genes is **reciprocal altruism,** the idea that animals help those who help them in return. Clearly, two individuals who cooperate with each other will prosper; however, reciprocal altruism can operate only if individuals can recognize one another and learn to help only those who return the favors. In other words, reciprocal altruism requires good sensory organs and a well-developed brain. (Perhaps we now understand why altruism is much more common in humans than in other species.)

The other acceptable explanation is **kin selection,** selection for a gene because it benefits the individual's relatives. For example, a gene could spread if it caused you to risk your life to protect your children. In a sense, such an act is altruistic; you are endangering yourself to help others, but because those others are your children, they share half of your genes, including perhaps the altruistic gene. Therefore, altruistic behavior toward your children helps spread your altruistic genes. Natural selection can favor altruism toward less close relatives—such as cousins, nephews, or nieces—if the benefits to them are enough greater than the cost to you (Dawkins, 1989; Hamilton, 1964; Trivers, 1985). In addition, a mechanism that caused you to behave altruistically toward your children might accidentally trigger you to help nonrelatives who looked or acted helpless or childlike.

Stop & Check

5. Many people believe the human appendix is useless. Should we therefore expect that it will grow smaller from one generation to the next?

6. What are two plausible ways for possible altruistic genes to spread in a population?

Check your answers on page 18.

Sociobiology

Sociobiology, or evolutionary psychology, deals with issues that concern the evolution of social behaviors, such as altruism. The emphasis is on *functional* explanations, as defined earlier (how a behavior might be useful and why natural selection would favor it). For example, why do males of so many species show more sexual jealousy than females do (M. I. Wilson & Daly, 1996)? Why do wolves live in packs and bears live singly? Why do males of some species help with infant care and males of other species do not?

Although sociobiologists make important contributions to our understanding, the field is subject to two major criticisms. First, functional explanations are often speculative. If we ask why male wrens share nesting and parental activities with the female and male grouse do not, it is relatively easy to devise a speculative explanation, but not everyone who proposes a speculation follows up on it with adequate field studies to test the idea. Second, sociobiological explanations sometimes imply that human behavior has evolved to be as it is, and therefore it should stay that way. For example, sociobiologists offer a plausible explanation for why mothers in all cultures contribute at least as much to childcare as fathers do, and generally much more: A mother can be sure that a baby is her own, whereas a father may not be equally certain. Sociobiologists also explain why men tend to be more interested than women are in having casual sex with multiple partners: Males sometimes spread their genes this way, whereas a female with many sex partners cannot have babies more frequently than a female with one partner (Buss, 1994). The objection many people raise, however, is that the way things *are* is not necessarily the same as the way they *should be.* Agreeing that men tend to be more promiscuous than women does not mean that we should encourage or condone such behavior. Indeed, various human societies have differing rules and expectations about sexual behavior. Even if our genes predispose men and women to behave differently, we still have great flexibility in acting on our predispositions.

Module 1.2

In Closing: Genes and Behavior

In the control of behavior, genes are neither all important nor irrelevant. Certain behaviors have a very high heritability; the ability to taste PTC is a clear, if not very important, example. Many other behaviors are influenced by many genes but are also subject to strong influence by experience. Our genes and our evolution make it possible for us to be what we are today, but they also give us the flexibility to change our behavior as circumstances warrant.

Summary

1. Genes are chemicals that maintain their integrity from one generation to the next and influence the development of the individual. A dominant gene affects development regardless of whether a person has pairs of that gene or only a single copy per cell. A recessive gene affects development only in the absence of the dominant gene. (p. 9)

2. Some behavioral differences demonstrate simple effects of dominant and recessive genes. More often, however, behavioral variations reflect the combined influences of many genes and many environmental factors. Heritability is an estimate of the amount of variation that is due to variation in genes as opposed to environmental variation. (p. 11)

3. The fact that some behavior shows high heritability for a given population does not necessarily indicate that it will show an equal heritability for a different population. It also does not deny the possibility that a change in the environment might significantly alter the behavioral outcome. (p. 11)

4. Genes influence behavior directly, by altering chemicals in the brain, and also indirectly, by affecting virtually any aspect of the body. (p. 12)

5. The process of evolution through natural selection is a logical necessity because mutations sometimes occur in genes, and individuals with certain sets of genes reproduce more successfully than others do. (p. 13)

6. Evolution spreads the genes that are associated with the individuals who have reproduced the most. (p. 15)

Answers to *Stop and Check* Questions

1. If your mother can taste PTC, we can make no predictions about your father. You may have inherited a gene from your mother that enables you to taste PTC, and because the gene is dominant, you need only one copy of the gene to taste PTC. However, if your mother cannot taste PTC, you must have inherited your ability to taste it from your father, so he must be a taster. (p. 11)

2. A sex-linked gene is on a sex chromosome (almost always the X chromosome). A sex-limited gene is on one of the other chromosomes, but it is activated by sex hormones and therefore makes its effects evident only in one sex or the other. (p. 11)

3. Heritability will be higher in the population who all share a good, supportive environment. The less variation that occurs in quality of environment, the greater the ability of hereditary differences to account for any differences in performance. (p. 12)

4. Keeping a child with the PKU gene on a strict low-phenylalanine diet prevents the mental retardation that the gene otherwise causes. (p. 12)

5. No. Failure to use or need a structure does not make it become smaller in the next generation. The appendix will shrink only if people with a gene for a smaller appendix reproduced more successfully than other people did. (p. 16)

6. Altruistic genes could spread because they facilitate care for one's kin or because they facilitate exchanges of favors with others (reciprocal altruism). (p. 18)

Thought Questions

1. Huntington's disease has a heritability of virtually 1. What human behaviors are you sure have a heritability of 0?

2. Certain conditions, including Alzheimer's disease, have a high heritability and ordinarily have their onset in old age. Genetic differences probably account for the fact that some people seem to age more slowly and more gracefully than others. Given that the genes affecting old age do not begin to show their effects *until* old age—long after people have stopped having children—how could evolution have any effect on such genes? Or should we assume that genes affecting only old people just drift at random and that evolution selects neither for nor against them?

The Use of Animals in Research

Certain ethical disputes seem likely to linger indefinitely, resistant to either agreement or compromise. One is abortion; another is the death penalty; still another is the use of animals for research. The animal research controversy is critical for biological psychology. As you will see throughout this book, most of what we know about the functioning of the nervous system stems from research done on laboratory animals. Some of that research is painful, stressful, or at least unpleasant for the animals. How shall we deal with the fact that on the one hand we want more knowledge and on the other hand we wish to minimize animal distress?

Reasons for Animal Research

Given that most biological psychologists are primarily interested in the human brain and human behavior, why do they study nonhuman animals? Here are four reasons.

1. *The underlying mechanisms of behavior are similar across species and sometimes are easier to study in a nonhuman species.* If you wanted to understand how a complex machine works, you might begin by examining a smaller, simpler machine that operates on the same principle. We also learn about brain-behavior relationships by starting with simpler cases. The brains and behavior of nonhuman vertebrates resemble those of humans in many aspects of their chemistry and anatomy (see Figure 1.12). Even invertebrate nerves follow the same basic principles as our own. Much research on nerve cells has been conducted on squid nerves, which are similar to human nerves but thicker and therefore easier to study.

2. *We are interested in animals for their own sake.* Humans are by nature curious. We want to understand why the Druids built Stonehenge, where the moon came from, how the rings of Saturn formed, and why certain animals do the strange things they do, regardless of whether or not such information turns out to have any practical applications.

3. *What we learn about animals sheds light on human evolution.* What is our place in nature? How did we come to be the way we are? One way of approaching such questions is by examining other species. Can we find any trace of language capacity in chimpanzees and other nonhuman species? How intelligent are monkeys, rats, and other species? Humans did not evolve from chimpanzees, monkeys, or rats, but we do share common ancestors with them, so studying them may provide important clues to our evolution.

4. *Certain experiments cannot use human subjects because of legal or ethical restrictions.* For example, investigators insert electrodes into the brain cells of rats and other animals to determine the relationship between brain activity and behavior. Such experiments answer questions that investigators cannot address in any other way. They also raise an ethical issue: If it is unacceptable to do such research on humans, should we not also object to using nonhumans? (Remember from Module 1.1: The physical basis of conscious experience is unknown. Do rats have the same mental life we do? None at all? Something in between? Clearly, we are making ethical decisions without full knowledge of what the animals experience.)

The Ethical Debate

In some cases, researchers observe animals in nature as a function of different times of day, different seasons of the year, changes in diet, and so forth. These procedures do not even inconvenience the animals and raise no ethical problems (unless you want to worry about invasion of privacy). In other experiments, however, including many discussed in this book, animals have been subjected to brain damage, electrode implantation, injections of drugs or hormones, and other unpleasant or harmful treatments. Many people regard such experimentation as cruelty to animals and have reacted either with peaceful (though vociferous) demonstrations or with more extreme tactics, such as breaking into research labs, stealing lab animals, vandalizing lab property, and even threatening to kill researchers (Schiermeier, 1998) (see Figure 1.13).

Animals are used in many kinds of research studies, some dealing with behavior and others with the functions of the nervous system.

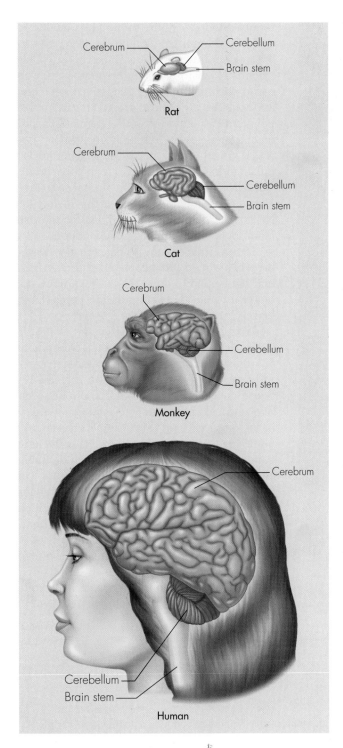

Figure 1.12 Brains of several species
The general plan and organization of the brain are similar for all mammals, even though the size varies from species to species.

The issues are indeed difficult. On the one hand, many laboratory animals undergo painful or debilitating procedures that are admittedly not intended for their own benefit. Anyone with a conscience (including scientists) is bothered by this fact. On the other hand, experimentation with animals has been critical to the medical research that led to methods for the prevention or treatment of polio, diabetes, measles, smallpox, massive burns, heart disease, and other serious conditions. Most Nobel Prizes in physiology or medicine have been awarded for research conducted on nonhuman animals. The hope of finding methods to treat or prevent AIDS and various brain diseases (such as Alzheimer's disease) depends largely on animal research. For many questions in biological psychology, our choice is to conduct research on animals or not to answer the questions at all (see Figure 1.13).

Opposition to animal research ranges considerably in degree. At one end are the moderates, the "minimalists" who agree that some animal research is acceptable but wish it to be minimized and regulated. That is, they accept some kinds of research but wish to prohibit others depending on the probable value of the research, the amount or type of distress to the animal, and perhaps the type of animal. (Most people have fewer qualms about hurting an insect, say, than about hurting a dolphin.)

At the other end are the "abolitionists," who see no room for compromise. Abolitionists maintain that all animals have the same rights as humans. They regard killing an animal as murder, regardless of whether the intention is to eat it, to use its fur, or to gain scientific knowledge. Keeping an animal (presumably even a pet) in a cage is, in their view, slavery. Because animals cannot give informed consent to an experiment, abolitionists insist it is wrong to use them in any experiment, regardless of the circumstances. According to one opponent of animal research, "We have no moral option but to bring this research to a halt. Completely. . . . We will not be satisfied until every cage is empty" (Regan, 1986, pp. 39–40). Advocates of this position sometimes claim that much animal research is extremely painful or that no animal research ever leads to important results. Note, however, that for a true abolitionist, none of those points really matter. The moral imperative remains that people have no right to use animals in research, even if it is highly useful, completely painless research.

Some abolitionists have opposed environmental protection groups as well. For example, red foxes, which humans introduced into California, so effectively rob bird nests that they have severely endangered several populations, including least terns and clapper rails. To protect the endangered birds, the U.S. Fish and Wildlife Service began trapping and killing red foxes in the areas where endangered birds breed. Their efforts were thwarted by a ballot initiative organized by animal rights activists, who argued that killing any animal is immoral even when the motive is to protect another species from extinction (Williams, 1999). Similar objections were raised when conservationists proposed to kill the pigs (again a human-introduced species) that were destroying the habitat of native Hawaiian wildlife.

At times in the animal rights dispute, people on

Figure 1.13   In defense of animal research
For many years, opponents of animal research have been protesting against experimentation with animals. This ad represents a reply by supporters of such research. (*Source: Courtesy of the Foundation for Biomedical Research*)

required to have an Institutional Animal Care and Use Committee, composed of veterinarians and community representatives as well as scientists, that evaluates proposed experiments, decides whether they are acceptable, and specifies procedures designed to minimize pain and discomfort. (Similar regulations and committees govern research on human subjects.) In addition, all research laboratories must abide by national laws requiring certain standards of cleanliness and animal care. Professional organizations such as the Society for Neuroscience publish guidelines for the use of animals in research (see Appendix B).

Other kinds of compromise are also possible. A survey of 372 people attending an animal rights march found that 51% supported a ten-point plan that included the items listed in Table 1.1 (Plous, 1998).

Is this sort of compromise satisfactory? The disagreement between animal researchers and the abolitionists who object even to carefully regulated research is not a dispute between good and evil; it is a dispute between two ethical positions: "Never knowingly harm another being" and "Sometimes a little harm leads to a greater good." On the one hand, permitting research has the undeniable consequence of inflicting pain or distress. On the other hand, banning the use of animals for human purposes means a great setback in medical research as well as the end of animal-to-human transplants (such as using pig heart valves to help people with heart diseases). For this reason, many victims of serious diseases have organized to oppose animal rights groups and to support animal research (Feeney, 1987).

both sides have taken shrill "us versus them" positions. Some defenders of animal research have claimed that such research is almost always useful and seldom painful, and some opponents have argued that the research is usually painful and never useful. In fact, the truth is messier (D. Blum, 1994): Much research is both useful and painful. Those of us who value both knowledge and animal life look for compromises instead of either–or solutions.

Nearly all animal researchers sympathize with the desire to minimize painful research. That is, just about everyone draws a line somewhere and says, "I will not do this experiment. The knowledge I might gain is not worth that much distress to the animals." To be sure, different researchers draw that line at different places.

Although it is often difficult to compare the probable value of proposed research with the probable distress to the animals, at least it is possible to compromise by letting a group of people decide rather than the experimenter alone. In the United States, every college or other research institution that receives federal funds is

Stop & Check

1. Describe reasons why biological psychologists conduct much of their research on nonhuman animals.

2. How does the "minimalist" position differ from the "abolitionist" position?

Check your answers on page 23.

In Closing: Humans and Animals

We began this chapter with a quote from the Nobel Prize–winning biologist, Niko Tinbergen. Tinbergen argued that no fundamental gulf separates humans from

Table 1.1 Some Items from a Proposed Compromise Between Animal Rights Activists and Researchers Studying Animals

If animal researchers will . . .	Then animal rights activists will . . .
Stop trying to portray animal rights activists as terrorists	Condemn all violent forms of activism, including arson, break-ins, vandalism, and bomb threats
Hold regular open houses at laboratories and address any problems that the public detects	Stop using exaggerated or outdated photographs from animal research that is no longer conducted
Refrain from forming political alliances with groups that favor animal use (e.g., hunters)	Refrain from forming political alliances with groups that are anti-science
Quit buying animals from random source dealers (i.e., animals not bred for research)	Quit claiming that biomedical researchers are responsible for families losing their pets
Acknowledge criticism respectfully, recognizing that activists and researchers share common ground	Express criticism respectfully, recognizing that activists and researchers share common ground

Source: Plous, 1998

other animal species. Because we are similar in many ways to other species, we can learn much about ourselves from animal studies. Also because of that similarity, we identify with animals and we wish not to inflict pain or distress upon them. Neuroscience researchers who have decided to conduct animal research have not, as a rule, taken this decision lightly. They want to minimize harm to animals, but they also want to increase knowledge. They believe it is better to inflict limited distress under controlled conditions than permit ignorance and disease to inflict much greater distress. We hope that at least most of the time we are making the right decision.

Summary

1. Researchers study animals because the mechanisms are sometimes easier to study in nonhumans, because they are interested in animal behavior for its own sake, because they want to understand the evolution of behavior, and because certain kinds of experiments are difficult or impossible with humans. (p. 19)

2. The ethics of using animals in research is controversial. Some research does inflict stress or pain on animals; however, many research questions can be investigated only through animal research. (p. 19)

3. Animal research today is conducted under legal and ethical controls that attempt to minimize animal distress. (p. 22)

Answers to *Stop and Check* Questions

1. Sometimes the mechanisms of behavior are easier to study in a nonhuman species. We are curious about animals for their own sake. We study animals to understand human evolution. Certain procedures are illegal or unethical with humans. (p. 22)

2. A "minimalist" wishes to limit animal research to studies with little discomfort and much potential value. An "abolitionist" wishes to eliminate all animal research, regardless of how the animals are treated or how much value the research might produce. (p. 22)

Module 1.4

Prospects for Further Study

This is by far the shortest module in the book; it offers advice about the possibilities if you want to consider a career in a field related to biological psychology.

The relevant careers fall into two categories: research and medicine. To pursue a career in research, one ordinarily needs a PhD, which could be in psychology, biology, neuroscience, neuropsychology, or other related fields. A few jobs are available in government-sponsored research laboratories, and more are available in industry, such as with drug companies. Most people with a PhD, however, hold college or university positions in which they do a combination of teaching and research. Depending on their interests, they might identify themselves as one of the following:

- *Behavioral neuroscientist* (almost synonyms: psychobiologist, biopsychologist, or physiological psychologist). Investigates how functioning of the brain and other organs influences behavior.

- *Neuroscientist.* Studies the anatomy, biochemistry, and physiology of the nervous system.

- *Neuropsychologist.* Conducts behavioral tests on people with brain damage or brain diseases to determine what the person can and cannot do and to monitor improvement or deterioration over time. Most neuropsychologists work in hospitals and clinics and have a mixture of psychological and medical training.

- *Psychophysiologist.* Measures heart rate, breathing rate, brain waves, and other body processes that change as a function of what someone is doing or what kind of information the person is processing.

- *Comparative psychologist* (almost synonyms: ethologist, animal behaviorist). Compares the behaviors of different species and tries to relate them to evolutionary histories and ecological niches.

- *Sociobiologist* (almost synonym: evolutionary psychologist). Relates behaviors, especially social behaviors, to the functions they have served and, therefore, the presumed selective pressures that caused them to evolve.

The medical fields require a medical degree (MD) plus about 4 years of additional specialized study and practice. Most people with an MD work in hospitals and clinics; those who work in hospitals affiliated with a medical school also teach and conduct research.

The related medical specialties are:

- *Neurologist.* Treats people with brain damage or diseases of the brain.

- *Neurosurgeon.* Performs brain surgery.

- *Psychiatrist.* Helps people with emotional distress or troublesome behaviors, sometimes using drugs or other medical procedures.

If you pursue a career in research or medicine, you need to stay up to date on new developments by attending conventions, consulting with colleagues, and reading the primary research journals, such as *Journal of Neuroscience, Neurology, Behavioral Neuroscience, Brain Research,* and *Archives of General Psychiatry.* However, what if you are entering a field on the outskirts of biological psychology or neuroscience, such as clinical psychology, school psychology, social work, or physical therapy? In that case, you probably don't want to wade through the most technical journal articles, but you should want to stay current on major developments in neuroscience research. After all, our understanding of psychology is becoming increasingly biological, and at a minimum, you want to converse intelligently with medical colleagues.

It used to be that I had no good recommendations other than buying new editions of this textbook every time it is published (!) or reading *Scientific American, American Scientist,* or *The Sciences*—excellent publications on science for the nonspecialist, including some neuroscience and psychology along with all the other fields. Those are still good recommendations, but beginning in 1999, there is now a comparable periodical devoted exclusively to neuroscience for the nonspecialist. The title is *Cerebrum,* published by the Dana Press, 745 Fifth Avenue, Suite 700, New York, NY 10151. Their Web site is http://www.dana.org and their e-mail address is danainfo@dana.org.

Terms

altruistic behavior (p. 15)

artificial selection (p. 13)

autosomal gene (p. 10)

biological psychology (p. 2)

chromosome (p. 9)

crossing over (p. 10)

deoxyribonucleic acid (DNA) (p. 9)

dominant (p. 9)

dualism (p. 5)

easy problems (p. 6)

enzyme (p. 9)

evolution (p. 13)

evolutionary explanation (p. 3)

fitness (p. 15)

functional explanation (p. 4)

gene (p. 9)

hard problem (p. 6)

heritability (p. 11)

heterozygous (p. 9)

homozygous (p. 9)

identity position (p. 6)

kin selection (p. 16)

Lamarckian evolution (p. 14)

materialism (p. 5)

mentalism (p. 5)

mind-body or *mind-brain problem* (p. 5)

monism (p. 5)

mutation (p. 11)

ontogenetic explanation (p. 3)

phenylketonuria (PKU) (p. 12)

physiological explanation (p. 3)

problem of other minds (p. 6)

recessive (p. 9)

reciprocal altruism (p. 16)

recombination (p. 10)

ribonucleic acid (RNA) (p. 9)

sex-limited gene (p. 10)

sex-linked gene (p. 10)

sociobiology (p. 16)

solipsism (p. 6)

X chromosome (p. 10)

Y chromosome (p. 10)

Suggestions for Further Reading

Blum, D. (1994). *The monkey wars.* New York: Oxford University Press. Informative and evenhanded account of the disputes between animal researchers and animal rights activists.

Dennett, D. C. (1991). *Consciousness explained.* Boston: Little, Brown. Although Dennett may or may not have explained consciousness, he has dealt with the mind-brain issue in a deep and provocative manner.

Gazzaniga, M. S. (1998). *The mind's past.* Berkeley: University of California Press. A noted neuroscientist's attempt to explain the physical origins of consciousness. This book includes a number of fascinating examples.

Shear, J. (Ed.). (1997). *Explaining consciousness—The "hard problem."* Cambridge, MA: MIT Press. A collection of articles by philosophers, psychologists, biologists, and physicists attempting to understand the relationship between mind and brain.

Weiner, J. (1999). *Time, love, memory.* New York: Knopf. Description of research on behavior genetics written for a popular audience.

Web Sites to Explore[3]

You can go to the Biological Psychology Study Center and click on these links. While there, you can also check for suggested articles available on InfoTrac. The Biological Psychology Internet address is: **http://psychology.wadsworth.com/book/kalatbiopsych7e/**

Set a bookmark for this site because you will find recommendations like this at the end of each chapter.

[3] Web sites arise and disappear without warning. The suggestions listed in this book were available at the time the book went to press; I cannot guarantee how long they will last.

http://www.nsplus.com/nsplus/insight/big3/conscious/2a.html
A statement on the history and current status of the mind-brain question with links to many related topics, such as machine consciousness.

http://www.imprint.co.uk/
This site highlights the *Journal of Consciousness Studies* and related publications and meetings.

http://home/triad.rr.com/theatre/swampman.htm
What if lightning struck a tree and accidentally arranged its molecules into a perfect copy of you? Would it be you? Would it be conscious? Think about the question and then read this insightful commentary.

http://mcb.harvard.edu/BioLink.html
This site has links to many other sites concerning genetics, evolution, and other biological fields.

http://oacu.od.nih.gov/index.htm
Includes regulations and recommendations for the humane use of animals in research.

Active Learner Link

Quiz for Chapter 1

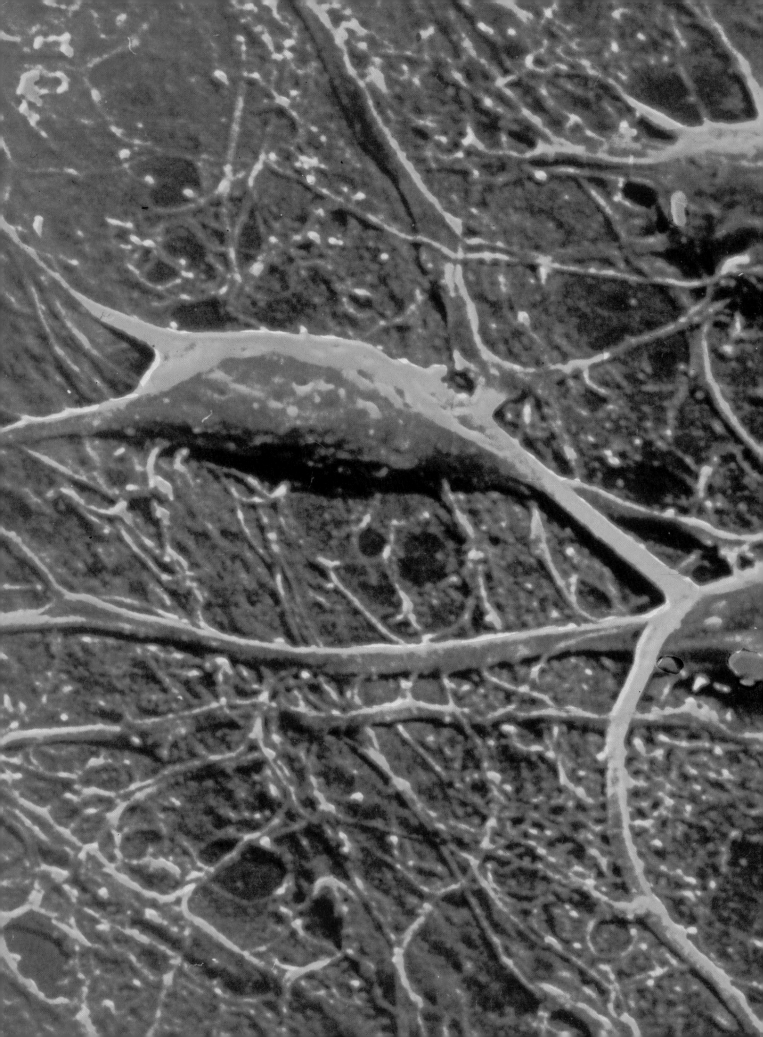

Nerve Cells and Nerve Impulses

2

Chapter Outline

Main Ideas

1. The nervous system is composed of two kinds of cells: neurons and glia. Only the neurons transmit impulses from one location to another.

2. A neuron has branches, known as axons and dendrites, which can increase or decrease their branching pattern as a function of experience, age, and chemical influences.

3. Many molecules in the bloodstream that can enter other body organs cannot enter the brain.

4. The action potential, an all-or-none change in the electrical potential across the membrane of a neuron, is caused by the sudden flow of sodium ions into the neuron and is followed by a flow of potassium ions out of the neuron.

5. Local neurons are small and do not have axons or action potentials. Instead, they convey information to nearby neurons by graded potentials.

A nervous system, composed of many individual cells, is in some regards like a society of people who work together and communicate with one another, or even like elements that form a chemical compound. In each case, the combination has properties and functions that are unlike those of its individual components. We begin our study of the nervous system by examining single cells; later, we try to understand the compounds of many cells acting together.

Advice: Parts of this chapter and the next require a knowledge of some basic chemical concepts such as *positively charged ions.* If you need to refresh your memory, read Appendix A.

Opposite:
An electron micrograph of neurons, magnified tens of thousands of times. The color is added artificially. For objects this small, it is impossible to focus light in order to obtain an image. It is possible to focus an electron beam, but electrons do not show color.

Module 2.1

The Cells of the Nervous System

Until the late 1800s, the best microscopic views of the nervous system revealed little detail about the organization of the brain. Without special staining techniques, the tiny cells, or *neurons,* of the brain are hard to distinguish from one another or from their background. Observers noted long, thin fibers between one neuron and another, but they could not determine whether each fiber stopped before the next cell or whether they actually merged. Then, in the late 1800s, Santiago Ramón y Cajal (see Digression 2.1) demonstrated that a single neuron does not merge with its neighbors. A small gap separates the tip of one neuron's fibers from the surface of the next neuron.

Philosophically, we can see the appeal of the once-popular concept that neurons merge. We each experience our consciousness as a single thing, not as the sum of separate parts. It seems right that all the cells in the brain should join together physically as one unit. Yet we now know that they do not. The adult human brain contains a great many neurons (Figure 2.1)—approximately 100 billion, according to one estimate (R. W. Williams & Herrup, 1988). (An accurate count would be more difficult than it is worth.) All those individual cells combine to produce unified experience and coordinated, organized behavior. Before we can begin to contemplate how they act together, we need to know a little about the properties of the individual cell.

Neurons and Glia

In Chapter 1, we examined some global issues, including the relationship between mind and brain and the evolution of behavior and consciousness. The global questions are difficult to answer, so researchers begin with smaller questions about the basic units of the nervous system and hope to build up to larger and larger issues.

The nervous system consists of two kinds of cells: neurons and glia. **Neurons** are cells that receive information and transmit it to other cells; they are what people usually mean when they refer to "nerve cells." Later, we examine the various types of glia and their functions. Because neurons resemble other body cells in many ways, we begin with the properties that all animal cells have in common.

The Structures of an Animal Cell

Figure 2.2 illustrates a neuron from the cerebellum of a mouse magnified × 23,000. It contains the same basic structures as most other animal cells, even though its size and shape are quite distinctive.

Every cell is surrounded by a **membrane** (often called a *plasma membrane*), a structure that separates the inside of the cell from the outside. It is composed of two layers of fat molecules that are free to flow around one another. (Figure 2.3 shows this arrangement in more detail.) Small uncharged chemicals, such as water, oxygen, and carbon dioxide, move rather freely across the membrane. A few charged ions, such as sodium, potassium, calcium, and chloride, can cross through specialized openings in the membrane called *protein channels.*

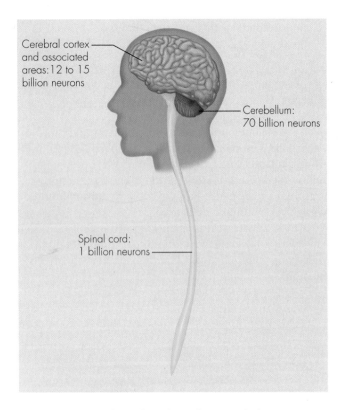

Figure 2.1 Estimated numbers of neurons in humans
Because of the small size of many neurons and the variation in cell density from one spot to another, obtaining an accurate count is difficult. *(Source: R. W. Williams & Herrup, 1988)*

Cerebral cortex and associated areas: 12 to 15 billion neurons

Cerebellum: 70 billion neurons

Spinal cord: 1 billion neurons

Santiago Ramón y Cajal

One of the major pioneers in the study of the nervous system—many rank him as the greatest of all—was the Spanish investigator Santiago Ramón y Cajal (1852–1934). Cajal's early career did not progress altogether smoothly. At one point, he was imprisoned in a solitary cell, limited to one meal a day, and taken out daily for public floggings . . . at the age of 10 . . . for the crime of not paying attention during his Latin class (Cajal, 1937). (And you thought *your* teachers were strict!)

Cajal wanted to become an artist, but his father, who believed he could never earn a living at art, insisted that he study medicine. Cajal managed to combine the two fields, becoming an outstanding anatomical researcher and illustrator.

His detailed drawings of the nervous system are still consulted today as a definitive source.

Before the late 1800s, microscopy could reveal few details about the nervous system. Then the Italian investigator Camillo Golgi discovered a method of using silver salts to stain nerve cells. For reasons unknown, this method completely stained some cells without affecting others at all. Consequently, it became possible to examine the structure of a single cell. Cajal used Golgi's methods but applied them to infant brains, in which the cells are smaller, more compact, and therefore easier to examine on a single slide. Cajal's research demonstrated the structure of nerve cells and the fact that they remain separate instead of merging into one another.

Most chemicals, however, cannot cross the membrane.

All animal cells (except red blood cells) have a **nucleus,** the structure that contains the chromosomes. A **mitochondrion** (pl.: mitochondria) is the structure where the cell performs metabolic activities, providing the energy that the cell requires for all its other activities. Mitochondria require fuel and oxygen to function. **Ribosomes** are the sites at which the cell synthesizes new protein molecules. Proteins provide building materials for the cell and facilitate various chemical reactions.

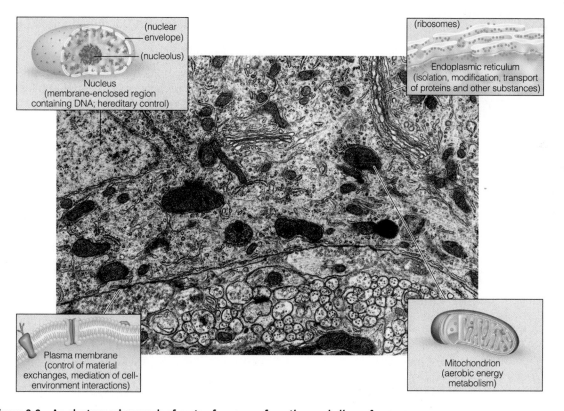

Figure 2.2 An electron micrograph of parts of a neuron from the cerebellum of a mouse
The nucleus, membrane, and other structures are characteristic of most animal cells. The plasma membrane is the border of the neuron. Magnification approximately × 23,000. (*Source: Micrograph courtesy of Dennis M. D. Landis*)

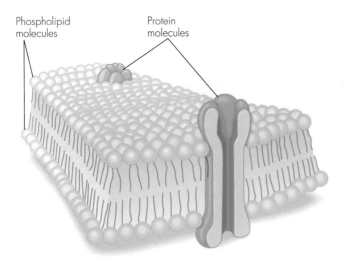

Figure 2.3   The membrane of a neuron
Embedded in the membrane are protein channels that permit certain ions to cross through the membrane at a controlled rate.

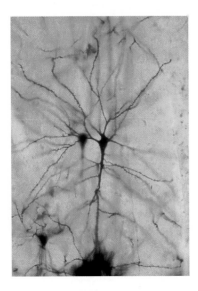

Figure 2.4   Neurons, stained to appear dark
Note the small fuzzy-looking spines on the dendrites.
(Source: Photo courtesy of Bob Jacobs, Colorado College)

Some ribosomes float freely within the cell; others are attached to the **endoplasmic reticulum,** a network of thin tubes that transport newly synthesized proteins to other locations.

The Structure of a Neuron

A neuron (Figure 2.4) contains a nucleus, a membrane, mitochondria, ribosomes, and the other structures typical of animal cells. The most distinctive structural feature of neurons is their shape.

Most neurons have these major components: dendrites, a cell body, an axon, and presynaptic terminals. For two examples, contrast the motor neuron in Figure 2.5 and the sensory neuron in Figure 2.6. A **motor neuron** receives excitation from other neurons and conducts impulses from its soma in the spinal cord to muscle or gland cells. Its dendrites enter the soma, and the axon exits from the soma. A **sensory neuron** is specialized at one end to be highly sensitive to a particular type of stimulation, such as touch information from the skin. Different kinds of sensory neurons have different structures; the one shown in Figure 2.6 is a neuron conducting touch information from the skin to the spinal cord. Its dendrites merge directly into the axon, and its soma is located on a little stalk off the main trunk.

The **dendrites** are branching fibers that get narrower as they extend from the cell body toward the periphery. (The term *dendrite* comes from a Greek root word meaning "tree"; a dendrite's shape resembles that of a tree.) The dendrites form the information-receiving pole of the neuron (Bodian, 1962). The dendrite's surface is lined with specialized *synaptic receptors,* at which the dendrite receives information from other neurons. (Chapter 3 focuses on the synapses.) The greater the surface area of a dendrite, the more information it can receive. Some dendrites branch widely and therefore have a large surface area. Some also contain **dendritic**

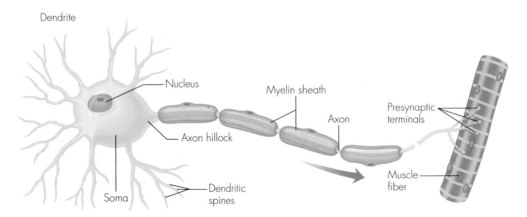

Figure 2.5   The components of a vertebrate motor neuron
The cell body of a motor neuron is located in the spinal cord. The various parts are not drawn to scale; in particular, a real axon is much longer in proportion to the size of the soma.

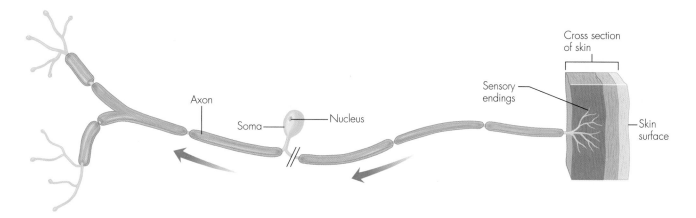

Figure 2.6 A vertebrate sensory neuron
Note that the soma is located on a stalk off the main trunk of the axon. (As in Figure 2.5, the various structures are not drawn to scale.)

spines, the short outgrowths that increase the surface area available for synapses (Figure 2.7).

The **cell body,** or **soma** (Greek for "body"; pl.: somata), contains the nucleus, ribosomes, mitochondria, and other structures found in most cells. Much of the metabolic work of the neuron occurs here. Cell bodies of neurons range in diameter from 0.005 mm to 0.1 mm in mammals and up to a full millimeter in certain invertebrates. Like the dendrites, the cell body is covered with synapses on its surface in many neurons.

The **axon** is a thin fiber of constant diameter, in most cases longer than the dendrites. (The term *axon*

comes from a Greek word meaning "axis.") The axon is the information-sender of the neuron, conveying an impulse toward either other neurons or a gland or muscle. Many vertebrate axons are covered with an insulating material called a **myelin sheath.** The axons of invertebrates do not have myelin sheaths.

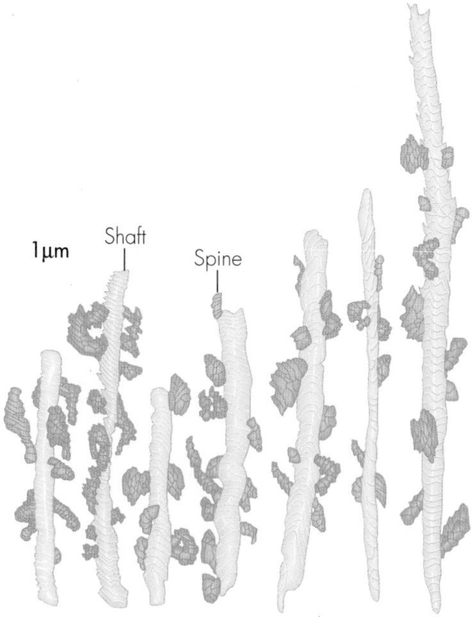

An axon has many branches, each of which swells at its tip, forming a **presynaptic terminal,** also known as a *bouton* or *end bulb*.[1] This is the point from which the axon releases chemicals that cross through the junction between one neuron and the next. Because synthesizing and using these chemicals require considerable energy, the presynaptic terminals have many mitochondria.

A neuron can have any number of dendrites, but it is limited to no more than one axon, which may have branches. (In most cases, branches break off from the trunk of the axon far from the cell body.) Some axons are amazingly long; for example, certain axons from your spinal cord extend all the way to your feet, a meter or so away. A **local neuron** is a small neuron with no axon or a very short one. It can convey information only to other neurons immediately adjacent to it.

Other terms associated with neurons are *afferent*, *efferent*, and *intrinsic*. An **afferent axon** brings information into a structure; an **efferent axon** carries information away from a structure. Every sensory neuron is an afferent to the rest of the nervous system; every motor neuron is an efferent from the nervous system. Within the nervous system, a given neuron is an efferent from the standpoint of one structure and an afferent from the standpoint of another. (Remember that *efferent* starts with *e*, as in *exit* from a room; *afferent* starts with *a*, as in *admission* to a room.) For example, an axon that is efferent from the thalamus may be

Figure 2.7 Dendritic spines
The dendrites of certain neurons are lined with spines, short outgrowths that receive specialized incoming information. That information apparently plays a key role in long-term changes in the neuron that mediate learning and memory. *(Source: K. M. Harris & Stevens, 1989)*

---

[1] Unfortunately, many structures in the nervous system have several names. As Candace Pert (1997, p. 64) has put it, "Scientists would rather use each other's toothbrushes than each other's terminology."

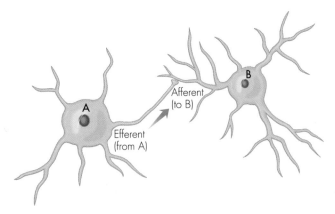

Figure 2.8   Cell structures and axons
It all depends on the point of view. An axon from A to B is an efferent axon from A and an afferent axon to B, just as a train from Washington to New York is exiting Washington and approaching New York.

afferent to the cerebral cortex (Figure 2.8). If a cell's dendrites and axon are entirely contained within a single structure, the cell is an interneuron or **intrinsic neuron** of that structure. For example, an intrinsic neuron of the thalamus has all its dendrites or axons within

the thalamus; it communicates only with other cells of the thalamus.

Variations Among Neurons

Neurons vary enormously in size, shape, and function. The shape of a given neuron determines its connections with other neurons and thereby determines how it contributes to the overall functioning of the nervous system. The wider the branching, the greater the number of possible connections with other neurons.

The function of a neuron is closely related to its shape (Figure 2.9). For example, the dendrites of the Purkinje cell of the cerebellum (Figure 2.9a) branch extremely widely within a single plane; this cell is capable of integrating an enormous amount of incoming information. The neurons in Figures 2.9c and 2.9e also have widely branching dendrites that receive and integrate information from many sources. By contrast, certain cells in the retina (Figure 2.9d) have only short branches of their dendrites and therefore pool input from only a few sources.

At one time, researchers believed that each neuron maintained its shape without change throughout life.

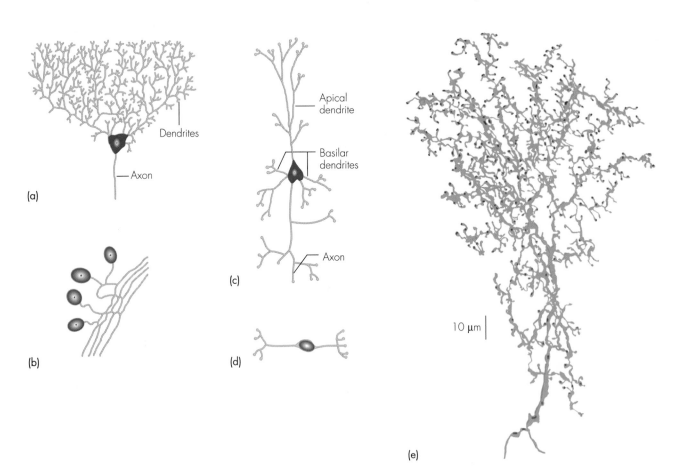

Figure 2.9   The diverse shapes of neurons
(**a**) Purkinje cell, a cell type found only in the cerebellum; (**b**) sensory neurons from skin to spinal cord; (**c**) pyramidal cell of the motor area of the cerebral cortex; (**d**) bipolar cell of retina of the eye; (**e**) Kenyon cell, from a honeybee. *(Source: Part (e) courtesy of R. G. Goss)*

We now know that new experiences modify a neuron's shape throughout life. Dale Purves and R. D. Hadley (1985) developed a method of injecting a dye that enabled them to examine the structure of a living neuron at different times, days to weeks apart. They demonstrated that some dendritic branches grow and extend, whereas others retract or disappear altogether (see Figure 2.10). Evidently, the anatomy of the brain is constantly plastic at the microscopic level.

Glia

Glia (or neuroglia), the other major components of the nervous system, do not transmit information over long distances as neurons do, although they exchange chemicals with adjacent neurons.

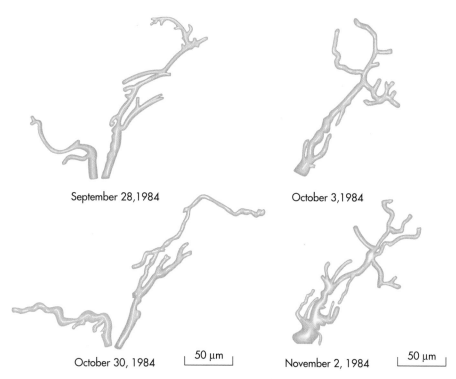

September 28, 1984

October 3, 1984

October 30, 1984 ⊢ 50 μm ⊣

November 2, 1984 ⊢ 50 μm ⊣

Figure 2.10   Changes over time in dendritic trees of two neurons
During a month, some branches elongated and others retracted. The shape of the neuron is in flux even during adulthood. *(Source: Purves & Hadley, 1985)*

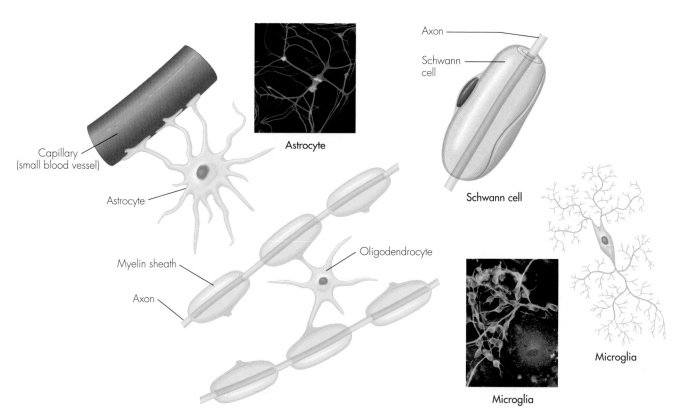

Capillary (small blood vessel)

Astrocyte

Astrocyte

Axon

Schwann cell

Schwann cell

Myelin sheath

Oligodendrocyte

Axon

Microglia

Microglia

Figure 2.11   Shapes of some glia cells
Oligodendrocytes produce myelin sheaths that insulate certain vertebrate axons in the central nervous system; Schwann cells have a similar function in the periphery. The oligodendrocyte is shown here forming a segment of myelin sheath for two axons; in fact, each oligodendrocyte forms such segments for 30 to 50 axons. Astrocytes pass chemicals back and forth between neurons and blood and among various neurons in an area. Microglia proliferate in areas of brain damage and remove toxic materials. Radial glia (not shown here) guide the migration of neurons during embryological development. Glia have other functions as well.

The term *glia,* derived from a Greek word meaning "glue," reflects early investigators' idea that glia were like glue that held the neurons together (Somjen, 1988). Although that concept is obsolete, the term remains. The average glia cell is about one-tenth the size of a neuron. However, because glia are about ten times more numerous than neurons in the human brain, they occupy about the same total space as the neurons (see Figure 2.11).

The functions of glia are numerous and not yet fully understood. One type of glia, the star-shaped glia called **astrocytes,** wrap around the presynaptic terminals of several axons, presumably a functionally related group, as shown in Figure 2.12. By taking up chemicals released by those axons and later releasing those chemicals back to the axons, an astrocyte helps synchronize the activity of the axons, enabling them to send messages in waves (Antanitus, 1998). Astrocytes also remove waste material, particularly that created when neurons die. **Oligodendrocytes** (OL-i-go-DEN-druh-sites) in the brain and spinal cord and **Schwann cells** in the periphery of the body are specialized types of glia that build the myelin sheaths that surround and insulate certain vertebrate axons. **Radial glia,** a type of astrocyte, guide the migration of neurons and the growth of their axons and dendrites during embryonic development. Schwann cells perform a related function after damage to axons in the periphery, guiding a regenerating axon to the appropriate target.

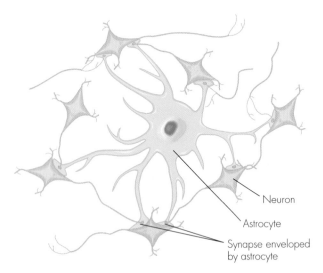

Figure 2.12   How an astrocyte can help synchronize associated axons
Branches of the astrocyte (in the center) surround the presynaptic terminals of several related axons. If a few of them are active at once, they release chemicals, some of which are absorbed by the astrocyte. The astrocyte then temporarily inhibits all the axons to which it is connected. When the inhibition ceases, all of the axons are primed to respond again in synchrony. *(Source: Based on Antanitus, 1998)*

Stop & Check

1. Identify the four major structures that compose a neuron.

2. Which kind of glia cell wraps around the synaptic terminals of axons?

Check your answers on page 36.

The Blood-Brain Barrier

Medical doctors sometimes find that a drug that they would like to administer cannot enter the brain. For example, certain chemotherapy drugs that fight cancer elsewhere in the body cannot get into the brain to attack brain cancers. Dopamine would be helpful in alleviating Parkinson's disease except that it is also unable to enter the brain. The mechanism that keeps most chemicals out of the vertebrate brain is known as the **blood-brain barrier.** Before we examine how it works, let us consider why we need it.

Why We Need a Blood-Brain Barrier

From time to time, viruses and other harmful substances enter the body. When a virus enters a cell, mechanisms within the cell extrude a virus particle through the cell membrane so that various cells of the immune system can find the virus. When the immune system cells attack the virus, they also kill the cell that contains it. In effect, the cell that exposes the virus through its membrane is committing suicide; it says, "Look, immune system, I'm infected with this virus. Kill me and save the others."

This plan works fine if the virus-infected cell is, say, a skin cell or a blood cell: The body can simply make a replacement. But the mature vertebrate brain does not easily replace damaged neurons. Some parts of the adult brain can make new neurons, but many do not, and no area can afford to lose many neurons. To minimize the risk, the body literally builds a wall along the sides of the brain's blood vessels. This wall keeps out most viruses, bacteria, and harmful chemicals.

"What happens if a virus does enter the brain?" you might ask. After all, certain viruses do break through the blood-brain barrier. The brain has ways to slow the reproduction of viruses (Levine et al., 1991) but not to kill them. Consequently, a virus that enters your nervous system probably remains with you for life. The herpes virus, for example, enters spinal-cord cells. No matter how much the immune system attacks the herpes virus outside the nervous system, virus particles remain in the spinal cord and can emerge years later to reinfect the rest of the body.

How the Blood-Brain Barrier Works

The blood-brain barrier (Figure 2.13) depends on the arrangement of endothelial cells that form the walls of the capillaries (Bundgaard, 1986; Rapoport & Robinson, 1986). In most parts of the body, such cells are separated by gaps large enough to allow the passage of large molecules. In the brain, the endothelial cells are joined so tightly that most molecules cannot pass between them.

Two categories of molecules can cross the blood-brain barrier passively (without the expenditure of energy): *small uncharged molecules,* such as oxygen and carbon dioxide, and *molecules that can dissolve in the fats of the capillary walls.* For example, most psychiatric drugs reach the brain because they dissolve in fats; so do many abused drugs, such as heroin, nicotine, and cannabinol (the active substance in marijuana). Heroin produces stronger effects on the brain than morphine does because heroin is more fat-soluble.

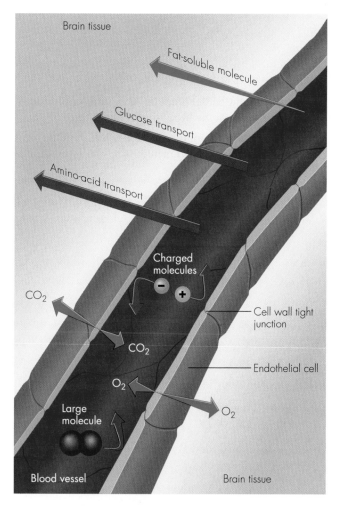

Figure 2.13 The blood-brain barrier
Most large molecules and electrically charged molecules cannot cross from the blood to the brain. A few small uncharged molecules such as O_2 and CO_2 can cross; so can certain fat-soluble molecules. Active transport systems pump glucose and certain amino acids across the membrane.

"If the blood-brain barrier is such a good defense," you might ask, "why don't we have similar walls around our other organs?" The answer is that the barrier that keeps out viruses also keeps out a number of useful chemicals, including most sources of nutrition. To get those chemicals into the brain requires an **active transport,** a protein-mediated process that expends energy to pump chemicals from the blood into the brain. Chemicals known to be actively transported into the brain include glucose (the brain's main fuel), amino acids (the building blocks of proteins), thiamine and other vitamins, and certain hormones (Brightman, 1997).

Stop & Check

3. What is one major advantage of having a blood-brain barrier?

4. What is a disadvantage of the blood-brain barrier?

5. Which chemicals cross the blood-brain barrier on their own?

6. Which chemicals cross the blood-brain barrier by active transport?

Check your answers on page 38.

The Nourishment of Vertebrate Neurons

Most cells use a wide variety of fuels, but vertebrate neurons depend heavily on **glucose,** a simple sugar, for their nutrition. (Cancer cells and the testis cells that make sperm also rely overwhelmingly on glucose.) The metabolic pathway that uses glucose requires oxygen; consequently, the neurons consume an enormous amount of oxygen compared with other body organs (Wong-Riley, 1989).

Why do neurons depend so heavily on glucose? Actually, they have the enzymes necessary to metabolize fats and several sugars. However, in most parts of the adult vertebrate nervous system, these other nutrients cannot cross the blood-brain barrier (Gjedde, 1984). When the blood-brain barrier is weak, as it is in infants, neurons can and do use other fuels. Also, at times of intense stimulation in a brain area, the neurons take one of the breakdown products of glucose metabolism, *lactate,* and metabolize it for further energy (Schurr, Miller, Payne, & Rigor, 1999).

Although neurons require glucose, a glucose shortage is rarely a problem. The liver can convert many carbohydrates, proteins, and fats into glucose, so almost any diet provides adequate glucose. An inability to *use* glucose can be a problem, however. Many chronic alcoholics have a diet deficient in vitamin B_1, **thiamine,** a chemical that is necessary for the use of glucose. Prolonged thiamine deficiency can lead to death of neurons and a condition called *Korsakoff's syndrome,* marked by severe memory impairments (Chapter 13).

In Closing: Neurons

What does the study of individual neurons tell us about behavior? Perhaps the main lesson is that our experience and behavior *do not* follow from the properties of any one neuron. Just as a chemist must know about atoms to make sense of compounds, a biological psychologist must know about cells to understand the nervous system. However, the nervous system is more than the sum of the individual cells, just as water is more than the sum of oxygen and hydrogen. Our behavior emerges from the communication among neurons.

Summary

1. In the late 1800s, Santiago Ramón y Cajal used newly discovered staining techniques to establish that the nervous system is composed of separate cells, now known as neurons. (p. 30)

2. Neurons receive information and convey it to other cells. The nervous system also contains *glia,* cells that serve many functions but do not transmit information over long distances. (pp. 30, 35)

3. Neurons have four major parts: a cell body, dendrites, an axon, and presynaptic terminals. Their shapes vary greatly depending on the function of the neuron and the connections that it makes with other cells. (p. 32)

4. Glia do not convey information over great distances, but they aid the functioning of neurons in many ways. (p. 35)

5. Because of the blood-brain barrier, many molecules, especially large ones, cannot enter the brain. (p. 36)

6. Adult neurons rely heavily on glucose, the only nutrient that can cross the blood-brain barrier. They need thiamine (vitamin B_1) to use glucose. (p. 37)

Answers to *Stop and Check* Questions

1. Dendrites, soma (cell body), axon, and presynaptic terminal (p. 36)

2. Astrocytes (p. 36)

3. The blood-brain barrier keeps out most viruses, bacteria, and other harmful substances. (p. 37)

4. The blood-brain barrier also keeps out most nutrients. (p. 37)

5. Small uncharged molecules and fat-soluble molecules can cross the blood-brain barrier. (p. 37)

6. Active transport enables glucose, amino acids, and certain vitamins and hormones to cross the blood-brain barrier. (p. 37)

The Nerve Impulse

Think about the axons that convey information from your feet's touch receptors toward your spinal cord and brain. If the axons could convey information by electrical conduction, they could transfer that information at the speed of light. However, given that your body is made of carbon compounds and not copper wire, the strength of the impulse would decay greatly on the way from your toes to your spinal cord and brain. You would experience a pinch on your shoulder much more strongly than a pinch on your abdomen, which in turn would feel much stronger than a pinch on your toes. Short people would feel toe pinches better than tall people could.

The way your axons actually function avoids these problems. Instead of simply conducting an electrical impulse, the axon regenerates an impulse at each point along the way, analogous to the way a burning string conveys a stimulus without loss of strength from its start to its finish. (Unlike a string, of course, an axon can transmit repeated impulses.)

Although the axon's method of transmitting an impulse prevents a pinch on your shoulder from feeling stronger than a pinch on your toes, it introduces a different problem: Because the axon transmits information at only a moderate speed (10–100 m/s), a pinch on your shoulder will reach your brain *sooner* than will a pinch on your toes. Now, if you get some friend to pinch you simultaneously on your shoulder and your toe, you probably will not notice that your brain received one stimulus before the other. In fact, if your friend pinches you *almost* simultaneously in two places, you probably will not be able to discern for sure which pinch came first. Your brain is not set up to register small differences in the time of arrival of touch messages. After all, why should it be? You almost never need to know whether a touch on one part of your body occurred slightly before or after a touch somewhere else.

In vision, however, your brain *does* need to know whether one stimulus began slightly before or after another one. If two adjacent spots on your retina—let's call them spots A and B—send impulses at almost the same time, an extremely small difference in timing of the impulses indicates whether a flash of light moved from A to B or from B to A. To detect movement as accurately as possible, your visual system compensates

for the fact that some parts of the retina are slightly closer to your brain than other parts are. Without some sort of compensation, simultaneous flashes arriving at two spots on your retina would reach your brain at different times, and you might perceive a flash of light moving from one spot to the other. What prevents that illusion is the fact that axons from more distant parts of your retina transmit impulses slightly faster than those closer to the brain (L. R. Stanford, 1987)!

In short, the properties of impulse conduction in an axon are well adapted to the exact needs for information transfer in the nervous system. Let us now examine the mechanics of impulse transmission in more detail.

The Resting Potential of the Neuron

The membrane of a neuron is specialized to control the exchange of chemicals between the inside and outside of the cell; it also maintains an electrical gradient necessary for neural signaling. All parts of a neuron are covered by a membrane about 8 nanometers (nm) thick (just less than 0.00001 mm), composed of two layers (an inner layer and an outer layer) of phospholipid molecules (molecules containing chains of fatty acids and a phosphate group). Embedded among the phospholipids are some cylindrical protein molecules (see Figure 2.3, p. 32). The structure of the membrane provides it with a good combination of flexibility and firmness and retards the flow of chemicals between the inside and the outside of the cell.

In the absence of any outside disturbance, the membrane maintains an electrical **polarization,** which means that the neuron inside the membrane has a slightly negative electrical potential with respect to the outside. In a resting neuron, this *electrical potential, or difference in voltage,* is called the **resting potential.**

The resting potential results from negatively charged proteins inside the cell and from the fact that positively charged sodium ions are more abundant outside than inside. The difference in distribution for various ions between the inside and outside of the membrane is called a **concentration gradient.** Sodium is more than ten times more concentrated outside the membrane than it is inside; potassium is more than twenty times more concentrated inside than outside (Guyton, 1974). However, because the body has far more total sodium ions than potassium ions, the concentration of sodium ions outside the membrane is far greater than the concentration of potassium ions inside the membrane. Thus, the outside of the cell is more positively charged and the inside more negatively charged.

Researchers can measure the resting potential by inserting a very thin *microelectrode* into the cell body, as Figure 2.14 shows. The diameter of the electrode must be as small as possible so that it can enter the cell without causing damage. By far the most common electrode is a fine glass tube filled with a concentrated salt solution and tapering to a tip diameter of 0.0005 mm or less. This electrode, inserted into the neuron, is connected to recording equipment. A reference electrode placed somewhere outside the cell completes the circuit. Connecting the electrodes to a voltmeter, we find that the neuron's interior has a negative potential relative to its exterior. The actual potential varies from one neuron to another; a typical level is -70 mV (millivolts), but can be less than -50 mV or as much as -90 mV.

The Forces Behind the Resting Potential

One mechanism that maintains the resting potential is the **selective permeability** of the neuron membrane, the ability of some molecules to pass much more freely through the membrane than others do. Oxygen, carbon dioxide, urea, and water cross in both directions at all times. Most larger or electrically charged ions and molecules cannot cross the membrane at all. However, a few biologically important ions, such as sodium, potassium, calcium, and chloride, cross through channels (or gates) in specialized proteins embedded in the membrane. Each of these ions travels through a different kind of channel, and the channels control the rate at which their ions pass. When the membrane is at rest, the potassium and chloride channels permit potassium and chloride ions to pass slowly, but the sodium channels are closed, preventing almost all sodium flow. These channels are shown in Figure 2.15. As we shall see later, certain kinds of stimulation can open the sodium channels.

What causes sodium ions to become so much more concentrated outside the neuron than inside it? The driving force is a protein complex called the **sodium-potassium pump,** which transports three sodium ions out of the cell while simultaneously drawing two potassium ions into the cell. Because both sodium and potassium ions carry a +1 electrical charge, the result is a net movement of positive ions out of the cell. The sodium-potassium pump is an active transport requiring energy.

The sodium-potassium pump is effective only because of the selective permeability of the membrane. Without the selective permeability, the sodium ions pumped out of the neuron would leak right back in again. As it is, the sodium ions pumped out stay out. However, some of the potassium ions pumped into the neuron do leak out, carrying a positive charge with them. That leakage increases the electrical gradient across the membrane, as shown in Figure 2.16.

The number of potassium ions inside the membrane reflects an equilibrium of competing forces. The concentration gradient for potassium tends to push potas-

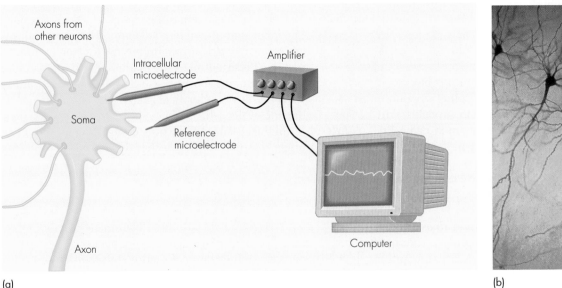
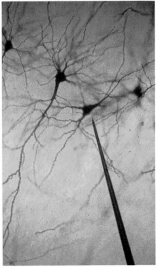

(a)

(b)

Figure 2.14 Methods for recording activity of a neuron
(**a**) Diagram of the apparatus and a sample recording. (**b**) A microelectrode and stained neurons magnified hundreds of times by a light microscope. *(Fritz Goro)*

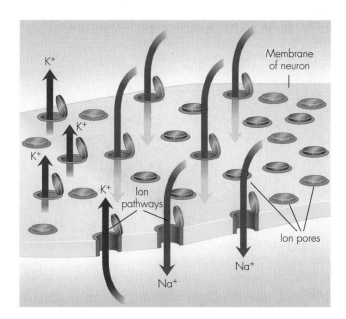

Figure 2.15 Ion channels in the membrane of a neuron
When a channel opens, it permits one kind of ion to cross the membrane. When it closes, it prevents passage of that ion.

sium out; that is, the numerous potassium ions inside the neuron are more likely to move out than the few potassium ions outside the neuron are likely to move in. However, the **electrical gradient,** the difference in positive and negative charges across the membrane, pushes potassium in the opposite direction: Because the inside of the cell is negatively charged in relation to the outside, potassium ions are attracted into the neuron. When the membrane is at rest, the concentration gradient and electrical gradient are almost in balance for potassium, but not exactly. If potassium could flow more freely, it would have a net flow outward.

In contrast, sodium tends to be driven into the neuron by both the concentration (more sodium outside, less inside) and the electrical gradient (positive charges more abundant outside than inside). Sodium ions remain mostly outside the cell because the sodium-potassium pump drives them out and because the sodium gates are so tightly closed.

Why a Resting Potential?

Presumably, evolution could have equipped us with neurons that

were electrically neutral at rest. The resting potential must provide enough benefit to justify the energy cost of the sodium-potassium pump. The advantage is that the resting potential prepares the neuron to respond rapidly to a stimulus. As we shall see in the next section, excitation of the neuron opens the sodium channels, enabling sodium to enter the cell explosively. Because the membrane did its work in advance by maintaining the concentration gradient for sodium, the cell is prepared to respond strongly and rapidly to a stimulus.

The resting potential of a neuron can be compared to a poised bow and arrow: An archer who pulls the bow in advance and then waits is ready to fire as soon as the appropriate moment comes. Evolution has applied the same strategy to the neuron.

Stop & Check

1. When the membrane is at rest, are the sodium ions more concentrated inside the cell or outside? Where are the potassium ions more concentrated?

2. When the membrane is at rest, what tends to drive the potassium ions out of the cell? What tends to draw them into the cell?

Check your answers on page 48.

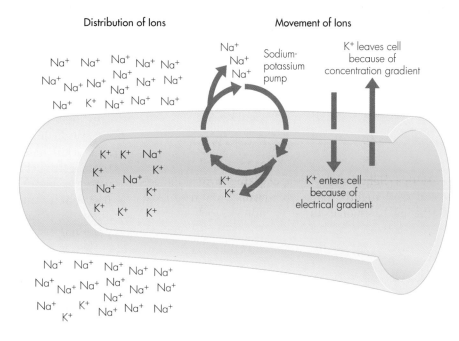

Figure 2.16 The sodium and potassium gradients for a resting membrane
Sodium ions are more concentrated outside the neuron; potassium ions are more concentrated inside. However, because the body has far more sodium than potassium, the total number of positive charges is greater outside the cell than inside. Protein and chloride ions (not shown) bear negative charges inside the cell. At rest, very few sodium ions cross the membrane except by the sodium-potassium pump. Potassium tends to flow into the cell because of an electrical gradient but tends to flow out because of the concentration gradient.

The Action Potential

The resting potential remains stable until the neuron is stimulated. Ordinarily, stimulation of the neuron takes place at synapses, which we consider in Chapter 3. In the laboratory, it is also possible to stimulate a neuron by inserting an electrode into it and applying current.

We can measure a neuron's potential with a micro-electrode, as shown in Figure 2.14b. When an axon's membrane is at rest, the recordings show a steady negative potential inside the axon. If we now use an additional electrode to apply a negative charge, we can further increase the negative charge inside the neuron. The change is called **hyperpolarization,** which means increased polarization. As soon as the artificial stimulation ceases, the charge returns to its original resting level. The recording looks like this:

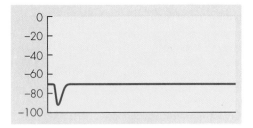

Now, let us apply a current for a slight **depolarization** of the neuron—that is, reduction of its polarization toward zero. If we apply a small depolarizing current, we get a result like this:

With a slightly stronger depolarizing current, the potential rises slightly higher, but again it returns to the resting level as soon as the stimulation ceases:

Now let us see what happens when we apply a still stronger current: Any stimulation beyond a certain level, called the **threshold of excitation,** produces a sudden, massive depolarization of the membrane. When the potential reaches the threshold, the membrane suddenly opens its sodium channels and permits a rapid, massive flow of ions across the membrane. The

potential then shoots up far beyond the strength of the stimulus:

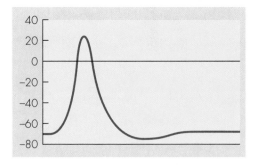

Any *subthreshold* stimulation produces a small response proportional to the amount of current. Any stimulation beyond the threshold, regardless of how far beyond, produces the same response, such as the one just shown. That response, a rapid depolarization and slight reversal of the usual polarization, is referred to as an **action potential.**

Stop & Check

3. What is the difference between a hyperpolarization and a depolarization?

4. What is the relationship between the threshold and an action potential?

Check your answers on page 48.

The Molecular Basis of the Action Potential

Remember that the sodium concentration is much higher outside the neuron than inside. In addition to this concentration gradient, sodium ions are attracted to the inside of the neuron by an electrical gradient because of the negative charge inside the neuron. If sodium ions were free to flow across the membrane, they would diffuse rapidly into the cell. Ordinarily, the membrane is almost impermeable to sodium, but during the action potential, its permeability increases sharply.

The membrane proteins that control sodium entry are **voltage-activated channels,** which are membrane channels whose permeability to sodium (or some other ion) depends on the voltage difference across the membrane. At the resting potential, the channels are closed. As the membrane becomes even slightly depolarized, the sodium channels begin to open and sodium flows more freely. If the depolarization is less than the threshold, sodium crosses the membrane only slightly more than usual. However, when the potential across the membrane reaches threshold, the sodium channels open wide enough to let sodium enter the cell rapidly. The entering sodium ions depolarize the cell still further, opening the sodium channels even wider. Sodium ions rush into the neuron explosively until the electrical potential across the membrane passes beyond zero to a reversed polarity, as shown in the following diagram:

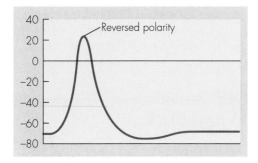

Compared to the total number of sodium ions in and around the axon, only a tiny percentage cross the membrane during an action potential. Even at the peak of the action potential, sodium ions continue to be far more concentrated outside the neuron than inside. An action potential increases the sodium concentration inside a neuron by less than 1% in most cases. Because of the persisting concentration gradient, sodium ions should still tend to diffuse into the cell. However, at the peak of the action potential, the sodium gates snap shut and cannot be opened again, even by a strong stimulation, for at least the next millisecond (ms) or so.

After the peak of the action potential, what brings the membrane back to its original state of polarization? The answer is *not* the sodium-potassium pump, which is simply too slow for this purpose. After the action potential is well underway, the potassium channels open and potassium ions flow out of the axon, carrying with them a positive charge (C. U. M. Smith, 1996). Potassium ions leave the axon simply because they are much more concentrated inside than outside and because they are no longer held inside by a negative charge. Because the potassium channels open wider than usual, enough potassium ions leave to drive the potential a bit beyond the normal resting level to a temporary hyperpolarization. Figure 2.17 summarizes the movements of ions during an action potential.

At the end of this process, the membrane has returned to its resting potential and everything is back to normal, except that the inside of the neuron has slightly more sodium ions and slightly fewer potassium ions than before. Eventually, the sodium-potassium pump restores the original distribution of ions, but that process takes time. In fact, if a series of action potentials occurs at a sufficiently rapid rate, the pump cannot keep up with the action, and sodium may begin to accumulate within the axon. If it accumulates long enough, the axon "fatigues" and stops firing action potentials. (Ordinarily, the synapses—discussed in Chapter 3—fatigue faster than the axon, so we seldom face a threat of excess sodium within the axon.)

For the neuron to function properly, sodium and potassium must flow across the membrane at just the right pace. Scorpion venom attacks the nervous system by keeping sodium channels open and closing potassium channels (Pappone & Cahalan, 1987; Strichartz, Rando, & Wang, 1987). As a result, the membrane goes into a prolonged depolarization that makes it useless for conveying information. **Local anesthetic** drugs, such as Novocain and Xylocaine, attach to the sodium channels of the membrane, preventing sodium ions from entering (Ragsdale, McPhee, Scheuer, & Catterall, 1994). In doing so, such drugs block action potentials in the affected area. If anesthetics are applied to sensory nerves carrying pain messages, they prevent the messages from reaching the brain. **General anesthetics**, such as ether and chloroform, decrease brain activity by opening certain potassium channels wider than usual (Patel et al., 1999). With the potassium channels wide

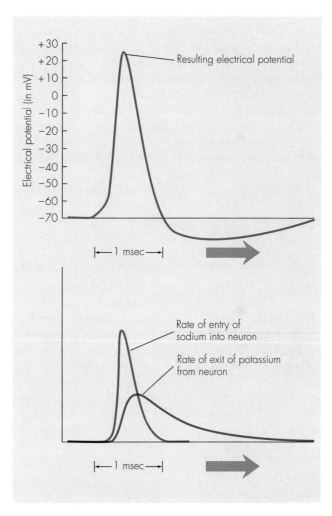

Figure 2.17 The movement of sodium and potassium ions during an action potential
Note that sodium ions cross during the peak of the action potential and that potassium ions cross later in the opposite direction, returning the membrane to its original polarization.

open, as soon as any stimulus starts to excite a neuron by opening sodium channels, potassium ions exit about as fast as the sodium ions enter, preventing most action potentials.

Stop & Check

5. During the rise of the action potential, do sodium ions move into the cell or out of it? Why?

6. As the membrane reaches the peak of the action potential, what ionic movement brings the potential down to the original resting potential?

Check your answers on page 48.

The All-or-None Law

Action potentials occur in axons, and they depend on the fact that axons have voltage-dependent sodium channels. That is, when the voltage reaches a certain level of depolarization (the threshold), these sodium channels open wide to let sodium enter rapidly, and the incoming sodium depolarizes the membrane still further. Dendrites and cell bodies can be depolarized, but they don't have the voltage-dependent sodium channels, so opening the channels a little, letting in a little sodium, doesn't cause them to open even more and let in still more sodium. Thus, dendrites and cell bodies don't produce action potentials.

Within a given axon, all action potentials are approximately equal in size, shape (amplitude), and velocity under normal circumstances. This is the **all-or-none law:** The size, amplitude, and velocity of an action potential are independent of the intensity of the stimulus that initiated it. By analogy, think about flushing a toilet: You have to make a press of at least a certain strength (the threshold), but pressing even harder does not make the toilet flush any faster or more vigorously.

As a consequence of this law, a neuron's messages are analogous to flicking a light on and off as a signal: The message is conveyed by the time sequence of impulses and pauses. For instance, an axon might signal "weak stimulus" by a low frequency of action potentials per second and "stronger stimulus" by a higher frequency.

The Refractory Period

While the electrical potential across the membrane is returning from its peak toward the resting point, it is still above the threshold. Why does the cell not produce another action potential during this period? Immediately after an action potential, the cell is in a **refractory period** during which it resists the production of further action potentials. In the first part of this period, the **absolute refractory period,** the sodium gates are firmly closed and the membrane cannot produce an action potential, regardless of the stimulation. During the second part, the **relative refractory period,** the sodium gates are reverting to their usual state, but the potassium gates remain open. Because of the free flow of potassium, a stronger than usual stimulus is necessary to initiate an action potential. Most of the axons that have been tested have an absolute refractory period of about 1 ms and a relative refractory period of another 2–4 ms.

Stop & Check

7. State the all-or-none law.

8. Does the all-or-none law apply to dendrites, somas, axons, or all three?

9. Suppose researchers find that axon A can produce up to 1000 action potentials per second (at least briefly, with maximum stimulation), but axon B can never produce more than 200 per second (regardless of the strength of the stimulus). What could we conclude about the refractory periods of the two axons?

Check your answers on page 48.

Propagation of the Action Potential

Up to this point, we have dealt with the action potential at one location on the axon. Now let us consider how it moves down the axon toward some other cell. Remember that it is important for axons to convey impulses without any loss of strength over distance.

In a motor neuron, an action potential begins on the **axon hillock,** a swelling where the axon exits the soma (Figure 2.5, p. 32). Each point along the membrane regenerates the action potential in much the same way that it was generated initially. During the action potential, sodium ions enter a point on the axon. Temporarily, that location is positively charged in comparison with neighboring areas along the axon. The positive ions flow down the axon and across the membrane, as shown in Figure 2.18. Other things being equal, the greater the diameter of the axon, the faster the ions flow (because of decreased resistance).

As sodium ions move down the axon, they slightly depolarize the adjacent areas of the membrane. The next area of the membrane is depolarized enough to reach its threshold and regenerate the action potential. In this manner, the action potential passes like a wave along the axon.

The term **propagation of the action potential** describes the transmission of an action potential down an axon. The propagation of an animal species is the production of babies; in a sense, the action potential gives birth to a new action potential at each point along the

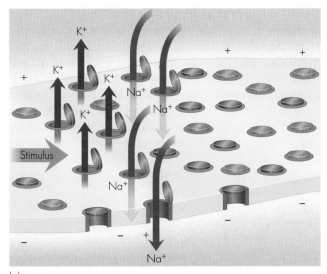

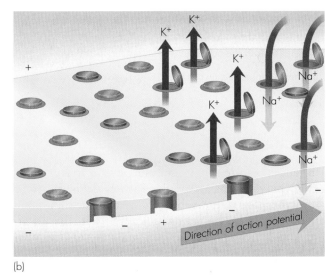

Figure 2.18
Current that enters an axon at the point of the action potential flows down the axon, thereby depolarizing adjacent areas of the membrane. The current flows more easily through relatively thick axons. Behind the area of sodium entry, potassium ions exit.

axon. In this manner, the action potential can be just as strong at the end of the axon as it was at the beginning. The action potential is much slower than electrical conduction because it requires the diffusion of sodium ions at successive points along the axon. Electrical conduction in a copper wire with free electrons travels at the speed of light, 300 million meters per second (m/s). In an axon, transmission relies on the flow of charged ions through a water medium. In thin axons, action potentials travel at a velocity of less than 1 m/s. In the thickest unmyelinated axons, action potentials reach a velocity of about 10 m/s. In axons surrounded by myelin, which we discuss in the next section, the velocity can be still greater.

Let us reexamine Figure 2.18 for a moment. What is to prevent the electrical charge from flowing in the di-

rection opposite that in which the action potential is traveling? Nothing. In fact, the electrical charge does flow in both directions. In that case, what prevents an action potential near the center of an axon from reinvading the areas that it has just passed? The answer is that the areas just passed are still in their refractory period.

The Myelin Sheath and Saltatory Conduction

As just noted, the maximum velocity of action potentials in the thickest unmyelinated axons of vertebrates is about 10 m/s. At that speed, an impulse from a giraffe's foot takes about 0.5 second to reach its brain. At the slower speeds of thinner unmyelinated axons, a giraffe's brain could be seconds out of date on what was happening to its feet. Myelin sheaths increase speed to facilitate quick, coordinated responses to stimuli.

Consider the following analogy. Suppose it is my job to carry written messages over a distance of 3 kilometers (km) without using any mechanical device. Taking each message and running with it would be analogous to the propagation of the action potential along an unmyelinated axon: They get the job done, but not very rapidly. I could try tying each message to a ball and throwing it, but I cannot throw a ball even close to 3 km. The ideal compromise is to station people at moderate distances along the 3 km and throw the message-bearing ball from person to person until it reaches its destination.

The principle behind **myelinated axons,** those covered with a myelin sheath, is the same. Myelinated axons, found only in vertebrates, are covered with a coating composed mostly of fats. The myelin sheath is interrupted at intervals of approximately 1 mm by short unmyelinated sections of axon called **nodes of Ranvier** (RAHN-vee-ay), as shown in Figure 2.19. Each node is only about 1 micrometer wide.

Suppose that an action potential is initiated at the axon hillock and propagated along the axon until it reaches the first myelin segment. The action potential cannot regenerate along the membrane between nodes because sodium channels are virtually absent in the areas between nodes (Catterall, 1984). After an action potential occurs at a node, sodium ions that enter the axon diffuse in both directions within the axon, repelling positive ions that were already present and thus pushing a chain of positive ions along the axon to the next node, where they regenerate the action potential (see Figure 2.20). This flow of ions is considerably faster than the regeneration of an action potential at each point along the axon; consequently, the transmission of impulses is faster in myelinated axons than in axons without myelin—in some cases, as fast as 120 m/s. The jumping of action potentials from node to node is referred to as **saltatory conduction,** from the Latin word *saltare,*

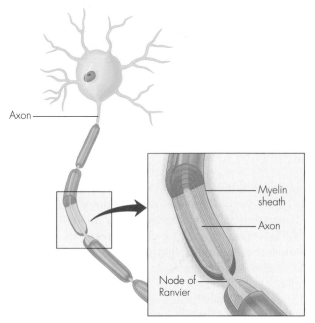

Axon

Myelin sheath

Axon

Node of Ranvier

Cutaway view of axon wrapped in myelin

Figure 2.19   An axon surrounded by a myelin sheath and interrupted by nodes of Ranvier
The inset shows a cross section through both the axon and the myelin sheath. Magnification approximately × 30,000. The anatomy is distorted here to show several nodes; in fact, the distance between nodes is generally about 100 times as large as the nodes themselves.

meaning "to jump." (The same root shows up in the word *somersault*.) In addition to providing very rapid conduction of impulses, saltatory conduction has the added benefit of conserving energy: Instead of admitting sodium ions at every point along the axon and then having to pump them out via the sodium-potassium

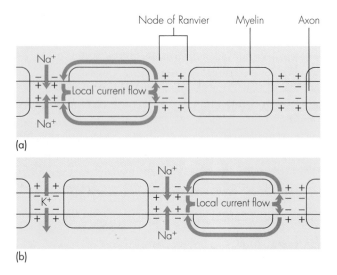

Node of Ranvier   Myelin   Axon

Na⁺

Local current flow

Na⁺

(a)

Na⁺

K⁺

Local current flow

Na⁺

(b)

Figure 2.20   Saltatory conduction in a myelinated axon
An action potential at the node triggers flow of current to the next node, where the membrane regenerates the action potential.

pump, a myelinated axon admits sodium only at its nodes.

Some diseases, including multiple sclerosis, destroy myelin sheaths, thereby slowing down action potentials or stopping them altogether. An axon that has lost its myelin is not the same as one that has never had any myelin. A myelinated axon develops sodium channels almost exclusively at the nodes (Waxman & Ritchie, 1985). After the axon loses its myelin, it still lacks sodium channels in the areas previously covered with myelin. Therefore, depolarization of the unmyelinated areas of axon does not produce an action potential.

Stop & Check

10. Distinguish between the absolute refractory period and the relative refractory period.

11. In a myelinated axon, how would the action potential be affected if the nodes were much closer together? How might it be affected if the nodes were much farther apart?

Check your answers on page 48.

Signaling Without Action Potentials

Unlike axons, dendrites and somata do not produce action potentials; they produce small depolarizations and hyperpolarizations, depending on the stimulation affecting them. The action potential, with its all-or-none law, starts at the beginning of the axon. The depolarizations and hyperpolarizations of the dendrites and soma do not follow the all-or-none law, but decay as they travel.

Small local neurons also do not produce action potentials because they have no axon and cannot transmit information to more distant cells. A local neuron receives information from other neurons in its immediate vicinity and produces **graded potentials,** membrane potentials that vary in magnitude and do not follow the all-or-none law. When a local neuron is stimulated, it depolarizes or hyperpolarizes in proportion to the intensity of the stimulus. The change in membrane potential is conducted to adjacent areas of the cell, gradually decaying as it travels.

Local neurons are somewhat difficult to study; it is difficult to insert an electrode into such a small cell without damaging it. A disproportionate amount of our knowledge, therefore, has come from large neurons (see Digression 2.2). A large neuron with a long axon is specialized to transmit messages over long distances, such as from the spinal cord to the muscles or from one part of the brain to another. Its dendrites receive information at one end of the cell, and its axon transmits information to a target at the other end. Local neurons do not have such a polarity between one end and the other; they can receive information at various points along their membrane and transmit it in either direction. In Chapter 6, we discuss in some detail a particular local neuron, the *horizontal cell*.

Module 2.2

In Closing: Neural Messages

In this chapter, we have examined what happens within a single neuron, as if each neuron acted independently. It does not, of course; all of its functions depend on communication with other neurons, as we consider in the next chapter. We may as well admit from the start, however, that neural communication is pretty amazing. Unlike human communication, in which a speaker sometimes presents a complicated message to an enormous audience, a neuron delivers only an action potential—a mere on/off message—to only that modest number of other neurons that receive branches of its axon. At various receiving neurons, an "on" message can be converted into either excitation or inhibition (yes/no). From this limited system, all of our behavior and experience emerge.

Summary

1. The inside of a resting neuron has a negative charge with respect to the outside. Sodium ions are actively pumped out of the neuron, and potassium ions are pumped in. Potassium ions are moderately free to flow across the membrane of the neuron, but the flow of sodium ions is greatly restricted. (p. 39)

2. When the charge across the membrane is reduced, sodium ions can flow more freely across the membrane. When the change in membrane potential is sufficient to reach the threshold of the neuron, sodium ions enter explosively, and the charge across the membrane is suddenly reduced and reversed. This event is known as the action potential. (p. 42)

3. The magnitude of the action potential is independent of the size of the stimulus that initiated it; this statement is the all-or-none law. (p. 44)

4. Immediately after an action potential, the membrane enters a refractory period during which it is resistant to starting another action potential. (p. 44)

5. The action potential is regenerated at successive points along the axon by sodium ions flowing through the core of the axon and then across the membrane. The action potential maintains a constant magnitude as it passes along the axon. (p. 44)

6. In axons that are covered with myelin, action potentials form only in the nodes between myelinated segments. Between the nodes, ions flow faster than through axons without myelin. (p. 45)

7. Many small local neurons transmit messages over relatively short distances by graded potentials that decay over time and space instead of by action potentials. (p. 46)

Answers to *Stop and Check* Questions

1. Sodium ions are more concentrated outside the cell; potassium is more concentrated inside. (p. 41)

2. When the membrane is at rest, the concentration gradient tends to drive potassium ions out of the cell; the electrical gradient draws them into the cell. The sodium-potassium pump also draws them into the cell. (p. 41)

3. A hyperpolarization is an exaggeration of the usual negative charge within a cell (to a more negative level than usual). A depolarization is a decrease in the amount of negative charge within the cell. (p. 42)

4. A depolarization that passes the threshold produces an action potential. One that falls short of the threshold does not produce an action potential. (p. 42)

5. During the action potential, sodium ions move into the cell. The voltage-dependent sodium gates have opened, so sodium can move freely. Sodium is attracted to the inside of the cell by both an electrical and a concentration gradient. (p. 44)

6. After the peak of the action potential, potassium ions exit the cell, driving the membrane back to the resting potential. (The sodium-potassium pump is not the answer here; it is too slow.) (p. 44)

7. According to the all-or-none law, the size and shape of the action potential are independent of the intensity of the stimulus that initiated it. That is, every depolarization beyond the threshold of excitation produces an action potential of about the same amplitude and velocity for a given axon. (p. 44)

8. The all-or-none law applies only to axons because only axons have action potentials. (p. 44)

9. Axon A must have a shorter absolute refractory period, about 1 ms, whereas B has a longer absolute refractory period, about 5 ms. (p. 44)

10. During the absolute refractory period, the sodium gates are locked and no amount of stimulation can produce another action potential. During the relative refractory period, a stronger than usual amount of stimulation is needed to produce an action potential. (p. 46)

11. If the nodes were closer, the action potential would travel more slowly. If they were much farther apart, the current might not be able to diffuse from one node to the next and still remain above threshold, so the action potentials might stop. (p. 46)

Thought Questions

1. Suppose that the threshold of a neuron were the same as the neuron's resting potential. What would happen? At what frequency would the cell produce action potentials?

2. In the laboratory, researchers can apply an electrical stimulus at any point along the axon, making action potentials travel in both directions from the point of stimulation. An action potential moving in the usual direction, away from the axon hillock, is said to be traveling in the *orthodromic* direction. An action potential traveling toward the axon hillock is traveling in the *antidromic* direction. If we started an orthodromic action potential at the axon hillock and an antidromic action potential at the opposite end of the axon, what would happen when they met at the center? Why? What research might make use of antidromic impulses?

3. If a drug partly blocks a membrane's potassium channels, how does it affect the action potential?

Chapter Ending
Key Terms and Activities

Terms

absolute refractory period (p. 44)

action potential (p. 42)

active transport (p. 37)

afferent axon (p. 33)

all-or-none law (p. 44)

astrocyte (p. 36)

axon (p. 33)

axon hillock (p. 44)

blood-brain barrier (p. 36)

cell body or *soma* (p. 33)

concentration gradient (p. 39)

dendrite (p. 32)

dendritic spine (p. 32)

depolarization (p. 42)

Suggestions for Further Reading

Kimelberg, H. K., & Norenberg, M. D. (1989, April). Astrocytes. *Scientific American, 260*(4), 66–76. An overview of the functions of glia.

Smith, C. U. M. (1996). *Elements of molecular neurobiology* (2nd ed.). New York: Wiley. A detailed treatment of the molecular biology of neurons, including both action potentials and synaptic activity.

Web Site to Explore

You can go to the Biological Psychology Study Center and click on this link. While there, you can also check for suggested articles available on InfoTrac. The Biological Psychology Internet address is: **http://psychology.wadsworth.com/book/kalatbiopsych7e/**

http://faculty.washington.edu/chudler/ap.html
A good, simple review of the basics about resting potentials and action potentials.

Active Learner Link

Animation: The Neuron and Neural Impulse
Quiz for Chapter 2

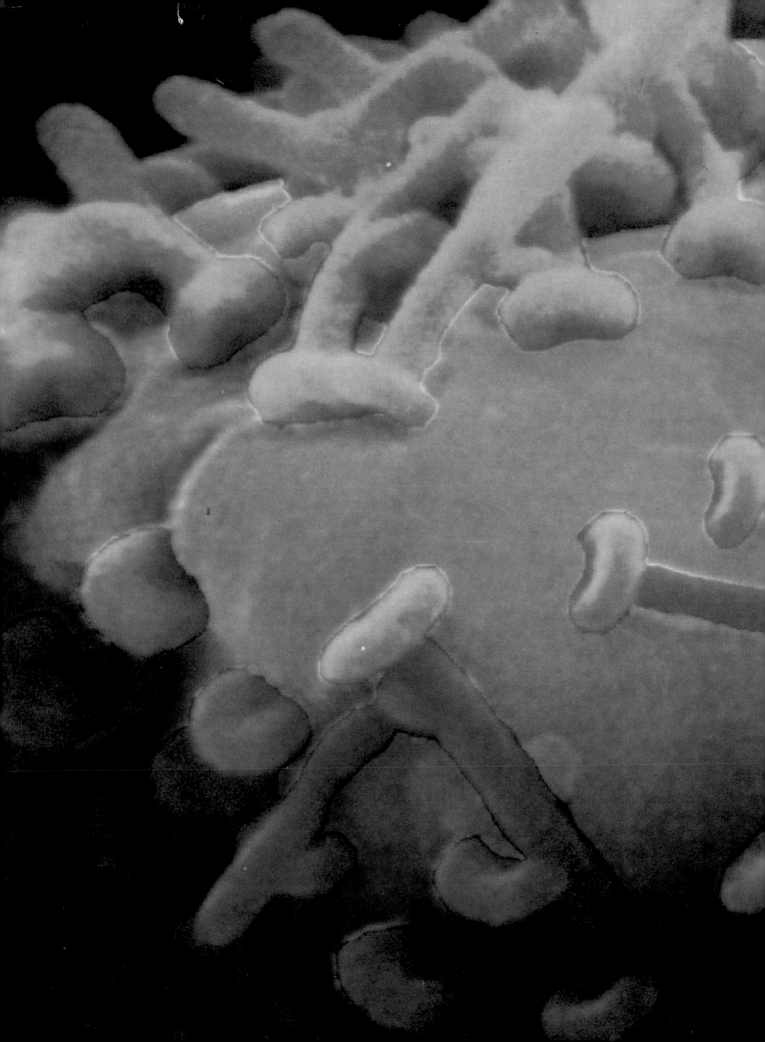

Communication Within the Body: Synapses and Hormones

Chapter Outline

Opposite:
This electron micrograph, with color added artificially, shows that the surface of a neuron is practically covered with synapses, the connections it receives from other neurons.

Main Ideas

1. At a synapse a neuron releases a chemical known as a neurotransmitter that excites or inhibits another cell.

2. A single release of neurotransmitter produces only a subthreshold response in the receiving cell. This response summates with other subthreshold responses to determine whether or not the cell produces an action potential.

3. Because different neurotransmitters contribute to behavior in different ways, many behavioral abnormalities can be traced to excessive or deficient transmission at a particular type of synapse.

4. Many of the drugs that affect behavior and experience do so by altering activity at synapses.

5. Hormones affect behavior either by attaching to receptors on the membrane of a cell or by altering the expression of the genes.

If you had to communicate with someone and you were not allowed to use speech or any other auditory information, what would you do? Chances are, your first choice would be a visual code, such as sign language or written words. If that failed, you might try some sort of touch code or a system of electrical impulses. You might not even think of communicating by passing chemicals back and forth. Chemical communication is, however, the primary method of communication for the neurons in your nervous system. Considering how well the human nervous system works, chemical communication is evidently a more versatile system than we might have guessed. Neurons communicate by transmitting chemicals at specialized junctions called *synapses*. The synapses are central to all comparison and integration of information in the brain.

The Concept of the Synapse

In the late 1800s Ramón y Cajal demonstrated that neurons do not physically merge into one another and that a narrow gap separates one from the next. As far as anyone knew, information might be transmitted across the gap in the same way that it was transmitted along an axon.

Then in 1906 Charles Scott Sherrington inferred that a specialized type of communication occurs at the gap between two neurons, which he labeled the **synapse.** Sherrington also deduced most of the major properties of the synapse. What makes his accomplishment particularly impressive is that he based his conclusions almost entirely on behavioral data. Decades later, when investigators developed techniques for measuring and recording neural processes, most of Sherrington's predictions turned out to be correct.

The Properties of Synapses

Sherrington conducted most of his experiments on **reflexes,** automatic responses to stimuli. In a leg flexion reflex, a sensory neuron excites a second neuron, which in turn excites a motor neuron, which excites a muscle, as Figure 3.1 shows. The circuit from sensory neuron to muscle response is called a **reflex arc.** Because a reflex depends on communication from one neuron to another—not just on the transmission of action potentials along an axon—Sherrington reasoned that the properties of a reflex might reveal some of the special properties of synapses.

In a typical experiment a dog was strapped into a harness suspended above the ground. Sherrington pinched one of the dog's feet; after a short delay the dog *flexed* (raised) the pinched leg and *extended* the others. Both the flexion and the extension were reflexive movements—automatic reactions to the stimulus. Furthermore Sherrington found the same movements after he made a cut that disconnected the spinal cord from the brain; evidently the flexion and extension were controlled by the spinal cord itself. In an intact animal the brain could modify the reflexive movements, but it was not necessary for their occurrence.

Sherrington observed several properties of reflexes suggesting that some special process must occur at the junctions between neurons: (1) Reflexes are slower than conduction along an axon; consequently, there must be some delay at the synapses. (2) Several weak stimuli presented at slightly different times or slightly different locations produce a stronger reflex than a single stimulus does. Therefore the synapse must be able to *summate* different stimuli. (3) When one set of muscles becomes excited, a different set becomes relaxed. Apparently, synapses are connected so that the excitation of one leads to a decreased excitation, or even an inhibition, of others. We consider each of these points in some detail.

Speed of a Reflex and Delayed Transmission at the Synapse

When Sherrington pinched a dog's foot, the dog flexed that leg after a short delay. During the delay an impulse had to travel up an axon from a skin receptor to the spinal cord, and then an impulse had to travel from the spinal cord back down the leg to a muscle. Sherrington measured the total distance that the impulse traveled from skin receptor to spinal cord to muscle and calculated the speed at which the impulse must have traveled to produce a muscle response after the measured delay. He found that the overall speed of conduction through the reflex arc was significantly slower than the known speed of conduction along an axon. Therefore, he deduced, transmission between one neuron and another at the synapse must be slower than transmission along an axon (see Figure 3.2).

Temporal Summation

Sherrington's work with reflex arcs suggested that repeated stimuli occurring within a brief time can have a cumulative effect. He referred to this phenomenon as **temporal summation.** When Sherrington pinched a dog's foot very lightly, the leg did not move. However, when he repeated the same light pinch several times in rapid succession, the leg flexed slightly. The more rapid the series of pinches, the greater the response. Sherrington surmised that a single pinch produced a synaptic transmission that was too weak to produce an action potential in the next cell. That is, the excitation

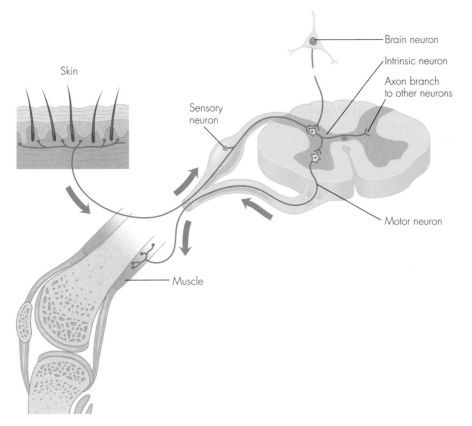

Figure 3.1 A reflex arc for leg flexion
The anatomy has been simplified to show the relationship among sensory neuron, intrinsic neuron, and motor neuron.

Skin

Sensory neuron

Muscle

Brain neuron

Intrinsic neuron

Axon branch to other neurons

Motor neuron

Note that this partial depolarization is a graded potential. Unlike action potentials, which are always depolarizations, graded potentials may be either depolarizations (excitatory) or hyperpolarizations (inhibitory). A graded depolarization is known as an **excitatory postsynaptic potential (EPSP).** Like an action potential, an EPSP results from sodium ions entering the cell (see Chapter 2). The synaptic activation opens sodium gates and increases the flow of sodium ions across the membrane. However, transmission at a single synapse does not open enough sodium gates to provoke an action potential. Unlike an action potential, an EPSP is a subthreshold event that decays over time and space; that is, its magnitude decreases as it travels along the membrane.

When Eccles stimulated the axon twice in close succession, two consecutive EPSPs were recorded in the postsynaptic cell. If the delay between EPSPs was short enough, temporal summation occurred; that is, the second EPSP added to what was left of the first one (point 2 in Figure 3.3). The summation of two EPSPs might or might not be enough to exceed the threshold of the postsynaptic cell depending on the size of the EPSP, the time between the two, and the threshold of the postsynaptic cell. In point 3 in Figure 3.3, three consecutive EPSPs combined to exceed the threshold and produce an action potential.

was less than the threshold of the cell that receives the message, the **postsynaptic neuron.** (The neuron that delivers the synaptic transmission is the **presynaptic neuron.**) Sherrington proposed that this subthreshold excitation begins to decay within a fraction of a second but is capable of combining with a second small excitation that quickly follows it. A rapid succession of pinches produces a series of weak activations at the synapse, each adding its effect to what was left of the previous excitations. If the excitations occur rapidly enough, they combine to exceed the threshold and therefore produce an action potential in the postsynaptic neuron.

Decades after Sherrington's studies it became possible to measure some of the single-cell properties he had inferred. To record the activity evoked in a neuron by synaptic input, researchers insert a microelectrode into the neuron to measure changes in the electrical potential across the membrane. Using this method John Eccles (1964) demonstrated temporal summation in single cells. He attached stimulating electrodes to some of the axons that formed synapses onto a neuron. He then recorded from the neuron while stimulating one or more of those axons. For example, after he had briefly stimulated an axon, Eccles recorded a slight depolarization of the membrane of the postsynaptic cell (point 1 in Figure 3.3).

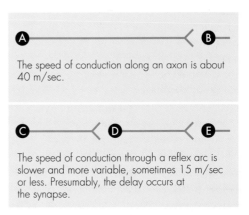

A————————————**B**

The speed of conduction along an axon is about 40 m/sec.

C————**D**————**E**

The speed of conduction through a reflex arc is slower and more variable, sometimes 15 m/sec or less. Presumably, the delay occurs at the synapse.

Figure 3.2 Sherrington's evidence for synaptic delay
An impulse traveling through a synapse in the spinal cord is slower than one traveling a similar distance along an uninterrupted axon.

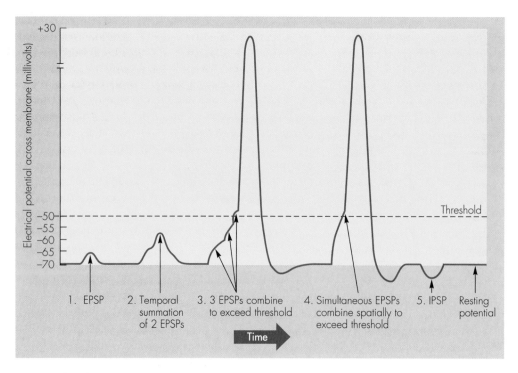

Figure 3.3   Recordings from a postsynaptic neuron during synaptic activation

Spatial Summation

Sherrington's work with reflex arcs also suggested that synapses have the property of **spatial summation:** Several synaptic inputs originating from separate locations can exert a cumulative effect on a neuron. Sherrington again began with a pinch that was too weak to elicit a response. But this time, instead of pinching the dog twice, he gave simultaneous pinches at two points on the foot. Although neither pinch alone elicited a response, the two together did. Sherrington concluded that pinching two points on the foot activated two sensory neurons, each of which sent an axon to the same target neuron. Excitation from either axon excited a synapse on that neuron, but one excitation was insufficient for an action potential. When both excitations were present at the same time, however, their combined effect exceeded the threshold for producing an action potential (see point 4 in Figure 3.3).

Again Eccles confirmed Sherrington's inference, demonstrating the spatial summation of EPSPs by recording from neurons. Note that temporal and spatial summation produce the same result: Either one generates an action potential in the postsynaptic cell (Figure 3.4).

Inhibitory Synapses

When Sherrington vigorously pinched a dog's foot, the flexor muscles of that leg contracted and so did the extensor muscles of the other three legs (see Figure 3.5). At the same time, the dog relaxed the extensor muscles of the stimulated leg and the flexor muscles of

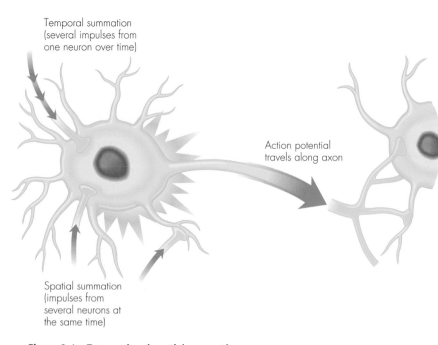

Figure 3.4   Temporal and spatial summation

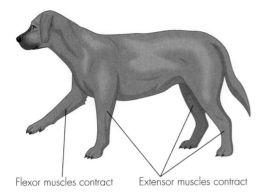

Figure 3.5 Antagonistic muscles
Flexor muscles draw an extremity toward the trunk of the body, whereas extensor muscles move an extremity away from the body.

larization of a membrane—called an **inhibitory postsynaptic potential**, or **IPSP**—resembles an EPSP in many ways. An IPSP occurs when synaptic input selectively opens the gates for potassium ions to leave the cell (carrying a positive charge with them) or for chloride ions to enter the cell (carrying a negative charge). Inhibition is more than just the absence of excitation; it is an active "brake" that can suppress excitatory responses.

Stop & Check

1. What evidence led Sherrington to conclude that transmission at a synapse is different from transmission along an axon?

2. What is the difference between temporal summation and spatial summation?

3. What was Sherrington's evidence for inhibition in the nervous system?

4. What ion gates in the membrane open during an EPSP? What gates open during an IPSP?

Check your answers on page 56.

the other legs. Sherrington's explanation for this series of coordinated and adaptive movements depended again on the synapses and in particular on the connections among neurons in the spinal cord: A pinch on the foot sends a message along a sensory neuron to an interneuron (an intermediate neuron) in the spinal cord, which in turn excites the motor neurons connected to the flexor muscles of that leg (Figure 3.6). Sherrington surmised that the interneuron also sends a message that decreases excitation of motor neurons connected to the extensor muscles in the same leg. He did not know whether the interneuron actually formed an inhibitory synapse onto the motor neuron to the extensor muscles or whether it simply decreased the amount of excitation. In either case the flexor and extensor muscles of the leg were prevented from contracting at the same time.

Eccles and other later researchers demonstrated that the interneuron actually has inhibitory synapses onto the motor neuron of the extensor muscle. At these synapses, input from the axon hyperpolarizes the postsynaptic cell, increasing the cell's negative charge and decreasing the probability of an action potential by moving the potential further from the threshold (point 5 in Figure 3.3). This temporary hyperpo-

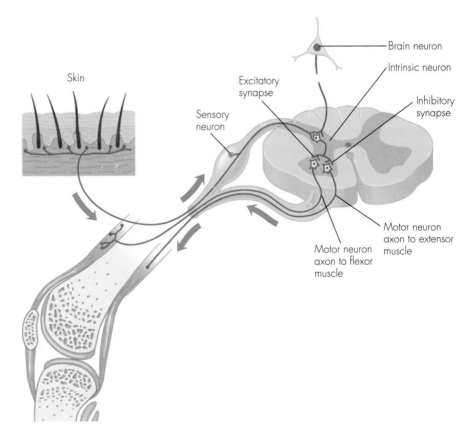

Figure 3.6 Sherrington's inference of inhibitory synapses
When a flexor muscle is excited, the probability of excitation decreases in the paired extensor muscle. Sherrington inferred that the interneuron that excited a motor neuron to the flexor muscle also inhibited a motor neuron connected to the extensor muscle.

Relationship Among EPSP, IPSP, and Action Potential

A neuron is rarely exposed to a single EPSP or IPSP at a time. A neuron may have thousands of synapses along its surface, some that excite the neuron and others that inhibit it. Any number and combination of synapses may be active at any time, yielding a continuing combination of temporal and spatial summation. The greater the number of EPSPs, the greater the probability of an action potential; the greater the number of IPSPs, the lower the probability of an action potential.

Moreover, some synapses are more influential than others because of their locations. EPSPs and IPSPs are graded potentials; they decrease in strength as they flow from their point of origin toward other parts of the neuron. A synapse located near the far end of a dendrite has only a weak effect on the cell; a synapse on the closer end of a dendrite has a much stronger effect (Soltesz, Smetters, & Mody, 1995).

In many neurons the EPSPs and IPSPs merely modify the frequency of action potentials that the neuron would fire spontaneously. That is, many neurons have a spontaneous firing rate, a periodic production of action potentials even without synaptic input. EPSPs increase the frequency of action potentials in these neurons, whereas IPSPs decrease it. For example, if the neuron's spontaneous firing rate is 10 per second, a steady stream of EPSPs might increase the rate to 15 or 20 or more, whereas a steady stream of IPSPs might decrease the rate to 5 or fewer action potentials per second.

Module 3.1

In Closing: The Neuron as Decision Maker

The neuron can be compared to a thermostat, a smoke detector, or any other device that detects something and triggers a response: When input reaches a certain level, the neuron triggers an action potential. That is, the synapses enable the postsynaptic neuron to integrate information. The EPSPs and IPSPs reaching a neuron at a given moment compete against one another, and the net result is a complicated, not exactly algebraic summation of the two effects. We could regard the summation of EPSPs and IPSPs as a "decision" because it determines whether or not the postsynaptic cell fires an action potential, but we should not imagine that any neuron decides between cereal and pancakes for breakfast. A great many neurons are involved in any behavior, and behavior depends on the whole neural network, not on a single neuron. Moreover, we cannot even assume, for instance, that an inhibitory synapse inhibits bodily activity. Activity at an inhibitory synapse may stop one neuron from inhibiting another neuron and thus yield a net excitation. Such disinhibition (inhibition of inhibition) is commonplace in the nervous system.

Summary

1. The synapse is the point of communication between two neurons. Charles S. Sherrington's observations of reflexes enabled him to infer the properties of synapses. (p. 52)

2. Because transmission through a reflex arc is slower than transmission through an equivalent length of axon, Sherrington concluded that there is a delay of transmission at the synapse. (p. 52)

3. Graded potentials (EPSPs and IPSPs) summate their effects. The summation of graded potentials from stimuli at different times is temporal summation. The summation of graded potentials from different locations is spatial summation. (p. 53)

4. A single stimulation at a synapse produces a brief graded potential in the postsynaptic cell. An excitatory graded potential (depolarizing) is an EPSP. An inhibitory graded potential (hyperpolarizing) is an IPSP. (pp. 53, 54)

5. An EPSP occurs when sodium gates open in the membrane; an IPSP occurs when potassium or chloride gates open. (pp. 53, 54)

6. At any time the EPSPs on a neuron compete with the IPSPs; the balance between the two determines the rate of firing of the neuron. (p. 56)

Answers to *Stop and Check* Questions

1. Sherrington found that the velocity of conduction through a reflex arc was significantly slower than the velocity of an action potential along an axon. Therefore some delay must occur at the junction between one neuron and the next. (p. 55)

2. Temporal summation is the combined effects of quickly repeated stimulation at a single synapse. Spatial summation is the combined effect of several nearly simultaneous stimulations at several synapses onto one neuron. (p. 55)

3. Sherrington found that a reflex that stimulates a flexor muscle sends a simultaneous message that inhibits nerves to the extensor muscles of the same limb. (p. 55)

4. During an EPSP, sodium gates open. During an IPSP, potassium or chloride gates open. (p. 55)

Thought Questions

1. When Sherrington measured the reaction time of a reflex (that is, the delay between stimulus and response), he found that the response occurred faster after a strong stimulus than after a weak one. How could you explain this finding? Remember that all action potentials—whether produced by strong or weak stimuli—travel at the same speed along a given axon.

2. A pinch on an animal's right hind foot leads to excitation of an interneuron that excites the motor neurons connected to the flexor muscles of that leg; the interneuron also inhibits the motor neurons connected to the extensor muscles of the leg. In addition this interneuron sends impulses that reach the motor neuron connected to the extensor muscles of the left hind leg. Would you expect the interneuron to excite or inhibit that motor neuron? (Hint: The connections are adaptive. When an animal lifts one leg, it must put additional weight on the other legs to maintain balance.)

3. Neuron X has a synapse onto neuron Y, and Y has a synapse onto Z. Presume that no other neurons or synapses are present. An experimenter finds that excitation of neuron X causes an action potential in neuron Z after a short delay. However, she determines that the synapse of X onto Y is inhibitory. Explain how the stimulation of X might produce excitation of Z.

Chemical Events at the Synapse

Although Charles Sherrington accurately inferred many properties of the synapse, he drew one conclusion that was wrong, or at least greatly overstated: Although he knew that synaptic transmission was slower than transmission along an axon, he thought it was still too fast to depend on a chemical process and therefore concluded that it must be electrical. We now know that although *some* synaptic transmission is indeed electrical, in most cases it relies on chemical processes that are much faster than Sherrington thought possible and far more versatile than anyone would have guessed.

The Discovery That Most Synaptic Transmission Is Chemical

T. R. Elliott, a young British scientist, reported in 1905 that the hormone *adrenaline* closely mimics the effects of the sympathetic nervous system, a set of nerves that control the internal organs (see Chapter 4). For example, stimulation of the sympathetic nerves accelerates the heartbeat, relaxes the stomach muscles, and dilates

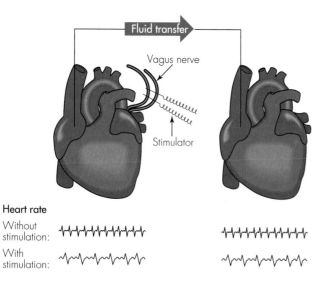

Heart rate

Without stimulation:

With stimulation:

Figure 3.7 Loewi's experiment demonstrating that nerves send messages by releasing chemicals
Loewi stimulated the vagus nerve to one frog's heart, decreasing the heartbeat. Then he transferred fluid from that heart to another frog's heart and observed a decrease in its heartbeat.

the pupils of the eyes. Applying adrenaline directly to the surface of the heart, the stomach, and the pupils produces those same effects. Elliott therefore suggested that the sympathetic nerves stimulate muscles by releasing adrenaline or a similar chemical and that synapses in general operate by releasing chemicals. Elliott's evidence was not decisive, however; perhaps adrenaline merely mimicked certain effects that are ordinarily produced by electrical stimulation. At the time, Sherrington's prestige was so great that most scientists ignored Elliott's results and continued to assume that synapses transmitted information by electrical impulses.

Otto Loewi, a German physiologist, was also attracted to the idea that synapses operate by releasing chemicals, but as he did not see how he could test the theory decisively, he set it aside. Then one night in 1920, he was aroused from sleep with a sudden idea. He wrote himself a note and went back to sleep. Unfortunately, the next morning he could not read his own writing. The following night at 3 A.M., when he awoke with the same idea, he rushed to the laboratory and performed the experiment at once.

He repeatedly stimulated the vagus nerve to a frog's heart, causing the heart rate to decrease. He then collected fluid from that heart, transferred it to a second frog's heart, and found that the second heart also decreased its rate of beating. (This experiment is illustrated in Figure 3.7.) In a later experiment Loewi stimulated the accelerator nerve to the first frog's heart, causing the heart rate to increase. When he collected fluid from that heart and transferred it to the second heart, the heart rate increased. That is, stimulating one nerve released something that inhibited heart rate, and stimulating a different nerve released something else that increased heart rate. Those somethings had to be chemicals, not loose electricity. Therefore, Loewi concluded, nerves send messages by releasing chemicals.

Loewi later remarked that if he had thought of this experiment in the light of day, he probably never would have tried it (Loewi, 1960). Even if synapses did release chemicals, his daytime reasoning went, there was little chance that they released enough of the chemicals to make collecting them easy. Fortunately, by the time he realized that the experiment was unlikely to work, he had already completed the research, for which he later won the Nobel Prize.

Although we now know that most synapses operate by transmitting chemicals, electrical synapses do exist. They occur mostly where it is important for two neurons to synchronize their activities exactly, such as synapses controlling rapid escape movements in certain fish and invertebrates.

The Sequence of Chemical Events at a Synapse

Many medical conditions and drugs affect behavior by altering neurotransmission. Consequently, understanding the chemical events occurring at a synapse is fundamental to much current research in biological psychology. The major events at a synapse are:

1. The neuron synthesizes chemicals that serve as neurotransmitters.

2. The neuron transports these chemicals to the axon terminals.

3. Action potentials travel down the axon.

4. At the presynaptic terminal an action potential causes calcium to enter the cell, thereby evoking the release of the neurotransmitters from the terminals and into the *synaptic cleft,* the space between the presynaptic and postsynaptic neurons.

5. The released molecules attach to receptors and alter the activity of the postsynaptic neuron.

6. The molecules separate from their receptors and (in some cases) are converted into inactive chemicals.

7. In some cells as many of the neurotransmitter molecules as possible are taken back into the presynaptic cell for recycling.

8. In some cells empty *vesicles* are returned to the cell body.

Figure 3.8 summarizes these steps. We shall discuss each step in more detail.

Types of Neurotransmitters

The chemicals that are released by one neuron at the synapse and that affect another are **neurotransmitters.** Each neuron synthesizes its neurotransmitters from materials in the blood. Neuroscientists believe that dozens of chemicals function as neurotransmitters in the brain, and research has been gradually adding to the list of known or suspected neurotransmitters (C. U. M. Smith, 1996). We shall consider many of these transmitters repeatedly; for now you can familiarize yourself with some of their names (see Figure 3.9). Some major categories are:

amino acids   acids containing an amine group (NH_2)

peptides   chains of amino acids (A long chain of amino acids is called a *polypeptide;* a still longer

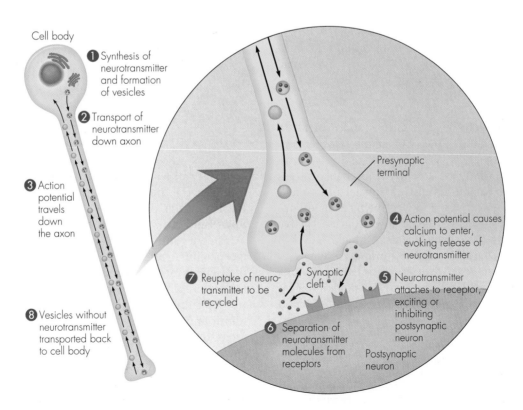

Figure 3.8   Some of the major events in transmission at a synapse

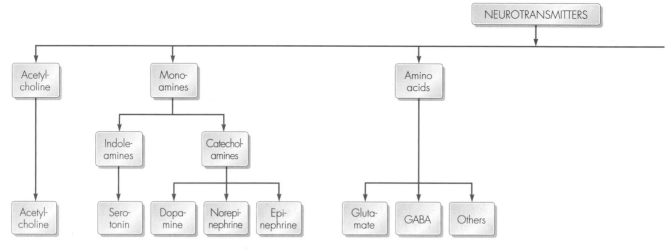

Figure 3.9   Some neurotransmitters

chain is a *protein*. The divisions between peptide, polypeptide, and protein are not firmly established.)

acetylcholine   (a one-member "family") a chemical similar to an amino acid, except that the NH_2 group has been replaced by an $N(CH_3)_3$ group

monoamines   nonacidic neurotransmitters containing an amine group (NH_2), **formed by a metabolic change of certain amino acids**

purines   a category of chemicals including adenosine and several of its derivatives

gases   specifically nitric oxide (NO) and possibly others

The chemicals used as neurotransmitters are a diverse lot. The most surprising is **nitric oxide** (chemical formula NO), a gas released by many small local neurons. (Do not confuse nitric oxide, NO, with nitrous oxide, N_2O, sometimes known as "laughing gas.") Nitric oxide is poisonous in large quantities and difficult to make by laboratory methods. Yet many neurons contain an enzyme that enables them to make this gas with relatively little energy. Nitric oxide probably serves many functions in the brain. One special function is that the nitric oxide released by active neurons dilates the blood vessels to increase blood flow to the most active areas of the brain (Dawson, Gonzalez-Zulueta, Kusel, & Dawson, 1998). One brain-scan technique, known as regional cerebral blood flow, measures relative amounts of blood flow to various brain areas. Nitric oxide is an important part of the explanation for why more blood flows to the active areas.

Synthesis of Transmitters

Every cell in the body uses chemical reactions to build some of the materials that it needs, converting substances provided by the diet into other chemicals necessary for normal functioning. The neuron is no exception, synthesizing its neurotransmitters from precursor molecules derived originally from foods.

Figure 3.10 illustrates the chemical steps in the synthesis of acetylcholine, serotonin, dopamine, epinephrine, and norepinephrine. Note the relationship among epinephrine, norepinephrine, and dopamine—three closely related compounds known as **catecholamines**, because they contain a catechol group and an amine group, as shown below:

Each pathway in Figure 3.10 begins with substances found in the diet. Acetylcholine, for example, is synthesized from choline, which is abundant in cauliflower and milk. The body can also make choline from lecithin, a component of egg yolks, liver, soybeans, butter, peanuts, and several other foods. The amino acids phenylalanine and tyrosine are precursors of dopamine, norepinephrine, and epinephrine.

The amino acid *tryptophan* is the precursor to serotonin, and a special "transport system" enables it to cross the blood-brain barrier. However, tryptophan shares its transport system with several other amino acids (including phenylalanine) that are almost always more prevalent in the diet. Thus, after a meal rich in protein, the level of tryptophan reaching the brain may

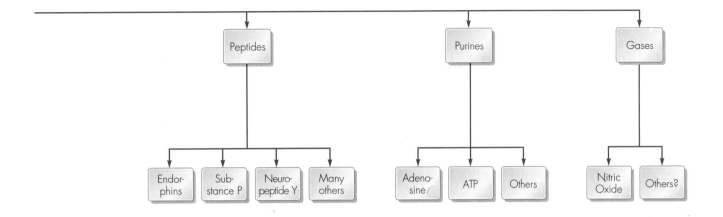

be low because of competition from the other amino acids. One way to increase the amount of tryptophan entering the brain is to eat carbohydrates with the protein. Carbohydrates increase release of the hormone *insulin*, which takes a number of competing amino acids out of the bloodstream and into cells throughout the body, thus decreasing the competition against tryptophan for entry into the brain (Wurtman, 1985).

Stop & Check

1. What was Loewi's evidence that neurotransmission depends on the release of chemicals?

2. Name the three catecholamine neurotransmitters.

Check your answers on page 66.

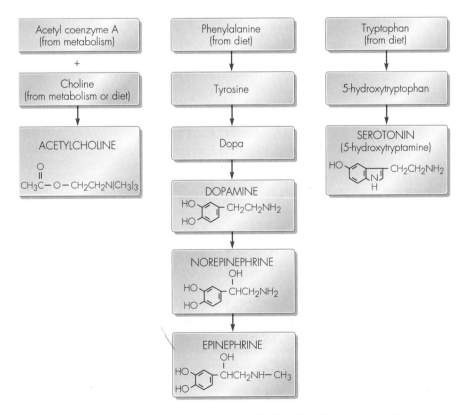

Figure 3.10 Steps in the synthesis of acetylcholine, dopamine, norepinephrine, epinephrine, and serotonin
Arrows represent chemical reactions.

Transport of Transmitters

Certain neurotransmitters, such as acetylcholine, are synthesized in the presynaptic terminal, close to where they are released. However, the larger neurotransmitters, including peptides, are synthesized in the cell body and transported from there down the axon to the terminal. The speed of transport varies from only 1 millimeter per day in thin axons to more than 100 mm per day in thicker ones.

Even at the highest speeds, transport from cell body to terminal may take hours or days in the longest axons. Consequently, after releasing peptides, neurons take a long time to replenish their supply. Furthermore, neurons reabsorb and recycle many of the nonpeptide transmitters, but not the peptides. For these reasons a neuron can exhaust its supply of a peptide relatively quickly, in contrast to other transmitters that can be released and re-released.

Release and Diffusion of Transmitters

The presynaptic terminal stores high concentrations of neurotransmitter molecules in **vesicles**, tiny nearly spherical packets (Figure 3.11). (Nitric oxide, the gaseous neurotransmitter mentioned earlier, is an exception to this rule. Neurons do not store nitric oxide for future use; they release it as soon as they synthesize it.) In addition to the neurotransmitter stored in vesicles, the presynaptic terminal also maintains substantial amounts outside the vesicles.

When an action potential reaches the end of an axon, the depolarization changes the voltage across the membrane and opens voltage-dependent calcium gates in the presynaptic terminal. As calcium flows through specialized channels into the presynaptic terminal, it causes the neuron to excrete neurotransmitter through its membrane and into the synaptic cleft between the presynaptic and postsynaptic neurons—a process called **exocytosis**. Exocytosis is quick, lasting a mere 1 or 2 milliseconds. The result is not the same every time; many action potentials fail to release any transmitter, and even those that succeed do not all release the same amount (Südhof, 1995).

After the presynaptic cell releases the neurotransmitter, the chemical diffuses across the synaptic cleft to the postsynaptic membrane, where it attaches to a receptor. The cleft is only 0.02 to 0.05 microns wide, and the neurotransmitter takes no more than 10 microseconds to diffuse across the cleft. The total delay in transmission across the synapse, including the time it takes for the presynaptic cell to release the neurotransmitter, is 2 milliseconds or less (A. R. Martin, 1977; Takeuchi, 1977).

The brain as a whole uses dozens of neurotransmitters, but no single neuron releases them all. For many years investigators believed that each neuron released just one neurotransmitter. This generalization is known as *Dale's principle,* after the first investigator to propose it. According to later studies it appears that many, perhaps most, neurons release two, three, or even more transmitters (Hökfelt, Johansson, & Goldstein, 1984). However, consistent with the general idea behind Dale's principle, each neuron, so far as we know, releases the same combination of transmitters from all branches of its axon. For example, if one branch of the axon releases glutamate and a peptide, then the other branches do also (Eccles, 1986).

Why does a neuron release a combination of transmitters instead of just one? The best guess is that the combination makes the neuron's message more complex. For example, one transmitter might quickly initiate a process and a second transmitter might either prolong it or end it (Jonas, Bischofberger, & Sandkühler, 1998).

Although a neuron releases only a limited number of neurotransmitters (generally at its terminal), it may receive and respond to a number of different neurotransmitters at various synapses (generally on its dendrites and soma). For example, it might respond to acetylcholine released at one synapse, serotonin at another synapse, GABA at still another, and so on.

Activation of Receptors of the Postsynaptic Cell

In English the term *fern* refers to a plant. In German *fern* means "far away." In French it means nothing at all. The meaning of any word depends on who hears it or reads it. Similarly, the meaning of a neurotransmitter depends on its receptor. For example, acetylcholine may excite one neuron, inhibit another, and have no effect at all on still another depending on those neurons' receptors.

A neurotransmitter receptor is a protein embedded in the membrane. When the neurotransmitter attaches to the active site of the receptor, the receptor can directly open a channel, or it can exert slower but longer lasting effects. For convenience we distinguish three major types of effects: ionotropic, metabotropic, and modulatory.

Ionotropic Effects Some neurotransmitters exert **ionotropic effects** on the postsynaptic neuron. This means that the neurotransmitter attaches to a receptor on the membrane, almost immediately opening the gates for some type of ion. For example, when the neurotransmitter *glutamate* attaches to certain receptors, it opens sodium gates, thereby enabling sodium ions to enter the postsynaptic cell. The sodium ions, bearing a positive

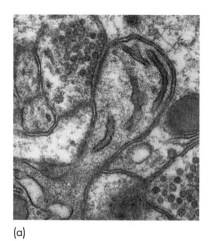
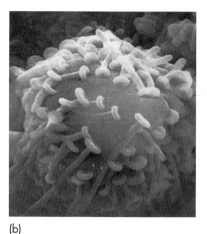

(a) (b)

Figure 3.11 Anatomy of a synapse
(a) An electron micrograph showing a synapse from the cerebellum of a mouse. Magnification × 93,000. The small round structures are vesicles. *(Source: Landis, 1987)* (b) Electron micrograph showing axon terminals onto the soma of a neuron. Magnification × 11,000. *(Source: E. R. Lewis, Everhart, & Zeevi, 1969)*

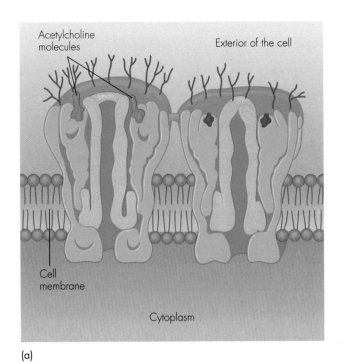

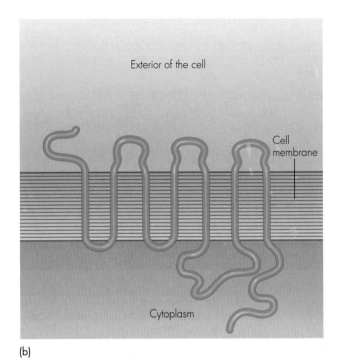

(a)

(b)

Figure 3.12 Neurotransmitter receptors
(**a**) Acetylcholine receptors embedded in a membrane. The receptors on the left have acetylcholine molecules attached to them; consequently, their ion pores are open. (**b**) A neurotransmitter receptor as it would look if folded out. *(Source: Part [a] adapted from Lindstrom, 1979)*

charge, partially depolarize the membrane. With a few exceptions (Fiorillo & Williams, 1998), glutamate is an *excitatory* neurotransmitter. In fact it is the most abundant excitatory transmitter in the vertebrate brain.

GABA is another neurotransmitter that exerts ionotropic effects, but its effects are almost always *inhibitory.* When GABA attaches to its receptors on the membrane, it opens chloride gates, enabling chloride ions, with their negative charge, to cross the membrane into the cell more rapidly than usual.

Acetylcholine exerts ionotropic effects at some synapses, which are known as *nicotinic* synapses because they can be stimulated by the drug *nicotine.* When acetylcholine attaches to one of these receptors, as shown in Figure 3.12, it slightly rotates the walls of the cylindrical channel into a position that lets sodium ions cross through the membrane (Unwin, 1995). Ionotropic effects are rapid but short-lived. Typically a neurotransmitter opens the ion channels within 10 ms after its release and keeps them open for less than 20 ms (North, 1989; Westbrook & Jahr, 1989). Ionotropic synapses are therefore useful for conveying information about visual and auditory stimulation, muscle movements, and other rapidly changing events.

Metabotropic Effects and Second Messenger Systems At certain other synapses neurotransmitters exert **metabotropic effects.** These effects take place by initiating a sequence of metabolic reactions that are slower and longer lasting than ionotropic effects. Metabotropic effects, which rely on the actions of a second messenger (as explained below), emerge 30 ms or more after the release of the transmitter (North, 1989). They may last seconds, minutes, or even hours.

When the neurotransmitter attaches to a metabotropic receptor, it alters the configuration of the rest of the protein, enabling a portion of the protein inside the neuron to react with other molecules, as described in Figure 3.13 (Levitzki, 1988; O'Dowd, Lefkowitz, & Caron, 1989). The neurotransmitter binds to a portion of the receptor molecule outside the membrane, bending the molecule, including a portion inside the membrane, and thereby activating a **G-protein,** which is a protein coupled to guanosine triphosphate (GTP), an energy-storing molecule. The activated G-protein in turn increases the concentration of a second messenger, such as cyclic adenosine monophosphate (cyclic AMP), inside the cell. Just as the "first messenger" (the neurotransmitter) carries a message to the postsynaptic cell, the **second messenger** carries a message to areas within the cell. The effect of the second messenger varies; it may open or close ion channels in the membrane or alter the production of proteins or activate a portion of a chromosome. Note the contrast: An ionotropic synapse has effects localized to one point on the membrane, whereas a metabotropic synapse, by way of its second

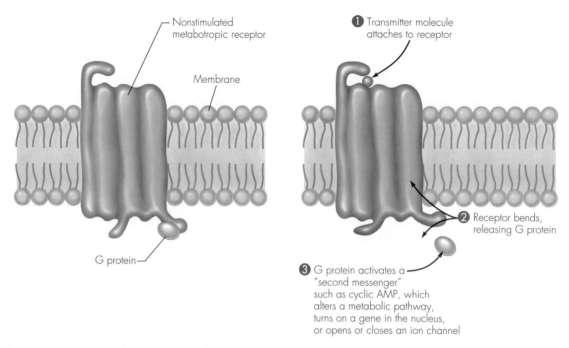

Figure 3.13 Sequence of events at a metabolic synapse, using a second messenger within the postsynaptic neuron

messenger, can influence activity in much or all of the postsynaptic cell.

Each of the heavily studied neurotransmitters (we can only guess about the others) interacts with several different kinds of receptors. For example, dopamine has at least five types of receptors, known as types D_1 through D_5. Similarly, glutamate, acetylcholine, serotonin, and the others have multiple receptors, in some cases including both ionotropic and metabotropic types. The different receptors have different functions in behavior, and therefore a drug or a genetic mutation that affects one receptor type may have specific effects on behavior.

Native South Americans cover arrow tips with curare, a poison that kills by blocking acetylcholine synapses at nerve-muscle junctions.

Neuromodulators A neurotransmitter is like a telephone line: It conveys a message directly and exclusively from the sender to the receiver. Hormones are more like a radio station: They convey a message to any receiver that happens to be tuned in to the right station. A **neuromodulator** is intermediate between a neurotransmitter and a hormone. Like a hormone, it conveys a message to any receiver that happens to be tuned in, but a neuromodulator is released in smaller volumes, closer to the target cells.

Neurons release neuromodulators generally but not necessarily at their terminals. The neuromodulators diffuse to other neurons in the region, perhaps even to the neuron that released them. They affect all those nearby cells that have receptors for them—that is, all the cells "tuned to the right station" (Vizi, 1984).

The distinction between a neurotransmitter and a neuromodulator is not sharp. After all, any chemical can diffuse away from its point of release and affect nearby cells. In most cases the neuromodulators have metabotropic effects and act by second messengers.

As a rule neuromodulators do not by themselves strongly excite or inhibit a neuron. This is why they are called "modulators"; they modulate (alter) the effect of neurotransmitters (Millhorn et al., 1989). For example, certain neuromodulators prolong or limit the effect of a neurotransmitter. Such neuromodulators are said to have a conditional effect: They produce an effect only when the neurotransmitter is present. Other neuromodulators have other effects, such as limiting the release of neurotransmitter from the presynaptic neuron.

3. When the action potential reaches the presynaptic terminal, which ion must enter the presynaptic terminal to evoke release of the neurotransmitter?

4. How do ionotropic and metabotropic synapses differ in speed and duration of effects?

5. Which type of synapse relies on second messengers?

Check your answers on page 66.

Inactivation and Reuptake of Neurotransmitters

A neurotransmitter does not normally linger at the postsynaptic membrane. If it did, it might continue exciting or inhibiting the postsynaptic neuron indefinitely. Various neurotransmitters are inactivated in different ways.

After acetylcholine activates a receptor, it is broken down by the enzyme **acetylcholinesterase** (a-SEE-til-ko-lih-NES-teh-raze) into two fragments: acetate and choline. The choline diffuses back to the presynaptic neuron, which takes it up and reconnects it with acetate already in the cell to form acetylcholine again. This recycling process is highly efficient but not perfect and not instantaneous. At any synapse, not just one using acetylcholine, a sufficiently rapid series of action potentials can release the neurotransmitter faster than the presynaptic cell resynthesizes it, thus bringing transmission to a halt (Liu & Tsien, 1995).

If the enzyme acetylcholinesterase is not present in adequate amounts, acetylcholine may remain at the synapse for an abnormally long time and continue to excite it. Drugs that block acetylcholinesterase can be useful for certain purposes. For example, myasthenia gravis is a condition associated with a deficit of transmission at acetylcholine synapses. One way to alleviate the symptoms is to give drugs that inhibit acetylcholinesterase, thereby prolonging the activity of acetylcholine.

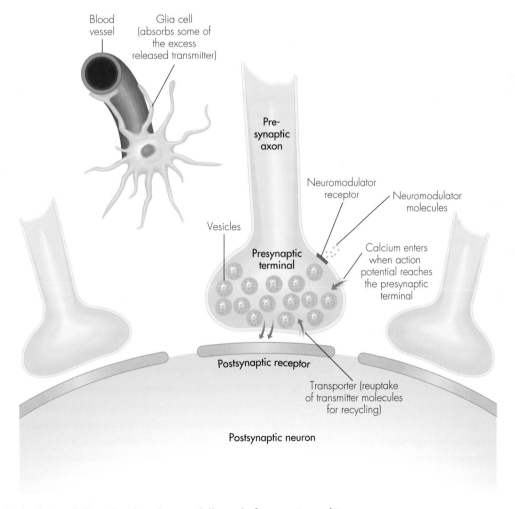

Figure 3.14 Factors influencing the release and disposal of a neurotransmitter
Neuromodulators can either increase or decrease the release of transmitter. The transporter molecule facilitates the recycling of transmitter for future use.

Serotonin and the catecholamines (DA, NE, and epinephrine) are not broken down into inactive fragments at the postsynaptic membrane, but simply detach from the receptor. The presynaptic neuron takes up most of these neurotransmitter molecules intact and reuses them. This process, called **reuptake,** occurs through special membrane proteins called **transporters.** Many of the familiar antidepressant drugs, such as fluoxetine (Prozac), act by blocking reuptake and thereby prolonging the effects of the neurotransmitter on its receptor. (We consider antidepressants in more detail in Chapter 15.)

Some of the serotonin and catecholamine molecules, either before or after reuptake, are converted into inactive chemicals that cannot stimulate the receptor. The enzymes that convert catecholamine transmitters into inactive chemicals are **COMT** (catechol-o-methyl-transferase) and **MAO** (monoamine oxidase), which affects serotonin as well as catecholamines. We return to MAO in the discussion of antidepressant drugs. Figure 3.14 summarizes the influences on release and disposal of a neurotransmitter.

Stop & Check

6. What happens to acetylcholine molecules after they stimulate a postsynaptic receptor?

7. What happens to serotonin and catecholamine molecules after they stimulate a postsynaptic receptor?

Check your answers on this page.

Module 3.2

In Closing: Neurotransmitters and Behavior

The brain uses a great many chemicals as neurotransmitters and neuromodulators, and each of the widely investigated neurotransmitters has more than one type of receptor. For example, acetylcholine has at least four types of nicotinic receptors and five types of muscarinic receptors (McCormick, 1989). Dopamine has at least five types of receptors (J. C. Schwartz, Giros, Martres, & Sokoloff, 1992), serotonin at least ten (Humphrey, Hartig, & Hoyer, 1993), and glutamate at least sixteen (Westbrook, 1994). In each case the transmitter itself activates all types of its receptor, although different receptors may respond to different drugs.

Why are there so many neurotransmitters and so many types of receptors? It is probably for the same reason that our alphabet has more than just three or four letters. The nervous system needs a large number of elements that can be combined in different ways to produce complex behavior. Different transmitters and different receptors play different roles in brain functioning and behavior. Indeed, one major reason people differ from one another in what we call "personality" may be that their neurotransmitter receptors differ.

Summary

1. Most synapses operate by transmitting a neurotransmitter from the presynaptic cell to the postsynaptic cell. (p. 58)

2. Many chemicals are used as neurotransmitters. As far as we know, each neuron releases the same combination of neurotransmitters from all branches of its axon. (p. 59)

3. At certain synapses a neurotransmitter exerts its effects by attaching to a receptor that opens the gates to allow a particular ion, such as sodium, to cross the membrane more readily. At other synapses a neurotransmitter may lead to slower but longer lasting changes inside the postsynaptic cell. (p. 62)

4. After a neurotransmitter has activated its receptor, some of the transmitter molecules reenter the presynaptic cell through transporter molecules in the membrane. This process, known as reuptake, enables the presynaptic cell to recycle its neurotransmitter. (p. 66)

Answers to *Stop and Check* Questions

1. When he stimulated a nerve that increased or decreased a frog's heart rate, he could withdraw some fluid from the area around the heart, transfer it to another frog's heart, and thereby increase or decrease its rate also. (p. 61)

2. Epinephrine, norepinephrine, and dopamine (p. 59)

3. Calcium (p. 65)

4. Ionotropic synapses act more quickly and more briefly. (p. 65)

5. Metabotropic synapses rely on the actions of a second messenger. (p. 65)

6. The enzyme acetylcholinesterase breaks acetylcholine molecules into two smaller molecules, acetate and choline, which are then reabsorbed by the presynaptic terminal. (p. 66)

7. Most serotonin and catecholamine molecules are reabsorbed by the presynaptic terminal. Some of their molecules are broken down into inactive chemicals which then float away in the blood. (p. 66)

Thought Questions

1. Suppose that axon A enters a ganglion (a cluster of neurons) and axon B leaves on the other side. An experimenter who stimulates A can shortly thereafter record an impulse traveling down B. We want to know whether B is just an extension of axon A or whether A formed an excitatory synapse on some neuron in the ganglion, whose axon is axon B. How could an experimenter determine the answer? You should be able to think of more than one good method. Presume that the anatomy within the ganglion is so complex that you cannot simply trace the course of an axon through it.

2. Transmission of visual and auditory information relies largely on ionotropic synapses. Why is ionotropic better than metabotropic for these purposes? For what purposes might metabotropic synapses be better?

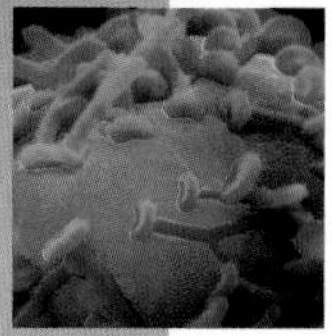

Module 3.3

Synapses, Abused Drugs, and Behavior

Neuroscientists study drugs for many reasons. An obvious one is that researchers want to find ways to combat drug abuse. Another obvious reason is that they want to develop better medications to combat anxiety, sleeplessness, depression, schizophrenia, and other disorders. (What is the difference between good drugs and bad ones? Not much; in fact many drugs that we regard as dangerous—including cocaine, morphine, and amphetamine—have medical uses as well. The difference between a good drug and a bad drug is largely a matter of the amount taken and the motivation for taking it.)

[handwritten note in margin: good starting ...]

An additional, perhaps less obvious, reason for studying drugs is that studying how drugs affect synapses helps us understand synapses and therefore helps us better understand the brain. For example, all the commonly abused drugs share certain effects on dopamine synapses. Investigating those effects may help us understand brain mechanisms of pleasure, habit formation, attention, or something else that is critical to addiction.

In this module we encounter many drugs that are derived from plants, such as nicotine from tobacco, coffee from coffee beans, opiates from the opiate poppy, cocaine from coca, and cannabis from marijuana. Why are our brains so sensitive to plant chemicals? One reason is that all animals, even invertebrates, use the same neurotransmitters as humans (Brownlee & Fairweather, 1999). Many plants have evolved chemicals that stimulate or inhibit animals' receptors. For example, many flowers have chemicals that attract insects to pollinate their flowers, and many plants have chemicals in their leaves that deter animals from eating them. Because all animals use the same transmitters, many plant chemicals that evolved to attract wasps or repel rabbits have strong effects on humans as well.

A second reason our brains respond to plant chemicals is that plants themselves use glutamate, acetylcholine, serotonin, and other "neurotransmitters" for their own purposes! In plants, of course, we cannot really call them neurotransmitters because plants do not have neurons. However, apparently these chemicals are important for some kind of communication among parts of the plant. For example, plants have ionotropic glutamate receptors very similar to those of humans (Lam et al., 1998). Even in humans most neurotransmitters have functions outside the nervous system, such as hormones that regulate digestion. Evidently a small number of chemicals have proved to be so well suited to conveying information that evolution has been very conservative in continuing to use them.

How Drugs Affect Synapses

A drug can either decrease or increase the effects of a neurotransmitter. A drug that blocks the effects of a neurotransmitter is called an **antagonist**; a drug that mimics or increases the effects is called an **agonist.** (*Antagonist,* meaning "enemy," is used in everyday speech, whereas *agonist* is seldom used except to describe drug effects. The term *agonist* is derived from a Greek word meaning "contestant"; an *antagonist* is an "antiagonist," or member of the opposing team.) Sometimes a drug is a *mixed agonist-antagonist,* meaning that it is an agonist for some behavioral effects of the neurotransmitter and an antagonist for others or is an agonist at some doses and an antagonist at others.

Drugs influence synaptic activity in many ways. As Figure 3.15 illustrates for a dopamine synapse, a drug can increase or decrease the synthesis of the neurotransmitter, cause it to leak from its vesicles, increase its release, decrease its reuptake, block its breakdown into inactive chemicals, or directly stimulate or block the postsynaptic receptors.

Investigators say that a drug has an **affinity** for a particular type of receptor if it binds to that receptor, fitting somewhat like a lock and key. Drugs vary in their affinities from strong to weak. The **efficacy** of a drug is its tendency to activate the receptor. So for example, a drug that binds tightly to a receptor but fails to stimulate it has a high affinity but a low efficacy. Such a drug is therefore an antagonist because, by occupying the receptor, it prevents the normal effects of the transmitter.

If you or people you know have ever taken tranquilizers, antidepressants, or other drugs, you may have noticed that the effectiveness and side effects vary from one person to another. Why? Part of the explanation is that each drug affects several kinds of synapse. For example, antipsychotic drugs block mostly dopamine receptors but also have smaller effects on other kinds of receptors, with different behavioral effects. Further-

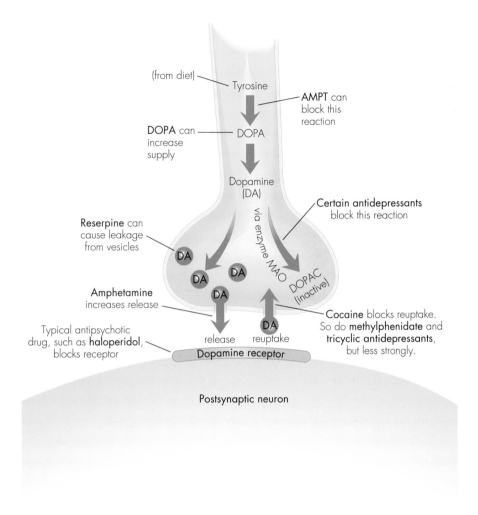

Figure 3.15 Events at a dopamine synapse and how certain drugs affect the process
Drugs can alter any stage of processing at a synapse, from synthesis of the neurotransmitter through release and reuptake.

Labels in figure:
(from diet) → Tyrosine
AMPT can block this reaction
DOPA can increase supply → DOPA
Dopamine (DA)
via enzyme MAO
Certain antidepressants block this reaction
Reserpine can cause leakage from vesicles
DOPAC (inactive)
Amphetamine increases release
Cocaine blocks reuptake. So do methylphenidate and tricyclic antidepressants, but less strongly.
Typical antipsychotic drug, such as haloperidol, blocks receptor
release   reuptake
Dopamine receptor
Postsynaptic neuron

more, for each neurotransmitter, the brain has several kinds of receptors, which also have different behavioral functions. People vary in their abundance of each kind of receptor, and some have genes that alter the shape and therefore effectiveness of particular receptors. So for example, one person might have a relatively large number of dopamine type D_4 receptors and relatively few D_1 or D_2 receptors, whereas someone else has more D_1, fewer D_4, and an average number of D_2 receptors. Therefore a drug that alters dopamine synapses can have noticeably different effects on the two people.

Synapses, Reinforcement, and Drug Use

Why are many drugs habit-forming or addictive? In fact we could ask the same question about gambling, video games, and many other powerful habits that do not involve drugs. The answers are incomplete, but the gist is that habit-forming or addictive behaviors have something to do with dopamine synapses. The story begins

with an accidental discovery by researchers who were trying to answer a much different question.

Electrical Self-Stimulation of the Brain

Decades ago two young scientists, James Olds and Peter Milner (1954), put rats in a situation in which they had to choose between turning left and turning right. Olds and Milner wanted to test whether stimulation of a particular brain area influences the direction in which the rat turns. However, they accidentally implanted the electrode in an unintended area of the brain, the septum. To their surprise, when the rat received the brain stimulation, it sometimes sat up, looked around, and sniffed, as if reacting to a favorable stimulus. Olds and Milner later placed rats in Skinner boxes, where they could produce **self-stimulation of the brain** by pressing a lever for electrical brain stimulation as a reinforcement (see Figure 3.16). Rats worked extremely vigorously to stimulate certain brain areas, in some cases pressing a lever 2000 times per hour until they collapsed from exhaustion (Olds, 1958).

The results of later experiments have indicated that brain stimulation is reinforcing almost exclusively in tracts of axons that release dopamine (Wise, 1996). Many other kinds of reinforcing experiences, ranging from sexual activity to video games, also stimulate the release of dopamine in several areas, especially the **nucleus accumbens,** a small subcortical area rich in dopamine receptors (Figure 3.17). Dopamine is an inhibitory transmitter in this area; reinforcement can also be achieved by decreasing the activity of glutamate, an excitatory transmitter here.

Many people have therefore regarded the nucleus accumbens as a pleasure area and dopamine as a pleasure

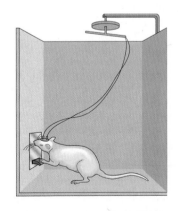

Figure 3.16 A rat pressing a lever for self-stimulation of its brain

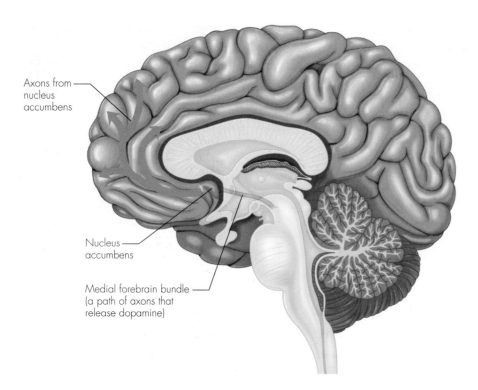

Axons from nucleus accumbens

Nucleus accumbens

Medial forebrain bundle (a path of axons that release dopamine)

Figure 3.17 Location of the nucleus accumbens in the human brain
A wide variety of procedures that yield reinforcement inhibit the activity of the nucleus accumbens. Therefore this area is considered essential for reinforcement or reward.

food presentation does (A. M. J. Young, Joseph, & Gray, 1993).

What, then, is the role of the dopamine synapses and the nucleus accumbens? At present the best hypothesis is that they relate to the attention-getting value of an event (Berridge & Robinson, 1998). Addictive drugs have a tremendous ability to dominate the user's attention and cravings, even if the drug experience is not dependably pleasant (Berridge & Robinson, 1995). Informative events, including both food and shock, are also attention-getting, whereas a fully expected event draws rather little attention.

We now examine some of the commonly abused drugs and their synaptic effects. At the end we consider the implications concerning synapses and their relationship to normal behavior and personality.

chemical. However, reinforcement is merely an event that causes an individual to repeat some act; the fact that you work for some outcome doesn't necessarily mean that you enjoy it. (Consider how hard you work to take your medicine, or to study for a test.) Several kinds of results conflict with the idea that dopamine release means pleasure:

- Food presented to a rat during the early stages of training evokes dopamine release; the same amount of food to a well-trained rat evokes very little dopamine release (Hollerman & Schultz, 1998). Evidently the dopamine relates not just to whether the event is pleasant, but to whether it is surprising or informative. From your own standpoint contrast how you react to a surprise present versus one you had expected to receive. Or consider how you might react to a flirtatious smile from someone who had never seemed to notice you before.

- After being given a drug that blocks dopamine synapses, the rat works less than usual for food, but when it gets it, the rat eats as vigorously as usual and shows the mouth and tongue movements that it ordinarily shows for a good-tasting food. So the dopamine blocker decreases the rat's tendency to work for food but doesn't change the pleasantness of the food.

- Unpleasant events, such as footshock, can elicit dopamine release in the nucleus accumbens, just as

Effects of Stimulant Drugs on Dopamine Synapses

Many highly addictive drugs are **stimulant drugs,** producing excitement, alertness, elevated mood, decreased fatigue, and sometimes increased motor activity. Each of these drugs increases activity at dopamine receptors, including those in the nucleus accumbens. Receptor types D_2, D_3, and D_4 are apparently more important for the reinforcing effects (R. A. Harris, Brodie, & Dunwiddie, 1992; Wise & Bozarth, 1987), whereas type D_1 is more important for the increased motor activity (Xu, Hu, Cooper, White, & Tonegawa, 1996).

Amphetamine stimulates dopamine synapses by increasing the release of dopamine from the presynaptic terminal. The presynaptic terminal ordinarily reabsorbs released dopamine through a protein called the *dopamine transporter.* Amphetamine apparently reverses the transporter, causing the cell to excrete dopamine instead of reabsorbing it (Giros, Jaber, Jones, Wightman, & Caron, 1996). **Cocaine** blocks the reuptake of dopamine, norepinephrine, and serotonin, thus prolonging their effects. Several kinds of evidence indicate that the behavioral effects of cocaine depend mainly on increasing dopamine effects and secondarily on serotonin effects (Rocha et al., 1998; Volkow, Wang, Fischman, et al., 1997). Because both amphetamine and cocaine increase dopamine activity, their behavioral effects are similar.

The effects of cocaine and amphetamine on dopamine synapses are intense but short-lived. By increasing the release of dopamine or decreasing its reuptake, the drugs increase the accumulation of dopamine in the synaptic cleft. However, the excess dopamine washes away from the synapse faster than the presynaptic cell can synthesize more dopamine. Furthermore the excess dopamine in the synaptic cleft activates autoreceptors on the presynaptic terminal, exerting a negative feedback effect that reduces further release of dopamine (North, 1992). The net result is that, within hours after taking amphetamine or cocaine, a user "crashes" into a depressed state.

The effects of stimulant drugs are also limited by the tolerance that a user develops. After someone has used cocaine repeatedly, the drug releases less dopamine and more of a transmitter called *dynorphin,* which counteracts the reinforcing properties of cocaine (Carlezon et al., 1998; Volkow, Wang, Fowler, et al., 1997). Similarly, after a rat has learned to press a lever to self-stimulate dopamine-releasing axons, further stimulation releases less and less dopamine (Garris et al., 1999). As noted before, repeated and predictable reinforcements become less attention-getting. Note the implication: Once a strong habit is formed, it can continue even with minimum reinforcement. In fact addicts often compensate by increasing the frequency or dosage of their drug use.

Methylphenidate (Ritalin), another stimulant drug, is often prescribed for people with **attention-deficit disorder (ADD),** a condition marked by impulsiveness and poor control of attention. Methylphenidate and cocaine both block the reuptake of dopamine at the same receptors in the brain. However, when people take a methylphenidate pill, its concentration in the brain increases gradually over an hour and then declines with a half-life of more than an hour and a half, in contrast to cocaine, which produces a four to five times faster rise and fall of effects (Volkow, Wang, & Fowler, 1997; Volkow, Wang, Fowler, et al., 1998). Therefore methylphenidate pills do not produce the sudden rush of excitement, the strong withdrawal effects, the cravings, or the addiction that are common with cocaine. In addition to its effects on dopamine, methylphenidate increases serotonin release. The benefits for people with ADD probably include improved attention due to the dopamine effects and a calming of activity due to serotonin effects (Gainetdinov et al., 1999).

Because dopamine is mostly an inhibitory transmitter, drugs that increase activity at dopamine synapses decrease the activity in much of the brain. Figure 3.18 shows the results of a PET scan, which measures relative amounts of activity in various brain areas (London et al., 1990) (see Methods 3.1). How, you might wonder, could drugs that decrease brain activity lead to behavioral arousal? One hypothesis is that high dopamine activity mostly decreases "background noise" in the brain and therefore increases the signal-to-noise ratio (Mattay et al., 1996).

Stimulant drugs are known primarily for their short-term effects, but repeated use of high doses can produce

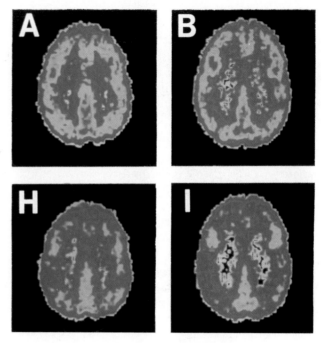

Figure 3.18 Effects of cocaine on the brain
Sometimes "your brain on drugs" is not like something in a frying pan, a popular analogy; it is more like something in the refrigerator. As these positron-emission tomography (PET) scans show, the brain has lower metabolism and lower overall activity under the influence of cocaine than it has ordinarily. Red indicates highest activity, followed by yellow, green, and blue. A and B represent brain activity under normal conditions; H and I show activity after a cocaine injection. *(Source: London et al., 1990)*

long-term, even permanent disruption of brain functioning. Cocaine users suffer lasting changes in brain metabolism and blood flow, thereby increasing their risk of stroke, epilepsy, and memory impairments (Strickland, Miller, Kowell, & Stein, 1998). The drug methylenedioxymethamphetamine (MDMA, or "ecstasy") stimulates the release of dopamine at low doses. At higher doses it also stimulates serotonin synapses, producing hallucinogenic effects similar to those of LSD. Unfortunately MDMA not only stimulates axons that release dopamine and serotonin, it also destroys them (McCann, Lowe, & Ricaurte, 1997), as shown in Figure 3.20. (At least it does so in rats and monkeys; we can only assume it does the same in humans.)

Stop **&** Check

1. How does amphetamine influence dopamine synapses?

2. How does cocaine influence dopamine synapses?

3. Why is methylphenidate generally less disruptive to behavior than cocaine is despite the drugs' similar mechanisms?

4. Does cocaine increase or decrease overall brain activity?

Check your answers on page 77.

PET Scans

Positron-emission tomography (PET) provides a high-resolution image of brain activity in a living brain by recording the emission of radioactivity from injected chemicals. First the person receives an injection of glucose or some other chemical with a radioactive label of ^{11}C, ^{18}F, or ^{15}O. These chemicals decay with half-lives of less than 2 hours. Because their half-lives are so short, the investigators must make them in a large device called a cyclotron and then use them almost immediately. Because cyclotrons are large and expensive, PET scans are available only at the largest research hospitals. When a radioactive label decays, releasing a positron, the positron immediately collides with a nearby electron, emitting two gamma rays in exactly opposite directions. The person's head is surrounded by a set of gamma ray detectors (Figure 3.19). When the detectors record two gamma rays at the same time, they identify a spot halfway between the detectors as the point of origin of the gamma rays. A computer uses this information to determine how many gamma rays are coming from each spot in the brain and therefore how much of the radioactive chemical is located in each area (Phelps & Mazziotta, 1985).

In a typical experiment the researchers give the person radioactively labeled glucose, which goes primarily to the most active areas of the brain. Then they present particular kinds of stimuli or ask the person to perform certain tasks and determine which brain areas become the most active.

Figure 3.19   A PET scanner
(No, it's not a state-of-the-art hairdo.) A person engages in a cognitive task while attached to this apparatus that records which areas of the brain become more active and by how much. Red indicates the greatest amount of activity followed by yellow, green, blue, and purple.
(Source: Burt Glinn/Magnum)

One disadvantage of the PET method is that it requires exposing the brain to a significant amount of radioactivity. No one should undergo repeated PET scans unless necessary for medical diagnosis.

Nicotine

Nicotine, a compound present in tobacco, has long been known to stimulate one type of acetylcholine receptor, conveniently known as the *nicotinic receptor,* which is found both in the central nervous system and at the nerve-muscle junction of skeletal muscles. Acetylcholine stimulation at other kinds of receptors is not reinforcing, but nicotinic receptors are abundant on dopamine-releasing neurons in the nucleus accumbens, so nicotine increases dopamine release there (Levin & Rose, 1995; Pontieri, Tanda, Orzi, & DiChiara, 1996). In fact nicotine activates mostly the same cells in the nucleus accumbens that cocaine does (Pich et al., 1997). One consequence of repeated exposure to nicotine, as demonstrated in rat studies, is that after the end of nicotine use, the nucleus accumbens cells responsible for reinforcement become less responsive than usual (Epping-Jordan, Watkins, Koob, & Markou, 1998). That is, many events, not just nicotine itself, become less reinforcing than they used to be. Some people who are trying to quit smoking find it helpful to take antidepressant drugs (S. M. Hall et al., 1998).

Opiates

Opiate drugs are derived from (or similar to those derived from) the opium poppy. Familiar opiates include morphine, heroin, and methadone. Opiates relax people, give them a sense of withdrawal from reality, and decrease their sensitivity to pain. Although opiates are known as highly addictive drugs, people who take them as painkillers under medical supervision almost never abuse them. Addiction is not simply a product of the drug; it depends on the person, his or her reasons for taking the drug, the dose, and even the social setting.

People smoked or injected morphine and other opiates for centuries before anyone knew how they affected the brain. Then Candace Pert and Solomon Snyder found that opiates attach to specific receptors in the brain (Pert & Snyder, 1973). It was a safe guess that vertebrates had not evolved such receptors just to enable us to become addicted to derivatives of the opium poppy; the brain must produce its own chemical that attaches to these receptors. And indeed, investigators soon found that the brain has a class of peptides now known as the *endorphins*—a contraction of *endo*-genous m*orphines.* One reason this discovery was exciting was that it indicated that opiates relieve pain in the brain, not just out in the skin or organs where people felt the pain. Also, this discovery implied that the brain may have a great many other peptides that regulate emotions and motivations. Much research has confirmed this hypothesis, and much remains to be learned about the brain's peptides.

Endorphin synapses may contribute directly to certain kinds of reinforcement (Nader, Bechara, Roberts, & van der Kooy, 1994), but they also act indirectly by way of dopamine. Endorphin synapses inhibit neurons that release GABA, a transmitter that inhibits dopamine release (North, 1992). Thus, through inhibition of an inhibitor, the net effect is to increase dopamine release.

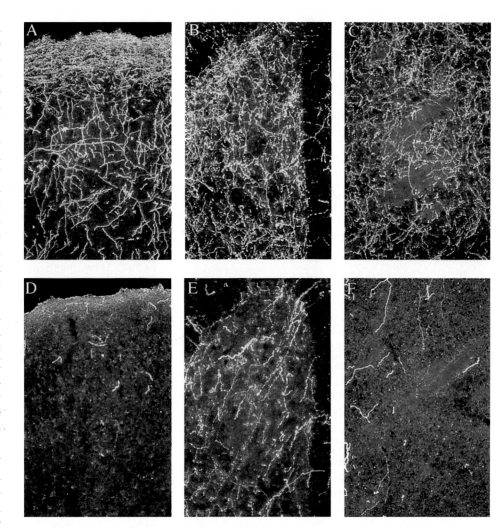

Figure 3.20 Brain damage produced by MDMA
These slices through monkey brains have been stained with a chemical that makes axons containing serotonin glow white. Photos in the top row are from a normal monkey; those below are from a monkey that was exposed to MDMA ("ecstasy") a year and a half earlier. Notice the decreased density of serotonin axons in the photos below. *(Source: McCann, Lowe, & Ricaurte, 1997)*

PCP

Phencyclidine (PCP, or "angel dust") is a commonly abused drug that, at low doses, produces intoxication and slurred speech, somewhat like the effects of alcohol. Larger doses produce hallucinations, thought disorders, loss of emotion, and memory loss. As we consider in Chapter 15, the symptoms of PCP abuse closely resemble schizophrenia.

PCP is an apparent exception to the rule that abused drugs increase activity at dopamine synapses. Rats will work to deliver phencyclidine to their brains even after dopamine synapses have been blocked (Carlezon & Wise, 1996). Instead PCP *inhibits certain kinds of glutamate receptors* (specifically known as NMDA-type glutamate receptors), including those located in the nucleus accum-

bens. Administration of phencyclidine to most brain areas produces a mixture of reinforcing and punishing effects, but in the nucleus accumbens it is reinforcing. Because glutamate axons converge on the same postsynaptic cells as dopamine axons, the simplest explanation is that reinforcement results from suppressed activity of those cells either by increasing dopamine (an inhibitory transmitter) or by decreasing glutamate (an excitatory transmitter).

Stop *&* Check

5. How does nicotine influence dopamine synapses?

6. How do opiates influence dopamine synapses?

7. What kind of synapse does phencyclidine (PCP) influence and how?

Check your answers on page 77.

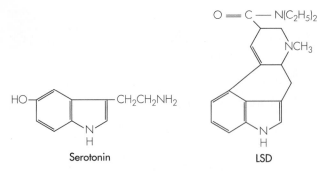

Figure 3.21 Resemblance of the neurotransmitter serotonin to LSD, a hallucinogenic drug

Marijuana

The leaves of the marijuana plant contain the chemical D^9-tetrahydrocannabinol (D^9-THC) and other **cannabinoids** (chemicals related to D^9-THC), which people absorb when they smoke or eat the leaves. The results may include an intensification of sensory experience and an illusion that time is passing very slowly. Marijuana users sometimes also experience impairments of attention, learning, and memory, especially the first few times they use the substance. Marijuana has been used medically to relieve pain or nausea and to combat glaucoma (an eye disorder), although its status as a medical drug remains in doubt in the United States.

Cannabinoids dissolve in the body's fats and leave the body very slowly. One consequence is that users seldom experience strong withdrawal effects after quitting the drug, as cocaine and opiate users do. Another consequence is that someone who uses marijuana can test positive for cannabinoids in the urine days or weeks later.

Marijuana users face certain health risks. Driving while under the influence of marijuana is analogous to driving under the influence of alcohol, and long-term marijuana smoking increases the risk of lung cancer, just as tobacco cigarettes do. However, marijuana users do not typically overdose as cocaine and opiate users do; even an unusually large dose of marijuana is unlikely to interfere with breathing or heartbeat.

For years investigators could not explain the effects of marijuana on the brain. They knew of a few effects on neuronal membranes, but found nothing spectacular until 1988, when they finally localized specific receptors for cannabinoids (Devane, Dysarz, Johnson, Melvin, & Howlett, 1988). Those receptors are abundant in the hippocampus, the basal ganglia, and the cerebellum (Herkenham, 1992; Herkenham, Lynn, de Costa, & Richfield, 1991). However, they are virtually absent from the medulla and the rest of the brain stem. That absence is significant because the medulla and brain stem include the centers that control breathing and heartbeat; we begin to understand why even large doses of marijuana do not threaten breathing or heartbeat.

Just as the discovery of opiate receptors in the brain led to a successful search for the brain's endogenous opiates, the discovery of cannabinoid receptors prompted investigators to search for a brain chemical that binds to cannabinoid receptors. The first such chemical to be found, **anandamide** (from the Sanskrit word *ananda*, meaning "bliss"), is found in both the skin and the brain and has at least one known function, which is to decrease pain (Calignano, LaRana, Giuffrida, & Piomelli, 1998; DiMarzo et al., 1995). However, the brain has abundant cannabinoid receptors but comparatively little anandamide, so it is probably not the main chemical to stimulate those receptors. Another possibility is *sn*-2 arachidonylglycerol, abbreviated **2-AG,** which the brain produces in larger quantities and which also binds to cannabinoid receptors (Stella, Schweitzer, & Piomelli, 1997). Why does your brain make marijuanalike chemicals? Little is known about the function of these chemicals in normal behavior, although one function is apparently to inhibit the serotonin type 3 (5-HT$_3$) synapses that are responsible for nausea (Fan, 1995). Marijuana has long been reported to reduce nausea; we now begin to understand why.

Hallucinogenic Drugs

Drugs that distort perception are called **hallucinogenic drugs.** Many hallucinogenic drugs, such as lysergic acid diethylamide (LSD), chemically resemble serotonin (see Figure 3.21) and stimulate serotonin type 2 (5-HT$_2$) receptors at inappropriate times or for longer than usual durations. Contrast this mode of action to that of amphetamine, which acts by releasing norepinephrine and dopamine from the presynaptic neurons. If the neurons have a low supply of these neurotransmitters, amphetamine is ineffective. In contrast, even after the complete removal of the neurons that release serotonin, LSD still exerts its full effect. It may even produce a greater-than-normal effect: After the removal of the serotonin-containing neurons, the postsynaptic neuron compensates by developing an increased number of serotonin receptors, making LSD more effective (B. L. Jacobs, 1987).

Note that we know *where* in the brain LSD exerts its effects, but not *why* those effects include hallucinations and other changes in perception. Presumably the 5-HT$_2$ receptors contribute in some way to perception, and an abnormal pattern of stimulation of those receptors leads to abnormal perceptions. But certainly we can explain the chemistry better than we can explain the psychological effects.

Caffeine

Caffeine, a drug found in coffee, tea, and many soft drinks, affects brain functioning in at least two ways. First, it increases heart rate but also constricts the blood vessels in the brain, thereby decreasing its blood sup-

Table 3.1 Summary of Some Drugs and Their Effects

Drugs	Main Effects on Behavior	Effect on Synapses
Amphetamine	Excitement, alertness, elevated mood, decreased fatigue	Increases release of dopamine and several other neurotransmitters
Cocaine	Excitement, alertness, elevated mood, decreased fatigue	Blocks reuptake of dopamine and several other neurotransmitters
Methylphenidate	Increased concentration	Blocks reuptake of dopamine and others, but more gradually than cocaine does
Nicotine	Mostly stimulant effects	Stimulates nicotinic-type acetylcholine receptor, which (among other effects) increases dopamine release in nucleus accumbens
Opiates	Relaxation, withdrawal, decreased pain	Stimulates endorphin receptors
Phencyclidine (PCP)	Intoxication, slurred speech. Higher doses: hallucinations, thought disorder, impaired memory and emotions	Inhibits NMDA-type glutamate receptors
Cannabinoids (marijuana)	Intensified sensory experiences, distorted sense of time, decreased pain and nausea	Excites receptors that also respond to anandamide and 2-AG
LSD	Distorted sensations	Stimulates serotonin type 2 receptors ($5\text{-}HT_2$)
Caffeine	Increased arousal, decreased headache, decreased sleep	Constricts blood vessels in brain, blocks adenosine (a transmitter that inhibits release of dopamine and acetylcholine)
Alcohol	Relaxation, decreased attention	Facilitates $GABA_A$ receptor, increases dopamine activity

ply. (Abstention from caffeine after repeated use increases blood flow to the brain and can cause a headache.) Second, caffeine interferes with the effects of the neurotransmitter adenosine. Adenosine acts at special receptors on the presynaptic terminal, inhibiting the release of dopamine and acetylcholine. By blocking the inhibitory effects of adenosine, caffeine increases the release of dopamine and acetylcholine (Silinsky, 1989).

Alcohol

Alcohol inhibits the flow of sodium across the membrane, expands the surface of membranes, decreases serotonin activity (Fils-Aime et al., 1996), facilitates response by the $GABA_A$ receptor (Mihic et al., 1997), blocks glutamate receptors (Tsai et al., 1998), and increases dopamine activity. No wonder it has so many diverse effects on behavior. In one strain of mice that ordinarily prefer alcohol to water, those with a mutation that deletes the dopamine D_2 receptor prefer water to alcohol (Phillips et al., 1998). That is, dopamine activity is important for the reinforcing value of alcohol,

as it is for so many other drugs. We consider alcohol abuse in Chapter 12.

Table 3.1 summarizes the effects of some commonly abused drugs.

Synapses, Reinforcement, and Personality

When researchers discovered that marijuana indirectly provokes increased dopamine activity in the nucleus accumbens, some people heralded this result as evidence that marijuana is similar to the more addictive drugs, such as cocaine and heroin. The flaw in that reasoning is that virtually *all* reinforcing experiences, not just addictive drugs, stimulate dopamine activity in the nucleus accumbens. For example, sexual excitement and orgasm depend on the release of dopamine at D_2 receptors (Giuliani & Ferrari, 1996; Hull et al., 1992). So does video game playing, at least in habitual players (Koepp et al., 1998). No doubt dopamine release could also be demonstrated in compulsive gamblers, sports

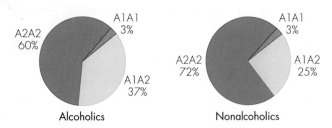

Figure 3.22 Relationship between D$_2$ receptor type and alcoholism
This figure summarizes the combined results of 15 studies, testing more than 1000 alcoholic adults and almost as many nonalcoholics. A higher percentage of the alcoholics have at least one A$_1$ type gene for the D$_2$ dopamine receptor. However, the contribution of this gene toward any alcoholic predisposition is obviously small. *(Source: Based on data of Noble et al., 1998)*

fans, and a great many others. Reinforcement is in the brain, not in the drug, and whatever is reinforcing to you can evoke dopamine release.

Might some change in your dopamine receptors influence your probability of trying drugs, gambling, or other risky behaviors? Indeed, might personality differences depend on variations in neurotransmitter receptors (Zuckerman, 1995)?

In 1990 researchers identified the gene that controls the development of the dopamine type D$_2$ receptor in humans. They also reported that people with the less common form of this gene, and therefore an alternative form of the D$_2$ receptor, were somewhat more likely than other people to develop severe alcoholism. Later research suggested that this gene is not specific to alcoholism, but instead increases the probability of a variety of pleasure-seeking behaviors, including alcohol consumption, other kinds of recreational drug use, overeating, and habitual gambling (Blum, Cull, Braverman, & Comings, 1996). Presumably the explanation is that, if the alternative form of the D$_2$ receptor is less sensitive than the usual form, then everyday experiences such as taking a walk or talking with friends might not be very reinforcing, so people might turn to drugs, gambling, sexual adventures, or other efforts to stimulate their D$_2$ receptors. However, the link between the alternative D$_2$ receptor and risky behaviors is a weak one (see Figure 3.22) (Goldman, Urbanek, Guenther, Robin, & Long, 1998; Noble et al., 1998). At most the gene controlling the D$_2$ receptor accounts for a small amount of behavioral variation.

Similarly researchers identified the gene that controls the D$_4$ receptor. Three studies found that people with an alternative form of the receptor have a stronger than average "novelty-seeking" aspect of personality as measured by a standardized personality test (Benjamin et al., 1996; Ebstein et al., 1996; Noble et al., 1998). Novelty seeking consists of being impulsive, exploratory, and quick-tempered. Other studies have found

that the alternative D$_4$ receptor is linked to an increased probability of schizophrenia (B. M. Cohen et al., 1999) and delusions (Serretti et al., 1998). However, several other studies failed to find a significant relationship between D$_4$ receptor types and various measures of personality (Jönsson et al., 1998; Pogue-Geile, Ferrell, Deka, Debski, & Manuck, 1998).

How should we interpret these small and inconsistent results? They suggest that variations in a single gene are but one contributor among many to resulting personality. Imagine by analogy 1000 chefs cooking a stew; some use 3 tablespoonfuls of tarragon and others use only 1. If they did everything else exactly the same, a gourmet might be able to detect which stews had more tarragon and which had less. But if they vary the other ingredients as well, and some chefs cook the stew longer or at a higher temperature, the stews may differ in so many ways that the effect of the tarragon is hard to notice. Something similar may be true for variations in neurotransmitter receptors: Our personalities depend on variations in many genes and experiences, as well as health and nutrition. Variations that result from a single gene may be present but hard to detect.

Module 3.3

In Closing: Drugs and Behavior

What do studies of drugs' mechanisms tell us in general about the basis of behavior? First, they tell us that drugs have much in common with one another, as well as with all sorts of other reinforcing events—they all increase dopamine (or decrease glutamate) activity in the nucleus accumbens. The effect on the nucleus accumbens probably relates more to attention than to pleasure. Second, studies of drugs tell us that individual differences in neurotransmitter receptors have the potential to alter our behavior, even what we call personality. According to current evidence no one receptor type by itself is responsible for huge variations in personality. However, we have large numbers of receptors, and the combined effects of many variations in receptors may indeed predispose different people to react differently to the experiences that mold their lives.

Summary

1. Drugs can act as agonists (facilitators) or antagonists (inhibitors) of a neurotransmitter by altering any step in the total sequence of transmission, from synthesis of the transmitter to its reuptake or breakdown following transmission. (p. 68)

2. Reinforcement depends to a great extent on the inhibition of cells in a few brain areas, including the nucleus accumbens. Reinforcing brain stimula-

tion, reinforcing experiences, and most self-administered drugs act largely by increasing the activity of axons that release dopamine (an inhibitory transmitter) at dopamine receptor types D_2, D_3, and D_4 in the nucleus accumbens. (p. 69)

3. Amphetamine acts mostly by increasing the release of dopamine. Cocaine and methylphenidate act by decreasing the reuptake of dopamine after its release. Opiate drugs stimulate endorphin synapses, which block GABA synapses, which would otherwise inhibit the release of dopamine. Phencyclidine inhibits glutamate synapses, which excite some of the same neurons that dopamine inhibits. (p. 70)

4. Marijuana, hallucinogens, caffeine, and alcohol also act by increasing or decreasing the activity at various kinds of synapses. Each has indirect ways of increasing dopamine release. (p. 74)

5. The genes responsible for dopamine receptor types D_2 and D_4 have been identified. People with the less common form of these genes produce altered, presumably less sensitive, receptors. A few studies have linked the alternative receptor forms to an increased probability of risk-taking and a novelty-seeking personality. Other personality dimensions may also relate to altered receptor types. So far, however, the research suggests only a weak relationship between any one receptor type and any identifiable personality trait. (p. 76)

Answers to *Stop and Check* Questions

1. Amphetamine causes the dopamine transporter to release dopamine instead of reabsorbing it. (p. 71)

2. Cocaine interferes with reuptake of released dopamine. (p. 71)

3. The effects of a methylphenidate pill develop and decline in the brain much more slowly than do those of cocaine. (p. 71)

4. Cocaine decreases total activity in the brain because it stimulates activity of dopamine, which is an inhibitory transmitter in most cases. (p. 71)

5. Nicotine excites acetylcholine receptors on neurons that release dopamine and thereby increases dopamine release. (p. 73)

6. Opiates stimulate endorphin synapses, which inhibit GABA synapses on certain cells that release dopamine. By inhibiting an inhibitor, opiates increase the release of dopamine. (p. 73)

7. Phencyclidine inhibits certain kinds of glutamate receptors. (p. 77)

Thought Questions

1. People who take methylphenidate (Ritalin) for control of attention-deficit disorder often report that, although the drug increases their arousal for a while, they feel a decrease in alertness and arousal a few hours later. Explain.

2. Some people who use MDMA ("ecstasy") report that after repeated use it becomes less effective. Offer an explanation other than the usual mechanisms of tolerance that apply to other drugs.

Module 3.4

Hormones and Behavior

If you want to tell your sister something personal, you tell her face to face or maybe even whisper in her ear. Neurotransmission at synapses, like personal communication, is delivered directly to the receptors in small amounts that other neurons nearby probably do not "overhear." In contrast suppose you are opening a new store and want to attract customers. You cannot speak individually to every potential customer. Instead you might place announcements on radio and television or in the newspaper. Hormones, like a public announcement, travel throughout the body, carrying a message to any cell that will listen.

A **hormone** is a chemical that is secreted by a gland and conveyed by the blood to other organs, whose activity it influences. **Figure 3.23** presents the major **endocrine** (hormone-producing) **glands**. Table 3.2 lists some important hormones and their principal effects. (The list is not complete; the body has an enormous number of hormones, including some that are present in small amounts with unknown effects.)

Hormones are particularly useful for coordinating long-lasting changes in multiple parts of the body. For example, in early spring, birds that are preparing to migrate secrete hormones with many effects: The birds change their eating and digestion to store extra fat—not enough to make flight difficult, but enough to provide the energy they need for a long journey. They also replace their old, faded feathers with brightly colored new ones; they start flying north; they start seeking mates; males start singing; and so forth.

For another example, fat cells release the hormone *leptin,* which we encounter in detail in Chapter 10. Leptin tells the brain how much fat the body has. So when leptin levels are high, appetite decreases, at least in individuals with normal sensitivity to leptin. When leptin levels are very low, the brain acts as if the body is starving: In addition to becoming hungry, the individual becomes inactive (to save energy) and shifts energy away from the reproductive system (also to save energy).

Hypothalamus
Pineal gland
Pituitary gland

Parathyroid glands
Thyroid glands
Thymus

Liver
Adrenal gland
Kidney
Pancreas

Ovary (in female)
Placenta (in female during pregnancy)

Testis (in male)

Figure 3.23 **Location of some of the major endocrine glands**
(Source: Starr & Taggart, 1989)

Stop & Check

1. Which has more long-lasting effects, a neurotransmitter or a hormone? Which has effects on more organs?

   Check your answers on page 83.

Mechanisms of Hormone Actions

Hormones exert many of their effects through mechanisms similar to those of metabotropic neurotransmitters or neuromodulators: They attach to receptors on

Table 3.2 Partial List of Hormone-Releasing Glands

Organ	Hormone	Hormone Functions
Hypothalamus	Various releasing hormones	Promote or inhibit release of various hormones by pituitary
Anterior pituitary	Thyroid-stimulating hormone (TSH)	Stimulates thyroid gland
	Luteinizing hormone (LH)	Increases production of progesterone (female), testosterone (male); stimulates ovulation
	Follicle-stimulating hormone (FSH)	Increases production of estrogen and maturation of ovum (female) and sperm production (male)
	ACTH	Increases secretion of steroid hormones by adrenal gland
	Prolactin	Increases milk production
	Growth hormone (GH), also known as somatotropin	Increases body growth, including the growth spurt during puberty
Posterior pituitary	Oxytocin	Controls uterine contractions, milk release, certain aspects of parental behavior, and sexual pleasure
	Vasopressin (also known as antidiuretic hormone)	Constricts blood vessels and raises blood pressure, decreases urine volume
Pineal	Melatonin	Increases sleepiness, influences sleep–wake cycle, also has role in onset of puberty
Thyroid	Thyoxine Triiodothyronine	Increase metabolic rate, growth, and maturation
Parathyroid	Parathyroid hormone	Increases blood calcium and decreases potassium
Adrenal cortex	Aldosterone	Reduces secretion of salts by the kidneys
	cortisol, corticosterone	Stimulate liver to elevate blood sugar, increase metabolism of proteins and fats
Adrenal medulla	Epinephrine, norepinephrine	Similar to effects of sympathetic nervous system
Pancreas	Insulin	Increases entry of glucose to cells and increases storage as fats
	Glucagon	Increases conversion of stored fats to blood glucose
Ovary	Estrogens	Promote female sexual characteristics
	Progesterone	Maintains pregnancy
Testis	Androgens	Promote sperm production, growth of pubic hair, and male sexual characteristics
Liver	Somatomedins	Stimulate growth
Kidney	Renin	Converts a blood protein into angiotensin, which regulates blood pressure and contributes to hypovolemic thirst
Thymus	Thymosin (and others)	Support immune responses
Fat cells	Leptin	Decreases appetite, increases activity, necessary for onset of puberty

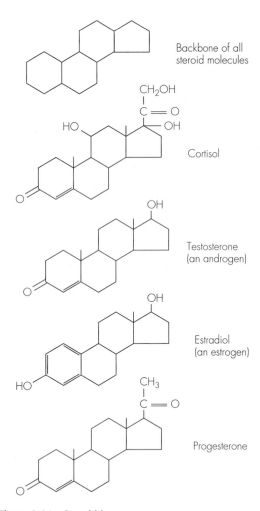

Figure 3.24　Steroid hormones
Note the similarity between the sex hormones testosterone and estradiol.

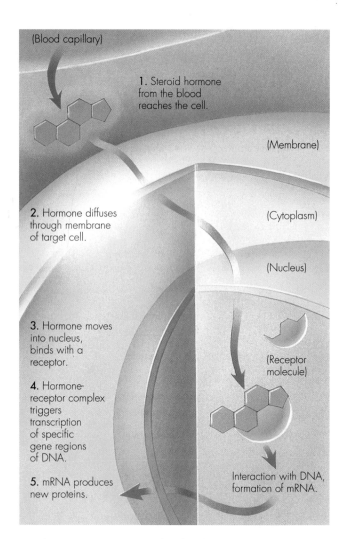

1. Steroid hormone from the blood reaches the cell.

(Blood capillary)

(Membrane)

2. Hormone diffuses through membrane of target cell.

(Cytoplasm)

(Nucleus)

3. Hormone moves into nucleus, binds with a receptor.

4. Hormone-receptor complex triggers transcription of specific gene regions of DNA.

(Receptor molecule)

5. mRNA produces new proteins.

Interaction with DNA, formation of mRNA.

Figure 3.25　One route of action for steroid hormones
The hormone enters a cell, binds with a receptor in the nucleus, and thereby activates particular genes. As a result the cell increases its production of specific proteins. (Steroid hormones also bind to receptors on the membrane, like peptide hormones.) *(Source: Starr & Taggart, 1989)*

the cell membrane, where they activate an enzyme that produces cyclic AMP or some other second messenger. In fact many chemicals—including epinephrine, norepinephrine, insulin, and oxytocin—serve as both neurotransmitters and hormones. We call a chemical a neurotransmitter or neuromodulator when it is released in small quantities close to its target cells; we call it a hormone when it is released in larger quantities that flow through the blood to targets throughout the body.

Dozens of hormones have been identified, and new ones continue to be discovered. Most fall into a few major classes. One class is composed of **protein hormones** and **peptide hormones,** composed of chains of amino acids. (Proteins are longer chains and peptides are shorter.) Insulin, one example of a protein hormone, facilitates the flow of glucose and other nutrients into the cells. A *glycoprotein* or *glycopeptide* is a chain of amino acids attached to a carbohydrate. Protein and peptide hormones attach to membrane receptors where they activate a second messenger within the cell—exactly the same process as at a metabotropic synapse.

Another major class, the **steroid hormones** contain four carbon rings, as Figure 3.24 shows. Steroids are de-rived from cholesterol; we are often warned about the risks of excessive cholesterol, but a moderate amount is necessary for generating these important hormones. Steroids exert their effects in two ways. First, they bind to membrane receptors, just as peptide and protein hormones do. Second, they enter cells and attach to receptors in the cytoplasm, which then move to the nucleus of the cell where they determine which genes will be expressed (see Figure 3.25). Two important steroids are cortisol, which is predominant in humans, and corticosterone, which is predominant in rodents. Released by the adrenal cortex in response to stressful experiences, these steroids increase the breakdown of fats and proteins (including muscle proteins) into chemicals the body can use for energy, including glucose. Thus they increase the body's ability to meet the needs of the immediate situation.

The "sex hormones"—estrogens, progesterone, and the androgens—are a special category of steroids, released mostly by the gonads (testis and ovary), although the adrenal glands also release a small amount. We generally refer to the **androgens,** a group that includes testosterone and several others, as "male hormones" because their level is much higher in men than in women. We refer to the **estrogens,** a group that includes estradiol and others, as "female hormones" because their level is much higher in women than in men. However, both types of hormones function in both sexes. **Progesterone,** among other functions, prepares the uterus for the implantation of a fertilized ovum and promotes the maintenance of pregnancy. Sex hormones have effects on the brain, the genitals, and other organs.

Genes that are activated by androgens or estrogens are called **sex-limited genes** because their effects are much stronger in one sex than in the other. For example, estrogen activates the genes responsible for breast development (much more in women than in men), and androgen activates the genes responsible for the growth of facial hair (much more in men than in women).

Testosterone, other androgens, and synthetic chemicals derived from them are known as **anabolic steroids** because they tend to build up muscles. They increase the synthesis of muscle proteins and enhance the size and strength of muscles, especially in those who exercise (Di Pasquale, 1997). (Cortisol is a *catabolic steroid* because it tends to break down muscles.) Some people, especially male athletes, take anabolic steroids to help develop their muscular strength. One such drug, *androstenedione,* is often taken as a pill but has doubtful effects, as the digestive system breaks down much or most of it before it has a chance to enter the blood.

You might assume that a drug that increases muscle strength has other masculinizing effects. However, the high levels of steroids produce negative feedback on the anterior pituitary, which secretes hormones that control the gonads. The result is breast growth, decreased testis size, increased cholesterol levels, and a high prevalence of depression (Pope & Katz, 1994). The use of anabolic steroids is dangerous and prohibited for those planning to compete in the Olympics and many other organized sports. A high-protein diet can accomplish some of the same goals as the drugs with fewer risks (Di Pasquale, 1997).

In addition to peptide and steroid hormones, other classes are thyroid hormones (released by the thyroid gland, all of them containing iodine) and monoamines (such as norepinephrine and dopamine). Several miscellaneous hormones do not fit into any of the described categories.

Stop & Check

2. Given the relationship between stress and cortisol and the effects of cortisol and testosterone on muscles, what do you predict would be the effect of stress on testosterone levels?

Check your answers on page 83.

Control of Hormone Release

Just as circulating hormones modify brain activity, hormones secreted by the brain control the secretion of many other hormones. The **pituitary gland,** attached to the hypothalamus, is sometimes called the "master gland" because its secretions influence so many other glands (see Figure 3.26). However, the hypothalamus controls the pituitary, so if any gland is the true master gland, it should be the hypothalamus. The pituitary consists of two distinct glands, the **anterior pituitary** and the **posterior pituitary,** which release different sets of hormones (Table 3.2, p. 79).

The posterior pituitary, composed of neural tissue, can be considered an extension of the hypothalamus. Neurons in the hypothalamus synthesize the hormones **oxytocin** and **vasopressin** (also known as antidiuretic hormone), plus much smaller amounts of other peptides (J. F. Morris & Pow, 1993). Hypothalamic cells then transport these hormones down their axons to their terminals in the posterior pituitary, as shown in Figure 3.27, which releases the hormones into the blood.

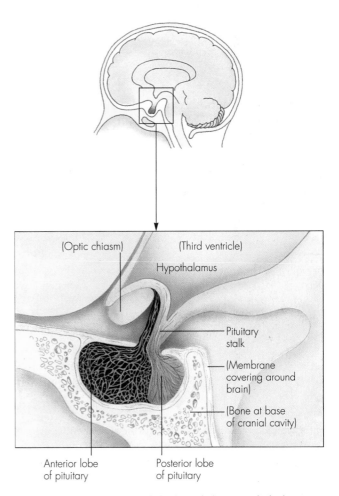

Figure 3.26 Location of the hypothalamus and pituitary gland in the human brain
(Source: Starr & Taggart, 1989)

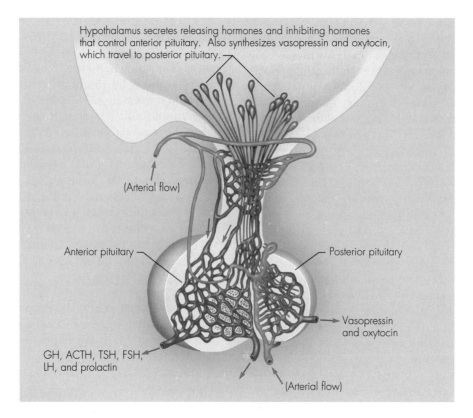

Figure 3.27 Pituitary hormones
The hypothalamus produces vasopressin and oxytocin, which travel to the posterior pituitary (really an extension of the hypothalamus). The posterior pituitary releases those hormones in response to neural signals. The hypothalamus also produces releasing hormones and inhibiting hormones, which travel to the anterior pituitary, where they control the release of six hormones synthesized there.

The anterior pituitary, composed of glandular tissue, synthesizes six hormones itself, although the hypothalamus controls their release (see Figure 3.27). The hypothalamus secretes **releasing hormones,** which flow through the blood to the anterior pituitary. There they stimulate or inhibit the release of six known hormones, five of which control the secretions of other endocrine organs:

Adrenocorticotropic hormone (ACTH)	Controls secretions of the adrenal cortex
Thyroid-stimulating hormone (TSH)	Controls secretions of the thyroid gland
Prolactin	Controls secretions of the mammary glands
Somatotropin, also known as growth hormone (GH)	Promotes growth throughout the body
Follicle-stimulating hormone (FSH)	
Luteinizing hormone (LH) (FSH and LH are known together as *gonadotropins* because they stimulate the gonads.)	Control secretions of the gonads

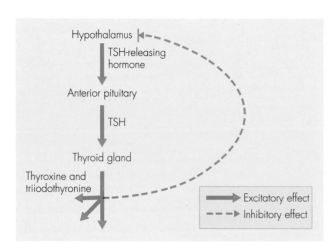

Figure 3.28 Negative feedback in the control of thyroid hormones
The hypothalamus secretes a releasing hormone that stimulates the anterior pituitary to release TSH, which stimulates the thyroid gland to release its hormones. Those hormones in turn act on the hypothalamus to decrease its secretion of the releasing hormone.

The hypothalamus maintains fairly constant circulating levels of certain hormones through a negative feedback system. For example, when the level of thyroid hormone is low, the hypothalamus releases *TSH-releasing hormone,* which stimulates the anterior pituitary to release TSH, which in turn causes the thyroid gland to secrete more thyroid hormones. After the level of thyroid hormones has risen, the hypothalamus decreases its release of TSH-releasing hormone (see Figure 3.28).

Stop & Check

3. Which part of the pituitary—anterior or posterior—is neural tissue, similar to the hypothalamus? Which part is glandular tissue and produces hormones that control the secretions by other endocrine organs?

Check your answers on this page.

Module 3.4

In Closing:
Hormones and the Nervous System

Many researchers believe that instead of talking about the nervous system, we should talk about the "neuroendocrine system," treating the nervous system and the endocrine system as a single indivisible unit. That is, hormones influence the nervous system and the nervous system controls the release of hormones; the two systems together produce communication throughout the body. While we are at it, others point out, the neuroendocrine system has much communication back and forth with the immune system, so maybe we should call it the "neuroimmunoendocrine system," admittedly a bit of a mouthful. Regardless of the term we use, the nervous system interacts strongly with these other systems, and hormones are important for many aspects of behavior. We encounter them especially in Chapters 10 (hunger and thirst), 11 (sex), and 12 (emotions).

Summary

1. Among the several types of hormones are peptide hormones and steroid hormones. Peptide hormones attach to membrane receptors and exert effects similar to those of neurotransmitters. Steroid hormones alter the expression of the genes. (p. 80)

2. The hypothalamus controls activity of the pituitary gland through both nerve impulses and releasing hormones. The pituitary in turn secretes hormones that alter the activity of other endocrine glands. (p. 81)

Answers to *Stop and Check* Questions

1. A hormone has more long-lasting effects. A hormone can affect many parts of the brain as well as other organs; a neurotransmitter affects only the neurons near its point of release. (p. 78)

2. Stress increases the release of cortisol, which breaks down muscles. Testosterone, which builds up muscles, declines during times of stress. (p. 81)

3. The posterior pituitary is neural tissue, like the hypothalamus. The anterior pituitary is glandular tissue and produces hormones that control several other endocrine organs. (p. 83)

Chapter Ending
Key Terms and Activities

Terms

acetylcholine (p. 60)

acetylcholinesterase (p. 65)

affinity (p. 68)

2-AG (p. 74)

agonist (p. 68)

amino acids (p. 59)

amphetamine (p. 70)

anabolic steroid (p. 81)

anandamide (p. 74)

androgen (p. 81)

antagonist (p. 68)

anterior pituitary (p. 81)

attention-deficit disorder (ADD) (p. 71)

caffeine (p. 74)

cannabinoids (p. 74)

catecholamine (p. 60)

cocaine (p. 70)

COMT (p. 66)

efficacy (p. 68)

endocrine gland (p. 78)

estrogen (p. 81)

excitatory postsynaptic potential (EPSP) (p. 53)

exocytosis (p. 61)

G-protein (p. 63)

hallucinogenic drugs (p. 74)

hormone (p. 78)

inhibitory postsynaptic potential (IPSP) (p. 55)

ionotropic effect (p. 62)

MAO (p. 66)

metabotropic effect (p. 63)

methylphenidate (p. 71)

monoamines (p. 60)

neuromodulator (p. 64)

neurotransmitter (p. 59)

nicotine (p. 72)

nitric oxide (p. 60)

nucleus accumbens (p. 69)

opiate drugs (p. 72)

oxytocin (p. 81)

peptide (p. 59)

peptide hormone (p. 80)

phencyclidine (PCP) (p. 73)

pituitary gland (p. 81)

positron-emission tomography (PET) (p. 72)

posterior pituitary (p. 81)

postsynaptic neuron (p. 53)

presynaptic neuron (p. 53)

progesterone (p. 81)

protein hormone (p. 80)

purines (p. 60)

reflex (p. 52)

reflex arc (p. 52)

releasing hormone (p. 82)

reuptake (p. 66)

second messenger (p. 63)

self-stimulation of the brain (p. 69)

sex-limited gene (p. 81)

spatial summation (p. 54)

spontaneous firing rate (p. 56)

steroid hormone (p. 80)

stimulant drugs (p. 70)

synapse (p. 52)

temporal summation (p. 52)

transporter (p. 66)

vasopressin (antidiuretic hormone) (p. 81)

vesicle (p. 61)

Suggestions for Further Reading

Julien, R. M. (1995). *A primer of drug action* (7th ed.). New York: Freeman. Extremely informative description of the effects of both legal and illegal drugs.

Levitan, I. B., & Kaczmarek, L. K. (1991). *The neuron.* New York: Oxford University Press. A thorough treatment of the mechanisms of synaptic communication.

Nelson, R. J. (1995). *An introduction to behavioral endocrinology.* Sunderland, MA: Sinauer Associates. An excellent, thorough text on hormones and behavior.

Zuckerman, M. (1995). Good and bad humors: Biochemical bases of personality and its disorders. *Psychological Science, 6,* 325–332. Discussion of how alterations in brain structures, transmitters, and receptors might contribute to variations in personality.

Web Sites to Explore

• You can go to the Biological Psychology Study Center and click on these links. While there, you can also check for suggested articles available on InfoTrac. The Biological Internet address is:
http://psychology.wadsworth.com/book/kalatbiopsych7e/

http://www.neurosci.tufts.edu/~rhammer/synapse1.html
Includes animations of neurotransmitter actions, plus an advertisement for a more elaborate animations program.

http://www.npaci.edu/features/98/Dec/index.html
A detailed model of an acetylcholine synapse onto a muscle.

http://psych.colorado.edu/~biopsych/jamey/synapse.html
Includes simple graphics of synapses and an extensive glossary.

http://www.rci.rutgers.edu/~lwh/drugs/
A complete textbook on *Drugs, Brain, and Behavior,* by C. R. Timmons and L. W. Hamilton. A good site to check for more information on drug effects.

http://www.med.upenn.edu/recovery/pros/opioids.html
Text specifically about heroin use and recovery.

http://www.nursing.uiowa.edu/sites/pedspain/Adjuvants/Ritalitt.htm
Information about methylphenidate (Ritalin).

http://www.nida.nih.gov/ResearchReports/Steroids/AnabolicSteroids.html
Good source of information about anabolic steroids.

Active Learner Link

Animation: Synaptic Transmission
Quiz for Chapter 3

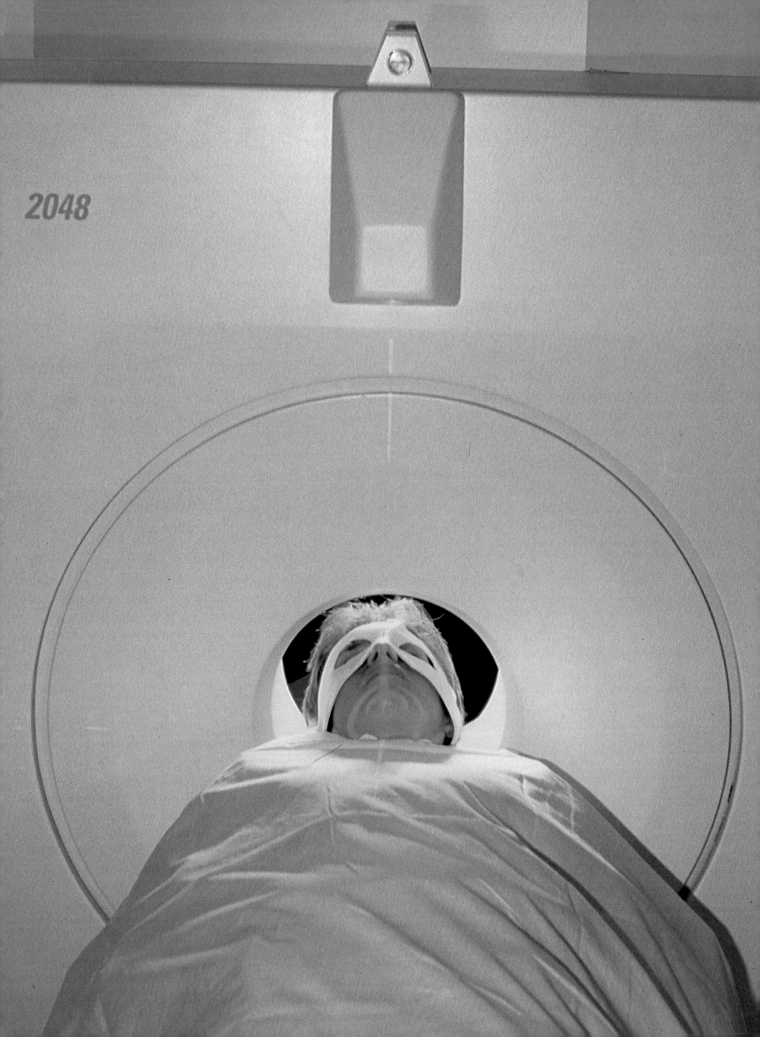

Chapter

4

Anatomy of the Nervous System

Main Ideas

1. Each part of the nervous system has specialized functions, although the parts work together to produce behavior. Damage to different areas results in different types of behavioral deficits.

2. The cerebral cortex, the largest structure in the mammalian brain, elaborately processes sensory information and provides for fine control of movement.

3. As research has identified the different functions of different brain areas, a difficult question has arisen concerning how the areas combine to produce unified experience and behavior.

Trying to learn **neuroanatomy** (the anatomy of the nervous system) from a book is like trying to learn geography from a road map. A map can tell you that Mystic, Georgia, is about 40 km north of Enigma, Georgia, and that the two cities are connected by a combination of roads including U.S. Route 129. Similarly a book can tell you that the habenula is about 4.6 mm from the interpeduncular nucleus in a rat's brain (slightly farther in a human brain) and that the two structures are connected by a set of axons known as the habenulopeduncular tract (also sometimes known as the fasciculus retroflexus). But these two little gems of information will seem both mysterious and enigmatic unless you are concerned with that part of Georgia or that area of the brain.

This chapter does not provide a detailed road map of the nervous system. It is more like a world globe, describing the large, basic structures (analogous to the continents) and some distinctive features of each. The focus is entirely on the nervous systems of vertebrates, especially mammals. Most of the illustrations are of the human brain, but its structure is similar to that of other mammals. Later chapters contain additional detail on specific parts of the brain in relation to particular behaviors.

Be prepared: This chapter contains more new terms than any other does. You should not expect to memorize all of the brain areas at once, and it will pay to review this chapter several times.

Opposite:
This woman is undergoing a PET scan, one of several methods for examining brain structure and activity in a living person.

Module 4.1

The Divisions of the Vertebrate Nervous System

Your nervous system consists of many structures, each with substructures made up of many neurons, each of which receives and makes many synapses. How do all those little parts work together to make one behaving unit, namely, you? Does each neuron have an independent function so that, for example, one cell recognizes your grandmother, another controls your desire for pizzas, and another makes you smile at babies? Do individual neurons send partial messages to some "monarch" center that adds up all the information into a single experience? Or does the brain operate as an undifferentiated whole, with each part doing the same thing as every other part?

The answer is "none of the above." Individual neurons have specialized functions, but the activity of a single cell by itself has no more meaning than the letter *h* does out of context. Different brain areas communicate with one another, but they do not funnel all their activity into any central processor or "little person in the head." Meaningful activity emerges from an enormous number of partly independent, partly interdependent processes occurring simultaneously throughout your nervous system. In this text we go back and forth between the special contributions of particular brain areas and the ways in which different areas communicate with one another and combine into functioning systems.

The vertebrate nervous system consists of the central nervous system and the peripheral nervous system (see Figure 4.1). The **central nervous system (CNS)** is the brain and the spinal cord, each of which includes a great many substructures. The **peripheral nervous system (PNS)**—the nerves outside the brain and spinal cord—has two divisions: The **somatic nervous system** consists of the nerves that convey messages from the sense organs to the CNS and from the CNS to the muscles and glands. The **autonomic nervous system** is a set of neurons that control the heart, the intestines, and other organs. This text focuses mostly on the central nervous system.

In this first module we examine key neuroanatomical terms and survey some large structures of the nervous system. In the second module we concentrate on the structures and functions of the cerebral cortex, the largest part of the mammalian central nervous system.

Some Terminology

To follow a road map, you first must understand the terms *north, south, east,* and *west.* But because the nervous system is a complex three-dimensional structure,

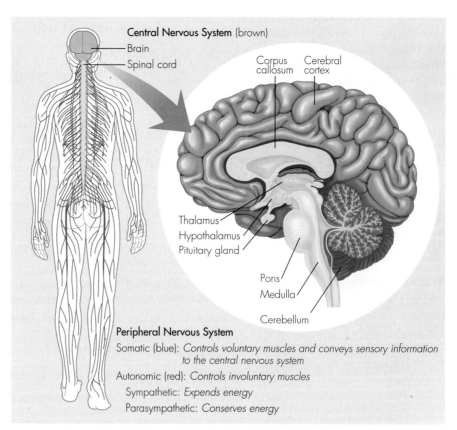

Central Nervous System (brown)
- Brain
- Spinal cord

Corpus callosum
Cerebral cortex
Thalamus
Hypothalamus
Pituitary gland
Pons
Medulla
Cerebellum

Peripheral Nervous System
Somatic (blue): *Controls voluntary muscles and conveys sensory information to the central nervous system*
Autonomic (red): *Controls involuntary muscles*
  Sympathetic: *Expends energy*
  Parasympathetic: *Conserves energy*

Figure 4.1 The human nervous system
Both the central nervous system and the peripheral nervous system have major subdivisions. The closeup of the brain shows the right hemisphere as seen from the midline.

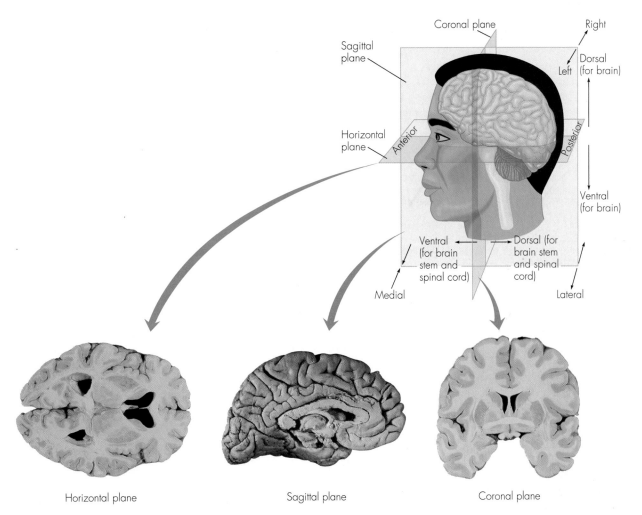

Figure 4.2 Terms for anatomical directions in the nervous system
In four-legged animals dorsal and ventral point in the same direction for the head as they do for the rest of the body. However, humans' upright posture has tilted the head relative to the spinal cord, so the dorsal and ventral directions of the head are not parallel to the dorsal and ventral directions of the spinal cord.

we need more terms to describe it. In Figure 4.2 and Table 4.1, note that **dorsal** means toward the back and **ventral** means toward the stomach. (One way to remember these terms is that a ventriloquist is literally a "stomach talker.") In a four-legged animal the top of the brain (with respect to gravity) is dorsal (on the same side as the animal's back), and the bottom of the brain is ventral (on the stomach side). When humans evolved an upright posture, the position of our head changed relative to the spinal cord. For convenience we still apply the terms *dorsal* and *ventral* to the same parts of the human brain as other vertebrate brains. Consequently the dorsal–ventral axis of the human brain is at right angles to the dorsal–ventral axis of the spinal cord.

Table 4.2 introduces some additional terminology that relates to clusters of neurons and anatomical structures of the brain. Such technical terms may be confusing at first, but they help investigators communicate clearly with one another. Tables 4.1 and 4.2 require careful study and review. After you think you have mastered the terms, check yourself with the following.

Stop & Check

1. What does *dorsal* mean, and what term is its opposite?

2. What term means *toward the side, away from the midline* and what term is its opposite?

3. If two structures are both on the left side of the body, they are _____ to each other. If one is on the left and the other is on the right, they are _____ to each other.

4. The bulges in the cerebral cortex are called _____; the grooves between them are called _____.

Check your answers on page 100.

The Spinal Cord

The **spinal cord** is the part of the CNS found within the spinal column; the spinal cord communicates with the sense organs and muscles below the level of the head. It

Table 4.1 Anatomical Terms Referring to Directions

Term	Definition
Dorsal	Toward the back, away from the ventral (stomach) side. The top of the brain is considered dorsal because it has that position in four-legged animals.
Ventral	Toward the stomach, away from the dorsal (back) side. (*Venter* is the Latin word for "belly." It also shows up in the word *ventriloquist*, literally meaning "stomach talker.")
Anterior	Toward the front end
Posterior	Toward the rear end
Superior	Above another part
Inferior	Below another part
Lateral	Toward the side, away from the midline
Medial	Toward the midline, away from the side
Proximal	Located close (approximate) to the point of origin or attachment
Distal	Located more distant from the point of origin or attachment
Ipsilateral	On the same side of the body (such as two parts on the left or two on the right)
Contralateral	On the opposite side of the body (one on the left and one on the right)
Coronal plane (or frontal plane)	A plane that shows brain structures as seen from the front
Sagittal plane	A plane that shows brain structures as seen from the side
Horizontal plane (or transverse plane)	A plane that shows brain structures as seen from above

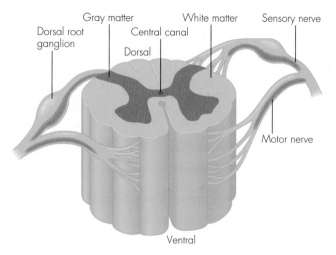

Gray matter White matter Sensory nerve
Dorsal root ganglion Central canal
Dorsal
Motor nerve
Ventral

Figure 4.3 Diagram of a cross section through the spinal cord
The dorsal root on each side conveys sensory information to the spinal cord; the ventral root conveys motor commands to the muscles.

is a segmented structure, and each segment has on each side both a sensory nerve and a motor nerve, as shown in Figures 4.3 and 4.4. The **Bell-Magendie law** refers to the observation that the entering dorsal roots carry sensory information and the exiting ventral roots carry motor information to the muscles and glands. (This was one of the first discoveries about the functions of the nervous system.) The cell bodies of the sensory neurons are located in clusters of neurons outside the spinal cord, called the **dorsal root ganglia**. (*Ganglia* is the plural of *ganglion*, a cluster of neurons.) Cell bodies of the motor neurons are located within the spinal cord.

In the cross section through the spinal cord shown in Figures 4.4 and 4.5, the H-shaped **gray matter** in the center of the cord is densely packed with cell bodies and dendrites. Many of the interneurons of the spinal cord (those that are neither sensory nor motor) send axons that leave the gray matter and travel toward the brain or to other parts of the spinal cord through the **white matter**, which is composed mostly of myelinated axons.

Each segment of the spinal cord sends sensory information to the brain and receives motor commands from the brain. All that information passes through tracts of axons in the spinal cord. If the spinal cord is

Table 4.2	Terms Referring to Parts of the Nervous System
Term	**Definition**
Lamina	A row or layer of cell bodies separated from other cell bodies by a layer of axons and dendrites
Column	A set of cells perpendicular to the surface of the cortex, with similar properties
Tract	A set of axons within the CNS, also known as a *projection*. If axons extend from cell bodies in structure A to synapses onto B, we say that the fibers "project" from A onto B.
Nerve	A set of axons in the periphery, either from the CNS to a muscle or gland or from a sensory organ to the CNS
Nucleus	A cluster of neuron cell bodies within the CNS
Ganglion	A cluster of neuron cell bodies, usually outside the CNS (as in the sympathetic nervous system)
Gyrus (pl.: gyri)	A protuberance on the surface of the brain
Sulcus (pl.: sulci)	A fold or groove that separates one gyrus from another
Fissure	A long, deep sulcus

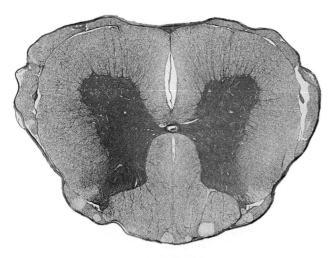

Figure 4.4 Photo of a cross section through the spinal cord
The H-shaped structure in the center is gray matter, composed largely of cell bodies. The surrounding white matter consists of axons. The axons are organized in tracts; some carry information from the brain and higher levels of the spinal cord downward, while others carry information from lower levels upward. (*Source: Manfred Kage/Peter Arnold, Inc.*)

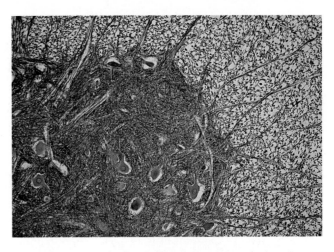

Figure 4.5 A section of gray matter of the spinal cord (lower left) and white matter surrounding it
Cell bodies and dendrites reside entirely in the gray matter. Axons travel from one area of gray matter to another in the white matter. (*Source: Manfred Kage/Peter Arnold, Inc.*)

cut at a given segment, the brain loses sensation from that segment and all segments below it; the brain also loses motor control over all parts of the body served by that segment and the lower ones.

The Autonomic Nervous System

The autonomic nervous system is a set of neurons that receives information from and sends commands to the heart, intestines, and other organs. It is comprised of two parts: the sympathetic and parasympathetic nervous systems (see Figure 4.6). The **sympathetic nervous system,** a network of nerves that prepare the body's organs for vigorous activity, consists of two paired chains of ganglia lying just to the left and right of the spinal cord in its central regions (the thoracic and lumbar areas) and connected by axons to the spinal cord. Sympathetic axons extend from the ganglia to the body's organs and activate them for "fight or flight"—increased breathing, increased heart rate, and decreased digestive activity. Because all of the sympathetic ganglia are closely linked, they often act as a single system, "in sympathy" with one another, although one part can be more active than the others. The sweat glands, the adrenal glands, the muscles that constrict blood vessels, and the muscles that erect the hairs of the skin have only sympathetic, not parasympathetic, input (see Digression 4.1).

The **parasympathetic nervous system** facilitates vegetative, nonemergency responses by the body's organs. The term *para* means "beside" or "related to," and parasympathetic activities are related to, and generally opposite to, sympathetic activities. For example, the sympathetic nervous system increases heart rate; the parasympathetic nervous system decreases it. The parasympathetic nervous system increases digestive activity; the sympathetic nervous system decreases it. Although the sympathetic and parasympathetic systems act in

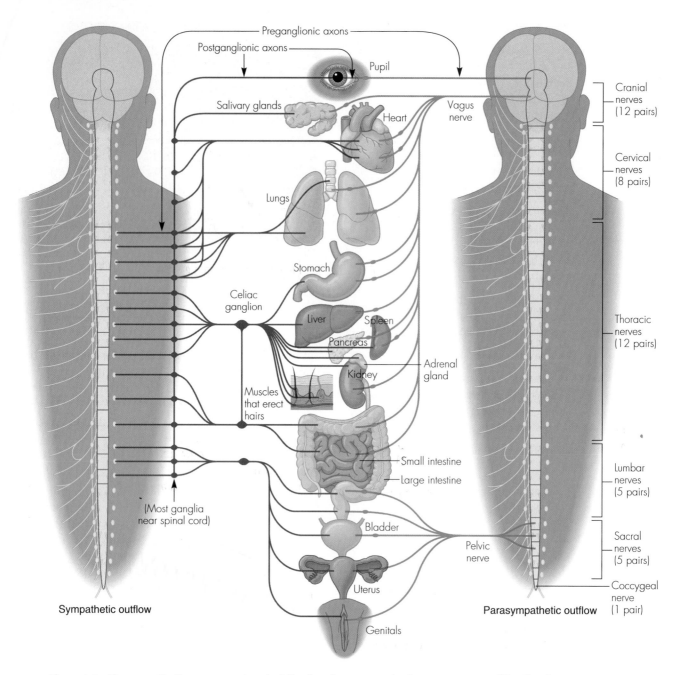

Figure 4.6 The sympathetic nervous system (red lines) and parasympathetic nervous system (blue lines)
Note that the adrenal glands and hair erector muscles receive sympathetic input only. *(Source: Starr & Taggart, 1989)*

opposition to one another, they are both constantly active to varying degrees, and some stimuli arouse parts of one system and parts of the other.

The parasympathetic nervous system is sometimes also known as the craniosacral system because it consists of the cranial nerves and nerves from the sacral spinal cord (Figure 4.6). Unlike the ganglia in the sympathetic system, the parasympathetic ganglia are not arranged in a chain near the spinal cord. Rather, long *preganglionic* axons extend from the spinal cord to parasympathetic ganglia close to each internal organ; shorter *postganglionic* fibers then extend from the para-

sympathetic ganglia into the organs themselves. Because the parasympathetic ganglia are not linked to one another, they act somewhat more independently than the sympathetic ganglia do. Parasympathetic activity decreases heart rate, increases digestive rate, and in general promotes energy-conserving, nonemergency functions.

The parasympathetic nervous system's postganglionic axons release the neurotransmitter acetylcholine. Most of the postganglionic synapses of the sympathetic nervous system use norepinephrine, although a few, such as the ones that control the sweat glands, use acetylcholine. Because the two systems use different transmitters,

Gooseflesh

Erection of the hairs, known as "gooseflesh" or "goose bumps," is controlled by the sympathetic nervous system. What does this response have to do with the fight-or-flight functions that are usually associated with the sympathetic nervous system?

Human body hairs are so short that erecting them accomplishes nothing of importance; the response is an evolutionary relic from ancient ancestors with furrier bodies. Erecting the hairs helps nonhuman mammals conserve their body warmth in a cold environment by increasing their insulation. It also serves several species as a defense against enemies in fight-or-flight

situations. Consider, for example, the Halloween cat or any other frightened, cornered animal; by erecting its hairs it looks larger and may thereby deter its opponent.

The porcupine's quills, which are an effective defense against potential predators, are actually modified body hairs. In a fight-or-flight situation, sympathetic nervous system activity leads to erection of the quills, just as it leads to erection of the hairs in other mammals (Richter & Langworthy, 1933). The behavior that makes the quills so useful, their erection in response to fear, evidently evolved before the quills themselves did.

---

certain drugs may excite or inhibit one system or the other. For example, over-the-counter cold remedies exert most of their effects either by blocking parasympathetic activity or by increasing sympathetic activity. This action is useful because the flow of sinus fluids is a parasympathetic response; thus, drugs that block the parasympathetic system inhibit sinus flow. The common side effects of cold remedies also stem from their prosympathetic, antiparasympathetic activities: They inhibit salivation and digestion and increase heart rate.

Stop & Check

5. Sensory nerves enter which side of the spinal cord, dorsal or ventral?

6. Which functions are controlled by the sympathetic nervous system? Which are controlled by the parasympathetic nervous system?

Check your answers on page 100.

The Hindbrain

The brain itself (as distinct from the spinal cord) consists of three major divisions: the hindbrain, the midbrain, and the forebrain (see Figure 4.7 and Table 4.3). Brain investigators unfortunately use a variety of terms synonymously. For example, instead of the English terms hindbrain, midbrain, and forebrain, some people prefer words with Greek roots: rhombencephalon,

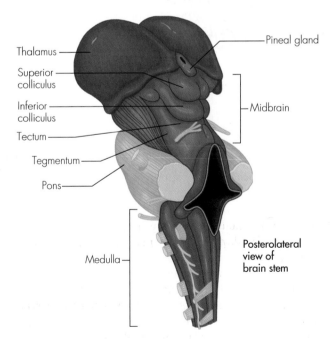

Figure 4.8   The human brain stem
This composite structure extends from the top of the spinal cord into the center of the forebrain. The pons, pineal gland, and colliculi are ordinarily surrounded by the cerebral cortex.

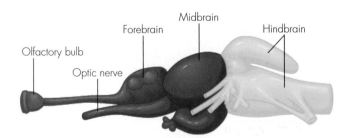

Figure 4.7   Three major divisions of the vertebrate brain
In a fish brain, as shown here, the forebrain, midbrain, and hindbrain are clearly visible as separate bulges. In adult mammals the forebrain grows so large that it surrounds the entire midbrain and part of the hindbrain.

Table 4.3 Major Divisions of the Vertebrate Brain

Area	Also Known as	Major Structures
Forebrain	Prosencephalon ("forward-brain")	
	Diencephalon ("between-brain")	Thalamus, hypothalamus
	Telencephalon ("end-brain")	Cerebral cortex, hippocampus, basal ganglia
Midbrain	Mesencephalon ("middle-brain")	Tectum, tegmentum, superior colliculus, inferior colliculus, substantia nigra
Hindbrain	Rhombencephalon (literally, "parallelogram-brain")	Medulla, pons, cerebellum
	Metencephalon ("afterbrain")	Pons, cerebellum
	Myelencephalon ("marrow-brain")	Medulla

mesencephalon, and prosencephalon. You may encounter those terms in other reading.

The **hindbrain,** the posterior part of the brain, consists of the medulla, the pons, and the cerebellum. The medulla and pons, the midbrain, and certain central structures of the forebrain constitute the **brain stem** (see Figure 4.8).

The **medulla,** or medulla oblongata, is just above the spinal cord and could be regarded as an enlarged, elaborated extension of the spinal cord, although it is located in the skull rather than in the spine. The medulla controls a number of vital reflexes—including breathing, heart rate, vomiting, salivation, coughing, and sneezing—through the **cranial nerves,** a set of nerves that control sensory and motor information of the head. Damage to the medulla is frequently fatal, and large doses of opiates can also be fatal because they suppress activity of the medulla.

Just as the lower parts of the body are connected to the spinal cord via sensory and motor nerves, the skin and muscles of the head and the internal organs are connected to the brain by 12 pairs of cranial nerves (one of each pair on the right of the brain and one on the left). Most cranial nerves have both sensory and motor components, although some include just one or the other (see Table 4.4). Each cranial nerve originates in a

nucleus (cluster of neurons) that integrates the sensory information and regulates the motor output. The cranial nerve nuclei for nerves V through XII are in the medulla and pons of the hindbrain. Those for cranial nerves I through IV are in the midbrain and forebrain (see Figure 4.9).

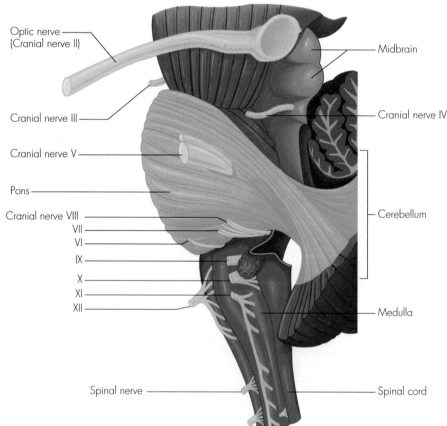

Figure 4.9 Cranial nerves II through XII
Note that cranial nerve I, the olfactory nerve, connects directly to the olfactory bulbs of the forebrain. *(Source: Based on Braus, 1960)*

Table 4.4 The Cranial Nerves

Number and Name	Function of Sensory Component	Function of Motor Component
I. Olfactory	Smell	(No motor nerve)
II. Optic	Vision	(No motor nerve)
III. Oculomotor	Sensations from eye muscles	Eye movements, pupil constriction
IV. Trochlear	Sensations from eye muscles	Eye movements
V. Trigeminal	Sensations from skin of face, nose, and mouth	Chewing, swallowing
VI. Abducens	Sensations from eye muscles	Eye movements
VII. Facial	Taste from the anterior two-thirds of the tongue, visceral sensations from head	Facial expressions, crying, salivation, and dilation of blood vessels in the head
VIII. Statoacoustic	Hearing, equilibrium	(No motor nerve)
IX. Glossopharyngeal	Taste and other sensations from throat and posterior third of tongue	Swallowing, salivation, dilation of blood vessels
X. Vagus	Taste and sensations from neck, thorax, and abdomen	Swallowing, control of larynx, parasympathetic nerves to heart and viscera
XI. Accessory	(no sensory nerve)	Movements of shoulders and head, parasympathetic to viscera
XII. Hypoglossal	Sensation from tongue muscles	Movement of tongue

The **pons** lies anterior and ventral to the medulla; like the medulla it contains nuclei for several cranial nerves. The term *pons* is Latin for "bridge"; the name reflects the fact that many axons in the pons cross from one side of the brain to the other.

The medulla and pons also contain the reticular formation and the raphe system. The **reticular formation** includes descending and ascending portions. The descending portion is one of several brain areas that control the motor areas of the spinal cord. The ascending portion sends output to much of the cerebral cortex, selectively increasing arousal and attention in one area or another (Guillery, Feig, & Lozsádi, 1998). The **raphe system** also sends axons to much of the forebrain, increasing or decreasing the brain's readiness to respond to stimuli (Mesulam, 1995).

The **cerebellum** is a large hindbrain structure with a great many deep folds. It has long been known for its contributions to the control of movement (see Chapter 8), and many textbooks, especially older ones, describe the cerebellum as important for "balance and coordination." True, people with cerebellar damage are clumsy and do lose their balance, but the functions of the cerebellum extend far beyond just balance and coordination. People with damage to the cerebellum have trouble shifting their attention back and forth between auditory and visual stimuli (Canavan, Sprengelmeyer, Diener, &

Hömberg, 1994). They also have problems with timing, including sensory timing. For example, they have trouble tapping a steady rhythm and trouble determining whether one rhythm is faster than another.

The Midbrain

As the name implies the **midbrain** is in the middle of the brain, although in adult mammals it is dwarfed and surrounded by the forebrain. In birds, reptiles, amphibians, and fish, the midbrain is a larger, more prominent structure. The roof of the midbrain is called the **tectum**. (*Tectum* is the Latin word for "roof"; the same root shows up in the geological term *plate tectonics*.) The two swellings on each side of the tectum are the **superior colliculus** and the **inferior colliculus** (see Figures 4.8 and 4.12), both are part of important routes for sensory information.

Under the tectum is the **tegmentum**, the intermediate level of the midbrain. (In Latin *tegmentum* means a "covering," such as a rug on the floor. The tegmentum covers several other midbrain structures, although it is covered by the tectum.) The tegmentum includes the nuclei for the third and fourth cranial nerves, parts of the reticular formation, and extensions of the pathways between the forebrain and the spinal cord or hindbrain.

Another midbrain structure is the substantia nigra, which gives rise to a dopamine-containing path that deteriorates in Parkinson's disease (see Chapter 8).

The Forebrain

The **forebrain** is the most anterior and most prominent part of the mammalian brain. The outer portion is the cerebral cortex. (*Cerebrum* is a Latin word meaning "brain"; *cortex* a Latin word meaning "bark" or "covering.") Under the cerebral cortex are other structures, including the thalamus, which provides the main source of input to the cerebral cortex. A set of structures known as the basal ganglia plays a major role in certain aspects of movement. A number of other interlinked structures, known as the **limbic system**, form a border (or *limbus*, the Latin word for "border") around the brain stem. These structures are particularly important for motivated and emotional behaviors, such as eating, drinking, sexual activity, anxiety, and aggression. The larger structures of the limbic system include the olfactory bulb, hypothalamus, hippocampus, amygdala, and cingulate gyrus of the cerebral cortex. Figure 4.10 shows the positions of these structures in three-dimensional perspective. Figures 4.11 and 4.12 show coronal and sagittal sections through the human brain (that is, sections showing structures as seen from the front and from the side). Figure 4.11 also includes a view of the ventral surface of the brain.

In describing the forebrain we begin with the subcortical areas; the next module focuses on the cerebral cortex. In later chapters we return to each of these areas as they become relevant.

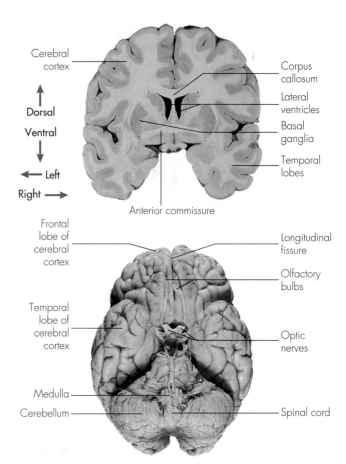

Figure 4.11 Two views of the human brain
Top: A coronal section. Note how the corpus callosum and anterior commissure provide communication between the left and right hemispheres. Bottom: The ventral surface. The optic nerves (cut here) extend to the eyes. (*Source: Photos courtesy of Dr. Dana Copeland*)

Thalamus

The thalamus and hypothalamus together form the *diencephalon,* a section distinct from the rest of the forebrain, which is known as the *telencephalon.* The **thalamus** is a structure in the center of the forebrain. The term is derived from a Greek word meaning "anteroom," "inner chamber," or "bridal bed." It resembles two avocados joined side by side, one in the left hemisphere and one in the right. Most sensory information goes first to the thalamus, which then processes it and sends the output to the cerebral cortex. The one clear exception to this rule is olfactory information, which progresses from the olfactory receptors to the olfactory bulbs and from the bulbs di-

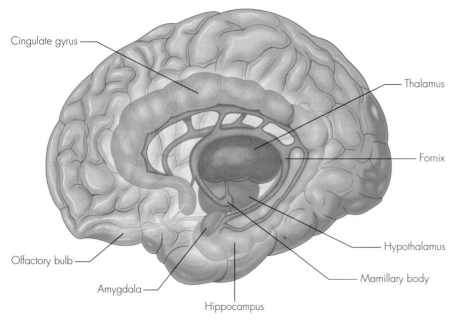

Figure 4.10   The limbic system is a set of subcortical structures that form a border (or limbus) around the brain stem

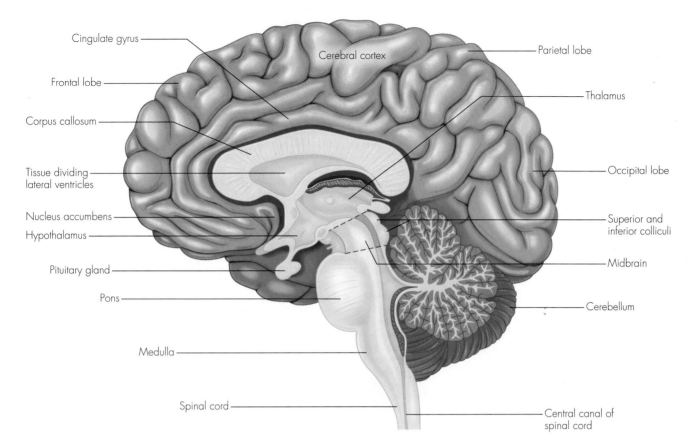

Figure 4.12 A sagittal section through the human brain
(Source: After Nieuwenhuys, Voogd, & vanHuijzen 1988)

rectly to the cerebral cortex without passing through the thalamus.

Many nuclei of the thalamus receive their primary input from one of the sensory systems, such as vision, and then transmit the information to a single area of the cerebral cortex, as in Figure 4.13, while also receiving feedback information from the same cortical area. Certain midline thalamic nuclei receive their input from several sources, including neighboring thalamic nuclei and several areas of the cortex; they then transmit information to other parts of the thalamus and multiple parts of the cortex. In other words some thalamic nuclei have simple, discrete functions such as vision; other thalamic nuclei convey more complex or general messages, such as arousal (Barth & MacDonald, 1996).

Hypothalamus

The **hypothalamus** is a small area near the base of the brain just ventral to the thalamus (see Figures 4.10 and 4.12). It has widespread connections with the rest of the forebrain and the midbrain. The hypothalamus contains a number of distinct nuclei, which we examine in Chapters 10 and 11. Partly through nerves and partly through hypothalamic hormones, the hypothalamus con-

veys messages to the pituitary gland, altering its release of hormones. Damage to a hypothalamic nucleus leads to abnormalities in one or more motivated behaviors, such as feeding, drinking, temperature regulation, sexual behavior, fighting, or activity level. Because of these spectacular effects, the rather small hypothalamus attracts a great deal of research attention.

Pituitary Gland

The **pituitary gland** is an endocrine (hormone-producing) gland attached to the base of the hypothalamus by a stalk that contains neurons, blood vessels, and connective tissue (see Figure 4.12). In response to messages from the hypothalamus, the pituitary synthesizes and releases hormones into the bloodstream, which carries them to other organs.

Basal Ganglia

The **basal ganglia,** a group of subcortical structures lateral to the thalamus, include three major structures: the caudate nucleus, the putamen, and the globus pallidus (see Figure 4.14). Some authorities include several other structures as well. The structure of the basal ganglia has been conserved through evolution, and the

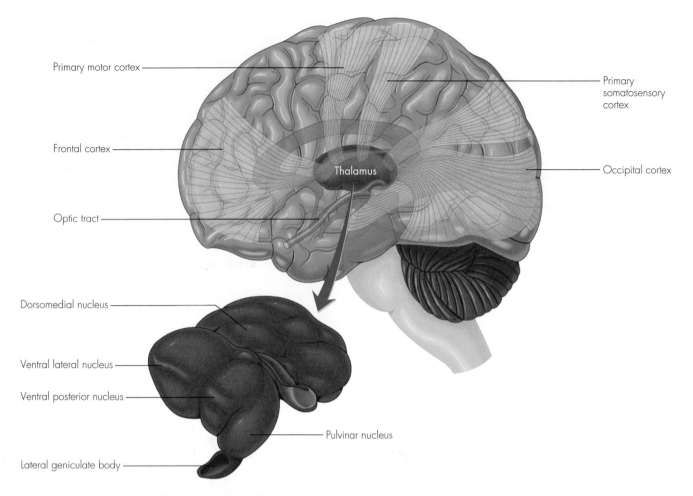

Figure 4.13   Routes of information from the thalamus to the cerebral cortex
Each thalamic nucleus projects its axons to a different location in the cortex. *(Source: After Nieuwenhuys, Voogd, & vanHuijzen, 1988)*

basic organization is about the same in mammals as in amphibians (Marin, Smeets, & González, 1998).

The basal ganglia have multiple subdivisions, each of which exchanges information with a different part of the cerebral cortex. The connections are most abundant with the frontal areas of the cortex, which are responsible for planning sequences of behavior and for certain aspects of memory and emotional expression (Graybiel, Aosaki, Flaherty, & Kimura, 1994). In conditions such as Parkinson's disease and Huntington's disease, in which the basal ganglia deteriorate, the most prominent symptoms are impairments of movement, but people also show depression, deficits of memory and reasoning, and attentional disorders.

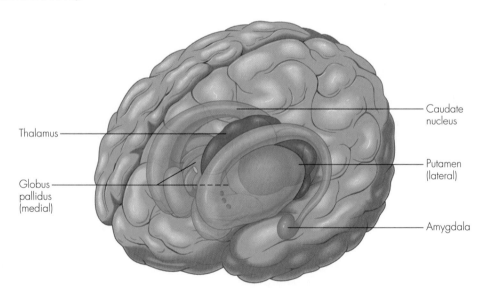

Figure 4.14   The basal ganglia
The thalamus is in the center, the basal ganglia are lateral to it, and the cerebral cortex is on the outside. *(Source: After Nieuwenhuys, Voogd, & vanHuijzen, 1988)*

Basal Forebrain

Several structures lie on the dorsal surface of the forebrain including the **nucleus basalis,** which receives input from the hypothalamus and basal ganglia, and sends axons that release acetylcholine to widespread areas in the cerebral cortex (Figure 4.15). We might regard the nucleus basalis as an intermediary between the emotional arousal of the hypothalamus and the information processing of the cerebral cortex. The nucleus basalis is a key part of the brain's system for arousal, wakefulness, and attention, as we consider in Chapter 9. Patients with Parkinson's disease and Alzheimer's disease have impairments of attention and intellect because of inactivity or deterioration of their nucleus basalis.

Hippocampus

The **hippocampus** (from a Latin word meaning "sea horse") is a large structure between the thalamus and the cerebral cortex, mostly toward the posterior of the forebrain, as shown in Figure 4.10. We consider the hippocampus in more detail in Chapter 12; the gist of that discussion is that the hippocampus is critical for storing certain kinds of memories, not all, and a debate continues about how best to describe the class of memories that depend on the hippocampus. People with hippocampal damage have trouble storing new memories, but they do not lose the memories they had from before damage to the hippocampus.

A major axon tract, the **fornix,** links the hippocampus with the hypothalamus and several other structures. The fornix was named after an ancient Roman arch that was a famous gathering place for prostitutes. That arch also gave us the word *fornication.* The fornix forms a large arch because it loops around the lateral ventricle that lies between the hippocampus and hypothalamus.

Stop & Check

7. Of the following, which are in the hindbrain, which in the midbrain, and which in the forebrain: basal ganglia, cerebellum, hippocampus, hypothalamus, medulla, pituitary gland, pons, substantia nigra, superior and inferior colliculi, tectum, tegmentum, thalamus?

8. Which subcortical area is the main source of input to the cerebral cortex?

Check your answers on page 101.

The Ventricles

The nervous system begins its development as a tube surrounding a fluid canal. The canal persists into adulthood as the **central canal,** a fluid-filled channel in the center of the spinal cord, and as the **ventricles,** four fluid-filled cavities within the brain. Each hemisphere contains one of the two large lateral ventricles (see Figure 4.16). Toward the posterior they connect to the third ventricle, which connects to the fourth ventricle in the medulla.

The ventricles and the central canal of the spinal cord contain **cerebrospinal fluid (CSF),** a clear fluid similar to blood plasma. CSF is formed by groups of cells, the *choroid plexus,* inside the four ventricles. It flows from the lateral ventricles to the third and then to the fourth ventricle. From the fourth ventricle some flows into the central canal of the spinal cord, but more goes through an opening into the thin spaces between the brain and the thin **meninges,** membranes that surround the brain and spinal cord. (Meningitis is an inflammation of the meninges surrounding the brain or spinal cord.) From one of those spaces, the subarachnoid space, CSF is gradually reabsorbed into the blood vessels of the brain.

Cerebrospinal fluid cushions the brain against mechanical shock when the head moves. It also provides buoyancy; just as a person weighs less in water than on land, cerebrospinal fluid helps support the weight of the brain. It also provides a reservoir of hormones and nutrition for the brain and spinal cord.

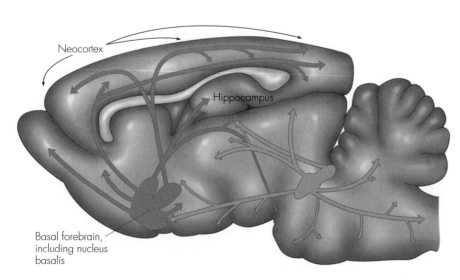

Figure 4.15 The basal forebrain
The nucleus basalis and other structures in this area send axons throughout the cortex, increasing its arousal and wakefulness through release of the neurotransmitter acetylcholine. *(Source: After Woolf, 1991)*

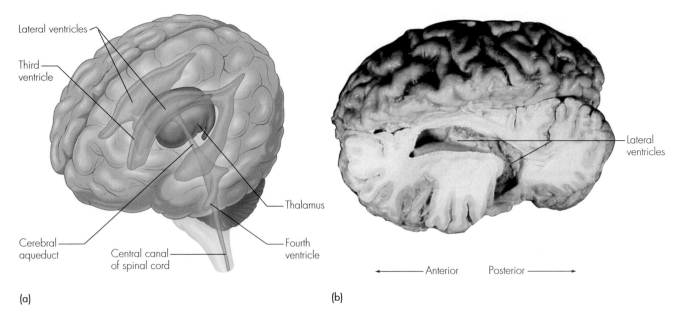

Figure 4.16 The cerebral ventricles
(**a**) Diagram showing positions of the four ventricles. (**b**) Photo of a human brain, viewed from above, with a horizontal cut through one hemisphere to show the position of the lateral ventricles. Note that the two parts of this figure are seen from different angles. *(Source: Photo courtesy of Dr. Dana Copeland)*

Sometimes the flow of CSF is obstructed and it accumulates within the ventricles or in the subarachnoid space, thus increasing the pressure on the brain. When this occurs in infants, the skull bones may spread, causing an overgrown head. This condition, known as *hydrocephalus* (HI-dro-SEFF-ah-luss), is usually associated with mental retardation.

Module 4.1

In Closing:
Structures of the Nervous System

The brain is a complex structure. This module has introduced a great many terms and facts; do not be discouraged if you have trouble remembering them. You didn't learn world geography all at one time either. It will help to refer back to this section to review the anatomy of certain structures as you encounter them again in later chapters. Gradually the material will become more familiar.

Summary

1. The main divisions of the vertebrate nervous system are the central nervous system and the peripheral nervous system. The central nervous system consists of the spinal cord, the hindbrain, the midbrain, and the forebrain. (p. 88)

2. Each segment of the spinal cord has a sensory nerve on each side and a motor nerve on each side.

Several spinal pathways convey information to the brain. (p. 89)

3. The sympathetic nervous system (one of the two divisions of the autonomic nervous system) activates the body's internal organs for vigorous activities. The parasympathetic system promotes digestion and other nonemergency processes. (p. 91)

4. The hindbrain consists of the medulla, pons, and cerebellum. The medulla and pons control breathing, heart rate, and other vital functions through the cranial nerves. The cerebellum contributes to movement. (p. 93)

5. The subcortical areas of the forebrain include the thalamus, hypothalamus, pituitary gland, basal ganglia, and hippocampus. (p. 96)

6. The cerebral cortex receives its sensory information, except for olfaction, from the thalamus. (p. 96)

Answers to *Stop and Check* Questions

1. *Dorsal* means toward the back, away from the stomach side. Its opposite is *ventral*. (p. 89)

2. Lateral; medial (p. 89)

3. Ipsilateral; contralateral (p. 89)

4. Gyri; sulci (p. 89)

5. Dorsal (p. 93)

6. The sympathetic nervous system prepares the organs for vigorous fight-or-flight activity. The para-

sympathetic system increases vegetative responses such as digestion. (p. 93)

7. Hindbrain: cerebellum, medulla, and pons. Midbrain: substantia nigra, superior and inferior colliculi, tectum, and tegmentum. Forebrain: basal ganglia, hippocampus, hypothalamus, pituitary, and thalamus. (p. 99)

8. Thalamus (p. 99)

Thought Question

The drug phenylephrine is sometimes prescribed for people suffering from a sudden loss of blood pressure or other medical disorders. It acts by stimulating norepinephrine synapses, including those that constrict blood vessels. One common side effect of this drug is goose bumps. Explain why. What other side effects might be likely?

The Cerebral Cortex

The forebrain consists of two cerebral hemispheres, one on the left side and one on the right (Figure 4.17). Each hemisphere is organized to receive sensory information, mostly from the contralateral (opposite) side of the body, and to control muscles, mostly on the contralateral side, through axons to the spinal cord and the cranial nerve nuclei.

The cellular layers on the outer surface of the cerebral hemispheres form gray matter known as the **cerebral cortex** (from the Latin word *cortex,* meaning "bark"). Large numbers of axons extend inward from the cortex, forming the white matter of the cerebral hemispheres (Figure 4.11). Neurons in each hemisphere communicate with neurons in the corresponding part of the other hemisphere through two bundles of axons, the **corpus callosum** (Figures 4.11, 4.12, and 4.17) and the smaller **anterior commissure** (Figure 4.11). (Several other commissures link subcortical structures.)

Organization of the Cerebral Cortex

The microscopic structure of the cells of the cerebral cortex varies substantially from one cortical area to an-

other. The differences in appearance relate to differences in function. Much research has been directed toward understanding the relationship between structure and function.

In humans and most other mammals, the cerebral cortex contains up to six distinct **laminae,** layers of cell bodies that are parallel to the surface of the cortex and separated from each other by layers of fibers (see Figure 4.18). The laminae vary in thickness and prominence from one part of the cortex to another, and a given lamina may be absent from certain areas. Lamina V, which sends long axons to the spinal cord and other distant areas, is thickest in the motor cortex, which has the greatest control of the muscles. Lamina IV, which receives axons from the various sensory nuclei of the thalamus, is prominent in all the primary sensory areas (visual, auditory, and somatosensory) but absent from the motor cortex. Anecdotal reports have found lamina IV to be even thicker than normal in the visual cortex of a person with photographic memory and in the auditory cortex of a musician with perfect pitch (Scheibel, 1984).

The cells of the cortex are also organized into **columns** of cells with similar properties, arranged perpendicular to the laminae. Figure 4.19 illustrates the

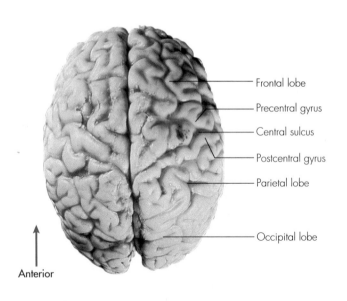

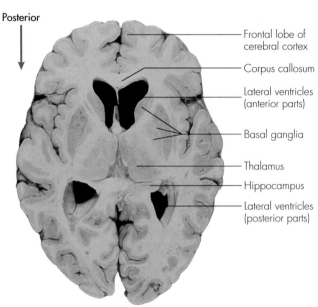

Posterior

Frontal lobe

Precentral gyrus

Central sulcus

Postcentral gyrus

Parietal lobe

Occipital lobe

Anterior

Frontal lobe of cerebral cortex

Corpus callosum

Lateral ventricles (anterior parts)

Basal ganglia

Thalamus

Hippocampus

Lateral ventricles (posterior parts)

Figure 4.17   Dorsal view of the brain surface and a horizontal section through the brain
(Source: Photos courtesy of Dr. Dana Copeland)

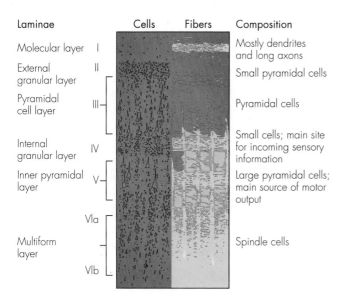

Laminae		Cells	Fibers	Composition
Molecular layer	I			Mostly dendrites and long axons
External granular layer	II			Small pyramidal cells
Pyramidal cell layer	III			Pyramidal cells
Internal granular layer	IV			Small cells; main site for incoming sensory information
Inner pyramidal layer	V			Large pyramidal cells; main source of motor output
Multiform layer	VIa			Spindle cells
	VIb			

Figure 4.18   The six laminae of the human cerebral cortex
(Source: Adapted from Ranson & Clark, 1959)

idea of columns, although in fact they do not all have such a straight shape. The cells within a given column have similar or related properties and many connections to one another. For example, if one cell in a given column responds to touch on the palm of the left hand, then the other cells in that column also respond to

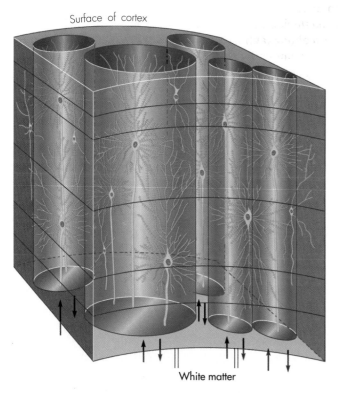

Surface of cortex

White matter

Figure 4.19   Columns in the cerebral cortex
Each column extends through several laminae. Neurons within a given column have similar properties. For example, in the somatosensory cortex all the neurons within a given column respond to stimulation of the same area of skin.

touch on the palm of the left hand. If one cell responds to a particular pattern of light at a particular location in the retina, then the other cells in the column respond to the same pattern of light in the same location.

We now turn to some of the specific parts of the cortex. We can distinguish 50 or more areas of the cerebral cortex based on differences in the thickness of the six laminae and on the appearance of cells and fibers within each lamina. For convenience, however, we group these areas into four *lobes* named for the skull bones that lie over them: occipital, parietal, temporal, and frontal.

The Occipital Lobe

The **occipital lobe,** located at the posterior (caudal) end of the cortex (see Figure 4.20), is the main target for axons from the thalamic nuclei that receive input from the visual pathways. The very posterior pole of the occipital lobe is known as the *primary visual cortex* or *striate cortex* because of its striped appearance in cross section. Destruction of any part of the striate cortex causes *cortical blindness* in the related part of the visual field. For example, extensive damage to the striate cortex of the right hemisphere causes blindness in the left visual field (the left side of the world from the viewer's perspective). A person with cortical blindness has normal eyes, normal pupillary reflexes, and some eye movements, but no pattern perception and not even visual imagery. People who suffer severe damage to the eyes become blind, but if they have an intact occipital cortex and if they had previous visual experience, they can still imagine visual scenes and can still have visual dreams (Sabo & Kirtley, 1982).

The Parietal Lobe

The **parietal lobe** lies between the occipital lobe and the **central sulcus,** which is one of the deepest grooves in the surface of the cortex (see Figure 4.20). The area just posterior to the central sulcus, called the **postcentral gyrus** or the *primary somatosensory cortex,* is the primary target for touch sensations and information from muscle-stretch receptors and joint receptors. **Brain** surgeons sometimes perform surgery using only local anesthesia (anesthetizing the scalp but leaving the brain awake). If during this process they lightly stimulate the postcentral gyrus in one hemisphere, people report "tingling" touch sensations on the opposite side of the body. The postcentral gyrus includes four bands of cells that run parallel to the central sulcus. Separate areas along each band receive simultaneous information from different parts of the body, as shown in Figure 4.21a (Nicolelis et al., 1998). Two of the bands receive mostly light-touch information, one receives deep-pressure information, and one receives a combination of both (Kaas,

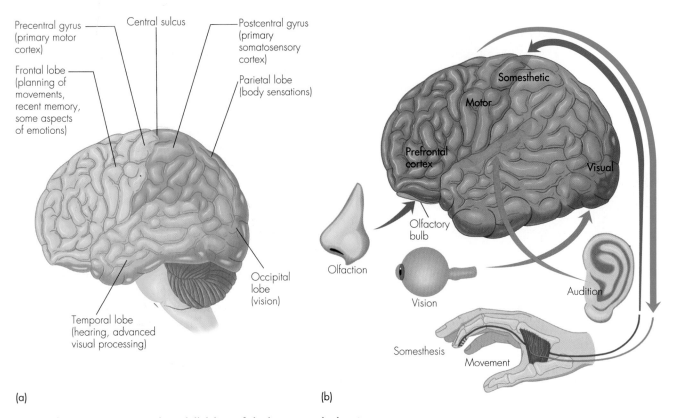

Figure 4.20 Some major subdivisions of the human cerebral cortex
(**a**) The four lobes: occipital, parietal, temporal, and frontal. (**b**) The primary sensory cortex for vision, hearing, and body sensations; the primary motor cortex; and the olfactory bulb, a noncortical area responsible for the sense of smell. *(Source for part [b]: T. W. Deacon, 1990a)*

Nelson, Sur, Lin, & Merzenich, 1979). In effect, the postcentral gyrus contains four separate representations of the body.

Information about touch and body location is important not only for its own sake but also for interpreting visual and auditory information. For example, if you see something in the upper left portion of the visual field, your brain needs to know which direction your eyes are turned, the position of your head, and the tilt of your body before it can determine the location of the object that you see and therefore the direction you should go if you want to approach or avoid it. The parietal lobe monitors all the information about eye, head, and body positions and passes it on to other brain areas that control movement (Gross & Graziano, 1995).

A fascinating symptom of right-hemisphere parietal lobe damage is **neglect,** a tendency to ignore the contralateral side of the body and world. (People with left-hemisphere damage do not strongly neglect the right side.) Neglect occurs after damage to the right parietal lobe, one part of the right frontal lobe, or the connection between those two areas (Burcham, Corwin, Stoll, & Reep, 1997). To get some understanding of the neglect phenomenon, make the following observations about yourself (or try it on your roommate): Fixate your eyes on some object and describe what you see. Note that you almost

TRY IT
YOUR
SELF

certainly described only what you saw in the center of your visual field. Now, *keeping your fixation on the same spot,* shift your attention up, down, left, and right and describe what you also see in the periphery. (For example, when you shift your attention down, you might describe the color of your clothing.) Most people find that they can shift their attention successfully and describe much that they neglected during their original report. The point of this demonstration is that people with unilateral parietal lobe damage show similar neglect for the entire left half of the visual field, describing only the right side of whatever they see (Driver & Mattingley, 1998). If someone urges them to attend to the left side, they can describe a little, but they find it as difficult to keep attending to the left side as you do to keep attending to the periphery of your vision. If they try to describe a familiar scene from memory, they describe only the right side, and if they try to draw something, they draw only its right side. They also generally ignore much of what they hear in the left ear and most of what they feel in the left hand, especially if they simultaneously feel something in the right hand. They may put clothes on only the right side of the body. So the problem is not an impairment of vision or other senses; it is impaired attention.

Various procedures can increase attention to the neglected side. For example, if you touch a right parietal

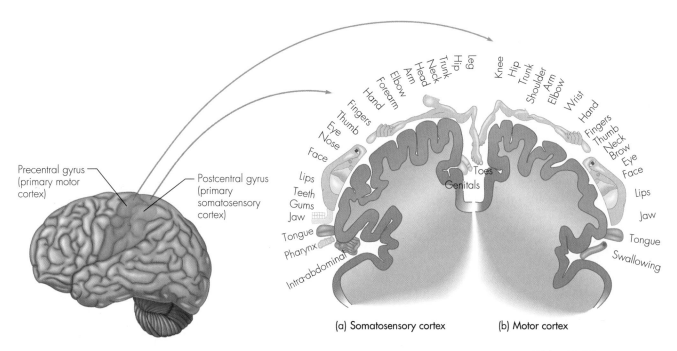

Figure 4.21 Approximate representation of sensory and motor information in the cortex
(**a**) Each location in the somatosensory cortex represents sensation from a different body part. (**b**) Each location in the motor cortex regulates movement of a different body part. *(Source: After Penfield & Rasmussen, 1950)*

lobe patient on the left hand and ask what it felt like, the usual answer is, "I felt nothing." However, if you cross that person's left hand under or over the right hand, then the same touch is more perceptible (Aglioti, Smania, & Peru, 1999) (see Figure 4.22). Also, if you ask the person to point to something in the left visual field, he or she will probably fail (Mattingley, Husain, Rorden, Kennard, & Driver, 1998). But success is more likely if the hand had already been even farther to the left, so the person can point to the object by moving the hand to the right. Again, the conclusion is that neglect

is not due to a loss of sensation, but a difficulty in directing attention to the left side.

The Temporal Lobe

The **temporal lobe** is the lateral portion of each hemisphere, near the temples (see Figure 4.20). It is the primary cortical target for auditory information. In humans the temporal lobe—the left temporal lobe for most people—is essential for understanding spoken language. The temporal lobe also contributes to some of the more complex aspects of vision, including perception of movement and recognition of faces. A tumor in the temporal lobe may give rise to elaborate auditory or visual hallucinations, whereas a tumor in the occipital lobe ordinarily evokes only simple sensations, such as flashes of light. In fact when psychiatric patients report hallucinations, brain scans detect extensive activity in the temporal lobes (Liddle, 1997; Pearlson, 1997).

The temporal lobes also play a part in emotional and motivational behaviors. Temporal lobe damage can lead to a set of behaviors known as the **Klüver-Bucy syndrome** (named for the investigators who first described it). Previously wild and aggressive monkeys fail to display normal fears and anxieties after temporal lobe damage (Klüver & Bucy, 1939). They put almost anything they find into their mouths and attempt to pick up snakes and lighted matches (which intact monkeys consistently avoid). Interpreting this behavior is difficult. For example, a monkey might handle a snake either because

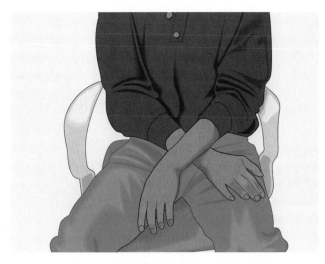

Figure 4.22 A simple way to reduce sensory neglect
Ordinarily someone with right parietal lobe damage neglects the left arm. However, if the left arm crosses over or under the right, attention to that arm increases.

The Rise and Fall of Prefrontal Lobotomies

In the late 1940s and early 1950s, about 40,000 prefrontal lobotomies were performed in the United States (Shutts, 1982). The surgery consists of damaging the prefrontal cortex or cutting the connections between the prefrontal cortex and the rest of the cortex. The impetus for the operation was a report that damaging the prefrontal cortex of laboratory primates had made them tamer without impairing their sensory or motor capacities in any striking way. It was reasoned that the same operation might help people who suffered from severe and otherwise untreatable psychiatric disorders.

The largest number of lobotomies in the United States were performed by Walter Freeman, a medical doctor who had never been trained in surgery. His techniques were amazingly crude,

even by the standards of the 1940s. (Sometimes he used an electric drill; sometimes a metal pick.) He performed many operations in his office or in other sites outside the hospital. (Freeman carried his equipment, such as it was, around with him in his car, which he called his "lobotomobile.")

Freeman and others became increasingly casual about deciding who should get a lobotomy. At first the technique was used only in cases of severe, untreatable schizophrenia. Lobotomy did calm some schizophrenic people, but the effects were usually disappointing, even by a generous interpretation. (We now know that the frontal lobes of many severe schizophrenics are partly shrunken and less active than normal; lobotomy was therefore damaging a structure that had already been impaired.) As time

---

it is no longer afraid (an emotional change) or because it no longer recognizes what a snake is (a cognitive change).

The Frontal Lobe

The **frontal lobe,** which contains the primary motor cortex and the prefrontal cortex, extends from the central sulcus to the anterior limit of the brain (see Figure 4.20). The posterior portion of the frontal lobe just anterior to the central sulcus, the **precentral gyrus,** is specialized for the control of fine movements, such as moving one finger at a time. Separate areas are responsible for different parts of the body (Figure 4.21b), mostly on the contralateral (opposite) side but with slight control of the ipsilateral (same) side, too.

The most anterior portion of the frontal lobe, the **prefrontal cortex,** is a large structure in species with a large overall cor-

tex, such as humans (see Figure 4.23). It is not the primary target for any single sensory system, but it receives information from all the sensory systems, including the interior of the body (Stuss & Benson, 1984). However, according to evidence so far, each sensory system pro-

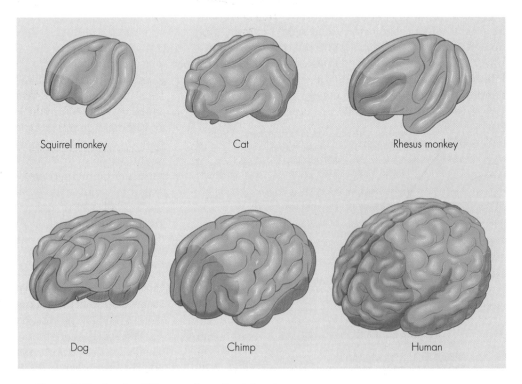

Figure 4.23 Species differences in prefrontal cortex
Note that the prefrontal cortex (blue area) constitutes a larger proportion of the human brain than of these other species. *(Source: After Fuster, 1989)*

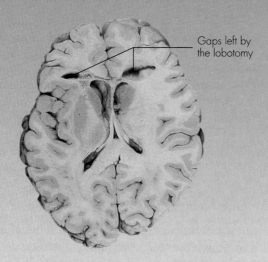

Gaps left by the lobotomy

A horizontal section of the brain of a person who had a prefrontal lobotomy many years earlier. The two holes in the frontal cortex are the visible results of the operation.
Source: (Photo courtesy of Dr. Dana Copeland)

went on Freeman lobotomized people with an assortment of other major and minor disorders, some of whom would in fact be considered normal by today's standards.

After effective drug therapies became available in the mid-1950s, physicians quickly and almost completely abandoned the use of lobotomy. Freeman, who had been praised by some of his colleagues and barely tolerated by others, lost his privilege to practice at most hospitals and faded into the same obscurity as lobotomy itself. Lobotomy has been an exceedingly rare operation since the mid-1950s (Lesse, 1984; Tippin & Henn, 1982).

Among the common consequences of prefrontal lobotomy were apathy, a loss of the ability to plan and take initiative, memory disorders (Chapter 13), distractibility, generally blunted emotions, and a loss of facial expression (Stuss & Benson, 1984). People with prefrontal damage lose their social inhibitions; they behave in a tactless, callous manner and ignore the rules of polite, civilized conduct. They may also seem impulsive, simply because they fail to calculate adequately the probable outcomes of their behaviors.

jects to different cell populations within the prefrontal cortex.

The prefrontal cortex was the target of **prefrontal lobotomies,** surgical disconnection of the prefrontal cortex from the rest of the brain, an infamous type of brain surgery that used to be conducted in attempts to control psychological disorders (see Digression 4.2). People with lobotomies generally lost their initiative and failed to inhibit socially unacceptable impulses. They also showed impairments in certain aspects of memory and in their facial expressions of emotion. However, the lobotomies added only superficially to our understanding of the prefrontal lobes. Later researchers, working with brain-damaged people and monkeys, have found that the prefrontal cortex is important for *working memory,* the ability to remember recent stimuli and events, such as where I parked the car today or what I was talking about before being interrupted (Goldman-Rakic, 1988). The prefrontal cortex is especially important for the **delayed-response task,** in which a stimulus appears briefly, and after some delay, the individual must respond to the remembered stimulus. The prefrontal cortex is much less important for reference memory, the ability to remember unchanging information, such as the fact that a green traffic light means "go" or that the summer Olympics occur once every 4 years.

The prefrontal cortex also contributes to the shifting of attention (Dias, Robbins, & Roberts, 1996). It monitors recent events, calculates possible actions in response to those events, ascertains from memory the probable outcomes of the actions, and determines the emotional value of each of those outcomes (Tucker, Luu, & Pribram, 1995). If all operates properly, the result is a good choice

of movements and a satisfying outcome. If the prefrontal cortex is damaged, however, the person may fail either to remember the likely outcomes or to imagine the emotional consequences. The result may be an incomplete or badly planned movement: The person showers with clothes on, shakes salt into the tea instead of onto the food, or pours water on the tube of toothpaste instead of on the toothbrush (M. F. Schwartz, 1995).

Stop & Check

1. If several neurons of the visual cortex all respond best when the retina is exposed to horizontal lines of light, then those neurons are probably to be found in the same _____.

2. Which lobe of the cerebral cortex includes the primary auditory cortex? the primary somatosensory cortex? the primary visual cortex? the primary motor cortex?

3. Damage to which part of the cortex is most likely to cause neglect of the left half of the body and the left half of the world?

Check your answers on page 112.

How Do the Pieces Work Together?

We have just considered a list of brain areas, each with its own function. And yet each of us has the sense of being a single person, not just a collection of many parts. The emergence of a unified experience from separate parts is a more complicated issue than it might at first seem.

Does the Brain Operate as a Whole or as a Collection of Parts?

Let's begin with an example, the role of the amygdala (Figure 4.14 on p. 98) in fear. (We consider this example in more detail in Chapter 12.) Almost any event that arouses fears or anxieties increases activity in the central nucleus of the amygdala, much more than in other brain areas. Furthermore, damage to the central amygdala causes a severe deficit in fears and anxieties. Mice with this kind of damage walk right up to a cat—something no normal mouse ever does. People with amygdala damage cannot even recognize other people's facial expressions of fear. They seem to have forgotten what fear even *means*. In many ways the central amygdala seems a powerful example of a brain area with a specialized function. So can we say that activity in the central amygdala *is* fear?

There is an important sense in which that question is unanswerable, at least by present methods. If we isolated a group of cells from the central amygdala, kept them alive and healthy in cell culture, and then stimulated them, would their activity be the experience of fear? We don't know; the cells would have no way to tell us!

Similarly, in the intact nervous system, the activity of the central amygdala may or may not *be* the conscious experience we call fear, but for it to have any consequences, that brain activity has to connect to the brain areas responsible for language, muscle actions, and autonomic activities. Ordinarily it also combines or competes with brain areas that register other emotions, motivations, and sensations. (For example, the fear response intensifies in the presence of pain but diminishes in the presence of a trusted companion.)

We could imagine the brain being organized either as an undifferentiated whole or as a collection of independent parts, each with a specialized function. The truth, however, lies somewhere between the two extremes. The relationship between the brain and its parts is somewhat like that between a sentence and the words that compose it: Each brain area has its own special function, just as each word does. If you damage any part of the brain or delete any word from a sentence, you lose part of the overall meaning. However, a single brain area can't do much by itself, any more than a single word can. The overall functioning of the brain or the meaning of a sentence derives both from the individual parts and from their connections to one another.

The evidence for specialization of parts is to be found throughout this text: After brain damage behavior deteriorates in a specific way depending on the location of the damage. What about the alternative viewpoint that the brain works as a whole in which all parts contribute equally? Karl Lashley (1929, 1950) supported this idea with evidence that when damage to the cerebral cortex impaired a rat's maze learning, the amount of damage was much more important than the location of the damage. The problem with drawing a strong conclusion from his study is that maze learning is a more complex task than it first appears. Solving a maze calls upon vision, touch, perception of body location, control of body movement, and sometimes even perception of sounds and odors. When researchers study other kinds of tasks, they often find that the location of the damage is indeed critical for predicting its effects.

The Binding Problem

Given that different brain areas have different functions, how do we put them together? In particular consider the sensory areas of the cerebral cortex. The primary visual area is in the occipital lobe, the primary auditory area is in the temporal lobe, and so forth. How does your brain combine various kinds of visual, auditory, tactile, and other information into a perception of a unified object?

Consider a few examples of the phenomena we need to explain:

- At a ventriloquist act you hear the ventriloquist's voice while you watch the dummy's mouth move and the dummy appears to be talking.

- If you watch film in which the picture is slightly out of synchrony with the sound, or a foreign-language film that was badly dubbed, you can tell that the sound does not match the picture.

- Here is a great demonstration, but you'll need a fake arm (available from almost any magic store). Position someone's arm parallel to a fake arm with a barrier between them so the person sees the fake arm and not the real one. Next, stroke simultaneously a finger of the fake hand and the corresponding finger of the real hand, as in Figure 4.24. Repeat this procedure several times with each finger and other parts of the hand. At each point the person sees you touching the fake hand while feeling you touch the same part of the real hand. After a minute or two, he or she will probably say that it feels as if the fake hand is real; that is, the brain attributes the touch sensations to the visible fake hand (Botvinick & Cohen, 1998). Finally, vigorously pinch the fake hand and watch the response! This effect doesn't always work. It works best if the person stares at the fake hand and cannot see the real hand at all.

The question of how the visual, auditory, and other areas of your brain influence one another to produce a combined perception of a single object is known as the **binding problem**. In an earlier era researchers thought that various kinds of sensory information converged onto what were known as the association areas of the

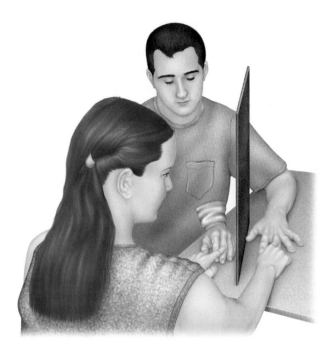

Figure 4.24 Demonstration of touch to "capture" vision
A person looks at a fake arm parallel to his or her actual arm, which is unseen. Someone simultaneously strokes corresponding parts of the fake and real hands. After a minute or two, the person begins to see the fake arm as being his or her own. In response to seeing a sudden pinch on the fake arm, the person will startle.

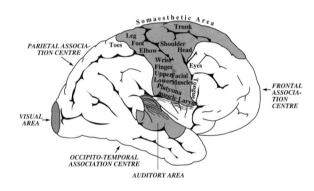

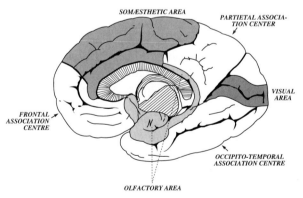

Figure 4.25 An old, somewhat misleading view of the cortex
Note the designation "association centre" in this illustration of the cortex in an old introductory psychology textbook (Hunter, 1923). Today's researchers are more likely to regard those areas as "additional sensory areas." They do not associate one kind of sensory information with another.

cortex (see Figure 4.25). Researchers had identified the primary sensory and motor areas because damage in those areas leads to blindness, hearing impairment, decreased muscle control, and so forth. But what was the function of the remaining areas, where damage caused no obvious loss of sensation or movement? Their guess was that those areas "associate," linking vision with hearing, hearing with touch, or current sensations with memories of previous experiences. This description fit a commonsense view of the mind: First the mind gets sensory information, then it thinks about it, then it acts.

However, later research found that the association areas do not link one kind of sensory information with another. Few if any cells in those areas respond to more than one sensory modality. For example, the association cortex next to the primary visual cortex consists of cells that provide more elaborate processing of visual information (Van Hoesen, 1993), the association area near the auditory cortex performs advanced auditory processing, and so on. Evidently the brain has no single site at which all kinds of information funnel to a central integrator—a "little person in the head." Whatever is the way that we bind vision, hearing, and other experiences into one, we do so in spite of physical separation of the brain's representations of the various senses.

One hypothesis that currently gets much attention is that binding of a perception depends on precisely simultaneous activity in various brain areas (Eckhorn et al., 1988; Gray, König, Engel, & Singer, 1989). For example, examine Figure 4.26. These figures are called "Mooney" faces after the investigator who first used them. Most people see a face in parts **b** and **c** but nothing in **a** or **d.** Flip the page upside down and they see faces in **a** and **d** but not in **b** or **c.** Some people fail to see a face at first, even if they view it in the correct position. Researchers found that when people saw a face and *recognized* it as a face, neurons in several areas of their visual cortex produced activity at a frequency varying from 30 to 80 action potentials per second—a frequency known as **gamma waves** (Rodriguez et al., 1999). The gamma waves were synchronized to the millisecond in various brain areas. When people failed to recognize a face, the gamma waves did not emerge.

Similarly, when a cat responds to a sudden stimulus, such as a bird that it both sees and hears, it has closely synchronized activity patterns in the occipital, parietal, and frontal areas of its cortex (Roelfsema, Engel, König, & Singer, 1997). At other times, when the cat is not

(a)   (b)

(c)   (d)

Figure 4.26 Four "Mooney" faces
Do you see any faces? Flip the page upside down and try
again. Large populations of neurons in the visual cortex
produce precisely synchronous activity when a person recognizes a pattern, but not when someone looks at the same
pattern and fails to recognize it.

attending to a single object, the activities in various
parts of its cortex are unsynchronized and out of phase.

What causes synchrony to develop? The process is
hardly well understood, but apparently synchrony
among distant parts of the cortex depends on coordination by an area in the inferior (lower) parietal cortex. Some people with bilateral (both-sided) parietal
lobe damage have trouble binding the different aspects of perception. For example, if they see a display
such as

they could report seeing a triangle and a square, one red
and one green, but would be almost as likely to call the
triangle green as the square (Robertson, Treisman,
Friedman-Hill, & Grabowecky, 1997). If they see a display such as

they would have trouble stating which circle was moving and which was not (Bernstein & Robertson, 1998).
In short they perceive shape, motion, and color, but they
do not bind them into a single perception. Such patients also take an unusually long time to shift attention
from one object to another (Husain, Shapiro, Martin, &
Kennard, 1997).

The results imply that exact synchrony of activity,
probably organized by the parietal lobe, is necessary for
perceptual binding. Note that the conclusion is *not* that
the inferior parietal cortex itself has the sensation of a
unified object; rather it somehow facilitates the ability
of the cortex as a whole to maintain synchrony and
thereby produce a unified sensation.

Curiously, after the great scientist Albert Einstein
(Figure 4.27) died, neuroscientists examined selected
areas of his brain in great detail and found that one area
was larger than normal and had an unusually high ratio
of glia to neurons. That area was the inferior parietal
cortex (M. C. Diamond, Scheibel, Murphy, & Harvey,
1985; Witelson, Kigar, & Harvey, 1999). We cannot
draw firm conclusions from a single case. Still . . .

However, even if researchers confirm that binding
different sensations depends on synchronized neural
activity, key questions remain. *Why* does synchrony of
various brain areas produce binding? (If a robot has
synchronous activity in two circuits, does it interpret
the activity in those circuits as representing a single object? Not necessarily.) We still do not understand how a
unified experience arises. If we can ever explain this
process, we shall have taken a major step toward resolving the mind-brain problem that we encountered in
Chapter 1.

Stop & Check

4. What is meant by the "binding problem" and what is the most
prominent hypothesis to explain it?

Check your answer on page 112.

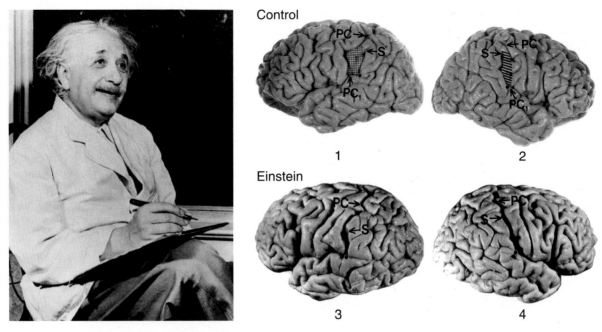

Figure 4.27 What makes a great brain great?
After the death of the great scientist Albert Einstein, researchers dissected his brain to look for clues to his genius. Although Einstein's brain was normal in total size, researchers noted some unusual aspects in its structure. Parts 1 and 2 show the left and right hemispheres of an average brain; the stippled (left) and hatched (right) sections are a brain area called the parietal operculum. Parts 3 and 4 show Einstein's brain; the parietal operculum is absent because the inferior parietal lobe has expanded beyond its usual boundaries, occupying the area where one ordinarily finds the parietal operculum. *(Sources: Historical Pictures Services, Chicago/FPG and Sandra F. Witelson)*

Module 4.2

In Closing:
Functions of the Cerebral Cortex

The human cerebral cortex is so large that we easily slip into thinking of it as "the" brain, with all of the rest of the brain almost trivial. In fact, only mammals have a true cerebral cortex, and even many mammals have only a small one. So subcortical areas by themselves can produce very complex behaviors . . . and a cerebral cortex by itself cannot do anything at all (because it would not be connected to any sense organs or muscles).

What, then, is the function of the cerebral cortex? The primary function seems to be one of elaborating sensory material. Even fish, which have no cerebral cortex, can see and hear and so forth, but they do not recognize and remember all the complex aspects of sensory stimuli that mammals do. In a television advertisement shown frequently in the late 1990s, one company said that it didn't make any products, but it made lots of products better. The same could be said for the cerebral cortex.

Summary

1. The cerebral cortex consists of six laminae (layers) of neurons. A given lamina may be absent from cer-

tain parts of the cortex. The cortex is organized into columns of cells arranged perpendicular to the laminae. (p. 102)

2. Most cortical areas have sensory, associational, and motor functions, although the degree of each varies. (p. 102)

3. The occipital lobe of the cortex is primarily responsible for vision. Damage to part of the occipital lobe leads to blindness in part of the visual field. (p. 103)

4. The parietal lobe processes body sensations. The postcentral gyrus contains four separate representations of the body. (p. 103)

5. The temporal lobe contributes to hearing and to complex aspects of vision. (p. 105)

6. The frontal lobe includes the precentral gyrus, which controls fine movements. It also includes the prefrontal cortex, which contributes to memories of current and recent stimuli, planning of movements, and regulation of emotional expressions. (p. 106)

7. Different brain areas have different functions, although no area can do anything by itself. (p. 108)

8. The binding problem is the question of how we connect activities in different brain areas, such as sights and sounds, even though the various brain areas do not all send their information to a single central processor. (p. 109)

9. The most prominent hypothesis to answer the binding problem is that the brain binds activity in different areas when those areas produce precisely synchronous waves of activity. Still, many questions remain. (p. 110)

produce unified perception and coordinated behavior. The most prominent hypothesis is that the brain binds activity in different areas when those areas produce precisely synchronized waves of activity. (p. 110)

Answers to *Stop and Check* Questions

1. Column (p. 107)
2. Temporal lobe; parietal lobe; occipital lobe; frontal lobe (p. 107)
3. The right parietal lobe (p. 107)
4. The binding problem is the question of how the brain combines activity in different brain areas to

Thought Question

When monkeys with Klüver-Bucy syndrome pick up lighted matches and snakes, we do not know whether they are displaying an emotional deficit or a difficulty identifying the object. What kind of research might help answer this question?

Chapter Ending
Key Terms and Activities

Terms

anterior (p. 90)

anterior commissure (p. 102)

autonomic nervous system (p. 88)

basal ganglia (p. 97)

Bell-Magendie law (p. 90)

binding problem (p. 108)

brain stem (p. 94)

central nervous system (CNS) (p. 88)

central canal (p. 99)

central sulcus (p. 103)

cerebellum (p. 95)

cerebral cortex (p. 102)

cerebrospinal fluid (CSF) (p. 99)

column (p. 91, 102)

contralateral (p. 90)

coronal plane (p. 90)

corpus callosum (p. 102)

cranial nerve (p. 94)

delayed-response task (p. 107)

distal (p. 90)

dorsal (p. 89)

dorsal root ganglion (p. 90)

fissure (p. 91)

forebrain (p. 96)

fornix (p. 99)

frontal lobe (p. 106)

gamma waves (p. 109)

ganglion (pl.: ganglia) (p. 91)

gray matter (p. 90)

gyrus (pl.: gyri) (p. 91)

hindbrain (p. 94)

hippocampus (p. 99)

horizontal plane (p. 90)

hypothalamus (p. 97)

inferior (p. 90)

inferior colliculus (p. 95)

ipsilateral (p. 90)

Klüver-Bucy syndrome (p. 105)

lamina (pl.: laminae) (p. 91, 102)

lateral (p. 90)

limbic system (p. 96)

medial (p. 90)

medulla (p. 94)

meninges (p. 99)

midbrain (p. 95)

neglect (p. 104)

nerve (p. 91)

neuroanatomy (p. 87)

nucleus (p. 91)

nucleus basalis (p. 99)

Suggestions for Further Reading

Calvin, W. H., & Ojemann, G. A. (1994). *Conversations with Neil's brain*. Reading, MA: Addison-Wesley. A discussion of brain anatomy and brain damage, written for a popular audience.

Hanaway, J., Woolsey, T. A., Gado, M. H., & Roberts, M. P., Jr. (1998). *The brain atlas*. Bethesda, MD: Fitzgerald Science Press. Outstanding illustrations of all parts of the human brain.

Heimer, L. (1995). *The human brain and spinal cord* (2nd ed.). New York: Springer-Verlag. Well-illustrated overview of the structure of the entire nervous system.

Klawans, H. L. (1988). *Toscanini's fumble and other tales of clinical neurology*. Chicago: Contemporary Books. Fascinating description of cases of human brain damage and other neurological conditions.

Web Sites to Explore

You can go to the Biological Psychology Study Center and click on these links. While there, you can also check for suggested articles available on InfoTrac. The Biological Psychology Internet address is:
http://psychology.wadsworth.com/book/kalatbiopsych7e/

http://www.biophysics.mcw.edu
Stunning images of the human brain, including movies that show the three-dimensional structure of the brain.

http://www.med.harvard.edu/AANLIB/home.html
The "whole brain atlas," which includes stunning photos of both normal and abnormal brain anatomy.

Active Learner Link

Quiz for Chapter 4

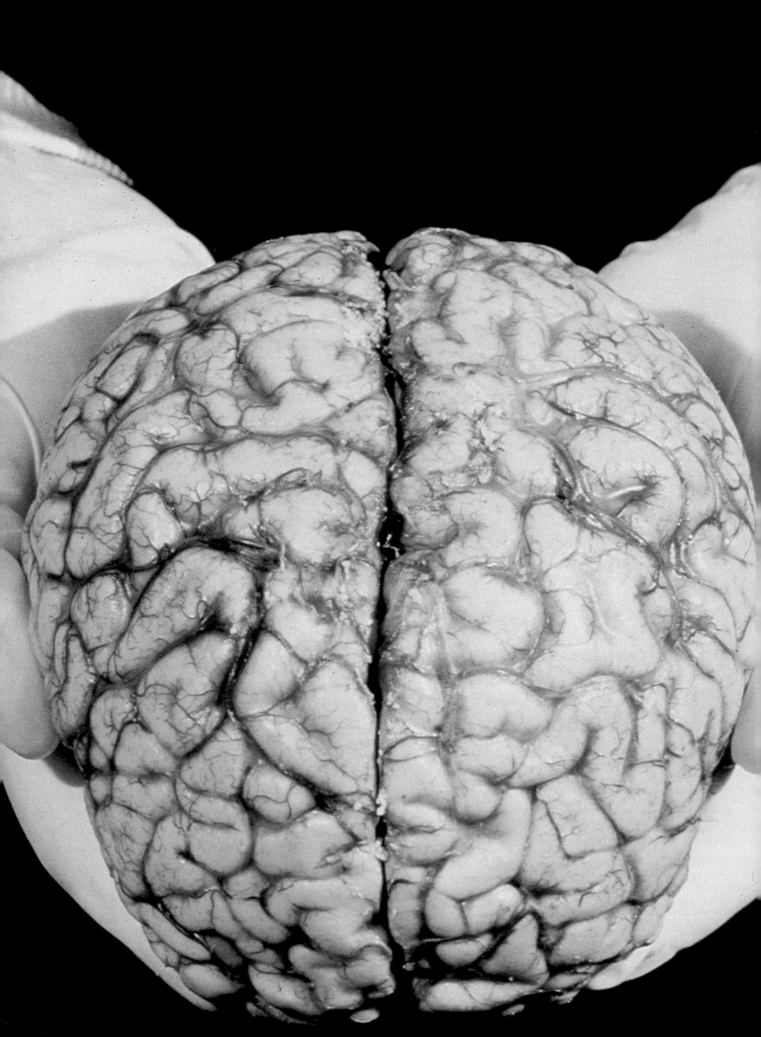

Development and Plasticity of the Brain

Chapter Outline

Main Ideas

1. The nervous system at first forms far more neurons than it needs and then eliminates those that do not establish suitable connections. It also forms more synapses than will survive and discards the less active ones.

2. Axons form connections by a combination of chemical attraction and the effects of experience. Experiences, especially early in life, can alter brain anatomy within limits.

3. The human brain can be damaged by a sharp blow, an interruption of blood flow, and several other types of injury. Therapies are now available to minimize the damage from a stroke if one acts quickly.

4. Many mechanisms contribute to recovery from brain damage, including restoration of undamaged neurons to full activity, regrowth of axons, readjustment of surviving synapses, and behavioral adjustments.

"Some assembly required." Have you ever bought a package containing those ominous words? Sometimes all you have to do is attach a few parts. But sometimes you face page after page of incomprehensible instructions. I remember putting together my daughter's bicycle and wondering how something that looked so simple could be so complicated.

The human nervous system requires an enormous amount of assembly, and the instructions are different from those of a bicycle. Instead of, "Put this piece here and that piece there," the instructions are, "Put these axons here and those dendrites there, and then wait to see what happens. Keep the connections that work the best, throw away the others, and then make new ones similar to the ones that you kept. Later, if those connections aren't working well, discard them and try new ones."

Therefore we say that the brain's anatomy is *plastic;* it is constantly changing, within limits. Major changes in brain anatomy occur during early development and continue to occur as a result of learning and in response to brain damage.

Opposite:
Different parts of the human brain grow and mature at different ages, but all parts continue developing in microscopic ways throughout life.

Module 5.1

Development of the Brain

As a college student you can probably perform many feats that you could not have done a few years ago: solve calculus problems, read a foreign language, or perhaps convincingly pretend that you understand James Joyce's novels. Have you developed these new skills because your brain has grown? No. Many neurons have changed in microscopic ways, but your brain hasn't actually grown.

Now think of all the things that 1- or 2-year-old children can do that they could not do at birth. Have *they* developed these new skills because of brain growth? To a large extent yes. Consider, for example, Jean Piaget's object permanence task, in which an observer shows a toy to an infant and then places it behind a barrier. Generally a child younger than 9 months old does not reach around the barrier to retrieve the toy (Figure 5.1). Why not? The biological explanation is that the prefrontal cortex is necessary for responding to a signal that appears and then disappears, and the synapses of the prefrontal cortex develop massively between the ages of 7 ½ and 12 months (Goldman-Rakic, 1987). The ability to solve the object permanence task requires developing certain neurons and synapses.

Behavioral development does not depend entirely on brain growth of course; it also requires microscopic readjustments in much the same way as an adult brain does. Furthermore, as we shall see, many processes of brain development depend on experience in complex ways that blur the distinction between learning and maturation. In this module we consider three major issues: the production of neurons, the growth of axons, and fine-tuning by experience.

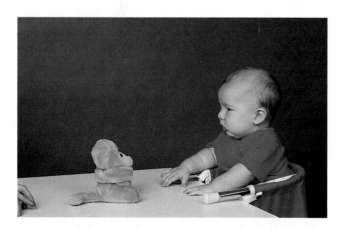

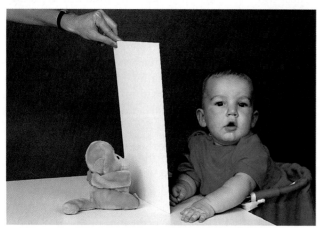

Figure 5.1 Piaget's object permanence task
An infant sees a toy and then an investigator places a barrier in front of the toy. Infants younger than about 9 months old fail to reach for the hidden toy. Tasks that require a response to a stimulus that is no longer present depend on the prefrontal cortex, a structure that is slow to mature. *(Source: Doug Goodman/Monkmeyer Press)*

Growth and Differentiation of the Vertebrate Brain

The human central nervous system begins to form when the embryo is about 2 weeks old. First the dorsal surface of the embryo thickens, and then long thin lips rise, curl, and merge, forming a neural tube surrounding a fluid-filled cavity (see Figure 5.2). As the tube sinks under the surface of the skin, the forward end enlarges and differentiates into the hindbrain, midbrain, and forebrain (see Figure 5.3); the rest becomes the spinal cord. The fluid-filled cavity within the neural tube becomes the central canal of the spinal cord and the four ventricles of the brain; the fluid is the cerebrospinal fluid (CSF). The developmental process is about the same in all vertebrates, varying mainly in speed, duration, and ultimately, size.

At birth, the average human brain weighs about 350 grams (g). Certain areas of the forebrain are immature for the first few weeks, as indicated by their low levels

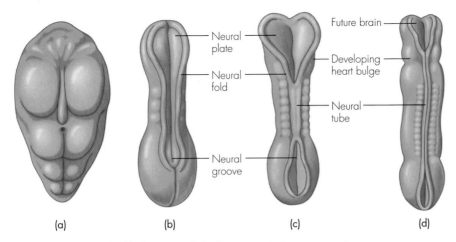

Figure 5.2 Early development of the human central nervous system
The brain and spinal cord begin as folding lips surrounding a fluid-filled canal. The stages shown occur at approximately age 2 to 3 weeks.

of glucose use. Development is rapid, however, and areas of the brain that are almost silent at birth approach adult patterns of arousal within 7 to 8 months (Chugani & Phelps, 1986). At the end of the first year, the brain weighs 1000 g, not much less than the adult weight of 1200 to 1400 g.

Growth and Development of Neurons

The development of the nervous system naturally includes the production and alteration of neurons. Neuroscientists distinguish four major stages in the development of neurons: proliferation, migration, differentiation, and myelination.

Proliferation is the production of new cells. Early in development cells lining the ventricles of the brain divide. Some of the new cells remain where they are, continuing to divide and redivide. Others become primitive neurons and glia that **migrate** (move) toward their eventual destinations in the brain. The process requires a precise chemical environment. Any gene or poison that interferes with proliferation or migration can produce problems ranging from mild cognitive deficits to severe mental retardation (Berger-Sweeney & Hohmann, 1997).

At first a primitive neuron looks like any other cell. Gradually the neuron **differentiates**, forming the axon and dendrites that provide its distinctive shape. The axon grows before the dendrites; in fact it grows while the neuron is migrating. (Some neurons leave an axon growing behind them like a tail.) When the neuron reaches its final location, dendrites begin to form, very slowly at first. Most dendritic growth occurs later, when incoming axons are due to arrive.

Not only does a neuron look different from other kinds of body cells, but neurons in different parts of the brain differ from one another in their shapes and chemical components. When and how does a neuron "de-

cide" which kind of neuron it is going to be? Evidently it is not a sudden all-or-none decision. In some cases, immature neurons experimentally transplanted from one part of the developing cortex to another develop all the properties characteristic of their new location (S. K. McConnell, 1992). However, immature neurons transplanted at a slightly later stage develop some of the properties of their new location while retaining some of the properties of neurons in their old location (Cohen-Tannoudji, Babinet, & Wassef, 1994). The result resembles the speech of immigrant children: Those who enter a country when very young may master the new language completely, whereas those entering at a slightly older age retain their original accent.

Finally, some vertebrate axons **myelinate,** as glia cells produce the insulating sheaths that increase transmission speed. In humans myelin forms first in the spinal cord and then in the hindbrain, midbrain, and forebrain. Unlike proliferation and migration of neurons, myelination continues for many years. A moderate amount of myelin is still forming at age 20, and in some brain areas it continues for additional decades (Benes, Turtle, Khan, & Farol, 1994).

Brain maturation requires not only the development of neurons but also the organization of brain areas. As the brain grows, what happens at the microscopic level? Anthony-Samuel LaMantia and Dale Purves (1989) created a way to stain and photograph the living brain of an infant mouse and then photograph the same area later in development. They found that the brain adds new subdivisions during at least the first 3 weeks of life. As Figure 5.4b shows, the olfactory bulb has *glomeruli,* analogous to the columns of the visual cortex. The glomeruli that are present in the first week of life expand over the next 2 weeks, and additional glomeruli also appear. Evidently the brain develops both by expanding old units and by adding new ones. A similar principle holds across species: Animals with large brains have many columns and specialized subdivisions within the cortex (Kaas, 1989; Killackey, 1990).

Stop & Check

1. What are proliferation and migration of neurons?

2. Are all glomeruli of the mouse olfactory bulb larger at age 3 weeks than at age 1 week? Why or why not?

Check your answers on page 130.

Determinants of Neuron Survival

Getting just the right number of neurons for each area of the nervous system is more complicated than it might seem. To be of any use, each neuron must receive axons from the right source and send its own axons to a cell in the right area. The various areas do not all develop at the same time, so in some cases the neurons in one area develop before any incoming axons have arrived or before any receptive sites are available for its own axons. If we examine a healthy adult nervous system, we find no leftover neurons that failed to make appropriate connections. How does the nervous system get the numbers to come out right?

Consider a specific example. The sympathetic nervous system chain sends axons to muscles and glands; each ganglion in the chain has exactly enough neurons to supply the muscles and glands in its area. Long ago one explanation was that the muscles sent chemical messages to the sympathetic ganglion to tell it how many neurons to form. One of the researchers who disconfirmed that hypothesis was Rita Levi-Montalcini. If you were going to plan life circumstances to encourage scientific success, you certainly would not have chosen anything like her early life. She was a young Italian Jewish woman at a time when the Nazis were persecuting and exterminating Jews. World War II was destroying the Italian economy, and almost no one encouraged women to pursue scientific or medical careers. Furthermore the research projects assigned to her as a young medical student were virtually impossible, as she described in her autobiography (Levi-Montalcini, 1988). Nevertheless she developed a love for research and eventually discovered that the muscles do not determine how many axons *form;* they determine how many *survive.*

When a neuron of the sympathetic nervous system forms a synapse onto an organ muscle, the muscle delivers a protein called **nerve growth factor (NGF)** that promotes the survival and growth of the axon (Levi-Montalcini, 1987). An axon that does not receive enough NGF degenerates, and its cell body dies. Each neuron starts life with a "suicide program": If its axon does not make contact with an appropriate postsynaptic cell by a certain age, the neuron kills itself through a process called **apoptosis,**[1] a programmed mechanism of cell death.

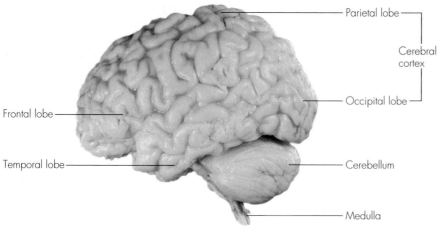

Figure 5.3 Human brain at five stages of development
The brain already shows an adult structure at birth, although it continues to grow during the first year or so. *(Source: Dana Copeland)*

---

[1] Apoptosis is based on the root word *ptosis,* pronounced "TOE-sis," and therefore some scholars insist that the second *p* in *apoptosis* should be silent. Others argue that *helicopter* is also derived from a root with a silent *p* (*pteron*), but we pronounce the *p* in *helicopter,* so we should also pronounce the *p* in *apoptosis.* Be prepared to hear and understand either pronunciation.

Apoptosis is distinct from *necrosis,* which is death caused by an injury or a toxic substance. NGF cancels the program for apoptosis; it is the postsynaptic cell's way of telling the incoming axon, "I'll be your partner. Don't kill yourself."

Nerve growth factor is a **neurotrophin,** a chemical that promotes the survival and activity of neurons. (The word *trophin* is derived from a Greek word for "nourishment.") In addition to NGF the nervous system responds to *brain-derived neurotrophic factor* (BDNF), *neurotrophins 3, 4/5,* and *6,* and others (Götz et al., 1993; Mendell, 1995). The neurotrophins act in several ways. First, early in development, they cause selected axons to survive and grow instead of submitting to apoptosis; different neurotrophins are active for different kinds of axons. Second, at later ages, new experiences cause neurons to secrete neurotrophins that increase the branching of incoming axons and thereby facilitate the mechanisms that store memories (Kesslak, So, Choi, Cotman, & Gomez-Pinilla, 1998; Kolb, Gorny, Côté, Ribeiro-da-Silva, & Cuello, 1997). Third, in response to nervous system injury, neurotrophins decrease pain and increase regrowth of damaged axons (Beck et al., 1995; Ren, Thomas, & Dubner, 1995; Tomac et al., 1995). Researchers hope to harness the power of neurotrophins to relieve certain diseases that attack the nervous system.

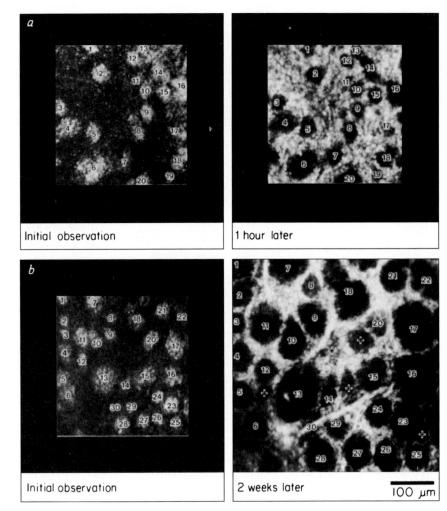

Figure 5.4 Sections of the olfactory bulbs of mice
Each number identifies a glomerulus, a cluster of neurons with similar properties. The initial observations (left) were taken in mice 4 to 6 days old. The later observations (right) were taken with a different staining procedure. In (**a**), note that the glomeruli change very little over a 1-hour delay. In (**b**), after a 2-week delay, the 30 original glomeruli have grown larger and 5 new glomeruli, indicated by +, have developed. The brain develops partly by expanding old units and partly by adding new units. *(Source: LaMantia & Purves, 1989)*

Not only the sympathetic ganglia but all areas of the developing nervous system initially overproduce neurons, in some cases developing two or three times as many as will actually survive into adulthood. Each part of the brain has a period of massive cell death, becoming littered with dead and dying cells (Figure 5.5). This loss of cells does not indicate that something is wrong; it is a natural part of development (Finlay & Pallas, 1989).

Why does the CNS produce more neurons than it needs? One possible explanation is that the extra neurons allow for error correction. Even if some axons fail to reach appropriate targets, enough others will. However, researchers find that axon growth is impressively accurate; axons seldom connect with inappropriate targets (Chalupa, 1998). A more likely explanation is that the extra neurons enable the CNS to match the number of incoming axons to the number of receiving cells. For example, when the motor neuron axons begin growing from the spinal cord toward the leg muscles, there is no way to predict exactly how many muscle fibers the leg will have. The spinal cord produces an abundance of neurons at the start and later discards the excess.

Stop  Check

3. What process enables the nervous system to have only as many axons as necessary to innervate the target neurons?

4. What class of chemicals prevents apoptosis?

5. At what age does a person have the greatest number of neurons—as an embryo, newborn, child, adolescent, or adult?

Check your answers on page 131.

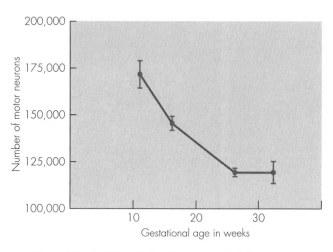

Figure 5.5 Cell loss during development of the nervous system
The graph shows the number of motor neurons in the ventral spinal cord of human fetuses. Note that the number of motor neurons is highest at 11 weeks and drops steadily until about 25 weeks, the age when motor neuron axons make synapses with muscles. Axons that fail to make synapses die. *(Source: Forger & Breedlove, 1987)*

Pathfinding by Axons

Suppose you operate a government office in Washington, D.C., and you want to install cables to send secret messages. You tell one employee to run a cable across the street to the Office of Bureaucratic Mismanagement. Because it is so near, you hardly give a thought to the problem of finding a route. Then you tell another employee to stretch a very long cable to the mayor's office in Truth or Consequences, New Mexico. Now you definitely have to worry about whether your employee will find an accurate, reasonably direct route.

The developing nervous system faces a similar problem because it sends some of its axons over enormous distances. How do axons find their way?

Chemical Pathfinding by Axons

A famous biologist, Paul Weiss (1924), conducted an experiment in which he grafted an extra leg to a salamander and then waited for axons to grow into it. (Such an experiment could never work with a mammal. Salamanders and other amphibians can regenerate parts of their bodies that mammals cannot. They also generate new axon branches to an extra grafted-on limb.) After the axons reached the muscles, the extra leg, positioned next to one of the hind legs, moved in perfect synchrony with the normal leg.

Weiss dismissed as unbelievable the idea that each axon had developed a branch that found its way to exactly the correct muscle in the extra limb. He suggested instead that the nerves attached to muscles at random and then sent a variety of messages, each one tuned to a different muscle. In other words it did not matter which axon was attached to which muscle. The muscles were like radios, each tuned to a different station: Each muscle received many signals but responded to only one.

Specificity of Axon Connections   Weiss was wrong. Later evidence supported the interpretation he considered impossible: The salamander's extra leg moved in synchrony with its neighbor because each axon had sent a branch that attached to exactly the correct muscle.

Since the time of Weiss's work, most of the research on axon growth has dealt with how sensory axons find their way to the correct targets in the brain. (The issues

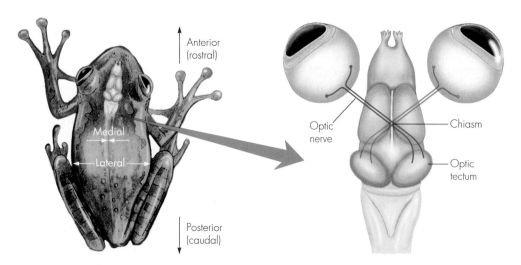

Figure 5.6 Connections from eye to brain in a frog
The optic tectum is a large structure in fish, amphibians, reptiles, and birds. Its location corresponds to the midbrain of mammals, but its function is more elaborate, analogous to what the cerebral cortex does in mammals. Note: Connections from eye to brain are different in humans, as described in Chapter 14. *(Source: After Romer, 1962)*

are the same as those for axons finding their way to muscles.) In one study Roger Sperry, a former student of Weiss, cut the optic nerves of some newts. In amphibians, unlike mammals, a damaged optic nerve grows back and contacts the *tectum,* the main visual area of fish, amphibians, reptiles, and birds (see Figure 5.6). Sperry found that when the new synapses formed, the newt regained normal vision.

Then Sperry (1943) repeated the experiment, but this time, after he cut each optic nerve, he rotated the eye by 180°. When the axons grew back to the tectum, which targets would they contact? Sperry found that the axons from what had originally been the dorsal side of the retina (which was now on the ventral side) grew back to the area responsible for vision in the dorsal side of the retina. Axons from what had once been the ventral side of the retina (now on the dorsal side) also grew back to their original targets. The newt now saw the world upside down and backward, responding to stimuli in the sky as if they were on the ground and to stimuli on the left as if they were on the right (see Figure 5.7). Each axon regenerated to the area of the tectum where it had originally been, presumably by following a chemical trail.

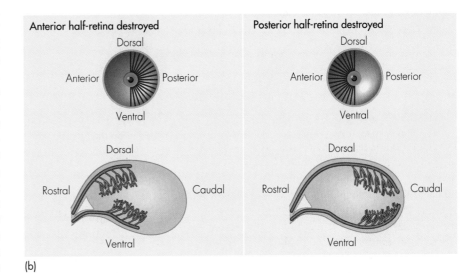

(a)

(b)

Figure 5.7 Summary of Sperry's experiment on nerve connections in newts
After he cut the optic nerve and inverted the eye, the optic nerve axons grew back to their original targets, not to the targets corresponding to the eye's current position.

Chemical Gradients The next question was: How specific a target might the axon have? Did an axon from the retina have to find the tectal cell with exactly the right chemical marker on its surface, like a key finding the right lock? Does the body have to synthesize a separate chemical marker for each of the billions of axons in the nervous system?

No. A growing axon follows a path of cell-surface molecules, attracted by some chemicals and repelled by others, in a process that steers the axon in approximately the correct direction (Tessier-Lavigne & Goodman, 1996). Some axons follow a trail based on one attractive chemical until they reach an intermediate location and then become insensitive to that chemical and follow a different attractant to their final target (Shirasaki, Katsumata, & Murakami, 1998; Wang & Tessier-Lavigne, 1999). When they reach their target,

neurotrophins determine how widely each axon spreads its branches (Inoue & Sanes, 1997). Finally, axons sort themselves over the surface of the target area by following a gradient of chemicals. For example, one chemical in the amphibian tectum is a protein known as TOP_{DV} (TOP for *top*ography; DV for *d*orso*v*entral). This protein is 30 times more concentrated in the axons of the dorsal retina than of the ventral retina and 10 times more concentrated in the ventral tectum than in the dorsal tectum. As axons from the retina grow toward the tectum, the retinal axons with the greatest concentration of TOP_{DV} connect to the tectal cells with the highest concentration of that chemical; the axons with the lowest concentration connect to the tectal cells with the lowest concentration. A similar gradient of another protein aligns the axons along the anterior–posterior axis (J. R. Sanes, 1993) (see Figure 5.8).

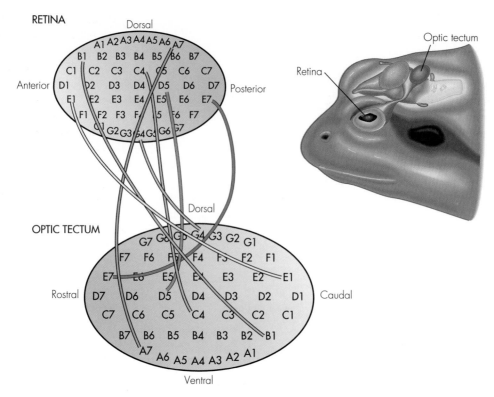

Figure 5.8 Retinal axons match up with neurons in the tectum by following two gradients
The protein TOP$_{DV}$ is concentrated mostly in the dorsal retina and the ventral tectum. Axons rich in TOP$_{DV}$ attach to tectal neurons that are also rich in that chemical. Similarly a second protein directs axons from the posterior retina to the rostral portion of the tectum.

Stop & Check

6. What was Sperry's evidence that axons grow to a specific target presumably by following a chemical gradient instead of attaching at random?

7. If all cells in the tectum of an amphibian produced the same amount of TOP$_{DV}$, what would be the effect on the attachment of axons to it?

Check your answers on page 131.

Competition Among Axons as a General Principle

As one might guess from the experiments just described, when axons initially reach their targets, each one forms synapses onto several target cells in approximately the correct location, and each target cell receives synapses from a large number of axons. Figure 5.9 summarizes the results: At first axons make tentative connections with many postsynaptic cells; gradually the postsynaptic cells strengthen some and reject others. (It's a little like dating.)

To some theorists these results suggest a general principle, which Gerald Edelman (1987) calls **neural Darwinism.** In Darwinian evolution gene mutations

and reassortments produce individuals with variations in their appearance and actions; natural selection favors some variations and weeds out the rest. Similarly, in the development of the nervous system, we start with more neurons and synapses than we keep. Synapses form haphazardly, and then a selection process keeps some and rejects others. In this manner the most successful axons and combinations survive; the others fail to sustain active synapses.

The principle of competition among axons is an important one, although we should use the analogy with Darwinian evolution cautiously. Mutations in the genes are random events, but trophic factors steer new axonal branches and synapses in the right direction. Still it is true that the most successful connections thrive at the expense of the less successful, as in Darwinian evolution.

Fine-Tuning by Experience

The genetic instructions for assembling your nervous system are only approximate. Because of the unpredictability of life, we have evolved the ability to redesign our brains (within limits) in response to our experience (Shatz, 1992). The plasticity of brain anatomy enables each of us to custom design a brain well adapted to the activities we most often encounter.

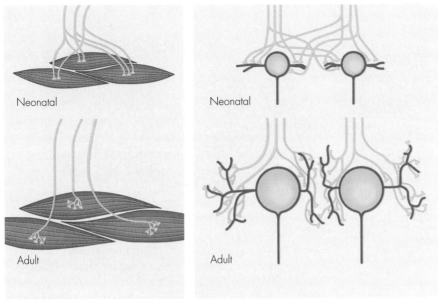

(a) Muscle fibers   (b) Sympathetic ganglion cells

Figure 5.9 Development by elimination of synapses
(**a**) Early in development each muscle fiber receives synapses from branches of several motor axons. The muscle fiber gradually strengthens its synapse with one axon and rejects the others. (However, an axon can form synapses with many muscle fibers.)
(**b**) Early in development neurons in the ganglia of the sympathetic nervous system receive synapses from many axons. Later each cell rejects the incoming axons from some neurons and accepts the axons from others. Although the cell as a whole may accept axons from numerous different neurons, typically each dendrite forms lasting synapses with only one axon. That axon may, however, form a great many branches and therefore a great many synapses onto that dendrite. *(Source: After Purves & Lichtman, 1980)*

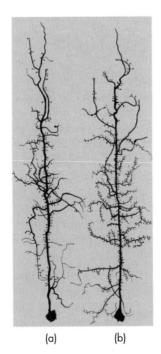

(a)   (b)

Figure 5.10 Effect of a stimulating environment on neuronal branching
(**a**) A jewel fish reared in isolation develops neurons with fewer branches. (**b**) A fish reared with others has more neuronal branches. *(Source: Richard Coss)*

Effects of Experience on Dendritic Branching

Let's start with a simple example. If you live in a complex and challenging environment, you need an elaborate nervous system. Ordinarily a laboratory rat lives in a simple and unchallenging environment—a small gray cage. Imagine by contrast a set of ten or so rats living together in a larger cage with a few little pieces of junk to explore or play with. Researchers sometimes call this an enriched environment, but it is enriched only in contrast to the usual rather sparse environment.

A rat in the more stimulating environment develops a thicker cortex, more dendritic branching, and improved performance on many tests of learning (Greenough, 1975; Rosenzweig & Bennett, 1996). Specific learning experiences also increase dendritic branching (Woolf, Zinnerman, & Johnson, 1999). An enriched environment enhances sprouting of axons and dendrites for species as remote as jewel fish (Coss & Globus, 1979) and honeybees (Coss, Brandon, & Globus, 1980) (see Figure 5.10). Humans with extensive education tend to have longer and more widely branched dendrites than less educated people do (Jacobs, Schall, & Scheibel, 1993). For the human data two explanations are likely: Learning does increase dendritic branching, but it is also probable that people who have already developed wide dendritic branching succeed in school and therefore stay longer.

Although the effects of environmental enrichment can occur at any time, some experiences produce bigger effects if they occur early. We can say that the brain is more plastic early than it is later. For example, young birds of certain species learn their song by selecting some elements out of a set of possible song components and discarding other possible elements (Marler & Nelson, 1992). In doing so they apparently magnify some dendritic branches and shrink others. One portion of a mynah bird's brain is essential to its ability to sing. (Mynah birds, like parrots and mockingbirds, excel at imitating other birds' songs.) In that brain area one kind of neuron has a great many *dendritic spines* (little outgrowths) early in the first year of life while the bird is learning many new songs. By the end of the first year, each of those neurons has fewer dendritic spines than it had at the start of the year, but the surviving spines are larger than they used to be (Figure 5.11). Evidently the multitude of tiny dendritic spines at the start of the year

Magnetoencephalography (MEG)

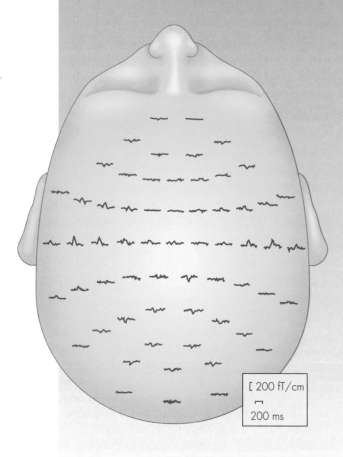

A **magnetoencephalograph (MEG)** measures the faint magnetic fields generated by brain activity (Hari, 1994). Magnetic detectors on the surface of the skull record the net activity over a fairly large area, so an MEG is imprecise in locating activity. However, it has excellent temporal resolution, showing changes from one millisecond to another.

For example, Figure 5.12 shows an MEG record comparing the responses of many brain areas to a brief tone heard in the right ear. The diagram represents a human head as viewed from above, with the nose at the top (Hari, 1994). Using MEG with more complicated tasks, such as naming a picture, researchers can identify the brain location that responds most quickly, the areas that respond slightly later, those that respond still later, and so on. In such a manner researchers can trace a wave of brain activity from its origin in one area to its processing in another (Salmelin, Hari, Lounasmaa, & Sams, 1994).

Figure 5.12 A result of magnetoencephalography, showing responses to a tone in the right ear
The nose is shown at the top. For each spot on the diagram, the display shows the changing response over a few hundred ms following the tone (note calibration at lower right). The tone evoked responses in many areas, with the largest responses in the temporal cortex, especially on the left side. (*Source: Hari, 1994*)

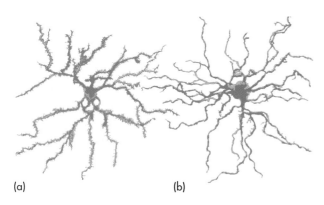

(a)   (b)

Figure 5.11 Dendritic spines in the song-control area of a mynah bird's brain
(**a**) Early in the bird's first year of life, the dendrites have an enormous number of tiny spines, each of them evidently corresponding to the enormous variety of potential song elements that the bird might learn. (**b**) About a year later the dendrites have far fewer spines, but the surviving spines have grown much larger. These presumably correspond to song elements that the bird has actually learned to produce. (*Source: Rausch & Scheich, 1982*)

made it possible for the bird to learn an unpredictable variety of new songs. By the end of the year, the mynah bird has learned many songs and strengthened the spines needed for those songs, but by losing other spines it has decreased its ability to learn additional songs.

Generation of New Neurons

Can the adult vertebrate brain generate any new neurons? The traditional belief, dating back to the work of Cajal in the late 1800s, was that vertebrate brains formed all their neurons during embryological development or during infancy at the latest. Gradually researchers found exceptions.

The first to be found was the olfactory receptors, which, because they are exposed to the outside world and its toxic chemicals, have a short life expectancy. A population of neurons in the nose remains immature throughout life. Periodically the neurons divide; one cell remains immature and the other develops into an olfactory receptor to replace one of the cells that is

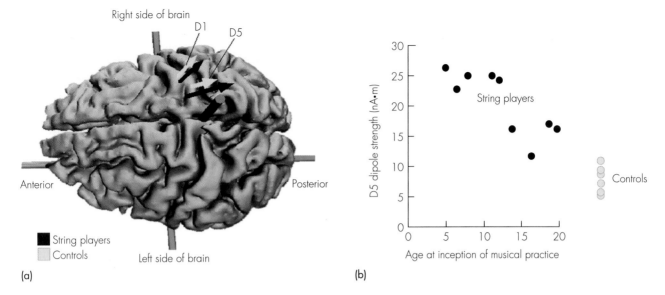

Figure 5.13 Expanded cortical representation of fingers on string players' left hand
(**a**) The yellow and black arrows show the dipole moments (an MEG measure of neuronal activity) in response to stimulation of the thumb (D1) and little finger (D5), superimposed on an MRI scan of a brain. The red bars merely show the left–right, dorsoventral, and anterior–posterior axes. Note that the representation of the left thumb is equal for string players and controls, but the representation of the fifth finger is significantly greater for the string players. Representations of the right hand, not shown in the figure, were equal for musicians and nonmusicians. (**b**) The brain representation of the little finger (D5) was greater in those who had started learning a stringed instrument early than in those who had started late. (*Source: Elbert, Pantev, Wienbruch, Rockstroh, & Taub, 1995*)

about to expire (Graziadei & deHan, 1973; Graziadei & Monti Graziadei, 1985). Later researchers also found a population of undifferentiated cells, called **stem cells,** in the interior of the brain that ordinarily do not divide and do not even act as neurons—they line the interior of the fluid-filled ventricles of the brain—but that sometimes generate daughter cells that migrate to the olfactory bulb and transform into glia cells or neurons (Johansson et al., 1999). Still later researchers have found the development of new neurons in the hippocampus in many species, including humans (Eriksson et al., 1998), even in aging animals (Kempermann, Kuhn, & Gage, 1998), and in some but not all parts of the cerebral cortex of monkeys (Gould, Reeves, Graziano, & Gross, 1999). The development of new neurons and probably their survival are enhanced by diverse experiences, and so the new neurons may play a role in learning and memory. However, we need much more research to clarify the role of newly formed neurons (Gould, Beylin, Tanapat, Reeves, & Shors, 1999; van Praag, Kempermann, & Gage, 1999).

Effects of Experience on Human Brain Structures

Particularly powerful evidence of the effects of early experience on brain development comes from studies of children with extensive early music training. Some people develop absolute pitch—the ability to hear a note and identify it, such as B flat or C sharp. Perhaps it is more accurate to say they "retain" the ability rather than "develop" it; many children have absolute

pitch, but nearly all lose it by adulthood. In any case almost every adult who shows this ability began extensive music training early, generally by age 6 or 7 (Takeuchi & Hulse, 1993). Adults who have absolute pitch also have larger than usual development in one area of the temporal cortex in the left hemisphere (Schlaug, Jäncke, Huang, & Steinmetz, 1995). If we assume that absolute pitch is the result of the early music training (rather than the cause of it), the extra development of the temporal cortex is also the result of the music training.

A related study used magnetoencephalography (MEG; see Methods 5.1) to compare the postcentral gyrus of nonmusicians to people who had extensive experience in playing stringed instruments, in most cases violin. As you may recall from Chapter 4, the postcentral gyrus is the primary somatosensory cortex, and each area along the gyrus responds to a particular area of the body. In string players, who use the left hand to finger the strings, the postcentral gyrus of the right hemisphere has a larger than usual area responding to sensations from the fingers of the left hand (Elbert, Pantev, Wienbruch, Rockstroh, & Taub, 1995). The left hemispheres had a normal-size area devoted to sensations from the right hand. As shown in Figure 5.13b, the area devoted to the left fingers was larger in those who began learning a stringed instrument early. However, those who started early had also continued for more years than those who started later; therefore we do not know whether the difference in brain structure depends on total years of study or on the age of starting.

Nevertheless it is clear that, within limits, practicing a skill can reorganize or restructure the brain.

Combinations of Chemical and Experiential Effects

The results discussed so far suggest a two-stage process. First axons find their approximate targets by following a chemical gradient, and then they strengthen some connections and discard others in response to experience. Like many generalizations about the nervous system, this one is not entirely correct. Even during early prenatal development, when axons are first reaching their destinations, they produce spontaneous action potentials, and if those are blocked, the axons fail to produce normal branches and connections (Catalano & Shatz, 1998).

What use could action potentials have during prenatal development, when the embryo has only very limited and not very meaningful experience? Consider an example: One part of the thalamus, the *lateral geniculate* (Figure 4.13, p. 98), receives its input from the retinas of the eyes. During prenatal development each lateral geniculate cell initially receives input from a number of retinal axons, which produce spontaneous action potentials. Repeated waves of activity sweep over the retina from one side to the other. Consequently, axons from adjacent areas of the retina are almost simultaneously activated. Each lateral geniculate cell selects a group of axons that are simultaneously active at this time; as a result it becomes responsive to a group of receptors adjacent to one another on the retina (Meister, Wong, Baylor, & Shatz, 1991).

Stop & Check

8. How does the brain of a lifelong string instrument player differ from that of most other people?

9. If axons from the retina were prevented from showing spontaneous activity during early development, what would be the probable effect on development of the lateral geniculate?

Check your answers on page 131.

Proportional Growth of Brain Areas

How did your developmental program determine how large to build your cerebral cortex, your medulla, your cerebellum, and so forth? The human brain is larger than that of most other mammals (Figure 5.14); did we need separate genes to double the size of one brain area, triple the size of another, and so forth?

Evidently not. The development of each brain area depends on two factors: the rate of production of new neurons per day and the number of days that the process continues. Although some brain areas grow faster than others, the rate and duration of development in one area are closely proportional to the rate and duration in the others.

Consider some data taken from a comparison across species. Figure 5.15 is a complicated graph, but the underlying idea is simple (Finlay & Darlington, 1995). For each line (such as neocortex), each point along the line represents one species. (Humans are the orange squares in the far right column for each of the ten lines.) Along the horizontal (x axis) are logarithms of the total volume of the brain. Along the vertical (y axis) are logarithms of the volume of each subarea, such as the neocortex. As you can see each area forms almost a straight line. In other words, if you know how large the total brain is, you can accurately predict the size of the neocortex, the cerebellum, the medulla, and so forth. The only major exception to this rule (not shown in the figure) is the olfactory bulb, which comprises a large percentage of some mammals' brains (such as rats') and only a tiny percentage of others'

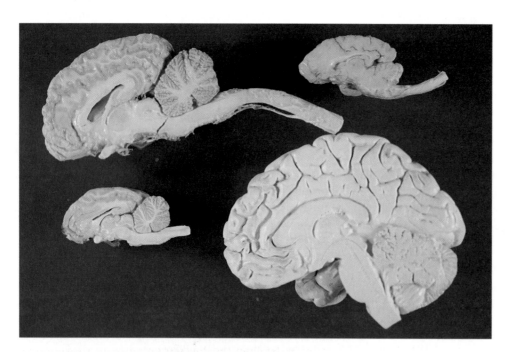

Figure 5.14 Comparison of mammalian brains
The human brain is the largest of those shown, although whales, dolphins, and elephants have still larger brains. All mammals have the same brain subareas in the same locations. Clockwise from top left: horse, dog, human, sheep.

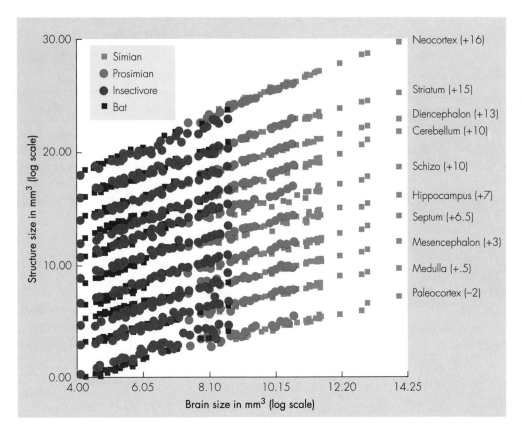

Figure 5.15   Relationship between total brain mass and mass of individual brain structures
Within a line each point represents the data for one species of placental (nonmarsupial) mammal; the points at the far right represent humans, which have the largest brains of the species studied. Each line represents a different part of the brain. The lines have been separated by adding or subtracting a constant from each; if the authors had not done so, the lines would be almost perfectly superimposed on one another, except for the neocortex.

Neocortex = cerebral cortex, including white matter and corpus callosum; striatum = caudate nucleus, putamen, and nucleus accumbens; diencephalon = thalamus, hypothalamus, and globus pallidus; schizocortex = parts of the medial temporal cortex; septum = an area ventral to the center of the corpus callosum; mesencephalon = the midbrain; paleocortex = anterior portion of the temporal lobe. *(Source: Finlay & Darlington, 1995)*

brains (such as humans'). The point of the graph is that different brain areas grow in parallel with one another; an increase in one area is linked to increases in others. For example, the main differences between human brains and chimpanzee brains are due to the fact that neuronal proliferation continues longer in humans (Rakic, 1998; Vrba, 1998).

(Do not misread Figure 5.15 as indicating that all brain components increase in *direct* proportion with one another; the graph is a logarithm-logarithm function. Because the cerebral cortex has a higher exponent than the other brain areas do, as overall brain mass increases, the percentage of the brain occupied by the cerebral cortex increases. However, it increases in an orderly, predictable way; the greater the total brain mass, the greater the percentage of it devoted to the cerebral cortex.)

The same principle applies to much of the variation in brain size among humans. That is, people with a larger cerebral cortex generally also have a larger cerebellum, medulla, hippocampus, and so forth. The genes, health, nutrition, and education that promote develop-

ment of one brain area also promote development of the others.

Is it therefore true that people with larger brains are more intelligent, as measured by, say, an IQ test? Theoretically we might expect a "yes" answer: If bigger is better, someone with a big brain has a larger than average cerebral cortex, hippocampus, and all other brain areas. Regardless of which areas contribute to which aspects of intelligence, someone with a large brain should have an advantage on all aspects.

For many years the available evidence failed to find an impressive correlation between brain volume and IQ scores (e.g., Passingham, 1979). However, those results were based on inaccurate estimates of brain size. Investigators either weighed the brains of recently deceased people (whose brains dry out and shrink) or they estimated brain sizes from the skull sizes. But brain sizes don't always match skull sizes. (They can't be larger, but they can be much smaller.) In a study using the modern MRI technique (Methods 5.2) to visualize and measure accurately the brains of living people, investigators measured the brains of 40 college students and found

MRI Scans

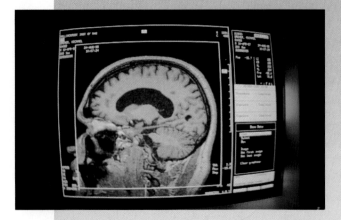

Figure 5.16 A view of a living brain generated by magnetic resonance imaging
Any atom with an odd-numbered atomic weight, such as hydrogen, has an inherent rotation. An outside magnetic field can align the axes of rotation. A radio frequency field can then make all these atoms move like tiny gyros. When the radio frequency field is turned off, the atomic nuclei release electromagnetic energy as they relax. By measuring that energy we can obtain an image of a structure such as the brain without damaging it. *(Dan McCoy/Rainbow)*

One method of examining the anatomy of a living brain is **magnetic resonance imaging (MRI),** also known as nuclear magnetic resonance (NMR). MRI produces images with a high degree of resolution without exposing the brain to radiation (Warach, 1995). This method is based on the fact that any atom with an odd-numbered atomic weight, such as hydrogen, has an axis of rotation. An MRI device applies a powerful magnetic field (about 25,000 times the magnetic field of the earth), thereby aligning all the axes of rotation. A brief radio frequency field can then tilt these axes. When the radio frequency field is turned off, the atomic nuclei release electromagnetic energy as they relax and return to their original axis. By measuring that energy, MRI devices form an image of the brain, such as the one in Figure 5.16. Most MRI scans are set to detect the energy released by the hydrogen atoms in water molecules, which are the most abundant molecules in the body. An MRI image can reveal structural defects such as enlargements or shrinkages of various brain areas. One drawback is that the person must lie with the head motionless in a very confining, noisy apparatus. The procedure is not suitable for fidgety people or those with a fear of enclosed places.

that the higher IQ students had larger brains on the average than did the lower IQ students (Willerman, Schultz, Rutledge, & Bigler, 1991).[2]

Do these results mean that IQ really is strongly related to brain size? Maybe; we need to see more data drawn from larger and more representative samples. Even if the results turn out to be replicable, a problem remains: Men have larger brains on average than women do, although men and women on average have the same IQ scores. Even low-IQ men have larger brains than high-IQ women. Part—but only part—of the resolution is brain-to-body ratio: Men are larger than women, so their brain-to-body ratio is similar to women's. But brain-to-body ratio isn't the whole story either. If it were, then short people would be more intelligent than tall people because they have a higher brain-to-body ratio. (In fact short people are not on average more intelligent.) The relationship between brain size and intelligence remains a puzzle.

Stop & Check

10. If you know the total volume of a mammal's brain, you can accurately predict the volume of its major components, such as the cerebral cortex. What conclusion follows from this observation?

11. Why did old studies find such a low correlation between human IQ and brain size? What advance in research methods led to a higher correlation?

Check your answers on page 131.

The Vulnerable Developing Brain

Brain development requires a complicated interplay of cells, chemicals, and timing that can easily go wrong. Frequently it is difficult to determine the cause of a brain abnormality or developmental behavior disorder (see Digression 5.1). In other cases it is possible to identify genes or chemicals that interfered with normal development. Researchers have identified hundreds of genetic mutations capable of impairing brain development (Thapar, Gottesman, Owen, O'Donovan, & McGuffin, 1994), and there are undoubtedly more to be discovered.

---

[2] A relationship between brain size and IQ tells us little about the relationship between genetics and IQ. Brain size does have a heritable component (Bartley, Jones, & Weinberger, 1997), but it also depends on health, nutrition, prenatal environment, and environmental enrichment—all factors that contribute as well to IQ.

Attention-Deficit Disorder: Mixed Abnormalities of Brain Development

A group of 5- to 7-year-old children left to themselves will be impulsive and highly active, with frequent shifts of attention from one activity to another. The same behaviors during school hours may earn a child a diagnosis of **attention-deficit/hyperactivity disorder (ADHD).** If they show the same behaviors without excess activity, they are given the diagnosis **attention-deficit disorder (ADD).** ADD or ADHD has become a common diagnosis, applied to approximately 5% of all children in the United States and a somewhat lower percentage in Europe. It affects more boys than girls, especially in early childhood. The diagnosis is, however, a fuzzy one. On the average, people with ADD do have some brain abnormalities, especially decreased activity in the frontal cortex, but the differences are small compared to most medical disorders. Granted, some children are so impulsive and have such short attention spans that no one would deny that they have problems. Others, however, are debatable cases—more rambunctious than most, but not necessarily disordered (Panksepp, 1998). Also, some children are mistakenly identified as ADD, although their real problem is inadequate sleep, family conflicts, allergies, or other problems unrelated to brain development.

ADD is generally diagnosed in childhood, usually based on behavior in school. Some children "outgrow" the problem in adolescence or early adulthood, but others continue to have academic and occupational problems throughout life, and sometimes also antisocial behaviors (Mannuzza, Klein, Bessler, Malloy, & LaPadula, 1998). No single cause has been identified, and ADD probably represents a cluster of several problems with different causes, including genetics, brain damage, malnutrition, exposure to lead or other toxins, and effects of the mother's smoking or using other drugs during pregnancy (Taylor, 1998). Whatever the original cause, people with ADD show several mild abnormalities of brain development, including decreased ability of the prefrontal cortex to inhibit inappropriate behaviors (Castellanos et al., 1996; Farone & Biederman, 1998). For example, people with ADD are particularly impaired on a task in which they receive one signal to make a response, sometimes followed quickly by a second signal to inhibit the response. ADD people usually make the response in spite of the signal to inhibit it (Rubia, Oosterlaan, Sergeant, Brandeis, & v. Leeuwen, 1998).

Decades ago physicians discovered that when they gave amphetamine to epileptic children to calm their seizures, it reduced the hyperactivity of some of those children. Physicians started using amphetamine to reduce hyperactivity, and still today the most common treatment for ADD is stimulant drugs such as methylphenidate (Ritalin) or amphetamine (Elia, Ambrosini, & Rapoport, 1999). The drugs increase attentiveness, improve social relationships, decrease impulsiveness, and moderately improve academic performance. As mentioned in Chapter 3, amphetamine and methylphenidate increase the availability of dopamine to the postsynaptic receptors. They produce their maximum effects on dopamine about 1 hour after someone takes a pill, and 1 hour is also the time of the maximum behavioral benefit, so researchers are confident that the pills affect behavior through dopamine activity (Volkow et al., 1998). The benefits wear off a few hours later.

Suppose you are in doubt about whether some child really has ADD. A physician prescribes a stimulant drug, and the child's behavior improves. Does the improvement imply that the child does have ADD? Not necessarily. One study found that stimulant drugs increase attention span even of normal children (Zahn, Rapoport, & Thompson, 1980).

The developing brain is more vulnerable than the mature brain is to the effects of malnutrition (Levitsky & Strupp, 1995), toxic chemicals, and infections. For example, impaired thyroid function in adulthood produces lethargy and decreased alertness, whereas a similar impairment in infancy produces permanent mental retardation and slowed body growth. (Thyroid deficiency was more widespread in the past because of inadequate iodine in the diet; today's table salt is almost always fortified with iodine.) Anesthetic drugs produce only a temporary loss of consciousness in adults; in infants, by suppressing synaptic activity of neurons still highly vulnerable to apoptosis, anesthetics result in the death of many neurons (Ikonomidou et al., 1999).

Exposure to alcohol also impairs the developing brain much more than it does the mature brain. The children of mothers who drink heavily during pregnancy may be born with **fetal alcohol syndrome,** a condition marked by decreased alertness, hyperactivity, varying degrees of mental retardation, motor problems, heart defects, and facial abnormalities (Figure 5.17). Dendrites tend to be short with few branches. When children with fetal alcohol syndrome reach adulthood, they have a high risk of alcoholism, drug dependence, depression, and other psychiatric disorders (Famy, Streissguth, & Unis, 1998). Researchers are not sure what amount of alcohol, if any, is safe to drink during pregnancy, and the risk probably depends on the stage of pregnancy as well as on the amount of alcohol. Even in children who do not show any facial or other visible abnormalities, the more the mother drank during pregnancy, the more impulsive the child and the

Figure 5.17 Child with fetal alcohol syndrome
Note the facial pattern. Many children exposed to smaller amounts of alcohol before birth have behavioral deficits without facial signs. *(Source: Ted Wood/Picture Group, Inc.)*

worse the school performance (Hunt, Streissguth, Kerr, & Carmichael-Olson, 1995).

Prenatal exposure to other substances can be harmful, too. Children of mothers who use cocaine during pregnancy have a slight decrease in IQ scores compared to normals and a somewhat greater decrease in language skills (Lester, LaGasse, & Seifer, 1998). The effects of cigarette smoking during pregnancy have not been as heavily investigated, but the available results indicate serious harm, possibly greater than that caused by cocaine. Children of mothers who smoked during pregnancy are at much increased risk of the following (Brennan, Grekin, & Mednick, 1999; Fergusson, Woodward, & Horwood, 1998; Finette, O'Neill, Vacek, & Albertini, 1998; Milberger, Biederman, Faraone, Chen, & Jones, 1996; Slotkin, 1998):

- Low weight at birth and many illnesses early in life
- Sudden infant death syndrome ("crib death")
- Long-term intellectual deficits
- Attention-deficit/hyperactivity disorder (ADHD)
- Impairments of the immune system
- Delinquency and crime later in life (sons especially)

In Chapter 12 we consider more thoroughly the link between prenatal nicotine and later antisocial behavior. The overall message obviously is that pregnant women should minimize their use of all drugs, even legal ones.

Module 5.1

In Closing: Brain Development

Considering the number of ways in which abnormal genes and chemicals can disrupt brain development, let alone the possible varieties of abnormal experience, it is a wonder that any of us develop normally. Evidently the system has enough redundancies or margin for error that we can function even if all of our connections do not develop quite perfectly. There are many ways for development to go wrong, but somehow the system usually manages to work.

Summary

1. In vertebrate embryos the central nervous system begins as a tube surrounding a fluid-filled cavity. Developing neurons proliferate, migrate, differentiate, and myelinate. (p. 116)

2. Initially the nervous system develops far more neurons than will actually survive. As they send out their axons, some make synaptic contacts with cells that release to them nerve growth factor or other neurotrophins. The neurons that receive neurotrophins survive; the others die. (p. 118)

3. Growing axons manage to find their way close to the right locations by following chemicals. (p. 120)

4. Axons attach themselves to a target area by arraying themselves over chemical gradients. (p. 121)

5. Variations in experience can alter overall brain growth and increase or decrease the amount of brain devoted to a particular sensory system. (p. 123)

6. The action potentials of an axon are important in synapse formation even at the earliest stages of development. (p. 126)

7. Among mammals the size of the brain as a whole correlates almost perfectly with the size of its major components. That is, the factors of health, nutrition, and genetics that control development of any one brain area also govern development of the other areas. (p. 126)

8. Among humans one study indicates a moderately large correlation between brain size and IQ. The meaning of this correlation is unclear for several reasons, including the confusing issue of why males and females differ in brain size but not in IQ. (p. 127)

9. The brain is vulnerable during early development; abnormalities of genes, nutrition, or the chemical environment can produce many behavioral disorders. (p. 128)

Answers to *Stop and Check* Questions

1. Proliferation is the formation of new neurons; migration is their movement from the point of origin to their final location. (p. 117)

2. The glomeruli that were present at age 1 week have grown by age 3 weeks, but some new ones have

formed. Therefore the 3-week-old mouse has some glomeruli that are smaller than some of those in the 1-week-old mouse. (p. 117)

3. The nervous system builds far more neurons than it needs and discards through apoptosis those that do not make lasting synapses. (p. 119)

4. Neurotrophins, such as nerve growth factor (p. 119)

5. The embryo has the most neurons. (p. 119)

6. Sperry found that if he cut a newt's eye and inverted it, axons grew back to their original targets, even though they were inappropriate to their new position on the eye. (p. 122)

7. Axons would attach haphazardly instead of arranging themselves according to their dorsoventral position on the retina. (p. 122)

8. In the somatosensory cortex of the right hemisphere, the area devoted to sensation from the fingers of the left hand (which touches the strings) is larger than normal. (p. 126)

9. The axons attach based on a chemical gradient but could not fine-tune the adjustment based on experience. Therefore the connections would be less precise. (p. 126)

10. All mammalian species have the same organization of the brain. The main differences among their brains are controlled by the number of cell divisions during brain development. (p. 128)

11. The old studies used inaccurate methods of estimating brain size. Newer studies use MRI scans to measure brain size in living people. (p. 128)

Thought Questions

1. Biologists can develop antibodies against nerve growth factor (that is, molecules that inactivate nerve growth factor). What would happen if someone injected such antibodies into a developing nervous system?

2. Based on material in this chapter, what is one reason a woman should avoid long-lasting anesthesia during delivery of a baby?

Module 5.2

Recovery of Function After Brain Damage

An American soldier who suffered a wound to the left hemisphere of his brain during the Korean War was at first unable to speak at all. Three months later he could speak in short fragments. When he was shown a letterhead, "New York University College of Medicine," and asked to read it, all he could say was, "Doctors— little doctors." Eight years later, when someone asked him again to read the letterhead, he replied, "Is there a catch? It says, 'New York University College of Medicine'" (Eidelberg & Stein, 1974).

Many people show behavioral recovery after brain damage, although the recovery is seldom if ever complete. Given that the mammalian nervous system replaces only a few lost neurons, and even those are only in certain locations, we face the theoretical question of how people recover from brain damage at all. We would like to understand the process so we can facilitate recovery and because studying recovery may yield insights into the functioning of the healthy brain.

Causes of Human Brain Damage

The human brain can be damaged in many ways, including tumors, infections, exposure to radiation or toxic substances, and degenerative conditions such as Parkinson's disease and Alzheimer's disease. In young adults the most common cause is **closed head injury,** a sharp blow to the head resulting from a fall, an automobile or motorcycle accident, a sports accident, an assault, or other sudden trauma that does not actually puncture the brain. The damage occurs partly because of rotational forces that drive brain tissue against the inside of the skull (see Digression 5.2). It also results from blood clots that interrupt normal blood flow to the brain (Kirkpatrick, Smielewski, Czosnyka, Menon, & Pickard, 1995). Many people, probably most, have suffered at least one closed head injury. Even a brief and

mild injury can sometimes produce noticeable long-term problems but usually does not (Satz et al., 1997). Repeated blows to the head, however, such as those suffered by professional boxers, produce serious losses of memory, reasoning, movement control, and emotional balance (Mendez, 1995) (see Figure 5.18).

A common cause of brain damage in older people (more rarely in the young) is temporary loss of normal blood flow to a brain area during a **stroke,** also known as a **cerebrovascular accident.** The more common type of stroke is **ischemia,** caused when a blood clot or other obstruction closes an artery; the less common type is **hemorrhage,** caused when an artery ruptures. The two types produce many of the same effects. Strokes vary in their severity from barely noticeable to immediately fatal. Figure 5.19 shows the brains of three people: one who died immediately after a stroke, one who survived for a long time after a stroke, and a victim of a bullet wound.

If one of your relatives had a stroke and you called a hospital, what advice would you probably get? As recently as the 1980s, the staff would have been in no great hurry to see the patient because they had little to

Figure 5.18 Effects of closed head injury
Although a single moderate trauma to the head ordinarily does not produce noticeable problems, repeated blows can cause slowness of speech and movement, as they did for boxer Muhammad Ali.

Digression 5.2

Why Don't Woodpeckers Get Concussions?

When a woodpecker strikes its bill against a tree, it repeatedly bangs its head against an unyielding object at a velocity of 6 to 7 meters per second (about 15 miles per hour). How does it escape brain injury?

P. R. A. May and associates (May, Fuster, Haber, & Hirschman, 1979) used slow-motion photography to observe the behavior of woodpeckers. They found that the bird often makes a pair of quick preliminary taps against the wood before a hard strike, much like a carpenter lining up a nail with a hammer. When it makes the hard strike, it does so in an almost perfectly straight line, keeping its neck rigid. The result is a near absence of rotational forces and consequent whiplash. The fact that woodpeck-

ers are so careful to avoid rotating their heads during impact supports the claim that rotational forces are a major factor in traumatic brain injuries.

The researchers suggested several implications for football players, race car drivers, and others who wear protective helmets. One is that the helmet would give more protection if it extended down to the shoulders, like the metal helmets worn by medieval knights. The advice for situations in which people do not wear helmets: If you anticipate an automobile accident or similar trauma, tuck your chin to your chest and tighten your neck muscles.

offer anyway. They were likely to recommend keeping the patient warm and providing tranquilizers or similar medications to lower blood pressure. We now know that those procedures actually made the condition worse. Today it is possible to reduce the effects of a stroke if physicians intervene quickly (Dávalos, Castillo, & Martinez-Vila, 1995).

Strokes kill neurons in two waves. First, cells in the immediate vicinity of the ischemia or hemorrhage die quickly. We still have little prospect of protecting those cells. Second, cells in the **penumbra** (Latin for "partial shadow"), the region that surrounds the immediate damage, are threatened and may die over the next few days or weeks (Ginsberg, 1995a; Hsu, Sik, Gallyas, Horváth, & Buzsáki, 1994; Jonas, 1995). Those cells may be protectable.

In ischemia, cells in the penumbra lose much of their oxygen and glucose supplies. In hemorrhage they are flooded with excess oxygen, calcium, and other blood products. After either ischemia or hemorrhage, penumbra cells are invaded by waste products from cells that are already dead or dying. Potassium ions

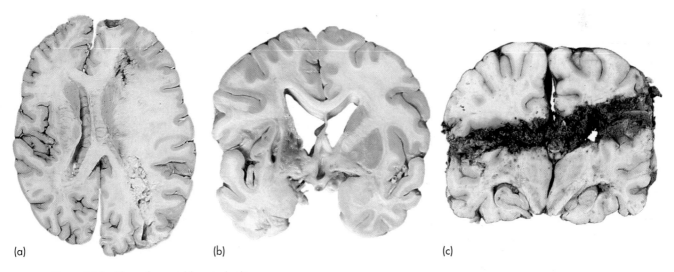

Figure 5.19 Three damaged human brains
(**a**) Brain of a person who died immediately after a stroke. Note the swelling on the right side. (**b**) Brain of a person who survived for a long time after a stroke. Note the cavities on the left side, where many cells were lost. (**c**) Brain of a person who suffered a gunshot wound and died immediately. *(Source: Courtesy of Dana Copeland)*

begin to accumulate outside neurons in the penumbra because the sodium-potassium pump does not have as much energy as usual. Edema (accumulation of fluid) forms because the blood-brain barrier has broken down. The combination of potassium and edema causes glia cells to dump much of the glutamate and other neurotransmitters that they had been storing (Billups & Attwell, 1996; Ginsberg, 1995b). The excess glutamate (an excitatory transmitter) overstimulates the neurons, making it even harder for their sodium-potassium pumps to keep pace. Sodium, calcium, and zinc ions gradually accumulate inside neurons. Exactly how they damage the cell is not fully clear, but one route is by interfering with the mitochondria, the cell's metabolic center (Stout, Raphael, Kanterewicz, Klann, & Reynolds, 1998). As neurons die, glia cells proliferate, removing waste products and dead neurons. Figure 5.20 summarizes this process. The main point of this figure is that both ischemia and hemorrhage kill neurons at least partly by overstimulating them.

To the extent that we understand stroke, we may be able to find ways to minimize its damage. The method now in wide use is to administer as quickly as possible a drug called **tissue plasminogen activator (tPA)**, which breaks up blood clots (Barinaga, 1996). This drug is of course recommended for ischemia but not for hemorrhage. In addition to dissolving blood clots, tPA has a mixture of helpful and harmful effects on the survival of damaged neurons (Kim, Park, Hong, & Koh, 1999).

Other methods, still in the experimental stage, attempt to prevent overstimulation by blocking glutamate synapses or by preventing calcium and other positive ions from entering neurons. So far, however, such methods have produced disappointing results (Lee, Zipfel, & Choi, 1999). Many researchers believe that ischemia kills cells partly by apoptosis—that is, by disturbing their environment enough that the cells activate their self-destruct programs. The evidence on whether apoptosis occurs is mixed (Colbourne, Sutherland, & Auer, 1999; Conti, Raghupathi, Trojanowski, & McIntosh, 1998), but

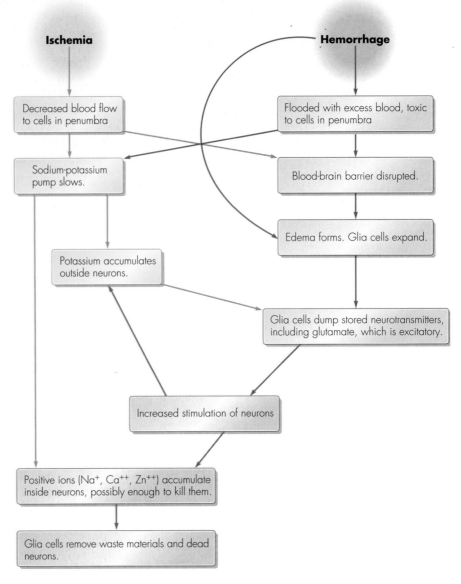

Figure 5.20 Mechanisms of neuron death after stroke
Procedures that can preserve neurons include removing the blood clot, blocking excitatory synapses, stimulating inhibitory synapses, blocking the flow of calcium and zinc, and cooling the brain.

if it does occur, it helps explain why blocking overstimulation has such disappointing results: Excess glutamate and calcium can kill cells by overstimulation, but deficient glutamate or calcium increases apoptosis. In studies of laboratory animals with strokes, a drug called *MK-801*, which blocks one type of glutamate receptor (the "NMDA" receptor), improves an animal's recovery if given early after the stroke but impairs recovery if given later (Barth, Grant, & Schallert, 1990).

In search of other approaches, researchers have tried using neurotrophins and other drugs that block apoptosis. Results have been favorable in animal trials using direct injection of the drugs into the brain, but application to humans is doubtful, because those drugs do not cross the blood-brain barrier (Barinaga, 1996; Choi-Lundberg et al., 1997; Levivier, Przedborski, Bencsics, & Kang, 1995; Schulz, Weller, & Moskowitz, 1999). Other procedures that have proved helpful in laboratory animal studies include drugs that trap free radicals (Schulz, Matthews, Jenkins, Brar, & Beal, 1995), food restriction (Bruce-Keller, Umberger, McFall, & Mattson, 1999), and cannabinoids—drugs similar to marijuana (Nagayama et al., 1999). The most effective laboratory method so far is to cool the brain. A cooled brain has less activity, lower energy needs, and less risk of over-stimulation than does a brain at normal temperature (Barone, Feuerstein, & White, 1997; Colbourne & Corbett, 1995). How well any of these methods may work with humans is unknown, however.

Stop & Check

1. In what ways does a stroke overstimulate neurons?

2. Why is tPA not recommended in cases of hemorrhage?

Check your answers on page 147.

Adjustments and Potential Recovery After Brain Damage

People with brain damage generally show some behavioral improvement, with most of the improvement occurring in the first month after the damage. Even after substantial improvement, however, the brain is not restored to what it had been. Someone who is functioning about normally may have to work harder than usual to achieve the same end and may deteriorate markedly after a couple of beers or a tiring effort (Fleet & Heilman, 1986).

As the person is recovering, what is changing in the brain? A simple assumption is that another part of the brain takes over the functions of the damaged area, but this assumption is valid only in a limited sense. When someone who has injured her left leg walks on her right leg and crutches, the arms and right leg are simply performing their own functions in a new way, not really taking over the function of the damaged leg. Similarly, after damage to the motor cortex in one hemisphere, the motor cortex of the remaining hemisphere develops some control of the ipsilateral limb (Chollet & Weiller, 1994). It is not really duplicating the function of the damaged area; it is merely improving the weak ipsilateral pathways that already existed.

Structural changes in the surviving neurons can partially restore lost functions, or the person can learn new ways to solve old problems. Let us consider some of the mechanisms of recovery.

Learned Adjustments in Behavior

Much of the recovery after brain damage is learned; the brain-damaged individual makes better use of unimpaired abilities. For example, someone who has lost vision in all but the center of the visual field may learn to move his or her head back and forth to compensate for the lack of peripheral vision (Marshall, 1985).

A brain-damaged person or animal may also learn to use abilities that at first appeared to be lost but actually were just impaired. For example, it is possible to eliminate most of the sensory information from a leg by cutting the sensory nerves from that leg to the spinal cord (see Figure 5.21). The animal loses sensation from the affected body parts, but it can still control the muscles. Such a limb is referred to as **deafferented,** because it has lost its afferent (sensory) input. Although the animal can still control the muscles of the deafferented limb, it seldom does. For example, monkeys with a deafferented limb do not spontaneously use it for walking, picking up objects, or any other voluntary behaviors (Taub & Berman, 1968). Investigators initially assumed that the monkey could not use the limb because of the lack of sensory feedback. In a later experiment, however, they cut the afferent nerves of both forelimbs; despite this more extensive damage, the monkey regained use of both deafferented limbs. It could walk moderately fast, climb upward or sideways on the walls of metal cages, and even pick up a raisin between its thumb and forefinger. Apparently a monkey fails to use one deafferented forelimb only because walking on three limbs is easier than moving the impaired limb. When both limbs are deafferented, the monkey is forced to use both.

Similarly many people with brain damage find it easier, especially at first, to struggle along without even trying to use an impaired ability. Many of them are capable of more than they are doing and more than they realize they can do. Therapy for brain-damaged people sometimes focuses on showing them how

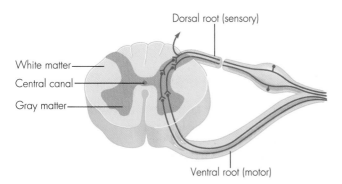

Figure 5.21 Cross section through the spinal cord
A cut through the dorsal root (as shown) deprives the animal of touch sensations from part of the body but leaves the motor nerves intact.

Labels in figure:
Dorsal root (sensory)
White matter
Central canal
Gray matter
Ventral root (motor)

Lesions

To study the behavioral functions of certain brain areas, researchers sometimes produce brain damage in laboratory animals, making a lesion (damage to a brain area) or an ablation (removal of part of the brain). To damage a structure not accessible from the surface, they use a stereotaxic instrument, a device for the precise placement of electrodes in the brain (Figure 5.22). By consulting a stereotaxic atlas (map) of the brain of some animal (such as a rat), a researcher can determine the location of a particular brain area with reference to the position of the ears, landmarks on the animal's skull (Figure 5.23), and so forth. Then the researcher drills a small hole in the skull, inserts the electrode, and carefully lowers it to the target area. Later the researcher passes a sufficient electrical current to damage the cells in that area.

Suppose someone makes a lesion in some brain area, finds that the animal stops eating, and concludes that the area is important for eating. "Wait a minute," you might ask. "How do we know the deficit wasn't caused by anesthetizing the animal, drilling a hole in its skull, and lowering an electrode through part of its brain to reach this target?" To test this possibility an experimenter produces a sham lesion in a control group, performing all the same procedures but without the electrical current. Any behavioral difference between the lesioned group and the sham-lesioned group must result from the lesion and not from inserting the electrode.

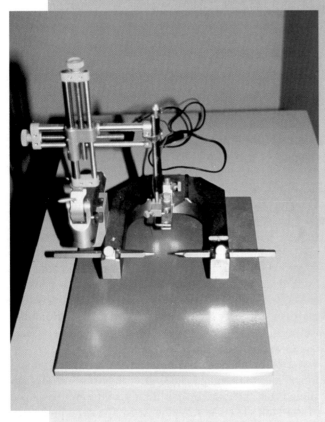

Figure 5.22   A stereotaxic instrument for locating brain areas in small animals
Using this device, researchers can insert an electrode to stimulate, record from, or damage any point in the brain.

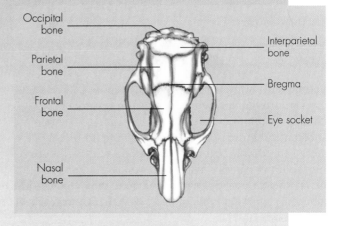

Figure 5.23   Skull bones of a rat
Bregma, the point where four bones meet on the top of the skull, is a useful landmark from which to locate areas of the brain.

much they already can do and encouraging them to practice those skills.

Diaschisis

Much research on brain-behavior relationships relies on analyzing the behavior of animals after damage to certain brain areas, as described in Methods 5.3. A behavioral deficit after brain damage reflects more than just the functions of the cells that were destroyed. Ordinarily, axons from each neuron provide stimulation that helps to keep other neurons active. When any neuron dies, the neurons that depended on it for input become less active. For example, after damage to an area in the right hemisphere, the corresponding area in the left hemisphere becomes temporarily less active also (Perani, Vallar, Paulesu, Alberoni, & Fazio, 1993). **Diaschisis** (di-AS-ki-sis, from a Greek term meaning "to shock throughout") refers to the decreased activity of surviving neurons after other neurons are damaged. For example, a lesion in the hypothalamus can lead to decreased activity in the cerebral cortex.

If diaschisis is an important contributor to behavioral deficits following brain damage, then stimulant drugs should promote recovery. In a series of experiments, D. M. Feeney and colleagues measured the behavioral effects of cortical damage in rats and cats. Depending on the location of the damage, the animals showed impairments in either coordinated movement or depth perception. Injecting amphetamine (which increases dopamine and norepinephrine activity) significantly enhanced the behaviors, and animals that practiced the behaviors under the influence of amphetamine showed long-lasting benefits. Injecting the drug haloperidol (which blocks most of the same synapses) impaired behavioral recovery (Feeney & Sutton, 1988; Feeney, Sutton, Boyeson, Hovda, & Dail, 1985; Hovda & Feeney, 1989; Sutton, Hovda, & Feeney, 1989).

These results imply that people who have had a stroke should be given stimulant drugs such as amphetamine, not immediately after the stroke, as with clot-busting drugs, but in the following days, when it is important for the person to use as much of the surviving brain as possible. Researchers have found that people's recovery from brain damage is enhanced by amphetamine if it is combined with physical therapy—that is, practice at the impaired skills (Feeney, Weisend, & Kline, 1993; Walker-Batson, Smith, Curtis, Unwin, & Greenlee, 1995). Recovery is impaired by tranquilizers, which among other effects decrease the release of dopamine and norepinephrine (L. B. Goldstein, 1993).

Stop & Check

3. Suppose someone has suffered a spinal cord injury that interrupts all sensation from the left arm. Now he or she uses only the right arm. Of the following, which is the most promising therapy: electrically stimulate the skin of the left arm, tie the right arm behind the person's back, or blindfold the person?

4. Following someone's brain damage, if you could direct amphetamine to one place in the brain, would you direct it to the cells that were damaged or somewhere else?

Check your answers on page 147.

The Regrowth of Axons

Although a destroyed cell body cannot be replaced, damaged axons do grow back under certain circumstances. A neuron of the peripheral nervous system has its cell body in the spinal cord and an axon that extends into the periphery. When such an axon is crushed, the degenerated portion grows back toward the periphery at a rate of about 1 mm per day. If it is myelinated, the regenerating axon follows the myelin path back to its original target. If the axon was cut instead of crushed, the myelin on the two sides of the cut may not line up correctly, and the regenerating axon may not have a sure path to follow. A sensory nerve finds its way to a sensory receptor, and a motor nerve finds its way to a muscle (Brushart, 1993); still, a motor nerve sometimes attaches to the wrong muscle, as Figure 5.24 illustrates.

Within the mature mammalian brain and spinal cord, damaged axons usually regenerate no more than a millimeter or two (Schwab, 1998). Therefore paralysis caused by spinal cord injury is permanent. However, in many kinds of fish, axons do regenerate across a cut spinal cord, far enough to restore nearly normal functioning (Bernstein & Gelderd, 1970; Rovainen, 1976; Scherer, 1986; Selzer, 1978). Why do damaged CNS axons regenerate so much better in fish than in mammals? Researchers have considered a number of possibilities. One is that a cut through the adult mammalian spinal cord results in too much scar tissue. A number of attempts have been made to inhibit the formation of scar tissue, but none has led to any reliable recovery from spinal cord damage (e.g., McMasters, 1962).

Another explanation is chemical. The myelin surrounding peripheral nerves secretes chemicals that help axons regenerate (Livesey et al., 1997), but the myelin in the central nervous system of mammals and birds (not fish) secretes proteins that inhibit axon growth (Fields, Schwab, & Silver, 1999; McClellan, 1998). Damaged axons regrow better in the young because less myelin has formed. The older the individual, the more myelin, and therefore the less potential for damaged axons to regrow. After CNS damage, the astrocytes that remove dead tissue also secrete proteins that inhibit axon regrowth (Davies et al., 1997). Injecting antibodies to the growth-inhibiting proteins enables many axons to regenerate after damage (Bregman et al., 1995; Thallmair et al., 1998). Another approach is to graft some peripheral glia into the CNS; this strategy also enables axons to regrow (Li, Field, & Raisman, 1998; Ramón-Cueto, Plant, Avila, & Bunge, 1998).

The hope is that someday such chemicals may help people recover from *hemiplegia*, one-sided paralysis caused by a cut part of the way through the spinal cord. (When the human spinal cord is cut all the way through, the separated halves pull so far apart that no axon could bridge the gap.) However, here is something to worry about: *Why* do CNS myelin and astrocytes secrete proteins that inhibit axon regrowth? Did we evolve such mechanisms because regrowing axons might connect to the wrong targets and do more harm than good? We have to await more research for the answers.

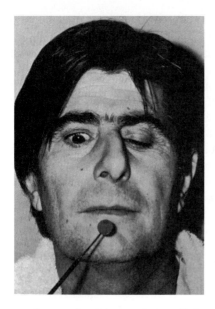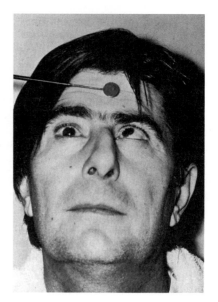

Figure 5.24 What can happen if damaged axons regenerate to incorrect muscles
Damaged axons to the muscles of the patient's right eye regenerated but attached incorrectly. When he looks down, his right eyelid opens wide instead of closing like the other eyelid. His eye movements are frequently misaimed, and he has trouble moving his right eye upward or to the left. *(Source: P. Thomas, 1988)*

Sprouting

After damage to a set of axons, the cells that had received input from them react to the loss by secreting neurotrophins (Van der Zee, Fawcett, & Diamond, 1992), which induce nearby uninjured axons to form new branches, or **collateral sprouts,** that attach to the vacant synapses (see Figure 5.25). Gradually over several months, the sprouts fill in most of the vacated synapses. For example, after loss of about half of the cells in a rat's *locus coeruleus* (a hindbrain area), the brain shows an enormous drop in the number of synapses that the locus coeruleus supplies to the forebrain. Over the next 6 months, the surviving axons sprout enough to restore almost completely normal input (Fritschy & Grzanna, 1992).

Sprouting is probably a normal condition, not one that occurs only after brain damage (Cotman & Nieto-Sampedro, 1982). The brain is constantly losing old synapses and sprouting new ones to replace them.

In some cases, when one axon is removed, an unrelated axon sprouts to occupy the vacant synapse. This kind of sprouting is probably either useless or harmful because it provides inappropriate information. In other cases, however, the sprouts come from closely related axons. For example, after damage to the connections to the left hippocampus from the left entorhinal cortex (the nearest part of the cerebral cortex), sprouts develop from the right entorhinal cortex. Their development takes a few days, about the same time as recovery of the behaviors (Kolb, 1995). Furthermore, after behavioral recovery has occurred, damage to the sprouted path from the right entorhinal cortex greatly impairs the behavior (Ramirez, McQuilkin, Carrigan, MacDonald, & Kelley, 1996). This result is probably the strongest evidence for the beneficial effects of sprouting.

Denervation Supersensitivity

A postsynaptic cell that is deprived of synaptic input for a long time becomes more sensitive to the neurotransmitter. For example, a normal

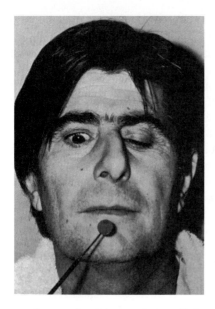

Figure 5.25 Collateral sprouting
A surviving axon grows a new branch to replace the synapses left vacant by a damaged axon.

At first — Loss of an axon — Sprouting to fill vacant synapses

Autoradiography

Just as an autograph is a person's signature, an autoradiograph is a chemical's signature. Investigators kill a laboratory animal and slice its brain into thin sections. Then they apply a radioactively labeled chemical to the slices. For the experiment shown in Figure 5.26, investigators used radioactively labeled spiroperidol, a drug that binds to dopamine type D_2 receptors. Then researchers place each section against a piece of X-ray film,

which records all the radioactivity that the labeled chemicals emit. From these data computers create a colored display in which red indicates the greatest amount of radioactive binding, followed by yellow, green, and blue. The red and yellow areas are those with the greatest amount of spiroperidol and therefore the greatest density of D_2 receptors.

muscle cell responds to the neurotransmitter acetylcholine only at the neuromuscular junction. If the axon is cut, or if it is inactive for days, the muscle cell builds additional receptors, becoming sensitive to acetylcholine over a wider area of its surface (Johns & Thesleff, 1961; Levitt-Gilmour & Salpeter, 1986). The same process occurs in neurons. Heightened sensitivity to a neurotransmitter after the destruction of an incoming axon is known as **denervation supersensitivity** (Glick, 1974). Heightened sensitivity as a result of inactivity by an incoming axon is called **disuse supersensitivity**. The mechanisms of supersensitivity include an increased number of receptors (Kostrzewa, 1995) and

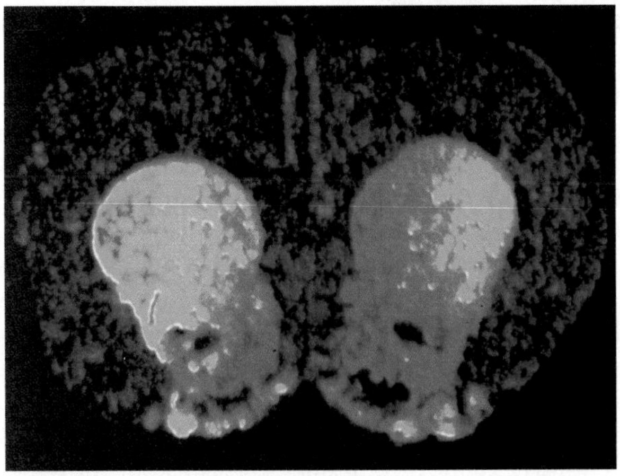

Figure 5.26 Responses of dopamine receptors to decreased input
In this autoradiography procedure, an injection of 6-OHDA destroyed dopamine axons in the hemisphere on the left. The increased amount of red and yellow on the left indicates more binding of the drug to D_2 receptors there. The conclusion is that after loss of dopamine axons, the left hemisphere developed more D_2 receptors. *(Source: LaHoste & Marshall, 1989)*

increased effectiveness of receptors, perhaps by changes in second-messenger systems.

One way to demonstrate denervation supersensitivity is to damage axons that release dopamine by use of the drug **6-hydroxydopamine (6-OHDA).** The neurons that release norepinephrine and dopamine recognize 6-OHDA as a related chemical, absorb it, and die after it is oxidized into toxic chemicals. As Figure 5.26 shows, after an injection of 6-OHDA to one side of the brain, postsynaptic cells react by increasing their number of dopamine receptors on that side (LaHoste & Marshall, 1989). Methods 5.4 describes autoradiography, the procedure used in that study.

Denervation supersensitivity contributes to recovery by increasing neurons' responses to the limited amount of dopamine that remains. In one study experimenters injected 6-OHDA on the left side of rats' brains, damaging dopamine-releasing axons on that side only (see Figure 5.27). They waited weeks for postsynaptic neurons to become supersensitive to dopamine. Then they injected the rats with either amphetamine or apomorphine. Amphetamine increases the release of dopamine by surviving axons. Because one side of the brain was lacking dopamine axons, the amphetamine stimulated only the intact right side of the brain, causing the rats to orient mostly toward stimuli on the left and therefore turn left. **Apomorphine** is a morphine derivative that directly stimulates dopamine receptors. Apomorphine could excite receptors on both sides of the brain, but because denervation supersensitivity had strengthened receptors on the left side, apomorphine had more effect on the left side of the brain so rats were more responsive to stimuli on the right, and therefore turned away from the damaged side of the brain (Marshall, Drew, & Neve, 1983). These results (shown in Figure 5.27) indicate that the denervated side of the brain has become supersensitive to dopamine and to drugs that stimulate dopamine receptors.

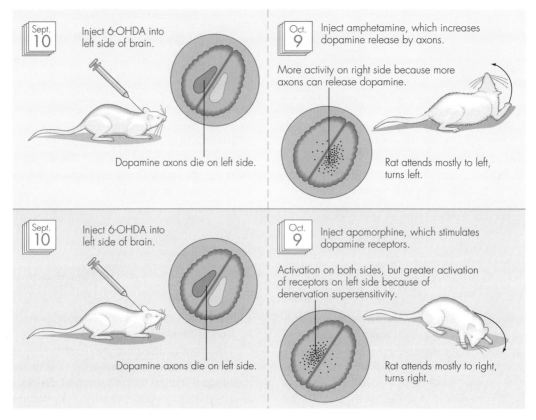

Figure 5.27 Demonstration of denervation supersensitivity
Injecting 6-OHDA destroys axons that release dopamine on one side of the brain. Later amphetamine stimulates only the intact side of the brain because it cannot cause axons to release dopamine on the damaged side. Apomorphine stimulates the damaged side more strongly because it directly stimulates dopamine receptors, which have become supersensitive on that side. *(Source: Based on data from Marshall, Drew, & Neve, 1983)*

Denervation supersensitivity helps explain why people can lose most of the axons in some pathways and still maintain nearly normal behavior (Sabel, 1997). After some of the axons are lost, the remaining axons increase their release of transmitters, and the receptors on the postsynaptic membrane develop denervation supersensitivity.

5. Collateral sprouting is a change in which—axons or dendritic receptors?

6. Denervation supersensitivity is a change in which—axons or dendritic receptors?

Check your answers on page 147.

Reorganized Sensory Representations and the Phantom Limb

As we saw earlier in this chapter, experiences can modify the connections within the cerebral cortex. Recall that after someone has played a stringed instrument for many years, the somatosensory cortex has an enlarged representation of the fingers of the left hand. Similarly, in Braille proofreaders, the brain representation of the index finger is measurably larger at the end of a workday than at the same time on a vacation day (Pascual-Leone, Wasserman, Sadato, & Hallett, 1995). Such changes may represent either collateral sprouting of axons or increased receptor sensitivity by the postsynaptic neurons. A slight reorganization of the cortex gives extra representation to the information that a person uses the most.

A more extensive reorganization of the brain can occur after an amputation. Reexamine Figure 4.21 (p. 105): Along the somatosensory cortex each section receives input from a different part of the body. Within the part of the cortex marked "fingers" in that figure, a closer examination reveals that each subarea responds more to one finger than to another. Figure 5.28 shows the arrangement for a monkey brain. In one study experimenters amputated finger 3 in an owl monkey. The cortical cells that previously responded to information from that finger now had no input. As time passed more and more of them became responsive to finger 2, finger 4, or part of the palm, until eventually the cortex had the pattern of responsiveness we see in Figure 5.28b (Kaas, Merzenich, & Killackey, 1983; Merzenich et al., 1984).

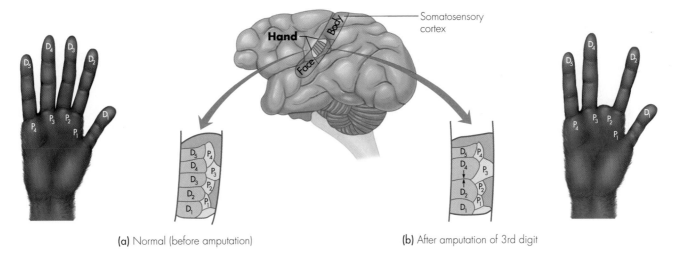

Figure 5.28 Somatosensory cortex of a monkey after a finger amputation
Note that the cortical area previously responsive to the third finger (D_3) becomes responsive to the second and fourth fingers (D_2 and D_4) and part of the palm (P_3). *(Source: Based on Kaas, Merzenich, & Killackey, 1983)*

What happens if an entire arm is amputated? For many years neuroscientists assumed that most of the cortex responsive to that arm became permanently silent because it was too far away from any other axons to evoke sprouting. Then came a surprise. Investigators recorded from the cerebral cortices of monkeys that had had a forelimb deafferented[3] 12 years previously and found that the large stretch of cortex previously responsive to the limb had become responsive to the face (Pons et al., 1991). How did such connections form? The altered responses in the cortex reflected changes that had occurred in several places. After loss of sensory input from the forelimb, the axons representing the forelimb degenerated, leaving vacant synaptic sites at several levels of the CNS. Axons representing the face sprouted into those sites in the spinal cord, brain stem, and thalamus (Florence & Kaas, 1995; E. G. Jones & Pons, 1998). (Or perhaps axons from the face may have already innervated those sites but were overwhelmed by the normal input. After removal of the normal input, the weaker synapses became stronger.) Also, lateral connections formed from the face-sensitive cortical areas into the previously hand-sensitive areas according to results from *histochemistry* (Florence, Taub, & Kaas, 1998) (see Methods 5.5).

Although the most detailed experiments have been with monkeys, brain scan studies confirm that the same processes occur with humans. Now consider what happens when cells in a reorganized cortex become activated. Previously they responded to an arm, and now they respond to stimulation on the face. But when they respond, does it feel like stimulation on the face or like stimulation on the arm?

The answer is that it still feels like the arm (Davis et

al., 1998). Physicians have long noted that many people with amputations experience a **phantom limb,** a continuing sensation of an amputated body part. That experience can range from occasional tingling to intense pain. It is possible to have a phantom hand, intestines, breast, penis, or anything else that has been amputated. Sometimes the phantom sensation fades within days or weeks, but sometimes it lasts a lifetime (Ramachandran & Hirstein, 1998).

Until the 1990s no one knew what caused phantom pains, and most believed that the sensations were coming from the stump of the amputated limb. Some physicians even performed additional amputations, removing more and more of the limb in a futile attempt to eliminate the phantom sensations. But modern methods have demonstrated that the greater the reorganization of the somatosensory cortex, the more likely and more intense the phantom sensations (Flor et al., 1995). For example, axons representing the face may come to activate the cortical area previously devoted to an amputated hand. Whenever the face is touched, the person still feels it on the face, but also feels a sensation in the phantom hand. It is even possible to map out which part of the face stimulates sensation in which part of the phantom hand (Aglioti, Smania, Atzei, & Berlucchi, 1997) (see Figure 5.29). Until a physician or researcher points out the connection, the person ordinarily does not notice that touching the face is what causes the phantom hand sensation.

The connection between phantom sensations and brain reorganization enables us to understand some otherwise puzzling observations. Note in Figure 4.21 (p. 105) that the part of the cortex responsive to the feet is immediately next to the part responsive to the genitals. Two patients, after amputation of the foot, not only continued to feel a phantom foot but reported feeling it especially during sexual arousal! One in fact

---

[3] Reminder: To *deafferent* is to cut the sensory nerves.

Histochemistry

Histology is the study of the structure of tissues. *Histochemistry* deals with the chemical components of tissues. One example is as follows: Investigators inject a chemical called horseradish peroxidase (HRP) into some cortical area of a laboratory animal. The axon terminals in that area absorb the chemical and transport it back to their cell bodies. Later, investigators take slices of the brain and treat it with a second chemical that reacts with HRP to form granules that are visible in a microscope. By finding those granules investigators can determine the point of origin for the axons that terminated where investigators had injected the HRP.

reported feeling orgasm not only in the genitals (as before) but now also in the phantom foot (Ramachandran & Blakeslee, 1998). Evidently the representation of the genitals had spread into the cortical area responsible for foot sensation. (These particular patients did not complain about their phantom sensations!)

If a phantom sensation is painful, is there any way to relieve it? In some cases, yes. Amputees who learn to use an artificial arm report that their phantom sensations and phantom pains gradually disappear (Lotze et al., 1999). Apparently they start attributing some sensations to the artificial arm, and as they do so they displace abnormal connections from the face.

In one study five people with painful phantom limbs who felt "as if fingernails were digging into the skin" sat with a tall mirror perpendicular to the chest, as shown in Figure 5.30, so that they saw a mirror image of their normal arm superimposed on the phantom limb that they felt. Four of them found that if they made a fist with the normal hand and then looked into the mirror while opening that hand, they felt the phantom hand opening also and the pain subsiding (Ramachandran, Rogers-Ramachandran, & Cobb, 1995). Evidently the combination of the visual experience and the tactile experience of the opposite hand had somehow altered the activity in the somatosensory cortex and reduced the phantom pain.

One important message from these studies is that connections in the brain remain plastic throughout life.

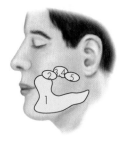

Figure 5.29 Sources of phantom sensation for one person
For this person stimulation in the areas marked on the cheek produced phantom sensations of digits one (thumb), two, four, and five. Stimulation on the shoulder also evoked phantom sensations of digits one, two, three, and five.
(Source: Ramachandran & Blakeslee, 1998)

Amputees who feel a phantom limb are likely to lose those phantom sensations if they learn to use an artificial arm.

Figure 5.30 A surprising method of relieving phantom pain
People with a phantom limb report sensation in the amputated limb—for example, pain as if fingernails were digging into the skin. By looking in a mirror placed as shown here, such a person can "see" the amputated limb (actually a reflection of the normal limb). If the normal limb moves, the phantom limb now also feels as if it is moving. If the normal fist relaxes, some people with a phantom limb feel their phantom fist relaxing, with consequent reduction of pain.

There are limits on the plasticity, certainly, but the limits are less strict than researchers once supposed.

Stop & Check

7. Is reorganization of the brain helpful or harmful?

Check your answer on page 147.

Effects of Age

As you might guess, very old people do not recover from brain damage as well as younger adults do. People gradually lose neurons throughout life; as they age beyond about 60, many people also begin to have some shrinkage of dendrites of the remaining neurons, at least in certain brain areas (Jacobs & Scheibel, 1993). The dendrites shrink more in people who become senile, and less or not at all—sometimes even expanding—in older people who remain alert (Buell & Coleman, 1981). Still, an older person who suffers brain damage is impaired in recovery by the fact that other cells are slowly dying off and by the fact that the remaining cells modify their branching less readily than they did at a younger age. As we grow old the brain simply becomes less plastic.

In fact someone who recovered from brain damage early in life may "unrecover" in old age. In one study investigators compared World War II veterans who suffered brain injuries during the war with veterans who suffered other kinds of injuries. In the 1950s, about 10 years after the war, while they were still young men, the brain-injured veterans scored almost as high as the others on the Army General Classification Test (a kind of IQ test). But by the 1980s, as they were approaching retirement age, the brain-injured men showed a significant decline in performance, while uninjured men maintained a steady performance (Corkin, Rosen, Sullivan, & Clegg, 1989) (see Figure 5.31). Evidently, when the brain is young it can compensate for damage, but as it grows older it has less margin for error and is less able to compensate even for damage that happened long ago.

Imagine how this principle might apply to a degenerative condition, such as Parkinson's disease. A young person might suffer several traumas to the brain, either from blows to the head or exposure to toxins, and compensate well enough so that the damage is not apparent. But in old age he or she deteriorates. The problem might seem new, but it is really the unmasking of an old problem (Schallert, 1983).

If recovery from brain damage is particularly poor in old age, you might expect it to be quite successful for the very young. Sometimes it is. According to the **Kennard**

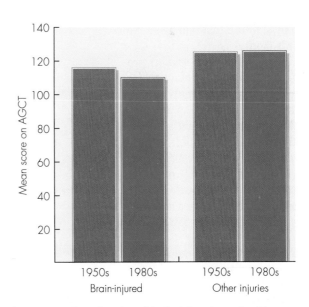

Figure 5.31 Deterioration of brain-injured men in old age
Brain-injured World War II veterans performed slightly below other veterans on IQ tests in the 1950s; they deteriorated significantly over the next 30 years, whereas the other veterans did not. *(Source: Based on data of Corkin, Rosen, Sullivan, & Clegg, 1989)*

principle, named after Margaret Kennard, who first stated it, recovery will be more extensive after brain damage early in life than after similar damage later (Kennard, 1938). For example, a 2-year-old who loses the entire left hemisphere will probably develop nearly normal speech, whereas an older child with similar damage will regain less speech. An adult will recover still less (Satz, Strauss, & Whitaker, 1990).

The problem with the Kennard principle is that it does not apply to all cases. The effects of early brain damage may be greater than, less than, or the same as the effects of later damage depending on the location of the damage and the tested behavior (Kolb, 1995). In some cases, especially if damage occurs prenatally or in the first half year of life, infants suffer far more severe consequences than adults. The young brain is more plastic than the old, but it is also more vulnerable. Early damage to one set of neurons can affect the survival and connections of other immature neurons.

For example, after one hemisphere of an infant rat brain is removed, the other hemisphere increases in thickness (Kolb, Sutherland, & Whishaw, 1983). Evidently neurons of one hemisphere compete with neurons of the other hemisphere; if one hemisphere is damaged, a greater percentage of cells in the opposite hemisphere can survive. In contrast, after removal of the anterior portion of the infant cortex, the posterior portion develops less than normal (Kolb & Holmes, 1983). Apparently the survival of neurons in the posterior cortex requires interaction with neurons in the anterior cortex, so damage to the anterior cortex affects the behavior of infant rats more than it does the behavior of adults.

Here is another example of early damage producing either excellent recovery or severe deficits depending on its location. Patricia Goldman, studying infant monkeys, found that damage to the **orbital frontal cortex** (an anterior area of the prefrontal cortex) produces deficits on the delayed alternation task, which requires alternating between choosing an object on the left and choosing an object on the right. This deficit is quite clear at age 1 year; however, by age 2 years the behavior improves considerably. Monkeys suffering the same brain damage at a later age show far less recovery (P. S. Goldman, 1976; E. A. Miller, Goldman, & Rosvold, 1973). Evidently early damage to the orbital frontal cortex prompts later developing areas to change their organization in a way that compensates for the damage.

In contrast, damage to the **dorsolateral prefrontal cortex** (an-

other area of the prefrontal cortex) of an infant monkey produces at first only a moderate deficit on the delayed alternation task. A year after the injury, it performs surprisingly well, almost as well as a normal 1-year-old monkey. When tested 2 years after the lesion, however, the brain-damaged monkey shows clear behavioral deficits (P. S. Goldman, 1971). That is, the behavioral deficit actually increases over time. The apparent explanation rests on the fact that the dorsolateral prefrontal cortex is slow to mature. The infant lesion produces little effect by age 1 year because a healthy dorsolateral prefrontal cortex does not do much at that age. But by age 2 years, when that area should start assuming some important functions, the damage begins to make a difference. Figure 5.32 summarizes these results. We return to this point in Chapter 15. Some investigators believe that schizophrenia is associated with early damage to the dorsolateral prefrontal cortex but that, because of the slow maturation of this area, the effects do not become fully evident until adolescence or early adulthood.

Stop *&* Check

8. After damage to a monkey's orbital prefrontal cortex in infancy, what are the consequences for behavior at 1 year and at 2 years?

9. After damage to a monkey's dorsolateral prefrontal cortex in infancy, what are the consequences for behavior at 1 year and at 2 years?

Check your answers on page 147.

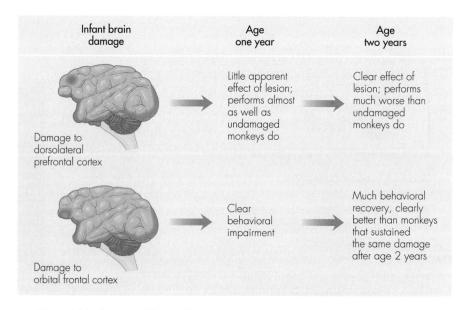

Infant brain damage	Age one year	Age two years
Damage to dorsolateral prefrontal cortex	Little apparent effect of lesion; performs almost as well as undamaged monkeys do	Clear effect of lesion; performs much worse than undamaged monkeys do
Damage to orbital frontal cortex	Clear behavioral impairment	Much behavioral recovery, clearly better than monkeys that sustained the same damage after age 2 years

Figure 5.32 Delayed effects of brain damage in infant monkeys
After damage to the dorsolateral prefrontal cortex, monkeys seem relatively unimpaired at age 1 year but are more severely impaired later, when this area ordinarily matures. After damage to the orbital frontal cortex, monkeys show a clear behavioral impairment at first but substantial recovery later. *(Source: Based on P. S. Goldman, 1976)*

Therapies

After someone suffers brain damage, physicians, physical therapists, and others try to help the person recover. Interventions to promote and guide brain plasticity may well be the therapy of the future; at present therapy consists mainly of supervised practice of the impaired behaviors.

Behavioral Interventions

You may fail to find your lost keys either because you accidentally threw them in the trash or because you left them in an odd place. Similarly, brain-damaged people and animals may seem to lack some skill either because they have destroyed it or because they cannot find it. Therapists help brain-damaged people find their lost skills or learn to use their remaining abilities more effectively. For example, some people with frontal lobe damage behave in socially inappropriate ways, using obscene language, failing to wash themselves, or making lewd overtures to strangers. Therapists may provide positive reinforcement for polite speech, good grooming, and self-restraint (McGlynn, 1990).

Similarly a brain-damaged animal that seems to have forgotten a learned skill may still retain it in some hidden manner. After damage to its visual cortex, a rat that previously had learned to approach a white card instead of a black card for food chose randomly between the two cards. Had the rat forgotten the discrimination completely? Evidently not, because it could much more easily relearn to approach the white card than learn to approach the black card (T. E. LeVere & Morlock, 1973). Apparently some of the original learning survived the brain damage (see Figure 5.33). Thomas LeVere (1975) proposed that such a lesion does not destroy the memory engram but merely impairs the rat's ability to find it.

Similarly humans who have suffered brain damage may have trouble accessing certain skills and memories. Just as a monkey that has no sensation in one arm may try to get by without using it, a person who has an impaired sensory system may try to do without it (T. E. LeVere, 1980). The task of physical therapists, occupational therapists, and speech therapists is to prod brain-damaged patients into practicing their impaired skills instead of ignoring them.

In an experiment that supports this approach to therapy, N. D. LeVere and T. E. LeVere (1982) trained rats with visual cortex lesions on a discrimination task that included both brightness and tactile cues. For one group of rats, the brightness and tactile stimuli were redundant; the rats could solve the problem by responding to either stimulus. This group solved the task rapidly but paid attention only to the tactile stimuli. If they were presented with only brightness stimuli, they responded randomly. For a second group of rats, the tactile stimuli were irrelevant; they could solve the problem only on the basis of brightness. This group took much longer than normal rats to solve the problem because their attention to the tactile stimuli distracted them from the relevant visual cues, but they did eventually solve it. In short, rats with visual cortex lesions can learn about visual stimuli, but they are impaired if other stimuli are available (N. Davis & LeVere, 1982). To help humans with similar brain damage, therapists should either simplify the problem by removing distracting stimuli or teach the individual to concentrate on the relevant stimuli.

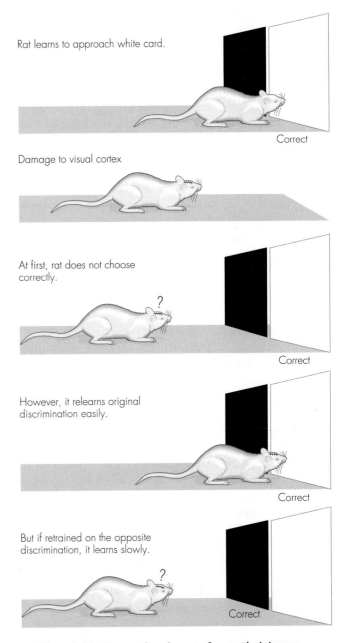

Figure 5.33 Memory impairment after cortical damage
Brain damage impairs retrieval of a memory but does not destroy it completely. *(Source: Based on T. E. LeVere & Morlock, 1973)*

Drugs

Several drugs have been shown to aid recovery from brain damage in animals. So far we do not know their effect on humans.

Nimodipine, a drug that prevents calcium from entering cells, improves memory for visual learning tasks in rats with visual cortex lesions (T. E. LeVere, 1993; T. E. LeVere, Ford, & Sandin, 1992). Calcium blockers administered before brain damage produce modest benefits, presumably by preventing a toxic rush of calcium into neurons. Calcium blockers produce greater benefits if administered after brain damage, presumably by improving cellular functioning.

Several studies indicate that **gangliosides** (a class of glycolipids—that is, combined carbohydrate and fat molecules) promote the restoration of damaged brains. The fact that they adhere to neuron membranes suggests that they contribute to the recognition of one neuron by another in development, guiding axons to the correct locations to form synapses. Daily injections of gangliosides aid the recovery of behavior after several kinds of brain damage (Cahn, Borziex, Aldinio, Toffano, & Cahn, 1989; Ramirez et al., 1987a, 1987b; Sabel, Slavin, & Stein, 1984). Exactly how they do so is not yet known.

In several studies of laboratory mammals, females have recovered better than males from some aspects of frontal cortex damage, and females recovered especially well if the damage occurred at the stage of their hormonal cycles when they had high levels of the hormone *progesterone* (Stein & Fulop, 1998). Progesterone has a variety of effects on the brain, but no one knows which are the relevant ones. Perhaps someday physicians will offer hormonal treatments for brain-damaged patients. It may also be worthwhile to schedule women for certain kinds of brain surgery on days when their progesterone levels are high.

Brain Grafts

One other approach to therapy is the almost Frankensteinian idea of replacing dead brain cells with healthy ones from a donor. We consider this possibility in Chapter 8 in the context of Parkinson's disease, where neural transplants have been tried most frequently. Here let the message be that the method is still in the experimental stage. It is possible to transplant neurons and keep them alive, and the brain has a weak immune system, so tissue rejection is not as serious a problem as it is for other organs. If a surgeon transplants fetal neurons, they sometimes grow and make suitable connections, and the procedure does provide measurable benefits. However, the surgery is difficult and the benefits, though real, are often disappointing. Researchers hope to improve the technique and find ways to improve the survival and growth of transplanted brain cells.

In Closing: Brain Damage and Recovery

In contrast to the multiple ways we have of replacing or temporarily compensating for the loss of blood or skin cells, our mechanisms of recovering from nervous system damage are less powerful. Even the responses that do occur, such as collateral sprouting of axons or reorganization of sensory representations, are helpful in some cases and harmful in others. It is tempting to speculate that we did not evolve many mechanisms of recovery from brain damage because, through most of our evolutionary history, a brain-damaged individual was not likely to survive long enough to recover. Today modern medicine keeps brain-damaged and spinal cord–damaged people alive for many years, and we need continuing research on how to improve artificially the recovery mechanisms that evolution has provided.

One measure of how far we have come is that the big question in this field is no longer *whether* we shall someday have good therapies for brain-damaged patients, but *what* those treatments will be. Will the answer be transplant of fetal tissues? Or implantation of neurotrophins or drugs with related effects that cross the blood-brain barrier or calcium blockers or gangliosides or yet other possibilities? Researchers do not have the answers now, but they have reason to be optimistic for the future.

Summary

1. Brain damage can occur in many ways, including strong or repeated blows to the head. Strokes, a common cause of brain damage in old age, kill neurons largely by overstimulation. Several methods can minimize the damage from stroke if they are applied quickly. (p. 132)

2. Much recovery from brain damage depends on learned changes in behavior to take advantage of the skills that remain. (p. 135)

3. After brain damage neurons that are remote from the site of damage may become inactive because they receive less input than usual. Behavioral recovery from brain damage depends partly on increased activity by these remote neurons; stimulant drugs can facilitate activity in surviving cells. (p. 136)

4. A cut axon may regenerate in the peripheral nervous system of a mammal and in either the central or peripheral nervous system of certain fish. Axons usually do not regenerate far in the adult mam-

malian CNS because of growth-inhibiting chemicals produced by central myelin. (p. 137)

5. When one set of axons dies, neighboring axons may under certain conditions sprout new branches to innervate the vacant synapses. (p. 138)

6. If many of the axons innervating a postsynaptic neuron die or become inactive, the neuron may become responsive to other axons. (p. 139)

7. The cortex and other areas change connections slightly to reflect changes in experience. They change connections more drastically after an amputation; for example, an area previously responsive to a hand may now respond to stimulation on the face or shoulder. (p. 140)

8. As a result of brain organization, many people with amputations report phantom sensations, such as touch or pain in the amputated limb. Those sensations are caused by stimulation in a body area that now connects to the cortex previously sensitive to the limb. (p. 141)

9. Recovery from brain damage may be better or worse in infants than in adults depending on a number of circumstances. (p. 143)

10. After early damage to the dorsolateral prefrontal cortex, behavior of monkeys seems normal at age 1 year (when the structure is immature anyway) but deteriorates at age 2 years (when it ordinarily becomes mature). (p. 144)

11. Therapy for brain-damaged people consists mostly of helping them practice the abilities that have been impaired but not destroyed. (p. 145)

12. Drugs that enhance memory or guide axonal growth promote recovery after certain kinds of brain damage. (p. 146)

Answers to *Stop and Check* Questions

1. In both ischemia and hemorrhage, glia cells dump stored neurotransmitters, including the excitatory transmitter glutamate. Also, the sodium-potassium pump slows, and positive ions accumulate inside the neurons. (p. 135)

2. The drug tPA breaks up blood clots, and the problem in hemorrhage is a ruptured blood vessel, not a blood clot. (p. 135)

3. Tie the right arm behind the back to force the person to use the impaired arm instead of only the normal arm. Stimulating the skin of the left arm would accomplish nothing, as the sensory receptors have no input to the CNS. Blindfolding would be either irrelevant or harmful (by decreasing the visual feedback from left-hand movements). (p. 137)

4. It is best to direct the amphetamine to the cells that had been receiving input from the damaged cells. Presumably the loss of input has produced diaschisis. (p. 137)

5. Axons (p. 140)

6. Dendritic receptors (p. 140)

7. The small-scale reorganization that enables increased representation of a violinist's or Braille reader's fingers is helpful. The larger scale reorganization that occurs after amputation is harmful. (p. 143)

8. A year after damage to a monkey's orbital prefrontal cortex, the monkey is impaired, but at 2 years it is largely recovered. (p. 144)

9. A year after damage to a monkey's dorsolateral prefrontal cortex, the monkey appears normal, but at 2 years it is deteriorated. (p. 144)

Thought Question

Ordinarily patients with Parkinson's disease move very slowly if at all. However, during an emergency (such as a fire in the building) they sometimes move rapidly and vigorously. Suggest a possible explanation.

Chapter Ending
Key Terms and Activities

Terms

ablation (p. 136)

apomorphine (p. 139)

apoptosis (p. 118)

attention-deficit disorder (ADD) (p. 129)

attention-deficit/hyperactivity disorder (ADHD) (p. 129)

closed head injury (p. 132)

collateral sprout (p. 138)

deafferent (p. 135)

denervation supersensitivity (p. 139)

diaschisis (p. 137)

differentiation (p. 117)

disuse supersensitivity (p. 139)

dorsolateral prefrontal cortex (p. 144)

edema (p. 134)

fetal alcohol syndrome (p. 129)

ganglioside (p. 146)

hemorrhage (p. 132)

6-hydroxydopamine (6-OHDA) (p. 139)

ischemia (p. 132)

Kennard principle (p. 143)

lesion (p. 136)

magnetic resonance imaging (MRI) (p. 128)

magnetoencephalograph (MEG) (p. 124)

migration (p. 117)

myelination (p. 117)

nerve growth factor (NGF) (p. 118)

neural Darwinism (p. 122)

neurotrophin (p. 119)

orbital frontal cortex (p. 144)

penumbra (p. 133)

phantom limb (p. 141)

proliferation (p. 117)

sham lesion (p. 136)

stem cells (p. 125)

stereotaxic instrument (p. 136)

stroke (or cerebrovascular accident) (p. 132)

tissue plasminogen activator (tPA) (p. 134)

Suggestions for Further Reading

DeMille, A. (1981). *Reprieve: A memoir.* Garden City, NY: Doubleday. A stroke victim's own account of her stroke and recovery from it with interpolated commentary by a neurologist, Fred Plum.

Levi-Montalcini, R. (1988). *In praise of imperfection.* New York: Basic Books. Autobiography by the discoverer of nerve growth factor.

Ramachandran, V. S., & Blakeslee, S. (1998). *Phantoms in the brain.* New York: Morrow. One of the most interesting and thought-provoking books ever written about human brain damage, including the phantom limb phenomenon.

Shatz, C. J. (1992, September). The developing brain. *Scientific American, 267*(3), 60–67. Excellent review of brain development by one of the leading researchers.

Web Sites to Explore

You can go to the Biological Psychology Study Center and click on these links. While there, you can also check for suggested articles available on InfoTrac. The Biological Psychology Internet address is:
http://psychology.wadsworth.com/book/kalatbiopsych7e/

http://www.cpdx.com/cpdx.abcns.htm
Information on several abnormalities of CNS development, including hydrocephalus and spina bifida.

http://www.chadd.org/
Includes answers to frequently asked questions about attention-deficit disorder.

http://www.stroke.org/
Information from the National Stroke Association.

Active Learner Link

Video: Developmental Psychopathology—Autism

Video: Neuroimaging

Quiz for Chapter 5

Chapter 6

Vision

Chapter Outline

Opposite:
Later in this chapter you will understand why this prairie falcon has tilted its head.

Main Ideas

1. Each sensory neuron conveys a particular type of experience; for example, anything that stimulates the optic nerve is perceived as light.

2. Vertebrate vision depends on two kinds of receptors: cones, which contribute to color vision, and rods, which do not.

3. Every cell in the visual system has a receptive field, an area of the visual world that can excite or inhibit it.

4. After visual information reaches the brain, concurrent pathways analyze different aspects, such as shape, color, and movement.

5. Neurons of the visual system establish approximately correct connections and properties through chemical gradients that are present before birth. However, visual experience can fine-tune or alter those properties, especially early in life.

Some years ago a graduate student taking his final oral exam for a PhD in psychology was asked, "How far can an ant see?" The student suddenly turned pale. He did not know the answer, and evidently he was supposed to. He mentally reviewed everything he had read about the compound eye of insects. Finally he gave up and admitted he did not know.

With an impish grin the professor told him, "Presumably, an ant can see 93 million miles—the distance to the sun." Yes, this was a trick question—a beaut as trick questions go. But it illustrates an important point: How far an ant can see, or how far you or I can see, depends on how far the light travels. We see because light strikes our eyes, not because we send out "sight rays." But that principle is far from intuitive. In fact it was not known until the Arab philosopher Ibn al-Haythem (965–1040) demonstrated that light rays bounce off any object in all directions, but we see only those rays that strike the retina perpendicularly (Gross, 1999). Even today a distressingly large number of college students believe that some energy comes out of their eyes when they see (Winer & Cottrell, 1996). The working of the sensory systems, especially vision, is quite complex and does not match our commonsense notions.

Module 6.1

Visual Coding and the Retinal Receptors

Imagine that you are a piece of iron. I admit that's not easy to do. A piece of iron doesn't have a brain, and even if it did, it would not have much experience. But try to imagine it anyway.

So there you are, sitting around doing nothing, as usual, when along comes a drop of water. What will be your perception of the water?

You will have the experience of rust. From your point of view, water is above all else *rustish*. Now return to your perspective as a human. You know that rustishness is not really a property of water itself, but of the way water interacts with iron.

The same is true of human perception. In vision, for example, when you look at the leaves of a tree, you perceive them as *green*. But green is no more a property of the leaves than rustish is a property of water. The greenness is what happens when the light bouncing off the leaves interacts with the neurons in the back of your eye and eventually with the neurons in your brain. In effect you color your own world; the greenness is in us—just as the rust is really in the piece of iron.

Reception, Transduction, and Coding

When any stimulus reaches any receptor, it starts a series of three steps that take us from stimulus to perception: reception, transduction, and coding (see Figure 6.1). **Reception** is simply the absorption of physical energy by the receptors. **Transduction** is the conversion of that physical energy to an electrochemical pattern in the neurons. **Coding** is the one-to-one correspondence between some aspect of the physical stimulus and some aspect of the nervous system activity. For example, molecules from a squeezed lemon strike receptors in the nose (reception); they lead to a chemical reaction that changes the polarization across the membrane of the receptor cell (transduction); and the resulting activity in that neuron and other neurons sends a distinctive message to the brain (coding). A fourth step, conscious awareness, can be distinguished because some stimuli that are received, transducted, and coded do not reach consciousness. Conscious awareness is not shown in Figure 6.1, however, mainly because no one is sure where to draw the arrow.

Each receptor is specialized to absorb one kind of

energy and transduce it into an electrochemical pattern in the brain. For example, visual receptors can absorb and respond to as little as a single photon of light and transduce it into a **receptor potential**, a local depolarization or hyperpolarization of a receptor membrane. The strength of the receptor potential determines the amount of excitation or inhibition the receptor delivers to the next neuron on the way to the brain.

From Neuronal Activity to Perception

After the information gets to the brain, how does the brain make sense of it? Let us consider what is *not* an answer. The 17th-century philosopher René Descartes believed that the brain's representation of a physical stimulus had to resemble the stimulus itself. That is, when you look at something, the nerves from the eye would project a picturelike pattern of impulses onto

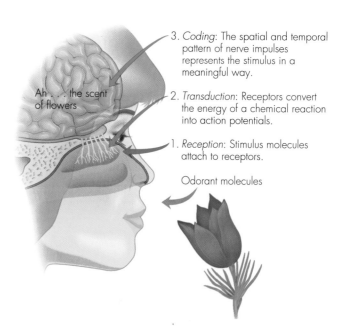

3. *Coding*: The spatial and temporal pattern of nerve impulses represents the stimulus in a meaningful way.

2. *Transduction*: Receptors convert the energy of a chemical reaction into action potentials.

1. *Reception*: Stimulus molecules attach to receptors.

Odorant molecules

Ah . . . the scent of flowers

Figure 6.1   Three steps in the sensation and perception of a stimulus
Vision, olfaction, and all other senses have the same three steps. Olfaction illustrates the point better because we are tempted to imagine that the brain somehow "sees" a copy of the visual image, and we are less tempted to make that mistake for olfaction.

your visual cortex. The problem with this theory is that it assumes a little person in the head who can look at the picture. There is no little person in the head, and even if there were, we would have to explain how he or she perceives the picture. (Maybe there is an even littler person inside that person's head?) One wonders whether the early scientists and philosophers might have avoided this error if they had started by studying olfaction instead of vision; we are less tempted to imagine that we create a little flower for a little person in the head to smell.

The main point is that the coding of visual information in your brain *does not duplicate* the shape of the object that you see. For example, when you see a table, the representation of the top of the table does not have to be on the top of your retina or on the top of your head.

General Principles of Sensory Coding

An important aspect of all sensory coding is *which* neurons are active. A given frequency of impulses may mean one thing when it occurs in one neuron and something quite different in another. In 1838 Johannes Müller described this basic insight as the **law of specific nerve energies.** Müller held that whatever excited a particular nerve established a special kind of energy unique to that nerve. In modern terms any activity by a particular nerve always conveys the same kind of information to the brain. The brain "sees" the activity of the optic nerve and "hears" the activity of the auditory nerve.

We can state the law of specific nerve energies another way: No nerve has the option of sending the message "high C note" at one time, "bright yellow" at another time, and "lemony smell" at yet another. It sends only one kind of message—action potentials. The brain somehow interprets the action potentials from the auditory nerve as sounds, the action potentials from the olfactory nerve as odors, and those from the optic nerve as light. (Admittedly the word *somehow* glosses over a deep mystery.)

If you poke your eye or rub it hard, you may see spots or flashes of light even if the room is totally dark. The reason is that the mechanical pressure excites receptors in the retina of the eye; anything that excites those receptors is perceived as light. (If you try this experiment, first remove any contact lenses. Then shut your eye and press gently on your eyeball.)

If it were possible to take the nerves from your eyes and ears and cross-transplant them so that the visual receptors were connected to the auditory nerve and vice versa, you would literally see sounds and hear lights. Perceptions depend on which neurons are active and how active each one is at a given time.

Although the law of specific nerve energies is fundamentally correct, we must add some important qualifications. First, cells with a spontaneous rate of firing

may signal one kind of stimulus by an increase in firing and a different kind by a decrease. For instance, a particular cell might signal "green" by increasing its firing rate and "red" by decreasing it.

Second, in some cases information depends on the timing of action potentials, not just their total number (Hopfield, 1995). Imagine a neuron that receives two incoming synapses designated A and B. Whether A fires a millisecond before or after B might tell a cell in the visual system the direction of movement. A similar difference might tell a cell in the auditory system whether a sound is coming from the left or from the right. Conceivably a cell might even recognize complex patterns based on the timing of inputs from a large number of synapses.

Third, the exact meaning of an impulse in a single neuron depends on which other neurons are active. Just as the meaning of the letter *h* depends on its context, the activity of a visual neuron might contribute to the sensation of green, yellow, or white depending on the activity of other neurons.

To understand how we perceive light and color, we begin with the reception and transduction by the receptors in the eyes.

Stop & Check

1. What is the law of specific nerve energies and how must it be modified because of modern knowledge of the nervous system?

Check your answer on page 162.

The Eye and Its Connections to the Brain

Light enters the eye through an opening in the center of the iris called the **pupil** (Figure 6.2). It is focused by the lens (adjustable) and cornea (not adjustable) and projected onto the **retina**, the rear surface of the eye, which is lined with visual receptors. Light from the left side of the world strikes the right half of the retina, and vice versa. Light from above strikes the bottom half of the retina and light from below strikes the top half. As in a camera the image is reversed. However, the inversion of the image poses no problems for the nervous system. Remember, the visual system does not simply duplicate the image. There is no more need to present the image right side up than there is for a computer to use the top of its memory bank to store commands for the top of the screen.

The Fovea

When you read or attend to any other detail of vision, you fixate the object on the portion of your retina with the greatest ability to resolve detail, known as the *macula*

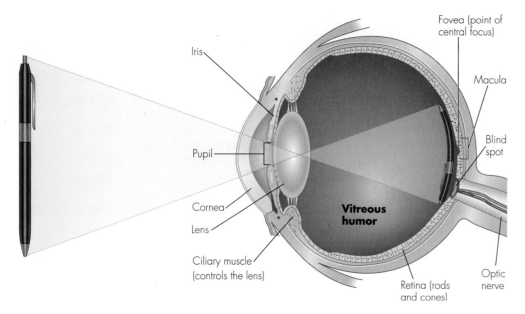

Figure 6.2 Cross section of the vertebrate eye
Note how an object in the visual field produces an inverted image on the retina.

Labels in figure: Iris, Pupil, Cornea, Lens, Ciliary muscle (controls the lens), Fovea (point of central focus), Macula, Blind spot, Vitreous humor, Optic nerve, Retina (rods and cones)

(Figure 6.2), an area measuring about 3 mm × 5 mm in the center of the retina. The most precise vision comes from the central portion of the macula, called the fovea (meaning "pit")—the area in the center of the human retina, specialized for acute, detailed vision. Because blood vessels and ganglion cell axons are almost absent near the fovea, it has the least impeded vision available. The tight packing of receptors also aids perception of detail.

Further aiding detailed vision, the human fovea has little or no convergence of receptors onto their postsynaptic cells, known as *bipolar cells.* Because the fovea has as many bipolar cells as receptors, the system can keep track of the exact location of any point of light. Toward the periphery, larger and larger numbers of receptors converge their inputs. As a result of this summation, the brain cannot discern the exact location or shape of a light source in the periphery. However, the summation enables perception of very faint lights in the periphery. In short, foveal vision has better *acuity* (sensitivity to detail), and peripheral vision has better sensitivity to dim light.

You have heard the expression "eyes like a hawk." In many bird species the eyes occupy most of the head, compared to only 5% of the head in humans. Furthermore many bird species have two foveas per eye, one pointing ahead and one pointing to the side (Wallman & Pettigrew, 1985). The extra foveas enable perception of detail in the periphery.

Hawks and other predatory birds have a greater density of visual receptors on the top half of their retinas (looking down) than they have on the bottom half (looking up). That arrangement is highly adaptive because predatory birds spend most of their day soaring high in the air looking down. However, when the bird lands and needs to see above it, it must turn its head, as Figure 6.3 shows (Waldvogel, 1990).

Conversely, in many prey species such as rats, the greater density of receptors is on the bottom half of the retina (Lund, Lund, & Wise, 1974). As a result they can see objects above them better than those below.

Figure 6.3 A behavioral consequence of how receptors are arranged on the retina
One owlet has turned its head almost upside down to see above itself. Birds of prey have a great density of receptors on the upper half of the retina, enabling them to see below them in great detail during flight. But they see objects above themselves very poorly, unless they turn their heads. Take another look at the prairie falcon at the start of this chapter. It is not a one-eyed bird; it is a bird that has tilted its head. Do you now understand why? *(Source: Chase Swift)*

Stop & Check

2. If you look at a faint star on a dark night, you sometimes find that you can see it better if you look slightly to the side of the star instead of straight at it. Why?

Check your answer on page 162.

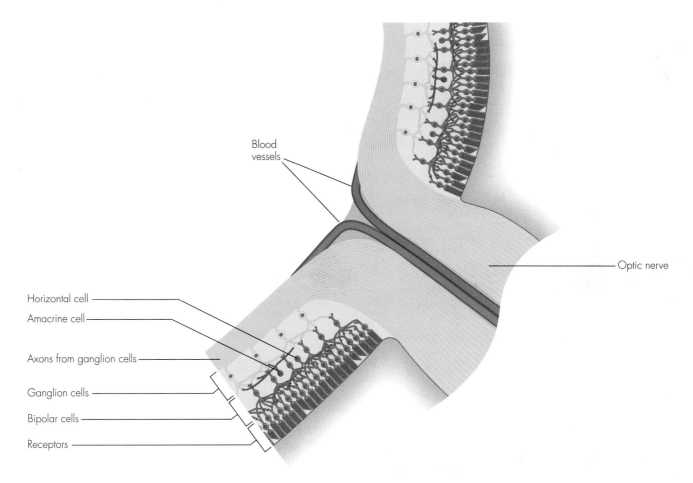

Blood vessels

Optic nerve

Horizontal cell

Amacrine cell

Axons from ganglion cells

Ganglion cells

Bipolar cells

Receptors

Figure 6.4 Visual path within the eyeball
The receptors send their messages to bipolar and horizontal cells, which in turn send messages to the amacrine and ganglion cells. The axons of the ganglion cells loop together to exit the eye at the blind spot. They form the optic nerve, which continues to the brain.

The Route Within the Retina

In a sense the retina is built inside out. If you or I were designing an eye, we would probably send the receptors' messages directly back to the brain. In the vertebrate retina, however, the receptors, located on the back of the eye, send their messages not toward the brain but to **bipolar cells,** neurons located closer to the center of the eye. The bipolar cells send their messages to **ganglion cells,** located still closer to the center of the eye. The ganglion cells' axons join one another, loop around, and travel back to the brain (see Figures 6.4 and 6.5).

One consequence of this anatomy is that light has to pass through the ganglion cells and bipolar cells before it reaches the receptors. However, because these cells are highly transparent, light passes through them without distortion. A more important consequence of the eye's anatomy is the *blind spot*. The ganglion cell axons band together to form the **optic nerve** (or optic tract), an axon bundle that exits through the back of the eye. The point at which it leaves (which is also where

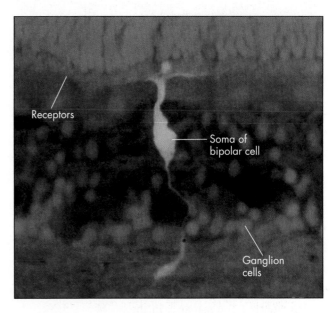

Receptors

Soma of bipolar cell

Ganglion cells

Figure 6.5 A bipolar cell from the retina of a carp, stained with Procion yellow
Bipolar cells get their name from the fact that a fibrous process is attached to each end (or pole) of the neuron. *(Source: Dowling, 1987)*

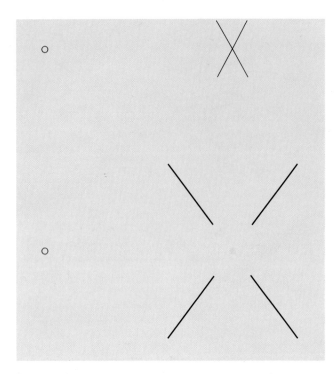

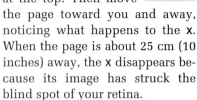

Figure 6.6 Two demonstrations of the blind spot of the retina
Close your left eye and focus your right eye on the o in the top part. Move the page toward you and away, noticing what happens to the x. At a distance of about 25 cm (10 inches), the x disappears. Now repeat this procedure with the bottom part. At that same distance what do you see?

some major blood vessels leave) is called the **blind spot** because it has no receptors.

Every person is therefore blind in part of each eye. You can demonstrate your own blind spot using Figure 6.6. Close your left eye and focus your right eye on the o at the top. Then move the page toward you and away, noticing what happens to the **x**. When the page is about 25 cm (10 inches) away, the **x** disappears because its image has struck the blind spot of your retina.

Now repeat the procedure with the lower part of the figure. When the page is again about 25 cm away from your eyes, what do you see? The *gap* disappears! But although you no longer see the gap, do you see something *inside* the gap? You might say that you see an **x** in the middle of the gap. Whether you actually *see* an **x** or just infer it is controversial, and it is possible that people literally fill in a gap under some circumstances and not

others (Dennett, 1991; DeWeerd, Gattass, Desimone, & Ungerleider, 1995; Ramachandran, 1992). Regardless of whether we call it an inference or a perception, it is your brain's own creation.

Some people have a much larger blind spot because glaucoma or another disease has destroyed receptors or parts of the optic nerve. Generally they do not notice their large blind spot any more than you notice your smaller one. Why not? Mainly, what they "see" in their blind areas is not blackness, but simply *nothing*—no sensation at all—the same as you see in your blind spot or out the back of your head.

Stop & Check

3. What makes the blind spot of the retina blind?

Check your answer on page 162.

Visual Receptors: Rods and Cones

The vertebrate retina contains two types of receptors: rods and cones (see Figure 6.7). The rods, which are most abundant in the periphery of the human retina, respond to faint light, but are bleached by bright light and thus not very useful in bright daylight. Cones, which are most abundant in and around the fovea, are less active in dim light but more useful in bright light. Color

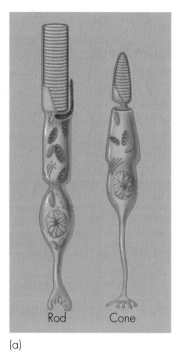

(a)

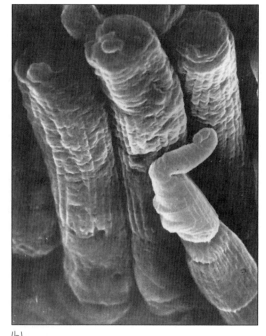

(b)

Figure 6.7 Structure of rod and cone
(a) Diagram of a rod and a cone. **(b)** Photo of rods and a cone, produced with a scanning electron microscope. Magnification × 7000. *(Source: Micrograph courtesy of E. R. Lewis, F. S. Werblin, & Y. Y. Zeevi)*

Table 6.1 Human Foveal Vision and Peripheral Vision

Characteristic	Foveal Vision	Peripheral Vision
Receptors	Cones in the fovea itself; cones and rods mix in the surrounding area	Proportion of rods increases toward the periphery; the extreme periphery has only rods
Convergence of receptors	Just a few receptors send their input to each postsynaptic cell	Increasing numbers of receptors send input to each postsynaptic cell
Brightness sensitivity	Useful for distinguishing among bright lights; responds poorly to faint lights	Responds well to faint lights; less useful for making distinctions in bright light
Sensitivity to detail	Detail vision is good because few receptors funnel their input to a postsynaptic cell	Detail vision is poor because so many receptors send their input to the same postsynaptic cell
Color vision	Good (many cones)	Poor (few cones)

vision, for species that have it, depends on the cones. The differences between foveal and peripheral vision are summarized in Table 6.1.

Both rods and cones contain **photopigments,** chemicals that release energy when struck by light. Photopigments consist of 11-*cis*-retinal (a derivative of vitamin A) bound to proteins called *opsins*. The 11-*cis*-retinal is stable in the dark; light energy converts it extremely quickly and efficiently to another form, all-*trans*-retinal (Wang, Schoenlein, Peteanu, Mathies, & Shank, 1994). (The light is absorbed in this process; it does not continue to bounce around in the eye.)

The conversion of 11-*cis*-retinal to all-*trans*-retinal changes hundreds of second-messenger molecules to their active state, ultimately closing the sodium channels in the cell membrane (Lamb & Pugh, 1990). The closing of sodium channels hyperpolarizes the receptor; the greater the light, the greater the hyperpolarization. Do not be confused by the fact that light inhibits the receptor cell. Receptors have inhibitory synapses

onto the next cells, the bipolar cells, and therefore the inhibition of receptor cells decreases the inhibition of the bipolar cells, producing an excitation.

Color Vision

Almost all vertebrates, including all tested mammals, have at least some cones in the retina (G. H. Jacobs, 1993). However, color vision requires comparing the responses of different kinds of cones. For example, rats, which have just one kind of cone (Neitz & Jacobs, 1986), cannot discriminate one color from another.

In the human visual system, the shortest visible wavelengths, about 400 nm (1 nm = nanometer, or 10^{-9} m), are perceived as violet; progressively longer wavelengths are perceived as blue, green, yellow, orange, and red, near 700 nm (Figure 6.8). Again, species differ; unlike humans the kestrel, a small hawk, can see ultraviolet light. Curiously, voles, small rodents that kestrels prey on, have urine and feces that reflect ultraviolet light (Viitala, Korpimäki, Palokangas, & Koivula, 1995), so kestrels probably use their ultraviolet vision to find prey.

Discrimination among colors poses a special coding problem for the nervous system. A cell in the visual system, like any other neuron, can vary only its frequency of action potentials or, in a cell with graded potentials, its membrane polarization. If the cell's response indicates brightness, then it cannot simultaneously signal color. Conversely, if

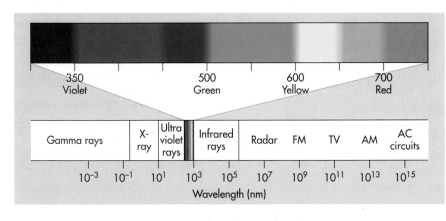

Figure 6.8 A beam of light separated into its wavelengths
Although the wavelengths vary over a continuum, we perceive them as several distinct colors.

each response indicates a different color, the cell cannot signal brightness. The inevitable conclusion is that no single neuron can simultaneously indicate brightness and color; our perceptions must depend on patterns of responses by a number of different neurons. Two major interpretations of color vision were described in the 1800s: the trichromatic theory and the opponent-process theory.

The Trichromatic (Young-Helmholtz) Theory

On theoretical grounds it has long been clear that color vision must depend on several kinds of receptors, each sensitive to different wavelengths. But how many kinds of receptors? People can distinguish red, green, yellow, blue, orange, pink, purple, greenish-blue, and so forth. Do we have a separate receptor for every distinguishable color? If not, how many receptor types do we have?

Long before biochemical methods were capable of distinguishing separate receptor types, researchers determined how many types must exist by using **psychophysical observations,** reports by observers concerning their perceptions of various stimuli. That is, they found that people could match any color by mixing appropriate amounts of just three wavelengths. Therefore researchers concluded that three kinds of receptors—we now call them cones—are sufficient to account for human color vision.

Based on such results Thomas Young proposed a theory, later modified by Hermann von Helmholtz and now known as the **trichromatic theory** of color vision, or the **Young-Helmholtz theory.** According to this theory we perceive color through the relative rates of response by three kinds of cones, each kind maximally sensitive to a different set of wavelengths. (*Trichromatic* means "three colors.") Figure 6.9 shows wavelength-sensitivity functions for the three cone types: *short-wavelength, medium-wavelength*, and *long-wavelength*. Note that each cone responds to a broad band of wavelengths, but to some wavelengths more than others.

According to the trichromatic theory, we discriminate among wavelengths by the ratio of activity across the three types of cones. For example, light at 500 nm excites the medium-wavelength cone to about 65% of its maximum, the long-wavelength receptor to 40% of its maximum, and the short-wavelength receptor to 10% or 15% of its maximum. This ratio of responses among the three cones determines a perception of blue-green. More intense light increases the activity of all three

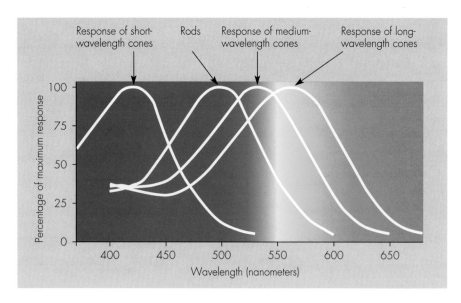

Figure 6.9 Response of rods and three kinds of cones to various wavelengths of light
Note that each kind responds somewhat to a wide range of wavelengths but best to wavelengths in a particular range. *(Source: Adapted from Bowmaker & Dartnall, 1980)*

cones but does not greatly alter the ratio of responses. That is, all receptors respond more strongly, but in the same proportions, so the color appears brighter, but still blue-green. When all three types of cones are equally active, we see white (or gray).

Note that any response by any one cone is ambiguous. For example, a low response rate by a middle-wavelength cone might indicate low-intensity 540-nm light or brighter 500-nm light or still brighter 460-nm light. A high response rate could indicate either bright light at 540 nm or bright white light, which includes 540 nm. The nervous system can determine the color and brightness of the light only by comparing the responses of the three types of cones.

Given the desirability of seeing all colors in all locations, we might suppose that all three kinds of cones are equally distributed over the central portion of the retina. In fact they are not. Long- and medium-wavelength cones are far more abundant than short-wavelength (blue) cones, and consequently it is easier to see tiny red, yellow, or green dots than blue dots (Roorda & Williams, 1999). Try this: Look at the dots in the display below, first at a close distance and then from greater and greater distances. You probably will notice that the blue dots look blue when close but appear black from a greater distance. The other colors are still visible when the blue is not.

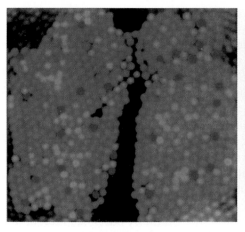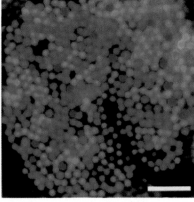

Figure 6.10 Distribution of cones in two human retinas
Investigators artificially colored these images of cones from two people's retinas, indicating the short-wavelength cones with blue, the medium-wavelength with green, and the long-wavelength with red. Note the difference between the two people, the relative rarity of short-wavelength cones, and the patchiness of the distributions. *(Source: Roorda & Williams, 1999)*

Furthermore the distribution of cones is patchy. Figure 6.10 shows the distribution of short-, medium-, and long-wavelength cones in two people's retinas, with blue, green, and red artificially added to distinguish the three cone types. Note how few short-wavelength cones are present. Note also the patches of all medium- or all long-wavelength cones. At a local level many areas of the retina lack the diversity of receptors needed for full color vision. Nevertheless, for objects of moderate size, we have no trouble identifying colors.

The Opponent-Process Theory

The trichromatic theory correctly predicted the discovery of three kinds of cones, but it does not easily explain all of the phenomena of color vision. For example, try the following demonstration: Stare at the dot in the center of Figure 6.11 under a bright light, without moving your eyes, for a full minute. (The brighter the light and the longer you stare, the stronger the effect.) Then look at a plain white surface, such as a wall or a blank sheet of paper. Keep your eyes steady. You will now see a **negative color afterimage,** a replacement of the red you had been staring at with green, green with red, yellow and blue with each other, and black and white with each other.

TRY IT
YOUR
SELF

To explain this and related phenomena, Ewald Hering, a 19th-century physiologist, proposed the **opponent-process theory:** We perceive color in terms of paired opposites: red versus green, yellow versus blue, and white versus black (Hurvich & Jameson, 1957). That is, there is no such thing as reddish green, greenish red, or yellowish blue. The brain has some mechanism that perceives color on a continuum from red to green and another from yellow to blue.

Modern researchers now understand what that system is: From the bipolar cells through the visual areas of the cerebral cortex, some neurons have inputs that enable red light to excite them and green light to inhibit them, or vice versa, or for blue to excite them and yellow to inhibit them (DeValois & Jacobs, 1968; Engel, 1999). Take, for example, a blue-yellow opponent bipolar cell, as shown in Figure 6.12. This bipolar cell responds best to short-wavelength (blue) light and is inhibited by either long-wavelength or medium-wavelength light, but most strongly by a mixture of both, which we see as yellow. Thus, whenever this cell becomes excited, it contributes to a blue perception; when inhibited, yellow. You can now understand how to explain negative color afterimages: After prolonged staring at something blue (short wavelengths), this bipolar cell has been depolarized extensively. If we remove the stimulus and put white in its place, the cell swings into a hyperpolarization, producing a sensation of yellow.

The Retinex Theory

Whereas the trichromatic theory correctly predicted the existence of three kinds of cones and explains some

Figure 6.11 Stimulus for demonstrating negative color afterimages
Stare at the dot in the center under bright light for about a minute and then look at a white field. You should see a red rose with green leaves.

aspects of color vision, and the opponent-process theory correctly predicted certain synaptic connections and explains negative color afterimages, both theories are unable to explain color constancy.

Color constancy is the ability to recognize the color of an object despite changes in lighting (Kennard, Lawden, Morland, & Ruddock, 1995; Zeki, 1980, 1983). If you put on green-tinted glasses or replace your white light bulb with a green-tinted one, you can still identify all the objects in the room. You will of course notice the greenish tint, but you still identify bananas as yellow, paper as white, walls as brown (or whatever), and so forth. You do so by comparing the color of one object with the color of another, in effect subtracting a fixed amount of green from each. Color constancy requires a comparison; if you focused the green light on just one object, it looks green regardless of its original color (see Figure 6.13). Similarly our perception of the brightness of an object depends on a comparison with other objects.

To account for color constancy, Edwin Land proposed the **retinex theory** (a combination of the words *retina* and *cortex*): When information from various parts of the retina reaches the cortex, the cortex compares each of the inputs to determine the brightness and color perception for each area (Land, Hubel, Livingstone, Perry, & Burns, 1983). For example, if the cortex notes a constant amount of green throughout a scene, it subtracts some green from each object to determine its true color. We consider the neurological basis for the retinex process later in this chapter.

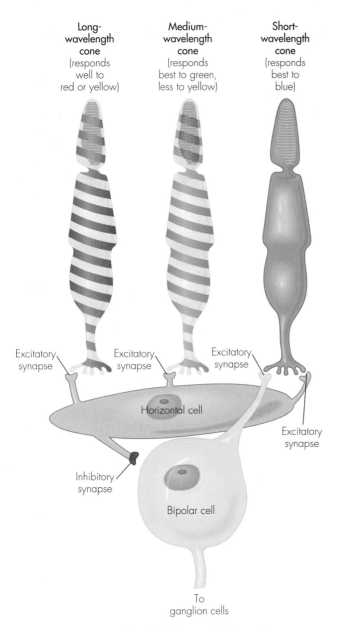

Figure 6.12 Possible wiring for one bipolar cell
Short-wavelength light (which we see as blue) excites the bipolar cell and (by way of the intermediate horizontal cell) also inhibits it. However, the excitation predominates, so blue light produces net excitation. Red, green, or yellow light inhibit this bipolar cell because they produce inhibition (through the horizontal cell) without any excitation. The strongest inhibition is from yellow light, which stimulates both the long- and medium-wavelength cones. Therefore we can describe this bipolar cell as excited by blue and inhibited by yellow. White light produces as much inhibition as excitation and therefore no net effect. (Actually, receptors excite by decreasing their usual inhibitory messages. Here we translate that double negative into excitation for simplicity.)

Figure 6.13 Color constancy
This photo was taken through a green filter. Note that you can identify the color of each object in the photo, including the White House. However, if you cover everything except the White House, it doesn't look white anymore; it looks green. According to the retinex theory, we perceive color when the cortex compares the inputs from various parts of the retina. In this case the cortex in effect subtracts a little green from each object because that is constant over the entire scene.

4. Suppose a bipolar cell received excitatory input from medium-wavelength cones and inhibitory input (through a horizontal cell) from all three kinds of cones. What color of light would most greatly excite the bipolar? What color would most greatly inhibit it?

5. When a television set is off, its screen appears gray. When you watch a program, parts of the screen appear black, even though more light is actually showing on the screen than when the set was off and the screen appeared gray. What accounts for the black perception?

Check your answers on page 162.

Color Vision Deficiency

A colleague once sent a survey to me and many other psychologists asking what discoveries psychologists had made. The encyclopedias are full of examples in astronomy, biology, chemistry, and physics, but they seldom designate any "discovery in psychology." What are psychologists' discoveries?

You might give that question some thought. A psychological discovery should be clearly part of psychology, formerly unknown, but now well established. You might devise your own list, but let me tell you my vote for the first real discovery in psychology: color blindness, or what is now called **color vision deficiency,** the inability to perceive color differences as most other people do. (Complete color blindness, the inability to perceive anything but shades of black and white, is rare.) Before color vision deficiency was discovered in the 1600s (Fletcher & Voke, 1985), people assumed that vision copies the objects we see. That is, if an object is round, we see the roundness; if it is yellow, we see the yellowness; if it is moving, we see the movement. Investigators *discovered* that it is possible to have otherwise satisfactory vision without seeing color.

We now recognize several types of color vision deficiency. For genetic reasons some people lack the long-wavelength, medium-wavelength, or short-wavelength cones. Some lack two kinds of cones (Nathans et al., 1989). Other people have all three types of cones but have low numbers or unusual forms of one of them.

In the most common form of color vision deficiency, people have trouble distinguishing red from green because of a gene that causes the long- and medium-wavelength cones to make the same photopigment instead of different ones. The gene causing this deficiency is on the X chromosome. About 8% of men are red-green color blind, compared with less than 1% of women (Bowmaker, 1998).

In Closing: Visual Receptors

I remember once explaining to my then-teenage son a newly discovered detail about the visual system, only to have him reply, "I didn't realize it would be so complicated. I thought the light strikes your eyes and then you see it." As you should now be starting to realize—and if not, the next module should convince you—vision requires extremely complicated processing. If you tried to build a robot with vision, you would quickly discover that shining light into its eyes accomplishes nothing unless its visual detectors are connected to devices that identify the useful information and use it to select the proper action. We have such devices in our brains, although we are still far from fully understanding them.

Summary

1. Each type of receptor transduces a particular kind of energy into a receptor potential, which is a hyperpolarization or depolarization of its membrane. (p. 152)

2. Sensory information is coded so that the brain can process it. The coded information bears no physical similarity to the stimuli it describes. (p. 152)

3. According to the law of specific nerve energies, the brain interprets any activity of a given sensory neuron as representing the sensory information to which that neuron is tuned. (p. 153)

4. Light passes through the pupil of a vertebrate eye and stimulates the receptors lining the retina at the back of the eye. (p. 153)

5. Visual acuity is greatest in the fovea, the central area of the retina. (p. 154)

6. Because so many receptors in the periphery converge their messages to their bipolar cells, our peripheral vision is highly sensitive to faint light but poorly sensitive to detail. (p. 154)

7. The axons from the retina loop around to form the optic tract, which exits from the eye at a point called the blind spot. (p. 155)

8. The retina has two kinds of receptors: rods and cones. Rods are more sensitive to faint light; cones are more useful in bright light. Rods are more numerous in the periphery of the eye, cones in the fovea. (p. 156)

9. Light stimulates the receptors by triggering a molecular change in 11-*cis*-retinal, releasing energy, and thereby activating second messengers within the cell. (p. 157)

10. According to the trichromatic (or Young-Helmholtz) theory of color vision, color perception begins with a given wavelength of light stimulating a distinctive ratio of responses by the three types of cones. (p. 158)

11. According to the opponent-process theory of color vision, visual system neurons beyond the receptors themselves respond with an increase in activity to indicate one color of light and a decrease to indicate the opposite color. The three pairs of opposites are red-green, yellow-blue, and white-black. (p. 159)

12. According to the retinex theory, the cortex compares the responses representing different parts of the retina to determine the brightness and color of each area. (p. 160)

13. For genetic reasons certain people are unable to distinguish one color from another. Red-green color blindness is the most common type. (p. 161)

Answers to *Stop and Check* Questions

1. The law of specific nerve energies is the principle that any impulse in a given nerve sends the same kind of message to the brain. Modifications are: (a) A neuron can send one message by an increase in response and a different response by a decrease. (b) Variations in the timing of responses can convey meaning. (c) The meaning of a neuron's response can depend on the context of other cells' responses. (p. 153)

2. If you look directly at a star, the light strikes the fovea, which has no rods and little or no convergence of receptors. If you look slightly to the side, the light hits a part of the retina that has some rods and is more sensitive to faint light. (p. 154)

3. The blind spot has no receptors because it is occupied by exiting axons and blood vessels. (p. 156)

4. It would be most excited by medium-wavelength (green) light. It would be inhibited by either long-wavelength (red) or short-wavelength (blue) light or by a combination of both. However, because the long-wavelength cones are far more abundant than the short-wavelength cones, the cell is mostly excited by green and inhibited by red. (p. 161)

5. The black experience arises by contrast with the other brighter areas. The contrast occurs by comparison within the cerebral cortex, as in the retinex principle of color vision. (p. 161)

Thought Question

How could you test for the presence of color vision in a bee? Examining the retina does not help; invertebrate receptors resemble neither rods nor cones. It is possible to train bees to approach one visual stimulus and not another. The difficulty is that if you trained some bees to approach, say, a yellow card and not a green card, you do not know whether they solved the problem by color or by brightness. Because brightness is different from physical intensity, you cannot equalize brightness by any physical measurement, nor can you assume that two colors that are equally bright to humans are also equally bright to bees. How might you get around the problem of brightness to study the possibility of color vision in bees?

The Neural Basis of Visual Perception

Before the discovery of color blindness, people assumed that anyone who saw an object at all saw everything about the object: its shape, its color, its movement. Because you have heard about color blindness since childhood, you may wonder why its discovery was so surprising. And yet you yourself may be surprised—as were late 20th-century psychologists—by the analogous phenomenon of *motion blindness*: Some people with otherwise satisfactory vision fail to detect that an object is moving, or at least have great trouble determining its direction and speed. "How could anyone see something and not see that it is moving?" you might ask. Your question is not very different from the question raised in the 1600s: "How could anyone see something without seeing what color it is?"

The fundamental fact about the visual cortex takes a little getting used to: You have neither a little person in the head nor a central processor that sees every aspect of a visual stimulus at once. Different parts of your cortex process different aspects of the visual stimulus somewhat independently of one another.

An Overview of the Mammalian Visual System

Let's begin with a general outline of the anatomy of the mammalian visual system and then examine certain stages in more detail. The rods and cones make synaptic contact with **horizontal cells** and bipolar cells (Figure 6.14). The horizontal cells make inhibitory contact onto bipolar cells, which in turn make synapses onto *amacrine cells* and ganglion cells. All these cells are within the eyeball.

The axons of the ganglion cells form the optic nerve, which leaves the retina and travels along the lower surface of the brain. The optic nerve from the left eye and the optic nerve from the right eye meet at the optic chiasm (Figure 6.15), where, in humans, half of the axons from each eye cross to the opposite side of the brain. The percentage of crossover varies from one species to another depending on the location of the eyes. In species with eyes on the sides of the head, such as rabbits and guinea pigs, nearly all the axons cross to the opposite side.

Most of the ganglion cell axons go to the **lateral geniculate nucleus,** a nucleus of the thalamus specialized for visual perception. (The term *geniculate* comes from the Latin root *genu*, meaning "knee." To *genuflect* is to bend the knee. In some species the lateral geniculate looks a little like a knee if you use some imagination.) Some axons go to the superior colliculus, and even fewer go to several other areas, including a section of the hypothalamus that controls the waking–sleeping schedule (see Chapter 9). At any rate most of the visual information goes to the lateral geniculate, which in turn sends its axons to the visual areas of the cerebral cortex.

The cerebral cortex has many visual areas with distinct functions and ways of analyzing visual information. However, the division of labor begins at the level of the ganglion cells, where several types of cells play different roles in perception. Those cells form different pathways that remain largely separate in the lateral geniculate and in the cerebral cortex. To understand the story of these different pathways, we need to begin with some general principles.

Stop & Check

1. Where does the optic nerve start and where does it end?

   Check your answer on page 180.

Mechanisms of Processing in the Visual System

The human retina contains roughly 120 million rods and 6 million cones. We cannot intelligently process 126 million independent messages; we need to extract the meaningful patterns, such as what the objects are, where they are, and whether they are moving.

Receptive Fields

The whole area of the world that you can see at any time is your **visual field.** The part that you see to your left is your left visual field; the part to your right is your right visual field. The part of the visual field to which any one neuron responds is that neuron's **receptive**

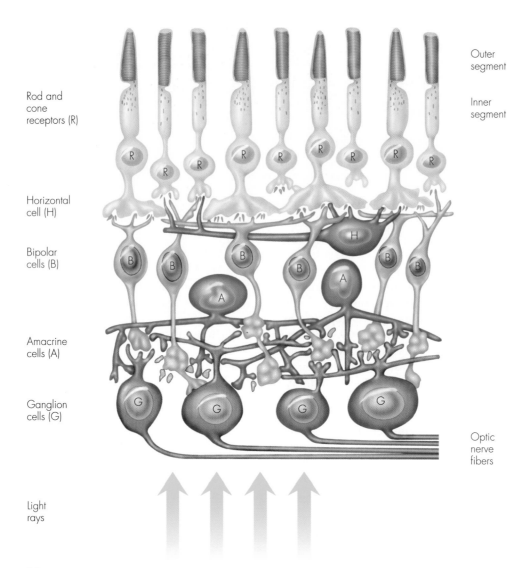

Rod and cone receptors (R)

Outer segment

Inner segment

Horizontal cell (H)

Bipolar cells (B)

Amacrine cells (A)

Ganglion cells (G)

Optic nerve fibers

Light rays

(a)

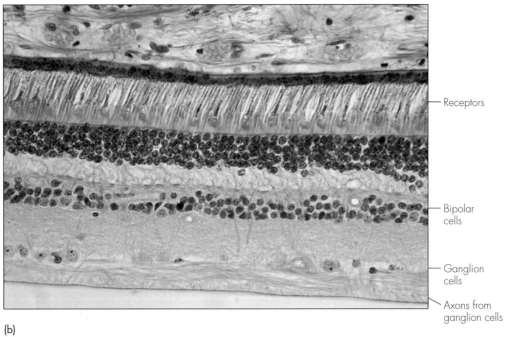

Receptors

Bipolar cells

Ganglion cells

Axons from ganglion cells

(b)

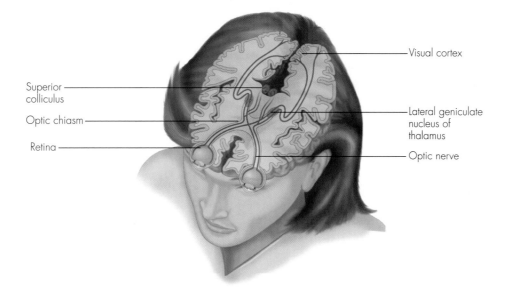

Figure 6.15 Major connections in the visual system of the brain
Part of the visual input goes to the thalamus and from there to the visual cortex. Another part of the visual input goes to the superior colliculus.

field.[1] For a receptor, the receptive field is simply the point in space from which light strikes the receptor. Because receptors connect to bipolar cells, which connect to ganglion cells and so forth, the receptive field of any of these other cells depends on its incoming synapses. For example, if a ganglion cell is connected to a group of receptors, the receptive field of the ganglion cell is a combination of the receptive fields of those receptors, as shown in Figure 6.16. Then the receptive fields of the ganglion cells converge to form the receptive fields of the next level of cells and so on. The connections from one neuron to another can be either excitatory or inhibitory, so receptive fields can have both excitatory and inhibitory regions.

To find a receptive field, an investigator can shine light in various locations while recording from some neuron. If light from some spot excites the neuron, then that location is part of the neuron's excitatory receptive field. If it inhibits activity, then the location is in the inhibitory receptive field.

Neuroscientists often informally say that a particular neuron in the visual system responds to a particular pattern of light. For example, "This cortical cell responds best to a green horizontal line." The investigator

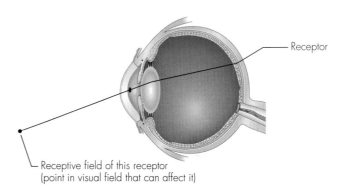

Receptor

Receptive field of this receptor
(point in visual field that can affect it)

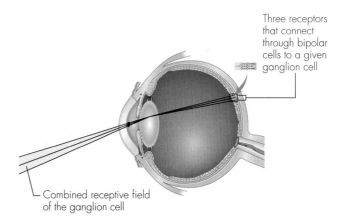

Three receptors that connect through bipolar cells to a given ganglion cell

Combined receptive field of the ganglion cell

Figure 6.16 Receptive fields
The receptive field of a receptor is simply the area of the visual field from which light strikes that receptor. For any other cell in the visual system, the receptive field is determined by which receptors connect to the cell in question.

---

[1] It is possible to describe the receptive field of a visual cell in two ways. The first is as a portion of the visual field, as just stated. The other is as a portion of the retina. Because every spot on the retina receives input from its own point in the visual field, the two ways are equivalent.

◀ **Figure 6.14 The vertebrate retina**
(a) Diagram of the neurons of the retina. The top of the figure is the back of the retina. All the optic nerve fibers group together and then turn around to exit through the back of the retina, in the "blind spot" of the eye. *(Source: Based on Dowling & Boycott, 1966)*
(b) Photo of a cross section through the retina. This section from the periphery of the retina has relatively few ganglion cells; a slice closer to the fovea would have a greater density.

does not mean that light shining on the neuron excites it. Rather the neuron is excited when light shines on its receptive field.

The receptive field of a ganglion cell can be described as a circular center with an antagonistic doughnut-shaped surround. That is, light in the center of the receptive field might be excitatory, with the surround inhibitory, or the opposite.

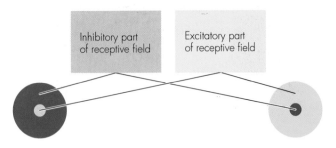

Lateral Inhibition

Neurons in the cerebral cortex have complicated receptive fields. Instead of simply being excited or inhibited by light, a cortical cell may respond to a complex pattern, such as a horizontal green line moving upward. Such receptive fields arise through combinations of excitatory and inhibitory synapses. One of the most basic examples is lateral inhibition.

Let's begin by considering part of the circuitry and then add more. The retina is lined with receptors (rods and cones). They have *inhibitory* synapses onto the bipolar cells and light *decreases* their output, but for simplicity's sake, instead of using double negatives, let's think of their output as excitation of the bipolar cells. That is, when light strikes one or more receptors, they excite the bipolars connected to them. Except in the fovea, bipolar cells are connected to multiple receptors (larger and larger numbers toward the periphery of the retina), as shown in Figure 6.4, p. 155; however, again for simplicity, let's imagine each receptor connected to just one bipolar:

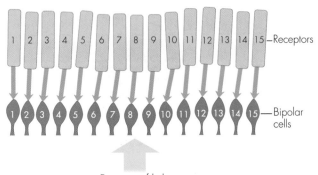

Direction of light

Now let's add the next element, the horizontal cells. Each receptor excites a horizontal cell, which *inhibits* the bipolar cells. Because the horizontal cell has a wide

spread, excitation of any receptor can inhibit a large group of bipolar cells. However, because the horizontal cell is a *local cell*, with no axon and no action potentials, its depolarization decays with distance. Mild excitation of, say, receptor 8 inhibits bipolars 7 through 9 most strongly, inhibits bipolars 6 and 10 a bit less, and so on. (The more intensely a receptor is excited, the greater the effect on the horizontal cell and therefore the greater the inhibition of the bipolar cells.)

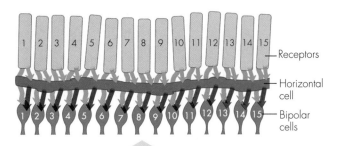

Direction of light

Now imagine what happens if light excites just receptors 6–10. These receptors excite bipolar cells 6–10 and the horizontal cell. So bipolar cells 6–10 receive both excitation and inhibition. The excitation from the receptors is stronger than the inhibition from the horizontal cell, so the bipolars receive net excitation.

However, although bipolar cells 6 through 10 receive equal excitation, they do not all receive the same amount of inhibition. Remember, the response of the horizontal cell decays over distance. Bipolar cells 7–9 are inhibited by receptors on both sides of them, but bipolar cells 6 and 10 are each inhibited by receptors on one side and not the other. That is, the bipolar cells on the edge of the excitation are inhibited less than those in the middle. Therefore the overall result is that bipolar cells 6 and 10 respond *more* than bipolars 7–9.

Now think about bipolar cell 5. What excitation does it receive? None. What inhibition? It is inhibited by the horizontal cell because of the excitation of receptor 6. Therefore bipolar 5, receiving inhibition but no excitation, responds even less than bipolars 1–4.

All these results illustrate **lateral inhibition,** the reduction of activity in one neuron by activity in neighboring neurons (Hartline, 1949). The main function of lateral inhibition is to heighten the contrast at borders. That is, when light falls on a surface, as shown on the next page, the bipolars just inside the border are most excited, and those outside the border are the least responsive.

You might (or might not) find this analogy helpful: If I place a wooden block on a surface of gelatin, the block depresses the gelatin beneath it while raising the surrounding surface (Figure 6.17a). The depression is

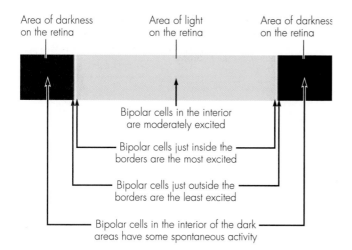

Area of darkness on the retina

Area of light on the retina

Area of darkness on the retina

Bipolar cells in the interior are moderately excited

Bipolar cells just inside the borders are the most excited

Bipolar cells just outside the borders are the least excited

Bipolar cells in the interior of the dark areas have some spontaneous activity

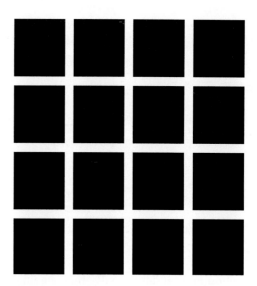

Figure 6.18   An illustration of lateral inhibition
Do you see dark diamonds at the "crossroads"?

analogous to the excitation of a neuron, and the rise in the surrounding gelatin is analogous to lateral inhibition of surrounding neurons. Then I place a second block next to the first. As the second block sinks into the gelatin, it slightly raises the first (Figure 6.17b). Finally, I try placing a row of blocks on the gelatin. The blocks at the beginning and end of the row sink deeper than the others (Figure 6.17c). Why? Because each block in the interior of the row is subject to upward pressure from both sides, whereas the blocks at the beginning and end of the row are subject to pressure from one side only.

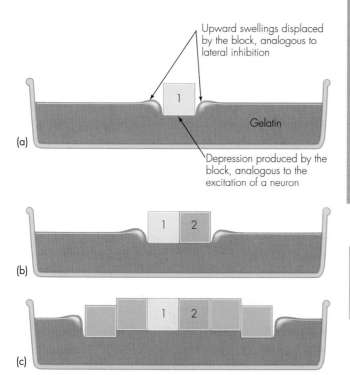

Upward swellings displaced by the block, analogous to lateral inhibition

Gelatin

(a)

Depression produced by the block, analogous to the excitation of a neuron

(b)

(c)

Figure 6.17   Blocks on a surface of gelatin, analogous to lateral inhibition
Each block pushes gelatin down and therefore pushes neighboring blocks up. Blocks at the edge are pushed up less than those in the center.

Stop & Check

2. As we progress from bipolar cells to ganglion cells to later cells in the visual system, are receptive fields ordinarily larger, smaller, or the same size? Why?

3. When light strikes a receptor, what effect does the receptor have on the bipolar cells (excitatory or inhibitory)? What effect does it have on horizontal cells? What effect does the horizontal cell have on bipolar cells?

4. If light strikes only one receptor, what is the net effect (excitatory or inhibitory) on the nearest bipolar cell that is directly connected to that receptor? What is the effect on other bipolar cells off to the sides? What causes that effect?

5. Examine Figure 6.18 above. You should see grayish diamonds at the crossroads among the black squares. Explain why.

Check your answers on pages 180.

Concurrent Pathways in the Visual System

Look out your window. Perhaps you see someone walking by. Although your perception of that person seems to be an integrated whole, different parts of your brain are analyzing different aspects. One set of neurons identifies the person's shape, another set concentrates on the colors, and another sees the speed and direction of movement (Livingstone, 1988; Livingstone & Hubel, 1988; Zeki & Shipp, 1988). Although the various pathways necessarily communicate with one another,

Table 6.2 Distinctions Between Parvocellular and Magnocellular Neurons

	Parvocellular Neurons	Magnocellular Neurons
Cell bodies	Smaller	Larger
Receptive fields	Smaller	Larger
Retinal location	In and near fovea	Throughout the retina
Color sensitive	Yes	No
Response	Sustained response; adapted for detailed analysis of stationary objects	Fast, sustained responses; adapted to detect movement and broad outlines of shape

they function more independently than we might have imagined.

In the Retina and Lateral Geniculate

Your visual pathway begins its division of labor before it reaches the cerebral cortex. Even at the level of the ganglion cells in the retina, different cells react differently to the same input.

Remember that the bipolar cells connect to ganglion cells, whose axons form the optic nerve. Most primate ganglion cells fall into two major categories (see Table 6.2): parvocellular and magnocellular (Shapley, 1995). The **parvocellular neurons,** with smaller cell bodies and small receptive fields, are located mostly in or near the fovea. (Parvocellular means "small celled," from the Latin root *parv*, meaning "small.") The **magnocellular neurons,** with larger cell bodies and receptive fields, are distributed fairly evenly throughout the retina. (Magnocellular means "large celled," from the Latin root *magn*, meaning "large." The same root appears in *magnify* and *magnificent*.) (A third category, the *koniocellular neurons*, are the least numerous, the least responsive, and the least understood.)

The parvocellular neurons have small receptive fields, so they are well suited to detect visual details. They are also highly sensitive to color, each excited by some colors and inhibited by others. The high sensitivity to detail and color reflects the fact that parvocellular cells are located mostly in and near the fovea, where we have many cones.

The magnocellular neurons, in contrast, have larger receptive fields and are not color sensitive. They respond strongly to moving stimuli and to large overall patterns, but not to details. Magnocellular neurons are found throughout the retina, including the periphery, where we are sensitive to movement but not to color or details.

Try this demonstration: Take a stack of small colored objects, pick one without looking at it, and slowly move it into the extreme periphery of your vision. When you can just

TRY IT YOUR SELF

barely see it, you cannot detect its shape or color, but if you shake it, you easily notice the movement.

Most magnocellular cells and apparently all parvocellular cells send their axons to the lateral geniculate nucleus of the thalamus. The parvocellular ganglion cells contact mostly small (parvocellular) cells of the lateral geniculate, whereas magnocellular ganglion cells contact mostly the larger (magnocellular) cells. Thus the two kinds of pathways remain fairly distinct.

The distinction between parvocellular and magnocellular pathways has certain implications for human vision (Livingstone, 1988; Livingstone & Hubel, 1988). For example, consider Figure 6.19. The artist used distinct colors to indicate shadows. The result does not look entirely realistic, and yet the shadows enable us to perceive depth about as well in the color version as in the black-and-white version. The reason is that the magnocellular pathway, which is important for depth perception, is sensitive to brightness and not color.

In the Cerebral Cortex

Most visual information from the lateral geniculate area of the thalamus goes first to the **primary visual cortex,** also known as area **V1** or as the *striate cortex* because of its striped appearance. It is the area of the cortex responsible for the first stage of visual processing. It responds to any kind of visual stimulus and is also active when people close their eyes and imagine visual stimuli (Kosslyn et al., 1999).

The primary visual cortex sends information to the **secondary visual cortex** (area **V2**), which conducts a second stage of visual processing and transmits the information to additional areas, as shown in Figure 6.20. The connections in the visual cortex are reciprocal; for example, V1 sends information to V2 and V2 returns information to V1. Each area also exchanges information with other cortical areas and the thalamus. Neuroscientists have distinguished 30 to 40 visual areas in the brain of a macaque monkey (Van Essen & Deyoe, 1995) and believe that the human brain has even more.

Figure 6.19 Role of lightness/darkness (but not color) in depth perception
The artist André Derain (1880–1954) showed depth with colored shadows in this portrait of painter Henri Matisse (1905). Although the painting does not look realistic, we perceive the depth easily because the magnocellular pathway (responsible for depth perception) is colorblind. Note that we perceive depth about equally well in the color and in the black-and-white version. *(Source: Tate Gallery, London/Art Resource, NY)*

Within the cerebral cortex, the parvocellular and magnocellular pathways split from two pathways into three. A mostly parvocellular pathway continues as a system sensitive to details of shape. A mostly magnocellular pathway has a ventral branch sensitive to movement and a dorsal branch important for integrating vision with action. A mixed parvocellular and magnocellular pathway is sensitive to brightness and color. Although the parvocellular cells and magnocellular cells lie side by side within this system, their responses do not mingle much (Ts'o & Gilbert, 1988).

Note in Figure 6.20 that although the shape, movement, and color/brightness pathways are separate, they all lead to the temporal cortex. The branch of the mostly magnocellular pathway associated with integrating vision with movement leads to the parietal cortex. Researchers refer collectively to the visual paths in the temporal cortex as the **ventral stream,** or the "what" pathway, because it is specialized for identifying and recognizing objects. The visual path in the parietal cortex is the **dorsal stream,** or the "where" or "how" pathway, because it helps the motor system find objects and determine how to move toward them, grasp them, and so forth. Although the parietal cortex has neurons sensitive to shape (Sereno & Maunsell, 1998), they cannot by themselves produce object recognition. People who have a damaged temporal cortex but an intact parietal cortex (damage to the ventral stream) cannot describe the size, shape, or location of the objects they see, although they accurately reach out to pick up the objects. When walking, they step over or go around the objects in their way—even though they cannot describe them in any way! In contrast people who have parietal cortex damage but an intact temporal cortex (damage to the ventral stream) can accurately describe what they see, but they cannot convert their vision into action. Although they can walk toward something they hear, they cannot walk toward something they see, nor can they reach out to grasp an object—even after describing its size, shape, and so forth (Goodale, 1996; Goodale, Milner, Jakobson, & Carey, 1991). In short, the ability to describe what we see is separate from the ability to do anything about it.

You will note a number of unfamiliar terms in Figure 6.20, including blobs and interblobs, thin stripes and thick stripes, referring to anatomical structures that stand out when stained in particular ways; they also receive different kinds of input and process them differently (Roe & Ts'o, 1995). Do not be too concerned about those details unless you plan to become a visual cortex researcher. The key point of Figure 6.20 is that the three paths are largely independent. Neurons within a given path connect mostly to other neurons in the same path. The anatomy therefore suggests that each path specializes in a different aspect of perception, such as shape, color, or movement.

Stop & Check

6. What are the differences between the magnocellular and parvocellular systems?

7. If you were in a darkened room and researchers wanted to "read your mind" just enough to know whether you were having visual fantasies, what could they do?

Check your answers on page 180.

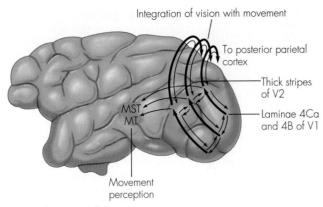

Integration of vision with movement

To posterior parietal cortex

Thick stripes of V2

MST MT

Laminae 4Ca and 4B of V1

Movement perception

(a) Mostly magnocellular path

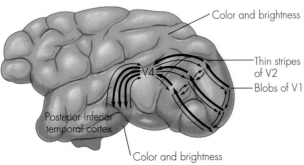

Color and brightness

Thin stripes of V2

V4

Blobs of V1

Posterior inferior temporal cortex

Color and brightness

(b) Mixed magnocellular/parvocellular path

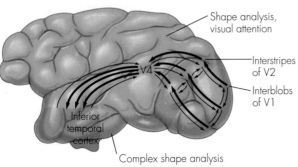

Shape analysis, visual attention

Interstripes of V2

V4

Interblobs of V1

Inferior temporal cortex

Complex shape analysis

(c) Mostly parvocellular path

Figure 6.20 Three visual pathways in the cerebral cortex
(a) A pathway originating mainly from magnocellular neurons. **(b)** A mixed magnocellular/parvocellular pathway. **(c)** A mainly parvocellular pathway. Neurons are heavily connected with other neurons in their own pathway but only sparsely connected with neurons of other pathways. Area V1 gets its primary input from the lateral geniculate nucleus of the thalamus; the other areas get some input from the thalamus but most from cortical areas. *(Sources: Based on DeYoe, Felleman, Van Essen, & McClendon, 1994; Ts'o & Roe, 1995; Van Essen & DeYoe, 1995)*

The Cerebral Cortex: The Shape Pathway

In the 1950s David Hubel and Torsten Wiesel (1959) began a research project in which they shone light patterns on the retina while recording from cells in a cat's or monkey's brain (see Methods 6.1). At first they presented just dots of light, using a slide projector and a

screen, and found little response by cortical cells. The first time they got a big response was when they were moving a slide into place. They quickly realized that the cell was responding to the edge of the slide and had a bar-shaped receptive field (Hubel & Wiesel, 1998). Their research, for which they received a Nobel Prize, has often been called "the research that launched a thousand microelectrodes" because it inspired so much further research. By now it has probably launched a million microelectrodes.

Hubel and Wiesel's Cell Types in the Primary Visual Cortex

Hubel and Wiesel distinguished several types of cells in the visual cortex. The receptive fields shown in Figure 6.21 are typical of **simple cells,** which are found exclusively in the primary visual cortex. The receptive field of a simple cell has fixed excitatory and inhibitory zones. The more light in the excitatory zone, the more the cell responds. The more light in the inhibitory zone, the less the cell responds. For example, Figure 6.21c shows a vertical receptive field for a simple cell. The cell's response decreases sharply if the bar of light is moved to the left or right or tilted from the vertical because light then strikes the inhibitory regions as well (see Figure 6.22). Most simple cells have bar-shaped or edge-shaped receptive fields, which may be at vertical, horizontal, or intermediate orientations.

Unlike simple cells, **complex cells,** located in either area V1 or V2, have receptive fields that cannot be mapped into fixed excitatory and inhibitory zones. A complex cell responds to a pattern of light in a particu-

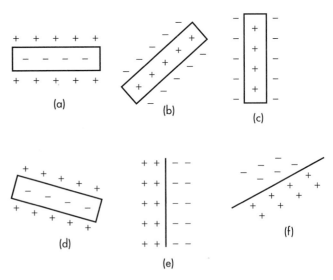

Figure 6.21 Typical receptive fields for simple visual cortex cells of cats and monkeys
Areas marked with a plus (+) are the excitatory receptive fields; areas marked with a minus (−) are the inhibitory receptive fields. *(Source: Based on Hubel & Wiesel, 1959)*

Microelectrode Recordings

David Hubel and Torsten Wiesel pioneered the use of microelectrode recordings to study the properties of individual neurons in the cerebral cortex. In this method investigators begin by anesthetizing an animal and drilling a small hole in the skull. Then they insert a thin electrode—either a fine metal wire insulated except at the tip or a narrow glass tube containing a salt solution and a metal wire. They direct the electrode either next to or into a single cell and then record its activity while they present various stimuli, such as patterns of light. Researchers use the results to determine what kinds of stimuli do and do not excite the cell.

lar orientation (for instance, a vertical bar) anywhere within its large receptive field, regardless of the exact location of the stimulus (see Figure 6.23). It responds most strongly to a stimulus moving perpendicular to its axis—for example, a vertical bar moving horizontally or a horizontal bar moving vertically. If a cell in the visual cortex responds to a bar-shaped pattern of light, the best way to classify the cell is to move the bar slightly in different directions. A cell that responds to the light in only one location is a simple cell; one that responds strongly to the light throughout a large area is a complex cell.

End-stopped, or **hypercomplex**, cells resemble complex cells with one additional feature: An end-stopped cell has a strong inhibitory area at one end of its bar-shaped receptive field. The cell responds to a bar-shaped pattern of light anywhere in its broad receptive field provided that the bar does not extend beyond a certain point (see Figure 6.24). Table 6.3 summarizes the properties of simple, complex, and end-stopped cells.

The Columnar Organization of the Visual Cortex

Cells having various properties are grouped together in the visual cortex in columns perpendicular to the surface (Hubel & Wiesel, 1977) (see Figure 4.19, p. 101). For example, cells within a given column respond either mostly to the left eye, mostly to the right eye, or to both eyes about equally. Also, cells within a given column respond best to lines of a single orientation.

Figure 6.25 shows what happens when an investigator lowers an electrode into the visual cortex and records from each cell that it reaches. Each red line represents a neuron and shows the angle of orientation of its receptive field. In electrode path A the first series of cells are all in one column and show the same orientation preferences. However, the end of path A invades a column with a different preferred orientation. Electrode path B, which is not perpendicular to the surface of the cortex, crosses through three columns and encounters cells with different properties. In short, the cells within a given column process similar information.

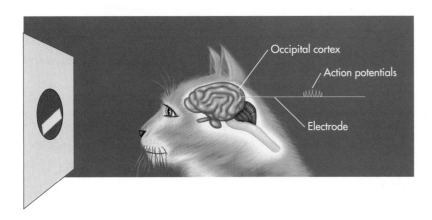
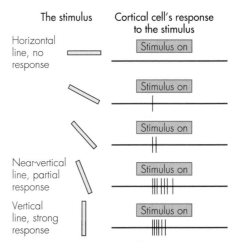

Figure 6.22   Responses of a cat's simple cell to a bar of light presented at varying angles
The short horizontal lines indicate when light is on. *(Source [right]: Adapted from Hubel & Wiesel, 1959)*

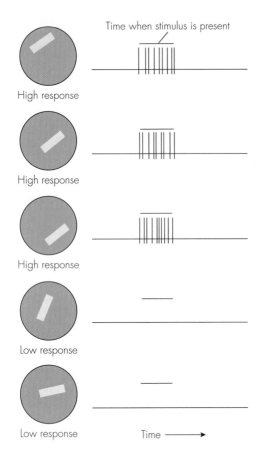

Figure 6.23 The receptive field of a complex cell in the visual cortex
It is like a simple cell in that its response depends on a bar of light's angle of orientation. It is unlike a simple cell in that its response is the same for a bar in any position within the receptive field.

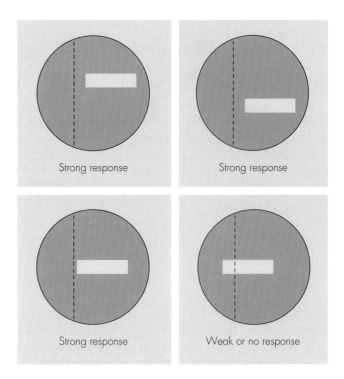

Figure 6.24 The receptive field of an end-stopped cell
The cell responds to a bar in a particular orientation (in this case horizontal) anywhere in its receptive field provided that the bar does not extend into a strongly inhibitory area.

Are Visual Cortex Cells Feature Detectors?

Given that neurons in areas V1 and V2 respond strongly to bar- or edge-shaped patterns, it seems natural to suppose that the activity of such a cell *is* (or at least is necessary for) the perception of a bar, line, or edge. That is, such cells might be **feature detectors**—neurons whose responses indicate the presence of a particular feature.

Supporting the concept of feature detectors is the fact that prolonged exposure to a given visual feature decreases sensitivity to that feature, as if one has fatigued the relevant detectors. For example, if you stare at a waterfall for a minute or more and then look away, the rocks and trees next to the waterfall appear to be flowing upward. This effect, the *waterfall illusion*, suggests that you have fatigued the neurons that detect downward motion, leaving unopposed the detectors that detect the opposite motion. You can see the same effect if you watch your computer screen scroll slowly for about a minute and then stare at an unmoving display.

TRY IT
YOUR
SELF

However, just as a medium-wavelength cone responds somewhat to the whole range of wavelengths, a cortical cell that responds best to one stimulus also responds to many others. The response of any cell is ambiguous unless it is compared to the responses of other cells.

Furthermore, Hubel and Wiesel tested only a limited range of stimuli. Later researchers have tried some other kinds of stimuli and found that a cortical cell that responds well to a single bar or line

also responds, generally even more strongly, to a sine-wave grating of bars or lines:

Different cortical neurons respond best to gratings of different spatial frequencies (i.e., wide bars or nar-

Table 6.3 Summary of Cells in the Primary Visual Cortex

Characteristic	Simple Cells	Complex Cells	End-Stopped Cells
Location	V1	V1 and V2	V1 and V2
Binocular input	Yes	Yes	Yes
Size of receptive field	Smallest	Medium	Largest
Receptive field	Bar- or edge-shaped, with fixed excitatory and inhibitory zones	Bar- or edge-shaped, without fixed excitatory or inhibitory zones; responds to stimulus anywhere in receptive field, especially if moving perpendicular to its axis	Same as complex cell, but with strong inhibitory zone at one end

row bars), and many are very precisely tuned—that is, they respond strongly to one frequency and hardly at all to a slightly higher or lower frequency (DeValois, Albrecht, & Thorell, 1982). Most visual researchers therefore believe that neurons in area V1 respond to spatial frequencies rather than to bars or edges. How do we translate a series of spatial frequencies into perception? From a mathematical standpoint, sine-wave spatial frequencies are easy to work with. In a branch of mathematics called Fourier analysis, it can be demonstrated that a combination of sine waves can produce an unlimited variety of other, more complicated patterns. For example, the graph shown at the top of the following display is the sum of the five sine waves below it:

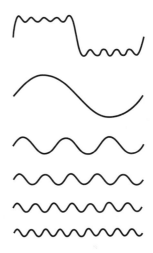

Therefore a series of spatial frequency detectors, some sensitive to horizontal patterns and others to vertical patterns, could represent anything anyone could see. Still, we obviously do not perceive the world as an assembly of sine waves, and the emergence of object perception remains a puzzle (Hughes, Nozawa, & Kitterle, 1996). Indeed the activities of areas V1 and V2 are probably preliminary steps that organize visual material and send it to more specialized areas that actually identify objects (Lennie, 1998).

Shape Analysis Beyond Areas V1 and V2

As visual information goes from the simple cells to the complex cells and then on to areas specialized for further shape analysis, the receptive fields become larger and more and more specialized. One important area for shape analysis is the inferior temporal cortex (see Figure 6.20). Because cells in this area have huge receptive fields, always including the foveal field of vision, their

Gray matter
White matter

Figure 6.25 Columns of neurons in the visual cortex
When an electrode passes perpendicular to the surface of the cortex (first part of A), it encounters a sequence of neurons responsive to the same orientation of a stimulus. (The colored lines show the preferred stimulus orientation for each cell.) When an electrode passes across columns (B, or second part of A), it encounters neurons responsive to different orientations. Column borders are shown here to make the point clear; no such borders are visible in the real cortex. *(Source: Hubel, 1963)*

responses provide almost no information about stimulus location. However, many of these cells do provide detailed information about stimulus shape, responding preferentially to such stimuli as a hand or a face (Desimone, 1991; Desimone, Albright, Gross, & Bruce, 1984). Their responses are insensitive to many distinctions that are critical for other cells. For example, some cells in the inferior temporal cortex respond about equally to a black square on a white background, a white square on a black background, and a square-shaped pattern of dots moving across a stationary pattern of dots (Sáry, Vogels, & Orban, 1993). Face-sensitive cells in macaque monkeys respond equally to a given face in left and right profiles. The ability of such cells to ignore changes in size and direction probably contributes to our capacity for **shape constancy**—the ability to recognize an object's shape even as it approaches or retreats or rotates.

Disorders of Object Recognition

Damage to the pattern pathway of the cortex should lead to specialized deficits in the ability to recognize objects. Neurologists have reported such cases for decades, although they frequently met with skepticism. Now that we understand *how* such specialized defects might arise, we find them easier to accept.

An inability to recognize objects despite otherwise satisfactory vision is called **visual agnosia** (meaning "visual lack of knowledge"). A brain-damaged person might be able to point to visual objects and slowly describe them but fail to recognize what they are. For example, one patient, when shown a key, said, "I don't know what that is; perhaps a file or a tool of some sort." When shown a stethoscope, he said that it was "a long cord with a round thing at the end." When he could not

identify a pipe, the examiner told him what it was. He then replied, "Yes, I can see it now," and pointed out the stem and bowl of the pipe. Then the examiner asked, "Suppose I told you that the last object was not really a pipe?" The patient replied, "I would take your word for it. Perhaps it's not really a pipe" (Rubens & Benson, 1971).

Among several specific types of agnosia, some people can recognize many kinds of complex objects but not faces, and others can recognize faces but not other kinds of objects. One closed-head injury patient could recognize faces of all kinds, including cartoons and face pictures made from objects (Figure 6.26). However, he could not recognize any of the individual objects that composed the face (Moscovitch, Winocur, & Behrmann, 1997).

The opposite disorder—ability to recognize other objects but not faces—is known as **prosopagnosia** (PROSS-oh-pag-NOH-see-ah). As a rule people with prosopagnosia can read and write, and they can recognize familiar people from their voices, so their problem is not an overall loss of vision or memory. When they look at a face, they can describe whether the person is old or young, male or female, but they cannot identify the person, and they are often unsure whether they have ever even seen the face before (Etcoff, Freeman, & Cave, 1991). However, some sort of subtle, unconscious recognition seems to remain. For example, if these patients are given a stack of photographs and asked to memorize which name goes with which face—"this is Ronald Reagan, this is Ronald MacDonald, this is Marilyn Monroe, this is Marilyn Manson . . ."—they memorize correct pairings faster than rearranged ones (Farah, O'Reilly, & Vecera, 1997).

Many people with prosopagnosia also have trouble

Figure 6.26 Faces made from other objects
One man, after a closed-head injury, could recognize these as faces and could point out the eyes, nose, and so forth, but could not identify any of the component objects. He was not even aware that the faces were composed of objects. *(Source: Moscovitch, Winocur, & Behrmann, 1997)*

fMRI Scans

Standard MRI scans (discussed in Methods 5.2, p. 128), record the energy released by water molecules and display details of brain anatomy smaller than a millimeter in diameter, but they don't show changes over time (because the brain has little net flow of water). A modified version of an MRI that enables researchers to view changes over time is **functional magnetic resonance imaging (fMRI)** (J. D. Cohen, Noll, & Schneider, 1993). The fMRI procedure takes advantage of the fact that hemoglobin (the blood protein that binds oxygen) slightly changes its responses to a magnetic field after it has released its oxygen. Because oxygen consumption increases in the brain areas with the greatest activity, researchers can set the fMRI scanner to distinguish between hemoglobin with oxygen and hemoglobin without oxygen and thereby measure the relative activity of various brain areas. Such images have spatial resolution of 1 or 2 mm (almost as good as standard MRI) and temporal resolution of less than a second (see Figure 6.27). Unlike a PET scan, the fMRI procedure does not expose the person to a radiation hazard. Researchers have just

begun to tap the potential of fMRI; it does not have enough resolution to enable neuroscientists to "watch people think," but it brings us closer than we have ever been before.

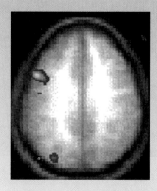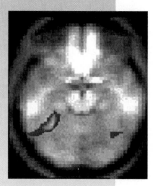

Figure 6.27 An fMRI scan of a human brain
An fMRI produces fairly detailed photos at rates up to about 1 per second. *(Source: Wagner, et al., 1998)*

recognizing different kinds of animals, plants, and cars (Farah, 1990). So the deficit is a general difficulty with complex visual discriminations and not exclusively a problem with faces. Typically, however, the people who cannot recognize faces can still read. Conversely, brain-damaged patients who lose the ability to read seldom complain of trouble in recognizing faces. Evidently the human brain has different mechanisms for

different kinds of pattern perception (Farah, Wilson, Drain, & Tanaka, 1998).

Functional MRI scans (as described in Methods 6.2) show that when people with intact brains recognize faces, activity increases in the inferior temporal cortex, in an area called the *fusiform gyrus* (Figure 6.28), and in part of the prefrontal cortex (McCarthy, Puce, Gore, & Allison, 1997; Ó Scalaidhe, Wilson, & Goldman-Rakic, 1997). The fusiform gyrus also responds to other complex figures that people learn to recognize. For example, when people are shown a series of "greebles," the unfamiliar-looking objects shown in Figure 6.29, at first they have trouble recognizing individual greebles, and the fusiform gyrus responds to them only weakly. As people gain familiarity with them and learn to recognize them, the fusiform gyrus becomes more and more active (Gauthier, Tarr, Anderson, Skudlarski, & Gore, 1999).

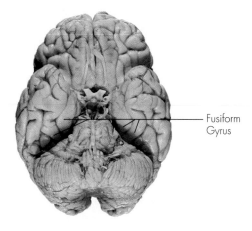

Fusiform Gyrus

Figure 6.28 The fusiform gyrus
This section of the inferior temporal lobe includes cells that become especially active during recognition of faces and similarly complex visual stimuli. *(Source: Courtesy of Dana Copeland)*

Stop & Check

8. How could a researcher determine whether a given neuron in the visual cortex was simple or complex?

9. What is prosopagnosia and what does its existence tell us about separate shape recognition systems in the visual cortex?

Check your answers on page 180.

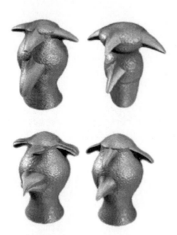

Figure 6.29 "Greebles"
When people are asked to recognize individual greebles or to sort them into "families" of related individuals, at first they have low accuracy. As they practice and improve, the fusiform gyrus becomes more responsive to greebles.
(Source: Gauthier, Tarr, Anderson, Skudlarski, & Gore, 1999)

The Cerebral Cortex: The Color Pathway

Color perception depends mostly on the parvocellular path, which predominates in and near the fovea. A path of cells highly sensitive to color emerges in parts of area V1 known as the *blobs*. (These blob-shaped clusters of neurons can be identified because a chemical called cytochrome oxidase stains them without staining other cells.) The blobs also have cells of the magnocellular path, which contribute to brightness perception. The cells in the blobs then send their output through particular parts of areas V2, V4, and the posterior inferior temporal cortex, as shown in Figure 6.20b.

Several investigators have found that either area V4 or a nearby area is particularly important for color constancy (Hadjikhani, Liu, Dale, Cavanagh, & Tootell, 1998; Zeki, McKeefry, Bartels, & Frackowiak, 1998). Recall from the discussion of the retinex theory that color constancy is the ability to recognize the color of an object even if the lighting changes. Monkeys with damage to area V4 can learn to pick up a yellow object to get food, but cannot find it if the overhead lighting is changed from white to blue (Wild, Butler, Carden, & Kulikowski, 1985). That is, they retain color vision but lose color constancy. In humans also, after damage to an area that straddles the temporal and parietal cortexes, perhaps corresponding to monkey area V4, people recognize and remember colors but lose their color constancy (Rüttiger et al., 1999).

In addition to a role in color vision, area V4 has cells that contribute to visual attention (Leopold & Logothetis, 1996). Animals with damage to V4 have trouble shifting their attention from the larger, brighter, or more prominent stimulus to any less prominent stimulus.

The Cerebral Cortex: The Motion and Depth Pathways

Many of the cells of the magnocellular pathway are specialized for **stereoscopic depth perception,** the ability to detect depth by differences in what the two eyes see. To illustrate, hold a finger in front of your eyes and look at it, first with just the left eye and then just the right eye. Try again, holding your finger at different distances. Note that the two eyes see your finger differently and that the closer your finger is to your face, the greater the difference between the two views. Certain cells in the magnocellular pathway detect the discrepancy between the two views, presumably mediating stereoscopic depth perception. When you look at something with just one eye, the same cells are almost unresponsive.

Structures Important for Motion Perception

A branch of the magnocellular pathway that is specialized for motion perception projects to an area in the middle of the temporal lobe, known as area **MT** (for middle-temporal cortex, also known as area **V5**), and to

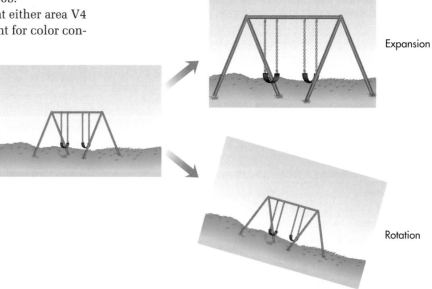

Expansion

Rotation

Figure 6.30 Stimuli that excite certain cells in the dorsal part of area MST
Cells in this area have large receptive fields. They do not respond if a single object moves but do respond if a whole scene expands, contracts, or rotates. That is, such cells respond if the observer moves forward or backward or tilts his or her head.

an adjacent region, area **MST** (medial superior temporal cortex) (see Figure 6.20). The cells in those areas respond selectively to the speed and direction of movement. For example, a particular cell might respond most vigorously to an object moving to the left at 15° of visual arc per second; another cell might respond best to something moving upward at 10° per second. Such cells are almost indifferent to *what* is moving; that is, they respond to a large or small, bright or dark object provided that it is moving in the correct direction at the correct speed (Albright, 1992; Lague, Raiguel, & Orban, 1993).

Especially in area MT, many cells respond best to moving borders within their receptive fields. Cells in the dorsal part of area **MST** respond best to the expansion, contraction, or rotation of a large visual scene, as illustrated in Figure 6.30. That kind of experience occurs when you move forward or backward or tilt your head. These two kinds of cells—the ones that record movement of single objects and the ones that record movement of the entire background—converge their messages onto neurons in the ventral part of area MST, where cells respond whenever an object moves in a certain direction *relative to its background* (K. Tanaka, Sugita, Moriya, & Saito, 1993) (see Figure 6.31).

A cell with such properties is enormously useful in determining the motion of objects. When you move your head from left to right, all the objects in your visual field move across your retina as if the world itself had moved right to left. (Go ahead and try it.) Yet when you do so, the world looks stationary. Indeed all the objects are stationary with respect to one another. But if, while you are moving your head from left to right, some object in your visual field really is moving, cells in the ventral part of area MST in your brain enable you to perceive that movement. Digression 6.1 describes another mechanism that prevents us from confusing eye movements with object movements.

Motion Blindness

Some brain-damaged people become **motion blind,** able to see objects but unable to determine whether they are moving or, if so, in which direction or how fast. Motion-blind people have trouble with the same tasks as monkeys with damage in area MT (Marcar, Zihl, & Cowey, 1997) and probably have damage in that same area (Greenlee, Lang, Mergner, & Seeger, 1995).

One motion-blind patient reported that she felt uncomfortable with people walking around because "people were suddenly here or there but I have not seen them moving." She could not cross a street without help: "When I'm looking at the car first, it seems far

Figure 6.31 Stimuli that excite certain cells in the ventral part of area MST
Cells in this area respond when an object moves relative to its background. They therefore react either when the background is steady and the object moves or when the object is steady and the background moves.

away. But then, when I want to cross the road, suddenly the car is very near." Even such a routine task as pouring coffee became difficult; the flowing liquid appeared to be frozen and unmoving, so she would not stop pouring until she had overfilled the cup (Zihl, von Cramon, & Mai, 1983).

Visual Attention

Recall that cells in the visual cortex receive their direct input from the lateral geniculate, but also receive feedback from other cortical cells. One consequence is that cells responding to one stimulus are partly suppressed when other cells are simultaneously responding to some other stimulus. Try the following: First, focus on the small *x* in the following display. Note that it is easy to perceive the letter *G* to the right. Then focus on the *x* in the second display. Note how much harder it is to see the same letter *G*, even though it is the same distance from the *x* as the first *G*.

TRY IT YOUR SELF

x   G   x H K G P W

Nevertheless you can direct attention to a particular area of your visual field, even without moving your eyes. In the following display, keep your eyes fixated on the central *x*. Then attend to the *G* at the right, and step by step shift your attention clockwise around the circle. Notice how you can indeed "see" different parts of the circle without moving your eyes.

Shifting attention takes about one-third of a second (Müller, Teder-Sälejärvi, & Hillyard, 1998) and is

```
        A
    Z       V
  W           R
  B     x     G
  N           K
    F   J   P
```

associated with increased activity in part of the parietal lobe, suggesting that this area helps direct attention (Gottlieb, Kusunoki, & Goldberg, 1998; Lumer, Friston, & Rees, 1998). The shift of attention increases neural activity in whichever cortical area responds to the attended area. That is, when you attend to the *G* in the display, activity increases in the part of your visual cortex that responds to a point a few degrees to the right of your fixation point. When you shift attention to a different part of your visual field, activity increases in a different part of your visual cortex (Kastner, De Weerd, Desimone, & Ungerleider, 1998; Tootell et al., 1998). Similarly, if you are told to pay attention to color or motion, activity increases in the areas of your visual cortex responsible for color or motion perception (Chawla, Rees, & Friston, 1999). In short, we have ways of increasing activity in the cortical areas that are most relevant to the task at hand.

The Binding Problem Revisited: Visual Consciousness

In Chapter 4 we encountered the unanswered question of how the brain produces a unified experience, even though different senses activate different brain areas. In this chapter we have seen that the same problem applies within a single sensory system. The visual cortex has separate paths for shape, color, and motion, with few links among them. So when you see a brown rabbit hopping, how does your visual cortex know that the brown, the rabbit shape, and the hopping are all part of the same object? And how and where does any of this visual processing become conscious?

I hasten to say that no one knows. But researchers are filling in a few pieces of the puzzle. One interesting piece is that consciousness of one aspect of a stimulus sometimes influences perception of another aspect. Examine the two degraded drawings in Figure 6.32. Most people perceive a face, at least after they look at the images for a while. If you perceive a face and flip between one image and the other, you will perceive the face as rotating in three dimensions. But someone who does not perceive a face perceives the flip from one image to the other as a meaningless two-dimensional flutter (Ramachandran, Armel, Foster, & Stoddard, 1998).

Another key point is that some visual processing takes place without being conscious. We infer, for ex-

ample, that visual processing is unconscious at least up to the level of the lateral geniculate. The evidence is this: If someone flashes a light in front of just one of your eyes in a dark room, you can detect the light, but you do not know which eye saw it. We are not conscious of which eye receives information. The information from the left eye is separate from that of the right eye as far as the lateral geniculate, but the two eyes merge information in the cortex. Because we are not conscious of which eye got the information, it is probably not the lateral geniculate that is conscious (Crick & Koch, 1995).

It is also possible to have a very limited amount of visual processing without *any* of it being conscious. For example, if you had damage to much of area V1 of your visual cortex, you would lose visual experience in much of what had been your visual field. If someone flashed a light in that blind field, you would insist that you saw nothing. However, if someone flashed a light and asked you to point to it or to turn your eyes toward it, you would be surprisingly accurate—surprising even to yourself (Bridgeman & Staggs, 1982; Weiskrantz, Warrington, Sanders, & Marshall, 1974). This ability to localize visual objects within an apparently blind visual field is called **blindsight**.

The explanation for blindsight remains controversial. Even after damage to the lateral geniculate or visual cortex, other branches of the optic nerve deliver some visual information to the superior colliculus (in the midbrain) and several other areas (Figure 6.15). Perhaps the superior colliculus controls unconscious visually guided movements (Cowey & Stoerig, 1995; Moore, Rodman, Repp, & Gross, 1995). However, if the superior colliculus were capable of doing so, we might expect all people with visual cortex damage to show blindsight. Some do, but many do not, and many who do show blindsight have it for only part of their "blind" visual

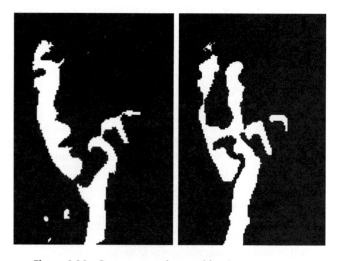

Figure 6.32 Do you recognize an object?
People who recognize this rough schematic drawing as a face interpret a flip from one face to the other as a three-dimensional rotation of the face. Those who don't see a face perceive only meaningless two-dimensional movement.
(Source: Ramachandran, Armel, Foster, & Stoddard, 1998)

Suppressed Vision During Eye Movements

The temporal cortex has cells that distinguish between moving objects and visual changes due to head movements. An additional mechanism prevents confusion or blurring during eye movements. Before the explanation, try this demonstration: Look at yourself in a mirror and focus on your left eye. Then shift your focus to your right eye. *(Please do this now.)* Did you see your eyes move? No, you did not. *(I said to try this. I bet you didn't. None of this is going to make any sense unless you try the demonstration!)*

TRY IT YOUR SELF

Why didn't you see your eyes move? Your first impulse is to say that the movement was too small or too fast. Wrong. Try looking at someone else's eyes while he or she focuses first on your left eye and then on your right. You *do* see the other person's eyes move. So an eye movement is neither too small nor too fast for you to see.

One reason why you do not see your own eyes move is that your brain actually shuts down its visual cortex during eye movements! In effect certain brain areas that monitor eye movements send the visual cortex the message, "We're about to move the eye muscles, so take a break for the next split second, or you will see nothing but a blur anyway." Regardless of what is in the visual field—in fact, even if the person is in total darkness—neural activity and blood flow in the visual cortex decrease during eye movements. The shutdown is especially prominent in the magnocellular pathway (Burr, Morrone, & Ross, 1994; Paus, Marrett, Worsley, & Evans, 1995).

---

field (Schärli, Harman, & Hogben, 1999; Wessinger, Fendrich, & Gazzaniga, 1997). An alternative explanation is that tiny islands of healthy tissue remain within an otherwise damaged visual cortex, not large enough to provide conscious perception, but nevertheless enough for blindsight (Fendrich, Wessinger, & Gazzaniga, 1992). Yet another possibility is that after damage to area V1, other cortical areas get enough visual input from the thalamus to produce blindsight (Moore, Rodman, & Gross, 1998). In any case the point is that a brain with no conscious vision can make a few useful responses to visual information.

As you will rightly infer, researchers do not yet understand much about visual consciousness. The dominant hypothesis is that consciousness is distributed over several cortical areas (Zeki, 1998). Perhaps we bind different aspects together because of synchronized simultaneous activity, as discussed in Chapter 4. Still, the fundamental basis of this process remains a challenge to future researchers.

Module 6.2

In Closing: Coordinating Separate Visual Pathways

The main points of this module have been as follows:

- Each cell in the visual system has a receptive field, a portion of the visual field to which it responds.

- Each cell in the visual system responds to specific features of a stimulus in its receptive field, such as shape, color, or movement.

- Separate pathways in the visual system attend to different aspects of the visual system.

- Certain kinds of brain damage can impair specific aspects of visual perception.

Another main point inherent in all of this is that a study of the physiology of individual cells in the brain may eventually tell us how we perceive visual scenes. The questions are daunting, but optimism runs high. Questions that were once the realm of philosophical speculation are now subject to scientific investigation.

Summary

1. The optic tracts of the two eyes join at the optic chiasm, where half of the axons from each eye cross to the opposite side of the brain. Most of the axons then travel to the lateral geniculate nucleus of the thalamus, which communicates with the visual cortex. (p. 163)

2. Each neuron in the visual system has a receptive field, an area of the visual field to which it is connected. Light in the receptive field excites or inhibits the neuron depending on the light's location, color, movement, and so forth. (p. 163)

3. Lateral inhibition is a mechanism by which stimulation in any area of the retina suppresses the responses in neighboring areas, thereby enhancing the contrast at light–dark borders. (p. 166)

4. The mammalian vertebrate visual system has a partial division of labor. In general the parvocellular system is specialized for perception of color and fine details; the magnocellular system is specialized

for perception of depth, movement, and overall patterns. (p. 168)

5. One system in the cerebral cortex is responsible for shape perception. Within the primary visual cortex, neuroscientists distinguish simple cells, which have a fixed excitatory and inhibitory field, from complex cells, which respond to a light pattern of a particular shape regardless of its exact location. End-stopped cells are similar to complex cells, except that they have a strong inhibitory field at one end. (p. 170)

6. Within the cortex, cells with similar properties cluster together in columns perpendicular to the surface of the cortex. (p. 171)

7. Neurons sensitive to shapes or other visual aspects may or may not act as feature detectors. In particular, cells of area V1 are highly responsive to spatial frequencies, even though we are not subjectively aware of spatial frequencies in our visual perception. (p. 172)

8. Damage to specific areas beyond the primary visual cortex can impair specific aspects of vision, such as facial recognition, color constancy, and motion perception. (pp. 174–177)

9. When two or more objects are present in the visual field, the cortex's response to one decreases its response to the other. However, a signal to attend to one of them increases that response. (p. 177)

10. Somehow we bind different aspects of visual sensation as a single object, even though shape, color, and motion are processed in different brain areas. Consciousness of some aspects of vision can influence perception of other aspects. Nevertheless, a limited amount of visual perception can occur without conscious awareness. (p. 178)

Answers to *Stop and Check* Questions

1. It starts with the ganglion cells in the eye. Most of its axons go to the lateral geniculate nucleus of the thalamus; smaller numbers go to the hypothalamus, superior colliculus, and elsewhere. (p. 163)

2. They become larger because each cell's receptive field is made by convergence of cells at an earlier level. (p. 167)

3. The receptor excites both the bipolar cells and the horizontal cell. The horizontal cell inhibits the same

bipolar cell that was excited plus additional bipolar cells in the surround. (p. 167)

4. It produces more excitation than inhibition for the nearest bipolar cells. For surrounding bipolar cells it produces only inhibition. The reason is that the receptor excites a horizontal cell, which inhibits all bipolar cells in the area. (p. 167)

5. In the parts of your retina that look at the long white arms, each neuron is maximally inhibited by input on two of its sides (either above and below or left and right). In the crossroads each neuron is maximally inhibited by input on all four sides. Therefore the response in the crossroads is decreased compared to that in the arms. (p. 167)

6. Neurons of the parvocellular system have small cell bodies with small receptive fields, are located mostly in and near the fovea, and are specialized for detailed and color vision. Neurons of the magnocellular system have large cell bodies with large receptive fields, are located in all parts of the retina, and are specialized for perception of large patterns and movement. (p. 169)

7. Researchers could use fMRI, EEG, or other recording methods to see whether activity was high in your primary visual cortex. (p. 169)

8. First identify a stimulus, such as a horizontal line, that stimulates the cell. Then shine the stimulus at several points in the cell's receptive field. If the cell responds only in one location, it is a simple cell. If it responds in several locations, it is a complex cell. (p. 175)

9. Prosopagnosia is the inability to recognize faces. Its existence implies that the cortical mechanism for identifying faces (and some other complex stimuli) is different from the mechanism for identifying words and many other visual stimuli. (p. 175)

Thought Question

After a receptor cell is stimulated, the bipolar cell receiving input from it shows an immediate burst of response. A fraction of a second later, the bipolar's response rate decreases, even though the stimulation from the receptor cell remains constant. How can you account for that decrease? (*Hint*: What does the horizontal cell do?)

Development of the Visual System

Suppose that you had lived all your life in the dark. And then today, for the first time, you came out into the light and looked around. Would you be able to make any sense of what you saw?

Presumably you did have this experience once—on the day you were born. We do not know how much sense babies make of what they see; presumably the world looks fairly mysterious to them. Yet within a few months to a year or so, they can recognize familiar faces, they can crawl toward toys they see, and they may even show signs of recognizing themselves in a mirror. How do they develop these impressive skills?

As we shall see, visual development depends on the formation and selection of synapses: Once axons get to approximately their correct targets, they form many synapses, only some of which survive. The selection of synapses depends partly on experience.

Infant Vision

When cartoonists show us an infant character, they draw the eyes large in proportion to the head. Infant eyes look large because they approach full size sooner

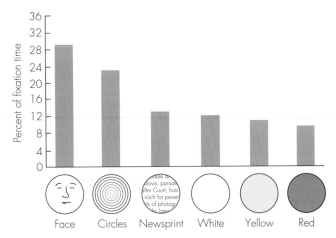

Figure 6.33 Amount of time infants spend looking at various patterns
Even in the first 2 days after birth, infants look more at faces and other complex patterns than at a plain color or incomprehensible newsprint. *(Source: Based on Fantz, 1963)*

than the rest of the head does. There is a good reason: Infant eyes form an enormous number of complex attachments to the brain. If the eyes grew substantially after making those attachments and then sent new axons to the brain, the brain would have to reorganize its connections continually to use the additional information.

Human newborns have better developed sensory capacities than psychologists once imagined. Newborns less than 2 days old spend more time looking at faces, circles, or stripes than at a patternless display (see Figure 6.33). However, because the receptors in and around the fovea are immature at birth (Abramov et al., 1982), infants see better in the periphery than in the center of vision.

Another special feature of infant vision is that infants have trouble shifting their attention. For example, infants less than 4 months old may stare at a highly attractive display, such as twirling dots on a computer screen, and be unable to shift their gaze (M. H. Johnson, Posner, & Rothbart, 1991). Occasionally they stare at an object until they begin crying in distress! Slightly older infants can look away from the most attractive display in the room, but they quickly shift their gaze back to it (Clohessy, Posner, Rothbart, & Veccra, 1991). Not until about age 6 months can an infant explore one object and then shift attention to something else.

To examine visual development in more detail, investigators turn to studies of animals. The research in this area has greatly expanded our understanding of brain development and has helped alleviate certain human abnormalities.

Effects of Experience on Visual Development

Developing axons of the visual system approach their targets by following chemical gradients, as discussed in Chapter 5. In newborn kittens and monkeys, the lateral geniculate and visual cortex already resemble those of adults (Gödecke & Bonhoeffer, 1996; Horton & Hocking, 1996), and they can develop many of their normal properties even if the eyes are damaged (Rakic & Lidow, 1995; Shatz, 1996). Normal experience is necessary, however, for fine-tuning the connections and even for maintaining the approximately correct connections that developed before birth.

Effects of Early Lack of Stimulation of One Eye

What would happen if an animal could see with one eye and not the other beginning early in life? For mammals with both eyes pointed in the same direction—cats and primates—most neurons in the visual cortex receive **binocular** input (stimulation from both eyes). As soon as a kitten opens its eyes at about age 9 days, each neuron responds to approximately corresponding areas in the two retinas—that is, areas that ordinarily focus on the same point in space (Figure 6.34).

If an experimenter sutures one eyelid shut so that a kitten sees with only the other eye for the first 4 to 6 weeks of life (see Figure 6.35a), cells in the visual cortex receive only infrequent random activity from the deprived eye and their synapses become unresponsive

to it (Rittenhouse, Shouval, Paradiso, & Bear, 1999). The kitten becomes almost blind in the deprived eye (Wiesel, 1982; Wiesel & Hubel, 1963).

Effects of Early Lack of Stimulation of Both Eyes

What happens if *both* eyes are kept shut for the first few weeks? We might expect the kitten to become blind in both eyes, but it does not (Figure 6.35b). Evidently, when one eye remains shut during early development, the active synapses from the open eye displace the inactive synapses from the closed eye. If neither eye is active, no axon displaces any other. For at least 3 weeks, the kitten's cortex remains normally responsive to both eyes. If the eyes remain shut still longer, the cortical responses become more sluggish and lose their crisp, sharp receptive fields (Crair, Gillespie, & Stryker, 1998). That is, to the extent that they respond at all, they respond to visual stimuli in many orientations.

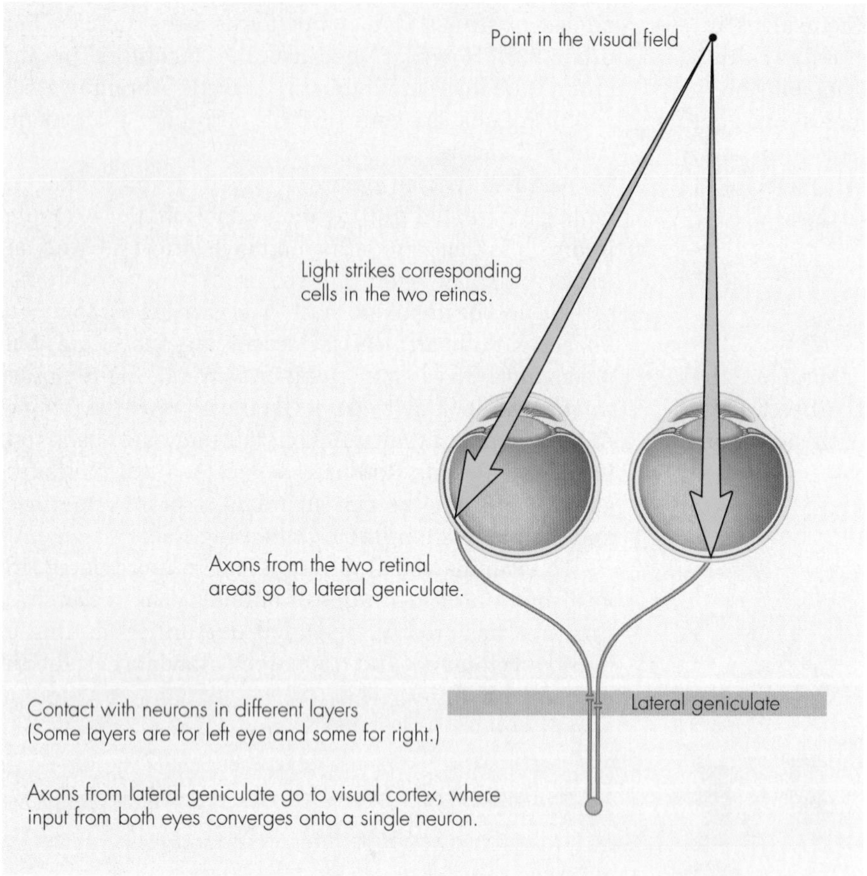

If someone were born blind and got to see later, would the new vision make any sense? Sometimes nature does this experiment. Some human infants are born blind because of a problem that can be corrected surgically; they have no visual experience until an operation, perhaps years later. After the operation they do respond somewhat to visual stimuli; for example, they can identify the brightness of a light and its approximate location. However, they have trouble identifying shapes or recognizing objects (Valvo, 1971). Presumably their cortical cells lack the sharply tuned receptive fields that make such recognition possible. Many such people find their newly gained vision to be almost useless and prefer to keep their eyes shut much of the time.

Because the effects of abnormal experiences on cortical development depend on age, researchers identify a **sensitive period** or **critical period,** a stage of development when experiences have a particularly strong and long-lasting influence. The length of the sensitive period varies from one species to another and from one part of the cortex to another (Crair & Malenka, 1995); it lasts a bit longer during complete visual deprivation—for

Figure 6.34 The anatomical basis for binocular vision in cats and primates
Light from a point in the visual field strikes one point in the left retina and another point in the right retina. Then those two retinal areas send their axons to separate layers of the lateral geniculate. In turn, neurons in the lateral geniculate send axons to the visual cortex, where the inputs from the two eyes finally converge onto a single cell. That cell is connected (via the lateral geniculate) with corresponding areas of the two retinas.

Labels in figure:
Point in the visual field
Light strikes corresponding cells in the two retinas.
Axons from the two retinal areas go to lateral geniculate.
Contact with neurons in different layers (Some layers are for left eye and some for right.)
Axons from lateral geniculate go to visual cortex, where input from both eyes converges onto a single neuron.
Lateral geniculate

example, if a kitten is kept in total darkness—than in the presence of limited experience (Kirkwood, Lee, & Bear, 1995). Experience after the sensitive period can also alter cortical neurons, but the effects are smaller and slower to develop (Darian-Smith & Gilbert, 1995; Sugita, 1996).

Stop & Check

1. What happens to neurons in a kitten's visual cortex if one of its eyes is closed during its early development? What if both eyes are closed?

Check your answers on page 186.

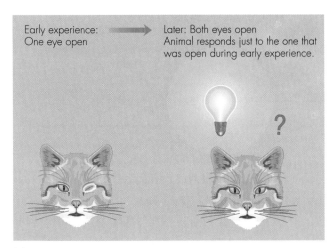

(a)

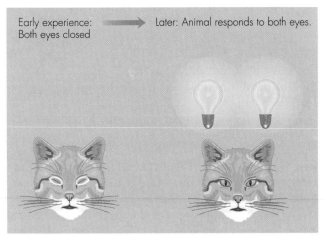

(b)

Figure 6.35 Effects of early visual deprivation
After deprivation of vision in one eye early in life, a kitten becomes responsive only to the active eye. After deprivation of vision in both eyes, it remains somewhat sensitive to both eyes, although responses gradually become sluggish and unselective. That is, cortical cells decrease their response to an inactive input, but they decrease it even more if an active input competes with the inactive one.

Restoration of Response After Early Deprivation of Vision

After the cortical neurons have become insensitive to the inactive eye, can experience restore their sensitivity? It depends. A cat that simply lives a normal life with both eyes open does not become responsive to the deprived eye. However, if the previously active eye is covered for a few months, the axons from that eye to the visual cortex shrink their branching, and the axons from the previously shut eye expand, restoring some responsiveness to both eyes (Antonini, Gillespie, Crair, & Stryker, 1998).

This animal research has clear relevance to the human condition called **lazy eye,** also known by the fancier term **amblyopia ex anopsia,** in which a child ignores the vision in one eye, sometimes even letting it drift in a different direction from the other eye. The animal results imply that the best way to facilitate normal vision in the ignored eye is to prevent the child from using the active eye. A physician puts a patch over the active eye, and the child gradually increases his or her attention to vision in the previously ignored eye. Eventually the child is permitted to use both eyes together. Although an eyepatch is likely to be most effective if it is used in early childhood, we do not know exactly how long the sensitive period lasts in humans.

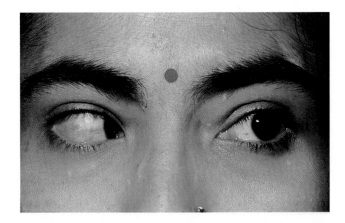

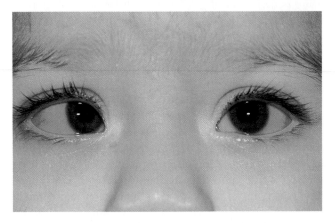

Two examples of "lazy eye."

Uncorrelated Stimulation in Both Eyes

Almost every neuron in the human visual cortex responds to approximately corresponding areas of both eyes. (Neurons that respond to the extreme left or extreme right of the visual field respond to only one eye.) By comparing the slightly different inputs from the two eyes, you achieve stereoscopic depth perception, a powerful method of perceiving distance.

Stereoscopic depth perception requires the brain to detect **retinal disparity,** the discrepancy between what the left eye sees and what the right eye sees. But how do cortical neurons adjust their connections to detect retinal disparity? Genetic instructions could not by themselves be sufficient; different individuals have slightly different head sizes, and the genes cannot know exactly how far apart the two eyes will be. The fine-tuning of binocular vision must depend on experience.

And indeed it does. Suppose an experimenter sets up a procedure in which a kitten can see with the left eye one day, the right eye the next day, and so forth. The kitten therefore receives the same amount of stimulation in both eyes, but it never sees with both eyes at the same time. After several weeks, almost every neuron in the visual cortex responds to one eye or the other, but not to both. The kitten therefore cannot detect retinal disparities and has no stereoscopic depth perception.

Similarly, suppose a kitten has defective or damaged eye muscles so that its two eyes cannot focus in the same direction at the same time. In this case both eyes are active simultaneously, but no neuron in the visual cortex gets the same message from both eyes at the same time. Again the result is that each neuron in the visual cortex chooses one eye or the other and becomes fully responsive to it, ignoring the other eye (Blake & Hirsch, 1975; Hubel & Wiesel, 1965).

A similar phenomenon occurs in humans. Certain children are born with **strabismus,** a condition in which the eyes do not point in the same direction. Such children do not develop stereoscopic depth perception; they perceive depth no better with two eyes than they do with one. Muscle surgery in adulthood to correct the strabismus does not improve their depth perception (Banks, Aslin, & Letson, 1975; D. E. Mitchell, 1980) presumably because the sensitive period for cortical development has passed.

The apparent mechanism is that each cortical cell increases its responsiveness to groups of axons with synchronized activity (Singer, 1986). For example, if a portion of the left retina frequently focuses on the same object as some portion of the right eye, then axons from those two retinal areas frequently carry synchronous messages, and a cortical cell strengthens its synapses with both axons. However, if the eye muscles are damaged, or if one eye at a time is always covered, the cortical cell does not receive simultaneous inputs from the two eyes, and it strengthens its synapses with axons from only one eye (usually the contralateral one).

Recall from Chapter 5 that postsynaptic cells promote the survival of certain axons by delivering nerve growth factor (NGF) or other neurotrophins. The same process apparently occurs in the visual cortex. In one experiment investigators closed one eye of infant ferrets. Ordinarily that procedure causes cells in the lateral geniculate and visual cortex to become responsive only to the open eye; however, when researchers supplied the brain with extra amounts of the neurotrophin NT-4, all cells remained responsive to both eyes (Riddle, Lo, & Katz, 1995). Apparently visual experience produces its effects by causing cortical neurons to release neurotrophins to only the active axons; if the brain is bathed in extra neurotrophins, all the axons survive equally, regardless of experience.

Stop & Check

2. What is "lazy eye" and how can it be treated?

3. What early experience is necessary to maintain binocular input to the neurons of the visual cortex?

4. Does an injection of NGF increase or decrease the effects of abnormal visual experience? Why?

Check your answers on page 186.

Early Exposure to a Limited Array of Patterns

If a kitten spends its entire early sensitive period wearing goggles with horizontal lines painted on them (Figure 6.36), nearly all its visual cortex cells become responsive to horizontal lines (Stryker & Sherk, 1975; Stryker, Sherk, Leventhal, & Hirsch, 1978). Even after months of later normal experience, the cat ignores vertical lines and objects (D. E. Mitchell, 1980).

What happens if human infants are exposed mainly to vertical or horizontal lines instead of both equally? You might wonder how such a bizarre thing could happen. No parents would let an experimenter subject their child to such a procedure, and it never happens accidentally in nature. Right?

Wrong. In fact, it probably happened to you! About 70% of all infants have **astigmatism,** a blurring of vision for lines in one direction (such as horizontal, vertical, or one of the diagonals). Astigmatism is caused by an asymmetric curvature of the eyes (Howland & Sayles, 1984). The prevalence of astigmatism declines to about 10% in 4-year-old children as a result of normal growth.

You can informally test yourself for astigmatism with Figure 6.37. Do the lines in some directions look faint or fuzzy? If so, rotate the page. You will notice that the appearance

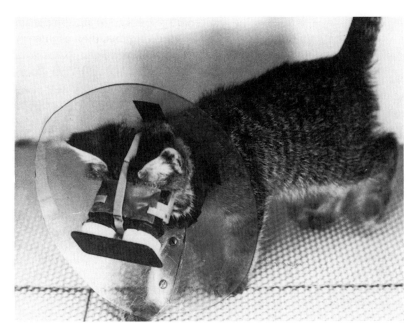

Figure 6.36 Procedure for restricting a kitten's visual experience during early development
For a few hours a day, the kitten wears goggles that show just one stimulus, such as horizontal stripes or diagonal stripes. For the rest of the day, the kitten stays with its mother in a dark room without the mask. *(Source: Photo courtesy of Helmut V. Hirsch)*

of the lines depends on their position. If you wear corrective lenses, try this demonstration with and without them. If you see a difference in the lines only without your lenses, then the lenses have corrected your astigmatism.

If your eyes had strong astigmatism during the sensitive period for the development of your visual cortex, you saw lines more clearly in one direction than in another direction. If your astigmatism was not

Figure 6.37 An informal test for astigmatism
Do the lines in one direction look darker or sharper than the other lines do? If so, notice what happens when you rotate either the page or your head. The lines really are identical; certain lines appear darker or sharper because of the shape of your eye. If you wear corrective lenses, try this demonstration both with and without your lenses.

corrected early, then the cells of your visual cortex probably became more responsive to the kind of lines you saw more clearly, and you will continue throughout life to see lines in other directions as slightly faint or blurry, even if your eyes are now perfectly spherical (Freedman & Thibos, 1975). However, if you began wearing corrective lenses before age 3 to 4 years, you thereby improved your adult vision (Friedburg & Klöppel, 1996). The moral of the story: Children should be tested for astigmatism early and given corrective lenses as soon as possible.

Lack of Seeing Objects in Motion

What happens if kittens grow up without seeing anything move? You can imagine the difficulty of arranging such a world; the kitten's head would move, even if nothing else did. Max Cynader and Garry Chernenko (1976) used an ingenious procedure: They raised kittens in an environment illuminated only by a strobe light that flashed eight times a second for 10 microseconds each. In effect the kittens' visual world was a series of still photographs. After 4 to 6 months in this odd environment, each kitten's visual cortex had neurons that responded normally to shapes but few neurons that responded strongly to moving stimuli. In short, the kittens had become motion blind.

Effects of Blindness on the Cortex

Finally, what happens if someone has no visual stimulation throughout the entire sensitive period? In one experiment kittens were reared without any visual experience. A section of their parietal lobe that ordinarily responds only to visual stimuli became responsive to auditory or touch stimuli, enabling the kittens to localize sounds with greater accuracy than normal cats do (Rauschecker, 1995).

Similarly, in people who become blind early in life, certain parts of the visual cortex become responsive to auditory and touch stimuli, including Braille symbols. The auditory and touch information invades more of the visual cortex in people who became blind at birth or in infancy than in those who became blind as teenagers or adults (L. G. Cohen et al., 1999). As discussed in Chapter 5, the brain is more plastic when young. Presumably this observation relates to the fact that people who begin learning Braille as adults do not become as adept as those who started in childhood.

In Closing: Developing Vision

The nature–nurture issue arises in one disguise or another in almost every area of psychology. In vision, consider what happens when you look out your window and see trees, people, and buildings. How did you know these objects were trees, people, and buildings? In fact, how did you know they were objects? How did you know which objects were close and which were distant? Were you born understanding vision (nature) or did you have to learn to understand it (nurture)? The main message of this module has been that understanding vision requires a complex mixture of nature and nurture. We are indeed born with a certain amount of understanding, but we need experience to maintain, improve, and refine it. As usual, the influences of heredity and environment are not fully separable.

Summary

1. Human infants have nearly normal peripheral vision at birth, but foveal vision matures later. In mammals the eyes approach their full size earlier than the rest of the head does. (p. 181)

2. The cells in the visual cortex of infant kittens have nearly normal properties. However, visual experience is necessary to maintain and fine-tune those properties. For example, if a kitten has visual experience in one eye and not in the other during the early sensitive period, its cortical neurons become responsive only to the open eye. (p. 182)

3. Cortical neurons become unresponsive to axons from the inactive eye mainly because of competition from axons from the active eye. If both eyes are closed, cortical cells remain somewhat responsive to axons from both eyes, although that response becomes sluggish and unselective as the weeks of deprivation continue. (p. 182)

4. If cortical cells have become unresponsive to an eye because it was inactive during the early sensitive period, normal visual experience later does not restore normal responsiveness. However, prolonged closure of the previously active eye can increase the response to the previously inactive eye. (p. 183)

5. Ordinarily most cortical neurons of cats and primates respond to portions of both retinas. However, if the two eyes are seldom open at the same

time during the sensitive period, or if they consistently focus in different directions, then each cortical neuron becomes responsive to the axons from just one eye and not the other. (p. 184)

6. If a kitten sees only horizontal or vertical lines during its sensitive period, most of the neurons in its visual cortex become responsive only to lines in that direction. For the same reason, children who have a strong astigmatism early in life may have a permanently decreased responsiveness to one kind of line or another. (p. 184)

7. Those who do not see motion early in life become permanently disabled at perceiving motion. (p. 185)

8. In people who are completely deprived of vision throughout early life, parts of the visual cortex become more responsive to auditory and tactile stimulation, enabling greater perception of Braille. (p. 185)

Answers to *Stop and Check* Questions

1. If one eye is closed during early development, the cortex becomes unresponsive to it. If both eyes are closed, cortical cells remain somewhat responsive to both eyes for several weeks and then gradually become sluggish and unselective in their responses. (p. 183)

2. "Lazy eye" is inattentiveness to one eye, in most cases an eye that does not move in conjunction with the other eye. It can be treated by closing or patching over the active eye, forcing the child to use the ignored eye. (p. 184)

3. To maintain binocular responsiveness, cortical cells must receive simultaneous activity from both eyes fixating on the same object at the same time. (p. 184)

4. NGF decreases the effects of abnormal experience by facilitating the survival of all axons. (p. 184)

Thought Questions

1. A rabbit has eyes on the sides of its head instead of in front. Would you expect rabbits to have many cells with binocular receptive fields—that is, cells that respond to both eyes? Why or why not?

2. Would you expect the cortical cells of a rabbit to be just as sensitive to the effects of experience as are the cells of cats and primates? Why or why not?

Chapter Ending
Key Terms and Activities

Terms

astigmatism (p. 184)

binocular (p. 182)

bipolar cell (p. 155)

blind spot (p. 156)

blindsight (p. 178)

coding (p. 152)

color constancy (p. 160)

color vision deficiency (p. 161)

complex cell (p. 170)

cone (p. 156)

dorsal stream (p. 169)

end-stopped cell (p. 171)

feature detector (p. 172)

fovea (p. 154)

functional magnetic resonance imaging (fMRI) (p. 175)

ganglion cell (p. 155)

horizontal cell (p. 163)

hypercomplex cell (p. 171)

inferior temporal cortex (p. 173)

lateral geniculate nucleus (p. 163)

lateral inhibition (p. 166)

law of specific nerve energies (p. 153)

lazy eye (or amblyopia ex anopsia) (p. 183)

magnocellular neuron (p. 168)

motion blindness (p. 177)

MST (p. 177)

MT (or area V5) (p. 176)

negative color afterimage (p. 159)

opponent-process theory (p. 159)

optic nerve (p. 155)

parvocellular neuron (p. 168)

photopigment (p. 157)

primary visual cortex (or area V1) (p. 168)

prosopagnosia (p. 174)

psychophysical observations (p. 158)

pupil (p. 153)

reception (p. 152)

receptive field (p. 163)

receptor potential (p. 152)

retina (p. 153)

retinal disparity (p. 184)

retinex theory (p. 160)

rod (p. 156)

secondary visual cortex (or area V2) (p. 168)

sensitive period or critical period (p. 182)

shape constancy (p. 174)

simple cell (p. 170)

stereoscopic depth perception (p. 176)

strabismus (p. 184)

transduction (p. 152)

trichromatic theory (or Young-Helmholtz theory) (p. 158)

ventral stream (p. 169)

visual agnosia (p. 174)

visual field (p. 163)

Suggestions for Further Reading

Gazzaniga, M. S. (Ed.). (1995). *The cognitive neurosciences.* Cambridge: MIT Press. A collection of 92 chapters by various researchers, including 14 chapters on various aspects of vision.

Hubel, D. H. (1988). *Eye, brain, and vision.* New York: Scientific American Library. Excellent source by cowinner of the Nobel Prize. See especially chapter 9.

Zeki, S. (1993). *A vision of the brain.* Oxford: Blackwell. Excellent discussion by a leading researcher.

Web Sites to Explore

You can go to the Biological Psychology Study Center and click on these links. While there, you can also check for suggested articles available on InfoTrac. The Biological Psychology Internet address is:
http://psychology.wadsworth.com/book/kalatbiopsych7e/

http://www.color-vision.com
Includes much information about color vision.

http://www.cim.mcgill/ca/~image529/TA529/Image529_98/projects97/31_Khurana/Visualcortex.html
Excellent graphics and information about the mammalian visual cortex.

http://www.psy.vanderbilt.edu/faculty/blake/Demos/TS/TS.html
Demonstrates how the visual system can use the coherent motion of many points to infer an object.

The Nonvisual Sensory Systems

Main Ideas

1. Our senses have evolved not to give us complete information about all the stimuli in the world but to give us the most useful information.

2. Different sensory systems code information in different ways. As a rule, the activity in a single sensory axon is ambiguous by itself; its meaning depends on its relationship to a pattern across a population of axons.

According to a Native American saying, "A pine needle fell. The eagle saw it. The deer heard it. The bear smelled it" (Herrero, 1985). Different species are sensitive to different kinds of information. Bees and many other insects can see short-wavelength (ultraviolet) light that humans cannot; conversely, humans see long-wavelength (red) light that insects cannot. Bats locate insect prey by echoes from sonar waves that they emit at 20,000 to 100,000 hertz (Hz, cycles per second), well above the range of adult human hearing (Griffin, Webster, & Michael, 1960). Certain cells in a frog's eyes respond selectively to small, dark, moving objects such as insects (Lettvin, Maturana, McCulloch, & Pitts, 1959). The ears of the green tree frog, *Hyla cinerea,* are highly sensitive to sounds at two frequencies—900 and 3000 Hz—the frequencies found in the adult male's mating call (Moss & Simmons, 1986).

Humans' visual and auditory abilities are broader and less specialized than those of frogs, perhaps because a wider range of stimuli is biologically more relevant to us than to them. However, humans too have important sensory specializations. For example, our sense of taste can alert us to the bitter taste of certain poisons even at very low concentrations (Richter, 1950; Schiffman & Erickson, 1971), whereas it has virtually no response to substances such as cellulose that are neither helpful nor harmful to us. Our olfactory systems are unresponsive to gases that would be useless for us to detect (nitrogen, for example) and highly responsive to such biologically useful stimuli as the smell of rotting meat. Thus this chapter concerns not how our sensory systems enable us to perceive reality, but how they process biologically useful information.

Opposite:
Smell, taste, hearing, and other senses receive less research attention than vision does, but they are essential to our lives.

Module 7.1

Audition

If a tree falls in a forest where no one is present to hear it, does it make a sound? The answer depends on what we mean by "sound." If we define sound simply as a vibration, then of course a falling tree makes a sound. However, we usually define sound as a psychological phenomenon, a vibration that some organism hears. By the standard definition, a vibration is not a sound unless someone hears it.

The human auditory system enables us to hear not only falling trees but also the birds singing in the branches and the wind blowing through the leaves. Some blind people learn to click their heels as they walk and use the echoes to locate obstructions. Our auditory systems are amazingly well adapted for detecting and interpreting useful information.

Sound and the Ear

Sound waves are periodic compressions of air, water, or other media. When a tree falls, both the tree and the ground vibrate, setting up sound waves in the air that strike the ears. If something hit the ground on the moon, where there is no air, people would not hear it—unless, perhaps, they put their ears to the ground.

Physical and Psychological Dimensions of Sound

Sound waves vary in amplitude and frequency. The **amplitude** of a sound wave is its intensity. A very intense compression of air, such as that produced by a bolt of lightning, produces sound waves of great amplitude, which a listener hears as great loudness. **Loudness,** the perception of intensity, is not the same as amplitude. If the amplitude of a sound doubles, its perceived loudness increases but it does not double. Many factors influence loudness; for example, a rapidly talking person sounds louder than slow music of the same physical amplitude. So if you complain that television advertisements sound louder than the program, no one should contradict you. Loudness is your perception, and if something *sounds* louder to you, it *is* louder.

The **frequency** of a sound is the number of compressions per second, measured in hertz (Hz, cycles per second). **Pitch** is a perception closely related to frequency. As a rule, the higher the frequency of a sound, the higher its pitch. Figure 7.1 illustrates the amplitude and frequency of sounds. The height of each wave corresponds to amplitude, and the number of waves per second corresponds to frequency.

Most adult humans can hear air vibrations ranging from about 15 Hz to somewhat less than 20,000 Hz. Children can hear high-frequency sounds much better than adults, whose ability to perceive high frequencies decreases with age and with exposure to loud noises (B. A. Schneider, Trehub, Morrongiello, & Thorpe, 1986). Mice and other small mammals can hear still higher pitches.

Structures of the Ear

Rube Goldberg (1883–1970) drew cartoons that featured enormously complicated, far-fetched inventions.

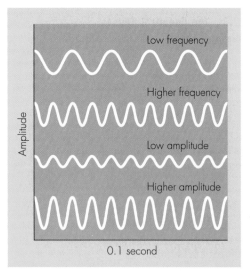

Figure 7.1   Four sound waves
The time between the peaks determines the frequency of the sound, which we experience as pitch. Here the top line represents five sound waves in 0.1 second, or 50 Hz—a very low-frequency sound that we experience as a very low pitch. The other three lines represent 100 Hz. The vertical extent of each line represents its amplitude or intensity, which we experience as loudness.

For example, a person's tread on the front doorstep would pull a string that raised a cat's tail, awakening the cat, which would then chase a bird that had been resting on a balance, which would swing up to strike a doorbell. The functioning of the ear may remind you of a Rube Goldberg device because sound waves are transduced into action potentials through a many-step, roundabout process. Unlike Goldberg's inventions, however, the ear actually works.

Anatomists distinguish among the outer ear, the middle ear, and the inner ear (see Figure 7.2). The outer ear includes the **pinna,** the familiar structure of flesh and cartilage attached to each side of the head. By altering the reflections of sound waves, the pinna helps us locate the source of a sound. Rabbits' large movable pinnas enable them to localize sound sources even more precisely.

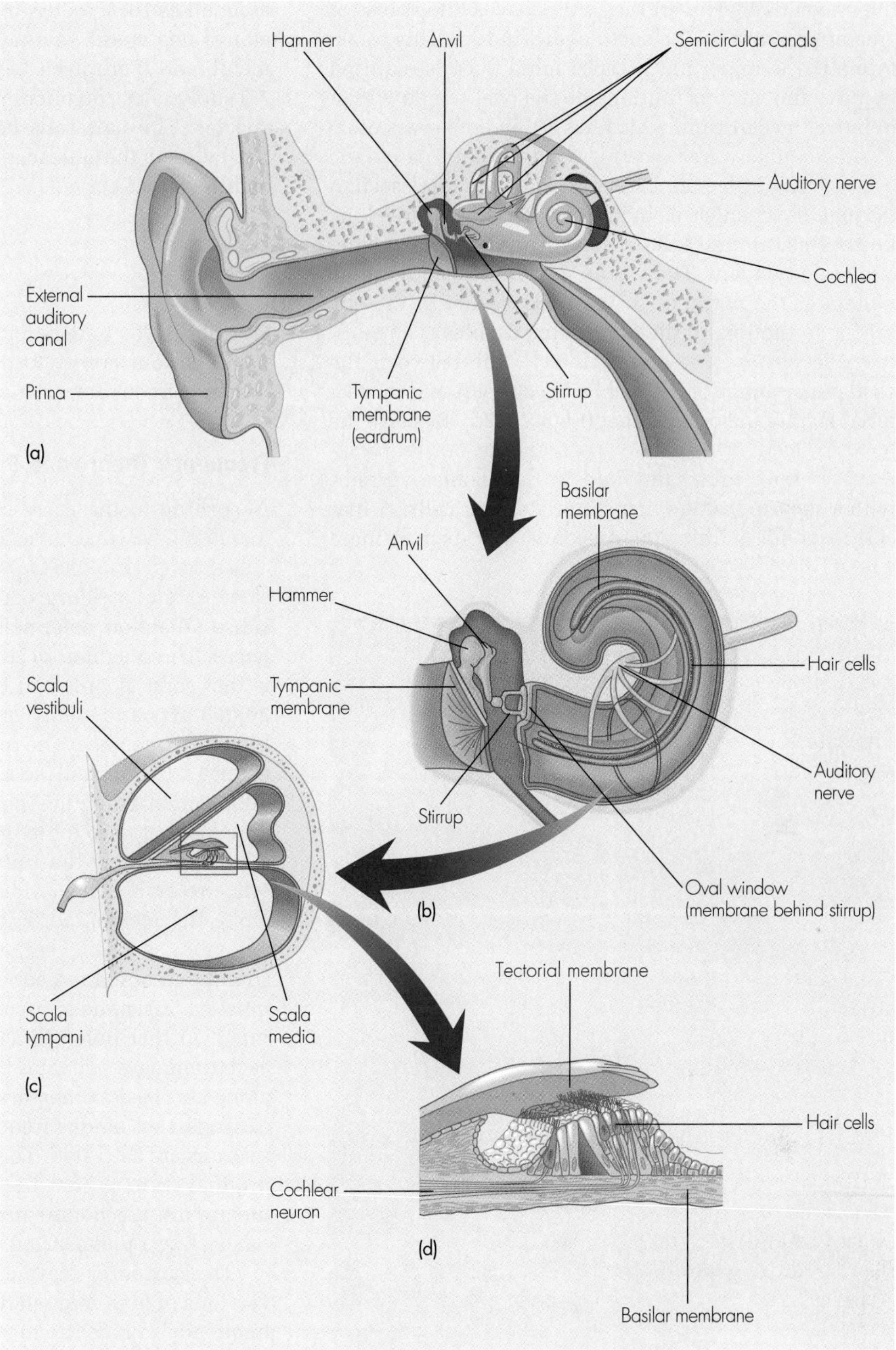

After sound waves pass through the auditory canal (Figure 7.2), they strike the **tympanic membrane,** or eardrum, in the middle ear. The tympanic membrane vibrates at the same frequency as the sound waves that strike it. The tympanic membrane is attached to three tiny bones that transmit the vibrations to the **oval window,** a membrane of the inner ear. These bones are sometimes known by their English names (hammer, anvil, and stirrup) and sometimes by their Latin names (malleus, incus, and stapes). The tympanic membrane is about 20 times larger than the footplate of

Figure 7.2 Structures of the ear
When sound waves strike the tympanic membrane in (**a**), they cause it to vibrate three tiny bones—the hammer, anvil, and stirrup—that convert the sound waves into stronger vibrations in the fluid-filled cochlea (**b**). Those vibrations displace the hair cells along the basilar membrane in the cochlea. (**c**) A cross section through the cochlea. The array of hair cells in the cochlea is known as the organ of Corti. (**d**) A closeup of the hair cells.

the stirrup, connected to the oval window. As in a hydraulic pump, the vibrations of the tympanic membrane are transformed into more forceful vibrations when they reach the smaller stirrup. The net effect of the system is to convert the sound waves into waves of greater pressure on the small oval window. This transformation is important because more force is required to move the viscous fluid inside the oval window than to move the eardrum, which has air on both sides of it.

In the inner ear is a snail-shaped structure called the **cochlea** (KOCK-lee-uh, Latin for "snail"). A cross section through the cochlea, as in Figure 7.2c, shows three long fluid-filled tunnels: the scala vestibuli, scala media, and scala tympani. The stirrup makes the oval window vibrate at the entrance to the scala vestibuli, thereby setting in motion all the fluid in the cochlea. The auditory receptors, known as **hair cells,** lie between the basilar membrane of the cochlea on one side and the tectorial membrane on the other (Figure 7.2d). Because the **tectorial membrane** is more rigid and the **basilar membrane** more flexible, the fluid in the cochlea vibrates with a shearing action that stimulates hair cells. A hair cell responds within microseconds to a displacement

as small as 10^{-10} meter (0.1 nanometer, about the diameter of one atom), thereby opening ion channels in its membrane (Fettiplace, 1990; Hudspeth, 1985). Figure 7.3 shows electron micrographs of the hair cells of three species. The hair cells have excitatory synapses onto the cells of the auditory nerve, which is part of the eighth cranial nerve.

Pitch Perception

Our ability to understand speech or enjoy music depends on our ability to differentiate among sounds of different frequencies. How do we do so?

Frequency Theory and Place Theory

According to the early **frequency theory,** the basilar membrane vibrates in synchrony with a sound, causing auditory nerve axons to produce action potentials at the same frequency. For example, a sound at 50 Hz would cause 50 action potentials per second in the auditory nerve. The downfall of this theory in its simplest form is that some people can distinguish frequencies up to 20,000 Hz, and many small animals can hear even higher frequencies. The refractory period of a neuron is about 1/1000 second, so a neuron can fire no more than 1000 action potentials per second, and it cannot keep up even that pace for long.

According to the **place theory,** the basilar membrane resembles the strings of a piano in that each area along the membrane is tuned to a specific frequency and vibrates whenever that frequency is present. (If you sound one note loud enough with a tuning fork or any musical instrument, you can make the piano string tuned to that note vibrate.) According to this theory, each frequency activates the hair cells at only one place along the basilar membrane, and the nervous system distinguishes among frequencies on the basis of which neurons are activated. The downfall of this theory in its original form is that the various parts of the basilar membrane are bound together, and no one part resonates like a piano string.

The currently prevalent theory combines modified versions of both frequency and place theories. For low-frequency sounds (up to at least 100 Hz—more than an octave below middle C in music), the basilar membrane does vibrate in synchrony with the sound waves (in accordance with the frequency theory), and auditory nerve axons generate one action potential per wave. Weak sounds activate few neurons, whereas stronger sounds activate more. Thus, at low frequencies, the frequency of impulses identifies the pitch, and the number of firing cells identifies the loudness.

No auditory neuron can fire in synchrony with a sound above 1000 Hz because of the refractory period; between 100 Hz and 1000 Hz, a neuron can fire in syn-

Figure 7.3 Hair cells from the auditory systems of three species
(**a, b**) Hair cells from a frog sacculus, an organ that detects ground-borne vibrations. (**c**) Hair cells from the cochlea of a cat. (**d**) Hair cells from the cochlea of a fence lizard. Kc = kinocilium, one of the components of a hair bundle.
(Source: Hudspeth, 1985)

chrony but frequently doesn't. At the lower part of this range, it occasionally misses a wave; at higher frequencies it fires on every second, third, fourth, or later wave. Its action potentials are phase-locked to the peaks of the sound waves (that is, they occur at the same phase in the sound wave), as illustrated here:

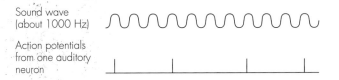

Other auditory neurons also produce action potentials that are phase-locked with peaks of the sound wave, but they can be out of phase with one another:

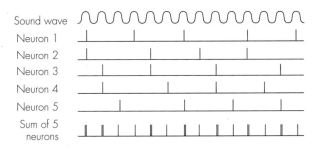

If we consider the auditory nerve as a whole, we find that each sound wave of moderately high fre-

quency produces a volley of impulses by various fibers; that is, with a tone of a few hundred Hz, each wave excites at least a few auditory neurons. According to the **volley principle** of pitch discrimination, the auditory nerve as a whole can have volleys of impulses up to about 5000 per second, even though no individual axon can approach that frequency by itself (Rose, Brugge, Anderson, & Hind, 1967). (Beyond about 5000 Hz even staggered volleys of impulses can't keep pace with the sound waves.) Neuroscientists assume that these volleys contribute to pitch perception, although no one knows quite how the brain uses the information.

Most human hearing takes place below 5000 Hz, the approximate limit of the volley principle. For example, middle C in music is only 264 Hz, and the highest key on a piano is 4224 Hz. Frequencies above 5000 Hz sound squeaky and play little role in music or speech. We do, nevertheless, hear them, using a mechanism similar to the place theory.

At its **base,** where the stirrup meets the cochlea, the basilar membrane is stiff and narrow (about 0.15 mm). It is wider (0.5 mm) and only one-hundredth as stiff at the other end of the cochlea, the **apex** (von Békésy, 1956; Yost & Nielsen, 1977) (see Figure 7.4). You may be surprised that the basilar membrane is narrowest at the base, where the cochlea itself is widest. At the base the cochlea has a wide bony shelf attached to the basilar membrane. When a vibration strikes the basilar membrane, it sets up a **traveling wave.** As the wave travels along the membrane, it produces some displacement at all points, but the amount of displacement varies because of differences in the thickness and stiffness of the membrane.

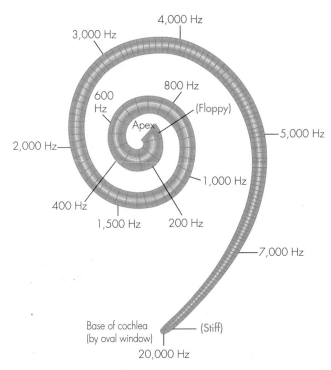

Figure 7.4 The basilar membrane of the human cochlea
High-frequency sounds produce their maximum displacement near the base. Low-frequency sounds produce their maximum displacement near the apex.

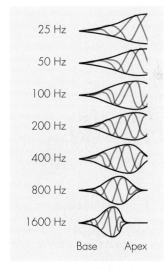

Figure 7.5 Traveling waves in the basilar membrane set up by different frequencies of sound
Note that the peak displacement is closer to the base of the cochlea for high frequencies and is toward the apex for lower frequencies. In reality the peak of each wave is much narrower than shown here.

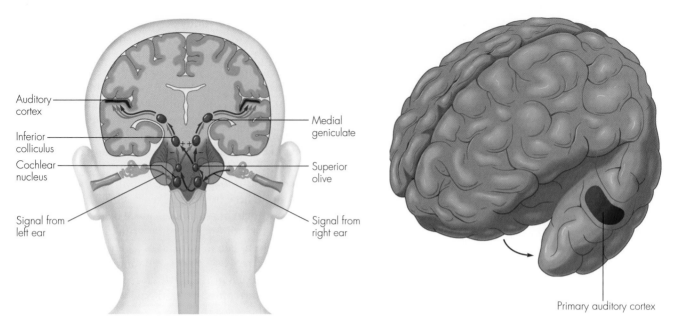

Figure 7.6 Route of auditory impulses from the receptors in the ear to the auditory cortex
The cochlear nucleus receives input from the ipsilateral ear only (the one on the same side of the head). All later stages have input originating from both ears.

Vibrations at different frequencies set up traveling waves that peak at different points along the basilar membrane, as shown in Figures 7.4 and 7.5. The traveling wave for a low-frequency vibration peaks at or near the apex, where the membrane is large and floppy. For progressively higher frequencies the point of maximum displacement is closer to the base. In fact the highest frequencies produce practically no displacement of the membrane near the apex. The waveforms in Figure 7.5 are drawn broadly to be easily visible. In healthy tissues, however, the waves are sharply defined, falling rapidly on both sides of the maximum displacement (Zwislocki, 1981). Only the neurons near the point of maximum displacement respond significantly to a tone.

Stop & Check

1. Through what mechanism do we perceive low-frequency sounds (up to about 100 Hz)?

2. How do we perceive middle-frequency sounds (100 to 5000 Hz)?

3. How do we perceive high-frequency sounds (above 5000 Hz)?

4. Which would stimulate a larger portion of the basilar membrane—a low-frequency sound or a high-frequency sound? Why?

Check your answers on page 198.

Pitch Perception in the Cerebral Cortex

Information from the auditory system passes through several subcortical structures, with an important cross-over between the superior olive and inferior colliculus that enables each hemisphere of the forebrain to get its major auditory input from the opposite ear (Glendenning, Baker, Hutson, & Masterton, 1992). The information ultimately reaches the primary auditory cortex in the temporal lobes, as shown in Figure 7.6. Within the primary auditory cortex, each cell responds best to one tone, and the cells preferring a given tone cluster together. That is, the auditory cortex provides a kind of map of the sounds—researchers call it a *tonotopic map*—so that the cortical area with the greatest response indicates what sound or sounds are heard. The general principle is the same for all mammals, but the studies would be more difficult to perform with humans. Figure 7.7 shows the results for gerbils (Scheich & Zuschratter, 1995).

Someone with massive damage to the primary visual cortex becomes blind. In contrast people with similar damage to the primary auditory cortex do not become deaf. They can hear and respond to simple sounds reasonably well unless the damage extends into subcortical brain areas (Tanaka, Kamo, Yoshida, & Yamadori, 1991). Damage to the primary auditory cortex mainly impairs people's ability to recognize combinations or sequences of sounds, such as in music or speech. Evidently the cortex is not necessary for all hearing, but just for advanced processing of it.

Just as the visual cortex has a ventral "what" pathway and a dorsal "where" pathway, the auditory cortex also has a ventral pathway in the prefrontal cortex representing what the sound represents and a dorsal pathway representing where it originated in space (Romanski, Tian, Mishkin, Goldman-Rakic, & Rauschecker, 1999). Apparently it is a general principle that the ner-

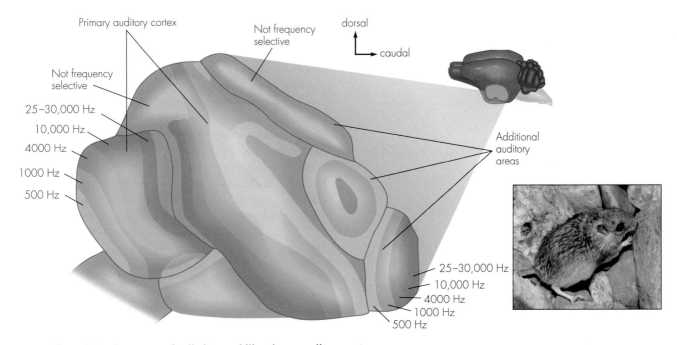

Figure 7.7 Responses of cells in a gerbil's primary auditory cortex
The color of each area indicates the approximate frequency of tone that produces the greatest response. Note that the neurons are arranged in a gradient, with cells responding to low-frequency tones at one end and cells responding to high-frequency tones at the other end. Note also that the gerbil cortex has several separate representations of the auditory world, each presumably serving a different function. *(Source: Adapted from Scheich & Zuschratter, 1995)*

vous system analyzes different aspects of a stimulus in different locations.

Hearing Loss

Complete deafness is rare. About 99% of hearing-impaired people can hear at least certain kinds of loud noises. We distinguish two categories of hearing impairment: conductive deafness and nerve deafness.

Conductive deafness, or **middle-ear deafness,** occurs if the bones of the middle ear fail to transmit sound waves properly to the cochlea. Such deafness can be caused by diseases, infections, or tumorous bone growth near the middle ear. Conductive deafness is sometimes temporary. If it persists, it can be corrected either by surgery or by hearing aids that amplify the stimulus. Because people with conductive deafness have a normal cochlea and auditory nerve, they hear their own voices, which can be conducted through the bones of the skull directly to the cochlea, bypassing the middle ear. Because they hear themselves and not others, they may complain that others are talking too softly.

Nerve deafness, or **inner-ear deafness,** results from damage to the cochlea, the hair cells, or the auditory nerve. It can occur in any degree and may be confined to one part of the cochlea, in which case someone cannot hear certain sound frequencies, such as the high frequencies. Hearing aids cannot compensate for extensive nerve damage, but they can be designed to help people who have lost receptors in a portion of the cochlea.

Nerve deafness can be inherited (Wang et al., 1998), or it can develop from a variety of prenatal problems or disorders of early childhood (Cremers & van Rijn, 1991; Robillard & Gersdorff, 1986), including:

- Exposure of one's mother to rubella (German measles), syphilis, or other diseases or toxins during pregnancy
- Inadequate oxygen to the brain at the time of birth
- Inadequate activity of the thyroid gland
- Certain diseases, including multiple sclerosis and meningitis
- Childhood reactions to certain drugs, including aspirin
- Repeated exposure to loud noises

Many people with nerve deafness experience **tinnitus** (tin-EYE-tus)—frequent or constant ringing in the ears. Tinnitus is common in old age, probably because so many older people have lost much of their high-frequency hearing. At least in some cases, tinnitus is due to a phenomenon like phantom limb, discussed in Chapter 5. Recall the example in which someone has an arm amputated, and then the axons reporting facial sensations invade the brain areas previously sensitive to the arm. Now stimulation of the face produces a sensation of a phantom arm. Similarly, damage to part of the cochlea is like an amputation; the brain no longer gets its normal input, and axons representing other parts of the body may invade a brain area previously responsive to sounds (in most cases high-frequency sounds).

Several patients have been reported who hear ringing in their ears whenever they move their jaws (Lockwood et al., 1998). Presumably axons representing the lower face invaded these patients' auditory cortex.

Stop & Check

5. What are the two major categories of hearing loss? For which type is a hearing aid generally more successful?

Check your answers on page 200.

Localization of Sounds

You are walking alone when suddenly you hear a loud noise. You want to know *what* produced the noise (friend or foe), but equally you want to know *where* the sound originated (so you can approach or escape it). Determining the direction and distance of a sound requires a comparison between the responses of the two ears—which are in effect just two points in space. And yet this system is accurate enough for you to turn almost immediately toward a sound, and for owls to locate mice in the middle of the night (Konishi, 1995).

One cue for localizing sound is the difference in intensity between the ears. For high-frequency sounds, with a wavelength shorter than the width of the head,

the head creates a *sound shadow* (Figure 7.8), making the sound louder for the closer ear. In adult humans this mechanism produces accurate sound localization for frequencies above 2000 to 3000 Hz. Another method of localization is the difference in *time of arrival* at the two ears. A sound coming from directly in front of a person reaches both ears at the same time. A sound coming directly from the side reaches the closer ear about 600 microseconds (ms) before the other. Sounds coming from intermediate locations reach the two ears at delays between 0 and 600 ms. Time of arrival is most useful for localizing sounds with a distinct, sudden onset. Most birds' alarm calls increase gradually in loudness, making them difficult for a predator to localize.

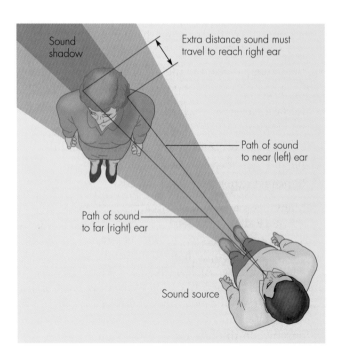

Figure 7.8 Differential loudness as a cue for sound localization
The sound shadow shown does not include the effects of diffraction, or "bending" of sound waves around the head.
(Source: After Lindsay & Norman, 1972)

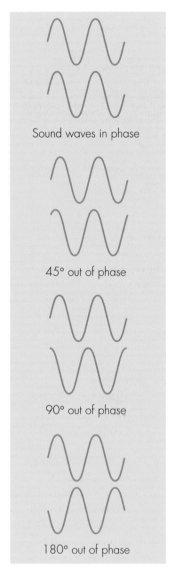

Figure 7.9 Sound waves can be in phase or out of phase
Sound waves that reach the two ears in phase are localized as coming from directly in front of (or behind) the hearer. The more out of phase the waves, the farther the sound source is from the body's midline.

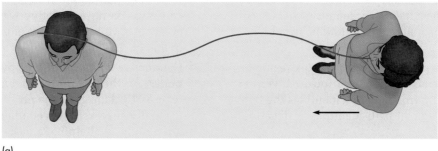

(a)

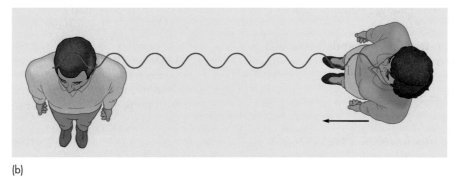

(b)

Figure 7.10 **Phase differences between the ears as a cue for sound localization**
Note that a low-frequency tone (**a**) arrives at the ears slightly out of phase. The ear for which the receptors fire first (here the person's left ear) is interpreted as being closer to the sound. If the difference in phase between the ears is small, then the sound source is close to the center of the body. However, with a high-frequency sound (**b**) the phase differences become ambiguous. The person cannot tell which sound wave in the left ear corresponds to which sound wave in the right ear.

Another cue is the *phase difference* between the ears. Every sound wave has phases with two consecutive peaks 360° apart. Figure 7.9 shows sound waves that are in phase and 45°, 90° or 180° out of phase. If a sound originates to the side of the head, the sound wave strikes the two ears out of phase, as shown in Figure 7.10. How much out of phase depends on the frequency of the sound and the size of the head. Phase differences provide information that is useful for localizing sounds with frequencies up to about 1500 Hz in humans.

In short, humans localize low frequencies by phase differences and high frequencies by loudness differences. We can localize a sound of any frequency by its time of onset if the onset is sudden enough.

The usefulness of phase differences and loudness differences depends on the size of the head (Masterton, Heffner, & Ravizza, 1969). Small animals such as mice, with their ears close together, detect neither phase differences nor loudness differences in low-frequency sounds. They are much better at localizing very high-frequency sounds (for which a small head casts a good sound shadow), and many species have evolved sensitivity to frequencies of 40,000 Hz or higher. Elephants, which can easily localize low-frequency sounds, have an upper hearing limit of just 10,000 Hz (Heffner & Heffner, 1982). These findings underscore a point made at the beginning of this chapter: Each species is most sensitive to the information that is most useful to it.

Stop *&* **Check**

6. Which method of sound localization is more effective for an animal with a small head? Which is more effective for an animal with a large head? Why?

Check your answers on page 200.

Module 7.1

In Closing: Functions of Hearing

Evolution has adapted the human auditory system to the highly complex process of language, and we sometimes forget that the original, primary function of hearing has to do with simpler but extremely important issues: What do I hear? Where is it? Is it coming closer? Is it a potential mate, a potential enemy, potential food, or something irrelevant? The organization of the auditory system is well suited to resolving these questions.

Summary

1. We detect the pitch of low-frequency sounds by the frequency of action potentials in the auditory system. At intermediate frequencies we detect volleys

of responses across many receptors. We detect the pitch of the highest frequency sounds by the area of greatest response along the basilar membrane. (p. 194)

2. Each cell in the primary auditory cortex responds best to a particular frequency of tones. A ventral pathway in the prefrontal cortex identifies the type of sound and a dorsal path identifies its location. (p. 196)

3. Deafness may result from damage to the nerve cells or to the bones that conduct sounds to the nerve cells. (p. 197)

4. We localize high-frequency sounds according to differences in loudness between the ears. We localize low-frequency sounds on the basis of differences in phase. (p. 198)

Answers to *Stop and Check* Questions

1. At low frequencies the basilar membrane vibrates in synchrony with the sound waves, and each responding axon in the auditory nerve sends one action potential per sound wave. (p. 196)

2. At intermediate frequencies no single axon fires an action potential for each sound wave, but different axons fire for different waves, and so a volley (group) of axons fires for each wave. (p. 196)

3. At high frequencies the sound sets up a traveling wave that causes maximum vibration at one point along the basilar membrane. The receptors attached at that point respond vigorously. (p. 196)

4. A low-frequency sound would stimulate all of the basilar membrane because the whole membrane vibrates in synchrony with a low-frequency sound. A

high-frequency sound would stimulate less of it because it sets up a traveling wave that produces a sharp peak in just one spot along the basilar membrane. (p. 196)

5. Conductive deafness (caused by problems with the bones of the middle ear) and nerve deafness (caused by damage to the nerves). Hearing aids are generally successful for conductive deafness; they are not always helpful in cases of nerve deafness. (p. 198)

6. Animals with a small head localize sounds mainly by differences in loudness, because the ears are not far enough apart for differences in onset time to be very large. Animals with a large head localize sounds mainly by differences in onset time, because their ears are far apart and well suited to noting differences in phase or onset time. (p. 199)

Thought Questions

1. Why do you suppose that the human auditory system evolved sensitivity to sounds in the range of 20 to 20,000 Hz instead of some other range of frequencies?

2. The text explains how we might distinguish loudness for low-frequency sounds. How might we distinguish loudness for a high-frequency tone?

3. The medial part of the superior olive (a structure in the medulla) is critical for sound localization based on phase differences. The lateral part of the superior olive is critical for localization based on loudness. Which part of the superior olive would you expect to be better developed in mice? In elephants?

Module 7.2

The Mechanical Senses

The next time you turn on your radio or stereo set, place your hand on its surface. The vibrations you feel in your hand are the same vibrations you hear.

If you practiced enough, could you learn to "hear" the vibrations with your fingers? No, they would remain just vibrations. If an earless species had enough time, might its vibration detectors evolve into sound detectors? Yes! In fact, that is what happened. Primitive animals had touch receptors that ultimately evolved into our organs of hearing. But we also retained receptors responsive to mechanical stimulation.

The *mechanical senses*—called that because they respond to pressure, bending, or other distortions of a receptor—include touch, pain, and other body sensations, as well as vestibular sensation, a system specialized to detect the position and movement of the head. Audition is a mechanical sense also because the hair cells are modified touch receptors. However, we have considered audition separately because of its complexity and great importance to humans.

Vestibular Sensation

Try this demonstration: Try to read this text while you jiggle your head up and down, back and forth. You will find that you can read it fairly easily. Now hold your head steady and jiggle the book up and down, back and forth. Suddenly you can hardly read it at all. Why?

When you move your head, the **vestibular organ** adjacent to the cochlea monitors each movement and directs compensatory movements of your eyes. When your head moves left, your eyes move right; when your head moves right, your eyes move left. Effortlessly you keep your eyes focused on what you want to see (Brandt, 1991). When you move the page, however, the vestibular organ cannot keep your eyes on target. Sensations from the vestibular organ detect the direction of tilt and the amount of acceleration of the head. We are seldom aware of our vestibular sensations except under unusual conditions such as riding a roller coaster; they are nevertheless critical for guiding eye movements and maintaining balance.

The anatomy of the vestibular organ, shown in Figure 7.11, consists of two *otolith organs* (the *saccule* and *utricle)* and three semicircular canals. Like the hearing receptors, the vestibular receptors are modified touch receptors. One otolith organ has a horizontal patch of hairs; the other has a vertical patch. Calcium carbonate particles called *otoliths* lie next to the hair cells. When the head tilts in different directions, the otoliths push against different sets of hair cells and excite them (Gresty, Bronstein, Brandt, & Dieterich, 1992).

The three **semicircular canals,** oriented in three different planes, are filled with a jellylike substance and lined with hair cells. An acceleration of the head in any plane causes the jellylike substance in one of these canals to push against the hair cells. Action potentials initiated by cells of the vestibular system travel through part of the eighth cranial nerve to the brain stem and cerebellum. (The eighth cranial nerve contains both an auditory component and a vestibular component.)

1. Someone with damage to the vestibular system has trouble reading street signs while walking. Why?

Check your answer on page 210.

Somatosensation

The **somatosensory system,** the sensation of the body and its movements, is not one sense but many. We can distinguish the shape of an object (discriminative touch), deep pressure, cold, warmth, pain, tickle (see Digression 7.1), and the position and movement of joints.

Somatosensory Receptors

The skin is packed with a variety of somatosensory receptors. Some of the major receptor types found in mammalian skin are shown in Figure 7.12; their probable functions are listed in Table 7.1 on page 204 (Iggo & Andres, 1982). However, each receptor contributes in

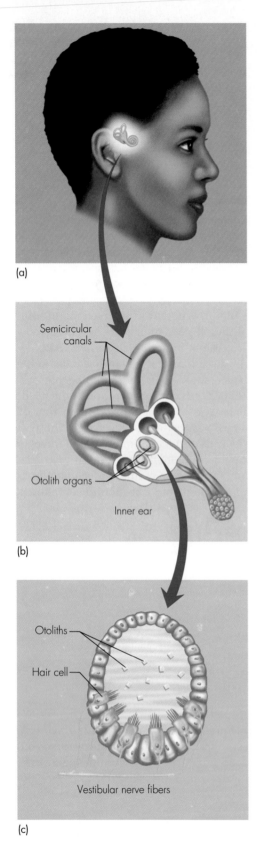

(a)

(b)

Semicircular canals

Otolith organs

Inner ear

(c)

Otoliths

Hair cell

Vestibular nerve fibers

Figure 7.11 Structures for vestibular sensation
(a) Location of the vestibular organs. (b) Structures of the vestibular organs. (c) Cross section through an otolith organ. Calcium carbonate particles, called otoliths, press against different hair cells depending on the direction of tilt and rate of acceleration of the head.

some degree to several kinds of somatosensory experience. Many respond to more than one kind of stimulus, such as touch and temperature. Others (not shown on the list) respond to deep stimulation, joint movement, or muscle movement.

A touch receptor may be a simple bare neuron ending (such as many pain receptors), an elaborated neuron ending (Ruffini endings and Meissner's corpuscles), or a bare ending surrounded by nonneural cells that modify its function (Pacinian corpuscles). Some of the more sensitive areas of skin, such as the fingertips, have as many as 350 touch cells per square millimeter of surface.

One example of a receptor is the Pacinian corpuscle, which detects sudden displacements or high-frequency vibrations on the skin (see Figure 7.13). Inside the onionlike outer structure is a neuron membrane. When mechanical pressure bends the membrane, its resistance to sodium flow decreases, and sodium ions enter, depolarizing the membrane (Loewenstein, 1960). Only a sudden or vibrating stimulus can bend the membrane; the onionlike outer structure provides mechanical support that resists gradual or constant pressure on the skin.

We need practice to use touch information effectively, just as we do for vision or hearing. In one study the whiskers of infant rats were trimmed daily until the rats were 45 days old. After their whiskers grew back, the rats learned to use them to feel surfaces and discriminate rough from smooth, but they never learned to distinguish one rough surface from another, as normally experienced rats do (Carvell & Simons, 1996).

Input to the Spinal Cord and the Brain

Information from touch receptors in the head enters the central nervous system (CNS) through the cranial nerves. Information from receptors below the head enters the spinal cord and passes toward the brain through the 31 spinal nerves (see Figure 7.14), including 8 cervical nerves, 12 thoracic nerves, 5 lumbar nerves, 5 sacral nerves, and 1 coccygeal nerve. Each spinal nerve has a sensory component and a motor component (to the muscles).

Each spinal nerve *innervates* (connects to) a limited area of the body. The skin area connected to a single sensory spinal nerve is called a dermatome (see Figure 7.15). For example, the third thoracic nerve (T3) innervates a strip of skin just above the nipples as well as the underarm area. But the borders between dermatomes are not so distinct as Figure 7.15 implies; there is actually an overlap of one-third to one-half between adjacent pairs.

The sensory information that enters the spinal cord travels in well-defined pathways toward the brain, with different kinds of information, such as touch and temperature, taking different routes and projecting to dif-

Tickle

Here is an example of an experience that we hardly understand at all: Why is there such a thing as tickling? If someone rapidly and repeatedly fingers your armpit, your neck, or the soles of your feet, you may start laughing. (People vary in how strongly they respond to tickle and which spots are most ticklish.) Chimpanzees respond to similar sensations with bursts of panting that resemble laughter. And yet tickling is unlike humor. Most people do not enjoy being tickled for very long, and certainly not by a stranger. If one joke makes you laugh, you are more likely than usual to laugh at the next joke. But after someone tickles you, you are neither more nor less likely than usual to laugh at a joke (Harris, 1999). So why do we laugh at all in response to tickle? For that matter, why do we laugh in response

to humor? We know that laughter serves as a social signal, telling others that you are likely to be playful or cooperative. But the underlying mechanisms of laughter are not well understood.

Why can't you tickle yourself? The answer may be similar to why you can't startle yourself. When you touch yourself, your brain compares the resulting stimulation to the "expected" stimulation and generates a relatively small response in the somatosensory cortex and elsewhere. When someone else touches you, the response is much stronger (Blakemore, Wolpert, & Frith, 1998). Evidently the brain gets messages from motor areas concerning what you are going to do, and those messages subtract from the touch sensations you actually receive.

---

ferent parts of the thalamus and cerebral cortex (Dykes, Sur, Merzenich, Kaas, & Nelson, 1981). The various areas of the somatosensory thalamus send their impulses to different areas of the somatosensory cortex, located in the parietal lobe. Two parallel strips in the somatosensory cortex respond mostly to touch on the skin; two other parallel strips respond mostly to deep pressure and movement of the joints and muscles

(Kaas, 1983). In short, various aspects of somatosensation remain at least partly separate all the way from the receptors to the cortex. Along each strip of somatosensory cortex, different subareas respond to different areas of the body; that is, the somatosensory cortex acts as a map of body location, as shown in Figure 4.21, p. 105.

The somatosensory cortex receives input primarily from the contralateral side of the body, although many

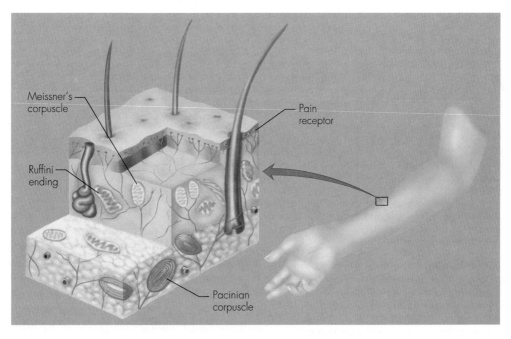

Figure 7.12 Some sensory receptors found in the skin, the human body's largest organ
Different receptor types respond to different stimuli, as described in Table 7.1.

Table 7.1 Somatosensory Receptors and Their Possible Functions

Receptor	Location	Responds to	Rate of Adaptation to a Prolonged Stimulus
Free nerve ending (unmyelinated or thinly myelinated fibers)	Around base of hairs and elsewhere in skin	Pain, warmth, cold	Uncertain
Hair-follicle receptors	Hair-covered skin	Movement of hairs	Rapid
Meissner's corpuscles	Hairless areas	Sudden displacement of skin; low-frequency vibration (flutter)	Rapid (?)
Pacinian corpuscles	Both hairy and hairless skin	Sudden displacement of skin; high-frequency vibration	Very rapid
Merkel's disks	Both hairy and hairless skin	Indentation of skin	Slow
Ruffini endings	Both hairy and hairless skin	Stretch of skin	Slow
Krause end bulbs	Hairless areas, perhaps including genitals; maybe some hairy areas	Uncertain	Uncertain

cells also receive input across the corpus callosum from the somatosensory cortex of the opposite hemisphere. Such crossed input enables somatosensory cortex cells to compare, for example, left-hand sensation and right-hand sensation (Iwamura, Iriki, & Tanaka, 1994). After damage to the somatosensory cortex, people generally experience an impairment of body perceptions. One patient with Alzheimer's disease, who had damage in the somatosensory cortex as well as elsewhere, had much trouble getting her clothes on correctly, and she could not point correctly in response to such directions as

"show me your elbow" or "point to my knee," although she pointed correctly to various nonbody objects in the room. When told to touch her elbow, her most frequent response was to feel her wrist and arm and suggest that the elbow was probably around there, somewhere. She acted as if she had only a blurry map of her own body parts (Sirigu, Grafman, Bressler, & Sunderland, 1991).

Stop *&* Check

2. In what way is somatosensation several senses instead of one?

Check your answer on page 210.

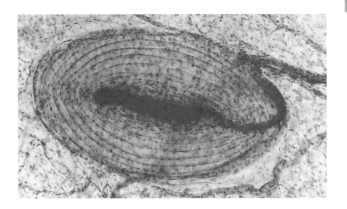

Figure 7.13 A Pacinian corpuscle
Pacinian corpuscles are a type of receptor that responds best to sudden displacement of the skin or to high-frequency vibrations. They respond only briefly to steady pressure on the skin. The onionlike outer structure provides a mechanical support to the neuron inside it so that a sudden stimulus can bend it but a sustained stimulus cannot. *(Source: Ed Reschke)*

Pain

Pain, the unpleasant emotion and sensation evoked by a harmful stimulus, alerts us to danger and grabs our attention (Eccleston & Crombez, 1999). People who are born insensitive to pain incur frequent injuries because they do not receive the early signals of harm. Some bite off the tips of their tongues, scorch their mouths by drinking very hot coffee, or expose their feet too long to the cold. Most of us shift position every few minutes without even thinking about it because we feel mild discomfort. People lacking a sense of pain generally do not feel even that discomfort, so they damage their bones and tendons by sitting or standing in one position for too long.

A woman with pain insensitivity once took a casserole out of the oven and carried it with her bare hands. Her husband screamed because the casserole was burning hot, but she calmly set it on their cardboard table. Not until the table burst into flames did she realize what a mistake she had made (Comings & Amromin, 1974).

Pain Neurons and Their Neurotransmitters

The term *pain* refers to a wide variety of sensations, ranging from sharp cuts to dull headaches (see Digression 7.2). Many kinds of pain depend on certain unmyelinated and thinly myelinated axons carrying information to the spinal cord and releasing a neurotransmitter

known as **substance P** (J. D. Levine, Fields, & Basbaum, 1993). Substance P is a neuromodulator or cotransmitter with glutamate in these neurons. A mild pain stimulus releases only glutamate; a stronger stimulus releases glutamate and substance P (Cao et al., 1998). Mice that lack receptors for substance P still react to painful stimuli (because they still have glutamate and its receptors), but if the painful stimulus becomes more intense, they continue to react as if it were mildly painful (DeFelipe et al., 1998).

What would you expect if an investigator injected substance P into an animal's spinal cord? The animal would whimper, scratch, bite, and show other indications of pain—not feeling pain in the spinal cord itself, but in the part of the body that sends information to that section of the spinal cord.

One way of increasing the release of substance P is

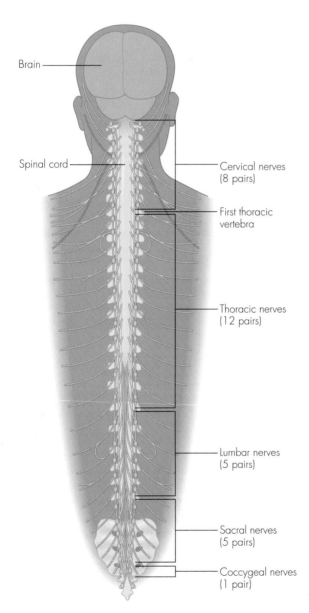

Figure 7.14   The human central nervous system (CNS)
Spinal nerves from each segment of the spinal cord exit through the correspondingly numbered opening between vertebrae. *(Source: Starr & Taggart, 1989)*

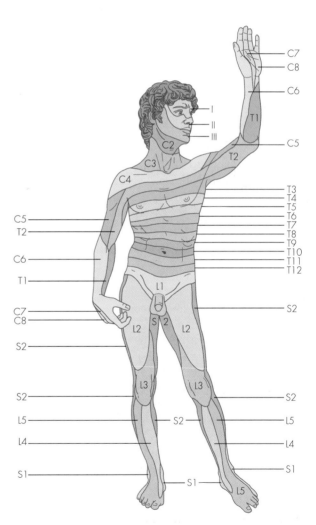

Figure 7.15   Dermatomes innervated by the 31 sensory spinal nerves
Areas I, II, and III of the face are not innervated by the spinal nerves, but instead by three branches of the fifth cranial nerve. Although this figure shows distinct borders, the dermatomes actually overlap one another by about one-third to one-half of their width.

Headaches

Most headaches are the result of tension in the neck muscles, sinus infections, anxiety or depression, sleeplessness, or withdrawal from caffeine. Such headaches can be treated with rest, aspirin, or in some cases antidepressant drugs or tranquilizers; they are not a cause for great concern. Less commonly a headache may be a sign of a serious medical problem, such as a brain tumor, encephalitis or other brain infection, a burst blood vessel, head injury, or migraine.

Here are a few questions to ask to determine whether a headache is probably a serious medical problem or probably a "don't worry about it" headache (S. Diamond, 1994; Pincus & Tucker, 1985):

- Have you had headaches like this before? (If yes, especially if you have had them occasionally for a year or more, your headache is almost certainly *not* a serious problem.)

- Is this headache the worst you have ever had? (If it is, it may be a serious problem.)

- Are you able to go to work or school in spite of the headaches? (If yes, the headache is probably not serious.)

- Does the headache awaken you when you are sleeping? (If it does, it might be serious.)

- Is the headache worse on some days than on others? (If it is worse during the week and not so bad on weekends, it is probably a tension headache.)

- Does your headache make you vomit? Lose consciousness? (If it does, it is a serious problem, perhaps migraine.)

- Have any of your relatives had similar headaches? (Most people with migraine headaches say yes.)

---

to inject **capsaicin,** a chemical that causes neurons containing substance P to release it suddenly. Injecting capsaicin causes an animal to react as it would to substance P itself (Gamse, Leeman, Holzer, & Lembeck, 1981; Jancsó, Kiraly, & Jancsó-Gábor, 1977; Yarsh, Farb, Leeman, & Jessell, 1979). Capsaicin also directly stimulates pain receptors that are sensitive to moderate heat—from about 43°C to 53°C (Caterina, Rosen, Tominaga, Brake, & Julius, 1999; Caterina et al., 1997). Capsaicin therefore induces a painful burning sensation, partly by releasing substance P and partly by stimulating heat receptors. However, as the pain subsides, a period of insensitivity to pain takes its place for two reasons. First, the neurons cannot synthesize substance P as fast as they released it, so their store is depleted. Second, if the dose of capsaicin is high enough, it damages the pain receptors as it stimulates them.

Capsaicin occurs in nature in jalapeños and other hot peppers. When you eat a hot pepper, the capsaicin stimulates heat receptors and causes neurons in your tongue to release substance P, giving you a sensation of pain or heat. After the heat sensation wears off, you experience a pleasant state of relief and decreased sensitivity to heat and pain on your tongue. Similarly capsaicin rubbed onto a sore shoulder, an arthritic joint, or other painful area produces a temporary burning sensation followed by a longer period of decreased pain. Do not, however, try eating hot peppers to help reduce pain in, say, your legs. Because little if any of the ingested capsaicin enters the blood, the capsaicin you eat

will not relieve your pain—unless it is your tongue that hurts (Karrer & Bartoshuk, 1991).

Stop & Check

3. Which neurotransmitters do pain neurons release?

4. What would happen to pain sensation if glutamate receptors were blocked? What happens after substance P receptors are blocked?

5. How do jalapeños produce a hot sensation?

Check your answers on page 210.

Pain and the Brain

The spinal cord neurons sensitive to pain send their information to certain thalamic nuclei that relay it to parts of the cerebral cortex. PET scans (see Methods 3.1, p. 72) disclose that people experiencing pain show increased activity in several cortical areas including the cingulate cortex and the somatosensory cortex (Craig, Bushnell, Zhang, & Blomqvist, 1994; Talbot et al., 1991) (see Figure 7.16). The projection to the cingulate cortex (see Figure 4.12, p. 97) is interesting because that area has long been linked to emotional responses. In one study surgeons probed the brains of people who were undergoing brain surgery. (Brain surgery can be done in waking people who have only the scalp anesthetized. The brain itself has no pain receptors.) When the surgeons applied painful heat or cold or pricked a patient's skin, they found increased activity in the cingulate cortex. However, direct stimulation of the cingulate cortex produced no report of pain (Hutchison, Davis, Lozano, Tasker, & Dostrovsky, 1999). Evidently cingulate cortex activity indicates the emotional content, not the painful sensation itself. Indeed much of the brain's response to pain appears to be an emotional response rather than strictly a sensation; the mere anticipation of pain excites many of the same brain areas as pain itself (Ploghaus et al., 1999).

Events That Limit Pain

How much pain someone feels is often poorly related to the amount of tissue damage. Some people complain of severe and lasting pain after a minor injury. However, athletes and soldiers sometimes ignore serious injuries until their competition or battle is over. An infant rat reacts vigorously to a burning stimulus when it is by itself, but reacts only slightly if it is next to its mother (Blass, Shide, Zaw-Mon, & Sorrentino, 1995).

To account for such phenomena, Ronald Melzack and P. D. Wall (1965) proposed a highly influential theory of pain known as the **gate theory.** According to this theory, certain areas of the spinal cord receive messages not only from pain receptors but also from other receptors in the skin and from axons descending from the brain. If these other inputs to the spinal cord are sufficiently active, they close the "gates" for the pain mes-

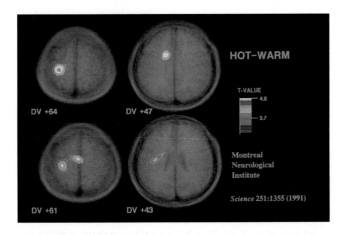

Figure 7.16 Representation of pain in the human brain

Investigators used PET scans and MRI data to record the activity of various brain areas during exposure to painful heat and to nonpainful warmth on the right arm. Then they subtracted the activity during warm stimulation from the activity during painful heat to find the activity due to pain itself. The areas marked in white showed the greatest response to pain, followed by the red, yellow, blue, and violet areas. Response was greatest in a portion of the somatosensory cortex contralateral to the stimulated arm. *(Source: Talbot et al., 1991)*

sages. In other words the brain can increase or decrease its own exposure to pain information.

Although Melzack and Wall's gate theory included certain details that turned out to be wrong, the general principle is valid: Nonpain stimuli can increase or decrease the intensity of pain. Much of that regulation takes place through **opioid mechanisms**—systems that are responsive to opiate drugs and similar chemicals. For centuries, although people used opiates to relieve pain, induce sleep, and stimulate pleasure, no one knew how they worked. Then, Candace Pert and Solomon Snyder (1973) found that morphine and related drugs bind specifically to certain brain receptors. The opiate receptors are concentrated in the same brain areas where substance P is concentrated (McLean, Skirboll, & Pert, 1985). Apparently opiate receptors inhibit the pain-producing effects of substance P (see Figure 7.17). The discovery of opiate receptors in the brain had exciting implications. First, it indicated that morphine and other opiates have their effects in the brain instead of pain receptors in the periphery. Second, it paved the way for a search for many other kinds of brain receptors.

Third, the discovery of opiate receptors implied that the brain must have its own opiatelike chemicals. Before long those substances were discovered. Two of them are peptide neurotransmitters: **met-enkephalin** and **leu-enkephalin**. (The term *enkephalin* refers to the fact that these chemicals were first found in the brain, or encephalon. The two enkephalins are the same except at one end, where met-enkephalin, a peptide, ends with the amino acid methionine and leu-enkephalin has the amino acid leucine.) Although the enkephalins have chemical structures very unlike morphine, they interact with the same receptors as morphine, as do several other brain chemicals, including *dynorphin*, *β-endorphin*, *a-neoendorphin*, and *nociceptin*. Collectively, these chemicals are known as **endorphins** (a contraction of *endogenous morphines*) because they are the brain's own morphines. Nociceptin, unlike the others, increases pain (Zaki & Evans, 1998).

Among the many roles of endorphins in behavior, the best documented one is **analgesia** (relief from pain). According to a theoretical review by Basbaum and Fields (1984), certain stimuli, particularly certain painful stimuli, activate neurons that release endorphins in the **periaqueductal gray area** and surrounding areas in the midbrain. Under the influence of the endorphins, the periaqueductal gray area excites cells in the medulla, and then the axons from both the medulla and the periaqueductal gray area itself send messages to appropriate areas of the spinal cord and brain stem, blocking the release of substance P and therefore decreasing pain (Reichling, Kwiat, & Basbaum, 1988; Terman, Shavitt, Lewis, Cannon, & Liebeskind, 1984). Figure 7.18 summarizes these effects.

Have you ever wondered why morphine and other

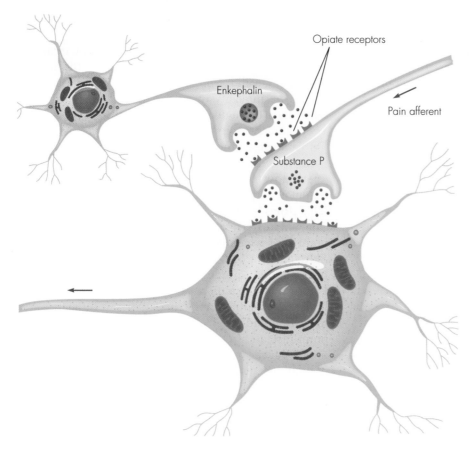

Opiate receptors

Enkephalin

Pain afferent

Substance P

Figure 7.17 Synapses responsible for pain and its inhibition
The pain afferent neuron releases substance P as its neurotransmitter. Another neuron releases enkephalin at presynaptic synapses; the enkephalin inhibits the release of substance P and therefore alleviates pain.

opiates relieve slow, dull pain but not sharp pain? For example, morphine relieves postsurgical pain, but it is not effective during the surgery itself. Also, patients under the influence of morphine to relieve postsurgical pain feel the sharp pain of a needle injection. The explanation is that sharp pain is carried in large-diameter pain fibers (with cell bodies larger than 40 μm), which are unaffected by endorphins, whereas dull pain is carried by smaller pain fibers (with cell bodies smaller than 30 μm), which do respond to endorphins (Taddese, Nah, & McCleskey, 1995).

Stimuli That Produce Analgesia

Both pleasant and unpleasant stimuli can release endorphins and thereby inhibit pain. Endorphins are released in a "runner's high" that many long-distance runners experience. They are also released during sexual activity and when one listens to the kinds of music that send a chill down your spine (Goldstein, 1980).

Certain kinds of painful stimuli also release endorphins, putting the brakes on further pain. Inescapable pain is especially potent at inhibiting further pain (Sutton et al., 1997). Presumably the evolutionary function

of this mechanism is that pain alerts the animal to danger, but if the animal can do nothing further about it, there is no advantage in a continued panic. (On the other hand, an animal that experiences inescapable pain may respond only feebly to later escapable pain, so this mechanism is sometimes disadvantageous.)

Some kinds of pain-induced and stress-induced analgesia depend on endorphin release and some do not. For example, exposure to intermittent or low-intensity continuous shock releases endorphins. We know that endorphins are necessary because the effect is blocked by naloxone, a drug that blocks opiate receptors. However, exposure to continuous, high-intensity shock also decreases pain sensitivity without inducing endorphin release (Terman & Liebeskind, 1986). Evidently animals have several mechanisms for inhibiting pain, not just the endorphin system.

Physicians and physical therapists sometimes try to control patients' pain with stimuli that release endorphins. Two examples are acupuncture, an ancient Chinese technique of gently twisting thin needles placed in the skin, and transcutaneous electrical nerve stimulation (TENS), a prolonged, mild electrical shock applied to the arms, legs, or back. TENS provides relief for more than half of the people in pain, with almost none of the side effects or risks associated with painkilling drugs (Pomeranz, 1989). Note that, because TENS decreases pain through nonpain stimulation, it supports the gate theory of pain.

The Pros and Cons of Morphine Analgesia

Suppose that a patient is suffering serious pain after surgery or from cancer. Should a physician prescribe enough morphine to suppress the pain? Or should the patient just suffer through it?

Some physicians hesitate to prescribe morphine, partly because of the fear of addiction. Actually, morphine taken under hospital conditions almost never becomes addictive. Very large doses of morphine can suppress breathing, but moderate doses do not pose that risk.

A more serious worry is that opiates temporarily

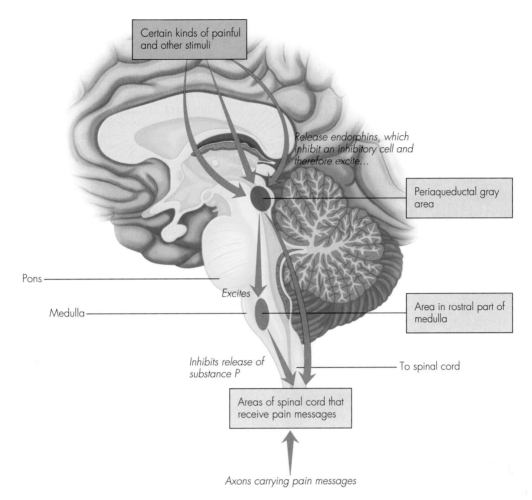

Certain kinds of painful and other stimuli

Release endorphins, which inhibit an inhibitory cell and therefore excite...

Periaqueductal gray area

Pons

Excites

Medulla

Area in rostral part of medulla

Inhibits release of substance P

To spinal cord

Areas of spinal cord that receive pain messages

Axons carrying pain messages

Figure 7.18   The periaqueductal gray area, where electrical stimulation relieves pain
Periaqueductal means "around the aqueduct," a passageway of cerebrospinal fluid between the third and fourth ventricles.

weaken the immune system and leave the body vulnerable to disease and even to the spread of cancer. That danger, however, lasts only days before the immune system returns to full force. Prolonged pain or stress, in contrast, weakens the immune system for much longer (Mogil, Sternberg, & Liebeskind, 1993). Morphine, by alleviating pain, in the long run actually strengthens the immune system and enhances the defenses against the spread of cancer (Page, Ben-Eliyahu, Yirmiya, & Liebeskind, 1993). Consequently vigorous efforts to relieve pain are beneficial to long-term recovery.

Stop & Check

6. How do opiates relieve pain?

7. Why does morphine relieve dull pain but not sharp pain?

8. If you wanted to determine whether some new pain-relief method acts through the same kind of synapses as opiates, what would be one simple way to do so?

Check your answers on page 210.

Sensitization of Pain

In addition to mechanisms of decreasing pain, the body has mechanisms that increase pain. If you have ever been sunburned, you probably remember how a mere touch, or a splash of hot water, felt severely painful. When a tissue becomes damaged and inflamed, it triggers the release of histamine, nerve growth factor, and other chemicals that help repair the damage. However, these chemicals also increase the number of sodium gates in nearby receptors, including pain receptors, and thereby facilitate action potentials in response to even weak stimuli (Devor, 1996; Tominaga et al., 1998). Even with no stimulus at all, action potentials arise spontaneously, producing a burning or stinging sensation. Inflammation also causes some touch receptors to start producing and releasing substance P, thereby acting as pain receptors (Neumann, Doubell, Leslie, & Woolf, 1996). Cells in the dorsal spinal cord also become sensitized, causing increased painful sensations even in areas remote from the damage (Malmberg, Chen, Tonegawa, & Basbaum, 1997). In short, pain is a complex phenomenon, with some mechanisms that inhibit it and others that exaggerate and prolong it.

In Closing: The Mechanical Senses

We humans generally pay so much attention to vision and hearing that we take our mechanical senses for granted. However, a mere moment's reflection should reveal how critical they are for survival. At every moment your vestibular sense tells you whether you are standing or falling; your sense of pain can tell you that you have in fact fallen. If you moved to a televisionlike universe with only vision and hearing, you might get by if you had already learned what all the sights and sounds mean. But it is hard to imagine how you could have learned their meaning without much previous experience of touch and pain.

Summary

1. The vestibular system is a sensory system that detects the position and acceleration of the head and adjusts body posture and eye movements accordingly. (p. 201)

2. The somatosensory system depends on a variety of receptors that are sensitive to different kinds of stimulation of the skin and internal tissues. The brain maintains several parallel somatosensory representations of the body. (p. 201)

3. Pain messages are transmitted by axons that release glutamate as their neurotransmitter for moderately painful stimuli and a combination of glutamate and substance P for stronger pains. (p. 205)

4. Capsaicin produces temporary pain by releasing substance P and by stimulating receptors for moderate heat. However, as that pain wears off, the individual becomes relatively insensitive to pain because the neurons need much time to restore their supply of substance P and because the heat receptors may have been weakened. (p. 206)

5. A certain harmful stimulus may give rise to a greater or lesser degree of pain depending on other current and recent stimuli. According to the gate theory of pain, other stimuli can close certain gates and block the transmission of pain. (p. 207)

6. Opiate drugs attach to the receptors that the brain uses for endorphins, transmitters that decrease pain sensations by blocking the release of substance P. (p. 207)

7. Both pleasant and unpleasant experiences can release endorphins and thereby decrease sensitivity to pain. (p. 208)

8. Although morphine by itself temporarily impairs the immune system, pain impairs it more. Morphine, by relieving pain, actually produces a net enhancement of the immune system. (p. 208)

9. Tissue damage activates the immune system, releasing chemicals that repair the damage but also sensitize receptors, making them overresponsive to further pain. (p. 209)

Answers to *Stop and Check* Questions

1. The vestibular system enables the brain to shift eye movements to compensate for changes in head position. Without feedback about head position, the person cannot correct the eye movements and gets the same experience as if an intact person were watching a jiggling book page. (p. 201)

2. We have several types of receptors, sensitive to touch, heat, and so forth, and different parts of the somatosensory cortex respond to different kinds of skin stimulation. (p. 204)

3. A mild pain stimulus releases glutamate. A stronger stimulus releases glutamate and substance P. (p. 206)

4. Blockage of glutamate receptors would eliminate pain sensations. (However, doing so would not be a good pain killing strategy. Glutamate is the most abundant transmitter in the brain, and blocking it would disrupt sensation, learning and memory, and many other functions.) Blocking substance P receptors can make intense pain feel like mild pain. (p. 206)

5. Jalapeños contain capsaicin, which causes pain neurons to release substance P, and also directly stimulates receptors that are sensitive to moderate heat. (p. 206)

6. Opiates stimulate endorphin synapses, which block the release of substance P. (p. 209)

7. Morphine and endorphins block activity in thin pain fibers, which convey dull pain, but do not affect thicker pain fibers, which convey sharp pain. (p. 209)

8. You could use the pain-relief technique with two groups of people, but first give one group naloxone, a drug that blocks endorphin synapses. If the new method works through endorphin synapses, naloxone should block its effects. If it works through some other method, naloxone should not prevent its effects. (p. 209)

Thought Questions

1. Why is the vestibular sense generally useless under conditions of weightlessness?

2. Sometimes you can temporarily relieve a pain by scratching the skin around the painful area. Explain how this procedure may work.

The Chemical Senses

Suppose you had the godlike power to create a new species of animal, but you could equip it with only one sensory system. Which sense would you give it?

Your first impulse might be to choose vision or hearing. After all, those senses are extremely valuable to humans. But an animal with only one sensory system is not going to be much like humans, is it? To have any chance of survival, it will probably have to be small and slow, maybe even one-celled. What sense will be most useful to such an animal?

Most theorists believe that the first sensory system of the earliest animals was a chemical sensitivity (G. H. Parker, 1922). A chemical sense enables a small animal to cope with the basics of finding food, identifying certain kinds of danger, and even locating mates.

Now imagine that you have to choose one of your senses to *lose*. Which one will it be? Most of us would not choose to lose vision, hearing, or touch. Losing pain sensitivity can be dangerous. You might choose to sacrifice your olfaction or taste.

Curious, isn't it? If an animal is going to survive with only one sense, it almost has to be a chemical sense, and yet to humans, who have many other well-developed senses, the chemical senses seem dispensable. Perhaps we underestimate their importance.

General Issues About Chemical Coding

Suppose you run a bakery and you need to send frequent messages to your supplier two blocks away. Suppose further that you can communicate only by ringing three large bells on the roof of your bakery. You would have to work out a code.

One possibility would be to label the three bells: The high-pitched bell means "I need flour." The medium-pitched bell means "I need sugar." And the low-pitched bell means "I need eggs." Then you simply ring the right bell at the right moment. The more you need something, the faster you ring the bell. We shall call this the *labeled-line code* because each bell has a single unchanging label. The problem is that this simple code can signal only flour, sugar, or eggs.

Another possibility would be to set up a code that depends on a relationship among the three bells. Ring-ing the high and medium bells equally means that you need flour. The medium and low bells together call for sugar; the high and low bells together call for eggs. Ringing all three together means you need vanilla extract. Ringing mostly the high bell while ringing the other two bells slightly means you need hazelnuts. And so forth. We call this the *across-fiber pattern code* because the meaning depends on the pattern across bells. This code is versatile and can be highly useful, unless we make it too complicated.

A sensory system could theoretically use either type of coding. In a system relying on the **labeled-line principle,** each receptor would respond to a limited range of stimuli and would send a direct line to the brain. In a system relying on the **across-fiber pattern principle,** each receptor responds to a wider range of stimuli and contributes to the perception of each of them. In other words a given level of response by a given sensory axon means little unless the brain knows what the other axons are doing at the same time (Erickson, 1982).

Vertebrate sensory systems probably do not have any pure labeled-line codes. In color perception we encountered an example of an across-fiber pattern code; each color-sensitive cell responds best to certain stimuli, but because it also responds to other stimuli, its message out of context is ambiguous. For example, a medium-wavelength cone might produce the same level of response to a moderately bright green light, a brighter blue light, or a white light. In auditory pitch perception the responses of the hair cell receptors are narrowly tuned, but even in this case the meaning of a particular receptor's response depends on the context: A given receptor may respond best to a certain high-frequency tone, but it also responds in phase with a number of low-frequency tones (as do all the other receptors). Each receptor also responds to white noise (static) and to various mixtures of tones. Auditory perception depends on a comparison of responses across all the receptors.

Similarly each taste and smell stimulus excites several kinds of receptors, and the meaning of a particular response by a particular receptor depends on the context of responses by other receptors. However, our understanding of the chemical senses is limited compared to the other senses. Even on basic questions of how we code tastes and smells or how many kinds of receptors we have, we cannot draw conclusions with the same confidence as with vision and hearing.

Stop  Check

1. Of the following, which use a labeled-line code and which use an across-fiber pattern code?
   a. A fire alarm
   b. A light switch
   c. The shift key plus another key on a computer or typewriter

Check your answers on page 220.

Taste

When we talk about the taste of food, we generally mean *flavor,* a combination of taste and smell. *Taste* refers to the stimulation of the taste buds. Most people who complain of losing their sense of taste actually have an impaired sense of smell, and a complete loss of taste is rare. In fact you don't need very many taste receptors to get a recognizable sensation. Even people who have suffered damage to most of the tongue continue to identify tastes accurately, although they report a loss of intensity (Lehman, Bartoshuk, Catalanotto, Kveton, & Lowlicht, 1995).

Taste Receptors

The receptors for taste are not true neurons but modified skin cells. Like neurons, taste receptors have excitable membranes and release neurotransmitters to excite neighboring neurons, which in turn transmit information to the brain. Like skin cells, however, taste receptors are gradually sloughed off and replaced, each one lasting about 10 to 14 days (Kinnamon, 1987).

Mammalian taste receptors are in **taste buds,** located in **papillae,** structures on the surface of the tongue (see Figure 7.19). A given papilla may contain any number of taste buds from none to ten or

more (Arvidson & Friberg, 1980), and each taste bud contains about 50 receptor cells.

In adult humans taste buds are located mainly along the outside edge of the tongue, with few or none in the center. You can demonstrate this principle as follows: Soak a small cotton swab in sugar water, salt water, or vinegar. Then touch it lightly on the center of your tongue, not too far toward the back. You will probably experience little taste. Then try it again on the edge of your tongue and notice how much stronger the taste is.

Now change the procedure a bit. Wash your mouth out with water and prepare a cotton swab as before. Touch the soaked portion to one edge of your tongue and then slowly stroke it to the center of your tongue.

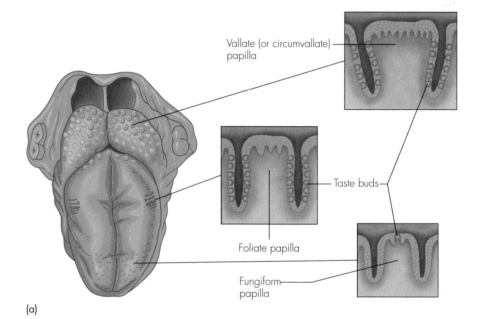

(a)

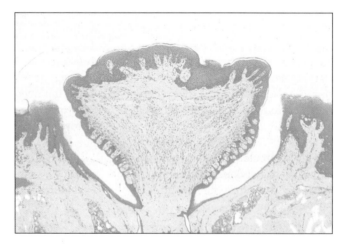

(b)

Figure 7.19   The organs of taste
(a) The tip, back, and sides of the tongue are covered with taste buds. Taste buds are located in papillae. (b) Photo showing cross section of a taste bud. Each taste bud contains about 50 receptor cells.

Now it will seem as if you are moving the taste to the center of your tongue. In fact you are getting only a touch sensation from the center of your tongue; you attribute the taste you had on the side of your tongue to every other spot you stroke (Bartoshuk, 1991).

How Many Kinds of Taste Receptors?

Traditionally people in Western society have thought of *sweet, sour, salty,* and *bitter* as the "primary" tastes. However, some tastes defy categorization in terms of these four labels (Schiffman & Erickson, 1980; Schiffman, McElroy, & Erickson, 1980). How could we determine how many kinds people have?

One way to answer this question is to find procedures that affect one kind of receptor without affecting others. For example, certain chemicals can alter the response of sweetness receptors without affecting other taste receptors (see Digression 7.3). Therefore we know there must be such a thing as a sweetness receptor.

Further evidence comes from studies of the following type: Soak your tongue for 15 seconds in a sour solution, such as unsweetened lemon juice. Then try tasting some other sour solution, such as dilute vinegar. You will find that the second solution tastes less sour than usual. Depending on the concentrations of the lemon juice and vinegar, the second solution may not taste sour at all. Decreased sensation from a repeated stimulus, called **adaptation**, presumably reflects the fatigue of receptors sensitive to sour tastes. Now try tasting something salty, sweet, or bitter. These substances taste about the same as usual. In short you experience very little **cross-adaptation**—reduced response to one taste after exposure to another (McBurney & Bartoshuk, 1973).

So we must have at least four kinds of taste receptors. But might we have more than four? Several kinds of evidence points to a separate taste for glutamate, which is a component of meats, meat broths, and monosodium glutamate (MSG). The taste of glutamate resembles that of unsalted chicken broth. Most people describe it as pleasant, at least in low concentrations. The English language did not have a word for this taste, but Japanese did, so English-speaking researchers have adopted the Japanese word, *umami.* Chemicals that interfere with salty tastes or other sensations do not interfere with umami (Scott & Plata-Salaman, 1991), and the responses of taste neurons to glutamate do not correlate strongly with responses to other taste stimuli (Kurihara & Kashiwayanagi, 1998).

Mechanisms of Taste Receptors

Neuroscientists have begun to identify and describe the taste receptors (Lindemann, 1996). One is the saltiness detector. Recall that a neuron produces an action potential when sodium ions cross its membrane. A saltiness receptor, which detects the presence of sodium, does not need a specialized membrane site sensitive to sodium. It simply permits sodium ions on the tongue to cross its membrane. The higher the concentration of sodium on the tongue, the greater the receptor's response. Chemicals such as amiloride, which prevents sodium from crossing the membrane, reduce the intensity of salty tastes (DeSimone, Heck, Mierson, & DeSimone, 1984; Schiffman, Lockhead, & Maes, 1983).

Sourness receptors operate on a different principle. When an acid binds to the receptor, it closes potassium channels, preventing potassium from leaving the cell. The result is an increased accumulation of positive charges within the neuron and therefore a depolarization of the membrane (Shirley & Persaud, 1990). Researchers have now identified and isolated the sourness receptor for study in more detail (Ugawa et al., 1998).

Sweetness, bitterness, and umami receptors operate much like a metabotropic synapse (Chapter 3). After a taste molecule binds to one of these receptors, it activates a G protein that releases a second messenger within the cell (Lindemann, 1996). It is possible that we have more than one kind of sweetness or bitterness receptor. For example, the substances that taste bitter have little in common chemically, except that nearly all are toxic. The umami receptor, the first taste receptor to be isolated and chemically identified, is similar but not identical in structure to one of the brain's metabotropic glutamate receptors (Chaudhari, Landin, & Roper, 2000).

Stop & Check

2. Suppose you find some new, unusual-tasting food. How could you determine whether we have a special receptor for that food or whether we taste it with a combination of the other known taste receptors?

3. If someone injected into your tongue some chemical that blocks the release of second messengers, what would be the effect on your taste experiences?

Check your answers on page 220.

Individual Differences in Taste

You may have been in a biology laboratory in which the instructor asked you to taste phenythiocarbamide (PTC) and then take samples home for your relatives to try. Some people taste it as bitter and some hardly taste it at all; the ability to taste it is controlled by a single dominant gene and therefore provides an interesting example for a genetics lab. (Did your instructor happen to mention that PTC is poisonous? Oh well. No harm if you didn't swallow very much of it.)

For Americans as a whole—the results differ by ethnic groups—about one-fourth hardly taste PTC at all

Miracle Berries and the Modification of Taste Receptors

Although the miracle berry of West Africa is practically tasteless, it temporarily changes the taste of other substances. Miracle berries contain a protein, *miraculin*, that modifies sweet receptors in such a way that they can be stimulated by acids (Bartoshuk, Gentile, Moskowitz, & Meiselman, 1974). If you ever get a chance to chew a miracle berry (and I do recommend it), for about the next half hour all acids (which are normally sour) will taste sweet, while continuing to taste sour as well.

Miraculin was, for a time, commercially available in the United States as a diet aid. The idea was that dieters could coat their tongue with a miraculin pill and then eat and drink unsweetened, slightly acidic substances. Such substances would taste sweet without providing many calories.

A colleague and I once spent an evening experimenting with miracle berries. We drank straight lemon juice, sauerkraut juice, even vinegar. All tasted extremely sweet. Somehow we forgot how acidic these substances are. We awoke the next day to find our mouths full of ulcers.

Other taste-modifying substances include an extract from the plant *Gymnema sylvestre*, which makes people temporarily insensitive to a great variety of sweet tastes (R. A. Frank, Mize, Kennedy, de los Santos, & Green, 1992), and the chemical *theophylline*, which reduces the bitterness of many substances (Kodama, Fukushima, & Sakata, 1978). After eating artichokes, some people report a sweet taste from water (Bartoshuk, Lee, & Scarpellino, 1972).

Have you ever tasted orange juice just after brushing your teeth? And did you wonder why something that usually tastes so good suddenly tasted so bad? Most toothpastes contain sodium lauryl sulfate, a chemical that intensifies bitter tastes while weakening sweet tastes (DeSimone, Heck, & Bartoshuk, 1980; Schiffman, 1983). Evidently it disrupts the membrane surfaces, preventing molecules from binding to sweetness receptors. Fortunately the effect wears off in a few minutes.

except in very high concentrations, one-half taste it as bitter, and one-fourth taste it as extremely bitter. People who taste PTC as extremely bitter, known as **supertasters,** have the largest number of *fungiform papillae* (the type near the tip of the tongue). They are also more sensitive than others are to nearly all other tastes. For that reason they are less likely than others to like the taste of black coffee, strong beer (such as Pilsner Urquell), hot peppers, tart fruits such as lemon and grapefruit, dark bread, and strong-tasting vegetables such as Brussels sprouts, cauliflower, cabbage, and radishes (Bartochuk, Duffy, Lucchina, Prutkin, & Fast, 1998; Drewnowski, Henderson, Shore, & Barratt-Fornell, 1998). On the average, supertasters tend to be thinner than others. (Do you hate all those tastes? Now you have an excuse: Maybe you are a supertaster!)

How Do We Perceive Tastes?

Although you may assume that the five kinds of receptors imply five labeled lines to the brain, research suggests a more complicated system (Hettinger & Frank, 1992). The receptors converge their input onto later cells in the taste system, each of which responds best to a particular taste, but somewhat to other tastes also.

The neurons that respond best to sweet substances are necessary for the perception of sweet tastes; in their absence, the remaining cells would not be able to dis-

tinguish sweetness from other tastes (D. V. Smith, VanBuskirk, Travers, & Bieber, 1983b). However, the "sweet-best" neurons by themselves are insufficient for perceiving sweets. If we examine *only* the responses of the sweet-best cells, we find ambiguous information (Scott, 1987). For example, a moderate level of response could indicate either a dilute sugar solution or a fairly concentrated salt solution. (Remember, the sweet-best cells respond somewhat to other stimuli also.) The brain can determine what the tongue is tasting only by comparing the responses of several kinds of taste neurons. In other words taste depends on a pattern of responses across fibers (R. P. Erickson, DiLorenzo, & Woodbury, 1994).

Taste Coding in the Brain

Information from the receptors in the anterior two-thirds of the tongue is carried to the brain along the chorda tympani, a branch of the seventh cranial nerve (the facial nerve). Taste information from the posterior tongue and the throat is carried along branches of the ninth and tenth cranial nerves. What do you suppose would happen if someone anesthetized your chorda tympani? You would no longer taste anything in the anterior part of your tongue, but you probably would not notice a change because you would still taste with the posterior part. However, the posterior part would be-

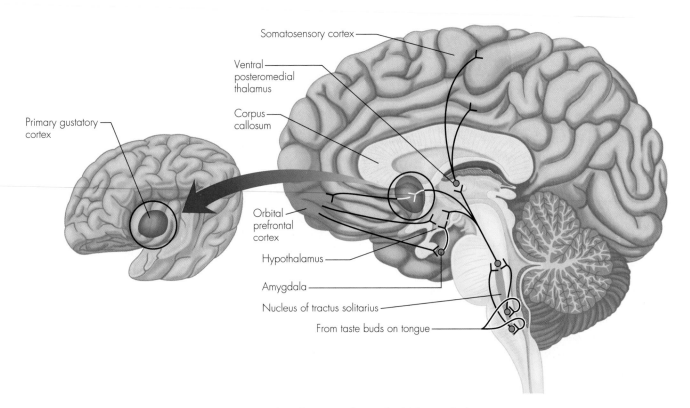

Figure 7.20 Major routes of impulses related to the sense of taste in the human brain
The thalamus and cerebral cortex receive impulses from both the left and the right sides of the tongue. *(Source: Based on Rolls, 1995)*

come much more sensitive to bitter tastes than before, somewhat more sensitive to most other tastes, and less sensitive to salt. Finally you might or might not—about 40% of people would—experience taste "phantoms," a little like the phantom limb experience discussed in Chapter 5 (Yanagisawa, Bartoshuk, Catalanotto, Karrer, & Kveton, 1998). That is, you might experience tastes even when nothing was on your tongue. Evidently the input from the anterior and posterior parts of your tongue interact in complex ways. Silencing the anterior part releases the posterior part from inhibition and causes it to report tastes more actively than before.

The taste nerves project to the **nucleus of the tractus solitarius (NTS),** a structure in the medulla (Travers, Pfaffmann, & Norgren, 1986). From the NTS, information branches out, reaching the pons, the lateral hypothalamus, the amygdala, the ventral-posterior thalamus, and two areas of the cerebral cortex, one responsible for taste and one responsible for the sense of touch on the tongue (Pritchard, Hamilton, Morse, & Norgren, 1986; Yamamoto, 1984). A few of these major connections are illustrated in Figure 7.20.

With any sensory system, the brain must determine not only what the stimulus is, but also what it means, and therefore whether to swallow it or spit it out. In rats, even cells in the NTS (the first stop in the brain) code the meaning of the taste and not just its physical identity. For example, rats deficient in sodium show an increased preference for salty tastes. Recordings from the NTS show that after rats become sodium deficient, salty substances excite cells that usually respond to sweets! We don't know whether the salty substance actually tastes sweet to the rat—although the results suggest that conclusion—but we do know that neurons of the medulla can classify the acceptability of the taste.

Conversely, a rat that has become nauseated after drinking sugar water decreases its preference for sugar, and its NTS now reacts to sugar almost like quinine, which is bitter. In short, if experience has shown a substance to be good for the rat, it starts to taste good; if experience has shown something to be dangerous, it starts to taste bad (Scott, 1992). Monkeys show similar results in their cerebral cortex, although not in their NTS.

Olfaction

Olfaction, the sense of smell, is the detection and recognition of chemicals in contact with the membranes inside the nose. In an ordinary day most of us pay little attention to what we smell, and the deodorant industry is dedicated to removing human body smells from our experience. Nevertheless olfaction is more important than we may realize. We rely on it for discriminating good from bad wine or edible from rotting meat. Natural gas companies add a strong odor to their gas so

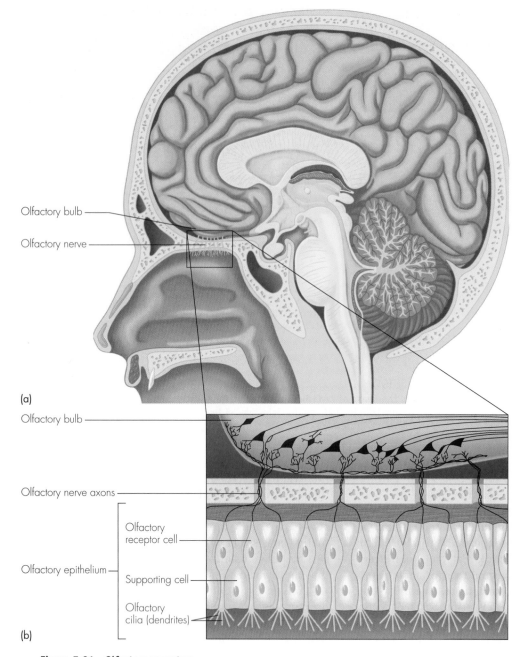

Olfactory bulb

Olfactory nerve

(a)

Olfactory bulb

Olfactory nerve axons

Olfactory epithelium

Olfactory receptor cell

Supporting cell

Olfactory cilia (dendrites)

(b)

Figure 7.21   Olfactory receptors
(**a**) Location of receptors in nasal cavity. (**b**) Closeup of olfactory cells.

that has the same odor sensitivities as the original (Nef, 1998).

The olfactory receptor sites are located on the cilia. Because odorant molecules must pass through a mucous fluid before they reach the receptors, we experience a delay—perhaps as long as 300 ms—between inhaling a substance and smelling it (Getchell & Getchell, 1987). After a chemical excites a receptor, further stimulation produces rapid adaptation (Kurahashi, Lowe, & Gold, 1994). To demonstrate this phenomenon, take a bottle of some harmless odorous chemical, such as lemon extract, and determine how far away you can hold the bottle and still smell it. Then hold it up to your nose and inhale deeply and repeatedly for a minute. Now test again: From how far away can you smell the extract? (Perhaps you can't even smell it next to your nose.)

TRY IT YOUR SELF

In all vertebrate species, the fundamental structure of an olfactory receptor is about the same as is the organization of the olfactory system in the brain (Eisthen, 1997). When an olfactory receptor is stimulated, its axon carries an impulse to the olfactory bulb (Figure 4.11, p. 96). Each odorous chemical excites only a limited part of the olfactory bulb. Evidently olfaction is coded in terms of which area of the olfactory bulb is excited. Chemicals that smell similar to one another excite almost the same areas, chemicals that smell very different excite different areas, and the results are practically the same from one individual to another (Rubin & Katz, 1999).

The olfactory bulb sends its axons to several other forebrain areas and especially activates parts of the pre-

that people can smell a leak in the gas line. Odors can call up an array of memories, often nostalgic ones.

Olfactory Receptors

The neurons responsible for smell are the **olfactory cells,** which line the olfactory epithelium in the rear of the nasal air passages (see Figure 7.21). In mammals each olfactory cell has cilia (threadlike dendrites) that extend from the cell body into the mucous surface of the nasal passage. Each olfactory receptor survives for a little over a month and then is replaced by a new cell

frontal cortex (Levy et al., 1997; Sobel et al., 1998). From there information connects to other areas that control feeding and reproduction, two kinds of behavior that are very sensitive to odors.

Stop & Check

4. Why does it take longer to notice a new odor than a light or sound?

Check your answer on page 220.

Behavioral Methods of Identifying Olfactory Receptors

How many kinds of olfactory receptors do we have? Two or three, or seven, or twenty, or what? Researchers answered the analogous question for color vision more than a century ago, using only behavioral observations. They found that, by mixing various amounts of three colors of light—say, red, green, and blue—they could match any other color that people can see. Researchers therefore concluded that we must have three, and probably only three, kinds of color receptors (which we now call cones).

We could imagine doing the same experiment for olfaction. Take a small number of odors—say, almond, lilac, and skunk—and test whether people can mix various proportions of those odors to match all other odors. If three odors are not enough, add more until eventually we can mix them to match every other possible odor. Because we do not know what the "primary odors" are (if indeed there are such things), we might have to do a great deal of trial-and-error testing to find the best set of odors to use. So far as we know, however, no one has ever tried such an experiment, or anyone who did try must have given up in discouragement.

A second approach is to study people who have trouble smelling one type of chemical. A general lack of olfaction is known as **anosmia;** the inability to smell a single chemical is a **specific anosmia.** For example, about 2% to 3% of all people are insensitive to the smell of isobutyric acid, the smelly component of sweat (Amoore, 1977). (They seldom complain about their disability.) Because people can lose the ability to smell just this one chemical, we may assume that there is a receptor specific to isobutyric acid. We might then search for additional specific anosmias on the theory that each specific anosmia represents the loss of a different type of receptor.

One investigator identified at least five other specific anosmias—musky, fishy, urinous, spermous, and malty—and less convincing evidence suggested 26 other possible specific anosmias (Amoore, 1977). But the more specific anosmias one finds, the more discouraging the task of being sure one has found all the possible types.

Biochemical Identification of Receptor Types

Ultimately the best way to determine the number of olfactory receptor types is to isolate the receptor molecules themselves. Linda Buck and Richard Axel (1991) identified in olfactory receptors a family of proteins, as shown in Figure 7.22. Like many neurotransmitter receptors, each of these proteins traverses the cell membrane seven times and responds to a chemical outside the cell (here an odorant molecule instead of a neurotransmitter) by triggering changes in a G protein inside the cell; the G protein then provokes chemical activities that lead to an action potential.

Olfactory receptor proteins occur only in the olfactory receptors, not elsewhere in the body. Moreover, different receptor cells have different receptor proteins. Buck and Axel identified 18 different receptor proteins, varying in their amino acid composition at certain sites (Figure 7.22). Other researchers since then have identified additional receptor proteins. The best estimate is that rats and mice have about a thousand types of olfactory receptors and that they devote about 1% of their total genes to coding olfactory receptors (Mombaerts, 1999). Humans have fewer olfactory receptors, but even we have hundreds.

Stop & Check

5. What is a specific anosmia?

6. How do olfactory receptors resemble metabotropic neurotransmitter receptors?

Check your answers on page 218.

Implications for Coding

We have only three kinds of cones and probably five kinds of taste receptors, so it was a surprise to find so many olfactory receptors. Having hundreds makes possible a great specialization of functions. To illustrate: Because we have only three kinds of cones with which to see a great variety of colors, each cone must contribute to almost every color perception. In olfaction we can afford to have receptors that respond to few stimuli. The response of one olfactory receptor might mean, "I smell a fatty acid with a straight chain of about three to five carbon atoms." The response of another receptor might mean, "I smell either a fatty acid or an aldehyde with a straight chain of about four to six carbon atoms." The responses of other cells could identify alcohols, alkanes, and so forth (Imamura, Mataga, & Mori, 1992; Mori, Mataga, & Imamura, 1992). In short the response of one receptor can identify the approximate nature of the molecule and the response of a larger population of receptors enables more precise recognition.

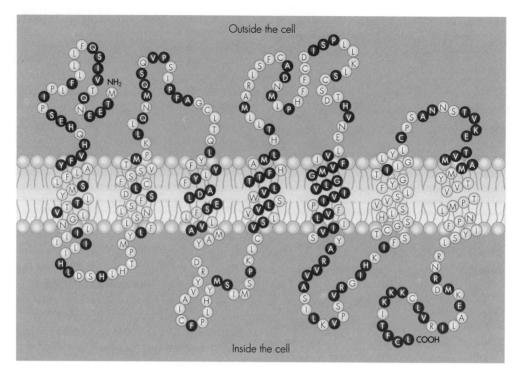

Figure 7.22 One of the olfactory receptor proteins
If you compare this protein with the synaptic receptor protein shown in Figure 3.12b (p. 63), you will notice great similarity. Each protein traverses the membrane seven times; each responds to a chemical outside the cell and triggers activity of a G protein inside the cell. The protein shown is one of a family; different olfactory receptors contain different proteins, each with a slightly different structure. Each of the little circles in this diagram represents one amino acid of the protein. The white circles represent amino acids that are the same in most of the olfactory receptor proteins; the purple circles represent amino acids that vary from one protein to another. *(Source: Based on Buck & Axel, 1991)*

The question may have occurred to you, "Why did evolution go to the bother of designing hundreds of different olfactory receptor types? After all, color vision gets by with just three types of cones." The main reason is that vision deals with light energy, which can be arranged along a single dimension, the wavelength. Olfaction deals with an enormous variety of airborne chemicals that are not arranged along any one continuum. To detect them all, we probably need a great variety of receptors. A secondary reason has to do with localization. In olfaction, space is no problem; we arrange our olfactory receptors over the entire surface of the nasal passages. In vision, however, the brain needs to determine precisely where on the retina some stimulus originates. Hundreds of different kinds of wavelength receptors could not be compacted into each spot on the retina.

Vomeronasal Sensation and Pheromones

An additional sense is important for most mammals, although less so for humans. The **vomeronasal organ (VNO)** is a set of receptors located near, but separate from, the olfactory receptors. Its receptors cross the cell membrane seven times, just like olfactory receptors. However, the VNO has relatively few types of receptors, those receptors have an entirely different amino

acid sequence from those of the olfactory system, and the VNO receptors maintain their response to a continued stimulus, instead of adapting to it as olfactory receptors do (Keverne, 1999).

Furthermore the VNO's role in behavior is more limited than that of the olfactory system. Predominantly the VNO controls responses to **pheromones,** which are chemicals released by an animal that affect the behavior of other members of the same species, especially sexually. Most mammals can determine from another individual's pheromones whether it is an infant, an adult male, a female in estrus (her fertile period), or a female not in estrus. Pheromones from a potential sex partner arouse sexual behaviors, and those from an infant influence maternal behavior, as we shall see in Chapter 11. In mice, pheromones from other females can delay puberty or stop the estrous cycle; pheromones from males can accelerate the onset of puberty or restore the estrous cycle (Bronson, 1974; Vandenbergh, 1987).

What about humans? Although the VNO is reasonably prominent in most mammals and easy to find in a human fetus, it is so small in adult humans that for years biologists doubted that it existed at all. Research has now established that many adults do have a small vomeronasal organ (Monti-Bloch, Jennings-White, Dolberg, & Berliner, 1994) (see Figure 7.23). However, re-

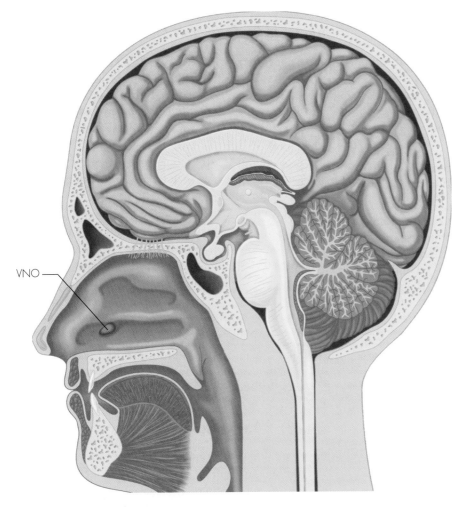

VNO

Figure 7.23 The human vomeronasal organ
This organ detects certain chemicals, especially those found on the human skin, but produces no conscious experience. Perhaps for that reason, researchers were slow to discover this organ.

Roizman, 1999). (They do not become synchronized if either of them is taking birth-control pills.) To test whether pheromones are responsible for the synchronization, researchers in two studies exposed young volunteer women to the underarm secretions of a donor woman. In both studies most of the women exposed to these secretions became synchronized to the donor woman's menstrual cycle (Preti, Cutler, Garcia, Huggins, & Lawley, 1986; Russell, Switz, & Thompson, 1980).

Another study dealt with the phenomenon that a woman who has an intimate relationship with a man tends to have more regular menstrual periods than other women do. One hypothesis is that the man's pheromones promote this regularity. In the study young women who were not sexually active were exposed daily to a man's underarm secretions. (Getting volunteers for a study like this isn't easy.) Gradually, over 14 weeks, most of these women's menstrual periods became more regular than before, with a mean of 29–30 days each (Cutler et al., 1986). In short, human body secretions apparently do act as pheromones, although the effects are more subtle than they are in nonhuman mammals, and the mechanism is still uncertain.

searchers have not yet found any receptors in the human VNO (Keverne, 1999).

Do humans respond to pheromones? The answer could be yes even if we do not have a functional VNO; in other species most pheromonal effects depend on the VNO, but some depend on the olfactory system (Johnston, 1998). Whichever organ is responsible, people do respond behaviorally to certain chemicals found in human skin which are usually described as "odorless." Exposure to these chemicals alters our skin temperature, sweating, and other autonomic responses (Monti-Bloch, Jennings-White, & Berliner, 1998), even though we are not conscious of the chemicals' odor or influence.

Several studies indicate a role of pheromones in human sexual behaviors, analogous to those in other mammals. One effect relates to the timing of women's menstrual cycles. Women who spend much time together find that their menstrual cycles become more synchronized (McClintock, 1971; Weller, Weller, Koresh-Kamin, & Ben-Shoshan, 1999; Weller, Weller, &

In Closing: Different Senses as Different Ways of Knowing the World

Ask the average person to describe his or her current environment, and you will probably get a description of what he or she sees and maybe a description of some sounds. If nonhumans could talk, most species would start by describing what they smell. A human, a dog, and a snail may be in the same place, but the environments they perceive are very different.

Humans don't have as many olfactory receptors as mice or dogs, and we seldom pay much attention to smells, but smells are nevertheless important for many aspects of our behavior. We don't meet new people by sniffing them, as dogs do, but we care about smells more than we generally realize.

Summary

1. Sensory information can be coded either in terms of a labeled-line system or in terms of an across-fiber pattern system. (p. 211)

2. Taste receptors are modified skin cells located in taste buds in papillae on the tongue. (p. 212)

3. According to current evidence, most researchers believe we have five kinds of taste receptors, sensitive to sweet, sour, salty, bitter, and umami (glutamate) tastes. (p. 213)

4. Salty receptors respond simply to sodium ions crossing the membrane. Sour receptors respond to a stimulus by blocking potassium channels. Sweet, bitter, and umami receptors act by a second messenger within the cell, similar to the way a metabotropic neurotransmitter receptor operates. (p. 213)

5. Some people, known as supertasters, have more fungiform papillae than other people do and are more sensitive to a great variety of tastes. They tend to avoid strong-tasting foods. (p. 214)

6. Brain neurons change their response to a taste to reflect its meaning. Sodium deficiency makes salt taste more pleasant; associating a taste with nausea makes it taste less pleasant. These changes in response occur even in the nucleus of the tractus solitarius (NTS) of rats, but not until the cortex in primates. (p. 215)

7. Olfactory receptors are proteins, each showing its strongest response to one chemical, weaker responses to similar chemicals, and little or no response to unrelated chemicals. Vertebrates have many olfactory receptor types, probably in the hundreds. (p. 216)

Answers to *Stop and Check* Questions

1. The shift key plus another is an example of an across-fiber pattern code. (The meaning of pressing one key depends on what else is pressed.) A fire alarm and a light switch are labeled lines; they convey only one message. (p. 212)

2. You could test for cross-adaptation. If the new taste cross-adapts with other tastes, then it uses the same receptors. If it does not cross-adapt, it may have a receptor of its own. (p. 213)

3. The chemical would block your experiences of sweet, bitter, and umami, but should not prevent you from tasting salty and sour. (p. 213)

4. An odorous chemical must diffuse through a mucous fluid before it can reach the olfactory receptors. (p. 217)

5. A specific anosmia is a less-than-normal sensitivity to a particular odorant. (p. 217)

6. Like metabotropic neurotransmitter receptors, an olfactory receptor acts through a G protein that triggers further events within the cell. (p. 217)

Thought Questions

1. In the English language, the letter *t* has no meaning out of context; its meaning depends on its relationship to other letters. Indeed, even a word, such as *to*, has little meaning except in its connection to other words. So is language a labeled-line system or an across-fiber pattern system?

2. Suppose a chemist synthesizes a new chemical which turns out to have an odor. Presumably we do not have a specialized receptor for that chemical. Explain how our receptors detect it.

Chapter Ending
Key Terms and Activities

Terms

across-fiber pattern principle (p. 211)

adaptation (p. 213)

amplitude (p. 192)

analgesia (p. 207)

anosmia (p. 217)

apex (p. 195)

base (p. 195)

basilar membrane (p. 194)

capsaicin (p. 206)

cochlea (p. 194)

conductive deafness (middle-ear deafness) (p. 197)

cross-adaptation (p. 213)

dermatome (p. 202)

endorphin (p. 207)

frequency (p. 192)

frequency theory (p. 194)

Suggestions for Further Reading

Beauchamp, G. K., & Bartoshuk, L. (1997). *Tasting and smelling.* San Diego: Academic Press. Excellent book covering receptors, psychophysics, and disorders of taste and smell.

Goldstein, E. B. (1996). *Sensation and perception* (4th ed.). Belmont, CA: Wadsworth. A general textbook on the sensory systems, emphasizing vision and hearing.

Hamill, O. P., & McBride, D. W., Jr. (1995). Mechanoreceptive membrane channels. *American Scientist, 83,* 30–37. Describes the mechanisms of various somatosensory receptors.

Pert, C. B. (1997). *Molecules of emotion.* New York: Simon & Schuster. Autobiographical statement by the woman who, as a graduate student, first demonstrated the opiate receptors.

Webster, D. B., Fay, R. R., & Popper, A. N. (Eds.). (1992). *The evolutionary biology of hearing.* New York: Springer Verlag. Collection of articles about hearing in humans and other species.

Web Sites to Explore

You can go to the Biological Psychology Study Center and click on these links. While there, you can also check for suggested articles available on InfoTrac. The Biological Psychology Internet address is:
http://psychology.wadsworth.com/book/kalatbiopsych7e/

http://www.marky.com/hearing/
Answers to frequently asked questions about deafness.

http://www.painnet.com/
Links to many kinds of information about pain and its control.

http://www.ampainsoc.org/
Information from the American Pain Society.

http://www.pbs.org/saf/3_ask/archive/qna/3294_peppers.html
Noted researcher Linda Bartoshuk answers frequently asked questions about taste.

http://www.olfactory.org/orf-link.html
Links to several sites concerning olfaction.

Active Learner Link

Quiz for Chapter 7

Movement

Chapter

8

Chapter Outline

Opposite:
Ultimately, the goal of all brain activity is to control movement—a far more complex process than it might seem.

Main Ideas

1. Movement depends on overall plans, not just connections between a stimulus and a muscle contraction.

2. Movements vary in sensitivity to feedback, skill, and variability in the face of obstacles.

3. Damage to different brain locations produces different kinds of movement impairment.

4. Brain damage that impairs movement also impairs cognitive processes. That is, control of movement is inseparably linked with cognition.

Before we get started, please try this: Get out a pencil and a sheet of paper, and put the pencil in your non-preferred hand. For example, if you are right-handed, put it in your left hand. Now with that hand draw a face in profile—that is, facing one direction or the other, but not straight ahead. *Please do this now.*

If you tried the demonstration, you probably notice that your drawing is much more childlike than usual. It is as if some part of your brain stored the way you used to draw as a young child. Now, if you are right-handed and therefore drew the face with your left hand, . . . why did you draw it facing to the right? At least I assume you did, because more than two-thirds of right-handers drawing with their left hand draw the profile facing right. Young children, age 5 or so, when drawing with the right hand almost always draw people and animals facing left, but when using the left hand almost always draw them facing right. So, *why* does this occur? The short answer is we don't know. The point is we have much to learn about the control of movement and how it relates to perception, motivation, and other functions.

The Control of Movement

Why do we have brains at all? Plants survive just fine without any need for a brain. So do sponges, which are animals, even if they don't act like it. But plants don't move, and neither do sponges. We do, and so do all other animals that have a brain. We need brains to control our behaviors, and our behaviors are movements.

"But wait," you might reply, "we need brains for other things too, don't we? Like seeing, hearing, finding food, talking, understanding what others say . . ."

Well, what would be the value of seeing and hearing if you couldn't do anything about them? Finding food is a movement. Talking is a movement. Understanding speech isn't a movement, but again it won't do you much good to understand speech unless you can do something about it. Imagine a great brain with no connection to any movement—like a computer with no connection to a monitor, printer, or anything else. No matter how powerful the internal processing, it would be useless.

Nevertheless most psychologists pay little attention to movement. The study of muscle contractions seems somehow less "psychological" than the study of visual perception, learning, social interactions, motivation, or emotion. And yet the rapid movements of a skilled typist, musician, or athlete require very complex brain activities. Understanding movement is a significant challenge for psychologists as well as biologists.

Muscles and Their Movements

All animal movement depends on the contraction of muscles. Vertebrate muscles fall into three categories (see Figure 8.1): **smooth muscles,** which control movements of internal organs; **skeletal,** or **striated, muscles,** which control movement of the body in relation to the environment; and **cardiac muscles** (the heart muscles), which have properties intermediate between those of smooth and skeletal muscles.

Each muscle is composed of many individual muscle fibers, as Figure 8.2 illustrates. A given axon may innervate more than one muscle fiber. For example, the eye muscles have a ratio of about one axon per three muscle fibers, and the biceps muscles of the arm have a ratio of one axon to more than a hundred fibers (Evarts, 1979). This difference enables eye movements to be more precise than biceps movements.

A **neuromuscular junction** is a synapse where a motor neuron axon meets a muscle fiber. In skeletal muscles every axon releases acetylcholine at the neuromuscular junction, and the acetylcholine always excites the muscle to contract. Each muscle can make just one movement—contraction—in just one direction. In the absence of excitation it relaxes, but it never moves actively in the opposite direction. Moving a leg or arm in two directions requires opposing sets of muscles, called **antagonistic muscles.** An arm, for example, has a **flexor** muscle that flexes or raises it and an **extensor** muscle that extends or straightens it (Figure 8.3). Walking, clapping hands, and other coordinated sequences require a regular alternation between contraction of one set of muscles and contraction of another.

Any deficit of acetylcholine or its receptors in the muscles can greatly impair movement. **Myasthenia gravis** (MY-us-THEE-nee-uh GRAHV-iss) is an *autoimmune disease* (one in which the immune system forms antibodies that attack the individual's own body). In myasthenia gravis the immune system attacks the acetylcholine receptors at neuromuscular junctions (Shah & Lisak, 1993). Myasthenia gravis causes the deaths of 2 or 3 people per 100,000 over the age of 75 each year; it seldom affects young people (Chandra, Bharucha, & Schoenberg, 1984).

The symptoms of myasthenia gravis are progressive weakness and rapid fatigue of the skeletal muscles. Here is what happens: Because the muscles have lost many of their acetylcholine receptors, the remaining receptors need the maximum amount of transmitter to move the muscles normally. After any motor neuron fires a few times in quick succession, later action potentials release less acetylcholine. A slight decline is no problem for healthy people, who have plenty of acetylcholine receptors. In people with myasthenia gravis, transmission at the neuromuscular junction is precarious at best, and even a slight decline in acetylcholine impairs movement (Drachman, 1978).

Myasthenia gravis can be treated with drugs that suppress the immune system (Shah & Lisak, 1993), but this approach leaves the patient vulnerable to other ill-

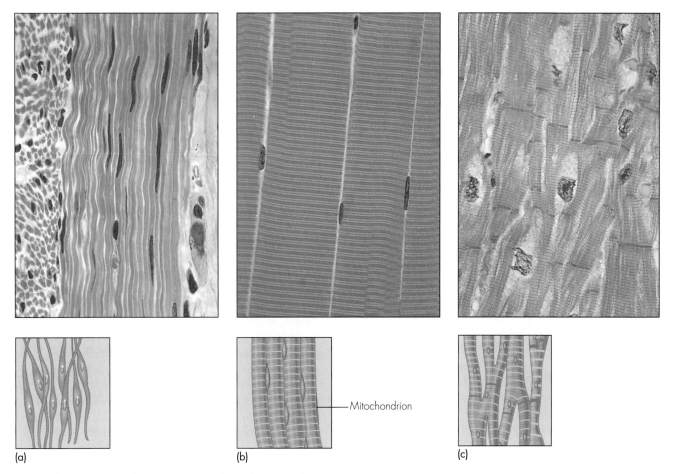

Figure 8.1   The three main types of vertebrate muscles
(a) Smooth muscle, found in the intestines and other organs, consists of long, thin cells. **(b)** Skeletal, or striated, muscle consists of long cylindrical fibers with stripes. **(c)** Cardiac muscle, found in the heart, consists of fibers that fuse together at various points. Because of these fusions, cardiac muscles contract together, not independently. *(Source: Illustrations after Starr & Taggart, 1989)*

nesses. So, many physicians prescribe drugs that inhibit acetylcholinesterase, the enzyme that breaks down acetylcholine. Inhibiting the breakdown of acetylcholine prolongs the action of acetylcholine at the neuromuscular junction. A physician must monitor the dose carefully, however, as too much acetylcholine is just as troublesome as too little.

Figure 8.2   An axon branching to innervate separate muscle fibers within a muscle
Movements can be much more precise where each axon innervates only a few fibers, as with eye muscles, than where it innervates many fibers, as with biceps muscles.

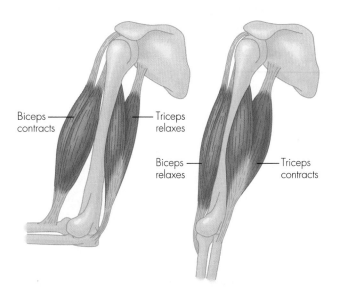

Figure 8.3   A pair of antagonistic muscles
The biceps of the arm is a flexor; the triceps is an extensor.
(Source: Starr & Taggart, 1989)

Fast and Slow Muscles

Imagine that you are a small fish. You are in constant danger of attack by larger fish, turtles, and birds; your only defense is your ability to swim away (Figure 8.4). The temperature of a fish is the same as the temperature of the water, and therefore you have a special problem in cold water. All muscle fibers contract more vigorously at high temperatures than at low temperatures. Therefore, at low temperatures, you will probably move more slowly than at higher temperatures, and you will be extremely vulnerable to attack by warm-blooded animals such as birds. Right? Strangely, no. A fish swims just as fast at low temperatures as it does at high temperatures. It maintains its swimming speed by recruiting more muscles at low temperatures (Rome, Loughna, & Goldspink, 1984).

A fish has three kinds of muscles: red, pink, and white. Red muscles produce rather slow movements, but they can respond almost indefinitely without fatigue, like the muscles you use for sitting or standing. White muscles produce the fastest movements, but they fatigue rapidly. Pink muscles are intermediate in both speed and fatigue. At high temperatures a fish relies mostly on its red muscles and a few pink muscles. At colder temperatures the fish relies more and more on its white muscles. By recruiting enough white muscles, the fish can maintain its usual swimming speed in all water temperatures, although it fatigues faster at low temperatures.

All right, you can stop imagining that you are a fish. In humans and other mammals, various kinds of muscle fibers are mixed together, not in separate bundles as in fish. Our muscle types are graded, from **fast-twitch fibers** that produce fast contractions but fatigue rapidly to **slow-twitch fibers** that produce less vigorous contractions without fatiguing (Hennig & Lømo, 1985). For standing, walking, and nonstrenuous activities, we rely on our slow-twitch and intermediate fibers. For running up a flight of stairs at full speed, we use more fast-twitch fibers. (And then we huff and puff.)

People have varying percentages of fast-twitch and slow-twitch fibers and can increase one type or the other depending on which ones they use. For example, investigators studied one group of male sprinters before and after a 3-month period of intensive training. The athletes increased their number of fast-twitch leg muscle fibers and decreased their slow-twitch fibers (Andersen, Klitgaard, & Saltin, 1994). Conversely, the Swedish ultramarathon runner Bertil Järlaker built up so many slow-twitch fibers in his legs that he once ran 3520 km (2188 mi) in 50 days (an average of 1.7 marathons per day) with only minimal signs of pain or fatigue (Sjöström, Friden, & Ekblom, 1987).

Figure 8.4 Temperature regulation and movement
Fish are "cold blooded," but many of their predators (such as this pelican) are not. At cold temperatures a fish must maintain its normal swimming speed, even though every muscle in its body contracts more slowly than usual. To do so a fish calls upon white muscles that it otherwise uses only for brief bursts of speed.

Stop & Check

1. Why can the eye muscles move with greater precision than the biceps muscles?

2. How does an acetylcholinesterase blocker help patients with myasthenia gravis?

3. How do fish manage to swim as fast in cold water as in warm water, even though each muscle contracts more vigorously in warm water?

4. In what way are fish movements impaired in cold water?

5. Why is an ultramarathoner like Bertil Järlaker probably mediocre or poor at short-distance races?

Check your answers on page 230.

Muscle Control by Proprioceptors

You are walking along on a slightly bumpy road. What happens if the messages from your spinal cord to your leg muscles are not exactly correct? You might set your foot down a little too hard or not quite hard enough. Nevertheless you adjust your posture almost immediately and maintain your balance without even thinking about it. How do you do that? A baby is lying on its back. You playfully tug its foot and then let go. At once the leg bounces back to its original position. How did that happen?

In both cases the mechanism is under the control of proprioceptors (see Figure 8.5). A **proprioceptor** is a receptor that is sensitive to the position or movement of a part of the body—in these cases a muscle. Muscle proprioceptors detect the stretch and tension of a muscle and send messages that enable the spinal cord to adjust its signals. When a muscle is stretched, the spinal cord sends a reflexive signal to contract that muscle. This **stretch reflex** is caused by a stretch; it does not result in a stretch.

One kind of proprioceptor is the **muscle spindle,** a receptor parallel to the muscle that responds to the stretch of the muscle (Merton, 1972; Miles & Evarts, 1979). Whenever the muscle spindle is stretched, its sensory nerve sends a message to a motor neuron in the spinal cord, which in turn sends a message back to the muscles surrounding the spindle, causing a contraction. Note that this reflex provides for negative feedback: When a muscle and its spindle are stretched, the spindle sends a message that results in a muscle contraction that opposes the stretch.

When you set your foot down on a slight bump on the road, your knee bends a bit, stretching the extensor muscles of that leg. The sensory nerves of the spindles send action potentials to the motor neuron in the spinal cord, and the motor neuron sends action potentials to the extensor muscle. Contraction of the extensor muscle straightens the leg, adjusting for the bump on the road.

A physician who asks you to cross your legs and then taps you just below the knee (Figure 8.6) is testing your stretch reflexes. The tap below the knee stretches the extensor muscles and their spindles, resulting in a message that jerks the lower leg upward.

Another proprioceptor, the **Golgi tendon organ,** responds to increases in muscle tension. Located in the tendons at opposite ends of a muscle, it acts as a brake against an excessively vigorous contraction. Some muscles are so strong that they could damage themselves if too many fibers contracted at once. Golgi tendon organs detect the tension that results during a muscle contraction. Their impulses travel to the spinal cord, where they inhibit the motor neurons through messages from interneurons. In short, a vigorous muscle contraction inhibits further contraction by activating the Golgi tendon organs.

The proprioceptors not only control important reflexes but also provide the brain with information about the location of body parts. If you have ever tried walking after your legs have "fallen asleep," you know how difficult it is to control movement without proprioception. One 19-year-old man suffered a complete loss of touch and proprioception from the neck down as a result of a virus that attacked his sensory neurons. For about a year

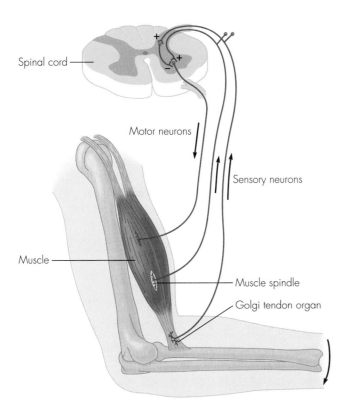

Figure 8.5 Two kinds of proprioceptors regulate the contraction of a muscle
When a muscle is stretched, the nerves from the muscle spindles transmit an increased frequency of impulses, resulting in a contraction of the surrounding muscle. Contraction of the muscle stimulates the Golgi tendon organ, which acts as a brake or shock absorber to prevent a contraction that is too quick or extreme.

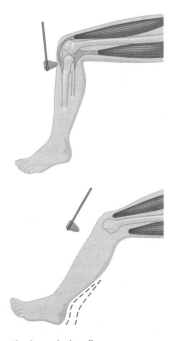

Figure 8.6 The knee-jerk reflex
This is one example of a stretch reflex.

afterward, he hardly moved a muscle. He still *could* move his muscles, but because of the lack of proprioception, he had no control of the distance, direction, or velocity of his movements, so he found it safer to make no movements at all. (Again, you may note parallels to the experience of having your legs fall asleep. The difference is that his loss of sensation included his entire body except the head and that it was permanent.) Over several years he gradually regained the ability to walk, write, and so forth, but only by watching every movement carefully. In a dim or dark room, he is still unable to control his movements (Cole, 1995). In short, do not underestimate the importance of your proprioceptors.

Stop & Check

6. If you hold your arm straight out and someone pulls it down slightly, it quickly bounces back. What proprioceptor is responsible?

7. What is the function of Golgi tendon organs?

Check your answers on page 230.

Units of Movement

The stretch reflex is a simple example of movement. More complex kinds include speaking, walking, threading a needle, and throwing a basketball through a hoop while off balance and trying to evade two defenders. In many ways these movements are different from one another, and they depend on different kinds of control by the nervous system.

Voluntary and Involuntary Movements

Reflexes are consistent automatic responses to stimuli. The stretch reflex is one example; another is the constriction of the pupil in response to bright light. Infants have several reflexes not seen in adults (Digression 8.1). We generally think of reflexes as *involuntary* because, although they are sensitive to external stimuli, they are not sensitive to reinforcements, punishments, and motivations.

Many behaviors are a complex mixture of voluntary and involuntary influences. Take swallowing, for example. You can voluntarily swallow or inhibit swallowing, but only within certain limits. Try to swallow ten times in a row voluntarily (without anything to drink). The first swallow is easy and the second is almost as easy. But before long you will find additional swallows difficult, unpleasant, eventually almost impossible. Now try to inhibit swallowing for as long as you can.

Chances are you will not last more than a minute or two. (You're not allowed to spit.)

Can you think of a purely voluntary movement—that is, one that is independent of external stimuli, with no unintentional components? The question probably sounds easy, and you suggest walking, talking, scratching your head. . . . However, most examples turn out to include involuntary components. Consider walking: When you walk, you automatically compensate for the bumps and irregularities in the road. You probably also swing your arms a bit, automatically, just as an involuntary consequence of walking.

Visual stimuli greatly facilitate walking, at least in certain people. A patient with Parkinson's disease ordinarily has great trouble walking but can walk surprisingly well when following a parade. Also, if someone marks lines across the floor at approximately one-step intervals, a Parkinson's patient can step across each line much more easily than when walking down an unmarked hall (Teitelbaum, Pellis, & Pellis, 1991). So is the walking voluntary or involuntary? Evidently it is a mixture of both: The person chooses to walk, but the stimuli of following a parade or crossing lines greatly facilitate the behavior. In short, the distinction between voluntary and involuntary is often blurry.

Movements with Different Sensitivity to Feedback

The military distinguishes between ballistic missiles and guided missiles. A ballistic missile is simply launched toward the target, like a thrown ball. Once the missile is launched, there is no way to correct its aim. A guided missile, however, detects the target location and adjusts its trajectory one way or the other to correct for error in the original aim.

Similarly some movements are ballistic and others are corrected by feedback. A **ballistic movement** is executed as a whole: Once initiated, it cannot be altered or its aim corrected. A reflex—a simple, automatic response to a stimulus, such as the stretch reflex or the contraction of the pupils in response to light—is a ballistic movement.

Completely ballistic movements are rare; most behaviors are subject to feedback correction. For example, when you thread a needle, you make a slight movement, check your aim, and then readjust the next movement. Similarly a singer who holds a single note for a prolonged time hears any unintentional wavering of the pitch and corrects it. The importance of the feedback becomes apparent if we distort it. Suppose we equip you with a device that records what you sing and then plays it back over earphones so that you hear what you sang 5 seconds ago. Now when you try to sing one note, you hear the error you made 5 seconds ago and try to correct it. But you will not start to hear your correction for another 5 seconds, and by that time you have overcorrected. The result is wild swings back and forth.

Infant Reflexes

Certain reflexes are present in infants but not in older children or adults. For example, if you place an object firmly in an infant's hand, the infant will reflexively grasp it tightly (the **grasp reflex**). If you stroke the sole of the foot, the infant will reflexively extend the big toe and fan the others (the **Babinski reflex**). If you touch the cheek of an awake infant, the head will turn toward the stimulated cheek and the infant will begin to suck (the **rooting reflex**). The rooting reflex is not a pure example of a reflex; its intensity depends on the infant's alertness, hunger, and so forth. Still, this reflex, like the others, is characteristic of infants and seldom present in healthy adults.

Although such reflexes fade away with time, their reflexive connections remain intact, not lost but suppressed by axons from the maturing brain. If the cerebral cortex is damaged, the infant reflexes are released from inhibition. In fact neurologists and other physicians frequently test adults for infant reflexes. A physician who strokes the sole of your foot during a physical exam is probably looking for evidence of brain damage. This is hardly the most dependable test, but it is among the easiest. If a stroke of the sole of your foot makes you fan your toes like a baby, there may be an impairment of your cerebral cortex.

Infant reflexes sometimes return temporarily if activity in the cerebral cortex is depressed by alcohol, carbon dioxide, or other chemicals. (You might try testing for infant reflexes in a friend who has consumed too much alcohol.)

Infants and children also have a stronger tendency than adults do to certain *allied reflexes*. If dust blows in your face, you will reflexively close your eyes and mouth and probably sneeze. These reflexes are *allied* in the sense that each of them tends to elicit the others. If you suddenly see a bright light—as when you emerge from a dark theater on a sunny afternoon— you will reflexively close your eyes and you may also close your mouth and perhaps sneeze. Some adults react this way; a higher percentage of young children do (Whitman & Packer, 1993).

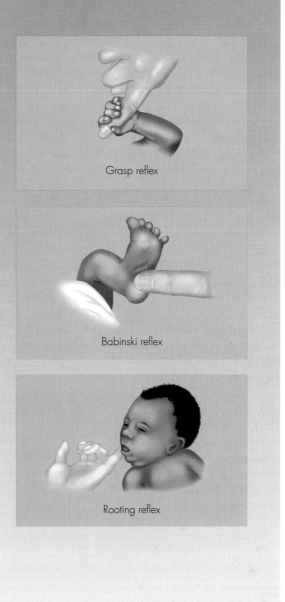

Grasp reflex

Babinski reflex

Rooting reflex

Sequences of Behaviors

Many of our behaviors consist of rapid sequences, as in speaking, writing, dancing, or playing a musical instrument. In certain cases we can attribute these sequences to **central pattern generators,** neural mechanisms in the spinal cord or elsewhere that generate rhythmic patterns of motor output. Examples include the spinal cord mechanisms that generate wing flapping in birds, fin movements in fish, and the repetitive shaking movements that a wet animal makes to dry itself off (often known as the "wet dog shake"). Although a stimulus

may activate a central pattern generator, it does not control the frequency of repetition of the alternating movements. For example, cats scratch themselves at a rate of three or four scratches per second, and this rhythm is generated by cells in the lumbar segments of the spinal cord (Deliagina, Orlovsky, & Pavlova, 1983). The rhythm is a constant, and it remains the same even if the spinal neurons are isolated from all cerebral input and even if the muscles are paralyzed. So it is clear that the spinal neurons generate the rhythm by themselves.

We refer to a fixed sequence of movements as a **motor program**. A central pattern generator produces a motor program, but so do other mechanisms that are not necessarily rhythmic. A motor program can be either learned or built into the nervous system. For an example of a built-in program, a mouse periodically grooms itself by sitting up, licking its paws, wiping its paws over its face, closing its eyes as the paws pass over them, licking the paws again, and so forth (Fentress, 1973). Once begun the sequence is predictable from beginning to end. In contrast many people develop learned yet very predictable motor sequences. An expert gymnast will produce a familiar pattern of movements as a smooth, coordinated whole; the same can be said for skilled typists, piano players, and so forth.

By comparing species we begin to understand how a motor program can be gained or lost through evolution. For example, if you hold a chicken several feet above the ground and then drop it, it will stretch its wings and flap them. Even chickens with featherless wings make the same movements, even though they fail to break their fall (Provine, 1979, 1981). Those chickens are, of course, genetically still programmed to fly. On the other hand, penguins, emus, and rheas, which have not used their wings for flight for millions of years, have lost the genes for flight movements and do not extend their wings when they are dropped (Provine, 1984).

Do humans have any built-in motor programs? Yawning is one example (Provine, 1986). A yawn consists of a prolonged open-mouth inhalation, often accompanied by stretching, and a shorter exhalation. Yawns are very consistent in duration, with a mean of just under 6 seconds.

Module 8.1

In Closing: Categories of Movement

Charles Sherrington described a motor neuron in the spinal cord as "the final common path." He meant that regardless of what sensory and motivational processes occupy the brain, the final result was always either a muscle contraction or the delay of a muscle contraction. However, a motor neuron and its associated muscle participate in a great many different kinds of movements, and we need many brain areas to control the different kinds.

Summary

1. Vertebrates have skeletal, cardiac, and smooth muscles. (p. 224)

2. Skeletal muscles range from slow muscles that do not fatigue to fast muscles that fatigue quickly. We rely on the slow muscles most of the time, but we recruit the fast muscles for brief periods of strenuous activity. (p. 226)

3. Proprioceptors are receptors sensitive to the position and movement of a part of the body. Two kinds of proprioceptors, muscle spindles and Golgi tendon organs, help regulate muscle movements. (p. 227)

4. Some movements, especially reflexes, proceed as a unit, with little if any guidance from sensory feedback. Other movements, such as threading a needle, are constantly guided and redirected by sensory feedback. (p. 228)

5. Someone who becomes skillful at a movement executes large sequences of the movement as a whole, with little dependence on moment-by-moment feedback. (p. 229)

Answers to *Stop and Check* Questions

1. Each axon to the biceps muscles innervates about a hundred fibers; therefore it is not possible to change the movement by just a few fibers more or less. In contrast an axon to the eye muscles innervates only about three fibers. (p. 226)

2. People with myasthenia gravis have fewer than normal receptors, so they need extra acetylcholine to maintain normal movement. Acetylcholinesterase breaks down acetylcholine after it stimulates a receptor on a muscle. So a drug that blocks acetylcholinesterase increases the amount of acetylcholine. (p. 226)

3. In cold water a fish recruits more muscles to compensate for the fact that each muscle contracts less vigorously. (p. 226)

4. Although a fish can move rapidly in cold water, it fatigues rapidly. (p. 226)

5. An ultramarathoner builds up large numbers of slow-twitch fibers at the expense of fast-twitch fibers. Therefore endurance is great but maximum speed is not. (p. 226)

6. The muscle spindle (p. 228)

7. The Golgi tendon organ responds to muscle tension and thereby prevents excessively strong muscle contractions. (p. 228)

Thought Question

Would you expect jaguars, cheetahs, and other great cats to have mostly slow-twitch, nonfatiguing muscles in their legs or mostly fast-twitch, quickly fatiguing muscles? What kinds of animals might have mostly the opposite kind of muscles?

Module 8.2

Brain Mechanisms of Movement

Suppose you stand up, walk across the room, sit at the piano, place your hands in position, and start to play. So far as you are consciously aware, you merely decide to perform this sequence of actions and then do it. However, much of your nervous system is devoted to making it happen. Furthermore different parts of your brain are responsible for different aspects of movement. Figure 8.7 outlines the major motor areas of the mammalian central nervous system. Don't get too bogged down in details at this point; we shall attend to each area in due course.

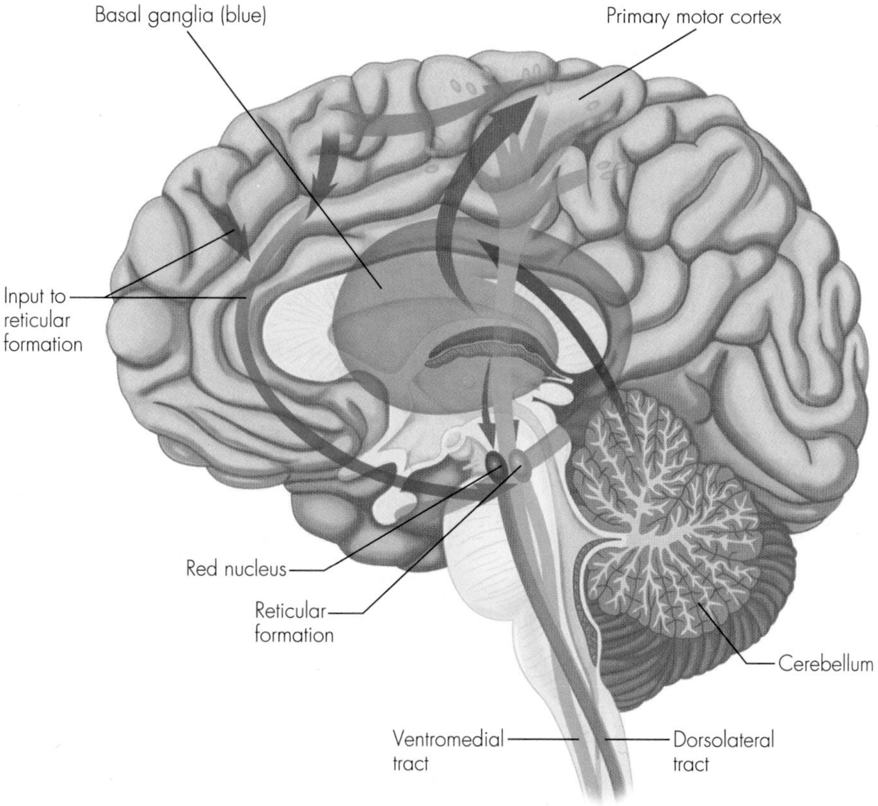

The Role of the Cerebral Cortex

Since the pioneering work of Gustav Fritsch and Eduard Hitzig (1870), neuroscientists have known that direct electrical stimulation of the **primary motor cortex,** the precentral gyrus of the frontal cortex, just anterior to the central sulcus (Figure 8.8), can elicit movements. However, the motor cortex has no direct connections to the muscles; it merely sends axons that turn on central pattern generators in the brain stem and spinal cord (Shik & Orlovsky, 1976). Diseases of the spinal cord can impair the control of movement in various ways (see Table 8.1).

Electrical stimulation of the motor cortex generally produces coordinated movement in several muscles, not isolated movement in a single muscle (Asanuma, 1981). In other words the cortex (unlike the spinal cord) is in charge of general movement plans, not individual muscle contractions. The cerebral cortex is particularly important in controlling complex actions. It contributes little to the control of coughing, sneezing, gagging, laughing, or crying (Rinn, 1984). Those behaviors are either reflexive or at least controlled by subcortical areas of the brain. (Perhaps this lack of cerebral control explains why it is hard to perform such actions voluntarily.)

Figure 8.9 (which repeats part of Figure 4.21, p. 105) shows a map of the body along the motor cortex. In general, stimulation of any spot in the motor cortex evokes movements in the body area shown next to it, on the opposite side of the body. For example, the brain area shown next to the hand is active during hand movements. However,

Basal ganglia (blue)

Primary motor cortex

Input to reticular formation

Red nucleus

Reticular formation

Cerebellum

Ventromedial tract

Dorsolateral tract

Figure 8.7 The major motor areas of the mammalian central nervous system
The cerebral cortex, especially the primary motor cortex, sends axons directly to the medulla and spinal cord. So do the red nucleus, reticular formation, and other brain stem areas. The medulla and spinal cord control muscle movements. The basal ganglia and cerebellum influence movement indirectly through their communication back and forth with the cerebral cortex and brain stem.

don't read this figure as implying that each spot in the motor cortex controls exactly one body area, much less that it controls just one muscle. Control is distributed over a population of cells, just as it is for sensation. (Remember the across-fiber pattern principle from Chapter 7.) For example, movement of any one finger or the wrist is associated with activity in a scattered population of cells, and the regions activated by one finger greatly overlap the regions activated by any other finger, as shown in Figure 8.10 (Sanes, Donoghue, Thangaraj, Edelman, & Warach, 1995). In one study researchers found that when they injected a drug to temporarily anesthetize a tiny spot in a monkey's motor cortex, they sometimes got peculiar results, such as paralyzing the second and fourth fingers but not the third (Schieber & Poliakov, 1998). So the motor cortex is organized more or less as a map of the body, but it is not a perfect, one-to-one map.

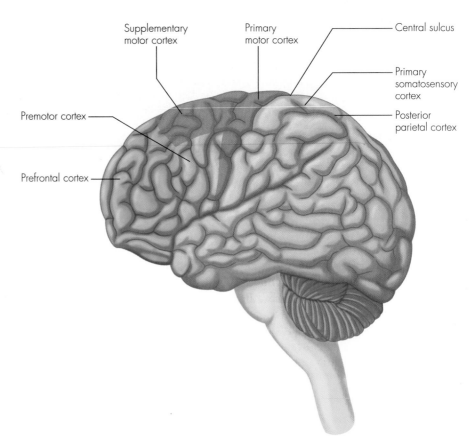

Figure 8.8   Principal areas of the motor cortex in the human brain
Cells in the premotor cortex and supplementary motor cortex are active during the planning of movements, even if the movements are never actually executed.

Areas Near the Primary Motor Cortex

A number of areas near the primary motor cortex also contribute to movement in diverse ways (see Figure 8.8). In the **posterior parietal cortex,** some neurons respond primarily to visual or somatosensory stimuli, some respond mostly to current or future movements, and some respond to a complicated mixture of the stimulus and the upcoming response (Shadlen & Newsome, 1996). You might think of the posterior parietal cortex as keeping track of the position of the body relative to the world (Snyder, Grieve, Brotchie, & Andersen, 1998). Contrast the effects of posterior parietal damage with those of occipital or temporal damage. People with posterior parietal damage can accurately describe what they see, but they have trouble converting their perception into action. Although they can walk toward something they hear, they cannot walk toward something they see, nor can they reach out to grasp something—even after describing its size, shape, and angle. In contrast, people with damage to certain parts of the occipital cortex cannot describe the size, shape, or location of the objects they see, but they can reach out and pick them up and when walking they step over or go around the objects in their way (Goodale, 1996; Goodale, Milner, Jakobson, & Carey, 1991). In short, the ability to describe what we see is separate from the influence of

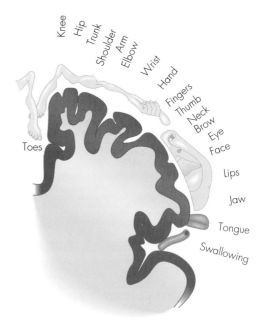

Figure 8.9   Map of body areas in the primary motor cortex
Stimulation at any point in the primary motor cortex is most likely to evoke movements in the body area shown. However, actual results are usually messier than this figure implies: For example, individual cells controlling one finger may be intermingled with cells controlling another finger.
(Source: Adapted from Penfield & Rasmussen, 1950)

Table 8.1 Some Disorders of the Spinal Column

Disorder	Description	Cause
Paralysis	Lack of voluntary movement in part of the body.	Damage to motor neurons in the spinal cord or their axons in the periphery.
Flaccid paralysis	Inability to move one part of the body voluntarily, accompanied by low muscle tone and weak reflexive movements.	Damage to motor neurons in the spinal cord. Can be temporary result of damage to axons from brain to spinal cord.
Spastic paralysis	Inability to move one part of the body voluntarily, although reflexive movements and tremors remain. Muscles are stiff and muscle tone is higher than normal. Reflexes are strong and jerky.	Damage to axons from the brain to the spinal cord. (Such damage initially causes flaccid paralysis, which eventually gives way to spastic paralysis.)
Paraplegia	Loss of sensation and voluntary muscle control in both legs. Reflexes remain in legs. Although no messages pass between the brain and the genitals, the genitals still respond reflexively to touch. Paraplegics feel nothing in their own genitals, but they can function sexually, satisfy their partners, and still experience orgasm (Money, 1967).	Cut through the spinal cord above the segments attached to the legs.
Quadriplegia	Loss of sensation and muscle control in all four extremities.	Cut through the spinal cord above the level controlling the arms.
Hemiplegia	Loss of sensation and muscle control in the arm and leg on one side.	Cut halfway through the spinal cord or (more commonly) damage to one of the hemispheres of the cerebral cortex.
Tabes dorsalis	Impaired sensation in the legs and pelvic region, impaired leg reflexes and walking, loss of bladder and bowel control.	Late stage of syphilis. Dorsal roots of the spinal cord deteriorate gradually.
Poliomyelitis	Paralysis.	Virus that damages cell bodies of motor neurons.
Amyotrophic lateral sclerosis (Lou Gehrig's disease)	Gradual weakness and paralysis, starting with the arms and later spreading to the legs. Both motor neurons and axons from the brain to the motor neurons are destroyed.	Unknown.

vision on movement, and we can lose either one without the other.

The primary somatosensory cortex is the main receiving area for touch and other body information, as mentioned in Chapter 7. It sends a substantial number of axons directly to the spinal cord and also provides the primary motor cortex with sensory information.

Cells in the prefrontal cortex, premotor cortex, and supplementary motor cortex are active during the planning of a movement. The **prefrontal cortex** responds mostly to the sensory signals that lead to a movement, including signals for movements to be made after a delay (Goldman-Rakic, Bates, & Chafee, 1992). The **pre-motor cortex** is most active during preparations for a movement and less active during the movement itself. It, too, responds to sensory stimuli, especially to visual stimuli from objects near the hands or the face (the parts of the body most likely to act on the information). Many of these cells continue to respond to those visual stimuli even when the lights are turned off—that is, they respond to temporary memories of the locations of objects (Graziano, Hu, & Gross, 1997).

In an experiment to contrast the contributions of the prefrontal cortex and the premotor cortex, monkeys were shown a red or green light, which signaled whether they would later have to touch the red or green pad to

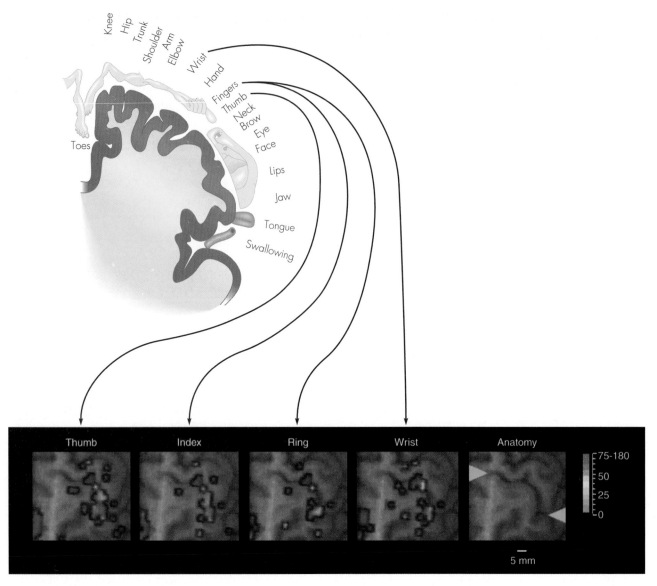

Figure 8.10 Motor cortex during movement of a finger or the wrist
In this functional MRI scan, red indicates the greatest activity, followed by yellow, green, and blue. Note that each movement activated a scattered population of cells and that the areas activated by any one part of the hand overlapped the areas activated by any other. The scan at the right (anatomy) shows a section of the central sulcus (between the two yellow arrows). The primary motor cortex is just anterior to the central sulcus. *(Source: Sanes, Donoghue, Thangaraj, Edelman, & Warach, 1995)*

get food. After a 1.25-second delay, the monkeys saw a second light, which meant that it was almost time to respond. They then had to wait between 1.25 seconds and 3.5 seconds before touching the correct pad to receive some juice as a reinforcement. (That is, the monkeys had to time their response correctly.) The initial stimulus (the red or green light) provoked activity mostly in the prefrontal cortex. The second stimulus (indicating that the monkey must wait at least another 1.25 seconds before responding) also provoked activity mostly in the prefrontal cortex. Toward the end of that delay, just before the movement, cells in the premotor cortex became active (DiPelligrino & Wise, 1991). Thus

preparation for a movement seems to consist of waves of activity, first in the prefrontal cortex, then in the premotor cortex, next mostly in the primary motor cortex, and ultimately in the spinal cord and the muscles.

The **supplementary motor cortex** is most active during preparations for a rapid series of movements, such as pushing, pulling, and then turning a stick. Many cells in this area are active only in preparation for one particular order of movements (Tanji & Shima, 1994). As Karl Lashley (1951) pointed out long ago, behaviors such as typing, dancing, speaking, and playing a musical instrument require such rapid alternations of actions that we must start each movement well before finishing the last one, sometimes two or three steps ahead. Damage to the supplementary motor cortex impairs the ability to organize smooth sequences of activities.

Stop *&* Check

1. How does the posterior parietal cortex contribute to movement? The prefrontal cortex? The premotor cortex? The supplementary motor cortex?

Check your answers on page 241.

Connections from the Brain to the Spinal Cord

All the messages from the brain must eventually reach the medulla and spinal cord, which control the muscles. The various outputs from the brain organize into two paths, the dorsolateral tract and the ventromedial tract.

The **dorsolateral tract** of the spinal cord is a set of axons from the primary motor cortex and surrounding areas and from the **red nucleus** of the midbrain (Figure 8.11). The paths from the motor cortex and the red nucleus control similar movements, but the motor cortex is more important for unrehearsed or very precise

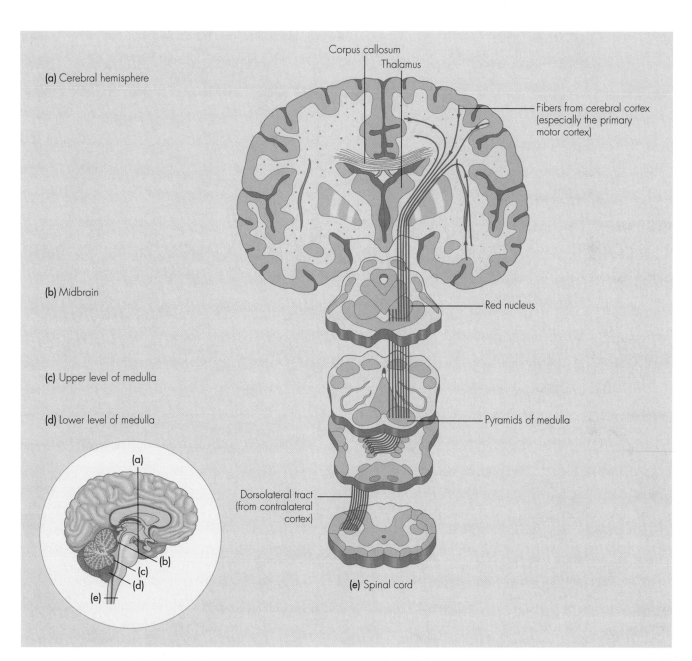

(a) Cerebral hemisphere

Corpus callosum
Thalamus

Fibers from cerebral cortex (especially the primary motor cortex)

(b) Midbrain

Red nucleus

(c) Upper level of medulla

(d) Lower level of medulla

Pyramids of medulla

Dorsolateral tract (from contralateral cortex)

(a)

(b)

(c)

(d)

(e)

(e) Spinal cord

Figure 8.11 The dorsolateral tract
This tract originates from the primary motor cortex, neighboring areas, and the red nucleus. It crosses from one side of the brain to the opposite side of the spinal cord and controls precise and discrete movements of the extremities, such as hands, fingers, and feet.

movements, such as playing an unfamiliar piece on the piano (Lorincz & Fabre-Thorpe, 1997; Onodera & Hicks, 1999). The dorsolateral tract axons extend without synaptic interruption to their target neurons in the spinal cord. In bulges of the medulla called *pyramids*, the dorsolateral tract crosses from one side of the brain to the opposite side of the spinal cord. (For that reason the dorsolateral tract is also called the pyramidal tract.) It controls movements in peripheral areas, such as the hands, fingers, and toes. People with damage to the primary motor cortex or its axons suffer at least a temporary loss of fine movements on the opposite side of the body.

The **ventromedial tract** includes many axons from the primary motor cortex and supplementary motor cortex and also some from many other parts of the cortex. It also includes axons that originate from the midbrain tectum, the reticular formation, and the **vestibular nucleus**, the brain area receiving input from the vestibular system described in Chapter 7 (see Figure 8.12). Axons of the ventromedial tract do not cross from one side of the nervous system to the other, although many of its axons have branches to both sides of the spinal cord. The ventromedial tract controls mainly the muscles of the neck, shoulders, and trunk (Kuypers, 1989). Note that these movements are necessarily bilat-

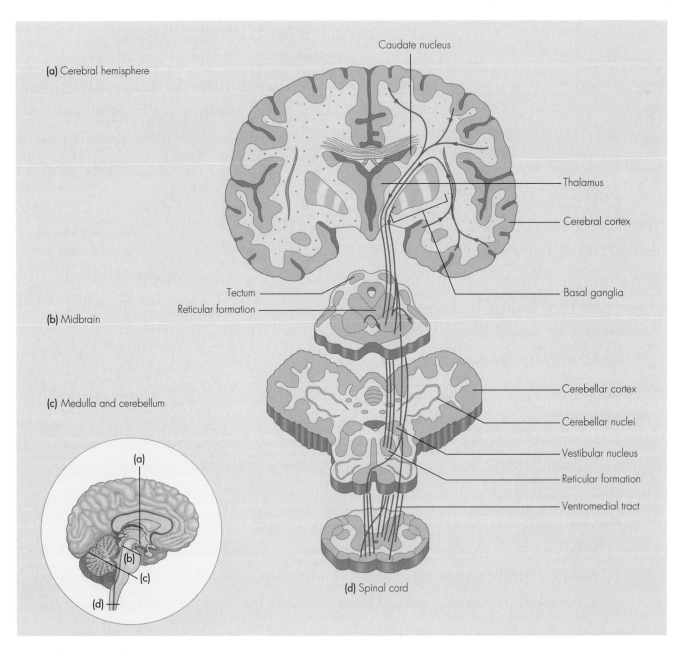

Figure 8.12 The ventromedial tract
This tract originates from many parts of the cerebral cortex and several areas of the midbrain and medulla. It produces bilateral control of trunk muscles for postural adjustments and bilateral movements such as standing, bending, turning, and walking.

eral; you can move your fingers on just one side, but if you move your neck, it has to move on both sides. Damage to the ventromedial tract impairs walking, turning, bending, standing up, and sitting down. Most movements rely on both dorsolateral and ventromedial tracts in cooperation with each other, not independently.

Stop & Check

2. What kinds of movements are controlled by the dorsolateral tract? By the ventromedial tract?

Check your answers on page 241.

The Role of the Cerebellum

The cerebellum is important for motor control, including learned motor responses. The term *cerebellum* is Latin for "little brain." The cerebellum contains more neurons than the rest of the brain combined (R. W. Williams & Herrup, 1988), and some of those neurons have broad branching with an enormous number of connections. So although the cerebellum is small physically, it is enormous in its potential for processing information.

The most obvious effect of cerebellar damage is trouble with rapid, ballistic movement sequences that require accurate aiming and timing. For example, people with cerebellar damage have trouble tapping a rhythm, pointing at a moving object, speaking, writing, typing, playing a musical instrument, most athletic activities, and even with simple alternating movements such as hand clapping. However, they have no particular trouble lifting weights because they do not need precise aim or timing.

The cerebellum is large in most species of birds, which have to time and aim their movements precisely, especially when landing after flight. The sloth, at the other extreme, is a mammal proverbial for its slowness. When M. G. Murphy and J. L. O'Leary (1973) made cerebellar lesions in sloths, they found no change in the animals' movements.

Here is one quick way to test how well someone's cerebellum is functioning: Ask the person to focus on one spot and then to move the eyes quickly to another spot. **Saccades** (sa-KAHDS), ballistic eye movements from one fixation point to another, depend on impulses from the cerebellum and the frontal cortex to the cranial nerves. A normal, healthy person's

eyes move from one fixation point to another by a single movement or by one large movement with a small correction at the end. Someone with cerebellar damage, however, has difficulty programming the angle and distance of eye movements (Dichgans, 1984). The eyes make many short movements until, by trial and error, they eventually focus on the intended spot.

Another test of cerebellar damage is the *finger-to-nose test*. The person is instructed to hold one arm straight out and then, at command, to touch his or her nose as quickly as possible. A normal person does so in three steps. First, the finger moves ballistically to a point just in front of the nose. This *move* function depends on the cerebellar cortex (the surface of the cerebellum), which sends messages to the nuclei (clusters of cell bodies in the interior of the cerebellum; see Figure 8.13). Second, the finger remains steady at that spot for a fraction of a second. This *hold* function depends on the nuclei alone (Kornhuber, 1974). Finally, the finger moves to the nose by a slower movement that does not depend on the cerebellum.

After damage to the cerebellar cortex, a person has trouble with the initial rapid movement. Either the finger stops too soon or it goes too far, striking the face. If certain cerebellar nuclei have been damaged, the person may have difficulty with the hold segment: The finger reaches a point just in front of the nose and then wavers wildly.

The symptoms of cerebellar damage markedly resemble those of intoxication. Drunken individuals as a rule are clumsy, their speech is slurred, and their eye movements are inaccurate. A police officer testing someone for drunkenness may use the finger-to-nose test or similar tests because the cerebellum is one of the first brain areas to show the effects of intoxication.

Evidence of a Broad Role

The cerebellum is not only a motor structure, and maybe not even primarily a motor structure. In one study functional MRI measured cerebellar activity while people performed several tasks with a single set of objects (Gao et al., 1996). When they simply lifted

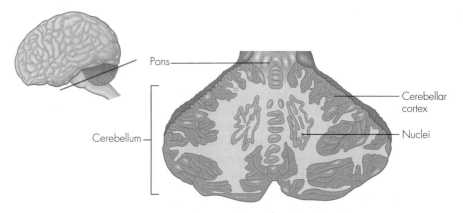

Figure 8.13 Location of the cerebellar nuclei relative to the cerebellar cortex

things, the cerebellum showed little activity. When they felt objects with both hands to decide whether they were the same or different, the cerebellum was much more active. The cerebellum even showed some activity when people held their hands steady and the experimenter rubbed an object across them. That is, the cerebellum responded to sensory stimuli that might guide movement, but not to movement by itself.

In another study people performed either a motor task or a visual attention task of silently counting squares or red shapes that appeared on a screen. According to fMRI scans, different parts of the cerebellum were active for the different tasks (Allen, Buxton, Wong, & Courchesne, 1997).

What, then, is the role of the cerebellum? We probably should not look for just one role. The cerebellum is a complex structure, and different areas may perform entirely different functions. Nevertheless Masao Ito (1984) proposed that one key role is to establish new motor programs that enable one to execute a sequence of actions as a whole instead of waiting for feedback. In Chapter 13 we consider the role of the cerebellum in classical conditioning. That is, the cerebellum helps you form motor habits, and it also may develop cognitive habits and skills.

Richard Ivry and his colleagues have emphasized the importance of the cerebellum for behaviors that depend on precise timing of fairly short intervals (up to about 1.5 seconds). Any sequence of rapid movements, including alternating movements, obviously requires timing. Many perceptual and cognitive tasks also require timing—for example, judging which of two visual stimuli is moving faster or listening to two pairs of tones and judging whether the delay was longer between the first pair or the second pair.

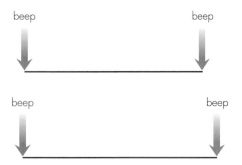

People who are accurate at one kind of timed movement, such as tapping a rhythm with a finger, tend also to be good at other timed movements, such as tapping a rhythm with a foot, and at judging which visual stimulus moved faster and which intertone delay was longer. People with cerebellar damage are impaired at all of these tasks, but unimpaired at controlling the force of a movement or at judging which tone is louder (Ivry & Diener, 1991; Keele & Ivry, 1990).

The cerebellum also appears critical for certain aspects of attention. For example, when people are given a signal to shift their attention to a particular visual location, most do so within 100 ms. (They become more accurate at detecting stimuli in that location, beginning 100 ms after the signal.) But people with cerebellar damage need a full second to shift their attention (Townsend et al., 1999).

So the cerebellum appears to be linked to habit formation, timing, certain aspects of attention, and maybe other functions. Are these really separate functions that just happen to be located in the same place? Or can we somehow reduce them all to a single theme? (For example, maybe shifting attention requires timing or aim. Or maybe quick shifting of attention is a kind of habit formation.) We don't have an answer now, but note that this unanswered question is really more psychological than neurological.

Cellular Organization

The cerebellum receives input from the spinal cord, from each of the sensory systems by way of the cranial nerve nuclei, and from the cerebral cortex. That information eventually reaches the cerebellar cortex, the surface of the cerebellum (see Figure 8.13).

Figure 8.14 shows the types and arrangements of neurons in the cerebellar cortex. The figure has more complexity than you can expect to understand all at once, but do note these main points:

- The neurons of the cerebellum are arranged in a very precise geometrical pattern, with multiple repetitions of the same units.
- The **Purkinje cells** are very flat cells in sequential planes.
- The **parallel fibers** are axons parallel to one another but perpendicular to the planes of the Purkinje cells.
- Action potentials in varying numbers of parallel fibers excite one Purkinje cell after another. Each of these Purkinje cells then transmits an inhibitory message to cells in the **nuclei of the cerebellum** (clusters of cell bodies in the interior of the cerebellum) and the vestibular nuclei in the brain stem, which in turn send information to the midbrain and the thalamus.
- Depending on which parallel fibers and how many of them are active, they might stimulate only the first few Purkinje cells or a long series of them. Because the parallel fibers' messages reach different Purkinje cells one after another, the greater the number of Purkinje cells excited, the greater their collective *duration* of response. That is, if the parallel fibers stimulate only the first few Purkinje cells, the result is a brief message to the target cells; if they stimulate more Purkinje cells, the message lasts longer. In short, the cellular anatomy is set up to control the duration of some output, which may be either a movement or a cognitive process (Raymond, Lisberger, & Mauk, 1996).

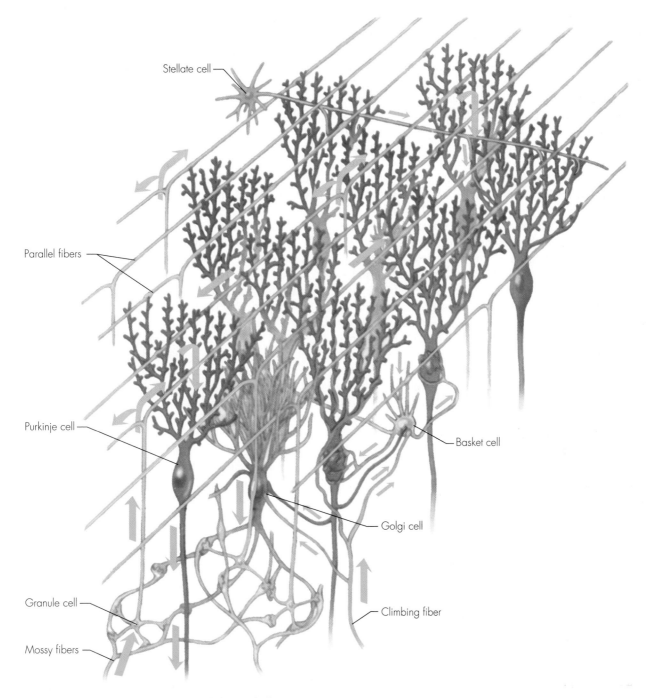

Stellate cell

Parallel fibers

Purkinje cell

Basket cell

Golgi cell

Granule cell

Climbing fiber

Mossy fibers

Figure 8.14 Cellular organization of the cerebellum
Parallel fibers (yellow) activate one Purkinje cell after another. Purkinje cells (red) inhibit a target cell in one of the nuclei of the cerebellum (not shown, but toward the bottom of the illustration). The more Purkinje cells that respond, the longer the target cell is inhibited. In this way the cerebellum controls the duration of a movement.

Stop & Check

3. Describe the shape and arrangement of Purkinje cells.

4. How are the parallel fibers arranged relative to one another and to the Purkinje cells?

5. If a larger number of parallel fibers are active, what is the effect on the collective output of the Purkinje cells?

6. Which aspect of behavior is most dependent on the output of Purkinje cells—strength or duration?

Check your answers on page 241.

The Role of the Basal Ganglia

The term **basal ganglia** applies collectively to a group of large subcortical structures in the forebrain (see Figure 8.15).[1] Various authorities differ in which structures they include as part of the basal ganglia, but everyone includes at least the **caudate nucleus,** the **putamen,** and the **globus pallidus.** Each of these areas exchanges information with the others and with the thalamus and cerebral cortex. The caudate nucleus and the putamen are receptive areas, receiving input from sensory areas of the thalamus and the cerebral cortex. The globus pallidus is the output area, sending information to the thalamus, which in turn sends it to the motor cortex and the prefrontal cortex (Hoover & Strick, 1993).

Damage to the basal ganglia invariably impairs movement, but the exact contribution of the basal ganglia is still unclear. One view is that the basal ganglia organize action sequences so they can be performed as automatic units or chunks (Graybiel, 1998). For example, when you are first learning to drive a car, you have to think about everything you do. After much experience, you can put on your turn signal, turn the wheel, change gears, and change speeds all at once, as a single smooth movement. The basal ganglia are important for habit learning of this type.

The basal ganglia also are active in selecting which response to make or inhibit. In one study investigators recorded activity from basal ganglia cells of patients who were undergoing brain surgery. (Brain surgery is sometimes performed on people who are awake, with only the scalp anesthetized.) When the patients were given a variety of signals, including signals to make or inhibit a simple finger response, the caudate nucleus showed much activity after a stimulus that called for an action, but only if the stimulus appeared infrequently. The more often the stimulus occurred, the less it excited the caudate nucleus. If it occurred on almost every trial, then the caudate nucleus started becoming active after a stimulus that called for *no* response (Kropotov & Etlinger, 1999).

In another study suggesting the same conclusion, people used a computer mouse to draw lines on a screen while researchers used PET scans to examine brain activity. Drawing a new line activated the basal ganglia and not the cerebellum. However, when people tried to retrace a line as accurately as possible, the cerebellum was much more active than the basal ganglia (Jueptner & Weiller, 1998). Again the basal ganglia seem critical for the selection of movements; the cerebellum is more important for accurate aim and using feedback to guide further behavior.

Some people are consistently clumsy, in many cases because of dysfunction in either the cerebellum or the basal ganglia. One study of very clumsy children found that those with cerebellar impairment were inaccurate in the timing of their movements, whereas those with basal ganglia impairments were inaccurate in their

---

[1] Ganglia is the plural of ganglion, so the term *basal ganglia* is a plural noun.

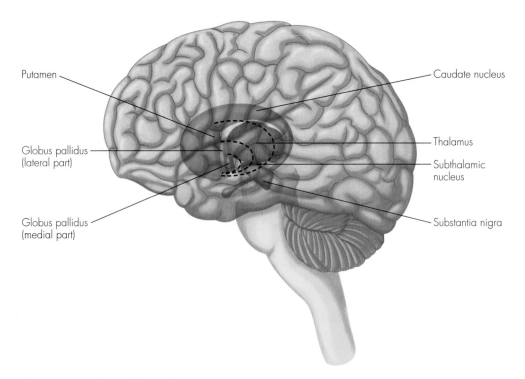

Figure 8.15 Location of the basal ganglia
The basal ganglia surround the thalamus and are surrounded by the cerebral cortex.

control of muscle force (Lundy-Ekman, Ivry, Keele, & Woollacott, 1991).

Stop & Check

7. How does the function of the basal ganglia differ from that of the cerebellum?

Check your answer on this page.

Module 8.2

In Closing: Possibilities for the Future

What good is all this information about motor systems? The obvious answers are simply that it is part of our overall understanding of the brain and that it helps us understand people with brain damage. Another answer is still a little far-fetched, but it is getting closer to being a possible reality: Some people become paralyzed because of spinal cord damage or muscle damage, even though their brains are intact. If we understood the brain systems well enough, we might be able to record from appropriate brain areas (to determine what movement the person is trying to make) and then connect the recording device to something that stimulates the muscles . . . or, if the muscles are damaged, connect the device to robotic arms and legs. That is, perhaps someone could build machinery that goes directly from brain activity to movement, bypassing the spinal cord. Researchers have already developed a system that works for rats, connecting cortical activity to simple movements of a robotic arm (Chapin, Moxon, Markowitz, & Nicolelis, 1999). At the pace that technology develops, it is hard to predict when or whether something similar might be possible for humans.

Summary

1. The primary motor cortex is the main source of brain input to the spinal cord. The spinal cord contains central pattern generators that actually control the muscles. (p. 231)

2. Areas near the primary motor cortex—including the prefrontal, premotor, and supplementary motor cortices—are active in detecting stimuli for movement and preparing for a movement. (p. 233)

3. The dorsolateral tract, which controls movements in the periphery of the body, has axons that cross from one side of the brain to the opposite side of the spinal cord. (p. 235)

4. The ventromedial tract controls bilateral movements near the midline of the body. (p. 236)

5. The cerebellum has multiple roles in behavior, including sensory functions related to perception of the timing or rhythm of stimuli. Its role in the control of movement is especially important for timing, aim, and correction of errors. (p. 237)

6. The cells of the cerebellum are arranged in a very regular pattern that enables them to produce outputs of well-controlled duration. (p. 238)

7. The basal ganglia are a group of large subcortical structures that are important for selecting and inhibiting particular movements. (p. 240)

Answers to *Stop and Check* Questions

1. The posterior parietal cortex is important for perception of the location of objects and the position of the body relative to the world, including those objects. The prefrontal cortex responds to sensory stimuli that call for some movement. The premotor cortex is active in preparation for a movement, immediately before the movement. The supplementary motor cortex is especially active in preparation for a rapid sequence of movements. (p. 235)

2. The dorsolateral tract controls detailed movements in the periphery on the contralateral side of the body. (For example, the dorsolateral tract from the left hemisphere controls the right side of the body.) The ventromedial tract controls the trunk muscles bilaterally. (p. 237)

3. A Purkinje cell branches widely within a single plane. Successive Purkinje cells are arranged as planes parallel to one another. (p. 239)

4. The parallel fibers are parallel to one another and perpendicular to the planes of the Purkinje cells. (p. 239)

5. As a larger number of parallel fibers become active, the Purkinje cells increase their duration of response. (p. 239)

6. Duration (p. 239)

7. The cerebellum is important for timing, aim, and correcting errors (using feedback to guide further behavior). The basal ganglia apparently contribute to selection of the correct movement to make and to the inhibition of inappropriate movements. (p. 241)

Thought Question

Human infants are at first limited to gross movements of the trunk, arms, and legs. The ability to move one finger at a time matures gradually over more than the first year. What hypothesis would you suggest about which brain areas controlling movement mature early and which ones mature later?

Module 8.3

Disorders of Movement

Even if your nervous system and muscles are completely healthy, you may sometimes find it difficult to move in the way you would like. For example, if you have just finished a bout of unusually strenuous exercise, your muscles may be so fatigued that you can hardly move them voluntarily, even though they keep twitching. Or if your legs "fall asleep" while you are sitting in an awkward position, you may stumble and even fall when you try to walk.

Certain neurological disorders produce exaggerated and lasting movement impairments. We consider two examples: Parkinson's disease and Huntington's disease.

Parkinson's Disease

The symptoms of **Parkinson's disease** are rigidity, muscle tremors, slow movements, and difficulty initiating physical and mental activity (M. T. V. Johnson et al., 1996;

Manfredi, Stocchi, & Vacca, 1995; Pillon et al., 1996). Most patients also become depressed at an early stage and many show cognitive deficits. These mental symptoms are probably part of the disease itself, not just a reaction to the muscle failures (Ouchi et al., 1999). Parkinson's disease strikes about 1 person per 100 above age 50, with a higher U.S. rate among Whites than Blacks (Chandra et al., 1984). It is much less common before age 50.

The immediate cause of Parkinson's disease is the gradual progressive death of neurons, especially in the substantia nigra and amygdala (Braak et al., 1995). Most research attention has focused on the substantia nigra neurons, which send axons, mostly dopamine releasing, to the caudate nucleus and putamen. People with Parkinson's disease lose dopamine-releasing axons, and the result is a net increase in the inhibitory output from the globus pallidus to the thalamus, and therefore decreased excitation from the thalamus to the cerebral cortex. Figure 8.16 summarizes these processes (Wich-

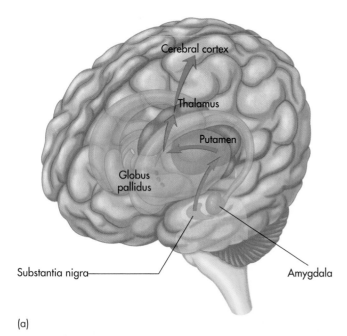

(a)

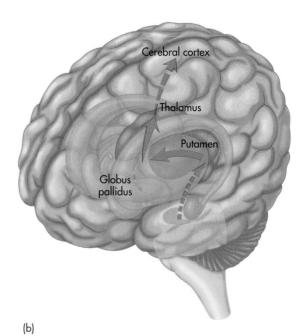

(b)

Figure 8.16 Connections from the substantia nigra: (a) normal and (b) in Parkinson's disease
Excitatory paths are shown in green; inhibitory are in red. The substantia nigra's axons inhibit the putamen. Axon loss increases excitatory communication to the globus pallidus. The result is increased inhibition from the globus pallidus to the thalamus and decreased excitation from the thalamus to the cerebral cortex. People with Parkinson's disease show decreased initiation of movement, slow and inaccurate movement, and psychological depression. *(Source: Based on Wichmann, Vitek, & DeLong, 1995)*

mann, Vitek, & DeLong, 1995). Some of the symptoms of Parkinson's disease may relate to the loss of arousal in the cerebral cortex that results from the weakened input. For example, most patients with Parkinson's disease have problems with memory and problem solving as well as movement.

Researchers estimate that the average person loses a little less than 1% of his or her substantia nigra neurons per year, beginning at around age 45. Most of us have enough to spare, but some people either start with a smaller number or lose them at a faster rate. If the number of surviving substantia nigra neurons declines to 20%–30% of normal, Parkinsonian symptoms begin (Knoll, 1993). The greater the cell loss, the more severe the symptoms.

Possible Causes

In the late 1990s the news media excitedly reported that researchers had located a gene that causes Parkinson's disease. The report was correct but misleading. Certain families include many members who develop Parkinson's disease early in life, and the responsible gene has indeed been identified (Kitada et al., 1998; Polymeropoulos et al., 1997). However, most cases of Parkinson's disease develop after age 50 in people not closely related to any other Parkinson's patients. One study examined Parkinson's patients who had twins. As shown in Figure 8.17, early-onset Parkinson's disease appears to have a strong genetic basis. The sample sizes are small; nevertheless it appears that if you have a monozygotic (MZ) twin who develops Parkinson's disease before age 50, you are at great risk too. If you have a dizygotic (DZ) twin who develops the disease early, your risk is not as great. However, if your twin develops Parkinson's disease *after* age 50, the risk is the same regardless of whether you are a monozygotic or dizygotic twin (Tanner et al., 1999). These results may understate the role of heredity in late-onset Parkinson's disease. In many cases MZ twins both develop Parkinson's disease, but one develops it much sooner than the other one (Piccini, Burn, Ceravolo, Maraganore, & Brooks, 1999). Thus, depending on when someone tested the twins, it would be possible to find results supporting different levels of heritability. Still, overall, the results imply that heritability is greater for early-onset than for late-onset

Parkinson's disease, and we should seek other influences for the late-onset condition.

But what other influences? Sometimes Parkinson's disease results from exposure to toxins. The first solid evidence was discovered by accident (Ballard, Tetrud, & Langston, 1985). In northern California in 1982, several people aged 22 to 42 developed symptoms of Parkinson's disease after using a drug similar to heroin. At first physicians resisted diagnosing Parkinson's disease because the patients were so young, but eventually the diagnosis became clear. Before the investigators could alert the community to the danger of the heroin substitute, many other users had developed symptoms ranging from mild to fatal (Tetrud, Langston, Garbe, & Ruttenber, 1989).

The substance responsible for the symptoms was **MPTP**, a chemical that the body converts to **MPP$^+$**, which accumulates in, and then destroys, neurons that release dopamine[2] (Nicklas, Saporito, Basma, Geller, & Heikkila, 1992). Postsynaptic neurons compensate for the dopamine loss by increasing their number of dopamine receptors (Chiueh, 1988) (see Figure 8.18). The symptoms of Parkinson's disease result partly from the decreased dopamine input and partly from the

---

[2] The full names of these chemicals are 1-methyl-4 phenyl-1,2,3,6-tetrahydropyridine and 1-methyl-4-phenylpyridinium ion. (Let's hear it for abbreviations!)

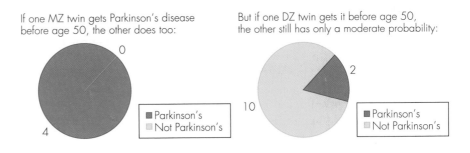

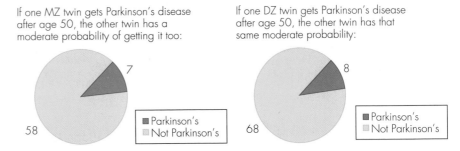

Figure 8.17 Probability of developing Parkinson's disease if you have a twin who developed the disease before or after age 50
Having a monozygotic (MZ) twin develop Parkinson's disease before age 50 means that you are very likely to get it too. A dizygotic (DZ) twin who gets it before age 50 does not pose the same risk. Therefore early-onset Parkinson's disease shows a strong genetic component. However, if your twin develops Parkinson's disease later (as is more common), your risk is the same regardless of whether you are a monozygotic or dizygotic twin. Therefore late-onset Parkinson's disease has little or no heritability. *(Source: Based on data of Tanner et al., 1999)*

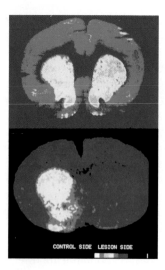

Figure 8.18 Results of injecting MPP⁺ into one hemisphere of the rat brain

The autoradiography above shows D₂ dopamine receptors; the one below shows axon terminals that contain dopamine. Red indicates the highest level of activity, followed by yellow, green, and blue. Note that the MPP⁺ greatly depleted the number of dopamine axons and that the number of D₂ receptors increased in response to this lack of input. However, the net result is a great decrease in dopamine activity. *(Source: Chiueh, 1988)*

jumpy overresponsiveness of the extra receptors (W. C. Miller & DeLong, 1988).

No one supposes that Parkinson's disease often results from illegal drugs. A more likely hypothesis is that people are sometimes exposed to MPTP or similar chemicals in polluted air or water. Certain herbicides and pesticides, including *paraquat*, are likely candidates (see Figure 8.19). One study of Parkinson's patients found that a higher than normal proportion had been exposed to large amounts of insecticides and herbicides (Butterfield, Valanis, Spencer, Lindeman, & Nutt, 1993). However, if exposure to a toxin were a common cause of Parkinson's disease, we should expect to find near epidemics in some geographic regions

and almost no cases elsewhere. The actual patchy distribution of the disease suggests that toxins are just one factor among several in causing the disease (C. A. D. Smith et al., 1992).

What else in people's way of life might influence the risk of Parkinson's disease? Several studies have compared the lifestyles of people who did and didn't develop Parkinson's disease. One factor that stands out is cigarette smoking: The people who smoked cigarettes had less chance of developing Parkinson's disease. (Read that sentence again.) Figure 8.20 shows the results for two groups, matched for age, sex, and race (Gorell, Rybicki, Johnson, & Peterson, 1999). Note that the group with Parkinson's disease includes more non-smokers and the group without Parkinson's disease includes more heavy smokers. Needless to say, cigarette smoking increases the risk of lung cancer and emphysema far more than it decreases the risk of Parkinson's disease, and no one should justify smoking for health reasons! Still, the results are theoretically interesting and suggest a need for research on exactly how cigarette smoking inhibits Parkinson's disease. Maybe nicotine acts as a neurotrophin (Fowler et al., 1996; Sershen, Toth, Lajtha, & Vizi, 1995).

In short, Parkinson's disease probably results from a mixture of causes. A gene is responsible for many cases of early-onset Parkinson's disease; exposure to toxins can increase risk; cigarette smoking apparently decreases risk; and researchers may later discover additional influences. Dopamine-containing neurons are evidently more vulnerable than most other neurons to damage from almost anything that impairs their metabolism (Zeevalk, Manzino, Hoppe, & Sonsalla, 1997), so we may well find a variety of causes that lead to the same result.

Stop & Check

1. Do monozygotic twins resemble each other more than dizygotic twins do for early-onset Parkinson's disease? For late-onset? What conclusion do these results imply?

2. How does MPTP exposure influence the likelihood of Parkinson's disease? What are the effects of cigarette smoking?

Check your answers on page 249.

L-Dopa Treatment

If Parkinson's disease results from a dopamine deficiency, then the goal of therapy should be to restore the missing dopamine. However, a dopamine pill would be ineffective because dopamine does not cross the blood-brain barrier. But L-dopa, a precursor to dopamine, does cross the barrier. Taken as a daily pill, L-dopa reaches the brain, where neurons convert it to

CH₃   CH₃   CH₃   CH₃

O₂CC₂H₅

MPPP   MPTP   MPP⁺   CH₃ Paraquat

Figure 8.19 The chemical structures of MPPP, MPTP, MPP⁺, and paraquat

Exposure to paraquat and similar herbicides and pesticides may increase the risk of Parkinson's disease.

dopamine. L-dopa is effective for most patients and continues to be the main treatment for Parkinson's disease. However, it is disappointing in several ways. First, its effectiveness varies, and for some patients it provides no relief at all. Second, it does not prevent the continued loss of neurons, so gradually it becomes less and less effective. Third, L-dopa enters not only the brain cells that need extra dopamine, but also others, producing harmful side effects that include nausea, restlessness, sleep problems, low blood pressure, stereotyped movements, hallucinations, and delusions. Generally the more severe the patient's symptoms, the more severe the side effects of L-dopa. In short, L-dopa is usually effective in the early to intermediate stages of Parkinson's disease but is less helpful in the later stages.

Why is L-dopa at best only moderately helpful and sometimes altogether ineffective? According to a very interesting hypothesis, the symptoms of Parkinson's disease do not result entirely from the loss of dopamine-releasing neurons. Many damaged dopamine neurons die, and others regenerate but remain somewhere in the middle between dying and regenerating, transformed instead into "orphan" cells that lack their usual connections (Willis & Armstrong, 1998). You might think of them as "zombie" cells, not exactly dead and not exactly alive either. Their axons lose their normal connections and swell up, accumulating dopamine and releasing it in random pulses far from their usual synapses. According to this view, Parkinsonian symptoms arise partly because dopamine does not reach the correct synapses at the correct times, but also partly because random leakage of dopamine reaches odd places at odd times. We shall await further research on this hypothesis, and if results support it, we may anticipate some new approaches to therapy.

Therapies Other Than L-Dopa

Given the limitations of L-dopa, researchers have sought alternatives and supplements. The following possibilities show promise (Dunnett & Björklund, 1999):

- Antioxidant drugs, which may decrease further damage

- Drugs that directly stimulate dopamine receptors

- Drugs that block glutamate (Recall from Chapter 3 that dopamine opposes the effects of glutamate; therefore a deficit of dopamine leads to excess glutamate activity.)

- Neurotrophins to promote survival and growth of the remaining neurons

- Drugs that decrease apoptosis (programmed cell death) of the remaining neurons

- High-frequency electrical stimulation of the globus pallidus, temporarily inactivating it (This procedure is especially effective for blocking tremor.)

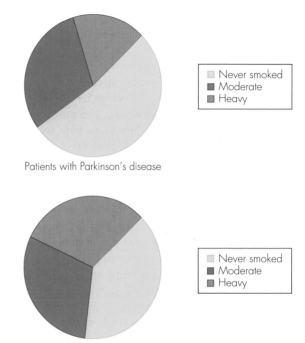

Figure 8.20 Smoking habits of people who did and did not develop Parkinson's disease
Note that the percentage of nonsmokers is higher among Parkinson's patients. The percentage of heavy smokers is higher among those without Parkinson's disease. *(Source: Based on results of Gorell, Rybicki, Johnson, & Peterson, 1999)*

- Surgical damage to the globus pallidus or parts of the thalamus (This procedure produces the same results as electrically inactivating the globus pallidus but is irreversible and therefore riskier.)

Nicotine may also be a possibility, regardless of whether it works as a neurotrophin or in other ways. Cigarette smoking is hazardous to health, but mainly because of the tars and carbon monoxide and other chemicals in cigarette smoke, not because of the nicotine. Administering nicotine by itself would not pose serious health risks in moderate doses; whether it would be effective is unknown.

Each approach has its limitations. The usual therapeutic strategy is to combine L-dopa with one or more additional treatments.

One more strategy is exciting with possibilities but still in the experimental stage. In a pioneering study M. J. Perlow and colleagues (1979) injected the chemical 6-OHDA into rats to make lesions in the substantia nigra in one hemisphere, producing Parkinson's-type symptoms in the opposite side of the body. After the movement abnormalities stabilized, the experimenters removed the substantia nigra from rat fetuses and transplanted them into the damaged brains. The grafts survived in 29 of the 30 recipients, making synapses in varying numbers. Four weeks later most recipients had recovered much of their normal movement. Control animals that suffered the same brain damage without receiving grafts showed little or no behavioral recovery.

If such surgery can work for rats, why not humans? The procedure is more feasible than it might sound at first. Perhaps because the blood-brain barrier protects the brain from foreign substances, the immune system is less active in the brain than elsewhere (Nicholas & Arnason, 1992), and physicians can give drugs to further suppress rejection of the transplanted tissue. However, the grafted brain tissue can make connections only if it is derived from a fetus.

Ordinarily scientists test any experimental procedure extensively with laboratory animals before trying it on humans, but in this case the temptation was too great. People in the late stages of Parkinson's disease are willing to try almost anything, and so are their families and physicians. After all, they have little to lose. But if surgeons are to transplant brain tissue, who will be the donors? Several early studies used tissue from the patient's own adrenal gland. Although that tissue is not composed of neurons, it produces and releases dopamine. Unfortunately the adrenal gland transplants seldom produced much benefit (see, for example, Backlund et al., 1985).

Another possibility is to transplant brain tissue from aborted fetuses. Fetal neurons transplanted into the brains of Parkinson's patients sometimes survive for years and do make synapses with the patient's own cells. However, not all of the transplanted cells survive, and at best the procedure produces only moderate relief of the patient's symptoms (Hauser et al., 1999; Lindvall, 1998). Furthermore the operation is difficult, requiring brain tissue from about six to eight aborted fetuses, age 6 to 9 weeks postconception. Many observers—even those who do not object to abortion itself—question whether the modest benefits are worth the effort. At best the procedure requires more research (Kupsch, Oertel, Earl, & Sautter, 1995).

One problem is that many of the transplanted cells do not survive or do not form effective synapses, and research on transplantation in rat brains shows that the success rate declines for recipients of advancing age. As mentioned in Chapter 5, aging brains are less plastic. They probably produce less neurotrophins than younger brains do. Researchers have found improved success of brain transplants in aging rats if the transplant includes not only fetal neurons but also a source of neurotrophins (Collier, Sortwell, & Daley, 1999). The same approach needs to be tried with humans, because human recipients are almost always old.

Another way to avoid using so many aborted fetuses is to grow cells in tissue culture, genetically alter them so that they produce large quantities of L-dopa, and then transplant them into the brain (Ljungberg, Stern, & Wilkin, 1999; Studer, Tabar, & McKay, 1998). That idea is particularly attractive if the cells grown in tissue cul-

ture are *stem cells,* immature cells that are capable of differentiating into a wide variety of other cell types depending on where they are in the body. It may be possible to nurture a population of stem cells that are capable of becoming neurons and glia and then deposit them into damaged brain areas (Wagner et al., 1999).

Yet another possibility is to transplant tissue from fetuses of another species. Although this idea may sound extreme, physicians have indeed transplanted substantia nigra tissue from the brains of pig fetuses into the brains of patients with Parkinson's disease. The investigators have not yet reported the amount of benefit, but a postmortem examination of one patient, who died 7 months after the transplant for unrelated reasons, found that substantial numbers of transplanted pig neurons survived and made synapses with the human neurons (Deacon et al., 1997). We eagerly await word on the long-term consequences of such surgery.

The research on brain transplants has raised yet another possibility for treatment. In several experiments the transplanted tissue failed to survive, but the recipient showed behavioral recovery anyway. Evidently the transplanted tissue releases trophic factors that stimulate axon and dendrite growth in the surrounding areas of the recipient's own brain (Bohn, Cupit, Marciano, & Gash, 1987; Dunnett, Ryan, Levin, Reynolds, & Bunch, 1987; Ensor, Morley, Redfern, & Miles, 1993). Further research has demonstrated that brain injections of neurotrophins can significantly benefit brain-damaged rats and monkeys, presumably by enhancing the growth of axons and dendrites (Gash et al., 1996; Kolb, Cote, Ribeiro-da-Silva, & Cuello, 1997). Unfortunately, because neurotrophins do not cross the blood-brain barrier, they must be implanted surgically. Still, researchers hope to find ways to get neurotrophins to the damaged areas of the brain (Granholm et al., 1998).

Stop & Check

3. What is the likely explanation for how L-dopa relieves the symptoms of Parkinson's disease?

4. In what ways is L-dopa treatment disappointing?

5. What are some other possible treatments?

Check your answers on page 249.

Huntington's Disease

Huntington's disease, also known as *Huntington disease* or *Huntington's chorea,* is a severe neurological disorder that strikes about 1 person in 10,000 in the United States (A. B. Young, 1995). Motor symptoms usually begin with jerky arm movements and then a facial twitch; later, tremors spread to other parts of the body and develop into purposeless writhing movements (M. A. Smith, Brandt, & Shadmehr, 2000). (*Chorea* comes from the same root as *choreography*; sometimes the writhing movements of chorea look a little like dancing.) Gradually the twitches, tremors, and writhing movements provide more and more interference with the person's walking, speech, and other voluntary movements. The ability to learn and improve new movements is especially limited (Willingham, Koroshetz, & Peterson, 1996). The disorder is associated with gradual, extensive brain damage, especially in the caudate nucleus, putamen, and globus pallidus, but also in the cerebral cortex (Tabrizi et al., 1999) (see Figure 8.21).

People with Huntington's disease also suffer psychological disorders, including depression, memory impairment, anxiety, hallucinations and delusions, poor judgment, alcoholism, drug abuse, and sexual disorders ranging from complete unresponsiveness to indiscriminate promiscuity (Shoulson, 1990). In some cases the psychological disorders develop before the motor disorders, and it is possible for someone in the early stages of Huntington's disease to be misdiagnosed as schizophrenic.

Huntington's disease most often appears between the ages of 30 and 50, although onset can occur at any time from childhood to old age. Once the symptoms emerge, both the psychological and the motor symptoms grow progressively worse over a period of about 15 years and culminate in death (Chase, Wexler, & Barbeau, 1979).

Heredity and Presymptomatic Testing

Huntington's disease is controlled by an autosomal dominant gene. A person with the gene eventually develops the disease and also transmits the gene to about half of his or her children. As a rule, a mutant gene that causes the loss of a function is recessive. The fact that the Huntington's gene is dominant implies that it produces the gain of some undesirable function.

Imagine that at the age of 20 you learn that one of your parents has Huntington's disease. You know that you have a 50% chance of developing it yourself, probably in about 20 years. In addition to your grief about your parent, your life will change in two ways. First, whenever you do something clumsy or experience a slight tremor anywhere in your body, you will fear that it signals the start of Huntington's disease. Second, if you had previously wanted to have children, now you worry that you would bring into the world children who might have to live through years of your deterioration and suffering, and who might eventually have to go through the same process themselves.

Investigators worked for many years to discover an accurate **presymptomatic test**—a way to identify which

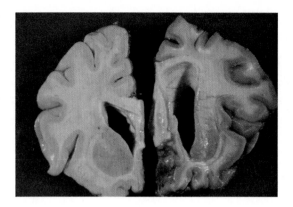

Figure 8.21   Brain of a normal person (left) and a person with Huntington's disease (right)
The angle of cut through the normal brain makes the lateral ventricle look larger in this photo than it actually is. Even so, note how much larger it is in the patient with Huntington's disease. The ventricles expand because of the loss of neurons. *(Source: Courtesy of Robert E. Schmidt, Washington University)*

young people are likely to develop the disease later. In the 1980s researchers established that the gene for Huntington's disease is on chromosome number 4, and in 1993 they identified the gene itself (Huntington's Disease Collaborative Research Group, 1993). Now it is possible to predict with almost 100% accuracy whether or not someone will get Huntington's disease just by examining the chromosomes. However, ask yourself: If you had a parent with Huntington's disease, would you want to have this chromosomes test? Many do; others decide they would rather live with uncertainty than run the risk of bad news.

Identification of the Huntington's disease gene facilitates research on the disease itself. In its normal form part of the gene includes a sequence of bases C-A-G (cytosine, adenine, guanine), repeated 11 to 24 times, sometimes a few more. In people with Huntington's disease, the sequence is repeated at least 36 times. People with 36–38 repeats may or may not get the disease and are likely to be rather old before they show symptoms. Those with 39–41 repeats are likely to get the disease, but might reach age 75 or 80 without it. Those with 42 or more repeats are evidently certain to get the disease, and the more repetitions they have, the earlier the probable onset, as shown in Figure 8.22 (Brinkman, Mezei, Theilmann, Almqvist, & Hayden, 1997). People with more than 50 repeats are likely to have even younger onset of symptoms, although too few cases have been found to present reliable statistics. In short, a chromosomal examination can predict not only whether a person will get Huntington's disease but also approximately when.

Identification of the gene for Huntington's disease led to discovery of the protein for which it codes, which has been designated **huntingtin.** Huntingtin occurs throughout the human body, although the mutant

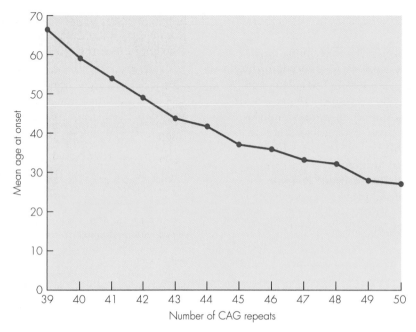

Figure 8.22   Relationship between CAG repeats and age of onset of Huntington's disease
Examination of someone's chromosomes can determine the number of CAG repeats in the gene for the huntingtin protein. The greater the number of CAG repeats, the earlier the probable onset. People with 36–38 repeats may also get the disease, but may not get it or may get it only in old age. The ages presented here are, of course, means. For a given individual a prediction can be made only as an approximation. *(Source: Based on data of Brinkmann, Mezei, Theilmann, Almqvist, & Hayden, 1997)*

form does no apparent harm except in the brain. Within the brain, the protein is found inside neurons and not on their membranes. Its normal function is still unknown, but the mutant form interferes with the expression of many of the genes of a neuron (Li, Cheng, Li, & Li, 1999). After investigators establish more clearly what the normal and mutant proteins do, the next step will be to use that information to devise methods of preventing or treating Huntington's disease.

 **Stop & Check**

6. What is a presymptomatic test?

7. What procedure enables physicians to predict who will or will not get Huntington's disease and estimate the age of onset?

Check your answers on page 249.

Module 8.3

In Closing: Heredity and Environment in Movement Disorders

Parkinson's disease and Huntington's disease illustrate the idea that genes influence behavior in different ways. Someone who examines the chromosomes can predict almost certainly who will and will not get Huntington's

disease and with moderate accuracy predict the age of getting it. A gene has also been identified for early-onset Parkinson's disease, but for late-onset Parkinson's disease, genetic factors play a smaller role, and researchers are looking for environmental influences instead of or in combination with the genes. In later chapters, especially Chapter 15, we shall discuss further disorders in which genes increase the risk of certain disorders, but we will not again encounter any disorder with such a strong heritability as Huntington's disease.

Summary

1. Parkinson's disease is characterized by impaired initiation of activity, slow and inaccurate movements, tremor, rigidity, and in most cases depression and cognitive deficits. It is associated with the degeneration of dopamine-containing axons from the substantia nigra to the caudate nucleus and putamen. (p. 242)

2. Early-onset Parkinson's disease has a strong hereditary basis, and the responsible gene has been identified. However, heredity plays only a small role in the more usual form of Parkinson's disease, with onset after age 50. (p. 243)

3. The chemical MPTP selectively damages neurons in the substantia nigra and leads to the symptoms of Parkinson's disease. Some cases of Parkinson's disease may result in part from exposure to toxins,

although toxins do not appear to be the full explanation. (p. 243)

4. The most common treatment for Parkinson's disease is L-dopa, which crosses the blood-brain barrier and enters neurons that convert it into dopamine. However, the effectiveness of L-dopa varies from one patient to another and is sometimes disappointing; it also produces unwelcome side effects. Many other treatments are in use or at least in the experimental stage, including transplant of fetal neurons into the damaged brain. (p. 244)

5. Huntington's disease is a hereditary condition marked by deterioration of motor control plus depression, memory impairment, and other cognitive disorders. Age of onset is usually between 30 and 50. (p. 246)

6. By examining chromosome 4, physicians can determine whether someone is likely to develop Huntington's disease later in life. The more CAG repeats in the gene, the earlier the likely onset of symptoms. (p. 247)

7. The gene responsible for Huntington's disease alters the structure of a protein, known as huntingtin, which affects many aspects of neural functioning, although the details remain unknown. (p. 247)

3. L-dopa enters the brain, where neurons convert it to dopamine, thus increasing the supply of a depleted neurotransmitter. (p. 246)

4. L-dopa is ineffective for some people and has only limited benefits for most others. It does not stop the loss of neurons. For people with severe Parkinson's disease, L-dopa produces fewer benefits and more severe side effects. (p. 246)

5. Other possible treatments include antioxidants, drugs that directly stimulate dopamine receptors, drugs that block glutamate, neurotrophins, drugs that decrease apoptosis, high-frequency electrical stimulation of the globus pallidus, and transplants of neurons from a fetus. (p. 246)

6. A presymptomatic test is a test given to people who do not yet show symptoms of a condition to predict which ones will eventually get it. (p. 248)

7. Physicians can examine human chromosome 4. In one identified gene they can count the number of consecutive repeats of the combination C-A-G. If the number is fewer than 36, the person will not get Huntington's disease. If the number is 36 or more, the larger the number, the more certain the person is to get the disease and the earlier he or she is likely to get it. (p. 248)

Answers to *Stop and Check* Questions

1. Monozygotic twins resemble each other more than dizygotic twins do for early-onset Parkinson's disease but not for late-onset. The conclusion is that early-onset Parkinson's disease is highly heritable and late-onset is not. (p. 244)

2. Exposure to MPTP can induce symptoms of Parkinson's disease. Cigarette smoking is correlated with decreased prevalence of the disease. (p. 244)

Thought Questions

1. Haloperidol is a drug that blocks dopamine synapses. What effect would haloperidol probably have in someone suffering from Parkinson's disease?

2. Neurologists assert that if people lived long enough, sooner or later everyone would get Parkinson's disease. Why?

Chapter Ending
Key Terms and Activities

Terms

antagonistic muscles (p. 224)

Babinski reflex (p. 229)

ballistic movement (p. 228)

basal ganglia (caudate nucleus, putamen, globus pallidus) (p. 240)

cardiac muscle (p. 224)

central pattern generator (p. 229)

cerebellar cortex (p. 238)

dorsolateral tract (p. 235)

extensor (p. 224)

fast-twitch fiber (p. 226)

flexor (p. 224)

Golgi tendon organ (p. 227)

grasp reflex (p. 229)

huntingtin (p. 247)

Huntington's disease (p. 246)

L-dopa (p. 244)

motor program (p. 229)

muscle spindle (p. 227)

MPTP, MPP$^+$ (p. 243)

myasthenia gravis (p. 224)

neuromuscular junction (p. 224)

nuclei of the cerebellum (p. 238)

parallel fibers (p. 238)

Parkinson's disease (p. 242)

posterior parietal cortex (p. 232)

prefrontal cortex (p. 233)

premotor cortex (p. 233)

presymptomatic test (p. 247)

primary motor cortex (p. 231)

proprioceptor (p. 227)

Purkinje cell (p. 238)

red nucleus (p. 235)

reflex (p. 228)

rooting reflex (p. 229)

saccade (p. 237)

skeletal muscle (or striated muscle) (p. 224)

slow-twitch fiber (p. 226)

smooth muscle (p. 224)

stretch reflex (p. 227)

supplementary motor cortex (p. 234)

ventromedial tract (p. 236)

vestibular nucleus (p. 236)

Suggestions for Further Reading

Cole, J. (1995). *Pride and a daily marathon.* Cambridge: MIT Press. Biography of a man who lost all his touch and proprioception from the neck down and eventually learned to control his movements strictly by vision.

Klawans, H. L. (1996). *Why Michael couldn't hit.* New York: Freeman. If you are at all interested in sports, you should find this book fascinating.

Lashley, K. S. (1951). The problem of serial order in behavior. In L. A. Jeffress (Ed.), *Cerebral mechanisms in behavior* (pp. 112–136). New York: Wiley. One of the true classic articles in psychology; thought-provoking appraisal of what a theory of movement needs to explain.

For more information about Parkinson's disease, contact the American Parkinson Disease Association, 1250 Hylan Blvd., Suite 4B, Staten Island, NY 10305.

For more information about Huntington's disease, contact the Huntington's Disease Society of America, 140 West 22nd St., Sixth Floor, New York, NY 10011–2420.

Web Sites to Explore

You can go to the Biological Psychology Study Center and click on these links. While there, you can also check for suggested articles available on InfoTrac. The Biological Psychology Internet address is:
http://psychology.wadsworth.com/book/kalatbiopsych7e/

http://www.umds.ac.uk/physiology/mcal/spinmain. html
For more information about muscle spindles.

http://pages.prodigy.net/stanley.way/myasthenia/
Includes links to sites with much information about myasthenia gravis.

http://www.loni.ucla.edu/data/monkey/movies.html
Excellent views of the anatomy of the basal ganglia and motor cortex. Click on each image for three-dimensional rotations.

http://neuroscience.about.com/msubDisPark.htm
Includes links to many sites concerning Parkinson's disease.

http://www.geocities.com/Pentagon/Base/1284/
Includes links to many sites concerning Huntington's disease.

Active Learner Link

Quiz for Chapter 8

Chapter 9

Rhythms of Wakefulness and Sleep

Chapter Outline

Opposite:
Rock hyraxes at a national park in Kenya.

Main Ideas

1. Wakefulness and sleep alternate on a cycle of approximately 24 hours. The body itself generates this cycle.

2. Sleep progresses through four stages, which differ in brain activity, heart rate, and other signs of arousal. A special type of sleep, known as paradoxical or REM sleep, is light in some ways and deep in others.

3. Areas in the brain stem and forebrain contribute to various aspects of arousal and sleep. Localized brain damage can result in prolonged sleep or wakefulness.

4. For a variety of reasons, many people do not sleep well enough to feel rested the following day.

5. Sleep and REM sleep in particular serve several functions, although much about their functions remains uncertain.

Every multicellular animal on Earth has daily rhythms of wakefulness and sleep, and if we are deprived of sleep, we suffer. But if life evolved on another planet with completely different conditions, could animals evolve life without a need for sleep? Imagine a planet that doesn't rotate on its axis. Some animals evolve adaptations to live in the light area, others in the dark area, and still others in the twilight zone separating light from dark. There would be no need for any animal to alternate active periods with inactive periods on any fixed schedule, and perhaps there would be no need at all for prolonged inactive periods similar to our sleep. If you were the astronaut who first discovered these non-sleeping animals, you might be surprised, but on other planets we should be ready for all kinds of surprises.

Now imagine that astronauts from that planet set out on their first voyage and happen to land on Earth. Imagine *their* surprise to discover animals like ourselves that alternate between active periods and long periods of almost complete inactivity, resembling death. To someone who hadn't seen sleep before, it would seem strange and mysterious indeed. For the purposes of this chapter, let us adopt their perspective and ask why animals as active as we are spend one-third of our lives doing so little.

Rhythms of Waking and Sleeping

You are, I suspect, not particularly surprised to learn that your body spontaneously generates its own rhythm of wakefulness and sleep. Psychologists of an earlier era, however, considered that idea revolutionary. Many of the behaviorists who dominated experimental psychology from about the 1920s through the 1950s believed that any change in an animal's behavior could be traced to some change in stimulation. For example, alternation between wakefulness and sleep must depend on something in the outside world, such as the cycle of sunrise and sunset or temperature fluctuations. The research of Curt Richter (1922) and others implied that the body generates its own cycles of activity and inactivity. Gradually the evidence became stronger that animals generate approximately 24-hour cycles of wakefulness and sleep even in an environment that was as constant as anyone could make it. The idea of self-generated wakefulness and sleep was an important step toward viewing animals as active producers of behaviors.

Endogenous Cycles

An animal that produced its behavior entirely in response to current stimuli would be at a serious disadvantage; in many cases an animal has to prepare for changes in sunlight and temperature before they occur. For example, most migratory birds start on their way toward their winter homes while the weather in their summer homes is still fairly warm. A bird that waited for the first frost would be in serious trouble. Similarly squirrels begin storing nuts and putting on extra layers of fat in preparation for winter long before food becomes scarce. Animals that mate during only one season of the year change extensively in both their anatomy and their behavior as the reproductive season approaches.

Animals' readiness for a change in seasons comes partly from internal mechanisms. For example, a migratory bird has several cues that tell it when to fly south for the winter, but after it reaches the tropics, it has no external cues to tell it when to fly north in the spring. (In the tropics the temperature doesn't change much from one time of year to another, and neither does the length of day or night.) Nevertheless it flies north at the right time. Even if it is kept in a cage with absolutely no cues to the season, it still becomes more active in the spring, and if it is released, it flies north (Gwinner, 1986). Evidently a mechanism somewhere in the bird's body generates a rhythm, an internal calendar, that prepares the bird for seasonal changes. We refer to that rhythm as an **endogenous circannual rhythm**. (*Endogenous* means "generated from within." *Circannual* comes from the Latin words *circum*, for "about," and *annum*, for "year.")

Similarly animals ranging from insects to humans produce **endogenous circadian rhythms**, rhythms that last about a day. (*Circadian* comes from *circum*, for "about," and *dies*, for "day.") Our most familiar endogenous circadian rhythm controls wakefulness and sleepiness. If you go without sleep all night—as most college students do, sooner or later—you feel sleepier and sleepier as the night goes on, until early morning. But as morning arrives, you actually begin to feel less sleepy. Evidently your urge to sleep depends largely on the time of day, not just how recently you have slept.

Figure 9.1 represents the activity of a flying squirrel kept in total darkness for 25 days. Each horizontal line represents one 24-hour day. A thickening in the line represents a period of activity by the animal. Even in this unchanging environment, the animal generates a regular rhythm of activity and sleep. The self-generated cycle may be slightly shorter than 24 hours, as in Figure 9.1, or slightly longer depending on whether the environment is constantly light or constantly dark and on whether the species is normally active in the light or in the dark (Carpenter & Grossberg, 1984). The cycle may also vary from one individual to another, even in the same environment. Nevertheless the rhythm is highly consistent for a given individual in a given environment, even though the environment provides no clues to time.

Mammals, including humans, have circadian rhythms in their waking and sleeping, frequency of eating and drinking, body temperature, secretion of certain hormones, volume of urination, sensitivity to certain drugs, and many other variables. For example, although we ordinarily think of human body temperature as 37°C, normal temperature fluctuates over the course of a day from a low of about 36.5°C in the middle of one's sleep to about 37.4°C in late afternoon or early evening (see Figure 9.2). Ordinarily all of these cycles stay in synchrony with one another, suggesting that they depend on a single master clock.

Setting and Resetting the Cycle

Although an animal's circadian rhythm persists in the absence of light, light is critical for periodically resetting the **biological clock,** the internal mechanism that underlies the rhythm. A biological clock is the internal mechanism for controlling a behavior that recurs on a regular schedule, such as sleep or migration. As an analogy, consider a wristwatch. I used to have a windup wristwatch that lost about 2 minutes per day. If I continued to wind the watch but never reset it, it would be an hour slow after a month. We could say that it had a **free-running rhythm** of 24 hours and 2 minutes—that is, a rhythm that occurs when no stimuli intervene to reset or alter it. The biological clock is similar to that wristwatch. Because its free-running rhythm is not exactly 24 hours, it has to be reset daily. The stimulus that resets it is often referred to by the German term **zeitgeber** (TSITE-gay-ber), meaning "time-giver." Light is the dominant zeitgeber for land animals (Rusak & Zucker, 1979). (The tides are a more important zeitgeber for many marine animals.) But light is not our only zeitgeber; others include strenuous exercise (Eastman, Hoese, Youngstedt, & Liu, 1995), noises, meals, and the temperature of the environment (Refinetti, 2000). So, for example, if you have moved to a new time zone or shifted to a new work schedule and you want to stay

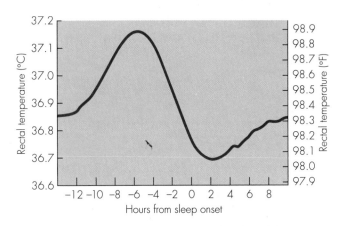

Figure 9.2 Mean rectal temperatures for nine adults
Body temperature reaches its low for the day about 2 hours after sleep onset; it reaches its peak about 6 hours before sleep onset. *(Source: Based on data of M. Morris, Lack, & Dawson, 1990)*

awake and alert longer than usual, expose yourself to bright lights, loud noises, and heavy exercise in the evening. But avoid them if you want to get to sleep at your normal time.

Duration of the Human Circadian Rhythm

It might seem simple to determine the duration of the human circadian rhythm: Put people in an environment with no cues to time and determine what waking-sleeping schedule they follow. But should we make that environment constantly bright, constantly dark, or what? Under constant bright lights people have trouble sleeping (and they complain about the experiment). In constant darkness they have trouble waking up (and again they complain about the experiment). In several studies people were allowed to turn on bright lights whenever they chose to be awake and turn them off when they wanted to sleep. Under these conditions most people followed a cycle closer to 25 than to 24 hours a day. The problem, which experimenters did not realize for years, was that bright light late in the day lengthens the circadian rhythm.

A better way to run the experiment is to provide light and darkness on a cycle that people cannot follow. Researchers had already known that most people can adjust to a 23- or 25-hour day, but not to a 22- or 28-hour day (Folkard, Hume, Minors, Waterhouse, & Watson, 1985; Kleitman, 1963). So later researchers kept 24 healthy adults for a month in rooms with an artificial 28-hour day. None of them could, in fact, synchronize to that schedule; they all therefore produced their own self-generated rhythms of alertness and body temperature. Those rhythms were all about the same from one person to another, with a mean of 24.2 hours (Czeisler et al., 1999). The human circadian rhythm therefore appears to last just slightly longer than 24 hours.

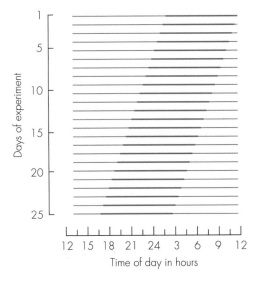

Figure 9.1 Activity record of a flying squirrel kept in constant darkness
The thickened segments indicate periods of activity as measured by a running wheel. Note that the free-running activity cycle lasts slightly less than 24 hours. *(Source: DeCoursey, 1960)*

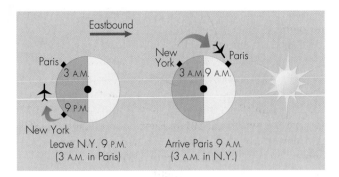

Figure 9.3 Jet lag
Eastern time is later than western time. People who travel six time zones east must wake up when their biological clocks say it is the middle of the night; when it is bedtime in the new time zone, their biological clocks say it is just late afternoon. In contrast, people who travel west get to stay up later at night and wake up later in the morning.

1. For a migratory bird, what is the advantage of having an endogenous circannual rhythm instead of relying on environmental cues to identify the season?

2. What stimulus is the most effective zeitgeber for humans?

3. What evidence indicates that humans have an internal biological clock?

Check your answers on page 260.

Resetting the Biological Clock

Our circadian rhythms have a period close to 24 hours, but they are hardly perfect. (Would you buy a clock that gained 0.2 hour per day?) We have to readjust our internal workings every day to stay in phase with the outside world. On weekends, when most of us are freer to set our own schedules, we expose ourselves to lights, noises, and activity at night, and then awaken late the next morning. By Monday morning, when the electric clock indicates 7 A.M., the biological clock is at about 5 A.M., and people stagger off to work or school without much pep (Moore-Ede,

Czeisler, & Richardson, 1983). People who travel across time zones or who work odd schedules have special problems in resetting their biological clocks.

Jet Lag

A disruption of biological rhythms due to crossing time zones is known as **jet lag**. (Before air travel, transatlantic travelers knew this phenomenon as "boat lag.") Most of us find it easier to adjust to crossing time zones going west than going east. Going west, we expose ourselves to bright lights and much activity at night, and then we stay awake late and awaken the next morning already partly adjusted to the new schedule. That is, we *phase-delay* our circadian rhythms. Going east, we have to go to sleep earlier and awaken earlier; we *phase-advance* (Figure 9.3).

Consider Figure 9.4. According to a study of major league baseball results in North America for three years, visiting teams that did not have to travel between one game and the next won 46% of their games. (Typically a visiting team plays a series of three or four games in one city, so it plays many games that do not require travel.) Teams that traveled east to west before the game did almost as well, winning 44% of the games. But teams that traveled west to east won only 37% of the games (Recht, Lew, & Schwartz, 1995). Clearly, traveling east puts people at a temporary disadvantage. Therefore, when a company sends a representative to an important meeting two or more times zones east from home, a wise policy is to get that representative to the destination at least a day or two before the meeting.

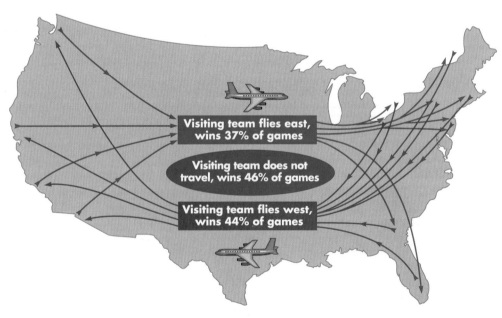

Figure 9.4 Effects of jet lag on visiting teams in North American major league baseball
Teams that had to travel from the West Coast to the East Coast before a game were less likely to win than were teams that traveled east to west or teams that stayed in the same city from one game to the next. *(Source: Based on data of Recht, Lew, & Schwartz, 1995)*

Shift Work

People who have to sleep irregularly—such as pilots and truck drivers, medical interns, and shift workers in certain factories—find that their duration of sleep depends on what time they go to sleep. When they have to go to sleep in the morning or early afternoon, they sleep only briefly, even though they have been awake for 16 hours or more (Frese & Harwich, 1984; Winfree, 1983).

People who work on a night shift, such as midnight to 8 A.M., sleep during the day. Even after months or years on such a schedule, many workers fail to adjust fully. They continue to feel groggy on the job, they do not sleep soundly during the day, and their body temperature continues to peak when they are trying to sleep in the day instead of while they are working at night. In general, night-shift workers perform less well and have more accidents than day workers.

Working at night does not reliably shift the circadian rhythm because the rhythm is reset by bright light much more effectively than by mere activity. Ordinary indoor lighting, around 150–180 lux, as found in most nighttime work settings, is only moderately effective in resetting the rhythm (Boivin, Duffy, Kronauer, & Czeisler, 1996), especially if the light is brighter during the day when the person tries to sleep. People adjust best to night work if they get to sleep in a very dark room during the day and if they are exposed to very bright lights at night, comparable to the noonday sun (Czeisler et al., 1990).

The Mechanisms of the Biological Clock

What mechanism within our body generates our circadian rhythm? And how does it work? Curt Richter (1967) found that the biological clock is insensitive to most forms of interference. Blind or deaf animals generate nearly normal circadian rhythms, although they drift out of phase with the external world because of the lack of zeitgebers. The circadian rhythm is surprisingly undisturbed by food or water deprivation, X rays, tranquilizers, alcohol, anesthesia, lack of oxygen, most kinds of brain damage, or the removal of any of the hormonal organs. Even an hour or so of induced hibernation often fails to reset the biological clock (Gibbs, 1983; Richter, 1975). Evidently the biological clock is a hardy, robust mechanism.

The Suprachiasmatic Nucleus (SCN)

The surest way to disrupt the biological clock is to damage one key area of the hypothalamus: the **suprachiasmatic** (soo-pruh-kie-as-MAT-ik) **nucleus,** abbreviated **SCN.** It gets its name from its location just above the optic chiasm (see Figure 9.5). The SCN exerts the main control over the circadian rhythms for sleep and temperature (Refinetti & Menaker, 1992). After damage to the SCN, the body still has rhythms, but they are less consistent and no longer synchronized to environmental patterns of light and dark.

The SCN generates circadian rhythms itself. If SCN neurons are disconnected from the rest of the brain or removed altogether and maintained in tissue culture, they continue to produce activity that follows a circadian rhythm (Earnest, Liang, Ratcliff, & Cassone, 1999; Inouye & Kawamura, 1979). Even a single isolated SCN cell can maintain a circadian rhythm, although it becomes less steady than a group of cells together (Herzog, Takahashi, & Block, 1998).

One group of experimenters discovered that some hamsters bear a mutant gene that causes them to produce not a 24-hour rhythm, but a 20-hour rhythm (Ralph & Menaker, 1988). They surgically removed the SCN from adult hamsters and then transplanted SCN tissue from hamster fetuses into the adults. When they transplanted SCN tissue from fetuses with a 20-hour rhythm, the recipients produced a 20-hour rhythm. When they transplanted tissue from fetuses with a 24-hour rhythm, the recipients produced a 24-hour rhythm (Ralph, Foster, Davis, & Menaker, 1990). That is, the rhythm followed the pace of the donor of SCN tissue, not that of the recipient brain.

Biochemically, how does the SCN produce circadian rhythms? Some of the answers stem from research that began with insects. Studies on the fruit fly *Drosophila* discovered genes that interact with the proteins they produce and produce a circadian rhythm (Shiromani, 1998). Two genes, known as *period* (abbreviated *per*) and *timeless* (*tim*), produce proteins that are present in only small amounts early in the morning. They increase throughout the day. By evening they reach a high level that makes the fly sleepy; that high level also feeds back to the genes to shut them down. During the night, the genes no longer produce those proteins and their concentration declines until the next morning, when the cycle begins anew. Furthermore light inactivates the *tim* protein, so extra light during the evening decreases the fly's sleepiness and delays the biological clock.

Why do we even care what goes on in flies? The answer is that after researchers knew how the system worked in flies, they looked for and found practically the same genes and practically the same proteins in mice and further demonstrated that the circadian rhythm of mice depends on those genes (Zheng et al., 1999). They also demonstrated that exposing the eyes to light sends a message that changes the expression of these genes in the SCN (M. E. Morris, Viswanathan, Kuhlman, Davis, & Weitz, 1998; Obrietan, Impey, & Storm, 1998). Evidently a great variety of animals, perhaps all of them, use variations on a single mechanism to control their circadian rhythms.

How Light Resets the SCN

Recall that the SCN is located just above the optic chiasm. A small branch of the optic nerve, known as the

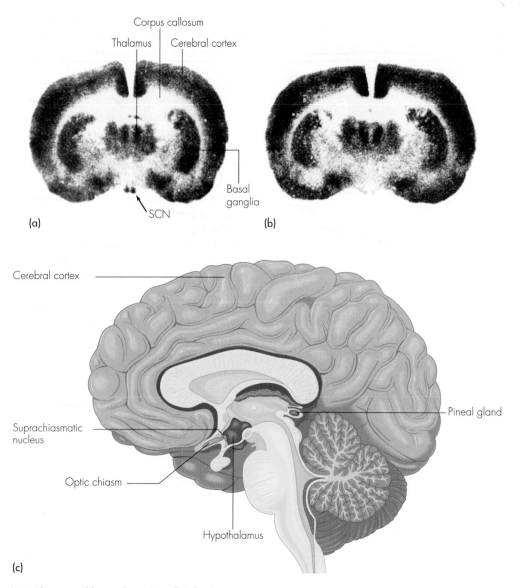

Corpus callosum

Thalamus | Cerebral cortex

Basal ganglia

SCN

(a)

(b)

Cerebral cortex

Pineal gland

Suprachiasmatic nucleus

Optic chiasm

Hypothalamus

(c)

Figure 9.5 The suprachiasmatic nucleus (SCN) of rats
The SCN is located at the base of the brain, just above the optic chiasm, which has torn off in these coronal sections through the plane of the anterior hypothalamus. Each rat was injected with radioactive 2-deoxyglucose, which is absorbed by the most active neurons. A high level of absorption of this chemical produces a dark appearance on the slide. Note that the level of activity in SCN neurons is much higher in section **(a)**, in which the rat was injected during the day, than it is in section **(b)**, in which the rat received the injection at night. *(Source: W. J. Schwartz & Gainer, 1977)* **(c)** A sagittal section through a human brain showing the location of the SCN and the pineal gland.

retinohypothalamic path, extends directly from the retina to the SCN in the hypothalamus. Axons of that path alter the SCN's settings.

Much about resetting the SCN remains mysterious, however. Mice with genetic defects that destroy nearly all their rods and cones nevertheless reset their biological clocks in synchrony with the light (Freedman et al., 1999; Lucas et al., 1999). Also, consider blind mole rats (Figure 9.6). Their eyes are covered with folds of skin and fur; they have neither eye muscles nor a lens with which to focus an image. They have fewer than 900 optic nerve axons, as compared with 100,000 in hamsters. Even a bright flash of light evokes no apparent behavior

and no measurable change in brain activity. Nevertheless light resets their circadian rhythms (de Jong, Hendriks, Sanyal, & Nevo, 1990). Evidently the mole rat's few visual receptors send the SCN enough information to act as a zeitgeber, even though none of the visual information reaches the cerebral cortex (David-Gray, Janssen, DeGrip, Nevo, & Foster, 1998).

Finally consider this odd experiment: Researchers kept people in very dim light for 4 days. Some of the participants were given 3 hours of bright light per day, but not light that they could see. The light was focused exclusively on the skin behind the knee! The participants' faces were shielded so they could not even see

Figure 9.6 A blind mole rat
Although blind mole rats are indeed blind in all other regards, they reset their circadian rhythms in response to light. *(Source: Courtesy of Eviatar Nevo)*

whether the light was on or off. Even this light reset people's circadian rhythms (Campbell & Murphy, 1998). Evidently light operates partly by blood-borne factors in addition to a direct route from the eyes to the SCN.

Stop & Check

4. Which brain area is most important for producing the circadian rhythm?

5. What evidence indicates that this area produces the rhythm itself?

6. How does light reset the biological clock?

Check your answers on page 260.

Melatonin

One way by which the SCN regulates waking and sleeping is by regulating production of **melatonin.** Melatonin is a hormone released by the **pineal gland,** an endocrine gland located just posterior to the thalamus (see Figure 9.5). Melatonin increases sleepiness. The human pineal gland secretes melatonin mostly at night, making us sleepy at that time. When people shift to a new time zone and start following a new schedule, they continue to feel sleepy at their old times until the melatonin rhythm shifts (Dijk & Cajochen, 1997). People who have pineal gland tumors or any other impairment of melatonin secretion experience great difficulty falling asleep, sometimes staying awake for days at a time (Haimov & Lavie, 1996).

Melatonin secretion usually starts to increase about 2 or 3 hours before bedtime. Taking a melatonin pill in the evening has little effect on sleepiness because the pineal gland produces melatonin at that time anyway. However, people who take melatonin at other times become sleepy within 2 hours (Haimov & Lavie, 1996).

Therefore some people take melatonin pills when they travel to a new time zone or start a new work schedule and need to sleep at an unaccustomed time.

Melatonin also feeds back to reset the biological clock through its effects on receptors in the SCN (Gillette & McArthur, 1996). A moderate dose of melatonin (0.5 mg) in the afternoon phase-advances the clock; that is, it makes the person get sleepy earlier in the evening and wake up earlier the next morning. Melatonin in the morning phase-delays the clock. However, these are long-term effects which do not account for the fact that melatonin induces sleepiness within a couple of hours after its onset.

Taking melatonin has become something of a fad. Its effect on sleep is well-established, although many people take melatonin who do not need it to sleep. Many have claimed that melatonin keeps people young, prevents cancer, and so forth, but the evidence for these claims is weak. Low pill doses (up to 0.3 mg/day) produce blood levels similar to those that occur naturally and therefore seem unlikely to do any harm. Larger doses seldom produce any unpleasant side effects with short-term use (up to 6 months). For longer term use, no one knows. Studies on laboratory animals indicate that long-term use can impair reproductive fertility and, if taken during pregnancy, harm the development of the fetus (Arendt, 1997; Weaver, 1997). No studies have been reported on long-term use by humans. Furthermore no government body regulates the production of melatonin, so the purity varies. The cautious advice therefore is to treat melatonin as a drug, not as a vitamin. Don't take it unless you need it.

In Closing: Sleep–Wake Cycles

Unlike an electric appliance that stays on until someone turns it off, the brain periodically turns itself on and off. Sleepiness is definitely not a voluntary or optional act. People who try to work when they are sleepy are prone to errors and injuries. Someone who sleeps well may not be altogether healthy or happy, but one who consistently fails to get enough sleep is almost certainly headed for troubles.

Summary

1. Animals, including humans, have internally generated rhythms of activity, lasting about 24 hours. Animals that hibernate or migrate also have internally generated rhythms lasting about a year. (p. 254)

2. Although the biological clock can continue to operate in constant light or constant darkness, the onset

of light at a particular time can reset the clock. (p. 255)

3. The biological clock can reset daily to match an external rhythm of light and darkness slightly different from 24 hours, but if the discrepancy exceeds about 2 hours, the biological clock generates its own rhythm instead of resetting. (p. 255)

4. It is easier for people to follow a cycle longer than 24 hours (as when traveling west) than to follow a cycle shorter than 24 hours (as when traveling east). (p. 256)

5. If people wish to work at night and sleep during the day, the best way to shift the circadian rhythm is to have bright lights at night and darkness during the day. (p. 257)

6. The suprachiasmatic nucleus (SCN), a part of the hypothalamus, generates the body's circadian rhythms for sleep and temperature. (p. 257)

7. The genes controlling the circadian rhythm are almost the same in mammals as in insects. At least in insects, and presumably in mammals too, the genes produce a protein that increases during the day and then feeds back to shut off the genes at night. (p. 257)

8. Light resets the biological clock partly by a branch of the optic nerve that extends to the SCN. However, light also acts on skin throughout the body, presumably sending a blood-borne factor to the SCN. (p. 257)

9. The SCN controls the body's rhythm partly by directing the release of melatonin by the pineal gland. The hormone melatonin increases sleepiness; if given at certain times of the day, it can also reset the circadian rhythm. (p. 259)

Answers to *Stop and Check* Questions

1. A bird that has migrated to the tropics for the winter will have no cue to identify spring. (The weather and length of day versus night are invariable through the year.) It therefore needs an endogenous mechanism to identify spring. (p. 256)

2. Light (p. 256)

3. People who have lived in an environment with a light/dark schedule much different from 24 hours fail to follow that schedule and instead become wakeful and sleepy on about a 24-hour basis. (p. 256)

4. The suprachiasmatic nucleus (SCN) (p. 259)

5. SCN cells produce a circadian rhythm of activity even if they are kept in cell culture isolated from the rest of the body. (p. 259)

6. A branch of the optic nerve, the retinohypothalamic path, conveys information about light to the SCN. The SCN also receives information about light from other sources too, presumably by blood-borne factors. If our mechanism works like that of *Drosophila,* the light inactivates a protein that builds up during the day. By decreasing that protein, light delays the onset of sleepiness. (p. 259)

Thought Questions

1. Is it possible for the onset of light to reset the circadian rhythms of a blind person? Explain.

2. Why would evolution have enabled blind mole rats to synchronize their SCN activity to light, even though they cannot see well enough to make any use of the light?

3. If you travel across several time zones to the east and want to use melatonin to help reset your circadian rhythm, at what time of day should you take it? What if you travel west?

Stages of Sleep and Brain Mechanisms

Suppose I buy a new radio. After I play it for 4 hours, it suddenly stops. To explain why, I try to discover whether the batteries are dead or whether the radio needs repair. Suppose I later discover that the radio always stops after playing for 4 hours, and that it will operate again a few hours later even without repairs or a battery change. I begin to suspect that the manufacturer designed it this way on purpose, perhaps to prevent me from wearing it out too fast or to prevent me from listening to the radio all day. I might then try to find the device that turns it off whenever I play it for 4 hours. Notice that I am now asking a new question. When I thought that the radio stopped because it needed repairs or new batteries, I had not thought to ask which device turned it off. I asked that question only when I thought of the stoppage as an active process.

Similarly, if we think of sleep as a passive cessation of activity, similar to catching one's breath after running a race, we do not ask which part of the brain is responsible for sleep. But if we think of sleep as a specialized state evolved to serve particular functions, we look for the devices that regulate it.

The Stages of Sleep

Most advances in scientific research result from improvements in our ability to measure something, and sleep research is no exception. In fact researchers never even suspected that sleep had separate stages, until they accidentally measured them.

The electroencephalograph (EEG), as described in Methods 9.1, records a gross average of the electrical potentials of the cells and fibers in a particular part of the brain by means of an electrode attached to the scalp (see Figures 9.7 and 9.8). It displays a net average of all the neurons' potentials. That is, if half increase their electrical potentials while the other half decrease, the EEG recording is flat. The EEG record rises or falls when cells fire in synchrony—doing the same thing at the same time. You might compare it to a record of the noise in a crowded football stadium: It shows only slight fluctuations until some event gets everyone yelling at once. The EEG provides an objective way for brain researchers to determine whether people are awake or asleep and to compare brain activity at different times of night.

Figure 9.9 shows the EEG and eye movements of a male college student during the various stages of sleep. Figure 9.9a begins with a period of relaxed wakefulness for comparison. Note the steady series of **alpha waves** at a frequency of 8 to 12 per second. Alpha waves are characteristic of the relaxed state, not of all wakefulness.

In Figure 9.9b the young man has just fallen asleep. During this period, called stage 1 sleep, the EEG is dominated by irregular, jagged, low-voltage waves. Overall brain activity is still fairly high, but it is declining. As Figure 9.9c shows, the most prominent characteristics of stage 2 are sleep spindles and K-complexes. A **sleep spindle** consists of 12- to 14-Hz waves during a burst that lasts at least half a second. A **K-complex** is a sharp high-amplitude negative wave followed by a smaller, slower positive wave. Sudden stimuli can evoke K-complexes during other stages of sleep (Bastien & Campbell, 1992), but they are most common in stage 2.

In each succeeding stage of sleep, heart rate, breathing rate, and brain activity are slower than in the previous stage, and the percentage of slow, large-amplitude waves increases (see Figures 9.9d and e). By stage 4 more than half the record includes large waves of at least a half-second duration. Stages 3 and 4 are known together as **slow-wave sleep (SWS)**.

Slow waves indicate that neuronal activity is highly synchronized. In stage 1 and in wakefulness, the cortex receives a great deal of input, much of it at high frequencies. Nearly all the neurons are active, but different populations of neurons are active at different times. Thus the EEG is full of short, rapid, choppy waves. By stage 4, however, sensory input to the cerebral cortex is greatly reduced, and the few remaining sources of input can synchronize many cells. As an analogy imagine that the barrage of stimuli arriving at the brain is like thousands of rocks dropped into a pond over the course of a minute: The resulting waves largely cancel one another out. The surface of the pond is choppy, with few large waves. By contrast, the result of just one rock dropping is fewer but larger waves, such as those in stage 4 sleep.

After stage 4, the person cycles back through stages 3 and 2. But then instead of stage 1, the person enters a

Electroencephalography (EEG)

A device called the **electroencephalograph (EEG)** records electrical activity of the brain through electrodes—generally no more than eight—attached to the scalp (see Figure 9.7). It enables investigators to make gross determinations of brain activity in humans and other animals without actually cutting into the skull. Electrodes are attached with glue or other adhesive to various locations on the scalp. The electrodes do not record the activity of any one neuron, but an average of the whole population of cells in the area under the electrode. The output of the electrodes is then amplified and recorded. An investigator can determine from EEG records whether the person is asleep, awake, or excited. Abnormalities in the EEG record may also suggest the presence of epilepsy, a tumor, or other medical problems in the region under a particular electrode.

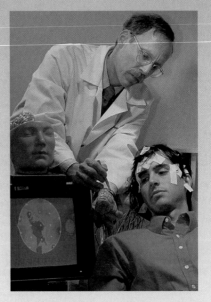

Figure 9.7   Electroencephalography
An electroencephalograph records the overall activity of neurons under each electrode, which is attached to the scalp.

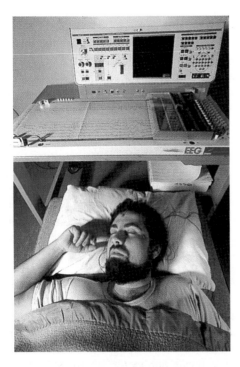

Figure 9.8   Sleeping person with electrodes in place on the scalp for recording brain activity
The printout above his head shows the readings from each electrode.

new stage, known as *rapid eye movement (REM)* sleep, which has special characteristics.

Stop & Check

1. What do long, slow waves on an EEG indicate?

Check your answer on page 272.

Paradoxical or REM Sleep

A person who has just fallen asleep enters stage 1 sleep. Later in the night people may or may not return to stage 1; usually they enter a related but very special stage, which two sets of researchers discovered accidentally in the 1950s.

In France, Michel Jouvet was trying to test the learning abilities of cats after complete removal of the cerebral cortex. To cope with the fact that decorticate mammals hardly move at all, Jouvet recorded slight movements of the muscles and EEGs from the hindbrain. During periods of apparent sleep, the cats had high levels of brain activity, but their neck muscles were completely relaxed. Jouvet named this phenomenon **paradoxical**

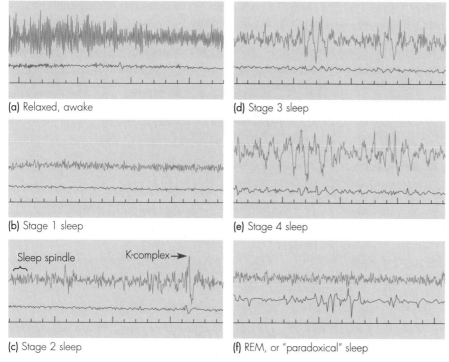

(a) Relaxed, awake

(b) Stage 1 sleep

(c) Stage 2 sleep

Sleep spindle   K-complex→

(d) Stage 3 sleep

(e) Stage 4 sleep

(f) REM, or "paradoxical" sleep

Figure 9.9 Polysomnograph records from a male college student
A polysomnograph includes records of EEG, eye movements, and sometimes other data, such as muscle tension or head movements. For each of these records, the top line is the EEG from one electrode on the scalp; the middle line is a record of eye movements; and the bottom line is a time marker, indicating 1-second units. Note the abundance of slow waves in stages 3 and 4. *(Source: Records provided by T. E. LeVere)*

sleep because it is in some ways the deepest sleep and in other ways the lightest. (The term *paradoxical* means "apparently self-contradictory.")

Meanwhile, in the United States Nathaniel Kleitman and Eugene Aserinsky were observing eye movements of sleeping people as a means of measuring depth of sleep, assuming simply that eye movements would decrease during sleep. At first they recorded only a few minutes of eye movements per hour, partly because the recording paper was expensive and partly because they did not expect to see anything interesting in the middle of the night anyway. When they occasionally found periods of eye movements in people who had been asleep for hours, the investigators assumed that something was wrong with their machines. Only after repeated careful measurements did they conclude that periods of rapid eye movements do exist during sleep (Dement, 1990). They called these periods **rapid eye movement (REM) sleep** (Aserinsky & Kleitman, 1955; Dement & Kleitman, 1957a) and soon concluded that REM sleep was synonymous with what Jouvet called *paradoxical sleep*. Researchers use the term *REM sleep* when referring to humans; most prefer the term *paradoxical sleep* for nonhumans because many species lack eye movements.

During paradoxical or REM sleep, the EEG shows irregular, low-voltage fast waves, which suggest a considerable amount of brain activity; in this regard REM

sleep is light. However, during REM sleep, the postural muscles of the body, such as those that support the head, are more relaxed than in any other stage; in this regard REM sleep is deep. This stage is also associated with erections in males and vaginal moistening in females. Heartrate, blood pressure, and breathing rate are more variable in REM than in stages 2 through 4. In short, REM sleep combines deep sleep, light sleep, and features that are difficult to classify as deep or light. Consequently it is best to avoid using the terms *deep* and *light* sleep.

In addition to its steady characteristics, REM sleep has certain intermittent characteristics, including facial twitches and the characteristic back-and-forth movements of the eyes. Figure 9.9f provides an example of the **polysomnograph**, a combination of EEG and eye-movement records, for a period of REM sleep. The EEG record is similar to that for stage 1 sleep, but notice how different the eye-movement records are. The stages other than REM are known as **non-REM (NREM) sleep**.

A person who falls asleep enters stage 1 and slowly progresses through stages 2, 3, and 4 in order, although loud noises or other intrusions can cause a reversal of stages or even an awakening. About 60 to 90 minutes after going to sleep, the person gradually begins to cycle back from stage 4 through stages 3 and 2 and then enters a period of REM sleep. The sequence repeats, with each complete cycle lasting about 90 minutes. Early in the night stages 3 and 4 predominate. Toward morning the duration of stage 4 grows shorter and the duration of REM sleep grows longer. Figure 9.10 shows typical sequences.

Initially after the discovery of REM, researchers believed it was closely linked with dreaming. William Dement and Nathaniel Kleitman (1957b) awakened adult volunteers during various stages of sleep and found that people awakened during REM sleep reported dreams 80% to 90% of the time. Later researchers, however, found that people awakened during NREM sleep also sometimes reported dreams and usually reported at least some kind of thought process. REM dreams are more likely than NREM dreams to include striking visual imagery and complicated plots, but not always. Some brain-damaged people continue to have REM sleep but do not report any dreams, and other people continue to report dreams despite no evidence of REM sleep (Solms, 1997). In short, REM tends to intensify dreams, but it is hardly synonymous with dreaming.

REM states are associated with "loose" associations or thinking. I can best explain this statement by describing a study. When people awaken, they do not become fully alert at once. (You may have noticed this tendency in yourself or your roommate!) A brain awakened from REM continues to have some REM characteristics, and a brain awakened from NREM continues to have NREM characteristics, as indicated by EEG recordings. In one study people who had just awakened from one type of sleep or the other read a word on a screen, then saw another set of letters, and had to identify as quickly as possible whether it was a real English word. For example,

First Word	Test Letters	Correct Response
LONG	SHORT	yes
THIEF	WRONG	yes
BICYCLE	FALARK	no

For people just awakened from NREM or people who had been awake for a long time, responses were fastest when the first word was strongly associated with the second word (such as LONG/SHORT). We say the first word "primed" the second—that is, made the viewer ready to perceive it. But for people just awakened from REM, responses were fastest when the first word was only *weakly* associated with the second word (such as THIEF/WRONG). Evidently in REM sleep each idea primes other ideas that are only loosely connected (Stickgold, Scott, Rittenhouse, & Hobson, 1999). For that reason REM dreams jump around in apparently haphazard ways.

Stop & Check

2. How can an investigator determine whether a sleeper is in REM sleep?

3. During which part of a night's sleep is REM most common?

4. How do the thought patterns of REM differ from those of NREM sleep?

Check your answers on page 272.

Brain Mechanisms of Wakefulness and Arousal

Recall that in Chapter 1 we encountered Chalmers's distinction between the "easy" and "hard" problems of consciousness. What he meant by the "easy" problems were such matters as, "Which brain areas increase overall alertness, and by what kinds of transmitters do they do so?" As you are about to see, that question is philosophically easy but scientifically more complicated than it might sound.

Brain Structures of Arousal

After a cut through the midbrain separates the forebrain and part of the midbrain from all the lower structures, an animal enters a prolonged state of sleep, as confirmed by the EEG, for the next week or so, and even after much recovery the animal shows only brief periods of wakefulness. The explanation might seem simple: The cut isolated the brain from the sensory stimuli that come up from the medulla and spinal cord. However, when a researcher cuts each of the individual tracts that enter the medulla and spinal cord, thus depriving the brain of almost all sensory input, the animal continues to have normal periods of wakefulness and sleep. Evidently cutting through the mid-

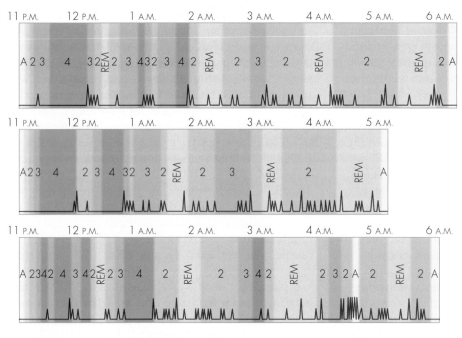

Figure 9.10 Sequence of sleep stages on three representative nights
Columns indicate awake (A) and sleep stages 2, 3, 4, and REM. Deflections in the line at the bottom of each chart indicate shifts in body position. Note that stage 4 sleep occurs mostly in the early part of the night's sleep, whereas REM sleep becomes more prevalent toward the end. *(Source: Based on Dement & Kleitman, 1957a)*

brain is more disruptive to wakefulness than is cutting all the sensory tracts.

A cut through the midbrain decreases arousal because it damages the **reticular formation,** a structure that extends from the medulla into the forebrain. The reticular formation contains some neurons with axons ascending into the brain and some with axons descending into the spinal cord. In Chapter 8 we encountered the neurons with descending axons. In 1949 Giuseppe Moruzzi and H. W. Magoun proposed that the reticular formation neurons with ascending axons are well suited to regulate arousal. The term *reticular* (based on the Latin word *rete*, meaning "net") describes the widespread, apparently haphazard connections among neurons in this system, although in fact they are more organized and have more specific functions than researchers once supposed (Young & Pigott, 1999). One part of the reticular formation that contributes to cortical arousal is known as the **pontomesencephalon** (Woolf, 1996). (The term derives from *pons* and *mesencephalon,* meaning "midbrain.") These neurons receive input from many sensory systems and generate spontaneous activity of their own. They send their axons to the thalamus and basal forebrain, as shown in Figure 9.11, releasing acetylcholine and glutamate and producing excitatory effects at synapses. The thalamus and basal forebrain relay arousal to widespread areas of the cortex. In the process the pontomesencephalon maintains cortical arousal during wakefulness and increases it in response to new or challenging tasks (Kinomura, Larsson, Gulyás, & Roland, 1996). Stimulation of the pontomesencephalon awakens a sleeping individual or increases alertness in someone already awake, shifting the EEG from long, slow waves to short waves at frequencies above 30 Hz (Munk, Roelfsema, König, Engel, & Singer, 1996). However, subsystems control different sensory modalities, so a stimulus sometimes arouses the visual or auditory areas independently of the others (Guillery, Feig, & Lozsádi, 1998).

However, today neither psychologists nor neuroscientists regard arousal as a single unitary process (Robbins & Everitt, 1995). Waking up, directing attention to a particular stimulus, preparing to store a memory, and increasing goal-directed effort are overlapping but different types of arousal, requiring many brain areas, as shown in Figure 9.11. For instance, the **locus coeruleus** (LOW-kus ser-ROO-lee-us, literally, "dark blue place"), a small structure in the pons, is almost completely inactive during sleep, and often even during waking, but emits bursts of impulses, releasing norepinephrine, in response to meaningful events. The output from the locus coeruleus causes recipient cells to activate genes that are important for storing information (Cirelli, Pompeiano, & Tononi, 1996). (The fact that the locus coeruleus is inactive during sleep helps explain why we quickly forget most dreams.)

Many cells in the **basal forebrain** (the area just ante-rior and dorsal to the hypothalamus) (see Figure 4.15, p. 99) provide axons to widespread areas of the thalamus and cerebral cortex. In most cases these axons release acetylcholine as their transmitter, and at most synapses the effect is excitatory (Mesulam, 1995; Szymusiak, 1995). Damage to the basal forebrain leads to decreased arousal, impaired learning and attention, and increased time spent in non-REM sleep. Because the basal forebrain is heavily damaged in Alzheimer's disease (Chapter 13), those patients have impairments of attention and memory.

In Figure 9.11 note that a couple of paths from the hypothalamus stimulate arousal by releasing histamine as their neurotransmitter (Lin, Hou, Sakai, & Jouvet, 1996). Antihistamine drugs, often used for allergies, produce drowsiness if they cross the blood-brain barrier.

Getting to Sleep

Sleep requires decreased arousal, and one important step is to decrease the temperature of the brain and the rest of the body's core. (Curiously a fever also increases sleepiness, but we usually sleep at night when our brains are cooler than during the day.) One of the best predictors of how fast someone will get to sleep is the amount of blood flow to the hands and feet (Kräuchi, Cajochen, Werth, & Wirz-Justice, 1999). People who shift much of their blood flow to the periphery (and therefore *warm* their hands and feet) expose more blood to the environment, which is presumably cooler than the inside of the body, and therefore they start to *cool* the core of the body. Just lying down helps shift blood flow to the periphery; melatonin helps as well. Many people with circulatory problems have trouble getting to sleep.

A second step is to decrease stimulation (Vellutti, 1997). Obviously, people who want to sleep find a quiet place, close their eyes, and in other ways decrease stimulation, although repetitive vestibular sensation, such as a gentle rocking motion, often helps people (especially babies) get to sleep.

Another important step is to inhibit the arousal systems that are excited by acetylcholine (Figure 9.11). One important inhibitor is **adenosine** (ah-DENN-o-seen). During metabolic activity, adenosine monophosphate (AMP) breaks down into adenosine; thus, when the brain is awake and active, adenosine accumulates. The neurons of the basal forebrain that are responsible for wakeful arousal (Figure 9.11) have adenosine receptors that inhibit them. In short, during wakefulness adenosine levels increase until they shut off the arousal neurons of the basal forebrain (Porkka-Heiskanen, 1999). During sleep adenosine levels decline. Caffeine (present in coffee, tea, and many soft drinks) increases arousal by inhibiting adenosine (Rainnie, Grunze, McCarley, & Greene, 1994). The message: Just as you might use caffeine to try to keep yourself awake, you might try

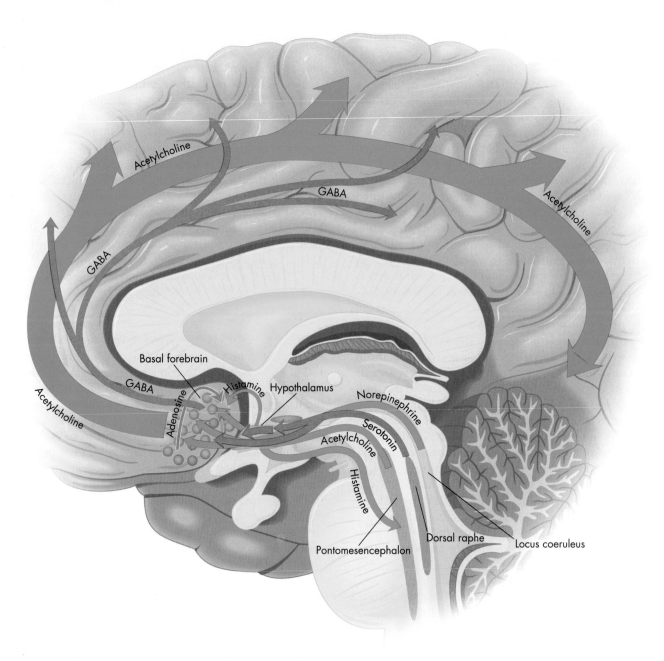

Figure 9.11 Brain mechanisms of sleeping and waking
Green arrows indicate excitatory connections; red arrows indicate inhibitory connections. Neurotransmitters are indicated where they are known. Although adenosine is shown as a small arrow, it is a metabolic product that builds up in the area, not something released by axons. *(Source: Based on Lin, Hou, Sakai, & Jouvet, 1996; Robbins & Everitt, 1995; and Szymusiak, 1995)*

decreasing your caffeine intake if you have trouble sleeping.

Prostaglandins are additional chemicals that promote sleep. Prostaglandins are chemicals present in much of the body; the immune system increases their concentration in response to infection. Like adenosine, prostaglandins build up during the day until they provoke sleep, and they decline during sleep (Ram et al., 1997). They stimulate a cluster of neurons that inhibit the hypothalamic cells that increase arousal (Scamell et al., 1998).

Getting to sleep is partly a matter of decreasing ac-

tivity in arousal areas, but it is also partly a matter of increasing activity in certain basal forebrain cells that send widespread axons releasing GABA, an inhibitory transmitter (Szymusiak, 1995) (see Figure 9.11). A lesion to these cells results in prolonged wakefulness, as do drugs that inhibit GABA. The sleep-related basal forebrain cells get much of their input from the anterior and preoptic areas of the hypothalamus (Sherin, Shiromani, McCarley, & Saper, 1996)—areas that are also important for temperature regulation, as we shall see in Chapter 10. One of the effects of fever is sleepiness, and the reason is that during a fever, the preoptic and ante-

Table 9.1 Brain Structures for Arousal and Sleep

Structure	Neurotransmitter(s) It Releases	Effects on Behavior
Pontomesencephalon	Acetylcholine, glutamate	Increases cortical arousal
Locus coeruleus	Norepinephrine	Increases information storage during wakefulness only
Basal forebrain		
Most cells	Acetylcholine	Excites thalamus and cortex; increases learning, attention; shifts sleep from NREM to REM
Other cells	GABA	Inhibits thalamus and cortex
Hypothalamus (parts)	Histamine	Increases arousal
Dorsal raphe and pons	Serotonin	Interrupts REM sleep

rior hypothalamus increase their output to the basal forebrain sleep-related cells.

Table 9.1 summarizes the effects of some key brain areas on arousal and sleep.

5. Examine Figure 9.11. Would damage to the dorsal raphe system increase or decrease sleep?

6. Why do most antihistamines make people drowsy?

7. How does caffeine increase arousal?

8. Why do people feel sleepy when they get sick? Give two reasons.

Check your answers on page 272.

Brain Function in REM Sleep

It might seem routine to use PET scans to determine which human brain areas increase their activity during REM sleep. But PET scans require an injection of a radioactive chemical. How are you going to give sleepers an injection without awakening them? Further, a PET scan yields a clear image only if the head remains motionless during data collection. If the person tosses or turns even slightly, the image is worthless.

To overcome these difficulties, researchers in two studies persuaded some young people to sleep with their heads firmly attached to masks that did not permit any movement. They also inserted a cannula (plastic tube) into each person's left arm so that they could inject radioactive chemicals at various times during the night. So imagine yourself in that setup. You have a cannula in your arm and your head is locked into position. Now try to sleep.

Because the researchers foresaw that it might be difficult to sleep under those conditions (!), they had the men go without sleep the entire night before. Someone who is tired enough can sleep even under trying circumstances. (Maybe.)

Now that you appreciate the heroic nature of the procedures, here are the results. During REM sleep, activity increased in the pons and the limbic system (which is important for emotional responses). Activity decreased in the primary visual cortex, the motor cortex, and the dorsolateral prefrontal cortex, but increased in parts of the parietal and temporal cortex (Braun et al., 1998; Maquet et al., 1996). In the next module we consider what these results imply about dreaming, but for now note that activity in the pons triggers the onset of REM sleep.

REM sleep is associated with a distinctive pattern of high-amplitude electrical potentials known as **PGO waves,** for pons-geniculate-occipital (see Figure 9.12). Waves of neural activity are detected first in the pons, shortly afterward in the lateral geniculate nucleus of the thalamus, and then in the occipital cortex (D. C. Brooks & Bizzi, 1963; Laurent, Cespuglio, & Jouvet, 1974). Each animal maintains a nearly constant amount of PGO waves per day. During a prolonged period of REM deprivation, PGO waves begin to emerge during sleep stages 2 to 4—when they do not normally occur—and even during wakefulness, often in association with strange behaviors, as if the animal were hallucinating. At the end of the deprivation period, when an animal is permitted to sleep without interruption, the REM periods have an unusually high density of PGO waves.

Besides originating the PGO waves, cells in the pons contribute to REM sleep by sending messages to the spinal cord, inhibiting the motor neurons that control the body's large muscles. After damage to the floor of the pons, a cat still has REM sleep periods, but its muscles

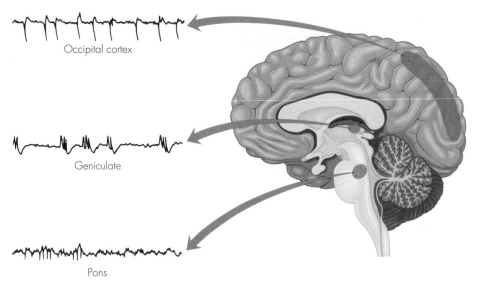

Occipital cortex

Geniculate

Pons

Figure 9.12 PGO waves
PGO waves start in the pons (P) and then show up in the lateral geniculate (G) and the occipital cortex (O). Each PGO wave is synchronized with an eye movement in REM sleep.

Figure 9.13 A cat with a lesion in the pons, wobbling about during REM sleep
Cells of an intact pons send inhibitory messages to the spinal cord neurons that control the large muscles.
(Source: Morrison, Sanford, Ball, Mann, & Ross, 1995)

are not relaxed. During REM it walks (though awkwardly), behaves as if it were chasing an imagined prey, jumps as if startled, and so forth (Morrison, Sanford, Ball, Mann, & Ross, 1995) (see Figure 9.13). Is the cat acting out its dreams? We do not know; the cat cannot tell us, but the strong suspicion is that the answer is yes. Evidently one function of the messages from the pons to the spinal cord is to prevent us from acting out our dreams.

REM sleep apparently depends on a relationship between the neurotransmitters serotonin and acetylcholine. Injections of the drug *carbachol*, which stimulates ACh synapses, quickly move a sleeper into REM sleep (Baghdoyan, Spotts, & Snyder, 1993). Note that acetylcholine is important for both wakefulness and REM sleep, two states that activate most of the brain. Serotonin, however, interrupts or shortens REM sleep (Boutrel, Franc, Hen, Hamon, & Adrien, 1999).

Abnormalities of Sleep

People who work long or irregular hours are especially likely to have sleep problems; so are people with psychiatric problems such as depression, schizophrenia, and substance abuse (Benca, Obermeyer, Thisted, & Gillin, 1992). But a great many otherwise healthy people also have at least occasional sleepless nights. Unsatisfactory sleep is a major cause of accidents on the job, comparable to the effects of drugs and alcohol.

Insomnia

How much sleep is enough? Some people get along fine with 6 hours of sleep per night. For others 8 hours may not be enough, especially if they awaken repeatedly during the night. The best gauge of **insomnia** is whether the person feels well rested the following day. Anyone who consistently feels tired during the day is not sleeping enough at night.

Insomnia can have many causes, including excessive noise, worries and stress, drugs and medications, pain, uncomfortable temperatures, sleeping in an unfamiliar place, or trying to fall asleep at the wrong time in one's circadian rhythm. It can also be the result of epilepsy, Parkinson's disease, brain tumors, depression, anxiety, or other neurological or psychiatric conditions. Some children suffer insomnia because they are milk-intolerant, and their parents, not realizing the intolerance, give them milk to drink right before bedtime (Horne, 1992). A friend of mine suffered insomnia for months until he realized that he dreaded going to sleep because he hated jogging as soon as he woke up in the morning. He switched his jogging time to late afternoon and no longer had any trouble sleeping. In short, before choosing a method of combating insomnia, try to identify the reasons for your sleep troubles.

It is convenient to distinguish three categories of insomnia: onset insomnia, maintenance insomnia, and termination insomnia. People with **onset insomnia** have trouble falling asleep. Those with **maintenance insomnia** awaken frequently during the night. And those with **termination insomnia** wake up too early and cannot get back to sleep. It is possible to have more than one of the three types.

Certain cases of insomnia are related to abnormalities of biological rhythms (MacFarlane, Cleghorn, & Brown, 1985a, 1985b). Ordinarily people fall asleep while their temperature is declining and awaken while it is rising, as in Figure 9.14a. Some people's body temperature rhythm is *phase delayed*, as in Figure 9.14b. If they try to fall asleep at the normal time, their body temperature is higher than normal for going to sleep. Such people are likely to experience onset insomnia (Morris et al., 1990). Other people's body temperature rhythm is *phase advanced*, as in Figure 9.14c. They are likely to suffer termination insomnia. Irregular fluctuations of circadian rhythms can cause maintenance insomnia.

REM sleep occurs mostly during the rising phase of the temperature cycle. For most people this is the second half of the night's sleep. For people with termination insomnia or anyone else who falls asleep after the temperature cycle has hit bottom, REM sleep may start soon after sleep begins (Czeisler, Weitzman, Moore-Ede, Zimmerman, & Knauer, 1980). Because depression is often associated with termination insomnia, most depressed people enter REM sleep earlier in the night than nondepressed people do (see Chapter 15).

Another cause of insomnia is, paradoxically, the use of tranquilizers as sleeping pills. Most sleeping pills operate partly by blocking the activity of norepinephrine, histamine, or other neurotransmitters that increase arousal.

Although tranquilizers may help a person fall asleep, taking such drugs a few times may cause dependence on them. Without the pills, the person goes into a withdrawal state that prevents sleep (Kales, Scharf, & Kales, 1978) and may react by taking the sleeping pills again, setting up a cycle from which it is difficult to escape.

Some tranquilizers are long-lasting; others are short-acting. Either kind poses problems. A long-lasting tranquilizer may not wear off by the next morning, leaving the person sleepy during the day. A short-acting tran-

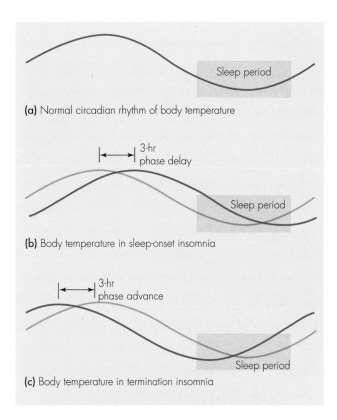

Figure 9.14 Insomnia and circadian rhythms
A delay in the circadian rhythm of body temperature is associated with onset insomnia; an advance, with termination insomnia.

quilizer may wear off during the night, causing the person to awaken early. In short, frequent use of tranquilizing sleeping pills is unwise.

Sleep Apnea

One special cause of insomnia is **sleep apnea,** the inability to breathe while sleeping. Many people breathe irregularly during REM sleep, and most people beyond age 45 have occasional periods of at least 9 seconds without breathing (Culebras, 1996). However, some people have such frequent breathless periods that they do not get enough oxygen, and some go a minute or more without breathing and then awaken, gasping for breath. Some do not remember awakening repeatedly during the night; they are aware only of feeling poorly rested the next morning. When sleep apnea occurs in infancy, it is one of the possible causes of *sudden infant death syndrome,* or "crib death." A family that is worried about sleep apnea in either a child or an adult can use devices that monitor the sleep and breathing and alert others when a problem occurs (White, Gibb, Wall, & Westbrook, 1995).

Obesity is one of several possible causes of sleep apnea. Some obese people, especially men, have narrower than normal airways and have to compensate by breathing more frequently or more vigorously than others do.

During sleep this compensation fails, and the sleep posture narrows the airways even more than usual (Mezzanotte, Tangel, & White, 1992). In other people, especially the elderly, sleep apnea results when brain mechanisms for respiration cease functioning during sleep.

People with sleep apnea are advised to lose weight and avoid alcohol and tranquilizers (which impair the breathing muscles). Medical options include surgery to remove tissue that obstructs the trachea (the breathing passage) or a mask that covers the nose and delivers air under enough pressure to keep the breathing passages open (see Figure 9.15).

Narcolepsy

Narcolepsy, a condition characterized by frequent unexpected periods of sleepiness during the day (Aldrich, 1998), strikes about 1 person in 1000, generally running in families (Mignot, 1998). Four symptoms are generally associated with narcolepsy, although many patients do not report all four:

1. Gradual or sudden attacks of extreme sleepiness during the day.

2. Occasional **cataplexy**—an attack of muscle weakness while the person remains awake. Cataplexy is often triggered by strong emotions, such as anger or great excitement. (One man suddenly collapsed during his own wedding ceremony!)

3. Sleep paralysis—a complete inability to move when falling asleep or waking up. Other people may experience sleep paralysis occasionally, but people with narcolepsy experience it more frequently.

4. *Hypnagogic hallucinations*—dreamlike experiences that the person has trouble distinguishing from reality, often occurring at the onset of sleep.

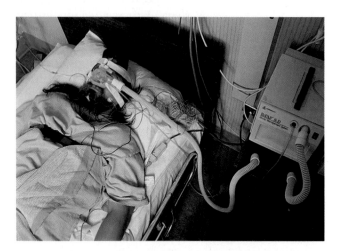

Figure 9.15   A Continuous Positive Airway Pressure (CPAP) mask
The mask fits snugly over the nose and delivers air at a fixed pressure, strong enough to keep the breathing passages open.

Each of these symptoms can be interpreted as an intrusion of a REM-like state into wakefulness; REM sleep is associated with muscle weakness (cataplexy), paralysis, and dreams (Mahowald & Schenck, 1992). Some people with narcolepsy have occasional periods of odd behaviors, as if they were acting out a dream—frying their socks, putting business files into the refrigerator, and so forth (Guilleminault, Heinzer, Mignot, & Black, 1998).

One explanation is that narcolepsy results from overactive acetylcholine synapses (Guilleminault et al., 1998). (Recall that acetylcholine is a neurotransmitter necessary for the onset of REM sleep.) Some of those acetylcholine synapses activate the areas of the pons that ordinarily send messages to the spinal cord to suppress muscle activity during REM. Sending these messages during the day produces cataplexy, one of the symptoms of narcolepsy (J. M. Siegel et al., 1991).

Theoretically we might imagine combating narcolepsy with acetylcholine blockers. In fact, the most common treatment is stimulant drugs, such as pemoline (Cylert) or methylphenidate (Ritalin), which increase wakefulness.

Periodic Limb Movement Disorder

Another factor occasionally linked to insomnia is **periodic limb movement disorder,** a repeated involuntary movement of the legs and sometimes arms (Edinger et al., 1992). Many people, perhaps most, experience an occasional involuntary kick, especially when starting to fall asleep. Leg movements are not a problem unless they become persistent. In some people, mostly middle-aged and older, the legs kick once every 20 to 30 seconds for a period of minutes or even hours, mostly during NREM sleep. Frequent or especially vigorous leg movements may awaken the person. In some cases tranquilizers help suppress the movements (Schenck & Mahowald, 1996).

REM Behavior Disorder

For most people the major postural muscles are relaxed and inactive during REM sleep. However, in an uncommon condition known as **REM behavior disorder,** people move around vigorously during their REM periods, apparently acting out their dreams. Many of their dreams are violent, and they may punch, kick, and leap about, often damaging property and injuring themselves or other people. Their dreams correspond to their movements; that is, they dream that they are kicking when they are actually kicking.

One study of people with REM sleep disorder found multiple areas of damage in the pons and midbrain (Culebras & Moore, 1989). Recall from the discussion of brain mechanisms of REM sleep that cells in the pons send messages to inhibit the spinal neurons that control large muscle movements; cats with damage to the pons appear to act out their dreams. The same is apparently true in humans.

Night Terrors, Sleep Talking, and Sleepwalking

Night terrors are experiences of intense anxiety from which a person awakens screaming in terror. A night terror should be distinguished from a nightmare, which is simply an unpleasant dream. Night terrors occur during NREM sleep and are far more common in children than in adults.

Many people, probably most, talk in their sleep occasionally. Unless someone hears you talking in your sleep and later tells you about it, you could talk in your sleep for years and never know about it. Sleep talking has about the same chance of occurring during REM sleep as during non-REM sleep (Arkin, Toth, Baker, & Hastey, 1970).

Sleepwalking runs in families, occurs mostly in children, especially ages 2 to 5, and is most common early in the night, during stage 3 or stage 4 sleep. (It does not occur during REM sleep because the large muscles are completely relaxed.) The causes are not known. Sleepwalking is generally harmless both to the sleepwalker and to others. No doubt you have heard people say, "You should never waken someone who is sleepwalking." In fact, it is not harmful or dangerous to awaken a sleepwalker, although the person is likely to feel very confused (Moorcroft, 1993).

In an individual case it is often difficult to distinguish sleepwalking from REM behavior disorder. One man pleaded "not guilty" to a charge of murder because he had been sleepwalking at the time and did not know what he was doing. The jury agreed with him, partly because he had a family history of sleepwalking. However, especially for a one-time event, it is difficult to know whether he was sleepwalking, subject to REM behavior disorder, or indeed even wide awake at the time (Broughton et al., 1994).

Module 9.2

In Closing: Stages of Sleep

In many cases scientific progress depends on drawing useful distinctions. Chemists divide the world into different elements, biologists divide life into different species, and medical doctors distinguish one disease from another. Similarly, psychologists try to recognize the most natural or useful distinctions among types of behavior or experience. The discovery of different stages of sleep was a major landmark in psychology because researchers found a previously unrecognized distinction that is both biologically and psychologically important. It also demonstrated that external measurements—in this case EEG recordings—can be used to identify internal experiences. We now take it largely for granted that an electrical or magnetic recording from the brain can tell us something about a person's experience, but it is worth pausing to note what a surprising discovery that was in its time.

Summary

1. Over the course of about 90 minutes, a sleeper goes through stages 1, 2, 3, and 4 and then back through stages 3 and 2 to a stage called REM, similar in most ways to stage 1. REM is characterized by rapid eye movements, much brain activity, complete relaxation of the trunk muscles, irregular breathing and heart rate, penile erection or vaginal lubrication, and a high probability of vivid dreams. (p. 261)

2. The brain has multiple systems for arousal. The pontomesencephalon, dorsal raphe, and parts of the hypothalamus control various cell clusters in the basal forebrain that send axons releasing acetylcholine throughout much of the forebrain. (p. 264)

3. The locus coeruleus is active almost exclusively in wakefulness and only in bursts triggered by meaningful events. It evidently facilitates attention and new learning. (p. 265)

4. Sleep is facilitated by decreased core body temperature, decreased stimulation, adenosine and prostaglandins which inhibit the arousal systems of the brain, and increased activity by certain clusters of basal forebrain cells that release GABA throughout much of the forebrain. (p. 265)

5. REM sleep is associated with increased activity in a number of brain areas, including the pons, limbic system, and parts of the parietal and temporal cortex. Activity decreases in the prefrontal cortex, the motor cortex, and the primary visual cortex. (p. 267)

6. REM sleep begins with PGO waves, waves of brain activity transmitted from the pons to the lateral geniculate to the occipital lobe. (p. 267)

7. Insomnia sometimes results from a shift in phase of the circadian rhythm of temperature in relation to the circadian rhythm of sleep and wakefulness. It can also result from difficulty in breathing while asleep, overuse of tranquilizers, and numerous other causes. (p. 268)

8. People with narcolepsy grow very sleepy during the day. Narcolepsy is associated with overactivity of acetylcholine synapses, presumably those responsible for REM sleep. (p. 270)

9. Among other sleep disorders are night terrors, sleep talking, sleepwalking, and REM behavior disorder. (p. 271)

Answers to *Stop and Check* Questions

1. Long, slow waves indicate a low level of activity, with much synchrony of response among neurons. (p. 262)

2. Examine EEG pattern and eye movements. (p. 264)

3. REM becomes more common toward the end of the night's sleep. (p. 264)

4. REM is associated with loose associations, with priming by words that are only weakly related. (p. 264)

5. Damage to the dorsal raphe increases sleep. Note that its axons inhibit the basal forebrain cells that send inhibitory messages to the rest of the cortex. Damaging the dorsal raphe decreases that inhibition and therefore leads to greater inhibition of the rest of the cortex. (p. 267)

6. Two paths from the hypothalamus—one to the basal forebrain and one to the pontomesencephalon—use histamine as their neurotransmitter to increase arousal. Antihistamines that cross the blood-brain barrier block those synapses. (p. 267)

7. Caffeine inhibits adenosine, which builds up during wakefulness and inhibits the arousal-inducing cells of the basal forebrain. (p. 267)

8. Illness arouses the immune system, which increases the prostaglandin levels. Prostaglandins stimulate brain areas that inhibit the arousal areas. Also, because of the fever that accompanies illness, the preoptic and anterior hypothalamus increase their stimulation of the basal forebrain cells that inhibit the cortex. (p. 267)

Thought Question

When cats are deprived of REM sleep for various periods and then permitted uninterrupted sleep, the amount of extra REM sleep increases for the first 25 to 30 days but does not increase further with a longer deprivation. What prevents the need from accumulating beyond that point? Consider PGO waves in your answer.

Why Sleep? Why REM? Why Dreams?

Why do you sleep? "That's easy," you reply. "It's because I get tired." Well, yes, of course, but why do you get so tired? When you tire your muscles or your brain, why can't you just relax and let your body do whatever repairs it has to do right then and there? Why set aside 7 or 8 hours in a row for inactivity? Does your body really need that much time each day to do repairs?

The Functions of Sleep

Sleep serves two major functions: to do repairs on the body and to conserve energy during a time of relative inefficiency. The two functions are certainly not in conflict, but some researchers put far more emphasis on one than the other, so we shall consider them as separate theories.

The Repair and Restoration Theory

According to the **repair and restoration theory of sleep,** the main function of sleep is to enable the body, especially the brain, to repair itself after the exertions of the day. One way to examine these restorative functions is to observe the effects of sleep deprivation. People who have gone without sleep for a week or more, either as an experiment or as a publicity stunt, have reported dizziness, impaired concentration, irritability, hand tremors, and hallucinations (Dement, 1972; L. C. Johnson, 1969). Prolonged sleep deprivation in animals, mostly rats, has produced more severe consequences, sometimes even death. One major difference is that the animals were forced to stay awake, whereas the human volunteers knew they could quit if necessary. (Stressors take a greater toll when they are unpredictable and uncontrollable.) During a few days of sleep deprivation, rats show increased body temperature, metabolic rate, and appetite, indicating that the body is working harder than usual. With still longer sleep deprivation, the immune system begins to fail, the animal loses its resistance to infection, and brain activity decreases (Everson, 1995; Rechtschaffen & Bergmann, 1995). Note that sleep ordinarily increases during illness; during sleep the body diverts energy away from other activities and toward increased function of the immune system.

However, the restorative functions of sleep are not analogous to catching your breath after running a race. If sleep were restorative in that simple sense, we should expect people to sleep significantly more after a day of great physical or mental exertion than after an uneventful day. But in fact heavy exertion increases sleep duration only slightly (Horne & Minard, 1985; Shapiro, Bortz, Mitchell, Bartel, & Jooste, 1981). How long we sleep does not depend on our activity level during the day.

Moreover, some people satisfy their restorative needs in far less than the customary 7 to 8 hours. Two men were reported to average only 3 hours of sleep per night and to awaken feeling refreshed (Jones & Oswald, 1968). A 70-year-old woman was reported to average only 1 hour of sleep per night; many nights she felt no need to sleep at all (Meddis, Pearson, & Langford, 1973).

The Evolutionary Theory

According to an alternative view (Kleitman, 1963; Webb, 1974), the function of sleep is similar to that of hibernation (see Digression 9.1)—to conserve energy. Hibernating animals decrease their heart rate, breathing rate, brain activity, and metabolism; they generate only enough body heat to avoid freezing. Hibernation is a true need; a ground squirrel that is prevented from hibernating can become as disturbed as a person who is prevented from sleeping. However, the function of hibernation is not to recover from a busy summer; it is simply to conserve energy when the environment is hostile.

Similarly, according to the **evolutionary theory of sleep,** we evolved a need to sleep to force us to conserve energy when we would be relatively inefficient. During sleep a mammal's body temperature decreases by 1 or 2 Celsius degrees, enough to save a small but noticeable amount of energy. During food shortages animals either increase their sleep time or decrease their body temperature during sleep (Berger & Phillips, 1995). The evolutionary theory does not deny that we need to sleep; it merely asserts that evolution built that need into us to compel us to conserve energy. It also does not deny that restorative functions occur during

Some Facts About Hibernation

1. Hibernation occurs in certain small mammals such as ground squirrels and bats. Whether or not bears hibernate is a matter of definition. Bears sleep most of the winter, but they do not lower their body temperatures the way small hibernating animals do.

2. Hamsters sometimes hibernate. If you keep your pet hamster in a cold, poorly lit place during the winter, and it appears to die, make sure that it is not just hibernating before you bury it!

3. Hibernation retards the aging process. Hamsters that spend longer times hibernating have proportionately longer life expectancies than other hamsters do (Lyman, O'Brien, Greene, & Papafrangos, 1981).

4. Hibernating animals produce a chemical that suppresses metabolism and temperature regulation. H. Swan and C. Schätte (1977) injected extracts from the brains of hibernating ground squirrels into the brains of rats, a nonhibernating species. The rats decreased their metabolism and body temperature. Similar brain extracts from nonhibernating ground squirrels had no apparent effect on the rats.

5. Hibernating animals come out of hibernation for a few hours every few days, raising their body temperature to about normal. However, they do not do much during these non-hibernating hours. In fact they spend most of the time sleeping (Barnes, 1996).

sleep, but it emphasizes that even if sleep did not serve restorative functions, we would benefit from it anyway as a means of saving energy.

The evolutionary theory predicts that species should vary in their sleep habits in accordance with how much time each day they must devote to the search for food, how safe they are from predators when they sleep, and other aspects of their way of life. In general the data support these predictions (Allison & Cicchetti, 1976; Campbell & Tobler, 1984). Most mammals that sleep many hours per day, such as cats and bats, eat nutrition-rich meals and face little threat of attack while they sleep. Many brief and fitful sleepers are herbivores (plant eaters) that need to graze much of the day to get enough food and need to be alert for predators even while they sleep (see Figure 9.16).

The two views of why we sleep are complementary and compatible. If we need to set aside time for repair and restoration, we may as well do it at times when we are inefficient at doing anything else. And if we are going to decrease body activity to conserve energy, we may as well use that inactive time for some repair and restoration. Which was the *original* function of sleep is a difficult question to answer.

Stop & Check

1. Some fish live in caves without light or in the deep ocean, which also has no light. What would the evolutionary theory of sleep predict about the sleep of these fish?

Check your answer on page 278.

The Functions of REM Sleep

From an evolutionary point of view, we look for the functions of a behavior. An average person spends about one-third of his or her life asleep and about one-fifth of sleep in REM, totaling about 600 hours of REM sleep per year. Presumably REM sleep serves some biological function. But what? To approach this question we can consider who gets more REM sleep than others and the effects of REM sleep deprivation. Then we consider a couple of hypotheses.

Individual and Species Differences

REM sleep is widespread in mammals and birds, indicating that the capacity for it is part of our ancient evolutionary heritage. Some species, however, have a great deal more than others; as a rule the species that get the most total sleep also have the highest percentage of REM sleep (J. M. Siegel, 1995). Cats spend up to 16 hours a day sleeping, much or most of it in REM sleep. Rabbits, guinea pigs, and sheep sleep much less and spend very little time in REM sleep.

Figure 9.17 demonstrates the relationship between age and REM sleep for humans; the trend is the same for other mammalian species. Infants get more REM and more total sleep than adults do, so the pattern remains that the more total sleep, the higher percentage of REM sleep. The abundance of REM sleep in infancy has led some researchers to suggest that it is important for modifying neuronal connections in response to early experience (Marks, Shaffery, Oksenberg, Speciale, & Roffward, 1995).

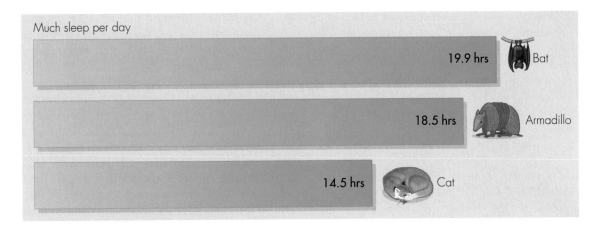

Much sleep per day

19.9 hrs — Bat

18.5 hrs — Armadillo

14.5 hrs — Cat

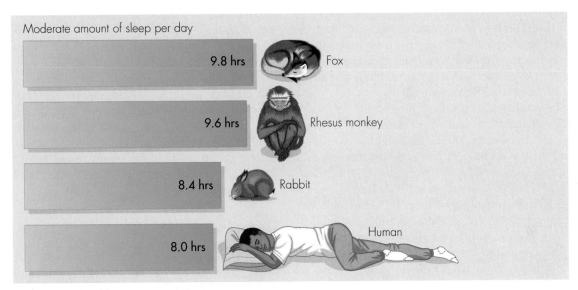

Moderate amount of sleep per day

9.8 hrs — Fox

9.6 hrs — Rhesus monkey

8.4 hrs — Rabbit

8.0 hrs — Human

Little sleep, easily aroused

3.9 hrs — Cow

3.8 hrs — Sheep

3.8 hrs — Goat

2.9 hrs — Horse

Figure 9.16 Hours of sleep per day for various animal species
Generally predators and others that are safe when they sleep tend to sleep a great deal; animals in danger of being attacked while they sleep spend less time asleep.

Among adult humans those who get the most sleep per night (9 or more hours) have the highest percentage of REM sleep, and those who get the least sleep (5 or fewer hours) have the lowest percentage of REM. Horne (1988) has therefore suggested that the more tightly guarded biological need is the one for NREM sleep and that much of REM sleep is optional.

The Effects of REM Sleep Deprivation

What would happen to someone who had almost no opportunity for REM sleep? William Dement (1960) observed the behavior of eight men who agreed to be deprived of REM sleep for 4 to 7 consecutive nights. During that period they slept only in a laboratory. Whenever the EEG and eye movements indicated that a given subject was entering REM sleep, an experimenter promptly awakened him and kept him awake for several minutes. The subject was then permitted to go back to sleep until he started REM sleep again.

Over the course of the 4 to 7 nights, the experimenters found that they had to awaken the subjects more and more frequently. On the first night an average subject had to be awakened 12 times. By the final night this figure had increased to 26 times. That is, the subjects had increased their attempts at REM sleep.

During the deprivation period most subjects reported mild, temporary personality changes, including irritability, increased anxiety, and impaired concentration. Five of the eight experienced increased appetite and weight gain. Control studies found that a similar number of awakenings not linked to REM sleep did not produce similar effects. The disturbances were therefore due to REM deprivation, not just to the total number of awakenings.

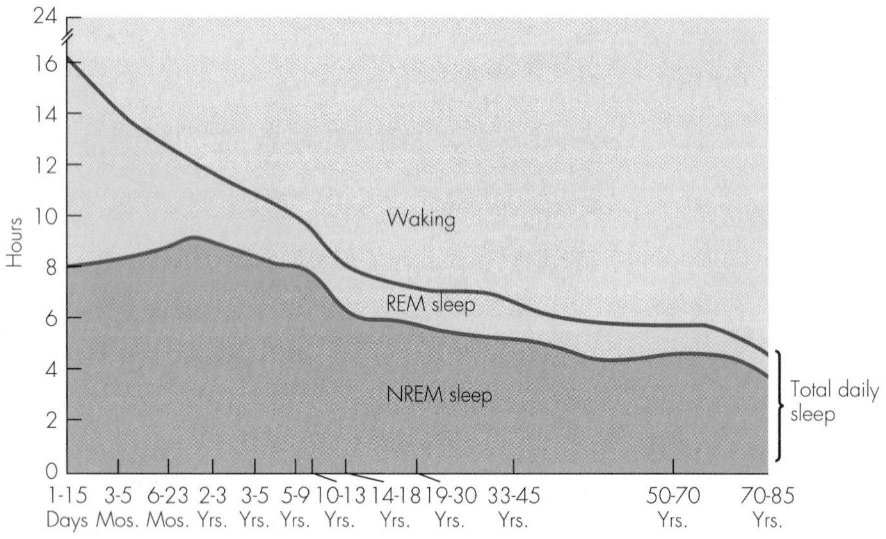

After the deprivation period seven subjects continued to sleep in the laboratory. During their first uninterrupted night, five of the seven spent more time than usual in REM sleep: 29% of the night, as compared with 19% before the deprivation. One subject showed no REM increase. (The investigators discarded the results from the seventh subject, who came to the laboratory drunk. Alcohol suppresses REM sleep, so results from this subject would be unreliable.)

Similar experiments have been done with laboratory animals, using longer periods of paradoxical sleep deprivation. Cats have been deprived of paradoxical sleep for up to 70 consecutive days (see Dement, Ferguson, Cohen, & Barchas, 1969). Do not imagine shifts of experimenters monitoring cats 24 hours a day and prodding them whenever they entered paradoxical sleep. Rather they kept each cat on a tiny island surrounded by water. As soon as the cat entered paradoxical sleep, its postural muscles relaxed, it lost its balance, and it fell into the water. It therefore awakened immediately after entering paradoxical sleep. This procedure impaired the cats' behavior and health severely, but note that the cats suffered not only sleep interruptions, but also disruption of body temperature from repeated plunges into cold water. The results are therefore hard to interpret.

Hypotheses

The results presented so far suggest that we need some REM sleep, especially if we sleep for a long time. Nevertheless the exact benefits of REM are not obvious.

One hypothesis is that REM is important for memory storage. A related idea is that REM helps the brain discard useless connections that formed accidentally during the day (Crick & Mitchison, 1983). Discarding useless connections would help the correct connections stand out by comparison, so the result could again be an improvement of memory.

Several kinds of evidence support a connection between REM and memory storage. Following a new learning experience, both humans and nonhumans increase their REM (or paradoxical) sleep, and those that increase it most are generally those that remember the new information best (C. Smith & Wong, 1991). However, REM is not necessary for all kinds of memory. In one study rats learned to swim to a platform that they could see and later remembered what to do even if they had been deprived of

Figure 9.17 Time spent by people of different ages in waking, REM sleep, and NREM sleep
REM sleep occupies about 8 hours a day in newborns but less than 2 hours in most adults. The sleep of infants is not quite like that of adults, however, and the criteria for identifying REM sleep are not the same. *(Source: Roffwarg, Muzio, & Dement, 1966)*

paradoxical sleep during the hours after training. However, those that had to learn to swim to a platform they could not see, just hidden by the surface of the murky water, did need paradoxical sleep, and if deprived of it, they forgot the location of the platform (C. Smith & Rose, 1997). In another study young adult humans who were deprived of REM had trouble remembering a motor skill (tracing a pattern as seen in a mirror) but did not forget a list of words. In contrast, people deprived of NREM sleep had trouble remembering the list of words but remembered the motor skill (Plihal & Born, 1997). That is, REM seems more important for strengthening memories of motor skills than for other types of memory.

Furthermore, memories are strengthened during NREM sleep as well as REM sleep. Researchers have found that the brain patterns that occur in rats as they learn some task are repeated during their next NREM period (Qin, McNaughton, Skaggs, & Barnes, 1997; Skaggs & McNaughton, 1996).

A more recent hypothesis sounds oddball just because we have for so long been looking for some glamorous role for REM sleep. But a nonglamorous role might be worth taking seriously: David Maurice (1998) has proposed that the primary role of REM is just to shake the eyeballs back and forth enough to get sufficient oxygen to the corneas of the eyes. The corneas, unlike the rest of the body, ordinarily get much of their oxygen supply directly from the surrounding air, not from the blood. They get some additional oxygen from the fluid behind them (Figure 6.2, p. 154), but when the eyes are motionless, that fluid can become stagnant. Moving the eyes even a little increases the oxygen supply to the corneas. Getting oxygen to the corneas is a bigger problem for those who sleep many hours at a time (precisely the ones who do get the most REM sleep). According to this view REM is a way of arousing a sleeper just enough to move the eyes back and forth a few times, and all the other manifestations of REM—including intense visual dreams—are accidental by-products. It's an interesting idea, worth further research.

Stop & Check

2. What kinds of individuals get more REM sleep than others? (Think in terms of age, species, and long versus short sleepers.)

Check your answer on page 278.

Biological Perspectives on Dreaming

What causes dreams? For decades psychologists were heavily influenced by Sigmund Freud's theory of dreams, which was based on the assumption that they reflect hidden and often unconscious wishes. Although Freud was certainly correct in asserting that dreams reflect the dreamer's personality and recent experiences, his theory of the mechanism of dreams depended on certain ideas about the nervous system that are now discarded (McCarley & Hobson, 1977). He believed, for example, that brain cells were inactive except when nerves from the periphery brought them energy. Freud was also hampered by relying on dream reports that his patients gave him hours or days after the dreams occurred.

The Activation-Synthesis Hypothesis

Contemporary investigators have offered several newer theories. According to the activation-synthesis hypothesis, during dreams various parts of the cortex are activated by the input arising from the pons plus whatever stimuli are present in the room, and the cortex synthesizes a story to make sense of all the activity (Hobson & McCarley, 1977; McCarley & Hoffman, 1981). According to a slightly different version of this hypothesis, the brain is aroused and ready to process information during REM sleep, but because the environment provides few stimuli, the sleeper processes information stored in memory, treating the stream of thought and imagery as if it were the real world (Antrobus, 1986).

While we sleep we do not completely lose contact with external stimuli. (For example, except in early childhood, we seldom roll out of bed.) We incorporate many external stimuli into our dreams, at least in a modified form: If water is dripping on your foot, you may dream about swimming or about walking in the rain. In addition, bursts of activity occur spontaneously in the visual, auditory, and motor cortexes and in various subcortical areas that contribute to motivation and emotion.

Occasional bursts of vestibular sensation are also common during REM sleep, perhaps because a sleeping person is generally lying down. According to the activation-synthesis hypothesis, the brain incorporates vestibular sensations into dreams of falling, flying, or spinning.

Have you ever dreamt that you were trying to move but couldn't? It is tempting to relate such dreams to the fact that the major postural muscles are virtually paralyzed during REM sleep: When you are dreaming you really *can't* move.

The main criticism of the activation-synthesis hypothesis is that it is too vague to be tested. We almost always sleep while lying down; why do we sometimes dream about flying or falling, but not at other times? Our major postural muscles are always paralyzed during REM; why don't we *always* dream of being paralyzed? Sometimes we dream about a sound because there really is a sound in the room, but more often we dream about a sound even though the room is as quiet as can be. Furthermore the activation-synthesis model assumes that the impetus for dreaming comes from the pons. Input from the pons does indeed generate the PGO waves that are central to REM. However, REM is not synonymous with dreaming. It is possible to have

REM without dreams (especially with certain kinds of brain damage) or to have dreams without REM.

A Clinico-Anatomical Hypothesis

An alternative view of the biology of dreams does not seem to have been given a name, but we shall tentatively label it the *clinico-anatomical hypothesis* because it was derived from clinical studies of dreaming by patients with various kinds of brain damage (Solms, 1997). According to this hypothesis dreams begin with arousing stimuli. In some cases those are actual stimuli in the environment, but in most cases they are generated from within, based on motivations and recent memories. Input from the pons (PGO waves) intensifies these stimuli but is not necessary and does not provide the content of dreams.

The brain, however, does not react to the arousing stimuli in its normal way. First, activity is suppressed in the primary visual cortex (area V1), so normal visual information cannot compete with the self-generated stimulation. Second, the primary motor cortex is suppressed, as are the motor neurons of the spinal cord, so arousal cannot lead to action. Third, activity is suppressed in the prefrontal cortex, which is important for working memory (memory of very recent events) and for certain processes loosely described as "use of knowledge." Consequently the dream is free to wander without the criticisms of "wait a minute; that's not possible!"

Meanwhile two cortical areas are active during dreams. One is the inferior (lower) part of the parietal cortex. Patients with damage here have problems with spatial perception and integration of body sensations with vision. They also report no dreams. The other important area is the visual area of the occipital cortex outside V1, plus the visual areas of the temporal lobe. People with damage here do report dreams, but the dreams include no visual content.

So the idea is that either internal or external stimulation activates parts of the parietal, occipital, and temporal cortex. No sensory input from V1 overrides the stimulation and no criticism from the prefrontal cortex censors it, so it develops into hallucinatory perceptions. This idea, like the activation-synthesis hypothesis, is vague and hard to test. It does have the advantage of being anchored on careful studies of patients, and it deserves much research consideration.

Module 9.3

In Closing: Our Limited Self-Understanding

I don't want to minimize how much we do understand about sleep, REM, and dreams, but it is noteworthy that we spend so much of our lives on activities that we still do not fully understand. Our lack of knowledge underscores a point about the biology of behavior: We evolved tendencies to behave in certain ways that lead to survival and reproduction. We do not need a conscious understanding of the reasons for our behavior for the behavior to do its job.

Summary

1. Sleep probably serves at least two functions: (a) repair and restoration and (b) conservation of energy during a period of relative inefficiency. (p. 273)

2. REM sleep is most common in individuals and species that sleep the most total hours. (p. 274)

3. People who are deprived of REM sleep become irritable and have trouble concentrating. After a period of REM deprivation, people compensate by spending more time than usual in REM sleep. (p. 276)

4. According to the activation-synthesis hypothesis, dreams are the brain's attempts to make sense of external stimuli and arousal that originate in the pons. (p. 277)

5. According to another hypothesis, dreams originate partly with external stimuli but mostly from the brain's own motivations, memories, and arousal. The stimulation often produces peculiar results because it does not have to compete with normal visual input and does not get censored by the prefrontal cortex. (p. 278)

Answers to *Stop and Check* Questions

1. The evolutionary theory would predict little if any sleep because these animals are equally efficient at all times of day and have no need to conserve energy at one time more than another. The fish might sleep, however, as a relic left over from ancestors that lived in the light—just as humans still erect our arm hairs in response to cold, a response that was useful for our hairier ancestors but not for us. (p. 274)

2. Much REM sleep is more typical of the young than the old, of those who get much sleep than those who get little, and of species that sleep much of the day and are unlikely to be attacked during their sleep. (p. 277)

Thought Question

Why would it be harder to deprive someone of just NREM sleep than just REM sleep?

Chapter Ending
Key Terms and Activities

Terms

activation-synthesis hypothesis (p. 277)

adenosine (p. 265)

alpha wave (p. 261)

basal forebrain (p. 265)

biological clock (p. 255)

cataplexy (p. 270)

electroencephalograph (EEG) (p. 262)

endogenous circadian rhythm (p. 254)

endogenous circannual rhythm (p. 254)

evolutionary theory of sleep (p. 273)

free-running rhythm (p. 255)

insomnia (p. 268)

jet lag (p. 256)

K-complex (p. 261)

locus coeruleus (p. 265)

maintenance insomnia (p. 269)

melatonin (p. 259)

narcolepsy (p. 270)

night terror (p. 271)

non-REM (NREM) sleep (p. 263)

onset insomnia (p. 269)

paradoxical sleep (p. 262)

periodic limb movement disorder (p. 270)

PGO wave (p. 267)

pineal gland (p. 259)

polysomnograph (p. 263)

pontomesencephalon (p. 265)

prostaglandin (p. 266)

rapid eye movement (REM) sleep (p. 263)

REM behavior disorder (p. 270)

repair and restoration theory of sleep (p. 273)

reticular formation (p. 265)

sleep apnea (p. 269)

sleep spindle (p. 261)

slow-wave sleep (SWS) (p. 261)

suprachiasmatic nucleus (SCN) (p. 257)

termination insomnia (p. 269)

zeitgeber (p. 255)

Suggestions for Further Reading

Culebras, A. (1996). *Clinical handbook of sleep disorders.* Boston: Butterworth-Heinemann. Discusses many kinds of sleep disorders.

Dement, W. C. (1992). *The sleepwatchers.* Stanford, CA: Stanford Alumni Association. Fascinating, entertaining account of sleep research by one of its leading pioneers.

Moorcroft, W. H. (1993). *Sleep, dreaming, & sleep disorders: An introduction.* (2nd ed.). New York: Lanham. For discussions of brain mechanisms and sleep disorders, see especially Chapters 4 and 8.

Refinetti, R. (2000). *Circadian physiology.* Boca Raton, FL: CRC Press. Marvelous summary of research on circadian rhythms and the relevance to human behavior.

Winson, J. (1990, November). The meaning of dreams. *Scientific American, 263*(5), 86–96. Discusses theories of the function of REM sleep and the meaning of dreams.

Suggested Web Sites

You can go to the Biological Psychology Study Center and click on these links. While there, you can also check for suggested articles available on InfoTrac. The Biological Psychology Internet address is: **http://psychology.wadsworth.com/book/kalatbiopsych7e/**

http://www.asda.org/sitelnks.html
Links to sites concerning several sleep disorders.

http://www.thesleepsite.com/
More information on sleep disorders.

http://www.dreamresearch.net
Research information about the content of dreams.

Active Learner Link

Quiz for Chapter 9

Chapter

The Regulation of Internal Body States

10

Chapter Outline

Main Ideas

1. Many physiological and behavioral processes maintain a near-constancy of certain body variables, and they anticipate as well as react to needs.

2. Mammals regulate body temperature by such physiological processes as shivering and by such behavioral processes as selecting an appropriate environment. Brain areas that control body temperature respond both to their own temperature and to the temperature of the skin and spinal cord.

3. Thirst responds to the osmotic pressure and total volume of the blood.

4. Hunger and satiety are regulated by several factors, including taste, stomach distention, the availability of glucose to the cells, and chemicals released by the fat cells.

What is life? Life can be defined in different ways depending on whether our interest is medical, legal, philosophical, or poetic. Biologically, what is necessary for life is *a coordinated set of chemical reactions.* Not all chemical reactions are alive, but without chemical reactions, or without precise regulation of those reactions, life as we know it stops.

Every chemical reaction in the body takes place in a water solution at a rate that depends on the identity and concentration of molecules in the water, the temperature of the solution, and the presence of contaminants. Much of our behavior is organized to keep the right chemicals in the right proportions and at the right temperature.

Opposite:
Life requires constant control of the body's water, fuel, and temperature.

Module 10.1

Temperature Regulation

An average college student expends about 2600 kilocalories (kcal) per day. Where do you suppose all that energy goes? To muscular exercise? Mental activity, perhaps? No. You use about 1700 kcal (roughly two-thirds of the total, and just less than what it takes to power a 100-watt light bulb) just for basal metabolism, the energy you use to maintain a constant body temperature while at rest (Burton, 1994). Reptiles and amphibians, which do not maintain a constant body temperature, need far less fuel than you do.

In short, temperature regulation is one of your body's top priorities, even if it is not one of your main topics of thought and conversation. I hope to convince you that it is more interesting than you had thought.

Homeostasis

Physiologist Walter B. Cannon (1929) introduced the term homeostasis (HO-mee-oh-STAY-sis) to refer to temperature regulation and other biological processes that keep certain body variables within a fixed range. To understand how a homeostatic process works, we can use the analogy of a thermostat in a house with both a heating and a cooling system. Someone fixes a set range of temperatures on the thermostat. When the temperature in the house drops below that range, the thermostat triggers the furnace to provide heat until the house temperature returns to the set range. When the temperature rises above the maximum of the range, the thermostat triggers the air conditioner to cool the house.

Similarly, homeostatic processes in animals trigger physiological and behavioral activities that keep certain variables within a set range. In many cases the range is so narrow that we refer to it as a set point, a single value that the body works to maintain. For example, if calcium is deficient in your diet and its concentration in the blood begins to fall below the set point of 0.16 g/L (grams per liter), storage deposits in your bones release additional calcium into the blood. If the calcium level in the blood rises above 0.16 g/L, part of the excess is stored in the bones and part is excreted. Analogous mechanisms maintain constant blood levels of water, oxygen, glucose, sodium chloride, protein, fat, and acidity (Cannon, 1929).

In the mammalian body, temperature regulation, thirst, and hunger are *nearly* homeostatic processes. They are not *exactly* homeostatic because they anticipate future needs as well as react to current needs (Appley, 1991). For example, in a frightening situation that might call for vigorous activity, you begin to sweat even before you start to move. (We call it "cold sweat.")

Set points for body temperature, body fat, and other variables are not quite fixed; they change with time of day, time of year, and other conditions (Mrosovsky, 1990). Set points also differ among species. Most mammals have a body temperature close to that of humans, 37°C, whereas birds are significantly warmer, generally around 41°C.

Controlling Body Temperature

Amphibians, reptiles, and most fish are poikilothermic (POY-kih-lo-THER-mik): Their body temperature is the same as the temperature of their environment. They can control their body temperature to some extent by selecting their location, but they lack physiological mechanisms of temperature regulation such as shivering and sweating. A few kinds of fish maintain a nearly constant temperature in the brain, though not in the rest of the body (Block, Finnerty, Stewart, & Kidd, 1993). Some poikilothermic animals have evolved adaptations to surviving in extreme temperatures, as discussed in Digression 10.1.

Mammals and birds are homeothermic: They use physiological mechanisms to maintain an almost constant body temperature despite large variations in the environmental temperature. Homeothermy requires effort and therefore fuel. An animal *generates* heat in proportion to its total mass; it *radiates* heat in proportion to its surface area. A small animal, such as a mouse or a hummingbird, has a high surface-to-volume ratio and therefore radiates heat rapidly. Such animals need a great deal of fuel each day to maintain their body temperature. Larger animals are better insulated against heat loss.

The Advantages of Constant Body Temperature

Why have we evolved mechanisms to control body temperature? Why is constant body temperature important enough to justify spending so much energy? Pri-

Surviving in Extreme Cold

As you may have heard, some people have had their bodies frozen immediately after death, with the intention that they be kept frozen until scientists have discovered (a) how to thaw a frozen body and bring it back to life and (b) how to cure the disease that killed these people.

What do you think? Good idea? If you had enough money, would you choose this route to possible life after death?

My advice is don't bother. Ice crystals form as soon as a human body freezes, and water expands as it freezes. Therefore the ice crystals tear apart the blood vessels and cell membranes. Even if scientists find cures for all the diseases and figure out how to thaw a human body successfully, what's the prospect that they will be able to repair almost every blood vessel and cell membrane in the body? It's always risky to say something is impossible, but this idea sounds pretty close to it.

Amazingly, however, some frogs, fish, and insects survive through northern Canadian winters despite temperatures near −40°.[a] How do they do it? Some insects and fish stock their blood with large amounts of glycerol and other antifreeze chemicals at the start of the winter, so they can get extremely cold without freezing. Wood frogs actually do freeze, but they have several mechanisms to reduce the damage. They start by withdrawing most fluid from their organs and blood vessels and

Companies will freeze a dead body with the prospect that future technologies can restore the person to life.

storing it in extracellular spaces. That way, ice crystals have plenty of room to expand when they do form, without tearing the blood vessels and cells. Also, they have chemicals that regulate ice crystal formation, so it occurs slowly and gradually throughout the body, not in chunks. Finally, they have enormous increases in blood-clotting capacity so that they can quickly repair any blood vessels that do rupture (Storey & Storey, 1999).

(If we used all those methods, could we freeze a human body without damage? Who knows? Maybe. But remember that if anyone does decide to try this, it's necessary to start all the treatments well before the person dies.)

---

[a] I didn't have to specify Fahrenheit or Celsius because −40°F is also −40°C.

marily, constant body temperature enables an animal to stay active even when the environment turns cold. Recall from Chapter 8 that a fish has trouble maintaining a high activity level at a low temperature. At a high temperature it can rely on its nonfatiguing slow-twitch muscle fibers; at lower temperatures it must recruit more and more of its rapidly fatiguing fast-twitch fibers. It can move rapidly even in the cold, but not for long. Birds and mammals, in contrast, keep their muscles warm at all times, regardless of air temperature.

Why did mammals evolve a body temperature of 37°C instead of 27° or 47° or any other possible value? We can answer this question two ways. First consider all the ways we have to heat ourselves or cool ourselves. If the air is cold and you need to heat yourself, you can:

- Find a warmer place. Many small animals burrow underground to keep warm.

- Put on more clothing, if you're a human, thereby increasing your insulation.

- Fluff out your fur, if you're a hairy mammal. (Actually you fluff out your "fur" even if you're hairless, although it doesn't do any good. When we humans get cold, we get goose bumps from erecting our hairs, even though our hairs are too short to provide any insulation.)

- Decrease blood flow to the skin, protecting the vital internal organs. You can afford to let your skin get cold, but not your heart or brain.

- Become more active, thereby generating more heat.

Figure 10.1 Behavioral regulation of body temperature
A 1-month-old emperor penguin chick is poorly insulated against Antarctic temperatures that may easily drop to −30°C or worse. However, when a hundred or more chicks huddle together tightly, they act in effect like one large well-insulated organism. As those on the outside get cold, they push their way to the inside, and the warm ones on the inside passively drift outward. (A nest of baby rodents acts much the same.) The process is so effective that a cluster of penguin chicks has to move frequently from one place to another, or it risks melting a hole in the ice and falling through!

- Shiver, thereby generating heat without moving.
- Huddle or cuddle with others. Most people are shy about hugging strangers to keep warm, but many animals are not (Figure 10.1). For example, spectacled eiders (birds in the duck family) spend their winters in the Arctic Ocean, most of which is covered with thick pack ice. However, with more than 150,000 eiders crowded into one tiny area, they not only keep one another warm but also maintain a 20-mile hole in the ice so they can dive for fish all winter long (Weidensaul, 1999).

However, if the air is warm and you need to cool yourself, your options are less effective:

- Find a cooler place (Figure 10.2).
- Become less active.
- Take off clothing or decrease fur thickness.

- Divert more blood to the skin for it to be cooled.
- Sweat. (Or pant if you're a species that doesn't sweat.)

All these mechanisms work if the air is cooler than the body. However, if the air is warmer than the body, then diverting more blood to the skin is useless, and decreased activity and clothing can only slow the rate at which you overheat, not actually cool you. If the air is above body temperature, your only defense is sweating, panting, or licking yourself (that is, cooling yourself through evaporation). But if you sweat much, you face the danger of losing too much body water. And if the air is humid as well as hot, sweating is useless. In short, you have more successful means of heating than of cooling yourself, and if you are going to maintain a constant body temperature, you benefit from a high temperature because you seldom need to cool yourself by much.

Remember that I said there are two explanations for why human body temperature is around 37°C. The first is that 37°C is close to the warmest temperatures we frequently face. The second is that animals gain an advantage by being as warm as they can. Other things being equal, an animal with a warmer body, and therefore warmer muscles, can run faster and with less fatigue than a cooler animal could. However, most proteins begin to break their bonds and lose their useful properties at temperatures above 40° or 41°C. It would be possible to evolve proteins that are stable at higher temperatures, but only by adding more stabilizing bonds. The enzymatic properties of proteins depend on the proteins' flexible structure, so making them rigid enough to withstand high temperatures would make them almost useless (Somero, 1996). In short, birds' body temperatures are probably about as high as possible for any kind of life based on proteins. Mammals are a little cooler, but not much.

Figure 10.2 One way to cope with the heat
Overheated animals, just like overheated people, look for the coolest spot they can find.

Reproductive cells require a somewhat cooler environment (Rommel, Pabst, & McLellan, 1998). Birds lay eggs and sit on them because the birds' internal temperature is too hot for the embryo. Similarly, in most male mammals the scrotum hangs outside the body because sperm production requires a temperature a bit cooler than the rest of the body. (A man who wears his undershorts too tight produces fewer healthy sperm cells.) Pregnant women are advised to avoid hot baths and anything else that would overheat a developing fetus.

Stop & Check

1. What is homeostasis?

2. What is the primary advantage of maintaining a constant body temperature?

3. What are two explanations for why we evolved a body temperature of about 37°C instead of some other temperature?

Check your answers on page 288.

Brain Mechanisms

All the physiological changes that defend body temperature—such as shivering, sweating, and changes in blood flow to the skin—depend predominantly on certain areas within the hypothalamus, a small structure at the base of the brain (see Figure 10.3). The hypothalamus contains a number of nuclei, each of which apparently serves a different function. Most critical for temperature control is the **preoptic area**, next to the anterior hypothalamus. (It is called *preoptic* because it is near the optic chiasm, where the optic nerves cross.)

The preoptic area monitors body temperature partly by monitoring its own temperature (D. O. Nelson & Prosser, 1981). When an experimenter heats the preoptic area, an animal pants or sweats, even in a cool environment. If the same area is cooled, the animal shivers, even in a warm room. These responses are not simply reflexive. An animal will also react to a heated or cooled preoptic area by pressing a lever or doing other work for cold air or hot air reinforcements (Satinoff, 1964).

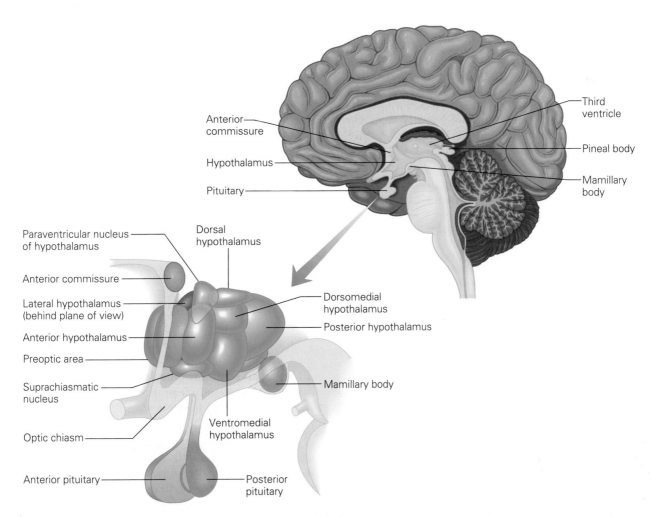

Figure 10.3   Major subdivisions of the hypothalamus and pituitary
(Source: After Nieuwenhuys, Voogd, & vanHuijzen, 1988)

Besides monitoring their own temperature, the cells of the preoptic area also receive input from temperature-sensitive receptors in the skin and spinal cord. The animal shivers most vigorously when both the preoptic area and the other receptors are cold; it sweats or pants most vigorously when both are hot.

Damage to the preoptic area impairs a mammal's ability to regulate temperature. It can no longer shiver, so its body temperature plummets in a cold environment (Satinoff, Valentino, & Teitelbaum, 1976). The preoptic area dominates temperature control, but temperature-sensitive cells also exist in other parts of the hypothalamus, elsewhere in the brain, and in the spinal cord. Fragmentary shivering and sweating can still occur after preoptic area damage.

Behavioral Mechanisms

Although the body temperature of fish, amphibians, and reptiles matches that of their surroundings, it seldom fluctuates wildly because they can choose their location within the environment. A desert lizard burrows into the ground in the middle of the day, when the surface is too hot, and again in the middle of the night, when the surface is too cold. On the surface, it moves from sun to shade as necessary to keep its temperature fairly constant.

Mammals, too, use behavioral means to regulate their body temperature. They do not sit on an icy surface shivering when they can build a nest or sweat and pant in the sun when they can find a shady spot. The more they can regulate their temperature behaviorally, the less they need to rely on physiological efforts (Refinetti & Carlisle, 1986a). If the physiological mechanisms fail, as they do after damage to the preoptic area of the hypothalamus, mammals can maintain a fairly constant body temperature by behavioral means alone, such as by seeking a warm or cold place or by pressing a lever to keep a heat lamp on (Satinoff & Rutstein, 1970; Van Zoeren & Stricker, 1977).

Fever

Bacterial and viral infections generally cause fever, an increase in body temperature. As a rule, the fever is not part of the illness; it is part of the body's defense against the illness. When the body is invaded by bacteria, viruses, fungi, or other foreign bodies, it mobilizes, among other things, its *leukocytes* (white blood cells) to attack them. The leukocytes release a protein called *interleukin-1*, which in turn causes the production of **prostaglandin E$_1$** and **prostaglandin E$_2$,** which then excite specific receptors in the preoptic area of the hypothalamus that direct the autonomic nervous system to raise body temperature (Scammell, Elmquist, Griffin, & Saper, 1996; Ushikubi et al., 1998). Prostaglandins also increase sleepiness, as we saw in Chapter 9.

Newborn rabbits, whose hypothalamus is immature, do not shiver in response to infections. If they are given a choice of environments, however, they select an unusually warm spot and thereby raise their body temperature (Satinoff, McEwen, & Williams, 1976). That is, they develop a fever by behavioral rather than physiological means. Fish and reptiles do the same if they can find a warm enough environment (Kluger, 1991). Again, the point is that fever is something the animal does to fight an infection.

Does fever do an animal any good? Certain types of bacteria grow less vigorously at high temperatures than at normal mammalian body temperatures. Other things being equal, developing a moderate fever increases an individual's chance of surviving a bacterial infection (Kluger, 1991). However, a fever of more than about 2.25°C above normal body temperature does more harm than good, and a 4° to 6°C fever can be fatal (Rommel et al., 1998).

Stop & Check

4. What evidence do we have that the preoptic area controls body temperature?

5. How can an animal regulate body temperature after damage to the preoptic area?

6. Suppose a drug interferes with the synthesis of prostaglandins. How would it affect fevers?

Check your answers on page 288.

Temperature Regulation and Behavior

When we are watching an animal's behavior and trying to interpret it, we can easily overlook the importance of temperature regulation. Let us consider two examples.

The Development of Animal Behavior

Over a number of years, psychologists observing the development of behavior in rats concluded that infant rats were incapable of certain behaviors—such as odor conditioning and certain controls of eating and drinking—and that the capacity for those behaviors developed at some point during the first weeks of life (a significant period of time in a rat's life). After extensive attempts to study the developmental psychology of such behaviors, researchers discovered that rats could perform them all in the first week of life, sometimes even on the first day, if the room was warm enough. The problem was simply that researchers generally work at "normal room temperature," perhaps 20°–23°C, which is comfortable for adult humans but dangerously cold for an isolated baby rat

Figure 10.4 The special difficulties of temperature regulation for a newborn rodent
A newborn rat has no hair, thin skin, and little body fat. If left exposed in a cool room, its body temperature quickly falls. This difficulty in regulating body temperature has impaired young rats' performance in many psychological experiments.

(see Figure 10.4). In a room kept above 30°C, infant rats' behavioral capacities improve markedly (Satinoff, 1991).

The Tonic Immobility Response

When a baby bird is grabbed by a predator, its first response is generally to adopt a position known as **tonic immobility,** limp and almost motionless (Figure 10.5). Observers say the chick is feigning death. We should not consider this act intentional, although immobility does decrease the probability of being attacked. After all, predators attack a prey only until it stops moving. The chick gains an advantage because the predator

Figure 10.5 The tonic immobility posture
When a predator captures a young chick, the chick adopts a frozen posture for at least a few seconds, sometimes as much as hours. When it moves again depends on changes in body temperature.

might drop it or give it some other opportunity to escape. Granted, the chances are not good, but any chance is better than none at all.

The chick may remain limp for seconds or for hours. Within limits, the longer, the better; if it starts moving again too soon, the predator will surely attack before the chick can escape. What determines how soon the chick stops feigning death? The answer is, simply, body temperature. A chick generates more body heat by moving than by sitting still, but moving also cools the chick by ventilation. A motionless chick gradually accumulates heat, unless the air is very cool. When its body temperature reaches 41.4°C (the normal body temperature of an adult chicken), it starts moving (Rovee-Collier, Kupersmidt, O'Brien, Collier, & Tepper, 1991). Moving incurs the risk of a possible attack by the predator, but staying still would incur the certain danger of overheating. The implication: Even when we are studying dynamic behaviors such as predator–prey relations, we should not forget the importance of temperature regulation.

In Closing: Temperature and Behavior

It has been said, only partly in jest, that shivering is a sign of stupidity. That is, the physiological mechanisms of temperature regulation (such as shivering and sweating) protect us when we have failed to find a place with a comfortable temperature or have worn too much or too little clothing. One of the key themes of this module has been the redundancy of mechanisms—the fact that the body has a variety of ways of accomplishing the same end. We shall see this theme again in the discussions of thirst and hunger.

Summary

1. Homeostasis is a tendency to maintain a body variable near a set point. Temperature, hunger, and thirst are almost homeostatic, but they anticipate future needs as well as reacting to current needs. (p. 282)

2. A constant body temperature enables a mammal or bird to move rapidly and without fatigue even when the air is cold. (p. 283)

3. A body temperature near 37°C has two advantages: It is usually higher than the air temperature, so we don't have to rely on our inefficient methods of cooling the body. And it keeps the body about as warm as possible without damaging proteins and therefore makes rapid muscle contractions possible. (p. 283)

4. The preoptic area of the hypothalamus is critical for temperature control. It monitors both its own temperature and that of the skin and spinal cord. (p. 285)

5. Even homeothermic animals rely partly on behavioral mechanisms for temperature regulation, especially in infancy and after damage to the preoptic area. (p. 286)

6. Fever is caused by the release of prostaglandins, which stimulate cells in the preoptic area. A moderate fever helps an animal combat an infection. (p. 286)

7. Temperature regulation often influences behaviors that seem unrelated to temperature; for example, infant mammals tested in a cool environment may fail to show their full behavioral capacities. (p. 286)

Answers to *Stop and Check* Questions

1. Homeostasis is a set of processes that keep certain body variables within a fixed range. (p. 285)

2. The primary advantage of a constant (high) body temperature is that it keeps the animal ready for rapid, prolonged muscle activity even if the air is cold. (p. 285)

3. One reason is that we have better mechanisms of heating ourselves than cooling ourselves, so it is best to have a body temperature close to the highest temperatures the environment often reaches. The second reason is that animals gain an advantage in being as warm as possible, and therefore as fast as possible, but proteins lose stability at temperatures above about 40° to 41°C. (p. 285)

4. Direct cooling or heating of the preoptic area leads to shivering or sweating. Also, damage to the preoptic area impairs physiological control of temperature. (p. 286)

5. It can regulate temperature through behavior, such as by finding a warmer or cooler place. (p. 286)

6. A drug that inhibited prostaglandin formation would lower fevers. Aspirin does, in fact, lower fever by that route. (p. 286)

Thought Question

Speculate on why birds have higher body temperatures than mammals.

Thirst

Water constitutes about 70% of the mammalian body. Because the concentration of chemicals in water determines the rate of all chemical reactions in the body, the water must be regulated within narrow limits. The body also needs enough fluid in the circulatory system to maintain normal blood pressure. People have been known to survive for weeks without food, but it is hard to survive long without water.

Mechanisms of Water Regulation

We don't have to be thirsty to drink. We drink the greatest amount during meals, partly to wash down the food and partly in anticipation of the solutes about to enter the body's fluids (Kraly, 1990). We also drink just because a beverage tastes good or because we want to socialize.

To maintain a constant amount of water in the body, we have to balance the water we lose with the water we take in. We take it in by drinking, of course, but also by eating. Leafy vegetables such as lettuce contain much water, and almost all foods yield some water during digestion. We lose water by urinating, defecating, and sweating. We also lose a little in every breath that we exhale and a little by evaporation from the eyes, the mouth, and other moist body surfaces.

Different species have adopted different strategies for balancing water intake and loss. Beavers and other species that live in or near the water drink plenty of water and eat moist foods; they excrete copious amounts of dilute urine and moist feces because they can afford to lose water. In contrast, many gerbils and other desert animals go through their entire lives without drinking; they gain enough water from their food and they have many adaptations to avoid losing water, including the fact that they excrete very dry feces and very concentrated urine. Unable to sweat they avoid the heat of the day by burrowing deep under the ground. Their highly convoluted nasal passages minimize the amount of water lost when they exhale.

We humans vary our strategy depending on circumstances. On the one hand, if you have ample supplies of tasty beverages, you can drink all you want and urinate the excess, as beavers do. (However, if you drink extensively without eating, as many alcoholics do, you may excrete enough body salts to harm yourself.) On the other hand, if you cannot find enough to drink, you will conserve your water, as gerbils do, mainly by decreasing the water in your urine. You will never be as good at this strategy as gerbils are, however. Humans can produce urine that is more concentrated than the blood, but not enormously more concentrated. (That's why you can't meet your needs by drinking ocean water.)

When your body needs water, it reacts not only with thirst but also with certain autonomic processes. The posterior pituitary (see Figure 10.3) releases a hormone called **vasopressin,** which raises blood pressure by constricting the blood vessels. (The term *vasopressin* comes from *vas*cular *press*ure.) The increased pressure helps compensate for the decreased volume. Vasopressin is also known as **antidiuretic hormone (ADH)** because it enables the kidneys to reabsorb water and therefore to secrete highly concentrated urine. (*Diuresis* means "urination.")

Stop & Check

1. If you lacked vasopressin, would you drink like a beaver or like a gerbil? Why?

Check your answers on page 293.

Osmotic Thirst

Although we speak about thirst as if it were a single entity, we experience one kind of thirst after an increase in the solute concentrations in the body and a different kind after a loss of overall fluid volume. Correspondingly, thirst researchers distinguish between *osmotic* thirst and *hypovolemic* thirst.

The combined concentration of all solutes in the body fluids remains at a nearly constant level of 0.15 M (molar) in mammals. (A concentration of 1.0 M has a number of grams of solute equal to the molecular weight

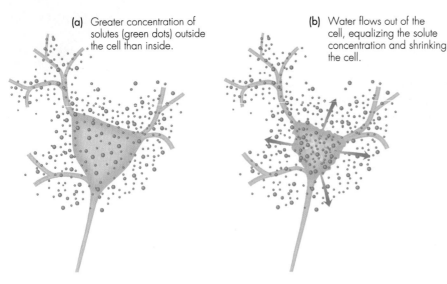

(a) Greater concentration of solutes (green dots) outside the cell than inside.

(b) Water flows out of the cell, equalizing the solute concentration and shrinking the cell.

Figure 10.6 The consequence of a difference in osmotic pressure
(a) A solute such as NaCl is more concentrated outside the cell than inside. **(b)** Water flows by osmosis out of the cell until the concentrations are equal. Neurons in certain brain areas detect their own dehydration and trigger thirst.

of that solute dissolved in 1 liter of solution.) This fixed concentration of solutes can be regarded as a set point, similar to the set point for temperature. Any deviation activates mechanisms that restore the concentration of solutes to the set point.

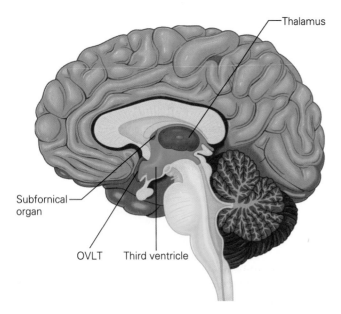

Thalamus

Subfornical organ

OVLT   Third ventricle

Figure 10.7 The brain's receptors for osmotic pressure and blood volume
These neurons are in areas surrounding the third ventricle of the brain, where no blood-brain barrier prevents blood-borne chemicals from entering the brain. The OVLT (organum vasculosum laminae terminalis) is the primary area for detecting osmotic pressure. The subfornical organ is the primary area for detecting blood volume. *(Source: Based in part on Weindl, 1973, and DeArmond, Fusco, & Dewey, 1974)*

The solutes inside and outside a cell produce an osmotic pressure, the tendency of water to flow across a semipermeable membrane from the area of low solute concentration to the area of higher concentration. A semipermeable membrane is one through which water can pass, but not solutes. The membrane surrounding a cell is almost a semipermeable membrane because water flows across it freely and various solutes flow either slowly or not at all between the *intracellular fluid* inside the cell and the *extracellular fluid* outside it. If you eat any salty food, sodium ions spread through the blood and the extracellular fluid but do not cross the membranes into cells. The result is a higher concentration of solutes outside the cells than inside. Whenever the solutes in the extracellular spaces become more concentrated than the intracellular fluid, the resulting osmotic pressure draws water from the cells into the extracellular fluid. Certain neurons detect their own loss of water and then trigger **osmotic thirst,** which helps restore the normal state (see Figure 10.6). The kidneys also excrete a more concentrated urine to rid the body of excess sodium.

How does the brain know when osmotic pressure is low? It gets part of the information from receptors around the third ventricle (Figure 10.7). These specialized areas are not protected by a blood-brain barrier; hence, they can detect chemicals circulating in the blood, including the overall solute concentration of the blood (Ramsay & Thrasher, 1990). The area principally responsible for detecting osmotic pressure is known as the **OVLT** (organum vasculosum laminae terminalis). The brain also gets information from receptors in the periphery, including the stomach, that detect high levels of sodium (Kraly, Kim, Dunham, & Tribuzio, 1995), enabling the brain to anticipate an osmotic need before the rest of the body actually experiences it.

Receptors in the OVLT, the stomach, and elsewhere relay their information to several parts of the hypothalamus, including the **supraoptic nucleus** and the **paraventricular nucleus,** which control the rate at which the posterior pituitary releases vasopressin. Receptors also relay information to the lateral preoptic area of the hypothalamus, where certain neurons control drinking. Many axons passing through the lateral preoptic area also contribute to drinking. A lesion in the lateral preoptic area impairs osmotic thirst partly by damage to cell bodies and partly by damage to passing axons (Saad, Luiz, Camargo, Renzi, & Manani, 1996).

Hypovolemic Thirst

Blood volume may drop sharply after a deep cut or internal hemorrhaging or after vomiting, diarrhea, or extensive sweating. When blood volume and pressure are too low, the blood cannot carry enough water and nutrients to the cells. The body's response is **hypovolemic** (HI-po-vo-LEE-mik) **thirst,** meaning thirst based on low volume. During hypovolemic thirst, the body needs to replenish not only its water but also the lost salts and other solutes.

After a loss of blood volume, an animal drinks more, but it will not drink much pure water, which would dilute its body fluids. It drinks much more if the water contains some salts (Stricker, 1969). If the animal is offered one container of pure water and another of excessively concentrated salt water, it alternates between the two to yield a mixture that matches the content of its blood.

Mechanisms

The body has two ways of detecting loss of blood volume (Epstein, 1990; Ramsay & Thrasher, 1990). First, **baroreceptors** attached to the large veins detect the pressure of blood returning to the heart. The second mechanism depends on hormones. When blood volume drops, the kidneys respond by releasing the hormone *renin*. Renin splits a portion off angiotensinogen, a large protein that circulates in the blood, to form angiotensin I, which certain enzymes convert to the hormone **angiotensin II,** which constricts the blood vessels, compensating for the drop in blood pressure (see Figure 10.8).

When angiotensin reaches the brain, it stimulates neurons in the **subfornical organ (SFO),** which, like the OVLT area, adjoins the third ventricle of the brain (see Figure 10.7). Also like the OVLT, the SFO lies outside the blood-brain barrier and is therefore well suited to monitor the blood. It relays information to the part of the preoptic area in the hypothalamus that directs drinking. Injecting angiotensin near the SFO increases drinking (Mangiapane & Simpson, 1980), and injecting a drug that blocks angiotensin II receptors inhibits drinking (Fregly & Rowland, 1991). These findings support the conclusion that angiotensin in the brain promotes certain types of thirst.

Angiotensin and baroreceptors have a **synergistic effect** (Epstein, 1983; Rowland, 1980). If two effects are synergistic, their combined effect is more than the sum of the two separate effects. That is, it may take less angiotensin to stimulate thirst if the baroreceptors also indicate low blood pressure than if they indicate normal blood pressure.

Table 10.1 summarizes the differences between osmotic thirst and hypovolemic thirst.

Figure 10.8 Hormonal response to hypovolemia

2. Would adding salt to the blood increase or decrease osmotic pressure on the cells?

3. Who would have a stronger preference for pure water—someone with osmotic thirst or someone with hypovolemic thirst?

Check your answers on page 293.

Sodium-Specific Cravings

Many people today limit their salt intake to control high blood pressure. However, although excessive salt can be harmful to people with high blood pressure, moderate amounts are necessary for life.

Individuals who have lost sodium and other solutes may experience a craving for salty tastes along with their hypovolemic thirst. For example, women with heavy menstrual flow often experience a craving for salty snacks. So do some athletes after extensive sweating. The salt craving develops automatically, as soon as the need exists (Richter, 1936). In contrast, specific hungers

Table 10.1 Comparison of Osmotic and Hypovolemic Thirst

Type of Thirst	Stimulus	Best Relieved by Drinking	Receptor Location	Hormone Influences
Osmotic thirst	High solute concentration outside cells causes loss of water from cells	Water	OVLT, a brain area adjoining the third ventricle	Accompanied by vasopressin secretion to conserve water
Hypovolemic thirst	Low blood volume	Water containing solutes	1. Baroreceptors, measuring blood flow returning to the heart 2. Subfornical organ, a brain area adjoining the third ventricle	Increased by angiotensin

for other vitamins and minerals have to be learned by trial and error (Rozin & Kalat, 1971).

Sodium hunger depends largely on hormones (Schulkin, 1991). When the body's sodium reserves are low, the adrenal glands produce the hormone **aldosterone,** which causes the kidneys, salivary glands, and sweat glands to conserve sodium and excrete more watery fluids than usual (Verrey & Beron, 1996). Aldosterone also triggers an increased preference for salty tastes. Decreased blood sodium also increases the blood concentrations of angiotensin II, another hormone that increases sodium hunger (Sato, Yada, & De Luca, 1996). The effects of aldosterone and angiotensin are strongly synergistic; either one alone produces a small increase in sodium intake, but together they produce a much greater effect (Sakai & Epstein, 1990; Stricker, 1983).

Exactly how aldosterone and angiotensin II provoke sodium cravings is not fully understood, and some of the research illustrates the difficulty of interpreting lesion studies. Decades ago researchers had found that rats with damage to the subfornical organ generally fail to show cravings when they were sodium deficient and therefore proposed that the SFO was one of the areas necessary for salt cravings. Perhaps aldosterone and angiotensin II exerted part of their effects there. Later, however, researchers demonstrated that SFO-damaged animals become so dehydrated (because of their failure to drink) that they had trouble displaying salt cravings. If enough water was put into their bodies, they could then show normal sodium appetite (Starbuck, Lane, & Fitts, 1997). The message is that a lesion can appear to impair one behavior just because it has impaired some other behavior that is necessary for the first one to occur.

Module 10.2

In Closing: The Psychology and Biology of Thirst

You may have thought that temperature regulation happens automatically and that water regulation depends on your behavior. You can see now that the distinction is not entirely correct. You control your body temperature partly by automatic means such as sweating or shivering, but also partly by behavioral means such as choosing a warm or a cool place. You control your body water partly by the behavior of drinking, but also by changes in kidney activity. If your kidneys cannot regulate your water and sodium adequately, your brain gets signals to change your drinking or sodium intake. In short, keeping your body's chemical reactions going depends on both skeletal and autonomic controls.

Summary

1. Different mammalian species have evolved different ways of maintaining body water, ranging from frequent drinking (beavers) to extreme conservation of fluids (gerbils). Humans alter their strategy depending on the availability of acceptable fluids. (p. 289)

2. An increase in the osmotic pressure of the blood draws water out of cells, causing osmotic thirst. Neurons in the OVLT, an area adjoining the third ventricle, detect changes in osmotic pressure and

send information to hypothalamic areas responsible for vasopressin secretion and for drinking. (p. 289)

3. Loss of blood volume causes hypovolemic thirst. Animals with hypovolemic thirst drink more water containing solutes than pure water. The subfornical organ is especially important for detecting changes in blood volume and sending information to trigger hypovolemic thirst. (p. 291)

4. Two stimuli have been identified for hypovolemic thirst: signals from the baroreceptors and the hormone angiotensin II, which increases when blood pressure falls. The two stimuli apparently act synergistically. (p. 291)

5. Loss of sodium salts from the body triggers sodium-specific cravings. The hormones aldosterone and angiotensin II synergistically stimulate such cravings. (p. 291)

Answers to *Stop and Check* Questions

1. If you lacked vasopressin, you would have to drink more like a beaver. You would not be able to conserve body water, so you would have to drink as much as possible all the time. (p. 289)

2. Adding salt to the blood would increase osmotic pressure in the cells because it would draw water from the cells into the blood. (p. 291)

3. The person with osmotic thirst would have a stronger preference for pure water. The one with hypovolemic thirst would drink more if the solution contained some salts. (p. 291)

Thought Questions

1. An injection of concentrated sodium chloride triggers osmotic thirst, but an injection of equally concentrated glucose does not. Why not?

2. Many women crave salt during menstruation or pregnancy. Why?

Module 10.3

Hunger

Any animal has to eat enough food to meet its needs, but different species have different strategies. Some snakes and other reptiles eat one huge meal (Figure 10.9) and then go without additional food for months, partly because the meal was so huge but also because they do not regulate body temperature and therefore do not need a constant supply of energy.

Bears never eat as much in a single gulp as that snake did in Figure 10.9, but they too eat as much as they can at one time. It is a sensible strategy because bears' main foods—fruits and nuts—are available in large quantities for short times and then become completely unavailable. So the bears eat all they can when they can to tide them over through times of starvation.

Small birds, at the other extreme of eating strategies, generally eat only what they need at the moment and store almost no fat at all. Such eating restraint is risky, as it requires finding tiny meals almost constantly. The advantage is that a bird that minimizes its weight maximizes its ability to fly away from predators (Figure 10.10). Even small birds can switch strategies, however, and eat larger meals when food is hard to find. They also eat larger meals (and get fat!) if there are no predators around (Gosler, Greenwood, & Perrins, 1995).

Humans vary in their strategy, but are intermediate between the bear and small bird extremes. We eat more than we need at the moment (unlike small birds), but eventually we quit (unlike bears). Choosing what to eat and deciding how much to eat are complicated and vitally important. Fortunately we don't have to make perfect decisions, and we have a wide array of learned and unlearned mechanisms to help in the process.

Figure 10.10   A great tit, a small European bird
Ordinarily, when food is abundant, tits eat just what they need each day and maintain very low fat reserves. When food is harder to find, they eat all they can and live off fat reserves between meals. During one era when their predators were scarce, tits started putting on more fat regardless of the food supplies.

Figure 10.9   A python swallowing a gazelle
The gazelle weighs about 50% more than the snake. Although some reptiles eat enormous meals, their energy needs are much lower than those of homeothermic animals. By the time this snake eats again, your total food intake will be vastly larger than a gazelle.

How the Digestive System Influences Food Selection

Before discussing hunger, let's quickly examine the digestive system, diagrammed in Figure 10.11. Its function is to break food down into smaller molecules that the cells can use. Digestion begins in the mouth, where food is mixed with saliva, which contains enzymes that help break down carbohydrates. Swallowed food travels down the esophagus to the stomach, where it is mixed with hydrochloric acid and several enzymes that digest proteins. Between the stomach and the intestines is a round sphincter muscle that periodically opens just briefly, allowing food to enter the intestines. Thus the stomach stores food as well as digests it.

Food then passes to the small intestine, which contains enzymes that help digest proteins, fats, and carbohydrates. It is also the main site for the absorption of digested foodstuffs into the bloodstream. Digested materials absorbed through the small intestine are car-

ried by the blood to body cells that use some of the nutrients and store the excess as glycogen, protein, or fat. Later these reserves are converted into glucose, the body's primary fuel, which is mobilized into the bloodstream. The large intestine absorbs water and minerals and lubricates the remaining materials to pass them as feces.

Enzymes and Consumption of Dairy Products

Newborn mammals survive entirely on mother's milk. Why do they stop nursing when they grow older? There are several reasons: The milk dries up, the mother pushes the infants away, and the infants grow large enough to try other foods. Moreover, after a certain age, most mammals lose their ability to metabolize lactose, the sugar in milk, because of declining levels of the intestinal enzyme lactase. From then on consumption of milk can cause gas, stomach cramps, or other distress (Rozin & Pelchat, 1988). Adult mammals can drink a little milk, as you may have noticed with a pet dog, but they generally limit their intake. The declining level of lactase may be an evolved mechanism to encourage weaning at the appropriate time.

Humans are the partial exception to this rule. Many adults have fairly high lactase levels and continue to consume milk, cheese, ice cream, and other dairy products throughout life. Worldwide, however, most adults cannot comfortably tolerate large amounts of milk products. About two-thirds of all adult humans, including almost all Southeast Asians, have low levels of lactase because of a recessive gene (Flatz, 1987). Most of these people can eat moderate amounts of dairy products (especially cheese and yogurt, which are easier to digest than milk) but develop cramps or gas pains if they consume too much. Figure 10.12 shows the worldwide distribution of lactose tolerance.

Other Influences on Food Selection

For a carnivore (meat eater), selecting a satisfactory diet is relatively simple; it eats any animal it can catch. A lion won't get vitamin deficient unless it eats vitamin-deficient zebras. However, herbivores (plant eaters) and omnivores (those that eat both meat and plants) must distinguish between edible and inedible substances and find a proper balance of vitamins and minerals. One way to do so is to learn from the experiences of others. For example, juvenile rats tend to imitate the food selections of their elders (Galef, 1992). Similarly children acquire the food preferences of their culture, even if they do not like every food their parents enjoy (Rozin, 1990).

But how did their parents learn what to eat? At some point some individuals had to learn for themselves. If you parachuted onto an uninhabited island

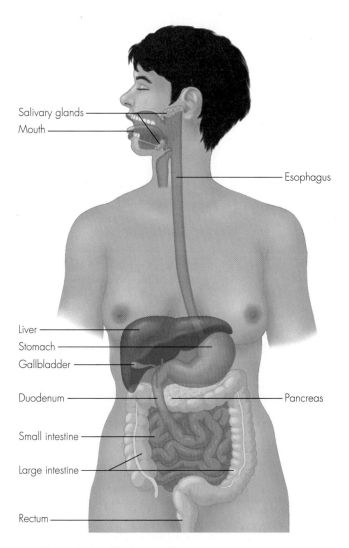

Figure 10.11 The human digestive system

Salivary glands
Mouth
Esophagus
Liver
Stomach
Gallbladder
Duodenum
Pancreas
Small intestine
Large intestine
Rectum

covered with unfamiliar plants, you would use a variety of behavioral strategies to select edible foods (Rozin & Vollmecke, 1986). First, you would let taste be your guide. You would select sweets, avoid bitter foods, and consume salty or sour foods in moderation. If you are a supertaster (Chapter 7), you will probably avoid most strong-tasting substances.

Second, you would prefer foods resembling familiar foods. After all, familiar foods are safe, and new foods may not be. What did you think of coffee the first time you tried it? Beer? Hot peppers? Most people do not like a strong new flavor the first time they try it.

Third, you would learn the consequences of eating each food you try. If you try something, especially something new, and then become ill, even hours later, your brain blames the illness on the food, and it won't taste good to you the next time you try it (Rozin & Kalat, 1971; Rozin & Zellner, 1985). This phenomenon is known as **conditioned taste aversions**. It is a robust phenomenon that occurs reliably after just a single pairing of food with illness, even if the illness came hours after the food (as it often does). In fact you will come to dislike a food that is followed by intestinal discomfort even if you consciously know that the nausea came from a thrill ride at the amusement park.

Stop & Check

1. Why do most Southeast Asian cooks not use milk and other dairy products?

Check your answer on page 307.

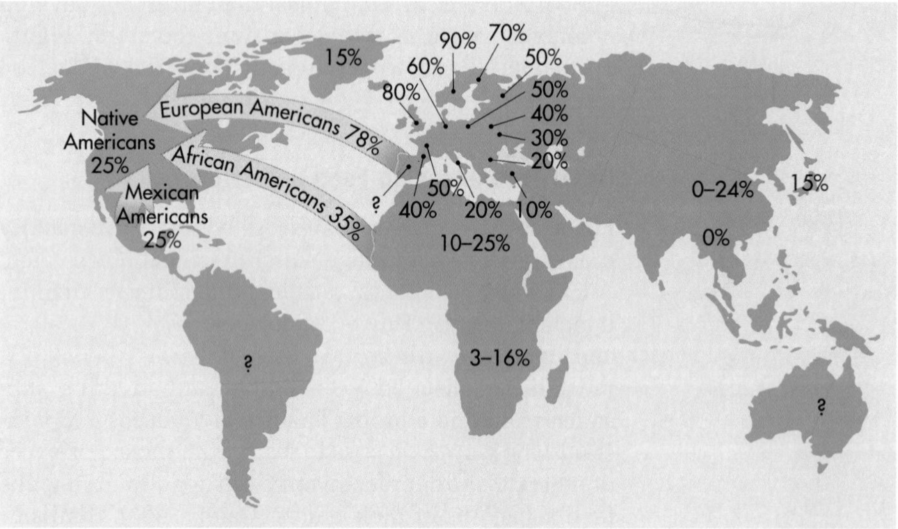

![Figure 10.12]

15% — 90% 70% — 50% — 50% — 40% — 30% — 20%

Native Americans 25%
European Americans 78%
African Americans 35%
Mexican Americans 25%

80% 60%
50% 40% 20% 10%
10–25%

0–24% 15%
0%

3–16%

Figure 10.12 Distribution of adult lactose tolerance
People in areas with high lactose tolerance (such as Scandinavia) are likely to enjoy milk, cheese, and other dairy products throughout their lives. People in areas with low tolerance (such as much of Asia) do not ordinarily consume milk or dairy products as adults. *(Source: Based on Flatz, 1987, and Rozin & Pelchat, 1988)*

How Taste and Digestion Control Hunger and Satiety

Eating is far too important to be entrusted to just one mechanism. Your brain gets messages from the mouth, the stomach, the intestines, and elsewhere indicating what to eat, how much, and when.

Oral Factors

You're a busy person, right? So if you could get all the nutrition you needed each day just by swallowing pills, would you do it? Most of us would refuse emphatically. Never mind how much time we would save; we *like* to taste and chew our foods. In fact many people like to taste and chew even when they are not hungry. Figure 10.13 shows a piece of 6500-year-old chewing gum made from birch-bark tar. Anthropologists aren't sure how the ancient people removed the sap to make the gum, and they aren't sure why anyone would chew something that tasted as bad as this gum probably did (Battersby, 1997). Clearly the urge to chew is strong.

If necessary, could you become satiated without tasting your food? In one experiment college students consumed lunch five days a week by swallowing one end of a rubber tube and then pushing a button to pump a liquid diet into the stomach (Jordan, 1969; Spiegel, 1973). (They were paid for participating.) After a few days of practice, each person established a consistent pattern, pumping in a constant volume of the liquid each day and maintaining a constant body weight. Most found the untasted meals unsatisfying, however, reporting a desire to taste or chew something (Jordan, 1969).

Although taste and other oral sensations contribute to the regulation of eating, they are not sufficient by themselves to end a meal. In **sham-feeding** experiments an animal is denied nutrition because everything it swallows leaks out of a tube connected to the esophagus or stomach. Under such conditions animals eat and swallow far more than normal. They may pause for a while, but then they eat again and again, never becoming satiated (G. P. Smith, 1998). In short, taste and other mouth sensations combine with other cues to produce satiety, but the taste and mouth cues alone are not sufficient.

Figure 10.13 Chewing gum from about 4500 B.C.
The gum, made from birch-bark tar, has small tooth marks indicating that it was chewed by a child or early teenager. *(Source: Battersby, 1997)*

The Stomach and Intestines

Ordinarily we end a meal before much of the food has reached the blood, much less the cells that need fuel. Do we stop eating simply because the stomach is full? Apparently yes, at least in many cases. In one experiment researchers attached an inflatable cuff at the connection between the stomach and the small intestine (Deutsch, Young, & Kalogeris, 1978). When they inflated the cuff, food could not pass from the stomach to the duodenum. They carefully ensured that the cuff was not traumatic to the animal and did not interfere with feeding. The key result was that, with the cuff inflated, an animal ate a normal-size meal and then stopped; that is, it could become satisfied even though the food did not leave the stomach. Evidently stomach distension is sufficient to produce satiety.

The stomach conveys satiety messages to the brain via the vagus nerve and the splanchnic nerves. The **vagus nerve** (cranial nerve X) conveys information about the stretching of the stomach walls, providing a major basis for satiety. The **splanchnic** (SPLANK-nik) **nerves** convey information about the nutrient contents of the stomach, carrying impulses from the thoracic and lumbar parts of the spinal cord to the digestive organs and from the digestive organs to the spinal cord (Deutsch & Ahn, 1986). Ordinarily the vagus nerve is more important for satiety, but the splanchnic nerves can serve the purpose if the vagus nerve is damaged (J. D. Davis, Smith, & Kung, 1994).

Is the stomach the *only* part of the digestive system important for satiety? Later researchers repeated the experiment with the inflatable cuff and replicated the result that a rat ate the same amount regardless of whether the cuff was open or closed, indicating that stomach distension is *sufficient* for satiety. However, when the cuff was open, much food passed to the duodenum before the end of the meal. The **duodenum** (DYOU-oh-DEE-num or dyuh-ODD-ehn-uhm) is the part of the small intestine adjoining the stomach; it is the first digestive site that absorbs a significant amount of nutrients. The rats in this experiment stopped eating when the duodenum was partly distended and the stomach was far from full (Seeley, Kaplan, & Grill, 1995). Evidently an eater can become satiated when food distends either the stomach or the duodenum.

Food infused directly to the duodenum of human volunteers produces reports of satiety (Lavin et al., 1996), and food infused to the duodenum of rats causes taste neurons in the pons to decrease their responsiveness to sweet tastes (Hajnal, Takenouchi, & Norgren, 1999). Curiously, sugars infused to the duodenum produce satiety much faster than fats do (Horn, Tordoff, & Friedman, 1996). Consequently both rats and humans on high-fat diets tend to overeat.

One way by which food in the duodenum inhibits appetite is by stimulating the duodenum to release the hormone **cholecystokinin** (ko-leh-SIS-teh-KI-nehn) **(CCK).** Injections of CCK do not delay a meal, but they decrease its size (Gibbs, Young, & Smith, 1973), partly because CCK closes the sphincter muscle between the stomach and the duodenum, causing the stomach to fill more quickly than it would have (McHugh & Moran, 1985; G. P. Smith & Gibbs, 1998). CCK is also a neuromodulator in the brain—actually the brain uses a shorter version of the CCK molecule—and in that role it also decreases eating. However, the CCK from the intestines does not cross the blood-brain barrier in significant quantities; certain brain neurons release CCK when they receive neural signals from the intestines. The fact that brain CCK and intestinal CCK have similar behavioral effects is an interesting coincidence suggesting that evolution uses the same chemicals in different places for similar purposes.

Stop & Check

2. What is the evidence that taste is not sufficient for satiety?

3. What is the evidence that stomach distension is sufficient for satiety?

4. What is the evidence that stomach distension, though sufficient, is not necessary for satiety?

5. What are two mechanisms by which CCK increases satiety?

Check your answers on pages 307–308.

Glucose, Insulin, and Glucagon

Much of the digested food that enters the bloodstream is in the form of glucose, which is an important source of energy for all parts of the body and by far the most important fuel of the brain. The blood's glucose level ordinarily remains almost constant (LeMagnen, 1981) because the liver can convert stored nutrients into glucose to keep blood glucose in homeostasis. What does vary is the amount of glucose the cells receive, and that amount depends on two pancreatic hormones: insulin and glucagon. **Insulin** enables

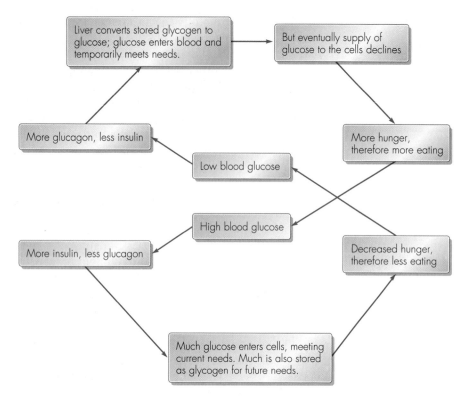

Figure 10.14   Insulin and glucagon feedback system
When glucose levels rise, the pancreas releases the hormone insulin, which causes cells to store the excess glucose as fats and glycogen. The entry of glucose into cells suppresses hunger. Lack of hunger leads to decreased eating, which lowers the glucose level; the pancreas releases glucagon, which stimulates the liver to convert stored glycogen into glucose, which enters the blood. The high ratio of glucagon to insulin also stimulates hunger, and the cycle repeats.

glucose to enter the cells, which may either use the glucose for current energy needs or store it as fat or glycogen. **Glucagon** has the reverse effect, stimulating the liver to convert stored glycogen to glucose, thus raising blood glucose levels. After a meal insulin levels rise, much glucose enters the cells, and appetite decreases. As time passes the blood glucose level falls, the pancreas releases more glucagon and less insulin, less glucose enters the cells, and hunger returns (Figure 10.14).

During or shortly after a meal, insulin levels rise, enabling the blood to supply the cells with glucose, and hunger levels drop. The insulin itself also reaches the brain and acts as a satiety hormone, decreasing hunger (Vanderweele, 1998). However, if the insulin level stays high for long, the body continues to move blood glucose into the cells, including the liver cells and fat cells that store it. Consequently the available blood glucose

begins to decline. For example, in late autumn migratory and hibernating species have constantly high insulin levels. They rapidly deposit much of each meal as fat and glycogen, grow hungry again, and continue gaining weight in preparation for a period without food (Figure 10.15).

When the insulin level is extremely low, as in people with diabetes, blood glucose levels may be three or more times the normal level, but little of it enters the cells (Figure 10.16). Diabetic people and animals eat more food than normal because their cells are starving (Lindberg, Coburn, & Stricker, 1984), but they excrete most of their glucose unused, so they lose weight. (Note the paradox that prolonged high or low insulin levels can increase eating, although for different reasons.)

People produce more insulin not only when they eat but also when they are getting ready to eat. Increased insulin before a meal prepares the body to let more glucose enter the cells and to store the excess part of the meal as fats. Obese people produce more insulin than do people of normal weight (W. G. Johnson & Wildman, 1983). Their high levels of insulin cause more food than normal to be stored as fat, and therefore their appetite returns soon after a meal (see Figure 10.15).

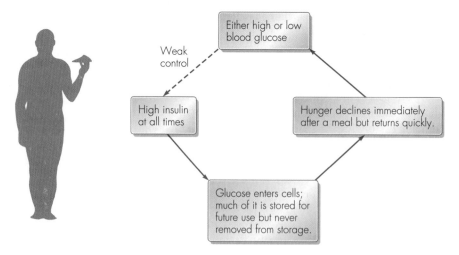

Figure 10.15   Effects of steadily high insulin levels on feeding
Even when the glucose level is low, insulin remains high and much of the blood glucose is stored as fats and glycogen. Consequently the blood's supply of glucose quickly drops and hunger returns.

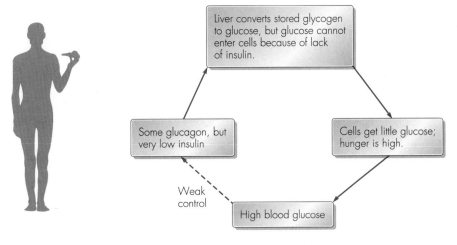

Figure 10.16 Untreated diabetics eat much but lose weight
Because of their low insulin levels, the glucose in their blood cannot enter the cells, either to be stored or to be used. Consequently they excrete glucose in their urine while their cells are starving.

Stop & Check

6. Why do people with very low insulin levels eat so much? Why do people with constantly high levels eat so much?

7. What would happen to someone's appetite if insulin levels and glucagon levels were both high?

Check your answers on page 308.

The Hypothalamus and Feeding Regulation

Damage to small areas of the hypothalamus can produce severe undereating or overeating. At one time researchers described the lateral hypothalamus as a feeding center and the ventromedial hypothalamus as a satiety center. We now regard that view as an oversimplification, and we seek a better understanding of how various areas contribute to the control of feeding.

The Lateral Hypothalamus

Several kinds of evidence indicate that the lateral hypothalamus is an important area for the control of feeding (Hoebel, 1988) (Figure 10.17). After damage here, an animal refuses food and water, grimacing and turning its head away as if the food were distasteful. The animal may starve to death unless it is force-fed, but if kept alive, it gradually recovers much of its ability to eat (see Figure 10.18). In an intact animal electrical stimulation of the lateral hypothalamus stimulates eating and responses that have previously been reinforced with food. That is, the stimulation increases food-seeking behav-

iors, not just chewing or some other reflex. Furthermore neurons in the lateral hypothalamus increase their activity when a hungry rat is offered food (see Methods 10.1).

One difficulty in interpreting these data is that any electrode that damages the lateral hypothalamus strikes not only the cell bodies in that area but also a number of dopamine-containing axons that happen to pass through. To deal with this problem, investigators developed several ways to damage just the axons or just the cells. For example, they may inject 6-hydroxydopamine (6-OHDA), which damages passing axons containing dopamine. Experiments of this type indicate that although damage to the dopamine-containing axons leaves an animal chronically inactive and unresponsive, it eats normally once it has food in its mouth (Berridge, Venier, & Robinson, 1989).

In other studies experimenters used chemicals that damage only the cell bodies, or induced lesions in very young rats, before the dopamine axons reach the lateral hypothalamus. The result was a major loss of feeding without loss of arousal and activity (Almli, Fisher, &

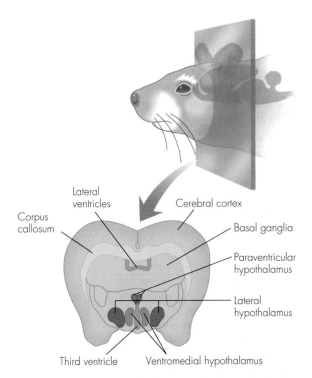

Figure 10.17 The lateral hypothalamus, ventromedial hypothalamus, and paraventricular hypothalamus
The side view above indicates the plane of the coronal section of the brain below. *(Source: After Hart, 1976)*

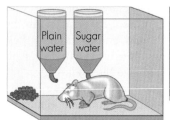

Stage 1. *Aphagia and adipsia.* Rat refuses all food and drink; must be force-fed to keep it alive.

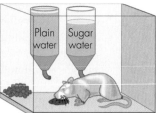

Stage 2. *Anorexia.* Rat eats a small amount of palatable foods and drinks sweetened water. It still does not eat enough to stay alive.

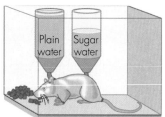

Stage 3. *Adipsia.* The rat eats enough to stay alive, though at a lower-than-normal body weight. It still refuses plain water.

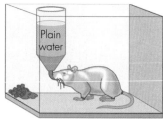

Stage 4. *Near-recovery.* The rat eats enough to stay alive, though at a lower-than-normal body weight. It drinks plain water, but only at mealtimes to wash down its food. Under slightly stressful conditions, such as in a cold room, the rat will return to an earlier stage of refusing food and water.

Figure 10.18 Recovery of feeding after damage to the lateral hypothalamus
At first the rat refuses all food and drink. If kept alive for several weeks or months by force-feeding, it gradually recovers its ability to eat and drink enough to stay alive. However, even at the final stage of recovery, its behavior is not the same as that of normal rats. *(Source: Based on Teitelbaum & Epstein, 1962)*

Hill, 1979; Grossman, Dacey, Halaris, Collier, & Routtenberg, 1978; Stricker, Swerdloff, & Zigmond, 1978). Evidently the cell bodies of the lateral hypothalamus contribute mainly to feeding, and the passing fibers contribute to overall arousal, activity, and reinforcement.

The question remains: *How* does the lateral hypothalamus contribute to feeding? It contributes in several ways (Hernandez, Murzi, Schwartz, & Hoebel, 1992) (see Figure 10.19). First, axons from the lateral hypothalamus extend to the NTS (nucleus of the tractus solitarius) in the medulla, part of the pathway responsive to taste (see p. 215). Information from the lateral hypothalamus modifies the activity of some of the NTS cells, either altering the taste sensation or increasing the salivation response to the tastes. Second, axons from the lateral hypothalamus extend into several forebrain structures, facilitating ingestion and swallowing, and causing cortical cells to increase their response to the taste, smell, or sight of food (Critchley & Rolls, 1996). Third, the lateral hypothalamus also activates a circuit that excites dopamine-containing cells, thereby initiating and reinforcing learned behaviors in a number of ways. Fourth, the lateral hypothalamus sends axons to the spinal cord, controlling autonomic responses such as digestive secretions (van den Pol, 1999).

After damage to the lateral hypothalamus, the animal has trouble digesting its foods.

Medial Areas of the Hypothalamus

Near the lateral hypothalamus is a set of areas that contribute very differently to feeding. Neuroscientists have known since the 1940s that a large lesion centered on the

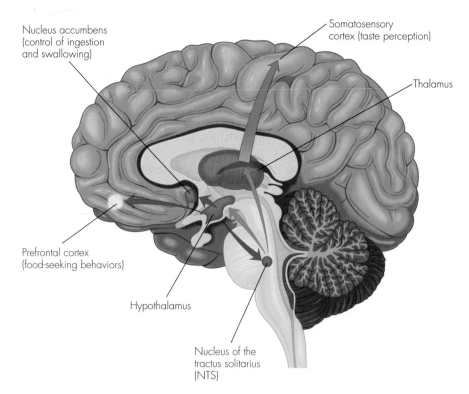

Figure 10.19 Pathways from the lateral hypothalamus
Axons from the lateral hypothalamus modify activity in several other brain areas, changing the response to taste, facilitating ingestion and swallowing, and increasing food-seeking behaviors. Also (not shown), the lateral hypothalamus controls stomach secretions.

Using Multiple Research Methods

Any conclusion demonstrated by any one research method in biological psychology is suspect. The method might have some hidden flaw, or the results might depend on some very particular set of conditions. However, if several studies using different methods converge on the same conclusion, the conclusion stands much firmer. For example, a lesion to the lateral hypothalamus produces decreased eating. It is possible to insert an electrode into the same location in another animal and pass a much briefer current, not enough to damage the cells but just enough to stimulate them. The result is increased feeding, as we would expect. If

the result had *not* been increased feeding, we would know that something was wrong, and researchers would have to reexamine their methods and assumptions. Also, it is possible to insert an electrode—again the same kind of electrode in the same location—but use it just for recording activity. Spontaneous increases in activity in that area correlate with increased feeding. When three methods converge on the same conclusion, we can increase our confidence. Note, however, that none of these studies tell us *how* activity in the lateral hypothalamus increases feeding. For that question, we need still further types of research.

ventromedial hypothalamus (VMH) leads to overeating and weight gain (see Figure 10.17). Some people with a tumor in that area have gained more than 10 kg (22 pounds) per month (Al-Rashid, 1971; Killeffer & Stern, 1970; Reeves & Plum, 1969). Rats with similar damage sometimes double or triple their weight (Figure 10.20). Eventually body weight levels off at a stable but high set point, and total food intake declines to nearly normal levels.

Although these symptoms have been known as the *ventromedial hypothalamic syndrome*, damage limited to the ventromedial hypothalamic nucleus itself does not consistently increase eating or body weight. To produce a large effect, the lesion must extend outside the ventromedial nucleus to invade nearby medial hypothalamic cells and axons. Excess eating and increased body weight can also result from damage to the ventral noradrenergic bundle (Figure 10.21), an ascending axon

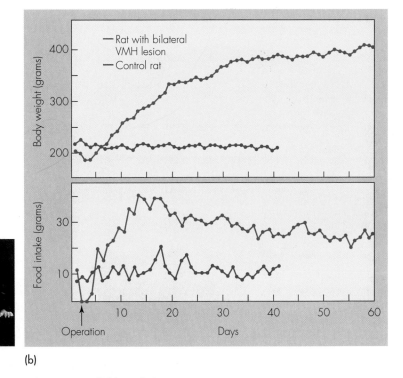

(a) (b)

Figure 10.20 The effects of damage to the ventromedial hypothalamus
(a) On the right is a normal rat. On the left is a rat after damage to the ventromedial hypothalamus. The brain-damaged rat may weigh up to three times as much as a normal rat. *(Source: Yoav Levy/Phototake)* **(b)** Changes in weight and eating in a rat after damage to the ventromedial hypothalamus. Within a few days after the operation, the rat begins eating much more than normal. As it gains weight, its eating decreases, although it remains above normal. *(Source: Adapted from Teitelbaum, 1961)*

pathway through the hypothalamus (Ahlskog & Hoebel, 1973; Ahlskog, Randall, & Hoebel, 1975; Gold, 1973).

Rats with damage in and around the ventromedial hypothalamus are finicky eaters. With a normal or sweetened diet, they overeat, sometimes eating day and night instead of sleeping. Yet they eat far less than normal on a bitter or otherwise untasty diet (Ferguson & Keesey, 1975; Teitelbaum, 1955). Consequently we cannot say that the rats show an overall increase in hunger. We should also not say that they lack satiety. They eat normal-size meals, demonstrating satiety at the normal time, but they eat more frequently than normal for several reasons (Hoebel & Hernandez, 1993). First, they have increased stomach motility and secretions, and their stomachs empty faster than normal. The faster the stomach empties, the sooner an animal is ready for its next meal. Second, the damage leads to a lasting increase in insulin production (King, Smith, & Frohman, 1984), so a larger than normal percentage of each meal is stored as fat. If animals with this kind of damage are prevented from overeating, they gain weight anyway! Mark Friedman and Edward Stricker (1976) have therefore proposed that the animal does not get fat because it overeats; rather it has to overeat because it stores so much fat and has little fuel left over for its current needs.

Rats with damage in the nearby **paraventricular nucleus (PVN)** of the hypothalamus also overeat, but for a different reason. Instead of eating more frequent meals, they eat larger meals, as if they were insensitive to the usual signals for ending a meal (Leibowitz, Hammer, & Chang, 1981). Table 10.2 summarizes the effects of lesions in several areas of the hypothalamus.

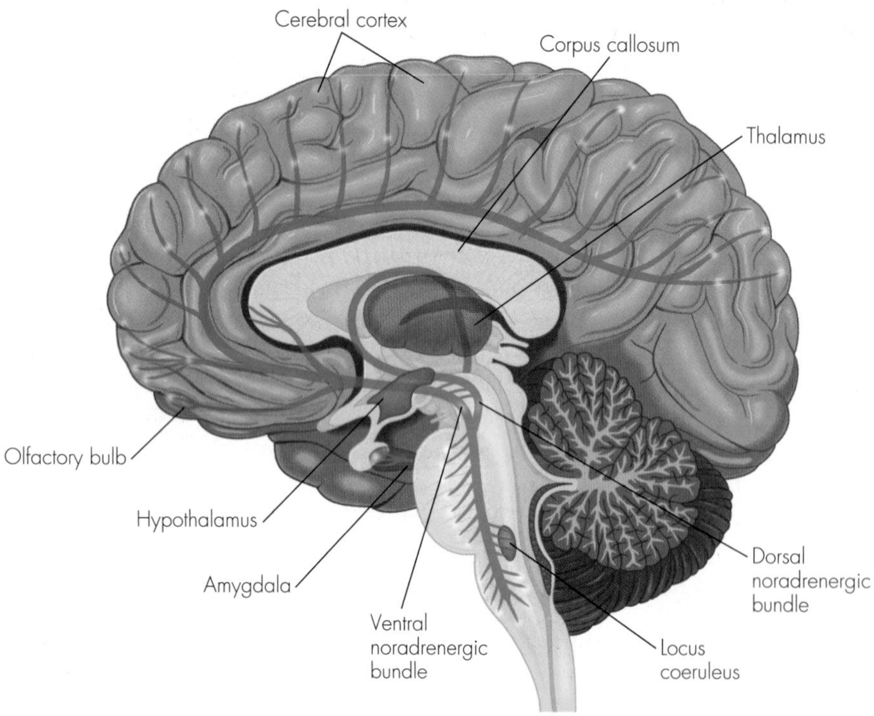

Stop & Check

8. What are the effects of damage to the cell bodies in the lateral hypothalamus? Of damage to the axons passing through the lateral hypothalamus?

9. In what way does eating increase after damage in and around the ventromedial hypothalamus? After damage to the paraventricular nucleus?

Check your answers on page 308.

Satiety Chemicals and Eating Disorders

Obesity is considered a medical condition, whereas anorexia and bulimia are considered psychiatric conditions. Nevertheless all eating disorders obviously depend on a combination of influences from biological predispositions and learned habits of dealing with food and exercise. That is, any eating disorder includes elements of both biology and psychology.

Through most of evolutionary time, people worried more about starvation than obesity. In fact the same is true for the whole animal kingdom, and animals are well equipped with mechanisms to guarantee that they eat enough, but less equipped with mechanisms to prevent overeating. Today people in prosperous countries have an abundance of tasty, high-calorie foods and a lifestyle that includes mobile phones, remote control television channel changers, and countless other labor-saving devices. As a result many people become obese to the point of endangering their health (Hill & Peters, 1998). Research on the physiology of satiety offers new hope for overcoming obesity.

Leptin

Figure 10.22 compares two normal mice to one mouse with a gene known (for obvious reasons) as *obese* (Zhang et al., 1994). After researchers located this gene, they identified a previously unknown peptide that the normal gene makes, now known as **leptin** (Halaas et al.,

Figure 10.21 Major norepinephrine pathways in the human brain
Damage to the ventral noradrenergic bundle leads to overeating and weight gain.
(Source: Based on Valzelli, 1980)

Cerebral cortex

Corpus callosum

Thalamus

Olfactory bulb

Hypothalamus

Amygdala

Ventral noradrenergic bundle

Locus coeruleus

Dorsal noradrenergic bundle

Table 10.2   Effects of Lesions in Certain Hypothalamic Areas

Hypothalamic Area	Effect of Lesion
Preoptic area	Deficit in physiological mechanisms of temperature regulation
Lateral preoptic area	Deficit in osmotic thirst due partly to damage to cells and partly to interruption of passing axons
Lateral hypothalamus	Undereating, weight loss, low insulin level (because of damage to cell bodies); underarousal, underresponsiveness (because of damage to passing axons)
Ventromedial hypothalamus	Increased meal frequency, weight gain, high insulin level
Paraventricular nucleus	Increased meal size, especially increased carbohydrate intake during the first meal of the active period of the day

1995). In genetically normal mammals (not just mice), fat cells throughout the body produce the peptide leptin: The more fat cells, the more leptin. Leptin circulates through the blood, notifying the rest of the body about the current fat supplies. Mice with the *obese* gene fail to produce leptin, and their bodies act as if they have no fat.

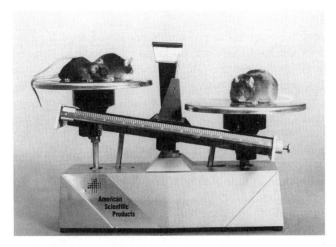

Figure 10.22   The effects of the obese gene on body weight in mice
A gene that has been located on a mouse chromosome leads to increased eating, decreased metabolic rate, and increased weight gain. *(Source: Zhang et al., 1994)*

Ordinarily, when leptin levels are high, animals act as if they have plenty of nutrition. They eat less (Campfield, Smith, Guisez, Devos, & Burn, 1995), become more active (Elias, Lee, et al., 1998), and increase the activity of their immune systems (Lord et al., 1998). (If you have enough fat supplies, you can afford to devote energy to your immune system. If you have no fat, you are starving and you have to conserve energy wherever you can.) In adolescence a certain level of leptin triggers the onset of puberty. (Again, if your fat supply is low, you don't have enough in reserve to start providing for a baby.) On the average, thinner people enter puberty later. However, an injection of leptin can trigger puberty even in very thin mice and presumably would in humans also (Chehab, Mounzih, Lu, & Lim, 1997).

Genetically obese mice do not make their own leptin, but after daily injections of leptin, they become more active and decrease their food intake and body weight (Pellymounter et al., 1995). As you might imagine, news of this research inspired many pharmaceutical companies to hope they could make a fortune by selling leptin. They worried about the potential for abuse: What if thin people (mainly women) took leptin to try to get still thinner and managed to starve themselves to death? But further research found that normal-weight mice did not starve in response to leptin. So leptin looked promising indeed.

Unfortunately almost all overweight people already have high levels of leptin (Considine et al., 1996). (Remember—the more fat, the more leptin.) A very few people, whose bodies do not produce leptin, do become extremely obese, just as the mice did, and they fail to enter puberty (Strobel, Issad, Camoin, Ozata, & Strosberg, 1998). That is, both their appetites and their reproductive systems act as if the body were starving. The fact that they consciously know they are fat has little effect.

If human obesity is seldom due to a lack of leptin, perhaps some people have an inadequate sensitivity to leptin. At least one family has been found with a hereditary defect in the gene controlling the leptin receptor; they become obese, as we would expect (Clément et al., 1998). Could physicians help overweight people lose weight by giving huge doses of leptin to overcome the problem of weak sensitivity to it? Maybe, but caution is necessary. Excess leptin levels increase the risk of diabetes and other medical problems (B. Cohen, Novick, & Rubinstein, 1996; Naggert et al., 1995). The search therefore turns to other chemicals related to satiety.

Neuropeptide Y

Leptin activates receptors in one part of the hypothalamus known as the *arcuate nucleus,* where it inhibits neurons that project to several parts of the hypothalamus (Broberger, De Lecea, Sutcliffe, & Hökfelt, 1998; Elias, Saper, et al., 1998). Those neurons release a neuromodulator peptide called **neuropeptide Y (NPY)** (Stephens et al., 1995) which (among other effects) powerfully inhibits the paraventricular nucleus (PVN) of the hypothalamus and therefore increases meal size. NPY is an abundant peptide, probably the most widespread peptide in the brain. When NPY inhibits the PVN, it produces the same effect as a lesion there: extreme overeating, as tastelessly illustrated in Figure 10.23 (Billington & Levine, 1992; Leibowitz & Alexander, 1991; Morley, Levine, Grace, & Kneip, 1985). Injection of NPY to other parts of the hypothalamus also increases feeding (Stanley & Gillard, 1994).

Let's review. Body fat produces leptin; leptin inhibits NPY release; NPY release inhibits PVN activity; and PVN activity inhibits feeding. Most people have trouble remembering and understanding double negatives, much less triple. Study Figure 10.24, but for most purposes it is enough to remember that leptin inhibits NPY and NPY increases feeding. Therefore mice that fail to produce leptin (the second column in Figure 10.24) overeat. Why do overweight humans overeat? Perhaps their leptin fails to inhibit NPY production; perhaps they have excess NPY or excess NPY receptors; perhaps something else is wrong. After researchers identify the problem, they will be better able to seek solutions.

Other Neuromodulators and Hormones

NPY has particularly powerful effects, but many other chemicals also influence feeding. Much of the research on these chemicals comes from studies using microdialysis, as described in Methods 10.2. Here is a list (probably not complete) of neuromodulators and hormones that act on the hypothalamus to increase or decrease eating (Friedman & Halaas, 1998; Plata-Salamán, 1998):

Increase Eating	Decrease Eating
Neuropeptide Y (NPY)	Cocaine- and amphetamine-related transcript (CART)
Peptide YY (PYY)	
Melanin-concentrating hormone (MCH)	Cholecystokinin (CCK)
	Corticotropin-releasing hormone (CRH)
Orexin A and orexin B (ORX)	
	α-Melanocyte-stimulating hormone (α-MSH)
Galanin	
Norepinephrine (NE)	Insulin
Agouti-related peptide (AgRP)	Glucagon-like peptide-1 (GLP-1)
	Bombesin
	Urocortin
	Serotonin (5-HT)
	Cytokines

Several general points about these lists are far more important than memorizing the names of chemicals. First, we can almost ignore species differences. The peptide *bombesin* occurs in amphibians but not mammals, the structure of insulin varies slightly from one species to another, and so on, but for the most part the same chemicals serve the same functions in all animals. For example, CCK increases satiety in both humans and snails (Morley, 1995).

Second, several chemicals serve related functions in the periphery and the brain. For example, the peripheral hormone glucagon mobilizes stored food for current use and therefore decreases the need to eat; the very similar peptide GLP-1 acts as a neuromodulator in the brain to decrease eating. CCK from the intestines closes the muscle between the stomach and intestines, thereby increasing stomach distension; CCK in the brain also inhibits feeding. The mechanisms are different but the outcome is the same. Evidently evolution has been conservative, using the same chemical repeatedly for related functions (Hoebel, 1988).

Third, note how many chemicals exert some control over feeding. Presumably they affect feeding in different ways, although researchers do not yet know many of the details. Here's one little item to ponder: Mice with a mutation of the serotonin 5-HT$_{2C}$ receptor maintain normal weight until middle age and then become obese (Nonogaki, Strack, Dallman, & Tecott, 1998). Will future research on that receptor help us understand

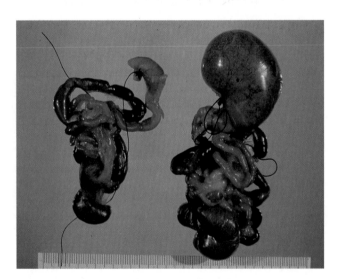

Figure 10.23 The effects of inhibiting the paraventricular nucleus of the hypothalamus
On the left is the digestive system of a normal rat. On the right is the digestive system of a rat that has had its paraventricular hypothalamus inhibited by injections of peptide YY, a neurotransmitter closely related to neuropeptide Y. The rat continued eating even though its stomach and intestines distended almost to the point of bursting. (All right, I admit this is a little bit disgusting.) *(Source: Morley, Levine, Grace, & Kneip, 1985)*

Microdialysis

In microdialysis an investigator implants into the brain a double fluid-filled tube with a thin membrane tip across which chemicals can diffuse. The experimenter slowly delivers some fluid through one tube, which exits through the other tube and brings with it some of the brain chemicals that have diffused across the membrane. In this manner researchers discover which neurotransmitters are released during eating and which are released at the point of satiation (e.g., Stanley, Schwartz, Hernandez, Leibowitz, & Hoebel, 1989).

why many people become obese in middle age? Will research on other neuromodulators and their receptors help us understand still other eating disorders?

One advantage of finding so many chemicals that affect eating is that researchers have many options about the kinds of drugs to develop. Most of the diet drugs developed so far act by stimulating serotonin receptor types 5-HT_{1B} and 5-HT_{2C} (Blundell & Halford, 1998). Future research has a wealth of possibilities to try—drugs that inhibit NPY, drugs that facilitate CCK, and on and on. However, all the different neurotransmitters ordinarily work together. For example, insulin and leptin combine forces to decrease NPY, PYY, and MCH production and to increase production of CART, α-MSH, and CRH (Elmquist, Elias, & Saper, 1999; Gardner, Rothwell, & Luheshi, 1998; Kristensen et al., 1998; Woods, Seeley, Porte, & Schwartz, 1998). When someone is overweight, does just one of these pathways go awry? Can we solve the problem by fixing just one kind of receptor? If not, the best weight-loss drug may be a combination of several chemicals.

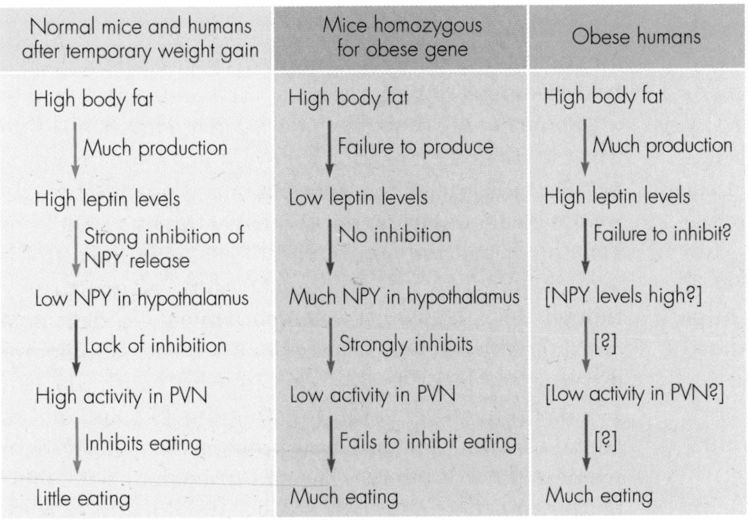

10. Why are leptin injections probably less helpful for overweight people than for obese mice?

11. What would be the effect on eating from a drug that blocks NPY receptors? One that blocks CCK receptors?

Check your answers on page 308.

Genetics, Metabolic Rate, and Body Weight

You have probably noticed that most thin parents have thin children and most heavy parents have heavy children. The resemblance no doubt relates in part to the family's food choices, but genetics also plays a major role. A Danish study found that the weights of 540 adopted children correlated much more strongly with that of their biological relatives than with that of their adoptive relatives (Stunkard et al., 1986). Overall, researchers estimate that human obesity has a heritability (see p. 11) of about .4 to .7 (Comuzzie & Allison, 1998).

However, the results indicate a large number of genes capable of affecting body weight, not just one major gene. (The multitude of genes should be no surprise, given the number of neuromodulators and hormones that contribute to satiety.) Genes can control body weight in many ways, including metabolic rate (Bogardus et al., 1986). People with higher metabolic rates produce more heat than others do and radiate it to their environment, thereby maintaining a low weight. People with lower metabolic rates generate less heat and conserve it better, therefore gaining weight even

Normal mice and humans after temporary weight gain	Mice homozygous for obese gene	Obese humans
High body fat	High body fat	High body fat
↓ Much production	↓ Failure to produce	↓ Much production
High leptin levels	Low leptin levels	High leptin levels
↓ Strong inhibition of NPY release	↓ No inhibition	↓ Failure to inhibit?
Low NPY in hypothalamus	Much NPY in hypothalamus	[NPY levels high?]
↓ Lack of inhibition	↓ Strongly inhibits	↓ [?]
High activity in PVN	Low activity in PVN	[Low activity in PVN?]
↓ Inhibits eating	↓ Fails to inhibit eating	↓ [?]
Little eating	Much eating	Much eating

Figure 10.24   Relation among weight, leptin, NPY, and eating
Ordinarily, high levels of body fat produce leptin, which inhibits eating. Obese mice fail to produce leptin. Obese humans produce leptin but fail to respond to it.

without overeating. As mentioned previously some families lack leptin, and others have ineffective leptin receptors. Perhaps researchers will find other families with abnormalities in other hormones and neuromodulators that affect eating.

However, genetic differences do not control how fat one gets; they only influence predispositions—that is, who is more likely to get fat, given a particular environment. Far more people are obese today than in the year 1900, and the reason has to be the changes in diet and lifestyle. (Evolution acts much more slowly.) Consider in particular the Native American Pima of Arizona and Mexico. Most are seriously overweight, and the difference between those who do and do not become overweight is genetic, probably because of several genes (Norman et al., 1998). However, a few decades ago very few were overweight. At that time they ate a diet of Sonoran Desert plants, which yield food only in brief seasons. The Pimas probably evolved an eating strategy like bears: Eat all you can when food is available because it will have to carry you through a period without food. Now, with a more typical U.S. diet that is equally available at all times, that strategy is maladaptive. In short, the Pimas' overweight depends on both the genes and the environment; either one by itself would not have this effect.

The same is true of anyone with a genetic predisposition to obesity. The genes may increase the likelihood of weight gain, but they don't force it. The actual results depend on the person's eating and exercise habits.

Weight-Loss Techniques

Losing weight permanently is like quitting smoking, quitting alcohol, or breaking any other strong habit: It is difficult, more people try than succeed, but it can be done.

A survey found that weight-loss specialists disagreed about many of their recommendations, but almost all agreed that anyone trying to lose weight should include increased exercise as part of the treatment package (M. B. Schwartz & Brownell, 1995). Exercise by itself won't remove much weight simply because human muscles are fairly efficient and do not use great amounts of energy. For example, walking 4.5 km (a little less than 3 miles) expends only about 150 kcal—the equivalent of a handful of potato chips (Burton, 1994). However, a regular pattern of exercise in combination with a good diet can be successful, and even for those who do not lose as much weight as they hoped, increased exercise lowers blood pressure, lowers cholesterol levels, and improves health, which was the ultimate goal, anyway (Campfield, Smith, & Burn, 1998).

Weight loss requires restraint of eating, a difficult habit to acquire in an era of all-you-can-eat buffets. Some people are helped by organized weight-loss programs in which they share encouragement and swap low-calorie recipes with others trying to lose weight.

Some are also helped by appetite-suppressant drugs. For years the most effective combination was "fen-phen": *fenfluramine,* which increases the release of serotonin and blocks its reuptake, and *phentermine,* which blocks reuptake of norepinephrine. Unfortunately fenfluramine too often produces medical complications, so it has been withdrawn from use. A replacement drug is *sibutramine* (Meridia), which blocks reuptake of both serotonin and norepinephrine. Investigators are also experimenting with drugs that inhibit absorption of dietary fat into the intestines, such as the drug orlistat (Xenical), which is now available (Campfield et al., 1998). Further research into the controls of satiety may make new drugs possible.

Anorexia and Bulimia

Overeating is hardly the only eating disorder. Inadequate eating can be just as dangerous or more so. People with anorexia nervosa are unwilling to eat as much as they need; they therefore become extremely thin and in some cases die. About 90% to 95% of people with anorexia are women. The condition usually begins in adolescence, much less often in the twenties, but once begun may continue for years.

People with anorexia are often interested in food; many enjoy cooking and the taste and smell of food. Their problem is not a lack of appetite but a fear of becoming fat or of losing self-control. Most people with anorexia are hardworking perfectionists who are amazingly active, unlike most other people on the verge of starvation. The perfectionism and driven activity resemble obsessive-compulsive behavior, and obsessive-compulsive disorder is common among the relatives of people with anorexia (Lilenfeld et al., 1998). Some people with anorexia also show signs of depression, and many have elevated levels of the hormone *cortisol,* as most depressed people do (Licinio, Wong, & Gold, 1996). However, antidepressant drugs are seldom effective treatments for anorexia.

Some people probably have a genetic predisposition that increases their chance of developing either anorexia or other disorders, but anorexia also depends heavily on the social environment (Walsh & Devlin, 1998). For example, most women of the Fiji Islands have traditionally been overweight by Western standards, although they themselves seemed content. In fact most considered a somewhat heavy body to be desirable, indicating an ability to do much physical work (Becker, 1995). Then, after the introduction of television on the islands, featuring mostly U.S. programs that glorify thin women, the Fiji women became discontent with their bodies and began trying to lose weight. Some even started forcing themselves to vomit (Becker & Burwell, 1999). None qualify for a diagnosis of anorexia nervosa—yet—but the influence of culture on extreme dieting seems clear.

Bulimia nervosa is a condition in which people (again, mostly women) alternate between dieting and overeating. Some (but not all) sometimes eat an enormous meal and then force themselves to vomit. People with bulimia tend to have higher than normal levels of peptide YY (PYY), a neuromodulator with effects similar to NPY (Kaye, Berrettini, Gwirtsman, & George, 1990). They have lower than normal levels of CCK (Brambilla et al., 1995) and signs of either decreased serotonin production or decreased receptor sensitivity for serotonin (Brewerton, 1995; Weltzin, Fernstrom, & Kaye, 1994). Both CCK and serotonin promote satiety, so decreased levels would provoke overeating.

Finding alterations in PYY, CCK, and serotonin does not tell us whether these chemical imbalances led to bulimia or whether bulimia led to changes in the neuromodulators. However, in one study investigators gave a tryptophan-deficient diet to ten women who had recovered from a history of bulimia. Tryptophan is the amino acid that the brain converts to serotonin, so a tryptophan-deficient diet lowers brain serotonin. The diet provoked mild depression and a sense that they could quickly lose control over their eating (K. A. Smith, Fairburn, & Cowen, 1999). The researchers suggested that dieting could sometimes decrease blood tryptophan and therefore decrease brain serotonin, triggering mood changes in certain vulnerable people.

Module 10.3

In Closing: The Multiple Controls of Hunger

Eating is controlled by a number of brain areas, which monitor blood glucose, stomach distention, duodenal contents, body weight, and many other variables. Because the system is so complex, it can produce errors in many ways. However, the complexity of the system also provides a kind of security, a bit like the checks and balances in some governments: If one part of the system makes a mistake, another part can counteract it. We notice people who choose a poor diet or eat the wrong amount. Perhaps we should be even more impressed by how many people eat more or less appropriately. The regulation of eating succeeds not in spite of its complexity, but because of it.

Summary

1. The ability to digest a food is one major determinant of preference for that food. For example, people who cannot digest lactose generally do not like to eat dairy products. (p. 295)

2. Other major determinants of food selection include innate preferences for certain tastes, a preference

for familiar foods, and the ability to learn about the consequences of foods. (p. 295)

3. People and animals eat partly for the sake of taste. However, a sham-feeding animal, which tastes its foods but does not absorb them, eats far more than normal. (p. 296)

4. Factors controlling hunger include distension of the stomach and intestines, secretion of CCK by the duodenum, and the availability of glucose and other nutrients to the cells. (p. 297)

5. The hormone insulin increases the entry of glucose to the cells, including cells that store nutrients for future use. Glucagon mobilizes stored fuel and converts it to glucose in the blood. Thus the combined influence of insulin and glucagon determines how much glucose is available at any time. (p. 297)

6. Damage to cells in the lateral hypothalamus leads to decreased eating and loss of weight by affecting taste, salivation, swallowing, food-seeking behaviors, and insulin. (p. 299)

7. Damage to the ventromedial hypothalamus and surrounding areas increases meal frequency; damage to the paraventricular nucleus of the hypothalamus increases meal size. Damage to either of these areas can lead to weight gain. (p. 300)

8. Ordinarily fat cells produce a protein called leptin, which inhibits hypothalamic secretion of neuropeptide Y (NPY) and thereby limits meal size. If an individual fails to produce leptin or if the leptin fails to inhibit NPY secretion, the result is overeating and obesity. (p. 302)

9. A number of other neurotransmitters also affect eating, although the details are not yet well understood. (p. 304)

10. For people as well as mice, genetic differences influence eating and weight gain. However, eating and weight also depend on the types and quantities of food available and the amount of exercise. Losing weight is difficult but possible. (p. 305)

11. Anorexia nervosa and bulimia nervosa are eating disorders that may be influenced by biological predispositions, although they also certainly depend on cultural pressures. (p. 306)

Answers to *Stop and Check* Questions

1. Most Southeast Asian adults lack the digestive enzyme lactase, which is needed to metabolize the sugar in milk. (p. 296)

2. When animals sham-feed (and all the food leaks out of the digestive system), they chew and taste their food but do not become satiated. (p. 297)

3. If a cuff is attached to the junction between the stomach and duodenum so that food cannot leave the stomach, an animal becomes satiated when the stomach is full. (p. 297)

4. If food can leave the stomach, an animal eats the same amount as if it can't leave the stomach. At the time it stops eating, the stomach is less full if it has been free to leave the stomach and enter the duodenum. (p. 297)

5. When the duodenum is distended, it releases CCK, which closes the sphincter muscle between the stomach and duodenum and therefore increases the rate at which the stomach becomes full. Also, neural signals from the intestines cause certain cells in the hippocampus to release CCK as a neuromodulator, and at its receptors it triggers decreased feeding. (pp. 297)

6. Those with very low levels, as in diabetes, cannot get glucose to enter their cells, and therefore they are constantly hungry. They pass much of their nutrition in the urine and feces. Those with constantly high levels deposit much of their glucose into fat and glycogen, so within a short time after a meal the supply of glucose drops. (p. 299)

7. When glucagon levels rise, stored glycogen is converted to glucose, which enters the blood. If insulin levels are high also, the glucose entering the blood is free to enter all the cells. So the result would be decreased appetite. (p. 299)

8. After damage to cell bodies in the lateral hypothalamus, cells in the NTS (in the medulla) and the forebrain become less responsive to the taste and other stimuli associated with food. Also, food becomes less reinforcing, and insulin levels drop. After damage to the axons passing through the lateral hypothalamus, the animal becomes less aroused and less active. (p. 302)

9. Animals with damage to the ventromedial hypothalamus eat more frequent meals. Animals with damage to the paraventricular nucleus of the hypothalamus eat larger meals. (p. 302)

10. Unlike obese mice, overweight people produce their own leptin in proportion to body fat; however, they are apparently insensitive to it. Also, very large amounts of leptin can induce diabetes. (p. 305)

11. A drug that blocks NPY receptors would decrease feeding. A drug that blocks CCK receptors would increase feeding. (p. 305)

Thought Question

For most people, insulin levels tend to be higher during the day than at night. Use this fact to explain why people grow hungry a few hours after a daytime meal but not so quickly at night.

Chapter Ending
Key Terms and Activities

Terms

aldosterone (p. 292)

angiotensin II (p. 291)

anorexia nervosa (p. 306)

baroreceptor (p. 291)

basal metabolism (p. 282)

bulimia nervosa (p. 307)

carnivore (p. 295)

cholecystokinin (CCK) (p. 297)

conditioned taste aversions (p. 296)

duodenum (p. 297)

glucagon (p. 298)

herbivore (p. 295)

homeostasis (p. 282)

homeothermic (p. 282)

hypovolemic thirst (p. 291)

insulin (p. 297)

lactase (p. 295)

lactose (p. 295)

lateral hypothalamus (p. 299)

lateral preoptic area (p. 290)

leptin (p. 302)

neuropeptide Y (NPY) (p. 303)

omnivore (p. 295)

osmotic pressure (p. 290)

osmotic thirst (p. 290)

OVLT (p. 290)

paraventricular nucleus (PVN) (p. 290, 302)

poikilothermic (p. 282)

preoptic area (p. 285)

prostaglandin E₁ and prostaglandin E₂ (p. 286)

set point (p. 282)

sham-feeding (p. 296)

splanchnic nerve (p. 297)

subfornical organ (SFO) (p. 291)

supraoptic nucleus (p. 290)

synergistic effect (p. 291)

tonic immobility (p. 287)

vagus nerve (p. 297)

vasopressin (also known as antidiuretic hormone, ADH) (p. 289)

ventromedial hypothalamus (VMH) (p. 301)

Suggestions for Further Reading

Capaldi, E. D. (Ed.). (1996). *Why we eat what we eat.* Washington, DC: American Psychological Association. Discusses the complex motivations that interact in eating and food selection.

Logue, A. W. (1991). *The psychology of eating and drinking* (2nd ed.). New York: W. H. Freeman. Discussion includes both normal eating and disorders such as anorexia nervosa and bulimia.

Smith, G. P. (Ed.). (1998). *Satiation: From gut to brain.* New York: Oxford University Press. Reviews research on mechanisms of satiety, mostly in the digestive system.

Widmaier, E. P. (1998). *Why geese don't get obese (and we do).* New York: W. H. Freeman. Lighthearted and often entertaining discussion of the physiology of eating, thirst, and temperature regulation.

Web Sites to Explore

You can go to the Biological Psychology Study Center and click on these links. While there, you can also check for suggested articles available on InfoTrac. The Biological Psychology Internet address is:
http://psychology.wadsworth.com/book/kalatbiopsych7e/

http://www.fed.cuhk.edu.hk/~johnson/misconceptions/concept_map/body_temperature.html
Simple graphics summarizing temperature regulation.

http://www.pencomputing.com/dim/links/scientific.html
Has links to many sites with scientific information about obesity.

http://www.mentalhealth.com/dis/p20-et01.html
Features information about anorexia nervosa.

Active Learner Link

Quiz for Chapter 10

Chapter 11

Reproductive Behaviors

Main Ideas

1. Sex hormones exert organizing and activating effects. Organizing effects during a sensitive period of early development permanently influence genital anatomy and the brain. Activating effects are transient and may occur at any time.

2. In mammals the presence or absence of testosterone determines whether the genitals and hypothalamus will develop in the male or the female manner, although for certain characteristics testosterone must first be converted to estradiol within the cell.

3. Sex hormones, including testosterone and estradiol, activate specific sexual, parental, and other behaviors.

4. Certain patterns of genes, hormones, and brain anatomy are related to differences in sexual identity and orientation, but how they interact with experience is not yet clear.

A powerful change comes over people around the time of adolescence. Their bodies change: breast growth and menstruation in females, beard growth and deepening of the voice in males, a growth spurt and onset of pubic hair in both. Their behavior changes, too. Instead of the occasional shy flirtations of preadolescence, suddenly people are preoccupied with sex. Just the sight of a special someone walking by can get the heart thumping.

Those changes are not unique to humans. It is a widespread rule that the time of sexual maturation of the body is also the time of increased interest in sexual behavior, and clearly hormones are a major controlling force. Many questions remain, however. For example, why do some people become sex offenders, and what can we do about it? Why are some people attracted to male partners and others to female partners? What makes people identify themselves as male or female? For such questions as these, hormones are certainly not the whole story. We shall consider the current state of knowledge, but the challenge to future researchers is to discover how the effects of hormones combine with those of experiences.

Opposite:
Humans may be the only species that plans parenthood, but all species, humans included, have a strong biological drive that can lead to parenthood.

The Effects
of Sex Hormones

Males secrete mostly the "male hormones" *(andro-gens)* and females the "female hormones" *(estrogens)*. If we injected female hormones into adult males and male hormones into adult females, could we make males act like females and females act like males? Researchers of the 1950s and 1960s, working with a variety of mammals and birds, were surprised to find that the answer was usually *no*. But the same hormones injected early in life had different, more profound effects.

Organizing Effects of Sex Hormones

We distinguish between the organizing and activating effects of sex hormones. The **organizing effects** of sex hormones occur mostly at a sensitive stage of development—shortly before and after birth in rats and well before birth in humans—and determine whether the brain and body will develop as a female or as a male. **Activating effects** can occur at any time in life, when a hormone temporarily activates a particular response. Activating effects on an organ may last hours, weeks, or even months longer than the hormone remains in an organ, but they do not last indefinitely. The distinction between the two kinds of effects is not absolute; early in life hormones exert activating effects even while they are organizing body development, and during puberty hormones can induce long-lasting structural changes as well as activating effects (Arnold & Breedlove, 1985; C. L. Williams, 1986).

Sex Differences in the Gonads and Hypothalamus

Sexual differentiation begins with the chromosomes, although it hardly ends there. A female mammal has an XX chromosome pattern; a male has XY. During an early stage of prenatal development in mammals, the **gonads** (reproductive organs) of every mammalian fetus are identical, and both male and female have a set of Müllerian ducts and a set of Wolffian ducts. The male's Y chromosome includes the **SRY** (sex region Y) **gene,** which causes the primitive gonads to develop into masculine structures called **testes,** the sperm-producing organs. (The Y chromosome is small and has few other genes.) The developing testes produce the hormone

testosterone (an androgen), which increases the growth of the testes, causing them to produce more testosterone, and so forth. Testosterone also causes the primitive **Wolffian ducts,** which are precursors to the male reproductive structures, to develop into *seminal vesicles* (saclike structures that store semen) and the *vas deferens* (a duct from the testis into the penis). A peptide hormone, *Müllerian inhibiting hormone (MIH),* causes degeneration of the **Müllerian ducts,** precursors to the female reproductive structures (oviducts, uterus, and upper vagina) (Graves, 1994). The result of all these testosterone-induced changes is the development of a penis and scrotum. A genetically female fetus (XX) would also develop male structures if she were exposed to large enough amounts of testosterone, but ordinarily she is not. Her gonads develop into **ovaries,** the egg-producing organs. Her Wolffian ducts degenerate, and her primitive Müllerian ducts develop and mature. Figure 11.1 shows the hormone-dependent development of male or female external genitals from the original unisex structures.

In addition to the obvious differences in the gonads and genitals, the sexes differ in the structure and function of several parts of the nervous system, especially the hypothalamus. One part of the medial preoptic hypothalamus, known as the **sexually dimorphic nucleus,** is larger in the male than in the female and is linked to male sexual behavior (Gorski, Gordon, Shryne, & Southam, 1978). Parts of the female hypothalamus, however, can generate a cyclic pattern of hormone release, as in the human menstrual cycle. The male hypothalamus cannot, and neither can the hypothalamus of a female who was exposed to extra testosterone early in life.

Sexual differentiation depends on the level of testosterone during a **sensitive period,** an early period when a hormone has a long-lasting effect. The human sensitive period for genital formation is about the third and fourth months of pregnancy (Money & Ehrhardt, 1972). In rats, which are less developed than humans are at birth, testosterone within the first few days controls development of the external genitals (G. W. Harris, 1964) and hypothalamus (Gorski et al., 1978), although it can continue producing effects on the hypothalamus even weeks later (Bloch & Mills, 1995; Bloch, Mills, & Gale, 1995). A female rat that is injected with testos-

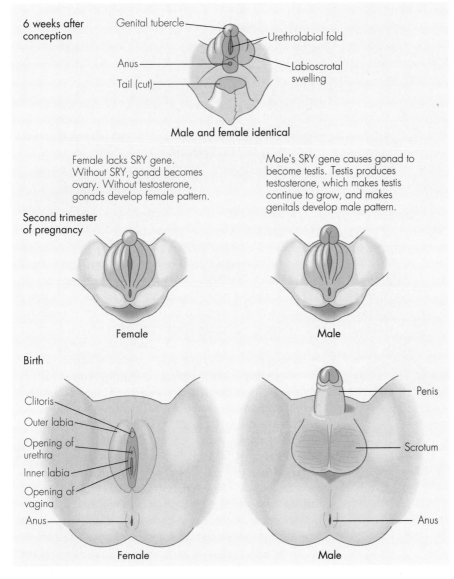

6 weeks after conception

Genital tubercle

Urethrolabial fold

Anus

Labioscrotal swelling

Tail (cut)

Male and female identical

Female lacks SRY gene. Without SRY, gonad becomes ovary. Without testosterone, gonads develop female pattern.

Male's SRY gene causes gonad to become testis. Testis produces testosterone, which makes testis continue to grow, and makes genitals develop male pattern.

Second trimester of pregnancy

Female

Male

Birth

Clitoris

Outer labia

Opening of urethra

Inner labia

Opening of vagina

Anus

Female

Penis

Scrotum

Anus

Male

Figure 11.1 Differentiation of human genitals
The male's SRY gene causes the gonad to become a testis, and the testis produces testosterone, which masculinizes development. In the absence of testosterone, development follows the female pattern. *(Source: Based on Netter, 1983)*

The overall mechanism is this: Nature's "default setting" is to make every mammal a female. Add early testosterone and the individual becomes a male; without testosterone it develops as a female. Adding early estradiol or other estrogens does not have the reverse effect. A male that is injected with estrogen still develops male genitals. The only way that a genetic male can develop a female appearance is if he is castrated or otherwise deprived of testosterone. (*Castration* is the removal of the testes.) Several species show variations on this pattern, as highlighted in Digression 11.1.

According to studies on rodents, testosterone exerts a major part of its effect on the hypothalamus through a surprising route: After it enters a neuron, it is converted to estradiol! Testosterone and estradiol are chemically very similar, as you can see in Figure 3.24 (p. 80). In organic chemistry a ring of six carbon atoms containing three double bonds is an *aromatic* compound. An enzyme found in the brain can *aromatize* testosterone into estradiol. Other androgens that cannot be aromatized into estrogens are less effective in masculinizing the hypothalamus. Moreover, drugs that prevent testosterone from being aromatized to estradiol block the organizing effects of testosterone on sexual development of the brain. Apparently androgens must be aromatized to estrogens to exert their organizing effects on the hypothalamus. Aromatase is particularly abundant in the early sensitive period in brain areas that become larger in males than in females; that is, aromatase occurs in the areas that are to be masculinized (Lauber, Sarasin, & Lichtensteiger, 1997).

Why, then, is the female not masculinized by her own estradiol? During the early sensitive period, immature mammals of many species have in their bloodstream a protein called **alpha-fetoprotein,** which is not present in adults (Gorski, 1980; MacLusky & Naftolin, 1981). Alpha-fetoprotein binds with estrogen and blocks it from leaving the bloodstream and entering the cells that are developing in this early period. Primates have other mechanisms for inactivating estrogen, such as breaking down estrogens into inactive substances. In any event

terone during the last few days before being born or the first few days afterward is partly masculinized, just as if the testosterone had been produced by her own body (Ward & Ward, 1985). Her clitoris grows larger than normal; her other reproductive structures look intermediate between female and male. At maturity her pituitary and ovaries produce steady levels of hormones instead of the cycles that are characteristic of females. Anatomically, certain parts of her hypothalamus appear more male than female. Her behavior is also masculinized: She mounts other females and makes copulatory thrusting movements rather than arching her back and allowing males to mount her. In short, early testosterone promotes the male pattern and inhibits the female pattern (Gorski, 1985; J. D. Wilson, George, & Griffin, 1981).

Sexual Differentiation in the Spotted Hyena

The spotted hyena provides exceptions to many of the general-izations we usually make about males and females (Glickman et al., 1992) (see Figure 11.2). On the average, female spotted hyenas are larger and more aggressive than males. The female's clitoris is as large as the male's penis and capable of erections like those of a penis. The female urinates through a canal in her clitoris. During puberty that canal enlarges enough for the male to insert his penis into it in sexual intercourse. Her babies are

Figure 11.2 A female spotted hyena pup
Note that her clitoris looks like a penis and that her labia are fused and swollen like a scrotum. Female spotted hyenas are exposed to large amounts of testosterone during prena-tal development. Their anatomy and their aggressive behav-ior become highly masculinized.

delivered through the canal in the clitoris. The first time a fe-male delivers, the babies rip through the wall of the clitoris, in most cases dying in the process and causing apparently severe pain to the mother. Later-born babies have a higher chance of survival, but even then, birth is a slow process with a higher chance of infant mortality than in most mammals (L. G. Frank, Weldele, & Glickman, 1995).

Why have female hyenas evolved so many of the traits we consider typically masculine at what appears to be a significant cost to both the mother and her babies? The explanation proba-bly relates to the ways in which hyenas fight one another for food. The dominant females and their young get first access to any food the pack finds, followed by the next most dominant females and their young, and so on. Groups of adult females form coalitions to improve or maintain their position. Adult males always leave their home pack and join another pack, where they remain permanently subordinate to all the female coali-tions. Beginning in infancy females spend their whole lives fighting for dominance. In male–female twin pairs, the female usually dominates her brother within the first 2 to 3 weeks (Smale, Holekamp, Weldele, Frank, & Glickman, 1995).

The physiological and ontogenetic explanation for the fe-males' behavior relates to hormones. During pregnancy the hyena mother's ovaries produce large amounts of androstenedione, the precursor chemical for both testosterone and estrogen. The placenta contains relatively large amounts of the enzyme that converts androstenedione to testosterone and small amounts of the enzyme that converts it to estrogen (Yalcinkaya et al., 1993). Therefore, at least at certain stages of development, the female fetus is exposed to much higher testosterone levels than are females of most other species.

testosterone is neither bound to alpha-fetoprotein nor metabolized; it is free to enter the cells, where enzymes convert it into estradiol. That is, testosterone is a way of getting estradiol into the cells when estradiol itself can-not leave the blood.

This explanation of testosterone's effects makes sense of an otherwise puzzling fact: Although normal amounts of estradiol have little effect on early develop-ment, an injection of a larger amount actually mas-culinizes a female's development. The reason is that normal amounts are bound to alpha-fetoprotein or me-tabolized, whereas a larger amount may exceed the body's capacity for inactivation; the excess can thus en-ter the cells and masculinize them.

Testosterone also exerts organizing effects on the nerves and muscles that control the penis. In most mammalian species a male has muscles in or near the penis that are either absent or very small in the area near the female's clitoris. These muscles receive their neural input from motor nuclei in the spinal cord that are present in males and either smaller or absent in fe-males. Early in development both male and female de-velop large numbers of neurons in these nuclei. The male's testosterone supports survival of these neurons; in the female the testosterone levels are lower and most of the neurons die (C. L. Jordan, Breedlove, & Arnold, 1982). A male also loses most of these neurons if he is treated with testosterone-blocking drugs during an early sensitive period (Grisham, Castro, Kashon, Ward, & Ward, 1992).

1. What would be the appearance of a mammal's external genitals if it were exposed to high levels of both androgens and estrogens during early development? What if it were exposed to low levels of both?

2. How would the external genitals appear on a genetic female that lacked alpha-fetoprotein?

3. If a genetic female were exposed to far higher than normal levels of estrogen during her early sensitive period, what would be the effect on her genital development? Why?

Check your answers on page 323.

Sex Differences in Nonreproductive Characteristics

Males and females obviously differ in their reproductive organs and sexual behaviors. But they also differ in many characteristics that are only indirectly related to reproduction. For example, males of most species tend to be larger and more prone to fighting than females are (Ellis, 1986). Females tend to live longer and to devote more attention to infant care. (Humans are among the few mammals in which the male helps care for the young.)

Many of these sex differences depend on prenatal hormones. For example, female monkeys exposed to testosterone during their sensitive period engage in more rough-and-tumble play than other females, are more aggressive, and make more threatening facial gestures (Quadagno, Briscoe, & Quadagno, 1977; W. C. Young, Goy, & Phoenix, 1964). Similar effects on play and aggressive behavior have been noted in dogs (Beach, Buehler, & Dunbar, 1982; Reinisch, 1981) and ferrets (Stockman, Callaghan, Gallagher, & Baum, 1986).

In humans, too, males and females differ in their patterns of play and aggression, even at an early age, although the role of early hormones is hard to determine. Girls who were exposed to elevated androgen levels during prenatal development (because of a gene that causes excess production of androgens from the adrenal gland) show more interest than their nonandrogenized sisters do in male-typical toys and activities such as football and other sports, electronics, auto mechanics, and hunting. They show little interest in sewing, dolls, fashion, jewelry, or other activities that interested their sisters (Berenbaum, 1999). None of these choices is "wrong"—plenty of women are more interested in sports than in fashion—but the large group difference suggests that the prenatal hormones exert lasting influences on psychological development.

Males and females also differ in several brain areas that have no direct relationship to sexual behavior. For example, women have a greater density of neurons in part of the temporal lobe that is important for language

(Witelson, Glezer, & Kigar, 1995). They also tend to have a larger corpus callosum in proportion to total brain size, presumably facilitating greater communication between the hemispheres (S. C. Johnson, Pinkston, Bigler, & Blatter, 1996).

Activating Effects of Sex Hormones

At any time in life, not just during an early sensitive period, current levels of testosterone or estradiol exert activating effects, temporarily modifying sexual or other activities. Behaviors can also influence hormonal secretions; Digression 11.2 describes one example.

Sexual Behavior in Rodents

After removal of the testes from a male rodent or the ovaries from a female, sexual behavior declines as the sex hormone levels in the blood decline. It may not disappear altogether, partly because the adrenal glands also produce steroid hormones. Injections of testosterone into a castrated male restore sexual behavior, as do injections of testosterone's two major metabolites, dihydrotestosterone and estradiol (M. J. Baum & Vreeburg, 1973). Estrogen followed by progesterone is the most effective combination for stimulating sexual behavior in a female (Glaser, Etgen, & Barfield, 1987).

Sex hormones activate sexual behavior partly by enhancing sensations. Estrogens enlarge the area of skin that excites the *pudendal nerve,* which transmits tactile stimulation from the pubic area to the brain (Komisaruk, Adler, & Hutchison, 1972). Sex hormones also facilitate sexual behavior by binding to receptors in the brain and thereby increasing neuronal activity, especially in the hypothalamus.

The ventromedial nucleus and the medial preoptic area (MPOA) of the hypothalamus are among the principal areas affected by sex hormones. Part of the MPOA is known as the *sexually dimorphic nucleus* because it is distinctly larger in males than in females. Stimulation of the MPOA increases male-typical sex behavior in males and female-typical sex behavior in females (Bloch, Butler, & Kohlert, 1996). Activity increases here (and in several other brain locations) during copulation (Heeb & Yahr, 1996).

Sex hormones prime the MPOA and several other brain areas to release dopamine, a neurotransmitter associated with reinforcement (Chapter 3). In normal rats (and presumably other species) MPOA neurons release dopamine strongly during sexual activity but not at other times (Hull, Eaton, Moses, & Lorrain, 1993). Castrated male rats have as much dopamine as other rats in their MPOA, but the presence of a receptive female does not evoke much release of dopamine, and these males do not attempt to copulate with the females (Hull, Du, Lorrain, & Matuszewich, 1997). In the female, MPOA

Behavior Influences Hormonal Secretions

The mating behavior of the ring-necked dove offers a striking example of how hormones and behavior interact. A newly mated pair of doves goes through a well-synchronized series of behaviors, as outlined in the following table:

	Male	Female
Day 1	Aggressive behavior	Nonaggressive behavior
Days 2–6	Courtship (nest coos)	Courtship (nest coos)
	Copulation	Copulation
	Nest building (brings twigs)	Nest building (arranges twigs)
Day 7		Lays two eggs
Next 2 weeks	Sits on eggs during middle of the day	Sits on eggs from late afternoon to next morning
Next 3 weeks	Tends and feeds chicks	Tends and feeds chicks

The behaviors of the male and female are tightly synchronized. If the female assumes the receptive posture too early, the male may copulate but then quickly deserts her (C. J. Erickson & Zenone, 1976). But properly timed copulation establishes a pair bond that keeps the couple together through the mating season and sometimes even into later years.

Both birds normally ignore nesting materials on day 1, begin to build a nest on day 2 or 3, and if the nest is not complete by day 6 or 7, work frantically on nest building at that time. Neither pays much attention to a nest with eggs before day 7, but they take turns sitting after that time. Both produce crop milk that they feed to chicks that hatch 14 days after the eggs are laid, but they do not provide milk if chicks hatch much earlier.

Although injections of certain hormones would induce any of the observed behaviors, it is also the case that each change in the birds' behavior induces a change in their hormone secretions. The sequence of behaviors depends on a system in which each behavior causes the production of hormones that prepare a bird for the next stage of behavior. On day 1 the male struts around and makes a cooing display. This behavior seems to excite the female; her ovaries increase production of estrogen (C. Erickson & Lehrman, 1964). By day 2 she is ready for courtship and soon after that for copulation. If a researcher simply injects an isolated female with estrogen, she is ready for courtship and copulation almost as soon as a male appears. Thus the function of the male's behavior on the first day is to stimulate the female's hormonal secretions. Meanwhile the male seems to be excited by observing the female on day 1; his androgen production increases. By day 2 he is ready for nest building.

A week of courtship and nest building causes the female to produce first estrogen and then a combination of estrogen and progesterone. If we give estrogen injections to an isolated female for a week, with additional progesterone on the last 2 days, she becomes ready to incubate eggs even if she has neither seen nor heard a male. Evidently courting and nesting experiences produce hormonal changes that prepare her for the next behavioral stage.

Similarly, 14 days of sitting on eggs (or of watching another bird sit on eggs) causes both males and females to produce the hormone prolactin, which stimulates the production of crop milk and disposes the birds to take care of the babies. If a dove is isolated from other birds and from nests and eggs, a researcher can still get it to care for babies by injecting it repeatedly with prolactin.

In short, one behavior causes a hormonal change, which disposes the bird toward a second behavior, which causes a further hormonal change, and so on to the end of the sequence (Lehrman, 1964; Martinez-Vargas & Erickson, 1973).

---

activity is primed by a combination of the hormones estradiol and oxytocin (Caldwell & Moe, 1999).

When the concentration of released dopamine is only moderately high, dopamine stimulates mostly type D_1 and the closely related D_5 receptors, which facilitate erection of the penis in the male (Hull et al., 1992) and sexually receptive postures in the female (Apostolakis et al., 1996). When the concentration of dopamine reaches a higher level, dopamine stimulates mostly type D_2 receptors, which lead to orgasm (Giuliani & Ferrari, 1996; Hull et al., 1992). The effects at D_1 and D_2 receptors tend to inhibit each other. As a result the early stages of sexual excitement are characterized by arousal but not orgasm; orgasm is followed by a decrease in arousal.

Sexual Behavior in Humans

Although current hormone levels are less critical for maintaining sexual behavior in humans than in other species, an influence is certainly present. Consequently it is possible to increase people's sexual arousal through hormones or to decrease it with hormone inhibitors in those with offensive sexual behaviors.

Effects on Men Among males, sexual excitement is generally highest when testosterone levels are highest, about ages 15 to 25. The hormone oxytocin also may contribute to sexual pleasure. The body releases enormous amounts of oxytocin during orgasm, more than tripling the usual concentration in the blood. Several studies support a relationship between oxytocin and sexual pleasure (M. R. Murphy, Checkley, Seckl, & Lightman, 1990).

Decreases in testosterone levels generally decrease sexual activity. After castration, for example, most men—though not all—report a decrease in sexual interest and activity (Carter, 1992). However, low testosterone is not the only basis for impotence, the inability to have an erection. Some men with normal testosterone levels are impotent, and giving them extra testosterone does not help (Carani et al., 1990).

Testosterone reduction has sometimes been tried as a means of controlling sex offenders—exhibitionists, rapists, child molesters, committers of incest, and so forth. Sex offenders are a diverse group. Most have about average testosterone levels (Lang, Flor-Henry, & Frenzel, 1990), and some actually have below average levels, although one study, limited mostly to child molesters, found levels above average (Rösler & Witztum, 1998). (The men in that study reported masturbating an average of 32 times per week—that is, about four or five times a day.) Even for sex offenders who do have high testosterone levels, the hormones do not explain their behaviors. (Many other men with high levels do not engage in offensive behaviors.) Nevertheless reducing the testosterone levels of sex offenders does reduce their sexual activities, just as it would for any other man.

Some sex offenders have been treated with *cyproterone*, a drug that blocks the binding of testosterone to receptors within cells. Others have been treated with *medroxyprogesterone*, which inhibits gonadotropin, the pituitary hormone that stimulates testosterone production. Within 4 to 8 weeks of treatment with either of these drugs, most sex offenders experience a decrease in sexual fantasies and offensive sexual behaviors. However, these drugs do not completely block testosterone production, and they sometimes fail to reduce the problem behaviors. They also produce unpleasant side effects, including depression, breast growth, weight gain, and blood clots, and their effects wear off quickly if someone stops taking the daily pills.

Therefore researchers have sought a more satisfactory testosterone-blocking procedure. A promising possibility is *triptorelin*, a long-lasting drug that blocks gonadotropin and therefore decreases testosterone production. In one study monthly injections of triptorelin decreased sex offenders' testosterone levels from 545 ng/dl to a mere 23 ng/dl. The drug also decreased deviant sexual fantasies and abnormal sexual behavior to zero in all participants (Rösler & Witztum, 1998).

Effects on Women A woman's hypothalamus and pituitary interact with the ovaries to produce the **menstrual cycle,** a periodic variation in hormones and fertility over the course of approximately 1 month (see Figure 11.3). After the end of a menstrual period, the anterior pituitary releases **follicle-stimulating hormone (FSH),** which promotes the growth of a follicle in the ovary. The follicle nurtures the *ovum* (egg cell) and produces estrogen. Toward the middle of the menstrual cycle, the follicle builds up more and more receptors to FSH; so even though the actual concentration of FSH in the blood is decreasing, its effects on the follicle increase. As a result the follicle produces increasing amounts of **estradiol,** which is a type of estrogen. (Estrogens and androgens are categories that include several individual hormones. Neither estrogen nor androgen is a specific chemical itself.)

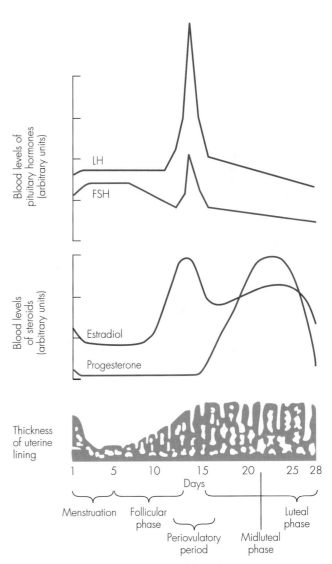

Figure 11.3 Blood levels of four hormones during the human menstrual cycle
Note that estrogen and progesterone are both at high levels during the midluteal phase, but drop sharply at menstruation, a short time later.

The increased release of estradiol causes an increased release of FSH as well as a sudden surge in the release of **luteinizing hormone (LH)** from the anterior pituitary (see the top graph in Figure 11.3). FSH and LH combine to cause the follicle to release an ovum.

The remnant of the follicle (now called the *corpus luteum*) releases the hormone progesterone, which prepares the uterus for the implantation of a fertilized ovum. Progesterone also inhibits the further release of LH. Toward the end of the menstrual cycle, the levels of LH, FSH, estradiol, and progesterone all decline. If the ovum is fertilized, the levels of estradiol and progesterone increase gradually throughout pregnancy. If the ovum is not fertilized, the lining of the uterus is cast off (menstruation), and the cycle begins again. Figure 11.4 summarizes the interactions between the pituitary and the ovary.

Birth-control pills prevent pregnancy by interfering with the usual feedback cycle between the ovaries and the pituitary. The most widely used birth-control pill, the *combination pill*, which contains both estrogen and progesterone, prevents the surge of FSH and LH that would otherwise release an ovum. The estrogen–progesterone combination also prevents an ovum, if released, from implanting in the uterus.

Changes in hormones over the menstrual cycle produce slight changes in women's sexual interest. The midway point, the **periovulatory period,** when ovulation occurs, is the time of maximum fertility and generally the highest estrogen levels. According to two studies women not taking birth-control pills initiate more sexual activity (either with a partner or by masturbation) during the periovulatory period than at other times during the month (Adams, Gold, & Burt, 1978; Udry & Morris, 1968) (see Figure 11.5). According to another study women rate an erotic video as more pleasant and arousing if they watch it during the periovulatory period than if they watch it at other times (Slob, Bax, Hop, Rowland, & van der Werff ten Bosch, 1996). These effects are small, though. Women are less dependent on their current hormone levels for sexual response than are females of other species.

Sex hormones also influence women's preferences in men's faces. Examine the faces in Figure 11.6. For each pair of faces, which do you regard as "more attractive"? Women:

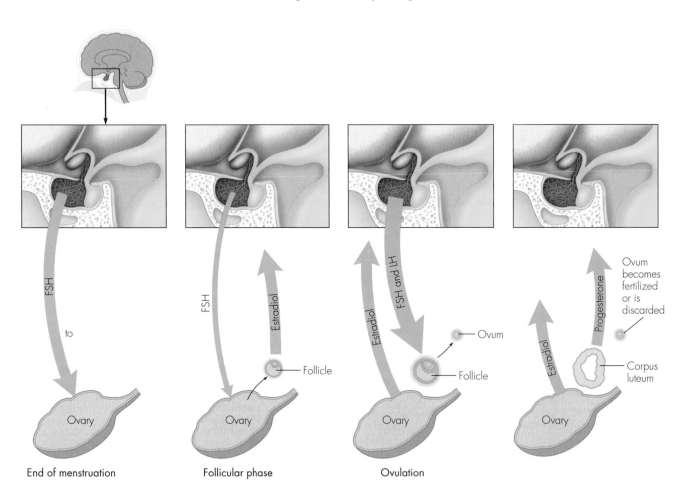

Figure 11.4 Interactions between the pituitary and the ovary
FSH from the pituitary stimulates the ovary to release and develop a follicle, which produces estradiol, triggering a release of a burst of FSH and LH from the pituitary. Those hormones cause the follicle to release its ovum and become a corpus luteum. The corpus luteum releases progesterone while the ovary releases estradiol.

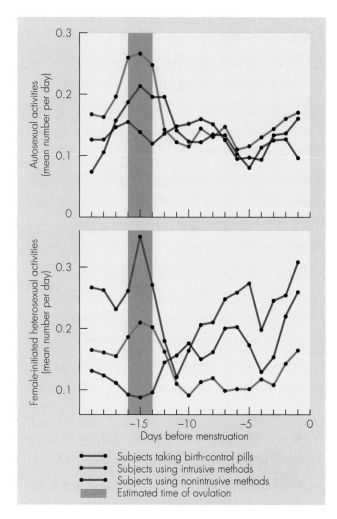

Figure 11.5 Female-initiated sexual activities during the monthly cycle
The top graph shows autosexual activities (masturbation and sexual fantasies); the bottom graph shows female-initiated activities with a male partner. "Intrusive" birth-control methods are diaphragm, foam, and condom; "nonintrusive" methods are IUD and vasectomy. Note that women other than pill users increase self-initiated sex activities when their estrogen levels peak. *(Source: Adams, Gold, & Burt, 1978)*

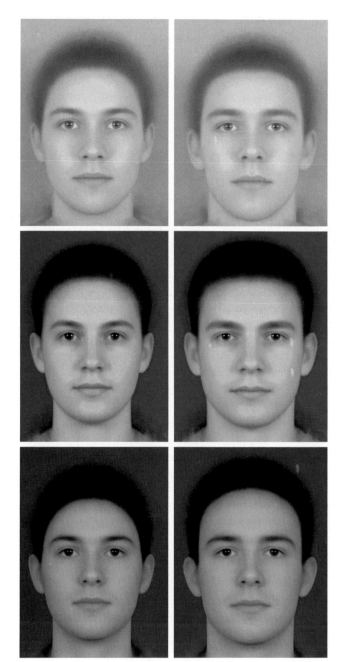

Figure 11.6 Male faces differing in apparent femininity or masculinity
Using a computer, women were able to change each face from relatively feminine (left faces) to relatively masculine (right faces). Women at different stages in their menstrual cycle had slightly different preferences. *(Source: Penton-Voak et al., 1999)*

For each pair, which would you prefer for a short-term sexual relationship? In one study, women not using oral contraceptives were presented with a computer that enabled them to modify each face to make it look more feminized (the left of each pair) or more masculinized (right). They adjusted the face until it looked most attractive. When they were asked specifically to show the face of the man they would prefer for a "short-term sexual relationship," women who were menstruating or in the luteal phase approaching menstruation usually adjusted the faces to look feminized. Women in the follicular phase (when estrogen and progesterone levels are rising and the probability of becoming pregnant is greatest) preferred a face closer to halfway between feminized and masculinized (Penton-Voak et al., 1999).

Women using oral contraceptives, whose hormones are kept more constant throughout the month, did not change their preferences from one time to another.

Nonsexual Behavior

Testosterone increases aggressive behavior in many species of mammals and birds. As a result males fight

Premenstrual Syndrome

You will probably never hear a woman describe menstruation as pleasant, but some react to it more strongly than others. Some women experience anxiety, irritability, and depression during the days just before menstruation, an experience known as **premenstrual syndrome (PMS)**. The symptoms are related in some way to the hormonal swings at this time, which include decreased estrogen and progesterone, increased cortisol (an adrenal hormone), and decreased activity of the neurotransmitters dopamine, serotonin, and norepinephrine (Taghavi et al., 1995; Van Goozen, Frijda, Wiegant, Endert, & Van de Poll, 1996).

Drugs that suppress the production of ovarian hormones reduce or abolish the symptoms for most sufferers. However, women with PMS have normal levels of estrogen and progesterone. For some reason they are reacting abnormally to normal changes in hormones (Schmidt, Nieman, Danaceau, Adams, & Rubinow, 1998). One hypothesis pertains to the metabolism of progesterone. Progesterone is metabolized into several other chemicals, including *allopregnenolone,* which produces antianxiety effects on the brain similar to those of tranquilizers. One study found that women with PMS had normal levels of progesterone but less than half the normal level of pregnenolone during the last couple of days before menstruation, although they had nearly normal levels of allopregnenolone at other times (Rapkin et al., 1997).

---

mostly during mating season, mostly in competition for mates. We shall consider this relationship further in Chapter 12 when we discuss aggressive behavior in general.

Estrogen and testosterone also produce activating effects on several brain systems with widespread functions. Estrogen stimulates a temporary growth of dendritic spines on dendrites in the hippocampus; the spines gradually retract after estrogen levels fall (Wooley & McEwen, 1993). Increased levels of estrogen also stimulate increased production of dopamine type D_2 receptors and serotonin type 5-HT_{2A} receptors in the nucleus accumbens, the prefrontal cortex, the olfactory cortex, and several other cortical areas (Fink, Sumner, Rosie, Grace, & Quinn, 1996). Those synapses contribute to sexual motivation and reinforcement, but also to other types of reinforcement and positive mood. Therefore increased estrogen would be linked to increased enjoyment of many activities, and decreased estrogen could lead to decreased enjoyment. Many women report unpleasant mood changes just after giving birth and during menopause, times of significant decreases in estrogen. Some women report irritability, discomfort, and depression just before menstruation (*premenstrual syndrome*), another time of decreased estrogen and other hormones (see Digression 11.3).

Increased estrogen improves verbal memory, memory of recent events, and fine motor skills, while producing a decline in spatial performance (such as arranging blocks to copy a pattern). Supporting evidence comes from studies of rats (Frye, 1995; O'Neal, Means, Poole, & Hamm, 1996), voles (Galea, Kavaliers, Os-

senkopp, & Hampson, 1995), and monkeys (Lacreuse, Herndon, Killiany, Rosene, & Moss, 1999) as well as humans, so the effect appears to be a robust one. In one human study women were tested on several tasks during their menstrual period, when estrogen and progesterone levels are low, and during the midluteal phase (see Figure 11.3), when estrogen and progesterone levels are high. When the estrogen and progesterone levels were high, women performed better on tests of manual dexterity and verbal fluency, but worse on spatial tasks (Kimura & Hampson, 1994). Figure 11.7 shows an example of a spatial task.

Additional evidence comes from studies of women after **menopause,** the time when women permanently stop menstruating. Those who take estrogen replacement treatments show better performance on memory

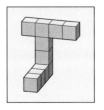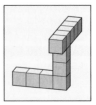

Figure 11.7 A spatial rotation task
People are presented with a series of pairs such as this one and asked whether the first figure could be rotated to match the second one. (Here the answer is *no.*) On the average, men perform better on this task than women, and women perform better while they are menstruating (and their sex hormone levels are low) than at other times. However, women perform verbal fluency and manual dexterity tasks better at other times than they do while menstruating.

tasks than do other women of the same age and education who are not taking estrogen (Resnick, Maki, Golski, Kraut, & Zonderman, 1998; Sherwin, 1997). Also, investigators have studied transsexuals undergoing procedures to switch from males to females. Those transsexuals who were taking estrogen treatments performed better than those not taking estrogen on tests of verbal memory (Miles, Green, Sanders, & Hines, 1998). All of these effects are small, however, so I do not recommend that women students plan their exam schedules to correspond to the right stage in the menstrual cycle.

Testosterone also influences cognition. Older men who have been given just enough extra testosterone to boost their levels back up to those typical of young men exhibit improved performance on spatial tasks (Janowsky, Oviatt, & Orwell, 1994). Again, the effect is small.

Why do sex hormones activate certain cognitive abilities? One speculation is that males of our species as well as many others tend to roam over a wider range than females and therefore need greater spatial abilities (Gaulin & FitzGerald, 1986). That hypothesis is testable to some degree; for example, the male–female difference on spatial tasks occurs in meadow voles (in which males roam more than females) but not in pine voles (in which the two sexes roam about equally). Still, in both rats and humans, males outperform females on spatial tasks only when females' estrogen levels are high; at other stages of the hormonal cycle, the sexes are about the same on spatial tasks. Why should estrogen *impair* spatial abilities? And why should it improve verbal memory and manual dexterity? Why should females need different abilities at different stages in their hormonal cycle? The answers are not obvious.

Stop & Check

4. How do cyproterone, medroxyprogesterone, and triptorelin decrease male sex drive?

5. At what time in a woman's menstrual cycle are her levels of estrogen and progesterone highest? When are they lowest?

6. What is the relationship between sex hormones and premenstrual syndrome?

Check your answers on page 323.

Puberty

Puberty, the onset of sexual maturity, usually begins at about age 12 to 13 for girls and a year later for boys in the United States. Because reproduction requires a great deal of energy, puberty does not begin until the body has enough energy reserves. On the average a girl experiences menarche (muh-NAR-kee), her first men-

struation, when she weighs about 47 kg (103 pounds). Girls who keep their weight very low, often because of ballet or athletic training, are slower than others to reach menarche and generally have more irregular menstrual cycles than other girls. Girls more than 30% overweight also have irregular cycles (Frisch, 1983, 1984).

Puberty starts when the hypothalamus begins to release *luteinizing hormone releasing hormone* at a rate of about one burst per hour. Once it begins it continues throughout the fertile period. This hormone stimulates the pituitary to secrete LH and FSH, which in turn stimulate the gonads to release estradiol in girls or testosterone in boys (B. D. Goldman, 1981). The sex hormones stimulate a growth spurt and induce the *secondary sexual characteristics*—breast development and broadening of the hips in women; lowering of the voice, broadening of the shoulders, and increased body hair in men.

Parental Behavior

In most species of mammals and birds, hormonal changes at the end of pregnancy prepare the mother for parental behavior. The mechanisms vary from one species to another. For example, pregnant monkeys become more and more interested in baby monkeys as their pregnancy progresses and their estrogen and progesterone levels increase (Maestripieri & Zehr, 1998). Rats, on the other hand, produce a pattern of hormones late in pregnancy that actually makes them *less* responsive than usual to infant rats (Mayer & Rosenblatt, 1984). After delivering the babies, however, mother rats as well as monkeys and all other species become very attentive, especially to their own young, largely because of a sudden surge of the hormones prolactin and oxytocin. Drugs that block oxytocin prevent a mother rat from gathering her young into the nest and nursing them (Pedersen, Caldwell, Walker, Ayers, & Mason, 1994). Other hormones promote other aspects of maternal behavior. In one study 30-day-old rats (just a week or so after weaning) were injected with mother rats' plasma that contained all the mothers' hormones. The young rats, especially the females, quickly showed typical rat parental behaviors toward still younger rats (Brunelli, Shindledecker, & Hofer, 1987). The hormones act by increasing activity in the medial preoptic area of the hypothalamus, and damage to this area eliminates rats' maternal behavior (J. R. Brown, Ye, Bronson, Dikkes, & Greenberg, 1996; Calamandrei & Keverne, 1994; Fleming & Korsmit, 1996; Numan & Numan, 1994) (see Figure 11.8). (This is the same preoptic area that is so important for temperature regulation, thirst, and sexual behavior. It's an important little area.)

Although maternal behavior depends on hormones for the first few days, it becomes less dependent at a later stage. If a female rat that has never been pregnant is left with some 5- to 10-day-old babies, she ignores them

Figure 11.8 Brain development and maternal behavior in mice
The mouse on the left shows normal maternal behavior. The one on the right has a genetic mutation that, among other effects, impairs the development of the preoptic area of the hypothalamus. *(Source: J. R. Brown, Ye, Bronson, Dikkes, & Goldberg, 1996)*

at first but gradually becomes more attentive. (Because the babies cannot survive without parental care, the experimenter must periodically replace them with new, healthy babies.) After about 6 days, the adoptive mother builds a nest, assembles the babies in the nest, licks them, and does everything else that a normal mother would, except nurse them. This experience-dependent behavior does not require hormonal changes and occurs even in rats that have had their ovaries removed (Mayer & Rosenblatt, 1979; Rosenblatt, 1967).

One thing that happens during this period of being with babies is that the mother becomes accustomed to their odors. Infant rats release some chemicals that stimulate the mother's vomeronasal organ, which responds to pheromones (see Chapter 7). We might imagine that evolution would have equipped infants with pheromones that elicit maternal behavior, but actually the effect on the vomeronasal organ interferes with maternal behavior. For a mother that has just gone through pregnancy, this interference does not matter; her hormones have primed her medial preoptic area so strongly that it overrides any objections from elsewhere in the brain. A female without hormonal priming, however, would reject the young unless she had a few days to become familiar with their smell (Del Cerro et al., 1995). Even for a normal mother, the familiarization helps to weaken the interference from the vomeronasal organ.

Why do mammals need two mechanisms for maternal behavior—one hormone-dependent and one not? In the early phase hormones compensate for the mother's lack of familiarity with the young. In the later phase experience maintains the maternal behavior even though the hormones start to decline (Rosenblatt, 1970).

What about the father's behavior? For most mammalian species the answer is simple: The father does not help care for the young. However, in species where the father does contribute, he undergoes hormonal changes similar to those of the mother. For example, in one species of dwarf hamster, males help with the young (unlike most other hamster species). In that species, as the female approaches the end of pregnancy, the male's

testosterone level increases, perhaps priming him to defend the nest vigorously. As soon as the mother delivers her babies, however, his testosterone levels drop and his prolactin levels increase. The result is nonaggressive parental behavior toward his young (Reburn & Wynne-Edwards, 1999).

Are hormones important for human parental behavior? Hormonal changes are necessary for a woman to nurse a baby, but otherwise, hormonal changes are not necessary to prepare anyone for infant care. After all, both men and never-pregnant women can adopt children and be excellent parents. It is possible that hormonal changes facilitate or increase some aspects of human parental behavior, but research data are not available on this point.

Stop *&* Check

7. What factors are responsible for maternal behavior shortly after rats give birth? What factors become more important in later days?

Check your answers on page 323.

Module 11.1

In Closing: Sex-Related Behaviors and Motivations

Why do humans and other animals engage in sexual and parental behaviors? "To pass on their genes and propagate the species," you may answer. Well, yes, the behaviors evolved to serve those purposes. However, in most cases the motivation for the sex act is simply that it feels good. It is hard to identify all the motivations that contribute to parental behavior, especially in nonhumans, but some of the motivation is, again, simply that it feels good. For example, a mother rat licks her babies all over shortly after their birth, providing them with stimulation that is essential for their survival. But the mother presumably does not know the value of the licking for the young; she licks them because she craves the salty taste of the fluid that covers them. She licks them much less if she has access to other salty fluids (Gubernick & Alberts, 1983). In short, animals need not understand the ultimate function of their reproductive behaviors; they have evolved mechanisms that cause them to enjoy and therefore perform the acts.

Summary

1. The organizing effects of a hormone are exerted during an early sensitive period and bring about relatively permanent alterations in anatomy or in the potential for function. (p. 312)

2. In the absence of sex hormones, an infant mammal develops the female pattern of genitals and hypothalamus. The addition of testosterone shifts development toward the male pattern. Extra estrogen, within normal limits, does not determine whether the individual looks male or female. (p. 313)

3. During early development testosterone is converted within certain cells to estradiol, which actually masculinizes the development of the hypothalamus. Estradiol in the blood does not masculinize development, either because it is bound to proteins in the blood or because it is metabolized. (p. 313)

4. In adulthood sex hormones can activate sex behaviors, partly by facilitating activity in the medial preoptic area and other parts of the hypothalamus. Dopamine acts at D_1 receptors to increase sexual arousal and at D_2 receptors to stimulate orgasm. (p. 315)

5. A woman's menstrual cycle depends on a feedback cycle that increases and then decreases the release of several hormones. In many species females are sexually responsive only when they are fertile. Women can respond sexually at any time in their cycle, although they may have a slight increase in sexual interest around the time of ovulation, when estrogen levels are highest. (p. 317)

6. Puberty begins when the hypothalamus starts to release bursts of luteinizing hormone releasing hormone. The onset of puberty is controlled by many factors, including body weight and social stimuli. (p. 321)

7. Hormones released around the time of giving birth facilitate maternal behavior in females of many mammalian species. Nevertheless mere prolonged exposure to young is also sufficient to induce parental behavior. Hormonal facilitation is not essential to human parental behavior. (p. 321)

Answers to *Stop and Check* Questions

1. A mammal exposed to high levels of both male and female hormones will appear male. One exposed to low levels of both will appear female. Genital development depends mostly on the presence or absence of androgens. (p. 315)

2. A female that lacked alpha-fetoprotein would be masculinized by her own estrogens. (p. 315)

3. Unusually high levels of estrogens could exceed the binding capacity of alpha-fetoprotein and therefore enter the cells and masculinize development. (p. 315)

4. Cyproterone prevents testosterone from binding to its receptors. Medroxyprogesterone and triptorelin block gonadotropin, the pituitary hormone that stimulates the testis to produce testosterone. Triptorelin blocks it more effectively and for a longer time. (p. 321)

5. Estrogen and progesterone are highest at the periovulatory phase; they are lowest during and just after menstruation. (p. 321)

6. Premenstrual syndrome is an abnormal reaction to the normal changes that occur in sex hormones. One hypothesis relates PMS to low levels of one metabolite of progesterone. (p. 321)

7. The early stage of rats' maternal behavior depends on a surge in the release of the hormones prolactin and oxytocin. A few days later her experience with the young decreases the vomeronasal responses that would tend to make her reject them. Experience with the young maintains maternal behavior after the hormone levels begin to drop. (p. 322)

Thought Questions

1. The pill RU-486 produces abortions by blocking the effects of progesterone. Explain how this process works.

2. The presence or absence of testosterone determines whether a mammal will differentiate as a male or a female; estrogens have no effect. In birds the story is the opposite: The presence or absence of estrogen is critical (Adkins & Adler, 1972). What problems would sex determination by estrogen create if that were the mechanism for mammals? Why do those problems not arise in birds? (*Hint*: Think about the difference between live birth and hatching from an egg.)

3. Antipsychotic drugs, such as haloperidol and chlorpromazine, block activity at dopamine synapses. What side effects might they have on sexual behavior?

Variations in Sexual Development and Orientation

The coral goby is a species of fish in which a male and a female tend their eggs and young together. If one of them dies, the survivor looks for a new partner. But it does not look very far. This is a very stay-at-home kind of fish. If it cannot easily find an available member of the opposite sex, but does find an unmated member of its own sex, it simply changes sex and mates with the neighbor. Male-to-female and female-to-male switches are equally common (Nakashima, Kuwamura, & Yogo, 1995).

Nothing quite like this happens in mammals, but it shows us that male and female are not altogether distinct categories. Certain people develop anatomies that are intermediate between male and female, anatomies that do not match their genetic sex, or psychological identities that do not match their anatomies. Some people develop a heterosexual orientation; others, a homosexual orientation. Variations are interesting for their own sake and for what they reveal about sexual development in general.

Sexual development is a very sensitive issue, so let us specify from the start: "Different" does not mean "abnormal," except in the statistical sense. People naturally differ in their sexual development just as they do in their height, weight, emotions, and memory.

Determinants of Gender Identity

Gender identity is how we identify sexually and what we call ourselves. The biological differences between males and females are *sex differences*; the differences that result from people's thinking about themselves as male or female are *gender differences.* To maintain this useful distinction, we should resist the growing trend to speak of the "gender" of dogs, fruit flies, and so forth. Gender identity is specifically a human characteristic.

Gender identity is related to, but not the same as, **gender role,** the activities and dispositions that a particular society encourages for one sex or the other. Someone can have a female gender identity while rejecting all or part of the female gender role. Gender roles are determined by culture and upbringing. For example, cooking is regarded as women's work in certain societies and as men's work in others. Gender identity is undoubtedly also shaped to a large degree by family experiences. From an early age a girl might be told, "You are a girl, and later if you decide to marry, you will marry a boy." She is dressed in girl's clothing and placed mostly in the company of other girls. Boys receive the reverse treatment.

And yet a few people are clearly dissatisfied with their assigned gender, some of them (transsexuals) to such a degree that they insist on a surgical sex change. Might a biological factor, such as prenatal hormones, influence gender identity? Several kinds of human cases shed light on this question, though we have no definitive answers.

Intersexes

Some people are not exactly male or female, but something intermediate (Haqq & Donahoe, 1998). For example, some XY males with a mutation in the SRY gene have poorly developed genitals. Some people are born with an XX chromosome pattern but an SRY gene that translocated from the father's Y chromosome onto some autosomal chromosome. Despite their XX chromosomes, they have either an ovary and a testis, or two testes, or a mixture of testis and ovary tissue on each side.

Others develop an intermediate appearance because of an atypical hormone pattern. Recall that testosterone masculinizes the development of the genitals and the hypothalamus during early development. If a genetic female is exposed to more testosterone than the average female but less than the average male, her appearance can be partly masculinized. A genetic male who has low levels of testosterone or low responsiveness to it may also develop intermediate between male and female.

For example, a genetically female fetus or (less often) her mother may have an adrenal gland that produces an excess of testosterone and other androgens. Decades ago some pregnant women took antimiscarriage drugs that mimicked some of the effects of testosterone. (Those drugs are no longer used.) In any of these cases, the result is ambiguous external anatomy, as Figure 11.9 illustrates. Note in the figure the structure that appears intermediate between a clitoris and a penis and the swellings that appear intermediate between labia and a scrotum.

Individuals whose genitals do not match the usual development for their genetic sex are referred to as **her-**

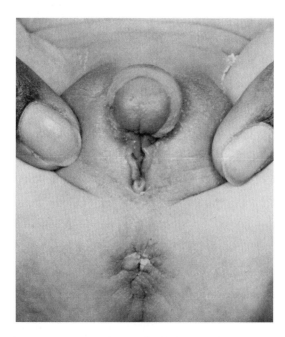

Figure 11.9 External genitals of a genetic female, age 3 months
Masculinized by excess androgens from the adrenal gland before birth, the infant shows the effects of the adrenogenital syndrome.

maphrodites (from Hermes and Aphrodite in Greek mythology). The *true hermaphrodite*, a rarity, has some normal testicular tissue and some normal ovarian tissue—for example, a testis on one side of the body and an ovary on the other. Individuals whose sexual development is intermediate or ambiguous, such as the one in Figure 11.9, are also sometimes called hermaphrodites, but more often called **intersexes** or pseudohermaphrodites. Most of them dislike the term *pseudohermaphrodite,* which sounds insulting, so we shall use the term *intersex.*

How common are intersexes? According to current estimates, at least 1 child in 100 in the United States is born with some degree of genital ambiguity, and 1 in 1000–2000 has enough ambiguity to make assignment as male or female uncertain (Dreger, 1998). However, no one should put great confidence in the accuracy of these estimates. Hospitals and physicians seldom keep records of such matters, and families also keep the information private. (Maintaining confidentiality is of course important, but one unfortunate consequence is that intersexed people have trouble finding others who have faced the same problems. The end of this chapter lists three support groups.)

When a baby is born with an intersex appearance, a decision must be made: Shall we call the child a boy or a girl? Ideally the label boy or girl should match what the person looks like, acts like, and feels like. Matching the chromosomes is less important because intersexes' chromosomes are a poor predictor of their eventual appearance and behavior.

Beginning in about the 1950s, medical doctors recommended the following: When in doubt, call the child a girl and perform surgery to make her look like a girl (see Dreger, 1998). It is difficult surgically to create a satisfactory artificial penis or to enlarge a small one. It is easier to create an artificial vagina or lengthen a short one. After the surgery, the child looks female, or close enough.

And she lives happily ever after, right? Well, physicians do very few long-term follow-ups on these people. Perhaps some are happy and we never hear from them, but virtually all adult intersexes who have said anything publicly have complained about their treatment. The surgically created or lengthened vagina may be satisfactory to a male partner, but it provides no sensation to the woman and requires frequent attention to prevent it from scarring over. Many intersexes wish they had their original "abnormal" penis/clitoris instead of the mutilated, insensitive structure left to them by a surgeon. Many develop a male gender identity despite being reared as females. Most of all, intersexes resent the deception. Historian Alice Dreger (1998) describes the case of one intersex:

> As a young person, [she] was told she had "twisted ovaries" that had to be removed; in fact, her testes were removed. At the age of twenty, "alone and scared in the stacks of a [medical] library," she discovered the truth of her condition. Then "the pieces finally fit together. But what fell apart was my relationship with both my family and physicians. It was not learning about chromosome or testes that caused enduring trauma, it was discovering that I had been told lies. I avoided all medical care for the next 18 years. . . . [T]he greatest source

This group of adult intersexed people have gathered to provide mutual support and to protest against the early surgical treatments they received. They requested that their names be used to emphasize their openness about their condition and to emphasize that intersexuality should not be considered shameful. They are from left to right: Martha Coventry, Max Beck, David Vandertie, Kristi Bruce, and Angela Moreno.

of anxiety is not our gonads or karyotype. It is shame and fear resulting from an environment in which our condition is so unacceptable that caretakers lie." (p. 192)

So how *should* such a child be reared? On that question, specialists do not agree. Some continue to insist that any child without a full-size penis should be surgically "corrected" to look like a female and then reared as a girl. A growing number, however, follow these recommendations (Diamond & Sigmundson, 1997):

- Be completely honest with the intersexed person and the family, and do nothing without their informed consent. (Some doctors in the past have conducted surgery on infants without even explaining what they were doing or why.)

- Identify the child as male or female based mainly on the predominant external appearance. That is, there should be no bias toward calling every intersex a female.

- Rear the child as consistently as possible, but be prepared that the intersexed person might later be sexually oriented toward males, females, both, or neither.

- Do *not* perform surgery to reduce the ambiguous penis/clitoris to the size of a normal clitoris. Such surgery impairs the person's erotic sensation and is at best premature, as no one knows how the child's sexual orientation will develop. If the intersexed person makes an informed request for such surgery in adulthood, then it is appropriate, but otherwise it should be avoided.

Testicular Feminization

Certain individuals with the typical male XY chromosome pattern have the genital appearance of a female. This condition is known as androgen insensitivity or testicular feminization. Although such individuals produce normal amounts of androgens (such as testosterone), their bodies lack the mechanism that enables it to bind to genes in a cell's nucleus. Consequently the cells are insensitive to androgens, and the external genitals develop almost like those of a normal female. Two abnormalities appear at puberty. First, in spite of breast development and broadening of the hips, menstruation does not begin because the body has two internal testes instead of ovaries and a uterus. (The vagina is short and leads to nothing.) Second, pubic hair does not develop because it depends on androgens in females as well as males (see Figure 11.10).

Someone with androgen insensitivity develops a clear female gender identity. Her gender identity should come as no surprise: She looks like a normal female, she has been raised unambiguously as a female, and her cells have been exposed only to estrogens since prenatal development. The only discrepancy is her genetic sex (XY).

Testicular feminization, like any other condition, comes in various degrees. Some look more male than female, but with a small penis, lack of body hair, and so forth.

Stop & Check

1. What would cause a genetic female (XX) to develop an intersex anatomy?

2. What would cause a genetic male (XY) to develop a feminized anatomy?

Check your answers on pages 331–332.

Discrepancies of Sexual Appearance

Most of the evidence from intersexes does not tell us anything indisputable about the roles of rearing and hormones in determining gender identity. From a scientific viewpoint the most decisive way to settle the issue would be to raise a completely normal male baby as a female or to raise a normal female baby as a male. If the process succeeded in producing an adult who was fully

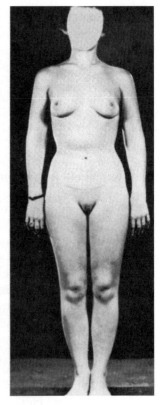

Figure 11.10   A woman with an XY chromosome pattern but insensitivity to androgens
Two undescended testes produce testosterone and other androgens, to which the body is insensitive. The testes and adrenal glands also produce estrogens that are responsible for the pubertal changes. *(Source: Federman, 1967)*

satisfied in the assigned role, we would know that upbringing determines gender identity and that hormones do not. Although no one would perform such an experiment intentionally, it is possible to study accidental events. Here, we shall consider examples in which children were apparently exposed to the hormonal pattern of one sex before birth and then reared as the other.

Penis Development Delayed Until Puberty In one community in the Dominican Republic with apparently much inbreeding, some genetic males have a genetic defect in the enzyme *5α-reductase 2*. That enzyme converts testosterone to *dihydrotestosterone*, an androgen that is more effective than testosterone for masculinizing the genitals. At birth the penis is so small that it looks like a slightly swollen clitoris, and the child is identified as female and reared as a girl. Nevertheless the testosterone level is that of a normal male and capable of masculinizing brain development. Later, at puberty, the sudden surge of testosterone causes significant penis growth.

Women: Imagine that at about age 12 years you had suddenly sprouted a penis and your family wanted to change your name from Juanita to Juan. Would you calmly say, "Yep, okay, I guess I'm a boy now"? Presumably not, but in nearly every case, the girl-turned-boy developed a clear male gender identity and directed his sexual interest toward females (Imperato-McGinley, Guerrero, Gautier, & Peterson, 1974). Remember, these were not "normal" girls; their brains had been exposed to male levels of testosterone from prenatal life onward. The report of these Dominican Republic families led researchers to look for additional cases, which they found in parts of Brazil and Turkey, again in isolated communities with much inbreeding. In both communities nearly all the children with 5α-reductase 2 deficiency were originally considered female but switched to male at puberty (Can et al., 1998; Mendonca et al., 1996).

One interpretation of these results is that the prenatal testosterone favored a male gender identity even in children who were reared as females. Another possibility is that gender identity is established by social influences during adolescence. In either case the results make it difficult to argue that early rearing experiences are the sole determinant of gender identity.

Stop & Check

3. What does the enzyme 5α-reductase do?

Check your answer on page 332.

Accidental Removal of the Penis Circumcision is the removal of the foreskin of the penis, a common procedure with newborn boys. One physician using an electrical procedure accidentally used too high a current and burned off the entire penis. The parents elected to rear the child as a female, with the appropriate corrective surgery. What makes this a particularly interesting case is that the child has a twin brother (whom the parents did not let the physician try to circumcise). If both twins developed satisfactory gender identities, one as a girl and the other as a boy, we would conclude that rearing was decisive in gender identity and that prenatal hormones were not.

Initial reports claimed that the child reared as a girl had a normal female gender identity, though she also had strong tomboyish tendencies (Money & Schwartz, 1978). However, by about age 10 she had figured out that something was wrong and that "she" was really a boy. She had preferred boys' activities and played only with boys' toys. She even tried urinating in a standing position, despite always making a mess. By age 14 she insisted that she wanted to live as a boy. At that time her (now his) father tearfully explained the earlier events. The child changed names and became known to and accepted by classmates as a boy; at age 25 he married a somewhat older woman and adopted her children. Clearly the biological predisposition had won out over the family's attempts to rear the child as a girl (Colapinto, 1997; Diamond & Sigmundson, 1997). Could a child who was exposed to the full pattern of male hormones prenatally ever be reared successfully as a female? Well, who knows? There aren't many cases in which it has been tried, and results probably vary (Bradley, Oliver, Chernick, & Zucker, 1998). The point is that no one should feel confident about such a switch, and it was a mistake to impose surgery and hormonal treatments to try to complete the feminization of this child.

Possible Biological Bases of Sexual Orientation

Why do some people prefer partners of the other sex and some prefer partners of their own sex? This topic is particularly troublesome because of the difficulty of separating scientific issues from social and political disputes. Most of our discussion will focus on male homosexuality, which is more common than female homosexuality and more heavily investigated.

Most people say that their sexual orientation "just happened," generally at an early age, and that they do not know how or why. Sexual orientation, like left- or right-handedness, is not something that people choose or that they can change easily.

Genetics

Studies of human behavior genetics often rely on comparisons of monozygotic and dizygotic twins. Logically, such evidence isn't perfect, but it's often the best available. Most studies of the genetics of sexual orientation have begun by advertising in gay or lesbian publications for homosexual men or women who have twins. Then they contacted the twins, not telling them how they got their names, and asked them to fill out a questionnaire. The questionnaire included diverse items to conceal the fact that the real interest was sexual orientation. Figure 11.11 shows the results for a pair of studies, one with men and one with women. Note that the probability of homosexuality is highest in monozygotic (identical) twins of the originally identified homosexual person, lower in dizygotic twins, and still lower in adopted brothers or sisters (Bailey & Pillard, 1991; Bailey, Pillard, Neale, & Agyei, 1993). Another study with a smaller sample found similar results (Whitam, Diamond, & Martin, 1993). Various studies have not agreed on whether a family with homosexual men is likely also to include homosexual women (Bailey & Bell, 1993; Bailey & Benishay, 1993; Bailey et al., 1999). That inconsistency is disappointing, because an answer would tell us whether the factors influencing sexual orientation are the same in men as in women.

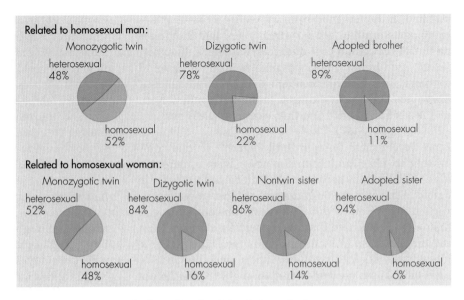

Figure 11.11 Sexual orientations in adult relatives of a homosexual man or woman
Note that the probability of a homosexual orientation is highest among monozygotic twins of a homosexual individual, lower among dizygotic twins, and still lower among adopted brothers or sisters. These data suggest a genetic contribution toward the development of sexual orientation. *(Source: Based on the data of Bailey & Pillard, 1991; Bailey, Pillard, Neale, & Agyei, 1993)*

Overall the results imply that genes influence sexual orientation. Note, however, two limitations:

- People who answer ads in gay and lesbian publications may or may not be typical of other homosexual people.
- If genetic factors completely determined sexual orientation, all pairs of identical twins would have the same sexual orientation. The frequent discrepancies indicate the importance of other unidentified influences. Of course, the explanation need not be the same for every individual.

One study that examined relatives beyond the immediate family found a higher incidence of homosexuality among the maternal relatives of homosexual men than among the paternal relatives (Hamer, Hu, Magnuson, Hu, & Pattatucci, 1993). These results suggest a relevant gene on the X chromosome, which a man necessarily receives from his mother. However, later studies have not replicated these results (Bailey et al., 1999; Rice, Anderson, Risch, & Ebers, 1999).

We should not assume that a gene correlated with sexual orientation necessarily exerts its effects by controlling the brain structures responsible for sexual behavior. We could imagine all sorts of indirect routes by which a gene might influence the way someone reacts

to various experiences or even modify physical appearance in such a way as to elicit different treatment by other people.

If certain genes promote a homosexual orientation, then why has evolution not selected strongly against those genes, which decrease the probability of reproduction? One possible explanation is that the genes might produce different effects in different people. For example, we could hypothesize a gene that increased the probability of homosexuality in boys and increased the fertility of their sisters. Another possibility is that homosexual men and women perhaps help their brothers or sisters to rear children and thereby perpetuate genes that the whole family shares (LeVay, 1993). So far, no research has tested either of these hypotheses.

Hormones

Given the importance of hormones for sexual behavior, it seems natural to look for their possible effects on sexual orientation. We can quickly dismiss the hypothesis that sexual orientation depends on adult hormone levels: Most homosexual men have testosterone and estrogen levels well within the same range as heterosexual men; most lesbian women also have hormone levels well within the typical female range.

A more plausible hypothesis is that sexual orientation depends on testosterone levels during a sensitive period of brain development, perhaps from the middle of the second month of pregnancy until the end of the fifth month in humans (Ellis & Ames, 1987). In studies of animals ranging from rats to pigs to zebra finches, males that were exposed to much-decreased levels of testosterone early in life have as adults shown sexual interest in other males (Adkins-Regan, 1988). Females exposed to extra testosterone during that period show an increased probability of attempting to mount sexual partners in the way that males typically do (see Figure 11.12).

However...
monal mani...
genitals. (H...
anatomically...
is one in w...
without mu...
ments rats in...
ful experienc...
for more tha...
Such stress i...
which cross...
tus's develop...
duce antitest...
Ward, 1986)....
alcohol as w...
(I. L. Ward, 1...
1994). Either...
males' behav...
of the hypoth...
As adults th...
male or fema...

Although...
males is alter...
tain other reg...
field (Meisel,...
ferent aspect...
nized at diffe...
different type...
the effects of j...
experiences a...
in isolation o...

Figure 11.12
The female wa...
sitive period;...
with androgens at adulthood. *(Source: Dörner, 1974)*

sponsivity only to males. Those reared with non-stressed males and females became sexually responsive to both males and females (Dunlap, Zadina, & Gougis, 1978; I. L. Ward & Reed, 1985).

With regard to human sexual orientation, the rat data are suggestive, but also have limitations:

- What is true of rats may not be true of humans. Hormonal influences on sexual behavior vary even between one primate species and another.

- The female sexual behaviors shown by the male rats in these studies (such as arching their backs) do not closely mimic human behaviors. Homosexual men are characterized by their preference for male partners, not necessarily by a preference for female postures or behaviors.

Despite their limitations, the rat studies suggest that investigators should examine any possible relationship between prenatal events and later sexual orientation. One approach is to ask the mothers of homosexual men whether they experienced any unusual stress during pregnancy. One researcher contacted 283 mothers of homosexual and heterosexual men, without letting them know why or how they had been chosen. The survey made no mention of sexual orientation; it merely asked about a variety of illnesses and stressors that the woman might have experienced before, during, or after pregnancy. The mothers of homosexual men reported a significantly greater number of stressful events, especially during the second trimester of pregnancy (Ellis, Ames, Peckham, & Burke, 1988). However, a similar study failed to find increased stress during pregnancies that produced homosexual sons (Bailey, Willerman, & Parks, 1991). Both studies are limited by their reliance on mothers' memories of pregnancies more than 20 years earlier. A more decisive (though much more difficult) procedure would be to measure stress during pregnancy and follow up later to identify the sexual orientation of the offspring. At this point the relationship between prenatal stress and human sexual orientation is uncertain.

What about the role of hormones in female homosexuality? In the 1950s and early 1960s, certain pregnant women took *diethylstilbestrol (DES)*, a synthetic estrogen, to prevent miscarriage or alleviate other problems. DES can exert masculinizing effects similar to those of testosterone. One study found that of 30 adult women whose mothers had taken DES during pregnancy, 7 reported some degree of homosexual or bisexual responsiveness. By comparison, only 1 of 30 women not prenatally exposed to DES reported any homosexual or bisexual responsiveness (Ehrhardt et al., 1985). These results suggest a role of prenatal hormones, though it could hardly be the sole influence.

One study looked at differences between homosexual and heterosexual women in a characteristic that differs between the sexes, although it has nothing to do with the sex act itself: Any brief click sound causes the inner ear to produce a weak clicking sound of its own, like an echo. On the average, women's ears produce a stronger click than men's ears do (although all these sounds are so faint that they need much amplification to be detected). Lesbian and bisexual women showed weaker clicks than heterosexual women, though stronger than heterosexual men (McFadden & Pasanen, 1998). That is, the results suggest a partial masculinization of the brain in some homosexual/bisexual women. (With women as with men, there is no reason to assume that one explanation fits all.)

Brain Anatomy

On the average, men's brains differ from women's in several ways, including the relative sizes of parts of the hypothalamus (Breedlove, 1992). Do the brains of homosexual men resemble those of heterosexual men or heterosexual women?

Current evidence shows results that vary from one brain area to another. The anterior commissure (see p. 98) is, on the average, larger in heterosexual women than in heterosexual men; in homosexual men it is at least as large as it is in women, perhaps even slightly larger (Gorski & Allen, 1992). The implications of this difference are unclear, as the anterior commissure has no known relationship to sexual behavior. The suprachiasmatic nucleus (SCN) is also larger in homosexual men than in heterosexual men (Swaab & Hofman, 1990). Recall from Chapter 9 that the SCN controls circadian rhythms. How might a difference in the SCN relate to sexual orientation? The answer is not clear, but male rats that are deprived of testosterone during early development also show abnormalities in the SCN, and their preference for male or female sexual partners varies with time of day. They make sexual advances toward both male and female partners early in their active period of the day, but mostly toward females as the day goes on (Swaab, Slob, Houtsmuller, Brand, & Zhou, 1995). Does human sexual behavior or orientation also vary depending on time of day? No research has been reported.

The most suggestive studies of brain differences concern a particular nucleus of the anterior hypothalamus, known as interstitial nucleus 3, which is generally more than twice as large in heterosexual men as in women. This area corresponds to part of the sexually dimorphic nucleus, mentioned on p. 312; it is important for male sexual behavior in rats. Simon LeVay (1991) examined interstitial nucleus 3 in 41 people who had died between the ages of 26 and 59. Of these, 16 were heterosexual men, 6 were heterosexual women, and 19 were homosexual men. All of the homosexual men, 6 of

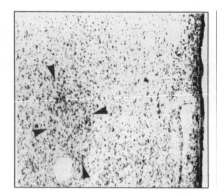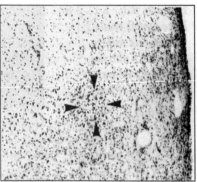

Figure 11.13   Typical sizes of interstitial nucleus 3 of the anterior hypothalamus
On the average, the volume of this structure was more than twice as large in a sample of heterosexual men (left) than it was in a sample of homosexual men (right), for whom it was about the same size as that in women. Animal studies have implicated this structure as important for male sexual activities. *(Source: LeVay, 1991)*

the 16 heterosexual men, and 1 of the 6 women had died of AIDS. LeVay found that the mean volume of interstitial nucleus 3 was 0.12 mm^3 in heterosexual men, 0.056 mm^3 in heterosexual women, and 0.051 mm^3 in homosexual men. Figure 11.13 shows typical cross sections for a heterosexual man and a homosexual man. Figure 11.14 shows the distribution of volumes for the three groups. Note that the difference between heterosexual men and the other two groups is fairly large and that the cause of death (AIDS versus other) has no clear relationship to the results.

These data have certain limitations. Although cause

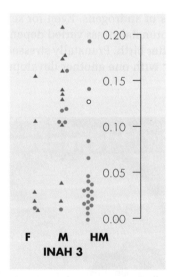

Figure 11.14   Distribution of volumes for interstitial nucleus 3 of the anterior hypothalamus
Samples are females (F), heterosexual males (M), and homosexual males (HM). Each filled circle represents a person who died of AIDS; each triangle represents a person who died from other causes. The one open circle represents a bisexual man who died of AIDS. *(Source: LeVay, 1991)*

of death does not apparently relate to brain structure for heterosexual men, it would nevertheless be helpful to examine the brains of homosexual men who died of causes other than AIDS. LeVay (1993) later examined the hypothalamus of a homosexual man who died of lung cancer; he had a small interstitial nucleus 3, like the homosexual men who died of AIDS. Still, it would be helpful to examine more cases.

A second limitation is that we do not know whether the apparent brain differences were present since early childhood or whether they developed in adulthood, perhaps a result of sexual activity instead of a cause. Some parts of the brain do change in size as a result of adult hormone levels, and changes as a result of experience may be possible also (Cooke, Tabibnia, & Breedlove, 1999). We need more research on this point.

A third point is that we do not know how interstitial nucleus 3 contributes to sexual behavior. Male rats with damage in this area decrease all sexual behaviors but do not change their preference among sexual partners (McGinnis, Williams, & Lumia, 1996). Male ferrets with damage here, however, do shift to preferring male partners (Baum, Tobet, Cherry, & Paredes, 1996; Kindon, Baum, & Paredes, 1996). We need to know more about the functions of this brain area in humans.

One final point: In Figure 11.14 note that, although the groups differ fairly substantially on average, they also overlap. Consequently the data do not indicate that the structure of the hypothalamus completely determines sexual orientation. At most it alters the probability of developing one orientation or another.

Stop & Check

4. What kind of experience in early development can cause a male rat to develop sexual responsiveness to other males and not to females? How does that experience probably produce its effects?

5. What differences have been reported, on the average, between the brains of homosexual and heterosexual men?

Check your answers on page 332.

In Closing: We Are Not All the Same

When Alfred Kinsey conducted the first massive surveys of human sexual behavior, he found that people varied enormously in their frequency of sexual acts, but each person considered his or her own frequency to be "normal." Many believed that sexual activity much more frequent than their own was excessive and abnormal, and might even lead to insanity (Kinsey, Pomeroy, & Martin, 1948; Kinsey, Pomeroy, Martin, & Gebhard, 1953).

How far have we come since then? People today are more aware of sexual diversity than they were in Kinsey's time and generally more accepting. Still, intolerance remains common. Biological research will not tell us how to treat one another, but it can help us understand how we come to be so different.

Summary

1. People can develop ambiguous genitals or genitals that don't match their chromosomal sex for several reasons. Intersexes are people who experienced a hormonal pattern intermediate between male and female during their prenatal sensitive period for sexual development. (p. 324)

2. Many intersexes do not develop a gender identity that clearly matches their assigned sex. Most resent the surgery that was imposed on them and especially the lack of opportunity to make an informed decision themselves. (p. 325)

3. Testicular feminization is a condition in which someone with XY chromosomes and internal testes lacks the mechanisms that enable testosterone to bind to receptors in the cells. Such people develop looking female and having a female gender identity. (p. 326)

4. In several parts of the world, some children have a gene that decreases their early production of dihydrotestosterone. Such a child looks female at birth and is considered a girl, but develops a penis at adolescence. Most such people then accept a male gender identity. (p. 327)

5. One genetic male was exposed to normal male hormones until infancy, when his penis was accidentally removed and then his testes intentionally removed. In spite of being reared as a girl, he had typically male interests and eventually insisted on a male gender identity. (p. 327)

6. Plausible biological explanations for homosexual orientation include genetics and prenatal hormones. Hormone levels in adulthood are within the normal range. (p. 327)

7. One part of the hypothalamus is structurally different, on the average, in homosexual men than in heterosexual men. Research does not yet tell us whether the brain difference led to the sexual orientation or whether sexual activities alter brain anatomy. (p. 330)

Answers to *Stop and Check* Questions

1. A genetic female whose adrenal gland produces much more than the usual amount of testosterone will develop an intersex appearance. (p. 326)

2. A genetic male with a gene that prevents testosterone from binding to its receptors will develop a female appearance. (p. 326)

3. The enzyme 5α-reductase catalyzes the conversion of testosterone to dihydrotestosterone, which is more effective in masculinizing the genitals. (p. 327)

4. Stressful experiences given to a rat late in her pregnancy can cause her male offspring to show a later preference for male partners. Evidently the stress increases the release of endorphins in the hypothalamus, and very high endorphin levels can block the effects of testosterone. (p. 331)

5. Interstitial nucleus 3 of the anterior hypothalamus is larger in the brains of heterosexual than homosexual men. (p. 331)

Thought Questions

1. On the average, intersexes have IQ scores in the 110 to 125 range, well above the mean for the population (Dalton, 1968; Ehrhardt & Money, 1967; Lewis, Money, & Epstein, 1968). One possible interpretation is that a hormonal pattern intermediate between male and female promotes great intellectual development. Another possibility is that intersexuality may be more common in intelligent families than in less intelligent ones or that the more intelligent families are more likely to bring their intersex children to an investigator's attention. What kind of study would be best for deciding among these hypotheses? (For one answer, see Money & Lewis, 1966.)

2. Recall LeVay's study of brain anatomy in heterosexual and homosexual men (p. 330). Certain critics have suggested that one or more of the men classified as "heterosexual" might actually have been homosexual or bisexual. If so, would that fact strengthen or weaken the overall conclusions?

Chapter Ending
Key Terms and Activities

Terms

activating effect (p. 312)

alpha-fetoprotein (p. 313)

androgen insensitivity (or testicular feminization) (p. 326)

estradiol (p. 317)

follicle-stimulating hormone (FSH) (p. 317)

gender identity (p. 324)

gender role (p. 324)

gonad (p. 312)

hermaphrodite (p. 324–325)

impotence (p. 317)

intersex (or pseudohermaphrodite) (p. 325)

luteinizing hormone (LH) (p. 318)

menarche (p. 321)

menopause (p. 320)

menstrual cycle (p. 317)

Müllerian duct (p. 312)

organizing effect (p. 312)

ovary (p. 312)

periovulatory period (p. 318)

premenstrual syndrome (PMS) (p. 320)

puberty (p. 321)

sensitive period (p. 312)

sexually dimorphic nucleus (p. 312)

SRY gene (p. 312)

testis (p. 312)

testosterone (p. 312)

Wolffian duct (p. 312)

Suggestions for Further Reading

Colapinto, J. (2000). *As nature made him: The boy who was raised as a girl.* New York: HarperCollins. Describes the boy whose penis was accidentally removed, as presented on page 327.

Diamond, J. (1997). *Why is sex fun?* New York: Basic Books. Human sexual behavior differs from that of other species in many ways and therefore raises many evolutionary issues, which this book addresses. For example, why do humans have sex at times when the woman cannot become pregnant? Why do women have menopause? Why don't men breast-feed their babies? And what good are men, anyway? If you haven't thought about such questions before, you should read this book.

Dreger, A. D. (1998). *Hermaphrodites and the medical invention of sex.* Cambridge, MA: Harvard University Press. A fascinating history of how the medical profession has treated and mistreated hermaphrodites.

LeVay, S. (1993). *The sexual brain.* Cambridge: MIT Press. Discusses the biological basis of sexual behaviors, including sexual orientation.

Support Groups

Ambiguous Genitalia Support Group
P. O. Box 313
Clements, CA 95227

American Educational Gender Information Service
P. O. Box 33724
Decatur, GA 30033–0724

Intersex Society of North America
P. O. Box 3070
Ann Arbor, MI 48106–3070

Web Sites to Explore

You can go to the Biological Psychology Study Center and click on these links. While there, you can also check for suggested articles available on InfoTrac. The Biological Psychology Internet address is:
http://psychology.wadsworth.com/book/kalatbiopsych7e/

http://www.indiana.edu/~sris/
Details the Kinsey Institute's research on human sexuality.

http://www.endosociety.org/pubaffai/factshee/premenstrual.htm
Presents information about premenstrual syndrome.

http://www.isna.org/
Site maintained by the Intersex Society of North America; presents information about intersexuality, ambiguous genitalia, etc.

Active Learner Link

Quiz for Chapter 11

Chapter 12

Emotional Behaviors

Main Ideas

1. Emotions are difficult to define and difficult to measure.

2. Although intense emotions, such as panic, interfere with good reasoning, moderate emotions are essential to making good decisions.

3. Stress activates the autonomic nervous system and the hypothalamus-pituitary-adrenal cortex axis. Both systems have many effects on health and well-being.

4. Aggressive behavior is associated with activity in parts of the hypothalamus and amygdala and with decreased serotonin turnover.

5. The amygdala appears to be critical for learned fears.

> Unfortunately, one of the most significant things ever said about emotion may be that everyone knows what it is until they are asked to define it.
>
> Joseph LeDoux (1996, p. 23)

Actually the situation is even worse than the opening quote implies. There are many items in physics that I don't know how to define correctly—magnetism, for one—that I could nevertheless measure. Emotions are not only difficult to define but also difficult to measure. For example, how would you determine how happy people are? Traditionally psychologists have asked people to rate themselves on a scale from "very happy" to "very unhappy." But how accurate are people's reports? We don't know. When South Americans rate their happiness much greater than Southeast Asians do, on the average, we don't know whether they are really happier or just using the rating scale differently.

The situation is starting to change, however, as researchers begin to get a better grasp of the biology of emotion. We are beginning to measure fear, anxiety, and even anger in ways that do not require self-reports, in ways that apply even to nonhumans. Research on emotion did not begin with a good definition of emotion, but eventually it may end with one.

Opposite:
Have you ever felt like strangling your computer? (This woman apparently does!)

What Is Emotion, Anyway? And What Good Is It?

Suppose researchers have discovered a new species—let's call it species X—and psychologists begin testing its abilities. They place food behind a green card and nothing behind a red card and find that after a few trials X always goes to the green card. So we conclude that X can learn and remember and that it has food motivation. Then researchers offer X a green card and a variety of gray cards; X still goes to the green, so it must have color vision and not just brightness discrimination. Next they let X touch a blue triangle which is extremely hot. X makes a loud sound and backs away. Then someone picks up the blue triangle (with padded gloves) and starts moving with it rapidly toward X. As soon as X sees this happening, it makes the same sound, turns, and starts moving rapidly away. Shall we conclude that it feels the emotion of fear?

If you said yes, now let me add: I said this was a new species, and so it is, but it's a new species of robot, not animal. Do you still think X feels emotions? Most people are willing to grant that the robot has learning, memory, food motivation, and color vision, but they won't agree that it has emotion. "It was just programmed to make that sound and move away from hot objects," they say. "It's not really *feeling* an emotion." (If such behavior isn't adequate evidence for emotion in a robot, is it adequate evidence for emotion in an animal?)

Is there anything a robot could do that would convince you it had emotions? Probably not. We are in the same situation as we were with consciousness in Chapter 1. Most people regard emotion as an internal conscious state. We confidently infer that other humans have emotions, and we infer emotions almost as confidently for chimpanzees, monkeys, dogs, and other mammals. About fish we are less certain; about insects we are doubtful; and when it comes to robots we just say no. But note that we never actually observe internal experiences, and therefore a scientific study is problematic, to say the least.

One possible approach, advocated by Antonio Damasio (1999), is to identify *emotions* as observable behaviors (such as running away) and to separate them from *feelings* (the private experiences). Scientific study would concentrate on the observable emotions and give them operational definitions. (An *operational defini-*tion specifies the operations one could use to produce something or measure it.) This suggestion has the virtue that it can lead to research progress.

Damasio further argues that it is no coincidence that we infer emotional feelings only when we also infer consciousness. He argues that emotional feelings occur only if consciousness is present. For example, people in a coma do not have emotions. Here is another example: People with an **absence seizure** (a type of epilepsy) have brief periods, less than a minute, when they stare blankly without talking or moving. Then they do something without any apparent purpose, such as walking down the hall and sitting in an unfamiliar room. Then, as suddenly as this state began, they suddenly "come to" and wonder where they are and what is happening. They have no recollections of the "absent" period, as if they were unconscious during that time. And relevant to the present point, they show no emotional expressions during the absent period. So apparently we need a certain level of consciousness and arousal to experience emotions. The reverse is less true. That is, we don't need to feel strong emotions to be conscious. However, the **limbic system**—the forebrain areas traditionally regarded as critical for emotion, which form a border around the brain stem—may be a more important part of normal consciousness than researchers had once believed (see Figure 12.1).

Although emotions may require some degree of consciousness, it is possible to have an emotion without being conscious of what caused it. As an experiment three hospital workers agreed to act in special ways toward one brain-damaged patient with severe memory problems. One was as pleasant as possible at all times; the second was neutral; the third was stern, refused all requests, and made the patient perform boring tasks. After 5 days, the patient was asked to look at photos of the three workers and try to identify them or say anything he knew about them. He said he did not recognize any of them. (Remember, he had severe memory problems.) Then he was asked which one he would approach as a possible friend or which one he would ask for help. He was asked this question repeatedly—it was possible to ask repeatedly because he never remembered being asked before—and he usually chose the photo of the "friendly" person and never chose the "unfriendly"

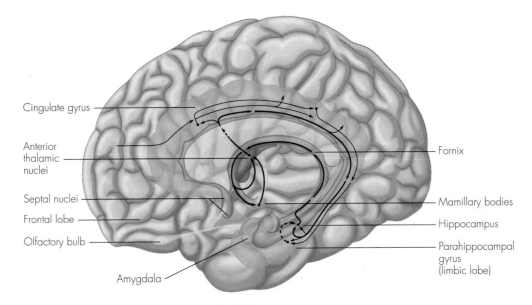

Figure 12.1 The limbic system
The limbic system is a group of structures in the interior of the brain. Here you see them as if you could look through a transparent exterior of the brain. *(Source: Based on MacLean, 1949)*

person in spite of the fact that the "unfriendly" person was a beautiful woman, smiling in the photograph (Tranel & Damasio, 1993). But he didn't know why he preferred one to the other.

Stop & Check

1. What do we learn about emotion by studying people with absence seizures?

2. What is the limbic system?

Check your answers on page 341.

Are Emotions Useful?

We sometimes advise one another to make decisions based on logic, not emotions. Spock, a character in the *Star Trek* series, was portrayed as extremely logical because he kept his emotions almost completely suppressed. Are we right in assuming that emotions get in the way of reasoning?

Extreme emotions can impair reasoning, but a lack of emotions doesn't help. Our most important decisions require a prediction of what will make us feel good or bad and what will make other people feel good or bad. In the words of Antonio Damasio (1999), "Inevitably, emotions are inseparable from the idea of good and evil" (p. 55).

People with certain kinds of prefrontal cortex damage have a striking loss of emotions, and the quality of their decision making suffers. Damasio (1994) exam-

ined a man who, as a result of prefrontal cortex damage, expressed almost no emotions. Nothing angered him; he was never very sad, even about his own brain damage; he never enjoyed anything very much, not even music. Far from being purely rational, he frequently made amazingly stupid decisions, losing his job, his marriage, and his savings. When tested in the laboratory, he had no trouble predicting the probable outcomes of various decisions. For example, when asked what would happen if he cashed a check and the bank teller handed him too much money, he knew the probable consequences of either returning it or walking away with it. But he admitted, "And after all this, I still wouldn't know what to do" (Damasio, 1994, p. 49). He could not even imagine feeling good or bad about various outcomes. He knew that one action would win him approval and another would get him in trouble, but it was not obvious to him that he would prefer approval to trouble!

Investigators also studied two young adults who had suffered prefrontal cortex damage in infancy (Anderson, Bechara, Damasio, Tranel, & Damasio, 1999). Not only did they make bad decisions, but apparently they never learned moral behavior. From childhood onward they frequently stole, lied, physically and verbally abused others, and failed to show any guilt. Neither had any friends and neither could keep a job. But both performed reasonably well on IQ tests.

Here is an experiment to explore further the role of emotions in decision making. People are given a "gambling" task in which they can draw one card at a time from four piles. They always win $100 in play money from decks A and B, $50 from C and D. However, some of the cards also have penalties:

Deck A

Gain $100;
one-half of all
cards also
have penalties
averaging $250

Deck B

Gain $100;
one-tenth of all
cards also
have penalties
of $1250

Deck C

Gain $50;
one-half of all
cards also
have penalties
averaging $50

Deck D

Gain $50;
one-tenth of all
cards also
have penalties
of $250

When you see all the payoffs laid out, you can easily calculate the best strategy: Pick cards only from decks C and D. In the experiment, however, people have to discover the payoffs by trial and error. Ordinarily, as people sample from all four decks, they gradually start showing signs of nervous tension whenever they draw a card from A or B, and they start shifting their preference toward C and D. People with damage to either the frontal cortex or the amygdala (part of the temporal lobe) show very limited signs of emotion. In this experiment they never develop any nervous tension associated with decks A and B, and they continue drawing from those decks (Bechara, Damasio, Damasio, & Lee, 1999). In short, people who can't anticipate the unpleasantness of likely outcomes tend to make bad decisions.

Stop & Check

3. Why do people with frontal cortex or amygdala damage make bad decisions?

Check your answer on page 341.

Emotions and Readiness for Action

When you feel a strong emotion, you are inclined to *do* something, and generally to do it intensely and vigorously. If you are afraid, you want to run away; if you are angry, you want to attack. If you are extremely happy, your response is a little less predictable, but still some sort of vigorous action is likely. What did you do the last time your team won a big game, especially if winning was a surprise? Did you jump, scream, hug all the people standing next to you?

Let's think for a moment about an apparent exception: You're lying in your bed at home when you hear an intruder break into the house. You might lie there frozen with fear, feeling a strong emotion but doing nothing. True, you are not moving at the moment, but your heart is racing. You might continue lying there, hoping the intruder will leave without noticing you, but you are ready to run away or to attack or to do whatever else the situation requires.

In short, it is hard to imagine an emotion without

some sort of body response based on the two branches of the autonomic nervous system: the sympathetic and the parasympathetic. The sympathetic nervous system prepares the body for brief, intense, vigorous responses usually characterized as "fight or flight." The parasympathetic nervous system increases digestion and other processes associated with conservation of energy and preparation for later events. (To review the structure of the sympathetic and parasympathetic nervous systems, see Figure 4.6, p. 92.) However, each situation calls for its own special mixture of sympathetic and parasympathetic arousal (Wolf, 1995). For example, running away from danger requires a different pattern of blood flow and other responses than does swimming away. Nausea includes increased sympathetic stimulation of the stomach (decreasing its contractions and secretions), but increased salivation and intestinal contractions, which are parasympathetic responses.

Exactly what is the relationship between the autonomic nervous system and emotions? Common sense holds that we first feel an emotion, which then causes changes in heart rate and so forth. However, according to the **James-Lange theory** (James, 1884), the autonomic arousal and skeletal actions come first; what we experience as an emotion is the label we give to our responses: I am afraid *because* I run away; I am angry *because* I attack.

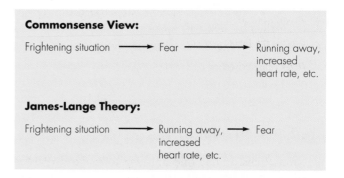

Commonsense View:

Frightening situation → Fear → Running away, increased heart rate, etc.

James-Lange Theory:

Frightening situation → Running away, increased heart rate, etc. → Fear

Note that the James-Lange theory has two key assumptions. The first is that the body's response comes first, before the emotion (which is just a perception of that response anyway). The second is that each discriminable emotion produces a different body response. That is, you can discern whether you are angry, frightened, disgusted, happy, sad, or whatever by perceiving what your body is doing.

Walter Cannon (1929), the physiologist most responsible for discovering the functions of the autonomic nervous system, challenged this view by arguing that the sympathetic nervous system (SNS) responds too slowly to be the cause of emotional states, and besides, it operates as a unit. Thus the SNS responds the same way to fear as to anger, and it cannot tell us which emotion we are feeling. According to the **Cannon-Bard theory,** an event, such as a frenzied killer running toward you with a chain saw, evokes the emotional experience and the physical arousal simultaneously but independently.

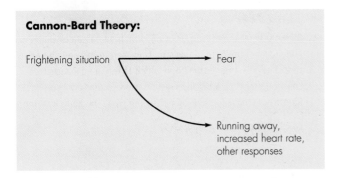

Cannon-Bard Theory:

Frightening situation → Fear

→ Running away, increased heart rate, other responses

Figure 12.2 Effect of facial expression on emotion
People who hold a pen in their teeth, and who are therefore forced to smile, are more likely to report amusement or humor than are people who hold a pen in their lips, who are therefore not smiling.

Later researchers found that Cannon overstated the degree to which the sympathetic nervous system operates the same with all emotions (Levenson, 1992). Furthermore the brain gets information not just from the sympathetic nervous system but from everything in the body that responds to a situation—the skeletal muscles, hormones, facial expressions, and so forth—and each of these responds differently to different emotional situations.

To test the James-Lange theory adequately, we need to know whether different emotions produce sensations that are different enough to define the experience. Most researchers report that the physiological differences among emotions are small and probably insufficient to identify one experience from another (Lang, 1994), but we don't have adequate data to say for sure. Ideally, imagine the following: I am placed in a series of situations designed to please me, frighten me, and anger me. Various devices attached to my body record my heart rate, blood pressure, skin temperature, muscle twitches, hormonal secretions, and so forth; wires are connected to devices attached to your body in another room so as to make your heart rate, blood pressure, and so forth the same as mine. Now you have the same physiological responses I do at the same time. Will you experience the same emotions I do? According to the James-Lange theory, yes, you will have exactly the same emotions I do! According to the Cannon-Bard theory, you might feel no emotion. According to yet another theory, the **Schachter-Singer theory,** the physiological changes would tell you how strong your emotion is, but you would need some cognitive appraisal (such as the sight of a bear charging you) to identify which emotion it is.

It would be a nice experiment in principle, but we don't have the technology to do it. Here's something on a much smaller scale that you can try with yourself or with any friends you can cajole into participating: Hold a pen in

your mouth, either with your teeth or with your lips, as shown in Figure 12.2. Now examine a page of comic strips in your newspaper. Mark each one + for very funny, ✓ for somewhat funny, or – for not funny. Most people rate cartoons funnier when holding a pen with their teeth—which forces a smile—than when holding it with their lips—which prevents a smile (Strack, Martin, & Stepper, 1988). That is, your perception of your body does influence your emotion, at least in this one way.

Another way to test the James-Lange theory would be to study people who lose sensations from their bodies and see what emotions they feel, if any. People who have endured spinal cord injuries lose sensation from parts of the body below the level of the damage. Many of them report decreased intensity of emotions, but certainly not a complete absence (Lowe & Carroll, 1985). However, they have not lost all sensation; they still receive information from everything above the level of the damage, including the cranial nerves, and they receive hormonal and other messages through the blood.

Perhaps more decisive are cases of **locked-in syndrome,** in which a person has damage in the ventral part of the brain stem, as shown in Figure 12.3. Such people continue to receive sensations (which travel through the dorsal brain stem), but they almost completely lose their output from the brain to the muscles. The only voluntary movements that remain are a few eye movements, and these people can learn to blink their eyes to spell out messages. We might imagine that the experience would be utter terror, but most patients report being remarkably tranquil—yes, frustrated and sad, but without the panic that an average person would feel if bound and gagged. Damasio's (1999) interpretation is that the person cannot send out any messages to make the muscles fidget, to cause "butterflies in the stomach," or to produce any other body changes, and therefore the brain receives messages of only tranquillity!

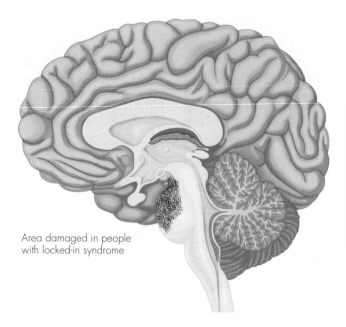

Figure 12.3 Brain damage that causes locked-in syndrome
People with damage in the ventral brain stem receive sensory input but lose almost all voluntary control of their muscles. They can communicate with others only by blinking their eyes.

Note that this interpretation requires a loop between the brain and the periphery:

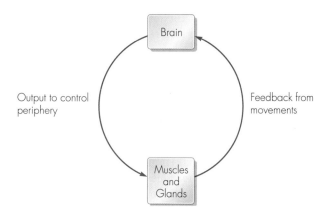

Here's one more patient whose behavior seems relevant to the James-Lange theory: A 16-year-old girl was undergoing brain surgery to remove an epileptic focus. As is often done, the surgeons conducted the surgery with only scalp anesthesia, so they could probe her brain while she was awake enough to report the results. (Sometimes surgeons stimulate a spot and the patient says, "Oh, that's the way I feel when I'm about to have one of my seizures." Then the surgeons know they are close to the epileptic focus.) When they stimulated one particular spot, she smiled. When they stimulated it again a bit more strongly, she laughed. They stimulated repeatedly, and each time she laughed. More to the point, not only did she laugh, but she always found a

reason for her laughter such as, "Oh you guys are so funny . . . standing around" (Fried, Wilson, MacDonald, & Behnke, 1998). She interpreted her body's response (laughter) as an emotion (amusement).

Stop & Check

4. Of the several theories of emotion, which one assumes that the body reacts rapidly to a new situation, before the person begins to experience an emotion? And which theory assumes that each emotion produces a distinctive sensation so that a person could identify the emotion just by perceiving what the body is doing?

Check your answers on page 341.

Module 12.1

In Closing: Emotions and the Mind

Occasionally students ask, "All of this biological psychology is fine, but what does it have to do with *real* psychology?" First, *all* of biological psychology is "real" psychology! But second, in the case of emotions, the relevance of biological investigations may be clearer than usual. Only by studying brain-damaged people with deficient emotions do we begin to understand how important emotions are to our lives. And the studies of the autonomic nervous system give us a powerful route to understanding what we really mean by *emotion*.

Summary

1. Most people understand the term *emotion* to imply an internal state which we can only infer in others, never observe. Science does better to concentrate on observable emotional behaviors. (p. 336)

2. When people appear to lack consciousness, as in the case of absence seizures, they also appear to lack emotions. Emotions may be integral to consciousness. (p. 336)

3. People with severely impaired emotions have trouble imagining which outcome they would prefer because they cannot imagine their emotional responses to those outcomes. Therefore they make poor decisions. (p. 337)

4. Emotional states activate parts of the autonomic nervous system. The sympathetic nervous system readies the body for vigorous movements, "fight or flight." The parasympathetic nervous system readies the body for energy conservation. (p. 338)

5. According to the James-Lange theory, emotion is one's perception of body changes. That is, the body

reacts first, before the experience of emotion, and each emotional state has its own distinctive sensation. (p. 338)

6. It is difficult to test the James-Lange theory definitively. However, people who cannot make any muscle movements (in the locked-in syndrome) have weakened emotions. Getting someone to smile or laugh induces a sensation of happiness or amusement. (p. 339)

Answers to *Stop and Check* Questions

1. People with absence seizures have brief periods when they seem to be unconscious. They move around purposelessly and fail to remember the episode later. They also fail to show emotions during these periods, so consciousness may be intimately linked with emotions. (p. 337)

2. The limbic system is a set of forebrain structures that surround the brain stem. It includes the hypothalamus, the amygdala, the hippocampus, and several other structures. The limbic system is particularly important for emotional behaviors. (p. 337)

3. People with frontal cortex or amygdala damage have much weakened emotions and cannot imagine how they will feel as a result of various outcomes. Therefore they do not get nervous when they are about to do something that will probably lead to a bad outcome. (p. 338)

4. In both cases it is the James-Lange theory. (p. 340)

Thought Question

You are sent as a psychologist-astronaut to the planet Zipton, which has animal life. However, the animals are made of silicon, not carbon, and their physiology is totally unlike ours. They do have learning, memory, vision, hearing, hunger, and sexual behaviors. Your task is to determine whether they also have emotions. How would you proceed?

Module 12.2

Stress and Health

In the early days of scientific medicine, physicians made little allowance for the relation of personality or emotions to health and disease. If someone became ill, the cause had to be structural, like a virus or bacterium. Today **behavioral medicine** emphasizes the effects on health of diet, smoking, exercise, stressful experiences, and other behaviors. We now accept the idea that emotions and other experiences influence people's illnesses and patterns of recovery. This view does not imply any mystical concept of "mind over matter"; stress and emotions are brain activities, after all.

Stress and the Autonomic Nervous System

The term *stress*, like the term *emotion,* is hard to define and hard to quantify. Many people use some variant of Hans Selye's (1979) definition that **stress** is the nonspecific response of the body to any demand made upon it. Selye included favorable events such as getting married or taking a new job as stressors, and indeed they can be stressful, but the stressors with the greatest effects on health are the unpleasant ones. Stress activates the autonomic nervous system rapidly and the hypothalamus-pituitary-adrenal cortex axis more slowly; both systems have major effects on health and well-being. We begin with the autonomic system. We have already considered the autonomic nervous system on pages 91–93, which you might want to review. Figure 12.4 provides a reminder of the anatomy.

Psychosomatic Illnesses

If the onset of an illness is influenced by someone's personality, emotions, or experiences, we call the illness *psychosomatic.* By that definition probably most illnesses are psychosomatic—and note that a psychosomatic illness is a real illness, not something imaginary. Many of the clearest examples of psychosomatic influences on illness include some aspect of autonomic nervous system activity.

Ulcers Beginning in the 1950s psychologists found evidence that stressful experiences can lead to ulcers. For example, rats were arranged in yoked pairs, in which one rat could run in a wheel to avoid shocks, but if it failed to run when it heard the warning signal, both it and its yoked partner received a shock to the tail. The rats without control of the shocks developed more ulcers than the rats with control (Weiss, 1971). Note that the sense of control or prediction was critical, not just the shocks themselves, as both rats received the same number of shocks at the same intensity. Rats with damage to the prefrontal cortex, like humans with such damage, don't show much emotional reactivity to events, as measured by hormone secretions and autonomic responses. And they don't get ulcers, even when exposed to the situations that cause ulcers in other rats (Sullivan & Gratton, 1999).

In experiments with monkeys, a monkey that could press a lever to avoid shocks ordinarily developed *more* ulcers than a monkey that could not (Brady, Porter, Conrad, & Mason, 1958). The difference between rats and monkeys reflects a difference in shock-avoidance learning. Monkeys become extremely good at pressing the lever to avoid shock—so good, in fact, that they almost never get shocks after the first hour of testing. Rats never become that good at avoiding shock. If a monkey continues to receive uncontrollable shocks, it too develops ulcers, just as a rat without control does (Foltz & Millett, 1964).

You might assume the ulcers develop during the shock-avoidance sessions. In fact they develop *during the rest periods* between shock sessions (Desiderato, MacKinnon, & Hissom, 1974). During the shock-avoidance sessions, the sympathetic nervous system increases heart rate and decreases stomach secretions and contractions. During the rest period, the parasympathetic nervous system input to the stomach, previously suppressed, undergoes a rebound increase in activation, leading to greater than normal stomach secretions and contractions. If there is no food to digest at the moment, what would happen? The stomach secretions attack the lining of the stomach itself, leading to ulcers.

All of this seemed reasonably well established, but in the 1980s researchers reported a bacterium that appeared to be associated with ulcers. Most people still have a bias that an explanation in terms of bacteria or viruses is better than one in terms of emotions, and the

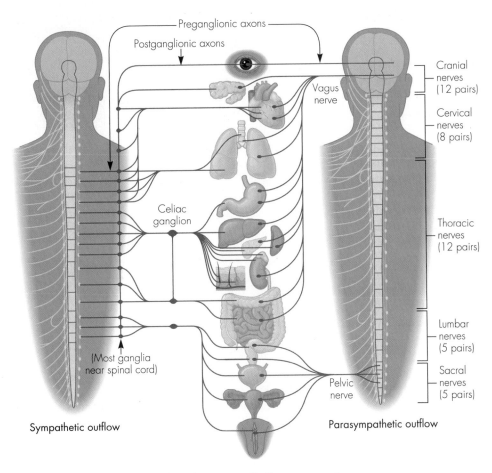

Preganglionic axons
Postganglionic axons
Vagus nerve
Celiac ganglion
(Most ganglia near spinal cord)

Cranial nerves (12 pairs)
Cervical nerves (8 pairs)
Thoracic nerves (12 pairs)
Lumbar nerves (5 pairs)
Sacral nerves (5 pairs)
Pelvic nerve

Sympathetic outflow   Parasympathetic outflow

Figure 12.4 The sympathetic and parasympathetic nervous systems
Review pages 91–93 for more information.

stress-based explanation of ulcers fell into neglect. Later, however, researchers found that only about 80% of ulcer patients have this bacterium in their stomach, and almost as many people *without* ulcers also have the bacterium. Furthermore antibacterial drugs are only slightly better at relieving ulcers than are placebos. In short, the bacterium is not the cause of ulcers, although it probably increases the risk. The psychosomatic explanation in terms of stress and the autonomic nervous system is back in business (Overmier & Murison, 1997).

Heart Disease   A number of studies have reported that heart disease is more common among people who are frequently hostile than among people who are relaxed and easygoing (Booth-Kewley & Friedman, 1987). However, researchers have not found the strong link we might expect between hostile emotions and high blood pressure or high heart rate (Jorgensen, Johnson, Kolodziej, & Schreer, 1996). Presumably the reason is that emotional influences on heart function are smaller and less consistent than those of genetics, diet, and exercise (T. Q. Miller, Smith, Turner, Guijarro, & Hallet, 1996).

A more dependable finding is that people who have strong social support—that is, friends and family to help them through their trying experiences—tend to keep their heart rate and blood pressure low, and therefore maintain better health than people without such support (Uchino, Cacioppo, & Kiecolt-Glaser, 1996). Presumably the social support acts by moderating influences that would otherwise produce excessive sympathetic nervous system arousal.

Voodoo Death and Related Phenomena

Almost everyone knows of someone with a strong will to live who survived well beyond others' expectations and of others who apparently "gave up" and died sooner than expected. An extreme case of the latter is *voodoo death*, in which a healthy person dies apparently just because he or she believes that a curse has destined death.

Such phenomena were generally ignored by scientists until Walter Cannon (1942) published a collection of reasonably well-documented reports of voodoo death. In a typical example a woman who ate a fruit and then learned that it had come from a taboo place died within hours. The common pattern in such cases was that the intended victims knew about the magic spells and believed that they were sure to die. Friends and relatives, who also believed in the hex, began to treat the victim as a dying person. Overwhelmed with dread and hopelessness, the victim refused food and water and died, usually within 24 to 48 hours. Similar examples occur in almost any society—not necessarily that people die because they believe they are hexed, but people with minor illnesses or injuries die because they expect to.

What is the cause of death in such cases? Curt Richter accidentally stumbled on a possible answer while studying the swimming abilities of rats. Why he cared about rat swimming, I don't know, but sometimes researchers experience *serendipity*, the process of stumbling upon something interesting while looking for something less interesting. Ordinarily rats can swim in turbulent warm water nonstop for 48 hours or more. However, a rat's whiskers are critical to its ability to find its way around, and Richter (1957a) found that a rat died quickly if he cut off its whiskers just before throwing it into the tank. It swam frantically for a minute or so and then suddenly sank to the bottom, dead. Richter found that under these conditions many, but not all, laboratory rats died quickly. Wild rats, which are more excitable, all died quickly under the same conditions. Autopsies showed that they had not drowned; their hearts had simply stopped beating.

Richter's explanation was that dewhiskering the rat and then suddenly throwing it into water greatly stimulated the rat's sympathetic nervous system and thus its heart rate. After the rat swam frantically for a minute or so and found no escape, its parasympathetic system became highly activated in rebound from the strong sympathetic activation. Massive parasympathetic response may have stopped the rat's heart altogether.

To confirm this explanation, Richter placed a rat in the water several times, rescuing it each time. Then he cut off the rat's whiskers and put it in the water again. The rescues apparently immunized the rat against extreme terror in this situation; it swam successfully for many hours. Richter's results suggest that certain cases of sudden death in a frightening situation may be due to excessive parasympathetic activity.

Does this explanation apply to many cases of heart attacks? Probably not. Most heart attacks begin when excessive sympathetic nervous system activity disrupts the normal rhythmic beating of the heart (Kamarck & Jennings, 1991). Excessive parasympathetic activity is probably a serious problem only under limited circumstances.

Stop & Check

1. Is the immediate cause of ulcer formation more likely to be increased sympathetic or parasympathetic input to the stomach?

2. Did Richter attribute sudden death (voodoo death) to increased sympathetic or parasympathetic input to the heart?

Check your answers on page 348.

Stress and the Hypothalamus-Pituitary-Adrenal Cortex Axis

Stress activates two body systems. One is the autonomic nervous system, which reacts quickly. The other is the **HPA axis**—the hypothalamus, pituitary gland, and adrenal cortex. Activation of the hypothalamus induces the anterior pituitary gland to secrete the hormone adrenocorticotropic hormone (**ACTH**), which in turn stimulates the human adrenal cortex to secrete **cortisol**, which elevates blood sugar and enhances metabolism (see Figure 12.5). (In rats it releases corticosterone instead.) Compared to the autonomic nervous

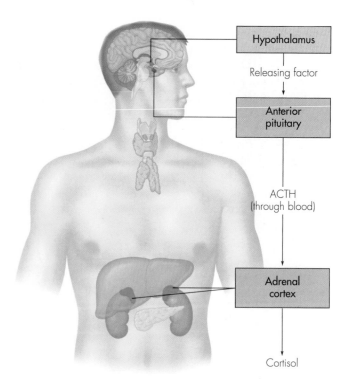

Figure 12.5 The hypothalamus-anterior pituitary-adrenal cortex axis
Prolonged stress leads to the secretion of the adrenal hormone cortisol, which elevates blood sugar and increases metabolism. These changes help the body sustain prolonged activity but at the expense of decreased immune system activity.

system, the HPA axis reacts more slowly, but it becomes increasingly important with prolonged stressors. For example, the government builds a toxic waste dump in your neighborhood; a loved one develops a chronic illness and requires almost constant care; your business is on the verge of failure and you face a constant worry of paying the bills.

Many researchers refer to cortisol as a "stress hormone" and even use measurements of cortisol level as an indication of someone's recent stress level. Cortisol helps the body mobilize its energies to fight a difficult situation and in the short run is beneficial to health. However, prolonged elevations of cortisol can become harmful. To see why, we start with an overview of the immune system.

The Immune System

The **immune system** consists of cells that protect the body against such intruders as viruses and bacteria. The immune system is like a police force: If it is too weak, the "criminals" (viruses and bacteria) run wild and create damage; if it becomes too strong or too unselective, it attacks "law-abiding citizens" (the body's own cells). When the immune system attacks normal cells, we call the result an *autoimmune disease*.

Leukocytes The most important elements of the immune system are the **leukocytes,** commonly known as white blood cells (Kiecolt-Glaser & Glaser, 1993; O'Leary, 1990). Leukocytes are produced in the bone marrow; they migrate to the thymus gland, the spleen, and the peripheral lymph nodes, which store and nurture them until some invader causes their release. The leukocytes patrol the blood and other body fluids, checking each cell. Every body cell has proteins on its surface, and your own body's surface proteins are as unique as your fingerprints. The leukocytes recognize the "self" proteins and spare those cells. But viruses, bacteria, and organ transplants have surface proteins and other molecules different from your own (nonself). We call these intruder molecules **antigens** (antibody-generator molecules). When a leukocyte finds an alien cell with antigens, it attacks.

The immune system's specific defense against an intruder begins with two kinds of cells: macrophages and B cells. A **macrophage** surrounds a bacterium or other intruder, digests it, and exposes its antigens on the macrophage's own surface. A **B cell** (a leukocyte that matures in the bone marrow) also attaches to an intruder and produces specific antibodies to attack the intruder's antigen. **Antibodies** are Y-shaped proteins that circulate in the blood, each kind specifically attaching to one kind of antigen, just as a key fits only one lock. The body develops antibodies against the particular antigens that it has encountered. If you ever had measles, for example, your immune system has developed antibodies against the measles virus and protects you against a further outbreak of the same disease. The strategy behind a vaccination is that introducing a weakened form of the virus causes the immune system to develop antibodies against the virus without actually getting the disease.

Another kind of leukocytes, the **T cells** (so named because they mature in the thymus), have two types. The cytotoxic T cells directly attack intruder cells; the helper T cells stimulate other T cells or B cells to multiply more rapidly. Some of the B cells become plasma cells that specialize in producing antibodies against the particular antigen that the original B cell encountered. Others differentiate into *memory cells,* which circulate in search of additional intruders like the first one. Figure 12.6 summarizes this process.

Natural Killer Cells Blood cells that attach to certain kinds of tumor cells and cells infected with viruses are known as **natural killer cells.** Natural killer cells are relatively nonspecific in their targets. Unlike an antibody

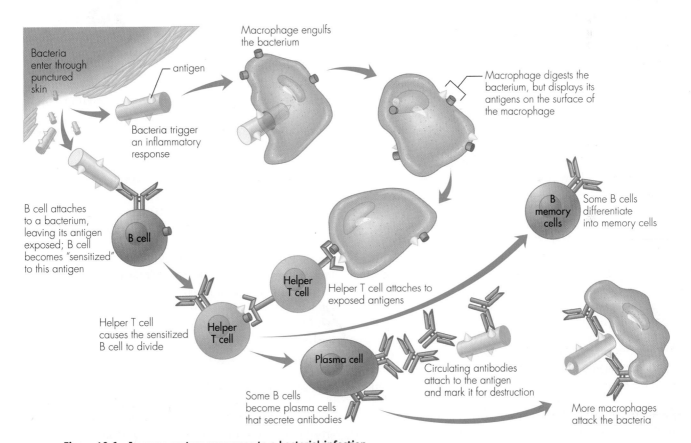

Figure 12.6 Immune system responses to a bacterial infection
A macrophage cell engulfs a bacterial cell and displays one of the bacteria's antigens on its surface. Meanwhile a B cell also binds to the bacteria and produces antibodies against the bacteria. A helper T cell attaches to both the macrophage and the B cell; it stimulates the B cell to generate copies of itself, called B memory cells, which immunize the body against future invasions by the same kind of bacteria.

or a T cell, each of which attacks only one kind of intruder, a natural killer cell can attack several kinds.

Cytokines When you feel sick, what are your usual symptoms? You will likely think of fever, sleepiness, lack of energy, and lack of appetite. You might not mention decreased sex drive, but that is a common symptom, too. All of these symptoms are brought about by **cytokines** (such as interleukin-1, or IL-1), chemicals released activate immune system cells to attack infections and also communicate with the brain to elicit anti-illness behaviors (Maier & Watkins, 1998). In a sense, cytokines are the immune system's way of telling the brain that the body is ill. Ordinarily only tiny amounts of cytokines cross the blood-brain barrier (although sometimes the blood-brain barrier is weakened during illness). Rather the cytokines in the periphery stimulate receptors on the vagus nerve (see Figure 4.9, p. 94), which relays a message to cells in the hypothalamus and hippocampus, which then release cytokines themselves. (You might think of it as something like sending a fax, where the original material doesn't travel, but the recipient makes a copy of it.)

The cytokines that are released in the brain instigate a variety of behaviors to attack the illness. Fever, as discussed in Chapter 10, is part of the body's defense against illness because most viruses do not thrive at high temperatures. Sleepiness, decreased muscle activity, and decreased sex drive are useful ways of conserving energy while the body is attacking the illness. Cytokines also decrease appetite. The usefulness of decreasing appetite is less obvious; we might guess that the body needs extra food to fight the illness. One explanation is that blood iron levels decline during fasting, and many viruses need iron. Another is that finding food is hard work for most animals; it might be better when sick to live off one's stored reserves for awhile.

Effects of Stress on the Immune System

Contrary to assumptions long held in biology, we now know that the nervous system has considerable control over the immune system. The study of this relationship, called **psychoneuroimmunology**, deals with the ways in which experiences, especially stressful ones, alter the immune system, and how the immune system in turn influences the central nervous system (O'Leary, 1990; Vollhardt, 1991).

The body reacts to different stressors in different ways. For example, it treats many powerful, inescapable, but temporary stressors like illnesses: It mobilizes the immune system and increases cytokine secretion. For instance, rats subjected to inescapable shocks develop a fever, increase their sleep, and decrease their appetite and sex drive. The same sometimes happens with people under much stress, such as people who are nervous about giving a public speech (Maier & Watkins, 1998).

Stress also activates the sympathetic nervous system and HPA axis. Brief activation of either system actually strengthens the immune response and thereby helps to attack viruses and even tumors (Benschop et al., 1995). The same is true for occasional bursts of emotion; even the "negative" emotions of fear and anger boost the activity of the immune system—briefly (Mayne, 1999).

What is harmful is *continued, long-term* anxiety, anger, or stress. A prolonged increase of cortisol directs energy toward increasing blood sugar and metabolism, but therefore away from synthesis of proteins, including the proteins of the immune system. For example, in 1979 at the Three Mile Island nuclear power plant, a major accident was barely contained. The people who continued to live in the vicinity during the next year had lower than normal levels of B cells, T cells, and natural killer cells. They also complained of emotional distress and showed impaired performance on a proofreading task (A. Baum, Gatchel, & Schaeffer, 1983; McKinnon, Weisse, Reynolds, Bowles, & Baum, 1989). A study of research scientists in the Antarctic found that a 9-month period of cold, darkness, and social isolation reduced T cell functioning to about half of normal levels (Tingate, Lugg, Muller, Stowe, & Pierson, 1997). Natural killer cells are suppressed in women whose husbands are dying of cancer, women whose husbands died within the past 6 months, and medical students going through an exam period (Glaser, Rice, Speicher, Stout, & Kiecolt-Glaser, 1986; Irwin, Daniels, Risch, Bloom, & Weiner, 1988).

In one study 276 volunteers filled out an extensive questionnaire about stressful life events before being injected with a moderate dose of common cold virus. (The idea was that those with the strongest immune responses could fight off the cold, but others would succumb.) People who reported stressful experiences lasting less than a month were not significantly more at risk for catching cold than were people who reported no stress. However, for people who reported stress lasting longer than a month, the longer it lasted, the greater the risk of illness (S. Cohen et al., 1998). Other studies have shown that stress is particularly destructive in people who simply resign themselves to it; the immune system is stronger, and therefore health is better, when people try to attack their problem and gain some sense of control (Olff, 1999).

Prolonged stress can be harmful in another way also. High cortisol levels increase the vulnerability of neurons in the hippocampus so that toxins or overstimulation will kill the neurons instead of just weakening them temporarily (Sapolsky, 1992). The hippocampus is important for learning and memory (Chapter 13), so a loss of neurons there can lead to serious behavioral problems. Furthermore hippocampal damage leads to increased cortisol levels, so a vicious cycle can develop:

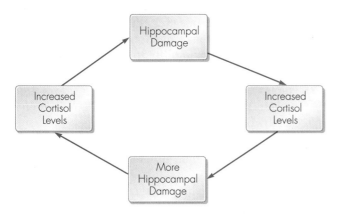

Aged people with the highest cortisol levels tend to be those with the smallest hippocampus and greatest memory problems (Lupien et al., 1998). Although the data do not tell us whether the problem started with cortisol or with hippocampal damage, the suggestion is that prolonged stress may have led to brain damage.

Stop & Check

3. What is the difference between an antigen and an antibody?

4. How do cytokines from the periphery influence brain activity?

5. What behavioral changes do cytokines stimulate?

6. True or false: Fear and anger are consistently harmful to health.

Check your answers on page 348.

Posttraumatic Stress Disorder

People have long recognized that many soldiers returning from battle are prone to continuing anxieties and fears. The condition has been known by such names as *battle fatigue* and *shell shock*; more recently it has been given the label **posttraumatic stress disorder (PTSD)**, which has become a somewhat common psychiatric diagnosis. PTSD occurs in some people who have had a traumatic experience of being severely injured or threatened or seeing other people harmed or killed. The symptoms, which last for months or years, include frequent distressing recollections (flashbacks) and nightmares about the traumatic event, avoidance of reminders of it, and exaggerated arousal in response to noises and other stimuli (American Psychiatric Association, 1994). It often occurs in soldiers who have seen their friends killed and who have nearly been killed themselves; it also occurs in rape victims, kidnap victims, torture victims, and others.

However, of all the people who endure severe traumas, some develop PTSD and others do not (McFarlane, 1997). For example, one night a man kidnapped three college cheerleaders, stuck them in the trunk of his car, and drove to an isolated location. There he left two in the trunk, dragged one out, raped her, and bludgeoned her to death. Then he returned to attack another of them. At that time the other two sprang out and escaped, hiding from him for the rest of the night. Eventually the rapist/murderer was convicted. The two surviving women had undergone the same dreadful ordeal, but only one of them developed PTSD. That one found herself unable to concentrate enough to complete her studies. She was impaired at work and chronically unable to relate romantically to men. She could not sleep, was terror-stricken by any reminder of the ordeal, and was constantly afraid that the attacker would escape from prison and attack her again. At one point she even got an apartment overlooking the state prison so she could watch to make sure there were no escapes. The other surviving woman, in contrast, completed her education, got a good job, got married, had children, and only occasionally thought about that terrible night (Krueger & Neff, 1995).

Why does a traumatic experience produce PTSD in some people and not in others? Researchers do not know, but presumably some people are more vulnerable than others before the trauma. Studies have found that most PTSD victims have a smaller than average hippocampus (Stein, Hanna, Koverola, Torchia, & McClarty, 1997). This result could represent a biological difference that predisposed these people to PTSD, or it could have developed after PTSD. (The only way to decide would be to test people before and after a severe trauma.) It might seem natural to assume that the relatively small hippocampus in PTSD victims represents damage from prolonged elevations in cortisol secretion. Indeed that scenario is possible; however, by the time PTSD victims are tested, most of them have significantly *lower* than normal cortisol levels (Yehuda, 1997). The low levels suggest another possibility: If some people have a lifelong pattern of low cortisol levels, well, cortisol is an important way of combating stress, so such people might be ill-equipped to withstand severe stress, and the stress might do them more damage than it does to most. Certainly much more research is needed, but the conclusion at present is that PTSD is not just a prolongation of the normal stress response.

Stop & Check

7. Name one way in which PTSD differs from a normal stress reaction.

Check your answer on page 348.

In Closing: Emotions and Body Reactions

Research on stress and health is often difficult to interpret. For example, it is sometimes difficult to determine which chemical changes in the brain are symptoms of stress and which are mechanisms of coping with stress (Stanford, 1995). Also, most research on stress and health does not distinguish between direct and indirect effects (S. Cohen & Williamson, 1991). For example, when we find that people with social support recover better from an illness than people without such support, is the difference due to effects of the autonomic and immune systems? Or is it that people with social support are likely to take their prescribed medicines and exercise and eat properly? Determining the relationship between experience and illness is a major long-term research challenge.

Summary

1. Stressful experiences activate the autonomic nervous system, with different responses for different stressors. The results can combine with other influences to affect health. For example, periods of inescapable, unpredictable shocks (rats) or intense work (monkeys) activate the sympathetic nerves that increase heart rate and decrease stomach secretions and contractions. During the rest periods immediately after these sessions, the parasympathetic nerves increase stomach secretions and contractions, increasing the risk of ulcers. (p. 342)

2. Heart disease is more common among people who are frequently hostile and less common in those with much social support. The mechanisms of these effects are not yet established. (p. 343)

3. Rat studies suggest that some cases of voodoo death or other sudden death could be due to strong parasympathetic inhibition of heart rate following a period of intense activation of heart rate by the sympathetic nervous system. (p. 343)

4. The immune system includes several kinds of leukocytes (white blood cells) that attack viruses, bacteria, and other alien cells. (p. 345)

5. In response to infection the immune system also releases cytokines that stimulate the vagus nerve, which in turn causes cells in the hypothalamus and hippocampus to release their own cytokines. Within the brain, cytokines increase fever and sleepiness and decrease appetite and sex drive. All these responses help fight disease. (p. 346)

6. Stressors activate the HPA axis—hypothalamus, pituitary gland, and adrenal cortex. The adrenal cortex secretes the hormone cortisol, which elevates blood sugar and metabolism. If prolonged, the increased cortisol directs energy away from synthesis of proteins, including those necessary for the immune system. Therefore prolonged stress increases one's vulnerability to viruses and bacteria. (p. 344)

7. The high cortisol levels associated with prolonged stress can also damage cells in the hippocampus, thereby impairing memory. (p. 346)

8. Posttraumatic stress disorder (PTSD) shows some special features that differentiate it from other stress. In particular, people with PTSD have, surprisingly, *lower* than normal cortisol levels. (p. 347)

Answers to *Stop and Check* Questions

1. Parasympathetic activity contributes to ulcer formation. During a period of high stress, the sympathetic nerves decrease stomach secretions and contractions. Ulcers form during the rest periods, when parasympathetic nerves increase the secretions and contractions. (p. 344)

2. Richter attributed sudden death (similar to voodoo death) to extreme parasympathetic inhibition of heart rate. (p. 344)

3. An antigen is a protein or other large molecule that identifies a cell as being part of the "self" or an "intruder." An antibody is a chemical that the immune system secretes to attack an antigen. (p. 347)

4. Cytokines stimulate receptors on the vagus nerve, which convey a message to cells in the hypothalamus and hippocampus, which then release cytokines themselves. (p. 347)

5. Cytokines influence neurons, especially in the hypothalamus, to increase fever and sleepiness and to decrease appetite and sex drive. (p. 347)

6. False. Fear, anger, or any other stressor impairs health if continued for a long time, but brief experiences arouse the sympathetic nervous system and enhance the activity of the immune system. (p. 347)

7. Ordinarily stress elevates cortisol levels. People with PTSD have lower than normal cortisol levels. (p. 347)

Thought Questions

1. If you believe you are at risk for ulcers, and you have just had an extremely stressful experience, what might you do to decrease the risk of ulcers?

2. If someone were unable to produce cytokines, what would be the consequences?

Attack and Escape Behaviors

Have you ever watched a cat play with a rat or mouse before killing it? Not all cats do, and some do only occasionally, but when one does, it kicks the rodent, bats it with its paws, tosses it in the air, and sometimes picks it up, shakes it, and carries it. Why? Is the cat sadistically tormenting its prey? No. Most of what we call its "play" behaviors are a compromise between attack and escape: When the rodent is facing away, the cat approaches; if the rodent turns around to face the cat, and especially if it bares its teeth, the cat bats it or kicks it defensively (Pellis et al., 1988). A cat that usually plays with its prey goes for a quick kill if the rodent is small and inactive or if the cat has been given tranquilizers to lower its anxiety. The same cat withdraws altogether if confronted with a large, menacing rodent (Adamec, Stark-Adamec, & Livingston, 1980; Biben, 1979; Pellis et al., 1988). In sum, a cat's responses range along a continuum from attack to escape, and a mixture of the two looks to us like play.

Most of the vigorous emotional behaviors we observe in animals fall into the categories of attack and escape, and it is no coincidence that we describe the sympathetic nervous system as the fight-or-flight system. These behaviors and their corresponding emotions—anger and fear—attract much interest both for neuroscience researchers and for clinical psychologists.

Attack Behaviors

In nonhuman animals the behavior called **affective attack** appears highly emotional. (Do not confuse *affective* with *effective. Affective* comes from the noun *affect,* meaning "emotion.") For example, a cat fighting or threatening another cat shrieks, erects its fur, and increases its heart rate and blood pressure. In contrast, a cat sometimes attacks and kills a mouse smoothly, swiftly, "unemotionally."

Similarly, human attack behavior may be wildly passionate or calm and detached. For example, a soldier in battle may feel no anger toward the enemy, and people sometimes make "cold-blooded" attacks for financial gain. Therefore we can hardly expect to find a single explanation for all aggressive behaviors.

What actually triggers an affective attack is usually some sort of pain or threat, but some individuals attack much more readily than others in response to a given situation, and an individual is more ready to attack at some times than at others. Hamsters provide the clearest demonstration. If a hamster is in its home territory and another hamster intrudes, the home hamster sniffs the intruder and ultimately attacks. Suppose the intruder leaves, and a little later another hamster intrudes. The home hamster attacks faster and more vigorously than before. The probability of attack remains elevated for 30 minutes or more after the first attack (Potegal, 1994). In other words, shortly after an attack, the hamster is primed for further attacks. You might say it's in a mood for a fight. During that period, activity increases in the corticomedial area of the amygdala, a structure in the temporal lobe (Potegal, Ferris, Hebert, Meyerhoff, & Skaredoff, 1996) (see Figure 12.7). In fact it is possible to bypass the experience and prime an attack by stimulating the corticomedial amygdala directly (Potegal, Hebert, DeCoster, & Meyerhoff, 1996).

We do not have equally good data on the role of the human amygdala in attack priming, but the behaviors are similar: After experiencing an insult or other provocation, people are more aggressive than usual for at least the next 5 to 20 minutes, and not just against the person who first provoked them (Potegal, 1994). After some stranger has irritated you, you might yell at your roommate or punch the wall. You have probably been told, "If you become angry, count to ten before you act." Counting to a few thousand would work better, but the idea is correct.

Heredity and Environment in Human Violence

Studies of aggressive, antisocial, and criminal behaviors have found that monozygotic twins resemble each other more closely than dizygotic twins do and that adopted children resemble their biological parents more closely than their adoptive parents (Mason & Frick, 1994). Such results suggest a possible genetic influence, but they do not distinguish between the effects of genetics and prenatal environment. (Families with a criminal record tend not to provide the best prenatal healthcare.) One prenatal factor of particular interest is the mother's smoking habits during pregnancy. Two

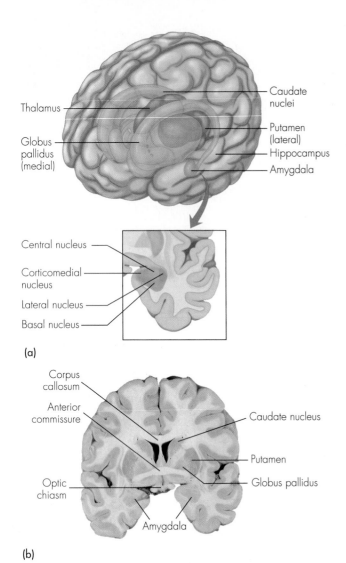

(a)

(b)

Figure 12.7 Location of amygdala in the human brain
The amygdala, located in the interior of the temporal lobe,
receives input from many cortical and subcortical areas. Part
(a) shows a blow-up of separate nuclei of the amygdala.
[Source: (a) After Nieuwenhuys, Voogd, & vanHuijzen, 1988,
and Hanaway, Woolsey, Gado, & Roberts, 1998. (b) Photo
courtesy of Dana Copeland]

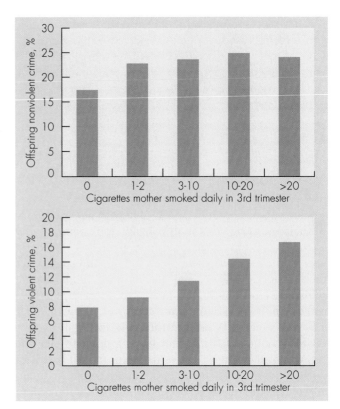

**Figure 12.8 Effects of maternal smoking on later crimi-
nal behavior by her sons**
The greater the number of cigarettes the mother smoked
during the third trimester of pregnancy, the greater the percentage of her sons eventually arrested for violent crimes.
(Source: Brennan, Grekin, & Mednick, 1999)

studies found that the more a woman smoked during
pregnancy, the more likely her son was to be arrested
for criminal activities in adolescence and early adulthood (Brennan, Grekin, & Mednick, 1999; Fergusson,
Woodward, & Horwood, 1998). The effect was particularly strong if the woman smoked *and* had complications during delivery (see Figure 12.8).

(A couple of thoughts: The correlation between smoking in pregnancy and later crime by the child doesn't appear to hold up well across cultures. There are some
countries in Europe where smoking is very common but
crime is not. On the other hand, within the United States,
the prevalence of smoking declined beginning in about
1970, and the crime rate fell for no known reason in the
1990s. Is there a connection? No one knows.)

Suppose genes exist that predispose a person to violence or criminality. How might these genes act? They
act in many ways, no doubt, including just by influencing body size (and therefore probability of winning a
fight). One study found that boys who are taller than
usual at age 3 years tend to be fearless and aggressive.
Apparently their aggressiveness becomes a habit because aggressive behavior at age 11 correlates more
strongly with how tall the boys were at 3 than with how
tall they are at 11 (Raine, Reynolds, Venables, Mednick,
& Farrington, 1998).

Genetic (or prenatal) influences interact with environmental influences in ways that researchers are just
beginning to explore. One study of adopted children
found the highest probability of aggressive behaviors
and conduct disorders among those who had biological
parents with criminal records *and* adoptive parents
with marital discord, depression, substance abuse, or
legal problems. A biological predisposition alone or a
troubled adoptive family by itself produced only moderate effects (Cadoret, Yates, Troughton, Woodworth, &
Stewart, 1995). A study of thousands of twins concluded that juvenile crimes and misbehaviors depended mainly on family environment because dizy-

gotic twins resembled each other almost as much as monozygotic twins. However, monozygotic twins resembled each other in *adult* crimes more than dizygotic twins did (Lyons et al., 1995). That is, the importance of predispositional factors (either genetic or prenatal) actually *increased* in adulthood, perhaps because adult twins have more ability to choose their own environments. A twin who is predisposed to aggressive behaviors will choose friends and activities consistent with similar tendencies and thereby magnify the effects of the predisposition.

Stop & Check

1. With regard to criminal behavior, adopted children resemble their biological relatives more closely than their adoptive relatives. One explanation for this observation is a genetic influence. What is the other?

2. What evidence suggests that criminal behavior depends on a combination of biological predisposition and family environment?

Check your answers on page 360.

Hormones

Most fighting among nonhuman animals is by males competing for mates or females defending their young. Male aggressive behavior depends heavily on testosterone, which is highest for adult males in the reproductive season. Castrated males and males during nonreproductive seasons fight much less (Goldstein, 1974; Moyer, 1974).

Similarly, throughout the world, men fight more often than women, get arrested for violent crimes more often, shout insults at each other more often, and so forth. Moreover the highest incidence of violence, as measured by crime statistics, is in men 15 to 25 years old, who have the highest levels of testosterone in the blood. The occasional studies that fail to find large sex differences in aggression generally fall into one of two categories. First, male–female differences tend to be smaller in studies of *self-reported* aggression or anger than in studies that actually observe aggressive behavior (Knight, Fabes, & Higgins, 1996). Second, women show about as much anger or aggression as men when they are seriously provoked. The difference is that some men pick fights for no apparent reason, whereas few women do (Bettencourt & Miller, 1996).

Among men of the same age, do those with the highest testosterone levels also have the highest rates of violent behavior? Yes, somewhat, although the differences are usually small (Brooks & Reddon, 1996; Dabbs, Carr, Frady, & Riad, 1995; Dabbs & Morris, 1990). Figure 12.9 shows the results of one typical study. Note

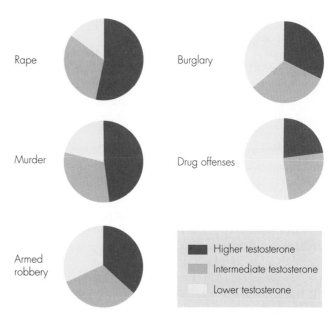

Figure 12.9   Testosterone levels for men convicted of various crimes
Men convicted of rape and murder have higher testosterone levels, on the average, than men convicted of burglary or drug offenses. (*Source: Based on Dabbs, Carr, Frady, & Riad, 1995*)

that men imprisoned for rape or murder include a large percentage with high testosterone levels; those imprisoned for nonviolent crimes had generally lower testosterone levels. Note also, however, that this effect is rather weak.

Temporal Lobe and Violence

As mentioned before, direct electrical stimulation of an animal's corticomedial amygdala can increase the probability of attack against an intruder. The same is true for stimulation of the ventromedial nucleus of the hypothalamus. Do not become confused: Yes, as we saw in the last two chapters, the ventromedial nucleus of the hypothalamus is important for control of eating and sexual behavior as well as aggressive behavior. Obviously we should not think of it as an "aggression area" or a "satiety area"; it contributes to many different behaviors.

At any rate, increased activity in the ventromedial hypothalamus increases the likelihood of attack, and testosterone exerts part of its effect on aggression by facilitating the activity in this area (Delville, Mansour, & Ferris, 1996). Stimulation of either the ventromedial hypothalamus itself or certain of the areas it controls in the brain stem can increase aggressive behavior. Depending on the exact location of the brain stimulation, the animal might attack another animal or might make a series of undirected growls and facial movements (A. Siegel & Pott, 1988) (see Figure 12.10).

Stimulation of the amygdala, an area in the temporal lobe (see Figure 12.7), can also lead to vigorous affective attacks. Animals with an epileptic *focus* (point of origin) in the amygdala often show an increase in aggressive behavior (Pinel, Treit, & Rovner, 1977). **Rabies,** which leads to furious, violent behavior, is a disease caused by a virus that attacks much of the brain but especially the temporal lobe (including the amygdala) (Lentz, Burrage, Smith, Crick, & Tignor, 1982). (*Rabies* is the Latin term for "rage.")

Damage to or removal of the amygdala usually leads to tameness and placidity. Monkeys with extensive damage in this area develop the *Klüver-Bucy syndrome,* as mentioned in Chapter 4. They attempt to pick up snakes, lighted matches, and other objects that they ordinarily avoid; male monkeys sink to the bottom of the dominance hierarchy because they do not react normally to other monkeys' threat gestures and other social signals (Rosvold, Mirsky, & Pribram, 1954). The basis for the Klüver-Bucy syndrome probably includes both impairment of emotional response and difficulty interpreting visual information.

Can irritation of the temporal lobe, such as in temporal lobe epilepsy, provoke violent behavior in humans as well? An epileptic attack occurs when a large group of neurons suddenly produces synchronous action potentials. When the epileptic focus is in the temporal lobe, the symptoms include hallucinations, lip smacking or other repetitive acts, and in certain cases emotional behaviors.

Here is a description of a patient with temporal lobe epilepsy who had sudden outbursts of unprovoked violent behavior (Mark & Ervin, 1970):

> Thomas was a 34-year-old engineer, who, at the age of 20, had suffered a ruptured peptic ulcer. The resulting internal bleeding deprived his brain of blood and produced brain damage. Although his intelligence and creativity were unimpaired, there were some serious changes in his behavior, including outbursts of violent rage, sometimes against strangers and sometimes against people he knew. Sometimes his episodes began when he was talking to his wife. He would then interpret something she said as an insult, throw her against the wall and attack her brutally for 5 to 6 minutes. After one of these attacks, he would go to sleep for a half hour and wake up feeling refreshed.
>
> Eventually, he was taken to a hospital, where epileptic activity was found in the temporal lobes of his cerebral cortex. For the next 7 months, he was given a combination of tranquilizers, antiepileptic drugs, and other medications. None of these treatments reduced his violent behavior. He had previously been treated by psychiatrists for 7 years without apparent effect. Eventually, he agreed to a surgical operation to destroy a small part of the amygdala on both sides of the brain. Afterwards, he had no more episodes of rage, although he continued to have periods of confusion and disordered thinking.

It is difficult to estimate how many people with temporal lobe epilepsy have violent outbursts because this kind of epilepsy is difficult to diagnose and violent behavior is difficult to measure (Volavka, 1990). In many instances antiepileptic drugs have shown promise in controlling episodic violent behavior.

Many people with damage in the prefrontal cortex also fight or threaten more frequently than other people or on less provocation (Giancola, 1995). However, people with prefrontal impairments have a general loss of inhibitions and a tendency toward many socially inappropriate behaviors, not just violent ones.

Serotonin Synapses and Aggressive Behavior

Several lines of evidence link low serotonin release with increased aggressive behavior.

Nonhuman Animals   Much of the earliest evidence for this conclusion came from studies on mice. Luigi Valzelli (1973) found that 4 weeks of social isolation induced a *decrease in serotonin turnover* in the brains of the male mice. **Turnover** is the amount of release and resynthesis of a neurotransmitter by presynaptic neurons. That is, a brain with low serotonin turnover might have a normal amount of serotonin, but the neurons fail to release it and synthesize new serotonin to take its

Figure 12.10   Effects of stimulation in the medial hypothalamus
Stimulation in some brain areas can lead to a full attack; in this case the result was undirected growling and facial expressions, a mere fragment of a normal attack. *(Source: Delgado, 1981)*

place. Turnover can be inferred from the concentration of 5-hydroxyindoleacetic acid (5-HIAA), a serotonin metabolite, in the blood, cerebrospinal fluid (CSF), or urine. When 5-HIAA levels are low, serotonin turnover is low.

Valzelli further found that when social isolation lowered a male mouse's serotonin turnover, it also induced increased aggressive behavior toward other males. If he placed two males with low serotonin turnover together, he could count on them to fight. Comparing different genetic strains of mice, he found that those with the lowest serotonin turnover fought the most (Valzelli & Bernasconi, 1979). Social isolation does not decrease serotonin turnover in female mice in any genetic strain, and it does not make the females aggressive. Later studies found excessive attack behaviors in mice that are deficient in one particular serotonin receptor, type 5-HT$_{1B}$ (Saudou et al., 1994).

In a fascinating natural-environment study, investigators measured 5-HIAA levels in 2-year-old male monkeys and then observed their behavior closely. The monkeys in the lowest quartile for 5-HIAA, and therefore the lowest quartile for serotonin turnover, were the most aggressive, had the greatest probability of attacking larger monkeys, and showed the greatest number of scars and wounds. Most of them died by the age of 6, whereas all monkeys in the highest quartile for serotonin turnover were still alive at 6 (Higley et al., 1996).

Why has natural selection not eliminated the genes for low serotonin turnover, given that most monkeys with low turnover die young? At this point one can only speculate. For example, maybe picking fights all the time is a high-risk, high-payoff strategy: Sure, if you pick a lot of fights, you'll probably get killed, but if you win enough to survive, you're on your way to being a very dominant male monkey and probably the father of a great many young. (It's a nice hypothesis, but we don't have data to test it yet.)

Neuroscientists are far from understanding the mechanisms that link low serotonin activity with aggressive behavior. However, it seems clear that the link is not specific to aggressive behavior, but more to something like impulsiveness (Brunner & Hen, 1997). Mice that lack one type of serotonin receptor, the 5-HT$_{1B}$ receptor, are not only more aggressive than other mice, they also develop a cocaine addiction faster than normal. In a maze they move "impulsively" from one arm to another without pausing at the choice points the way other mice do. And if given a choice between pressing one lever to get a small reward in 4 seconds or a different lever to get a larger reward after 20 seconds, they are more likely than normal mice to choose the quicker but smaller reward. In short, they seem to act without sufficiently pondering the probable outcomes.

Humans Numerous studies have found low serotonin turnover in people with a history of violent behavior, including people convicted of arson and other violent

crimes (Virkkunen, Nuutila, Goodwin, & Linnoila, 1987) and people who commit or attempt suicide by violent means (G. L. Brown et al., 1982; Edman, Åsberg, Levander, & Schalling, 1986; Mann, Arango, & Underwood, 1990; Pandey et al., 1995). Serotonin turnover varies by 5% to 10% from one time of year to another; one study in Belgium found that suicide rates were highest in spring, when serotonin turnover was lowest, and lowest in fall and winter, when serotonin turnover was highest (Maes et al., 1995).

Even if we do not fully understand how low serotonin activity predisposes to violence, we may be able to use the measurements to make some useful predictions. For example, one study of children and adolescents with a history of aggressive behavior found that those with the lowest serotonin turnover were most likely to get into trouble for additional aggressive behavior during the following 2 years (Kruesi et al., 1992). Follow-up studies on people convicted of violent crimes or arson found that, after their release from prison, those with lower serotonin turnover had a greater probability of committing other violent crimes (Virkkunen, DeJong, Bartko, Goodwin, & Linnoila, 1989; Virkkunen, Eggert, Rawlings, & Linnoila, 1996). A follow-up study of people who had survived suicide attempts found that low serotonin turnover levels predicted additional suicide attempts within the next 5 years (Roy, DeJong, & Linnoila, 1989) (see Figure 12.11). Thus we can imagine mental hospitals using blood tests to identify the patients who need to be watched most carefully for suicidal tendencies and possibly using medications to increase serotonin activity. We can also imagine courts or parole boards using blood tests to help them decide how dangerous it might be to release someone. Whether we *want* our courts to base their decisions on such information is another question, but they *could*, and their predictions might be more accurate than what they have today.

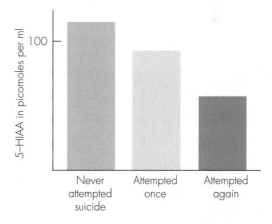

Figure 12.11 Levels of 5-HIAA in the CSF of depressed people
Measurements for the two suicide-attempting groups were taken after the first attempt. Low levels of 5-HIAA indicate low serotonin turnover. *(Source: Based on results of Roy, DeJong, & Linnoila, 1989)*

Panic Disorder

We may be able to learn more about the physiology of anxiety by studying clinical conditions associated with excess anxiety. Panic disorder afflicts about 1% of all adults (Robins et al., 1984). Sufferers have occasional attacks of extreme fear, breathlessness, heart palpitations, fatigue, and dizziness. From these symptoms, it would seem natural to assume that the problem is an overresponsive sympathetic nervous system. However, direct measurements of sympathetic nerves indicate that people sub-

ject to panic disorder have normal sympathetic nervous activity at most times and that even during a panic attack the sympathetic nerves are not as highly aroused as one might guess (Wilkinson et al., 1998).

One interpretation of panic disorder is that people misinterpret respiratory signals in the brain and react as if they were suffocating (Klein, 1993). One of the surest ways to trigger a panic attack in a susceptible person is to increase the blood

---

It is possible to alter serotonin synthesis by changes in diet. Neurons synthesize serotonin from tryptophan, an amino acid found in proteins, though seldom in large amounts. (Milk and turkey have relatively high levels.) Tryptophan crosses the blood-brain barrier by an active transport channel that it shares with other large amino acids, such as phenylalanine. Thus a diet high in the other amino acids but low in tryptophan impairs the brain's ability to synthesize serotonin. One study found that many young men on such a diet showed an increase in aggressive behavior a few hours after eating (Moeller et al., 1996). Under the circumstances it would seem prudent for anyone with aggressive or suicidal tendencies to reduce consumption of aspartame (NutraSweet), which is 50% phenylalanine, and maize (American corn), which is high in phenylalanine and low in tryptophan (Lytle, Messing, Fisher, & Phebus, 1975).

If procedures that decrease serotonin increase violence, we might predict that drugs that increase serotonin would decrease violence, including suicide. So far, however, researchers have found only slight benefits from such drugs (Montgomery, 1997).

We shall get to depression in Chapter 15, but if you already know something about depression, you may note a problem: Depression is also linked to low serotonin activity (or at least, drugs that increase serotonin activity often relieve depression), but most depressed people are not violent. If some treatment suddenly lowered your serotonin level, would you at once become violent or depressed? The answer is, "it depends"—always a good answer in psychology. If you had a previous history or predisposition toward either violence or depression, the drop in serotonin level would probably trigger a renewed bout. If you had a history of obsessive-compulsive disorder, the serotonin drop might aggravate that tendency as well (Greist, Jefferson, Kobak, Katzelnick, & Serlin, 1995). You might become more impul-

sive and therefore more prone to accidents (Kaplan, Muldoon, Manuck, & Mann, 1997). Serotonin activity apparently has something to do with suppressing unwelcome behaviors, but not everyone has the same impulses in need of suppression.

Stop & Check

3. How can one measure the amount of serotonin turnover in the brain?

4. What change in diet can alter the production of serotonin?

Check your answers on page 360.

Escape Behaviors

We distinguish two escape emotions: fear and anxiety. Fear is a temporary experience, like what you feel in a small boat with a storm approaching. If you escape from the danger, the fear is gone. Anxiety is longer lasting and less escapable. For example, you might feel anxiety about your future or about being in crowds.

Anxiety, like almost anything else, can be helpful or harmful depending on its degree. If you had no anxiety, you might take excessive risks. However, if you had severe anxiety, you might be too paralyzed by it to take the slightest venture, even to take a step out your front door. Digression 12.1 discusses panic disorder, a condition linked to excess anxiety.

Fear, Enhanced Fears, and the Amygdala

Do we have any built-in, unlearned fears? Yes, at least one: Loud noises frighten everyone, even newborn babies. The only apparent exceptions to this rule are deaf levels of lactate and carbon dioxide. Those levels sometimes rise enough during exercise or stress to resemble the levels that occur in suffocation; people who are subject to panic attacks often respond as if they were in fact suffocating, especially in situations that decrease their sense of control (Sanderson, Rapee, & Barlow, 1989). Interestingly, cigarette smoking has been found to increase the risk of developing panic disorder (Breslau & Klein, 1999).

Many people experiencing a panic attack aggravate the problem by **hyperventilating** (breathing more often or more deeply than they need to). Taking a deep breath or two can often be a good way of calming oneself, but prolonged hyperventilation lowers the levels of carbon dioxide and phosphates in the blood and therefore decreases activity of the vagus nerve,

which controls heart rate (George et al., 1989). Then any stress or other event that elevates blood CO_2 will produce a very large *percentage* increase in CO_2 and in turn a sharp rise in heart rate.

People with panic disorder can be treated with drugs, psychotherapy, or both. We might guess that tranquilizers would be effective because of their ability to suppress anxiety, but the results are usually better with antidepressants (Pollack, Otto, Worthington, Manfro, & Wolkow, 1998). Psychotherapy helps sufferers break the cycle of panic attacks leading to hyperventilation and then further attacks. It also helps them decrease their fear of their own panic attacks. (Sometimes people fear that a panic attack will lead to a heart attack, so the start of a panic attack becomes something to panic about.)

people. The response to an unexpected loud noise, known as the **startle reflex,** is extremely fast: Auditory information goes first to the cochlear nucleus in the medulla and from there directly to an area in the pons that commands the tensing of the muscles, especially the neck muscles. (Tensing the neck muscles is a protective reaction especially important because the neck is so vulnerable to injury.) Information reaches the pons within 3 to 8 milliseconds after a loud noise, and the full startle reflex occurs within two-tenths of a second (Yeomans & Frankland, 1996).

Although you don't learn your fear of loud noises, your current mood or past experiences can modify your reaction. You will respond more vigorously if you are already tense, as when you are walking alone through an unfamiliar neighborhood at night. People with post-traumatic stress disorder, who are certainly known for their intense anxiety, show a much stronger than normal startle reflex (Grillon, Morgan, Davis, & Southwick, 1998).

Here's a demonstration you can try on a cooperative roommate or friend. Dim the lights and ask your friend to close his or her eyes while you slowly read the following:

Imagine you are walking . . . alone . . . at night. You are walking through a part of town where you have never been before, and suddenly you realize you have lost your way. You're not sure you want to stop and ask someone for directions, and anyway, you don't see anyone, so you try to find your way by yourself. You walk down a street, hoping to see something familiar, but the street gets darker. Suddenly the only street light goes out. It's so dark you can hardly see one step in front of yourself. But you can't stay where you are, so you keep walking. Now you hear footsteps. They're growing louder. You realize someone is walking behind you. They're still

pretty far away, but the footsteps are growing closer. You decide to step off the sidewalk and hope the other person passes. So you're just standing there. But now you realize you're not alone. Someone else is standing right next to you! . . . [Pause.]

Now slam a shoe or other object onto a table or other object as hard as you can to make a sudden loud noise.

If you build the suspense well, your friend may jump and scream and refuse to participate in any more of your psychology demonstrations. For comparison you might try making the same loud noise for someone else without reading the story. The point is that a loud noise always produces some startle response, but if someone is already tense or frightened, the noise produces an even greater startle response.

Psychologists can measure the enhancement of a startle reflex as a gauge of fear or anxiety in nonhumans as well as humans. Typically investigators first measure an animal's muscular responses to a loud noise. Then they repeatedly pair a stimulus, such as a light, with shock. Finally they present the light just before the loud noise and determine how much more the animal jumps after the combination of stimuli than after the noise alone. (A control group is tested with a light stimulus that has not been paired with shock. We need to be sure that the effect of the light-plus-noise combination is due to what the animal has learned about the light.) Results of such studies consistently show that after animals have learned an association between a stimulus and shock, that stimulus becomes a fear signal; presenting the stimulus just before a loud noise enhances the animal's response to the noise. Conversely, a stimulus previously associated with pleasant stimuli can become a safety signal that decreases the startle reflex (Schmid, Koch, & Schnitzler, 1995).

By measuring the enhancement of the startle reflex,

People's choices of activities depend in part on how easily they develop anxiety.

normal startle reflex after a loud noise, but it shows no enhanced startle reflex if it gets a fear signal before the loud noise. In one typical study rats were repeatedly exposed to a light followed by shock and then tested for their responses to bursts of loud noise, with or without the light. Intact rats showed a moderate startle reflex to the loud noise and an enhanced response if the light (fear stimulus) preceded the noise. However, rats with damage at any point along the path from the central amygdala to the hindbrain showed a startle reflex to the loud noise but no enhancement by the fear stimulus (Hitchcock & Davis, 1991). Other studies confirm that damage to the amygdala reduces or eliminates learned or enhanced fears (Campeau & Davis, 1995; Lee, Walker, & Davis, 1996; Phillips & LeDoux, 1992; B. J. Young & Leaton, 1996).

In other experiments, experimenters gave rats unpleasant experiences—footshock in one experiment and smaller than usual reward in another—and then infused lidocaine (an anesthetic drug) into the amygdala of just one hemisphere or the other. The suppression of amygdala activity impaired rats' memory of the unpleasant event; that is, when the rats were returned to the testing apparatus, they behaved like rats that had not been shocked or rats that had continued receiving their customary large rewards for operant activities. Curiously, in both studies, suppression of the amygdala in the right hemisphere produced a bigger effect than suppression of the left amygdala (Coleman-Mesches, Salinas, & McGaugh, 1996; Mesches & McGaugh, 1995).

The Human Amygdala

The amygdala appears to be central to the human experience of anxiety as well. Several studies used PET scans or fMRI scans to measure brain activity while people looked at photos of faces. Photos of people showing emotional expressions evoked much greater amygdala responses than did neutral faces. Photos of fearful faces evoked activity in different areas of the amygdala than did happy faces, and in some studies the fearful faces evoked stronger activity (Breiter et al., 1996; Büchel, Morris, Dolan, & Friston, 1998; Hamann, Ely, Grafton, & Kilts, 1999; Morris et al., 1996). If people saw the same photo repeatedly, it excited the amygdala strongly the first time, but much less on later occasions (Breiter et al., 1996; Büchel et al., 1998). That result for the amygdala corresponds to the experience of a person as a whole: You are likely to react strongly the first time you see a photo of a frightened person, but not the tenth time.

People with a rare genetic disorder known as *Urbach-Wiethe disease* suffer a gradual atrophy (dying away) of the amygdala as calcium accumulates there. People with this disorder have almost no experience of fear. For example, they approach other people indiscriminately instead of trying to choose friendly and trust-

investigators have determined the role of various brain areas in learned fears. One key area is the amygdala (see Figures 12.7 and 12.12). Many cells in the amygdala, especially in the basolateral and central nuclei, get input from more than one sensory modality, such as vision and pain or hearing and pain, so the circuitry is well suited to establishing conditioned fears (Uwano, Nishijo, Ono, & Tamura, 1995).

Output from the amygdala to the hypothalamus controls autonomic fear responses, such as increased blood pressure. Output from the amygdala to the prefrontal cortex modifies cortical interpretation of potentially frightening stimuli (Garcia, Vouimba, Baudry, & Thompson, 1999). The amygdala also has axons to an area called the *central gray* in the midbrain, which in turn sends axons to the nucleus in the pons that controls the startle reflex (Fendt, Koch, & Schnitzler, 1996). By this relay the amygdala can enhance the startle reflex, increasing freezing, flinching, and other skeletal responses (LeDoux, Iwata, Cicchetti, & Reis, 1988). Figure 12.12 shows the connections.

A rat with damage to the amygdala still shows a

worthy people (Adolphs, Tranel, & Damasio, 1998). They also don't show strong dislikes, even in a nonsocial context. Imagine that you're rating the attractiveness of a series of drawings. Most people rate some as pleasant and others as unpleasant, maybe even ugly. But people with damage to the amygdala rate almost all of them as almost equally pleasant (Adolphs & Tranel, 1999).

Such people also have trouble recognizing facial expressions of fearfulness in others. (Presumably it is hard for someone who feels little fear to identify with someone else's.) One woman with this condition had no trouble recognizing faces, but if she looked at photos of people with different emotional expressions, she had much trouble identifying the fearful expressions and a little trouble with the angry and surprised expressions (Adolphs, Tranel, Damasio, & Damasio, 1994). When asked to rate the apparent intensity of the emotional expressions, she rated the intensity in the frightened, angry, or surprised faces much lower than any other observer did. Finally, when she was asked to draw faces showing certain emotions (Figure 12.13), she made good drawings of a happy, sad, surprised, disgusted, and angry face. However, when asked to draw an "afraid" face, she refused at first, saying she did not know what such a face would look like. When the researcher insisted that she try, she drew someone crawling away with hair on end (as cartoonists often indicate fear). Certainly she seemed much less able to imagine fear than any other emotional state (Adolphs, Tranel, Damasio, & Damasio, 1995).

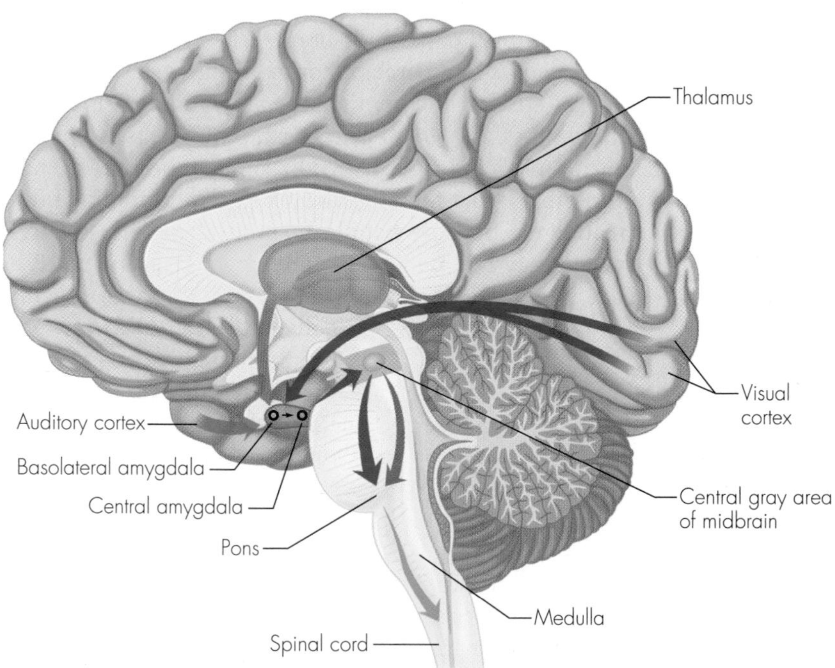

Stop & Check

5. Does hyperventilation tend to alleviate or aggravate panic attack?

6. What brain mechanism enables the startle reflex to be so fast?

7. How could a researcher use the startle reflex to determine whether some stimulus causes a person fear?

8. What kind of person has trouble recognizing fear expressions in other people?

Check your answers on page 360.

Anxiety-Reducing Drugs

CCK (cholecystokinin) is one of the important excitatory neuromodulators in the amygdala, and GABA (gamma amino butyric acid) is clearly the main inhibitory transmitter. Injections of CCK-stimulating drugs into the amygdala enhance the startle reflex (Frankland, Josselyn, Bradwejn, Vaccarino, & Yeomans, 1997), and injections of GABA-blockers can induce an outright panic (Strzelczuk & Romaniuk, 1996). In principle one could reduce anxiety either by blocking CCK or by increasing GABA activity. Most of the drugs that have been marketed so far have all been GABA facilitators, but research with rats indicates that CCK-blockers may have potential also (Adamec, Shallow, & Budgell, 1997).

Decades ago **barbiturates** were the class of tranquilizers (anxiety reducers) most widely used. Although barbiturates are effective, they have two significant drawbacks: They are strongly habit forming, and it is fairly easy to take a fatal overdose, either intentionally or accidentally, especially by combining barbiturates with alcohol.

Today the most commonly used tranquilizers are the **benzodiazepines** (BEN-zo-die-AZ-uh-peens), such as diazepam (trade name Valium), chlordiazepoxide (Librium), and alprazolam (Xanax), all of which can be taken as pills. Like many other drugs, benzodiazepines were found to be effective long before anyone knew how they worked. Then, in the late 1970s and early 1980s, investigators discovered specific benzodiazepine binding sites in the CNS.

Figure 12.12 Amygdala and connections relevant to learned fears
Cells in the lateral and basolateral parts of the amygdala receive visual and auditory information and then send messages to the central amygdala, which then sends its output to the central gray area of the midbrain, which relays the information to a nucleus in the pons responsible for the startle reflex. Damage at any point along the route from amygdala to pons interferes with learned fears, although only damage to the pons would block the startle reflex itself.

Thalamus

Visual cortex

Auditory cortex

Basolateral amygdala

Central amygdala

Pons

Central gray area of midbrain

Medulla

Spinal cord

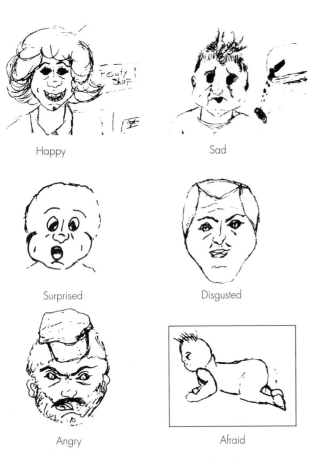

Happy

Sad

Surprised

Disgusted

Angry

Afraid

Figure 12.13 Drawings by a woman with a damaged amygdala
Note that her drawings of emotional expressions are fairly realistic and convincing except for fear. She at first declined to draw a fearful expression because, she said, she could not imagine it. When urged to try, she used the fact that frightened people try to escape, and she remembered that frightened people are often depicted with their hair on end, at least in cartoons. (*Source: Adolphs, Tranel, Damasio, & Damasio, 1995. Copyright Oxford University Press*)

The receptors are part of the **GABA$_A$ receptor complex,** which includes a site that binds the neurotransmitter GABA as well as sites that bind other chemicals that modify the sensitivity of the GABA site (see Figure 12.14). (The brain also has other kinds of GABA receptors, such as GABA$_B$, with different behavioral effects.)

The heart of the GABA$_A$ receptor complex is a chloride channel. When open, it permits chloride ions (Cl$^-$) to cross the membrane into the neuron, hyperpolarizing the cell. (That is, the synapse is inhibitory.) Surrounding the chloride channel are four units, each containing one or more sites sensitive to GABA. Three of those four units (labeled α in Figure 12.14) also contain a benzodiazepine binding site. When a benzodiazepine molecule attaches, it neither opens nor closes the chloride channel by itself, but it alters the shape of the receptor so that the GABA attaches more easily and binds more tightly (Macdonald, Weddle, & Gross, 1986). Benzodiazepines thus facilitate the effects of GABA. Alcohol also binds to the receptor and facilitates GABA binding (see Digression 12.2).

GABA has a wide variety of effects in the brain. Benzodiazepines exert their antianxiety effects in the amygdala and the hypothalamus. A minute amount of benzodiazepines injected directly to a rat's amygdala decreases learned shock-avoidance behaviors (Pesold & Treit, 1995), relaxes the muscles, and increases social interactions with unfamiliar partners (Sanders & Shekhar, 1995). However, people don't take benzodiazepines as injections to the amygdala; they take them as pills, so the drug goes to all parts of the brain. When the drug reaches the thalamus and cerebral cortex, it induces sleepiness, blocks epileptic convulsions, and impairs memory (Rudolph et al., 1999). The mixture of effects is a problem. Some people take benzodiazepines to decrease anxiety; others take them as sleeping pills or antiepileptic treatments, but few people need all three effects, and presumably no one wants the memory impairment. Researchers hope to develop drugs that are more specifically targeted to GABA receptors in particular brain areas, thereby producing more limited behavioral effects (Tallman, Cassella, White, & Gallager, 1999).

Other naturally occurring chemicals bind to the same sites as benzodiazepines. One such chemical is the protein **diazepam-binding inhibitor (DBI),** which blocks the behavioral effects of diazepam and other benzodiazepines (Guidotti et al., 1983). This and several related proteins are also known as **endozepines,** a contraction of "endogenous benzodiazepine,"

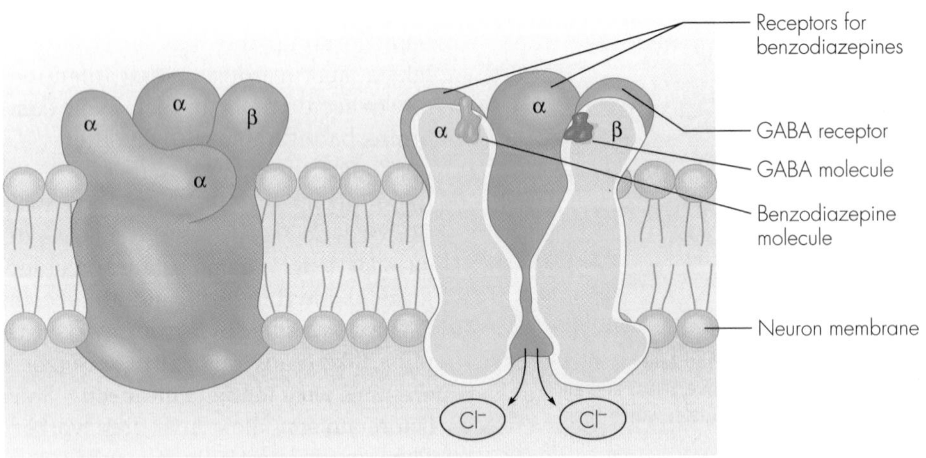

Receptors for benzodiazepines

GABA receptor

GABA molecule

Benzodiazepine molecule

Neuron membrane

Cl$^-$ Cl$^-$

Figure 12.14 The GABA$_A$ receptor complex
Of its four receptor sites sensitive to GABA, the three α sites are also sensitive to benzodiazepines. (*Source: Based on Guidotti, Ferrero, Fujimoto, Santi, & Costa, 1986*)

The Relationship Between Alcohol and Tranquilizers

Ethyl alcohol, the beverage alcohol, has behavioral effects similar to those of benzodiazepine tranquilizers. It decreases anxiety and behavioral inhibitions based on the threat of punishment. Moreover a combination of alcohol and tranquilizers depresses body activities and brain functioning more severely than either drug alone would. (A combination of alcohol and tranquilizers can be fatal.) Furthermore alcohol, benzodiazepines, and barbiturates all exhibit the phenomenon of cross-tolerance: An individual who has used one of the drugs enough to develop a tolerance to it will show a partial tolerance to other depressant drugs as well.

Alcohol promotes the flow of chloride ions through the $GABA_A$ receptor complex, just as tranquilizers do (Suzdak et al., 1986), probably by facilitating the binding of GABA to its receptors. Alcohol influences the brain in other ways as well, but the effects on GABA are responsible for alcohol's antianxiety and intoxicating effects. Drugs that block the effects of alcohol on the $GABA_A$ receptor complex also block most of alcohol's behavioral effects. One experimental drug, known as Ro15-4513, is particularly effective in this regard (Sudzak et al., 1986). Besides affecting the $GABA_A$ receptor complex, Ro15-4513 blocks the effects of alcohol on motor coordination, its depressant action on the brain, and its ability to reduce anxiety (Becker, 1988; Hoffman, Tabakoff, Szabo, Suzdak, & Paul, 1987; Ticku & Kulkarni, 1988) (see Figure 12.15).

Could Ro15-4513 be useful as a "sobering-up" pill or as a treatment to help people who want to stop drinking alcohol? Hoffman-LaRoche, the company that discovered it, eventually concluded that the drug would be too risky. People who relied on the pill might think they were sober and try to drive home

when they were still somewhat impaired. Furthermore giving such a pill to alcoholics could easily backfire. Alcoholics generally drink to get drunk; a pill that decreased their feeling of intoxication would probably lead them to drink even more. Ro15-4513 reverses the behavioral effects of moderate alcohol doses, but a large dose can still be a health hazard or even fatal (Poling, Schlinger, & Blakely, 1988). For these reasons Ro15-4513 is used only in experimental laboratories.

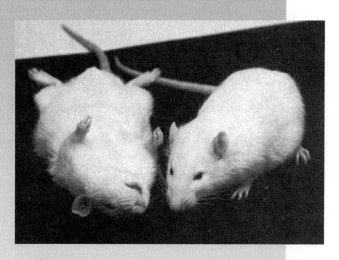

Figure 12.15   Two rats that were given the same amount of alcohol
The one on the right was later given the experimental drug Ro15-4513. Within 2 minutes, its performance on motor tasks improved significantly. *(Source: Photo courtesy of Jules Asher)*

although their effects are actually the opposite to those of benzodiazepines. So really an endozepine is an endogenous *anti*-benzodiazepine. Indeed GABA, which decreases anxiety, also decreases the release of endozepines (Patte et al., 1999). Why do our brains secrete endozepines and thereby increase our level of fears and anxieties? At this point we do not know, but presumably the "right" level of fear varies from time to time, and these chemicals may have a role in regulating that level.

9. What would be the effect of benzodiazepines on someone who had no GABA?

Check your answer on page 360.

In Closing: Understanding Emotions and Doing Something About Them

Today we understand the physiology of violence and fearfulness far better than we used to, but clearly we have a long way to go. Suppose we do make major advances; what then? Let's imagine some possibilities (with the admitted risk of being completely wrong): Suppose we could take a blood sample—measuring 5-HIAA or whatever—plus an fMRI scan and a few other measurements, and then use these measurements to predict someone's probability of violent crime. And suppose we could make that prediction much more accurately than psychologists can currently predict people's violent behavior. Shall we then use that information to make decisions on who stays in prison and who gets out on parole? Shall we go a step further and use brain tests to identify people who are likely to commit violent crimes? If so, shall we take steps to prevent crimes before they even occur—such as maybe genetic engineering or whatever other methods researchers might devise?

And what about anxiety? Today we have antianxiety drugs that work moderately well. Suppose research advances to the point that we could modulate people's anxiety precisely without undesirable side effects. Would it be a good idea to use these new methods to assure that everyone had the "right" anxiety level—not too much, not too little? Future research will give us new options and opportunities; deciding what to do with them is another matter.

Summary

1. Either a provoking experience, such as fighting, or the direct stimulation of the corticomedial area of the amygdala can produce a temporarily heightened readiness to attack. (p. 349)

2. There is evidence that genetic or prenatal influences can alter the tendency toward violent behavior in conjunction with family environment and other experiences. (p. 349)

3. Testosterone can increase the readiness to attack. (p. 349)

4. Parts of the hypothalamus and amygdala are especially important for aggressive behavior. Stimulation in these areas can increase attack behaviors; damage can lead to placidity and failure to attack. (p. 351)

5. Low serotonin turnover is associated with an increased likelihood of impulsive behavior, sometimes including violence. (p. 352)

6. Researchers measure enhancement of the startle reflex as an indication of anxiety or learned fears. (p. 355)

7. The startle reflex itself depends on activity in the pons. Enhancement of the startle reflex through learning depends on the amygdala. (p. 356)

8. People and nonhuman animals with damage to the amygdala lose much of their fear or anxiety. People with such damage also have trouble recognizing facial expressions of fear. (p. 356)

9. Tranquilizers decrease fear by facilitating the binding of the neurotransmitter GABA to the GABA$_A$ receptors, especially in the amygdala. (p. 357)

Thought Question

Much of the play behavior of a cat can be analyzed into attack and escape components. Is the same true for children's play?

Chapter Ending
Key Terms and Activities

Terms

absence seizure (p. 336)

ACTH (p. 344)

affective attack (p. 349)

antibody (p. 345)

antigen (p. 345)

B cell (p. 345)

barbiturate (p. 357)

behavioral medicine (p. 342)

benzodiazepine (p. 357)

Cannon-Bard theory (p. 339)

cortisol (p. 344)

cross-tolerance (p. 359)

cytokines (p. 346)

diazepam-binding inhibitor (DBI) or endozepine (p. 358)

$GABA_A$ receptor complex (p. 358)

HPA axis (p. 344)

5-hydroxyindoleacetic acid (5-HIAA) (p. 353)

hyperventilation (p. 355)

immune system (p. 344)

James-Lange theory (p. 338)

leukocyte (p. 345)

limbic system (p. 336)

locked-in syndrome (p. 339)

macrophage (p. 345)

natural killer cell (p. 345)

panic disorder (p. 354)

posttraumatic stress disorder (PTSD) (p. 347)

psychoneuroimmunology (p. 346)

rabies (p. 352)

Schachter-Singer theory (p. 339)

startle reflex (p. 355)

stress (p. 342)

T cell (p. 345)

turnover (p. 352)

Suggestions for Further Reading

Damasio, A. (1999). *The feeling of what happens.* New York: Harcourt Brace. A neurologist's account of the connection between emotion and consciousness. Highly recommended.

Kagan, J. (1994). *Galen's prophecy.* New York: Basic Books. Insightful discussion of human emotion and temperament.

LeDoux, J. (1996). *The emotional brain.* New York: Simon & Schuster. Discusses the role of the amygdala and other brain areas in emotional behaviors.

Leonard, B. E., & Miller, K. (Eds.). (1995). *Stress, the immune system, and psychiatry.* Chichester: Wiley. Presents research on how the nervous system affects the immune system.

Niehoff, D. (1999). *The biology of violence.* New York: Free Press. Discusses research on the neural and hormonal mechanisms of aggressive behavior.

Web Sites to Explore

You can go to the Biological Psychology Study Center and click on these links. While there, you can also check for suggested articles available on InfoTrac. The Biological Psychology Internet address is: **http:// psychology.wadsworth.com/book/kalatbiopsych7e/**

http://www.stressless.com/AboutSL/StressLinks.cfm
Includes links to many sites dealing with stress and stress relief.

http://marlin.utmb.edu/~nkeele/index.html
One researcher describes his own studies of the amygdala and provides links to other sites.

http://www.arf.org/isd/pim/benzo.html
Information on benzodiazepines.

Active Learner Link

Quiz for Chapter 12

Chapter Outline

Main Ideas

1. To understand the physiology of learning, we must answer two questions: What changes occur in a single cell during learning, and how do changed cells work together to produce adaptive behavior?

2. Psychologists distinguish among several types of memory, each of which can be impaired by a different kind of brain damage.

3. During learning, a variety of changes occur that are either brief or permanent and that either facilitate or decrease the activity at particular synapses.

Suppose you type something on your computer and then store it. A year later you come back, click on the correct file name, and retrieve what you wrote. How did the computer remember what to do?

That question is really two questions. One is: How does the computer store a representation of the keys that you typed? To explain how that happened, we need to understand the physics of the silicon chips inside your computer. The second question is: How does the computer convert all those on and off messages on silicon chips into the array on your computer screen? To answer that question, we need to understand the computer's wiring diagram.

Similarly, when we try to explain how you remember some experience, we are really answering two questions. One is: How did a pattern of sensory information create lasting changes in the input–output properties of some of your neurons? That question concerns the biophysics of the neuron. The second question is: After certain neurons change certain properties, how does the nervous system as a whole produce the appropriate behavior? That question concerns the wiring diagram. Learning requires changes in individual cells, but what happens in a single cell may be very different from how the organism learns as a whole.

We shall begin this chapter by considering how the various areas of the nervous system interact to produce learning and memory. In the second module we turn to the more detailed physiology of how experience changes the properties of the individual cells and synapses.

Opposite:
Maze learning is but one of the many types of learning. Results from one type do not necessarily apply to another.

Learning, Memory, Amnesia, and Brain Functioning

Suppose you lost the ability to form long-lasting memories. You can remember what you just did and what someone just said to you, but you remember nothing that happened earlier. It's as if you just awakened from a long sleep. So you write on a sheet of paper, "Just now, for the first time, I have suddenly become conscious!" A little later you forget this experience, too. So far as you can tell, you have just now emerged into consciousness after a long sleeplike period. You look at this sheet of paper on which you wrote about becoming conscious, but you don't remember writing it. How odd! You must have written something about being conscious during a time when in fact you were not! Irritated, you cross off that statement and write anew, "*NOW* I am for the first time conscious!" And a minute later you cross that one off and write it again. And again. Eventually someone finds this sheet of paper on which you have repeatedly written and crossed out statements about suddenly being conscious for the first time.

Sound far-fetched? It really happened to a patient known as "C" who developed severe memory impairments after encephalitis damaged his temporal cortex (B. A. Wilson, Baddeley, & Kapur, 1995). Life without memory is very unlike life as the rest of us know it; indeed, it is almost no life at all.

Localized Representations of Memory

What is the brain's physical representation of learning and memory? One early, influential idea was that it might be a strengthened connection between two brain areas. The Russian physiologist Ivan Pavlov pioneered the investigation of what we now call **classical conditioning** (Figure 13.1a), in which pairing two stimuli changes the response to one of them (Pavlov, 1927). Ordinarily the experimenter starts by presenting a **conditioned stimulus (CS),** which initially elicits no response of note, and then presents the **unconditioned stimulus (UCS),** which automatically elicits the **unconditioned response (UCR).** After some pairings of the CS and the UCS (perhaps just one or two pairings, perhaps many), the individual begins making a new, learned response to the CS, called a **conditioned response (CR).** In his original experiments Pavlov presented a dog with a sound (CS) followed by meat (UCS), which stimulated the dog to salivate (UCR). After many such pairings, the sound alone (CS) stimulated the dog to salivate (CR). In that case and many others, the CR resembles the UCR, but in some cases it does not. For example, if a CS is paired with shock, the shock elicits screaming and jumping, but the CS elicits a freezing response.

In **operant conditioning** an individual's response is followed by a reinforcement or punishment (Figure 13.1b). A **reinforcement** is any event that increases the future probability of the response; a **punishment** is an event that suppresses the frequency of the response. For example, when a rat enters one arm of a maze and finds Froot Loops cereal (a potent reinforcement for a rat), the probability of its entering that arm again increases. If it receives a shock instead, the probability decreases.

Some cases of learning are difficult to label as classical or operant. For example, after a male songbird hears the song of his own species during his first few months, he imitates it the following year. The song that he heard was not paired with any other stimulus, as in classical conditioning. He learned the song without reinforcements or punishments, so we can't call it operant conditioning either. That is, animals have specialized methods of learning other than classical and operant conditioning (Rozin & Kalat, 1971; Rozin & Schull, 1988).

Lashley's Search for the Engram

Pavlov believed that classical conditioning reflected a strengthened connection between a brain area that represents CS activity and a brain area that represents UCS activity. That strengthened connection lets any excitation of the CS center flow to the UCS center, evoking the unconditioned response (Figure 13.2). Karl Lashley set out to test this hypothesis. He said that he was searching for the **engram**—the physical representation of what has been learned. (A connection between two brain areas would be one example of an engram but is hardly the only possibility.)

Lashley reasoned that if learning depends on new or strengthened connections between two brain areas, a knife cut somewhere in the brain should interrupt that connection and abolish the learned response. He trained

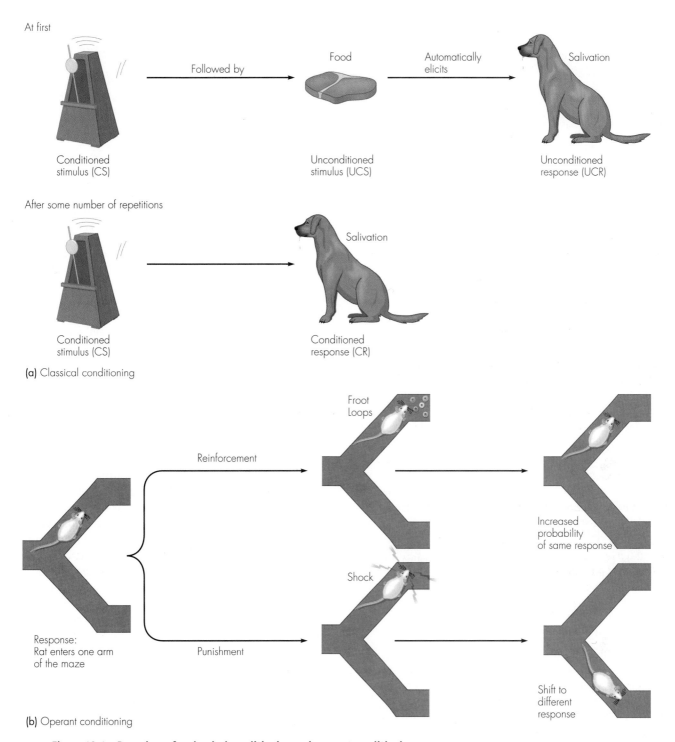

(a) Classical conditioning

(b) Operant conditioning

Figure 13.1 Procedures for classical conditioning and operant conditioning
(a) In classical conditioning two stimuli (CS and UCS) are presented at certain times regardless of what the learner does.
(b) In operant conditioning the learner's behavior controls the presentation of reinforcement or punishment.

rats on a variety of mazes and a brightness discrimination task and then made one or more deep cuts in varying locations in their cerebral cortexes (Lashley, 1929, 1950) (see Figure 13.3). However, no knife cut significantly impaired the rats' performances. Evidently the types of learning that he studied did not depend on connections across the cortex.

Lashley also tested whether any portion of the cerebral cortex is more important than others for learning. He trained rats on mazes before or after he removed large portions of the cortex. The lesions impaired performance, but the amount of retardation depended more on the amount of brain damage than on its location. Learning and memory apparently did not rely on a

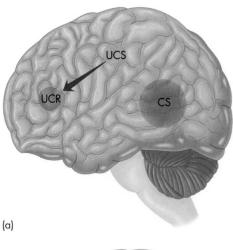

(a)

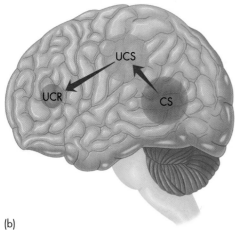

(b)

Figure 13.2 Pavlov's view of the physiology of learning
Initially **(a)** the UCS excites the UCS center, which then excites the UCR center. The CS excites the CS center, which elicits no response of interest. After training **(b)**, excitation in the CS center flows to the UCS center, thus eliciting the same response as the UCS.

single cortical area. Lashley therefore proposed two principles about the nervous system:

- **equipotentiality**—all parts of the cortex contribute equally to complex behaviors such as learning; any part of the cortex can substitute for any other.

- **mass action**—the cortex works as a whole, and the more cortex the better.

Note, however, another interpretation of Lashley's results: Maze learning and visual discrimination learning are more complex tasks than they might appear. A rat finding its way to food must attend to visual and tactile stimuli, the location of its body, the position of its head, auditory and olfactory cues if available, and so forth. The whole cortex participates, but each area could be contributing in a different way.

Eventually researchers discovered that Lashley's conclusions reflected two unnecessary assumptions: (a) that the cerebral cortex is the best place to search for an engram and (b) that all kinds of memory are physiolog-

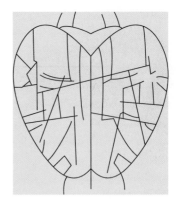

Figure 13.3 Cuts that Lashley made in the brains of various rats
He found that no cut or combination of cuts interfered with a rat's memory of a maze. *(Source: Adapted from Lashley, 1950)*

ically the same. As we shall see, investigators who discarded these assumptions came to different conclusions.

The Modern Search for the Engram

Richard F. Thompson and his colleagues used a simpler task than Lashley's and sought the engram of memory not in the cerebral cortex but in the cerebellum, a structure that Masao Ito (1984) had identified as a likely organ of learning.

Thompson and his colleagues studied classical conditioning of eyelid responses in rabbits. They presented first a tone (CS) and then a puff of air (UCS) to the cornea of the rabbit's eye. At first a rabbit blinked at the air puff but not at the tone; after repeated pairings, classical conditioning occurred and the rabbit blinked at the tone also. Investigators recorded the activity in various brain cells to determine which ones changed their responses during learning.

Thompson and other investigators consistently found changes in cells of one nucleus of the cerebellum, the **lateral interpositus nucleus (LIP).** At the start of training, those cells showed very little response to the tone, but as learning proceeded, the cells' responses increased (Thompson, 1986). The fact that damaging a brain area prevented a learned response does not necessarily mean that the learning took place in that area. Imagine a sequence of brain areas:

If learning occurs in any one of them (say, area D), we could record changes in D and in every area after it. And we could prevent learning by damaging any of the areas that send information to D. How, then, can anyone determine where learning occurs?

Thompson and his colleagues reasoned that if learning occurred in D, then E, F, and so on have to be active

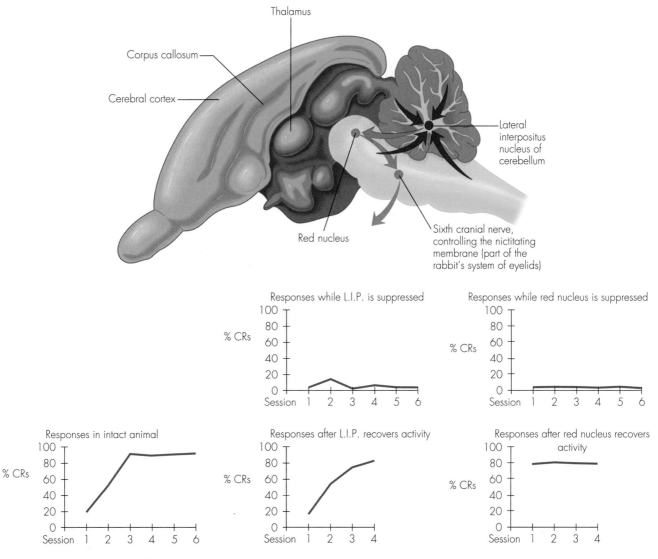

Figure 13.4 Localization of an engram
Rabbits were trained on classical conditioning of an eyelid response. Temporary suppression of activity in the lateral interpositus nucleus of a rabbit blocked all indications of learning. After the suppression wore off, the rabbits learned as slowly as rabbits with no previous training. Temporary suppression of activity in the red nucleus blocked the response during the period of suppression, but the learned response appeared as soon as the red nucleus recovered from the suppression. *(Source: Based on the experiments of Clark & Lavond, 1993, and Krupa, Thompson, & Thompson, 1993)*

to pass the information along to the muscles, but they wouldn't have to be active for learning itself to occur. (Everything up to D would have to be active, of course, just to get the information to D.) To investigate the role of the LIP, investigators temporarily suppressed activity in that nucleus at the start of training, either by cooling it or by injecting a drug into it. Then they presented the CS and UCS as usual and found no learning. Then they waited for the effects of the cooling or the drugs to wear off and continued training. At that point the rabbits began to learn, but they learned *at the same speed as animals that had received no previous training.* Evidently the LIP had to be active for learning to occur.

But did learning actually occur in the LIP, or does this area just relay the information to some other area where learning occurs? In the next experiments investigators suppressed activity in the red nucleus, a midbrain motor area that receives input from the cerebellum: When the red nucleus was suppressed, the rabbits showed no responses during training. However, as soon as the red nucleus had recovered from the cooling or drugs, the rabbits showed strong learned responses to the tone (Clark & Lavond, 1993; Krupa, Thompson, & Thompson, 1993). In other words suppressing the red nucleus temporarily prevented the response but did not prevent learning. The researchers concluded, therefore, that the learning occurred in the LIP. (The LIP was the last structure in the sequence that had to be awake for learning to occur.) Figure 13.4 summarizes these experiments. Later experiments demonstrated that synapses in the LIP increase their responsiveness to incoming stimuli during learning (Tracy, Thompson, Krupa, & Thompson, 1998).

The mechanisms for this type of conditioning are probably the same in humans. In one study PET scans revealed that classical conditioning of the eye blink in young adults produced increased activity in the cerebellum, red nucleus, and several other areas (Logan & Grafton, 1995). People who have damage in the cerebellum are impaired at eye-blink conditioning (Woodruff-Pak, Papka, & Ivry, 1996).

Stop & Check

1. Thompson found a localizable engram, whereas Lashley did not. What key differences in procedures or assumptions were probably responsible for their different results?

2. What evidence indicates that the red nucleus is necessary for performance of a conditioned response but not for learning the response?

Check your answers on page 380.

Types of Memory

Although much of classical conditioning probably depends on the cerebellum, many other kinds of learning and memory do not. You will recall from Chapter 6 that different parts of the brain contribute to different aspects of visual perception. The same principle holds for memory, and much of our progress in understanding the physiology of memory has come from progress in distinguishing among different types of memory.

Short-Term and Long-Term Memory

Donald Hebb (1949) reasoned that no one mechanism could account for all the phenomena of learning. We can form memories almost instantaneously, and some last a lifetime. Hebb considered it unlikely that any chemical process could occur fast enough to account for immediate memory yet remain stable enough to provide permanent memory. He therefore distinguished between **short-term memory,** of events that have just occurred, **and long-term memory,** of events from previous times. Several types of evidence validate such a distinction:

- Short-term and long-term memory have somewhat different properties. For illustration, read these seven letters and then repeat them from memory: CYXGMBF. Now try eight: OBGSFKIE. Then nine: RJNWSCFPT. If you are like most adults, you can hold about seven

TRY IT YOUR SELF

items in short-term memory but not more. You also forget the list quickly unless you constantly rehearse it. (Even if you correctly repeated the first set of letters, you have probably already forgotten it.) In contrast you can store vast amounts of information in your long-term memory without removing old memories to make room for the new.

- With short-term memory, once you have forgotten something, it is lost forever. For example, do you remember that first set of letters you read in the previous paragraph? No? What if I told you that it was either CYGXBMF or CYXGMBF. Did that help? Probably not. With long-term memory, however, you might think you have forgotten something and yet find that some hint helps you reconstruct it. For example, try naming all your high-school teachers. After you have named all you can, you will be able to name still more if someone shows you photos and tells you the teachers' initials.

- People with certain kinds of brain damage show specialized kinds of memory loss, such as impaired formation of new long-term memories despite normal short-term memory. We shall examine some cases later in this chapter.

Consolidation of Long-Term Memories

According to Hebb's (1949) original theory, any memory that stayed in short-term storage long enough would be gradually **consolidated** (strengthened) into a long-term memory. Hebb guessed that a short-term memory might be represented by a *reverberating circuit* of neuronal activity in the brain, with a self-exciting loop of neurons (Figure 13.5). If the reverberating circuit remained active long enough, some permanent chemical or structural change would occur.

However, later researchers found that simply rehearsing something in short-term memory is no guarantee of forming a long-term memory. Think about your

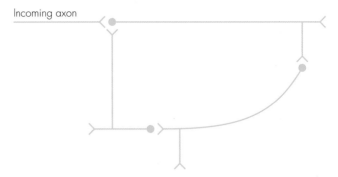

Figure 13.5 A hypothetical reverberating circuit
According to Hebb, a series of neurons might excite one another approximately as shown, thus maintaining a trace of some stimulation long enough to form a more permanent storage.

high-school experiences. You probably spent hours trying to memorize names and dates for a history test, and now you can hardly remember any of them. Yet you clearly remember the first time that special person smiled at you, the time you said something foolish in class and people laughed at you, the time you won a major honor, the frightening moment when you heard that a friend was hurt in a car accident. You didn't have to rehearse any of those events; you formed strong memories almost at once. Why? Because they were meaningful and emotional. Psychologists call these events "flashbulb memories."

How does the emotional response enhance consolidation? Remember from Chapter 12 that stressful or emotionally exciting experiences increase the secretion of epinephrine (adrenaline) and cortisol. Epinephrine from the periphery does not cross the blood-brain barrier but stimulates receptors on the vagus nerve (cranial nerve X), which carries excitation to cells in the brain stem, which in turn activate the amygdala (Williams, Men, Clayton, & Gold, 1998). Cortisol also activates the amygdala. Research on humans as well as laboratory animals has demonstrated that direct injections of epinephrine or cortisol enhance the storage and consolidation of recent experiences (Cahill & McGaugh, 1998). The same is true for direct stimulation of the vagus nerve or direct stimulation of the amygdala (Akirav & Richter-Levin, 1999; Clark, Naritoku, Smith, Browning, & Jensen, 1999). So excitement enhances memory by stimulating hormones that directly or indirectly activate the amygdala. The amygdala in turn stimulates the hippocampus and cerebral cortex, which are both important for memory storage. However, excessive or prolonged stress, with correspondingly prolonged cortisol, impairs memory (deQuervain, Roozendaal, & McGaugh, 1998; Newcomer et al., 1999).

After damage in and around the amygdala, both humans and nonhumans can still store memories, but emotional arousal does not enhance the storage. For example, imagine yourself memorizing a long list of words. Most are normal everyday words, but a few are emotionally charged "taboo" words such as *penis* or *bitch*. An hour later you won't remember all of the words, but you will remember most of the taboo words. Patients with damage in or near the amygdala are no more likely to remember the taboo words than any others (LaBar & Phelps, 1998).

A Modified Theory: Working Memory

Hebb believed that short-term memory was a temporary holding station on the way to long-term memory. Later researchers modified this view. Not everything in your temporary storage passes into long-term memory, nor should it. A. D. Baddeley and G. J. Hitch (1994) introduced the term **working memory** to emphasize that temporary storage is not just a station on the way to long-term memory; it is the way we store information while we are working with it or attending to it.

Here is a task you can use to test working memory. Read the list of words below to someone else, or have someone read them to you. After each word, say *the previous word*. That is, when you hear the first word, say nothing. When you hear the second word, say the first word. And so forth. Here is the list (you could use any list, of course):

> peach, apple, blueberry, melon, orange, mango, banana, lemon, papaya, fig, plum, tangerine, grape

Now do it again, but this time say *what was two words back*. That is, say nothing after the first two words; after the third say the first word and so forth. You begin to see that holding material in working memory isn't always easy.

Baddeley and Hitch distinguished three components of working memory:

- a **phonological loop,** which stores auditory information, including words;

- a **visuospatial sketchpad,** which stores visual information; and

- the **central executive,** which directs attention toward one stimulus or another and determines which items will be stored in working memory.

They distinguished the phonological loop from the visuospatial sketchpad because verbal memory seems to be in many ways independent of visual memory. If you try to memorize a long list of words or a long list of pictures, you will find that one gets confused with another. But if you memorize a mixture of words and pictures, the words and pictures do not interfere with each other (Hale, Myerson, Rhee, Weiss, & Abrams, 1996). Presumably we also have working memory for touch, smell, and taste, but less is known about those stores.

One common test of working memory that can be used with either humans or nonhumans is the **delayed response task,** in which one must respond to a stimulus that was heard or seen a short while earlier. For example, a light shines above one of several doors. The light goes off, a delay ensues, and then the individual has to go to the door where it saw the light. The delay can be increased or decreased to test the limits of working memory. Many studies have found that when humans or other mammals perform a delayed response task, cells in the prefrontal cortex maintain high activity during the delay, presumably because they are storing the memory (Courtney, Ungerleider, Keil, & Haxby, 1997; Rainer, Asaad, & Miller, 1998; Romo, Brody, Hernández, & Lemus, 1999). People with prefrontal damage are impaired on delayed response tasks (Chao & Knight, 1998).

In one series of experiments, a monkey was trained to stare at a fixation point on a screen. A light flashed elsewhere on the screen. To get a reward, the monkey had to continue staring straight ahead until the fixation point disappeared and then move its eyes to where the light had flashed several seconds before. Each location of the to-be-remembered light activated a different population of cells in the monkey's prefrontal cortex. For example, a light directly above the fixation point activated one set of cells; a light directly to the right activated a different set. Those cells remained active until the monkey's response (Goldman-Rakic, 1995a). Monkeys with damage to the prefrontal cortex showed a severe deficit in performance on these tasks, although they performed normally on tasks that required them to move their eyes toward a light without a delay. Monkeys with damage to tiny areas of the prefrontal cortex were impaired in their working memory for certain locations only; for example, monkeys with damage in one area had trouble remembering a light to the right of fixation, and those with damage in another area had trouble remembering a light to the left (Goldman-Rakic, 1994). This result implies that different cell populations store temporary memories of different locations or different stimuli.

Baddeley and Hitch's concept of the central executive is difficult to investigate because the concept itself is imprecise. Researchers generally study it with tasks that require divided attention—such as carrying on a conversation while watching for a complex pattern on a computer screen—like the job of an air-traffic controller. One study using functional MRI found that simultaneously performing a verbal task and a visuospatial task activated the prefrontal cortex far more than either task did by itself (D'Esposito et al., 1995). People with damage in the prefrontal cortex have trouble on all kinds of working memory tasks, especially if they have to shift attention between one task and another (Cummings, 1995).

Stop & Check

3. How does epinephrine enhance memory storage? Epinephrine and cortisol enhance emotionally charged memories by activating which brain area?

4. Name the three components of working memory.

Check your answers on page 380.

The Hippocampus and Amnesia

Amnesia is memory loss. Some people have such serious memory deficits that they cannot even remember that they have just finished a meal. One patient ate lunch, about 20 minutes later was offered a second lunch and ate that too, and then another 20 minutes

later started on a third lunch and ate most of it. A few minutes later he said he would like to "go for a walk and get a good meal" (Rozin, Dow, Moscovitch, & Rajaram, 1998). Many kinds of brain damage can produce amnesia, but one of the most powerful kinds is damage to the hippocampus.

Memory Loss After Hippocampal Damage

In 1953 a man known as H. M. suffered from such frequent and severe epileptic seizures that he had to quit his job. When he consistently failed to respond to antiepileptic drugs, he and his neurosurgeon became desperate to try almost anything. Because his seizures originated from disordered activity in the hippocampus (see Figure 13.6), the neurosurgeon removed that structure from both hemispheres, as well as several neighboring structures in the temporal cortex. At the time researchers had done almost no animal studies of the hippocampus, and no one knew what to expect after the surgery. As events turned out, even though the operation greatly reduced H. M.'s seizures, he almost certainly would have preferred to remain epileptic (Milner, 1959; Penfield & Milner, 1958; Scoville & Milner, 1957).

After the surgery H. M.'s personality and intellect remained intact; his IQ score even increased slightly, presumably because of the decrease in epileptic interference. However, he suffered a massive **anterograde amnesia** (loss of memories for events that happened after brain damage). He could form short-term memories but very few new long-term memories. He also suffered a moderate **retrograde amnesia** (loss of memory for events that occurred shortly before brain damage). That is, he had some trouble recalling events that happened within 1 to 3 years before the operation.

For example, after the operation he could not learn his way to the hospital bathroom. After reading a story he could not describe what had happened in it. He could read a magazine repeatedly without losing interest. He lived with his parents, and when they moved to a new address, he needed about 8 years to memorize the floor plan, but even then he could not find his way home from a distance of more than two blocks (Milner, Corkin, & Teuber, 1968).

In one test Brenda Milner (1959) asked H. M. to remember the number 584. After a 15-minute delay without distractions, he recalled it correctly, explaining, "It's easy. You just remember 8. You see, 5, 8, and 4 add to 17. You remember 8, subtract it from 17, and it leaves 9. Divide 9 in half and you get 5 and 4, and there you are, 584. Easy." A moment later, after his attention had shifted to another subject, he had forgotten both the number and the complicated line of thought he had associated with it.

In 1980 he moved to a nursing home. Four years later, he could not say where he lived or who cared for him. Although he watched the news on television every

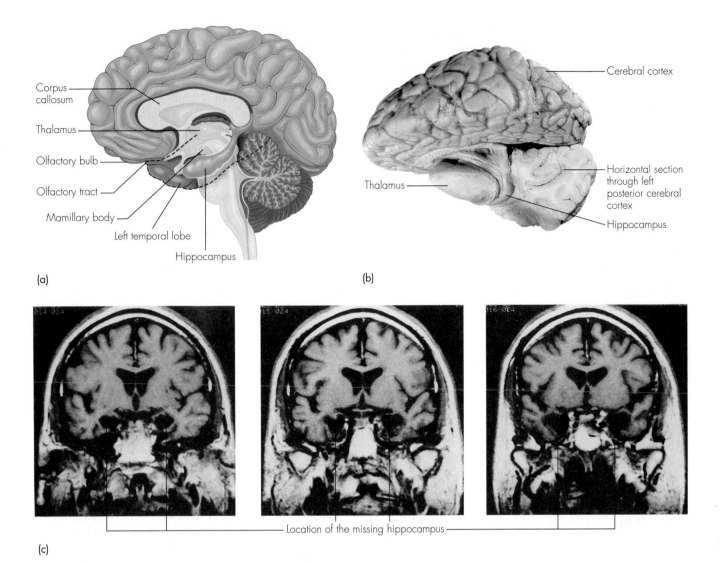

Figure 13.6 The hippocampus
(a) Location of the hippocampus in the human brain. The hippocampus is in the interior of the temporal lobe, so the left hippocampus is closer to the viewer than the rest of this plane; the right hippocampus is behind the plane. **(b)** Photo of a human brain from above. The right hemisphere is intact. The top part of the left hemisphere has been cut away to show how the hippocampus loops over (dorsal to) the thalamus, posterior to it, and then below (ventral to) it. *(Source: Photo courtesy of Dana Copeland)* **(c)** MRI scan of the brain of H. M., showing absence of the hippocampus. Note the large size of this lesion. *(Source: Photo courtesy of David Amaral and Suzanne Corkin)*

night, he could recall only a few fragments of events since 1953. For several years after the operation, whenever he was asked his age and the date, he answered "27" and "1953." After a few years he started guessing wildly, generally underestimating his age by 10 years or more and missing the date by as much as 43 years (Corkin, 1984).

Although H. M. has enormous trouble learning new facts and keeping track of current events, he acquires new skills without apparent difficulty. For example, he has learned how to pass his finger through a small maze, read mirror writing, and solve the Tower of Hanoi puzzle shown in Figure 13.7 (N. J. Cohen, Eichenbaum, Deacedo, & Corkin, 1985). He does not *remember* learning these skills, however. In fact he says

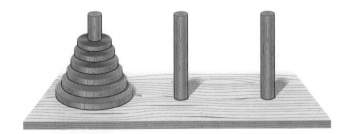

Figure 13.7 The Tower of Hanoi puzzle
The task is to transfer all the disks to another peg, moving just one at a time, without ever placing a larger disk on top of a smaller disk. H. M. has learned to solve this problem, although he says that he does not remember ever seeing it before.

he does not remember seeing the maze or the puzzle before. That is, he has impaired **declarative memory**, the ability to state a memory in words, but intact **procedural memory**, the development of motor skills.

He also shows much more *implicit* than *explicit* memory. **Explicit memory** is deliberate recall of information that one recognizes as a memory. It is tested by such questions as "What did you do last night?" or "Who were the main characters in the last novel you read?" **Implicit memory** is the influence of recent experience on behavior, even if one does not realize that one is using memory. For example, recall the patient described in Chapter 12 (p. 336) who could not recognize three people in photos, but when asked which one he would approach for a favor, always chose the one who had been friendly to him. He didn't know why he chose that person because he didn't consciously remember any of them. This behavior is an example of implicit memory.

In summary, H. M. has:

- Moderate retrograde amnesia (impaired memory of events that occurred 1 to 3 years before his operation)
- Normal short-term or working memory
- Severe anterograde amnesia for declarative memory
- Intact procedural memory
- Better implicit than explicit memory

Theories of the Function of the Hippocampus

Exactly how does the hippocampus contribute to memory? H. M. did not lose old memories from before his damage, and neither do other patients with hippocampal damage. Studies on rats and mice confirm that the hippocampus is important for storing long-term memories, but once they are well consolidated, they depend on the cerebral cortex and not the hippocampus (Bontempi, Laurent-Demir, Destrade, & Jaffard, 1999).

Still the hippocampus is more important for storing some kinds of information than others—remember, H. M. could learn new procedures much better than new facts. Researchers have been trying to describe exactly which kinds of memory are most dependent on the hippocampus, and the question has proved to be more difficult than it might sound.

The Hippocampus and Declarative Memory One hypothesis is that the hippocampus is critical for declarative, explicit memory (Squire, 1992). Certainly that hypothesis fits well with the data for H. M. and several other patients with hippocampal damage. However, one problem is that hippocampal damage also sometimes impairs implicit memory (Chun & Phelps, 1999). A more serious problem is that hippocampal damage impairs some, not all, memory in nonhuman animals even though they cannot explicitly "declare" any of their memories.

Can we at least say that hippocampal damage impairs nonhumans on tasks that resemble humans' declarative memories? Consider one example, usually studied in monkeys: In a **delayed matching-to-sample task,** an animal sees an object (the sample) and then, after a delay, gets a choice between two objects, from which it must choose the one that matches the sample. In the **delayed nonmatching-to-sample task,** the procedure is the same except that the animal must choose the object that is different from the sample (Figure 13.8). In both cases the task is to recognize which stimulus is familiar and which is new.

These tasks can be described as declarative memory, and hippocampal damage strongly impairs performance of them (Zola et al., 2000). The monkey is indicating, "This is like [or unlike] the object I just saw." Unfortunately for theorists, performance varies enormously with what seem like minor changes in procedure. For example, if a monkey always has to choose between a red triangle and a blue square, damage to the prefrontal cortex impairs performance, but hippocampal damage does not. If a monkey has to choose between different objects every time, damage to either the hippocampus or the prefrontal cortex greatly impairs performance (Aggleton, Blindt, & Rawlins, 1989). So the hippocampus is necessary for one version of the task and not the other, even though both appear to be declarative.

The Hippocampus and Spatial Memory Another hypothesis is that the hippocampus is especially important for spatial memories. Electrical recordings have indicated that many neurons in a rat's hippocampus are tuned to particular spatial locations, responding best when an animal is in a particular place (O'Keefe & Burgess, 1996) or looking in a particular direction (Dudchenko & Taube, 1997; Rolls, 1996).

Monkey lifts sample object to get food.

Food is under the new object.

Figure 13.8   Procedure for delayed nonmatching-to-sample task

In one study researchers conducted PET scans on the brains of London taxi drivers as they answered questions such as, "What's the shortest legal route from the Carlton Tower Hotel to the Sherlock Holmes Museum?" (London taxi drivers are very well trained and almost always answered correctly.) Answering these route questions activated their hippocampus much more than did answering nonspatial questions (Maguire, Frackowiak, & Frith, 1997).

Consider a couple of nonhuman tasks that require the hippocampus. A **radial maze** has eight or more arms, some of which have a bit of food or other reinforcement at the end (Figure 13.9). A rat placed in the center can find food by exploring each arm once and only once. In a typical variation it might have to learn that the arms with a rough floor never have food or that the arms pointing toward the window never have food. So a rat can make a mistake either by entering a never-correct arm or by entering a correct arm twice.

The task is analogous to the following, which you could try on yourself: Try to name as many cities as possible that you have visited in the last year. You could err by omitting a city you had visited, naming a city you did not visit, or naming one city twice—forgetting that you had already named it. **TRY IT YOUR SELF**

Rats with damage to the hippocampus seldom enter the never-correct arms, but they often enter a correct arm twice. That is, they forget which arms they have already tried (Jarrard, Okaichi, Steward, & Goldschmidt, 1984; Olton & Papas, 1979; Olton, Walker, & Gage, 1978). It would be as if you kept naming the same two or three cities repeatedly. We might consider this task declarative memory, but note that it also taps spatial memory.

Hippocampal damage also impairs performance on the **Morris search task,** in which a rat must swim through murky water to find a rest platform that is just under the surface (Figure 13.10). (Rats work vigorously to escape water. Humans are about the only mammals that swim recreationally, other than the obvious ones like otters and dolphins.) A rat with hippocampal damage finds the platform, but unlike normal rats, it has trouble remembering the location from one trial to the next, and therefore its escape times do not improve much (Jarrard, 1995). Again, this is a spatial memory.

Particularly compelling evidence for the role of the hippocampus in spatial memory comes from comparisons of closely related species that differ in their spatial memory. Clark's nutcracker, a member of the jay family in western North America, lives year-round at high altitudes. During the summer and fall, it buries tens of thousands of seeds in thousands of locations. Unlike squirrels, which bury nuts but often cannot find them, nutcrackers return to their hiding places in the winter and find enough to survive when no other food is available. Pinyon jays, which live at slightly lower elevations, also in western North America, bury less food and depend on it less to survive the winter. Scrub jays and Mexican jays, living at still lower altitudes, depend even less on stored food. Researchers have found that of these four species, the Clark's nutcrackers have the largest hippocampus and perform best on radial mazes and other laboratory tests of spatial memory. Pinyon jays are second best in both respects. On nonspatial tasks, such as color memory, size of hippocampus does not correlate with success (Basil, Kamil, Balda, & Fite, 1996; Olson, Kamil, Balda, & Nims, 1995) (see Figure 13.11). In short, the species comparisons support a link between the hippocampus and spatial memory.

However, although hippocampal damage consistently impairs spatial memory performance, it sometimes

Figure 13.9 A radial maze
Food is in some arms but not in others. A rat that reenters one arm before trying other arms has made an error of spatial working memory.

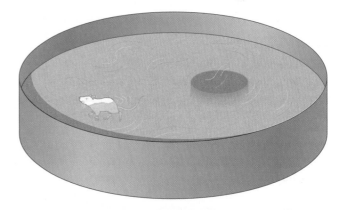

Figure 13.10 The Morris search task
A rat is placed in murky water. A platform that would provide support is submerged so the rat cannot see it. Rats with hippocampal damage have trouble remembering the location of the platform.

Species	Reliance on Stored Food	Size of Hippocampus Relative to Rest of Brain	Performance on Laboratory Tests of Spatial Memory	Performance on Laboratory Tests of Color Memory
Clark's nutcracker	Lives high in mountains; stores food in summer and relies on finding it to survive the winter.	Largest	Best	Slightly worse
Pinyon jay	Lives at fairly high altitude; depends on stored food to survive the winter.	Second largest	Second best	Slightly better
Scrub jay	Stores some food but less dependent on it.	Smaller	Less good	Slightly worse
Mexican jay	Stores some food but less dependent on it.	Smaller	Less good	Slightly better

Figure 13.11 Hippocampus and spatial memory in jays
Of four species of the jay family, all living in western North America, the species that rely most heavily on stored food to get through the winter have the largest hippocampus and perform best on laboratory tests of spatial memory. They have no consistent advantage on nonspatial memory. *(Source: Based on results of Basil, Kamil, Balda, & Fite, 1996, and Olson, Kamil, Balda, & Nims, 1995)*

also impairs performance on tasks with no apparent spatial component (e.g., Wan, Pang, & Olton, 1994). Researchers have found that even while an animal is performing a single task, some parts of the hippocampus code spatial information and others code nonspatial aspects of the task (Hampson, Simeral, & Deadwyler, 1999). Thus the hippocampus is important for spatial tasks but not exclusively for spatial tasks.

The Hippocampus and Configural Learning The third prominent hypothesis is that the hippocampus is necessary for **configural learning,** in which the meaning of a stimulus depends on what other stimuli are paired with it. For example, after a rat with hippocampal damage has learned that stimulus A signals food and B does

also, it has great trouble learning that a configuration of A and B together means *no food.* Similarly, people with hippocampal damage can learn to choose a square over a triangle and a triangle over a circle. But they become lost if they now have to learn to choose the circle over the square (Rickard & Grafman, 1998):

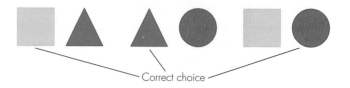

Many researchers interpreted these results to mean that the hippocampus is especially important for dealing with configurations of stimuli. However, later researchers have argued that configurations have no special status. Hippocampal damage impairs configural learning only because such learning is usually complicated and difficult. It also can impair nonconfigural learning if it is made difficult enough. For example, someone with hippocampal damage can learn one or two object discriminations easily enough:

but has trouble remembering six such discriminations simultaneously (Reed & Squire, 1999):

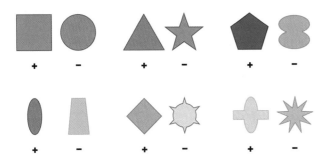

The Hippocampus and Binding Memories The hippocampus is more important for some kinds of memory than others, but researchers do not yet have a consensus on the types of memory it serves. Whether or not performance depends on the hippocampus varies with a number of procedural details that might appear irrelevant. In one study hippocampal disruption impaired memory if a rat was choosing between two large goal boxes, but not if it was choosing between small goal boxes (Cassaday & Rawlins, 1995). These tasks sound about the same to you and me, but evidently they are not the same for a rat.

Most do agree, however, that the hippocampus is important for consolidating memories. According to Larry Squire ("Interview with Larry Squire," 1998) the hippocampus "holds together the various sites in the neocortex that constitute a memory" (p. 780). The hippocampus receives input from many parts of the cortex and sends output to equally diverse areas. Its input comes not from any of the primary sensory areas, such as area V1 (see p. 170), but from secondary and tertiary sensory areas that have already processed the information heavily. According to Moscovitch (1995) the hippocampus receives only information that has already become conscious. (Obviously a difficult hypothesis to test!) Consciousness requires binding different kinds of sensory information, and the connections to the hippocampus make it well suited to help link such information as an object's shape and its spatial location (Rolls, 1996). After those links are established, the brain may be able to use a stimulus

"reminder" of an experience to reconstruct the full experience.

Stop & Check

5. What is the difference between anterograde and retrograde amnesia?

6. Which types of memory are least impaired in H. M.?

7. What are four views of the contribution of the hippocampus to memory formation?

Check your answers on page 380.

Other Types of Brain Damage and Amnesia

Learning and memory depend on many brain areas, and different kinds of brain damage produce different types of amnesia. Here we examine two more disorders: Korsakoff's syndrome and Alzheimer's disease.

Korsakoff's Syndrome and Other Prefrontal Damage

Korsakoff's syndrome, also known as *Wernicke-Korsakoff syndrome,* is brain damage caused by prolonged thiamine deficiency. Severe thiamine deficiency occurs mostly in chronic alcoholics who go for weeks at a time on a diet of nothing but alcoholic beverages, which contain carbohydrates but no vitamins. The brain needs thiamine (vitamin B₁) to metabolize glucose, its primary fuel. Prolonged thiamine deficiency leads to a loss or shrinkage of neurons throughout the brain, especially in the mamillary bodies (part of the hypothalamus) and in the dorsomedial thalamus, a nucleus that sends axons to the prefrontal cortex (Squire, Amaral, & Press, 1990; Victor, Adams, & Collins, 1971). Therefore the symptoms of Korsakoff's syndrome are similar to those of people with damage to the prefrontal cortex, including apathy, confusion, and both retrograde and anterograde amnesia. Hospitals in large cities report about 1 person with Korsakoff's syndrome per 1000 admissions. Treatment with thiamine sometimes helps, but the longer someone has been thiamine deficient, the poorer the outlook.

To illustrate one aspect of memory in Korsakoff's syndrome, try this demonstration. Here are the first three letters of some words. For each, fill in letters to make any complete word:

met _____ pro _____ con _____

per_____ thi_____ def _____

(Please try the demonstration before reading further.)

Each of these three-letter combinations can start many English words; *pro-*, *con-*, and *per-* start well over

50 each. Did you happen to fill in any of the following—*metabolize, prolonged, confusion, person, thiamine, deficient*? Those six words were in the paragraph just before the demonstration. After you had read those words, you were *primed* to think of them. Priming, one type of implicit memory, is the phenomenon that seeing or hearing words temporarily increases one's probability of using them. Patients with Korsakoff's syndrome sometimes read a list of words and then show strong priming effects on a fill-in-the-rest-of-the-word task, even though they don't remember even seeing a list of words, much less remember what the words were (Schacter, 1985). That is, like H. M., people with Korsakoff's syndrome show better implicit than explicit memory.

Korsakoff's patients and other patients with frontal lobe damage have difficulties in reasoning about their memories, such as deciding the order of events (Moscovitch, 1992). Suppose I ask, "Which happened to you most recently—graduation from high school, getting your first driver's license, or reading Chapter 2 of *Biological Psychology*?" You reason it out: "I started driving during my junior year of high school so that came before graduation. *Biological Psychology* is one of my college texts, so I started reading it after high school." A person with frontal lobe damage has trouble with even this simple kind of reasoning.

A distinctive symptom of Korsakoff's syndrome is confabulation, in which the patient takes a guess at the answer and then accepts that guess as if it were a memory. For questions about the patient's own life, the guess is almost always an answer that was true in the past, but not now, such as, "I went dancing last night." Some patients, though not all, are consistent in their confabulations. For example, when asked how long he had been in the hospital, one patient always responded, "Since yesterday" (Burgess & McNeil, 1999). Much of the problem seems to be that patients have trouble inhibiting an answer they have previously made. In one study patients were shown a series of photos and then shown some additional photos and asked which ones matched photos in that series.

Examine series of pictures

Then: Was this
picture in the
series you just
saw?

Yes   No

They did reasonably well up to this point. Then they were shown a second series of photos and again were asked which of several new photos matched the ones in the series they just saw.

Examine series of pictures

Then: Was this
picture in the
series you just
saw?

Yes   No   Yes
(incorrect)

The patients generally said "yes" to photos that had been on the first list even though they were not on the second (Schnider & Ptak, 1999). They were unable to suppress an answer that was correct previously.

The tendency to confabulate produces a fascinating influence on the strategies for studying. Suppose you had to learn a long list of three-word sentences such as: "Medicine cured hiccups" and "Tourist desired snapshot." Would you simply reread the list many times? Or would you alternate between reading the list and testing yourself?

Medicine cured _____.

Tourist desired _____.

Almost everyone learns better the second way. Completing the sentences forces you to be more active and calls your attention to the items you have not yet learned. Korsakoff's patients, however, learn much better the first way, by reading the list over and over. The reason is, when they test themselves, they confabulate. ("*Medicine cured headache. Tourist desired passport.*") Then they remember their confabulation instead of the correct answer (Hamann & Squire, 1995).

Alzheimer's Disease

Another cause of severe memory loss is Alzheimer's (AHLTZ-hime-ers) disease, which starts with minor forgetfulness, but progresses to serious memory loss, confusion, depression, restlessness, hallucinations, delusions, sleeplessness, and loss of appetite (Cummings & Victoroff, 1990). Most older people experience minor forgetfulness and some decrease in cortical and hippocampal functioning, but Alzheimer's disease is far more severe (Morrison & Hof, 1997). Alzheimer's disease occasionally strikes people younger than age 40. It becomes more common with age, affecting almost 5% of people in the 65–74-year range and almost 50% of people over 85 (D. A. Evans et al., 1989).

At the start people with Alzheimer's disease typically have trouble remembering their own actions. For example, Daniel Schacter (1983) reported playing golf with an Alzheimer's patient who remembered the rules and jargon of the game correctly but could not remember how many strokes he took on any hole. Five times he teed off, waited for the other player to tee off, and then teed off again, having forgotten his first shot.

As with H. M. and Korsakoff's patients, Alzheimer's patients have better procedural than declarative memory. They learn new hand skills but then are surprised by their good performance on what they consider an unfamiliar task (Gabrieli, Corkin, Mickel, & Growdon, 1993). Alzheimer's patients also show a bigger deficit on explicit than on implicit memory, although they also have moderate impairments on implicit memory as well (Meiran & Jelicic, 1995), probably because of impaired attention (Randolph, Tierney, & Chase, 1995).

The first clue to the genetics of Alzheimer's was the fact that people with *Down syndrome* (a type of mental retardation) almost invariably get Alzheimer's disease if they survive into middle age (Lott, 1982). Down syndrome is caused by having three copies of chromosome 21 rather than the usual two copies. That fact led investigators to examine chromosome 21, where in fact they did find a gene linked to many cases of early-onset Alzheimer's disease (Goate et al., 1991; Murrell, Farlow, Ghetti, & Benson, 1991). Later researchers found a gene on chromosome 14 that is responsible for 70% of early-onset Alzheimer's disease (Schellenberg et al., 1992; Sherrington et al., 1995), a less common gene for the early-onset disease on chromosome 1 (Levy-Lahad et al., 1995), and a gene on chromosome 19 that is responsible for many cases of late-onset Alzheimer's, with onset after age 60 to 65 (Corder et al., 1993; Pericak-Vance et al., 1991; Strittmatter & Roses, 1995). All of these genes lead to the accumulation of amyloid deposits in the brain. Brain cells contain a large protein called *amyloid precursor protein,* which is *cleaved* (broken) to form a smaller protein. In the majority of people, it is mostly cleaved to form a protein of 40 amino acids, called $A\beta_{40}$, which does little harm and presumably serves some useful function. However, in people with any of the genes for Alzheimer's disease, amyloid precursor protein is cleaved mostly to a slightly longer protein, having 42 amino acids, **amyloid beta protein 42** ($A\beta_{42}$), which accumulates in the brain and impairs the functions of neurons and glia cells. Alzheimer's patients also accumulate an abnormal form of the *tau* protein that forms part of the intracellular support structure of neurons; most research has focused on $A\beta_{42}$, but tau may be part of the problem as well (Hardy, Duff, Hardy, Perez-Tur, & Hutton, 1998).

For years a debate raged about whether the accumulation of amyloid and tau were causes of Alzheimer's disease or just results of some other underlying cause. More researchers now believe that accumulation of these chemicals is part of the cause. Amyloid deposits produce widespread atrophy (wasting away) of the cerebral cortex, hippocampus, and other areas, as Figure 13.12 shows (Hyman, Van Hoesen, Damasio, & Barnes, 1984). As neurons die or shrink (see Figure 13.13), discarded parts form tangles and plaques, as Figure 13.14 illustrates (Rogers & Morrison, 1985). **Tangles** are structures formed from degenerating neuronal cell bodies and **plaques** are structures formed from degenerating axons and dendrites. One of the most heavily damaged areas is the entorhinal cortex, which communicates extensively with the hippocampus (Van Hoesen, Hyman, & Damasio, 1991). Another area of consistent damage is the basal forebrain, whose cells arouse the rest of the cortex by releasing acetylcholine (as discussed in Chapter 9). In rats, damage to the basal forebrain produces various deficits that are best summarized as impaired attention (Baxter, Bucci, Gorman, Wiley, & Gallagher, 1995; McGaughy, Kaiser, & Sarter, 1996), and the behavioral problems of Alzheimer's disease could also be described that way.

What can we do to prevent or alleviate Alzheimer's disease? For years medicine had little to offer. Then researchers found that elevating patients' blood glucose enhanced their memory. That result would seem logical, as the brain depends on glucose for nutrition. However, as you remember from Chapter 10, an increase in blood glucose leads to an increase in insulin secretion, and later researchers have found that insulin enhances memory much more than glucose alone does (Craft et al., 1999). Exactly what insulin does in the brain is still unknown.

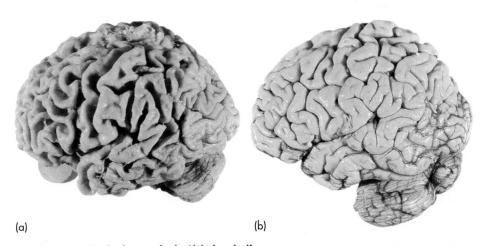

(a)

(b)

Figure 13.12 Brain atrophy in Alzheimer's disease
The cerebral cortex of an Alzheimer's patient **(a)** has gyri that are clearly shrunken in comparison with those of a normal person **(b)**. *(Source: Photos courtesy of Dr. Robert D. Terry)*

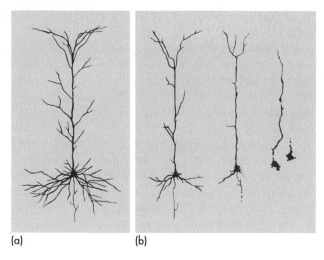

(a)   (b)

Figure 13.13 Neuronal degeneration in Alzheimer's disease
(a) A cell in the prefrontal cortex of a normal human;
(b) cells from the same area of cortex in Alzheimer's disease patients at various stages of deterioration. Note the shrinkage of the dendritic tree. *(Source: After Scheibel, 1983)*

Another possibility is to give drugs that stimulate acetylcholine receptors. (Remember, one of the main areas damaged is the basal forebrain, which arouses brain activity via axons containing acetylcholine.) Those drugs can be enhanced by other drugs that prolong acetylcholine release (McDonald, Willard, Wenk, & Crawley, 1998).

Researchers also are evaluating new ways to block Aβ₄₂ production and stimulate surviving cells to become more active (Selkoe, 1999). Even diet shows some prospects. Research with rats indicates that a diet rich in antioxidants guards against a variety of brain degeneration diseases. So eat your spinach and strawberries, and take a vitamin E pill (Joseph et al., 1998).

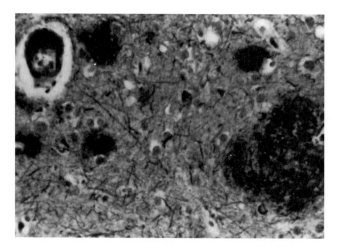

Figure 13.14 Cerebral cortex of an Alzheimer's patient
The grayish areas are plaques. Magnification x 160. *(Source: From Rogers & Morrison, 1985)*

Finally, research with mice suggests this fascinating possibility: One genetic strain of mice, the PDAPP mouse, overproduces Aβ₄₂ and develops symptoms resembling human Alzheimer's disease. Researchers found that if they injected small amounts of Aβ₄₂ into young mice, their immune system attacked it, the immune system continued attacking Aβ₄₂, and the mice avoided Alzheimer's-type symptoms later (Schenk et al., 1999).

What Amnesic Patients Teach Us

The study of amnesic patients reveals that people do not lose all aspects of memory equally. A patient with great difficulty establishing new memories may be able to remember events from long ago, and someone with greatly impaired factual memory may be able to learn new skills reasonably well. Evidently people have several somewhat independent kinds of memory that depend on different brain areas.

Stop & Check

8. Most people learn a list better if they alternate between studying the list and testing their memory of it. What kind of patient learns best by studying without testing themselves? Why?

9. What is Aβ₄₂ and how does it relate to Alzheimer's disease?

Check your answers on page 380.

Infant Amnesia

We conclude this module with brief reflections on **infant amnesia,** the phenomenon that adults remember very few events from their earliest years. Long-term memories do form during this period; for example, a child turning 4 may be able to describe the birthday party when he or she turned 3. Even 6-month-old children sometimes remember how to play with some toy that they haven't seen for 3 months or more (Rovee-Collier, 1997). Nevertheless, within a few years, we forget almost everything that happened before about age 4 or 5 (Howe & Courage, 1997).

According to one hypothesis early declarative memories are weak because the hippocampus is slow to mature (Moscovitch, 1985). To evaluate this hypothesis investigators tested children of several ages on tasks that in rats are known to depend on the hippocampus. For example, they built a radial maze of human dimensions, in which children had to explore each arm to get rewards, remembering which arms they had already visited on a given day (Figure 13.15). Investigators also built a version of the Morris search task (Figure 13.16); however, instead of asking the children to swim through

Figure 13.15 Radial maze for children
Children could find rewards by visiting each arm once and only once. Good performance requires working memory for spatial information and is known to depend on the hippocampus. *(Source: From Overman, Pate, Moore, & Peuster, 1996)*

murky water to find the platform, they had the children wade through little pieces of Styrofoam. On both of these tasks, the performance of children less than 7 years old was impaired compared to that of older children (Overman, Pate, Moore, & Peuster, 1996). This evidence suggests that poor declarative memory for early experiences may reflect slow development of the hippocampus.

Still, if the hippocampus is mature enough for a 4-year-old to remember what happened at age 3, why isn't it mature enough for a 10-year-old to remember what happened at age 4? Infant amnesia continues to elude explanation.

Figure 13.16 Adaptation of the Morris search task for children
Unlike rats, which have to swim through murky water to find the platform, children wade through little pieces of Styrofoam. *(Source: From Overman, Pate, Moore, & Peuster, 1996)*

Module 13.1

In Closing: Different Types of Memory

"Overall intelligence," as measured by an IQ test, is a convenient fiction. It is convenient because, under most circumstances, people who are good at one kind of intellectual task are also good at other kinds, so an overall test score makes useful predictions. However, it is a fiction because different kinds of abilities rely on different brain processes, and it is possible to damage one without another. Even memory is composed of separate abilities, and it is possible to lose one type or aspect of memory without impairing others. The study of amnesia shows how the brain operates as a series of partly independent mechanisms serving specific purposes.

Summary

1. Ivan Pavlov suggested that learning depends on the growth of a connection between two brain areas. Karl Lashley showed that learning does *not* depend on new connections across the cerebral cortex. (p. 364)

2. Later researchers have demonstrated that, in certain cases, classical conditioning takes place in small areas within the cerebellum. More complex learning undoubtedly requires more widespread changes. (p. 366)

3. Psychologists distinguish between short-term memory and long-term memory. Short-term memory holds only a small amount of information and

retains it only briefly unless it is constantly rehearsed. Long-term memory retains vast amounts of material indefinitely, but recalling this information sometimes requires great effort. (p. 368)

4. The consolidation of short-term memories into long-term memories depends more on arousal than on the mere passage of time. Arousing events increase the release of epinephrine and cortisol, which directly or indirectly stimulate the amygdala. The amygdala enhances activity in the hippocampus and cerebral cortex. (p. 368)

5. Working memory, a modern alternative to the concept of short-term memory, stores information temporarily while one is using it. The prefrontal cortex and other areas can store working memories through repetitive cellular activity. (p. 369)

6. People with damage to the hippocampus, such as the patient H. M., have great trouble forming new long-term declarative memories, although they can still recall events from before the damage and can still form new procedural memories. (p. 370)

7. The hippocampus is important for some kinds of learning and memory but not all. In humans it appears to be important for declarative memory, but the declarative versus procedural distinction is hard to state unambiguously and hard to apply to nonhumans. The hippocampus is particularly important for spatial memory and for much of nonspatial memory also. Hippocampal damage impairs configural learning and also other kinds of learning if they are difficult enough. (p. 372)

8. Patients with Korsakoff's syndrome or other types of prefrontal damage have impairments of memory, including difficulty drawing inferences from memories. They often fill in their memory gaps with confabulations, which they then remember as if they were true. (p. 375)

9. Alzheimer's disease is a progressive disease, most common in old age, that is characterized by a severe impairment of memory and attention. It is caused partly by the deposition of amyloid in the brain. Several genes increase the deposition of amyloid. (p. 376)

10. It is not known why most people forget the events of early childhood. Some memory deficits in childhood suggest a relationship to slow development of the hippocampus, but young children form memories that last many months, so it is not clear why those memories cannot last still longer. (p. 378)

Answers to *Stop and Check* Questions

1. Thompson studied a different, probably simpler type of learning. Also, he looked in the cerebellum instead of the cerebral cortex. (p. 368)

2. If the red nucleus is inactivated during training, the animal makes no conditioned responses during the training, so the red nucleus is necessary for the response. However, as soon as the red nucleus recovers, the animal can show conditioned responses at once, without any further training, so learning occurred while the red nucleus was inactivated. (p. 368)

3. Epinephrine stimulates receptors on the vagus nerve, which excites cells in the brain stem, which in turn activate the amygdala. Epinephrine and cortisol both enhance emotional memories by stimulating the amygdala. (p. 370)

4. The components of working memory are the phonological loop, the visuospatial sketchpad, and the central executive. (p. 370)

5. Retrograde amnesia is forgetting events before brain damage; anterograde amnesia is failing to store memories of events after brain damage. (p. 375)

6. H. M. is least impaired on short-term memory, procedural memory, implicit memory, and memory of events that occurred more than 1–3 years before his surgery. (p. 375)

7. Various theorists emphasize the importance of the hippocampus for declarative memory, spatial memory, configural learning, and binding memory traces from different cortical areas. (p. 375)

8. Patients with Korsakoff's syndrome learn best if they don't test themselves, because when they do test themselves, they confabulate answers and later remember their confabulations instead of the correct answers. (p. 378)

9. $A\beta_{42}$ is a protein that accumulates in the brains of patients with Alzheimer's disease and causes the growth of plaques and tangles. (p. 378)

Thought Questions

1. Lashley sought to find the engram, the physiological representation of learning. In general terms how would you recognize an engram if you saw one? That is, what would someone have to demonstrate before you could conclude that a particular change in the nervous system was really an engram?

2. Benzodiazepine tranquilizers impair memory. Use what you have learned in this chapter and the previous one to propose an explanation.

Storing Information in the Nervous System

When you see, hear, or do something, your experience probably leaves many traces in your nervous system. Which of these traces are important for memory?

If I walk through a field, are the footprints that I leave "memories"? How about the mud that I pick up on my shoes? If the police wanted to know who walked across that field, a forensics expert could check my shoes to answer the question. And yet we would not call these physical traces memories in the usual sense.

Similarly, when a pattern of activity passes through the brain, it leaves a path of physical changes, but not everything that changes is really a memory. The task of finding how the brain stores memories is a little like searching for the proverbial needle in a haystack, and researchers have explored many avenues that seemed promising for a while but now seem fruitless (see Digression 13.1).

Learning and the Hebbian Synapse

Ivan Pavlov's concept of classical conditioning lent itself readily to theorizing about the physiological basis of learning. As we have already seen, Pavlov's theories inspired Karl Lashley's unsuccessful search for new connections across the cerebral cortex. They also stimulated Donald Hebb to propose a mechanism for change at a synapse.

Hebb suggested that when the axon of neuron A "repeatedly or persistently takes part in firing [cell B], some growth process or metabolic change takes place in one or both cells" that increases the subsequent ability of axon A to excite cell B (Hebb, 1949, p. 62). In other words an axon that has successfully stimulated cell B in the past becomes even more successful in the future.

Consider how this process relates to classical conditioning. Suppose that axon A initially excites cell B slightly, and axon C excites B more strongly. If A and C fire together, their combined effect on B may produce an action potential. You might think of axon A as the CS and axon C as the UCS. Pairing activity in axons A and C causes an increased effect of A on B in the future. Hebb was noncommittal about whether the change occurred in axon A, cell B, or both.

A synapse that increases in effectiveness because of simultaneous activity in the presynaptic and postsynaptic neurons is called a **Hebbian synapse**. In Chapter 5 we encountered many examples of this type of synapse; in the development of the nervous system, postsynaptic neurons increase their responsiveness to combinations of axons that are active at the same time as one another (and therefore at the same time as the postsynaptic neuron). Such synapses may also be critical for many kinds of associative learning. Neuroscientists have discovered much about the mechanisms of Hebbian (or almost Hebbian) synapses.

Single-Cell Mechanisms of Invertebrate Behavior Change

We can imagine many possible physiological mechanisms for learning and memory. If we are going to look for a needle in a haystack, a good strategy is to look in a small haystack. Therefore many researchers have turned to studies of invertebrates. The nervous system of an invertebrate is organized differently from that of a vertebrate, but the general chemistry of the neuron, the principles of the action potential, and even the neurotransmitters are the same. If we identify the physical basis of learning and memory in an invertebrate, we cannot assume that vertebrates use the same mechanism, but at least we have a good hypothesis of what

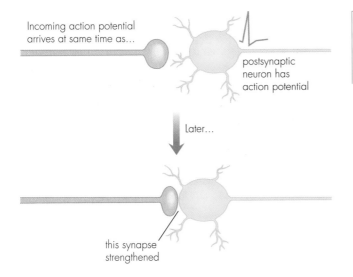

Incoming action potential arrives at same time as...

postsynaptic neuron has action potential

Later...

this synapse strengthened

Blind Alleys and Abandoned Mines in Research

Textbook authors, myself included, write mostly about successful research, the studies that led to our current understanding of a field. You may get the impression that science progresses in a smooth fashion, that each study leads to the next, and that each investigator simply contributes to an ever-accumulating body of knowledge. However, if you look at the old journals or textbooks in a field, you will find discussions of various "promising" or "exciting" findings that we disregard today. Scientific research does not progress in a straight line from ignorance to enlightenment; it explores one direction after another, a little like a rat in a complex maze, abandoning the arms that lead nowhere and pursuing those that lead further. Many promising lines of research turn out to be blind alleys.

The problem with the maze analogy is that an investigator seldom runs into a wall that clearly identifies the end of a route. Perhaps a better analogy is a prospector digging in one location after another, never entirely certain whether to abandon an unprofitable spot or to keep digging just a little longer. Many once-exciting lines of research in the physiology of learning are now of little more than historical interest. Here are three examples.

1. Wilder Penfield sometimes performed brain surgery for severe epilepsy on conscious patients who had only scalp anesthesia. When he applied a brief, weak electrical stimulus to part of the brain, the patient could describe the experience that the stimulation evoked. Stimulation of the temporal cortex sometimes evoked vivid descriptions such as:

I feel as though I were in the bathroom at school.

I see myself at the corner of Jacob and Washington in South Bend, Indiana.

I remember myself at the railroad station in Vanceburg, Kentucky; it is winter and the wind is blowing outside, and I am waiting for a train.

Penfield (1955; Penfield & Perot, 1963) suggested that each neuron in the temporal cortex stores a particular memory, almost like a videotape of one's life. However, it is doubtful that the brain stimulation actually evoked old memories. Stimulation very rarely elicited a memory of a specific event, more often evoking vague sights and sounds or repeated experiences such as "seeing a bed" or "hearing a choir sing 'White Christmas.'" Stimulation almost never elicited memories of doing anything—just of seeing and hearing. Also, some patients reported events that they had never actually experienced, such as being chased by a robber or seeing Christ descend from the sky. In short, the stimulation produced something more like a dream than an accurate memory.

2. G. A. Horridge (1962) apparently demonstrated that decapitated cockroaches can learn. First he cut the connections between a cockroach's head and the rest of its body. Then he suspended the cockroach so that its legs dangled just above a surface of water. An electrical circuit was arranged as Figure 13.17 shows so that the roach's leg received a shock whenever it touched the water. Each experimental roach was paired with a control roach

might work. (Biologists have long used this strategy for studying genetics, embryology, and other biological processes.)

Aplysia as an Experimental Animal

Aplysia, a marine invertebrate related to the common slug, has become a popular animal for studies of the physiology of learning (see Figure 13.18). It has fewer neurons than any vertebrate, and many are large (up to 1 mm in diameter) and therefore easy to study. Moreover, unlike vertebrates, *Aplysia* has neurons that are virtually identical from one individual to another so that, after an experimenter identifies the properties of the *R2* cell in one specimen, other experimenters can find the same cell in their own animals and can carry the studies further or relate that neuron to other identified neurons.

Much of the research on *Aplysia* concerns changes in behavior as a result of experience. Some of those

Figure 13.18 *Aplysia,* **or sea hare, a marine mollusk**
A full-grown animal is a little larger than the average human hand.

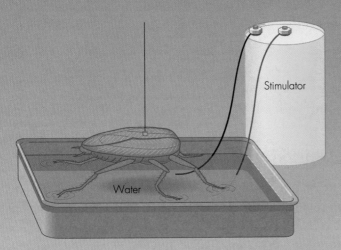

Figure 13.17 Learning in a headless cockroach?
The decapitated cockroach is suspended just above the water; it receives a shock whenever its hind leg touches the water. A cockroach in the control group gets a shock whenever the first roach does regardless of its own behavior. According to some reports, the experimental roach learned to keep its leg out of the water. *(Source: After Horridge, 1962)*

that got a leg shock whenever the first roach did; only the experimental roach had any control over the shock, however. (This kind of experiment is known as a "yoked-control" design.)

Over 5 to 10 minutes, roaches in the experimental group "learned" a response of tucking the leg under the body to avoid shocks. Roaches in the control group did not, on the average, change their leg position during the training period. Thus the changed response apparently qualifies as learning and not as some accidental by-product of the shocks.

These experiments initially seemed a promising way to study

learning in a very simple nervous system, a single cockroach ganglion (Eisenstein & Cohen, 1965). Unfortunately, decapitated cockroaches learn slowly, and the results vary sharply from one individual to another, limiting the usefulness of the results. After a few studies in the 1960s and early 1970s, interest in this line of research faded.

3. In the 1960s and early 1970s, several investigators proposed that each memory is coded as a specific molecule, probably RNA or protein. The boldest test of that hypothesis was an attempt to transfer memories chemically from one individual to another. James McConnell (1962) reported that, when planaria (flatworms) cannibalized other planaria that had been classically conditioned to respond to a light, they apparently "remembered" what the cannibalized planaria had learned. (At least they learned the response faster than planaria generally do.)

Inspired by that report, other investigators trained rats to approach a clicking sound for food (Babich, Jacobson, Bubash, & Jacobson, 1965). After the rats were well trained, the experimenters ground up their brains, extracted RNA, and injected it into untrained rats. The recipient rats learned to approach the clicking sound faster than rats in the control group did.

That report led to a sudden flurry of experiments on the transfer of training by brain extracts. In *some* of these experiments, rats that received brain extracts from a trained group showed apparent memory of the task, whereas those that received extracts from an untrained group did not (Dyal, 1971; Fjerdingstad, 1973).

The results were inconsistent and unreplicable, however, even within a single laboratory (L. T. Smith, 1975). Many laboratories failed to find any hint of a transfer effect. By the mid-1970s most biological psychologists saw no point in continuing such research.

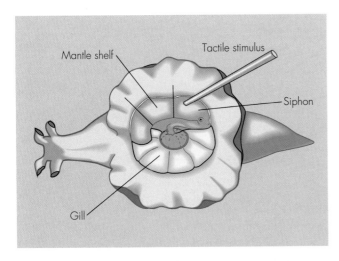

Figure 13.19 Touching an *Aplysia* causes a withdrawal response
The sensory and motor neurons controlling this reaction have been identified and studied.

changes may seem simple, and it is a matter of definition whether we call them *learning* or use the broader term *plasticity*. One commonly studied behavior is the withdrawal response: If someone touches the siphon, mantle, or gill of an *Aplysia* (Figure 13.19), the animal vigorously withdraws the irritated structure. Investigators have traced the neural path from the touch receptors through various identifiable interneurons to the motor neurons that direct the withdrawal response. Using this neural pathway, investigators have studied such phenomena as habituation and sensitization.

Habituation in *Aplysia*

Habituation is a decrease in response to a stimulus that is presented repeatedly and accompanied by no change in other stimuli. For example, if your clock chimes on the hour, you notice it less after many repetitions. Habituation can be demonstrated in an *Aplysia* by repeatedly

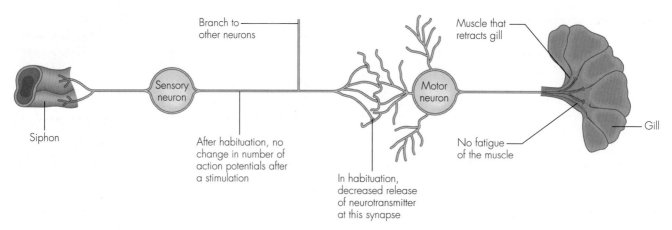

Figure 13.20 **Habituation of the gill-withdrawal reflex in *Aplysia***
Touching the siphon causes a withdrawal of the gill. After many repetitions the response habituates (declines) because of decreased transmission at the synapse between the sensory neuron and the motor neuron. *(Source: After Castellucci, Pinsker, Kupfermann, & Kandel, 1970)*

stimulating its gills with a brief jet of seawater. At first it withdraws its gills, but after many repetitions it stops responding. In explaining this phenomenon we can eliminate muscle fatigue because, even after habituation has occurred, direct stimulation of the motor neuron produces a full-sized muscle contraction (Kupfermann, Castellucci, Pinsker, & Kandel, 1970). We can also rule out a change in the firing rate of the sensory neuron. The sensory neuron still gives a full, normal response to stimulation; it merely fails to excite the motor neuron as

much as before (Kupfermann et al., 1970). We are therefore left with the conclusion that habituation in *Aplysia* depends on a change in the synapse between the sensory neuron and the motor neuron (Figure 13.20).

Sensitization in *Aplysia*

If you receive an unexpected, intense shock, you will probably react sharply to any loud sounds, sharp pinches, and other sudden stimuli in the next few days. This

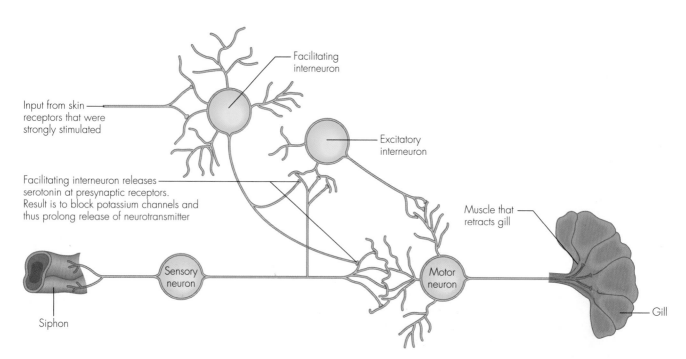

Figure 13.21 **Sensitization of the withdrawal response in Aplysia**
Stimulation of the sensory neuron ordinarily excites the motor neuron, partly by a direct path and partly by stimulation of an excitatory interneuron. Stimulation of a facilitating interneuron releases serotonin to the presynaptic receptors on the sensory neuron, blocking potassium channels and thereby prolonging the release of neurotransmitter. This effect can be long-lasting. *(Source: After Kandel & Schwartz, 1982)*

phenomenon is **sensitization,** an increase in response to mild stimuli as a result of previous exposure to more intense stimuli. Similarly a strong stimulus almost anywhere on *Aplysia's* skin can intensify later withdrawal responses to a touch.

Researchers have traced sensitization to changes at identified synapses (Cleary, Hammer, & Byrne, 1989; Dale, Schacher, & Kandel, 1988; Kandel & Schwartz, 1982), as shown in Figure 13.21. Strong stimulation anywhere on the skin excites a particular *facilitating interneuron,* which has axons that release serotonin (5-HT) onto the presynaptic terminals of many sensory neurons. These are called *presynaptic receptors.* When serotonin attaches to these receptors, it closes potassium channels in the membrane. As you will recall from Chapter 2, potassium flows out of the neuron after the peak of the action potential; the exit of potassium restores the neuron to its usual polarization. When serotonin blocks the potassium channels, the effect is a prolonged action potential in the presynaptic cell and therefore more transmitter release. If the sensitizing stimulus is repeated, the sensory neuron synthesizes new proteins that produce long-term sensitization (Schacher, Castellucci, & Kandel, 1988).

The research on *Aplysia* shows us that behavioral change can be based on increases or decreases in the activity at identifiable synapses. Learning need not rely on the same mechanisms in all situations in all species, however. Additional research may discover different mechanisms of learning.

Stop & Check

1. How can a Hebbian synapse account for the basic phenomena of classical conditioning?

2. What are the advantages of research on *Aplysia* as compared with vertebrates?

3. When serotonin blocks potassium channels on the presynaptic terminal, what is the effect on transmission?

Check your answers on page 389.

Long-Term Potentiation in Mammals

What cellular mechanisms account for learning in vertebrates? Since the time of Sherrington and Cajal, most neuroscientists have assumed that learning depends on some kind of change at the synapses, but the first evidence for that conclusion came from studies of hippocampal neurons in the 1970s (Bliss & Lømo, 1973). The phenomenon, known as **long-term potentiation (LTP),** is this: One or more axons connected to some dendrite bombard it with a brief but rapid series of

stimuli—such as 100 synaptic excitations per second for 1 to 4 seconds. The burst of intense stimulation leaves the synapses potentiated (more responsive to new input of the same type) for minutes, days, or weeks.

LTP shows three properties that make it an attractive candidate for the cellular basis of learning and memory:

- **specificity**—If some of the synapses onto a cell have been highly active and others have not, only the active ones become strengthened.

- **cooperativity**—Nearly simultaneous stimulation by two or more axons produces LTP, whereas stimulation by just one produces it weakly if at all. That is, if axons A and D are repeatedly active together, while axons B and C are usually inactive, the synapses of A and D become strengthened and those of B and C remain the same or become weaker (Sejnowski, Chattarji, & Stanton, 1990).

- **associativity**—Pairing a weak input with a strong input enhances later response to the weak input. In this regard the synapses subject to LTP are like Hebbian synapses, except that LTP requires only the depolarization of a dendrite, not necessarily an action potential.

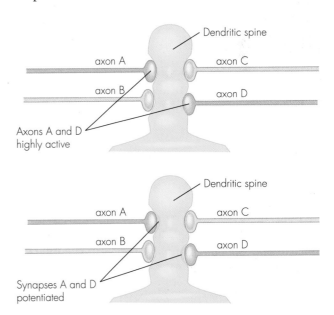

The opposite change, long-term depression, also occurs in both the hippocampus (Kerr & Abraham, 1995) and the cerebellum (Ito, 1989). **Long-term depression (LTD)** is a prolonged decrease in response to a synaptic input that has been repeatedly paired with some other input, generally at a low frequency.

Biochemical Mechanisms

Determining how LTP or LTD occurs has been a huge research challenge because each neuron receives many incoming synapses—often in the tens of thousands—and each synapse is extremely small. Isolating the chemical changes at any one synapse has taken an enormous amount of careful and creative research, and many of the details are still uncertain. Nevertheless a consensus has emerged on the basic points (Malenka & Nicoll, 1999). The mechanisms vary somewhat among brain areas (Bortolotto et al., 1999; Weisskopf, Bauer, & LeDoux, 1999); we shall discuss LTP in the hippocampus, where it is easiest to demonstrate and where its mechanisms have been most extensively studied.

In every known case LTP depends on changes at glutamate synapses. Glutamate is by far the brain's most abundant transmitter, and the brain has several types of glutamate receptors (Nakanishi, 1992). In past chapters you have seen that neuroscientists identify different dopamine receptors by number, such as D_1 and D_2, and different GABA receptors by letter, such as $GABA_A$. For glutamate they have named the different receptors after drugs that stimulate them. Here we are interested in two kinds: the AMPA and NMDA type glutamate receptors. The **AMPA receptor** is ordinarily excited only by glutamate, but it can also respond to a drug called α-amino-3-hydroxy-5-methyl-4-isoxazolepropionic acid (quite a mouthful). The **NMDA receptor** is also ordinarily excited only by glutamate, but it can respond to a drug called N-methyl-D-aspartate.

Both of these are ionotropic receptors; that is, when they are stimulated, they open a channel to let one or more kinds of ion enter the postsynaptic cell. The AMPA receptor opens sodium channels, and it is similar to the other synaptic receptors we have considered in past chapters. The NMDA receptor, however, is of a type we have not previously discussed: It responds to its transmitter, glutamate, *only when the membrane is already at least partly depolarized.* Ordinarily, when glutamate attaches to an NMDA receptor, the ion channel is blocked by magnesium ions so that no other ions can pass. Glutamate opens the channel only if the magnesium leaves, and the best way to remove the magnesium is to depolarize the membrane (see Figure 13.22).

Now suppose the axon that releases glutamate is active repeatedly. Better yet, let's have two axons active repeatedly, attached to the same dendrite. So many sodium ions enter through the AMPA channels that the dendrite

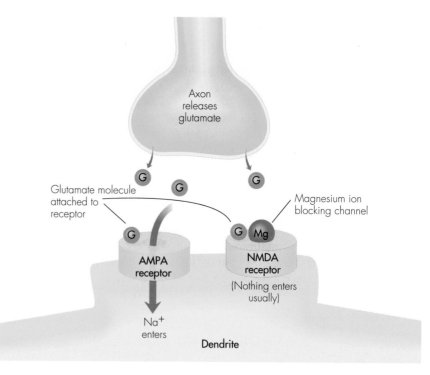

Figure 13.22 The AMPA and NMDA receptors, before LTP
Glutamate attaches to both receptors. At the AMPA receptor it opens a channel to let sodium ions enter. At the NMDA receptor it binds but usually fails to open the channel, which is blocked by magnesium ions.

becomes significantly depolarized. (It does not produce an action potential; remember, only axons produce action potentials.) The depolarization of the dendrite displaces the magnesium molecules, enabling glutamate to open the NMDA channel. Both sodium and calcium enter through the NMDA channel (see Figure 13.23).

The entry of calcium is the key to the later changes. When calcium enters through the NMDA channel, it activates many other chemicals inside the dendrite. It temporarily activates some genes that are otherwise inactive (Meberg, Barnes, McNaughton, & Routtenberg, 1993) and alters the activities of more than a hundred other known chemicals within the dendrite (Sanes & Lichtman, 1999). The net result is *to increase the later responsiveness of the receptors to glutamate.*

Exactly how does calcium enhance the later responsiveness at synapses? It activates certain genes and particularly activates a protein called CaMKII (α-calcium-calmodulin-dependent proteinkinase II), leading to the following effects:

- The structure of the AMPA receptor changes, becoming more responsive to glutamate.

- Some NMDA receptors change into AMPA receptors (which respond more strongly to glutamate than NMDA receptors do).

- The dendrite may build more AMPA receptors or move them into a better position.

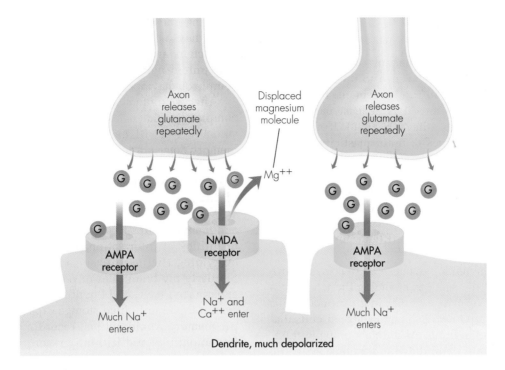

Figure 13.23 The AMPA and NMDA receptors during LTP
If one or (better) more AMPA receptors have been repeatedly stimulated, enough sodium enters to largely depolarize the dendrite's membrane. Doing so displaces the magnesium ions and therefore enables glutamate to stimulate the NMDA receptor. Both sodium and calcium enter through the NMDA receptor's channel.

• The dendrite may make more branches, thus forming additional synapses with the same axon (Engert & Bonhoeffer, 1999; Toni, Buchs, Nikonenko, Bron, & Muller, 1999) (see Figure 13.24). Recall from Chapter 5 that enriched experience also leads to increased dendritic branching.

Let's summarize: When glutamate massively stimulates AMPA receptors, the resulting depolarization enables glutamate also to stimulate nearby NMDA receptors. Stimulation of the NMDA receptors lets calcium enter the cell, where it sets into motion a series of changes that potentiate the dendrite's future re-

sponsiveness to glutamate by increasing either the number of AMPA receptors or their responsiveness. It is possible that the incoming axons change their properties also.

Once LTP has been established, it no longer depends on NMDA synapses. Drugs that block NMDA synapses prevent the *establishment* of LTP, but they do not interfere with the *maintenance* of LTP that was already established (Gustafsson & Wigström, 1990). In other words, once the NMDA receptors have potentiated the AMPA receptors, they stay potentiated.

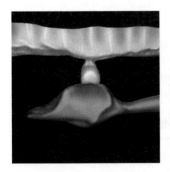 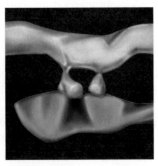

Figure 13.24 One way in which LTP occurs
In some cases the dendrite makes new branches, which attach to branches of the same axon, thus increasing the overall stimulation. *(Source: Based on Barinaga, 1999)*

Stop & Check

4. Before LTP: In the normal state what is the effect of glutamate at the AMPA receptors? At the NMDA receptors?

5. During the formation of LTP: When a burst of intense stimulation releases much more glutamate than usual at two or more incoming axons, what is the effect of the glutamate at the AMPA receptors? At the NMDA receptors? Which ions enter at the NMDA receptors?

6. After LTP has formed: After the neuron has gone through LTP, what is now the effect of glutamate at the AMPA receptors? At the NMDA receptors?

Check your answers on page 389.

LTP and Behavior

How important is LTP for learning? Is it "the" basis for learning, one of several mechanisms, or just a laboratory curiosity with little relevance to the real world? Neuroscientists are not in full agreement, but an increasing percentage believe it is at least part of the mechanism for learning (Stevens, 1998). It may contribute also to other types of brain plasticity that we don't ordinarily regard as learning. For example, recall from Chapter 6 that special kinds of visual experience can alter connections in the visual system only during a sensitive period of development. A drug that blocks NMDA receptors blocks the effects of visual experience during the sensitive period (Kleinschmidt, Bear, & Singer, 1987).

Obviously, changing a synapse or two in the hippocampus is not the same as changing the whole animal's behavior. However, a change in the hippocampus may be the first step toward changing large circuits that include much of the brain. As animals undergo training, LTP occurs rapidly in the hippocampus; 90 to 180 minutes later, one can detect LTP also in parts of the cerebral cortex (Izquierdo, 1995). The hippocampus may store memories temporarily and then transfer them elsewhere, perhaps directing their storage in several places (Nagahara, Otto, & Gallagher, 1995).

One of the key reasons for studying LTP is that understanding the biochemistry of learning may enable researchers to understand what could impair or improve memory. Mice with genes that cause abnormalities of the NMDA receptor have difficulties in learning; those with genes causing extra production of NMDA receptors have better than normal memory (Tang et al., 1999). A wide variety of drugs that interfere with LTP also block learning, whereas drugs that facilitate LTP enhance learning (Izquierdo & Medina, 1995). Some of these drugs directly affect calcium, which is important for LTP. Calcium channels apparently become somewhat "leaky" in old age, resulting in higher than normal resting levels of calcium within neurons. Too much calcium flow into the neurons is just as harmful as too little; LTP requires abundant calcium flow at just the right times, with no flow at others. In aged mammals drugs that partially block calcium channels can enhance learning and memory (Deyo, Straube, & Disterhoft, 1989). Potentially drugs with similar effects may someday be available for human use.

Module 13.2

In Closing: The Physiology of Memory

In this module we examined mechanisms such as LTP, which seem remote from the complex behaviors we call learning and memory. And indeed they are remote; changing one synapse would have little impact by itself. It has to be part of a large interacting network, and researchers are far from understanding how we combine untold numbers of changed synapses to produce complex behaviors.

After we understand the workings of memory more completely, what can we do with the information? Presumably we will help people overcome or prevent memory deterioration; we can expect much better therapies for Alzheimer's disease and so forth. Should we also look forward to improving memory for normal people? Would you like to have a super-memory?

Maybe, but let's be cautious. Even though I could add memory chips to my computer to store ever-larger quantities of information, I still don't want to keep everything I write or every e-mail message I receive. Similarly my brain doesn't record a memory of every experience I have, and I'm not sure I would want it to, even if it had unlimited storage capacity. The ideal super-memory would not just record more and more information; it would faithfully record what we need to remember.

Summary

1. A Hebbian synapse is one that is strengthened if it is active at the same time that the postsynaptic neuron produces an action potential. (p. 381)

2. Habituation of the gill-withdrawal reflex in *Aplysia* depends on a mechanism that decreases the release of transmitter from a particular presynaptic neuron. (p. 382)

3. Sensitization of the gill-withdrawal reflex in *Aplysia* occurs when serotonin blocks potassium channels in a presynaptic neuron and thereby prolongs the release of transmitter from that neuron. (p. 383)

4. Long-term potentiation (LTP) is an enhancement of response at certain synapses because of a brief but intense series of stimuli delivered to a neuron, generally by two or more axons delivering simultaneous inputs. LTP occurs in many brain areas and is particularly prominent in the hippocampus. (p. 385)

5. LTP in hippocampal neurons occurs as follows: Repeated glutamate excitation of AMPA receptors depolarizes the membrane. The depolarization removes magnesium ions that had been blocking NMDA receptors. Glutamate is then able to excite the NMDA receptors, opening a channel for calcium ions to enter the neuron. (p. 386)

6. When calcium enters through the NMDA-controlled channels, it activates a protein that alters the structure of AMPA receptors, converts some NMDA receptors to AMPA receptors, builds more AMPA receptors, and increases the growth of dendritic branches. All these changes increase the later

responsiveness of the dendrite to incoming glutamate. (p. 386)

7. Procedures that enhance or impair LTP have similar effects on certain kinds of learning. Research on LTP may lead to drugs that help improve memory. (p. 388)

Answers to *Stop and Check* Questions

1. In a Hebbian synapse pairing the activity of a weaker (CS) axon with a stronger (UCS) axon produces an action potential and in the process strengthens the response of the cell to the CS axon. On later trials it will produce a bigger depolarization of the postsynaptic cell, which we can regard as a conditioned response. (p. 385)

2. *Aplysia* has fewer cells than vertebrates, and the cells and connections are virtually identical from one individual to another. Therefore researchers can work out the mechanisms of behavior in great detail. (p. 385)

3. Blocking potassium channels prolongs the action potential and therefore prolongs the release of neurotransmitter, producing an increased response. (p. 385)

4. Before LTP, glutamate stimulates AMPA receptors but usually has little effect at the NMDA receptors because magnesium blocks them. (p. 387)

5. During the formation of LTP, the massive glutamate input strongly stimulates the AMPA receptors, thus depolarizing the dendrite. This depolarization enables glutamate to excite the NMDA receptors also. Both calcium and sodium enter there. (p. 387)

6. After LTP has been established, glutamate stimulates the AMPA receptors more than before. At the NMDA receptors it is again usually ineffective. (p. 387)

Thought Question

If a synapse has already developed LTP once, should it be easier or more difficult to get it to develop LTP again? Why?

Chapter Ending
Key Terms and Activities

Terms

Alzheimer's disease (p. 376)

amnesia (p. 370)

AMPA receptor (p. 386)

amyloid beta protein 42 (Aβ$_{42}$) (p. 377)

anterograde amnesia (p. 370)

associativity (p. 385)

central executive (p. 369)

classical conditioning (p. 364)

conditioned response (CR) (p. 364)

conditioned stimulus (CS) (p. 364)

confabulation (p. 376)

configural learning (p. 374)

consolidation (p. 368)

cooperativity (p. 385)

declarative memory (p. 372)

delayed matching-to-sample task (p. 372)

delayed nonmatching-to-sample task (p. 372)

delayed response task (p. 369)

engram (p. 364)

equipotentiality (p. 366)

explicit memory (p. 372)

habituation (p. 382)

Hebbian synapse (p. 381)

implicit memory (p. 372)

infant amnesia (p. 378)

Korsakoff's syndrome (p. 375)

lateral interpositus nucleus (LIP) (p. 366)

long-term depression (p. 385)

long-term memory (p. 368)

long-term potentiation (LTP) (p. 385)

mass action (p. 366)

Morris search task (p. 373)

NMDA receptor (p. 386)

operant conditioning (p. 364)

Suggestions for Further Reading

Cohen, N. J., & Eichenbaum, H. (1993). *Memory, amnesia, and the hippocampal system.* Cambridge: MIT Press. Discussion of memory impairments, especially as they relate to the hippocampus.

Martinez, J. L., Jr., & Derrick, B. E. (1996). Long-term potentiation and learning. *Annual Review of Psychology, 47,* 173–203. Good review of research on LTP and its relationship to learning.

McGaugh, J. L., Bermúdez-Rattoni, F., & Prado-Alcalá, R. A. (1995). *Plasticity in the central nervous system.* Mahwah, NJ: Erlbaum. A collection of chapters on many topics related to the physiology of memory.

Web Sites to Explore

You can go to the Biological Psychology Study Center and click on these links. While there, you can also check for suggested articles available on InfoTrac. The Biological Psychology Internet address is: **http://psychology.wadsworth.com/book/kalatbiopsych7e/**

http://www.alzforum.org/members/index.html
Excellent site for information about Alzheimer's disease.

http://rprcsgi.rprc.washington.edu/neuronames/ interim/hippocampus.html
Shows excellent illustrations of the hippocampus.

Active Learner Link

Video: Tom with Alzheimer's Disease

Quiz for Chapter 13

Lateralization and Language

Chapter Outline

Main Ideas

1. The left and right hemispheres of the brain communicate through the corpus callosum. After damage to the corpus callosum, each hemisphere has access to information from the opposite half of the body and from the opposite visual field.

2. In most people the left hemisphere is specialized for language and analytical processing. The right hemisphere is specialized for certain complex visual-spatial tasks and synthetic processing.

3. The language specializations of the human brain are enormous elaborations of features that are present in other primates.

4. Abnormalities of the left hemisphere can lead to a great variety of specific language impairments.

Your brain consists of a multitude of neurons, but unlike a society of people who act together at times but still remain independent, the neurons produce a single consciousness. Although your brain parts are many, you experience yourself as a unity.

What happens if connections among brain areas are broken? After damage to the corpus callosum, people act as if they have two fields of awareness—separate "minds," if you wish. With damage to certain areas of the left hemisphere, people lose their language abilities, while remaining unimpaired in other ways. Studies of such people offer fascinating clues about how the brain operates and raise equally fascinating unanswered questions.

Opposite:
Sign language, speech, and writing all reflect the same specializations of the human brain.

Module 14.1

Lateralization of Function

The left hemisphere of the cerebral cortex is connected to skin receptors and muscles mainly on the right side of the body. It sees only the right half of the world. The right hemisphere is connected to sensory receptors and muscles mainly on the left half of the body. It sees only the left half of the world.

Each hemisphere has limited sensory input and motor control on its own side of the body, and both hemispheres can control the muscles of the face and trunk. The degree of ipsilateral control (of the same side of the body) varies from one individual to another. *Why* all vertebrates evolved so that each hemisphere controls the contralateral (opposite) side of the body, no one knows. Perhaps there *is* no reason. By analogy, we can imagine a city in which all the doors have their hinges on the left. Why? No special reason; the first housebuilder put hinges on the left and everyone else copied. Maybe the earliest brains just happened to have contralateral control, and because it worked well enough, evolution never changed it. I admit that explanation is not very convincing. You are welcome to think of a better one.

At any rate, the left and right hemispheres exchange information through a set of axons called the **corpus callosum** (Figure 14.1; see also Figures 4.11 and 4.12) and through the anterior commissure, the hippocampal commissure, and a couple of other small commissures. Information that initially enters one hemisphere crosses to the opposite hemisphere with only a brief delay.

The two hemispheres are not simply mirror images of each other. In most humans the left hemisphere is specialized for language; the functions of the right hemisphere are more difficult to summarize, as we shall see later in this chapter. Such division of labor between the two hemispheres is known as **lateralization**. If you had no corpus callosum, your left hemisphere could talk only about the information from the right side of your body, and your right hemisphere could react only to information from the left. Because of the corpus callosum, however, each hemisphere receives information from both sides. Only after damage to the corpus callosum (or to one hemisphere) do we see the effects of lateralization.

Before we can discuss lateralization in any detail, we must consider the relation of the eyes to the brain. The connections from the left and right eyes to the left and right hemispheres are more complex than you might expect.

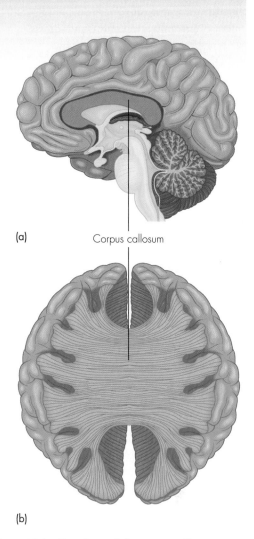

(a)

Corpus callosum

(b)

Figure 14.1 Two views of the corpus callosum
The corpus callosum is a large set of axons conveying information between the two hemispheres. **(a)** A sagittal section through the human brain. **(b)** A dissection (viewed from above) in which gray matter has been removed to expose the corpus callosum.

Visual and Auditory Connections to the Hemispheres

The hemispheres are connected to the eyes in such a way that each hemisphere gets input from the opposite half of the visual world; that is, the left hemisphere sees the right side of the world and the right hemisphere sees the left side. In rabbits and other species that have their eyes far to the side of the head, the connections from eye to brain are easy to describe: The left eye connects to the right hemisphere and the right eye connects to the left hemisphere. *Your eyes are not connected to the brain in this way.* Both of your eyes face forward. You can see the left side of the world almost as well with your right eye as you can with your left eye.

Figure 14.2 illustrates the connections from the eyes to the brain in humans. Vision starts with stimulation of the receptors that line the *retina* on the back of each eye. When light from the **visual field**—what is visible at any moment—enters the eyes, light from the right visual field shines onto the left half of both retinas, and light from the left visual field shines onto the right half of both retinas. The left half of *each* retina connects to the left hemisphere, which therefore sees the right visual field. Similarly the right half of each retina connects to the right hemisphere, which sees the left visual field. A small vertical strip down the center of each retina, covering about 5° of visual arc, connects to both hemispheres (Innocenti, 1980). In Figure 14.2 note how half of the axons from each eye cross to the opposite side of the brain at a place called the **optic chiasm** (literally, the optic "cross").

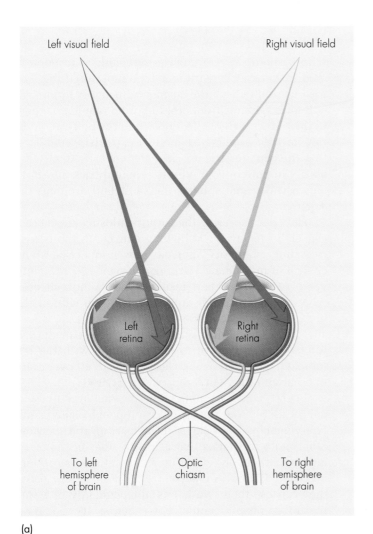

(a)

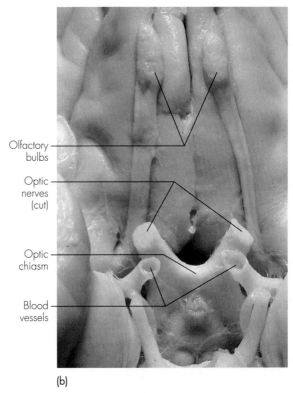

(b)

Figure 14.2 Connections from the eyes to the human brain
(a) Route of visual input to the two hemispheres of the brain. Note that the left hemisphere is connected to the left half of each retina and thus gets visual input from the right half of the world; the opposite is true of the right hemisphere. **(b)** Closeup of olfactory bulbs and the optic chiasm. At the optic chiasm, axons from the right half of the left retina cross to the right hemisphere, and axons from the left half of the right retina cross to the left hemisphere. *(Source: Photo courtesy of Dana Copeland)*

Epilepsy

Epilepsy is a condition characterized by repeated episodes of excessive, synchronized neural activity—that is, many neurons producing action potentials at the same time—mainly because of decreased release of the inhibitory neurotransmitter GABA (During, Ryder, & Spencer, 1995). It can result from a variety of causes, including genetics, birth injury or other trauma, infection in the brain, exposure to toxic substances, and brain tumors. All of the genes that cause epilepsy do so by altering voltage-gated ion channels in neuronal membranes; other types of epilepsy are less well understood (McNamara, 1999). Epilepsy

of genetic origin is likely to begin during childhood or adolescence; epilepsy from other causes can begin at any age. About 1%–2% of all people have epilepsy.

Epilepsy can produce a variety of symptoms depending on which parts of the brain are affected and for how long. Two categories are *generalized seizures* and *partial seizures*. A **generalized seizure** spreads quickly across neurons over a large portion of both hemispheres of the brain. In the most spectacular form, a **grand mal seizure,** the person makes sudden, repetitive jerking movements of the head and limbs for a period of seconds

---

Right visual field→ left half of each retina→ left hemisphere

Left visual field→ right half of each retina→ right hemisphere

Although information about each visual field projects to just one side of the cerebral cortex, the auditory system handles information differently. Each ear receives sound waves from just one side of the head, but each sends the information to both sides of the brain, because any part of the brain that contributes to localizing sounds must receive input from both ears. However, when the two ears receive different information, each hemisphere does pay more attention to the ear on the opposite side (Hugdahl, 1996).

Stop & Check

1. Why is the left hemisphere of the brain connected to only the right eye in rabbits but to parts of both eyes in humans?

2. In humans, light from the right visual field shines on the _____ half of each retina, which sends its axons to the _____ hemisphere of the brain.

Check your answers on page 404.

Cutting the Corpus Callosum

Damage to the corpus callosum prevents the exchange of information between the two hemispheres. Occasionally surgeons sever the corpus callosum as a therapy for severe epilepsy (see Digression 14.1). Epilepsy usually can be controlled with drugs, but someone

with frequent, severe seizures who fails to respond to medication may be willing to try almost anything. The idea behind cutting the corpus callosum is to prevent epileptic seizures from crossing from one hemisphere to the other, so they affect only half the body. In addition to this predicted benefit, a surprising bonus is that the seizures become less frequent. Evidently the ability of epileptic activity to rebound back and forth between the hemispheres increases and prolongs the seizures.

How does severing the corpus callosum affect other aspects of behavior? Following damage to the corpus callosum, laboratory animals show normal sensation, control of movement, learning and memory, and motivated behaviors. Their responses are abnormal only when sensory stimuli are limited to one side of the body. For example, if they see something in the left visual field, they can reach out to it only with the left forepaw. If they learn to do something with the left forepaw, they then have to learn the skill all over again to do it with the right forepaw (Sperry, 1961).

People who have undergone damage to the corpus callosum, referred to as **split-brain people**, show similar tendencies. They can still walk, swim, and carry out other motor activities that use both sides of the body, although their coordination is sometimes slow and awkward (Zaidel & Sperry, 1977). For certain tasks, they can use their two hands independently in a way that other people cannot. For example, try drawing **C** with your left hand while simultaneously drawing **U** with your right hand. Most people find this task difficult, but split-brain people do it with ease because each hemisphere acts independently (Franz, Eliassen, Ivry, & Gazzaniga, 1996).

TRY IT YOUR SELF

or minutes and then collapses into exhaustion and sleep. In a **petit mal seizure** (or *absence seizure*), the person stares unresponsively for about 15 to 20 seconds, making few movements except for eye blinking or a drooping of the head. Observers may not even be aware of the seizure, and sometimes the affected person may not be either. The person may, however, be confused and forget what just happened.

In contrast to a generalized seizure, a **partial seizure** begins in a focus (point of origin) somewhere in the brain and then spreads to nearby areas. Depending on the location of the focus, someone with a partial seizure may experience a variety of sensations or involuntary movements, such as a tingling hand or a shaking leg. Sometimes the effect spreads, as when a twitch starts in a finger and moves up the arm. The person remains conscious but may become confused. A partial seizure with a focus in the temporal lobe is known as a *partial seizure with*

complex symptomatology or a *temporal lobe seizure* or a *psychomotor seizure*. Such seizures produce only slight movements, such as lip smacking or chewing, but can lead to complex psychological states, including anxiety, laughter, repetitive thoughts, dreamlike hallucinations, or déjà vu experiences.

Over the years medical researchers have developed a large array of antiepileptic drugs, which act mostly by blocking sodium flow across the membrane or by enhancing the effects of GABA. More than 90% of epileptic patients respond well enough to drugs to live a reasonably normal life. Some suffer only the inconvenience of taking a daily pill. A few, however, continue to have frequent seizures despite medication. As a last resort, physicians consider removing the focus surgically.

Split-brain people suffer little or no impairment of overall intellectual performance or motivation. However, careful experiments by Roger Sperry and his students (Nebes, 1974) revealed subtle behavioral effects when stimuli were limited to one side of the body or the other. In a typical experiment a split-brain patient stared straight ahead as words or pictures were flashed on either side of a screen (see Figure 14.3). Information that went to one hemisphere could not cross to the other because of the damage to the corpus callosum. The information stayed on the screen long enough to be visible, but not long enough for the person to move his or her eyes.

If the experimenter then asked the person to point to the object that had just been shown or named, the person could point with the left hand only to what the right hemisphere had seen, and could point with the right hand only to what the left hemisphere had seen. The two halves of the brain had different information, and they could not communicate to share that information.

For most people, the ability to speak depends on the left hemisphere of the cerebral cortex (see Methods 14.1), although the right hemisphere also understands much speech (Levy, 1983). When a display was flashed in the right visual field, thus going to the left hemisphere, a split-brain person could name the object easily. But when it was flashed in the left visual field, going to the right hemisphere, the person usually could neither name nor describe it. I say "usually" because a small amount of information travels between the hemispheres through several smaller commissures, as shown in Figure 14.4, and some split-brain patients get enough information to identify a few of the objects they see (Berlucchi, Mangun, & Gazzaniga, 1997; Forster & Corballis, 2000). Nevertheless even a patient who could not name the object would correctly point to it with the left hand. The person sometimes even said, "I don't know," while pointing to the correct choice. (Of course, a split-brain person who watched the left hand point out an object could then name it.)

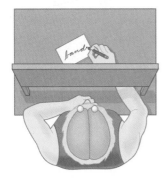

Figure 14.3 Effects of damage to the corpus callosum
When the word "hatband" is flashed on a screen, a woman with a split brain can report only what her left hemisphere saw, "band." However, with her left hand, she can point to a hat, which is what the right hemisphere saw.

Stop & Check

3. Can a split-brain person name an object after feeling it with the left hand? With the right hand? Explain.

4. After a split-brain person sees something in the left visual field, how can he or she describe or identify the object?

Check your answers on page 404.

Testing Hemispheric Dominance for Speech

Several methods are available to test which hemisphere is dominant for speech in a person with a normal corpus callosum. One is the **Wada test,** named after its inventor. A physician injects sodium amytal, a barbiturate tranquilizer, into the carotid artery on one side of the head. The drug puts that side of the brain to sleep, enabling researchers to test the capacities of the other hemisphere. For example, a person with left-hemisphere dominance for speech continues speaking after a sodium amytal injection to the right hemisphere, but not after an injection to the left hemisphere. The Wada test gives highly accurate information about lateralization, but the procedure is difficult, risky, and sometimes even fatal.

A less accurate, but easier and safer, test is the **dichotic listening task,** in which a person wears earphones that present different words to the two ears at the same time. The person tries to say either or both words. Ordinarily someone with left-hemisphere dominance for language identifies mostly the words heard in the right ear; someone with right-hemisphere dominance identifies mostly words heard in the left ear.

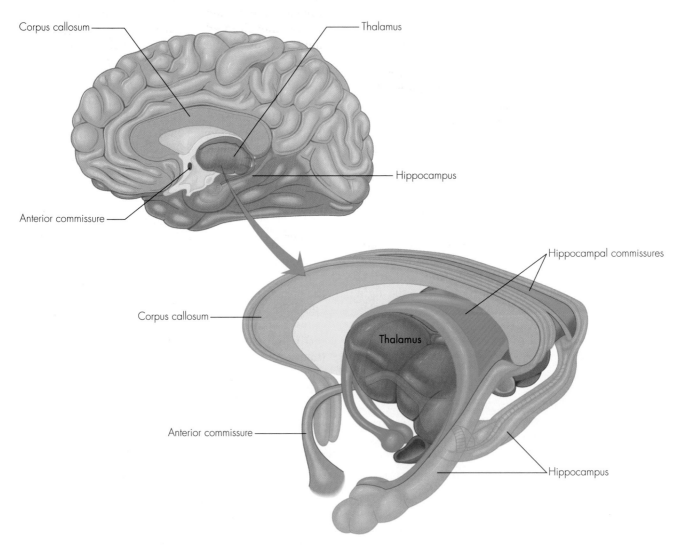

Figure 14.4   The anterior commissure and hippocampal commissures
These commissures allow for the exchange of information between the two hemispheres, as does the larger corpus callosum.
(Source: Based on Nieuwenhuys, Voogd, & vanHuijzen, 1988, and others)

Split Hemispheres: Competition and Cooperation

Each hemisphere of a split-brain person can process information and respond independently of the other. Indeed the hemispheres seem at times to act like separate people sharing one body. One split-brain person sometimes found himself buttoning his shirt with one hand while unbuttoning it with the other. Another split-brain person picked up a newspaper with the right hand, only to have the left hand (controlled by the less verbal hemisphere) put it down. Repeatedly the right hand picked it up; an equal number of times, the left hand put it down, until finally the left hand threw it to the floor (Preilowski, 1975).

One split-brain person—or rather, his left hemisphere—described his experience as follows (Dimond, 1979, p. 211):

> If I'm reading, I can hold the book in my right hand; it's a lot easier to sit on my left hand, than to hold it with both hands.... You tell your hand—I'm going to turn so many pages in a book—turn three pages—then somehow the left hand will pick up two pages and you're at page 5, or whatever. It's better to let it go, pick it up with the right hand, and then turn to the right page. With your right hand, you correct what the left has done.

Such conflicts are more common soon after surgery than later. The severed halves of the corpus callosum do not grow back together, but the brain learns to use the other smaller connections between the left and right hemispheres (Myers & Sperry, 1985). The left hemisphere somehow suppresses the right hemisphere's interference and simply takes control for some situations. In other situations the hemispheres learn to cooperate. A split-brain person who was tested with the standard apparatus shown in Figure 14.3 became able to name what he saw in the left visual field, but only when the answers were restricted to two possibilities (such as yes/no or true/false) and only when he was allowed to correct himself immediately after making a guess. For example, when something was flashed in the left visual field, the experimenter might ask, "Was it a letter of the alphabet?" The left (speaking) hemisphere would take a guess: "Yes." If that guess was incorrect, the right hemisphere, which knew the correct answer, would then make the face frown. (Both hemispheres can control facial muscles on both sides of the face.) The left hemisphere, feeling the frown, would say, "Oh, I'm sorry, I meant 'no.'"

In another experiment a split-brain patient saw two words flashed at once, one on each side. He was then asked to draw a picture of what he had read. Each hemisphere saw a full word, but the two words could combine to make a different word. For example,

Left Visual Field (Right Hemisphere)	Right Visual Field (Left Hemisphere)
hot	dog
honey	moon
sky	scraper
rain	bow

With the right hand, he almost always drew what he had seen in the right visual field (left hemisphere), such as *dog* or *moon*. However, with the left hand, he sometimes drew a literal combination of the two words. For example, after seeing *hot* and *dog*, he drew a dog that was overheated, not a wiener on a bun, and after seeing *sky* and *scraper*, he drew a sky and a scraper (see Figure 14.5). The right hemisphere, which predominantly controls the left hand, drew what it saw in the left visual field (*hot* or *sky*). Ordinarily the left hemisphere doesn't control the left hand, but through the bilateral mechanisms of the ventromedial spinal pathway (described in Chapter 8), it can move the left hand clumsily, and evidently enough to add what it saw in the right visual field (*dog* or *scraper*). However, neither hemisphere could combine the words into one concept (Kingstone & Gazzaniga, 1995).

The Right Hemisphere

When investigators discovered that the left hemisphere controls speech, most psychologists thought the right hemisphere was something like a vice president, supporting the "major" hemisphere but always subordinate to it. Later studies indicated that the right hemisphere has its own specialized functions.

For example, the right hemisphere is crucial for the emotional content of speech. People who have suffered damage to the right hemisphere speak with little inflection or expression (Shapiro & Danly, 1985), do not understand the emotions that other people express through tone of voice (Tucker, 1981), and usually fail to understand humor and sarcasm.

SCRAPER-SKY

Figure 14.5 Left-hand drawing by a split-brain patient
He saw the word *sky* in the left visual field and *scraper* in the right visual field. His left hemisphere controlled the left hand enough to draw a scraper and his right hemisphere controlled it enough to draw a sky. Neither hemisphere could combine the two words to make the emergent concept *skyscraper*. (Source: Kingstone & Gazzaniga, 1995)

(a)

(b)

Figure 14.6   Half of a smiling face combined with half of a neutral face
Which looks happier to you—**(a)** the one with a smile on your left or **(b)** the one with a smile on your right? Your answer may suggest which hemisphere of your brain is dominant for interpreting emotional expressions. *(Source: Levy, Heller, Banich, & Burton, 1983)*

The hemispheres also have different contributions to emotion in general. Several kinds of studies indicate that happiness activates mostly the left hemisphere, whereas fear and anger activate mostly the right (Canli, 1999; Wiedemann et al., 1999). However, the right hemisphere is dominant for recognizing emotions in others, including both pleasant and unpleasant emotions. In a split-brain person, the right hemisphere does better than the left at recognizing whether two photographs show the same or different emotions (Stone, Nisenson, Eliassen, & Gazzaniga, 1996). Similar results have been found for split-brain monkeys (Vermeire, Hamilton, & Erdmann, 1998). Moreover, according to Jerre Levy and her colleagues' studies of brain-intact people, when the left and right hemispheres perceive different emotions in someone's face, the response of the right hemisphere dominates. For example, examine the faces in Figure 14.6. Each of these combines half of a smiling face with half of a neutral face. Which looks happier to you: face (a) or face (b)? Most people choose face (a), with the smile on the viewer's left (Heller & Levy, 1981; Hoptman & Levy, 1988). Similarly a frown on the viewer's left looks sadder than a frown on the viewer's right (Sackeim, Putz, Vingiano, Coleman, & McElhiney, 1988). Remember, what you see in your left visual field directly activates your right hemisphere.

The right hemisphere also appears to be more adept than the left at comprehending overall visual patterns, including spatial relationships. For example, one young woman with damage to her posterior right hemisphere had great trouble finding her way around, even in fa-

TRY IT
YOUR
SELF

miliar areas. To reach a destination, she needed directions with specific visual details, such as, "Walk to the corner where you see a building with a statue in front of it. Then turn left and go to the corner that has a flagpole and turn right. . . ." Each of these directions had to include an unmistakable feature; if the instruction was "go to the city government building—that's the one with a tower," she could easily go to a very different building that happened to have a tower (Clarke, Assal, & deTribolet, 1993).

How can we best describe the difference in functions between the hemispheres? According to Robert Ornstein (1997), the left hemisphere focuses more on details and the right hemisphere more on overall patterns. Recall the difference between the parvocellular (detailed shape) and magnocellular (overall patterns and movement) paths of the visual cortex, described in Chapter 6: Much research indicates that the parvocellular path is stronger in the left hemisphere and the magnocellular path is stronger in the right (Roth & Hellige, 1998). One result is that the right hemisphere is better at spatial processing. For example, split-brain patients can arrange puzzle pieces more accurately with the left hand than with the right and can use the left hand better for drawing a box, a bicycle, and similar objects. Also, in one study brain-intact people examined visual stimuli such as the one in Figure 14.7, in which many repetitions of a small let-

B   B
B   B
B   B
B   B
B B B B B B B
B   B
B   B
B   B
B   B

Figure 14.7   Stimulus to test analytical and holistic perception
When people were told to name the large composite letter, they had more activity in the right hemisphere. When told to name the small component letters, they had more activity in the left hemisphere. *(Source: Based on Fink et al., 1996)*

ter compose a different large letter. When they were asked to identify the small letters (in this case B), activity increased in the left hemisphere, but when they were asked to identify the large overall letter (H), activity was greater in the right hemisphere (Fink et al., 1996).

But the difference goes beyond vision: The left hemisphere tends to understand language more literally, and therefore people with right-hemisphere damage often miss the "big picture" of what someone is saying. For example, such people often fail to understand jokes (Ornstein, 1997).

The right hemisphere is also more active for music perception (Zatorre, 1979). However, what determines hemispheric dominance is not just the stimulus itself, but what the brain does with the stimulus. For example, the Thai language is one of many "tonal" languages, in which a rising, falling, or steady tone of a vowel changes the meaning of a word. So the sound has a singing quality that is not typical of most European languages. When an English-speaking person listens to Thai, the two hemispheres are about equally dominant, treating the speech almost like music. But for a native Thai speaker, the left hemisphere is dominant, treating the same stimulus as speech (Van Lancker & Fromkin, 1973).

Table 14.1 summarizes some key differences between the left and right hemispheres.

Stop & Check

5. Which hemisphere is dominant for each of the following in most people: speech, expressions of happiness, expressions of anger and fear, emotional inflection of speech, interpreting other people's emotional expressions, spatial relationships, perceiving overall patterns?

Check your answers on page 404.

Hemispheric Specializations in Intact Brains

The differences between the two hemispheres also can be demonstrated in people without brain damage. Most of these differences are, however, small trends.

Here is one demonstration you can try yourself: Tap with a pencil in your right hand on a sheet of paper as many times as you can in 1 minute and then count the tap marks. Rest, and repeat with your left hand. Then repeat with both hands while you talk at the same time. Compare results to find out how much faster you tapped when you weren't talking. For most right-handers, talking decreases the tapping rate with the right hand more than with the left hand (Kinsbourne & McMurray, 1975). Evidently it is more difficult to do two things at once when both activities depend on the same hemisphere.

Development of Lateralization and Handedness

Because in most people language depends primarily on the left hemisphere, it is natural to ask whether the hemispheres differ anatomically. If so, is the difference present before speech develops or does it develop later? What is the relationship between handedness and hemispheric dominance for speech?

Anatomical Differences Between the Hemispheres

The human brain is specialized to attend to language sounds. If you listen to a repeated syllable ("*pack pack pack pack . . .* ") and then suddenly the vowel sound changes (" *. . . pack pack pack peck . . .* "), the change will catch your attention, as one could detect by recording larger evoked responses from your scalp. Changing from *pack* to *peck* also increases the evoked response

Table 14.1	Differences in Function Between the Two Hemispheres	
	Contributions of Left Hemisphere	**Contributions of Right Hemisphere**
Speech	Production and most comprehension	Emotional inflections; understanding humor, sarcasm, other emotional content
Other Sounds		Music perception
Emotions	Expressions of happiness	Expressions of fear, anger, disgust; interpreting others' emotional expressions
Vision	Details; more activity by parvocellular path	Overall pattern; more activity by magnocellular path; spatial processing, such as arranging puzzle pieces or drawing a picture

from a baby, even a premature infant born only 30 weeks after conception (Cheour-Luhtanen et al., 1996). Evidently humans attend to language sounds from the start.

But do the hemispheres differ from the start? Norman Geschwind and Walter Levitsky (1968) found that one section of the temporal cortex, called the **planum temporale** (PLAY-num tem-poh-RAH-lee), is larger in the left hemisphere for 65% of people (Figure 14.8). Sandra Witelson and Wazir Pallie (1973) examined the brains of infants who died before age 3 months and found that the left planum temporale was larger in 12 of 14—on the average, about twice as large. Later studies using MRI scans found that healthy 5- to 12-year-old children with the biggest ratio of left to right planum temporale performed best on language tests, whereas children with nearly equal hemispheres were better on certain nonverbal tasks (Leonard et al., 1996). People who suffer damage to the left hemisphere in infancy eventually develop less language than those with equal damage to the right hemisphere (Stark & McGregor, 1997). In short, the left hemisphere is specialized for language from the start, in most people.

Maturation of the Corpus Callosum

The corpus callosum matures gradually over the first 5 to 10 years of human life (Trevarthen, 1974). The developmental process is not a matter of growing new axons, but of selecting certain axons and discarding others. At an early stage the brain generates far more axons in the corpus callosum than it will have at maturity (Ivy & Killackey, 1981; Killackey & Chalupa, 1986). The reason is that any two neurons connected by the corpus callosum need to have corresponding functions. For example, a neuron in the left hemisphere that responds to light in the very center of the retina should be con-

nected to a right-hemisphere neuron that responds to light in the same location. During early embryonic development, the genes cannot specify exactly where those two neurons will be. Therefore many connections are made across the corpus callosum, but only those axons that happen to connect very similar cells survive (Innocenti & Caminiti, 1980).

Because the connections take years to develop their mature adult pattern, the behavior of young children in some situations resembles that of split-brain adults. An infant who has one arm restrained will not reach across the midline of the body to pick up a toy on the other side before about age 17 weeks. Evidently, in younger children, each hemisphere has too little access to information from the opposite hemisphere (Provine & Westerman, 1979).

In one study 3- and 5-year-old children were asked to feel two fabrics, either with one hand at two times or with two hands at the same time, and say whether the materials felt the same or different. The 5-year-olds did equally well with one hand or with two. The 3-year-olds made 90% more errors with two hands than with one (Galin, Johnstone, Nakell, & Herron, 1979). The likely interpretation is that the corpus callosum matures sufficiently between ages 3 and 5 to facilitate the comparison of stimuli between the two hands.

Development Without a Corpus Callosum

Rarely, the corpus callosum fails to form or forms incompletely, possibly for genetic reasons, although not necessarily. People born without a corpus callosum are unlike people who have it cut later in life. First, whatever prevented formation of the corpus callosum undoubtedly affects brain development in other ways. Second, the absence or near absence of the corpus cal-

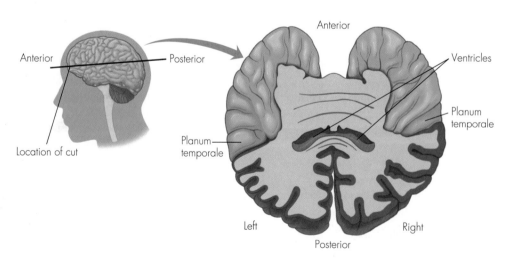

Figure 14.8 Horizontal section through a human brain
This cut, taken just above the surface of the temporal lobe, shows the planum temporale, an area that is critical for speech comprehension. Note that it is substantially larger in the left hemisphere than in the right hemisphere. *(Source: Geschwind & Levitsky, 1968)*

losum induces the remaining brain areas to develop abnormally.

People born without a corpus callosum can perform some tasks that split-brain patients fail. They can verbally describe what they feel with either hand and what they see in either visual field; they can also feel one object with the left hand and another with the right hand and say whether they are the same or different (Bruyer et al., 1985; Sanders, 1989). How do they do so? They do not use their right hemisphere for speech (Lassonde, Bryden, & Demers, 1990). Rather each hemisphere develops pathways connecting it to both sides of the body, enabling the left (speaking) hemisphere to feel both the left and right hands. Also, the brain's other commissures become larger than usual. In addition to the corpus callosum, people have the **anterior commissure** (Figure 4.11, p. 96, and Figure 14.4, p. 398), which connects the anterior parts of the cerebral cortex, the **hippocampal commissure,** which connects the left and right hippocampi (Figure 14.4), and the smaller *posterior commissure* (not shown in Figure 14.4). The extra development of these other commissures partly compensates for the lack of a corpus callosum.

Stop & Check

6. A child born without a corpus callosum can name something felt with the left hand, but an adult who suffered damage to the corpus callosum cannot. What are two likely explanations?

Check your answers on page 404.

Handedness and Language Dominance

About 10% of all people are either left handed or ambidextrous. (Most left-handers are somewhat ambidextrous.) Of all the surviving prehistoric drawings and paintings that show people using tools, more than 90% show the tool in the right hand (Coren & Porac, 1977). Chimpanzees, monkeys, and even rats and mice also show arm preferences, although much less strongly than humans do. Thus, right-handedness appears to be part of our ancient heritage, not a recent development. Curiously, octopuses do not show an arm preference (Mather, 1998).

Although the brains of left- and right-handed people are different, they are not mirror images. For about 99% of right-handed people, the left hemisphere is strongly dominant for speech, and a right-hander who loses speech after left-hemisphere damage cannot regain it except by recovered activity in the left hemisphere (Heiss, Kessler, Thiel, Ghaemi, & Karbe, 1999). Most left-handers have a mixture of left- and right-hemisphere control of speech, but dominance by the left side. Very few have strong right-hemisphere dominance (Loring et al., 1990), although some show language impairments after damage to either hemisphere (Basso & Rusconi, 1998). The corpus callosum (especially the anterior corpus callosum) is thicker in left-handers than in right-handers (Moffat, Hampson, & Lee, 1998). Presumably, the larger corpus callosum is needed for communication between the left-hemisphere language areas and the right-hemisphere areas controlling the left hand.

Avoiding Overstatements

The research on left-brain/right-brain differences has become popular and sometimes leads to unscientific assertions. Occasionally you may hear someone say something like, "I don't do well in science because it is a left-brain subject and I am a right-brain person." That kind of statement is based on two reasonable premises and one that is doubtful. The scientific ones are (a) that the left hemisphere is specialized for verbal or analytic processing and the right hemisphere is specialized for nonverbal or synthetic processing and (b) that certain tasks evoke greater activity in one hemisphere than in the other. The doubtful premise is that any individual habitually relies on one hemisphere or the other.

What evidence do you suppose someone has for believing, "I am a right-brain person"? Did he or she undergo an MRI or PET scan to determine which hemisphere was larger or more active? Not likely. Generally, when people say, "I am right-brained," they mean that they perform better on creative tasks than on logical tasks. Therefore, the statement really means, "I do poorly in science because I do poorly in science."

In fact only the very simplest tasks activate just one hemisphere. Here is the evidence, which is a bit complicated: Suppose you are asked to tap your finger as soon as you see a flash of light. If you tap with your right finger, you will respond faster when you see a flash of light in the right visual field, and if you tap with your left finger, you will respond faster to a flash in the left visual field. The reason is when you use a finger on the same side of the body as the flash of light, the information doesn't have to cross the corpus callosum. Crossing the corpus callosum takes only a few milliseconds, but even that short delay is measurable. Now suppose we do the same kind of experiment but make the task slightly more complicated. Instead of tapping for any light you see, you tap for just certain kinds of light, so you have to process the information in some way before tapping your finger. The result is that you will tap a bit more slowly, and your reaction time won't depend on which finger is tapping or which visual field sees the stimulus (Forster & Corballis, 2000). The reason is that even a slightly difficult task requires you to use both hemispheres anyway, so it doesn't matter whether the light started in one hemisphere or the other. The same is true in general: Almost any task that is complicated enough to be interesting requires cooperation by both hemispheres.

Module 14.1

In Closing: One Brain, Two Hemispheres

Imagine that someone asks you a question to which you honestly reply that you do not know, while your left hand points to the correct answer. It must be an unsettling experience. A split-brain person acts at times like two people—two spheres of consciousness. A brain-intact person acts and feels like a unity. How does a split-brain person feel? We don't know. When we ask, only the left hemisphere can answer, and *it* feels like a unity, but we don't know how the other hemisphere feels. As is so often true when we deal with the mind-brain relationship, many answers are elusive.

Summary

1. The corpus callosum is a set of axons connecting the two hemispheres of the brain. (p. 394)

2. The left hemisphere controls speech in most people, and each hemisphere controls mostly the hand on the opposite side, sees the opposite side of the world, and feels the opposite side of the body. (p. 394)

3. In humans the left visual field projects onto the right half of each retina, which sends axons to the right hemisphere. The right visual field projects onto the left half of each retina, which sends axons to the left hemisphere. (p. 395)

4. After damage to the corpus callosum, each hemisphere can respond quickly and accurately to questions about the information that reaches it directly and can slowly answer a few questions about information on the other side if it crosses the anterior commissure or one of the other small commissures. (p. 397)

5. Although the two hemispheres of a split-brain person are sometimes in conflict, they find many ways to cooperate and to cue each other. (p. 399)

6. The right hemisphere is dominant for the emotional inflections of speech and for interpreting other people's emotional expressions in either speech or facial expression. The right hemisphere also controls one's own expressions of fear, anger, and disgust. In vision and other modalities, it attends mostly to overall patterns, in contrast to the left hemisphere, which is better for details. (p. 399)

7. The left and right hemispheres differ anatomically even during infancy. Young children have some trouble comparing information from the left and right hands because the corpus callosum is not fully mature. (p. 401)

8. In a child born without a corpus callosum, the rest of the brain develops in unusual ways, and the child does not show the same deficits as an adult who sustains damage to the corpus callosum. (p. 402)

9. The brain of a left-handed person is not simply a mirror image of a right-hander's brain. Most left-handers have left-hemisphere or mixed dominance for speech; few have strong right-hemisphere dominance for speech. (p. 403)

10. Both left and right hemispheres contribute to all but the simplest behaviors. (p. 403)

Answers to *Stop and Check* Questions

1. In rabbits the right eye is far to the side of the head and sees only the right visual field. In humans the eyes point straight ahead and half of each eye sees the right visual field. (p. 396)

2. Left; left (p. 396)

3. A split-brain person cannot describe something after feeling it with the left hand, but can with the right. The right hand sends its information to the left hemisphere, which is dominant for language in most people. The left hand sends its information to the right hemisphere, which cannot speak. (p. 397)

4. After seeing something in the left visual field, a split-brain person could point to the correct answer with the left hand. (p. 397)

5. The left hemisphere is dominant for speech and expressing happiness; the right hemisphere is dominant for all the other items listed. (p. 401)

6. In children born without a corpus callosum, the left hemisphere develops more than the usual connections with the left hand, and the anterior commissure and other commissures grow larger than usual. (p. 403)

Thought Question

When a person born without a corpus callosum moves the fingers of one hand, he or she also is likely to move the fingers of the other hand involuntarily. What possible explanation can you suggest?

Evolution and Physiology of Language

Communication is widespread among animals through visual, auditory, tactile, or chemical (pheromonal) displays. Even insects such as bees, ants, and wasps signal one another. But human language is different because of its **productivity,** its ability to produce new signals to represent new ideas. That is, certain monkeys have one call to indicate "eagle or hawk in the air—take cover" and another to indicate "beware—snake on the ground." But they have no way to indicate "snake in the tree above you" or "eagle standing on the ground." Humans can discuss all sorts of new events, inventing new words and combinations whenever we need them.

Did we evolve this ability out of nothing or from some precursor already present in other species? Why do we have language, whereas other species have at most a rudimentary hint of it? And what brain specializations make language possible? We consider these questions in order.

Nonhuman Precursors of Language

Evolution rarely makes something totally new. Nearly all differences among species are modifications of an old structure. Bat wings are modified arms, porcupine quills are modified hairs, and so forth. So we would expect human language to be a modification of something we can detect in our closest relatives, chimpanzees, at least in a small degree or under special circumstances. After all, more than 99% of human genes are the same as those of chimpanzees (King & Wilson, 1975).

Common Chimpanzees

After many early, unsuccessful attempts to teach chimpanzees to speak, researchers achieved better results by teaching them American Sign Language or other visual systems (B. T. Gardner & Gardner, 1975; Premack & Premack, 1972) (see Figure 14.9). In one version chimps learned to press keys bearing symbols to type messages on a computer (Rumbaugh, 1977). For example, they could make requests (such as "Please machine give apple" or "Please machine turn on movie"). They also learned to type messages to other chimps ("Please share your chocolate").

Is this use of symbols really language? Not necessarily. For example, when I insert my ATM card into a machine and enter my four-digit PIN, I don't really understand those four digits to mean "Please machine give money." Similarly, when a chimpanzee punches four symbols on a machine, it may not understand them to mean "Please machine give apple." Symbols are like language only if the user can recombine them to make new sentences. The chimps' use of symbols differed from language in several regards (Rumbaugh, 1990; Terrace, Petitto, Sanders, & Bever, 1979):

- The chimpanzees seldom used the symbols in new, original combinations (as even very young children do).

- The chimpanzees used their symbols almost always to request, only rarely to describe.

- The chimpanzees produced requests far better than they seemed to understand anyone else's requests. In contrast, young children can understand far more than they can say. If you studied a foreign language, presumably you understand many sentences that you could not correctly state yourself. (If you look up how to say something in a foreign-language phrase book, but then can't understand the reply, you don't really understand the language.)

Bonobos

Such observations made psychologists skeptical about chimpanzee language. Then some surprising results emerged from studies of a rare endangered species, *Pan paniscus,* known as the bonobo or the pygmy chimpanzee (a misleading name because they are practically the same size as common chimpanzees).

Bonobos have a social order resembling that of humans in several regards. Males and females form strong, sometimes lasting, personal attachments. They often copulate face-to-face. The female is sexually responsive at almost all times and not just during her fertile period. Unlike most other primates, the males contribute significantly to infant care. Adults often share food with

Figure 14.9 One attempt to teach chimpanzees language
One of the Premacks' chimps, Elizabeth, reacts to colored plastic chips that read "Not Elizabeth banana insert—Elizabeth apple wash." *(Source: Photo courtesy of Ann Premack)*

one another. They stand comfortably on their hind legs. In short, they resemble humans more than any other primates do.

In the mid-1980s Sue Savage-Rumbaugh, Duane Rumbaugh, and their associates began trying to teach a female bonobo named Matata to press symbols that light up when touched; each symbol represents a word (see Figure 14.10). Although Matata made little progress, her infant son Kanzi learned just by watching her attempts. When given a chance to use the symbol board, he quickly excelled, even though he had never been formally trained. Soon researchers noticed that Kanzi understood a fair amount of spoken language. For example, whenever anyone said the word "light," Kanzi would flip the light switch. By age 5½, he understood about 150 English words and could respond to such complex, unfamiliar spoken commands as "Throw your ball in the river" and "Go to the refrigerator and get out a tomato" (Savage-Rumbaugh, 1990; Savage-Rumbaugh, Sevcik, Brakke, & Rumbaugh, 1992). Since then Kanzi has demonstrated language comprehension comparable to that of a 2- to 2½-year-old child (Savage-Rumbaugh et al., 1993).

Kanzi and his younger sister Mulika use symbols in several ways that resemble humans more than they resemble common chimpanzees (Savage-Rumbaugh, 1991; Savage-Rumbaugh et al., 1993):

- They understand more than they can produce.
- They use symbols to name and describe objects even when they are not requesting them.
- They request items that they do not see, such as "bubbles" (I want to play with the bubble-blower) or "car trailer" (drive me in the car to the trailer).
- They occasionally use the symbols to describe past events. Kanzi once punched the symbols "Matata bite" to explain the cut that he had received on his hand an hour earlier.
- They frequently make original, creative requests. For example, after Kanzi learned to press symbols to ask someone to play "chase" with him, he asked one person to chase another person while he watched!

Why have Kanzi and Mulika developed such impressive skills where other chimpanzees failed? One likely explanation is a species difference: Perhaps bonobos have more language potential than common chimpanzees. A second explanation is that Kanzi and Mulika began language training when young, unlike the chimpanzees in most other studies. A third reason pertains to the method of training: Perhaps learning by observation and imitation promotes better understanding

Figure 14.10 Language tests for Kanzi, a bonobo *(Pan paniscus)*
He listens to questions through the earphones and points to answers on a board. The experimenter with him does not know what the questions are or what answers are expected. *(Source: From Georgia State University's Language Research Center, operated with the Yerkes Primate Center of Emory. Photo courtesy of Duane Rumbaugh)*

than the formal training methods of previous studies (Savage-Rumbaugh et al., 1992).

Stop *&* Check

1. In what ways do common chimpanzees' use of symbols differ from language?

2. What are three likely explanations for why the bonobos made more language progress than common chimpanzees?

Check your answers on page 419.

Nonprimates

What about nonprimate species? Dolphins have learned to respond to a system of gestures and sounds, each representing one word. For example, after the command "Right hoop left Frisbee fetch," a dolphin takes the Frisbee on the left to the hoop on the right (Herman, Pack, & Morrel-Samuels, 1993). A dolphin responds correctly to new combinations of old words, but only if the result is meaningful. For example, the first time that a dolphin is given the command "Person hoop fetch," it takes the hoop to the person. But when told "Person water fetch," it does nothing (because it has no way to take water to the person). Note that this system offers the dolphins no opportunity or incentive to produce language. They cannot tell humans to take the Frisbee to the hoop (Savage-Rumbaugh, 1993).

Spectacular results have been reported for Alex, an African gray parrot (Figure 14.11). Parrots are, of course, famous for imitating human sounds; Irene Pepperberg was the first to argue that parrots can use sounds meaningfully. She kept Alex in a stimulating environment and taught him to say words in conjunction with specific objects. First she and the other trainers would say a word many times and then offer rewards if Alex approximated the same sound. Here is an excerpt from a conversation with Alex early in training (Pepperberg, 1981, p. 142):

Pepperberg: Pasta! (*Takes pasta.*) Pasta! (*Alex stretches from his perch, appears to reach for pasta.*)

Alex: Pa!

Pepperberg: Better . . . what is it?

Alex: Pah-ah.

Pepperberg: Better!

Alex: Pah-ta.

Pepperberg: Okay, here's the pasta. Good try.

Although pasta was used in this example, Pepperberg generally used toys. For example, if Alex said "paper," "wood," or "key," she would give him what he asked for. In no case did she reward him for saying "paper" or "wood" by giving him a piece of food.

Alex made gradual progress, learning to give spoken answers to spoken questions. He was shown a tray of 12 small objects and then asked such questions as "What color is the key?" (answer: "green") and "What object is gray?" (answer: "circle"). In one test he gave the correct answer to 39 of 48 questions. Even many of his incorrect answers were almost correct. In one case he was asked the color of the block and he responded with the color of the rock (Pepperberg, 1993). He also can answer questions of the form "How many blue key?" in which he has to examine ten to fourteen objects, count the blue keys among objects of two shapes and two colors, and then say the answer, ranging from one to six (Pepperberg, 1994).

Is Alex actually learning language? Pepperberg simply refers to his performance as "language-like." She says that she is using the research to study the bird's concept formation, not his language capacities. Still, Alex has made far more progress than most of us would have thought possible.

What do we learn from studies of nonhuman language abilities? At a practical level we may gain some insights into how best to teach language to those who do not learn it easily, such as brain-damaged people or autistic children. At a more theoretical level, these

Figure 14.11 Language tests for Alex, a gray parrot
Alex has apparently learned to converse about objects in simple English—for example, giving the correct answer to "What color is the circle?" He receives no food rewards. *(Source: David Carter)*

studies call attention to the difficulty of defining language: The main reason that we have such trouble deciding whether chimpanzees or parrots have language is that we have not specified exactly what language is.

With regard to the question we started with, it appears that bonobos have some potential for language learning, so human language evolved from a precursor that was present in the ancient ancestor from which both species derived. What we still don't know is what that precursor ability was doing. Do bonobos, and perhaps other primates, have some language-type abilities because they use it for communication? Perhaps so; the ability for spoken language probably evolved from early communication by gestures (Corballis, 1999). (Gestures are still important for communication; ask someone what a spiral is and then watch their hands move!)

However, the current use of some ability can be very different from the original use. For example, computers were originally invented to make mathematical calculations. Today most people use them for writing papers, exchanging e-mail, and browsing the Internet. If you looked just at current use, you might not guess the original use. Similarly it is possible that language evolved from brain circuits devoted to organizing movement or to some other noncommunicational function.

How Did Humans Evolve Language?

Assuming that humans evolved language from a precursor present in other primates, the question remains: Why did we evolve language? You may think the answer is obvious: "Look at all the ways in which language is useful ... " True, but if it's so useful, why didn't other primates (which after all have some precursor abilities) also evolve language? If it's possible to teach a parrot a little language, why don't parrots in the wild have a language? In fact why don't all sorts of animals have at least simple languages? Most theories fall into two main categories: (a) we evolved language as a by-product of overall brain development and (b) we evolved it as an extra part of the brain.

Language as a Product of Overall Intelligence

The simplest view is that humans evolved big brains, and therefore great intelligence, and when brains and intelligence become great enough, language appears as an accidental by-product. Language is an important part of human intelligence, so it is natural to think of language and intelligence as closely related. There are, however, a number of problems with assuming that language is just a by-product of overall brain development.

First Problem: Unclear Relationship Between Brain and Intelligence If language is a by-product of overall brain development, maybe chimpanzees' brains are just not

quite big enough for language. If we take this idea seriously, we run into difficulties. Elephants' brains are four times the size of ours, and sperm whales' brains are twice as big as elephants'. But neither has language—at least none that we can decipher and none that guides their behavior in any visible way.

An alternative view is that intelligence depends on brain-to-body ratio. Figure 14.12 illustrates the relationship between logarithm of body mass and logarithm of brain mass for various vertebrates (Jerison, 1985). Note that the species we regard as most intelligent—ourselves, ahem, for example—have larger brains in proportion to body size than do the species we consider less impressive—frogs, for example. However, as soon as you try to define exactly what you mean by animal intelligence, you will find that it is a very slippery issue (Macphail, 1985). For now let's not even worry about that one. Humans, it turns out, do *not* have the highest brain-to-body ratio of all species. That honor goes to the squirrel monkey, whose brain constitutes 5% of the monkey's total weight. The human brain weighs only 2% of our total weight. Even the elephant-nose fish, which you might keep in a tropical fish aquarium, beats us in percentage (Figure 14.13). Its brain weighs a mere 0.3 g (as compared to our 1200 to 1400 g), but that's 3% of the total weight of the fish (Nilsson, 1999). So, are squirrel monkeys and elephant-nose fish more intelligent than we are? I don't know, but my guess is that brain-to-body ratio is misleading.

Consider also the **chihuahua problem:** Among dogs, chihuahuas have the highest brain-to-body ratio simply because they were selected for small bodies (Deacon, 1997). Are chihuahuas the smartest of dogs? Again, I don't know, but if they are, it's going to be news to most people. In short, intelligence, as we define it, is not a simple outcome of either overall brain size or brain-to-body ratio.

Stop & Check

3. Why are both brain size and brain-to-body ratio unsatisfactory explanations for intelligence?

Check your answer on page 419.

Second Problem: People with Full-Sized Brains and Impaired Language If language is a product of overall brain development, then people with full-sized brains, no brain damage, and normal overall intelligence should necessarily have normal language. However, not all do. In one family, 16 of 30 people over three generations show severe language deficits despite normal intelligence in other regards. Because of a dominant gene, which has been located and identified, the affected people have serious troubles in pronunciation

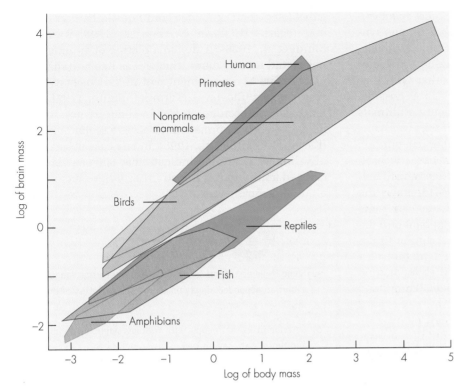

Figure 14.12 Relationship of brain mass to body mass across species
Each species is one point within one of the polygons. In general, log of body mass is a good predictor of log of brain mass. Note that primates in general and humans in particular have a large brain mass in proportion to body mass. *(Source: Adapted from Jerison, 1985)*

and virtually all other aspects of language (Fisher, Vargha-Khadem, Watkins, Monaco, & Pembrey, 1998; Gopnik & Crago, 1991). They fail to master even the simplest grammatical rules, as shown in the following dialogue about making plurals:

Experimenter	Respondent
This is a wug; these are . . .	How should I know? *[Later]* These are wug.
This is a zat; these are . . .	These are zacko.
This is a sas; these are . . .	These are sasss. *[Not sasses]*

In another test experimenters presented sentences and asked whether each sentence was correct, and if not, how to improve it. People in this family accepted many ungrammatical sentences while labeling many correct sentences as incorrect. (Evidently they were just guessing.) When they tried to correct a sentence, their results were often odd. For example:

Original Item	Attempted Correction
The boy eats three cookie.	The boys eat four cookie.

In short, a genetic condition that affects brain development can seriously impair language without necessarily impairing other aspects of intelligence.

Third Problem: Williams Syndrome

What about the reverse pattern? Could someone be mentally retarded in most ways and nevertheless have good language? Psychologists long assumed that such a pattern was impossible, that language learning requires good overall intelligence.

And then in the 1960s, psychologists discovered a rare condition, affecting about 1 person in 20,000 to 30,000, called **Williams syndrome,** characterized by mental retardation in most regards but skillful use of language. The cause is a deletion of several genes from chromosome 7 (Frangiskakis et al., 1996), leading to abnormal development of the posterior portions of the cerebral cortex and several subcortical areas (Bellugi, Lichtenberger, Mills, Galaburda, & Korenberg, 1999). Affected people are unable to learn the simple skills needed to take care of themselves; they have impaired attention, planning, problem solving, use of numbers, visuomotor skills (such as copying a drawing), and spatial perception (such as finding their way home). Even as adults they require constant supervision and cannot hold even an unskilled job.

Nevertheless they are close to normal in several other regards. One is their ability to interpret facial expressions, such as relaxed or worried, serious or playful, flirtatious or uninterested (Tager-Flusberg, Boshart, & Baron-Cohen, 1998). Another is social behavior, such as friendliness and openness toward other people. Still another is music, such as the ability to clap a complex

Figure 14.13 An elephant-nose fish
The brain of this odd-looking fish weighs 0.3 g (0.01 ounce), which is 3% of the weight of the whole fish—a vastly higher percentage than most other fish and higher even than humans. What this fish does with so much brain, we don't know, but it may relate to the fish's unusual ability to detect electrical fields.

rhythm (Levitin & Bellugi, 1998). Their most spectacular skill is language. Not all people with Williams syndrome have good language abilities (Jarrold, Baddeley, & Hewes, 1998), but some are quite amazing, especially considering their impairments of many other skills. For example, if asked to "name as many animals as possible in the next minute," most people list familiar animals such as dog, horse, and squirrel. People with Williams syndrome list about the same total number in a minute, but their list includes odd examples, such as weasel, newt, ibex, unicorn, yak, koala, and triceratops (Bellugi, Wang, & Jernigan, 1994). Figure 14.14 shows the result when a young woman with Williams syndrome and an IQ of 49 was asked to draw an elephant and describe it. Contrast her almost poetic description to the unrecognizable drawing. When shown a picture of a frog in a jar and asked to tell a story about it, one Williams syndrome teenager with an IQ of 50 produced the following:

> Once upon a time when it was dark at night . . . the boy had a frog. The boy was looking at the frog . . . sitting on the chair, on the table, and the dog was looking through . . . looking up to the frog in a jar. That night he slept and slept for a long time, the dog did. But, the frog was not gonna go to sleep. And when the frog went out . . . the boy and the dog were still sleeping. The next morning it was beautiful in the morning. It was bright and the sun was nice and warm. Then suddenly when he opened his eyes . . . he looked at the jar and then suddenly the frog was not there. The jar was empty. There was no frog to found (whispered). (Bellugi et al., 1999, p. 199)

I don't want to overstate the case. People with Williams syndrome have some language abnormalities. Their language development is slow in early childhood, and although many of them make spectacular gains later, their grammar continues to be odd in several regards (Clahsen & Almazen, 1998; Karmiloff-Smith et al., 1998). If shown a picture of an unfamiliar object and told its name, they are as likely to think the name refers to a prominent part of the object as to the whole object (Stevens & Karmiloff-Smith, 1997). Their language has been compared in some regards to what happens when a normal adult learns a second language (Karmiloff-Smith et al., 1998). In any case observations of Williams syndrome indicate that language is a specialized ability that is not strictly a by-product of overall intelligence.

Stop & Check

4. Name three arguments against the hypothesis that language evolution depended simply on the overall evolution of brain and intelligence.

5. Describe tasks that people with Williams syndrome do poorly and those that they do well.

Check your answers on page 419.

Language as a Special Module

An alternative view is that language evolved as an extra brain module, a new specialization. This presumed module has been forcefully described by Noam Chomsky (1980) and Steven Pinker (1994) as a **language acquisition device,** a built-in mechanism for acquiring language. The main evidence for this view is the amazing ease with which most children develop language. The hearing children of deaf parents gain language almost on schedule despite hearing nothing from their own parents (Lenneberg, 1969). Deaf children quickly learn sign language, and if no one teaches them a sign language, they invent one of their own and teach it to one another (Goldin-Meadow, McNeill, & Singleton, 1996; Goldin-Meadow & Mylander, 1998).

Advocates of the language acquisition device concept sometimes go beyond saying that children learn language readily, saying instead that people are *born* with language; all they have to do is to fill in the words and details. Chomsky defends this idea with the **poverty of the stimulus argument:** Children do not hear many examples of some of the grammatical structures they acquire, and therefore they could not learn them. For example, even young children will phrase the question

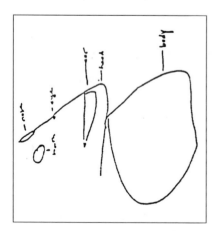

Figure 14.14 A drawing and a description of an elephant by a young woman with Williams syndrome
The labels on the drawing were provided by the investigator, based on what the woman said she was drawing. *(Source: Bellugi, Wang, & Jernigan, 1994)*

> And what an elephant is, it is one of the animals. And what the elephant does, it lives in the jungle. It can also live in the zoo. And what it has, it has long gray ears, fan ears, ears that can blow in the wind. It has a long trunk that can pick up grass, or pick up hay . . . If they're in a bad mood it can be terrible . . . If the elephant gets mad it could stomp; it could charge, like a bull can charge. They have long big tusks. They can damage a car . . . it could be dangerous. When they're in a pinch, when they're in a bad mood it can be terrible. You don't want an elephant as a pet. You want a cat or a dog or a bird . . .

"Is the boy who is unhappy watching Mickey Mouse?"

instead of

"Is the boy who unhappy is watching Mickey Mouse?"

Chomsky maintains that children have not had enough opportunity to learn that grammatical rule, so they must be born knowing it. The rebuttal to Chomsky's argument is that children can learn any of humanity's thousands of languages depending on where they live, and it is implausible that they could be born knowing the diverse grammars of all languages (Deacon, 1997; Seidenberg, 1997).

Most researchers agree that humans have specially evolved *something* that enables them to learn language easily. What that something is, we don't know. It may not even be a separate brain module, depending on what one means by "module." If one means an independent capacity added on, like a speech synthesizer attached to a computer, then language is not really a separate module. In the next section we consider the brain structures of language, but the gist is that much of the brain is reorganized to produce language and much participates in language, not just one or two new brain areas.

So back to the original question: Why did humans evolve language, whereas no other species did? The honest answer is that we don't know, but language is probably not a by-product of evolving overall intelligence. In fact the opposite is easier to imagine: Selective pressure for social interactions among people, including those between parents and children, favored the evolution of language, and as language improved, overall intelligence developed as a by-product of language (Deacon, 1992, 1997).

Is There a Critical Period for Language Learning?

If humans are specially adapted to learn language, perhaps we are adapted to learn best during a critical period early in life, just as sparrows learn their song best during an early period. One way to test this hypothesis is to see whether people learn a second language better if they start young. The consistent result is that adults are better than children at memorizing the vocabulary of a second language, but children are much more likely to master the pronunciation and the more unfamiliar aspects of the grammar. (For example, the difference between *a* and *the* in English is difficult for adult Chinese speakers, whose native language doesn't use articles.) However, there is no cutoff at a particular age; starting at age 2 is better than 4, 4 is better than 6, even 13 is better than 16 (Harley & Wang, 1997; Weber-Fox & Neville, 1996). For someone who has studied a language a little and developed only slight skill in it, the

brain hardly treats it as language at all. The brain areas usually activated by the first language hardly respond to the new language (Neville et al., 1998). However, if someone learns a second language well, it activates the same language areas as the first (Paradis, 1998), and the amount of language-area activation depends on the degree of mastery of the second language, *not on the age of starting it* (Perani et al., 1998). Thus the data on second-language learning are ambiguous with regard to a critical period.

Another way to test the critical-period idea is to study people who were not exposed to language at all during infancy. There are a few cases of children who lived in the wild, raised by wolves or whatever, who were later found and returned to human society. The result is that they were limited in their language learning, but these results are difficult to interpret for many obvious reasons.

Clearer data come from studies of deaf children who at first were not exposed to other deaf children or to sign language. If their deafness was profound enough that they could not learn spoken language, they were effectively isolated from all language. Here the result is clear: The earlier a child has a chance to learn sign language, the more skilled he or she will become. Those who begin late never catch up to those who began when young. In fact deaf people who begin sign language late (say, after 12) never catch up to hearing people who study it as a second language, even if they too begin it late (Harley & Wang, 1997). In other words it's important to learn some language early. If you do, you can learn another language later, but if you don't learn any language when you're young, you will be forever disadvantaged.

Stop & Check

6. What is the poverty of the stimulus argument, and what is one argument against it?

7. If you learn a second language late in life, does it activate the same brain area as the first language or a different one?

8. What is the strongest evidence in favor of a critical period for language learning?

Check your answers on page 419.

Effects of Brain Damage on Language

Although chimpanzees and African gray parrots may learn an approximation of language, it does not come easily for them. In contrast, almost every healthy child develops language. Human cultures vary enormously in their use of tools, but even technologically primitive cultures have complicated, sometimes very complicated, languages (Pinker, 1996). Evidently the human brain is specialized to make language learning easy. Most of our knowledge about the brain mechanisms of language has come from studies of brain-damaged people.

Broca's Aphasia

In 1861 a patient who had been mute for 30 years was treated for gangrene by the French surgeon Paul Broca. When the man died 5 days later, Broca did an autopsy and found a lesion in the frontal cortex. In later years Broca examined the brains of additional patients whose only problem had been aphasia (severe language impairment); in nearly all cases he found damage that included this same area, a small part of the frontal lobe of the left cerebral cortex near the motor cortex, which is now known as Broca's area (Figure 14.15). The usual cause was a stroke (an interruption of blood flow to part of the brain). Broca published his results in 1865, slightly later than papers by other French physicians, Marc and Gustave Dax, which also pointed to the left hemisphere as the seat of language abilities (Finger & Roe, 1996). Broca is given the credit, however, because his description was more detailed and more convincing. The discovery that language depends on a specific part of the left hemisphere was the first demonstration linking a behavior to a brain area, but it was at first resisted because of its apparent similarity to the discredited pseudoscience of phrenology (Digression 14.2). Its acceptance paved the way for all later studies of specialized functions of brain areas.

We now know that damage limited to Broca's area produces only a minor or brief language impairment; serious deficits occur only with extensive damage that extends beyond Broca's area to other cortical and subcortical structures. Damage to Broca's area and surrounding areas is associated specifically with Broca's aphasia or *nonfluent aphasia*, characterized most prominently by impaired language production (Geschwind, 1970, 1972). For many years neurologists asserted that people with Broca's aphasia had normal language comprehension; later studies found that both production and comprehension are normal in some ways but show deficits when the meaning of a sentence depends on prepositions, word endings, or unusual word order—in short, whenever the meaning of the sentence is difficult to understand.

Difficulty in Language Production People with Broca's aphasia speak slowly and inarticulately, and they have trouble writing and gesturing (Cicone, Wapner, Foldi, Zurif, & Gardner, 1979). The left frontal cortex is just as important for the sign language of the deaf (Neville et al., 1998), and deaf people with Broca's aphasia have trouble producing sign language, although they can use their hands well in other ways (Hickok, Bellugi, & Klima, 1996).

People with Broca's aphasia speak meaningfully but omit pronouns, prepositions, conjunctions, helper verbs, quantifiers, and tense and number endings. These omitted words and endings are known as the *closed class* of grammatical forms because a language rarely adds new prepositions, conjunctions, and the like. In contrast, new nouns and verbs (the *open class*) enter a language frequently. People with Broca's aphasia use nouns and verbs more easily than closed-class words. They find it difficult to repeat a phrase such as "No ifs, ands, or buts," although they can successfully repeat "The general commands the army." Furthermore patients who cannot read aloud "To be or not to be" can read "Two bee oar knot two bee" (H. Gardner & Zurif, 1975). Clearly the trouble is with the word meanings, not just pronunciation.

Problems in Comprehending Grammatical Words and Devices People with Broca's aphasia have trouble understanding the same kinds of words that they have trouble speaking, such as prepositions and conjunctions, and sentences with complex grammar, such as "The girl that the boy is chasing is tall" (Zurif, 1980). Sometimes the meaning of a sentence depends on relational words and grammatical devices, and sometimes it does not. You might try taking some paragraph and deleting all the prepositions, conjunctions, articles, and word endings to see how it might appear to someone with Broca's aphasia. Here is an example, taken from Chapter 1 of this text:

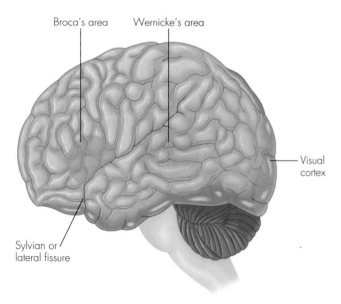

Figure 14.15 Some major language areas of the cerebral cortex
In most people only the left hemisphere is specialized for language.

Broca's area
Wernicke's area
Visual cortex
Sylvian or lateral fissure

Phrenology

In the 1800s Franz Joseph Gall observed some people with an excellent verbal memory who had bulging, protruding eyes. He inferred that verbal memory depended on a part of the brain right behind the eyes that could grow very large and push the eyes forward. Gall then identified other people with unusual talents or personalities and examined their skulls for evidence of bulges or depressions. His process of relating skull anatomy to behavioral capacities is known as **phrenology**. Figure 14.16 is a typical phrenological map of the human skull.

The central problem with phrenology was that the phrenologists did not test their hypotheses carefully. When they found even one person with an unusual personality, they would look for a bump or depression on the skull and identify the underlying brain area as important for that aspect of personality. If they had examined more people, they would have learned that various people with similar personalities do not have similar bumps and depressions on their skulls.

Phrenology gave brain localization a bad reputation, and some people even today disparage brain localization as "mere phrenology." Different brain areas do have different functions, however, which can be identified through careful research.

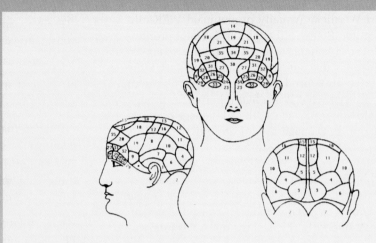

Affective Faculties

Propensities
? Desire to live
• Alimentiveness
1 Destructiveness
2 Amativeness
3 Philoprogenitiveness
4 Adhesiveness
5 Inhabitiveness
6 Combativeness
7 Secretiveness
8 Acquisitiveness
9 Constructiveness

Sentiments
10 Cautiousness
11 Approbativeness
12 Self-esteem
13 Benevolence
14 Reverence
15 Firmness
16 Conscientiousness
17 Hope
18 Marvelousness
19 Ideality
20 Mirthfulness
21 Imitation

Intellectual Faculties

Perceptive
22 Individuality
23 Configuration
24 Size
25 Weight and resistance
26 Coloring
27 Locality
28 Order
29 Calculation
30 Eventuality
31 Time
32 Tune
33 Language

Reflective
34 Comparison
35 Causality

Figure 14.16   A phrenologist's map of the brain
Neuroscientists today also try to localize functions in the brain, but they use more careful methods and they study such functions as vision and hearing, not secretiveness and marvelousness. *(Source: Spurzheim, 1908)*

Biological psychology is ~~the~~ study ~~of the~~ physiological, evolutionary, ~~and~~ developmental mechanisms ~~of~~ behavior ~~and~~ experience. ~~Much of it is~~ devoted ~~to~~ studying brain functions. Figure ~~1.1~~ offers ~~a~~ view ~~of the~~ human brain ~~from the~~ top (~~what~~ neuroscientists call ~~a~~ dorsal view) ~~and from the~~ bottom (~~a~~ ventral view). ~~The~~ labels point ~~to a few~~ important areas, ~~which will~~ become ~~more~~ familiar as ~~you~~ proceed ~~through this~~ text. ~~As we~~ inspect ~~each~~ brain area, ~~we~~ find ~~that it~~ has recognizable subareas ~~and~~ sub-subareas.

Still, people with Broca's aphasia have not totally lost their knowledge of grammar. For example, they generally recognize that something is wrong with the sentence "He written has songs," even if they cannot say how to improve it (Wulfeck & Bates, 1991). The speech patterns of English-speaking people with Broca's aphasia differ from those of, say, Germans or Italians, because even after brain damage, people use the word order that is normal for their language. When comprehension depends on word endings or other grammatical devices, people with Broca's aphasia are impaired, but their performance is not random. In many ways their comprehension resembles that of normal people who are greatly distracted (Blackwell & Bates, 1995).

Wernicke's Aphasia

In 1874 Carl Wernicke (usually pronounced WER-nih-kee in the United States, although the German pronunciation is VER-nih-keh), a 26-year-old junior assistant in a German hospital, discovered that damage in part of the left temporal cortex produced language impairment very different from what Broca had reported. Although patients could speak and write, their language comprehension was poor. Damage in and around **Wernicke's area** (Figure 14.15), located near the auditory part of the cerebral cortex, produces **Wernicke's aphasia**, characterized by impaired ability to remember the names of objects and impaired language comprehension. It is also sometimes known as *fluent aphasia* because the person can still speak smoothly. Typical results are as follows:

1. *Articulate speech.* In contrast to Broca's aphasics, Wernicke's aphasics speak clearly and fluently, except when they pause to try to think of the name of something.

2. *Difficulty finding the right word.* People suffering from Wernicke's aphasia have **anomia** (ay-NOME-ee-uh), difficulty recalling the names of objects. Sometimes they make up names or substitute one name for another, and sometimes they use vague or roundabout expressions such as "the thing that we used to do with the thing that was like the other one." Such expressions no doubt mean something to the speaker, but pity the poor listener. When they do manage to find some of the right words, they arrange them improperly, such as, "The Astros listened to the radio tonight" (instead of "I listened to the Astros on the radio tonight") (R. C. Martin & Blossom-Stach, 1986).

3. *Poor language comprehension.* Wernicke's aphasics have great trouble understanding both spoken and written speech. Although many sentences are clear enough without prepositions, word endings, and grammar (which confuse Broca's aphasics), very few sentences make sense without nouns and verbs (which trouble Wernicke's patients).

The following conversation is between a woman with Wernicke's aphasia and a speech therapist trying to teach her the names of some objects. (The Duke University Department of Speech Pathology and Audiology provided this dialogue.)

Therapist: (*Holding picture of an apron*) Can you name that one?

Woman: Um . . . you see I can't, I can I can barely do; he would give me sort of umm . . .

T: A clue?

W: That's right . . . just a like, just a . . .

T: You mean, like, "You wear that when you wash dishes or when you cook a meal . . . "?

W: Yeah, something like that.

T: Okay, and what is it? You wear it around your waist, and you cook . . .

W: Cook. Umm, umm, see I can't remember.

T: It's an apron.

W: Apron, apron, that's it, apron.

T: (*Holding another picture*) That you wear when you're getting ready for bed after a shower.

W: Oh, I think that he put under different, something different. We had something, you know, umm, you know.

T: A different way of doing it?

W: No, umm . . . umm . . . (*Pause*)

T: It's actually a bathrobe.

W: Bathrobe. Uh, we didn't call it that, we called it something else.

T: Smoking jacket?

W: No, I think we called it, uh . . .

T: Lounging . . . ?

W: No, no, something, in fact, we called it just . . . (*Pause*)

T: Robe?

W: Robe. Or something like that.

Table 14.2 contrasts Broca's aphasia and Wernicke's aphasia.

Beyond Broca and Wernicke

The discussion of aphasia so far may have implied that language production and the use of complex grammar depend on areas in the frontal cortex (Broca's area and surrounding regions) and that language comprehension and naming depend on temporal cortex regions (including Wernicke's area). But that view is an oversimplification (Caramazza, 1995). According to PET and fMRI studies (see Methods 3.1, p. 72, and Methods 6.2, p. 175), speaking increases activity in much of the frontal, temporal, and parietal cortex in the left hemisphere and in parts of the left thalamus and basal ganglia (Wallesch, Henriksen, Kornhuber, & Paulson, 1985) (see Figure 14.17). Reading a sentence aloud also causes widespread activity in Broca's area, Wernicke's area, other surrounding areas, and to a lesser extent, in the corresponding areas of the right hemisphere (Just, Carpenter, Keller, Eddy, & Thulborn, 1996).

Table 14.2 Broca's Aphasia and Wernicke's Aphasia

Type	Pronunciation	Content of Speech	Comprehension
Broca's aphasia	Very poor	Mostly nouns and verbs; omits prepositions and other grammatical connectives	Impaired if the meaning depends on prepositions, grammar, or unusual word order
Wernicke's aphasia	Unimpaired	Grammatical but sometimes non-sensical; has trouble finding the right word, especially names of objects	Seriously impaired

Furthermore the brain areas activated by a task depend on more details of the procedure than we might imagine. Consider, for example, reading aloud. That sounds like a simple enough task, and we might imagine that neurologists could assign it to a particular brain area. All right, try this: Here is a list of European birds that are probably unfamiliar to you. Read the list aloud: *capercaillie, gyrfalcon, goshawk, chukar, chough.*

My point is that in English we frequently encounter

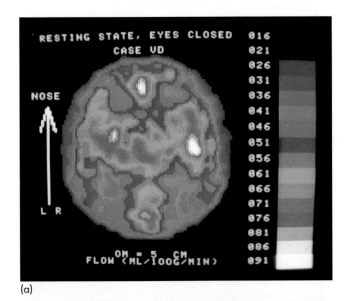

(a)

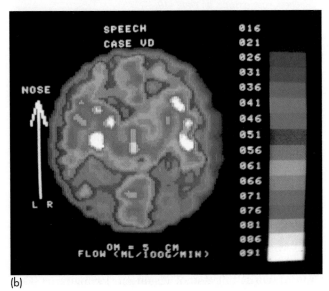

(b)

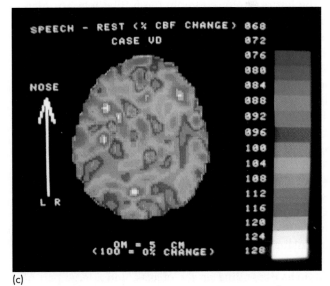

(c)

Figure 14.17 Records showing blood flow for a normal adult
Red indicates the highest level of activity, followed by yellow, green, and blue. **(a)** Blood flow to the brain at rest. **(b)** Blood flow while subject describes a magazine story. **(c)** Difference between **(b)** and **(a)**. The results in **(c)** indicate which brain areas increased their activity during language production. Note the increased activity in many areas of the brain, especially on the left side. *(Source: Wallesch, Henriksen, Kornhuber, & Paulson, 1985)*

words that we don't know how to pronounce. In particular, how did you pronounce *chough*? Did you think it would rhyme with *though, through, cough, rough, dough,* or *bough*? You didn't know, and you had to guess—probably incorrectly. (It rhymes with *rough.*) In contrast, Italian and many other languages are consistently phonetic; the spelling tells you exactly how to say a word, and a correct pronunciation tells you how to spell it. As a result, Italian children learn to read sooner than English-speaking children do, and even in adulthood they read faster. Also—and I'm finally getting to the point—reading aloud activates less of the brain for Italian speakers than it does for English speakers (Paulesu et al., 2000). Reading English requires more work, and often requires double-checking ("Did I say that word right?"), a step that isn't necessary in Italian.

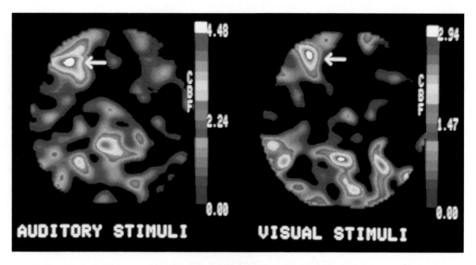

Figure 14.18 Brain areas activated by thinking of a use for an object
For the scan on the left, people heard words; for the scan on the right, they read them. In both cases the PET scan shows which brain areas were activated more by stating a use for a word (such as cake–eat) than by merely repeating the word (cake–cake). Note that for both hearing and reading, activity increased markedly in the left anterior frontal cortex (marked with arrows). *(Source: Petersen, Fox, Posner, Mintun, & Raichle, 1988)*

Two studies examined cortical responses while people looked at pictures and named the images. Both studies found that naming any object activated parts of the temporal lobe corresponding approximately to Wernicke's area. Additional areas also became active depending on the kind of object and what the person imagined doing with it. According to one study, naming people activated the anterior area of the temporal lobe, naming animals activated a posterior area, and naming tools activated a still more posterior area (Damasio, Grabowski, Tranel, Hichwa, & Damasio, 1996). The other study found that naming animals activated part of the occipital lobe, whereas naming tools activated part of the left premotor cortex in the frontal lobe (A. Martin, Wiggs, Ungerleider, & Haxby, 1996). These studies used different methods, so the results should not be considered contradictory.

Figure 14.18 shows the results of a study in which people heard or read the names of objects and then either repeated the words or stated a use for the objects (such as *hammer–pound* or *cake–eat*). Stating a use for the word activated frontal cortex areas that were not affected by simply repeating the word (Petersen, Fox, Posner, Mintun, & Raichle, 1988; Posner, Petersen, Fox, & Raichle, 1988). Presumably, when people think of a function, they activate the motor or premotor areas that would enable them to perform that function. The figure indicates that the frontal cortex treats spoken and written language in virtually the same way.

The important point is that naming activates different areas depending on the objects, and a large part of the cortex contributes to naming in one way or another. That is, the human brain is not just a larger chimpanzee brain plus a language module; a great amount of the brain had to be reorganized to make language happen.

Stop & Check

9. Describe the speech production of people with Broca's aphasia and those with Wernicke's aphasia.

10. Describe the speech comprehension of people with Broca's aphasia and those with Wernicke's aphasia.

11. Why does reading aloud require more of the brain in English speakers than Italian speakers?

Check your answers on page 419.

Dyslexia

Dyslexia is a specific impairment of reading in a person with adequate vision and adequate skills in other academic areas. There is no single abnormality associated with all cases of dyslexia any more than there is a single cause of headache or backache.

Many people with dyslexia apparently have relatively unresponsive magnocellular paths in the visual system (Livingstone, Rosen, Drislane, & Galaburda, 1991). Recall from Chapter 6 that the magnocellular path deals with overall patterns and moving objects. Many people with dyslexia have impaired perception not only of words but also of visual motion patterns (Cornelissen, Richardson, Mason, Fowler, & Stein, 1995; Eden et al., 1996; B. J. Evans, Drasdo, & Richards, 1994). However, the effects vary considerably from one individual to another.

The evidence also suggests an altered organization of the left and right hemispheres. As a rule a dyslexic person is more likely to have a bilaterally symmetrical cerebral cortex, whereas in other people the planum temporale and certain other areas are larger in the left hemisphere (Hynd & Semrud-Clikeman, 1989). In some dyslexic people certain language-related areas are actually larger in the right hemisphere (Duara et al., 1991). How this pattern relates to the magnocellular deficit is unclear, however, because in most people the magnocellular system tends to be more dominant in the right hemisphere (Roth & Hellige, 1998).

Dyslexia is often associated with perceptual abnormalities in several modalities, not just vision. For example, imagine yourself feeling a pattern of narrow ridges and grooves, such as the grooves on an old-fashioned record album except straight instead of curved. Your task is to decide whether the ridges run parallel to your finger or perpendicular to it. Then you are to feel another pattern of ridges and grooves and say whether they are wider or narrower than the first. Many people with dyslexia perform well below average on this task. Incidentally, people with attention deficit disorder perform about normally, so the problem is specific to dyslexia (Grant, Zangaladze, Thiagarajah, & Sathian, 1999). In short, dyslexia is a general problem, not just something about vision.

Yet another explanation of dyslexia relates it to a difference in attention. Here is a demonstration. Focus your eyes on the central dot in each display below and, without moving your eyes back and forth, try to read the middle letter of each three-letter display:

```
       NOE  •
             •  TWC
      WSH  •
             •  EYO
     CTN  •
             •  ONT
     HCW  •
             •  OHW
   IEY  •
           •  WCI
  HNO  •
         •  SIY
```

If you are like most people, you found it easier to read the letters close to the fixation point and probably perceived those on the right more easily than those on the left. The tendency to read better to the right may be a function of our long experience in reading from left to right; several studies disagree on whether the same tendency occurs in people reading Hebrew and Farsi, which are printed right to left (Brysbaert, Vitu, & Schroyens, 1996; Faust, Kravetz, & Babkoff, 1993; Malamed & Zaidel, 1993; Pollatsek, Bolozky, Well, & Rayner, 1981).

For most people adding a letter at the fixation point generates little interference with nearby letters but major interference with remotely placed letters. For example, the H does not mask the W in this display:

but it does mask the N in this display:

(We are talking about letters flashed briefly on a screen. The interference is less impressive when you can stare at letters on a page.)

Now, it turns out that the results I just described apply to most people, but not to all. For a certain minority a letter at the fixation point produces noticeable interference for an immediately adjacent letter (like the W in the HW display), but less than the normal amount of interference for a remote letter (like the N in the H　N display). People showing this pattern suffer from dyslexia! When people with certain kinds of dyslexia focus on one letter, it blocks perception of the immediately adjacent letters, but permits perception of a letter farther to the right (Geiger, Lettvin, & Zegarra-Moran, 1992). So when they focus on a word, they are worse than average at reading it, but better than average at perceiving letters 5° to 10° to the right of fixation. That kind of attentional focus could certainly confuse attempts at reading and is presumably related to the slow reading speed associated with dyslexia (De Luca, Di Page, Judica, Spinelli, & Zoccolotti, 1999). Figure 14.19 shows the mean results for normal readers and for people with dyslexia.

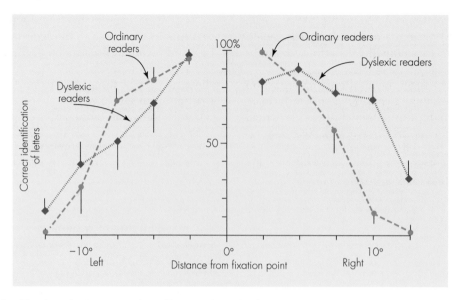

Figure 14.19 Identification of a letter at various distances from the fixation point
Normal readers identify a letter most accurately when it is closest to the fixation point, and their accuracy drops steadily as letters become more remote from that point. Many people with dyslexia show a small impairment for letters just to the right of the fixation point, yet they are substantially more accurate than normal readers are in identifying letters 5° to 10° to the right of fixation. *(Source: Based on Geiger, Lettvin, & Zegarra-Moran, 1992)*

For people with this abnormality, an effective treatment might be to teach them to attend to just one word at a time. Some dyslexic children and adults have been told to place over the page that they are reading a sheet of paper with a window cut out of it that is large enough to expose just one word. In 3 months 15 dyslexic children improved their reading skills by 1.22 grade levels (Geiger, Lettvin, & Fahle, 1994). Four dyslexic adults also made spectacular progress; one advanced from a third-grade to a tenth-grade reading level in 4 months (Geiger et al., 1992). After about the first 3 weeks of practice, they no longer needed the special cut-out sheet of paper.

One final twist: Of the four dyslexic adults who went through this process, three decided that they would rather return to being dyslexic! While dyslexic, they could attend to several tasks at once, such as talking to someone, listening to news on the radio, creating a work of art, and so forth. When they learned to read one word at a time, they found themselves able to perform only one task at a time, and they missed their old way of life. In short, their reading skills were tied to their overall attentional strategies.

Stop & Check

12. What is the evidence that dyslexia represents a dysfunction of more than just vision?

Check your answer on page 419.

In Closing: Language and the Brain

Perhaps the best summary of dyslexia is also the best summary of language impairments in general: Language and reading are sufficiently complicated that people can become impaired in many ways for many reasons. Language is not simply a by-product of overall intelligence, but it is hardly independent of other intellectual functions either.

Summary

1. Chimpanzees can learn to communicate through gestures or nonvocal symbols, although their output does not closely resemble human language. Bonobos have made far more language progress than common chimpanzees because of species differences, early onset of training, and different training methods. (p. 405)

2. Even an African gray parrot has shown surprising language abilities, so the primate type of brain is apparently not necessary for language. (p. 407)

3. The hypothesis that language emerged as a by-product of overall intelligence or brain size faces several major problems: Intelligence is not a simple correlate of brain size; some people have full-sized

brains but impaired language; and people with Williams syndrome have nearly normal language despite mental retardation. (p. 408)

4. The alternative hypothesis that language evolved as a special module is more appealing, although the meaning of "special module" is far from clear. People are specialized to learn language easily, but the whole brain is reorganized for that purpose, not just one or two areas. (p. 410)

5. The best evidence for a critical period for language development is the observation that deaf children learn sign language much better if they start early than if their first opportunity comes later in life. However, there does not appear to be a sudden loss of language capacity at any particular age. (p. 411)

6. People with Broca's aphasia have difficulty speaking and writing. They find prepositions, conjunctions, and other grammatical connectives especially difficult. They also fail to understand speech when its meaning depends on grammatical connectives, sentence structure, or word order. (p. 412)

7. People with Wernicke's aphasia have trouble understanding speech and recalling the names of objects. (p. 414)

8. Language activates many brain areas, and the more difficult a language task, the more active the brain becomes. Naming objects activates different brain areas depending on the type of object. (p. 414)

9. People with reading impairments apparently have a variety of abnormalities in brain structure, perception, and attention. (p. 416)

Answers to *Stop and Check* Questions

1. The chimpanzees seldom arranged the symbols into new combinations, seldom used them to describe anything (only to request), and produced symbols better than they understood anyone else's use of the symbols. (p. 407)

2. Bonobos may be more predisposed to language than common chimpanzees. The bonobos started training at an earlier age. They learned by imitation instead of formal training techniques. (p. 407)

3. If we define intelligence in terms of human-type intelligence, including language, there are species with larger overall brain volume or with a larger brain-to-body ratio that lack language. (p. 408)

4. First, overall intelligence, as defined by humans, has no simple relationship to brain size. Second, some people have normal brain size but very poor language. Third, some people are mentally retarded

but nevertheless develop nearly normal language. (p. 410)

5. Poor: self-care skills, attention, planning, problem solving, numbers, visual-motor skills, and spatial perception. Relatively good: language, interpretation of facial expressions, social behaviors, some aspects of music. (p. 410)

6. The poverty of the stimulus argument is the claim that children say complex sentences without adequate opportunity to learn them, so they must be born with an innate grammar. The argument against this idea is that grammatical rules vary among languages, and children could not be born prepared for all the grammars they might have to learn. (p. 411)

7. If you learn a second language well, it activates the same brain areas as your first language regardless of the age at which you learned it. (p. 411)

8. Deaf children who are not exposed to sign language until later in life (and who did not learn spoken language either while they were young) never become as proficient at it as those who started younger. (p. 411)

9. People with Broca's aphasia speak slowly and with poor pronunciation, but their speech includes nouns and verbs. They omit prepositions, conjunctions, and other grammatical words that have no meaning out of context. People with Wernicke's aphasia speak fluently and grammatically, but omit most nouns and verbs and therefore make little sense to others. (p. 416)

10. People with Broca's aphasia understand most speech unless the meaning depends on grammatical devices or complex sentence construction. People with Wernicke's aphasia understand little speech. (p. 416)

11. Reading English requires more of the brain because it is more difficult; Italian is spelled phonetically and English is not. (p. 416)

12. People with dyslexia have impaired identification of objects by touch. Also, they can improve their reading by learning to shift their attention to one part of the visual field instead of distributing it. (p. 418)

Thought Questions

1. Most people with Broca's aphasia suffer from partial paralysis on the right side of the body. Most people with Wernicke's aphasia do not. Why?

2. In a syndrome called *word blindness*, a person loses the ability to read (even single letters), although the person can still see and speak. What is a possible neurological explanation?

Chapter Ending
Key Terms and Activities

Terms

anomia (p. 414)

anterior commissure (p. 403)

aphasia (p. 412)

Broca's aphasia (p. 412)

Broca's area (p. 412)

chihuahua problem (p. 408)

corpus callosum (p. 394)

dichotic listening task (p. 398)

dyslexia (p. 416)

epilepsy (p. 396)

generalized seizure (p. 396)

grand mal seizure (p. 396)

hippocampal commissure (p. 403)

language acquisition device (p. 410)

lateralization (p. 394)

optic chiasm (p. 395)

partial seizure (p. 397)

petit mal seizure (or absence seizure) (p. 397)

phrenology (p. 413)

planum temporale (p. 402)

poverty of the stimulus argument (p. 410)

productivity (p. 405)

split-brain people (p. 396)

visual field (p. 395)

Wada test (p. 398)

Wernicke's aphasia (p. 414)

Wernicke's area (p. 414)

Williams syndrome (p. 409)

Suggestions for Further Reading

Deacon, T. (1997). *The symbolic species.* New York: Norton. Deep analysis of the evolution of language and intelligence.

Krasnegor, N. A., Rumbaugh, D. M., Schiefelbusch, R. L., & Studdert-Kennedy, M. (1991). *Biological and behavioral determinants of language development.* Hillsdale, NJ: Erlbaum. Features chapters on language learning by chimpanzees, children, and language-impaired people.

Ornstein, R. (1997). *The right mind.* New York: Harcourt Brace. Very readable description of split-brain research and the differences between the left and right hemispheres.

Pinker, S. (1994). *The language instinct.* New York: Morrow. Discussion of both behavioral and biological aspects of language.

Web Sites to Explore

You can go to the Biological Psychology Study Center and click on these links. While there, you can also check for suggested articles available on InfoTrac. The Biological Psychology Internet address is: **http://psychology.wadsworth.com/book/kalatbiopsych7e/**

http://www.aphasia.org/
Home page of the National Aphasia Association, with links to research and support groups.

http://www.strokefamily.org/
Information about recovering speech after a stroke.

http://www.blockbonobofoundation.org/blinks.htm
Information about bonobos.

http://www.uic.edu/depts/mcne/founders
Photos and short biographies of Broca, Wernicke, and other prominent early neurologists.

http://www.bda-dyslexia.org.uk
Information about dyslexia.

Active Learner Link

Animation: Right Brain/Left Brain
Simulation: Hemispheric Specialization
Quiz for Chapter 14

SCHIZOPHRENIE : HEBEPHRENE

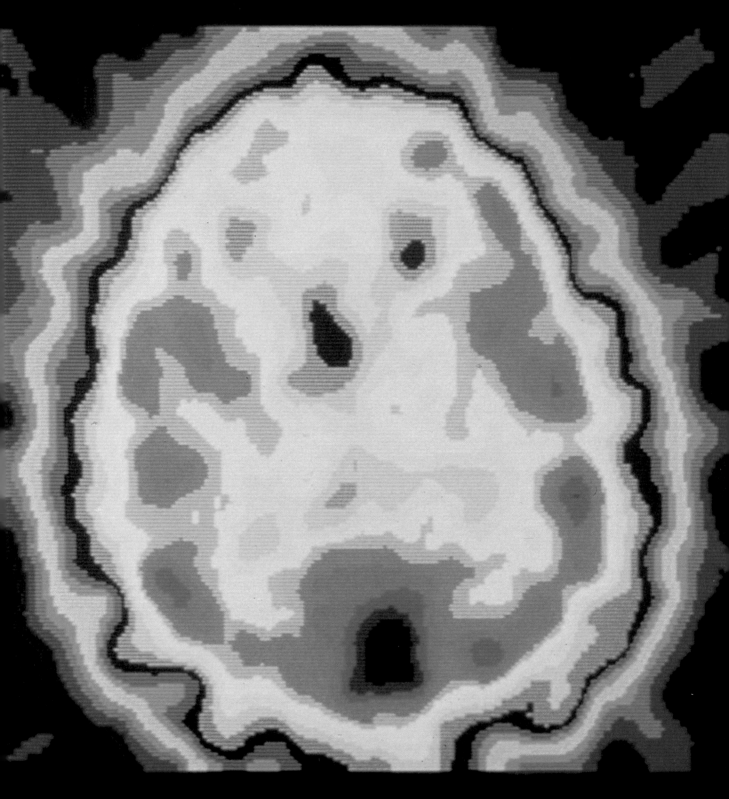

METHIONINE C11

Chapter Outline

Main Ideas

1. Psychological disorders result from a combination of biological and environmental influences.

2. Some people have genetic predispositions that increase their risk of alcoholism. Researchers continue to investigate how those genes act and how they interact with experience.

3. Various drugs used for treating depression and schizophrenia alter transmission at various synapses. The drugs' effectiveness suggests that the disorders may be caused in part by problems affecting particular neurotransmitters.

4. A number of nonpharmaceutical biological treatments are also effective against certain kinds of mood disorder, including electroconvulsive shock, changes in sleep patterns, exposure to bright light, and lithium salts.

5. Schizophrenia may be the result of genetic or other problems that impair early development of the brain.

What is mental illness? Is it a disease analogous to tuberculosis or influenza? Or is it a normal reaction to abnormal experiences? We can find examples that fit either of these extremes, but according to the biological view of mental illness, most cases are a combination of biological and experiential influences. Because of genetics, prenatal environment, or other predispositions, some people are more likely than others to develop substance abuse, depression, schizophrenia, or other disorders. The exact outcome, however, depends on the environment. To take an obvious example, you couldn't become an alcoholic if you lived in a country that had no alcohol.

In this chapter, the emphasis is strongly on the biological components of mental illnesses; *Biological Psychology* is, after all, the title of the book. But this emphasis does not imply that other aspects are unimportant.

Opposite:
This PET scan of an unmedicated person with schizophrenia shows less than the normal amount of activity in the prefrontal cortex.

Module 15.1

Alcoholism

The American Psychiatric Association (1994), in its *Diagnostic and Statistical Manual* (4th ed.), defines **substance abuse** as a maladaptive pattern of substance use leading to clinically significant impairment or distress (p. 182). Almost any substance can be abused. Back in the 1970s there were people trying to get "high" from nutmeg, banana peels . . . . I even knew one man who injected mayonnaise. In this module we focus on one common type of substance abuse, alcoholism. **Alcoholism** or **alcohol dependence** produces significant harm to people's lives, and those people find themselves continuing to drink in excess even after deciding to quit or to decrease their drinking (see Figure 15.1).

An enormous amount of damage can be attributed directly to alcohol abuse as a result of lost jobs, broken families, accidents caused by drunk drivers, and so forth. Alcohol also compounds other problems. An estimated 25% to 40% of hospital patients have problems caused by, or recovery delayed by, alcohol abuse (Holden, 1987), and clinical psychologists spend about one-fourth of their time dealing with people who are suffering in part from alcohol or other substance problems (Cummings, 1979). Heavy alcohol use has also been linked to deterioration of the prefrontal cortex in middle-aged men (Pfefferbaum, Sullivan, Rosenbloom, Mathalon, & Lim, 1998).

Genetics

Many people insist "I am not an alcoholic" because they don't drink every day, sometimes drink without getting drunk, and manage to hold a successful job in spite of their drinking. However, being an alcoholic does not require severe deterioration; many people have drinking problems only on weekends or during some weeks and not others. The deciding factor is whether the alcohol is interfering with the person's life.

No two alcoholics are quite alike; still, researchers find it useful to distinguish two major types of alcoholism (Brown, Babor, Litt, & Kranzler, 1994; Devor, Abell, Hoffman, Tabakoff, & Cloninger, 1994):

Type I (or Type A) *Alcoholism:*	**Type II** (or Type B) *Alcoholism:*
less dependence on genetics	stronger genetic basis
develops gradually over years	rapid, early onset (usually by age 25)
men and women about equally	overwhelmingly men
generally less severe	more severe
	more associated with criminality

Figure 15.1 Alcoholism
One feature of alcoholism is that a person wants to reduce or stop drinking but consistently fails. Seeking the help of others is often effective.

Type I alcoholism apparently develops more as a reaction to troubling experiences than from any strong biological predisposition. We concentrate therefore on Type II alcoholism, not because it is necessarily more important, but because it is more relevant to the topic of this book.

Recall from Chapter 12 that low serotonin turnover is associated with impulsive behavior, which can include violence. Low serotonin turnover is highly characteristic of Type II alcoholics (Fils-Aime et al., 1996), as is a history of impulsive and violent behaviors (Virkkunen et al., 1994). Not only does impulsiveness predispose someone to overindulge in alcohol, but research on rats demonstrates that alcohol increases impulsive behavior, such as choosing a small immediate reward instead of a larger delayed reward (Poulos, Parker, & Lê, 1998). In short, alcohol, impulsiveness, and low serotonin turnover are all closely interlinked.

Given that low serotonin turnover itself is known to have a strong genetic basis, it is not surprising that Type II alcoholism appears to have a genetic contribution. Most alcoholics have close relatives who also abuse alcohol or other drugs (Bierut et al., 1998). This evidence, of course, does not distinguish between the effects of heredity and environment. A stronger line of evidence comes from the finding that monozygotic twins have greater concordance for alcohol abuse than do dizygotic twins. One study estimated a .55 heritability for alcoholism (True et al., 1999). Additional evidence is that biological children of alcoholics have an increased risk of alcoholism themselves, even if they are adopted by nonalcoholics (Cloninger, Bohman, & Sigvardsson, 1981; Vaillant & Milofsky, 1982). However, this evidence is subject to the criticism that the mother may have been drinking during pregnancy, and thus the resemblance of children to biological parents could reflect prenatal environment. Overall, most researchers believe genetics is a contributing factor, although disagreement continues about the strength of that influence (Cadoret, Troughton, & Woodworth, 1994).

The risk of alcoholism probably depends on many genes. For one example, recall from Chapter 3 that researchers have suggested a link between impulsive pleasure-seeking behavior (including alcohol abuse) and genes causing less responsive forms of the dopamine type D_2 and D_4 receptors, which are known to be important for reinforcement. Those reports have been difficult to replicate (e.g., Heinz et al., 1996), so the contribution of those genes to alcoholism appears weak at best. Still, the idea is appealing because Type II alcoholism is strongly associated with impulsive behaviors of many kinds.

Why is Type II alcoholism so much more common in men than in women? Presumably male hormones interact in some way with the genes and other influences on alcoholism, but no one knows the details.

Stop & Check

1. Which type of alcoholism has a stronger genetic basis? Which type has earlier onset?

2. What is one way in which a gene might influence the probability of alcoholism?

Check your answers on page 427.

Alcohol Metabolism and Antabuse

Although much of the genetic basis of alcoholism must relate to impulsiveness, one genetic effect relates specifically to the way the body metabolizes alcohol. After a person drinks ethyl alcohol (drinking alcohol, as opposed to methyl alcohol or isopropyl alcohol), enzymes in the liver metabolize it to **acetaldehyde,** a poisonous substance. An enzyme then converts acetaldehyde to **acetic acid,** a chemical that the body can use as a source of energy:

$$\text{Ethyl alcohol} \longrightarrow \text{Acetaldehyde} \xrightarrow{\text{Acetaldehyde dehydrogenase}} \text{Acetic acid}$$

Some people have an abnormal gene for acetaldehyde dehydrogenase, so they metabolize acetaldehyde more slowly. If they drink much alcohol, they accumulate acetaldehyde, which can produce flushing of the face, increased heart rate, nausea, headache, abdominal pain, and difficult breathing. Repeated exposure can cause cirrhosis of the liver and damage to other organs. As you can imagine, people who can't metabolize acetaldehyde to acetic acid are less likely than other people to abuse alcohol. About half of the people in China and Japan have the gene that slows acetaldehyde metabolism; that gene may help explain why relatively few people in those countries develop alcohol abuse (Tu & Israel, 1995) (see Figure 15.2). In other words one gene that affects alcohol abuse produces its direct effects in the liver, not in the brain.

The drug *disulfiram,* which goes by the trade name Antabuse, antagonizes the effects of the enzyme acetaldehyde dehydrogenase by binding to its copper ion. Like many drugs, its effects were discovered by accident. The workers in one rubber-manufacturing plant found that when they got the chemical on their skin, they developed dermatitis (Schwartz & Tulipan, 1933). If they inhaled it, they couldn't drink alcohol without getting sick because they accumulated acetaldehyde. Soon therapists tried using disulfiram (Antabuse) as a drug, hoping that alcoholics would associate alcohol with illness and stop drinking.

Most studies find that Antabuse is only moderately effective (Hughes & Cook, 1997). When it works at all, it

Figure 15.2 Robin Kalat (the author's daughter) finds an alcohol vending machine in Tokyo
Japan has traditionally had a relatively relaxed attitude about preventing people from buying alcohol, presumably because severe alcoholism has been uncommon. One reason is that many Japanese people cannot quickly metabolize acetaldehyde to acetic acid. However, in 2000, increasing alcohol abuse prompted Japan to ban public alcohol vending machines.

acts as a supplement to the alcoholic's own commitment to stop drinking. By taking a daily pill and thinking about the illness that could follow a drink of alcohol, the person reaffirms a decision to abstain. In that case, of course, it doesn't matter whether the pill really contains Antabuse or not; someone who never drinks will never experience

the threatened illness (Fuller & Roth, 1979). Those who do drink in spite of taking the pill do become ill, but unfortunately are as likely to quit taking the pill as to quit drinking alcohol. Antabuse treatment is more effective if steps are taken to urge continued use of the drug, such as by having friends or relatives make sure the person takes the pill daily (Azrin, Sisson, Meyers, & Godley, 1982).

Stop & Check

3. Who would be likely to drink more alcohol—someone who metabolizes acetaldehyde to acetic acid rapidly or one who metabolizes it slowly?

4. How does Antabuse work?

Check your answers on page 427.

Risk Factors for Alcohol Abuse

The more severe someone's alcohol problem, and the longer it has lasted, the harder it is to quit. Many researchers have tried to identify alcoholism as early as possible in hopes of intervening to prevent a serious problem.

Most of the research follows this design: First identify a group of sons of alcoholic fathers. Generally, researchers study sons who are in their late teens or early twenties, who have started drinking alcohol but have not yet become problem drinkers. Because of the strong familial tendency of alcoholism, they expect that some of these young men are future alcoholics. (Researchers have focused on men instead of women because almost all Type II alcoholics are men. They study sons of alcoholic fathers instead of mothers to increase the chance that they will see genetic instead of prenatal influences.) The researchers identify other young men of the same age with similar drinking habits but no alcoholic relatives. They then compare the way the two groups react toward alcohol. The idea is that any behavior more common in the sons of alcoholics is probably a predictor of future alcoholism (see Figure 15.3).

This method has led to two major findings:

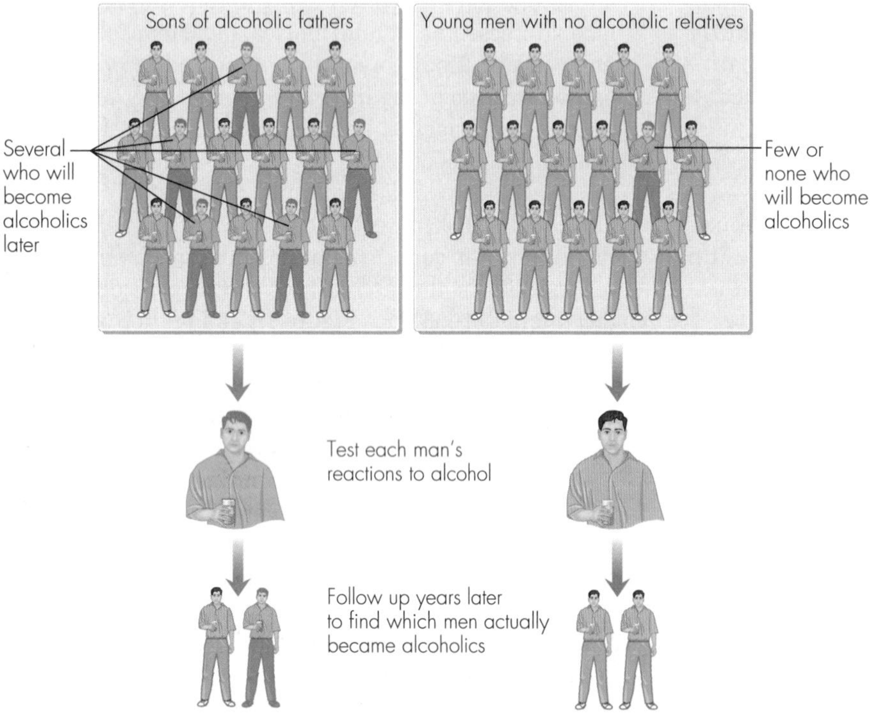

Figure 15.3 Design for studies of predisposition to alcoholism
Sons of alcoholic fathers are compared to other young men of the same age and same current drinking habits. Any behavior that is more common in the first group is presumably a predictor of later alcoholism.

Sons of alcoholic fathers

Young men with no alcoholic relatives

Several who will become alcoholics later

Few or none who will become alcoholics

Test each man's reactions to alcohol

Follow up years later to find which men actually became alcoholics

- Sons of alcoholics show *less* than average intoxication after drinking a small to moderate amount of alcohol. They report feeling less drunk, they show less body sway, and they register less change on an EEG (Schuckit & Smith, 1996; Volavka et al., 1996). Presumably a man who begins to feel tipsy after a drink or two stops at that point; one who "holds his liquor well" continues drinking, perhaps to the point of impairing judgment. A follow-up study found that men who report low intoxication after moderate drinking are much more likely than others to become alcohol abusers within the next 8 years (Schuckit & Smith, 1996).

- Sons of alcoholics also experience more than average relief from tension after drinking alcohol (Levenson, Oyama, & Meek, 1987). That is, in a difficult situation, alcohol decreases stress for most people, but it decreases it even more for sons of alcoholics.

In short, the combination that puts someone at greatest risk for alcoholism is to feel much relief from stress but not much intoxication after drinking a moderate amount of alcohol. Such people can be identified. Now the question is whether it is possible to steer them toward moderate drinking or abstention by intervening soon enough.

Stop & Check

5. What are two ways in which sons of alcoholics differ, on average, from sons of nonalcoholics?

Check your answer on this page.

Module 15.1

In Closing: Alcoholism and Addiction

Each addiction has some special features that set it apart from the others. For example, alcoholism is different from cocaine or heroin abuse because alcohol is legal and tolerated if it is used in moderation; it is also different because we metabolize alcohol into acetic acid, which is a source of energy. In other ways, however, all addictions have much in common. Most people who abuse one drug abuse other drugs also (Tsuang et al., 1998). Gambling has much in common with alcoholism and other substance abuse, although gambling introduces no substance into the body. Even habitual video-game playing and Internet use can be regarded as addictions if they become so excessive that they interfere with other activities. So we should beware of attributing the addictive properties of alcohol or anything else to the pharmacological properties of the substance itself. The addiction isn't in the drug; it's in the user.

Summary

1. Type I alcoholism has a slower onset, is usually less severe, and affects men and women about equally. Type II alcoholism starts faster and sooner, is more severe, affects mostly men, and is sometimes associated with criminality. (p. 424)

2. Type II alcoholism is usually related to overall impulsiveness and low serotonin turnover. (p. 425)

3. Ethyl alcohol is metabolized to acetaldehyde, which is then metabolized to acetic acid. People who, for genetic reasons, do that second step relatively slowly tend to become ill after drinking and therefore are unlikely to drink heavily. (p. 425)

4. Antabuse, a drug sometimes used as a supplemental treatment for alcoholics, blocks the conversion of acetaldehyde to acetic acid. (p. 425)

5. Sons of alcoholics are less likely than other young men of the same age to show signs of intoxication after moderate drinking and are more likely to report significant relief from stress after drinking. (p. 426)

Answers to *Stop and Check* Questions

1. For both parts of the question, Type II. (p. 425)

2. A gene might alter the structure of a dopamine receptor, thus changing someone's response to reinforcing events. (p. 425)

3. People who metabolize it rapidly would be more likely to drink alcohol because they suffer fewer unpleasant effects. (p. 426)

4. Antabuse blocks the enzyme that converts acetaldehyde to acetic acid and therefore makes people sick if they drink alcohol. Potentially it could teach people an aversion to alcohol, but more often it works as a way for the person to make a daily recommitment to abstain from drinking. (p. 426)

5. Sons of alcoholics show less intoxication, including less body sway, after drinking a moderate amount of alcohol. They also show greater relief from stress after drinking alcohol. (p. 427)

Thought Question

Genes can affect the probability of alcohol abuse by altering the metabolism of acetaldehyde and possibly by altering dopamine receptors that are important for reinforcement. What other possible routes could you imagine for a gene to affect alcoholism?

Module 15.2

Mood Disorders

Depression can be easy to diagnose in many cases. Depressed people act depressed; they look depressed (Figure 15.4); they even tell you they are depressed. However, in many other cases diagnosis is more difficult than you might imagine. People can act depressed because of hormonal problems or brain tumors. Many people have depression mixed with substance abuse, anxiety, schizophrenia, and so forth. Textbooks describe each disorder as a separate, discrete entity, but many cases don't fall neatly into categories (Kendler, Karkowski, & Walsh, 1998). The consequence for research is sometimes inconsistent results; different samples of depressed patients may differ substantially from one another.

Major Depressive Disorder

Almost everyone feels somewhat depressed at times—sad, discouraged, lacking in energy. The differences between ordinary and major depression depend on intensity and duration. According to DSM-IV (American Psychiatric Association, 1994), people with a **major depression** feel sad and helpless every day for weeks at a time. They have little energy, feel worthless, contemplate suicide, have trouble sleeping, cannot concentrate, get little pleasure from sex or food, and in many cases can hardly even imagine being happy

Figure 15.4 The face of depression
Depressed people show their condition in their face, their walk, their voice, their whole mannerism.

again. Major depression is diagnosed about twice as often in women as in men. It can occur at any time from adolescence to old age (only rarely in children), with a peak frequency in the 25–44-year age range. According to a survey of more than 8000 U.S. adults, about 19% of all people suffer psychiatrically significant depression at least once in their lives (Kessler et al., 1994).

Genetics

Depression tends to run in families (Erlenmeyer-Kimling et al., 1997), and adopted children resemble their biological parents more than their adoptive parents with regard to depression (Wender et al., 1986). However, the degree of family resemblance depends on the type of depression. If you have relatives who had a severe, long-lasting depression beginning before age 30, your risk of depression is increased much more than if your relatives had a milder depression later in life (Kendler, Gardner, & Prescott, 1999; Lyons et al., 1998).

A family history of depression also increases your risk more strongly if you are female (Bierut et al., 1999). Why that is true is uncertain. Childhood depression is about equally common (actually, equally uncommon) in boys and girls; beginning at puberty, depression is more common in females than males in all cultures for which we have data (Cyranowski, Frank, Young, & Shear, 2000; Silberg et al., 1999). The extra vulnerability of women is found even when researchers survey a town for undiagnosed cases, so it is not just a result of women seeking treatment more often than men. However, the probability of depression does not correlate strongly with hormone levels (Roca, Schmidt, & Rubinow, 1999). (Neither does PMS, as you may recall from Chapter 11.) The sex difference in depression remains unexplained.

So far, researchers have not located a single gene that is strongly linked to depression, despite serious efforts (e.g., McQuillin, Lawrence, Kalsi, Chen, & Gurling, 1999). It is likely that several genes increase the risk of depression, or perhaps increase the risk of *some sort* of disorder that might actually manifest itself as depression, alcoholism, anxiety disorder, and so forth, depending on environmental influences.

Triggering Depressed Episodes

Depression offers a classic example of the interaction between heredity and environment. Most depressed people can point to a life event that seemed to precipitate or aggravate their depression. Most also have evidence of genetic or other biological predispositions to depression. The most severe episodes occur when someone who has always been a little depressed, perhaps because of a biological predisposition, then has a traumatic experience. For example, after the California earthquake of 1989, almost everyone in the area became temporarily depressed, but those who had already been somewhat depressed before the earthquake became more severely depressed and remained depressed longer than the others (Nolen-Hoeksema & Morrow, 1991).

Depression is generally episodic, not constant. Someone may feel normal for weeks, months, or years, and then something triggers a new episode of depression. For example, a certain amount of depression is common just after giving birth. Most women experience the blues for a day or two after delivery because of pain, emotional upheaval, the inconvenience of hospital care, and the hormonal changes. About 20% experience a moderately serious **postpartum depression**— that is, a depression after giving birth. About 1 woman in 1000 enters a more serious, long-lasting depression (Hopkins, Marcus, & Campbell, 1984). In most cases, however, they had already suffered several previous episodes of depression; the postpartum changes aggravated, but didn't really cause, depression (Schöpf, Bryois, Jonquière, & Le, 1984).

Stop & Check

1. More women than men suffer from major depression. Why is it *unlikely* that female hormones are responsible for this difference?

Check your answer on page 437.

Abnormalities of Hemispheric Dominance

Studies of normal people have found a fairly strong relationship between happy mood and increased activity in the left prefrontal cortex (Jacobs & Snyder, 1996). Most depressed people have decreased activity in the left and increased activity in the right prefrontal cortex (Davidson, 1984; Starkstein & Robinson, 1986). Here's something you can try: Ask someone to solve a cognitive problem, such as "See how many words you can think of that start with *hu*-" or "Try to remember all the ingredients you've ever seen on a pizza." Then unobtrusively watch the person's eye movements. Most people gaze to the right, but most depressed people gaze to the left (Lenhart & Katkin, 1986).

TRY IT YOURSELF

Many people become seriously depressed after left-hemisphere damage; fewer do after right-hemisphere damage (Bolla-Wilson, Robinson, Starkstein, Boston, & Price, 1989). In rare cases people with right-hemisphere damage become manic, the opposite of depressed (Robinson, Boston, Starkstein, & Price, 1988). We shall return to this point when we discuss the effects of electroconvulsive shock to the left or right hemisphere.

Viruses

A few cases of depression may be linked to a viral infection. As recently as the 1980s, Borna disease was known only as an infection of European farm animals. Gradually investigators discovered that a much greater variety of species are vulnerable, over a much wider geographical range. In severe cases the virus is fatal; in milder cases **Borna disease** is noted mostly by its behavioral effects, such as periods of frantic activity alternating with periods of inactivity (see Figure 15.5).

Many viruses are passed between humans and other species, although the effects on humans may be quite different, or even undetectable. In 1985 investigators

Figure 15.5 Symptoms of Borna disease
Farm animals infected with Borna disease have periods of frantic activity alternating with inactivity, much like a person with bipolar disorder. **(top)** Horse with Borna disease. **(bottom)** Same horse after recovery. *(Source: Bode & Ludwig, 1997)*

Accidental Discoveries of Psychiatric Drugs

We like to think that basic science comes first and that applied science or technology later applies the discoveries of basic science to solve practical problems. Yet the history of drug therapies, particularly in psychiatry, includes many examples of useful drugs stumbled upon by accident that researchers then had to study to explain their success.

Disulfiram, for example, was originally used in the manufacture of rubber. Someone noticed that workers in a certain rubber factory developed a distaste for alcohol and traced the cause to disulfiram, which had altered the workers' metabolism so they became ill after drinking any alcohol. Disulfiram, now better known by the trade name Antabuse, is often prescribed for people who are trying to avoid alcohol.

Iproniazid was originally marketed as rocket fuel. Eventually someone discovered that it was useful therapy for tuberculosis. Later, while experimenting on its effects in treating tuberculosis, someone discovered that it was an effective antidepressant (Klerman, 1975).

The use of bromides to control epilepsy was originally based

on a theory, but the theory was all wrong (Friedlander, 1986; Levitt, 1975). People in the 1800s who believed that masturbation caused epilepsy thought that bromides reduced sexual drive. Therefore, the reasoning went, bromides should reduce epilepsy. It turns out that bromides do relieve epilepsy, but for altogether different reasons.

For decades the search for new psychiatric drugs was a matter of haphazardly testing as many chemicals as possible, first on laboratory animals and then on humans. For example, investigators looking for new tranquilizers would seek out drugs that decreased rats' avoidance of stimuli associated with shock. (A drug that decreased avoidance presumably decreased fear.) Today, because we largely understand how tranquilizers and other drugs affect synapses, drug researchers no longer have to test nearly so many compounds on animals. They start by synthesizing chemicals with properties similar to those of drugs already in use, evaluating new chemicals in test tubes or tissue samples until they find one with a potential for stronger or more specific effects on neurotransmission.

reported the results of a blood test given to 370 people (Amsterdam et al., 1985). Only 12 people tested positive for Borna disease virus, but *all 12 were suffering from major depression or bipolar disorder.* These 12 were a small percentage of the 265 depressed people tested; still, *none* of the 105 undepressed people had the virus.

During the 1990s thousands of people were tested in Europe, Asia, and North America. The Borna virus was found in about 2% of normal people, 30% of severely depressed patients, and 13% to 14% of people with chronic brain diseases (Bode, Ferszt, & Czech, 1993; Bode, Riegel, Lange, & Ludwig, 1992). However, later studies found the Borna virus in people with other psychiatric diseases as well as depression (Herzog et al., 1997). Evidently the Borna virus predisposes people to psychiatric difficulties, but not necessarily depression.

Antidepressant Drugs

It is logical to assume that investigators would first figure out the causes of a psychological disorder and then develop a treatment to address it. But the opposite sequence has been more common: First investigators find a drug or other therapy that seems helpful, and then they infer what the underlying cause of the disorder must have been. Like many other psychiatric drugs, the

early antidepressants were discovered by accident (see Digression 15.1).

The antidepressant drugs fall into four major categories: tricyclics, MAOIs, selective serotonin reuptake inhibitors, and atypical antidepressants (see Figure 15.6). The **tricyclics** (such as imipramine, trade name Tofranil) operate by preventing the presynaptic neuron from reabsorbing serotonin or catecholamines after releasing them; thus, the neurotransmitters remain longer in the synaptic cleft and continue stimulating the postsynaptic cell. However, the tricyclics also block histamine receptors, acetylcholine receptors, and certain

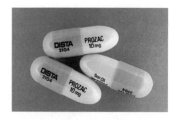

Figure 15.6 Fluoxetine (Prozac) pills
Tricyclic drugs block the reuptake of catecholamines and serotonin by presynaptic terminals. Monoamine oxidase inhibitors block the breakdown of catecholamines and serotonin after their release into the synaptic cleft. Selective serotonin reuptake inhibitors, such as Prozac, have effects that are more limited to a single neurotransmitter.

sodium channels (Horst & Preskorn, 1998). As mentioned in Chapter 9, blocking histamine produces drowsiness. Blocking acetylcholine leads to dry mouth and difficulty urinating. Blocking sodium channels causes heart irregularities, among other problems. Many people have to limit their use of tricyclics because of the side effects.

The **monoamine oxidase inhibitors (MAOIs)** (such as phenelzine, trade name Nardil) block the enzyme monoamine oxidase (MAO), a presynaptic terminal enzyme that metabolizes catecholamines and serotonin into inactive forms. When MAOIs block this enzyme, the presynaptic terminal has more of its transmitter available for release. The tricyclics are usually more effective, but MAOIs help many patients who do not respond to tricyclics (Thase, Trivedi, & Rush, 1995). People taking MAOIs must avoid foods containing tyramine, including cheese, raisins, liver, pickles, licorice, and a long list of others. Tyramine combines effects with MAOIs to increase blood pressure, sometimes fatally.

The **selective serotonin reuptake inhibitors (SSRIs)** are similar to tricyclics, but specific to the neurotransmitter serotonin. For example, fluoxetine (trade name Prozac) blocks the reuptake of serotonin by the presynaptic terminal. SSRIs produce only mild side effects, mainly mild nausea or headache (Feighner et al., 1991). However, they sometimes produce nervousness and are not recommended for patients with both depression and anxiety. Other common SSRIs include sertraline (Zoloft), fluvoxamine (Luvox), citalopram (Celexa), and paroxetine (Paxil or Seroxat).

The **atypical antidepressants** are a miscellaneous group of drugs with antidepressant effects but only mild side effects (Horst & Preskorn, 1998). They are often effective for patients who failed to respond to the other drugs. One atypical antidepressant is bupropion (Wellbutrin), which inhibits reuptake of dopamine and to some extent norepinephrine, but not serotonin. A second is venlaxafine, which mostly inhibits the reuptake of serotonin, but also somewhat that of norepinephrine and slightly that of dopamine. A third is nefazodone, which specifically blocks serotonin type 2A receptors and also weakly blocks reuptake of serotonin and norepinephrine. Figure 15.7 summarizes the mechanisms of tricyclics, MAOIs, and SSRIs.

Most or all antidepressants have delayed effects that limit the excitation of the postsynaptic cell. One such effect is to decrease the sensitivity of the postsynaptic receptors. Recall from Chapter 5 the concept of disuse supersensitivity: A receptor that receives little

input becomes more sensitive to future input. The opposite is also true: A receptor that receives excess input decreases its sensitivity. A second effect depends on a special kind of receptor that we have not encountered earlier in this text, called an *autoreceptor*. An **autoreceptor** is a negative feedback receptor on the presynaptic terminal. After an axon releases much of its neurotransmitter, some of the molecules come back to stimulate the autoreceptors, which then decrease further release of the neurotransmitter. **In other words any increase in transmitter release is followed by a decrease. In effect the autoreceptors put on the brakes** (see Figure 15.8). When antidepressant drugs prolong the presence of serotonin or other transmitters in the synapse, the extra molecules stimulate the autoreceptors and thereby decrease further release.

Implications for the Physiology of Depression   Now that we know what kinds of drugs relieve depression, we can infer what brain abnormalities produce depression, right? Unfortunately it is not that simple. We can draw two apparent conclusions: (a) Mood depends on the effects of a combination of transmitters, not just one. (b) Different depressed people have somewhat different transmitter abnormalities. Beyond these generalities, the conclusions become less certain.

One major problem is the time course of the drugs' effectiveness. The effect of an antidepressant drug on serotonin and catecholamine synapses reaches its peak

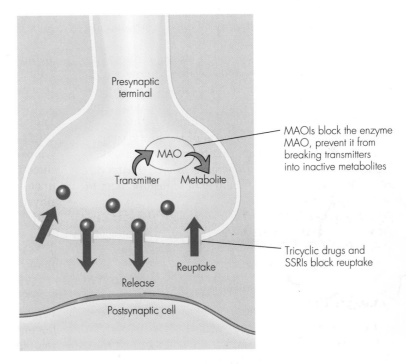

Figure 15.7   Routes of action of antidepressants
Tricyclics block the reuptake of dopamine, norepinephrine, or serotonin. SSRIs specifically block the reuptake of serotonin. MAOIs block the enzyme MAO, which converts dopamine, norepinephrine, or serotonin into inactive chemicals. Atypical antidepressants have varying effects.

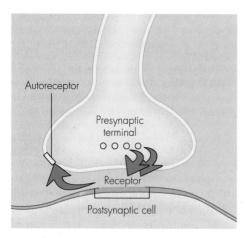

Figure 15.8 An autoreceptor
After an axon releases a neurotransmitter, some of the molecules attach to autoreceptors on the presynaptic terminal itself, feeding back to decrease further release of the transmitter.

within hours. In contrast, the behavioral benefits build up over 2 or 3 weeks. One study found that most benefits occurring in less than 2 weeks are placebo effects; the patients continue reporting the benefits even if the physician substitutes an inactive pill (Stewart et al., 1998). Contrast this situation to that of methylphenidate (Ritalin) for attention deficit disorder: peak effect on the synapses in 60 minutes; peak effect on behavior in 60 minutes (Volkow et al., 1998). So the known effects of antidepressant drugs on the synapses may be an important step, but it can hardly be the full explanation for the drugs' benefits.

Repeated use of antidepressant drugs produces numerous long-term effects, and we don't know which one is critical. However, here is a promising candidate: Repeated use of antidepressants leads to increased production and release of a neurotrophin called *brain-derived neurotrophic factor* in parts of the hippocampus and cerebral cortex (Duman, Heninger, & Nestler, 1997). These are areas known to decrease in size during depression, so the neurotrophin may help restore them to normal size and function.

Stop **&** Check

2. What are the effects of tricyclic drugs?

3. What are the effects of MAOIs?

4. What are the effects of SSRIs?

5. What are the atypical antidepressants?

6. What is the major difficulty in understanding how all the antidepressant drugs relieve depression?

Check your answers on page 437.

Other Therapies

Antidepressant drugs have provided safe, effective, relatively inexpensive help for a great many people, but only about two-thirds of all patients get a measurable benefit. Cognitive psychotherapy helps also, but again for only about two-thirds of patients. Placebos (inactive drugs) also benefit one-third to one-half of all patients, so it appears that much of the benefit of both drugs and psychotherapy is a **placebo effect**—a benefit due to the expectation of improvement or the mere passage of time. The advantage of psychotherapy is that it is more likely than drugs to produce long-lasting relief (M. D. Evans et al., 1992); many people who take the drugs have a relapse within a few months after they stop the drugs. However, drugs are cheaper and far less time-consuming.

Given that neither drugs nor psychotherapy is fully satisfactory, the search continues for new and improved treatments. St. John's wort, an herb, is an effective antidepressant with an unknown means of action. Being a natural substance does not make it safe, however; its side effects include gastrointestinal distress, sedation, and painful sensitivity to bright lights (Wong, Smith, & Boon, 1998). The traditional Chinese procedure of acupuncture has also shown some potential in fighting depression, also by unknown means (Allen, Schnyer, & Hitt, 1998). Other antidepressant treatments include electroconvulsive therapy and sleep alterations.

Electroconvulsive Therapy (ECT) Treatment through an electrically induced seizure, known as **electroconvulsive therapy (ECT)**, has had a stormy history (Fink, 1985). It originated with the observation that people with both epilepsy and schizophrenia sometimes have a decrease in the symptoms of one when they have an increase in the symptoms of the other (Trimble & Thompson, 1986). In the 1930s a Hungarian physician, Ladislas Meduna, tried to relieve schizophrenia by inducing convulsive seizures. Soon other physicians were doing the same, using a large dose of insulin to induce the seizures. Insulin shock is a dreadful experience, however, and difficult to control. An Italian physician, Ugo Cerletti, after years of experimentation with animals, developed a method of inducing seizures with an electric shock through the head (Cerletti & Bini, 1938). Electroconvulsive therapy is quick, and most patients awaken calmly and do not remember it.

When ECT proved to be an unreliable treatment for schizophrenia, you might guess that psychiatrists would abandon it. Instead they tried it for other mental hospital patients, even though they had no theoretical reason to expect success. ECT did indeed seem helpful for many depressed patients and soon became a common treatment. Its overuse and misuse, especially during the 1950s, earned it a bad reputation. Some patients were given ECT hundreds of times without their consent, even when it was ineffective.

When antidepressant drugs became available in the late 1950s, the use of ECT declined rapidly. However, as it became clear in the 1970s that not all depressed patients respond well to the drugs, ECT made a partial comeback. It is used only with informed consent, usually for patients who have not responded to antidepressant drugs (Scovern & Kilmann, 1980; Weiner, 1979). It is also sometimes recommended for patients with strong suicidal tendencies because it works faster than antidepressant drugs: Feeling better in 1 week instead of 2 may be the difference between life and death.

ECT is usually applied every other day for about 2 weeks, sometimes more. Patients are given muscle relaxants or anesthetics to minimize discomfort and the possibility of injury (Figure 15.9). Because the shock is less intense than in earlier years, the risk of provoking a heart attack is low except in elderly patients.

The most common side effect of ECT is memory loss, but if physicians administer the shock to the right hemisphere only, the antidepressant effects occur without memory impairment (McElhiney et al., 1995). (Recall that right-hemisphere activity is more associated with unpleasant mood.) Because depression is associated with decreased activity of the left hemisphere, right-hemisphere ECT may either promote a better balance of activity between the two hemispheres or somehow enhance activity in the left hemisphere.

Medical commissions in both the United States and Great Britain have concluded that ECT is safe and effective (M. Fink, 1985). However, about half of those who respond well to ECT relapse into depression within 6 months unless they are given drugs or other therapies in the meantime (Riddle & Scott, 1995).

More than half a century after the introduction of ECT, no one is yet sure how it relieves depression. It stimulates the production of additional dopamine type D_1 and D_2 receptors in the nucleus accumbens (S. Smith, Lindefors, Hurd, & Sharp, 1995), decreases the number of norepinephrine receptors at postsynaptic cells (Kellar & Stockmeier, 1986; Lerer & Shapira, 1986), and exerts a wide variety of other effects. We do not know, however, which effect is critical.

A more recent, similar treatment is repetitive transcranial magnetic stimulation. An intense magnetic field is applied to the scalp, temporarily disabling all the neurons just below the magnet. This procedure resembles ECT both in its level of effectiveness and in the fact that no one knows why it is effective (George et al., 1997).

Altered Sleep Patterns Most depressed people, especially those who are middle aged or older, experience sleep abnormalities that suggest a disorder of their bio-

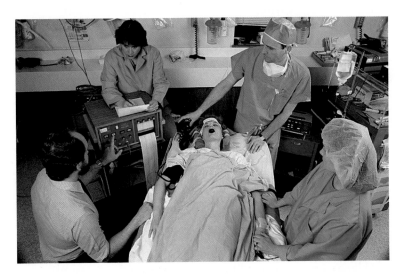

Figure 15.9   Electroconvulsive therapy (ECT)
In contrast to the practices of an earlier era, ECT today is administered with muscle relaxants or anesthetics to minimize discomfort. It can be used only if the patient gives informed consent.

logical rhythms. Recall from Chapter 9 that a normal undepressed person who goes to bed at the normal time first enters REM sleep about 80 minutes after falling asleep; the amount of REM sleep remains low for the first half of the night and increases in the second half. That trend is controlled by the time of day, not by how long the person has been asleep. Someone who goes to sleep later than usual on a given night is likely to enter REM sleep more rapidly because REM sleep is related to circadian rhythms (see Figure 15.10). REM sleep occupies a small percentage of total sleep while body temperature is declining and a larger percentage while body temperature is rising (Czeisler, Weitzman, Moore-Ede, Zimmerman, & Knauer, 1980).

Most depressed people enter REM sleep within 45 minutes after going to bed at their normal time, but for them body temperature may already be starting to rise at that time, as Figure 15.10 illustrates. Most depressed people sleep restlessly, awaken early, and cannot get back to sleep. During the day, they feel drowsy. As they recover from depression, their sleep improves also (Dew et al., 1996).

One promising treatment for depression is to have the person go to sleep earlier than usual, in phase with the temperature cycle. Sleep begins at, say, 6 P.M., when the temperature cycle is at about the point it is in undepressed people at 11 P.M.; after 8 hours of sleep, the person awakens at 2 A.M. On each succeeding night the person goes to sleep half an hour later, until bedtime is at 11 P.M. or some other satisfactory point. In short, therapists treat the depressed patient like someone who is having trouble adjusting to a change in time zones. The result is a relief from depression that lasts for months (Sack, Nurnberger, Rosenthal, Ashburn, & Wehr, 1985).

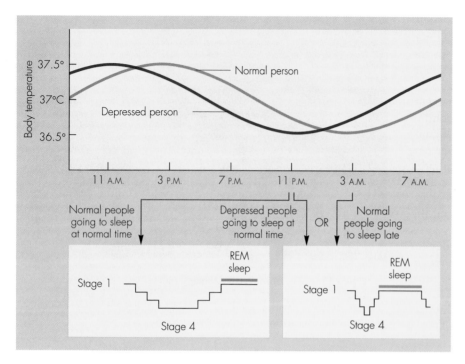

Figure 15.10 Sleep, REM, and the circadian rhythm of body temperature
Nondepressed people going to bed at their normal time get much stage 4 sleep for the first few hours and increasing amounts of REM sleep later in the night. Most depressed people have their circadian rhythms advanced by several hours; when they go to sleep at 11 P.M., they sleep as a normal person does at about 3 A.M. *(Source: Bottom graphs adapted from Hobson, 1989)*

Stop & Check

7. For what kinds of patients is ECT recommended?

8. What change in sleep habits sometimes relieves depression?

Check your answers on page 437.

Bipolar Disorder

Depression is either a unipolar or a bipolar disorder. People with **unipolar disorder** experience only one pole, or extreme; they vary between feeling normal and feeling depressed. People with **bipolar disorder**—formerly known as **manic-depressive disorder**—alternate between the two poles of depression and its opposite, mania. **Mania** is characterized by restless activity, excitement, laughter, self-confidence, rambling speech, and loss of inhibitions. In extreme cases manic people are dangerous to themselves and others. Figure 15.11 represents the rise and fall of a manic episode in one hospitalized patient.

A cycle from depression to mania and back to depression again may last only days or for a year or more (Bunney, Murphy, Goodwin, & Borge, 1972). About 1% of people have at least a mild case of bipolar disorder at some time in life, with an average age of onset in the early twenties (Craddock & Jones, 1999).

The rate of glucose metabolism is a good indicator of overall brain activity. As Figure 15.12 shows, glucose use is higher than normal during mania and lower than normal during depression (Baxter et al., 1985). What causes the change from one state to the other is unknown. Bipolar patients do have some brain abnormalities, including a larger than normal amygdala (Strakowski et al., 1999). As mentioned in Chapter 12, the amygdala is an important area for emotions.

Genetics

Several lines of evidence suggest a hereditary basis for bipolar disorder (Craddock & Jones, 1999). If one monozygotic twin has bipolar disorder, the other has at least a 50% chance of getting it also, whereas dizygotic twins, brothers, sisters, and children have about a 5% to 10% probability. Adopted children who develop bipolar disorder are more likely to have biological than adoptive relatives with mood disorders.

Modern methods of biochemical analysis have enabled researchers to identify the genes responsible for Huntington's disease, Alzheimer's disease, and many other conditions. Research on bipolar disorder has yielded apparent linkage to genes on several chromosomes (Blackwood et al., 1996; Egeland et al., 1987; Freimer et al., 1996; Ginns et al., 1996). However, researchers have not yet located a specific gene linked to the disorder.

Treatments

The first successful treatment to be discovered for bipolar disorder was **lithium** salts, which continue to be used for bipolar disorder and for certain cases in which a person alternates regularly between depression and normal mood. The effectiveness of lithium was discovered accidentally by an Australian investigator, J. F. Cade, who believed that uric acid might relieve mania and depression. Cade mixed uric acid with a lithium salt to help it dissolve and then gave the solution to patients. It was indeed helpful, although investigators eventually realized that lithium was the effective agent, not uric acid.

Lithium stabilizes the mood of a bipolar patient, preventing a relapse into either mania or depression. The use of lithium must be regulated carefully; the correct dose is both safe and effective, but a slightly higher dose is toxic (Schou, 1997). How lithium relieves bipolar disorder is

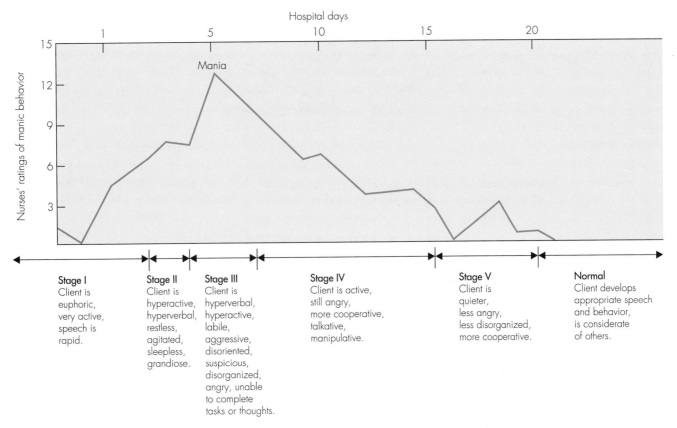

Figure 15.11 Observations of a 3-week manic episode *(Source: After Janosik & Davies, 1987)*

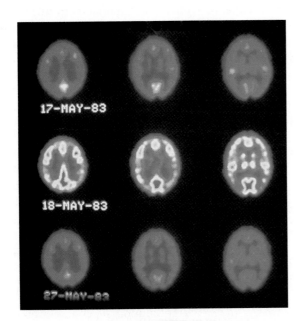

Figure 15.12 PET scans for a bipolar patient
Horizontal planes through three levels of the brain are shown for each day. On May 17 and May 27, when the patient was depressed, brain metabolic rates were low. On May 18, when the patient was in a cheerful, hypomanic mood, the brain metabolic rate was high. Red indicates the highest metabolic rate, followed by yellow, green, and blue. *(Source: Courtesy of L. R. Baxter, Jr.)*

still not known (Manji & Lenox, 1998). Therapeutic doses of lithium produce complex effects on several second-messenger systems and thereby affect activity in many neuronal pathways (Manji, Potter, & Lenox, 1995). Presumably these effects somehow bring fluctuating brain systems into stability, but the details are unknown.

The other common treatment for bipolar disorder is the use of anticonvulsant drugs such as valproic acid (trade names Depakene, Depakote, and others). Bipolar disorder is not a type of epilepsy, but the drugs have multiple effects. One key effect is to block certain second-messenger systems. High levels of omega-3 fatty acids also block those second-messenger systems, and they too are effective treatments for some bipolar patients (Stoll et al., 1999). In short, the emerging pattern is that treatments for bipolar disorder act at the level of the second messengers.

Stop *&* Check

9. What are two common treatments for bipolar disorder?

Check your answer on page 437.

Seasonal Affective Disorder

Another form of depression is **seasonal affective disorder,** conveniently abbreviated **SAD,** which is depression

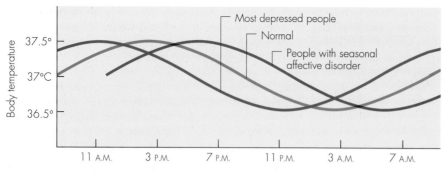

Figure 15.13 Circadian rhythms for normal, depressed, and SAD people
Note that SAD patients are phase delayed while most other depressed patients are
phase advanced.

that regularly recurs during a particular season, such as winter. SAD occurs mostly in regions near the poles, where the winter nights are very long, but it occurs in moderate climates also. Most people feel happier and more active in the summer, when there are many hours of sunlight, than in winter (Madden, Heath, Rosenthal, & Martin, 1996). SAD appears to be an exaggeration of this common tendency. It is seldom severe, and most people with SAD don't even seek a therapist, much less hospitalization. Consequently, statistics about its prevalence are probably underestimates.

In many ways SAD differs from other types of depression; for example, SAD patients have phase-delayed sleep and temperature rhythms, unlike most other depressed patients, whose rhythms are phase advanced (Teicher et al., 1997) (see Figure 15.13).

It is possible to treat SAD with very bright lights (for example, 2500 lux) for an hour or more each day. The bright light treatment is effective in morning, afternoon, or evening, but most research indicates that it has its strongest effect if presented in the morning (Eastman, Young, Fogg, Liu, & Meaden, 1998; Lewy et al., 1998; Terman, Terman, & Ross, 1998).

Researchers do not yet know what causes seasonal affective disorder or why bright light alleviates it. The most likely hypotheses are that bright light affects serotonin synapses and that it alters circadian rhythms. Regardless of how it works, it produces bigger, more reliable benefits than either antidepressant drugs or psychotherapy does for other types of depression. Consequently some therapists have begun recommending bright light therapy for nonseasonal depression, even though no research has yet been done for that application (Wirz-Justice, 1998).

Stop & Check

10. In what parts of the world are people most likely to experience seasonal affective disorder?

Check your answer on page 437.

In Closing: The Biology of Mood Swings

Do you feel sad because of events that have happened to you or because of your brain chemistry? According to biological psychologists, that is a meaningless question. Your experiences *are* changes in your brain state; you cannot have one without the other. The better question is: Are some people more likely than others to become depressed because of a preexisting condition in their brain structure or chemistry? The answer to that one is "probably." It is difficult to get from "probably" to "definitely" because it is difficult to do research on human moods. At each stage in life, brain structure and chemistry alter one's reactions to events, and experience in turn alters the brain, affecting the reaction to the next event. Studying an adult brain has the same challenge as watching only a few minutes in the middle of a complex movie and trying to guess how events led up to that point.

Summary

1. People with major depression feel sad, helpless, and lacking in energy for weeks at a time. For most, depression occurs as a series of episodes, each triggered by life events or biological changes. (p. 428)

2. Depression shows a strong family tendency, especially for women, implying a genetic contribution. However, the responsible genes have not yet been located. (p. 428)

3. Most severe cases of depression are an interaction between a biological predisposition and life events that trigger an episode. (p. 429)

4. Depression is associated with decreased activity in the left hemisphere of the cortex. (p. 429)

5. Four kinds of antidepressant drugs are in wide use. Tricyclics block reuptake of serotonin and catecholamines but produce strong side effects. MAOIs

block an enzyme that breaks down catecholamines and serotonin. SSRIs block reuptake of serotonin. Atypical antidepressants are a miscellaneous group with diverse effects. (p. 430)

6. The antidepressants alter synaptic activity quickly, but their effects on behavior build up over weeks. Researchers do not yet know the critical influences that develop during that delay. (p. 431)

7. Other therapies for depression include cognitive psychotherapy, electroconvulsive therapy, and altered sleep patterns. Each has its own pattern of benefits. (p. 432)

8. People with bipolar disorder alternate between two extremes: depression and mania. Bipolar disorder has a probable genetic basis. Effective therapies include lithium salts and certain anticonvulsant drugs, which act by altering activity of second messengers. (p. 434)

9. Seasonal affective disorder is marked by recurrent depression during one season of the year. Exposure to bright lights is usually effective in treating it. (p. 435)

Answers to *Stop and Check* Questions

1. Among women, hormone levels do not correlate with probability of depression. Also, nearly all women who suffer major depression after giving birth have had previous bouts of depression not in conjunction with hormonal changes. (p. 429)

2. Tricyclic drugs block reuptake of serotonin and catecholamines. They also block histamine receptors, acetylcholine receptors, and certain sodium channels, thereby producing unpleasant side effects. (p. 432)

3. MAOIs block the enzyme MAO, which breaks down catecholamines and serotonin. The result is increased availability of these transmitters. (p. 432)

4. SSRIs selectively inhibit the reuptake of serotonin. (p. 432)

5. Atypical antidepressants are a miscellaneous group of antidepressants that do not fall into any of the other groups. They have diverse effects on serotonin and other synapses. (p. 432)

6. The antidepressants produce their known effects on the synapses quickly, but their behavioral benefits develop gradually over 2 to 3 weeks. (p. 432)

7. ECT is recommended for depressed people who did not respond to other therapies and for those who are an immediate suicide risk (because ECT acts faster than other therapies). (p. 434)

8. Getting depressed people to go to bed earlier sometimes relieves depression. (p. 434)

9. The common treatments for bipolar disorder are lithium salts and certain anticonvulsant drugs. (p. 435)

10. Seasonal affective disorder is more common toward the poles, where the difference between summer and winter is greatest. (p. 436)

Thought Questions

1. Some people have suggested that ECT relieves depression by causing people to forget the events that caused it. What evidence opposes this hypothesis?

2. Certain people suffer from what they describe as "post-Christmas depression," a feeling of letdown after all the excitement of the holiday season. What other explanation can you offer?

Schizophrenia

Here is a conversation between two people diagnosed with schizophrenia (Haley, 1959, p. 321):

A: Do you work at the air base?

B: You know what I think of work. I'm 33 in June, do you mind?

A: June?

B: 33 years old in June. This stuff goes out the window after I live this, uh—leave this hospital. So I can't get my vocal cords back. So I lay off cigarettes. I'm in a spatial condition, from outer space myself. . . .

A: I'm a real spaceship from across.

B: A lot of people talk that way, like crazy, but "Believe It or Not," by Ripley, take it or leave it—alone—it's in the *Examiner*, it's in the comic section, "Believe It or Not," by Ripley, Robert E. Ripley, Believe it or not, but we don't have to believe anything, unless I feel like it. Every little rosette—too much alone.

A: Yeah, it could be possible.

B: I'm a civilian seaman.

A: Could be possible. I take my bath in the ocean.

B: Bathing stinks. You know why? 'Cause you can't quit when you feel like it. You're in the service.

People with schizophrenia say and do things that other people (including other people with schizophrenia) find difficult to understand. The causes of the disorder are still not well understood, but they apparently include a large biological component.

Characteristics

According to DSM-IV, **schizophrenia** is a disorder characterized both by deteriorating ability to function in everyday life and by some combination of hallucinations, delusions, thought disorder, movement disorder, and inappropriate emotional expressions (American Psychiatric Association, 1994). The symptoms vary greatly. Hallucinations and delusions are prominent for some; thought disorders are dominant for others; some

have clear signs of brain damage, but others do not. In short, you could easily find several people who have all been diagnosed with schizophrenia who nevertheless have almost nothing in common (Andreasen, 1999). What we call schizophrenia may turn out to be more than one disorder, and the confusion among disorders may be responsible for the often conflicting research results.

Schizophrenia was originally called *dementia praecox*, which is Latin for "premature deterioration of the mind." In 1911 Eugen Bleuler introduced the term *schizophrenia*, which has become the established term even though it confuses many people. Although schizophrenia is Greek for "split mind," it is *not* the same thing as *multiple personality*, a condition in which someone alternates among different personalities and identities. A person with schizophrenia has only one personality. What Bleuler meant by *schizophrenia* was a split between the emotional and intellectual aspects of the person: The person's emotional expression or lack of it seems unconnected with current experiences. For example, the person might giggle or cry for no apparent reason or listen to bad news and show no response. Not all patients show this detachment of emotion from intellect, but the term lives on.

Behavioral Symptoms

Schizophrenia is characterized by **positive symptoms** (behaviors that are present that should be absent) and **negative symptoms** (behaviors that are absent that should be present). The typical negative symptoms are weak social interactions, emotional expression, speech, and working memory. Negative symptoms tend to be stable over time and difficult to treat. Positive symptoms, which are more sporadic, fall into two clusters that do not correlate strongly with each other (Andreasen, Arndt, Alliger, Miller, & Flaum, 1995). The *psychotic* cluster consists of **delusions** (unfounded beliefs, such as the conviction that one is being persecuted or that outer space aliens are trying to control one's behavior) and **hallucinations** (abnormal sensory experiences, such as hearing voices when no one else is speaking). PET scans have determined that hallucinations occur during periods of increased activity in the thalamus, hippocampus, basal ganglia, and prefrontal cortex (Silbersweig et al., 1995) (see Figure 15.14).

The *disorganized* cluster of positive symptoms consists of inappropriate emotions (expressing great happiness or sadness for no apparent reason), bizarre behaviors, and thought disorder. The most typical thought disorder of schizophrenia is a difficulty understanding and using abstract concepts. For example, a schizophrenic person would take literally a proverb such as, "When the cat's away, the mice will play." Schizophrenic people also organize their thoughts loosely, as in a dream.

Of all these symptoms, which if any is the primary or central problem? According to Nancy Andreasen (1999), one of the leading investigators of schizophrenia, the main problem is disordered thoughts, which result from abnormal interactions between the cortex and the thalamus and cerebellum. The disordered thinking may result in hallucinations and delusions, but those are not the fundamental problem.

Schizophrenia can be either acute or chronic. An acute condition has a sudden onset and good prospects for recovery. A chronic condition has a gradual onset and a long-term course. In other words some people have permanent schizophrenia, whereas others have one or two episodes followed by a return to normality with no need for further treatment (Wiersma, Nienhuis, Slooff, & Giel, 1998).

Before antischizophrenic drugs became available in the mid-1950s, most schizophrenic people were confined to mental hospitals, where they generally deteriorated for the rest of their lives. Today many people with schizophrenia manage to live normally with the aid of drugs and outpatient treatment, and many others live normal lives most of the time, with an occasional need for hospitalization.

Demographic Data

Schizophrenia is difficult to diagnose. Many people have mild cases, and others have disorders that resemble schizophrenia (see Digression 15.2). Consequently statistics on the prevalence of schizophrenia cannot be precise. One survey of U.S. adults reported that about 1.3% of all people suffer from schizophrenia at some point in their lives (Kendler, Gallagher, Abelson, & Kessler, 1996). Many others, perhaps another 1% of the population, develop a milder *schizoid* condition.

However, schizophrenia is less common in young people today than in previous generations, and many countries have reported a gradual decline in prevalence since about the mid-1900s (Suvisaari, Haukka, Tanskanen, & Lönnqvist, 1999). No one knows why. It's an odd situation: Our society is doing something right, and we don't know what.

Schizophrenia occurs in all ethnic groups and all parts of the world, although it is 10 to 100 times more common in the United States and Europe than in most Third World countries (Torrey, 1986). Part of that discrepancy could be due to differences in diagnostic standards and recordkeeping, but there are other possibilities. Within the United States, schizophrenia is more common for those born in crowded cities than for those born in small towns or on farms (Torrey, Bowler, & Clark, 1997), and small towns and farms are more typical of Third World countries. Also, in the United States or Europe, someone with schizophrenia is likely to live with parents or other immediate family members. Sooner or later, almost anyone with full-time responsibility for a schizophrenic relative loses patience, and the resultant hostile expressions, known to psychiatrists as expressed emotion, seriously aggravate the condition (Butzlaff & Hooley, 1998). In more traditional cultures, notably India and the Arab countries, a large extended family takes care of any schizophrenic relative; caregivers seldom lose their patience; and even when schizophrenia does occur, it is mild compared to U.S. standards (El-Islam, 1982; Leff et al., 1987).

Lifetime prevalence of schizophrenia is about equal for men and women, but the usual age of onset is early tewnties for men, late tewnties for women. Some women have their first onset around the age of menopause, age

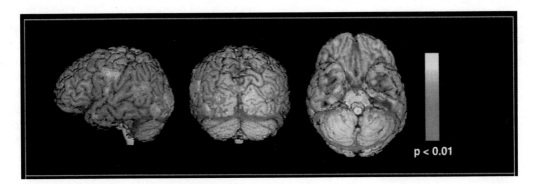

Figure 15.14 Brain areas activated during hallucinations
Researchers made PET scans of the brain of a schizophrenic patient during both auditory and visual hallucinations and compared activity to his resting state. Yellow indicates areas of greatest activation, and red is next greatest. Note the widespread areas of activation; note also the lack of activation in Broca's area, where we might have expected activity if the hallucinations were due to inner speech. *(Source: Silbersweig et al., 1995)*

Differential Diagnosis of Psychological Disorders

Suppose you're a psychiatrist and you meet a patient who has recently deteriorated in everyday functioning and has hallucinations, delusions, thought disorder, and disorganized speech. You are ready to enter a diagnosis of schizophrenia and begin treatment, right?

Not so fast. According to DSM-IV (American Psychiatric Association, 1994), before making a diagnosis of schizophrenia one must first rule out other conditions that might produce similar symptoms. A differential diagnosis is one that identifies a condition as distinct from other conditions with similar symptoms. Here are a few conditions that can resemble schizophrenia and be misdiagnosed:

- *Mood disorder with psychotic features*: Depressed people sometimes have hallucinations and delusions, especially delusions of guilt or failure.

- *Prolonged substance abuse*: Hallucinations and delusions can result from drug abuse, especially if someone uses large amounts over weeks or months. Drugs likely to pro-

duce such effects include amphetamine, methamphetamine, cocaine, LSD, and phencyclidine ("angel dust"). Even marijuana intoxication can sometimes resemble schizophrenia (Emrich, Leweke, & Schneider, 1997). Substance abuse is more likely than schizophrenia to produce temporary symptoms and more likely to produce visual hallucinations.

- *Brain damage*: Lesions to the temporal or prefrontal cortex can produce symptoms resembling schizophrenia. Presumably no competent therapist would confuse schizophrenia with the effects of a stroke, but one might easily overlook the possibility of a brain tumor.

- *Undetected hearing deficits*: Sometimes someone who is starting to have trouble hearing thinks that everyone else is whispering and therefore starts to worry, "They're whispering because they're talking about me!" If someone's only problem is delusions of persecution, it is wise to check the person's hearing.

45–50. The reasons for this difference are unknown; one hypothesis is that estrogen has some protective effect against schizophrenia (Häfner et al., 1998).

Childhood-onset schizophrenia is much less common and may have different causes. Unlike the adult-onset version, childhood schizophrenia is associated with identifiable genetic abnormalities (Burgess et al., 1998) and gradually increasing brain damage (Rapoport et al., 1999). The brain abnormalities are also more severe, as a rule (Nopoulos, Giedd, Andreasen, & Rapoport, 1998).

Stop & Check

1. Why are hallucinations considered a "positive symptom"?

2. Has schizophrenia been increasing, decreasing, or staying the same in prevalence?

Check your answers on page 450

Genetics

In the first edition of this textbook, published in 1981, I concluded that "heredity is a very important determinant of schizophrenia" (Kalat, 1981, p. 462). It seemed to me, as to others, that the remaining task for researchers was to fill in the details of how many genes contributed, where they were on the chromosomes, and how they influenced behavior. Over the years further evidence hasn't fallen into place as neatly as expected. Heredity still looks like a contributor to schizophrenia, but we are less sure how important it is. Let's consider the evidence for a genetic contribution and the problems with that evidence.

Twin Studies

The closer your biological relationship to someone with schizophrenia, the greater your own probability of schizophrenia, as shown in Figure 15.15 (Gottesman, 1991). One of the most important points in Figure 15.15 is that having a monozygotic twin with schizophrenia increases the risk far more than does a dizygotic twin with schizophrenia, as many other studies have confirmed (Cardno et al., 1999). For monozygotic twins there is about a 50% concordance (agreement) for schizophrenia (varying from one study to another), as compared to a 15% to 20% concordance for dizygotic twins. Furthermore twin pairs who are really monozygotic, but thought they weren't, are more concordant for schizophrenia than twin pairs who thought they were, but really aren't (Kendler, 1983). That is, *being* monozygotic is more critical than *being treated as* monozygotic.

- *Huntington's disease*: The symptoms of Huntington's disease include hallucinations, delusions, and disordered thinking. Ordinarily the motor symptoms come first and the psychotic thinking develops only in the late stages of the disease, but sometimes the psychological symptoms become prominent before the motor impairments do. And after all, one type of schizophrenia, called *catatonic schizophrenia,* includes motor abnormalities, so a mixture of psychological and motor symptoms could represent either schizophrenia or Huntington's disease. A family medical history usually calls attention to the possibility of Huntington's disease, but some people are adopted or don't know their family's medical history.

- *Nutritional abnormalities*: Niacin deficiency can produce hallucinations and delusions (Hoffer, 1973); so can prolonged deficiency of vitamin C or an allergy to milk proteins (not the same thing as lactose intolerance). Some people cannot tolerate wheat gluten or other proteins and react with hallucinations and delusions (Reichelt, Seim, & Reichelt, 1996). Most psychiatrists consider dietary deficiencies or allergies to be a rare cause of schizophrenic reactions, but if we almost never test for the possibility, how do we know?

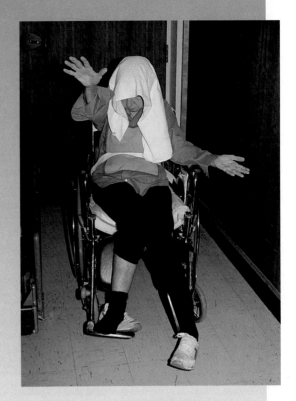

Person with catatonic schizophrenia.

The high concordance for monozygotic twins has long been taken as strong evidence for a genetic influence. However, note three problems:

- Monozygotic twins have only about 50% concordance, not 100%. Clearly, heredity can't be the only factor. Monozygotic twins could sometimes differ because a gene is activated in one individual and suppressed in another (Tsujita et al., 1998), or they could differ because of some environmental influence.

- As mentioned in Chapter 1, most monozygotic twins develop in a single placenta, whereas dizygotic twins always develop in separate placentas. It is therefore possible that part of what we have been attributing to genetics might instead be due to similarity of prenatal environment.

- In Figure 15.15 note the greater similarity between dizygotic twins than between siblings. Dizygotic twins have the same genetic resemblance as siblings, but greater environmental similarity, including that of prenatal and early postnatal life.

Adopted Children Who Develop Schizophrenia

When an adopted child develops schizophrenia, schizophrenia is more probable among the biological relatives than the adopting relatives. One Danish study found schizophrenia in 12.5% of the immediate biological relatives and none of the adopting relatives (Kety et al., 1994). Note in Figure 15.15 that children of a schizophrenic mother have a 17% chance of schizophrenia, even if adopted by nonschizophrenic parents.

Those results suggest a genetic basis, but they are also consistent with a prenatal influence. Consider a pregnant woman with schizophrenia. Yes, she passes her genes to her child, but she also provides a less than ideal prenatal environment. Most women with schizophrenia have low income, smoke and drink during pregnancy, and fail to get medical care during pregnancy. Many have a poor diet. If their children develop schizophrenia, we cannot be sure that the influence is genetic.

Potentially More Decisive Evidence

In rare cases an adopted child has a paternal half-sibling who is also adopted. Paternal half-siblings have the same father but different mothers and therefore different prenatal environments. One study found 63 adopted schizophrenics whose paternal half-siblings were adopted by other families. Of the 63 half-siblings, 8 had schizophrenia also—a concordance well above the approximately 1% prevalence of schizophrenia in the population (Kety, 1977). The results therefore seem

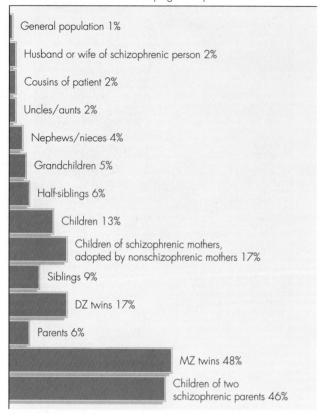

Percent developing schizophrenia

General population 1%

Husband or wife of schizophrenic person 2%

Cousins of patient 2%

Uncles/aunts 2%

Nephews/nieces 4%

Grandchildren 5%

Half-siblings 6%

Children 13%

Children of schizophrenic mothers, adopted by nonschizophrenic mothers 17%

Siblings 9%

DZ twins 17%

Parents 6%

MZ twins 48%

Children of two schizophrenic parents 46%

Figure 15.15 Probabilities of developing schizophrenia
The closer the genetic relationship to someone with schizophrenia, the higher the probability of developing it oneself.
(Source: Based on data from I. I. Gottesman, 1991)

like strong support for a genetic influence—except that two women putting their babies up for adoption after having had sex with the same man, presumably nonmarital sex, probably have much in common with each other and with the man, including smoking habits, drinking habits, health habits, and so forth.

Here is another kind of evidence that appears at first to support a genetic influence: Suppose one monozygotic twin has schizophrenia and the other twin does not, and later both twins become parents. Then researchers report that the children of the twin without schizophrenia have "almost the same risk of schizophrenia" as do the children of the twin with schizophrenia (Gottesman & Bertelson, 1989; Kringlen & Cramer, 1989). That is, the percentage having schizophrenia does not differ significantly for the two groups. The interpretation has been that both twins inherited genes that predispose to schizophrenia. For some reason one twin developed schizophrenia and the other didn't, yet both had the same chance to pass the genes to their children. If schizophrenia were caused by an environmental factor, presumably the twin without schizophrenia would have no way to pass it to his or her children.

In principle such evidence could be convincing. However, let's look more closely at the data. For the two studies combined, the results are as follows:

- Children of the twin with schizophrenia: 5 of 36 developed schizophrenia themselves.

- Children of the twin without schizophrenia: 5 of 61 developed schizophrenia themselves.

Contrary to the authors' conclusion, the trend is that the twins without schizophrenia were *less* likely to pass it to their children (as well as being more likely to have children overall). True, the difference between the two groups is not statistically significant, but only because the sample sizes were small. In short, no conclusion is justified.

Efforts to Locate a Gene

As you can see, the evidence based on family resemblance is suggestive but inconclusive. There are reasons to question a strong role of genetics. One is the fact mentioned earlier that schizophrenia has declined in prevalence in many countries since about the mid-1900s. If it were based solely on genetics, we could not have seen such a rapid decline.

The strongest evidence for a genetic influence would be to locate a gene that is consistently linked with schizophrenia. Recall from earlier chapters that researchers have located genes that are strongly linked with Huntington's disease and Alzheimer's disease. Many researchers have sought to locate a gene for schizophrenia, but so far none of the reported links have been replicable. Techniques of biochemical genetics have become very powerful, and if schizophrenia were linked to a single gene, we could expect someone to have found it by now. One careful study of all the chromosomes, comparing 126 people with schizophrenia to 143 without, found no genetic marker that was strongly linked with schizophrenia (Levinson et al., 1998). A similar study found several genes with possible links to schizophrenia, but again nothing with a very strong link (Blouin et al., 1998).

What shall we conclude? One possibility is that our diagnoses of schizophrenia are just too sloppy for genetic purposes; clinicians are diagnosing schizophrenia in people who don't have it and failing to diagnose it in many who do. Another possibility is that schizophrenia depends on some combination of genes. A worst-case scenario for researchers would be something like "there are nine risk genes, and if you have at least three of them, you are likely to get schizophrenia." Such a complex pattern would be monstrous to demonstrate.

And of course, the other possibility is that some people develop schizophrenia because of genetics, others because of prenatal or early postnatal environment, and still others because of a combination of genetic and environmental factors. If so, it might be difficult to locate the relevant genes just because they would not be linked to schizophrenia consistently enough. About the only point we can conclude with confidence is this: Schizophrenia is not a single-gene disorder like Huntington's disease.

Stop & Check

3. The higher concordance between monozygotic than dizygotic twins implies a probable genetic basis for schizophrenia. What other interpretation is possible?

4. The fact that adopted children who develop schizophrenia usually have biological relatives with schizophrenia implies a probable genetic basis. What other interpretation is possible?

Check your answers on page 450.

The Neurodevelopmental Hypothesis

According to the **neurodevelopmental hypothesis** now popular among biomedical researchers, schizophrenia is based on abnormalities in the prenatal (before birth) or neonatal (newborn) development of the nervous system, which lead to subtle but important abnormalities of brain anatomy and major abnormalities in behavior (Weinberger, 1996). The hypothesis holds that stressful experiences can aggravate the symptoms and that supportive relatives and friends can decrease them, but environmental factors by themselves do not cause schizophrenia.

The argument for the neurodevelopmental hypothesis is that (a) in addition to genetics, several kinds of prenatal or neonatal abnormalities that impair brain development are linked to later schizophrenia; (b) people with schizophrenia have a number of minor brain abnormalities that apparently originate early in life; and (c) it is plausible that certain abnormalities of early brain development could produce behavioral abnormalities in adulthood.

Prenatal and Neonatal Abnormalities of Development

Many people with schizophrenia had problems before or shortly after birth that could have affected their brain development, including poor nutrition during pregnancy (Dalman, Allebeck, Cullberg, Grunewald, & Köstler, 1999), premature birth or low birth weight (P. B. Jones, Rantakallio, Hartikainen, Isohanni, & Sipila, 1998), and complications during delivery, such as excessive bleeding or prolonged labor (Hultman, Öhman, Cnattingius, Wieselgren, & Lindström, 1997; Verdoux et al., 1997).

Schizophrenia also has been linked to problems in early or middle pregnancy. During the winter of 1944–1945, near the end of World War II, Germany blockaded the Netherlands, which depended heavily on imported food. The Dutch people endured a near-starvation diet until the Allies liberated them in May. Women who were in the earliest stage of pregnancy during the starvation period gave birth to a high percentage of babies who later developed schizophrenia (Susser et al., 1996).

If a mother is Rh-negative and her baby is Rh-positive, a small amount of the baby's Rh-positive blood factor may, beginning in the second trimester, leak into the mother's blood supply, triggering an immunological rejection response. The response is weak with the woman's first Rh-positive baby but stronger during later pregnancies, and it is more intense with boy than girl babies. Second- and later-born boy babies with Rh incompatibility have an increased risk of hearing deficits, mental retardation, and several other problems, and about twice the usual probability of schizophrenia (Hollister, Laing, & Mednick, 1996).

Further evidence that the risk may be traced to prenatal difficulties stems from the **season-of-birth effect:** the tendency for people born in winter to have a slightly (5% to 8%) greater probability of developing schizophrenia than people born at other times of the year. This tendency occurs only in nontropical climates (where the weather changes by season) and is particularly pronounced for schizophrenic people who have no schizophrenic relatives and those born in large cities (Torrey, Miller, Rawlings, & Yolken, 1997).

What might account for the season-of-birth effect? One possibility is complications of delivery or early nutrition. Another is viral infection. Viral epidemics are most common in the fall. Therefore, the reasoning goes, many pregnant women become infected in the fall with a virus that impairs a crucial stage of brain development in a baby who will be born in the winter. A virus that affects the mother does not cross the placenta into the fetus's brain, but it does give the mother a fever, and heat can damage the fetal brain. A mere 1.5°C fever slows the division of fetal neurons and a 3°C fever kills them (Laburn, 1996). (Exercise during pregnancy does *not* overheat the abdomen and is not dangerous to the fetus. Hot baths and saunas are risky, however.)

To test the possible role of viral infections, investigators have asked whether the season-of-birth effect is particularly strong in years of a major fall epidemic. The results have been inconsistent and weak (Mednick, Machon, & Huttunen, 1990; Morgan et al., 1997; Westergaard, Mortensen, Pedersen, Wohlfahrt, & Melbye, 1999). The ideal evidence would be to examine which individual women had infections during their pregnancy, the stage at which they had them, the fevers they developed, and later the percentage of their children who developed schizophrenia. However, no one has records of this type, as most women who get influenza don't consult a physician.

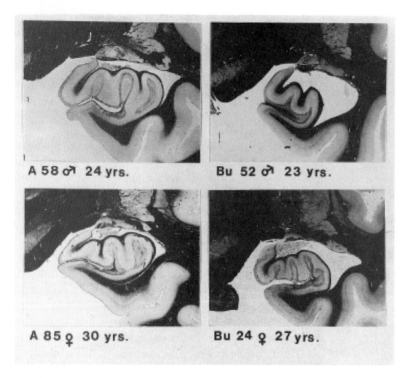

Figure 15.16 The hippocampus of normal people (left) and people with schizophrenia (right)
Notice the atrophy of the brains on the right. *(Source: Bogerts, Meertz, & Schönfeldt-Bausch, 1985; photos courtesy of B. Bogerts)*

Mild Brain Abnormalities

In accord with the neurodevelopmental hypothesis, some (not all) people with schizophrenia show mild abnormalities of brain anatomy. MRI scans indicate that in people with schizophrenia, the prefrontal cortex, temporal cortex, hippocampus, and amygdala are a few percent smaller than normal, especially in the left hemisphere (Velakoulis et al., 1999; Wright et al., 2000) (see Figure 15.16). The ventricles (fluid-filled spaces within the brain) are larger than normal (Wolkin et al., 1998; Wright et al., 2000) (see Figure 15.17). Brain anatomy is generally most abnormal in people with the greatest behavioral deficits and the earliest onset of symptoms.

Lateralization is also different from the normal pattern. In most people the left hemisphere is slightly larger than the right, especially in the planum temporale of the temporal lobe, but in schizophrenic people the right hemi-sphere is slightly larger (Kwon et al., 1999). Schizophrenic people have lower than normal overall activity in the left hemisphere (Gur & Chin, 1999) and are more likely than other people to be left-handed (Satz & Green, 1999). All these results suggest a subtle change in early brain development.

On a variety of neuropsychological tests, schizophrenic patients tend to show deficits of memory and attention similar to those of people with damage to the temporal or prefrontal cortex (Park, Holzman, & Goldman-Rakic, 1995) (see Methods 15.1). The areas with the most consistent signs of abnormality are those that mature most slowly, such as the dorsolateral prefrontal cortex (Pearlson, Petty, Ross, & Tien, 1996). The dorsolateral prefrontal cortex increases its activity during working memory tasks for most people, but not for people with schizophrenia (Berman, Torrey, Daniel, & Weinberger, 1992; Fletcher et al., 1998). People with schizophrenia also have fewer than the normal number of synapses in the prefrontal cortex (Glantz & Lewis, 1997, 2000). As you might expect, people with schizophrenia perform poorly at working memory tasks (Goldberg, Weinberger, Berman, Pliskin, & Podd, 1987; Spindler, Sullivan, Menon, Lim, & Pfefferbaum, 1997).

At a microscopic level the most reliable finding is that cell bodies are smaller than normal, especially in the hippocampus and prefrontal cortex (Rajkowska, Selemon, & Goldman-Rakic, 1998; Selemon, Rajkowska, & Goldman-Rakic, 1995; Weinberger, 1999). Also, some neurons fail to arrange themselves in the neat, orderly

Ventricles

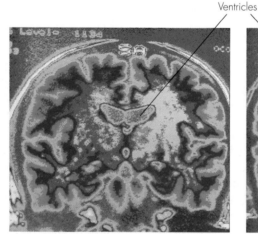 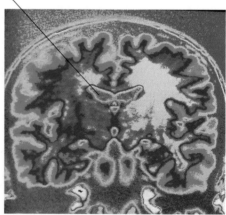

Figure 15.17 Coronal sections for identical twins
The twin on the left has schizophrenia; the twin on the right does not. Note that the ventricles (near the center of each brain) are larger in the twin with schizophrenia. *(Source: Photos courtesy of E. F. Torrey & M. F. Casanova/NIMH)*

The Wisconsin Card Sorting Task

Neuropsychologists use many behavioral tests to measure the functioning of the prefrontal cortex. One is the Wisconsin Card Sorting Task. A person is handed a shuffled deck of cards that differ in number, color, and shape of objects—for example, three red circles, five blue triangles, four green squares. First the person is asked to sort them by one rule, such as separate them by color. Then the rule changes, and the person is supposed to

sort them by a different rule, such as number. Shifting to a new rule requires suppressing the old one and evokes activity in the prefrontal cortex (Konishi et al., 1998). People with damage to the prefrontal cortex can sort by whichever rule is first, but then they have trouble shifting to a new rule. People with schizophrenia have the same difficulty.

manner typical of normal brains (Benes & Bird, 1987) (see Figure 15.18). The details of abnormal development remain to be established, but it is noteworthy that many schizophrenic patients have abnormal amounts of cell recognition molecules that guide the migration of neurons and axons during early development (Honer et al., 1997; Poltorak et al., 1997).

The brain damage associated with schizophrenia is not *progressive*. That is, it does not increase as the person ages, as it does for Parkinson's disease or Huntington's disease. Both IQ scores and brain measurements of older schizophrenic patients are similar to those of younger patients (Andreasen, Swayze, et al., 1990; Censits, Ragland, Gur, & Gur, 1997; Russell, Munro, Jones, Hemsley, & Murray, 1997; Selemon et al., 1995). Furthermore schizophrenic brains have no proliferation of glia cells, which ordinarily increase when neurons die (Benes, 1995; Lim et al., 1998). Evidently the brain abnormalities of schizophrenia develop early in life and then remain fairly steady.

Early Development and Later Psychopathology

One question may have struck you by now. How can we reconcile the evidence for abnormalities of early brain development with the fact that the symptoms of schizophrenia usually become prominent between ages 20 and 30? The time course may not be so puzzling as it seems at first (Weinberger, 1996). The areas that most consistently show signs of abnormality, mainly the prefrontal cortex, mature most slowly (Lewis, 1997; Sowell, Thompson, Holmes, Jernigan, & Toga, 1999). The dorsolateral prefrontal cortex probably doesn't reach adult levels of competence until at least the late teens. As discussed in Chapter 5, infant monkeys with damage in the dorsolateral prefrontal cortex behave normally at first and gradually become impaired later, when the dorsolateral prefrontal cortex would ordinarily become mature. Similar damage in human infants

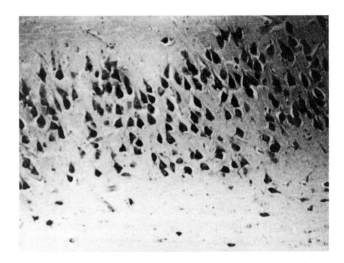
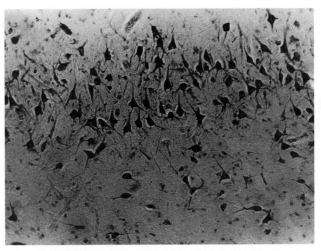

Figure 15.18 Hippocampal disorganization in schizophrenia
Neurons of a normal person (top) show an orderly arrangement; those of someone with schizophrenia (bottom) appear more haphazard and disorganized. *(Source: Photos courtesy of Arnold Scheibel)*

might produce only minor problems in childhood but increasing impairments in late adolescence and young adulthood.

The current status of the neurodevelopmental hypothesis is best described as plausible, but not firmly established. Many studies link schizophrenia to probable prenatal damage and mild brain abnormalities, but the effects are small, vary from one sample of patients to another, and are often subject to alternative interpretations (Weinberger, 1996). Additional research will be necessary to test the hypothesis more thoroughly.

Stop & Check

5. What is the season-of-birth effect?

6. If schizophrenia is due to abnormal brain development, why do behavioral symptoms not become apparent until later in life?

Check your answers on page 450.

Neurotransmitters and Drugs

As presented earlier in this module, researchers once stated confidently that schizophrenia was a genetic disorder, but the evidence hasn't solidified that position as neatly as expected. Something similar has happened regarding neurotransmitters. Researchers were once convinced—and many still are—that schizophrenia is due to excess activity at dopamine synapses. But again, this view faces problems that haven't gone away. We consider the evidence for the dopamine hypothesis, the problems with that hypothesis, and then an alternative.

The Dopamine Hypothesis

According to the dopamine hypothesis of schizophrenia, schizophrenia results from excess activity at certain dopamine synapses. The main evidence for this hypothesis comes from studies of drugs that relieve or aggravate the symptoms of schizophrenia.

Antipsychotic Drugs The most persuasive evidence for the dopamine hypothesis comes from studies of drugs that relieve schizophrenia. In the 1950s psychiatrists were surprised to discover that one tranquilizer, chlorpromazine (trade name Thorazine), frequently relieves the positive symptoms of schizophrenia. Previously most schizophrenic patients who entered a mental hospital never left. Chlorpromazine and related drugs halt the course of the disease in many cases if treatment begins early. Often a patient must continue taking the drug, much as a diabetic patient continues taking insulin, although some patients recover and have no more need for the medication. About one-fourth of schizophrenic patients do not benefit from the drugs, and the prospects for benefit are worse among those who deteriorated severely before starting treatment.

Researchers later discovered that most other antipsychotic or neuroleptic drugs (drugs that tend to relieve schizophrenia and similar conditions) belong to two chemical families: the phenothiazines, which include chlorpromazine, and the butyrophenones, which include haloperidol (trade name Haldol). Figure 15.19 illustrates the correlation between the therapeutic effects of various drugs and their ability to block postsynaptic dopamine receptors. For each drug researchers determined the mean dose prescribed for schizophrenic patients (displayed along the horizontal axis) and the amount needed to block dopamine receptors (displayed along the vertical axis). As the figure shows, the drugs that are most effective against schizophrenia (and therefore used in the smallest doses) are the most effective at blocking dopamine receptors (Seeman, Lee, Chau-Wong, & Wong, 1976).

Drugs That Can Provoke Schizophrenic Symptoms Large, frequent doses of certain drugs can induce substance-induced psychotic disorder, characterized by hallucinations and delusions (positive symptoms of schizophrenia). Among the drugs that commonly produce these symptoms are amphetamine, methamphetamine, and cocaine, all of which increase the activity at dopamine synapses, as noted in Chapter 3. LSD also produces psychotic symptoms; LSD is best known for its effects on serotonin synapses, but it also increases activity at dopamine synapses. The main differences between drug-induced psychosis and schizophrenia are that the drug-induced states often include visual hallucinations, whereas schizophrenia usually doesn't, and that drug-induced psychosis is usually temporary (Ellinwood, 1969; Sato, 1992). Also, these drugs usually induce only positive, not negative, symptoms.

Additional Support for the Dopamine Hypothesis It has long been noted that stress exacerbates (makes worse) schizophrenia. Even mild stressors, such as loud noise, can exacerbate the symptoms temporarily. Researchers have found that stressors increase the release of dopamine in the prefrontal cortex, an area that most theorists believe to be key for understanding schizophrenia. Furthermore stress-induced impairments of behavior can be relieved by dopamine-blocking drugs, such as haloperidol (Arnsten & Goldman-Rakic, 1998).

Problems with the Dopamine Hypothesis Recall from the depression module that antidepressant drugs alter the activity at dopamine and serotonin synapses quickly, but improve mood only after 2 or 3 weeks of treatment. The same issue arises for schizophrenia: Antipsychotic drugs block dopamine synapses within minutes, but their effects on behavior build up gradually over 2 or 3 weeks.

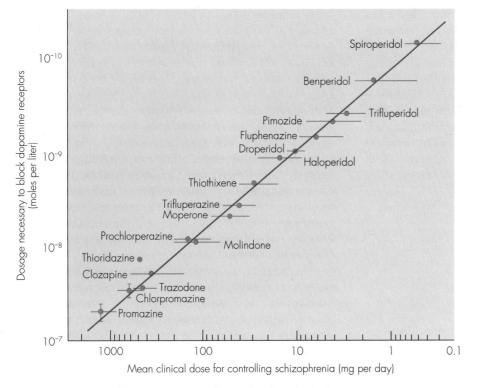

Figure 15.19 Dopamine-blocking effects of antipsychotic drugs
Drugs are arranged along the horizontal axis in terms of the average daily dose prescribed for schizophrenic patients. (Horizontal lines indicate common ranges of dosage.) Note that *larger* doses are to the left and *smaller* doses are to the right so that *more effective* drugs are to the right. (Less is needed of a more effective drug to achieve the same effect.) Along the vertical axis is a measurement of the amount of each drug required to achieve a certain degree of blockage of postsynaptic dopamine receptors. Again, *larger* doses are toward the bottom and *smaller* doses are toward the top so that the drugs on top are *more effective* in blocking dopamine synapses. A drug's effectiveness in blocking dopamine synapses is almost perfectly correlated with its ability to control schizophrenia. *(Source: Seeman, Lee, Chau-Wong, & Wong, 1976)*

So blocking dopamine synapses may be an important first step for an antipsychotic drug, but clearly something else must be happening in those 2 or 3 weeks.

Furthermore, direct measurements of dopamine and its metabolites generally find approximately normal levels in people with schizophrenia (Jaskiw & Weinberger, 1992). Studies of dopamine receptors have yielded complicated results. The density of dopamine type D_2 receptors is about normal in schizophrenic people, but that of type D_1 is below normal, and the levels of D_3 and D_4 are above normal (Gurevich et al., 1997; Murray et al., 1995; Okubo et al., 1997). So far, researchers have found no relationship between schizophrenia and the genes that code for dopamine receptors. In short, the drug

data suggest some relationship to dopamine or its receptors, but direct measurements find no convincing abnormality.

The Glutamate Hypothesis

According to an alternative possibility, the glutamate hypothesis of schizophrenia, the underlying problem is deficient activity at certain glutamate synapses, especially in the prefrontal cortex. In many brain areas dopamine inhibits glutamate release, or glutamate stimulates neurons that inhibit dopamine release, or glutamate excites neurons that dopamine inhibits. Therefore increased dopamine would produce about the same effects as decreased glutamate, and drugs that block dopamine increase glutamate effects. So the antipsychotic effects of drugs like chlorpromazine and haloperidol are equally compatible with the dopamine hypothesis (too much dopamine, which needs to be blocked) or the glutamate hypothesis (too little glutamate, which needs to be enhanced).

The glutamate hypothesis is supported by data from the effects of the drug phencyclidine, measurements of glutamate activity in the brain, and the possible effectiveness of certain glutamate-enhancing drugs as antipsychotic drugs.

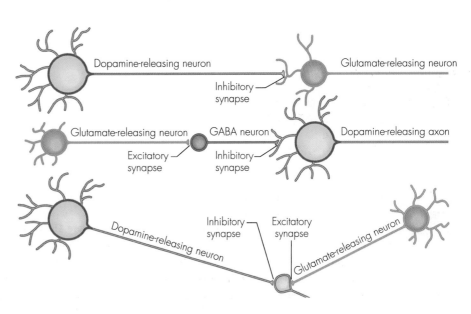

The Effects of Phencyclidine Recall that dopamine-stimulating drugs such as amphetamine and cocaine can induce positive symptoms of schizophrenia. **Phencyclidine (PCP)** ("angel dust"), a drug that inhibits glutamate type NMDA receptors, produces both positive and negative symptoms of schizophrenia, mimicking schizophrenia even more closely. Studies on monkeys show that it impairs the functioning of the prefrontal cortex, including the activity at dopamine synapses (Jentsch et al., 1997). PCP is a good model for schizophrenia in other regards also (Farber, Newcomer, & Olney, 1999; Olney & Farber, 1995):

- PCP and the related drug *ketamine* produce little if any psychotic response in preadolescents. Just as the symptoms of schizophrenia usually begin to emerge well after puberty, so do the psychotic effects of PCP and ketamine.

- LSD, amphetamine, and cocaine produce temporary schizophrenic symptoms in almost anyone, and not much worse in people with a history of schizophrenia than in anyone else. However, for someone who has recovered from schizophrenia, PCP induces a long-lasting relapse.

Measurements of Glutamate Researchers have found that the brains of schizophrenic people release lower than normal amounts of glutamate in the prefrontal cortex and hippocampus (Akbarian et al., 1995; Tsai et al., 1995).

Also, measurements of the RNA molecules associated with certain genes indicate deficient expression of glutamate receptors in the temporal lobe, hippocampus, and prefrontal cortex of schizophrenic patients. The amount of deficiency of those receptors correlates highly with deterioration of memory and reasoning (Hirsch, Das, Garey, & de Belleroche, 1997). These findings are consistent with the glutamate hypothesis, but much more research is needed.

Drugs That Enhance Glutamate Activity It might seem that the best test of the glutamate hypothesis would be to administer glutamate itself. However, recall from Chapter 5 how strokes kill neurons—by overstimulating glutamate synapses. An overall increase in glutamate to the brain would be extremely risky.

However, glutamate affects several types of receptors, and it may be possible to find drugs that act just at the appropriate synapses in the prefrontal cortex. One drug, with the not-very-catchy name *LY 354740*, which selectively stimulates one type of metabotropic glutamate receptor, blocks the behavioral effects of PCP on rats and prevents its disruption of activity in the prefrontal cortex (Moghaddam & Adams, 1998). That drug has not yet been tried with humans. Another possibility is the amino acid glycine. The type-NMDA gluta-

mate receptor has a primary site that is activated by glutamate but also a secondary cotransmitter site that is activated by glycine (see Figure 15.20). Glycine by itself does not activate the receptor, but it increases the effectiveness of glutamate. Thus an increase in glycine can gently increase the activity at NMDA synapses without the risk of overstimulating glutamate throughout the brain. Researchers have found that although glycine is not an effective antipsychotic drug by itself, it increases the effects of other antipsychotic drugs, especially with regard to negative symptoms (Heresco-Levy et al., 1999). Cycloserine, a drug that attaches less strongly to the glycine site but crosses the blood-brain barrier more easily, also improves the effectiveness of antipsychotic drugs, especially for negative symptoms (Goff et al., 1999).

So, what is the status of the dopamine and glutamate hypotheses? The evidence to date does not fully confirm or reject either of them. We need more research, especially with regard to the glutamate hypothesis, which arose more recently and has received less attention so far.

Stop & Check

7. How fast do antipsychotic drugs affect dopamine synapses? How fast do they alter behavior?

8. What drugs induce mainly the positive symptoms of schizophrenia? What drug can induce both positive and negative symptoms?

9. Why are so many drug results equally compatible with the dopamine hypothesis and the glutamate hypothesis?

Check your answers on page 450.

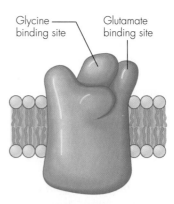

Figure 15.20 An NMDA glutamate receptor
NMDA glutamate receptors have a primary binding site for glutamate but also a secondary binding site for glycine. Glycine by itself does not activate the receptor, but it increases the effect of glutamate. Cycloserine also attaches to the glycine site, about half as effectively as glycine.

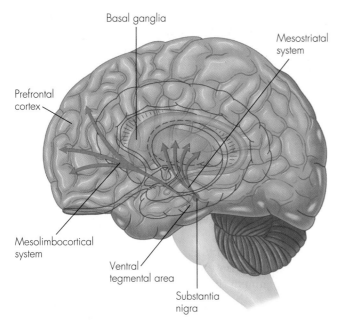

Figure 15.21 Two major dopamine pathways
The mesolimbocortical system is apparently responsible for the symptoms of schizophrenia; the path to the basal ganglia is probably responsible for tardive dyskinesia, a movement disorder. *(Source: Adapted from Valzelli, 1980)*

The Search for Improved Drugs

The commonly used antipsychotic drugs block dopamine receptors throughout the brain. Presumably the benefits result from effects on the dopamine neurons in the **mesolimbocortical system,** a set of neurons that project from the midbrain tegmentum to the limbic system. However, the drugs also block dopamine neurons in other locations, including those in the basal ganglia (see Figure 15.21). The result is an unpleasant side effect called **tardive dyskinesia** (TARD-eev dis-kih-NEE-zhee-uh), characterized by tremors and other involuntary movements that develop gradually over periods ranging from a few days of medication to more than 20 years (Kiriakakis, Bhatia, Quinn, & Marsden, 1998). Tardive dyskinesia may result from denervation supersensitivity (Chapter 5): Prolonged blockage of dopamine transmission causes the postsynaptic neurons to increase in sensitivity and respond vigorously to even small amounts of dopamine. After receptors in the basal ganglia become supersensitive, even slight stimulation causes bursts of involuntary movements.

Once tardive dyskinesia emerges, it can last for years even if the person quits the drug (Kiriakakis et al., 1998). Consequently the best strategy is to prevent it from starting. Certain new drugs called **atypical antipsychotics,** such as clozapine, alleviate schizophrenia while seldom if ever produce movement problems (see Figure 15.22). Compared to most other antipsychotic drugs, clozapine has less effect on dopamine type D_2 receptors, but stronger effects on type D_4 receptors and

serotonin type 5-HT$_2$ receptors (Meltzer, Matsubara, & Lee, 1989; Mrzljak et al., 1996; Roth, Willins, Kristiansen, & Kroeze, 1999). It also produces different benefits. Whereas most antipsychotic drugs reduce hallucinations and delusions but seldom help with the negative symptoms, clozapine helps to relieve both positive and negative symptoms (Stip, 2000). Unfortunately, clozapine produces side effects of its own, including a decrease in white blood cells, leaving the person vulnerable to infection. People taking clozapine therefore need frequent, somewhat expensive blood tests. Some new atypical antipsychotic drugs, such as olanzapine and quetiapine, produce benefits similar to clozapine's with less impairment of white blood cells (Beaumont, 2000). More research is needed to find the best drug treatments for schizophrenia.

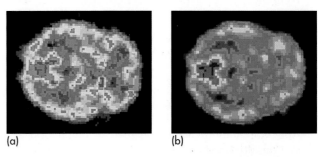

Figure 15.22 PET scans of a patient with schizophrenia
These PET scans of a patient with schizophrenia **(a)** taking clozapine and **(b)** during a period off the drug, demonstrate that clozapine increases brain activity in many brain areas. (Red indicates the highest activity, followed by yellow, green, and blue.) Clozapine helps relieve both positive and negative symptoms.

Module 15.3

In Closing: The Fascination of Schizophrenia

A good mystery novel presents an array of clues, mixing important clues with irrelevant information, and the reader's challenge is to figure out who committed the crime. Schizophrenia research is similar, except that we want to know *what* is to blame, not *who*. As with a mystery novel, we have to sort through an enormous number of clues and false leads, looking for a pattern. One difference is that, unlike the reader of a mystery novel, we have the option of collecting new evidence of our own.

I trust it is clear to you that researchers have not yet solved the mystery of schizophrenia. But it should also be clear that they have made progress. The hypotheses they are considering today are almost certainly not completely correct, but they have much more evidence behind them than the hypotheses of decades past. The future looks exciting for this area of research.

Summary

1. Positive symptoms of schizophrenia (characteristics not present in most other people) include hallucinations, delusions, inappropriate emotions, bizarre behaviors, and thought disorder. (p. 438)

2. Negative symptoms (normal characteristics absent in people with schizophrenia) include deficits of social interaction, emotional expression, and speech. (p. 438)

3. Studies of twins and adopted children imply a genetic predisposition to schizophrenia. However, concordance between monozygotic twins is only about 50%, not 100%, and prevalence of the disorder has declined since the mid-1900s, so schizophrenia cannot be purely a genetic disorder. (p. 440)

4. The evidence does not tell us how much of the predisposition is due to genetics and how much is due to prenatal environment. So far, researchers have not located any gene that is strongly linked with schizophrenia. (p. 442)

5. According to the neurodevelopmental hypothesis, either genes or difficulties early in life impair brain development in ways that lead to behavioral abnormalities beginning in early adulthood. (p. 443)

6. The probability of schizophrenia is higher than average for those who were subjected to prenatal malnutrition, Rh incompatibility, or maternal fever. (p. 443)

7. Some people with schizophrenia show mild abnormalities of early brain development, which do not increase during adulthood. (p. 444)

8. Parts of the prefrontal cortex are very slow to mature. It is plausible that early disruption of those areas might produce behavioral symptoms that become manifest as schizophrenia in young adults. (p. 445)

9. According to the dopamine hypothesis, schizophrenia is due to excess dopamine activity. The main support for this hypothesis is that drugs that block dopamine synapses reduce the positive symptoms of schizophrenia, and that drugs that increase dopamine activity can induce the positive symptoms. However, direct measurements of dopamine and its receptors have not strongly supported this theory. (p. 446)

10. According to the glutamate hypothesis, the problem is deficient glutamate activity. Evidence supporting this view is that phencyclidine, which blocks NMDA glutamate synapses, produces both positive and negative symptoms of schizophrenia, especially in people predisposed to schizophrenia. (p. 447)

11. Prolonged use of antipsychotic drugs may produce tardive dyskinesia, a movement disorder. The atypical antipsychotic drug clozapine relieves both positive and negative symptoms without producing tardive dyskinesia, but it produces other dangerous side effects of its own. (p. 449)

Answers to *Stop and Check* Questions

1. Hallucinations are considered a positive symptom because they are present when they should be absent. A "positive" symptom is not a "good" symptom. (p. 440)

2. Schizophrenia has been decreasing in prevalence. (p. 440)

3. Monozygotic twins could resemble each other partly because they shared more of their prenatal environment than did dizygotic twins. (p. 443)

4. A biological mother can influence her child's development through prenatal environment as well as genetics, even if the child is adopted early. (p. 443)

5. The season-of-birth effect is the observation that schizophrenia is slightly more common among people who were born in the winter. (p. 446)

6. Parts of the prefrontal cortex are very slow to reach maturity; therefore early disruption of this area's development might not produce any symptoms early in life, when the prefrontal cortex is contributing little anyway. (p. 446)

7. They alter dopamine synaptic activity within minutes. They take 2 to 3 weeks to alter behavior. (p. 448)

8. Amphetamine, cocaine, and LSD in large doses induce positive symptoms, such as hallucinations and delusions. Phencyclidine induces both positive and negative symptoms. (p. 448)

9. Dopamine inhibits glutamate cells in many areas, and glutamate stimulates neurons that inhibit dopamine. Therefore the effects of increasing dopamine are similar to those of decreasing glutamate. (p. 448)

Thought Questions

1. With some illnesses, a patient who at first fails to respond is offered higher and higher doses of medication. However, if a schizophrenic patient does not respond to antipsychotic drugs, it is generally not a good idea to increase them. Why not?

2. Long-term use of antipsychotic drugs can induce tardive dyskinesia. However, if a person with tardive dyskinesia stops taking the drugs, the symptoms actually grow worse, at least temporarily. Why?

3. Why might it sometimes be difficult to find effective drugs for someone who suffers from both depression and schizophrenia?

Chapter Ending
Key Terms and Activities

Terms

acetaldehyde (p. 425)

acetic acid (p. 425)

acute (p. 439)

alcoholism (or alcohol dependence) (p. 424)

Antabuse (p. 425)

antipsychotic (or neuroleptic) drug (p. 446)

atypical antidepressants (p. 431)

atypical antipsychotics (p. 449)

autoreceptor (p. 431)

bipolar disorder (or manic-depressive disorder) (p. 434)

Borna disease (p. 429)

butyrophenone (p. 446)

chlorpromazine (p. 446)

chronic (p. 439)

concordance (p. 440)

delusion (p. 438)

differential diagnosis (p. 440)

dopamine hypothesis of schizophrenia (p. 446)

electroconvulsive therapy (ECT) (p. 432)

expressed emotion (p. 439)

glutamate hypothesis of schizophrenia (p. 447)

hallucination (p. 438)

lithium (p. 434)

major depression (p. 428)

mania (p. 434)

mesolimbocortical system (p. 449)

monoamine oxidase inhibitors (MAOIs) (p. 431)

negative symptom (p. 438)

neurodevelopmental hypothesis (p. 443)

paternal half-siblings (p. 441)

phencyclidine (PCP) (p. 448)

phenothiazine (p. 446)

placebo effect (p. 432)

positive symptom (p. 438)

postpartum depression (p. 429)

schizophrenia (p. 438)

seasonal affective disorder (SAD) (p. 435)

season-of-birth effect (p. 443)

selective serotonin reuptake inhibitors (SSRIs) (p. 431)

substance abuse (p. 424)

substance-induced psychotic disorder (p. 446)

tardive dyskinesia (p. 449)

thought disorder (p. 439)

tricyclic (p. 430)

Type I alcoholism (p. 424)

Type II alcoholism (p. 424)

unipolar disorder (p. 434)

Suggestions for Further Reading

Andreasen, N. C. (1994). *Schizophrenia: From mind to molecule.* Washington, DC: American Psychiatric Press. Discusses the behavior, biology, and treatment of schizophrenia.

Waddington, J. L., & Buckley, P. F. (1996). *The neurodevelopmental basis of schizophrenia.* Austin, TX: Landes Co. Discusses season-of-birth effect and possible roles of viruses, obstetric complications, and other early influences on the later development of schizophrenia.

Web Sites to Explore

You can go to the Biological Psychology Study Center and click on these links. While there, you can also check for suggested articles available on InfoTrac. The Biological Psychology Internet address is:
http://psychology.wadsworth.com/book/kalatbiopsych7e/

http://www.alcoholism.net/
Information about alcoholism.

http://www.depression.com/
News articles and links to other information about depression.

http://www.sltbr.org/
Includes information about light treatment for seasonal affective disorder.

http://www.schizophrenia.com/
Links to support groups and further information about schizophrenia.

http://www.futur.com/
More research information about schizophrenia.

Active Learner Link

Video: Mary with Bipolar Disorder

Video: Frontal Neglect and the Wisconsin Card Sorting Task

Video: Schizophrenia

Video: Patients with Schizophrenia

Video: Evelyn and Barbara with Major Depression

Quiz for Chapter 15

Appendix A

Brief, Basic Chemistry

Main Ideas

1. All matter is composed of a limited number of elements that combine in endless ways.

2. Atoms, the component parts of an element, consist of protons, neutrons, and electrons. Most atoms can gain or lose electrons, or share them with other atoms.

3. The chemistry of life is predominantly the chemistry of carbon compounds.

Introduction

To understand certain aspects of biological psychology, particularly the action potential and the molecular mechanisms of synaptic transmission, you need to know a little about chemistry. If you have taken a high school or college course and remember the material reasonably well, you should have no trouble with the chemistry in this text. If your knowledge of chemistry is pretty hazy, this appendix will help. (If you plan to take other courses in biological psychology, you should study as much biology and chemistry as possible.)

Elements and Compounds

If you look around, you will see an enormous variety of materials—dirt, water, wood, plastic, metal, cloth, glass, your own body. Every object is composed of a small number of basic building blocks. If a piece of wood catches fire, it breaks down into ashes, gases, and water vapor. The same is true of your body. An investigator could take those ashes, gases, and water and break them down by chemical and electrical means into carbon, oxygen, hydrogen, nitrogen, and a few other materials. Eventually, however, the investigator arrives at a set of materials that cannot be broken down further: Pure carbon or pure oxygen, for example, cannot be converted into anything simpler, at least not by ordinary chemical means. (High-power bombardment with subatomic particles is another story.) The matter we see is composed of elements (materials that cannot be broken down into other materials) and compounds (materials made up by combining elements).

Chemists have found 92 elements in nature, and they have constructed more in the laboratory. (Actually, one of the 92—technetium—is so rare as to be virtually unknown in nature.) Figure A.1, the periodic table, lists each of these elements. Of these, only a few are important for life on Earth. Table A.1 shows the elements commonly found in the human body.

Note that each element has a one- or two-letter abbreviation, such as O for oxygen, H for hydrogen, and Ca for calcium. These are internationally accepted symbols that facilitate communication among chemists who speak different languages. For example, element number 19 is called potassium in English, potassio in Italian, kālijs in Latvian, and draslík in Czech. But chemists in all countries use the symbol K (from *kalium,* the Latin word for "potassium"). Similarly, the symbol for sodium is Na (from *natrium,* the Latin word for "sodium"), and the symbol for iron is Fe (from the Latin word *ferrum*).

A compound is represented by the symbols for the elements that compose it. For example, NaCl stands for sodium chloride (common table salt). H_2O, the symbol for water, indicates that water consists of two parts of hydrogen and one part of oxygen.

Atoms and Molecules

A block of iron can be chopped finer and finer until it is divided into tiny pieces that cannot be broken down any further. These pieces are called atoms. Every element is composed of atoms. A compound, such as water, can also be divided into tinier and tinier pieces. The smallest possible piece of a compound is called a molecule. A molecule of water can be further decomposed into two atoms of hydrogen and one atom of oxygen, but when that happens the compound is broken

and is no longer water. A molecule is the smallest piece of a compound that retains the properties of the compound.

An atom is composed of subatomic particles, including protons, neutrons, and electrons. A proton has a positive electrical charge, a neutron has a neutral charge, and an electron has a negative charge. The nucleus of an atom—its center—contains one or more protons plus a number of neutrons. Electrons are found in the space around the nucleus. Because an atom has the same number of protons as electrons, the electrical charges balance out. (Ions, which we shall consider in a moment, have an imbalance of positive and negative charges.)

The difference between one element and another is in the number of protons in the nucleus of the atom. Hydrogen has just one proton, for example, and oxygen has eight. The number of protons is the atomic number of the element; in the periodic table it is recorded at the

Table A.1 The Elements That Compose Almost All of the Human Body

Element	Symbol	Percentage by Weight in Human Body
Oxygen	O	65
Carbon	C	18
Hydrogen	H	10
Nitrogen	N	3
Calcium	Ca	2
Phosphorus	P	1.1
Potassium	K	0.35
Sulfur	S	0.25
Sodium	Na	0.15
Chlorine	Cl	0.15
Magnesium	Mg	0.05
Iron	Fe	Trace
Copper	Cu	Trace
Iodine	I	Trace
Fluorine	F	Trace
Manganese	Mn	Trace
Zinc	Zn	Trace
Selenium	Se	Trace
Molybdenum	Mo	Trace

Periodic Table of the Elements

Figure A.1 The periodic table of chemistry

It is called "periodic" because certain properties show up at periodic intervals. For example, the column from lithium down consists of metals that readily form salts. The column at the far right consists of gases that do not readily form compounds. Elements 110–118 have only tentative names and symbols.

top of the square for each element. The number at the bottom is the element's **atomic weight,** which indicates the weight of an atom relative to the weight of one proton. A proton has a weight of one unit, a neutron has a weight just trivially greater than one, and an electron has a weight just trivially greater than zero. The atomic weight of the element is the number of protons in the atom plus the average number of neutrons. For example, most hydrogen atoms have one proton and no neutrons; a few atoms per thousand have one or two neutrons, giving an average atomic weight of 1.008. Sodium ions have 11 protons; most also have 12 neutrons, and the atomic weight is slightly less than 23. (Can you figure out the number of neutrons in the average potassium atom? Refer to Figure A.1.)

Ions and Chemical Bonds

An atom that has gained or lost one or more electrons is called an **ion.** For example, if sodium and chloride come together, the sodium atoms readily lose one electron each and the chloride atoms gain one each. The result is a set of positively charged sodium ions (indicated Na^+) and negatively charged chloride ions (Cl^-). Potassium atoms, like sodium atoms, tend to lose an electron and to become positively charged ions (K^+); calcium ions tend to lose two electrons and gain a double positive charge (Ca^{++}).

Because positive charges attract negative charges, sodium ions attract chloride ions. When dry, sodium and chloride form a crystal structure, as Figure A.2 shows. (In water solution, the two kinds of ions move about haphazardly, occasionally attracting one another

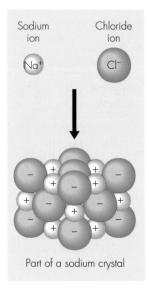

Figure A.2   The crystal structure of sodium chloride
Each sodium ion is surrounded by chloride ions, and each chloride ion is surrounded by sodium ions; no ion is bound to any other single ion in particular.

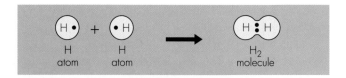

Figure A.3   Structure of a hydrogen molecule
A hydrogen atom has one electron; in the compound the two atoms share the two electrons equally.

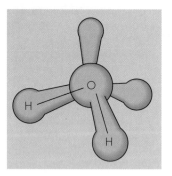

Figure A.4   Structure of a water molecule
The oxygen atom shares a pair of electrons with each hydrogen atom. Oxygen holds the electrons more tightly, making the oxygen part of the molecule more negatively charged than the hydrogen part of the molecule.

but then pulling apart.) The attraction of positive ions for negative ions forms an **ionic bond.** In other cases, instead of transferring an electron from one atom to another, some pairs of atoms share electrons with each other, forming a **covalent bond.** For example, two hydrogen atoms bind, as shown in Figure A.3, and two hydrogen atoms bind with an oxygen atom, as shown in Figure A.4. Atoms that are attached by a covalent bond cannot move independently of one another.

Reactions of Carbon Atoms

Living organisms depend on the enormously versatile compounds of carbon. Because of the importance of these compounds for life, the chemistry of carbon is known as organic chemistry.

Carbon atoms form covalent bonds with hydrogen, oxygen, and a number of other elements. They also form covalent bonds with other carbon atoms. Two carbon atoms may share from one to three pairs of electrons. Such bonds can be indicated as follows:

C—C   Two atoms share one pair of electrons.
C=C   Two atoms share two pairs of electrons.
C≡C   Two atoms share three pairs of electrons.

Each carbon atom ordinarily forms four covalent bonds, either with other carbon atoms, with hydrogen atoms, or with other atoms. Many biologically important compounds include long chains of carbon compounds linked to one another, such as:

H—C—C—C—OH (with H atoms on each carbon)

H—C=C—C=C—C=C—H (with H atoms)

Note that each carbon atom has a total of four bonds, counting each double bond as two. In some molecules, the carbon chain loops around to form a ring:

Ringed structures are common in organic chemistry. To simplify the diagrams chemists often omit the hydrogen atoms. You can simply assume that each carbon atom in the diagram has four covalent bonds and that all the bonds not shown are with hydrogen atoms. To further simplify the diagrams, chemists often omit the carbon atoms themselves, showing only the carbon-to-carbon bonds. For example, the two molecules shown in the previous diagram might be rendered as follows:

If a particular carbon atom has a bond with some atom other than hydrogen, the diagram shows the exception. For example, in each of the two molecules diagrammed below, one carbon has a bond with an oxygen atom, which in turn has a bond with a hydrogen atom. All the bonds that are not shown are carbon–hydrogen bonds.

Figure A.5 illustrates some carbon compounds that are critical for animal life. Purines and pyrimidines form the central structure of DNA and RNA, the chemicals responsible for heredity. Proteins, fats, and carbohydrates are the primary types of fuel that the body uses. Figure A.6 displays the chemical structures of seven neurotransmitters that are extensively discussed in this text.

Chemical Reactions in the Body

A living organism is an immensely complicated, coordinated set of chemical reactions. Life requires that the rate of each reaction be carefully regulated. In many cases one reaction produces a chemical that enters into another reaction, which produces another chemical that enters into another reaction, and so forth. If any one of those reactions is too rapid compared to the others, the chemical it produces will accumulate to possibly harmful levels. If a reaction is too slow, it will not

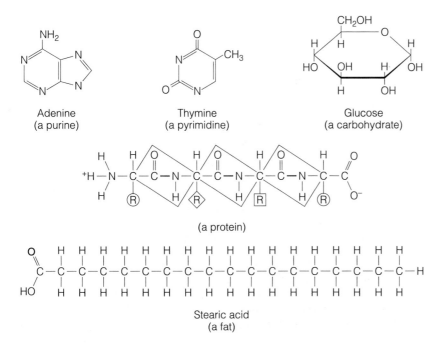

Figure A.5 Structures of some important biological molecules
The R in the protein represents a point of attachment for various chains that differ from one amino acid to another. Actual proteins are much longer than the chemical shown here.

Adenine (a purine)

Thymine (a pyrimidine)

Glucose (a carbohydrate)

(a protein)

Stearic acid (a fat)

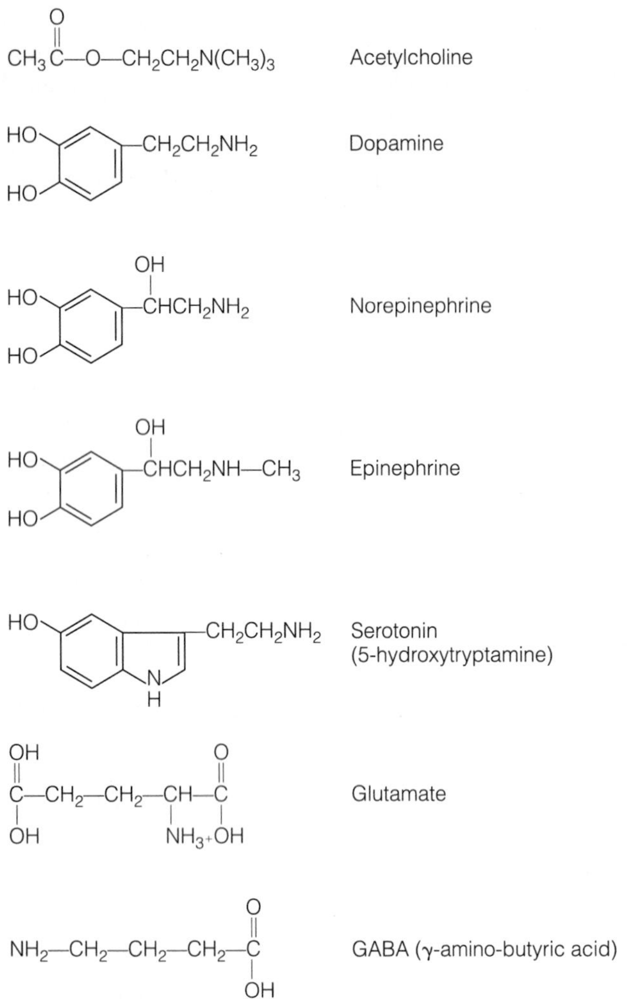

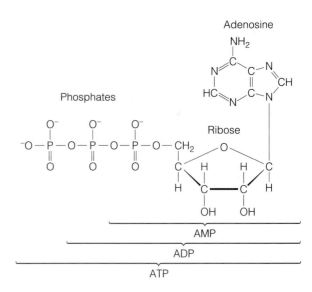

Figure A.7 ATP, composed of adenosine, ribose, and three phosphates
ATP can lose one phosphate group to form ADP (adenosine diphosphate) and then lose another one to form AMP (adenosine monophosphate). Each time it breaks off a phosphate group, it releases energy.

Acetylcholine

Dopamine

Norepinephrine

Epinephrine

Serotonin (5-hydroxytryptamine)

Glutamate

GABA (γ-amino-butyric acid)

Figure A.6 Chemical structures of seven abundant neurotransmitters

produce enough product and the next reaction will be stalled.

Enzymes are proteins that control the rate of chemical reactions. Each reaction is controlled by a particular enzyme. Enzymes are a type of catalyst. A catalyst is any chemical that facilitates a reaction among other chemicals, without being altered itself in the process.

The Role of ATP

The body relies on **ATP (adenosine triphosphate)** as its main way of sending energy where it is needed (Figure A.7). Much of the energy derived from food goes into forming ATP molecules that eventually provide energy for the muscles and other body parts.

ATP consists of adenosine bound to ribose and three phosphate groups (PO_3). Phosphates form high-energy covalent bonds. That is, a large amount of energy is required to form the bonds and a large amount of energy is released when they break. ATP can break off one or two of its three phosphates to provide energy.

Summary

1. Matter is composed of 92 elements that combine to form an endless variety of compounds. (p. 454)

2. An atom is the smallest piece of an element. A molecule is the smallest piece of a compound that maintains the properties of the compound. (p. 454)

3. The atoms of some elements can gain or lose an electron, thus becoming ions. Positively charged ions attract negatively charged ions, forming an ionic bond. In some cases two or more atoms may share electrons, thus forming a covalent bond. (p. 456)

4. The principal carrier of energy in the body is a chemical called ATP. (p. 458)

Terms

atom (p. 454)

atomic number (p. 454)

atomic weight (p. 456)

ATP (adenosine triphosphate) (p. 458)

compound (p. 454)

covalent bond (p. 456)

element (p. 454)

enzyme (p. 458)

ion (p. 456)

ionic bond (p. 456)

molecule (p. 454)

Society for Neuroscience Policies on the Use of Animals and Human Subjects in Neuroscience Research

Policy on the Use of Animals in Neuroscience Research

The Policy on the Use of Animals in Neuroscience Research affects a number of the Society's functions that involve making decisions about animal research conducted by individual members. These include the scheduling of scientific presentations at the Annual Meeting, the review and publication of original research papers in *The Journal of Neuroscience,* and the defense of members whose ethical use of animals in research is questioned by antivivisectionists. The responsibility for implementing the policy in each of these areas will rest with the relevant administrative body (Program Committee, Publications Committee, Editorial Board, and Committee on Animals in Research, respectively), in consultation with Council.

Introduction

The Society for Neuroscience, as a professional society for basic and clinical researchers in neuroscience, endorses and supports the appropriate and responsible use of animals as experimental subjects. Knowledge generated by neuroscience research on animals has led to important advances in the understanding of diseases and disorders that affect the nervous system and in the development of better treatments that reduce suffering in humans and animals. This knowledge also makes a critical contribution to our understanding of ourselves, the complexities of our brains, and what makes us human. Continued progress in understanding how the brain works and further advances in treating and curing disorders of the nervous system require investigation of complex functions at all levels in the living nervous system. Because no adequate alternatives exist, much of this research must be done on animal subjects. The Society takes the position that neuroscientists have an obligation to contribute to this progress through responsible and humane research on animals.

Several functions of the Society are related to the use of animals in research. A number of these involve decisions about research conducted by individual members of the Society, including the scheduling of scientific presentations at the Annual Meeting, the review and publication of original research papers in *The Journal of Neuroscience,* and the defense of members whose ethical use of animals in research is questioned by antivivisectionists. Each of these functions, by establishing explicit support of the Society for the research of individual members, defines a relationship between the Society and its members. The purpose of this document is to outline the policy that guides that relationship. Compliance with the following policy will be an important factor in determining the suitability of research for presentation at the Annual Meeting or for publication in *The Journal of Neuroscience,* and in situations where the Society is asked to provide public and active support for a member whose use of animals in research has been questioned.

General Policy

Neuroscience research uses complicated, often invasive methods, each of which is associated with different problems, risks, and specific technical considerations. An experimental method that would be deemed inappropriate for one kind of research may be the method of choice for another kind of research. It is therefore impossible for the Society to define specific policies and procedures for the care and use of all research animals and for the design and conduct of every neuroscience experiment.

The U.S. *Public Health Service Policy on Humane Care and Use of Laboratory Animals* (PHS Policy) and the *Guide for the Care and Use of Laboratory Animals* (the Guide) describe a set of general policies and procedures designed to ensure the humane and appropriate use of live vertebrate animals in all forms of biomedical research. The Society finds the policies and procedures set forth in the PHS Policy and the Guide to be both necessary and sufficient to ensure a high standard of animal care and use and adopts them as its official "Policy on the Use of Animals in Neuroscience Research" (Society Policy). All Society members are expected to conduct their animal research in compliance with the Society Policy and are required to verify that they have done so when submitting abstracts for presentation at the Annual Meeting or manuscripts for publication in

The Journal of Neuroscience. Adherence to the Society Policy is also an important step toward receiving help from the Society in responding to questions about a member's use of animals in research. A complete description of the Society's policy and procedures for defending members whose research comes under attack is given in the Society's *Handbook for the Use of Animals in Neuroscience Research.*

Local Committee Review

An important element of the Society Policy is the establishment of a local committee that is charged with reviewing and approving all proposed animal care and use procedures. In addition to scientists experienced in research involving animals and a veterinarian, the membership of this local committee should include an individual who is not affiliated with the member's institution in any other way. In reviewing a proposed use of animals, the committee should evaluate the adequacy of institutional policies, animal husbandry, veterinary care, and the physical plant. Specific attention should be paid to proposed procedures for animal procurement, quarantine and stabilization, separation by species, disease diagnosis and treatment, anesthesia and analgesia, surgery and postsurgical care, and euthanasia. The review committee also should ensure that procedures involving live vertebrate animals are designed and performed with due consideration of their relevance to human or animal health, the advancement of knowledge, or the good of society. This review and approval of a member's use of live vertebrate animals in research by a local committee is an essential component of the Society Policy. Assistance in developing appropriate animal care and use procedures and establishing a local review committee can be obtained from the documents listed here and from the Society.

Other Laws, Regulations, and Policies

In addition to complying with the policy described above, Regular Members (i.e., North American residents) of the Society must also adhere to all relevant national, state, or local laws and/or regulations that govern their use of animals in neuroscience research. Thus, U.S. members must observe the U.S. Animal Welfare Act (as amended in 1985) and its implementing regulations from the U.S. Department of Agriculture. Canadian members must abide by the *Guide to the Care and Use of Experimental Animals,* and members in Mexico must comply with the *Reglamento de la Ley General de Salud en Materia de Investigacion para la Salud* of the Secretaria de Salud (published on Jan. 6, 1987). Similarly, in addition to complying with the laws and regulations of their home countries, Foreign Members of the Society should adhere to the official Society Policy outlined here.

Recommended References

"Anesthesia and paralysis in experimental animals." *Visual Neuroscience,* 1:421–426. 1984.

The Biomedical Investigator's Handbook for Researchers Using Animal Models. 1987. Foundation for Biomedical Research, 818 Connecticut Ave., N.W., Suite 303, Washington, D.C. 20006.

Guide for the Care and Use of Laboratory Animals, 7th edition. 1996. NRC (National Research Council), Institute of Laboratory Animal Resources, National Academy of Sciences, 2101 Constitution Ave., N.W., Washington, D.C. 20418.

Guide to the Care and Use of Experimental Animals, 2nd edition, vol. 1. 1993. Canadian Council on Animal Care, 350 Albert St., Suite 315, Ottawa, Ontario, Canada K1R 1B1.

Handbook for the Use of Animals in Neuroscience Research. 1991. Society for Neuroscience, 11 Dupont Circle, N.W., Suite 500, Washington, D.C. 20036.

OPRR Public Health Service Policy on Humane Care and Use of Laboratory Animals (revised Sept. 1986). Office for Protection from Research Risks, NIH, 6100 Executive Blvd., Suite 3B01-MSC 7507, Rockville, MD 20892-7507.

Preparation and Maintenance of Higher Mammals During Neuroscience Experiments. Report of a National Institutes of Health Workshop. NIH Publication No. 91-3207, March 1991. National Eye Institute, Bldg. 31, Rm. 6A47, Bethesda, MD 20892.

Seventh Title of the Regulations of the General Law of Health, Regarding Health Research. In: *Laws and Codes of Mexico.* Published in the Porrua Collection, 12th updated edition, pp. 430–431. Porrua Publishers, Mexico, 1995.

The following principles, based largely on the PHS *Policy on Humane Care and Use of Laboratory Animals,* can be a useful guide in the design and implementation of experimental procedures involving laboratory animals.

Animals selected for a procedure should be of an appropriate species and quality and the minimum number required to obtain valid results.

Proper use of animals, including the avoidance or minimization of discomfort, distress, and pain, when consistent with sound scientific practices, is imperative.

Procedures with animals that may cause more than momentary or slight pain or distress should be performed with appropriate sedation, analgesia, or anesthesia. Surgical or other painful procedures should not be performed on unanesthetized animals paralyzed by chemical agents.

Postoperative care of animals shall be such as to minimize discomfort and pain and, in any case, shall be equivalent to accepted practices in schools of veterinary medicine.

Animals that would otherwise suffer severe or chronic pain or distress that cannot be relieved should be painlessly killed at the end of the procedure or, if appropriate, during the procedure. If the study requires the death of the animal, the animal must be killed in a humane manner.

Living conditions should be appropriate for the species and contribute to the animals' health and comfort. Normally, the housing, feeding, and care of all animals used for biomedical purposes must be directed by a veterinarian or other scientist trained and experienced in the proper care, handling, and use of the species being maintained or studied. In any case, appropriate veterinary care shall be provided.

Exceptions to these principles require careful consideration and should only be made by an appropriate review group such as an institutional animal care and use committee.

Policy on the Use of Human Subjects in Neuroscience Research

Experimental procedures involving human subjects must have been conducted in conformance with the policies and principles contained in the Federal Policy for the Protection of Human Subjects (United States Office of Science and Technology Policy) and in the Declaration of Helsinki. When publishing a paper in *The Journal of Neuroscience* or submitting an abstract for presentation at the Annual Meeting, authors must sign a statement of compliance with this policy.

Recommended References

Declaration of Helsinki. (Adopted in 1964 by the 18th World Medical Assembly in Helsinki, Finland, and revised by the 29th World Medical Assembly in Tokyo in 1975.) In: *The Main Issue in Bioethics Revised Edition.* Andrew C. Varga, Ed. New York: Paulist Press, 1984.

Federal Policy for the Protection of Human Subjects; Notices and Rules. *Federal Register.* Vol. 56, No. 117 (June 18, 1991), pp. 28002–28007.

http://www.apa.org/science/anguide.html
This Web site presents the ethical guidelines adopted by the Anerican Psychological Association. They are largely similar to those of the Neuroscience Society.

References

Numbers in parentheses following citations indicate the chapter in which a reference is cited.

Abramov, I., Gordon, J., Hendrickson, A., Hainline, L., Dobson, V., & LaBossiere, E. (1982). The retina of the newborn human infant. *Science, 217,* 265–267. (6)

Adamec, R. E., Shallow, T., & Budgell, J. (1997). Blockade of CCK$_B$ but not CCK$_A$ receptors before and after the stress of predator exposure prevents lasting increases in anxiety-like behavior: Implications for anxiety associated with posttraumatic stress disorder. *Behavioral Neuroscience, 111,* 435–449. (12)

Adamec, R. E., Stark-Adamec, C., & Livingston, K. E. (1980). The development of predatory aggression and defense in the domestic cat (*Felis catus*): 3. Effects on development of hunger between 180 and 365 days of age. *Behavioral and Neural Biology, 30,* 435–447. (12)

Adams, D. B., Gold, A. R., & Burt, A. D. (1978). Rise in female-initiated sexual activity at ovulation and its suppression by oral contraceptives. *New England Journal of Medicine, 299,* 1145–1150. (11)

Adkins, E. K., & Adler, N. T. (1972). Hormonal control of behavior in the Japanese quail. *Journal of Comparative and Physiological Psychology, 81,* 27–36. (11)

Adkins-Regan, E. (1988). Sex hormones and sexual orientation in animals. *Psychobiology, 16,* 335–347. (11)

Adolphs, R., & Tranel, D. (1999). Preferences for visual stimuli following amygdala damage. *Journal of Cognitive Neuroscience, 11,* 610–616. (12)

Adolphs, R., Tranel, D., & Damasio, A. R. (1998). The human amygdala in social judgment. *Nature, 393,* 470–474. (12)

Adolphs, R., Tranel, D., Damasio, H., & Damasio, A. (1994). Impaired recognition of emotion in facial expressions following bilateral damage to the human amygdala. *Nature, 372,* 669–672. (12)

Adolphs, R., Tranel, D., Damasio, H., & Damasio, A. (1995). Fear and the human amygdala. *Journal of Neuroscience, 15,* 5879–5891. (12)

Aggleton, J. P., Blindt, H. S., & Rawlins, J. N. P. (1989). Effects of amygdaloid and amygdaloid-hippocampal lesions on object recognition and spatial working memory in rats. *Behavioral Neuroscience, 103,* 962–974. (13)

Aglioti, S., Smania, N., Atzei, A., & Berlucchi, G. (1997). Spatiotemporal properties of the pattern of evoked phantom sensations in a left index amputee patient. *Behavioral Neuroscience, 111,* 867–872. (5)

Aglioti, S., Smania, N., & Peru, A. (1999). Frames of reference for mapping tactile stimuli in brain-damaged patients. *Journal of Cognitive Neuroscience, 11,* 67–79. (4)

Ahlskog, J. E., & Hoebel, B. G. (1973). Overeating and obesity from damage to a noradrenergic system in the brain. *Science, 182,* 166–169. (10)

Ahlskog, J. E., Randall, P. K., & Hoebel, B. G. (1975). Hypothalamic hyperphagia: Dissociation form hyperphagia following destruction of noradrenergic neurons. *Science, 190,* 399–401. (10)

Akbarian, S., Kim, J. J., Potkin, S. G., Hagman, J. O., Tafazzoli, A., Bunney, W. E., Jr., & Jones, E. G. (1995). Gene expression for glutamic acid decarboxylase is reduced without loss of neurons in prefrontal cortex of schizophrenics. *Archives of General Psychiatry, 52,* 258–266. (15)

Akirav, I., & Richter-Levin, G. (1999). Biphasic modulation of hippocampal plasticity by behavioral stress and basolateral amygdala stimulation in the rat. *Journal of Neuroscience, 19,* 10530–10535. (13)

Albright, T. D. (1992). Form-cue invariant motion processing in primate visual cortex. *Science, 255,* 1141–1143. (6)

Aldrich, M. S. (1998). Diagnostic aspects of narcolepsy. *Neurology, 50*(Suppl. 1), S2-S7. (9)

Allen, G., Buxton, R. B., Wong, E. C., & Courchesne, E. (1997). Attentional activation of the cerebellum independent of motor involvement. *Science, 275,* 1940–1943. (8)

Allen, J. J. B, Schnyer, R. N., & Hitt, S. K. (1998). The efficacy of acupuncture in the treatment of major depression in women. *Psychological Science, 9,* 397–401. (15)

Allison, T., & Cicchetti, D. V. (1976). Sleep in mammals: Ecological and constitutional correlates. *Science, 194,* 732–734. (9)

Almli, C. R., Fisher, R. S., & Hill, D. L. (1979). Lateral hypothalamus destruction in infant rats produces consummatory deficits without sensory neglect or attenuated arousal. *Experimental Neurology, 66,* 146–157. (10)

Al-Rashid, R. A. (1971). Hypothalamic syndrome in acute childhood leukemia. *Clinical Pediatrics, 10,* 53–54. (10)

American Psychiatric Association. (1994). *Diagnostic and statistical manual of mental disorders* (4th ed.). Washington, DC: American Psychiatric Association. (12, 15)

Amoore, J. E. (1977). Specific anosmia and the concept of primary odors. *Chemical Senses and Flavor, 2,* 267–281. (7)

Amsterdam, J. D., Winokur, A., Dyson, W., Herzog, S., Gonzalez, F., Rott, R., & Koprowski, H. (1985). Borna disease virus. *Archives of General Psychiatry, 42,* 1093–1096. (15)

Andersen, J. L., Klitgaard, H., & Saltin, B. (1994). Myosin heavy chain isoforms in single fibres from m. vastus lateralis of sprinters: Influence of training. *Acta Physiologica Scandinavica, 151,* 135–142. (8)

Anderson, S. W., Bechara, A., Damasio, H., Tranel, D., & Damasio, A. R. (1999). Impairment of social and moral behavior related to early damage in human prefrontal cortex. *Nature Neuroscience, 2,* 1032–1037. (12)

Andreasen, N. C. (1999). A unitary model of schizophrenia. *Archives of General Psychiatry, 56,* 781–787. (15)

Andreasen, N. C., Arndt, S., Alliger, R., Miller, D., & Flaum, M. (1995). Symptoms of schizophrenia: Methods, meanings, and mechanisms. *Archives of General Psychiatry, 52,* 341–351. (15)

Andreasen, N. C., Swayze, V. W., II, Flaum, M., Yates, W. R., Arndt, S., & McChesney, C. (1990). Ventricular enlargement in schizophrenia evaluated with computed tomographic scanning. *Archives of General Psychiatry, 47,* 1008–1015. (15)

Antanitus, D. S. (1998). A theory of cortical neuron-astrocyte interaction. *Neuroscientist, 4,* 154–159. (2)

Antonini, A., Gillespie, D. C., Crair, M. C., & Stryker, M. P. (1998). Morphology of single geniculocortical afferents and functional recovery of the visual cortex after reverse monocular deprivation in the kitten. *Journal of Neuroscience, 18,* 9896–9909. (6)

Antrobus, J. S. (1986). Dreaming: Cortical activation and perceptual thresholds. *Journal of Mind and Behavior, 7,* 193–211. (9)

Apostolakis, E. M., Garai, J., Fox, C., Smith, C. L., Watson, S. J., Clark, J. H., & O'Malley, B. W. (1996). Dopaminergic regulation of progesterone receptors: Brain D5 dopamine receptors mediate induction of lordosis by D1-like agonists in rats. *Journal of Neuroscience, 16,* 4823–4834. (11)

Appley, M. H. (1991). Motivation, equilibrium, and stress. In R. Dienstbier (Ed.), *Nebraska Symposium on Motivation 1990* (pp. 1–67). Lincoln: University of Nebraska Press. (10)

Arendt, J. (1997). Safety of melatonin in long-term use(?). *Journal of Biological Rhythms, 12,* 673–681. (9)

Arkin, A. M., Toth, M. F., Baker, J., & Hastey, J. M. (1970). The frequency of sleep talking in the laboratory among chronic sleep talkers and good dream recallers. *Journal of Nervous and Mental Disease, 151,* 369–374. (9)

Arnold, A. P., & Breedlove, S. M. (1985). Organizational and activational effects of sex steroids on brain and behavior: A reanalysis. *Hormones and Behavior, 19,* 469–498. (11)

Arnsten, A. F. T., & Goldman-Rakic, P. S. (1998). Noise stress impairs prefrontal cortical cognitive function in monkeys. *Archives of General Psychiatry, 55,* 362–368. (15)

Arvidson, K., & Friberg, U. (1980). Human taste: Response and taste bud number in fungiform papillae. *Science, 209,* 807–808. (7)

Asanuma, H. (1981). The pyramidal tract. In V. B. Brooks (Ed.), *Handbook of physiology: Section 1: The nervous system, Volume 2. Motor control* (Pt. 1, pp. 703–733). Bethesda, MD: American Physiological Society. (8)

Aserinsky, E., & Kleitman, N. (1955). Two types of ocular motility occurring in sleep. *Journal of Applied Physiology, 8,* 1–10. (9)

Azrin, N. H., Sisson, R. W., Meyers, R., & Godley, M. (1982). Alcoholism treatment by disulfiram and community reinforcement therapy. *Journal of Behavior Therapy and Experimental Psychiatry, 13,* 105–112. (15)

Babich, F. R., Jacobson, A. L., Bubash, S., & Jacobson, A. (1965). Transfer of a response to naive rats by injection of ribonucleic acid extracted from trained rats. *Science, 149,* 656–657. (13)

Backlund, E.-O., Granberg, P.-O., Hamberger, B., Sedvall, G., Seiger, A., & Olson, L. (1985). Transplantation of adrenal medullary tissue to striatum in Parkinsonism. In A. Björklund & U. Stenevi (Eds.), *Neural grafting in the mammalian CNS* (pp. 551–556). Amsterdam: Elsevier. (8)

Baddeley, A. D., & Hitch, G. J. (1994). Developments in the concept of working memory. *Neuropsychology, 8,* 485–493. (13)

Baghdoyan, H. A., Spotts, J. L., & Snyder, S. G. (1993). Simultaneous pontine and basal forebrain microinjections of carbachol suppress REM sleep. *Journal of Neuroscience, 13,* 229–242. (9)

Bailey, J. M., & Bell, A. P. (1993). Familiality of female and male homosexuality. *Behavior Genetics, 23,* 313–322. (11)

Bailey, J. M., & Benishay, D. S. (1993). Familial aggregation of female sexual orientation. *American Journal of Psychiatry, 150,* 272–277. (11)

Bailey, J. M., & Pillard, R. C. (1991). A genetic study of male sexual orientation. *Archives of General Psychiatry, 48,* 1089–1096. (11)

Bailey, J. M., Pillard, R. C., Dawood, K., Miller, M. B., Farrer, L. A., Trivedi, S., & Murphy, R. L. (1999). A family history study of male sexual orientation using three independent samples. *Behavior Genetics, 29,* 79–86. (11)

Bailey, J. M., Pillard, R. C., Neale, M. C., & Agyei, Y. (1993). Heritable factors influence sexual orientation in women. *Archives of General Psychiatry, 50,* 217–223. (11)

Bailey, J. M., Willerman, L., & Parks, C. (1991). A test of the maternal stress theory of human male homosexuality. *Archives of Sexual Behavior, 20,* 277–293. (11)

Ballard, P. A., Tetrud, J. W., & Langston, J. W. (1985). Permanent human parkinsonism due to 1-methyl-4-phenyl-1,2,3,6-tetrahydropyridine (MPTP). *Neurology, 35,* 949–956. (8)

Banks, M. S., Aslin, R. N., & Letson, R. D. (1975). Sensitive period for the development of human binocular vision. *Science, 190,* 675–677. (6)

Barinaga, M. (1996). Finding new

drugs to treat stroke. *Science, 272,* 664–666. (5)

Barnes, B. M. (1996, Sept./Oct.). Sang froid. *The Sciences, 36*(5), 13–14. (9)

Barone, F. C., Feuerstein, G. Z., & White, R. F. (1997). Brain cooling during transient focal ischemia provides complete neuroprotection. *Neuroscience and Biobehavioral Reviews, 21,* 31–44. (5)

Barth, D. S., & MacDonald, K. D. (1996). Thalamic modulation of high-frequency oscillating potentials in auditory cortex. *Nature, 383,* 78–81. (4)

Barth, T. M., Grant, M. L., & Schallert, T. (1990). Effects of MK-801 on recovery from sensorimotor cortex lesions. *Stroke, 21*(Suppl. III), III-153-III-157. (5)

Bartley, A. J., Jones, D. W., & Weinberger, D. R. (1997). Genetic variability of human brain size and cortical gyral patterns. *Brain, 120,* 257–269. (5)

Bartoshuk, L. M. (1991). Taste, smell, and pleasure. In R. C. Bolles (Ed.), *The hedonics of taste* (pp. 15–28). Hillsdale, NJ: Lawrence Erlbaum. (7)

Bartoshuk, L. M., Duffy, V. B., Lucchina, L. A., Prutkin, J., & Fast, K. (1998). PROP (6-*n*-propylthiouracil) supertasters and the saltiness of NaCl. *Annals of the New York Academy of Sciences, 855,* 793–796. (7)

Bartoshuk, L. M., Gentile, R. L., Moskowitz, H. R., & Meiselman, H. L. (1974). Sweet taste induced by miracle fruit (*Synsephalum dulcificum*). *Physiology & Behavior, 12,* 449–456. (7)

Bartoshuk, L. M., Lee, C.-H., & Scarpellino, R. (1972). Sweet taste of water induced by artichoke (*Cynara scolymus*). *Science, 178,* 988–990. (7)

Basbaum, A. I., & Fields, H. L. (1984). Endogenous pain control systems: Brainstem spinal pathways and endorphin circuitry. *Annual Review of Neuroscience, 7,* 309–338. (7)

Basil, J. A., Kamil, A. C., Balda, R. P., & Fite, K. V. (1996). Differences in hippocampal volume among food storing corvids. *Brain, Behavior and Evolution, 47,* 156–164. (13)

Basso, A., & Rusconi, M. L. (1998). Aphasia in left-handers. In P. Coppens, Y. Lebrun, & A. Basso (Eds.), *Aphasia in atypical populations* (pp. 1–34). Mahwah, NJ: Erlbaum. (14)

Bastien, C., & Campbell, K. (1992). The evoked K-complex: All-or-none phenomenon? *Sleep, 15,* 236–245. (9)

Battersby, S. (1997). Plus c'est le même chews. *Nature, 385,* 679. (10)

Baum, A., Gatchel, R. J., & Schaeffer, M. A. (1983). Emotional, behavioral, and physiological effects of chronic stresss at Three Mile Island. *Journal of Consulting & Clinical Psychology, 51,* 565–582. (12)

Baum, M. J., Tobet, S. A., Cherry, J. A., & Paredes, R. G. (1996). Estrogenic control of preoptic area development in a carnivore, the ferret. *Cellular and Molecular Neurobiology, 16,* 117–128. (11)

Baum, M. J., & Vreeburg, J. T. M. (1973). Copulation in castrated male rats following combined treatment with estradiol and dihydrotestosterone. *Science, 182,* 283–285. (11)

Baxter, L. R., Phelps, M. E., Mazziotta, J. C., Schwartz, J. M., Gerner, R. H., Selin, C. E., & Sumida, R. M. (1985). Cerebral metabolic rates for glucose in mood disorders. *Archives of General Psychiatry, 42,* 441–447. (15)

Baxter, M. G., Bucci, D. J., Gorman, L. K., Wiley, R. G., & Gallagher, M. (1995). Selective immunotoxic lesions of basal forebrain cholinergic cells: Effects on learning and memory in rats. *Behavioral Neuroscience, 109,* 714–722. (13)

Beach, F. A., Buehler, M. G., & Dunbar, I. F. (1982). Competitive behavior in male, female, and pseudohermaphroditic female dogs. *Journal of Comparative and Physiological Psychology, 96,* 855–874. (11)

Beaumont, G. (2000). Antipsychotics— The future of schizophrenia treatment. *Current Medical Research and Opinion, 16,* 37–42. (15)

Bechara, A., Damasio, H., Damasio, A. R., & Lee, G. P. (1999). Different contributions of the human amygdala and ventromedial prefrontal cortex to decision-making. *Journal of Neuroscience, 19,* 5473–5481. (12)

Beck, K. D., Valverde, J., Alexi, T., Poulsen, K., Moffat, B., Vandlen, R. A., Rosenthal, A., & Hefti, F. (1995). Mesencephalic dopaminergic neurons protected by GDNF from axotomy-induced degeneration in the adult brain. *Nature, 373,* 339–341. (5)

Becker, A. E. (1995). *Body, self, and society: The view from Fiji.* Philadelphia: University of Pennsylvania Press. (10)

Becker, A. E., & Burwell, R. A. (1999). *Acculturation and disordered eating in Fiji.* Paper presented at the meeting of the American Psychiatric Association. (10)

Becker, H. C. (1988). Effects of the imidazobenzodiazepine Ro15-4513 on the stimulant and depressant actions of ethanol on spontaneous locomotor activity. *Life Sciences, 43,* 643–650. (12)

Békésy, G. —See von Békésy, G.

Bellugi, U., Lichtenberger, L., Mills, D., Galaburda, A., & Korenberg, J. R. (1999). Bridging cognition, the brain and molecular genetics: Evidence from Williams syndrome. *Trends in Neurosciences, 22,* 197–207. (14)

Bellugi, U., Wang, P. P., & Jernigan, T. L. (1994). Williams syndrome: An unusual neuropsychological profile. In S. H. Broman & J. Grafman (Eds.), *Atypical cognitive deficits in developmental disorders* (pp. 23–56). Hillsdale, NJ: Lawrence Erlbaum. (14)

Benca, R. M., Obermeyer, W. H., Thisted, R. A., & Gillin, J. C. (1992). Sleep and psychiatric disorders. *Archives of General Psychiatry, 49,* 651–668. (9)

Benes, F. M. (1995). Is there a neuroanatomic basis for schizophrenia? An old question revisited. *The Neuroscientist, 1,* 104–115. (15)

Benes, F. M., & Bird, E. D. (1987). An analysis of the arrangement of neurons in the cingulate cortex of schizophrenic patients. *Archives of General Psychiatry, 44,* 608–616. (15)

Benes, F. M., Turtle, M., Khan, Y., & Farol, P. (1994). Myelination of a key relay zone in the hippocampal formation occurs in the human brain during childhood, adolescence, and adulthood. *Archives of General Psychiatry, 51,* 477–484. (5)

Benjamin, J., Li, L., Patterson, C., Greenberg, B. D., Murphy, D. L., & Hamer, D. H. (1996). Population and familial association between the D4 dopamine receptor gene and measures of Novelty Seeking. *Nature Genetics, 12,* 81–84. (3)

Benschop, R. J., Godaert, G. L. R., Geenen, R., Brosschot, J. F., DeSmet, M. B. M., Olff, M., Heijnen, C. J., & Beilleux, R. E. (1995). Relationships between cardiovascular and immunologic changes in an experimental stress model. *Psychological Medicine, 25,* 323–327. (12)

Berenbaum, S. A. (1999). Effects of early androgens on sex-typed activities and interests in adolescents with congenital adrenal hyperplasia. *Hormones and Behavior, 35,* 102–110. (11)

Berger, R. J., & Phillips, N. H. (1995). Energy conservation and sleep. *Behavioural Brain Research, 69,* 65–73. (9)

Berger-Sweeney, J., & Hohmann, C. F. (1997). Behavioral consequences of abnormal cortical development: Insights into developmental disabilities. *Behavioural Brain Research, 86,* 121–142. (5)

Berlucchi, G., Mangun, G. R., & Gazzaniga, M. S. (1997). Visuospatial attention and the split brain. *News in Physiological Sciences, 12,* 226–231. (14)

Berman, K. F., Torrey, E. F., Daniel, D. G., & Weinberger, D. R. (1992). Regional cerebral blood flow in monozygotic twins discordant and concordant for schizophrenia. *Archives of General Psychiatry, 49,* 927–934. (15)

Bernstein, J. J., & Gelderd, J. B. (1970). Regeneration of the long spinal tracts in the goldfish. *Brain Research, 20,* 33–38. (5)

Bernstein, L. J., & Robertson, L. C. (1998). Illusory conjunctions of color and motion with shape following bilateral parietal lesions. *Psychological Science, 9,* 167–175. (4)

Berridge, K. C., & Robinson, T. E. (1995). The mind of an addicted brain: Neural sensitization of wanting versus liking. *Current Directions in Psychological Science, 4,* 71–76. (3)

Berridge, K. C., & Robinson, T. E. (1998). What is the role of dopamine in reward: Hedonic impact, reward learning, or incentive salience? *Brain Research Reviews, 28,* 309–369. (3)

Berridge, K. C., Venier, I. L., & Robinson, T. E. (1989). Taste reactivity analysis of 6-hydroxydopamine-induced aphagia: Implications for arousal and anhedonia hypotheses of dopamine function. *Behavioral Neuroscience, 103,* 36–45. (10)

Bettencourt, B. A., & Miller, N. (1996). Gender differences in aggression as a function of provocation: A meta-analysis. *Psychological Bulletin, 119,* 422–447. (12)

Biben, M. (1979). Predation and predatory play behaviour of domestic cats. *Animal Behaviour, 27,* 81–94. (12)

Bierut, L. J., Dinwiddie, S. H., Begleiter, H., Crowe, R. R., Hesselbrock, V., Nurnberger, J. I., Jr., Porjesz, B., Schuckit, M. A., & Reich, T. (1998). Familial transmission of substance dependence: Alcohol, marijuana, cocaine, and habitual smoking. *Archives of General Psychiatry, 55,* 982–988. (15)

Bierut, L. J., Heath, A. C., Bucholz, K. K., Dinwiddie, S. H., Madden, P. A. F., Statham, D. J., Dunne, M. P., & Martin, N. G. (1999). Major depressive disorder in a community-based twin sample. *Archives of General Psychiatry, 56,* 557–563. (15)

Billington, C. J., & Levine, A. S. (1992). Hypothalamic neuropeptide Y regulation of feeding and energy metabolism. *Current Opinion in Neurobiology, 2,* 847–851. (10)

Billups, B., & Attwell, D. (1996). Modulation of non-vesicular glutamate release by pH. *Nature, 379,* 171–174. (5)

Blackwell, A., & Bates, E. (1995). Inducing agrammatic profiles in normals: Evidence for the selective vulnerability of morphology under cognitive resource limitation. *Journal of Cognitive Neuroscience, 7,* 228–257. (14)

Blackwood, D. H. R., He, L., Morris, S. W., McLean, A., Whitton, C., Thomson, M., Walker, M. T., Woodburn, K., Sharp, C. M., Wright, A. F., Shibasaki, Y., St. Clair, D. M., Porteous, D. J., & Muir, W. J. (1996). A locus for bipolar affective disorder on chromosome 4p. *Nature Genetics, 12,* 427–430. (15)

Blake, R., & Hirsch, H. V. B. (1975). Deficits in binocular depth perception in cats after alternating monocular deprivation. *Science, 190,* 1114–1116. (6)

Blakemore, S.-J., Wolpert, D. M., & Frith, C. D. (1998). Central cancellation of self-produced tickle sensation. *Nature Neuroscience, 1,* 635–640. (7)

Blass, E. M., Shide, D. J., Zaw-Mon, C., & Sorrentino, J. (1995). Mother as shield: Differential effects of contact and nursing on pain responsivity in infant rats—Evidence for nonopioid mediation. *Behavioral Neuroscience, 109,* 342–353. (7)

Bliss, T. V. P., & Lømo, T. (1973). Long-lasting potentiation of synaptic transmission in the dentate area of the anaesthetized rabbit following stimulation of the perforant path. *Journal of Physiology* (London), *232,* 331–356. (13)

Bloch, G. J., Butler, P. C., & Kohlert, J. G. (1996). Galanin microinjected into the medial preoptic nucleus facilitates female- and male-typical sexual behaviors in the female rat. *Physiology & Behavior, 59,* 1147–1154. (11)

Bloch, G. J., & Mills, R. (1995). Prepubertal testosterone treatment of neonatally gonadectomized male rats: Defeminization and masculinization of behavioral and endocrine function in adulthood. *Neuroscience and Biobehavioral Reviews, 19,* 187–200. (11)

Bloch, G. J., Mills, R., & Gale, S. (1995). Prepubertal testosterone treatment of female rats: Defeminization of behavioral and endocrine function in adulthood. *Neuroscience and Biobehavioral Reviews, 19,* 177–186. (11)

Block, B. A., Finnerty, J. R., Stewart, A. F. R., & Kidd, J. (1993). Evolution of endothermy in fish: Mapping physiological traits on a molecular phylogeny. *Science, 260,* 210–214. (10)

Blouin, J.-L., Dombroski, B. A., Nath, S. K., Lasseter, V. K., Wolyniec, P. S., Nestadt, G., Thornquist, M., Ullrich, G., McGrath, J., Kasch, L., Lamacz, M., Thomas, M. G., Gehrig, C., Radhakrishna, U.,

Snyder, S. E., Balk, S. E., Neufeld, K., Swartz, K. L., DeMarchi, N., Papadimitriou, G. N., Dikeos, D. G., Stefanis, C. N., Chakravarti, A., Childs, B., Housman, D. E., Kazazian, H. H., Antonarakis, S. E., & Pulver, A. E. (1998). Schizophrenia susceptibility loci on chromosomes 13q32 and 8p21. *Nature Genetics, 20,* 70–73. (15)

Blum, D. (1994). *The monkey wars.* New York: Oxford University Press. (1)

Blum, K., Cull, J. G., Braverman, E. R., & Comings, D. E. (1996). Reward deficiency syndrome. *American Scientist, 84,* 132–145. (3)

Blundell, J. E., & Halford, J. C. G. (1998). Serotonin and appetite regulation. *CNS Drugs, 9,* 473–495. (10)

Bode, L., Ferszt, R., & Czech, G. (1993). Borna disease virus infection and affective disorders in man. *Archives of Virology,* (Suppl. 7), 159–167. (15)

Bode, L., & Ludwig, H. (1997). Clinical similarities and close genetic relationship of human and animal Borna disease virus. *Archives of Virology* (Suppl. 13), 167–182. (15)

Bode, L., Riegel, S., Lange, W., & Ludwig, H. (1992). Human infections with Borna disease virus: Seroprevalence in patients with chronic diseases and healthy individuals. *Journal of Medical Virology, 36,* 309–315. (15)

Bodian, D. (1962). The generalized vertebrate neuron. *Science, 137,* 323–326. (2)

Bogerts, B., Meertz, E., & Schönfeldt-Bausch, R. (1985). Basal ganglia and limbic system pathology in schizophrenia. *Archives of General Psychiatry, 42,* 784–791. (15)

Bohn, M. C., Cupit, L., Marciano, F., & Gash, D. M. (1987). Adrenal medulla grafts enhance recovery of striatal dopaminergic fibers. *Science, 237,* 913–916. (8)

Boivin, D. B., Duffy, J. F., Kronauer, R. E., & Czeisler, C. A. (1996). Dose-response relationships for resetting of human circadian clock by light. *Nature, 379,* 540–542. (9)

Bolla-Wilson, K., Robinson, R. G., Starkstein, S. E., Boston, J., & Price, T. R. (1989). Lateralization of dementia of depression in stroke patients. *American Journal of Psychiatry, 146,* 627–634. (15)

Bontempi, B., Laurent-Demir, C., Destrade, C., & Jaffard, R. (1999). Time-dependent reorganization of brain circuitry underlying long-term memory storage. *Nature, 400,* 671–675. (13)

Booth-Kewley, S., & Friedman, H. S. (1987). Psychological predictors of heart disease: A quantitative review. *Psychological Bulletin, 101,* 343–362. (12)

Bortolotto, Z. A., Clarke, V. R. J., Delany, C. M., Parry, M. C., Smolders, I., Vignes, M., Ho, K. H., Miu, P., Brinton, B. T., Fantaske, R., Ogden, A., Gates, M., Ornstein, P. L., Lodge, D., Bleakman, D., & Collingridge, G. L. (1999). Kainate receptors are involved in synaptic plasticity. *Nature, 402,* 297–301. (13)

Botvinick, M., & Cohen, J. (1998). Rubber hands "feel" touch that eyes see. *Nature, 391,* 756. (4)

Boutrel, B., Franc, B., Hen, R., Hamon, M., & Adrien, J. (1999). Key role of 5-HT$_{1B}$ receptors in the regulation of paradoxical sleep as evidenced in 5-HT$_{1B}$ knock-out mice. *Journal of Neuroscience, 19,* 3204–3212. (9)

Bowmaker, J. K. (1998). Visual pigments and molecular genetics of color blindness. *News in Physiological Sciences, 13,* 63–69. (6)

Bowmaker, J. K., & Dartnall, H. J. A. (1980). Visual pigments of rods and cones in a human retina. *Journal of Physiology* (London), *298,* 501–511. (6)

Bradley, S. J., Oliver, G. D., Chernick, A. B., & Zucker, K. J. (1998). Experiment of nature: Ablatio penis at 2 months, sex reassignment at 7 months, and a psychosexual follow-up in young adulthood. *Pediatrics, 102,* p. e9. (11) Available at: http://www.pediatrics.org/cgi/content/full/102/1/e9

Brady, J. V., Porter, R. W., Conrad, D. G., & Mason, J. W. (1958). Avoidance behavior and the development of gastroduodenal ulcers. *Journal of the Experimental Analysis of Behavior, 1,* 69–72. (12)

Brambilla, F., Brunetta, M., Draisci, A., Peirone, A., Perna, G., Sacerdote, P., Manfredi, B., & Panerai, A. E. (1995). T-lymphocyte concentrations of cholecystokinin-8 and beta-endorphin in eating

disorders: II. Bulimia nervosa. *Psychiatry Research, 59,* 51–56. (10)

Brandt, T. (1991). Man in motion: Historical and clinical aspects of vestibular function. *Brain, 114,* 2159–2174. (7)

Braun, A. R., Balkin, T. J., Wesensten, N. J., Guadry, F., Carson, R. E., Varga, M., Baldwin, P., Belenky, G., & Herscovitch, P. (1998). Dissociated pattern of activity in visual cortices and their projections during human rapid eye movement sleep. *Science, 279,* 91–95. (9)

Braus, H. (1960). *Anatomie des Menschen, 3. Band: Periphere Leistungsbahnen II. Centrales Nervensystem, Sinnesorgane. 2. Auflage* [Human anatomy: Vol. 3. Peripheral pathways II. Central nervous system, sensory organs (2nd ed.)]. Berlin: Springer-Verlag. (4)

Breedlove, S. M. (1992). Sexual dimorphism in the vertebrate nervous system. *Journal of Neuroscience, 12,* 4133–4142. (11)

Bregman, B. S., Kunkel-Bagden, E., Schnell, L., Dai, H. N., Gao, D., & Schwab, M. E. (1995). Recovery from spinal cord injury mediated by antibodies to neurite growth inhibitors. *Nature, 378,* 498–501. (5)

Breiter, H. C., Etcoff, N. L., Whalen, P. J., Kennedy, W. A., Rauch, S. L., Buckner, R. L., Strauss, M. M., Hyman, S. E., & Rosen, B. R. (1996). Response and habituation of the human amygdala during visual processing of facial expression. *Neuron, 17,* 875–887. (12)

Brennan, P. A., Grekin, E. R., & Mednick, S. A. (1999). Maternal smoking during pregnancy and adult male criminal outcomes. *Archives of General Psychiatry, 56,* 215–219. (5, 12)

Breslau, N., & Klein, D. F. (1999). Smoking and panic attack. *Archives of General Psychiatry, 56,* 1141–1147. (12)

Brewerton, T. D. (1995). Toward a unified theory of serotonin dysregulation in eating and related disorders. *Psychoneuroendocrinology, 20,* 561–590. (10)

Bridgeman, B., & Staggs, D. (1982). Plasticity in human blindsight. *Vision Research, 22,* 1199–1203. (6)

Brightman, M. W. (1997). Blood-brain barrier: Penetration by solutes and cells. In G. Adelman & B. H. Smith (Eds.), *Elsevier encyclopedia of neuroscience.* New York: Elsevier. (2)

Brinkmann, R. R., Mezei, M. M., Theilmann, J., Almqvist, E., & Hayden, M. R. (1997). The likelihood of being affected with Huntington disease by a particular age, for a specific CAG size. *American Journal of Human Genetics, 60,* 1202–1210. (8)

Broberger, C., De Lecea, L., Sutcliffe, J. G., & Hökfelt, T. (1998). Hypocretin/orexin- and melanin-concentrating hormone-expressing cells form distinct populations in the rodent hypothalamus: Relationship to the neuropeptide Y and agouti gene-related protein systems. *Journal of Comparative Neurology, 402,* 460–474. (10)

Bronson, F. H. (1974). Pheromonal influences on reproductive activities in rodents. In M. C. Birch (Ed.), *Pheromones* (pp. 344–365). Amsterdam: North Holland. (7)

Brooks, D. C., & Bizzi, E. (1963). Brain stem electrical activity during deep sleep. *Archives Italiennes de Biologie, 101,* 648–665. (9)

Brooks, J. H., & Reddon, J. R. (1996). Serum testosterone in violent and nonviolent young offenders. *Journal of Clinical Psychology, 52,* 475–483. (12)

Broughton, R., Billlings, R., Cartwright, R., Doucette, D., Edmeads, J., Edwardh, M., Ervin, F., Orchard, B., Hill, R., & Turrell, G. (1994). Homicidal somnambulism: A case report. *Sleep, 17,* 253–264. (9)

Brown, G. L., Ebert, M. H., Goyer, P. F., Jimerson, D. C., Klein, W. J., Bunney, W. E., & Goodwin, F. K. (1982). Aggression, suicide, and serotonin: Relationships of CSF amine metabolites. *American Journal of Psychiatry, 139,* 741–746. (12)

Brown, J., Babor, T. F., Litt, M. D., & Kranzler, H. R. (1994). The type A/type B distinction. *Annals of the New York Academy of Sciences, 708,* 23–33. (12)

Brown, J. R., Ye, H., Bronson, R. T., Dikkes, P., & Greenberg, M. E. (1996). A defect in nurturing in mice lacking the immediate early gene *fos* B. *Cell, 86,* 297–309. (11)

Brownlee, D. J. A., & Fairweather, I. (1999). Exploring the neurotransmitter labyrinth in nematodes. *Trends in Neurosciences, 22,* 16–24. (3)

Bruce-Keller, A. J., Umberger, G., McFall, R., & Mattson, M. P. (1999). Food restriction reduces brain damage and improves behavioral outcome following excitotoxic and metabolic insults. *Annals of Neurology, 45,* 8–15. (5)

Brunelli, S. A., Shindledecker, R. D., & Hofer, M. A. (1987). Behavioral responses of juvenile rats (*Rattus norvegicus*) to neonates after infusion of maternal blood plasma. *Journal of Comparative Psychology, 101,* 47–59. (11)

Brunner, D., & Hen, R. (1997). Insights into the neurobiology of impulsive behavior from serotonin receptor knockout mice. *Annals of the New York Academy of Sciences, 836,* 81–105. (12)

Brushart, T. M. E. (1993). Motor axons preferentially reinnervate motor pathways. *Journal of Neuroscience, 13,* 2730–2738. (5)

Bruyer, R., Dupuis, M., Ophoven, E., Rectem, D., & Reynaert, C. (1985). Anatomical and behavioral study of a case of asymptomatic callosal agenesis. *Cortex, 21,* 417–430. (14)

Brysbaert, M., Vitu, F., & Schroyens, W. (1996). The right visual field advantage and the optimal viewing position effect: On the relation between foveal and parafoveal word recognition. *Neuropsychology, 10,* 385–395. (14)

Büchel, C., Morris, J., Dolan, R. J., & Friston, K. J. (1998). Brain systems mediating aversive conditioning: An event-related fMRI study. *Neuron, 20,* 947–957. (12)

Buck, L., & Axel, R. (1991). A novel multigene family may encode odorant receptors: A molecular basis for odor recognition. *Cell, 65,* 175–187. (7)

Buell, S. J., & Coleman, P. D. (1981). Quantitative evidence for selective dendritic growth in normal human aging but not in senile dementia. *Brain Research, 214,* 23–41. (5)

Bundgaard, M. (1986). Pathways across the vertebrate blood-brain barrier: Morphological viewpoints. *Annals of the New York Academy of Sciences, 481,* 7–19. (2)

Bunney, W. E., Jr., Murphy, D. L., Goodwin, F. K., & Borge, G. F. (1972). The "switch process" in manic-depressive illness. *Archives of General Psychiatry, 27,* 295–302. (15)

Burcham, K. J., Corwin, J. V., Stoll, M. L., & Reep, R. L. (1997). Disconnection of medial agranular and posterior parietal cortex produces multimodal neglect in rats. *Behavioural Brain Research, 86,* 41–47. (4)

Burgess, C. E., Lindblad, K., Sigransky, E., Yuan, Q.-P., Long, R. T., Breschel, T., Ross, C. A., McInnis, M., Lee, P., Ginns, E., Lenane, M., Kumra, S., Jacobsen, L., Rapoport, J., & Schalling, M. (1998). Large CAG/CTG repeats are associated with childhood-onset schizophrenia. *Molecular Psychiatry, 3,* 321–327. (15)

Burgess, P. W., & McNeil, J. E. (1999). Content-specific confabulation. *Cortex, 35,* 163–182. (13)

Burr, D. C., Morrone, M. C., & Ross, J. (1994). Selective suppression of the magnocellular visual pathway during saccadic eye movements. *Nature, 371,* 511–513. (6)

Burton, R. F. (1994). *Physiology by numbers.* Cambridge, England: Cambridge University Press. (10)

Buss, D. M. (1994). The strategies of human mating. *American Scientist, 82,* 238–249. (1)

Butterfield, P. G., Valanis, B. G., Spencer, P. S., Lindeman, C. A., & Nutt, J. G. (1993). Environmental antecedents of young-onset Parkinson's disease. *Neurology, 43,* 1150–1158. (8)

Butzlaff, R. L., & Hooley, J. M. (1998). Expressed emotion and psychiatric relapse. *Archives of General Psychiatry, 55,* 547–552. (15)

Cadoret, R., Troughton, E., & Woodworth, G. (1994). Evidence of heterogeneity of genetic effect in Iowa adoption studies. *Annals of the New York Academy of Sciences, 708,* 59–71. (15)

Cadoret, R. J., Yates, W. R., Troughton, E., Woodworth, G., & Steward, M. A. (1995). Genetic-environmental interaction in the genesis of aggressivity and conduct disorders. *Archives of General Psychiatry, 52,* 916–924. (12)

Cahill, L., & McGaugh, J. L. (1998). Mechanisms of emotional arousal and lasting declarative memory. *Trends in Neurosciences, 21,* 294–299. (13)

Cahn, R., Borziex, M.-G., Aldinio, C., Toffano, G., & Cahn, J. (1989). Influence of monosialoganglioside inner ester on neurologic recovery after global cerebral ischemia in monkeys. *Stroke, 20,* 652–656. (5)

Cajal, S. R. (1937). Recollections of my life. *Memoirs of the American Philosophical Society, 8.* (Original work published 1901–1917) (2)

Calamandrei, G., & Keverne, E. B. (1994). Differential expression of *fos* protein in the brain of female mice dependent on pup sensory cues and maternal experience. *Behavioral Neuroscience, 108,* 113–120. (11)

Caldwell, J. D., & Moe, B. D. (1999). Conjugated estradiol increases female sexual receptivity in response to oxytocin infused into the medial preoptic area and medial basal hypothalamus. *Hormones and Behavior, 35,* 38–46. (11)

Calignano, A., LaRana, G., Giuffrida, A., & Piomelli, D. (1998). Control of pain initiation by endogenous cannabinoids. *Nature, 394,* 277–281. (3)

Campbell, S. S., & Murphy, P. J. (1998). Extraocular circadian phototransduction in humans. *Science, 279,* 396–399. (9)

Campbell, S. S., & Tobler, I. (1984). Animal sleep: A review of sleep duration across phylogeny. *Neuroscience & Biobehavioral Reviews, 8,* 269–300. (9)

Campeau, S., & Davis, M. (1995). Involvement of the central nucleus and basolateral complex of the amygdala in fear conditioning measured with fear-potentiated startle in rats trained concurrently with auditory and visual conditioned stimuli. *Journal of Neuroscience, 15,* 2301–2311. (12)

Campfield, L. A., Smith, F. J., & Burn, P. (1998). Strategies and potential molecular targets for obesity treatment. *Science, 280,* 1383–1387. (10)

Campfield, L. A., Smith, F. J., Guisez, Y., Devos, R., & Burn, P. (1995). Recombinant mouse OB protein: Evidence for a peripheral signal linking adiposity and central neural networks. *Science, 269,* 546–552. (10)

Can, S., Zhu, Y.-S., Cai, L.-Q., Ling, Q., Katz, M. D., Akgun, S., Shackleton, C. H. L., & Imperato-McGinley, J. (1998). The identification of 5α-reductase 2 and 17β-hydrosteroid dehydrogenase-3 gene defects in male pseudohermaphrodites from a Turkish kindred. *Journal of Clinical Endocrinology and Metabolism, 83,* 560–569. (11)

Canavan, A. G. M., Sprengelmeyer, R., Diener, H.-C., & Hömberg, V. (1994). Conditional associative learning is impaired in cerebellar disease in humans. *Behavioral Neuroscience, 108,* 475–485. (4)

Canli, T. (1999). Hemispheric asymmetry in the experience of emotion: A perspective from functional imaging. *Neuroscientist, 5,* 201–207. (14)

Cannon, W. B. (1927). The James-Lange theory of emotion. *American Journal of Psychology, 39,* 106–124. (12)

Cannon, W. B. (1929). Organization for physiological homeostasis. *Physiological Reviews, 9,* 399–431. (10)

Cannon, W. B. (1942). "Voodoo" death. *American Anthropologist, 44,* 169–181. (12)

Cao, Y. Q., Mantyh, P. W., Carlson, E. J., Gillespie, A.-M., Epstein, C. J., & Basbaum, A. I. (1998). Primary afferent tachykinins are required to experience moderate to intense pain. *Nature, 392,* 390–394. (7)

Caramazza, A. (1995). Interview with Alfonso Caramazza. *Journal of Cognitive Neuroscience, 7,* 303–309. (14)

Carani, C., Zini, D., Baldini, A., Della Casa, L., Ghizzani, A., & Marrama, P. (1990). Effects of androgen treatment in impotent men with normal and low levels of free testosterone. *Archives of Sexual Behavior, 19,* 223–234. (11)

Cardno, A. G., Marshall, E. J., Coid, B., Macdonald, A. M., Ribchester, T. R., Davies, N. J., Venturi, P., Jones, L. A., Lewis, S. W., Sham, P. C., Gottesman, I. I., Farmer, A. E., McGuffin, P., Reveley, A. M., & Murray, R. M. (1999). Heritability estimates for psychotic disorders. *Archives of General Psychiatry, 56,* 162–168. (15)

Carlezon, W. A., Jr., Thome, J., Olson, V. G., Lane-Ladd, S. B., Brodkin, E. S., Hiroi, N., Duman, R. S., Neve, R. L., & Nestler, E. J. (1998). Regulation of cocaine reward by CREB. *Science, 282,* 2272–2275. (3)

Carlezon, W. A., Jr., & Wise, R. A. (1996). Rewarding actions of phencyclidine and related drugs in nucleus accumbens shell and frontal cortex. *Journal of Neuroscience, 16,* 3112–3122. (3)

Carpenter, G. A., & Grossberg, S. (1984). A neural theory of circadian rhythms: Aschoff's rule in diurnal and nocturnal mammals. *American Journal of Physiology, 247,* R1067-R1082. (9)

Carter, C. S. (1992). Hormonal influences on human sexual behavior. In J. B. Becker, S. M. Breedlove, & D. Crews (Eds.), *Behavioral endocrinology* (pp. 131–142). Cambridge, MA: MIT Press. (11)

Carvell, G. E., & Simons, D. J. (1996). Abnormal tactile experience early in life disrupts active touch. *Journal of Neuroscience, 16,* 2750–2757. (7)

Cassaday, H. J., & Rawlins, J. N. P. (1995). Fornix-fimbria section and working memory deficits in rats: Stimulus complexity and stimulus size. *Behavioral Neuroscience, 109,* 594–606. (13)

Castellanos, F. X., Giedd, J. N., Marsh, W. L., Hamburger, S. D., Vaituzis, A. C., Dickstein, D. P., Sarfatti, S. E., Vauss, Y. C., Snell, J. W., Rajapakse, J. C., & Rapoport, J. L. (1996). Quantitative brain magnetic resonance imaging in attention-deficit hyperactivity disorder. *Archives of General Psychiatry, 53,* 607–616. (5)

Castellucci, V. F., Pinsker, H., Kupfermann, I., & Kandel, E. (1970). Neuronal mechanisms of habituation and dishabituation of the gill-withdrawal reflex in *Aplysia. Science, 167,* 1745–1748. (13)

Catalano, S. M., & Shatz, C. J. (1998). Activity-dependent cortical target selection by thalamic axons. *Science, 281,* 559–562. (5)

Catchpole, C. K., & Slater, P. J. B. (1995). *Bird song: Biological themes and variations.*

Cambridge, England: Cambridge University Press. (1)

Caterina, M. J., Rosen, T. A., Tominaga, M., Brake, A. J., & Julius, D. (1999). A capsaicin-receptor homologue with a high threshold for noxious heat. *Nature, 398,* 436–441. (7)

Caterina, M. J., Schumacher, M. A., Tominaga, M., Rosen, T. A., Levine, J. D., & Julius, D. (1997). The capsaicin receptor: A heat-activated ion channel in the pain pathway. *Nature, 389,* 816–824. (7)

Catterall, W. A. (1984). The molecular basis of neuronal excitability. *Science, 223,* 653–661. (2)

Celebrini, S., & Newsome, W. T. (1995). Microstimulation of extrastriate area MST influences performance on a direction discrimination task. *Journal of Neurophysiology, 73,* 437–448. (6)

Censits, D. M., Ragland, J. D., Gur, R. C., & Gur, R. E. (1997). Neuropsychological evidence supporting a neurodevelopmental model of schizophrenia: A longitudinal study. *Schizophrenia Research, 24,* 289–298. (15)

Cerletti, U., & Bini, L. (1938). L'Elettroshock [Electroshock]. *Archivio Generale di Neurologia e Psichiatria e Psicoanalisi, 19,* 266–268. (15)

Chakos, M. H., Ma, J., Alvir, J., Woerner, M. G., Koreen, A., Geisler, S., Mayerhoff, D., Sobel, S., Kane, J. M., Borenstein, M., & Lieberman, J. A. (1996). Incidence and correlates of tardive dyskinesia in first episode of schizophrenia. *Archives of General Psychiatry, 53,* 313–319. (16)

Chalmers, D. J. (1995). Facing up to the problem of consciousness. *Journal of Consciousness Studies, 2,* 200–219. (1)

Chalupa, L. M. (1998). Cell death and the establishment of specific connections. In M. S. Gazzaniga & J. S. Altman (Eds.), *Brain and mind: Evolutionary perspectives* (pp. 49–53). Strasbourg, France: Human Frontier Science Program. (5)

Chandra, V., Bharucha, N. E., & Schoenberg, B. S. (1984). Mortality data for the U.S. for deaths due to and related to twenty neurologic diseases. *Neuroepidemiology, 3,* 149–168. (8)

Chao, L. L., & Knight, R. T. (1998). Contribution of human prefrontal cortex to delay performance. *Journal of Cognitive Neuroscience, 10,* 167–177. (13)

Chapin, J. K., Moxon, K. A., Markowitz, R. S., & Nicolelis, M. A. L. (1999). Real-time control of a robot arm using simultaneously recorded neurons in the motor cortex. *Nature Neuroscience, 2,* 664–670. (8)

Chase, T. N., Wexler, N. S., & Barbeau, A. (1979). *Advances in neurology: Vol. 23. Huntington's disease.* New York: Raven. (8)

Chaudhari, N., Landin, A. M., & Roper, S. D. (2000). A metabotropic glutamate receptor variant functions as a taste receptor. *Nature Neuroscience, 3,* 113–119. (7)

Chawla, D., Rees, G., & Friston, K. J. (1999). The physiological basis of attentional modulation in extrastriate visual areas. *Nature Neuroscience, 2,* 671–676. (6)

Chehab, F. F., Mounzih, K., Lu, R., & Lim, M. E. (1997). Early onset of reproductive function in normal female mice treated with leptin. *Science, 275,* 88–90. (10)

Chen, Y., Levy, D. L., Nakayama, K., Matthysse, S., Palafox, G., & Holzman, P. S. (1999). Dependence of impaired eye tracking on deficient velocity discrimination in schizophrenia. *Archives of General Psychiatry, 56,* 155–161. (15)

Cheour-Luhtanen, M., Alho, K., Sainio, K., Rinne, T., Reinikainen, K., Pohjavuoir, M., Renlund, M., Aaltonen, O., Eerola, O., & Näätänen, R. (1996). The ontogenetically earliest discriminative response of the human brain. *Psychophysiology, 33,* 478–481. (14)

Chiueh, C. C. (1988). Dopamine in the extrapyramidal motor function: A study based upon the MPTP-induced primate model of Parkinsonism. *Annals of the New York Academy of Sciences, 515,* 226–248. (8)

Choi-Lundberg, D. L., Lin, Q., Chang, Y.-N., Chiang, Y. L., Hay, C. M., Mohajeri, H., Davidson, B. L., & Bohn, M. C. (1997). Dopaminergic neurons protected from degeneration by GDNF gene therapy. *Science, 275,* 838–841. (5)

Chollet, F., & Weiller, C. (1994). Imaging recovery of function following brain injury. *Current Opinion in Neurobiology, 4,* 226–230. (5)

Chomsky, N. (1980). *Rules and representations.* New York: Columbia University Press. (14)

Chugani, H. T., & Phelps, M. E. (1986). Maturational changes in cerebral function in infants determined by ^{18}FDG positron emission tomography. *Science, 231,* 840–843. (5)

Chun, M. M., & Phelps, E. A. (1999). Memory deficits for implicit contextual information in amnesic subjects with hippocampal damage. *Nature Neuroscience, 2,* 844–847. (13)

Churchland, P. S. (1996). The hornswoggle problem. *Journal of Consciousness, 3,* 402–408. (1)

Cicone, N., Wapner, W., Foldi, N. S., Zurif, E., & Gardner, H. (1979). The relation between gesture and language in aphasic communication. *Brain and Language, 8,* 324–349. (14)

Cirelli, C., Pompeiano, M., & Tononi, G. (1996). Neuronal gene expression in the waking state: A role for the locus coeruleus. *Science, 274,* 1211–1215. (9)

Clahsen, H., & Almazen, M. (1998). Syntax and morphology in Williams syndrome. *Cognition, 68,* 167–198. (14)

Clark, K. B., Naritoku, D. K., Smith, D. C., Browning, R. A., & Jensen, R. A. (1999). Enhanced recognition memory following vagus nerve stimulation in human subjects. *Nature Neuroscience, 2,* 94–98. (13)

Clark, R. E., & Lavond, D. G. (1993). Reversible lesions of the red nucleus during acquisition and retention of a classically conditioned behavior in rabbits. *Behavioral Neuroscience, 107,* 264–270. (13)

Clarke, S., Assal, G., & deTribolet, N. (1993). Left hemisphere strategies in visual recognition, topographical orientation and time planning. *Neuropsychologia, 31,* 99–113. (14)

Cleary, L. J., Hammer, M., & Byrne, J. H. (1989). Insights into the cellular mechanisms of short-term sensitization in *Aplysia.* In T. J. Carew & D. B. Kelley (Eds.), *Perspectives in neural systems and behavior* (pp. 105–119). New York: Alan R. Liss. (13)

Clément, K., Vaisse, C., Lahlou, N., Cabrol, S., Pelloux, V., Cassuto, D., Gourmelen, M., Dina, C., Chambaz, J., Lacorte, J.-M., Basdevant, A., Bougnères, P., Lebouc, Y., Froguel, P., & Guy-Grand, B. (1998). A mutation in the human leptin receptor gene causes obesity and pituitary dysfunction. *Nature, 392*, 398–401. (10)

Clohessy, A. B., Posner, M. I., Rothbart, M. K., & Veccra, S. P. (1991). The development of inhibition of return in early infancy. *Journal of Cognitive Neuroscience, 3*, 345–350. (6)

Cloninger, C. R., Bohman, M., & Sigvardsson, S. (1981). Inheritance of alcohol abuse: Cross-fostering of adopted men. *Archives of General Psychiatry, 38*, 861–868. (15)

Clutton-Brock, T. H., O'Riain, M. J., Brotherton, P. N. M., Gaynor, D., Kansky, R., Griffin, A. S., & Manser, M. (1999). Selfish sentinels in cooperative mammals. *Science, 284*, 1640–1644. (1)

Cohen, B., Novick, D., & Rubinstein, M. (1996). Modulation of insulin activities by leptin. *Science, 274*, 1185–1188. (10)

Cohen, B. M., Ennulat, D. J., Centorrino, F., Matthysse, S., Konieczna, H., Chu, H.-M., & Cherkerzian, S. (1999). Polymorphisms of the dopamine D$_4$ receptor and response to antipsychotic drugs. *Psychopharmacology, 141*, 6–10. (3)

Cohen, J. D., Noll, D. C., & Schneider, W. (1993). Functional magnetic resonance imaging: Overview and methods for psychological research. *Behavior Research Methods, Instruments, & Computers, 25*, 101–113. (1, 6)

Cohen, L. G., Weeks, R. A., Sadato, N., Celnik, P., Ishii, K., & Hallett, M. (1999). Period of susceptibility for cross-modal plasticity in the blind. *Annals of Neurology, 45*, 451–460. (6)

Cohen, N. J., Eichenbaum, H., Deacedo, B. S., & Corkin, S. (1985). Different memory systems underlying acquisition of procedural and declarative knowledge. *Annals of the New York Academy of Sciences, 444*, 54–71. (13)

Cohen, S., Frank, E., Doyle, W. J., Skoner, D. P., Rabin, B. S., & Swaltney, J. M., Jr. (1998). Types of stressors that increase susceptibility to the common cold in healthy adults. *Health Psychology, 17*, 214–223. (12)

Cohen, S., & Williamson, G. M. (1991). Stress and infectious disease in humans. *Psychological Bulletin, 109*, 5–24. (12)

Cohen-Tannoudji, M., Babinet, C., & Wassef, M. (1994). Early determination of a mouse somatosensory cortex marker. *Nature, 368*, 460–463. (5)

Colapinto, J. (1997, December 11). The true story of John/Joan. *Rolling Stone*, pp. 54–97. (11)

Colbourne, F., & Corbett, D. (1995). Delayed postischemic hypothermia: A six-month survival study using behavioral and histological assessments of neuroprotection. *Journal of Neuroscience, 15*, 7250–7260. (5)

Colbourne, F., Sutherland, G. R., & Auer, R. N. (1999). Electron microscopic evidence against apoptosis as the mechanism of neuronal death in global ischemia. *Journal of Neuroscience, 19*, 4200–4210. (5)

Cole, J. (1995). *Pride and a daily marathon*. Cambridge, MA: MIT Press. (8)

Coleman-Mesches, K., Salinas, J. A., & McGaugh, J. L. (1996). Unilateral amygdala inactivation after training attenuates memory for reduced reward. *Behavioural Brain Research, 77*, 175–180. (12)

Collier, T. J., Sortwell, C. E., & Daley, B. F. (1999). Diminished viability, growth, and behavioral efficacy of fetal dopamine neuron grafts in aging rats with long-term dopamine depletion: An argument for neurotrophic supplementation. *Journal of Neuroscience, 19*, 5563–5573. (8)

Comings, D. E., & Amromin, G. D. (1974). Autosomal dominant insensitivity to pain with hyperplastic myelinopathy and autosomal dominant indifference to pain. *Neurology, 24*, 838–848. (7)

Comuzzie, A. G., & Allison, D. B. (1998). The search for human obesity genes. *Science, 280*, 1374–1377. (10)

Considine, R. V., Sinha, M. K., Heiman, M. L., Kriauciunas, A., Stephens, T. W., Nyce, M. R., Ohannesian, J. P., Maarco, C. C., McKee, L. J., Bauer, T. L., & Caro, J. F. (1996). Serum immunoreactive-leptin concentrations in normal-weight and obese humans. *New England Journal of Medicine, 334*, 292–295. (10)

Conti, A. C., Raghupathi, R., Trojanowski, J. Q., & McIntosh, T. K. (1998). Experimental brain injury induces regionally distinct apoptosis during the acute and delayed post-traumatic period. *Journal of Neuroscience, 18*, 5663–5672. (5)

Cooke, B. M., Tabibnia, G., & Breedlove, S. M. (1999). A brain sexual dimorphism controlled by adult circulating androgens. *Proceedings of the National Academy of Sciences (U.S.A.), 96*, 7538–7540. (11)

Corballis, M. C. (1999). The gestural origins of language. *American Scientist, 87*, 138–145. (14)

Corder, E. H., Saunders, A. M., Strittmatter, W. J., Schmechel, D. E., Gaskell, P. C., Small, G. W., Roses, A. D., Haines, J. L., & Pericak-Vance, M. A. (1993). Gene dose of apolipoprotein E type 4 allele and the risk of Alzheimer's disease in late onset families. *Science, 261*, 921–923. (13)

Coren, S., & Porac, C. (1977). Fifty centuries of right-handedness: The historical record. *Science, 198*, 631–632. (14)

Corkin, S. (1984). Lasting consequences of bilateral medial temporal lobectomy: Clinical course and experimental findings in H. M. *Seminars in Neurology, 4*, 249–259. (13)

Corkin, S., Amaral, D. G., González, R. G., Johnson, K. A., & Hyman, B. T. (1997). H. M.'s medial temporal lobe lesion: Findings from magnetic resonance imaging. *Journal of Neuroscience, 17*, 3964–3979. (13)

Corkin, S., Rosen, T. J., Sullivan, E. V., & Clegg, R. A. (1989). Penetrating head injury in young adulthood exacerbates cognitive decline in later years. *Journal of Neuroscience, 9*, 3876–3883. (5)

Cornelissen, P., Richardson, A., Mason, A., Fowler, S., & Stein, J. (1995). Contrast sensitivity and coherent motion detection measured at photopic luminance levels in dyslexics and controls.

Vision Research, 35, 1483–1494. (14)

Coss, R. G., Brandon, J. G., & Globus, A. (1980). Changes in morphology of dendritic spines on honeybee calycal interneurons associated with cumulative nursing and foraging experiences. *Brain Research, 192,* 49–59. (5)

Coss, R. G., & Globus, A. (1979). Social experience affects the development of dendritic spines and branches on tectal interneurons in the jewel fish. *Developmental Psychobiology, 12,* 347–358. (5)

Cotman, C. W., & Nieto-Sampedro, M. (1982). Brain function, synapse renewal, and plasticity. *Annual Review of Psychology, 33,* 371–401. (5)

Courtney, S. M., Ungerleider, L. G., Keil, K., & Haxby, J. V. (1997). Transient and sustained activity in a distributed neural system for human working memory. *Nature, 386,* 608–611. (13)

Cowey, A., & Stoerig, P. (1995). Blindsight in monkeys. *Nature, 373,* 247–249. (6)

Crabbe, J. C., Wahlsten, D., & Dudek, B. C. (1999). Genetics of mouse behavior: Interactions with laboratory environment. *Science, 284,* 1670–1672. (1)

Craddock, N., & Jones, I. (1999). Genetics of bipolar disorder. *Journal of Medical Genetics, 36,* 585–594. (15)

Craft, S., Asthana, S., Newcomer, J. W., Wilkinson, C. W., Matos, I. T., Baker, L. D., Cherrier, M., Lofgreen, C., Latandresse, S., Petrova, A., Plymate, S., Raskind, M., Grimwood, K., & Veith, R. C. (1999). Enhancement of memory in Alzheimer's disease with insulin and somatostatin, but not glucose. *Archives of General Psychiatry, 56,* 1135–1140. (13)

Craig, A. D., Bushnell, M. C., Zhang, E.-T., & Blomqvist, A. (1994). A thalamic nucleus specific for pain and temperature sensation. *Nature, 372,* 770–773. (7)

Crair, M. C., Gillespie, D. C., & Stryker, M. P. (1998). The role of visual experience in the development of columns in cat visual cortex. *Science, 279,* 566–570. (6)

Cremers, C. W. R. J., & van Rijn, P. M. (1991). Acquired causes of deafness in childhood. *Annals of the New York Academy of Sciences, 630,* 197–202. (7)

Crick, F., & Koch, C. (1995). Are we aware of neural activity in primary visual cortex? *Nature, 375,* 121–123. (6)

Crick, F., & Mitchison, G. (1983). The function of dream sleep. *Nature, 304,* 111–114. (9)

Critchley, H. D., & Rolls, E. T. (1996). Hunger and satiety modify the responses of olfactory and visual neurons in the primate orbitofrontal cortex. *Journal of Neurophysiology, 75,* 1673–1686. (10)

Culebras, A. (1996). *Clinical handbook of sleep disorders.* Boston: Butterworth-Heinemann. (9)

Culebras, A., & Moore, J. T. (1989). Magnetic resonance findings in REM sleep behavior disorder. *Neurology, 39,* 1519–1523. (9)

Cummings, J. L. (1995). Anatomic and behavioral aspects of frontal-subcortical circuits. *Annals of the New York Academy of Sciences, 769,* 1–13. (13)

Cummings, J. L., & Victoroff, J. I. (1990). Noncognitive neuropsychiatric syndromes in Alzheimer's disease. *Neuropsychiatry, Neuropsychology, & Behavioral Neurology, 3,* 140–158. (13)

Cummings, N. A. (1979). Turning bread into stones: Our modern antimiracle. *American Psychologist, 34,* 1119–1129. (15)

Cutler, W. B., Preti, G., Krieger, A., Huggins, G. R., Garcia, C. R., & Lawley, H. J. (1986). Human axillary secretions influence women's menstrual cycles: The role of donor extract from men. *Hormones and Behavior, 20,* 463–473. (7)

Cynader, M., & Chernenko, G. (1976). Abolition of direction selectivity in the visual cortex of the cat. *Science, 193,* 504–505. (6)

Cyranowski, J. M., Frank, E., Young, E., & Shear, K. (2000). Adolescent onset of the gender difference in lifetime rates of major depression. *Archives of General Psychiatry, 57,* 21–27. (15)

Czeisler, C. A., Duffy, J. F., Shanahan, T. L., Brown, E. N., Mitchell, J. F., Rimmer, D. W., Ronda, J. M., Silva, E. J., Allan, J. S., Emens, J. S., Dijk, D.-J., & Kronauer, R. E. (1999). Stability, precision, and near-24-hour period of the human circadian pacemaker. *Science, 284,* 2177–2181. (9)

Czeisler, C. A., Johnson, M. P., Duffy, J. F., Brown, E. N., Ronda, J. M., & Kronauer, R. E. (1990). Exposure to bright light and darkness to treat physiologic maladaptation to night work. *New England Journal of Medicine, 322,* 1253–1259. (9)

Czeisler, C. A., Weitzman, E. D., Moore-Ede, M. C., Zimmerman, J. C., & Knauer, R. S. (1980). Human sleep: Its duration and organization depend on its circadian phase. *Science, 210,* 1264–1267. (15)

Dabbs, J. M., Jr., Carr, T. S., Frady, R. L., & Riad, J. K. (1995). Testosterone, crime, and misbehavior among 692 male prison inmates. *Personality and Individual Differences, 18,* 627–633. (12)

Dabbs, J. M., & Morris, R. (1990). Testosterone, social class, and antisocial behavior in a sample of 4,462 men. *Psychological Science, 1,* 209–211. (12)

Dale, N., Schacher, S., & Kandel, E. R. (1988). Long-term facilitation in *Aplysia* involves increase in transmitter release. *Science, 239,* 282–285. (13)

Dalman, C., Allebeck, P., Cullberg, J., Grunewald, C., & Köstler, M. (1999). Obstetric complications and the risk of schizophrenia. *Archives of General Psychiatry, 56,* 234–240. (15)

Dalton, K. (1968). Ante-natal progesterone and intelligence. *British Journal of Psychiatry, 114,* 1377–1382. (11)

Damasio, A. (1999). *The feeling of what happens.* New York: Harcourt Brace. (12)

Damasio, A. R. (1994). *Descartes' error.* New York: Putnam's Sons. (12)

Damasio, H., Grabowski, T. J., Tranel, D., Hichwa, R. D., & Damasio, A. R. (1996). A neural basis for lexical retrieval. *Nature, 380,* 499–505. (14)

Darian-Smith, C., & Gilbert, C. D. (1995). Topographic reorganization in the striate cortex of the adult cat and monkey is cortically mediated. *Journal of Neuroscience, 15,* 1631–1647. (6)

Darwin, C. (1859). *The origin of species.* New York: D. Appleton. (1)

Dávalos, A., Castillo, J., & Martinez-Vila, E. (1995). Delay in neurological attention and stroke outcome. *Stroke, 26,* 2233–2237. (5)

David-Gray, Z. K., Janssen, J. W. H., DeGrip, W. J., Nevo, E., & Foster, R. G. (1998). Light detection in a "blind" animal. *Nature Neuroscience, 1,* 655–656. (9)

Davidson, R. J. (1984). Affect, cognition, and hemispheric specialization. In C. E. Izard, J. Kagan, & R. B. Zajonc (Eds.), *Emotions, cognition, & behavior* (pp. 320–365). Cambridge, England: Cambridge University Press. (15)

Davies, S. J. A., Fitch, M. T., Memberg, S. P., Hall, A. K., Raisman, G., & Silver, J. (1997). Regeneration of adult axons in white matter tracts of the central nervous system. *Nature, 390,* 680–683. (5)

Davis, J. D., Smith, G. P., & Kung, T. M. (1994). Abdominal vagotomy alters the structure of the ingestive behavior of rats ingesting liquid diet. *Behavioral Neuroscience, 108,* 767–779. (10)

Davis, K. D., Kiss, Z. H. T., Luo, L., Tasker, R. R., Lozano, A. M., & Dostrovsky, J. O. (1998). Phantom sensations generated by thalamic microstimulation. *Nature, 391,* 385–387. (5)

Davis, N., & LeVere, T. E. (1982). Recovery of function after brain damage: The question of individual behaviors or functionality. *Experimental Neurology, 75,* 68–78. (5)

Dawkins, R. (1989). *The selfish gene* (new edition). Oxford, England: Oxford University Press. (1)

Dawson, T. M., Gonzalez-Zulueta, M., Kusel, J., & Dawson, V. L. (1998). Nitric oxide: Diverse actions in the central and peripheral nervous system. *Neuroscientist, 4,* 96–112. (3)

Deacon, T., Schumacher, J., Dinsmore, J., Thomas, C., Palmer, P., Kott, S., Edge, A., Penney, D., Kassissieh, S., Dempsey, P., & Isacson, O. (1997). Histological evidence of fetal pig neural cell survival after transplantation into a patient with Parkinson's disease. *Nature Medicine, 3,* 350–353. (8)

Deacon, T. W. (1990). Problems of ontogeny and phylogeny in brain-size evolution. *International Journal of Primatology, 11,* 237–282. (4)

Deacon, T. W. (1992). Brain-language coevolution. In J. A. Hawkins & M. Gell-Mann (Eds.), *The evolution of human languages* (pp. 49–83). Reading, MA: Addison-Wesley. (14)

Deacon, T. W. (1997). *The symbolic species.* New York: W. W. Norton (14)

DeArmond, S. J., Fusco, M. M., & Dewey, M. M. (1974). *Structure of the human brain.* New York: Oxford University Press. (10)

DeCoursey, P. (1960). Phase control of activity in a rodent. *Cold Spring Harbor symposia on quantitative biology, 25,* 49–55. (9)

DeFelipe, C., Herrero, J. F., O'Brien, J. A., Palmer, J. A., Doyle, C. A., Smith, A. J. H., Laird, J. M. A., Belmonte, C., Cervero, F., & Hunt, S. P. (1998). Altered nociception, analgesia and aggression in mice lacking the receptor for substance P. *Nature, 392,* 394–397. (7)

de Jong, W. W., Hendriks, W., Sanyal, S., & Nevo, E. (1990). The eye of the blind mole rat (*Spalax ehrenbergi*): Regressive evolution at the molecular level. In E. Nevo & O. A. Reig (Eds.), *Evolution of subterranean mammals at the organismal and molecular levels* (pp. 383–395). New York: Alan R. Liss (9)

Del Cerro, M. C. R., Perez Izquierdo, M. A., Rosenblatt, J. S., Johnson, B. M., Pacheco, P., & Komisaruk, B. R. (1995). Brain 2-deoxyglucose levels related to maternal behavior-inducing stimuli in the rat. *Brain Research, 696,* 213–220. (11)

Delgado, J. M. R. (1981). Neuronal constellations in aggressive behavior. In L. Valzelli & L. Morgese (Eds.), *Aggression and violence: A psycho/biological and clinical approach* (pp. 82–98). Milan, Italy: Edizioni Saint Vincent. (12)

Deliagina, T. G., Orlovsky, G. N., & Pavlova, G. A. (1983). The capacity for generation of rhythmic oscillations is distributed in the lumbosacral spinal cord of the cat. *Experimental Brain Research, 53,* 81–90. (8)

De Luca, M., Di Page, E., Judica, A., Spinelli, D., & Zoccolotti, P. (1999). Eye movement patterns in linguistic and non-linguistic tasks in developmental surface dyslexia. *Neuropsychologia, 37,* 1407–1420. (14)

Delville, Y., Mansour, K. M., & Ferris, C. F. (1996). Testosterone facilitates aggression by modulating vasopressin receptors in the hypothalamus. *Physiology & Behavior, 60,* 25–29. (12)

Dement, W. (1960). The effect of dream deprivation. *Science, 131,* 1705–1707. (9)

Dement, W. (1972). *Some must watch while some must sleep.* San Francisco: W. H. Freeman. (9)

Dement, W. C. (1990). A personal history of sleep disorders medicine. *Journal of Clinical Neurophysiology, 7,* 17–47. (9)

Dement, W., Ferguson, J., Cohen, H., & Barchas, J. (1969). Non-chemical methods and data using a biochemical model: The REM quanta. In A. J. Mandell & M. P. Mandell (Eds.), *Psychochemical research in man* (pp. 275–325). New York: Academic Press. (9)

Dement, W., & Kleitman, N. (1957a). Cyclic variations in EEG during sleep and their relation to eye movements, body motility, and dreaming. *Electroencephalography and Clinical Neurophysiology, 9,* 673–690. (9)

Dement, W., & Kleitman, N. (1957b). The relation of eye movements during sleep to dream activity: An objective method for the study of dreaming. *Journal of Experimental Psychology, 53,* 339–346. (9)

Dennett, D. C. (1991). *Consciousness explained.* Boston, MA: Little, Brown, and Co. (1, 6)

Dennett, D. C. (1996). Facing backwards on the problem of consciousness. *Journal of Consciousness, 3,* 4–6. (1)

deQuervain, D. J.-F., Roozendaal, B., & McGaugh, J. L. (1998). Stress and glucocorticoids impair retrieval of long-term spatial memory. *Nature, 394,* 787–790. (13)

Desiderato, O., MacKinnon, J. R., & Hissom, H. (1974). Development of gastric ulcers in rats following stress termination. *Journal of Comparative and Physioloigcal Psychology, 87,* 208–214. (12)

DeSimone, J. A., Heck, G. L., & Bartoshuk, L. M. (1980). Surface active taste modifiers: A comparison of the physical and psychophysical properties of gymnemic acid and sodium lauryl sulfate. *Chemical Senses, 5,* 317–330. (7)

DeSimone, J. A., Heck, G. L., Mierson, S., & DeSimone, S. K. (1984). The active ion transport properties of canine lingual epithelia in vitro. *Journal of General Physiology, 83,* 633–656. (7)

Desimone, R. (1991). Face-selective cells in the temporal cortex of monkeys. *Journal of Cognitive Neuroscience, 3,* 1–8. (6)

Desimone, R., Albright, T. D., Gross, C. G., & Bruce, C. (1984). Stimulus-selective properties of inferior temporal neurons in the macaque. *Journal of Neuroscience, 4,* 2051–2062. (6)

D'Esposito, M., Detre, J. A., Alsop, D. C., Shin, R. K., Atlas, S., & Grossman, M. (1995). The neural basis of the central executive system of working memory. *Nature, 378,* 279–281. (13)

Deutsch, J. A., & Ahn, S. J. (1986). The splanchnic nerve and food intake regulation. *Behavioral and Neural Biology, 45,* 43–47. (10)

Deutsch, J. A., Young, W. G., & Kalogeris, T. J. (1978). The stomach signals satiety. *Science, 201,* 165–167. (10)

DeValois, R. L., Albrecht, D. G., & Thorell, L. G. (1982). Spatial frequency selectivity of cells in macaque visual cortex. *Vision Research, 22,* 545–559. (5)

DeValois, R. L., & Jacobs, G. H. (1968). Primate color vision. *Science, 162,* 533–540. (6)

Devane, W. A., Dysarz, F. A. III, Johnson, M. R., Melvin, L. S., & Howlett, A. C. (1988). Determination and characterization of a cannabinoid receptor in rat brain. *Molecular Pharmacology, 34,* 605–613. (3)

Devor, E. J., Abell, C. W., Hoffman, P. L., Tabakoff, B., & Cloninger, C. R. (1994). Platelet MAO activity in Type I and Type II alcoholism. *Annals of the New York Academy of Sciences, 708,* 119–128. (15)

Devor, M. (1996). Pain mechanisms. *The Neuroscientist, 2,* 233–244. (7)

Dew, M. A., Reynolds, C. F. III, Buysse, D. J., Houck, P. R., Hoch, C. C., Monk, T. H., & Kupfer, D. J. (1996). Electroencephalographic sleep profiles during depression.

Archives of General Psychiatry, 53, 148–156. (15)

DeWeerd, P., Gattass, R., Desimone, R., & Ungerleider, L. G. (1995). Responses of cells in monkey visual cortex during perceptual filling-in of an artificial scotoma. *Nature, 377,* 731–734. (6)

Deyo, R., Straube, K. T., & Disterhoft, J. F. (1989). Nimodipine facilitates associative learning in aging rabbits. *Science, 243,* 809–811. (13)

DeYoe, E. A., Felleman, D. J., Van Essen, D. C., & McClendon, E. (1994). Multiple processing streams in occipitotemporal visual cortex. *Nature, 371,* 151–154. (6)

Diamond, M., & Sigmundson, H. K. (1997). Management of intersexuality: Guidelines for dealing with persons with ambiguous genitalia. *Archives of Pediatrics and Adolescent Medicine, 151,* 1046–1050. (11)

Diamond, M. C., Scheibel, A. B., Murphy, G. M., & Harvey, T. (1985). On the brain of a scientist: Albert Einstein. *Experimental Neurology, 88,* 198–204. (4)

Diamond, S. (1994). Head pain. *Clinical Symposia, 46*(3), 1–34. (7)

Dias, R., Robbins, T. W., & Roberts, A. C. (1996). Dissociation in prefrontal cortex of affective and attentional shifts. *Nature, 380,* 69–72. (4)

Dichgans, J. (1984). Clinical symptoms of cerebellar dysfunction and their topodiagnostic significance. *Human Neurobiology, 2,* 269–279. (8)

Dijk, D.-J., & Cajochen, C. (1997). Melatonin and the circadian regulation of sleep initiation, consolidation, structure, and the sleep EEG. *Journal of Biological Rhythms, 12,* 627–635. (9)

DiMarzo, V., Fontana, A., Cadas, H., Schinelli, S., Cimino, G., Schwartz, J.-C., & Piomelli, D. (1994). Formation and inactivation of endogenous cannabinoid anandamide in central neurons. *Nature, 372,* 686–691. (3)

Dimond, S. J. (1979). Symmetry and asymmetry in the vertebrate brain. In D. A. Oakley & H. C. Plotkin (Eds.), *Brain, behaviour, and evolution* (pp. 189–218). London: Methuen. (14)

Di Pasquale, M. (1997). *Amino acids and proteins for the athlete: The*

anabolic edge. Boca Raton, FL: CRC Press. (3)

DiPelligrino, G., & Wise, S. P. (1991). A neurophysiological comparison of three distinct regions of the primate frontal lobe. *Brain, 114,* 951–978. (8)

Dörner, G. (1974). Sex-hormone-dependent brain differentiation and sexual functions. In G. Dörner (Ed.), *Endocrinology of sex* (pp. 30–37). Leipzig: J. A. Barth. (11)

Dowling, J. E. (1987). *The retina.* Cambridge, MA: Harvard University Press. (6)

Dowling, J. E., & Boycott, B. B. (1966). Organization of the primate retina. *Proceedings of the Royal Society of London, B, 166,* 80–111. (6)

Drachman, D. B. (1978). Myasthenia gravis. *New England Journal of Medicine, 298,* 136–142, 186–193. (8)

Dreger, A. D. (1998). *Hermaphrodites and the medical invention of sex.* Cambridge, MA: Harvard University Press. (11)

Drewnowski, A., Henderson, S. A., Shore, A. B., & Barratt-Fornell, A. (1998). Sensory responses to 6-*n*-propylthiouracil (PROP) or sucrose solutions and food preferences in young women. *Annals of the New York Academy of Sciences, 855,* 797–801. (7)

Driver, J., & Mattingley, J. B. (1998). Parietal neglect and visual awareness. *Nature Neuroscience, 1,* 17–22. (4)

Duara, R., Kushch, A., Gross-Glenn, K., Barker, W. W., Jallad, B., Pascal, S., Loewenstein, D. A., Sheldon, J., Rabin, M., Levin, B., & Lubs, H. (1991). Neuroanatomic differences between dyslexic and normal readers on magnetic resonance imaging scans. *Archives of Neurology, 48,* 410–416. (14)

Dudchenko, P. A., & Taube, J. S. (1997). Correlation between head direction cell activity and spatial behavior on a radial arm maze. *Behavioral Neuroscience, 111,* 3–19. (13)

Duman, R. S., Heninger, G. R., & Nestler, E. J. (1997). A molecular and cellular theory of depression. *Archives of General Psychiatry, 54,* 597–606. (15)

Dunlap, J. L., Zadina, J. E., & Gougis, G. (1978). Prenatal stress interacts with prepubertal social isolation to reduce male copulatory behavior. *Physiology and Behavior, 21,* 873–875. (11)

Dunnett, S. B., & Björklund, A. (1999). Prospects for new restorative and neuroprotective treatments in Parkinson's disease. *Nature, 399*(Suppl.), A32–A39. (8)

Dunnett, S. B., Ryan, C. N., Levin, P. D., Reynolds, M., & Bunch, S. T. (1987). Functional consequences of embryonic neocortex transplanted to rats with prefrontal cortex lesions. *Behavioral Neuroscience, 101,* 489–503. (8)

During, M. J., Ryder, K. M., & Spencer, D. D. (1995). Hippocampal GABA transporter function in temporal-lobe epilepsy. *Nature, 376,* 174–177. (14)

Dyal, J. A. (1971). Transfer of behavioral bias: Reality and specificity. In E. J. Fjerdingstad (Ed.), *Chemical transfer of learned information* (pp. 219–263). New York: American Elsevier. (13)

Dykes, R. W., Sur, M., Merzenich, M. M., Kaas, J. H., & Nelson, R. J. (1981). Regional segregation of neurons responding to quickly adapting, slowly adapting, deep and Pacinian receptors within thalamic ventroposterior lateral and ventroposterior inferior nuclei in the squirrel monkey (*Saimiri sciureus*). *Neuroscience, 6,* 1687–1692. (7)

Earnest, D. J., Liang, F.-Q., Ratcliff, M., & Cassone, V. M. (1999). Immortal time: Circadian clock properties of rat suprachiasmatic cell lines. *Science, 283,* 693–695. (9)

Eastman, C. I., Hoese, E. K., Youngstedt, S. D., & Liu, L. (1995). Phase-shifting human circadian rhythms with exercise during the night shift. *Physiology & Behavior, 58,* 1287–1291. (9)

Eastman, C. I., Young, M. A., Fogg, L. F., Liu, L., & Meaden, P. M. (1998). Bright light treatment of winter depression. *Archives of General Psychiatry, 55,* 883–889. (15)

Ebstein, R. P., Novick, O., Umansky, R., Priel, B., Osher, Y., Blaine, D., Bennett, E. R., Nemanov, L., Katz, M., & Belmaker, R. H. (1996). Dopamine D4 receptor (*D4DR*) exon III polymorphism associated with the personality trait of Novelty Seeking. *Nature Genetics, 12,* 78–80. (3)

Eccles, J. C. (1964). *The physiology of synapses.* Berlin: Springer-Verlag. (3)

Eccles, J. C. (1986). Chemical transmission and Dale's principle. In T. Hökfelt, K. Fuxe, & B. Pernow (Eds.), *Progress in brain research* (Vol. 68, pp. 3–13). Amsterdam: Elsevier. (3)

Eccleston, C., & Crombez, G. (1999). Pain demands attention: A cognitive-affective model of the interruptive function of pain. *Psychological Bulletin, 125,* 356–366. (7)

Eckhorn, R., Bauer, R., Jordan, W., Brosch, M., Kruse, W., Munk, M., & Reitboeck, H. J. (1988). Coherent oscillations: A mechanism of feature linking in the visual cortex? *Biological Cybernetics, 60,* 121–130. (4)

Edelman, G. M. (1987). *Neural Darwinism.* New York: Basic Books. (5)

Eden, G. F., VanMeter, J. W., Rumsey, J. M., Maisog, J. M., Woods, R. P., & Zeffiro, T. A. (1996). Abnormal processing of visual motion in dyslexia revealed by functional brain imaging. *Nature, 382,* 66–69. (14)

Edinger, J. D., McCall, W. V., Marsh, G. R., Radtke, R. A., Erwin, C. W., & Lininger, A. (1992). Periodic limb movement variability in older DIMS patients across consecutive nights of home monitoring. *Sleep, 15,* 156–161. (9)

Edman, G., Åsberg, M., Levander, S., & Schalling, D. (1986). Skin conductance habituation and cerebrospinal fluid 5-hydroxyindoleacetic acid in suicidal patients. *Archives of General Psychiatry, 43,* 586–592. (12)

Egeland, J. A., Gerhard, D. S., Pauls, D. L., Sussex, J. N., Kidd, K. K., Allen, C. R., Hostetter, A. M., & Housman, D. E. (1987). Bipolar affective disorders linked to DNA markers on chromosome 11. *Nature, 325,* 783–787. (15)

Ehrhardt, A. A., Meyer-Bahlburg, H. F. L., Rosen, L. R., Feldman, J. F., Veridiano, N. P., Zimmerman, I., & McEwen, B. S. (1985). Sexual orientation after prenatal exposure to exogenous estrogen. *Archives of Sexual Behavior, 14,* 57–77. (11)

Ehrhardt, A. A., & Money, J. (1967). Progestin-induced hermaphroditism: IQ and psychosexual identity in a study of ten girls. *Journal of Sex Research, 3,* 83–100. (11)

Eidelberg, E., & Stein, D. G. (1974). Functional recovery after lesions of the nervous system. *Neurosciences Research Program Bulletin, 12,* 191–303. (5)

Eisenstein, E. M., & Cohen, M. J. (1965). Learning in an isolated prothoracic insect ganglion. *Animal Behaviour, 13,* 104–108. (13)

Eisthen, H. L. (1997). Evolution of vertebrate olfactory systems. *Brain, Behavior and Evolution, 50,* 222–233. (7)

Elbert, T., Pantev, C., Wienbruch, C., Rockstroh, B., & Taub, E. (1995). Increased cortical representation of the fingers of the left hand in string players. *Science, 270,* 305–307. (5)

Elia, J., Ambrosini, P. J., & Rapoport, J. L. (1999). Treatment of attention-deficit hyperactivity disorder. *New England Journal of Medicine, 340,* 780–788. (5)

Elias, C. F., Lee, C., Kelly, J., Aschkenazi, C., Ahima, R. S., Couceyro, P. R., Kuhar, M. J., Saper, C. B., & Elmquist, J. K. (1998a). Leptin activates hypothalamic CART neurons projecting to the spinal cord. *Neuron, 21,* 1375–1385. (10)

Elias, C. F., Saper, C. B., Maratos-Flier, E., Tritos, N. A., Lee, C., Kelly, J., Tatro, J. B., Hoffman, G. E., Ollmann, M. M., Barsh, G. S., Sakurai, T., Yanagisawa, M., & Elmquist, J. K. (1998b). Chemically defined projections linking the mediobasal hypothalamus and the lateral hypothalamic area. *Journal of Comparative Neurology, 402,* 442–459. (10)

El-Islam, M. F. (1982). Rehabilitation of schizophrenics by the extended family. *Acta Psychiatrica Scandinavica, 65,* 112–119. (15)

Ellinwood, E. H., Jr. (1969). Amphetamine psychosis: A multi-dimensional process. *Seminars in Psychiatry, 1,* 208–226. (16)

Elliott, T. R. (1905). The action of adrenalin. *Journal of Physiology* (London), *32,* 401–467. (3)

Ellis, L. (1986). Evidence of neuroandrogenic etiology of sex roles from a combined analysis of human, nonhuman primate and nonprimate mammalian studies. *Personality and Individual Differences, 7*, 519–552. (11)

Ellis, L., & Ames, M. A. (1987). Neurohormonal functioning and sexual orientation: A theory of homosexuality-heterosexuality. *Psychological Bulletin, 101*, 233–258. (11)

Ellis, L., Ames, M. A., Peckham, W., & Burke, D. (1988). Sexual orientation of human offspring may be altered by severe maternal stress during pregnancy. *Journal of Sex Research, 25*, 152–157. (11)

Elmquist, J. K., Elias, C. F., & Saper, C. B. (1999). From lesions to leptin: Hypothalamic control of food intake and body weight. *Neuron, 22*, 221–232. (10)

Emrich, H. M., Leweke, F. M., & Schneider, U. (1997). Towards a cannabinoid hypothesis of schizophrenia: Cognitive impairments due to dysregulation of the endogenous cannabinoid system. *Pharmacology Biochemistry and Behavior, 56*, 803–807. (15)

Engel, S. A. (1999). Using neuroimaging to measure mental representations: Finding color-opponent neurons in visual cortex. *Current Directions in Psychological Science, 8*, 23–27. (6)

Engert, F., & Bonhoeffer, T. (1999). Dendritic spine changes associated with hippocampal long-term synaptic plasticity. *Nature, 399*, 66–70. (13)

Ensor, D. M., Morley, J. S., Redfern, R. M., & Miles, J. B. (1993). The activity of an analogue of MPF (β-endorphin 28-31) in a rat model of Parkinson's disease. *Brain Research, 610*, 166–168. (8)

Epping-Jordan, M. P., Watkins, S. S., Koob, G. F., & Markou, A. (1998). Dramatic decreases in brain reward function during nicotine withdrawal. *Nature, 393*, 76–79. (3)

Epstein, A. N. (1983). The neuropsychology of drinking behavior. In E. Satinoff & P. Teitelbaum (Eds.), *Handbook of behavioral neurobiology: Vol. 6. Motivation* (pp. 367–423). New York: Plenum. (10)

Epstein, A. N. (1990). Prospectus: Thirst and salt appetite. In E. M. Stricker (Ed.), *Handbook of behavioral neurobiology: Vol. 10. Neurobiology of food and fluid intake* (pp. 489–512). New York: Plenum. (10)

Erickson, C., & Lehrman, D. (1964). Effect of castration of male ring doves upon ovarian activity of females. *Journal of Comparative and Physiological Psychology, 58*, 164–166. (11)

Erickson, C. J., & Zenone, P. G. (1976). Courtship differences in male ring doves: Avoidance of cuckoldry? *Science, 192*, 1353–1354. (11)

Erickson, R. P. (1982). The across-fiber pattern theory: An organizing principle for molar neural function. *Contributions to Sensory Physiology, 6*, 79–110. (7)

Erickson, R. P., DiLorenzo, P. M., & Woodbury, M. A. (1994). Classification of taste responses in brain stem: Membership in fuzzy sets. *Journal of Neurophysiology, 71*, 2139–2150. (7)

Eriksson, P. S., Perfilieva, E., Björk-Eriksson, T., Alborn, A.-M., Nordborg, C., Peterson, D. A., & Gage, F. H. (1998). Neurogenesis in the adult human hippocampus. *Nature Medicine, 4*, 1313–1317. (5)

Erlenmeyer-Kimling, L., Adamo, U. H., Rock, D., Roberts, S. A., Bassett, A. S., Squires-Wheeler, E., Cornblatt, B. A., Endicott, J., Pape, S., & Gottesman, I. I. (1997). The New York high-risk project. *Archives of General Psychiatry, 54*, 1096–1102. (15)

Etcoff, N. L., Freeman, R., & Cave, K. R. (1991). Can we lose memories of faces? Content specificity and awareness in a prosopagnosic. *Journal of Cognitive Neuroscience, 3*, 25–41. (6)

Evans, B. J. W., Drasdo, N., & Richards, I. L. (1994). An investigation of some sensory and refractive visual factors in dyslexia. *Vision Research, 34*, 1913–1926. (14)

Evans, D. A., Funkenstein, H. H., Albert, M. S., Scherr, P. A., Cook, N. R., Chown, M. J., Hebert, L. E., Hennekens, C. H., & Taylor, J. O. (1989). Prevalence of Alzheimer's disease in a community population of older persons. *Journal of the American Medical Association, 262*, 2551–2556. (13)

Evans, M. D., Hollon, S. D., DeRubeis, R. J., Piasecki, J. M., Grove, W. M., Garvey, M. J., & Tuason, V. B. (1992). Differential relapse following cognitive therapy and pharmacotherapy for depression. *Archives of General Psychiatry, 49*, 802–808. (15)

Evarts, E. V. (1979). Brain mechanisms of movement. *Scientific American, 241*(3), 164–179. (8)

Everson, C. A. (1995). Functional consequences of sustained sleep deprivation in the rat. *Behavioural Brain Research, 69*, 43–54. (9)

Famy, C., Streissguth, A. P., & Unis, A. S. (1998). Mental illness in adults with fetal alcohol syndrome or fetal alcohol effects. *American Journal of Psychiatry, 155*, 552–554. (5)

Fan, P. (1995). Cannabinoid agonists inhibit the activation of 5-HT3 receptors in rat nodose ganglion neurons. *Journal of Neurophysiology, 73*, 907–910. (3)

Fantz, R. L. (1963). Pattern vision in newborn infants. *Science, 140*, 296–297. (6)

Farah, M. J. (1990). *Visual agnosia.* Cambridge, MA: MIT Press. (6)

Farah, M. J., O'Reilly, R. C., & Vecera, S. P. (1997). The neural correlates of perceptual awareness: Evidence from covert recognition in prosopagnosia. In J. D. Cohen & J. W. Schooler (Eds.), *Scientific approaches to consciousness* (pp. 357–371). Mahwah, NJ: Lawrence Erlbaum Associates. (6)

Farah, M. J., Wilson, K. D., Drain, M., & Tanaka, J. N. (1998). What is "special" about face perception? *Psychological Review, 105*, 482–498. (6)

Faraone, S. V., & Biederman, J. (1998). Neurobiology of attention-deficit hyperactivity disorder. *Biological Psychiatry, 44*, 951–958. (5)

Farber, N. B., Newcomer, J. W., & Olney, J. W. (1999). Glycine agonists: What can they teach us about schizophrenia? *Archives of General Psychiatry, 56*, 13–17. (15)

Faust, M., Kravetz, S., & Babkoff, H. (1993). Hemispheric specialization or reading habits: Evidence from lexical decision research with Hebrew words and sentences. *Brain and Language, 44*, 254–263. (14)

Federman, D. D. (1967). *Abnormal sexual development.* Philadelphia, PA: W. B. Saunders. (11)

Feeney, D. M. (1987). Human rights and animal welfare. *American Psychologist, 42*, 593–599. (1)

Feeney, D. M., & Baron, J.-C. (1986). Diaschisis. *Stroke, 17*, 817–830. (15)

Feeney, D. M., & Sutton, R. L. (1988). Catecholamines and recovery of function after brain damage. In D. G. Stein & B. A. Sabel (Eds.), *Pharmacological approaches to the treatment of brain and spinal cord injury* (pp. 121–142). New York: Plenum. (5)

Feeney, D. M., Sutton, R. L., Boyeson, M. G., Hovda, D. A., & Dail, W. G. (1985). The locus coeruleus and cerebral metabolism: Recovery of function after cerebral injury. *Physiological Psychology, 13*, 197–203. (5)

Feeney, D. M., Weisend, M. P., & Kline, A. E. (1993). Noradrenergic pharmacotherapy, intracerebral infusion and adrenal transplantation promote functional recovery after cortical damage. *Journal of Neural Transplantation & Plasticity, 4*, 199–213. (5)

Feighner, J. P., Gardner, E. A., Johnston, J. A., Batey, S. R., Khayrallah, M. A., Ascher, J. A., & Lineberry, C. G. (1991). Double-blind comparison of bupropion and fluoxetine in depressed outpatients. *Journal of Clinical Psychiatry, 52*, 329–335. (15)

Fendrich, R., Wessinger, C. M., & Gazzaniga, M. S. (1992). Residual vision in a scotoma: Implications for blindsight. *Science, 258*, 1489–1491. (6)

Fendt, M., Koch, M., & Schnitzler, H.-U. (1996). Lesions of the central gray block conditioned fear as measured with the potentiated startle paradigm. *Behavioural Brain Research, 74*, 127–134. (12)

Fentress, J. C. (1973). Development of grooming in mice with amputated forelimbs. *Science, 179*, 704–705. (8)

Ferguson, N. B. L., & Keesey, R. E. (1975). Effect of a quinine-adulterated diet upon body weight maintenance in male rats with ventromedial hypothalamic le-sions. *Journal of Comparative and Physiological Psychology, 89*, 478–488. (10)

Fergusson, D. M., Woodward, L. J., & Horwood, J. (1998). Maternal smoking during pregnancy and psychiatric adjustment in late adolescence. *Archives of General Psychiatry, 55*, 721–727. (5, 12)

Fettiplace, R. (1990). Transduction and tuning in auditory hair cells. *Seminars in the Neurosciences, 2*, 33–40. (7)

Fields, R. D., Schwab, M. E., & Silver, J. (1999). Does CNS myelin inhibit axon regeneration? *Neuroscientist, 5*, 12–18. (5)

Fils-Aime, M.-L., Eckardt, M. J., George, D. T., Brown, G. L., Mefford, I., & Linnoila, M. (1996). Early-onset alcoholics have lower cerebrospinal fluid 5-hydroxyindoleacetic acid levels than late-onset alcoholics. *Archives of General Psychiatry, 53*, 211–216. (15)

Finette, B. A., O'Neill, J. P., Vacek, P. M., & Albertini, R. J. (1998). Gene mutations with characteristic deletions in cord blood T lymphocytes associated with passive maternal exposure to tobacco smoke. *Nature Medicine, 4*, 1144–1151. (5)

Finger, S., & Roe, D. (1996). Gustave Dax and the early history of cerebral dominance. *Archives of Neurology, 53*, 806–813. (14)

Fink, G., Sumner, B. E. H., Rosie, R., Grace, O., & Quinn, J. P. (1996). Estrogen control of central neurotransmission: Effect on mood, mental state, and memory. *Cellular and Molecular Neurobiology, 16*, 325–344. (11)

Fink, G. R., Halligan, P. W., Marshall, J. C., Frith, C. D., Frackowiak, R. S. J., & Dolan, R. J. (1996). Where in the brain does visual attention select the forest and the trees? *Nature, 382*, 626–628. (14)

Fink, M. (1985). Convulsive therapy: Fifty years of progress. *Convulsive Therapy, 1*, 204–216. (15)

Finlay, B. L., & Darlington, R. B. (1995). Linked regularities in the development and evolution of mammalian brains. *Science, 268*, 1578–1584. (5)

Finlay, B. L., & Pallas, S. L. (1989). Control of cell number in the developing mammalian visual system. *Progress in Neurobiology, 32*, 207–234. (5)

Fiorillo, C. D., & Williams, J. T. (1998). Glutamate mediates an inhibitory postsynaptic potential in dopamine neurons. *Nature, 394*, 78–82. (3)

Fisher, S. E., Vargha-Khadem, F., Watkins, K. E., Monaco, A. P., & Pembrey, M. E. (1998). Localisation of a gene implicated in a severe speech and language disorder. *Nature Genetics, 18*, 168–170. (14)

Fjerdingstad, E. J. (1973). Transfer of learning in rodents and fish. In W. B. Essman & S. Nakajima (Eds.), *Current biochemical approaches to learning and memory* (pp. 73–98). Flushing, NY: Spectrum. (13)

Flatz, G. (1987). Genetics of lactose digestion in humans. *Advances in Human Genetics, 16*, 1–77. (10)

Fleet, W. S., & Heilman, K. M. (1986). The fatigue effect in hemispatial neglect. *Neurology, 36*(Suppl. 1), 258. (5)

Fleming, A. S., & Korsmit, M. (1996). Plasticity in the maternal circuit: Effects of maternal experience on fos-lir in hypothalamic, limbic, and cortical structures in the postpartum rat. *Behavioral Neuroscience, 110*, 567–582. (11)

Fletcher, P. C., McKenna, P. J., Frith, C. D., Grasby, P. M., Friston, K. J., & Dolan, R. J. (1998). Brain activations in schizophrenia during a graded memory task studied with functional neuroimaging. *Archives of General Psychiatry, 55*, 1001–1008. (15)

Fletcher, R., & Voke, J. (1985). *Defective colour vision.* Bristol, England: Adam Hilger. (6)

Flor, H., Elbert, T., Knecht, S., Wienbruch, C., Pantev, C., Birbaumer, N., Larbig, W., & Taub, E. (1995). Phantom-limb pain as a perceptual correlate of cortical reorganization following arm amputation. *Nature, 375*, 482–484. (5)

Florence, S. L., Taub, H. B., & Kaas, J. H. (1998). Large-scale sprouting of cortical connections after peripheral injury in adult macaque monkeys. *Science, 282*, 1117–1121. (5)

Folkard, S., Hume, K. I., Minors, D. S., Waterhouse, J. M., & Watson, F. L. (1985). Independence of the circadian rhythm in alertness from the sleep/wake cycle. *Nature, 313*, 678–679. (9)

Foltz, E. L., & Millett, F. E. (1964). Experimental psychosomatic disease states in monkeys: I. Peptic ulcer—"executive monkeys." *Journal of Surgical Research, 4*, 445–453. (12)

Forger, N. G., & Breedlove, S. M. (1987). Motoneuronal death during human fetal development. *Journal of Comparative Neurology, 264*, 118–122. (5)

Forster, B., & Corballis, M. C. (2000). Interhemispheric transfer of colour and shape information in the presence and absence of the corpus callosum. *Neuropsychologia, 38*, 32–45. (14)

Fowler, J. S., Volkow, N. D., Wang, G.-J., Pappas, N., Logan, J., MacGregor, R., Alexoff, D., Shea, C., Schlyer, D., Wolf, A. P., Warner, D., Zezulkova, I., & Cilento, R. (1996). Inhibition of monoamine oxidase B in the brains of smokers. *Nature, 379*, 733–736. (8)

Frangiskakis, J. M., Ewart, A. K., Morris, C. A., Mervis, C. B., Bertrand, J., Robinson, B. F., Klein, B. P., Ensing, G. J., Everett, L.A., Green, E. D., Pröschel, C., Gutowski, N. J., Noble, M., Atkinson, D. L., Odelberg, S. J., & Keating, M. T. (1996). LIM-kinase 1 hemizygosity implicated in impaired visuospatial constructive cognition. *Cell, 86*, 59–69. (14)

Frank, L. G., Weldele, M. L., & Glickman, S. E. (1995). Masculinization costs in hyaenas. *Nature, 377*, 584–585. (11)

Frank, R. A., Mize, S. J. S., Kennedy, L. M., de los Santos, H. C., & Green, S. J. (1992). The effect of *Gymnema sylvestre* extracts on the sweetness of eight sweeteners. *Chemical Senses, 17*, 461–479. (7)

Frankland, P. W., Josselyn, S. A., Bradwejn, J., Vaccarino, F. J., & Yeomans, J. S. (1997). Activation of amygdala cholecystokinin$_B$ receptors potentiates the acoustic startle response in the rat. *Journal of Neuroscience, 17*, 1838–1847. (12)

Frankland, P. W., & Ralph, M. R. (1995). Circadian modulation in the rat acoustic startle circuit. *Behavioral Neuroscience, 109*, 43–48. (12)

Franz, E. A., Eliassen, J. C., Ivry, R. B., & Gazzaniga, M. S. (1996). Dissociation of spatial and temporal coupling in the bimanual movements of callosotomy patients. *Psychological Science, 7*, 306–310. (14)

Freedman, M. S., Lucas, R. J., Soni, B., von Schantz, M., Muñoz, M., David-Gray, Z., & Foster, R. (1999). Regulation of mammalian circadian behavior by non-rod, non-cone, ocular photoreceptors. *Science, 284*, 502–504. (9)

Freedman, R. D., & Thibos, L. N. (1975). Contrast sensitivity in humans with abnormal visual experience. *Journal of Physiology, 247*, 687–710. (6)

Fregly, M. J., & Rowland, N. E. (1991). Effect of a nonpeptide angiotensin II receptor antagonist, DuP 753, on angiotensin-related water intake in rats. *Brain Research Bulletin, 27*, 97–100. (10)

Freimer, N. B., Reus, V. I., Escamilla, M. A., McInnes, L. A., Spesny, M., Leon, P., Service, S. K., Smith, L. B., Silva, S., Rojas, E., Gallegos, A., Meza, L., Fournier, E., Baharloo, S., Blankenship, K., Tyler, D. J., Batki, S., Vinogradov, S., Weissenbach, J., Barondes, S. H., & Sandkuijl, L. A. (1996). Genetic mapping using haplotype, association and linkage methods suggests a locus for severe bipolar disorder (BP1) at 18q22-q23. *Nature Genetics, 12*, 436–441. (15)

Frese, M., & Harwich, C. (1984). Shiftwork and the length and quality of sleep. *Journal of Occupational Medicine, 26*, 561–566. (9)

Fried, I., Wilson, C. L., MacDonald, K. A., & Behnke, E. J. (1998). Electric current stimulates laughter. *Nature, 391*, 650. (12)

Friedburg, D., & Klöppel, K. P. (1996). Frühzeitige Korrektion von Hyperopie und Astigmatismus bie Kindern führt zu besserer Entwicklung des Sehschärfe. *Klinische Monatsblatt der Augenheilkunde, 209*, 21–24. (6)

Friedlander, W. J. (1986). Who was "the father of bromide treatment of epilepsy"? *Archives of Neurology, 43*, 505–507. (15)

Friedman, J. M., & Halaas, J. L. (1998). Leptin and the regulation of body weight in mammals. *Nature, 395*, 763–770. (10)

Friedman, M. I., & Stricker, E. M. (1976). The physiological psychology of hunger: A physiological perspective. *Psychological Review, 83*, 409–431. (10)

Frisch, R. E. (1983). Fatness, puberty, and fertility: The effects of nutrition and physical training on menarche and ovulation. In J. Brooks-Gunn & A. C. Petersen (Eds.), *Girls at puberty* (pp. 29–49). New York: Plenum. (11)

Frisch, R. E. (1984). Body fat, puberty and fertility. *Biological Reviews, 59*, 161–188. (11)

Fritsch, G., & Hitzig, E. (1870). Über die elektrische Erregbarkeit des Grosshirns [Concerning the electrical stimulability of the cerebrum]. *Archiv für Anatomie Physiologie und Wissenschaftliche Medicin*, 300–332. (8)

Fritschy, J.-M., & Grzanna, R. (1992). Degeneration of rat locus coeruleus neurons is not accompanied by an irreversible loss of ascending projections. *Annals of the New York Academy of Sciences, 648*, 275–278. (5)

Frye, C. A. (1995). Estrus-associated decrements in a water maze task are limited to acquisition. *Physiology & Behavior, 57*, 5–14. (11)

Fuller, R. K., & Roth, H. P. (1979). Disulfiram for the treatment of alcoholism: An evaluation in 128 men. *Annals of Internal Medicine, 90*, 901–904. (15)

Fuster, J. M. (1989). *The prefrontal cortex* (2nd ed.). New York: Raven Press. (4)

Gabrieli, J. D. E., McGlinchey-Berroth, R., Carrillo, M. C., Gluck, M. A., Cermak, L. S., & Disterhoft, J. F. (1995). Intact delay-eyeblink classical conditioning in amnesia. *Behavioral Neuroscience, 109*, 819–827. (13)

Gainetdinov, R. R., Wetsel, W. C., Jones, S. R., Levin, E. D., Jaber, M., & Caron, M. G. (1999). Role of serotonin in the paradoxical calming effect of psychostimulants on hyperactivity. *Science, 283*, 397–401. (3)

Galea, L. A. M., Kavaliers, M., Ossenkopp, K.-P., & Hampson, E. (1995). Gonadal hormone levels and spatial learning performance in the Morris water maze in male and female meadow voles, *Micro-*

tus pennsylvanicus. Hormones & Behavior, 29, 106–125. (11)

Galef, B. G., Jr. (1992). Weaning from mother's milk to solid foods: The developmental psychobiology of self-selection of foods by rats. *Annals of the New York Academy of Sciences, 662,* 37–52. (10)

Galin, D., Johnstone, J., Nakell, L., & Herron, J. (1979). Development of the capacity for tactile information transfer between hemispheres in normal children. *Science, 204,* 1330–1332. (14)

Gamse, R., Leeman, S. E., Holzer, P., & Lembeck, F. (1981). Differential effects of capsaicin on the content of somatostatin, substance P, and neurotensin in the nervous system of the rat. *Naunyn-Schmiedeberg's Archives of Pharmacology, 317,* 140–148. (7)

Gao, J.-H., Parsons, L. M., Bower, J. M., Xiong, J., Li, J., & Fox, P. T. (1996). Cerebellum implicated in sensory acquisition and discrimination rather than motor control. *Science, 272,* 545–547. (8)

Garcia, R., Vouimba, R.-M., Baudry, M., & Thompson, R. F. (1999). The amygdala modulates prefrontal cortex activity relative to conditioned fear. *Nature, 402,* 294–296. (12)

Gardner, B. T., & Gardner, R. A. (1975). Evidence for sentence constituents in the early utterances of child and chimpanzee. *Journal of Experimental Psychology: General, 104,* 244–267. (14)

Gardner, H., & Zurif, E. B. (1975). *Bee* but not *be*: Oral reading of single words in aphasia and alexia. *Neuropsychologia, 13,* 181–190. (14)

Gardner, J. D., Rothwell, N. J., & Luheshi, G. N. (1998). Leptin affects food intake via CRF-receptor-mediated pathways. *Nature Neuroscience, 1,* 103. (10)

Garris, P. A., Kilpatrick, M., Bunin, M. A., Michael, D., Walker, Q. D., & Wightman, R. M. (1999). Dissociation of dopamine release in the nucleus accumbens from intracranial self-stimulation. *Nature, 398,* 67–69. (3)

Gash, D. M., Zhang, Z., Ovadia, A., Cass, W. A., Yi, A., Simmerman, L., Russell, D., Martin, D., Lapchak, P. A., Collins, F., Hoffer, B. J., & Gerhardt, G. A. (1996). Functional recovery in parkinson-

ian monkeys treated with GDNF. *Nature, 380,* 252–255. (8)

Gaulin, S. J. C., & FitzGerald, R. W. (1986). Sex differences in spatial ability: An evolutionary hypothesis and test. *American Naturalist, 127,* 74–88. (11)

Gauthier, I., Tarr, M. J., Anderson, A. W., Skudlarski, P., & Gore, J. C. (1999). Activation of the middle fusiform "face area" increases with experience in recognizing novel objects. *Nature Neuroscience, 2,* 568–573. (6)

Gaze, R. M., & Sharma, S. C. (1970). Axial differences in the reinnervation of the goldfish optic tectum by regenerating optic fibers. *Experimental Brain Research, 10,* 171–181. (5)

Gazzaniga, M. S., LeDoux, J. E., & Wilson, D. H. (1977). Language, praxis, and the right hemisphere: Clues to some mechanisms of consciousness. *Neurology, 27,* 1144–1147. (14)

Geiger, G., Lettvin, J. Y., & Fahle, M. (1994). Dyslexic children learn a new visual strategy for reading: A controlled experiment. *Vision Research, 34,* 1223–1233. (14)

Geiger, G., Lettvin, J. Y., & Zegarra-Moran, O. (1992). Task-determined strategies of visual process. *Cognitive Brain Research, 1,* 39–52. (14)

George, D. T., Nutt, D. J., Walker, W. V., Porges, S. W., Adinoff, B., & Linnoila, M. (1989). Lactate and hyperventilation substantially attenuate vagal tone in normal volunteers. *Archives of General Psychiatry, 46,* 153–156. (12)

George, M. S., Wasserman, E. M., Kimbrell, T. A., Little, J. T., Williams, W. E., Danielson, A. L., Greenberg, B. D., Hallett, M., & Post, R. M. (1997). Mood improvement following daily left prefrontal repetitive transcranial magnetic stimulation in patients with depression: A placebo-controlled crossover trial. *American Journal of Psychiatry, 154,* 1752–1756. (15)

Geschwind, N. (1970). The organization of language and the brain. *Science, 170,* 940–944. (14)

Geschwind, N. (1972). Language and the brain. *Scientific American, 226*(4), 76–83. (14)

Geschwind, N., & Levitsky, W. (1968).

Human brain: Left-right asymmetries in temporal speech region. *Science, 161,* 186–187. (14)

Giancola, P. R. (1995). Evidence for dorsolateral and orbital prefrontal cortical involvement in the expression of aggressive behavior. *Aggressive Behavior, 21,* 431–450. (12)

Gibbs, F. P. (1983). Temperature dependence of the hamster circadian pacemaker. *American Journal of Physiology, 244,* R607–R610. (9)

Gibbs, J., Young, R. C., & Smith, G. P. (1973). Cholecystokinin decreases food intake in rats. *Journal of Comparative and Physiological Psychology, 84,* 488–495. (10)

Gillette, M. U., & McArthur, A. J. (1996). Circadian actions of melatonin at the suprachiasmatic nucleus. *Behavioural Brain Research, 73,* 135–139. (9)

Ginns, E. I., Ott, J., Egeland, J. A., Allen, C. R., Fann, C. S. J., Pauls, D. L., Weissenbach, J., Carulli, J. P., Falls, K. M., Keith, T. P., & Paul, S. M. (1996). A genome-wide search for chromosomal loci linked to bipolar affective disorder in the Old Order Amish. *Nature Genetics, 12,* 431–435. (15)

Ginsberg, M. D. (1995a). Neuroprotection in brain ischemia: An update (Part I). *The Neuroscientist, 1,* 95–103. (5)

Ginsberg, M. D. (1995b). Neuroprotection in brain ischemia: An update (Part II). *The Neuroscientist, 1,* 164–175. (5)

Giros, B., Jaber, M., Jones, S. R., Wightman, R. M., & Caron, M. G. (1996). Hyperlocomotion and indifference to cocaine and amphetamine in mice lacking the dopamine transporter. *Nature, 379,* 606–612. (3)

Giuliani, D., & Ferrari, F. (1996). Differential behavioral response to dopamine D_2 agonists by sexually naive, sexually active, and sexually inactive male rats. *Behavioral Neuroscience, 110,* 802–808. (3, 11)

Gjedde, A. (1984). Blood-brain transfer of galactose in experimental galactosemia, with special reference to the competitive interaction between galactose and glucose. *Journal of Neurochemistry, 43,* 1654–1662. (2)

Glantz, L. A., & Lewis, D. A. (1997).

Reduction of synaptophysin immunoreactivity in the prefrontal cortex of subjects with schizophrenia. *Archives of General Psychiatry, 54,* 660–669. (15)

Glantz, L. A., & Lewis, D. A. (2000). Decreased dendritic spine density on prefrontal cortical pyramidal neurons in schizophrenia. *Archives of General Psychiatry, 57,* 65–73. (15)

Glaser, J. H., Etgen, A. M., & Barfield, R. J. (1987). Temporal aspects of ventromedial hypothalamic progesterone action in the facilitation of estrous behavior in the female rat. *Behavioral Neuroscience, 101,* 534–545. (11)

Glaser, R., Rice, J., Speicher, C. E., Stout, J. C., & Kiecolt-Glaser, J. K. (1986). Stress depresses interferon production by leukocytes concomitant with a decrease in natural killer cell activity. *Behavioral Neuroscience, 100,* 675–678. (12)

Glendenning, K. K., Baker, B. N., Hutson, K. A., & Masterton, R. B. (1992). Acoustic chiasm V: Inhibition and excitation in the ipsilateral and contralateral projections of LSO. *Journal of Comparative Neurology, 319,* 100–122. (7)

Glick, S. D. (1974). Changes in drug sensitivity and mechanisms of functional recovery following brain damage. In D. G. Stein, J. J. Rosen, & N. Butters (Eds.), *Plasticity and recovery of function in the central nervous system* (pp. 339–372). New York: Academic Press. (5)

Glickman, S. E., Frank, L. G., Licht, P., Yalcinkaya, T., Siiteri, P. K., & Davidson, J. (1992). Sexual differentiation of the female spotted hyena: One of nature's experiments. *Annals of the New York Academy of Sciences, 662,* 135–159. (11)

Goate, A., Chartier-Harlin, M. C., Mullan, M., Brown, J., Crawford, F., Fidani, L., Giuffra, L., Haynes, A., Irving, N., James, L., Mant, R., Newton, P., Rooke, K., Roques, P., Talbot, C., Pericak-Vance, M., Roses, A., Williamson, R., Rossor, M., Owen, M., & Hardy, J. (1991). Segregation of a missense mutation in the amyloid precursor protein gene with familial Alzheimer's disease. *Nature, 349,* 704–706. (13)

Gödecke, I., & Bonhoeffer, T. (1996). Development of identical orientation maps for two eyes without common visual experience. *Nature, 379,* 251–254. (6)

Goff, D. C., Tsai, G., Levitt, J., Amico, E., Manoach, D., Schoenfeld, D. A., Hayden, D. L., McCarlety, R., & Coyle, J. T. (1999). A placebo-controlled trial of D-cycloserine added to conventional neuroleptics in patients with schizophrenia. *Archives of General Psychiatry, 56,* 21–27. (15)

Gold, R. M. (1973). Hypothalamic obesity: The myth of the ventromedial hypothalamus. *Science, 182,* 488–490. (10)

Goldberg, T. E., Weinberger, D. R., Berman, K. F., Pliskin, N. H., & Podd, M. H. (1987). Further evidence for dementia of the prefrontal type in schizophrenia? *Archives of General Psychiatry, 44,* 1008–1014. (15)

Goldin-Meadow, S., McNeill, D., & Singleton, J. (1996). Silence is liberating: Removing the handcuffs on grammatical expression in the manual modality. *Psychological Review, 103,* 34–55. (14)

Goldin-Meadow, S., & Mylander, C. (1998). Spontaneous sign systems created by deaf children in two cultures. *Nature, 391,* 279–281. (14)

Goldman, B. D. (1981). Puberty. In N. T. Adler (Ed.), *Neuroendocrinology of reproduction* (pp. 229–239). New York: Plenum. (11)

Goldman, P. S. (1971). Functional development of the prefrontal cortex in early life and the problem of neuronal plasticity. *Experimental Neurology, 32,* 366–387. (5)

Goldman, P. S. (1976). The role of experience in recovery of function following orbital prefrontal lesions in infant monkeys. *Neuropsychologia, 14,* 401–412. (5)

Goldman-Rakic, P. S. (1987). Development of cortical circuitry and cognitive function. *Child Development, 58,* 601–622. (5)

Goldman-Rakic, P. S. (1988). Topography of cognition: Parallel distributed networks in primate association cortex. *Annual Review of Neuroscience, 11,* 137–156. (inside cover, 4)

Goldman-Rakic, P. S. (1994). Specification of higher cortical functions. In S. H. Broman & J. Grafman (Eds.), *Atypical cognitive deficits in developmental disorders* (pp. 3–17). Hillsdale, NJ: Lawrence Erlbaum. (13)

Goldman-Rakic, P. S. (1995). Cellular basis of working memory. *Neuron, 14,* 477–485. (13)

Goldman-Rakic, P. S., Bates, J. F., & Chafee, M. V. (1992). The prefrontal cortex and internally generated motor acts. *Current Opinion in Neurobiology, 2,* 830–835. (8)

Goldstein, A. (1980). Thrills in response to music and other stimuli. *Physiological Psychology, 8,* 126–129. (7)

Goldstein, L. B. (1993). Basic and clinical studies of pharmacologic effects on recovery from brain injury. *Journal of Neural Transplantation & Plasticity, 4,* 175–192. (5)

Goldstein, M. (1974). Brain research and violent behavior. *Archives of Neurology, 30,* 1–35. (12)

Goodale, M. A. (1996). Visuomotor modules in the vertebrate brain. *Canadian Journal of Physiology and Pharmacology, 74,* 390–400. (6, 8)

Goodale, M. A., Milner, A. D., Jakobson, L. S., & Carey, D. P. (1991). A neurological dissociation between perceiving objects and grasping them. *Nature, 349,* 154–156. (6, 8)

Gopnik, M., & Crago, M. B. (1991). Familial aggregation of a developmental language disorder. *Cognition, 39,* 1–50. (14)

Gorell, J. M., Rybicki, B. A., Johnson, C. C., & Peterson, E. L. (1999). Smoking and Parkinson's disease: A dose-response relationship. *Neurology, 52,* 115–119. (8)

Gorski, R. A. (1980). Sexual differentiation of the brain. In D. T. Krieger & J. C. Hughes (Eds.), *Neuroendocrinology* (pp. 215–222). Sunderland, MA: Sinauer. (11)

Gorski, R. A. (1985). The 13th J. A. F. Stevenson memorial lecture. Sexual differentiation of the brain: Possible mechanisms and implications. *Canadian Journal of Physiology and Pharmacology, 63,* 577–594. (11)

Gorski, R. A., & Allen, L. S. (1992). Sexual orientation and the size of the anterior commissure in the human brain. *Proceedings of the*

National Academy of Sciences, U.S.A., 89, 7199–7202. (11)

Gorski, R. A., Gordon, J. H., Shryne, J. E., & Southam, A. M. (1978). Evidence for a morphological sex difference within the medial preoptic area of the rat brain. *Brain Research, 148,* 333–346. (11)

Gosler, A. G., Greenwood, J. J. D., & Perrins, C. (1995). Predation risk and the cost of being fat. *Nature, 377,* 621–623. (10)

Gottesman, I. I. (1991). *Schizophrenia genesis.* New York: W. H. Freeman. (15)

Gottesman, I. I., & Bertelson, A. (1989). Confirming unexpressed genotypes for schizophrenia. *Archives of General Psychiatry, 46,* 867–872. (15)

Gottlieb, J. P., Kusunoki, M., & Goldberg, M. E. (1998). The representation of salience in monkey parietal cortex. *Nature, 391,* 481–484. (6)

Götz, R., Köster, R., Winkler, C., Raulf, F., Lottspeich, F., Schartl, M., & Thoenen, H. (1993). Neurotrophin-6 is a new member of the nerve growth factor family. *Nature, 372,* 266–269. (5)

Gould, E., Beylin, A., Tanapat, P., Reeves, A., & Shors, T. J. (1999). Learning enhances adult neurogenesis in the hippocampal formation. *Nature Neuroscience, 2,* 260–265. (5)

Gould, E., Reeves, A. J., Graziano, M. S. A., & Gross, C. G. (1999). Neurogenesis in the neocortex of adult primates. *Science, 286,* 548–552. (5)

Granholm, A. C., Albeck, D., Backman, C., Curtis, M., Ebendal, T., Friden, P., Henry, M., Hoffer, B., Kordower, J., Rose, G. M., Soderstrom, S., & Bartus, R. T. (1998). A non-invasive system for delivering neural growth factors across the blood-brain barrier: A review. *Reviews in the Neurosciences, 9,* 31–55. (8)

Grant, A. C., Zangaladze, A., Thiagarajah, M. C., & Sathian, K. (1999). Tactile perception in developmental dyslexia: A psychophysical study using gratings. *Neuropsychologia, 37,* 1201–1211. (14)

Graves, J. A. M. (1994). Mammalian sex-determining genes. In R. V. Short & E. Balaban (Eds.), *The differences between the sexes* (pp. 397–418). Cambridge, England: Cambridge University Press. (11)

Gray, C. M., König, P., Engel, A. K., & Singer, W. (1989). Oscillatory responses in cat visual cortex exhibit inter-columnar synchronization which reflects global stimulus properties. *Nature, 338,* 334–337. (4)

Graybiel, A. M. (1998). The basal ganglia and chunking of action repertoires. *Neurobiology of Learning and Memory, 70,* 119–136. (8)

Graybiel, A. M., Aosaki, T., Flaherty, A. W., & Kimura, M. (1994). The basal ganglia and adaptive motor control. *Science, 265,* 1826–1831. (4)

Graziadei, P. P. C., & deHan, R. S. (1973). Neuronal regeneration in frog olfactory system. *Journal of Cell Biology, 59,* 525–530. (5)

Graziadei, P. P. C., & Monti Graziadei, G. A. (1985). Neurogenesis and plasticity of the olfactory sensory neurons. *Annals of the New York Academy of Sciences, 457,* 127–142. (5)

Graziano, M. S. A., Hu, X. T., & Gross, C. G. (1997). Coding the locations of objects in the dark. *Science, 277,* 239–241. (8)

Greenlee, M. W., Lang, H.-J., Mergner, T., & Seeger, W. (1995). Visual short-term memory of stimulus velocity in patients with unilateral posterior brain damage. *Journal of Neuroscience, 15,* 2287–2300. (6)

Greenough, W. T. (1975). Experiential modification of the developing brain. *American Scientist, 63,* 37–46. (5)

Greist, J. H., Jefferson, J. W., Kobak, K. A., Katzelnick, D. J., & Serlin, R. C. (1995). Efficacy and tolerability of serotonin transport inhibitors in obsessive-compulsive disorder. *Archives of General Psychiatry, 52,* 53–60. (12)

Gresty, M. A., Bronstein, A. M., Brandt, T., & Dieterich, M. (1992). Neurology of otolith function. *Brain, 115,* 647–673. (7)

Griffin, D. R., Webster, F. A., & Michael, C. R. (1960). The echolocation of flying insects by bats. *Animal Behaviour, 8,* 141–154. (7)

Grillon, C., Morgan, C. A. III, Davis, M., & Southwick, S. M. (1998). Effect of darkness on acoustic startle in Vietnam veterans with PTSD. *American Journal of Psychiatry, 155,* 812–817. (12)

Grisham, W., Castro, J. M., Kashon, M. L., Ward, I. L., & Ward, O. B. (1992). Prenatal flutamide alters sexually dimorphic nuclei in the spinal cord of male rats. *Brain Research, 578,* 69–74. (11)

Gross, C. G. (1999). The fire that comes from the eye. *The Neuroscientist, 5,* 58–64. (6)

Gross, C. G., & Graziano, M. S. A. (1995). Multiple representations of space in the brain. *The Neuroscientist, 1,* 43–50. (4)

Grossman, S. P., Dacey, D., Halaris, A. E., Collier, T., & Routtenberg, A. (1978). Aphagia and adipsia after preferential destruction of nerve cell bodies in hypothalamus. *Science, 202,* 537–539. (10)

Gubernick, D. J., & Alberts, J. R. (1983). Maternal licking of young: Resource exchange and proximate controls. *Physiology & Behavior, 31,* 593–601. (11)

Guidotti, A., Ferrero, P., Fujimoto, M., Santi, R. M., & Costa, E. (1986). Studies on endogenous ligands (endocoids) for the benzodiazepine/beta carboline binding sites. *Advances in Biochemical Pharmacology, 41,* 137–148. (12)

Guidotti, A., Forchetti, C. M., Corda, M. G., Konkel, D., Bennett, C. D., & Costa, E. (1983). Isolation, characterization, and purification to homogeneity of an endogenous polypeptide with agonistic action on benzodiazepine receptors. *Proceedings of the National Academy of Sciences, U.S.A., 80,* 3531–3535. (12)

Guilleminault, C., Heinzer, R., Mignot, E., & Black, J. (1998). Investigations into the neurologic basis of narcolepsy. *Neurology, 50*(Suppl. 1), S8–S15. (9)

Guillery, R. W., Feig, S. L., & Lozsádi, D. A. (1998). Paying attention to the thalamic reticular nucleus. *Trends in Neurosciences, 21,* 28–32. (4, 9)

Gur, R. E., & Chin, S. (1999). Laterality in functional brain imaging studies of schizophrenia. *Schizophrenia Bulletin, 25,* 141–156. (15)

Gurevich, E. V., Bordelon, Y., Shapiro, R. M., Arnold, S. E., Gur, R. E., & Joyce, J. N. (1997). Mesolimbic dopamine D_3 receptors and use of antipsychotics in patients with schizophrenia. *Archives of General Psychiatry, 54,* 225–232. (15)

Gustafsson, B., & Wigström, H. (1990). Basic features of long-term potentiation in the hippocampus. *Seminars in the Neurosciences, 2,* 321–333. (13)

Guyton, A. C. (1974). *Function of the human body* (4th ed.). Philadelphia: Saunders. (2)

Gwinner, E. (1986). Circannual rhythms in the control of avian rhythms. *Advances in the Study of Behavior, 16,* 191–228. (9)

Hadjikhani, N., Liu, A. K., Dale, A. M., Cavanagh, P., & Tootell, R. B. H. (1998). Retinotopy and color sensitivity in human visual cortical area V8. *Nature Neuroscience, 1,* 235–241. (6)

Häfner, H., an der Heiden, W., Behrens, S., Gattaz, W. F., Hambrecht, M., Löffler, W., Maurer, K., Munk-Jørgensen, P., Nowotny, B., Riecher-Rössler, A., & Stein, A. (1998). Causes and consequences of the gender difference in age of onset of schizophrenia. *Schizophrenia Bulletin, 24,* 99–113. (15)

Haimov, I., & Lavie, P. (1996). Melatonin—A soporific hormone. *Current Directions in Psychological Science, 5,* 106–111. (9)

Hajnal, A., Takenouchi, K., & Norgren, R. (1999). Effect of intraduodenal lipid on parabrachial gustatory coding in awake rats. *Journal of Neuroscience, 19,* 7182–7190. (10)

Halaas, J. L, Gajiwala, K. S., Maffei, M., Cohen, S. L., Chait, B. T., Rabinowitz, D., Lallone, R. L., Burley, S. K., & Friedman, J. M. (1995). Weight-reducing effects of the plasma protein encoded by the *obese* gene. *Science, 269,* 543–546. (10)

Hale, S., Myerson, J., Rhee, S. H., Weiss, C. S., & Abrams, R. A. (1996). Selective interference with the maintenance of location information in working memory. *Neuropsychology, 10,* 228–240. (13)

Haley, J. (1959). An interactional description of schizophrenia. *Psychiatry, 22,* 321–332. (15)

Hall, S. M., Reus, V. I., Muñoz, R. F., Sees, K. L., Humfleet, G., Hartz, D. T., Frederick, S., & Triffleman, E. (1998). Nortriptyline and cogni-tive-behavioral therapy in the treatment of cigarette smoking. *Archives of General Psychiatry, 55,* 683–690. (3)

Hamann, S. B., Ely, T. D., Grafton, S. T., & Kilts, C. D. (1999). Amygdala activity related to enhanced memory for pleasant and aversive stimuli. *Nature Neuroscience, 2,* 289–293. (12)

Hamann, S. B., & Squire, L. R. (1995). On the acquisition of new declarative knowledge in amnesia. *Behavioral Neuroscience, 109,* 1027–1044. (13)

Hamer, D. H., Hu, S., Magnuson, V. L., Hu, N., & Pattatucci, A. M. L. (1993). A linkage between DNA markers on the X chromosome and male sexual orientation. *Science, 261,* 321–327. (11)

Hamilton, W. D. (1964). The genetical evolution of social behavior (I and II). *Journal of Theoretical Biology, 7,* 1–16; 17–52. (1)

Hampson, R. E., Simeral, J. D., & Deadwyler, S. A. (1999). Distribution of spatial and nonspatial information in dorsal hippocampus. *Nature, 402,* 610–614. (13)

Hanaway, J., Woolsey, T. A., Gado, M. H., & Roberts, M. P., Jr. (1998). *The brain atlas.* Bethesda, MD: Fitzgerald Science Press. (12)

Haqq, C. M., & Donahoe, P. K. (1998). Regulation of sexual dimorphism in mammals. *Physiological Reviews, 78,* 1–33. (11)

Hardy, J., Duff, K., Hardy, K. G., Perez-Tur, J., & Hutton, M. (1998). Genetic dissection of Alzheimer's disease and related dementias: Amyloid and its relationship to tau. *Nature Neuroscience, 1,* 355–358. (13)

Hari, R. (1994). Human cortical functions revealed by magneto-encephalography. *Progress in Brain Research, 100,* 163–168. (5)

Harley, B., & Wang, W. (1997). The critical period hypothesis: Where are we now? In A. M. B. deGroot & J. F. Knoll (Eds.), *Tutorials in bilingualism* (pp. 19–51). Mahwah, NJ: Erlbaum. (14)

Harris, C. R. (1999, July–August). The mystery of ticklish laughter. *American Scientist, 87*(4), 344–351. (7)

Harris, G. W. (1964). Sex hormones, brain development and brain function. *Endocrinology, 75,* 627–648. (11)

Harris, K. M., & Stevens, J. K. (1989). Dendritic spines of CA1 pyramidal cells in the rat hippocampus: Serial electron microscopy with reference to their biophysical characteristics. *Journal of Neuroscience, 9,* 2982–2997. (2)

Harris, R. A., Brodie, M. S., & Dunwiddie, T. V. (1992). Possible substrates of ethanol reinforcement: GABA and dopamine. *Annals of the New York Academy of Sciences, 654,* 61–69. (3)

Hart, B. L. (Ed.). (1976). *Experimental psychobiology.* San Francisco: W. H. Freeman. (10)

Hartline, H. K. (1949). Inhibition of activity of visual receptors by illuminating nearby retinal areas in the limulus eye. *Federation Proceedings, 8,* 69. (6)

Hauser, R. A., Freeman, T. B., Snow, B. J., Nauert, M., Gauger, L., Kordower, J. H., & Olanow, W. (1999). Long-term evaluation of bilateral fetal nigral transplantation in Parkinson disease. *Archives of Neurology, 56,* 179–187. (8)

Hebb, D. O. (1949). *Organization of behavior.* New York: Wiley. (inside cover, 13)

Heeb, M. M., & Yahr, P. (1996). C-Fos immunoreactivity in the sexually dimorphic area of the hypothalamus and related brain regions of male gerbils after exposure to sex-related stimuli or performance of specific sexual behaviors. *Neuroscience, 72,* 1049–1071. (11)

Heffner, R. S., & Heffner, H. E. (1982). Hearing in the elephant (*Elephas maximus*): Absolute sensitivity, frequency discrimination, and sound localization. *Journal of Comparative and Physiological Psychology, 96,* 926–944. (7)

Heinz, A., Dufeu, P., Kuhn, S., Dettling, M., Gräf, K., Kürten, I., Rommelspacher, H., & Schmidt, L. G. (1996). Psychopathological and behavioral correlates of dopaminergic sensitivity in alcohol-dependent patients. *Archives of General Psychiatry, 53,* 1123–1128. (15)

Heiss, W.-D., Kessler, J., Thiel, A., Ghaemi, M., & Karbe, H. (1999). Differential capacity of left and right hemispheric areas for compensation of poststroke aphasia. *Annals of Neurology, 45,* 430–438. (14)

Heller, W., & Levy, J. (1981). Perception and expression of emotion in right-handers and left-handers. *Neuropsychologia, 19,* 263–272. (14)

Hennig, R., & Lømo, T. (1985). Firing patterns of motor units in normal rats. *Nature, 314,* 164–166. (8)

Heresco-Levy, U., Javitt, D. C., Ermilov, M., Mordel, C., Silipo, G., & Lichtenstein, M. (1999). Efficacy of high-dose glycine in the treatment of enduring negative symptoms of schizophrenia. *Archives of General Psychiatry, 56,* 29–36. (15)

Herkenham, M. (1992). Cannabinoid receptor localization in brain: Relationship to motor and reward systems. *Annals of the New York Academy of Sciences, 654,* 19–32. (3)

Herkenham, M., Lynn, A. B., de Costa, B. R., & Richfield, E. K. (1991). Neuronal localization of cannabinoid receptors in the basal ganglia of the rat. *Brain Research, 547,* 267–274. (3)

Herman, L. M., Pack, A. A., & Morrel-Samuels, P. (1993). Representational and conceptual skills of dolphins. In H. L. Roitblat, L. M. Herman, & P. E. Nachtigall (Eds.), *Language and communication: Comparative perspectives* (pp. 403–442). Hillsdale, NJ: Lawrence Erlbaum. (14)

Hernandez, L., Murzi, E., Schwartz, D. H., & Hoebel, B. G. (1992). Electrophysiological and neurochemical approach to a hierarchical feeding organization. In P. Bjorntorp & B. N. Brodoff (Eds.), *Obesity* (pp. 171–183). Philadelphia, PA: J. B. Lippincott. (10)

Herrero, S. (1985). *Bear attacks: Their causes and avoidance.* Piscataway, NJ: Winchester. (7)

Herzog, E. D., Takahashi, J. S., & Block, G. D. (1998). *Clock* controls circadian period in isolated suprachiasmatic nucleus neurons. *Nature Neuroscience, 1,* 708–713. (9)

Herzog, S., Pfeuffer, I., Haberzettl, K., Feldmann, H., Frese, K., Bechter, K., & Richt, J. A. (1997). Molecular characterization of Borna disease virus from naturally infected animals and possible links to human disorders. *Archives of Virology* (Suppl. 13), 183–190. (15)

Hickok, G., Bellugi, U., & Klima, E. S. (1996). The neurobiology of sign language and its implications for the neural basis of language. *Nature, 381,* 699–702. (14)

Higley, J. D., Mehlman, P. T., Higley, S. B., Fernald, B., Vickers, J., Lindell, S. G., Taub, D. M., Suomi, S. J., & Linnoila, M. (1996). Excessive mortality in young free-ranging male nonhuman primates with low cerebrospinal fluid 5-hydroxyindoleacetic acid concentrations. *Archives of General Psychiatry, 53,* 537–543. (12)

Hill, J. O., & Peters, J. C. (1998). Environmental contributions to the obesity epidemic. *Science, 280,* 1371–1374. (10)

Hirsch, S. R., Das, I., Garey, L. J., & de Belleroche, J. (1997). A pivotal role for glutamate in the pathogenesis of schizophrenia, and its cognitive dysfunction. *Pharmacology Biochemistry and Behavior, 56,* 797–802. (15)

Hitchcock, J. M., & Davis, M. (1991). Efferent pathway of the amygdala involved in conditioned fear as measured with the fear-potentiated startle paradigm. *Behavioral Neuroscience, 105,* 826–842. (12)

Hobson, J. A. (1989). *Sleep.* New York: Scientific American Library. (15)

Hobson, J. A., & McCarley, R. W. (1977). The brain as a dream state generator: An activation-synthesis hypothesis of the dream process. *American Journal of Psychiatry, 134,* 1335–1348. (9)

Hoebel, B. G. (1988). Neuroscience and motivation: Pathways and peptides that define motivational systems. In R. C. Atkinson, R. J. Herrnstein, G. Lindzey, & R. D. Luce (Eds.), *Stevens' handbook of experimental psychology* (2nd ed.) (pp. 547–625). New York: John Wiley. (10)

Hoebel, B. G., & Hernandez, L. (1993). Basic neural mechanisms of feeding and weight regulation. In A. J. Stunkard & T. A. Wadden (Eds.), *Obesity: Theory and therapy* (2nd ed.) (pp. 43–62). New York: Raven Press. (10)

Hoffer, A. (1973). Mechanism of action of nicotinic acid and nicotinamide in the treatment of schizophrenia. In D. Hawkins & L. Pauling (Eds.), *Orthomolecular psychiatry* (pp. 202–262). San Francisco: W. H. Freeman. (15)

Hoffman, P. L., Tabakoff, B., Szabó, G., Suzdak, P. D., & Paul, S. M. (1987). Effect of an imidazobenzodiazepine, Ro15-4513, on the incoordination and hypothermia produced by ethanol and pentobarbital. *Life Sciences, 41,* 611–619. (12)

Hökfelt, T., Johansson, O., & Goldstein, M. (1984). Chemical anatomy of the brain. *Science, 225,* 1326–1334. (3)

Holden, C. (1987). Is alcoholism treatment effective? *Science, 236,* 20–22. (15)

Hollerman, J., & Schultz, W. (1998). Dopamine neurons report an error in the temporal prediction of reward during learning. *Nature Neuroscience, 1,* 304–309. (3)

Hollister, J. M., Laing, P., & Mednick, S. A. (1996). Rhesus incompatibility as a risk factor for schizophrenia in male adults. *Archives of General Psychiatry, 53,* 19–24. (15)

Honer, W. G., Falkai, P., Young, C., Wang, T., Xie, J., Bonner, J., Hu, L., Boulianne, G. L., Luo, Z., & Trimble, W. S. (1997). Cingulate cortex synaptic terminal proteins and neural cell adhesion molecules in schizophrenia. *Neuroscience, 78,* 99–110. (15)

Hoover, J. E., & Strick, P. L. (1993). Multiple output channels in the basal ganglia. *Science, 259,* 819–821. (8)

Hopfield, J. J. (1995). Pattern recognition computation using action potential timing for stimulus representation. *Nature, 376,* 33–36. (6)

Hopkins, J., Marcus, M., & Campbell, S. B. (1984). Postpartum depression: A critical review. *Psychological Bulletin, 95,* 498–515. (15)

Hoptman, M. J., & Levy, J. (1988). Perceptual asymmetries in left- and right-handers for cartoon and real faces. *Brain & Cognition, 8,* 178–188. (14)

Horn, C. C., Tordoff, M. G., & Friedman, M. I. (1996). Does ingested fat produce satiety? *American Journal of Physiology, 270,* R761–R765. (10)

Horne, J. A. (1988). *Why we sleep.* Oxford, England: Oxford University Press. (9)

Horne, J. A. (1992). Sleep and its disorders in children. *Journal of*

Child Psychology & Psychiatry & Allied Disorders, 33, 473–487. (9)

Horne, J. A., & Minard, A. (1985). Sleep and sleepiness following a behaviourally "active" day. *Ergonomics, 28,* 567–575. (9)

Horridge, G. A. (1962). Learning of leg position by the ventral nerve cord in headless insects. *Proceedings of the Royal Society of London,* B, *157,* 33–52. (13)

Horst, W. D., & Preskorn, S. H. (1998). Mechanisms of action and clinical characteristics of three atypical antidepressants: Venlafaxine, nefazodone, bupropion. *Journal of Affective Disorders, 51,* 237–254. (15)

Horton, J. C., & Hocking, D. R. (1996). An adult-like pattern of ocular dominance columns in striate cortex of newborn monkeys prior to visual experience. *Journal of Neuroscience, 16,* 1791–1807. (6)

Hovda, D. A., & Feeney, D. M. (1989). Amphetamine-induced recovery of visual cliff performance after bilateral visual cortex ablation in cats: Measurements of depth perception thresholds. *Behavioral Neuroscience, 103,* 574–584. (5)

Howe, M. L., & Courage, M. L. (1993). The emergence and early development of autobiographical memory. *Psychological Review, 104,* 499–523. (13)

Howland, H. C., & Sayles, N. (1984). Photorefractive measurements of astigmatism in infants and young children. *Investigative Ophthalmology and Visual Science, 25,* 93–102. (6)

Hsu, M., Sik, A., Gallyas, F., Horváth, Z., & Buzsáki, G. (1994). Short-term and long-term changes in the postischemic hippocampus. *Annals of the New York Academy of Sciences, 743,* 121–140. (5)

Hubel, D. H. (1963, November). The visual cortex of the brain. *Scientific American, 209*(5), 54–62. (6)

Hubel, D. H., & Wiesel, T. N. (1959). Receptive fields of single neurons in the cat's striate cortex. *Journal of Physiology, 148,* 574–591. (6)

Hubel, D. H., & Wiesel, T. N. (1965). Binocular interaction in striate cortex of kittens reared with artificial squint. *Journal of Neurophysiology, 28,* 1041–1059. (6)

Hubel, D. H., & Wiesel, T. N. (1977). Functional architecture of macaque monkey visual cortex. *Proceedings of the Royal Society of London,* B, *198,* 1–59. (6)

Hubel, D. H., & Wiesel, T. N. (1998). Early exploration of the visual cortex. *Neuron, 20,* 401–412. (6)

Hudspeth, A. J. (1985). The cellular basis of hearing: The biophysics of hair cells. *Science, 230,* 745–752. (7)

Hugdahl, K. (1996). Brain laterality—beyond the basics. *European Psychologist, 1,* 206–220. (14)

Hughes, H. C., Nozawa, G., & Kitterle, F. (1996). Global precedence, spatial frequency channels, and the statistics of natural images. *Journal of Cognitive Neuroscience, 8,* 197–230. (6)

Hughes, J. C., & Cook, C. C. H. (1997). The efficacy of disulfiram: A review of outcome studies. *Addiction, 92,* 381–395. (15)

Hull, E. M., Du, J., Lorrain, D. S., & Matuszewich, L. (1997). Testosterone, preoptic dopamine, and copulation in male rats. *Brain Research Bulletin, 44,* 327–333. (11)

Hull, E. M., Eaton, R. C., Markowski, V. P., Moses, J., Lumley, L. A., & Loucks, J. A. (1992). Opposite influence of medial preoptic D_1 and D_2 receptors on genital reflexes: Implications for copulation. *Life Sciences, 51,* 1705–1713. (3, 11)

Hull, E. M., Eaton, R. C., Moses, J., & Lorrain, D. (1993). Copulation increases dopamine activity in the medial preoptic area of male rats. *Life Sciences, 52,* 935–940. (11)

Hultman, C. M., Öhman, A., Cnattingius, S., Wieselgren, I.-M., & Lindström, L. H. (1997). Prenatal and neonatal risk factors for schizophrenia. *British Journal of Psychiatry, 170,* 128–133. (15)

Humphrey, P. P. A., Hartig, P., & Hoyer, D. (1993). A proposed new nomenclature for 5-HT receptors. *Trends in Pharmacological Sciences, 14,* 233–236. (3)

Hunt, E., Streissguth, A. P., Kerr, B., & Carmichael-Olson, H. (1995). Mothers' alcohol consumption during pregnancy: Effects on spatial-visual reasoning in 14-year-old children. *Psychological Science, 6,* 339–342. (5)

Hunter, W. S. (1923). *General psychology* (rev. ed.). Chicago: University of Chicago Press. (4)

Huntington's Disease Collaborative Research Group. (1993). A novel gene containing a trinucleotide repeat that is expanded and unstable on Huntington's disease chromosomes. *Cell, 72,* 971–983. (8)

Hurvich, L. M., & Jameson, D. (1957). An opponent-process theory of color vision. *Psychological Review, 64,* 384–404. (6)

Husain, M., Shapiro, K., Martin, J., & Kennard, C. (1997). Abnormal temporal dynamics of visual attention in spatial neglect patients. *Nature, 385,* 154–156. (4)

Hutchison, W. D., Davis, K. D., Lozano, A. M., Tasker, R. R., & Dostrovsky, J. O. (1999). Pain-related neurons in the human cingulate cortex. *Nature Neuroscience, 2,* 403–405. (7)

Hyman, B. T., Van Hoesen, G. W., Damasio, A. R., & Barnes, C. L. (1984). Alzheimer's disease: Cell-specific pathology isolates the hippocampal formation. *Science, 225,* 1168–1170. (13)

Hynd, G. W., & Semrud-Clikeman, M. (1989). Dyslexia and brain morphology. *Psychological Bulletin, 106,* 447–482. (14)

Iggo, A., & Andres, K. H. (1982). Morphology of cutaneous receptors. *Annual Review of Neuroscience, 5,* 1–31. (7)

Ikonomidou, C., Bosch, F., Miksa, M., Bittigau, P., Vöckler, J., Dikranian, K., Tenkova, T. I., Stefovska, V., Turski, L., & Olney, J. W. (1999). Blockade of NMDA receptors and apoptotic neurodegeneration in the developing brain. *Science, 283,* 70–74. (5)

Imamura, K., Mataga, N., & Mori, K. (1992). Coding of odor molecules by mitral/tufted cells in rabbit olfactory bulb: I. Aliphatic compounds. *Journal of Neurophysiology, 68,* 1986–2002. (7)

Imperato-McGinley, J., Guerrero, L., Gautier, T., & Peterson, R. E. (1974). Steroid 5 alpha-reductase deficiency in man: An inherited form of male pseudohermaphroditism. *Science, 186,* 1213–1215. (11)

Innocenti, G. M. (1980). The primary visual pathway through the corpus callosum: Morphological and functional aspects in the cat. *Archives Italiennes de Biologie, 118,* 124–188. (14)

Innocenti, G. M., & Caminiti, R. (1980). Postnatal shaping of callosal connections from sensory areas. *Experimental Brain Research, 38,* 381–394. (14)

Inoue, A., & Sanes, J. R. (1997). Lamina-specific connectivity in the brain: Regulation by N-cadherin, neurotrophins, and glycoconjugates. *Science, 276,* 1428–1431. (5)

Inouye, S. T., & Kawamura, H. (1979). Persistence of circadian rhythmicity in a mammalian hypothalamic "island" containing the suprachiasmatic nucleus. *Proceedings of the National Academy of Sciences, U.S.A., 76,* 5962–5966. (9)

"Interview with Larry R. Squire." (1998). *Journal of Cognitive Neuroscience, 10,* 778–782. (13)

Irwin, M., Daniels, M., Risch, S. C., Bloom, E., & Weiner, H. (1988). Plasma cortisol and natural killer cell activity during bereavement. *Biological Psychiatry, 24,* 173–178. (12)

Ito, M. (1984). *The cerebellum and neural control.* New York: Raven. (8, 13)

Ito, M. (1989). Long-term depression. *Annual Review of Neuroscience, 12,* 85–102. (13)

Ivry, R. B., & Diener, H. C. (1991). Impaired velocity perception in patients with lesions of the cerebellum. *Journal of Cognitive Neuroscience, 3,* 355–366. (8)

Ivy, G. O., & Killackey, H. P. (1981). The ontogeny of the distribution of callosal projection neurons in the rat parietal cortex. *Journal of Comparative Neurology, 195,* 367–389. (14)

Iwamura, Y., Iriki, A., & Tanaka, M. (1994). Bilateral hand representation in the postcentral somatosensory cortex. *Nature, 369,* 554–556. (7)

Izquierdo, I. (1995). Role of the hippocampus, amygdala, and entorhinal cortex in memory storage and expression. In J. L. McGaugh, F. Bermúdez-Rattoni, & R. A. Prado-Alcalá (Eds.), *Plasticity in the central nervous system* (pp. 41–56). Mahwah, NJ: Lawrence Erlbaum. (13)

Izquierdo, I., & Medina, J. H. (1995). Correlation between the pharmacology of long-term potentiation and the pharmacology of memory. *Neurobiology of Learning and Memory, 63,* 19–32. (13)

Jacobs, B., Schall, M., & Scheibel, A. B. (1993). A quantitative dendritic analysis of Wernicke's area in humans: II. Gender, hemispheric, and environmental factors. *Journal of Comparataive Neurology, 327,* 97–111. (5)

Jacobs, B., & Scheibel, A. B. (1993). A quantitative dendritic analysis of Wernicke's area in humans: I. Lifespan changes. *Journal of Comparative Neurology, 327,* 83–96. (5)

Jacobs, B. L. (1987). How hallucinogenic drugs work. *American Scientist, 75,* 386–392. (3)

Jacobs, G. D., & Snyder, D. (1996). Frontal brain asymmetry predicts affective style in men. *Behavioral Neuroscience, 110,* 3–6. (15)

Jacobs, G. H. (1993). The distribution and nature of colour vision among the mammals. *Biological Reviews, 68,* 413–471. (6)

James, W. (1884). What is an emotion? *Mind, 9,* 188–205. (12)

Jancsó, G., Kiraly, E., & Jancsó-Gábor, A. (1977). Pharmacologically induced selective degeneration of chemosensitive primary sensory neurones. *Nature, 270,* 741–743. (7)

Janosik, E. H., & Davies, J. L. (1986). *Psychiatric mental health nursing.* Boston: Jones & Bartlett. (15)

Janowsky, J. S., Oviatt, S. K., & Orwell, E. S. (1994). Testosterone influences spatial cognition in older men. *Behavioral Neuroscience, 108,* 325–332. (11)

Jarrard, L. E. (1995). What does the hippocampus really do? *Behavioural Brain Research, 71,* 1–10. (13)

Jarrard, L. E., Okaichi, H., Steward, O., & Goldschmidt, R. B. (1984). On the role of hippocampal connections in the performance of place and cue tasks: Comparisons with damage to hippocampus. *Behavioral Neuroscience, 98,* 946–954. (13)

Jarrold, C., Baddeley, A. D., & Hewes, A. K. (1998). Verbal and nonverbal abilities in the Williams syndrome phenotype: Evidence for diverging developmental trajectories. *Journal of Child Psychology and Psychiatry and Allied Disciplines, 39,* 511–523. (14)

Jaskiw, G. E., & Weinberger, D. R. (1992). Dopamine and schizophrenia—a cortically corrective perspective. *Seminars in the Neurosciences, 4,* 179–188. (15)

Jentsch, J. D., Redmond, D. E., Jr., Elsworth, J. D., Taylor, J. R., Youngren, K. D., & Roth, R. H. (1997). Enduring cognitive deficits and cortical dopamine dysfunction in monkeys after long-term administration of phencyclidine. *Science, 277,* 953–955. (15)

Jerison, H. J. (1985). Animal intelligence as encephalization. *Philosophical Transactions of the Royal Society of London,* B, *308,* 21–35. (14)

Johansson, C. B., Momma, S., Clarke, D. L., Risling, M., Lendahl, U., & Frisén, J. (1999). Identification of a neural stem cell in the adult mammalian central nervous system. *Cell, 96,* 25–34. (5)

Johns, T. R., & Thesleff, S. (1961). Effects of motor inactivation on the chemical sensitivity of skeletal muscle. *Acta Physiologica Scandinavica, 51,* 136–141. (5)

Johnson, L. C. (1969). Physiological and psychological changes following total sleep deprivation. In A. Kales (Ed.), *Sleep: Physiology & pathology* (pp. 206–220). Philadelphia: Lippincott. (9)

Johnson, M. H., Posner, M. I., & Rothbart, M. K. (1991). Components of visual orienting in early infancy: Contingency learning, anticipatory looking, and disengaging. *Journal of Cognitive Neuroscience, 3,* 335–344. (6)

Johnson, M. T. V., Kipnis, A. N., Coltz, J. D., Gupta, A., Silverstein, P., Zwiebel, F., & Ebner, T. J. (1996). Effects of levodopa and viscosity on the velocity and accuracy of visually guided tracking in Parkinson's disease. *Brain, 119,* 801–813. (8)

Johnson, S. C., Pinkston, J. B., Bigler, E. D., & Blatter, D. D. (1996). Corpus callosum morphology in normal controls and traumatic brain injury: Sex differences, mechanisms of injury, and neuropsychological correlates.

Neuropsychology, 10, 408–415. (11)

Johnson, W. G., & Wildman, H. E. (1983). Influence of external and covert food stimuli on insulin secretion in obese and normal subjects. *Behavioral Neuroscience, 97,* 1025–1028. (10)

Johnston, R. E. (1998). Pheromones, the vomeronasal system, and communication. *Annals of the New York Academy of Sciences, 855,* 333–348. (7)

Jonas, P., Bischofberger, J., & Sand-kühler, J. (1998). Corelease of two fast neurotransmitters at a central synapse. *Science, 281,* 419–424. (3)

Jonas, S. (1995). Prophylactic pharma-cologic neuroprotection against focal cerebral ischemia. *Annals of the New York Academy of Sciences, 765,* 21–25. (5)

Jones, E. G., & Pons, T. P. (1998). Thalamic and brainstem contribu-tions to large-scale plasticity of primate somatosensory cortex. *Science, 282,* 1121–1125. (5)

Jones, H. S., & Oswald, I. (1968). Two cases of healthy insomnia. *Elec-troencephalography and Clinical Neurophysiology, 24,* 378–380. (9)

Jones, P. B., Rantakallio, P., Harti-kainen, A.-L., Isohanni, M., & Sipila, P. (1998). Schizophrenia as a long-term outcome of preg-nancy, delivery, and perinatal complications: A 28-year follow-up of the 1966 North Finland general population birth cohort. *American Journal of Psychiatry, 155,* 355–364. (15)

Jönsson, E. G., Nöthen, M. M., Gus-tavsson, J. P., Neidt, H., Forslund, K., Mattila-Evenden, M., Rylan-der, G., Propping, P., & Åsberg, M. (1998). Lack of association be-tween dopamine D$_4$ receptor gene and personality traits. *Psychologi-cal Medicine, 28,* 985–989. (3)

Jordan, C. L., Breedlove, M., & Arnold, A. P. (1982). Sexual di-morphism and the influence of neonatal androgen in the dorsolat-eral motor nucleus of the rat lum-bar spinal cord. *Brain Research, 249,* 309–314. (11)

Jordan, H. A. (1969). Voluntary intra-gastric feeding. *Journal of Comparative and Physiological Psychology, 68,* 498–506. (10)

Jorgensen, R. S., Johnson, B. T.,

Kolodziej, M. E., & Schreer, G. E. (1996). Elevated blood pressure and personality: A meta-analytic review. *Psychological Bulletin, 120,* 293–320. (12)

Joseph, J. A., Shukitt-Hale, B., Denisova, N. A., Prior, R. L., Cao, G., Martin, A., Taglialatela, G., & Bickford, P. C. (1998). Long-term dietary strawberry, spinach, or vitamin E supplementation re-tards the onset of age-related neu-ronal signal-transduction and cognitive behavioral deficits. *Journal of Neuroscience, 18,* 8047–8055. (13)

Jueptner, M., & Weiller, C. (1998). A review of differences between basal ganglia and cerebellar con-trol of movements as revealed by functional imaging studies. *Brain, 121,* 1437–1449. (8)

Just, M. A., Carpenter, P. A., Keller, T. A., Eddy, W. F., & Thulborn, K. R. (1996). Brain activation modulated by sentence compre-hension. *Science, 274,* 114–116. (14)

Kaas, J. H. (1983). What, if anything, is SI? Organization of first somato-sensory area of cortex. *Physiologi-cal Reviews, 63,* 206–231. (7)

Kaas, J. H. (1989). Why does the brain have so many visual areas? *Jour-nal of Cognitive Neuroscience, 1,* 121–135. (5)

Kaas, J. H., Merzenich, M. M., & Kil-lackey, H. P. (1983). The reorgani-zation of somatosensory cortex following peripheral nerve dam-age in adult and developing mam-mals. *Annual Review of Neuroscience, 6,* 325–356. (5)

Kaas, J. H., Nelson, R. J., Sur, M., Lin, C.-S., & Merzenich, M. M. (1979). Multiple representations of the body within the primary somato-sensory cortex of primates. *Science, 204,* 521–523. (4)

Kalat, J. W. (1981). *Biological psy-chology* (1st ed.). Belmont, CA: Wadsworth. (15)

Kales, A., Scharf, M. B., & Kales, J. D. (1978). Rebound insomnia: A new clinical syndrome. *Science, 201,* 1039–1041. (9)

Kamarck, T., & Jennings, J. R. (1991). Biobehavioral factors in sudden cardiac death. *Psychological Bulletin, 109,* 42–75. (12)

Kandel, E. R., & Schwartz, J. H.

(1982). Molecular biology of learn-ing: Modulation of transmitter release. *Science, 218,* 433–443. (13)

Kaplan, J. R., Muldoon, M. F., Manuck, S. B., & Mann, J. J. (1997). Assess-ing the observed relationship between low cholesterol and vio-lence-related mortality. *Annals of the New York Academy of Sci-ences, 836,* 57–80. (12)

Karmiloff-Smith, A., Tyler, L. K., Voice, K., Sims, K., Udwin, O., Howlin, P., & Davies, M. (1998). Linguistic dissociations in Williams syndrome: Evaluating receptive syntax in on-line and off-line tasks. *Neuropsychologia, 36,* 343–351. (14)

Karrer, T., & Bartoshuk, L. (1991). Capsaicin desensitization and recovery on the human tongue. *Physiology & Behavior, 49,* 757–764. (7)

Kastner, S., DeWeerd, P., Desimone, R., & Ungerleider, L. G. (1998). Mechanisms of directed attention in the human extrastriate cortex as revealed by functional MRI. *Science, 282,* 108–111. (6)

Kaye, W. H., Berrettini, W., Gwirts-man, H., & George, D. T. (1990). Altered cerebrospinal fluid neuro-peptide Y and peptide YY im-munoreactivity in anorexia and bulimia nervosa. *Archives of Gen-eral Psychiatry, 47,* 548–556. (10)

Keele, S. W., & Ivry, R. (1990). Does the cerebellum provide a common computation for diverse tasks? *Annals of the New York Academy of Sciences, 608,* 179–207. (8)

Kellar, K. J., & Stockmeier, C. A. (1986). Effects of electroconvul-sive shock and serotonin axon lesions on beta-adrenergic and serotonin-2 receptors in rat brain. *Annals of the New York Academy of Sciences, 462,* 76–90. (15)

Kempermann, G., Kuhn, H. G., & Gage, F. H. (1998). Experience-induced neurogenesis in the senescent dentate gyrus. *Journal of Neuroscience, 18,* 3206–3212. (5)

Kendler, K. S. (1983). Overview: A current perspective on twin stud-ies of schizophrenia. *American Journal of Psychiatry, 140,* 1413–1425. (15)

Kendler, K. S., Gallagher, T. J., Abel-son, J. M., & Kessler, R. C. (1996).

Lifetime prevalence, demographic risk factors, and diagnostic validity of nonaffective psychosis as assessed in a U.S. community sample. *Archives of General Psychiatry, 53,* 1022–1031. (15)

Kendler, K. S., Gardner, C. O., & Prescott, C. A. (1999). Clinical characteristics of major depression that predict risk of depression in relatives. *Archives of General Psychiatry, 56,* 322–327. (15)

Kendler, K. S., Karkowski, L. M., & Walsh, D. (1998). The structure of psychosis. *Archives of General Psychiatry, 55,* 492–499. (15)

Kennard, C., Lawden, M., Morland, A. B., & Ruddock, K. H. (1995). Colour identification and colour constancy are impaired in a patient with incomplete achromatopsia associated with prestriate cortical lesions. *Proceedings of the Royal Society of London,* B, *260,* 169–175. (6)

Kennard, M. A. (1938). Reorganization of motor function in the cerebral cortex of monkeys deprived of motor and premotor areas in infancy. *Journal of Neurophysiology, 1,* 477–496. (5)

Kerr, D. S., & Abraham, W. C. (1995). Cooperative interactions among afferents govern the induction of homosynaptic long-term depression in the hippocampus. *Proceedings of the National Academy of Sciences (U.S.A.), 92,* 11637–11641. (13)

Kesslak, J. P., So, V., Choi, J., Cotman, C. W., & Gomez-Pinilla, F. (1998). Learning upregulates brain-derived neurotrophic factor messenger ribonucleic acid: A mechanism to facilitate encoding and circuit maintenance? *Behavioral Neuroscience, 112,* 1012–1019. (5)

Kessler, R. C., McGonagle, K. A., Zhao, S., Nelson, C. B., Hughes, M., Eshleman, S., Wittchen, H.-U., & Kendler, K. S. (1994). Lifetime and 12-month prevalence of *DSM-III-R* psychiatric disorders in the United States. *Archives of General Psychiatry, 51,* 8–19. (15)

Kety, S. S. (1977). Genetic aspects of schizophrenia: Observations on the biological and adoptive relatives of adoptees who became schizophrenic. In E. S. Gershon, R. H. Belmaker, S. S. Kety, &

M. Rosenbaum (Eds.), *The impact of biology on modern psychiatry* (pp. 195–206). New York: Spectum Publication (15)

Kety, S. S., Wender, P. H., Jacobson, B., Ingraham, L. J., Jansson, L., Faber, B., & Kinney, D. K. (1994). Mental illness in the biological and adoptive relatives of schizophrenic adoptees. *Archives of General Psychiatry, 51,* 442–455. (15)

Keverne, E. B. (1999). The vomeronasal organ. *Science, 286,* 716–720. (7)

Kiecolt-Glaser, J. K., & Glaser, R. (1993). Mind and immunity. In D. Goleman & J. Gurin (Eds.), *Mind/body medicine* (pp. 39–61). Yonkers, NY: Consumer Reports Books. (12)

Killackey, H. P. (1990). Neocortical expansion: An attempt toward relating phylogeny and ontogeny. *Journal of Cognitive Neuroscience, 2,* 1–17. (5)

Killackey, H. P., & Chalupa, L. M. (1986). Ontogenetic change in the distribution of callosal projection neurons in the postcentral gyrus of the fetal rhesus monkey. *Journal of Comparative Neurology, 244,* 331–348. (14)

Killeffer, F. A., & Stern, W. E. (1970). Chronic effects of hypothalamic injury. *Archives of Neurology, 22,* 419–429. (10)

Kim, Y.-H., Park, J.-H., Hong, S. H., & Koh, J.-Y. (1999). Nonproteolytic neuroprotection by human recombinant tissue plasminogen activator. *Science, 284,* 647–650. (5)

Kimura, D., & Hampson, E. (1994). Cognitive pattern in men and women is influenced by fluctuations in sex hormones. *Current Directions in Psychological Science, 3,* 57–61. (11)

Kindon, H. A., Baum, M. J., & Paredes, R. J. (1996). Medial preoptic/anterior hypothalamic lesions induce a female-typical profile of sexual partner preference in male ferrets. *Hormones and Behavior, 30,* 514–527. (11)

King, B. M., Smith, R. L., & Frohman, L. A. (1984). Hyperinsulinemia in rats with ventromedial hypothalamic lesions: Role of hyperphagia. *Behavioral Neuroscience, 98,* 152–155. (10)

King, C.-L., & Wilson, A. C. (1975).

Evolution at two levels in humans and chimpanzees. Science, 188, 107–116. (14)

Kingstone, A., & Gazzaniga, M. S. (1995). Subcortical transfer of higher order information: More illusory than real? *Neuropsychology, 9,* 321–328. (14)

Kinnamon, J. C. (1987). Organization and innervation of taste buds. In T. E. Finger & W. L. Silver (Eds.), *Neurobiology of taste and smell* (pp. 277–297). New York: John Wiley. (7)

Kinomura, S., Larsson, J., Gulyás, B., & Roland, P. E. (1996). Activation by attention of the human reticular formation and thalamic intralaminar nuclei. *Science, 271,* 512–515. (9)

Kinsbourne, M., & McMurray, J. (1975). The effect of cerebral dominance on time sharing between speaking and tapping by preschool children. *Child Development, 46,* 240–242. (14)

Kinsey, A. C., Pomeroy, W. B., & Martin, C. E. (1948). *Sexual behavior in the human male.* Philadelphia: Saunders. (11)

Kinsey, A. C., Pomeroy, W. B., Martin, C. E., & Gebhard, P. H. (1953). *Sexual behavior in the human female.* Philadelphia: Saunders. (11)

Kiriakakis, V., Bhatia, K. P., Quinn, N. P., & Marsden, C. D. (1998). The natural history of tardive dyskinesia: A long-term follow-up study of 107 cases. *Brain, 121,* 2053–2066. (15)

Kirkpatrick, P. J., Smielewski, P., Czosnyka, M., Menon, D. K., & Pickard, J. D. (1995). Near-infrared spectroscopy in patients with head injury. *Journal of Neurosurgery, 83,* 963–970. (5)

Kirkwood, A., Lee, H.-K., & Bear, M. F. (1995). Co-regulation of long-term potentiation and experience-dependent synaptic plasticity in visual cortex by age and experience. *Nature, 375,* 328–331. (6)

Kitada, T., Asakawa, S., Hattori, N., Matsumine, H., Yamamura, Y., Minoshima, S., Yokochi, M., Mizuno, Y., & Shimizu, N. (1998). Mutations in the *parkin* gene cause autosomal recessive juvenile parkinsonism. *Nature, 392,* 605–608. (8)

Klein, D. F. (1993). False suffocation alarms, spontaneous panics, and related conditions. *Archives of General Psychiatry, 50,* 306–317. (12)

Kleinschmidt, A., Bear, M. F., & Singer, W. (1987). Blockade of "NMDA" receptors disrupts experience-dependent plasticity of kitten striate cortex. *Science, 238,* 355–358. (13)

Kleitman, N. (1963). *Sleep and wakefulness* (rev. ed.). Chicago: University of Chicago Press. (9)

Klerman, G. L. (1975). Relationships between preclinical testing and therapeutic evaluation of antidepressive drugs: The importance of new animal models for theory and practice. In A. Sudilovsky, S. Gershon, & B. Beer (Eds.), *Predictability in psychopharmacology* (pp. 159–178). New York: Raven. (15)

Kluger, M. J. (1991). Fever: Role of pyrogens and cryogens. *Physiological Reviews, 71,* 93–127. (10)

Klüver, H., & Bucy, P. C. (1939). Preliminary analysis of functions of the temporal lobes in monkeys. *Archives of Neurology and Psychiatry, 42,* 979–1000. (4)

Knight, G. P., Fabes, R. A., & Higgins, D. A. (1996). Concerns about drawing causal inferences from meta-analyses: An example in the study of gender differences in aggression. *Psychological Bulletin, 119,* 410–421. (12)

Knoll, J. (1993). The pharmacological basis of the beneficial effects of (−) deprenyl (selegiline) in Parkinson's and Alzheimer's diseases. *Journal of Neural Transmission,* (Suppl. 40), 69–91. (8)

Kodama, J., Fukushima, M., & Sakata, T. (1978). Impaired taste discrimination against quinine following chronic administration of theophylline in rats. *Physiology & Behavior, 20,* 151–155. (7)

Koepp, M. J., Gunn, R. N., Lawrence, A. D., Cunningham, V. J., Dagher, A., Jones, T., Brooks, D. J., Bench, C. J., & Grasby, P. M. (1998). Evidence for striatal dopamine release during a video game. *Nature, 393,* 266–268. (3)

Kolb, B. (1995). *Brain plasticity and behavior.* Mahwah, NJ: Lawrence Erlbaum. (5)

Kolb, B., Côté, S., Ribeiro-da-Silva, A., & Cuello, A. C. (1997). Nerve growth factor treatment prevents dendritic atrophy and promotes recovery of function after cortical injury. *Neuroscience, 76,* 1139–1151. (8)

Kolb, B., Gorny, G., Côté, S., Ribeiro-da-Silva, A., & Cuello, A. C. (1997). Nerve growth factor stimulates growth of cortical pyramidal neurons in young adult rats. *Brain Research, 751,* 289–294. (5)

Kolb, B., & Holmes, C. (1983). Neonatal motor cortex lesions in the rat: Absence of sparing of motor behaviors and impaired spatial learning concurrent with abnormal cerebral morphogenesis. *Behavioral Neuroscience, 97,* 697–709. (5)

Kolb, B., Sutherland, R. J., & Whishaw, I. Q. (1983). Abnormalities in cortical and subcortical morphology after neonatal neocortical lesions in rats. *Experimental Neurology, 79,* 223–244. (5)

Komisaruk, B. R., Adler, N. T., & Hutchison, J. (1972). Genital sensory field: Enlargement by estrogen treatment in female rats. *Science, 178,* 1295–1298. (11)

Konishi, M. (1995). Neural mechanisms of auditory image formation. In M. S. Gazzaniga (Ed.), *The cognitive neurosciences* (pp. 269–277). Cambridge, MA: MIT Press. (7)

Konishi, S., Nakajima, K., Uchida, I., Kameyama, M., Nakahara, K., Sekihara, K., & Miyashita, Y. (1998). Transient activation of inferior prefrontal cortex during cognitive set shifting. *Nature Neuroscience, 1,* 80–84. (15)

Kornhuber, H. H. (1974). Cerebral cortex, cerebellum, and basal ganglia: An introduction to their motor functions. In F. O. Schmitt & F. G. Worden (Eds.), *The neurosciences: Third study program* (pp. 267–280). Cambridge, MA: MIT Press. (8)

Kosslyn, S. M., Pascual-Leone, A., Felician, O., Camposano, S., Kennan, J. P., Thompson, W. L., Ganis, G., Sukel, K. E., & Alpert, N. M. (1999). The role of area 17 in visual imagery: Convergent evidence from PET and rTMS. *Science, 284,* 167–170. (6)

Kostrzewa, R. M. (1995). Dopamine receptor supersensitivity. *Neuroscience and Biobehavioral Reviews, 19,* 1–17. (5)

Kraly, F. S. (1990). Drinking elicited by eating. *Progress in Psychobiology and Physiological Psychology, 14,* 67–133. (10)

Kraly, F. S., Kim, Y.-M., Dunham, L. M., & Tribuzio, R. A. (1995). Drinking after intragastric NaCl without increase in systemic plasma osmolality in rats. *American Journal of Physiology, 269,* R1085–R1092. (10)

Kräuchi, K., Cajochen, C., Werth, E., & Wirz-Justice, A. (1999). Warm feet promote the rapid onset of sleep. *Nature, 401,* 36–37. (9)

Kringlen, E., & Cramer, G. (1989). Offspring of monozygotic twins discordant for schizophrenia. *Archives of General Psychiatry, 46,* 873–877. (15)

Kristensen, P., Judge, M. E., Thim, L., Ribel, U., Christjansen, K. N., Wulff, B. S., Clausen, J. T., Jensen, P. B., Madsen, O. D., Vrang, N., Larsen, P. J., & Hastrup, S. (1998). Hypothalamic CART is a new anorectic peptide regulated by leptin. *Nature, 393,* 72–76. (10)

Kropotov, J. D., & Etlinger, S. C. (1999). Selection of actions in the basal ganglia-thalamocortical circuits: Review and model. *International Journal of Psychophysiology, 31,* 197–217. (8)

Krueger, B., & Neff, J. (1995, January 29). As killer dies, 2 women find diverging paths to peace. *News & Observer* (Raleigh, NC), pp. 1A, 4A. (12)

Kruesi, M. J. P., Hibbs, E. D., Zahn, T. P., Keysor, C. S., Hamburger, S. D., Bartko, J. J., & Rapoport, J. L. (1992). A 2-year prospective follow-up of children and adolescents with disruptive behavior disorders. *Archives of General Psychiatry, 49,* 429–435. (12)

Krupa, D. J., Thompson, J. K., & Thompson, R. F. (1993). Localization of a memory trace in the mammalian brain. *Science, 260,* 989–991. (13)

Kupfermann, I., Castellucci, V., Pinsker, H., & Kandel, E. (1970). Neuronal correlates of habituation and dishabituation of the gill withdrawal reflex in *Aplysia. Science, 167,* 1743–1745. (13)

Kupsch, A., Oertel, W. H., Earl, C. D.,

& Sautter, J. (1995). Neuronal transplantation and neurotrophic factors in the treatment of Parkinson's disease—update February 1995. *Journal of Neural Transmission* (Suppl. 46), 193–207. (8)

Kurahashi, T., Lowe, G., & Gold, G. H. (1994). Suppression of odorant responses by odorants in olfactory receptor cells. *Science, 265,* 118–120. (7)

Kurihara, K., & Kashiwayanagi, M. (1998). Introductory remarks on umami taste. *Annals of the New York Academy of Sciences, 855,* 393–397. (7)

Kuypers, H. G. J. M. (1989). Motor system organization. In G. Adelman (Ed.), *Neuroscience year* (pp. 107–110). Boston: Birkhäuser. (8)

Kwon, J. S., McCarley, R. W., Hirayasu, Y., Anderson, J. E., Fischer, I. A., Kikinis, R., Jolesz, F. A., & Shenton, M. E. (1999). Left planum temporale volume reduction in schizophrenia. *Archives of General Psychiatry, 56,* 142–148. (15)

LaBar, K. S., & Phelps, E. A. (1998). Arousal-mediated memory consolidation: Role of the medial temporal lobe in humans. *Psychological Science, 9,* 490–493. (13)

Laburn, H. P. (1996). How does the fetus cope with thermal challenges? *News in Physiological Sciences, 11,* 96–100. (15)

Lacreuse, A., Herndon, J. G., Killiany, R. J., Rosene, D. L., & Moss, M. B. (1999). Spatial cognition in rhesus monkeys: Male superiority declines with age. *Hormones and Behavior, 36,* 70–76. (11)

Lague, L., Raiguel, S., & Orban, G. A. (1993). Speed and direction selectivity of macaque middle temporal neurons. *Journal of Neurophysiology, 69,* 19–39. (6)

LaHoste, G. J., & Marshall, J. F. (1989). Non-additivity of D_2 receptor proliferation induced by dopamine denervation and chronic selective antagonist administration: Evidence from quantitative autoradiography indicates a single mechanism of action. *Brain Research, 502,* 223–232. (5)

Lam, H.-M., Chiu, J., Hsieh, M.-H., Meisel, L., Oliveira, I. C., Shin, M., & Coruzzi, G. (1998). Gluta-mate-receptor genes in plants. *Nature, 396,* 125–126. (3)

LaMantia, A.-S., & Purves, D. (1989). Development of glomerular pattern visualized in the olfactory bulbs of living mice. *Nature, 341,* 646–649. (5)

Lamb, T. D., & Pugh, E. N., Jr. (1990). Physiology of transduction and adaptation in rod and cone photoreceptors. *Seminars in the Neurosciences, 2,* 3–13. (6)

Land, E. H., Hubel, D. H., Livingstone, M. S., Perry, S. H., & Burns, M. M. (1983). Colour-generating interactions across the corpus callosum. *Nature, 303,* 616–618. (6)

Landis, D. M. D. (1987). Initial junctions between developing parallel fibers and Purkinje cells are different from mature synaptic junctions. *Journal of Comparative Neurology, 260,* 513–525. (3)

Lang, P. J. (1994). The varieties of emotional experience: A meditation on James-Lange theory. *Psychological Review, 101,* 211–221. (12)

Lang, R. A., Flor-Henry, P., & Frenzel, R. R. (1990). Sex hormone profiles in pedophilic and incestuous men. *Annals of Sex Research, 3,* 59–74. (11)

Lashley, K. S. (1929). *Brain mechanisms and intelligence.* Chicago: University of Chicago Press. (4, 13)

Lashley, K. S. (1930). Basic neural mechanisms in behavior. *Psychological Review, 37,* 1–24. (4, 13) (inside cover)

Lashley, K. S. (1950). In search of the engram. *Symposia of the Society for Experimental Biology, 4,* 454–482. (4, 13)

Lashley, K. S. (1951). The problem of serial order in behavior. In L. A. Jeffress (Ed.), *Cerebral mechanisms in behavior* (pp. 112–136). New York: John Wiley & Sons. (8)

Lassonde, M., Bryden, M. P., & Demers, P. (1990). The corpus callosum and cerebral speech lateralization. *Brain and Language, 38,* 195–206. (14)

Lauber, M. E., Sarasin, A., & Lichtensteiger, W. (1997). Transient sex differences of aromatase (CYP19) mRNA expression in the developing rat brain. *Neuroendocrinology, 66,* 173–180. (11)

Laurent, J.-P., Cespuglio, R., & Jouvet, M. (1974). Dèlimitation des voies ascendantes de l'activité ponto-géniculo-occipitale chez le chat [Demarcation of the ascending paths of ponto-geniculo-occipital activity in the cat]. *Brain Research, 65,* 29–52. (9)

Lavin, J. H., Wittert, G., Sun, W.-M., Horowitz, M., Morley, J. E., & Read, N. W. (1996). Appetite regulation by carbohydrate: Role of blood glucose and gastrointestinal hormones. *American Journal of Physiology, 271,* E209–E214. (10)

LeDoux, J. (1996). *The emotional brain.* New York: Simon & Schuster. (12)

LeDoux, J. E., Iwata, J., Cicchetti, P., & Reis, D. J. (1988). Different projections of the central amygdaloid nucleus mediate autonomic and behavioral correlates of conditioned fear. *Journal of Neuroscience, 8,* 2517–2529. (12)

Lee, J.-M., Zipfel, G. J., & Choi, D. W. (1999). The changing landscape of ischaemic brain injury mechanisms. *Nature, 399*(Suppl.), A7–A14. (5)

Lee, Y., Walker, D., & Davis, M. (1996). Lack of a temporal gradient of retrograde amnesia following NMDA-induced lesions of the basolateral amygdala assessed with the fear-potentiated startle paradigm. *Behavioral Neuroscience, 110,* 836–839. (12)

Leff, J., Wig, N. N., Chosh, A., Bedi, H., Menon, D. K., Kuipers, L., Korten, A., Ernberg, G., Day, R., Sartorius, N., & Jablensky, A. (1987). Expressed emotion and schizophrenia in North India: III. Influence of relatives' expressed emotion on the course of schizophrenia in Changigarh. *British Journal of Psychiatry, 151,* 166–173. (15)

Lehman, C. D., Bartoshuk, L. M., Catalanotto, F. C., Kveton, J. F., & Lowlicht, R. A. (1995). Effect of anesthesia of the chorda tympani nerve on taste perception in humans. *Physiology & Behavior, 57,* 943–951. (7)

Lehrman, D. S. (1964). The reproductive behavior of ring doves. *Scientific American, 211*(5), 48–54. (11)

Leibowitz, S. F., & Alexander, J. T. (1991). Analysis of neuropeptide Y-induced feeding: Dissociation of Y_1 and Y_2 receptor effects on natural meal patterns. *Peptides, 12,* 1251–1260. (10)

Leibowitz, S. F., Hammer, N. J., & Chang, K. (1981). Hypothalamic paraventricular nucleus lesions produce overeating and obesity in the rat. *Physiology & Behavior, 27,* 1031–1040. (10)

LeMagnen, J. (1981). The metabolic basis of dual periodicity of feeding in rats. *Behavioral and Brain Sciences, 4,* 561–607. (10)

Lenhart, R. E., & Katkin, E. S. (1986). Psychophysiological evidence for cerebral laterality effects in a high-risk sample of students with subsyndromal bipolar depressive disorder. *American Journal of Psychiatry, 143,* 602–607. (15)

Lenneberg, E. H. (1969). On explaining language. *Science, 164,* 635–643. (14)

Lennie, P. (1998). Single units and visual cortical organization. *Perception, 27,* 889–935. (5)

Lentz, T. L., Burrage, T. G., Smith, A. L., Crick, J., & Tignor, G. H. (1982). Is the acetylcholine receptor a rabies virus receptor? *Science, 215,* 182–184. (12)

Leonard, C. M., Lombardino, L. J., Mercado, L. R., Browd, S. R., Breier, J. I., & Agee, O. F. (1996). Cerebral asymmetry and cognitive development in children: A magnetic resonance imaging study. *Psychological Science, 7,* 89–95. (14)

Leopold, D. A., & Logothetis, N. K. (1996). Activity changes in early visual cortex reflect monkeys' percepts during binocular rivalry. *Nature, 379,* 549–553. (6)

Lerer, B., & Shapira, B. (1986). Neurochemical mechanisms of mood stabilization. *Annals of the New York Academy of Sciences, 462,* 367–375. (15)

Lesse, S. (1984). Psychosurgery. *American Journal of Psychotherapy, 38,* 224–228. (4)

Lester, B. M., LaGasse, L. L., & Seifer, R. (1998). Cocaine exposure and children: The meaning of subtle effects. *Science, 282,* 633–634. (5)

Lettvin, J. Y., Maturana, H. R., McCulloch, W. S., & Pitts, W. H. (1959). What the frog's eye tells the frog's brain. *Proceedings of the Institute of Radio Engineers, 47,* 1940–1951. (7)

LeVay, S. (1991). A difference in hypothalamic structure between heterosexual and homosexual men. *Science, 253,* 1034–1037. (11)

LeVay, S. (1993). *The sexual brain.* Cambridge, MA: MIT Press. (11)

Levenson, R. W. (1992). Autonomic nervous system differences among emotions. *Psychological Science, 3,* 23–27. (12)

Levenson, R. W., Oyama, O. N., & Meek, P. S. (1987). Greater reinforcement from alcohol for those at risk: Parental risk, personality risk, and sex. *Journal of Abnormal Psychology, 96,* 242–253. (15)

LeVere, N. D., & LeVere, T. E. (1982). Recovery of function after brain damage: Support for the compensation theory of the behavioral deficit. *Physiological Psychology, 10,* 165–174. (5)

LeVere, T. E. (1975). Neural stability, sparing and behavioral recovery following brain damage. *Psychological Review, 82,* 344–358. (5)

LeVere, T. E. (1980). Recovery of function after brain damage: A theory of the behavioral deficit. *Physiological Psychology, 8,* 297–308. (5)

LeVere, T. E. (1993). Recovery of function after brain damage: The effects of nimodipine on the chronic behavioral deficit. *Psychobiology, 21,* 125–129. (5)

LeVere, T. E., Ford, K., & Sandin, M. (1992). Recovery of function after brain damage: The benefits of diets supplemented with the calcium channel blocker nimodipine. *Psychobiology, 20,* 219–222. (5)

LeVere, T. E., & Morlock, G. W. (1973). Nature of visual recovery following posterior neodecortication in the hooded rat. *Journal of Comparative and Physiological Psychology, 83,* 62–67. (5)

Levi-Montalcini, R. (1987). The nerve growth factor 35 years later. *Science, 237,* 1154–1162. (5)

Levi-Montalcini, R. (1988). *In praise of imperfection.* New York: Basic books. (5)

Levin, E. D., & Rose, J. E. (1995). Acute and chronic nicotine interactions with dopamine systems and working memory performance. *Annals of the New York Academy of Sciences, 757,* 245–252. (3)

Levine, B., Hardwick, J. M., Trapp, B. D., Crawford, T. O., Bollinger, R. C., & Griffin, D. E. (1991). Antibody-mediated clearance of alphavirus infection from neurons. *Science, 254,* 856–860. (2)

Levine, J. D., Fields, H. L., & Basbaum, A. I. (1993). Peptides and the primary afferent nociceptor. *Journal of Neuroscience, 13,* 2273–2286. (7)

Levinson, D. F., Mahtani, M. M., Nancarrow, D. J., Brown, D. M., Kruglyak, L., Kirby, A., Hayward, N. K., Crowe, R. R., Andreasen, N. C., Black, D. W., Silverman, J. M., Endicott, J., Sharpe, L., Mohs, R. C., Siever, L. J., Walters, M. K., Lennon, D. P., Jones, H. L., Nertney, D. A., Daly, M. J., Gladis, M., & Mowry, B. J. (1998). Genome scan of schizophrenia. *American Journal of Psychiatry, 155,* 741–750. (15)

Levitin, D. J., & Bellugi, U. (1998). Musical abilities in individuals with Williams syndrome. *Music Perception, 15,* 357–389. (14)

Levitsky, D. A., & Strupp, B. J. (1995). Malnutrition and the brain: Changing concepts, changing concerns. *Journal of Nutrition, 125*(Suppl. 8), S2212–S2220. (5)

Levitt, R. A. (1975). *Psychopharmacology.* Washington, DC: Hemisphere. (15)

Levitt-Gilmour, T. A., & Salpeter, M. M. (1986). Gradient of extrajunctional acetylcholine receptors early after denervation of mammalian muscle. *Journal of Neuroscience, 6,* 1606–1612. (5)

Levitzki, A. (1988). From epinephrine to cyclic AMP. *Science, 241,* 800–806. (3)

Levivier, M., Przedborski, S., Bencsics, C., & Kang, U. J. (1995). Intrastriatal implantation of fibroblasts genetically engineered to produce brain-derived neurotrophic factor prevents degeneration of dopaminergic neurons in a rat model of Parkinson's disease. *Journal of Neuroscience, 15,* 7810–7820. (5)

Levy, J. (1983). Language, cognition, and the right hemisphere: A response to Gazzaniga. *American Psychologist, 38,* 538–541. (14)

Levy, J., Heller, W., Banich, M. T., & Burton, L. A. (1983). Asymmetry of perception in free viewing of chimeric faces. *Brain and Cognition, 2,* 404–419. (14)

Levy, L. M., Henkin, R. I., Hutter, A., Lin, C. S., Martins, D., & Shellinger, D. (1997). Functional MRI of human olfaction. *Journal of Computer Assisted Tomography, 21,* 849–856. (7)

Lewis, D. A. (1997). Development of the prefrontal cortex during adolescence: Insights into vulnerable neural circuits in schizophrenia. *Neuropsychopharmacology, 16,* 385–398. (15)

Lewis, V. G., Money, J., & Epstein, R. (1968). Concordance of verbal and nonverbal ability in the adrenogenital syndrome. *Johns Hopkins Medical Journal, 122,* 192–195. (11)

Lewy, A. J., Bauer, V. K., Cutler, N. L., Sack, R. L., Ahmed, S., Thomas, K. H., Blood, M. L., & Jackson, J. M. L. (1998). Morning vs. evening light treatment of patients with winter depression. *Archives of General Psychiatry, 55,* 890–896. (15)

Li, S.-H., Cheng, A. L., Li, H., & Li, X.-J. (1999). Cellular defects and altered gene expression in PC12 cells stably expressing mutant huntingtin. *Journal of Neuroscience, 19,* 5159–5172. (8)

Li, Y., Field, P. M., & Raisman, G. (1998). Regeneration of adult rat corticospinal axons induced by transplanted olfactory ensheathing cells. *Journal of Neuroscience, 18,* 10514–10524. (5)

Licinio, J., Wong, M. L., & Gold, P. W. (1996). The hypothalamic-pituitary-adrenal axis in anorexia nervosa. *Psychiatry Research, 62,* 75–83. (10)

Liddle, P. F. (1997). Dynamic neuroimaging with PET, SPET or fMRI. *International Review of Psychiatry, 9,* 331–337. (4)

Lilenfeld, L. R., Kaye, W. H., Greeno, C. G., Merikangas, K. R., Plotnicov, K., Pollice, C., Rao, R., Strober, M., Bulik, C. M., & Nagy, L. (1998). A controlled family study of anorexia nervosa and bulimia nervosa. *Archives of General Psychiatry, 55,* 603–610. (10)

Lim, K. O., Adalsteinsson, E., Spielman, D., Sullivan, E. V., Rosenbloom, M. J., & Pfefferbaum, A. (1998). Proton magnetic resonance spectroscopic imaging of cortical gray and white matter in schizophrenia. *Archives of General Psychiatry, 55,* 346–352. (15)

Lin, J.-S., Hou, Y., Sakai, K., & Jouvet, M. (1996). Histaminergic descending inputs to the mesopontine tegmentum and their role in the control of cortical activation and wakefulness in the cat. *Journal of Neuroscience, 16,* 1523–1537. (9)

Lindberg, N. O., Coburn, C., & Stricker, E. M. (1984). Increased feeding by rats after subdiabetogenic streptozotocin treatment: A role for insulin in satiety. *Behavioral Neuroscience, 98,* 138–145. (10)

Lindemann, B. (1996). Taste reception. *Physiological Reviews, 76,* 719–766. (7)

Lindsay, P. H., & Norman, D. A. (1972). *Human information processing.* New York: Academic Press. (7)

Lindstrom, J. (1979). Autoimmune response to acetylcholine receptors in myasthenia gravis and its animal model. *Advances in Immunology, 27,* 1–50. (3)

Lindvall, O. (1998). Update on fetal transplantation: The Swedish experience. *Movement Disorders, 13*(Suppl. 1), 83–87. (8)

Liu, G., & Tsien, R. W. (1995). Properties of synaptic transmission at single hippocampal synaptic boutons. *Nature, 375,* 404–408. (3)

Livesey, F. J., O'Brien, J. A., Li, M., Smith, A. G., Murphy, L. J., & Hunt, S. P. (1997). A Schwann cell mitogen accompanying regeneration of motor neurons. *Nature, 390,* 614–618. (5)

Livingstone, M. S. (1988, January). Art, illusion and the visual system. *Scientific American, 258*(1), 78–85. (6)

Livingstone, M. S., & Hubel, D. (1988). Segregation of form, color, movement, and depth: Anatomy, physiology, and perception. *Science, 240,* 740–749. (6)

Livingstone, M. S., Rosen, G. D., Drislane, F. W., & Galaburda, A. M. (1991). Physiological and anatomical evidence for a magnocellular defect in developmental dyslexia. *Proceedings of the National Academy of Sciences (U.S.A.), 88,* 7943–7947. (14)

Ljungberg, M. C., Stern, G., & Wilkin, G. P. (1999). Survival of genetically engineered, adult-derived rat astrocytes grafted into the 6-hydroxydopamine lesioned adult rat striatum. *Brain Research, 816,* 29–37. (8)

Lockwood, A. H., Salvi, R. J., Coad, M. L., Towsley, M. L., Wack, D. S., & Murphy, B. W. (1998). The functional neuroanatomy of tinnitus: Evidence for limbic system links and neural plasticity. *Neurology, 50,* 114–120. (7)

Loewenstein, W. R. (1960, August). Biological transducers. *Scientific American, 203*(2), 98–108. (7)

Loewi, O. (1960). An autobiographic sketch. *Perspectives in Biology, 4,* 3–25. (3)

Logan, C. G., & Grafton, S. T. (1995). Functional anatomy of human eyeblink conditioning determined with regional cerebral glucose metabolism and positron-emission tomography. *Proceedings of the National Academy of Sciences (U.S.A.), 92,* 7500–7504. (13)

London, E. D., Cascella, N. G., Wong, D. F., Phillips, R. L., Dannals, R. F., Links, J. M., Herning, R., Grayson, R., Jaffe, J. H., & Wagner, H. N. (1990). Cocaine-induced reduction of glucose utilization in human brain. *Archives of General Psychiatry, 47,* 567–574. (3)

Lord, G. M., Matarese, G., Howard, J. K., Baker, R. J., Bloom, S. R., & Lechler, R. I. (1998). Leptin modulates the T-cell immune response and reverses starvation-induced immunosuppression. *Nature, 394,* 897–901. (10)

Lorincz, E., & Fabre-Thorpe, M. (1997). Effect of pairing red nucleus and motor thalamic lesions on reaching toward moving targets in cats. *Behavioral Neuroscience, 111,* 892–907. (8)

Loring, D. W., Meador, K. J., Lee, G. P., Murro, A. M., Smith, J. R., Flanigin, H. F., Gallagher, B. B., & King, D. W. (1990). Cerebral language lateralization: Evidence from intracarotid amobarbital testing. *Neuropsychologia, 28,* 831–838. (14)

Lott, I. T. (1982). Down's syndrome, aging, and Alzheimer's disease: A clinical review. *Annals of the New York Academy of Sciences, 396,* 15–27. (13)

Lotze, M., Grodd, W., Birbaumer, N., Erb, M., Huse, E., & Flor, H. (1999). Does use of a myoelectric prosthesis prevent cortical reorganization and phantom limb pain? *Nature Neuroscience, 2,* 501–502. (5)

Lowe, J., & Carroll, D. (1985). The effects of spinal injury on the intensity of emotional experience. *British Journal of Clinical Psychology, 24,* 135–136. (12)

Lucas, R. J., Freedman, M. S., Muñoz, M., Garcia-Fernández, J.-M., & Foster, R. G. (1999). Regulation of the mammalian pineal by non-rod, non-cone ocular photoreceptors. *Science, 284,* 505–507. (9)

Lumer, E. D., Friston, K. J., & Rees, G. (1998). Neural correlates of perceptual rivalry in the human brain. *Science, 280,* 1930–1934. (6)

Lund, R. D., Lund, J. S., & Wise, R. P. (1974). The organization of the retinal projection to the dorsal lateral geniculate nucleus in pigmented and albino rats. *Journal of Comparative Neurology, 158,* 383–404. (6)

Lundy-Ekman, L., Ivry, R., Keele, S., & Woollacott, M. (1991). Timing and force control deficits in clumsy children. *Journal of Cognitive Neuroscience, 3,* 367–376. (8)

Lupien, S. J., de Leon, M., de Santi, S., Convit, A., Tarshish, C., Nair, N. P. V., Thakur, M., McEwen, B. S., Hauger, R. L., & Meaney, M. J. (1998). Cortisol levels during human aging predict hippocampal atrophy and memory deficits. *Nature Neuroscience, 1,* 69–73. (12)

Lykken, D. T., McGue, M., Tellegen, A., & Bouchard, T. J. (1992). Emergenesis: Genetic traits that may not run in families. *American Psychologist, 47,* 1565–1577. (1)

Lyman, C. P., O'Brien, R. C., Greene, G. C., & Papafrangos, E. D. (1981). Hibernation and longevity in the Turkish hamster *Mesocricetus brandti. Science, 212,* 668–670. (9)

Lyons, M. J., Eisen, S. A., Goldberg, J., True, W., Lin, N., Meyer, J. M., Toomey, R., Faraone, S. V., Merla-Ramos, M., & Tsuang, M. T. (1998). A registry-based twin study of depression in men. *Archives of General Psychiatry, 55,* 468–472. (15)

Lyons, M. J., True, W. R., Eisen, S. A., Goldberg, J., Meyer, J. M., Faraone, S. V., Eaves, L. J., & Tsuang, M. T. (1995). Differential heritability of adult and juvenile antisocial traits. *Archives of General Psychiatry, 52,* 906–915. (12)

Lytle, L. D., Messing, R. B., Fisher, L., & Phebus, L. (1975). Effects of long-term corn consumption on brain serotonin and the response to electric shock. *Science, 190,* 692–694. (12)

Macdonald, R. L., Weddle, M. G., & Gross, R. A. (1986). Benzodiazepine, β-carboline, and barbiturate actions on GABA responses. *Advances in Biochemical Psychopharmacology, 41,* 67–78. (12)

MacFarlane, J. G., Cleghorn, J. M., & Brown, G. M. (1985a). Melatonin and core temperature rhythms in chronic insomnia. In G. M. Brown & S. D. Wainwright (Eds.), *The pineal gland: Endocrine aspects* (pp. 301–306). New York: Pergamon. (9)

MacFarlane, J. G., Cleghorn, J. M., & Brown, G. M. (1985b, September). *Circadian rhythms in chronic insomnia.* Paper presented at the 4th World Congress of *Biological Psychiatry,* Philadelphia. (9)

MacLean, P. D. (1949). Psychosomatic disease and the "visceral brain": Recent developments bearing on the Papez theory of emotion. *Psychosomatic Medicine, 11,* 338–353. (12)

MacLusky, N. J., & Naftolin, F. (1981). Sexual differentiation of the central nervous system. *Science, 211,* 1294–1303. (11)

Macphail, E. M. (1985). Vertebrate intelligence: The null hypothesis. *Philosophical Transactions of the Royal Society of London*, B, *308,* 37–51. (14)

Madden, P. A. F., Heath, A. C., Rosenthal, N. E., & Martin, N. G. (1996). Seasonal changes in mood and behavior. *Archives of General Psychiatry, 53,* 47–55. (15)

Maes, M., Scharpé, S., Verkerk, R., D'Hondt, P., Peeters, D., Cosyns, P., Thompson, P., De Meyer, F., Wauters, A., & Neels, H. (1995). Seasonal availability in plasma L-tryptophan availability in healthy volunteers. *Archives of General Psychiatry, 52,* 937–946. (12)

Maestripieri, D., & Zehr, J. L. (1998). Maternal responsiveness increases during pregnancy and after estrogen treatment in macaques. *Hormones and Behavior, 34,* 223–230. (11)

Maguire, E. A., Frackowiak, R. S. J., &

Frith, C. D. (1997). Recalling routes around London: Activation of the right hippocampus in taxi drivers. *Journal of Neuroscience, 17,* 7103–7110. (13)

Mahowald, M. W., & Schenck, C. H. (1992). Dissociated states of wakefulness and sleep. *Neurology, 42*(Suppl. 6), 44–52. (9)

Maier, S. F., & Watkins, L. R. (1998). Cytokines for psychologists: Implications of bidirectional immune-to-brain communication for understanding behavior, mood, and cognition. *Psychological Review, 105,* 83–107. (12)

Malamed, F., & Zaidel, E. (1993). Language and task effects on lateralized word recognition. *Brain and Language, 45,* 70–85. (14)

Malenka, R. C., & Nicoll, R. A. (1999). Long-term potentiation—A decade of progress? *Science, 285,* 1870–1874. (13)

Malmberg, A. B., Chen, C., Tonegawa, S., & Basbaum, A. I. (1997). Preserved acute pain and reduced neuropathic pain in mice lacking PKCγ. *Science, 278,* 179–283. (7)

Manfredi, M., Stocchi, F., & Vacca, L. (1995). Differential diagnosis of parkinsonism. *Journal of Neural Transmission,* (Suppl. 45), 1–9. (8)

Mangiapane, M. L., & Simpson, J. B. (1980). Subfornical organ: Forebrain site of pressor and dipsogenic action of angiotensin II. *American Journal of Physiology, 239,* R382–R389. (10)

Manji, H. K., & Lenox, R. H. (1998). Lithium: A molecular transducer of mood-stabilization in the treatment of bipolar disorders. *Neuropsychopharmacology, 19,* 161–166. (15)

Manji, H. K., Potter, W. Z., & Lenox, R. H. (1995). Signal transduction pathways. *Archives of General Psychiatry, 52,* 531–543. (15)

Mann, J. J., Arango, V., & Underwood, M. D. (1990). Serotonin and suicidal behavior. *Annals of the New York Academy of Sciences, 600,* 476–485. (12)

Mannuzza, S., Klein, R. G., Bessler, A., Malloy, P., & LaPadula, M. (1998). Adult psychiatric status of hyperactive boys grown up. *American Journal of Psychiatry, 155,* 493–498. (5)

Maquet, P., Peters, J.-M., Aerts, J., Delfiore, G., Degueldre, C., Luxen, A., & Franck, G. (1996). Functional neuroanatomy of human rapid-eye-movement sleep and dreaming. *Nature, 383*, 163–166. (9)

Marcar, V. L., Zihl, J., & Cowey, A. (1997). Comparing the visual deficits of a motion blind patient with the visual deficits of monkeys with area MT removed. *Neuropsychologia, 35*, 1459–1465. (6)

Marin, O., Smeets, W. J. A. J., & González, A. (1998). Evolution of the basal ganglia in tetrapods: A new perspective based on recent studies in amphibians. *Trends in Neurosciences, 21*, 487–494. (4)

Mark, V. H., & Ervin, F. R. (1970). *Violence and the brain*. New York: Harper & Row. (12)

Marks, G. A., Shaffery, J. P., Oksenberg, A., Speciale, S. G., & Roffwarg, H. P. (1995). A functional role for REM sleep in brain maturation. *Behavioural Brain Research, 69*, 1–11. (9)

Marler, P., & Nelson, D. (1992). Neuroselection and song learning in birds: Species universals in a culturally transmitted behavior. *Seminars in the Neurosciences, 4*, 415–423. (5)

Marshall, J. F. (1985). Neural plasticity and recovery of function after brain injury. *International Review of Neurobiology, 26*, 201–247. (5)

Marshall, J. F., Drew, M. C., & Neve, K. A. (1983). Recovery of function after mesotelencephalic dopaminergic injury in senescence. *Brain Research, 259*, 249–260. (5)

Martin, A., Wiggs, C. L., Ungerleider, L. G., & Haxby, J. V. (1996). Neural correlates of category-specific knowledge. *Nature, 379*, 649–652. (14)

Martin, A. R. (1977). Junctional transmission: II. Presynaptic mechanisms. In E. R. Kandel (Ed.), *Handbook of physiology* (Sect. 1, Vol. 1, Pt. 1, pp. 329–355). Bethesda, MD: American Physiological Society. (3)

Martin, R. C., & Blossom-Stach, C. (1986). Evidence of syntactic deficits in a fluent aphasic. *Brain and Language, 28*, 196–234. (14)

Martinez-Vargas, M. C., & Erickson, C. J. (1973). Some social and hormonal determinants of nest-building behaviour in the ring dove (*Streptopelia risoria*). *Behaviour, 45*, 12–37. (11)

Mason, D. A., & Frick, P. J. (1994). The heritability of antisocial behavior: A meta-analysis of twin and adoption studies. *Journal of Psychopathology and Behavioral Assessment, 16*, 301–323. (12)

Masterton, B., Heffner, H., & Ravizza, R. (1969). The evolution of human hearing. *Journal of the Acoustical Society of America, 45*, 966–985. (7)

Mather, J. A. (1998). How do octopuses use their arms? *Journal of Comparative Psychology, 112*, 306–316. (14)

Mattay, V. S., Berman, K. F., Ostrem, J. L., Esposito, G., Van Horn, J. D., Bigelow, L. B., & Weinberger, D. R. (1996). Dextroamphetamine enhances "neural network-specific" physiological signals: A positron-emission tomography rCBF study. *Journal of Neuroscience, 15*, 4816–4822. (3)

Mattingley, J. B., Husain, M., Rorden, C., Kennard, C., & Driver, J. (1998). Motor role of human inferior parietal lobe revealed in unilateral neglect patients. *Nature, 392*, 179–182. (4)

Maurice, D. M. (1998). The Von Sallmann lecture of 1996: An ophthalmological explanation of REM sleep. *Experimental Eye Research, 66*, 139–145. (9)

May, P. R. A., Fuster, J. M., Haber, J., & Hirschman, A. (1979). Woodpecker drilling behavior: An endorsement of the rotational theory of impact brain injury. *Archives of Neurology, 36*, 370–373. (5)

Mayer, A. D., & Rosenblatt, J. S. (1979). Hormonal influences during the ontogeny of maternal behavior in female rats. *Journal of Comparative and Physiological Psychology, 93*, 879–898. (11)

Mayer, A. D., & Rosenblatt, J. S. (1984). Postpartum changes in maternal responsiveness and nest defense in *Rattus norvegicus*. *Journal of Comparative Psychology, 98*, 177–188. (11)

Mayne, T. J. (1999). Negative affect and health: The importance of being earnest. *Cognition and Emotion, 13*, 601–635. (12)

McBurney, D. H., & Bartoshuk, L. M. (1973). Interactions between stimuli with different taste qualities. *Physiology & Behavior, 10*, 1101–1106. (7)

McCann, U. D., Lowe, K. A., & Ricaurte, G. A. (1997). Long-lasting effects of recreational drugs of abuse on the central nervous system. *The Neuroscientist, 3*, 399–411. (3)

McCarley, R. W., & Hobson, J. A. (1977). The neurobiological origins of psychoanalytic dream theory. *American Journal of Psychiatry, 134*, 1211–1221. (9)

McCarley, R. W., & Hoffman, E. (1981). REM sleep, dreams, and the activation-synthesis hypothesis. *American Journal of Psychiatry, 138*, 904–912. (9)

McCarthy, G., Puce, A., Gore, J. C., & Allison, T. (1997). Face-specific processing in the human fusiform gyrus. *Journal of Cognitive Neuroscience, 9*, 605–610. (6)

McClellan, A. D. (1998). Spinal cord injury: Lessons from locomotor recovery and axonal regeneration in lower vertebrates. *The Neuroscientist, 4*, 250–263. (5)

McClintock, M. K. (1971). Menstrual synchrony and suppression. *Nature, 229*, 244–245. (7)

McConnell, J. V. (1962). Memory transfer through cannibalism in planarians. *Journal of Neuropsychiatry, 3*(Suppl. 1), 42–48. (13)

McConnell, S. K. (1992). The genesis of neuronal diversity during development of cerebral cortex. *Seminars in the Neurosciences, 4*, 347–356. (5)

McCormick, D. A. (1989). Acetylcholine: Distribution, receptors, and actions. *Seminars in the Neurosciences, 1*, 91–101. (3)

McDonald, M. P., Willard, L. B., Wenk, G. L., & Crawley, J. N. (1998). Coadministration of galanin antagonist M40 with a muscarinic M$_1$ agonist improves delayed nonmatching to position choice accuracy in rats with cholinergic lesions. *Journal of Neuroscience, 18*, 5078–5085. (13)

McElhiney, M. C., Moody, B. J., Steif, B. L., Prudic, J., Devanand, D. P., Nobler, M. S., & Sackeim, H. A. (1995). Autobiographical memory and mood: Effects of electroconvulsive therapy. *Neuropsychology, 9*, 501–517. (15)

McFadden, D., & Pasanen, E. G.

(1998). Comparison of the auditory systems of heterosexuals and homosexuals: Click-evoked otoacoustic emissions. *Proceedings of the National Academy of Sciences (U.S.A.), 95,* 2709–2713. (11)

McFarlane, A. C. (1997). The prevalence and longitudinal course of PTSD. *Annals of the New York Academy of Sciences, 821,* 10–23. (12)

McGaughy, J., Kaiser, T., & Sarter, M. (1996). Behavioral vigilance following infusions of 192 IgG-saporin into the basal forebrain: Selectivity of the behavioral impairment and relation to cortical AChE-positive fiber density. *Behavioral Neuroscience, 110,* 247–265. (13)

McGinnis, M. Y., Williams, G. W., & Lumia, A. R. (1996). Inhibition of male sex behavior by androgen receptor blockade in preoptic area or hypothalamus, but not amygdala or septum. *Physiology & Behavior, 60,* 783–789. (11)

McGlynn, S. M. (1990). Behavioral approaches to neuropsychological rehabilitation. *Psychological Bulletin, 108,* 420–441. (5)

McHugh, P. R., & Moran, T. H. (1985). The stomach: A conception of its dynamic role in satiety. *Progress in Psychobiology and Physiological Psychology, 11,* 197–232. (10)

McKinnon, W., Weisse, C. S., Reynolds, C. P., Bowles, C. A., & Baum, A. (1989). Chronic stress, leukocyte-subpopulations, and humoral response to latent viruses. *Health Psychology, 8,* 389–402. (12)

McLean, S., Skirboll, L. R., & Pert, C. B. (1985). Comparison of substance P and enkephalin distribution in rat brain: An overview using radioimmunocytochemistry. *Neuroscience, 14,* 837–852. (7)

McMasters, R. E. (1962). Regeneration of the spinal cord in the rat: Effects of Piromen and ACTH upon the regenerative capacity. *Journal of Comparative Neurology, 119,* 113–121. (5)

McNamara, J. O. (1999). Emerging insights into the genesis of epilepsy. *Nature, 399*(Suppl.), A15–A22. (14)

McQuillin, A., Lawrence, J., Kalsi, G., Chen, A., & Gurling, H. (1999). No allelic association between bipolar affective disorder and the tryptophan hydroxylase gene. *Archives of General Psychiatry, 56,* 99–100. (15)

Meberg, P. J., Barnes, C. A., McNaughton, B. L., & Routtenberg, A. (1993). Protein kinase C and F1/GAP-43 gene expression in hippocampus inversely related to synaptic enhancement lasting 3 days. *Proceedings of the National Academy of Sciences, 90,* 12050–12054. (13)

Meddis, R., Pearson, A. J. D., & Langford, G. (1973). An extreme case of healthy insomnia. *EEG and Clinical Neurophysiology, 35,* 213–214. (9)

Mednick, S. A., Machon, R. A., & Huttunen, M. O. (1990). An update on the Helsinki influenza project. *Archives of General Psychiatry, 47,* 292. (15)

Meiran, N., & Jelicic, M. (1995). Implicit memory in Alzheimer's disease: A meta-analysis. *Neuropsychology, 9,* 291–303. (13)

Meisel, R. L., Dohanich, G. P., & Ward, I. L. (1979). Effects of prenatal stress on avoidance acquisition, open-field performance and lordotic behavior in male rats. *Physiology & Behavior, 22,* 527–530. (11)

Meister, M., Wong, R. O. L., Baylor, D. A., & Shatz, C. J. (1991). Synchronous bursts of action potentials in ganglion cells of the developing mammalian retina. *Science, 252,* 939–943. (5)

Meltzer, H. Y., Matsubara, S., & Lee, J.-C. (1989). Classification of typical and atypical antipsychotic drugs on the basis of dopamine D-1, D-2 and serotonin$_2$ pK$_i$ values. *Journal of Pharmacology and Experimental Therapeutics, 251,* 238–246. (15)

Melzack, R., & Wall, P. D. (1965). Pain mechanisms: A new theory. *Science, 150,* 971–979. (7)

Mendell, L. M. (1995). Neurotrophic factors and the specification of neural function. *The Neuroscientist, 1,* 26–34. (5)

Mendez, M. F. (1995). The neuropsychiatric aspects of boxing. *International Journal of Psychiatry in Medicine, 25,* 249–262. (5)

Mendonca, B. B., Inacio, M., Costa, E. M. F., Arnhold, I. J. P., Silva, F. A. Q., Nicolau, W., Bloise, W., Russell, D. W., & Wilson, J. D. (1996). Male pseudohermaphroditism due to steroid 5α-reductase 2 deficiency. *Medicine, 75,* 64–76. (11)

Merton, P. A. (1972). How we control the contraction of our muscles. *Scientific American, 226*(5), 30–37. (8)

Merzenich, M. M., Nelson, R. J., Stryker, M. P., Cynader, M. S., Schoppman, A., & Zook, J. M. (1984). Somatosensory cortical map changes following digit amputation in adult monkeys. *Journal of Comparative Neurology, 224,* 591–605. (5)

Mesches, K. C., & McGaugh, J. L. (1995). Differential effects of pretraining inactivation of the right or left amygdala on retention of inhibitory avoidance training. *Behavioral Neuroscience, 109,* 642–647. (12)

Mesulam, M.-M. (1995). Cholinergic pathways and the ascending reticular activating system of the human brain. *Annals of the New York Academy of Sciences, 757,* 169–179. (4)

Mezzanotte, W. S., Tangel, D. J., & White, D. P. (1992). Waking genioglossal electromyogram in sleep apnea patients versus normal controls (a neuromuscular compensatory mechanism). *Journal of Clinical Investigation, 89,* 1571–1579. (9)

Mignot, E. (1998). Genetic and familial aspects of narcolepsy. *Neurology, 50*(Suppl. 1), S16–S22. (9)

Mihic, S. J., Ye, Q., Wick, M. J., Koltchine, V. V., Krasowski, M. D., Finn, S. E., Mascia, M. P., Valenzuela, C. F., Hanson, K. K., Greenblatt, E. P., Harris, R. A., & Harrison, N. L. (1997). Sites of alcohol and volatile anaesthetic action on GABA$_A$ and glycine receptors. *Nature, 389,* 385–389. (3)

Milberger, S., Biederman, J., Faraone, S. V., Chen, L., & Jones, J. (1996). Is maternal smoking during pregnancy a risk factor for attention deficit hyperactivity disorder in children? *American Journal of Psychiatry, 153,* 1138–1142. (5)

Miles, C., Green, R., Sanders, G., & Hines, M. (1998). Estrogen and memory in a transsexual population. *Hormones and Behavior, 34*, 199–208. (11)

Miles, F. A., & Evarts, E. V. (1979). Concepts of motor organization. *Annual Review of Psychology, 30*, 327–362. (8)

Miller, E. A., Goldman, P. S., & Rosvold, H. E. (1973). Delayed recovery of function following orbital prefrontal lesions in infant monkeys. *Science, 182*, 304–306. (5)

Miller, T. Q., Smith, T. W., Turner, C. W., Guijarro, M. L., & Hallet, A. J. (1996). A meta-analytic review of research on hostility and physical health. *Psychological Bulletin, 119*, 322–348. (12)

Miller, W. C., & DeLong, M. R. (1988). Parkinsonian symptomatology: An anatomical and physiological analysis. *Annals of the New York Academy of Sciences, 515*, 287–302. (8)

Millhorn, D. E., Bayliss, D. A., Erickson, J. T., Gallman, E. A., Szymeczek, C. L., Czyzyk-Krzeska, M., & Dean, J. B. (1989). Cellular and molecular mechanisms of chemical synaptic transmission. *American Journal of Physiology, 257* (6, Part 1), L289–L310. (3)

Milner, B. (1959). The memory defect in bilateral hippocampal lesions. *Psychiatric Research Reports, 11*, 43–58. (13)

Milner, B., Corkin, S., & Teuber, H.-L. (1968). Further analysis of the hippocampal amnesic syndrome: 14-year follow-up study of H. M. *Neuropsychologia, 6*, 215–234. (13)

Moeller, F. G., Dougherty, D. M., Swann, A. C., Collins, D., Davis, C. M., & Cherek, D. R. (1996). Tryptophan depletion and aggressive responding in healthy males. *Psychopharmacology, 126*, 97–103. (12)

Moffat, S. D., Hampson, E., & Lee, D. H. (1998). Morphology of the planum temporale and corpus callosum in left-handers with evidence of left and right hemisphere speech representation. *Brain, 121*, 2369–2379. (14)

Moghaddam, B., & Adams, B. W. (1998). Reversal of phencyclidine effects by a group II metabotropic glutamate receptor agonist in rats. *Science, 281*, 1349–1352. (15)

Mogil, J. S., Sternberg, W. F., & Liebeskind, J. C. (1993). Studies of pain, stress and immunity. In C. R. Chapman & K. M. Foley (Eds.), *Current & emerging issues in cancer pain: Research & practice* (pp. 31–47). New York: Raven Press. (7)

Mombaerts, P. (1999). Seven-transmembrane proteins as odorant and chemosensory receptors. *Science, 286*, 707–711. (7)

Money, J. (1967). Sexual problems of the chronically ill. In C. W. Wahl (Ed.), *Sexual problems: Diagnosis and treatment in medical practice* (pp. 266–287). New York: Free Press. (8)

Money, J., & Ehrhardt, A. A. (1972). *Man & woman, boy & girl*. Baltimore, MD: Johns Hopkins University Press. (11)

Money, J., & Lewis, V. (1966). IQ, genetics and accelerated growth: Adrenogenital syndrome. *Bulletin of the Johns Hopkins Hospital, 118*, 365–373. (11)

Money, J., & Schwartz, M. (1978). Biosocial determinants of gender identity differentiation and development. In J. B. Hutchison (Ed.), *Biological determinants of sexual behaviour* (pp. 765–784). Chichester, England: John Wiley. (11)

Montgomery, S. A. (1997). Suicide and antidepressants. *Annals of the New York Academy of Sciences, 836*, 329–338. (12)

Monti-Bloch, L., Jennings-White, C., & Berliner, D. L. (1998). The human vomeronasal system: A review. *Annals of the New York Academy of Sciences, 855*, 373–389. (7)

Monti-Bloch, L., Jennings-White, C., Dolberg, D. S., & Berliner, D. L. (1994). The human vomeronasal system. *Psychoneuroendocrinology, 19*, 673–686. (7)

Moorcroft, W. H. (1993). *Sleep, dreaming, & sleep disorders* (2nd ed.). Lanham, MD: University Press of America. (9)

Moore, T., Rodman, H. R., & Gross, C. G. (1998). Man, monkey, and blindsight. *The Neuroscientist, 4*, 227–230. (6)

Moore, T., Rodman, H. R., Repp, A. B., & Gross, C. G. (1995). Localization of visual stimuli after striate cortex damage in monkeys: Parallels with human blindsight. *Proceedings of the National Academy of Sciences U.S.A., 92*, 8215–8218. (6)

Moore-Ede, M. C., Czeisler, C. A., & Richardson, G. S. (1983). Circadian timekeeping in health and disease. *New England Journal of Medicine, 309*, 469–476. (9)

Morgan, V., Castle, D., Page, A., Fazio, S., Gurrin, L., Burton, P., Montgomery, P., & Jablensky, A. (1997). Influenza epidemics and incidence of schizophrenia, affective disorders and mental retardation in Western Australia: No evidence of a major effect. *Schizophrenia Research, 26*, 25–39. (15)

Mori, K., Mataga, N., & Imamura, K. (1992). Differential specificities of single mitral cells in rabbit olfactory bulb for a homologous series of fatty acid odor molecules. *Journal of Neurophysiology, 67*, 786–789. (7)

Morley, J. E. (1995). The role of peptides in appetite regulation across species. *American Zoologist, 35*, 437–445. (10)

Morley, J. E., Levine, A. S., Grace, M., & Kneip, J. (1985). Peptide YY (PYY), a potent orexigenic agent. *Brain Research, 341*, 200–203. (10)

Morris, J. F., & Pow, D. V. (1993). New anatomical insights into the inputs and outputs from hypothalamic magnocellular neurons. *Annals of the New York Academy of Sciences, 689*, 16–33. (3)

Morris, J. S., Frith, C. D., Perrett, D. I., Rowland, D., Young, A. W., Calder, A. J., & Dolan, R. J. (1996). A differential neural response in the human amygdala to fearful and happy expressions. *Nature, 383*, 812–815. (12)

Morris, M., Lack, L., & Dawson, D. (1990). Sleep-onset insomniacs have delayed temperature rhythms. *Sleep, 13*, 1–14. (9)

Morris, M. E., Viswanathan, N., Kuhlman, S., Davis, F. C., & Weitz, C. J. (1998). A screen for genes induced in the suprachiasmatic nucleus by light. *Science, 279*, 1544–1547. (9)

Morrison, A. R., Sanford, L. D., Ball, W. A., Mann, G. L., & Ross, R. J. (1995). Stimulus-elicited behavior in rapid eye movement sleep without atonia. *Behavioral Neuroscience, 109*, 972–979. (9)

Morrison, J. H., & Hof, P. R. (1997).

Life and death of neurons in the aging brain. *Science, 278,* 412–419. (13)

Moruzzi, G., & Magoun, H. W. (1949). Brain stem reticular formation and activation of the EEG. *Electroencephalography and Clinical Neurophysiology, 1,* 455–473. (9)

Moscovitch, M. (1985). Memory from infancy to old age: Implications for theories of normal and pathological memory. *Annals of the New York Academy of Sciences, 444,* 78–96. (13)

Moscovitch, M. (1992). Memory and working-with-memory: A component process model based on modules and central systems. *Journal of Cognitive Neuroscience, 4,* 257–267. (13)

Moscovitch, M. (1995). Recovered consciousness hypothesis concerning modularity and episodic memory. *Journal of Clinical and Experimental Neuropsychology, 17,* 276–290. (13)

Moscovitch, M., Winocur, G., & Behrmann, M. (1997). What is special about face recognition? Nineteen experiments on a person with visual object agnosia and dyslexia but normal face recognition. *Journal of Cognitive Neuroscience, 9,* 555–604. (6)

Moss, C. F., & Simmons, A. M. (1986). Frequency selectivity of hearing in the green treefrog, *Hyla cinerea. Journal of Comparative Physiology, A, 159,* 257–266. (7)

Moyer, K. E. (1974). Sex differences in aggression. In R. C. Friedman, R. M. Richart, & R. L. VandeWiele (Eds.), *Sex differences in behavior* (pp. 335–372). New York: Wiley. (12)

Mrosovsky, N. (1990). *Rheostasis: The physiology of change.* New York: Oxford University Press. (10)

Mrzljak, L., Bergson, C., Pappy, M., Huff, R., Levenson, R., & Goldman-Rakic, P. S. (1996). Localization of dopamine D4 receptors in GABAergic neurons of the primate brain. *Nature, 381,* 245–248. (15)

Müller, M. M., Teder-Sälejärvi, W., & Hillyard, S. A. (1998). The time course of cortical facilitation during cued shifts of spatial attention. *Nature Neuroscience, 1,* 631–634. (6)

Munk, M. H. J., Roelfsema, P. R., König, P., Engel, A. K., & Singer, W. (1996). Role of reticular activation in the modulation of intracortical synchronization. *Science, 272,* 271–274. (9)

Murphy, M. G., & O'Leary, J. L. (1973). Hanging and climbing functions in raccoon and sloth after total cerebellectomy. *Archives of Neurology, 28,* 111–117. (8)

Murphy, M. R., Checkley, S. A., Seckl, J. R., & Lightman, S. L. (1990). Naloxone inhibits oxytocin release at orgasm in man. *Journal of Clinical Endocrinology and Metabolism, 71,* 1056–1058. (11)

Murray, A. M., Hyde, T. M., Knable, M. B., Herman, M. M., Bigelow, L. B., Carter, J. M., Weinberger, D. R., & Kleinman, J. E. (1995). Distribution of putative D4 dopamine receptors in postmortem striatum from patients with schizophrenia. *Journal of Neuroscience, 15,* 2186–2191. (15)

Murrell, J., Farlow, M., Ghetti, B., & Benson, M. D. (1991). A mutation in the amyloid precursor protein associated with hereditary Alzheimer's disease. *Science, 254,* 97–99. (13)

Myers, J. J., & Sperry, R. W. (1985). Interhemispheric communication after section of the forebrain commissures. *Cortex, 21,* 249–260. (14)

Nagahara, A. H., Otto, T., & Gallagher, M. (1995). Entorhinal-perirhinal lesions impair performance of rats on two versions of place learning in the Morris water maze. *Behavioral Neuroscience, 109,* 3–9. (13)

Nagayama, T., Sinor, A. D., Simon, R. P., Chen, J., Graham, S. H., Jin, K., & Greenberg, D. A. (1999). Cannabinoids and neuroprotection in global and focal cerebral ischemia and in neuronal cultures. *Journal of Neuroscience, 19,* 2987–2995. (5)

Nagel, T. (1974). What is it like to be a bat? *The Philosophical Review, 83,* 435–450. (1)

Nakanishi, S. (1992). Molecular diversity of glutamate receptors and implications for brain function. *Science, 258,* 597–603. (13)

Nakashima, Y., Kuwamura, T., & Yogo, Y. (1995). Why be a both-ways sex changer? *Ethology, 101,* 301–307. (11)

Nathans, J., Davenport, C. M., Maumenee, I. H., Lewis, R. A., Hejtmancik, J. F., Litt, M., Lovrien, E., Weleber, R., Bachynski, B., Zwas, F., Klingaman, R., & Fishman, G. (1989). Molecular genetics of human blue cone monochromacy. *Science, 245,* 831–838. (6)

Nebes, R. D. (1974). Hemispheric specialization in commissurotomized man. *Psychological Bulletin, 81,* 1–14. (14)

Nef, P. (1998). How we smell: The molecular and cellular bases of olfaction. *News in Physiological Sciences, 13,* 1–5. (7)

Neitz, J., & Jacobs, G. H. (1986). Reexamination of spectral mechanisms in the rat (*Rattus norvegicus*). *Journal of Comparative Psychology, 100,* 21–29. (6)

Nelson, D. O., & Prosser, C. L. (1981). Intracellular recordings from thermosensitive preoptic neurons. *Science, 213,* 787–789. (10)

Netter, F. H. (1983). *CIBA collection of medical illustrations: Vol. 1. Nervous system.* New York: CIBA. (11)

Neumann, S., Doubell, T. P., Leslie, T., & Woolf, C. J. (1996). Inflammatory pain hypersensitivity mediated by phenotypic switch in myelinated primary sensory neurons. *Nature, 384,* 360–364. (7)

Neville, H. J., Bavelier, D., Corina, D., Rauschecker, J., Karni, A., Lalwani, A., Braun, A., Clark, V., Jezzard, P., & Turner, R. (1998). Cerebral organization for language in deaf and hearing subjects: Biological constraints and effects of experience. *Proceedings of the National Academy of Sciences (U.S.A.), 95,* 922–929. (14)

Newcomer, J. W., Selke, G., Melson, A. K., Hershey, T., Craft, S., Richards, K., & Alderson, A. L. (1999). Decreased memory performance in healthy humans induced by stress-level cortisol treatment. *Archives of General Psychiatry, 56,* 527–533. (13)

Nicholas, M. K., & Arnason, B. G. W. (1992). Immunologic responses in central nervous system transplantation. *Seminars in the Neurosciences, 4,* 273–283. (8)

Nicklas, W. J., Saporito, M., Basma, A., Geller, H. M., & Heikkila, R. E. (1992). Mitochondrial mechanisms of neurotoxicity. *Annals of the New York Academy of Sciences, 648,* 28–36. (8)

Nicolelis, M. A. L., Ghazanfar, A. A., Stambaugh, C. R., Oliveira, L. M. O., Laubach, M., Chapin, J. K., Nelson, R. J., & Kaas, J. H. (1998). Simultaneous encoding of tactile information by three primate cortical areas. *Nature Neuroscience, 1,* 621–630. (4)

Nieuwenhuys, R., Voogd, J., & van-Huijzen, C. (1988). *The human central nervous system* (3rd rev. ed.). Berlin: Springer-Verlag. (4, 10, 12, 14)

Nilsson, G. E. (1999, December). The cost of a brain. *Natural History, 108,* 66–73. (14)

Noble, E. P., Ozkaragoz, T. Z., Ritchie, T. L., Zhang, X., Belin, T. R., & Sparkes, R. S. (1998). D_2 and D_4 dopamine receptor polymorphisms and personality. *American Journal of Medical Genetics, 81,* 257–267. (3)

Nolen-Hoeksema, S., & Morrow, J. (1991). A prospective study of depression and posttraumatic stress symptoms after a natural disaster: The Loma Prieta earthquake. *Journal of Personality and Social Psychology, 61,* 115–121. (15)

Nonogaki, K., Strack, A. M., Dallman, M. F., & Tecott, L. H. (1998). Leptin-independent hyperphagia and type 2 diabetes in mice with a mutated serotonin 5-HT$_{2C}$ receptor gene. *Nature Medicine, 4,* 1152–1156. (10)

Nopoulos, P. C., Giedd, J. N., Andreasen, N. C., & Rapoport, J. L. (1998). Frequency and severity of enlarged cavum septi pellucidi in childhood-onset schizophrenia. *American Journal of Psychiatry, 155,* 1074–1079. (15)

Norman, R. A., Tataranni, P. A., Pratley, R., Thompson, D. B., Hanson, R. L., Prochazka, M., Baier, L., Ehm, M. G., Sakul, H., Foroud, T., Garvey, W. T., Burns, D., Knowler, W. C., Bennett, P. H., Bogardus, C., & Ravussin, E. (1998). Autosomal genomic scan for loci linked to obesity and energy metabolism in Pima Indians. *American Journal of Human Genetics, 62,* 659–668. (10)

North, R. A. (1989). Neurotransmitters and their receptors: From the clone to the clinic. *Seminars in the Neurosciences, 1,* 81–90. (3)

North, R. A. (1992). Cellular actions of opiates and cocaine. *Annals of the New York Academy of Sciences, 654,* 1–6. (3)

Numan, M., & Numan, M. J. (1994). Expression of fos-like immunoreactivity in the preoptic area of maternally behaving virgin rats. *Behavioral Neuroscience, 108,* 379–394. (11)

Ó Scalaidhe, S. P., Wilson, F. A. W., & Goldman-Rakic, P. S. (1997). Areal segregation of face-processing neurons in prefrontal cortex. *Science, 278,* 1135–1138. (6)

Obrietan, K., Impey, S., & Storm, D. R. (1998). Light and circadian rhythmicity regulate MAP kinase activation in the suprachiasmatic nuclei. *Nature Neuroscience, 1,* 693–700. (9)

O'Dowd, B. F., Lefkowitz, R. J., & Caron, M. G. (1989). Structure of the adrenergic and related receptors. *Annual Review of Neuroscience, 12,* 67–83. (3)

O'Keefe, J., & Burgess, N. (1996). Geometric determinants of the place fields of hippocampal neurons. *Nature, 381,* 425–434. (13)

Okubo, Y., Suhara, T., Suzuki, K., Kobayashi, K., Inoue, O., Terasaki, O., Someya, Y., Sassa, T., Sudo, Y., Matsushima, E., Iyo, M., Tateno, Y., & Toru, M. (1997). Decreased prefrontal dopamine D_1 receptors in schizophrenia revealed by PET. *Nature, 385,* 634–636. (15)

Olds, J. (1958). Satiation effects in self-stimulation of the brain. *Journal of Comparative and Physiological Psychology, 51,* 675–678. (3)

Olds, J., & Milner, P. (1954). Positive reinforcement produced by electrical stimulation of the septal area and other regions of the rat brain. *Journal of Comparative and Physiological Psychology, 47,* 419–428. (3)

O'Leary, A. (1990). Stress, emotion, and human immune function. *Psychological Bulletin, 108,* 363–382. (12)

Olff, M. (1999). Stress, depression and immunity: The role of defense and coping styles. *Psychiatry Research, 85,* 7–15. (12)

Olney, J. W., & Farber, N. B. (1995). Glutamate receptor dysfunction and schizophrenia. *Archives of General Psychiatry, 52,* 998–1007. (15)

Olson, D. J., Kamil, A. C., Balda, R. P., & Nims, P. J. (1995). Performance of four seed-caching corvid species in operant tests of nonspatial and spatial memory. *Journal of Comparative Psychology, 109,* 173–181. (13)

Olton, D. S., & Papas, B. C. (1979). Spatial memory and hippocampal function. *Neuropsychologia, 17,* 669–682. (13)

Olton, D. S., Walker, J. A., & Gage, F. H. (1978). Hippocampal connections and spatial discrimination. *Brain Research, 139,* 295–308. (13)

O'Neal, M. F., Means, L. W., Poole, M. C., & Hamm, R. J. (1996). Estrogen affects performance of ovariectomized rats in a two-choice water-escape working memory task. *Psychoneuroendocrinology, 21,* 51–65. (11)

Onodera, S., & Hicks, T. P. (1999). Evolution of the motor system: Why the elephant's trunk works like a human's hand. *The Neuroscientist, 5,* 217–226. (8)

Ornstein, R. (1997). *The right mind.* New York: Harcourt Brace. (14)

Ouchi, Y., Yoshikawa, E., Okada, H., Futatsubashi, M., Sekine, Y., Iyo, M., & Sakamoto, M. (1999). Alterations in binding site density of dopamine transporter in the striatum, orbitofrontal cortex, and amygdala in early Parkinson's disease: Compartment analysis for β-CFT binding with positron emission tomography. *Annals of Neurology, 45,* 601–610. (8)

Overman, W. H., Pate, B. J., Moore, K., & Peuster, A. (1996). Ontogeny of place learning in children as measured in the radial arm maze, Morris search task, and open field task. *Behavioral Neuroscience, 110,* 1205–1228. (13)

Overmier, J. B., & Murison, R. (1997). Animal models reveal the "psych" in the psychosomatics of peptic ulcer. *Current Directions in Psychological Science, 6,* 180–184. (12)

Page, G. G., Ben-Eliyahu, S., Yirmiya, R., & Liebeskind, J. C. (1993).

Morphine attenuates surgery-induced enhancement of metastatic colonization in rats. *Pain, 54,* 21–28. (7)

Pandey, G. N., Pandey, S. C., Dwivedi, Y., Sharma, R. P., Janicak, P. G., & Davis, J. M. (1995). Platelet serotonin-2A receptors: A potential biological marker for suicidal behavior. *American Journal of Psychiatry, 152,* 850–855. (12)

Panksepp, J. (1998). Attention deficit hyperactivity disorders, psychostimulants, and intolerance of childhood playfulness: A tragedy in the making? *Current Directions in Psychological Science, 7,* 91–98. (5)

Pappone, P. A., & Cahalan, M. D. (1987). *Pandinus imperator* scorpion venom blocks voltage-gated potassium channels in nerve fibers. *Journal of Neuroscience, 7,* 3300–3305. (2)

Paradis, M. (1998). Aphasia in bilinguals: How atypical is it? In P. Coppens, Y. Lebrun, & A. Basso (Eds.), *Aphasia in atypical populations* (pp. 35–66). Mahwah, NJ: Erlbaum. (14)

Park, S., Holzman, P. S., & Goldman-Rakic, P. S. (1995). Spatial working memory deficits in the relatives of schizophrenic patients. *Archives of General Psychiatry, 52,* 821–828. (15)

Parker, G. H. (1922). *Smell, taste, and allied senses in the vertebrates.* Philadelphia: Lippincott. (7)

Pascual-Leone, A., Wasserman, E. M., Sadato, N., & Hallett, M. (1995). The role of reading activity on the modulation of motor cortical outputs to the reading hand in Braille readers. *Annals of Neurology, 38,* 910–915. (5)

Passingham, R. E. (1979). Brain size and intelligence in man. *Brain, Behavior, and Evolution, 16,* 253–270. (5)

Patel, A. J., Honoré, E., Lesage, F., Fink, M., Romey, G., & Lazdunski, M. (1999). Inhalation anesthetics activate two-pore-domain background K+ channels. *Nature Neuroscience, 2,* 422–426. (2)

Patte, C., Gandolfo, P., Leprince, J., Thoumas, J. L., Fontaine, M., Vaudry, H., & Tonon, M. C. (1999). GABA inhibits endozepine release from cultured rat astrocytes. *Glia, 25,* 404–411. (12)

Paulesu, E., McCrory, E., Fazio, F., Mononcello, L., Brunswick, N., Cappa, S.F., Cotelli, M., Cossu, G., Corte, F., Lorusso, M., Pesenti, S., Gallagher, A., Perani, D., Price, C., Frith, C. D., & Frith, U. (2000). A cultural effect on brain function. *Nature Neuroscience, 3,* 91–96. (14)

Paus, T., Marrett, S., Worsley, K. J., & Evans, A. C. (1995). Extraretinal modulation of cerebral blood flow in the human visual cortex: Implications for saccadic suppression. *Journal of Neurophysiology, 74,* 2179–2183. (6)

Pavlov, I. P. (1927). *Conditioned reflexes.* Oxford, England: Oxford University Press. (13)

Pearlson, G. D. (1997). Superior temporal gyrus and planum temporale in schizophrenia: A selective review. *Progress in Neuro-Psychopharmacology and Biological Psychiatry, 21,* 1203–1229. (4)

Pearlson, G. D., Petty, R. G., Ross, C. A., & Tien, A. Y. (1996). Schizophrenia—A disease of heteromodal association cortex. *Neuropsychopharmacology, 14,* 1–17. (15)

Pedersen,, C. A., Caldwell, J. D., Walker, C., Ayers, G., & Mason, G. A. (1994). Oxytocin activates the postpartum onset of rat maternal behavior in the ventral tegmentum and medial preoptic areas. *Behavioral Neuroscience, 108,* 1163–1171. (11)

Pellis, S. M., O'Brien, D. P., Pellis, V. C., Teitelbaum, P., Wolgin, D. L., & Kennedy, S. (1988). Escalation of feline predation along a gradient from avoidance through "play" to killing. *Behavioral Neuroscience, 102,* 760–777. (12)

Pellymounter, M. A., Cullen, M. J., Baker, M. B., Hecht, R., Winters, D., Boone, T., & Collins, F. (1995). Effects of the *obese* gene product on body weight regulation in *ob/ob* mice. *Science, 269,* 540–543. (10)

Penfield, W. (1955). The permanent record of the stream of consciousness. *Acta Psychologica, 11,* 47–69. (13)

Penfield, W., & Milner, B. (1958). Memory deficit produced by bilateral lesions in the hippocampal zone. *Archives of Neurology and Psychiatry, 79,* 475–497. (13)

Penfield, W., & Perot, P. (1963). The brain's record of auditory and visual experience. *Brain, 86,* 595–696. (13)

Penfield, W., & Rasmussen, T. (1950). *The cerebral cortex of man.* New York: Macmillan. (4, 8)

Penton-Voak, I. S., Perrett, D. I., Castles, D. L., Kobayashi, T., Burt, D. M., Murray, L. K., & Minamisawa, R. (1999). Menstrual cycle alters face preference. *Nature, 399,* 741–742. (11)

Pepperberg, I. M. (1993). Cognition and communication in an African Grey parrot (*Psittacus erithacus*): Studies on a nonhuman, nonprimate, nonmammalian subject. In H. L. Roitblat, L. M. Herman, & P. E. Nachtigall (Eds.), *Language and communication: Comparative perspectives* (pp. 221–248). Hillsdale, NJ: Lawrence Erlbaum. (14)

Pepperberg, I. M. (1994). Numerical competence in an African gray parrot (*Psittacus erithacus*). *Journal of Comparative Psychology, 108,* 36–44. (14)

Perani, D., Paulesu, E., Galles, N. S., Dupoux, E., Dehaene, S., Bettinardi, V., Cappa, S. F., Fazio, F., & Mehler, J. (1998). The bilingual brain: Proficiency and age of acquisition of the second language. *Brain, 121,* 1841–1852. (14)

Perani, D., Vallar, G., Paulesu, E., Alberoni, M., & Fazio, F. (1993). Left and right hemisphere contributions to recovery form neglect after right hemisphere damage—An [18F]FDG PET study of two cases. *Neuropsychologia, 31,* 115–125. (5)

Pericak-Vance, M. A., Bebout, J. L., Gaskell, P. C., Jr., Yamaoka, L. H., Hung, W.-Y., Alberts, M. J., Walker, A. P., Bartlett, R. J., Haynes, C. A., Welsh, K. A., Earl, N. L., Heyman, A., Clark, C. M., & Roses, A. D. (1991). Linkage studies in familial Alzheimer disease: Evidence for chromosome 19 linkage. *American Journal of Human Genetics, 48,* 1034–1050. (13)

Perlow, M. J., Freed, W. J., Hoffer, B. J., Seiger, A., Olson, L., & Wyatt, R. J. (1979). Brain grafts reduce motor abnormalities produced by destruction of nigrostriatal dopamine system. *Science, 204,* 643–647. (8)

Pert, C. B. (1997). *Molecules of emotion.* New York: Touchstone. (2)

Pert, C. B., & Snyder, S. H. (1973). The opiate receptor: Demonstration in nervous tissue. *Science, 179,* 1011–1014. (3, 7)

Pesold, C., & Treit, D. (1995). The central and basolateral amygdala differentially mediate the anxiolytic effect of benzodiazepines. *Brain Research, 671,* 213–221. (12)

Petersen, S. E., Fox, P. T., Posner, M. I., Mintun, M., & Raichle, M. E. (1988). Positron emission tomographic studies of the cortical anatomy of single-word processing. *Nature, 331,* 585–589. (14)

Pfefferbaum, A., Sullivan, E. V., Rosenbloom, M. J., Mathalon, D. H., & Lim, K. O. (1998). A controlled study of cortical gray matter and ventricular changes in alcoholic men over a 5-year interval. *Archives of General Psychiatry, 55,* 905–912. (15)

Phelps, M. E., & Mazziotta, J. C. (1985). Positron emission tomography: Human brain function and biochemistry. *Science, 228,* 799–809. (1, 3)

Phillips, R. G., & LeDoux, J. E. (1992). Differential contribution of amygdala and hippocampus to cued and contextual fear conditioning. *Behavioral Neuroscience, 106,* 274–285. (12)

Phillips, T. J., Brown, K. J., Burkhart-Kasch, S., Wenger, C. D., Kelly, M. A., Rubinstein, M., Grandy, D. K., & Low, M. J. (1998). Alcohol preference and sensitivity are markedly reduced in mice lacking dopamine D_2 receptors. *Nature Neuroscience, 1,* 610–615. (3)

Piccini, P., Burn, D. J., Ceravolo, R., Maraganore, D., & Brooks, D. J. (1999). The role of inheritance in sporadic Parkinson's disease: Evidence from a longitudinal study of dopaminergic function in twins. *Annals of Neurology, 45,* 577–582. (8)

Pich, E. M., Pagliusi, S. R., Tessari, M., Talabot-Ayer, D., van Huijsduijnen, R. H., & Chiamulera, C. (1997). Common neural substrates for the addictive properties of nicotine and cocaine. *Science, 275,* 83–86. (3)

Pillon, B., Ertle, S., Deweer, B., Sarazin, M., Agid, Y., & Dubois, B. (1996). Memory for spatial location is affected in Parkinson's disease. *Neuropsychologia, 34,* 77–85. (8)

Pincus, J. H., & Tucker, G. J. (1985). *Behavioral neurology* (3rd ed.). New York: Oxford University Press. (7)

Pinel, J. P. J., Treit, D., & Rovner, L. I. (1977). Temporal lobe aggression in rats. *Science, 197,* 1088–1089. (12)

Pinker, S. (1994). *The language instinct.* New York: Harper-Collins. (14)

Pinker, S. (1996). Facts about human language relevant to its evolution. In J.-P. Changeux & J. Chavaillon (Eds.), *Origins of the human brain* (pp. 262–283). Oxford, England: Clarendon Press. (14)

Plata-Salamán, C. R. (1998). Cytokines and feeding. *News in Physiological Sciences, 13,* 298–304. (10)

Plihal, W., & Born, J. (1997). Effects of early and late nocturnal sleep on declarative and procedural memory. *Journal of Cognitive Neuroscience, 9,* 534–547. (9)

Ploghaus, A., Tracey, I., Gati, J. S., Clare, S., Menon, R. S., Matthews, P. M., & Rawlins, J. N. P. (1999). Dissociating pain from its anticipation in the human brain. *Science, 284,* 1979–1981. (7)

Plomin, R., Corley, R., DeFries, J. C., & Fulker, D. (1990). Individual differences in television viewing in early childhood: Nature as well as nurture. *Psychological Science, 1,* 371–377. (1)

Plomin, R., Owen, M. J., & McGuffin, P. (1994). The genetic basis of complex human behaviors. *Science, 264,* 1733–1739. (1)

Plous, S. (1998). Signs of change within the animal rights movement: Results from a follow-up survey of activists. *Journal of Comparative Psychology, 112,* 48–54. (1)

Pogue-Geile, M., Ferrell, R., Deka, R., Debski, T., & Manuck, S. (1998). Human novelty-seeking personality traits and dopamine D_4 receptor polymorphisms: A twin and genetic association study. *American Journal of Medical Genetics, 81,* 44–48. (3)

Poling, A., Schlinger, H., & Blakely, E. (1988). Failure of the partial inverse benzodiazepine agonist Ro15-4513 to block the lethal effects of ethanol in rats. *Pharmacology Biochemistry & Behavior, 31,* 945–947. (12)

Pollack, M. H., Otto, M. W., Worthington, J. J., Manfro, G. G., & Wolkow, R. (1998). Sertraline in the treatment of panic disorder. *Archives of General Psychiatry, 55,* 1010–1016. (12)

Pollatsek, A., Bolozky, S., Well, A. D., & Rayner, K. (1981). Asymmetries in the perceptual span for Israeli readers. *Brain and Language, 14,* 174–180. (14)

Poltorak, M., Wright, R., Hemperly, J. J., Torrey, E. F., Issa, F., Wyatt, R. J., & Freed, W. J. (1997). Monozygotic twins discordant for schizophrenia are discordant for N-CAM and L1 in CSF. *Brain Research, 751,* 152–154. (15)

Polymeropoulos, M. H., Lavedan, C., Leroy, E., Ide, S. E., Dehejia, A., Dutra, A., Pike, B., Root, H., Rubenstein, J., Boyer, R., Stenroos, E. S., Chandrasekharappa, S., Athanassiadou, A., Papapetropoulos, T., Johnson, W. G., Lazzarini, A. M., Duvoisin, R. C., Di Iorio, G., Golbe, L. I., & Nussbaum, R. L. (1997). Mutation in the α-synuclein gene identified in families with Parkinson's disease. *Science, 276,* 2045–2050. (8)

Pomeranz, B. H. (1989). Transcutaneous electrical nerve stimulation (TENS). In G. Adelman (Ed.), *Neuroscience year* (pp. 161–164). Boston: Birkhäuser. (7)

Pons, T. P., Garraghty, P. E., Ommaya, A. K., Kaas, J. H., Taub, E., & Mishkin, M. (1991). Massive cortical reorganization after sensory deafferentation in adult macaques. *Science, 252,* 1857–1860. (5)

Pontieri, F. E., Tanda, G., Orzi, F., & DiChiara, G. (1996). Effects of nicotine on the nucleus accumbens and similarity to those of addictive drugs. *Nature, 382,* 255–257. (3)

Pope, H. G., & Katz, D. L. (1994). Psychiatric and medical effects of anabolic-androgenic steroid use. *Archives of General Psychiatry, 51,* 375–382. (3)

Porkka-Heiskanen, T. (1999). Adenosine in sleep and wakefulness. *Annals of Medicine, 31,* 125–129. (9)

Posner, M. I., Petersen, S. E., Fox, P. T., & Raichle, M. E. (1988). Localization of cognitive operations in the human brain. *Science, 240,* 1627–1631. (14)

Posner, S. F., Baker, L., Heath, A., & Martin, N. G. (1996). Social contact, social attitudes, and twin similarity. *Behavior Genetics, 26,* 123–133. (1)

Potegal, M. (1994). Aggressive arousal: The amygdala connection. In M. Potegal & J. F. Knutson (Eds.), *The dynamics of aggression* (pp. 73–111). Hillsdale, NJ: Lawrence Erlbaum. (12)

Potegal, M., Ferris, C., Hebert, M., Meyerhoff, J. M., & Skaredoff, L. (1996). Attack priming in female Syrian golden hamsters is associated with a *c-fos* coupled process within the corticomedial amygdala. *Neuroscience, 75,* 869–880. (12)

Potegal, M., Hebert, M., DeCoster, M., & Meyerhoff, J. L. (1996). Brief, high-frequency stimulation of the corticomedial amygdala induces a delayed and prolonged increase of aggressiveness in male Syrian golden hamsters. *Behavioral Neuroscience, 110,* 401–412. (12)

Poulos, C. X., Parker, J. L., & Lê, D. A. (1998). Increased impulsivity after injected alcohol predicts later alcohol consumption in rats: Evidence for "loss-of-control drinking" and marked individual differences. *Behavioral Neuroscience, 112,* 1247–1257. (15)

Preilowski, B. (1975). Bilateral motor interaction: Perceptual-motor performance of partial and complete split-brain patients. In K. J. Zülch, O. Creutzfeldt, & G. C. Galbraith (Eds.), *Cerebral localization* (pp. 115–132). New York: Springer Verlag. (14)

Premack, A. J., & Premack, D. (1972). Teaching language to an ape. *Scientific American, 227*(4), 92–99. (14)

Preti, G., Cutler, W. B., Garcia, C. R., Huggins, G. R., & Lawley, H. J. (1986). Human axillary secretions influence women's menstrual cycles: The role of donor extract of females. *Hormones and Behavior, 20,* 474–482. (7)

Pritchard, T. C., Hamilton, R. B., Morse, J. R., & Norgren, R. (1986). Projections of thalamic gustatory and lingual areas in the monkey, *Macaca fascicularis. Journal of Comparative Neurology, 244,* 213–228. (7)

Provine, R. R. (1979). "Wing-flapping" develops in wingless chicks. *Behavioral and Neural Biology, 27,* 233–237. (8)

Provine, R. R. (1981). Wing-flapping develops in chickens made flightless by feather mutations. *Developmental Psychobiology, 14,* 481–486. (8)

Provine, R. R. (1984). Wing-flapping during development and evolution. *American Scientist, 72,* 448–455. (8)

Provine, R. R. (1986). Yawning as a stereotyped action pattern and releasing stimulus. *Ethology, 72,* 109–122. (8)

Provine, R. R., & Westerman, J. A. (1979). Crossing the midline: Limits of early eye-hand behavior. *Child Development, 50,* 437–441. (14)

Purves, D., & Hadley, R. D. (1985). Changes in the dendritic branching of adult mammalian neurones revealed by repeated imaging *in situ. Nature, 315,* 404–406. (2)

Purves, D., & Lichtman, J. W. (1980). Elimination of synapses in the developing nervous system. *Science, 210,* 153–157. (5)

Quadagno, D. M., Briscoe, R., & Quadagno, J. S. (1977). Effect of perinatal gonadal hormones on selected nonsexual behavior patterns: A critical assessment of the non-human and human literature. *Psychological Bulletin, 84,* 62–80. (11)

Qin, Y.-L., McNaughton, B. L., Skaggs, W. E., & Barnes, C. A. (1997). Memory reprocessing in corticocortical and hippocampocortical neuronal ensembles. *Philosophical Transactions of the Royal Society of London,* B, *352,* 1525–1533. (9)

Ragsdale, D. S., McPhee, J. C., Scheuer, T., & Catterall, W. A. (1994). Molecular determinants of state-dependent block of Na^+ channels by local anesthetics. *Science, 265,* 1724–1728. (2)

Raine, A., Reynolds, C., Venables, P. H., Mednick, S. A., & Farrington, D. P. (1998). Fearlessness, stimulation-seeking, and large body size at age 3 as early predispositions to childhood aggression at age 11 years. *Archives of General Psychiatry, 55,* 745–751. (12)

Rainer, G., Asaad, W. F., & Miller, E. K. (1998). Selective representation of relevant information by neurons in the primate prefrontal cortex. *Nature, 393,* 577–579. (13)

Rainnie, D. G., Grunze, H. C. R., McCarley, R. W., & Greene, R. W. (1994). Adenosine inhibition of mesopontine cholinergic neurons: Implications for EEG arousal. *Science, 263,* 689–692. (9)

Rajkowska, G., Selemon, L. D., & Goldman-Rakic, P. S. (1998). Neuronal and glial somal size in the prefrontal cortex. *Archives of General Psychiatry, 55,* 215–224. (15)

Rakic, P. (1998). Cortical development and evolution. In M. S. Gazzaniga & J. S. Altman (Eds.), *Brain and mind: Evolutionary perspectives* (pp. 34–40). Strasbourg, France: Human Frontier Science Program. (5)

Rakic, P., & Lidow, M. S. (1995). Distribution and density of monoamine receptors in the primate visual cortex devoid of retinal input from early embryonic stages. *Journal of Neuroscience, 15,* 2561–2574. (6)

Ralph, M. R., Foster, R. G., Davis, F. C., & Menaker, M. (1990). Transplanted suprachiasmatic nucleus determines circadian period. *Science, 247,* 975–978. (9)

Ralph, M. R., & Menaker, M. (1988). A mutation of the circadian system in golden hamsters. *Science, 241,* 1225–1227. (9)

Ram, A., Pandey, H. P., Matsumura, H., Kasahara-Orita, K., Nakajima, T., Takahata, R., Satoh, S., Terao, A., & Hayaishi, O. (1997). CSF levels of prostaglandins, especially the level of prostaglandin D_2, are correlated with increasing propensity towards sleep in rats. *Brain Research, 751,* 81–89. (9)

Ramachandran, V. S. (1992). Filling in gaps in perception: Part 1. *Current Directions in Psychological Science, 1,* 199–205. (6)

Ramachandran, V. S., Armel, C., Foster, C., & Stoddard, R. (1998). Object recognition can drive motion perception. *Nature, 395,* 852–853. (6)

Ramachandran, V. S., & Blakeslee, S. (1998). *Phantoms in the brain.* New York: Morrow. (5)

Ramachandran, V. S., & Hirstein, W. (1998). The perception of phantom limbs: The D. O. Hebb lecture. *Brain, 121,* 1603–1630. (5)

Ramachandran, V. S., Rogers-Ramachandran, D., & Cobb, S. (1995). Touching the phantom limb. *Nature, 377,* 489–490. (5)

Ramirez, J. J., Fass, B., Karpiak, S. E., & Steward, O. (1987a). Ganglioside treatments reduce locomotor hyperactivity after bilateral lesions of the entorhinal cortex. *Neuroscience Letters, 75,* 283–287. (5)

Ramirez, J. J., Fass, B., Kilfoil, T., Henschel, B., Grones, W., & Karpiak, S. E. (1987b). Ganglioside-induced enhancement of behavioral recovery after bilateral lesions of the entorhinal cortex. *Brain Research, 414,* 85–90. (5)

Ramirez, J. J., McQuilkin, M., Carrigan, T., MacDonald, K., & Kelley, M. S. (1996). Progressive entorhinal cortex lesions accelerate hippocampal sprouting and spare spatial memory in rats. *Proceedings of the National Academy of Sciences, U.S.A., 93,* 15512–15517. (5)

Ramón-Cueto, A., Plant, G. W., Avila, J., & Bunge, M. B. (1998). Long-distance axonal regeneration in the transected adult rat spinal cord is promoted by olfactory ensheathing glia transplants. *Journal of Neuroscinece, 18,* 3803–3815. (5)

Ramsay, D. J., & Thrasher, T. N. (1990). Thirst and water balance. In E. M. Stricker (Ed.), *Handbook of behavioral neurobiology: Vol. 10: Neurobiology of food and fluid intake* (pp. 353–386). New York: Plenum Press. (10)

Randolph, C., Tierney, M. C., & Chase, T. N. (1995). Implicit memory in Alzheimer's disease. *Journal of Clinical and Experimental Neuropsychology, 17,* 343–351. (13)

Ranson, S. W., & Clark, S. L. (1959). *The anatomy of the nervous system: Its development and function* (10th ed.). Philadelphia: W. B. Saunders Co. (4)

Rapkin, A. J., Morgan, M., Goldman, L., Brann, D. W., Simone, D., & Mahesh, V. B. (1997). Progesterone metabolite allopregnanolone in women with premenstrual syndrome. *Obstetrics & Gynecology, 90,* 709–714. (11)

Rapoport, J. L., Giedd, J. N., Blumenthal, J., Hamburger, S., Jeffries, N., Fernandez, T., Nicolson, R., Bedwell, J., Lenane, M., Zijdenbos, A., Paus, T., & Evans, A. (1999). Progressive cortical change during adolescence in childhood-onset schizophrenia. *Archives of General Psychiatry, 56,* 649–654. (15)

Rapoport, S. I., & Robinson, P. J. (1986). Tight-junctional modification as the basis of osmotic opening of the blood-brain barrier. *Annals of the New York Academy of Sciences, 481,* 250–267. (2)

Rausch, G., & Scheich, H. (1982). Dendritic spine loss and enlargement during maturation of the speech control system in the mynah bird (*Gracula religiosa*). *Neuroscience Letters, 29,* 129–133. (5)

Rauschecker, J. P. (1995). Developmental plasticity and memory. *Behavioural Brain Research, 66,* 7–12. (6)

Rauschecker, J. P., Tian, B., & Hauser, M. (1995). Processing of complex sounds in the macaque nonprimary auditory cortex. *Science, 268,* 111–114. (7)

Raymond, J. L., Lisberger, S. G., & Mauk, M. D. (1996). The cerebellum: A neuronal learning machine? *Science, 272,* 1126–1131. (8)

Reburn, C. J., & Wynne-Edwards, K. E. (1999). Hormonal changes in males of a naturally biparental and a uniparental mammal. *Hormones and Behavior, 35,* 163–176. (11)

Recht, L. D., Lew, R. A., & Schwartz, W. J. (1995). Baseball teams beaten by jet lag. *Nature, 377,* 583. (9)

Rechtschaffen, A., & Bergmann, B. M. (1995). Sleep deprivation in the rat by the disk-over-water method. *Behavioural Brain Research, 69,* 55–63. (9)

Reed, J. M., & Squire, L. R. (1999). Impaired transverse patterning in human amnesia is a special case of impaired memory for two-choice discrimination tasks. *Behavioral Neuroscience, 113,* 3–9. (13)

Reeves, A. G., & Plum, F. (1969). Hyperphagia, rage, and dementia accompanying a ventromedial hypothalamic neoplasm. *Archives of Neurology, 20,* 616–624. (10)

Refinetti, R. (2000). *Circadian physiology.* Boca Raton, FL: CRC Press. (9)

Refinetti, R., & Carlisle, H. J. (1986). Complementary nature of heat production and heat intake during behavioral thermoregulation in the rat. *Behavioral and Neural Biology, 46,* 64–70. (10)

Refinetti, R., & Menaker, M. (1992). The circadian rhythm of body temperature. *Physiology & Behavior, 51,* 613–637. (9)

Regan, T. (1986). The rights of humans and other animals. *Acta Physiologica Scandinavica, 128*(Suppl. 554), 33–40. (1)

Reichelt, K. L., Seim, A. R., & Reichelt, W. H. (1996). Could schizophrenia be reasonably explained by Dohan's hypothesis on genetic interaction with a dietary peptide overload? *Progress in Neuro-Psychopharmacology & Biological Psychiatry, 20,* 1083–1114. (15)

Reichling, D. B., Kwiat, G. C., & Basbaum, A. I. (1988). Anatomy, physiology, and pharmacology of the periaqueductal gray contribution to antinociceptive controls. In H. L. Fields & J.-M. Besson (Eds.), *Progress in brain research* (Vol. 77, pp. 31–46). Amsterdam: Elsevier. (7)

Reinisch, J. M. (1981). Prenatal exposure to synthetic progestins increases potential for aggression in humans. *Science, 211,* 1171–1173. (11)

Ren, K., Thomas, D. A., & Dubner, R. (1995). Nerve growth factor alleviates a painful peripheral neuropathy in rats. *Brain Research, 699,* 286–292. (5)

Resnick, S. M., Maki, P. M., Golski, S., Kraut, M. A., & Zonderman, A. B. (1998). Effects of estrogen replacement therapy on PET cerebral blood flow and neuropsychological performance. *Hormones and Behavior, 34,* 171–182. (11)

Reynolds, C. A., Baker, L. A., & Pedersen, N. L. (1996). Models of spouse similarity: Applications to fluid ability measured in twins and their spouses. *Behavior Genetics, 26,* 73–88. (1)

Rice, G., Anderson, C., Risch, N., & Ebers, G. (1999). Male homosexuality: Absence of linkage to microsatellite markers at Xq28. *Science, 284,* 665–667. (11)

Richter, C. P. (1922). A behavioristic study of the activity of the rat. *Comparative Psychology Monographs, 1,* 1–55. (9)

Richter, C. P. (1936). Increased salt appetite in adrenalectomized rats. *American Journal of Physiology, 115,* 155–161. (10)

Richter, C. P. (1950). Taste and solubility of toxic compounds in poisoning of rats and humans. *Journal of Comparative and Physiological Psychology, 43,* 358–374. (7)

Richter, C. P. (1957). On the phenomenon of sudden death in animals and man. *Psychosomatic Medicine, 19,* 191–198. (12)

Richter, C. P. (1967). Psychopathology of periodic behavior in animals and man. In J. Zubin & H. F. Hunt (Eds.), *Comparative psychopathology* (pp. 205–227). New York: Grune & Stratton. (9)

Richter, C. P. (1975). Deep hypothermia and its effect on the 24-hour clock of rats and hamsters. *Johns Hopkins Medical Journal, 136,* 1–10. (9)

Richter, C. P., & Langworthy, O. R. (1933). The quill mechanism of the porcupine. *Journal für Psychologie und Neurologie, 45,* 143–153. (4)

Rickard, T. C., & Grafman, J. (1998). Losing their configural mind: Amnesic patients fail on transverse patterning. *Journal of Cognitive Neuroscience, 10,* 509–524. (13)

Riddle, D. R., Lo, D. C., & Katz, L. C. (1995). NT-4-mediated rescue of lateral geniculate neurons from effects of monocular deprivation. *Nature, 378,* 189–191. (6)

Riddle, W. J. R., & Scott, A. I. F. (1995). Relapse after successful electroconvulsive therapy: The use and impact of continuation antidepressant drug treatment. *Human Psychopharmacology, 10,* 201–205. (15)

Rinn, W. E. (1984). The neuropsychology of facial expression: A review of the neurological and psychological mechanisms for producing facial expressions. *Psychological Bulletin, 95,* 52–77. (8)

Rittenhouse, C. D., Shouval, H. Z., Paradiso, M. A., & Bear, M. F. (1999). Monocular deprivation induces homosynaptic long-term depression in visual cortex. *Nature, 397,* 347–350. (6)

Robbins, T. W., & Everitt, B. J. (1995). Arousal systems and attention. In M. S. Gazzaniga (Ed.), *The cognitive Neurosciences* (pp. 703–720). Cambridge, MA: MIT Press. (9)

Robertson, L., Treisman, A., Friedman-Hill, S., & Grabowecky, M. (1997). The interaction of spatial and object pathways: Evidence from Balint's syndrome. *Journal of Cognitive Neuropsychology, 9,* 295–317. (4)

Robillard, T. A. J., & Gersdorff, M. C. H. (1986). Prevention of pre- and perinatal acquired hearing defects: Part I. Study of causes. *Journal of Auditory Research, 26,* 207–237. (7)

Robinson, R. G., Boston, J. D., Starkstein, S. E., & Price, T. R. (1988). Comparison of mania and depression after brain injury: Causal factors. *American Journal of Psychiatry, 145,* 172–178. (15)

Roca, C. A., Schmidt, P. J., & Rubinow, D. R. (1999). Gonadal steroids and affective illness. *Neuroscientist, 5,* 227–237. (15)

Rocha, B. A., Fumagalli, F., Gainetdinov, R. R., Jones, S. R., Ator, R., Giros, B., Miller, G. W., & Caron, M. G. (1998). Cocaine self-administration in dopamine-transporter knockout mice. *Nature Neuroscience, 1,* 132–137. (3)

Rodriguez, E., George, N., Lachaux, J.-P., Martinerie, J., Renault, B., & Varela, F. J. (1999). Perception's shadow: Long-distance synchronization of human brain activity. *Nature, 397,* 430–433. (4)

Roe, A. W., & Ts'o, D. Y. (1995). Visual topography in primate V2: Multiple representation across functional stripes. *Journal of Neuroscience, 15,* 3689–3715. (6)

Roelfsema, P. R., Engel, A. K., König, P., & Singer, W. (1997). Visuomotor integration is associated with zero time-lag synchronization among cortical areas. *Nature, 385,* 157–161. (4)

Roffwarg, H. P., Muzio, J. N., & Dement, W. C. (1966). Ontogenetic development of human sleep-dream cycle. *Science, 152,* 604–609. (9)

Rogers, J., & Morrison, J. H. (1985). Quantitative morphology and regional and laminar distributions of senile plaques in Alzheimer's disease. *Journal of Neuroscience, 5,* 2801–2808. (13)

Rolls, E. T. (1995). Central taste anatomy and neurophysiology. In R. L. Doty (Ed.), *Handbook of olfaction and gustation* (pp. 549–573). New York: Dekker. (7)

Rolls, E. T. (1996a) The representation of space in the primate hippocampus, and its relation to memory. In K. Ishikawa, J. L. McGaugh, and H. Sakata (Eds.), *Brain processes and memory* (pp. 203–227). Amsterdam: Elsevier. (13)

Rolls, E. T. (1996b). A theory of hippocampal function in memory. *Hippocampus, 6,* 601–620. (13)

Romanski, L. M., Tian, B., Mishkin, M., Goldman-Rakic, P. S., & Rauschecker, J. P. (1999). Dual streams of auditory afferents target multiple domains in the primate prefrontal cortex. *Nature Neuroscience, 2,* 1131–1136. (7)

Rome, L. C., Loughna, P. T., & Goldspink, G. (1984). Muscle fiber activity in carp as a function of swimming speed and muscle temperature. *American Journal of Psychiatry, 247,* R272–R279. (8)

Romer, A. S. (1962). *The vertebrate body.* Philadelphia, PA: Saunders. (5)

Rommel, S. A., Pabst, D. A., & McLellan, W. A. (1998). Reproductive thermoregulation in marine mammals. *American Scientist, 86,* 440–448. (10)

Romo, R., Brody, C. D., Hernández, A., & Lemus, L. (1999). Neuronal correlates of parametric working memory in the prefrontal cortex. *Nature, 399,* 470–473. (13)

Roorda, A., & Williams, D. R. (1999). The arrangement of the three cone classes in the living human eye. *Nature, 397,* 520–522. (6)

Rose, J. E., Brugge, J. F., Anderson, D. J., & Hind, J. E. (1967). Phase-locked response to low-frequency tones in single auditory nerve fibers of the squirrel monkey. *Journal of Neurophysiology, 30,* 769–793. (7)

Rosenberg, D. R., & Keshavan, M. S.

(1998). Toward a neurodevelopmental model of obsessive-compulsive disorder. *Biological Psychiatry, 43,* 623–640. (12)

Rosenblatt, J. S. (1967). Nonhormonal basis of maternal behavior in the rat. *Science, 156,* 1512–1514. (11)

Rosenblatt, J. S. (1970). Views on the onset and maintenance of maternal behavior in the rat. In L. R. Aronson, E. Tobach, D. S. Lehrman, & J. S. Rosenblatt (Eds.), *Development and evolution of behavior* (pp. 489–515). San Francisco: W. H. Freeman. (11)

Rosenstein, D. L., Kalogeris, K. T., Kalafut, M., Malley, J., & Rubinow, D. R. (1996). Peripheral measures of arginine, vasopressin, atrial natriuretic peptide and adrenocorticotropic hormone in premenstrual syndrome. *Psychoneuroendocrinology, 21,* 347–359. (11)

Rosenzweig, M. R., & Bennett, E. L. (1996). Psychobiology of plasticity: Effects of training and experience on brain and behavior. *Behavioural Brain Research, 78,* 57–65. (5)

Rösler, A., & Witztum, E. (1998). Treatment of men with paraphilia with a long-acting analogue of gonadotropin-releasing hormone. *New England Journal of Medicine, 338,* 416–422. (11)

Rosvold, H. E., Mirsky, A. F., & Pribram, K. H. (1954). Influence of amygdalectomy on social behavior in monkeys. *Journal of Comparative and Physiological Psychology, 47,* 173–178. (12)

Roth, B. L., Willins, D. L., Kristiansen, K., & Kroeze, W. K. (1999). Activation is hallucinogenic and antagonism is therapeutic: Role of 5-HT$_{2A}$ receptors in atypical antipsychotic drug actions. *Neuroscientist, 5,* 254–262. (15)

Roth, E. C., & Hellige, J. B. (1998). Spatial processing and hemispheric asymmetry: Contributions of the transient/magnocellular visual system. *Journal of Cognitive Neuroscience, 10,* 472–484. (14)

Rovainen, C. M. (1976). Regeneration of Müller and Mauthner axons after spinal transection in larval lampreys. *Journal of Comparative Neurology, 168,* 545–554. (5)

Rovee-Collier, C. (1997). Dissociations in infant memory: Rethinking the development of explicit and implicit memory. *Psychological Review, 104,* 467–498. (13)

Rovee-Collier, C., Kupersmidt, J., O'Brien, L., Collier, G., & Tepper, V. (1991). Behavioral thermoregulation and immobilization: Conflicting demands for survival. *Journal of Comparative Psychology, 105,* 232–242. (10)

Rowland, N. (1980). Drinking behavior: Physiological, neurological, and environmental factors. In T. M. Toates & T. R. Halliday (Eds.), *Analysis of motivational processes* (pp. 39–59). London: Academic Press. (10)

Roy, A., DeJong, J., & Linnoila, M. (1989). Cerebrospinal fluid monoamine metabolites and suicidal behavior in depressed patients. *Archives of General Psychiatry, 46,* 609–612. (12)

Rozin, P. (1990). Getting to like the burn of chili pepper. In B. G. Green, J. R. Mason, & M. R. Kare (Eds.), *Chemical senses,* (Vol. 2, pp. 231–269). New York: Marcel Dekker. (10)

Rozin, P., Dow, S., Moscovitch, M., & Rajaram, S. (1998). What causes humans to begin and end a meal? A role for memory for what has been eaten, as evidenced by a study of multiple meal eating in amnesic patients. *Psychological Science, 9,* 392–396. (13)

Rozin, P., & Kalat, J. W. (1971). Specific hungers and poison avoidance as adaptive specializations of learning. *Psychological Review, 78,* 459–486. (10, 13)

Rozin, P., & Pelchat, M. L. (1988). Memories of mammaries: Adaptations to weaning from milk. *Progress in Psychobiology and Physiological Psychology, 13,* 1–29. (10)

Rozin, P., & Schull, J. (1988). The adaptive-evolutionary point of view in experimental psychology. In R. C. Atkinson, R. J. Herrnstein, G. Lindzey, & R. D. Luce (Eds.), *Stevens' handbook of experimental psychology (2nd ed.): Vol. 1. Perception and motivation* (pp. 503–546). New York: Wiley (13)

Rozin, P., & Vollmecke, T. A. (1986). Food likes and dislikes. *Annual Review of Nutrition, 6,* 433–456. (10)

Rozin, P., & Zellner, D. (1985). The role of Pavlovian conditioning in the acquisition of food likes and dislikes. *Annals of the New York Academy of Sciences, 443,* 189–202. (10)

Rubens, A. B., & Benson, D. F. (1971). Associative visual agnosia. *Archives of Neurology, 24,* 305–316. (6)

Rubia, K., Oosterlaan, J., Sergeant, J. A., Brandeis, D., & v. Leeuwen, T. (1998). Inhibitory dysfunction in hyperactive boys. *Behavioural Brain Research, 94,* 25–32. (5)

Rubin, B. D., & Katz, L. C. (1999). Optical imaging of odorant representations in the mammalian olfactory bulb. *Neuron, 23,* 499–511. (7)

Rudolph, U., Crestani, F., Benke, D., Brünig, I., Benson, J. A., Fritschy, J.-M., Martin, J. R., Bluethmann, H., & Möhler, H. (1999). Benzodiazepine actions mediated by specific γ-aminobutyric acid$_A$ receptor subtypes. *Nature, 401,* 796–800. (12)

Rumbaugh, D. M. (Ed.). (1977). *Language learning by a chimpanzee: The Lana Project.* New York: Academic Press. (14)

Rumbaugh, D. M. (1990). Comparative psychology and the great apes: Their competency in learning, language, and numbers. *Psychological Record, 40,* 15–39. (14)

Rusak, B., & Zucker, I. (1979). Neural regulation of circadian rhythms. *Physiological Reviews, 59,* 449–526. (9)

Russell, A. J., Munro, J. C., Jones, P. B., Hemsley, D. R., & Murray, R. M. (1997). Schizophrenia and the myth of intellectual decline. *American Journal of Psychiatry, 154,* 635–639. (15)

Russell, M. J., Switz, G. M., & Thompson, K. (1980). Olfactory influences on the human menstrual cycle. *Pharmacology, Biochemistry, and Behavior, 13,* 737–738. (7)

Rüttiger, L., Braun, D. I., Gegenfurtner, K. R., Petersen, D., Schönle, P., & Sharpe, L. T. (1999). Selective color constancy deficits after circumscribed unilateral brain lesions. *Journal of Neuroscience, 19,* 3094–3106. (6)

Saad, W. A., Luiz, A. C., Camargo, L. A. A., Renzi, A., & Manani, J. V. (1996). The lateral preoptic area plays a dual role in the regulation of thirst in the rat. *Brain Research Bulletin, 39,* 171–176. (10)

Sabel, B. A. (1997). Unrecognized potential of surviving neurons: Within-systems plasticity, recovery of function, and the hypothesis of minimal residual structure. *The Neuroscientist, 3,* 366–370. (5)

Sabel, B. A., Slavin, M. D., & Stein, D. G. (1984). GM$_1$ ganglioside treatment facilitates behavioral recovery from bilateral brain damage. *Science, 225,* 340–342. (5)

Sabo, K. T., & Kirtley, D. D. (1982). Objects and activities in the dreams of the blind. *International Journal of Rehabilitation Research, 5,* 241–242. (4)

Sack, D. A., Nurnberger, J., Rosenthal, N. E., Ashburn, E., & Wehr, T. A. (1985). Potentiation of antidepressant medications by phase advance of the sleep-wake cycle. *American Journal of Psychiatry, 142,* 606–608. (15)

Sackeim, H. A., Putz, E., Vingiano, W., Coleman, E., & McElhiney, M. (1988). Lateralization in the processing of emotionally laden information: I. Normal functioning. *Neuropsychiatry, Neuropsychology, and Behavioral Neurology, 1,* 97–110. (14)

Sakai, R. R., & Epstein, A. N. (1990). Dependence of adrenalectomy-induced sodium appetite on the action of angiotensin II in the brain of the rat. *Behavioral Neuroscience, 104,* 167–176. (10)

Salmelin, R., Hari, R., Lounasmaa, O. V., & Sams, M. (1994). Dynamics of brain activation during picture naming. *Nature, 368,* 463–465. (5)

Sanders, R. J. (1989). Sentence comprehension following agenesis of the corpus callosum. *Brain and Language, 37,* 59–72. (14)

Sanders, S. K., & Shekhar, A. (1995). Anxiolytic effects of chlordiazepoxide blocked by injection of GABA$_A$ and benzodiazepine receptor antagonists in the region of the anterior basolateral amygdala of rats. *Biological Psychiatry, 37,* 473–476. (12)

Sanderson, W. C., Rapee, R. M., & Barlow, D. H. (1989). The influence of an illusion of control on panic attacks induced via inhalation of 5.5% carbon dioxide-

enriched air. *Archives of General Psychiatry, 46,* 157–162. (12)

Sanes, J. N., Donoghue, J. P., Thangaraj, V., Edelman, R. R., & Warach, S. (1995). Shared neural substrates controlling hand movements in human motor cortex. *Science, 268,* 1775–1777. (8)

Sanes, J. R. (1993). Topographic maps and molecular gradients. *Current Opinion in Neurobiology, 3,* 67–74. (5)

Sanes, J. R., & Lichtman, J. W. (1999). Can molecules explain long-term potentiation? *Nature Neuroscience, 2,* 597–604. (13)

Sapolsky, R. M. (1992). *Stress, the aging brain, and the mechanisms of neuron death.* Cambridge, MA: MIT Press. (12)

Sáry, G., Vogels, R., & Orban, G. A. (1993). Cue-invariant shape selectivity of macaque inferior temporal neurons. *Science, 260,* 995–997. (6)

Satinoff, E. (1964). Behavioral thermoregulation in response to local cooling of the rat brain. *American Journal of Physiology, 206,* 1389–1394. (10)

Satinoff, E. (1991). Developmental aspects of behavioral and reflexive thermoregulation. In H. N. Shanir, G. A. Barr, & M. A. Hofer (Eds.), *Developmental psychobiology: New methods and changing concepts* (pp. 169–188). New York: Oxford University Press. (10)

Satinoff, E., McEwen, G. N., Jr., & Williams, B. A. (1976). Behavioral fever in newborn rabbits. *Science, 193,* 1139–1140. (10)

Satinoff, E., & Rutstein, J. (1970). Behavioral thermoregulation in rats with anterior hypothalamic lesions. *Journal of Comparative and Physiological Psychology, 71,* 77–82. (10)

Satinoff, E., Valentino, D., & Teitelbaum, P. (1976). Thermoregulatory cold-defense deficits in rats with preoptic/anterior hypothalamic lesions. *Brain Research Bulletin, 1,* 553–565. (10)

Sato, M. (1992). A lasting vulnerability to psychosis in patients with previous methamphetamine psychosis. *Annals of the New York Academy of Sciences, 654,* 160–170. (15)

Sato, M. A., Yada, M. M., & De Luca, L. A., Jr. (1996). Antagonism of

the renin-angiotensin system and water deprivation-induced NaCl intake in rats. *Physiology & Behavior, 60,* 1099–1104. (10)

Satz, P., & Green, M. F. (1999). Atypical handedness in schizophrenia: Some methodological and theoretical issues. *Schizophrenia Bulletin, 25,* 63–78. (15)

Satz, P., Strauss, E., & Whitaker, H. (1990). The ontogeny of hemispheric specialization: Some old hypotheses revisited. *Brain and Language, 38,* 596–614. (5)

Satz, P., Zaucha, K., McCleary, C., Light, R., Asarnow, R., & Becker, D. (1997). Mild head injury in children and adolescents: A review of studies (1970–1995). *Psychological Bulletin, 122,* 107–131. (5)

Saudou, F., Amara, D. A., Dierich, A., LeMeur, M., Ramboz, S., Segu, L., Buhot, M.-C., & Hen, R. (1994). Enhanced aggressive behavior in mice lacking 5-HT$_{1B}$ receptor. *Science, 265,* 1875–1878. (12)

Savage-Rumbaugh, E. S. (1990). Language acquisition in a nonhuman species: Implications for the innateness debate. *Developmental Psychobiology, 23,* 599–620. (14)

Savage-Rumbaugh, E. S. (1991). Language learning in the bonobo: How and why they learn. In N. A. Kresnegor, D. M. Rumbaugh, R. L. Schiefelbusch, & M. Studdert-Kennedy (Eds.), *Biological and behavioral determinants of language development* (pp. 209–233). Hillsdale, NJ: Lawrence Erlbaum. (14)

Savage-Rumbaugh, E. S. (1993). Language learnability in man, ape, and dolphin. In H. L. Roitblat, L. M. Herman, & P. E. Nachtigall (Eds.), *Language and communication: Comparative perspectives* (pp. 457–473). Hillsdale, NJ: Lawrence Erlbaum. (14)

Savage-Rumbaugh, E. S., Murphy, J., Sevcik, R. A., Brakke, K. E., Williams, S. L., & Rumbaugh, D. M. (1993). Language comprehension in ape and child. *Monographs of the Society for Research in Child Development, 58*(Serial no. 233). (14)

Savage-Rumbaugh, E. S., Sevcik, R. A., Brakke, K. E., & Rumbaugh, D. M. (1992). Symbols: Their communicative use, communication, and combination by bonobos (*Pan paniscus*). In L. P. Lipsitt & C. Rovee-Collier (Eds.), *Advances in infancy research* (Vol. 7, pp. 221–278). Norwood, NJ: Ablex. (14)

Scamell, T., Gerashchenko, D., Urade, Y., Onoe, H., Saper, C., & Hayaishi, O. (1998). Activation of ventrolateral preoptic neurons by the somnogen prostaglandin D_2. *Proceedings of the National Academy of Sciences (U.S.A.), 95,* 7754–7759. (9)

Scammell, T. E., Elmquist, J. K., Griffin, J. D., & Saper, C. B. (1996). Ventromedial preoptic prostaglandin-E_2 activates fever-producing autonomic pathways. *Journal of Neuroscience, 16,* 6246–6254. (10)

Schacher, S., Castellucci, V. F., & Kandel, E. R. (1988). cAMP evokes long-term facilitation in *Aplysia* sensory neurons that requires new protein synthesis. *Science, 240,* 1667–1669. (13)

Schacter, D. L. (1983). Amnesia observed: Remembering and forgetting in a natural environment. *Journal of Abnormal Psychology, 92,* 236–242. (13)

Schacter, D. L. (1985). Priming of old and new knowledge in amnesic patients and normal subjects. *Annals of the New York Academy of Sciences, 444,* 41–53. (13)

Schallert, T. (1983). Sensorimotor impairment and recovery of function in brain-damaged rats: Reappearance of symptoms during old age. *Behavioral Neuroscience, 97,* 159–164. (5)

Schärli, H., Harman, A. M., & Hogben, J. H. (1999). Blindsight in subjects with homonymous visual field defects. *Journal of Cognitive Neuroscience, 11,* 52–66. (6)

Scheibel, A. B. (1983). Dendritic changes. In B. Reisberg (Ed.), *Alzheimer's disease* (pp. 69–73). New York: Free Press. (13)

Scheibel, A. B. (1984). A dendritic correlate of human speech. In N. Geschwind & A. M. Galaburda (Eds.), *Cerebral dominance* (pp. 43–52). Cambridge, MA: Harvard University Press. (4)

Scheich, H., & Zuschratter, W. (1995). Mapping of stimulus features and meaning in gerbil auditory cortex with 2-deoxyglucose and c-fos antibodies. *Behavioural Brain Research, 66,* 195–205. (7)

Schellenberg, G. D., Bird, T. D., Wijsman, E. M., Orr, H. T., Anderson, L., Nemens, E., White, J. A., Bonnycastle, L., Weber, J. L., Alonso, M. E., Potter, H., Heston, L. L., & Martin, G. M. (1992). Genetic linkage evidence for a familial Alzheimer's disease locus on chromosome 14. *Science, 258,* 668–671. (13)

Schenck, C. H., & Mahowald, M. W. (1996). Long-term, nightly benzodiazepine treatment of injurious parasomnias and other disorders of disrupted nocturnal sleep in 170 adults. *American Journal of Medicine, 100,* 333–337. (9)

Schenk, D., Barbour, R., Dunn, W., Gordon, G., Grajeda, H., Guido, T., Hu, K., Huang, J., Johnson-Wood, K., Khan, K., Kholodenko, D., Lee, M., Liao, Z., Lieberburg, I., Motter, R., Mutter, L., Soriano, F., Shopp, G., Vasquez, N., Vandevert, C., Walker, S., Wogulis, M., Yednock, T., Games, D., & Seubert, P. (1999). Immunization with amyloid-β attenuates Alzheimer-disease-like pathology in the PDAPP mouse. *Nature, 400,* 173–177. (13)

Scherer, S. S. (1986). Reinnervation of the extraocular muscles in goldfish is nonselective. *Journal of Neuroscience, 6,* 764–773. (5)

Schieber, M. H., & Poliakov, A. V. (1998). Partial inactivation of the primary motor cortex hand area: Effects on individuated finger movements. *Journal of Neuroscience, 18,* 9038–9054. (8)

Schiermeier, Q. (1998). Animal rights activists turn the screw. *Nature, 396,* 505. (1)

Schiffman, S. S. (1983). Taste and smell in disease. *New England Journal of Medicine, 308,* 1275–1279, 1337–1343. (7)

Schiffman, S. S., & Erickson, R. P. (1971). A psychophysical model for gustatory quality. *Physiology & Behavior, 7,* 617–633. (7)

Schiffman, S. S., & Erickson, R. P. (1980). The issue of primary tastes versus a taste continuum. *Neuroscience & Biobehavioral Reviews, 4,* 109–117. (7)

Schiffman, S. S., Lockhead, E., & Maes, F. W. (1983). Amiloride reduces the taste intensity of Na^+ and Li^+ salts and sweeteners. *Proceedings of the National Academy of Sciences, U.S.A., 80,* 6136–6140. (7)

Schiffman, S. S., McElroy, A. E., & Erickson, R. P. (1980). The range of taste quality of sodium salts. *Physiology & Behavior, 24,* 217–224. (7)

Schlaug, G., Jäncke, L., Huang, Y., & Steinmetz, H. (1995). In vivo evidence of structural brain asymmetry in musicians. *Science, 267,* 699–701. (5)

Schmid, A., Koch, M., & Schnitzler, H.-U. (1995). Conditioned pleasure attenuates the startle response in rats. *Neurobiology of Learning and Memory, 64,* 1–3. (12)

Schmidt, P. J., Nieman, L. K., Danaceau, M. A., Adams, L. F., & Rubinow, D. R. (1998). Differential behavioral effects of gonadal steroids in women with and in those without premenstrual syndrome. *New England Journal of Medicine, 338,* 209–216. (11)

Schneider, B. A., Trehub, S. E., Morrongiello, B. A., & Thorpe, L. A. (1986). Auditory sensitivity in preschool children. *Journal of the Acoustical Society of America, 79,* 447–452. (7)

Schnider, A., & Ptak, R. (1999). Spontaneous confabulators fail to suppress currently irrelevant memory traces. *Nature Neuroscience, 2,* 677–681. (13)

Schöpf, J., Bryois, C., Jonquière, M., & Le, P. K. (1984). On the nosology of severe psychiatric post-partum disorders. *European Archives of Psychiatry and Neurological Sciences, 234,* 54–63. (15)

Schou, M. (1997). Forty years of lithium treatment. *Archives of General Psychiatry, 54,* 9–13. (15)

Schuckit, M. A., & Smith, T. L. (1996). An 8-year follow-up of 450 sons of alcoholic and control subjects. *Archives of General Psychiatry, 53,* 202–210. (15)

Schulkin, J. (1991). *Sodium hunger: The search for a salty taste.* Cambridge, England: Cambridge University Press. (10)

Schulz, J. B., Matthews, R. T., Jenkins, B. G., Brar, P., & Beal, M. F. (1995). Improved therapeutic window for treatment of histotoxic hypoxia with a free radical spin trap. *Journal of Cerebral*

Blood Flow and Metabolism, 15, 948–952. (5)

Schulz, J. B., Weller, M., & Moskowitz, M. A. (1999). Caspases as treatment targets in stroke and neurodegenerative diseases. *Annals of Neurology, 45,* 421–429. (5)

Schurr, A., Miller, J. J., Payne, R. S., & Rigor, B. M. (1999). An increase in lactate output by brain tissue serves to meet the energy needs of glutamate-activated neurons. *Journal of Neuroscience, 19,* 34–39. (2)

Schwab, M. E. (1998). Regenerative nerve fiber growth in the adult central nervous system. *News in Physiological Sciences, 13,* 294–298. (5)

Schwartz, J. C., Giros, B., Martres, M.-P., & Sokoloff, P. (1992). The dopamine receptor family: Molecular biology and pharmacology. *Seminars in the Neurosciences, 4,* 99–108. (3)

Schwartz, L., & Tulipan, L. (1933). An outbreak of dermatitis among workers in a rubber manufacturing plant. *Public Health Reports, 48,* 809–814. (15)

Schwartz, M. B., & Brownell, K. D. (1995). Matching individuals to weight loss treatments: A survey of obesity experts. *Journal of Consulting and Clinical Psychology, 63,* 149–153. (10)

Schwartz, M. F. (1995). Re-examining the role of executive functions in routine action production. *Annals of the New York Academy of Sciences, 769,* 321–335. (4)

Schwartz, W. J., & Gainer, H. (1977). Suprachiasmatic nucleus: Use of ^{14}C-labeled deoxyglucose uptake as a functional marker. *Science, 197,* 1089–1091. (9)

Scott, T. R. (1987). Coding in the gustatory system. In T. E. Finger & W. L. Silver (Eds.), *Neurobiology of taste and smell* (pp. 355–378). New York: John Wiley. (7)

Scott, T. R. (1992). Taste: The neural basis of body wisdom. In A. P. Simopoulos (Ed.), *Nutritional triggers for health and in disease* (pp. 1–39). Basel: Karger. (7)

Scott, T. R., & Plata-Salaman, C. R. (1991). Coding of taste quality. In T. V. Getchell et al. (Eds.), *Smell and taste in health and disease* (pp. 345–368). New York: Raven. (7)

Scovern, A. W., & Kilmann, P. R. (1980). Status of electroconvulsive therapy: Review of the outcome literature. *Psychological Bulletin, 87,* 260–303. (15)

Scoville, W. B., & Milner, B. (1957). Loss of recent memory after bilateral hippocampal lesions. *Journal of Neurology, Neurosurgery, and Psychiatry, 20,* 11–21. (13)

Searle, J. R. (1992). *The rediscovery of the mind.* Cambridge, MA: MIT Press. (1)

Seeley, R. J., Kaplan, J. M., & Grill, H. J. (1995). Effect of occluding the pylorus on intraoral intake: A test of the gastric hypothesis of meal termination. *Physiology & Behavior, 58,* 245–249. (10)

Seeman, P., Lee, T., Chau-Wong, M., & Wong, K. (1976). Antipsychotic drug doses and neuroleptic/dopamine receptors. *Nature, 261,* 717–719. (15)

Seidenberg, M. S. (1997). Language acquisition and use: Learning and applying probabilistic constraints. *Science, 275,* 1599–1603. (14)

Sejnowski, T. J., Chattarji, S., & Stanton, P. K. (1990). Homosynaptic long-term depression in hippocampus and neocortex. *Seminars in the Neurosciences, 2,* 355–363. (13)

Selemon, L. D., Rajkowska, G., & Goldman-Rakic, P. S. (1995). Abnormally high neuronal density in the schizophrenic cortex. *Archives of General Psychiatry, 52,* 805–818. (15)

Selkoe, D. J. (1999). Translating cell biology into therapeutic advances in Alzheimer's disease. *Nature, 399*(Suppl.), A23–A31. (13)

Selye, H. (1979). Stress, cancer, and the mind. In J. Taché, H. Selye, & S. B. Day (Eds.), *Cancer, stress, and death* (pp. 11–27). New York: Plenum. (12)

Selzer, M. E. (1978). Mechanisms of functional recovery and regeneration after spinal cord transection in larval sea lamprey. *Journal of Physiology, 277,* 395–408. (5)

Sereno, A. B., & Maunsell, J. H. R. (1998). Shape selectivity in primate lateral intraparietal cortex. *Nature, 395,* 500–503. (6)

Serretti, A., Macciardi, F., Cusin, C., Lattuada, E., Lilli, R., & Smeraldi, E. (1998). Dopamine receptor D$_4$ gene is associated with delusional symptomatology in mood disorders. *Psychiatry Research, 80,* 129–136. (3)

Sershen, H., Toth, E., Lajtha, A., & Vizi, E. S. (1995). Nicotine effects on presynaptic receptor interactions. *Annals of the New York Academy of Sciences, 757,* 238–244. (8)

Shadlen, M. N., & Newsome, W. T. (1996). Motion perception: Seeing and deciding. *Proceedings of the National Academy of Sciences, U.S.A., 93,* 628–633. (8)

Shah, A., & Lisak, R. P. (1993). Immunopharmacologic therapy in myasthenia gravis. *Clinical Neuropharmacology, 16,* 97–103. (8)

Shapiro, B. E., & Danly, M. (1985). The role of the right hemisphere in the control of speech prosody in propositional and affective contexts. *Brain and Language, 25,* 19–36. (14)

Shapiro, C. M., Bortz, R., Mitchell, D., Bartel, P., & Jooste, P. (1981). Slow-wave sleep: A recovery period after exercise. *Science, 214,* 1253–1254. (9)

Shapley, R. (1995). Parallel neural pathways and visual function. In M. S. Gazzaniga (Ed.), *The cognitive neurosciences* (pp. 315–324). Cambridge, MA: MIT Press. (6)

Shatz, C. J. (1992, September). The developing brain. *Scientific American, 267*(9), 60–67. (5)

Shatz, C. J. (1996). Emergence of order in visual-system development. *Proceedings of the National Academy of Sciences, U.S.A., 93,* 602–608. (6)

Sherin, J. E., Shiromani, P. J., McCarley, R. W., & Saper, C. B. (1996). Activation of ventrolateral preoptic neurons during sleep. *Science, 271,* 216–219. (9)

Sherrington, C. S. (1906). *The integrative action of the nervous system.* New York: Scribner's. (2nd ed.). New Haven, CT: Yale University Press, 1947. (3)

Sherrington, R., Rogaev, E. I., Liang, Y., Rogaeva, E. A., Levesque, G., Ikeda, M., Chi, H., Lin, C., Li, G., Holman, K., Tsuda, T., Mar, L., Foncin, J.-F., Bruni, A. C., Montesi, M. P., Sorbi, S., Rainero, I., Pinessi, L., Nee, L., Chumakov, I., Pollen, D., Brookes, A., Sanseau, P., Polinsky, R. J., Wasco, W., DaSilva, H. A. R., Haines, J. L.,

Pericak-Vance, M. A., Tanzi, R. E., Roses, A. D., Fraser, P. E., Rommens, J. M., & St. George-Hyslop, P. H. (1995). Cloning of a gene bearing missense mutations in early-onset familial Alzheimer's disease. *Nature, 375,* 754–760. (13)

Sherwin, B. (1997). Estrogen effects on cognition in menopausal women. *Neurology, 48,* S21–S26. (11)

Shik, M. L., & Orlovsky, G. N. (1976). Neurophysiology of locomotor automatism. *Physiological Reviews, 56,* 465–501. (8)

Shirasaki, R., Katsumata, R., & Murakami, F. (1998). Change in chemoattractant responsiveness of developing axons at an intermediate target. *Science, 279,* 105–107. (5)

Shirley, S. G., & Persaud, K. C. (1990). The biochemistry of vertebrate olfaction and taste. *Seminars in the Neurosciences, 2,* 59–68. (7)

Shiromani, P. J. (1998). Sleep circuitry, regulation, and function: Lessons from c-fos, leptin, and timeless. *Progress in Psychobiology and Physiological Psychology, 17,* 67–90. (9)

Shoulson, I. (1990). Huntington's disease: Cognitive and psychiatric features. *Neuropsychiatry, Neuropsychology, and Behavioral Neurology, 3,* 15–22. (8)

Shutts, D. (1982). *Lobotomy: Resort to the knife.* New York: Van Nostrand Reinhold. (4)

Siegel, A., & Pott, C. B. (1988). Neural substrates of aggression and flight in the cat. *Progress in Neurobiology, 31,* 261–283. (12)

Siegel, J. M. (1995). Phylogeny and the function of REM sleep. *Behavioural Brain Research, 69,* 29–34. (9)

Siegel, J. M., Nienhuis, R., Fahringer, H. M., Paul, R., Shiromani, P., Dement, W. C., Mignot, E., & Chiu, C. (1991). Neuronal activity in narcolepsy: Identification of cataplexy-related cells in the medial medulla. *Science, 252,* 1315–1318. (9)

Silberg, J., Pickles, A., Rutter, M., Hewitt, J., Simonoff, E., Maes, H., Carbonneau, R., Murrelle, L., Foley, D., & Eaves, L. (1999). The influence of genetic factors and life stress on depression among adolescent girls. *Archives of General Psychiatry, 56,* 225–232. (15)

Silbersweig, D. A., Stern, E., Frith, C., Cahill, C., Holmes, A., Grootoonk, S., Seaward, J., McKenna, P., Chua, S. E. Schnorr, L., Jones, T., & Frackowiak, R. S. J. (1995). A functional neuroanatomy of hallucinations in schizophrenia. *Nature, 378,* 176–179. (15)

Silinsky, E. M. (1989). Adenosine derivatives and neuronal function. *Seminars in the Neurosciences, 1,* 155–165. (3)

Singer, W. (1986). Neuronal activity as a shaping factor in postnatal development of visual cortex. In W. T. Greenough & J. M. Jusaska (Eds.), *Developmental neuropsychobiology* (pp. 271–293). Orlando, FL: Academic Press. (6)

Sirigu, A., Grafman, J., Bressler, K., & Sunderland, T. (1991). Multiple representations contribute to body knowledge processing. Evidence from a case of autopagnosia. *Brain, 114,* 629–642. (7)

Sjöström, M., Friden, J., & Ekblom, B. (1987). Endurance, what is it? Muscle morphology after an extremely long distance run. *Acta Physiologica Scandinavica, 130,* 513–520. (8)

Skaggs, W. E., & McNaughton, B. L. (1996). Replay of neuronal firing sequences in rat hippocampus during sleep following spatial experience. *Science, 271,* 1870–1873. (9)

Slob, A. K., Bax, C. M., Hop, W. C. J., Rowland, D. L., & van der Werff ten Bosch, J. J. (1996). Sexual arousability and the menstrual cycle. *Psychoneuroendocrinology, 21,* 545–558. (11)

Slotkin, T. A. (1998). Fetal nicotine or cocaine exposure: Which is worse? *Journal of Pharmacology and Experimental Therapeutics, 285,* 931–945. (5)

Smale, L., Holekamp, K. E., Weldele, M., Frank, L. G., & Glickman, S. E. (1995). Competition and cooperation between litter-mates in the spotted hyaena, *Crocuta crocuta. Animal Behaviour, 50,* 671–682. (11)

Smith, C., & Rose, G. M. (1997). Post-training paradoxical sleep in rats is increased after spatial learning in the Morris water maze. *Behavioral Neuroscience, 111,* 1197–1204. (9)

Smith, C., & Wong, P. T. P. (1991).

Paradoxical sleep increases predict successful learning in a complex operant task. *Behavioral Neuroscience, 105,* 282–288. (9)

Smith, C. A. D., Gough, A. C., Leigh, P. N., Summers, B. A., Harding, A. E., Maranganore, D. M., Sturman, S. G., Schapira, A. H. V., Williams, A. C., Spurr, N. K., & Wolf, C. R. (1992). Debrisoquine hydroxylase gene polymorphism and susceptibility to Parkinson's disease. *Lancet, 339,* 1375–1377. (8)

Smith, C. U. M. (1996). *Elements of molecular neurobiology.* Chichester, England: John Wiley. (2, 3)

Smith, D. V., VanBuskirk, R. L., Travers, J. B., & Bieber, S. L. (1983). Coding of taste stimuli by hamster brain stem neurons. *Journal of Neurophysiology, 50,* 541–558. (7)

Smith, G. P. (1998). Pregastric and gastric satiety. In G. P. Smith (Ed.), *Satiation: From gut to brain* (pp. 10–39). New York: Oxford University Press. (10)

Smith, G. P., & Gibbs, J. (1998). The satiating effects of cholecystokinin and bombesin-like peptides. In G. P. Smith (Ed.), *Satiation: From gut to brain* (pp. 97–125). New York: Oxford University Press. (10)

Smith, K. A., Fairburn, C. G., & Cowen, P. J. (1999). Symptomatic relapse in bulimia nervosa following acute tryptophan depletion. *Archives of General Psychiatry, 56,* 171–176. (10)

Smith, L. T. (1975). The interanimal transfer phenomenon: A review. *Psychological Bulletin, 81,* 1078–1095. (13)

Smith, M. A., Brandt, J., & Shadmehr, R. (2000). Motor disorder in Huntington's disease begins as a dysfunction in error feedback control. *Nature, 403,* 544–549. (8)

Smith, S., Lindefors, N., Hurd, Y., & Sharp, T. (1995). Electroconvulsive shock increases dopamine D$_1$ and D$_2$ receptor mRNA in the nucleus accumbens of the rat. *Psychopharmacology, 120,* 333–340. (15)

Snyder, L. H., Grieve, K. L., Brotchie, P., & Andersen, R. A. (1998). Separate body- and world-referenced representations of visual space in parietal cortex. *Nature, 394,* 887–891. (8)

Sobel, N., Prabhakaran, V., Demond, J. E., Glover, G. H., Goode, R. L.,

Sullivan, E. V., & Gabrieli, J. D. E. (1998). Sniffing and smelling: Separate subsystems in the human olfactory cortex. *Nature, 392,* 282–286. (7)

Solms, M. (1997). *The neuropsychology of dreams.* Mahwah, NJ: Erlbaum. (9)

Solms, M. (in press). Dreaming and REM sleep are controlled by different brain mechanisms. *Behavioral and Brain Sciences.* (9)

Soltesz, I., Smetters, D. K., & Mody, I. (1995). Tonic inhibition originates from synapses close to the soma. *Nature, 14,* 1273–1283. (3)

Somero, G. N. (1996). Temperature and proteins: Little things can mean a lot. *News in Physiological Sciences, 11,* 72–77. (10)

Somjen, G. G. (1988). Nervenkitt: Notes on the history of the concept of neuroglia. *Glia, 1,* 2–9. (2)

Sowell, E. R., Thompson, P. M., Holmes, C. J., Jernigan, T. L., & Toga, A. W. (1999). *In vivo* evidence for post-adolescent brain maturation in frontal and striatal regions. *Nature Neuroscience, 2,* 859–861. (15)

Sperry, R. W. (1943). Visuomotor coordination in the newt (*Triturus viridescens*) after regeneration of the optic nerve. *Journal of Comparative Neurology, 79,* 33–55. (5)

Sperry, R. W. (1961). Cerebral organization and behavior. *Science, 133,* 1749–1757. (14)

Spiegel, T. A. (1973). Caloric regulation of food intake in man. *Journal of Comparative and Physiological Psychology, 84,* 24–37. (10)

Spindler, K. A., Sullivan, E. V., Menon, V., Lim, K. O., & Pfefferbaum, A. (1997). Deficits in multiple systems of working memory in schizophrenia. *Schizophrenia Research, 27,* 1–10. (15)

Spurzheim, J. G. (1908). *Phrenology* (rev. ed.) Philadelphia: Lippincott. (14)

Squire, L. R. (1992). Memory and the hippocampus: A synthesis from findings with rats, monkeys, and humans. *Psychological Review, 99,* 195–231. (13)

Squire, L. R., Amaral, D. G., & Press, G. A. (1990). Magnetic resonance imaging of the hippocampal formation and mammillary nuclei distinguish medial temporal lobe and diencephalic amnesia.

Journal of Neuroscience, 10, 3106–3117. (13)

Stanford, L. R. (1987). Conduction velocity variations minimize conduction time differences among retinal ganglion cell axons. *Science, 238,* 358–360. (2)

Stanford, S. C. (1995). Central noradrenergic neurones and stress. *Pharmacology & Therapeutics, 68,* 297–342. (12)

Stanley, B. G., & Gillard, E. R. (1994). Hypothalamic neuropeptide Y and the regulation of eating behavior and body weight. *Current Directions in Psychological Science, 3,* 9–15. (10)

Stanley, B. G., Schwartz, D. H., Hernandez, L., Leibowitz, S. F., & Hoebel, B. G. (1989). Patterns of extracellular 5-hydroxyindoleacetic acid (5-HIAA) in the paraventricular hypothalamus (PVN): Relation to circadian rhythm and deprivation-induced eating behavior. *Pharmacology, Biochemistry, & Behavior, 33,* 257–260. (10)

Starbuck, E. M., Lane, J. R., & Fitts, D. A. (1997). Interaction of hydration and subfornical organ lesions in sodium-depletion induced salt appetite. *Behavioral Neuroscience, 111,* 206–213. (10)

Stark, R. E., & McGregor, K. K. (1997). Follow-up study of a right- and a left-hemispherectomized child: Implications for localization and impairment of language in children. *Brain and Language, 60,* 222–242. (14)

Starkstein, S. E., & Robinson, R. G. (1986). Cerebral lateralization in depression. *American Journal of Psychiatry, 143,* 1631. (15)

Starr, C., & Taggart, R. (1989). *Biology: The unity and diversity of life.* Pacific Grove, CA: Brooks/Cole. (3, 4, 7, 8)

Stein, D. G., & Fulop, Z. L. (1998). Progesterone and recovery after traumatic brain injury: An overview. *Neuroscientist, 4,* 435–442. (5)

Stein, M. B., Hanna, C., Koverola, C., Torchia, M., & McClarty, B. (1997). Structural brain changes in PTSD. *Annals of the New York Academy of Sciences, 821,* 76–82. (12)

Stella, N., Schweitzer, P., & Piomelli, D. (1997). A second endogenous cannabinoid that modulates long-

term potentiation. *Nature, 382,* 677–678. (3)

Stephens, T. W., Basinski, M., Bristow, P. K., Bue-Valleskey, J. M., Burgett, S. G., Craft, L., Hale, J., Hoffman, J., Hsiung, H. M., Kriauciunas, A., MacKellar, W., Rosteck, P. R., Jr., Schoner, B., Smith, D., Tinsley, F. C., Zhang, W.-Y., & Heiman, M. (1995). The role of neuropeptide Y in the antiobesity action of the *obese* gene product. *Nature, 377,* 530–532. (10)

Stevens, C. F. (1998). A million dollar question: Does LTP = memory? *Neuron, 20,* 1–2. (13)

Stevens, T., & Karmiloff-Smith, A. (1997). Word learning in a special population: Do individuals with Williams syndrome obey lexical constraints? *Journal of Child Language, 24,* 737–765. (14)

Stewart, J. W., Quitkin, F. M., McGrath, P. J., Amsterdam, J., Fava, M., Fawcett, J., Reimherr, F., Rosenbaum, J., Beasley, C., & Roback, P. (1998). Use of pattern analysis to predict differential relapse of remitted patients with major depression during 1 year of treatment with fluoxetine or placebo. *Archives of General Psychiatry, 55,* 334–343. (15)

Stickgold, R., Scott, L., Rittenhouse, C., & Hobson, J. A. (1999). Sleep-induced changes in associative memory. *Journal of Cognitive Neuroscience, 11,* 182–193. (9)

Stip, E. (2000). Novel antipsychotics: Issues and controversies. Typicality of atypical antipsychotics. *Journal of Psychiatry & Neuroscience, 25,* 137–153. (15)

Stockman, E. R., Callaghan, R. S., Gallagher, C. A., & Baum, M. J. (1986). Sexual differentiation of play behavior in the ferret. *Behavioral Neuroscience, 100,* 563–568. (11)

Stoll, A. L., Severus, W. E., Freeman, M. P., Rueter, S., Zboyan, H. A., Diamond, E., Cross, K. K., & Marangell, L. B. (1999). Omega 3 fatty acids in bipolar disorder. *Archives of General Psychiatry, 56,* 407–412. (15)

Stone, V. E., Nisenson, L., Eliassen, J. C., & Gazzaniga, M. S. (1996). Left hemisphere representations of emotional facial expressions. *Neuropsychologia, 34,* 23–29. (14)

Storey, K. B., & Storey, J. M. (1999, May/June). Lifestyles of the cold and frozen. *The Sciences, 39*(3), 33–37. (10)

Stout, A. K., Raphael, H. M., Kanterewicz, B. I., Klann, E., & Reynolds, I. J. (1998). Glutamate-induced neuron death requires mitochondrial calcium uptake. *Nature Neuroscience, 1,* 366–373. (5)

Strack, F., Martin, L. L., & Stepper, S. (1988). Inhibiting and facilitating conditions of the human smile: A nonobtrusive test of the facial feedback hypothesis. *Journal of Personality and Social Psychology, 54,* 768–777. (12)

Strakowski, S. M., Del Bello, M. P., Sax, K. W., Zimmerman, M. E., Shear, P. K., Hawkins, J. M., & Larson, E. R. (1999). Brain magnetic resonance imaging of structural abnormalities in bipolar disorder. *Archives of General Psychiatry, 56,* 254–260. (15)

Strichartz, G., Rando, T., & Wang, G. K. (1987). An integrated view of the molecular toxinology of sodium channel gating in excitable cells. *Annual Review of Neuroscience, 10,* 237–267. (2)

Stricker, E. M. (1969). Osmoregulation and volume regulation in rats: Inhibition of hypovolemic thirst by water. *American Journal of Physiology, 217,* 98–105. (10)

Stricker, E. M. (1983). Thirst and sodium appetite after colloid treatment in rats: Role of the renin-angiotensin-aldosterone system. *Behavioral Neuroscience, 97,* 725–737. (10)

Stricker, E. M., Swerdloff, A. F., & Zigmond, M. J. (1978). Intrahypothalamic injections of kainic acid produce feeding and drinking deficits in rats. *Brain Research, 158,* 470–473. (10)

Strickland, T. L., Miller, B. L., Kowell, A., & Stein, R. (1998). Neurobiology of cocaine-induced organic brain impairment: Contributions from functional neuroimaging. *Neuropsychology Review, 8,* 1–9. (3)

Strittmatter, W. J., & Roses, A. D. (1995). Apolipoprotein E: Emerging story in the pathogenesis of Alzheimer's disease. *The Neuroscientist, 1,* 298–306. (13)

Strobel, A., Issad, T., Camoin, L., Ozata, M., & Strosberg, A. D. (1998). A leptin missense mutation associated with hypogo-

nadism and morbid obesity. *Nature Genetics, 18,* 213–215. (10)

Stryker, M. P., & Sherk, H. (1975). Modification of cortical orientation selectivity in the cat by restricted visual experience: A reexamination. *Science, 190,* 904–906. (6)

Stryker, M. P., Sherk, H., Leventhal, A. G., & Hirsch, H. V. B. (1978). Physiological consequences for the cat's visual cortex of effectively restricting early visual experience with oriented contours. *Journal of Neurophysiology, 41,* 896–909. (6)

Strzelczuk, M., & Romaniuk, A. (1996). Fear induced by the blockade of GABA$_A$-ergic transmission in the hypothalamus of the cat: Behavioral and neurochemical study. *Behavioural Brain Research, 72,* 63–71. (12)

Studer, L., Tabar, V., & McKay, R. D. G. (1998). Transplantation of expanded mesencephalic precursors leads to recovery in parkinsonian rats. *Nature Neuroscience, 1,* 290–295. (8)

Stunkard, A. J., Sorensen, T. I. A., Hanis, C., Teasdale, T. W., Chakraborty, R., Schull, W. J., & Schulsinger, F. (1986). An adoption study of human obesity. *New England Journal of Medicine, 314,* 193–198. (10)

Stuss, D. T., & Benson, D. F. (1984). Neuropsychological studies of the frontal lobes. *Psychological Bulletin, 95,* 3–28. (4)

Südhof, T. C. (1995). The synaptic vesicle cycle: A cascade of protein-protein interactions. *Nature, 375,* 645–653. (3)

Sugita, Y. (1996). Global plasticity in adult visual cortex following reversal of visual input. *Nature, 380,* 523–526. (6)

Sullivan, R. M., & Gratton, A. (1999). Lateralized effects of medial prefrontal cortex lesions on neuroendocrine and autonomic stress responses in rats. *Journal of Neuroscience, 19,* 2834–2840. (12)

Susser, E., Neugebauer, R., Hoek, H. W., Brown, A. S., Lin, S., Labovitz, D., & Gorman, J. M. (1996). Schizophrenia after prenatal famine. *Archives of General Psychiatry, 53,* 25–31. (15)

Sutton, L. C., Lea, E., Will, M. J., Schwartz, B. A., Hartley, C. E.,

Poole, J. C., Watkins, L. R., & Maier, S. F. (1997). Inescapable shock-induced potentiation of morphine analgesia. *Behavioral Neuroscience, 111,* 1105–1113. (7)

Sutton, R. L., Hovda, D. A., & Feeney, D. M. (1989). Amphetamine accelerates recovery of locomotor function following bilateral frontal cortex ablation in rats. *Behavioral Neuroscience, 103,* 837–841. (5)

Suvisaari, J. M., Haukka, J. K., Tanskanen, A. J., & Lönnqvist, J. K. (1999). Decline in the incidence of schizophrenia in Finnish cohorts born from 1954 to 1965. *Archives of General Psychiatry, 56,* 733–740. (15)

Suzdak, P. D., Glowa, J. R., Crawley, J. N., Schwartz, R. D., Skolnick, P., & Paul, S. M. (1986). A selective imidazobenzodiazepine antagonist of ethanol in the rat. *Science, 234,* 1243–1247. (12)

Swaab, D. F., & Hofman, M. A. (1990). An enlarged suprachiasmatic nucleus in homosexual men. *Brain Research, 537,* 141–148. (11)

Swaab, D. F., Slob, A. K., Houtsmuller, E. J., Brand, T., & Zhou, J. N. (1995). Increased number of vasopressin neurons in the suprachiasmatic nucleus (SCN) of "bisexual" adult male rats following perinatal treatment with the aromatase blocker ATD. *Developmental Brain Research, 85,* 273–279. (11)

Swan, H., & Schatte, C. (1977). Antimetabolic extract from the brain of the hibernating ground squirrel, *Citellus tridecemlineatus. Science, 195,* 84–85. (9)

Szymusiak, R. (1995). Magnocellular nuclei of the basal forebrain: Substrates of sleep and arousal regulation. *Sleep, 18,* 478–500. (9)

Tabrizi, S. J., Cleeter, M. W. J., Xuereb, J., Taanman, J.-W., Cooper, J. M., & Schapira, A. H. V. (1999). Biochemical abnormalities and excitotoxicity in Huntington's disease brain. *Annals of Neurology, 45,* 25–32. (8)

Taddese, A., Nah, S. Y., & McCleskey, E. W. (1995). Selective opioid inhibition of small nociceptive neurons. *Science, 270,* 1366–1369. (7)

Tager-Flusberg, H., Boshart, J., & Baron-Cohen, S. (1998). Reading the windows to the soul: Evidence of domain-specific sparing in Williams syndrome. *Journal of Cognitive Neuroscience, 10,* 631–639. (14)

Taghavi, E., Menkes, D. B., Howard, R. C., Mason, P. A., Shaw, J. P., & Spears, G. F. S. (1995). Premenstrual syndrome: A double-blind controlled trial of desipramine and methylscopolamine. *International Clinical Psychopharmacology, 10,* 119–122. (11)

Takeuchi, A. (1977). Junctional transmission: I. Postsynaptic mechanisms. In E. R. Kandel (Ed.), *Handbook of physiology Section 1: Neurophysiology, Vol. 1. Cellular biology of neurons* (Pt. 1, pp. 295–327). Bethesda, MD: American Physiological Society. (3)

Takeuchi, A. H., & Hulse, S. H. (1993). Absolute pitch. *Psychological Bulletin, 113,* 345–361. (5)

Talbot, J. D., Marrett, S., Evans, A. C., Meyer, E., Bushnell, M. C., & Duncan, G. H. (1991). Multiple representations of pain in human cerebral cortex. *Science, 251,* 1355–1358. (7)

Tallman, J. F., Cassella, J. V., White, G., & Gallager, D. W. (1999). GABA$_A$ receptors: Diversity and its implications for CNS disease. *The Neuroscientist, 5,* 351–361. (12)

Tanaka, K., Sugita, Y., Moriya, M., & Saito, H.-A. (1993). Analysis of object motion in the ventral part of the medial superior temporal area of the macaque visual cortex. *Journal of Neurophysiology, 69,* 128–142. (6)

Tanaka, Y., Kamo, T., Yoshida, M., & Yamadori, A. (1991). "So-called" cortical deafness. *Brain, 114,* 2385–2401. (7)

Tang, Y.-P., Shimizu, E., Dube, G. R., Rampon, C., Kerchner, G. A., Zhuo, M., Liu, G., & Tsien, J. Z. (1999). Genetic enhancement of learning and memory in mice. *Nature, 401,* 63–69. (13)

Tanji, J., & Shima, K. (1994). Role for supplementary motor area cells in planning several movements ahead. *Nature, 371,* 413–416. (8)

Tanner, C. M., Ottman, R., Goldman, S. M., Ellenberg, J., Chan, P., Mayeux, R., & Langston, J. W. (1999). Parkinson disease in twins: An etiologic study. *Journal*

of the American Medical Association, 281, 341–346. (8)

Taub, E., & Berman, A. J. (1968). Movement and learning in the absence of sensory feedback. In S. J. Freedman (Ed.), *The neuropsychology of spatially oriented behavior* (pp. 173–192). Homewood, IL: Dorsey. (5)

Taylor, E. (1998). Clinical foundations of hyperactivity research. *Behavioural Brain Research, 94,* 11–24. (5)

Teicher, M. H., Glod, C. A., Magnus, E., Harper, D., Benson, G., Krueger, K., & McGreenery, C. E. (1997). Circadian rest-activity disturbances in seasonal affective disorder. *Archives of General Psychiatry, 54,* 124–130. (15)

Teitelbaum, P. (1955). Sensory control of hypothalamic hyperphagia. *Journal of Comparative and Physiological Psychology, 48,* 156–163. (10)

Teitelbaum, P. (1961). Disturbances in feeding and drinking behavior after hypothalamic lesions. In M. R. Jones (Ed.), *Nebraska Symposia on Motivation 1961* (pp. 39–69). Lincoln: University of Nebraska Press. (10)

Teitelbaum, P., & Epstein, A. N. (1962). The lateral hypothalamic syndrome. *Psychological Review, 69,* 74–90. (10)

Teitelbaum, P., Pellis, V. C., & Pellis, S. M. (1991). Can allied reflexes promote the integration of a robot's behavior? In J. A. Meyer & S. W. Wilson (Eds.), *From animals to animats: Simulation of animal behavior* (pp. 97–104). Cambridge, MA: MIT Press/Bradford Books. (8)

Terman, G. W., & Liebeskind, J. C. (1986). Relation of stress-induced analgesia to stimulation-produced analgesia. *Annals of the New York Academy of Sciences, 467,* 300–308. (7)

Terman, G. W., Shavitt, Y., Lewis, J. W., Cannon, J. T., & Liebeskind, J. C. (1984). Intrinsic mechanisms of pain inhibition: Activation by stress. *Science, 226,* 1270–1277. (7)

Terman, M., Terman, J. S., & Ross, D. C. (1998). A controlled trial of timed bright light and negative air ionization for treatment of winter depression. *Archives of General Psychiatry, 55,* 875–882. (15)

Terrace, H. S., Petitto, L. A., Sanders,

R. J., & Bever, T. G. (1979). Can an ape create a sentence? *Science, 206,* 891–902. (14)

Tessier-Lavigne, M., & Goodman, C. S. (1996). The molecular biology of axon guidance. *Science, 274,* 1123–1133. (5)

Tetrud, J. W., Langston, J. W., Garbe, P. L., & Ruttenber, A. J. (1989). Mild parkinsonism in persons exposed to 1-methyl-4-phenyl-1,2,3,6-tetrahydropyridine (MPTP). *Neurology, 39,* 1483–1487. (8)

Thaker, G. K., Ross, D. E., Cassady, S. L., Adami, H. M., LaPorte, D., Medoff, D. R., & Lahti, A. (1998). Smooth pursuit eye movements to extraretinal motion signals. *Archives of General Psychiatry, 55,* 830–836. (15)

Thallmair, M., Metz, G. A. S., Z'Graggen, W. J., Raineteau, O., Kartje, G. L., & Schwab, M. E. (1998). Neurite growth inhibitors restrict plasticity and functional recovery following corticospinal tract lesions. *Nature Neuroscience, 1,* 124–131. (5)

Thapar, A., Gottesman, I. I., Owen, M. J., O'Donovan, M. C., & McGuffin, P. (1994). The genetics of mental retardation. *British Journal of Psychiatry, 164,* 747–758. (5)

Thase, M. E., Trivedi, M. H., & Rush, A. J. (1995). MAOIs in the contemporary treatment of depression. *Neuropsychopharmacology, 12,* 185–219. (15)

Thomas, P. K. (1988). Clinical aspects of PNS regeneration. In S. G. Waxman (Ed.), *Advances in neurology* (Vol. 47, pp. 9–29). New York: Raven Press. (5)

Thompson, R. F. (1986). The neurobiology of learning and memory. *Science, 233,* 941–947. (13)

Ticku, M. K., & Kulkarni, S. K. (1988). Molecular interactions of ethanol with GABAergic system and potential of Ro15-4513 as an ethanol antagonist. *Pharmacology Biochemistry & Behavior, 30,* 501–510. (12)

Tinbergen, N. (1951). *The study of instinct.* Oxford, England: Oxford University Press. (1)

Tinbergen, N. (1973). The search for animal roots of human behavior. In N. Tinbergen, *The animal in its world* (Vol. 2, pp. 161–174). Cambridge, MA: Harvard University Press. (1)

Tingate, T. R., Lugg, D. J., Muller, H. K., Stowe, R. P., & Pierson, D. L. (1997). Antarctic isolation: Immune and viral studies. *Immunology and Cell Biology, 75,* 275–283. (12)

Tippin, J., & Henn, F. A. (1982). Modified leukotomy in the treatment of intractable obsessional neurosis. *American Journal of Psychiatry, 139,* 1601–1603. (4)

Tomac, A., Lindqvist, E., Lin, L.-F. H., Ögren, S. O., Young, D., Hoffer, B. J., & Olson, L. (1995). Protection and repair of the nigrostriatal dopaminergic system by GDNF *in vivo. Nature, 373,* 335–339. (5)

Tominaga, M., Caterina, M. J., Malmberg, A. B., Rosen, T. A., Gilbert, H., Skinner, K., Raumann, B. E., Basbaum, A. I., & Julius, D. (1998). The cloned capsaicin receptor integrates multiple pain-producing stimuli. *Neuron, 21,* 531–543. (7)

Toni, N., Buchs, P.-A., Nikonenko, I., Bron, C. R., & Muller, D. (1999). LTP promotes formation of multiple spine synapses between a single axon terminal and a dendrite. *Nature, 402,* 421–425. (13)

Tootell, R. B. H., Hadjikhani, N., Hall, E. K., Marrett, S., Vanduffel, W., Vaughan, J. T., & Dale, A. M. (1998). The retinotopy of visual spatial attention. *Neuron, 21,* 1409–1422. (6)

Torrey, E. F. (1986). Geographic variations in schizophrenia. In C. Shagass, R. C. Josiassen, W. H. Bridger, K. J. Weiss, D. Stoff, & G. M. Simpson (Eds.), *Biological psychiatry 1985* (pp. 1080–1082). New York: Elsevier. (15)

Torrey, E. F., Bowler, A. E., & Clark, K. (1997). Urban birth and residence as risk factors for psychoses: An analysis of 1880 data. *Schizophrenia Research, 25,* 169–176. (15)

Torrey, E. F., Miller, J., Rawlings, R., & Yolken, R. H. (1997). Seasonality of births in schizophrenia and bipolar disorder: A review of the literature. *Schizophrenia Research, 28,* 1–38. (15)

Townsend, J., Courchesne, E., Covington, J., Westerfield, M., Harris, N. S., Lyden, P., Lowry, T. P., & Press, G. A. (1999). Spatial attention deficits in patients with acquired or developmental cerebellar abnormality. *Journal of Neuroscience, 19,* 5632–5643. (8)

Tracy, J. A., Thompson, J. K., Krupa, D. J., & Thompson, R. F. (1998). Evidence of plasticity in the pontocerebellar conditioned stimulus pathway during classical conditioning of the eyeblink response in the rabbit. *Behavioral Neuroscience, 112,* 267–285. (13)

Tranel, D., & Damasio, A. (1993). The covert learning of affective valence does not require structures in hippocampal system or amygdala. *Journal of Cognitive Neuroscience, 5,* 79–88. (12)

Travers, S. P., Pfaffmann, C., & Norgren, R. (1986). Convergence of lingual and palatal gustatory neural activity in the nucleus of the solitary tract. *Brain Research, 365,* 305–320. (7)

Trevarthen, C. (1974). Cerebral embryology and the split brain. In M. Kinsbourne & W. L. Smith (Eds.), *Hemispheric disconnection and cerebral function* (pp. 208–236). Springfield, IL: Charles C Thomas. (14)

Trimble, M. R., & Thompson, P. J. (1986). Neuropsychological and behavioral sequelae of spontaneous seizures. *Annals of the New York Academy of Sciences, 462,* 284–292. (15)

Trivers, R. L. (1985). *Social evolution.* Menlo Park: Benjamin/Cummings. (1)

True, W. R., Xian, H., Scherer, J. F., Madden, P. A. F., Bucholz, K. K., Heath, A. C., Eisen, S. A., Lyons, M. J., Goldberg, J., & Tsuang, M. (1999). Common genetic vulnerability for nicotine and alcohol dependence in men. *Archives of General Psychiatry, 56,* 655–661. (15)

Tsai, G., Passani, L. A., Slusher, B. S., Carter, R., Baer, L., Kleinman, J. E., & Coyle, J. T. (1995). Abnormal excitatory neurotransmitter metabolism in schizophrenic brains. *Archives of General Psychiatry, 52,* 829–836. (15)

Tsai, G. E., Ragan, P., Chang, R., Chen, S., Linnoila, M. I., & Coyle, J. T. (1998). Increased glutamatergic neurotransmission and oxidative stress after alcohol withdrawal. *American Journal of Psychiatry, 155,* 726–732. (3)

Ts'o, D. Y., & Gilbert, C. D. (1988). The organization of chromatic and spatial interactions in the primate striate cortex. *Journal of Neuroscience, 8,* 1712–1727. (6)

Ts'o, D. Y., & Roe, A. W. (1995). Functional compartments in visual cortex: Segregation and interaction. In M. S. Gazzaniga (Ed.), *The cognitive neurosciences* (pp. 325–337). Cambridge, MA: MIT Press. (6)

Tsuang, M. T., Lyons, M. J., Meyer, J. M., Doyle, T., Eisen, S. A., Goldberg, J., True, W., Lin, N., Toomey, R., & Eaves, L. (1998). Co-occurrence of abuse of different drugs in men. *Archives of General Psychiatry, 55,* 967–972. (15)

Tsujita, T., Niikawa, N., Yamashita, H., Imamura, A., Hamada, A., Nakane, Y., & Okazaki, Y. (1998). Genomic discordance between monozygotic twins discordant for schizophrenia. *American Journal of Psychiatry, 155,* 422–424. (15)

Tu, G. C., & Israel, Y. (1995). Alcohol consumption by Orientals in North America is predicted largely by a single gene. *Behavior Genetics, 25,* 59–65. (15)

Tucker, D. M. (1981). Lateral brain function, emotion, and conceptualization. *Psychological Bulletin, 89,* 19–46. (14)

Tucker, D. M., Luu, P., & Pribram, K. H. (1995). Social and emotional self-regulation. *Annals of the New York Academy of Sciences, 769,* 213–239. (4)

Tzourio, C., Rocca, W. A., Breteler, M. M., Baldereschi, M., Dartigues, J.-F., Lopez-Pousa, S., Manubens-Bertran, J.-M., & Alpérovitch, A. (1997). Smoking and Parkinson's disease: An age-dependent risk effect? *Neurology, 49,* 1267–1272. (8)

Uchino, B. N., Cacioppo, J. T., & Kiecolt-Glaser, J. K. (1996). The relationship between social support and physiological processes: A review with emphasis on underlying mechanisms and implications for health. *Psychological Bulletin, 119,* 488–531. (12)

Udry, J. R., & Morris, N. M. (1968). Distribution of coitus in the menstrual cycle. *Nature, 220,* 593–596. (11)

Ugawa, S., Minami, Y., Guo, W., Saishin, Y., Takatsuji, K., Yamamoto, T., Tohyama, M., &

Shimada, S. (1998). Receptor that leaves a sour taste in the mouth. *Nature, 395,* 555–556. (7)

Unwin, N. (1995). Acetylcholine receptor channel imaged in the open state. *Nature, 373,* 37–43. (3)

Ushikubi, F., Segi, E., Sugimoto, Y., Murata, T., Matsuoka, T., Kobayashi, T., Hizaki, H., Tuboi, K., Katsuyama, M., Ichikawa, A., Tanaka, T., Yoshida, N., & Narumiya, S. (1998). Impaired febrile response in mice lacking the prostaglandin E receptor subtype EP$_3$. *Nature, 395,* 281–284. (10)

Uwano, T., Nishijo, H., Ono, T., & Tamura, R. (1995). Neuronal responsiveness to various sensory stimuli, and associative learning in the rat amygdala. *Neuroscience, 68,* 339–361. (12)

Vaillant, G. E., & Milofsky, E. S. (1982). The etiology of alcoholism: A prospective viewpoint. *American Psychologist, 37,* 494–503. (15)

Valvo, A. (1971). *Sight restoration after long-term blindness.* New York: American Foundation for the Blind. (6)

Valzelli, L. (1973). The "isolation syndrome" in mice. *Psychopharmacologia, 31,* 305–320. (12)

Valzelli, L. (1980). *An approach to neuroanatomical and neurochemical psychophysiology.* Torino, Italy: C. G. Edizioni Medico Scientifiche. (10, 15)

Valzelli, L., & Bernasconi, S. (1979). Aggressiveness by isolation and brain serotonin turnover changes in different strains of mice. *Neuropsychobiology, 5,* 129–135. (12)

Vandenbergh, J. G. (1987). Regulation of puberty and its consequences on population dynamics of mice. *American Zoologist, 27,* 891–898. (7)

van den Pol, A. N. (1999). Hypothalamic hypocretin (orexin): Robust innervation of the spinal cord. *Journal of Neuroscience, 19,* 3171–3182. (10)

Vanderweele, D. A. (1998). Insulin as a satiating signal. In G. P. Smith (Ed.), *Satiation: From gut to brain* (pp. 198–216). New York: Oxford University Press. (10)

Van der Zee, C. E. E. M., Fawcett, J., & Diamond, J. (1992). Antibody to NGF inhibits collateral sprouting of septohippocampal fibers following entorhinal cortex lesion in adult rats. *Journal of Comparative Neurology, 326,* 91–100. (5)

Van Essen, D. C., & DeYoe, E. A. (1995). Concurrent processing in the primate visual cortex. In M. S. Gazzaniga (Ed.), *The cognitive neurosciences* (pp. 383–400). Cambridge, MA: MIT Press. (6)

Van Goozen, S. H. M., Frijda, N. H., Wiegant, V. M., Endert, E., & Van de Poll, N. E. (1996). The premenstrual phase and reactions to aversive events: A study of hormonal influences on emotionality. *Psychoneuroendocrinology, 21,* 479–497. (11)

Van Hoesen, G. W. (1993). The modern concept of association cortex. *Current Opinion in Neurobiology, 3,* 150–154. (4)

Van Hoesen, G. W., Hyman, B. T., & Damasio, A. R. (1991). Entorhinal cortex pathology in Alzheimer's disease. *Hippocampus, 1,* 1–8. (13)

Van Lancker, D., & Fromkin, V. A. (1973). Hemispheric specialization for pitch and "tone": Evidence from Thai. *Journal of Phonetics, 1,* 101–109. (14)

van Praag, H., Kempermann, G., & Gage, F. H. (1999). Running increases cell proliferation and neurogenesis in the adult mouse dentate gyrus. *Nature Neuroscience, 2,* 266–270. (5)

Van Zoeren, J. G., & Stricker, E. M. (1977). Effects of preoptic, lateral hypothalamic, or dopamine-depleting lesions on behavioral thermoregulation in rats exposed to the cold. *Journal of Comparative and Physiological Psychology, 91,* 989–999. (10)

Velakoulis, D., Pantelis, C., McGorry, P. D., Dudgeon, P., Brewer, W., Cook, M., Desmond, P., Bridle, N., Tierney, P., Murrie, V., Singh, B., & Copolov, D. (1999). Hippocampal volume in first-episode psychoses and chronic schizophrenia. *Archives of General Psychiatry, 56,* 133–140. (15)

Vellutti, R. A. (1997). Interactions between sleep and sensory physiology. *Journal of Sleep Research, 6,* 61–77. (9)

Verdoux, H., Geddes, J. R., Takei, N., Lawrie, S. M., Bovet, P., Eagles, J. M., Heun, R., McCreadie, R. G., McNeil, T. F., O'Callaghan, E., Stöber, G., Williger, U., Wright, P., & Murray, R. M. (1997). Obstetric complications and age at onset in schizophrenia: An international collaborative meta-analysis of individual patient data. *American Journal of Psychiatry, 154,* 1220–1227. (15)

Vermeire, B. A., Hamilton, C. R., & Erdmann, A. L. (1998). Right-hemispheric superiority in split-brain monkeys for learning and remembering facial discriminations. *Behavioral Neuroscience, 112,* 1048–1061. (14)

Verrey, F., & Beron, J. (1996). Activation and supply of channels and pumps by aldosterone. *News in Physiological Sciences, 11,* 126–133. (10)

Victor, M., Adams, R. D., & Collins, G. H. (1971). *The Wernicke-Korsakoff syndrome.* Philadelphia: F. A. Davis. (13)

Viitala, J., Korpimäki, E., Palokangas, P., & Koivula, M. (1995). Attraction of kestrels to vole scent marks visible in ultraviolet light. *Nature, 373,* 425–427. (6)

Virkkunen, M., DeJong, J., Bartko, J., Goodwin, F. K., & Linnoila, M. (1989). Relationship of psychobiological variables to recidivism in violent offenders and impulsive fire setters. *Archives of General Psychiatry, 46,* 600–603. (12)

Virkkunen, M., Eggert, M., Rawlings, R., & Linnoila, M. (1996). A prospective follow-up study of alcoholic violent offenders and fire setters. *Archives of General Psychiatry, 53,* 523–529. (12)

Virkkunen, M., Nuutila, A., Goodwin, F. K., & Linnoila, M. (1987). Cerebrospinal fluid monoamine metabolite levels in male arsonists. *Archives of General Psychiatry, 44,* 241–247. (12)

Virkkunen, M., Rawlings, R., Tokola, R., Poland, R. E., Guidotti, A., Nemeroff, C., Bissette, G., Kalogeras, K., Karonen, S.-L., & Linnoila, M. (1994). CSF biochemistries, glucose metabolism, and diurnal activity rhythms in alcoholic, violent offenders, fire setters, and healthy volunteers. *Archives of General Psychiatry, 51,* 20–27. (15)

Vizi, E. S. (1984). *Non-synaptic interactions between neurons: Modula-*

tion of neurochemical transmission. Chichester, England: John Wiley. (3)

Volavka, J. (1990). Aggression, electroencephalography, and evoked potentials: A critical review. *Neuropsychiatry, Neuropsychology, and Behavioral Neurology, 3*, 249–259. (12)

Volavka, J., Czobor, P., Goodwin, D. W., Gabrielli, W. F., Penick, E. C., Mednick, S. A., Jensen, P., Knop, J., & Schulsinger, F. (1996). The electroencephalogram after alcohol administration in high-risk men and the development of alcohol use disorders 10 years later. *Archives of General Psychiatry, 53*, 258–263. (15)

Volkow, N. D., Wang, G.-J., Fischman, M. W., Foltin, R. W., Fowler, J. S., Abumrad, N. N., Vitkum, S., Logan, J., Gatley, S. J., Pappas, N., Hitzemann, R., & Shea, C. E. (1997). Relationship between subjective effects of cocaine and dopamine transporter occupancy. *Nature, 386*, 827–830. (3, 5, 15)

Volkow, N. D., Wang, G.-J., & Fowler, J. S. (1997). Imaging studies of cocaine in the human brain and studies of the cocaine addict. *Annals of the New York Academy of Sciences, 820*, 41–55. (3)

Volkow, N. D., Wang, G.-J., Fowler, J. S., Gatley, S. J., Logan, J., Ding, Y.-S., Hitzemann, R., & Pappas, N. (1998). Dopamine transporter occupancies in the human brain induced by therapeutic doses of oral methylphenidate. *American Journal of Psychiatry, 155*, 1325–1331. (3, 5)

Volkow, N. D., Wang, G.-J., Fowler, J. S., Logan, J., Gatley, S. J., Hitzemann, R., Chen, A. D., Dewey, S. L., & Pappas, N. (1997). Decreased striatal dopaminergic responsiveness in detoxified cocaine-dependent subjects. *Nature, 386*, 830–833. (3)

Vollhardt, L. T. (1991). Psychoneuroimmunology: A literature review. *American Journal of Orthopsychiatry, 61*, 35–47. (12)

von Békésy, G. (1956). Current status of theories of hearing. *Science, 123*, 779–783. (7)

Vrba, E. S. (1998). Multiphasic growth models and the evolution of prolonged growth exemplified by human brain evolution. *Journal of*

Theoretical Biology, 190, 227–239. (5)

Wagner, A. D., Schacter, D. L., Rotte, M., Koutstaal, W., Maril, A., Dale, A. M., Rosen, B. R., & Buckner, R. L. (1998). Building memories: Remembering and forgetting of verbal experiences as predicted by brain activity. *Science, 281*, 1188–1191. (13)

Wagner, J., Åkerud, P., Castro, D. S., Holm, P. C., Canab, J. M., Snyder, E. Y., Perlman, T., & Arenas, E. (1999). Induction of a midbrain dopaminergic phenotype in *Nurr*1-overexpressing neural stem cells by type 1 astrocytes. *Nature Biotechnology, 17*, 653–659. (8)

Waisbren, S. R., Brown, M. J., de Sonneville, L. M. J., & Levy, H. L. (1994). Review of neuropsychological functioning in treated phenylketonuria: An information-processing approach. *Acta Paediatrica, 83*(Suppl. 407), 98–103. (1)

Waldvogel, J. A. (1990). The bird's eye view. *American Scientist, 78*, 342–353. (6)

Walker-Batson, D., Smith, P., Curtis, S., Unwin, H., & Greenlee, R. (1995). Amphetamine paired with physical therapy accelerates motor recovery after stroke: Further evidence. *Stroke, 26*, 2254–2259. (5)

Waller, N. G., Kojetin, B. A., Bouchard, T. J., Jr, Lykken, D. T., & Tellegen, A. (1990). Genetic and environmental influences on religious interests, attitudes, and values: A study of twins reared apart and together. *Psychological Science, 1*, 138–142. (1)

Wallesch, C.-W., Henriksen, L., Kornhuber, H.-H., & Paulson, O. B. (1985). Observations on regional cerebral blood flow in cortical and subcortical structures during language production in normal man. *Brain and Language, 25*, 224–233. (14)

Wallman, J., & Pettigrew, J. D. (1985). Conjugate and disjunctive saccades in two avian species with contrasting oculomotor strategies. *Journal of Neuroscience, 5*, 1418–1428. (6)

Walsh, B. T., & Devlin, M. J. (1998). Eating disorders: Progress and problems. *Science, 280*, 1387–1390. (10)

Wan, R.-Q., Pang, K., & Olton, D. S.

(1994). Hippocampal and amygdaloid involvement in nonspatial and spatial working memory in rats: Effects of delay and interference. *Behavioral Neuroscience, 108*, 866–882. (13)

Wang, A., Liang, Y., Fridell, R. A., Probst, F. J., Wilcox, E. R., Touchman, J. W., Morton, C. C., Morell, R. J., Noben-Trauth, K., Camper, S. A., & Friedman, T. B. (1998). Associations of unconventional myosin *MYO15* mutations with human nonsyndromic deafness *DFNB3*. *Science, 280*, 1447–1451. (7)

Wang, H., & Tessier-Lavigne, M. (1999). *En passant* neurotrophic action of an intermediate axonal target in the developing mammalian CNS. *Nature, 401*, 765–769. (5)

Wang, Q., Schoenlein, R. W., Peteanu, L. A., Mathies, R. A., & Shank, C. V. (1994). Vibrationally coherent photochemistry in the femtosecond primary event of vision. *Science, 266*, 422–424. (6)

Wang, T., Okano, Y., Eisensmith, R., Huang, S. Z., Zeng, Y. T., Wilson, H. Y. L., & Woo, S. L. (1989). Molecular genetics of phenylketonuria in Orientals: Linkage disequilibrium between a termination mutation and haplotype 4 of the phenylalanine hydroxylase gene. *American Journal of Human Genetics, 45*, 675–680. (1)

Warach, S. (1995). Mapping brain pathophysiology and higher cortical function with magnetic resonance imaging. *The Neuroscientist, 1*, 221–235. (5)

Ward, I. L. (1977). Exogenous androgen activates female behavior in noncopulating, prenatally stressed male rats. *Journal of Comparative and Physiological Psychology, 91*, 465–471. (11)

Ward, I. L., & Reed, J. (1985). Prenatal stress and prepubertal social rearing conditions interact to determine sexual behavior in male rats. *Behavioral Neuroscience, 99*, 301–309. (11)

Ward, I. L., Ward, B., Winn, R. J., & Bielawski, D. (1994). Male and female sexual behavior potential of male rats prenatally exposed to the influence of alcohol, stress, or both factors. *Behavioral Neuroscience, 108*, 1188–1195. (11)

Ward, I. L., & Ward, O. B. (1985). Sexual behavior differentiation: Effects of prenatal manipulations in rats. In N. Adler, D. Pfaff, & R. W. Goy (Eds.), *Handbook of behavioral neurobiology*, Vol. 7 (pp. 77–98). New York: Plenum. (11)

Ward, O. B., Monaghan, E. P., & Ward, I. L. (1986). Naltrexone blocks the effects of prenatal stress on sexual behavior differentiation in male rats. *Pharmacology Biochemistry & Behavior, 25*, 573–576. (11)

Waxman, S. G., & Ritchie, J. M. (1985). Organization of ion channels in the myelinated nerve fiber. *Science, 228*, 1502–1507. (2)

Weaver, D. R. (1997). Reproductive safety of melatonin: A "wonder drug" to wonder about. *Journal of Biological Rhythms, 12*, 682–689. (9)

Webb, W. B. (1974). Sleep as an adaptive response. *Perceptual and Motor Skills, 38*, 1023–1027. (9)

Weber-Fox, C. M., & Neville, H. J. (1996). Maturational constraints on functional specializations for language processing: ERP and behavioral evidence in bilingual speakers. *Journal of Cognitive Neuroscience, 8*, 231–256. (14)

Weidensaul, S. (1999). *Living on the wind.* New York: North Point Press. (10)

Weinberger, D. R. (1996). On the plausibility of "the neurodevelopmental hypothesis" of schizophrenia. *Neuropsychopharmacology, 14*, 1S–11S. (15)

Weinberger, D. R. (1999). Cell biology of the hippocampal formation in schizophrenia. *Biological Psychiatry, 45*, 395–402. (15)

Weindl, A. (1973). Neuroendocrine aspects of circumventricular organs. In W. F. Ganong & L. Martini (Eds.), *Frontiers in neuroendocrinology 1973* (pp. 3–32). New York: Oxford University Press. (10)

Weiner, R. D. (1979). The psychiatric use of electrically induced seizures. *American Journal of Psychiatry, 136*, 1507–1517. (15)

Weiskrantz, L., Warrington, E. K., Sanders, M. D., & Marshall, J. (1974). Visual capacity in the hemianopic field following a restricted occipital ablation. *Brain, 97*, 709–728. (6)

Weiss, J. M. (1971). Effects of coping behavior in different warning signal conditions on stress pathology in rats. *Journal of Comparative and Physiological Psychology, 77*, 1–13. (12)

Weiss, P. (1924). Die funktion transplantierter amphibienextremitäten. Aufstellung einer resonanztheorie der motorischen nerventätigkeit auf grund abstimmter endorgane [The function of transplanted amphibian limbs. Presentation of a resonance theory of motor nerve action upon tuned end organs]. *Archiv für Mikroskopische Anatomie und Entwicklungsmechanik, 102*, 635–672. (5)

Weisskopf, M. G., Bauer, E. P., & LeDoux, J. E. (1999). L-type voltage-gated calcium channels mediate NMDA-independent associative long-term potentiation at thalamic input synapses to the amygdala. *Journal of Neuroscience, 19*, 10512–10519. (13)

Weller, L., Weller, A., Koresh-Kamin, H., & Ben-Shoshan, R. (1999). Menstrual synchrony in a sample of working women. *Psychoneuroendocrinology, 24*, 449–459. (7)

Weller, L., Weller, A., & Roizman, S. (1999). Human menstrual synchrony in families and among close friends: Examining the importance of mutual exposure. *Journal of Comparative Psychology, 113*, 261–268. (7)

Wender, P. H., Kety, S. S., Rosenthal, D., Schulsinger, F., Ortmann, J., & Lunde, I. (1986). Psychiatric disorders in the biological and adoptive families of adopted individuals with affective disorders. *Archives of General Psychiatry, 43*, 923–929. (15)

Wessinger, C. M., Fendrich, R., & Gazzaniga, M. S. (1997). Islands of residual vision in hemianopic patients. *Journal of Cognitive Neuropsychology, 9*, 203–221. (6)

Westergaard, T., Mortensen, P. B., Pedersen, C. B., Wohlfahrt, J., & Melbye, M. (1999). Exposure to prenatal and childhood infections and the risk of schizophrenia. *Archives of General Psychiatry, 56*, 993–998. (15)

Westbrook, G. L. (1994). Glutamate receptor update. *Current Opinion in Neurobiology, 4*, 337–346. (3)

Westbrook, G. L., & Jahr, C. E. (1989). Glutamate receptors in excitatory neurotransmission. *Seminars in the Neurosciences, 1*, 103–114. (3)

Whitam, F. L., Diamond, M., & Martin, J. (1993). Homosexual orientation in twins: A report on 61 pairs and three triplet sets. *Archives of Sexual Behavior, 22*, 187–206. (11)

White, D. P., Gibb, T. J., Wall, J. M., & Westbrook, P. R. (1995). Assessment of accuracy and analysis time of a novel device to monitor sleep and breathing in the home. *Sleep, 18*, 115–126. (9)

Whitman, B. W., & Packer, R. J. (1993). The photic sneeze reflex: Literature review and discussion. *Neurology, 43*, 868–871. (8)

Wichmann, T., Vitek, J. L., & DeLong, M. R. (1995). Parkinson's disease and the basal ganglia: Lessons from the laboratory and from neurosurgery. *The Neuroscientist, 1*, 236–244. (8)

Wiedemann, G., Pauli, P., Dengler, W., Lutzenberger, W., Birbaumer, N., & Buchkremer, G. (1999). Frontal brain asymmetry as a biological substrate of emotions in patients with panic disorders. *Archives of General Psychiatry, 56*, 78–84. (14)

Wiersma, D., Nienhuis, F. J., Slooff, C. J., & Giel, R. (1998). Natural course of schizophrenic disorders: A 15-year follow-up of a Dutch incidence cohort. *Schizophrenia Bulletin, 24*, 75–85. (15)

Wiesel, T. N. (1982). Postnatal development of the visual cortex and the influence of environment. *Nature, 299*, 583–591. (6)

Wiesel, T. N., & Hubel, D. H. (1963). Single-cell responses in striate cortex of kittens deprived of vision in one eye. *Journal of Neurophysiology, 26*, 1003–1017. (6)

Wiggins, S., Whyte, P., Huggins, M., Adam, S., Theilman, J., Bloch, M., Sheps, S. B., Schechter, M. T., & Hayden, M. R., for the Canadian collaborative study of predictive testing. (1992). The psychological consequences of predictive testing for Huntington's disease. *New England Journal of Medicine, 327*, 1401–1405. (8)

Wild, H. M., Butler, S. R., Carden, D., & Kulikowski, J. J. (1985). Primate cortical area V4 important for colour constancy but not wavelength discrimination. *Nature, 313*, 133–135. (6)

Wilkinson, D. J. C., Thompson, J. M., Lambert, G. W., Jennings, G. L., Schwarz, R. G., Jefferys, D., Turner, A. G., & Esler, M. D. (1998). Sympathetic activity in patients with panic disorder at rest, under laboratory mental stress, and during panic attacks. *Archives of General Psychiatry, 55*, 511–520. (12)

Willerman, L., Schultz, R., Rutledge, J. N., & Bigler, E. D. (1991). *In vivo* brain size and intelligence. *Intelligence, 15*, 223–228. (5)

Williams, C. L. (1986). A reevaluation of the concept of separable periods of organizational and activational actions of estrogens in development of brain and behavior. *Annals of the New York Academy of Sciences, 474*, 282–292. (11)

Williams, C. L., Men, D., Clayton, E. C., & Gold, P. E. (1998). Norepinephrine release in the amygdala after systemic injection of epinephrine or escapable footshock: Contribution of the nucleus of the solitary tract. *Behavioral Neuroscience, 112*, 1414–1422. (13)

Williams, R. W., & Herrup, K. (1988). The control of neuron number. *Annual Review of Neuroscience, 11*, 423–453. (2, 8)

Williams, T. (1999, May–June). Management by majority. *Audubon, 101*(3), 40–49. (1)

Willingham, D. B., Koroshetz, W. J., & Peterson, E. W. (1996). Motor skills have diverse neural bases: Spared and impaired skill acquisition in Huntington's disease. *Neuropsychology, 10*, 315–321. (8)

Willis, G. L., & Armstrong, S. M. (1998). Orphan neurones and amine excess: The functional neuropathology of Parkinsonism and neuropsychiatric disease, *Brain Research Reviews, 27*, 177–242. (8)

Wilson, B. A., Baddeley, A. D., & Kapur, N. (1995). Dense amnesia in a professional musician following herpes simplex virus encephalitis. *Journal of Clinical and Experimental Neuropsychology, 17*, 668–681. (13)

Wilson, D. S., & Sober, E. (1994). Reintroducing group selection to the human behavioral sciences. *Behavioral and Brain Sciences, 17*, 585–654. (1)

Wilson, J. D., George, F. W., & Griffin, J. E. (1981). The hormonal control of sexual development. *Science, 211*, 1278–1284. (11)

Wilson, M. I., & Daly, M. (1996). Male sexual proprietariness and violence against wives. *Current Directions in Psychological Science, 5*, 2–7. (1)

Winer, G. A., & Cottrell, J. E. (1996). Does anything leave the eye when we see? Extramission beliefs of children and adults. *Current Directions in Psychological Science, 5*, 137–142. (6)

Winfree, A. T. (1983). Impact of a circadian clock on the timing of human sleep. *American Journal of Physiology, 245*, R497–R504. (9)

Wirz-Justice, A. (1998). Beginning to see the light. *Archives of General Psychiatry, 55*, 861–862. (15)

Wise, R. A. (1996). Addictive drugs and brain stimulation reward. *Annual Review of Neuroscience, 19*, 319–340. (3)

Wise, R. A., & Bozarth, M. A. (1987). A psychomotor stimulant theory of addiction. *Psychological Review, 94*, 469–492. (3)

Witelson, S. F., Glezer, I. I., & Kigar, D. L. (1995). Women have greater density of neurons in posterior temporal cortex. *Journal of Neuroscience, 15*, 3418–3428. (11)

Witelson, S. F., Kigar, D. L., & Harvey, T. (1999). The exceptional brain of Albert Einstein. *Lancet, 353*, 2149–2153. (4)

Witelson, S. F., & Pallie, W. (1973). Left hemisphere specialization for language in the newborn: Neuroanatomical evidence of asymmetry. *Brain, 96*, 641–646. (14)

Wolf, S. (1995). Dogmas that have hindered understanding. *Integrative Physiological and Behavioral Science, 30*, 3–4. (12)

Wolkin, A., Rusinek, H., Vaid, G., Arena, L., Lafargue, T., Sanfilipo, M., Loneragan, C., Lautin, A., & Rotrosen, J. (1998). Structural magnetic resonance image averaging in schizophrenia. *American Journal of Psychiatry, 155*, 1064–1073. (15)

Wong, A. H. C., Smith, M., & Boon, H. S. (1998). Herbal remedies in psychiatric practice. *Archives of General Psychiatry, 55*, 1033–1044. (15)

Wong-Riley, M. T. T. (1989). Cytochrome oxidase: An endogenous metabolic marker for neuronal activity. *Trends in Neurosciences, 12*, 94–101. (2)

Woodruff-Pak, D. S., Papka, M., & Ivry, R. B. (1996). Cerebellar involvement in eyeblink classical conditioning in humans. *Neuropsychology, 10*, 443–458. (13)

Woods, S. C., Seeley, R. J., Porte, D., Jr., & Schwartz, M. W. (1998). Signals that regulate food intake and energy homeostasis. *Science, 280*, 1378–1383. (10)

Woodworth, R. S. (1934). *Psychology* (3rd ed.). New York: Henry Holt and Company. (2)

Wooley, C. S., & McEwen, B. S. (1993). Roles of estradiol and progesterone in regulation of hippocampal dendritic spine density during the estrous cycle in the rat. *Journal of Comparative Neurology, 336*, 293–306. (11)

Woolf, N. J. (1991). Cholinergic systems in mammalian brain and spinal cord. *Progress in Neurobiology, 37*, 475–524. (4)

Woolf, N. J. (1996). Global and serial neurons form a hierarchically arranged interface proposed to underlie memory and cognition. *Neuroscience, 74*, 625–651. (9)

Woolf, N. J., Zinnerman, M. D., & Johnson, G. V. W. (1999). Hippocampal microtubule-associated protein-2 alterations with contextual memory. *Brain Research, 821*, 241–249. (5)

Wright, I. C., Rabe-Hesketh, S., Woodruff, P. W. R., David, A. S., Murray, R. M., & Bullmore, E. T. (2000). Meta-analysis of regional brain volumes in schizophrenia. *American Journal of Psychiatry, 157*, 16–25. (15)

Wulfeck, B., & Bates, E. (1991). Differential sensitivity to errors of agreement and word order in Broca's aphasia. *Journal of Cognitive Neuroscience, 3*, 258–272. (14)

Wurtman, J. J. (1985). Neurotransmitter control of carbohydrate consumption. *Annals of the New York Academy of Sciences, 443*, 145–151. (3)

Xu, M., Hu, X.-T., Cooper, D. C., White, F. J., & Tonegawa, S. (1996). A genetic approach to study mechanisms of cocaine action. *Annals of the New York Academy of Sciences, 801,* 51–63. (3)

Yalcinkaya, T. M., Siiteri, P. K., Vigne, J.-L., Licht, P., Pavgi, S., Frank, L. G., & Glickman, S. E. (1993). A mechanism for virilization of female spotted hyenas in utero. *Science, 260,* 1929–1931. (11)

Yamamoto, T. (1984). Taste responses of cortical neurons. *Progress in Neurobiology, 23,* 273–315. (7)

Yanagisawa, K., Bartoshuk, L. M., Catalanotto, F. A., Karrer, T. A., & Kveton, J. F. (1998). Anesthesia of the chorda tympani nerve and taste phantoms. *Physiology & Behavior, 63,* 329–335. (7)

Yarsh, T. L., Farb, D. H., Leeman, S. E., & Jessell, T. M. (1979). Intrathecal capsaicin depletes substance P in the rat spinal cord and produces prolonged thermal analgesia. *Science, 206,* 481–483. (7)

Yehuda, R. (1997). Sensitization of the hypothalamic-pituitary-adrenal axis in posttraumatic stress disorder. *Annals of the New York Academy of Sciences, 821,* 57–75. (12)

Yeomans, J. S., & Frankland, P. W. (1996). The acoustic startle reflex: Neurons and connections. *Brain Research Reviews, 21,* 301–314. (12)

Yost, W. A., & Nielsen, D. W. (1977). *Fundamentals of hearing.* New York: Holt, Rinehart, & Winston. (7)

Young, A. B. (1995). Huntington's disease: Lessons from and for molecular neuroscience. *The Neuroscientist, 1,* 51–58. (8)

Young, A. M. J., Joseph, M. H., & Gray, J. A. (1993). Latent inhibition of conditioned dopamine release in rat nucleus accumbens. *Neuroscience, 54,* 5–9. (3)

Young, B. J., & Leaton, R. N. (1996).

Amygdala central nucleus lesions attenuate acoustic startle stimulus-evoked heart rate changes in rats. *Behavioral Neuroscience, 110,* 228–237. (12)

Young, G. B., & Pigott, S. E. (1999). Neurobiological basis of consciousness. *Archives of Neurology, 56,* 153–157. (9)

Young, W. C., Goy, R. W., & Phoenix, C. H. (1964). Hormones and sexual behavior. *Science, 143,* 212–218. (11)

Zahn, T. P., Rapoport, J. L., & Thompson, C. L. (1980). Autonomic and behavioral effects of dextroamphetamine and placebo in normal and hyperactive prepubertal boys. *Journal of Abnormal Child Psychology, 8,* 145–160. (5)

Zaidel, D., & Sperry, R. W. (1977). Some long-term motor effects of cerebral commissurotomy in man. *Neuropsychologia, 15,* 193–204. (14)

Zaki, P. A., & Evans, C. J. (1998). ORL-1: An awkward child of the opioid receptor family. *Neuroscientist, 4,* 172–184. (7)

Zatorre, R. J. (1979). Recognition of dichotic melodies by musicians and nonmusicians. *Neuropsychologia, 17,* 607–617. (14)

Zeevalk, G. D., Manzino, L., Hoppe, J., & Sonsalla, P. (1997). In vivo vulnerability of dopamine neurons to inhibition of energy metabolism. *European Journal of Pharmacology, 320,* 111–119. (8)

Zeki, S. (1980). The representation of colours in the cerebral cortex. *Nature, 284,* 412–418. (6)

Zeki, S. (1983). Colour coding in the cerebral cortex: The responses of wavelength-selective and colour-coded cells in monkey visual cortex to changes in wavelength composition. *Neuroscience, 9,* 767–781. (6)

Zeki, S. (1998). Parallel processing, asynchronous perception, and a distributed system of consciousness in vision. *Neuroscientist, 4,* 365–372. (6)

Zeki, S., McKeefry, D. J., Bartels, A., & Frackowiak, R. S. J. (1998). Has a new color area been discovered? *Nature Neuroscience, 1,* 335. (6)

Zeki, S., & Shipp, S. (1988). The functional logic of cortical connections. *Nature, 335,* 311–317. (6)

Zhang, Y., Proenca, R., Maffei, M., Barone, M., Leopold, L., & Friedman, J. M. (1994). Positional cloning of the mouse *obese* gene and its human homologue. *Nature, 372,* 425–432. (10)

Zheng, B., Larkin, D. W., Albrecht, U., Sun, Z. S., Sage, M., Eichele, G., Lee, C. C., & Bradley, A. (1999). The *mPer2* gene encodes a functional component of the mammalian circadian clock. *Nature, 400,* 169–173. (9)

Zihl, J., von Cramon, D., & Mai, N. (1983). Selective disturbance of movement vision after bilateral brain damage. *Brain, 106,* 313–340. (6)

Zola, S. M., Squire, L. R., Teng, E., Stefanacci, L., Buffalo, E. A., & Clark, R. E. (2000). Impaired recognition memory in monkeys after damage limited to the hippocampal region. *Journal of Neuroscience, 20,* 451–463. (13)

Zuckerman, M. (1995). Good and bad humors: Biochemical bases of personality and its disorders. *Psychological Science, 6,* 325–332. (3)

Zurif, E. B. (1980). Language mechanisms: A neuropsychological perspective. *American Scientist, 68,* 305–311. (14)

Zwislocki, J. J. (1981). Sound analysis in the ear: A history of discoveries. *American Scientist, 69,* 184–192. (7)

Credits

Chapter 1: 5: Figure 1.5 from Descartes', *Treatise on Man.*

Chapter 2: 33: Figure 2.7 from "Dendritic Spines of CA1 Pyramidal Cells in the Rat Hippocampus: Serial Electron Microscopy with Reference to their Biophysical Characteristics," by K. M. Harris and J. K. Stevens, 1989, *Journal of Neuroscience, 9,* pp. 2982–2997. Copyright © 1989 Society for Neuroscience. Reprinted by permission. **34:** Figure 2.9, Part e, from R. G. Coss, *Brain Research,* October 1982. Reprinted by permission of R. G. Coss. **35:** Figure 2.10 reprinted by permission from "Changes in Dendritic Branching of Adult Mammalian Neurons Revealed by Repeated Imaging in Situ," by D. Purves and R. D. Hadley, *Nature, 315,* pp. 404–406. Copyright © 1985 Macmillan Magazines Ltd. Reprinted by permission of D. Purves and Macmillan Magazines Ltd.

Chapter 3: 63: Figure 3.12a, adapted from "Autoimmune Response to Acetylcholine Receptors in Myasthenia Gravis and Its Animal Model," by J. Lindstrom. In H. G. Kunkel and F. J. Dixon, Eds., *Advances in Immunology, 27,* p. 10. Copyright © 1979 Academic Press. Reprinted by permission. **70:** Figure 3.17 from *Clinical Symposia,* Vol. 48, No. 1, 1996.

Chapter 4: 92: Figure 4.6 adapted from *Biology: The Unity and Diversity of Life,* 5th Edition, by C. Starr and R. Taggart, p. 340. Copyright © 1989 Brooks Cole. All rights reserved. **99:** Figure 4.15 adapted from "Cholinergic Systems in Mammalian Brain and Spinal Chord," by N. J. Woolf, *Progress in Neurobiology, 37,* pp. 475–524, 1991. Reprinted by permission of the author. **103:** Figure 4.18 from *The Anatomy of the Nervous System* by S. W. Ranson and S. L. Clark, 1959. Reprinted by permission of W. B. Saunders Co. **104:** Figure 4.20b from "Problems of Ontogeny and Phylogeny in Brain-Size Evolution," by T. W. Deacon, 1990, *Journal of Primatology, 11,* pp. 237–282. Copyright © 1990 Plenum Publishing. Reprinted by permission. **105:** Figure 4.21 adapted from *The Cerebral Cortex of Man* by W. Penfield and T. Rasmussen. Copyright © 1950 Macmillan Publishing Co., Inc. Renewed 1978 by Theodore Rasmussen. Reprinted by permission. **106:** Figure 4.23 after *The Prefrontal Cortex* by J. M. Fuster, 1989. Copyright 1989 Raven Press. Reprinted by permission.

Chapter 5: 120: Figure 5.5 from "Motoneuronal Death in the Human Fetus," by N. G. Forger and S. M. Breedlove, *Journal of Comparative Neurology, 264,* pp. 118–122. Copyright © 1987 Alan R. Liss, Inc. Reprinted by permission of N. G. Forger. **123:** Figure 5.9 from "Elimination of Synapses in the Developing Nervous System," by D. Purves and J. W. Lichtman, 1980, *Science, 210,* pp. 153–157. Copyright © 1980 by the AAAS. Reprinted by permission. **124:** Figure 5.12 reprinted from *Neuroscience: From the Molecular to the Cognitive,* by R. Hari, 1994, p. 165, with kind permission from Elsevier Science-NL, Sara Burgerhartstraat 25, 1055 KV Amsterdam, The Netherlands. **125:** Figure 5.13 reprinted with permission from "Increased Cortical Representation of the Fingers of the Left Hand in String Players," by T. Elbert, C. Pantev, C. Wienbruch, B. Rockstroh, and E. Taub, *Science, 270,* pp. 305–307. Copyright © 1995 American Association for the Advancement of Science. **127:** Figure 5.15 reprinted with permission from "Linked Regularities in the Development and Evolution of Mammalian Brains," by B. L. Finlay and R. B. Darlington, 1995, *Science, 268,* pp. 1578–1584. Copyright © 1995 American Association for the Advancement of Science. **141:** Figure 5.28 redrawn by permission from *The Annual Review of Neuroscience, Volume 6,* copyright 1983 by Annual Reviews, Inc. Used by permission of Annual Reviews, Inc. and Jon H. Kaas. **142:** Figure 5.29 from *Phantoms in the Brain,* by V. S. Ramchandran, M.D., Ph.D., and Sandra Blakeslee. Copyright © 1998 by V. S. Ramchandran and Sandra Blakeslee. Used by permission of William Morrow and Company, Inc.

Chapter 6: 164: Figure 6.14a, based on "Organization of the Primate Retina," by J. E. Dowling and B. B. Boycott, *Proceedings of the Royal Society of London,* B, 1966, 166, pp. 80–111. Used by permission of the Royal Society of London and John Dowling. **158:** Figure 6.9 adapted from "Visual Pigments of Rods and Cones in a Human Retina," by J. K. Bowmaker and H. J. A. Dartnall, *Journal of Physiology,* 298, pp. 501–511. Reprinted by permission. **171:** Figure 6.22, from "Receptive Fields of Single Neurons in the Cat's Striate Cortex," by D. H. Hubel and T. N. Wiesel, 1959, *Journal of Physiology, 148,* pp. 574–591. Copyright Cambridge University Press, UK. Reprinted by permission. **173:** Figure 6.25 from "The Visual Cortex of the Brain," by David H. Hubel, November 1963, *Scientific American, 209,* 5, p. 62. Copyright © Scientific American, Inc.

Chapter 7: 197: Figure 7.7 adapted from "Mapping of Stimulus Features and Meaning in Gerbil Auditory Cortex with 2-Deoxyglucose and c-Fos Antibodies," by H. Scheich and W. Zuschratter, *Behavioral Brain Research, 66,* pp. 195–205. Copyright © 1995 with kind permission from Elsevier Science-NL, Sara Burgerhartstraat 25, 1055 KV Amsterdam, The Netherlands. **205:** Figure 7.14 from *Biology: The Unity and Diversity of Life,* 5th Edition, by C. Starr and R. Taggart, p. 338. Copyright © 1989 Wadsworth Publishing Co. Reprinted by permission.

Chapter 8: 225: Figure 8.3 from *Biology: The Unity and Diversity of Life,* 5th Edition, by C. Starr and R. Taggart, p. 331. Copyright © 1989 Wadsworth Publishing Company. Reprinted by permission. **244:** Figure 8.18 from "Dopamine in the Extrapyramidal Motor Function: A Study Based Upon the MPTP-Induced Primate Model of Parkinsonism," by C. C. Chiueh, 1988, *Annals of the New York Academy of Sciences, 515,* p. 223. Reprinted by permission.

Chapter 9: 255: Figure 9.1 from "Phase Control of Activity in a Rodent," by P. J. DeCoursey, *Cold Spring Harbor Symposia on Quantitative Biology,* 1960, 25:49–55. Reprinted by permission of Cold Spring Harbor Laboratory and P. J. DeCoursey. **255:** Figure 9.2 from "Sleep-Onset Insomniacs Have Delayed Temperature Rhythms," by M. Morris, L. Lack, and D. Dawson, *Sleep,* 1990, *13*:1–14. Reprinted by permission. **263:** Figure 9.9 polysomnograph records provided by T. E. LeVere. **276:** Figure 9.17 from "Ontogenetic Development of Human Sleep-Dream Cycle," by H. P. Roffwarg, J. N. Muzio, and W. C. Dement, *Science,* 1966, *152*:604–609. Copyright 1966 by the AAAS. Reprinted by permission.

Chapter 10: 301: Figure 10.20 reprinted by permission of the University of Nebraska Press from "Disturbances in Feeding and Drinking Behavior After Hypothalamic Lesions," by P. Teitelbaum, pp. 39–69, in M. R. Jones, Ed., 1961, *Nebraska Symposium on Motivation.* Copyright © 1961 by the University of Nebraska Press. Copyright © renewed 1989 by the University of Nebraska Press.

Chapter 11: 319: Figure 11.5 from "Rise in Female-Initiated Sexual Activity at Ovulation and its Suppression by Oral Contraceptives," by D. B. Adams, A. R. Gold and A. D. Burt, 1978, *New England Journal of Medicine, 299,* pp. 1145–1150. Reprinted by permission from *The New England Journal of Medicine.* **330:** Figure 11.13 reprinted with permission from "A Difference in Hypothalamic Structure Between Heterosexual and Homosexual Men," by S. LeVay, *Science, 253,* pp. 1034–1037. Copyright © 1991 American Association for the Advancement of Science. **330:** Figure 11.14 reprinted with permission from "A Difference in Hypothalamic Structure Between Heterosexual and Homosexual Men," by S. LeVay, *Science, 253,* pp. 1034–1037. Copyright © 1991 American Association for the Advancement of Science.

Chapter 12: 350: Figure 12.8 from "Maternal Smoking During Pregnancy and Adult Male Criminal Outcomes," by P. A. Brennan, E. R. Grekin, and S. A. Mednick, *Archives of General Psychiatry, 56,* pp. 215–219. Copyrighted1999, American Medical Association. Reprinted by permission. **358:** Figure 12.13 from "Fear and the Human Amygdala," by R. Adolphs, D. Tranel, H. Damasio, and A. Damasio, *Journal of Neuroscience, 15,* pp. 5879–5891. Copyright © 1995 Oxford University Press. Reprinted by permission.

Chapter 13: 378: Figure 13.13 after "Dendritic Changes," by A. B. Scheibel, p. 70. In B. Reisberg, Ed., *Alzheimer's Disease,* 1983, Free Press. **383:** Figure 13.19 based on "Learning of Leg Position by the Ventral Nerve Cord in Headless Insects," by G. A. Horridge, *Proceedings of the Royal Society of London,* B, 1962, 157, pp. 33–52. Used by permission of the Royal Society of London and G. A. Horridge. **384:** Figure 13.20 redrawn from "Neuronal Mechanisms of Habituation and Dishabituation of the Gill-Withdrawal Reflex in Aplysia," by V. Castellucci, H. Pinsker, I. Kupfermann, and E. R. Kandel, *Science,* 1970, *167,* pp. 1745–1748. Copyright © 1970 by the AAAS. Used by permission of AAAS and V. Castellucci.

Chapter 14: 399: Figure 14.5 from "Subcortical Transfer of Higher Order Information: More Illusory than Real?" by A. Kingstone and M. S. Gazzaniga, 1995, *Neuropsychology, 9,* pp. 321–328. Copyright © 1995 by the American Psychological Association. Reprinted with permission. **402:** Figure 14.8 from "Human Brain: Left-Right Asymmetries in Temporal Speech Region," by N. Geschwind and W. Levitsky, 1968, *Science, 161,* pp. 186–187. Copyright © 1968 by the AAAS. Reprinted by permission of AAAS and N. Geschwind. **410:** Figure 14.14 from "Williams Syndrome: An Unusual Neuropsychological Profile," by U. Bellugi, P. P. Wang, and T. L. Jernigan. In S. H. Broman and J. Grafman, Eds., *Atypical Cognitive Deficits in Developmental Disorders.* Copyright © 1987 Lawrence Erlbaum. Reprinted by permission. **418:** Figure 14.19 reprinted from "Task-Determined Strategies of Visual Process," by G. Geiger, J. Y. Lettvin, and O. Zegarra-Moran, 1992, *Cognitive Brain Research, 1,* pp. 39–52, 1992 with kind permission of Elsevier Science-NL, Sara Burgerhartstraat 25, 1055 KV Amsterdam, The Netherlands.

Chapter 15: 434: Figure 15.10 bottom graphs adapted from *Sleep* by J. Allan Hobson, Scientific American Library, 1989. Reprinted by permission of W. H. Freeman and Company. **435:** Figure 15.11 from *Psychiatric Mental Health Nursing* by E. Janosik and J. Davies, p. 173. Copyright © 1986 Boston: Jones and Bartlett Publishers. Reprinted with permission. **447:** Figure 15.19 from "Antipsychotic Drug Doses and Neuroleptic/Dopamine Receptors," by P. Seeman, T. Lee, M. Chau-Wong, and K. Wong, 1976, *Nature, 261,* pp. 717–719. Copyright © 1976 Macmillan Magazines Limited. Reprinted by permission of Nature and Phillip Seeman.

Appendix B: 459: Excerpts from "Policies on the Use of Animals and Human Subjects in Neuroscience Research," Society for Neuroscience. Reprinted by permission.

Endsheet Quotations: Andreasen, N. C.: personal communication. **Beach, F. A.,** 1988, "In memoriam: Frank A. Beach." *Hormones and Behavior, 22,* 419–443; and personal communication. **Cannon, W. B.,** 1945, *The way of an investigator.* New York: Norton. **Dement, W. C.,** 1972, *Some must watch while some must sleep.* San Francisco: W. H. Freeman. **Geschwind, N.,** 1965, "Disconnexion syndromes in animals and man." *Brain, 88,* 237–294, 585–644. **Goldman-Rakic, P. S.,** 1988, "Topography of cognition: Parallel distributed networks in primate association cortex." *Annual Review of Neuroscience, 11,* 137–156 (p. 152). **Hebb, D. O.,** 1949, *Organization of behavior,* p. xiii. New York: John Wiley & Sons. **Hubel, D.:** personal communication. **Ito, M.:** personal communication. **Kandel, E. R.:** personal communication. **Lashley, K. S.,** 1930, "Basic neural mechanisms in behavior." *Psychology Review, 37,* 1–24. **Levi-Montalcini, R.,** 1988, *In praise of imperfection,* p. 94. New York: Basic Books. **Levy, J.:** personal communication.

McGaugh, J. L.: personal communication. **Ramón y Cajal,** S., 1937, "Recollections of my life." *Memoirs of the American Philosophical Society,* 8, parts 1 and 2. **Richter, C. P.:** personal communication. **Rumbaugh, D.,** and **S. Savage-Rumbaugh:** personal communication. **Shatz, C. J.:** personal communication. **Sherrington, C. S.,** 1941, *Man on his nature,* p. 104. New York: Macmillan. **Sperry, R. W.,** 1975, "In search of psyche." In F. G. Worden, J. P. Swazey, & G. Adelman, Eds., *The neurosciences: Paths of discovery,* pp. 425–434. Cambridge, MA: MIT Press. **Squire, L. R.:** personal communication. **Wiesel, T. N.,** 1982, "Postnatal development of the visual cortex and the influence of environment." *Nature, 299,* 583–591.

Photo Credits

Chapter 1: 0, Courtesy of the Cincinnati Zoo; **2,** both, Courtesy of Dr. Dana Copeland; **3,** top left, © Dan McCoy/Rainbow; **3,** top right, © Steve Maslowski/Photo Researchers; **3,** bottom left, © Chase Swift/CORBIS; **3,** bottom right, © Alisa Crandall/CORBIS; **4,** top, © Frank Siteman/Stock Boston; **4,** bottom left, © Paul Freed/Animals Animals; **4,** bottom right, © Chris Hellier/CORBIS; **13,** Courtesy of Professor Bruce Dudek; **15,** top, © F. J. Hierschel/Okapia/Photo Researchers; **15,** bottom, © Owen Franken/Stock Boston; **16,** © Nigel J. Dennis; Gallo Images/ CORBIS; **20,** top left, © Gontier/ Photo Researchers; **20,** left center, © David M. Barron/Animals Animals; **20,** left bottom, © Hank Morgan/Science Sources/ Photo Researchers; **20,** right top, © G. J. Bernard/Animals Animals; **20,** right bottom, © Frans Lanting/Photo Researchers; **22,** Courtesy of the Foundation for Medical Research.

Chapter 2: 28, © Secchi-Lecaque/Roussel-UCLAF/CNRI/SPL/Photo Researchers; **31,** Courtesy of Dennis M. D. Landis; **32,** Photo courtesy of Bob Jacobs, Colorado College; **35,** both, © Nancy Kedersha/UCLA/SLP/ Photo Researchers; **40,** © Fritz Goro.

Chapter 3: 50, © Omikron/Science Source/Photo Researchers; **62,** left, Micrograph courtesy of Dennis M. D. Landis; **62,** right, From "Studying neural organization in Aplysia with the scanning electron micrograph" by E. R. Lewis et al., *Science,* 1969, 165:1142. Copyright 1969 by the AAAS. Reprinted with permission of AAS and E. R. Lewis; **64,** © Victor Englebert/ Photo Researchers; **71,** From "Cocaine-induced reduction of glucose utilization in human brain" by E. D. London et al., *Archives of General Psychiatry,* 1990, 47:5670574. Copyright 1990, American Medical Association. Used by permission of AMA and E. D. London; **72,** © Burt Glinn/Magnum; **73,** Figure 1, p. 401, from McCann, U. D. Lowe, K. A. and Ricaurte, G. A. (1997). Long-lasting effects of recreational drugs of abuse on the central nervous system. *The Neuroscientist, 3,* 399-411. Reprinted by permission of the authors.

Chapter 4: 86, © Hank Morgan/Rainbow; **89,** left, Courtesy of Dr. Dana Copeland; **89,** middle, © Lester V. Bergman/CORBIS; **89,** right, Courtesy of Dr. Dana Copeland; **91,** both, © Manfred Kage/Peter Arnold, Inc.; **96,** both, Courtesy of Dr. Dana Copeland; **100,** Courtesy of Dr. Dana Copeland; **102,** both, Courtesy of Dr. Dana Copeland; **105,** © Carolyn Iverson/Photo Researchers; **107,** Courtesy of Dr. Dana Copeland; **110,** Figure 2.2, page 391, of commentary by W. Singer referring to article: E. Rodriguez et al. (1999). Perception's shadow: long-distance synchronization of human brain activity. *Nature, 397,* 430-433. Used with permission of the author; **111,** left © Stock Montage; **111,** right (all), Figure 2, p. 2151, From Witelson, S. F., Kigar, D. L. & Harvey T. (1999). The exceptional brain of Albert Einstein, *Lancet, 353,* 2149-2153.

Chapter 5: 114, © Geoff Tompkinson/SPL/ Photo Researchers; **116,** both, © Goodman/Monkmeyer; **118,** Courtesy of Dr. Dana Copeland; **119,** Anthony-Samuel LaMantia and Dale Purves (1989), Development of glomerular pattern visualized in the olfactory bulbs of living mice. *Nature 341:*646-649; **126,** Photo by David Hinds; **128,** © Roger Ressmeyer/CORBIS; **130,** © David Wells/CORBIS; **132,** left, © Bettmann/ CORBIS; **132,** right, © Reuters Newmedia Inc/CORBIS; **133,** all, Courtesy of Dr. Dana Copeland; **136,** Provided by James W. Kalat ; **138,** From "Clinical aspects of PNS regeneration" by K. Thomas in S. G. Waxman, Ed., *Advances in neurological disease, vol. 47: Functional recovery in neurological disease,* 1988, Raven Press. Reprinted by permission of Raven Press and K. Thomas. Photos by Michael D. Sanders; **142,** © Genevieve Naylor/CORBIS.

Chapter 6: 150, © Tom McHugh/Photo Researchers; **154,** © Chase Smith; **155,** From *The Retina* by John E. Dowling, 1987, Belknap Press of Harvard University Press. Micrograph by M. Tachibana and A. Kaneko. Reprinted by permission of John E. Dowling; **156,** Micrograph courtesy of E. R. Lewis, F. S. Werblin, and Y. Y. Zeevi **159,** top, Figure 3, p. 522, from Roorda, A., and Williams, D. R. (1999). The arrangement of the three cone classes in the living human eye. *Nature, 397,* 520-522; **159,** bottom, West Rim Emterprises; **160,** © Don Carl Steffen/Photo Researchers; **164,** © Ed Reschke; **169,** both, © Tate Gallery, London/ Art Resource, NY; © 2000 Artists Right Society ARS, New York, ADAGP, Paris; **174,** all, © Erich Lessing/Art Resource, NY; **175,** top, Courtesy of Anthony Wagner; **175,** bottom, Courtesy of Dr. Dana Copeland; **176,** Figure 1a, p. 569, from Gauthier, I., Tarr, M. J., Anderson, A. W., Skudlarski, Pl, & Gore, J. C. (1999). Activation of the middle fusiform "face area" increases with experience in recognizing novel objects. *Nature Neuroscience, 2,* 568-573; **178,** "Object recognition can drive motive

perception" by V. S. Ramachandran, C. Armel, C. Foster, and R. Stoddard, *Nature,* 1998, *395:*852-853; **183,** top, © Biophoto Associates/Science Source/Photo Researchers; **183,** bottom, © Sue Ford/ Science Source/Photo Researchers; **185,** Courtesy of Helmut V. Hirsch.

Chapter 7: 190, © Owen Franken/CORBIS; **197,** © Eric and David Hosking/CORBIS; **204,** © Ed Reschke; **207,** From "Multiple representations of pain in human cerebral cortex," *Science, 251:*1355-1358. Used by permission of Jeanne D. Talbot, Universitè de Montreal; **212,** © SIU/ Peter Arnold, Inc.

Chapter 8: 222, © F. Willingham; **225,** all, © Ed Reschke; **226,** © Bill Curtsinger; **234,** From "Shared neural substrates controlling hand movements in human motor cortex," by J. Sanes, J. Donoghue, V. Thangaraj, R. Edelman, & S. Warach, *Science,* 1995, *268:*1774-1778. Copyright 1995 by AAAS. Reprinted by permission of AAAS and J. Sanes; **244,** From "Dopamine in the extrapyramidal motor function: A study based upon the MPTP-induced primate model of Parkinsonism" by C. C. Chiueh, 1998, *Annals of the New York Academy of Sciences, 515:*226-248. Reprinted by permission of the New York Academy of Sciences and C. C. Chiueh; **247,** Courtesy of Robert E. Schmidt, Washington University.

Chapter 9: 258, © Norbert Wu; **259,** © Eviatar Nevo; **262,** both, © Richard Nowitz/ Photo Researchers; **268,** From Morrison, A. R., Sanford, L. D., Ball, W. A., Mann, G. L. and Ross, R. J. (1995), "Stimulus-elicited behavior in rapid eye movement sleep without atonia." *Behavioral Neuroscience, 109,* 972-979; **270,** © Russell D. Curtis/Photo Researchers.

Chapter 10: 280, © Betty K. Bruce/Animals Animals; **283,** Courtesy of Trans-Time, Inc.; **284,** top, © Johnny Johnson/ Animals Animals; **284,** bottom, AP/ Wide World Photos; **287,** © A. Cosmos Blank/ NAS/ Photo Researchers; **294,** left, © Gunter Ziesler/ Bruce Coleman; **294,** right, © Stephen Dalton/ Photo Researchers; **297,** Stephen Battersby; **301,** © Yoav Levy/ Phototake; **303,** John Sholtis/The Rockefeller University **304,** From "Peptide YY PYY, a potent orexigenic agent," by J. E. Morley, A. S. Levine, M. Grace and J. Kneip, *Brain Research,* 1985, *341,* 200–203.

Chapter 11: 310, © Art Wolfe; **314,** Courtesy of Kay E. Holekamp; **319,** Figure 1, p. 741, from I. S. Penton-Voak, D. I. Perrett, D. L. Castles, T. Kobayashi, D. M. Burt, L. K. Murray, & R. Minamisawa. (1999). Menstrual cycle alters face preference. *Nature, 399,* 741-742; **322,** From "A defect in nurturing in mice lacking the immediate early gene fosB," by Brown, J. R., Ye H., Bronson, R. T., Dikkes, P., and Greenberg, M. E., *Cell,* 86, 297-309; **325,** top, "Man-Woman/Boy-Girl," 1972/John Money & Enke Erhardt, Baltimore/John Hopkins University Press; **325,** bottom,

Courtesy of Intersex Society of North America; **326,** From *Abnormal Sexual Development* by D. D. Federman, 1967, Used by permission of W. B. Saunders Company; **329,** From "Sex-hormone-dependent brain differentiation and sexual functions" by G. Dorner, in G. Dorner (ed.), *Endocrinology of sex.* Copyright 1975 by permission of Johann Ambrosius Barth; **330,** From "A difference in hypothalamic structure between heterosexual and homosexual men," by LeVay, S. (1991). *Science,* 253, 1034-1037. Copyright 1991 by the AAAS.

Chapter 12: 334, © R. W. Jones/ CORBIS; **339,** both, © Kathleen Olson; **350,** Courtesy of Dr. Dana Copeland; **352,** From "Neuronal constellations in aggressive behavior" by Jose Delgado, in L. Valzellis and L. Morgese (eds.) *Aggression and violence: A psycho/biological and clinical approach,* Edizioni Saint Vincent, 1981. Used by permission of Jose Delgado; **359,** Courtesy of Jules Asher. From "New Drug Counters Alcohol Intoxication" by G. Kolata, 1986, *Science,* 234:1199. Copyright 1986 by the AAAS. Used by permission of AAAS; **356,** © Joe McBride/STONE.

Chapter 13: 362, © Georg Gerster/Photo Researchers; **371,** top, Courtesy of Dr. Dana Copeland; **371,** bottom, Courtesy of David Amaral and Suzanne Corkin; **373,** © Hank Morgan/Photo Researchers; **374,** top, © D. Robert Franz/ The Wildlife Collection; **374,** middle top, © Dale and Marian Zimmerman/Animals Animals; **374,** middle bottom and bottom, © Tom Vezo/ The Wildlife Collection; **377,** both, Courtesy of Dr. Robert D. Terry, Department of Neurosciences, School of Medicine, University of California at San Diego; **378,** From "Quantitative morphology and regional and laminar distributions of senile plaques in Alzheimerís disease," by J. Rogers and J. H. Morrison, *Journal of Neuroscience,* 1985, 5:2801-2808. Copyright 1985 by the Society for Neuroscience. Photo courtesy of Dr. Joseph Rogers. Reprinted by permission of Dr. Joseph Rogers; **379,** both, From "Ontogeny of place learning in children as measure in the radial arm maze, Morris search task, and open field task," by Overman, W. H., Pate, B. J., Moore, K. and Peuster, A. *Behavioral Neuroscience, 110,* 1205-1228. Copyright 1996 by the American Psychological Association; **383,** © H. Chaumeton/ Nature.

Chapter 14: 392, © Michael Newman/ PhotoEdit; **395,** Courtesy of Dr. Dana Copeland; **400,** From "Asymmetry of perception in free viewing of chimeric faces" by J. Levy, W. Heller, M. T. Banich and L. A. Burton, *Brain and Cognition,* 1983, 2:404–419. Used by permission of Academic Press; **406,** top, Courtesy of Ann Premack; **406,** bottom, From Georgia State University's Language Research Center, operated with Yerkes Primate Center of Emory. Photo courtesy of Duane Rumbaugh; **407,** David Carter; **409,** © Michael Dick/Animals Animals.

Theme Index

Consciousness and Mind–Brain Relationship

abused drugs, 70–75
binding, 108–110
biological explanations of behavior, 3–5
emotions and consciousness, 336–338
experience, brain chemistry, and depression, 436
hippocampus and binding, 375
law of specific nerve energies, 152–153
many neurons but one consciousness, 30
neglect, 104–105
nonhumans, consciousness in, 7
organization of brain areas, 88, 108
perceptual coding, 152–153, 211, 214, 217–218
philosophical positions, 2, 5–7
psychosomatic illness, 342–344
self-stimulation of the brain, 69–70
split brain, 396–399
visual consciousness and binding, 178–179

Human Abnormalities

absence seizure, 336
alcoholism, 424–427
Alzheimer's disease, 376–378
amnesia after hippocampal damage, 370–372
anorexia, 306
attention-deficit disorder, 129
bipolar disorder, 434–435
blindsight, 178
Broca's aphasia, 412–414
bulimia, 307
closed head injury, 132
clumsiness, 240–241
color constancy, loss of, 176
corpus callosum, failure of development, 402–403
cortical blindness, 103
deafness, 197–198
depression, 428–434
diabetes, 298
dyslexia, 416–418
emotions, loss of, 337–338
epilepsy, 396–397
fetal alcohol syndrome, 129–130
hallucinations, 105
heart disease, 343

Huntington's disease, 246–248
hydrocephalus, 100
insomnia, 268–269
Klüver-Bucy syndrome, 105
Korsakoff's syndrome, 375–376
locked-in syndrome, 339
motion blindness, 177
myasthenia gravis, 224
narcolepsy, 270
neglect, 104–105
night terrors, 271
obesity, 302–306
pain insensitivity, 204–205
panic disorder, 354–355
Parkinson's disease, 242–246
periodic limb movement disorder, 270
phantom limb, 140–143
posttraumatic stress disorder, 347
prefrontal lobotomies, 106–107
prosopagnosia, 174
REM behavior disorder, 270
seasonal affective disorder, 435–436
schizophrenia, 438–449
sleep apnea, 269–270
sleeptalking and sleepwalking, 271
split brain, 396–399
stroke, 132–135
tinnitus, 197–198
ulcers, 342–343
Urbach-Wiethe disease, 356
violent behavior, 349–354
visual agnosia, 174
voodoo death, 343
Wernicke's aphasia, 414
Williams syndrome, 409

Nature–Nurture

alcoholism, genetics of, 424–427
altruism, 16
Alzheimer's disease, genetics of, 377
anorexia, 306
bipolar disorder, genetics of, 434
color-vision deficiency, genetics of, 161
corpus callosum, maturation of, 402
dairy products, consumption of, 295–296

depression, genetics of, 428
direct and indirect genetic effects, 12–13
dominance for language, 401–403
early blindness, 185
early chemical environment, 128–130
evolution of behavior, 13–16
evolutionary and functional explanations, 3–5
experience and brain development, 122–126
experience and visual development, 181–185
gender identity, 324–327
growth and development of brain, 116–122
heritability estimates, 11–12
Huntington's disease, genetics of, 247–248
infant vision, 181
intersexes, 324–326
language capacity, 405–411
Mendelian genetics, 9–12
obesity, 305–306
Parkinson's disease, genetics of, 243–244
personality, genetics of, 75–76
phenylketonuria, 12
schizophrenia, genetics of, 440–443
schizophrenia, prenatal environment and, 443–446
sex-linked and sex-limited genes, 10–11
sexual maturation, 312–315
sexual orientation, 327–331
sociobiology, 16–17
supertasters, 213–214
temperature and infant behaviors, 286–287
violent behavior, 349–351

Research Methods

autoradiography, 139
fMRI scans, 175
histochemistry, 142
lesions, 136
magnetoencephalography, 124
microdialysis, 305
microelectrode recordings, 171
MRI scans, 128
multiple methods, 301
PET scans, 72
testing hemispheric dominance, 398
Wisconsin Card Sorting Task, 445

Species Comparisons

animals in research, 19–23
auditory localization, 199
brain structures, 126–128
brain-to-body ratio, 408–409
cerebellum, 237
circadian and circannual rhythms, 254–255, 258–259
consciousness in nonhumans, 7
dorsal and ventral, 89
drinking, 289
eating, 294

evolutionary and functional explanations, 3–5
eye-to-brain connections, 163, 186
eyes, 154, 157
food selection, 295
gooseflesh and porcupine quills, 93
hearing range, 191, 192
hibernation, 274
hormones, 80
language capacity, 405–408
learning mechanisms, 381–385
memory and hippocampus, 373–374
midbrain, 95
movement speed and fatigue, 226
neurotransmitters, 68
obesity, 303
regeneration of limbs, 120
regeneration of spinal cord axons, 137
sexual behavior, hormonal dependence of, 315–321
sexual maturation in hyenas, 314
sleep, 273–276
strabismus, 184
temperature regulation, 282–286
visual sensitive periods, 182

Try It Yourself

astigmatism, 184
binding vision and touch, 108
blind spot in eye, 156
Broca's aphasia, 412–413
consciousness, inference of, 7
dyslexia, 417
enhancement of startle reflex, 355
facial expressions and emotions, 339
gaze direction, 429
hemispheric specializations, 396, 401
hippocampus-dependent memory, 373
hormones and partner preference, 318–319
implicit memory, 375
lateralization of emotional interpretation, 400
law of specific nerve energies, 153
left and right hemispheres, 396, 401
neglect, 104
olfactory adaptation, 216
opponent processes in color vision, 159
peripheral vision, 168
profile drawing, 223
short-term memory, 368
short-wavelength cones, sparsity of, 158
suppressed vision during eye movements, 179
taste adaptation, 213
taste bud localization, 212
time of touch, perception of, 39
vestibular functions, 201
visual attention, 177
voluntary and involuntary movements, 228
working memory, 369

Name Index

Subject Glossary/Index

Amplitude intensity of a sound or other stimulus, 192

Amputated limbs
brain reorganization and, 140–141, *141*
phantom limb phenomenon and, 141–143, *142, 143*

Amygdala, *98, 108, 349, 350*
aggressive behavior and, 351–352
anxiety and, 356–357
bipolar disorder and, 434
effects of damage to, 356–357, *358*
fear responses and, 356, *357*
memory and, 369

Amyloid beta protein 42 (Aβ$_{42}$), protein with 42 amino acids, which accumulates in the brain and impairs the functions of neurons and glia cells, leading to Alzheimer's disease, 377

Amyloid precursor protein, 377

Amyotrophic lateral sclerosis, *233*

Anabolic steroid is a steroid chemical, especially a derivative of testosterone, that tends to build up muscles , 81

Analgesia is relief from pain, 207
morphine, 208–209
stimuli that produce, 208

Anandamide naturally occurring brain chemical that binds to the same receptors as cannabinoids, 74

Anatomical terminology, 88–89, *90, 91*

Androgen class of steroid hormones that are more abundant in males than in females for most species, *79, 81, 312, 313*

Androgen insensitivity condition in which a person lacks the mechanism that enables androgens to bind to genes in a cell's nucleus, 326, *326*

Androstenedione, 81

Angiotensin II hormone that constricts the blood vessels, contributing to hypovolemic thirst, 291

Animal research, 19–23, *20*
ethics of, 19, 21–22, *23*
neuroscientific policies on, 459–461
reasons for, 19, *21*

Animals
altruistic behavior in, 16, *16*
brain-to-body ratio of, 408, *409*
cell structure in, 30–32, *31*
eating strategies among, 294, *294*
evolutionary relationships among, 13, *14*
serotonin turnover in, 352–353

sleep hours per day for, *275*
temperature regulation in, 282–287
See also Mammals

Anomia difficulty recalling the names of objects, 414

Anorexia nervosa condition characterized by unwillingness to eat, severe weight loss, and sometimes death, 306, 309

Anosmia general lack of olfaction, 217

Antabuse trade name for disulfiram, a drug that helps people break an alcohol habit by impairing their ability to convert acetaldehyde to acetic acid, 425–426

Antagonist drug that blocks the effects of a neurotransmitter, 68

Antagonistic muscles pairs of muscles that move a limb in opposite directions (for example, extensor and flexor), 224, *225*

Anterior is toward the front end, *90*

Anterior commissure set of axons connecting the two cerebral hemispheres; smaller than the corpus callosum, *96, 102, 398, 403*

Anterior pituitary portion of the pituitary gland, *79*, 81

Anterograde amnesia loss of memory for events that happened after brain damage, 370

Antibody Y-shaped protein that fits onto an antigen and weakens it or marks it for destruction, 345

Anticonvulsant drugs, 435

Antidepressant drugs, 430–432, *430, 431, 432*
categories of, 430–431
discovery of, 430
physiological implications of, 431–432

Antidiuretic hormone (ADH) pituitary hormone that raises blood pressure and enables the kidneys to reabsorb water and therefore to secrete highly concentrated urine, 289

Antidromic direction, 48

Antigen protein on the surface of a microorganism in response to which the immune system generates antibodies, 345

Antipsychotic drug that relieves schizophrenia, 446, *447*

Anxiety
amygdala and, 356–357
drugs for reducing, 357–359
panic disorder and, 354–355
See also Fear

Apex one end of the cochlea,

farthest from the point where the stirrup meets the cochlea, 195, *195*

Aphasia severe impairment of language, 412–414, *415*

Aplysia, 382–385, *383, 384, 385*

Apomorphine morphine derivative that stimulates dopamine receptors, 139

Apoptosis developmental program by which a neuron kills itself at a certain age unless inhibited from doing so, 118–119, 134

Arcuate nucleus, 303

Aromatase, 313

Arousal
brain structures of, 264–265, *266, 267*
decreasing for sleep, 265–267
See also Wakefulness/sleep cycles

Artificial selection change in the frequencies of various genes in a population because of a breeder's selection of desired individuals for mating purposes, 13

Aspartame, 12

Association areas of the cortex, 108–110, *109*

Associativity tendency for pairing a weak input with a stronger input to enhance the later effectiveness of the weaker input, 385

Astigmatism blurring of vision for lines in one direction because of the nonspherical shape of the eye, 184–185, *185*

Astrocyte (astroglia) relatively large star-shaped glia cell, 36, *36*

Atom piece of an element that cannot be divided any further, 453

Atomic number is the number of protons in the nucleus of an atom, 453

Atomic weight number indicating the weight of an atom relative to a weight of one for a proton, 455

ATP (adenosine triphosphate) a compound that stores energy; also used as a neuromodulator, 457, *457*

Attack behaviors, 349–354

Attention, visual, 177–178

Attention-deficit disorder (ADD) condition marked by impulsiveness and poor control of attention, 71, 129, 148

Attention-deficit/hyperactivity disorder (ADHD) condition marked by excesses of impulsiveness, activity, and shifts of attention, 129

Attraction
influence of sex hormones on, 318–319, *319*
See also Reproductive behaviors

Atypical antidepressants miscellaneous group of drugs with antidepressant effects but only mild side effects, 431

Atypical antipsychotics drugs that block dopamine activity in the pathways to the prefrontal cortex, especially at dopamine type D$_4$ receptors, but have little effect on the D$_2$ receptors, and also block serotonin type 5-HT$_2$ receptors, 449

Audition, 192–200
auditory cortex and, 196–197, *196, 197*
ear structure and, 192–194
hearing loss and, 197–198
lateralization and, 396, 401, *401*
localization of sounds and, 198–199, *198, 199*
nature of sound and, 192
pitch perception and, 194–197
psychological disorders and, 440
Web site on, 221

Autoimmune diseases, 224, 344

Autonomic nervous system set of neurons that regulates functioning of the internal organs, 88, *88*, 91–93, *92, 343*
emotions and, 338–339
stress and, 342–344

Autoradiography, 139

Autoreceptor presynaptic receptor that is stimulated by the neurotransmitter released by the presynaptic cell itself, feeding back to decrease further release of the transmitter, 431, *432*

Autosomal gene is a gene on any of the chromosomes other than the sex chromosomes (X and Y), 10

Axon hillock swelling of the soma, the point where the axon begins, *32, 44*

Axons single thin fibers of constant diameter that extend from a neuron, 33–34, *34*
astrocytes and, 36, *36*
chemical pathfinding by, 120–122
collateral sprouting of, 138, *138*
impulse transmission in, 39
myelinated, 45–46
nodes of Ranvier and, 45, *46*
principle of competition among, 122, *123*
regrowth of, 137, *138*
specificity of connections between, 120–121

B cell type of leukocyte that matures in the bone marrow; attaches to an intruder and produces specific antibodies to attack the intruder's antigen, 345, *345*

Babinski reflex is the reflexive flexion of the big toe when the sole of the foot is stimulated, 229

Ballistic movement is motion that proceeds as a single organized unit that cannot be redirected once it begins, 228

Barbiturates class of drugs sometimes used as tranquilizers, 357

Baroreceptor is a receptor that detects the blood pressure in the largest blood veins, 291

Basal forebrain is the forebrain area anterior and dorsal to the hypothalamus; includes cell clusters that promote wakefulness and other cell clusters that promote sleep, 99, *99*, 265, *267*

Basal ganglia set of subcortical forebrain structures lateral to the hypothalamus including the caudate nucleus, putamen, and globus pallidus, 97–98, *98*, 240–241, *240*

Basal metabolism rate of energy use while the body is at rest, used largely for maintaining a constant body temperature, 282

Base is the part of the tympanic membrane closest to the stirrup, 195, *195*

Basilar membrane is the floor of the scala media, within the cochlea, *193*, 194, 195–196, *195*

Battle fatigue, 347

Behavior
aggressive, 319–320, 349–354
altruistic, 15–16
biological explanations of, 3–5
body temperature and, 286–287
brain damage and adjustments in, 135–136
drugs and, 76
evolution of, 13–17
genetics and, 12–13
hormones and, 78–83
long-term potentiation and, 388
motor sequences of, 229–230
neurotransmitters and, 66
schizophrenic, 438–439
violent, 349–354

Behavioral interventions, 145, *145*

Behavioral medicine field that includes the influence of eating and drinking habits, smoking, stress, exercise, and other behavioral variables on health, 342

Behavioral neuroscientist, 24

Bell-Magendie law observation that the dorsal roots of the spinal cord carry sensory information and that the ventral roots carry motor information toward the muscles and glands, 90

Benzodiazepines is a class of widely used antianxiety drugs, 357–358

Binding problem question of how the visual, auditory, and other areas of the brain influence one another to produce a combined perception of a single object, 108–110
visual consciousness and, 178–179, *178*

Binocular vision is based on the simultaneous stimulation of two eyes, 182, *182*

Biological clock internal mechanism for controlling rhythmic variations in a behavior, 255, *255*
jet lag and, 256, *256*
mechanisms of, 257–259
resetting, 255, 256–257
shift work and, 257
suprachiasmatic nucleus and, 257–259, *258*, *259*
Web sites on, 279

Biological psychology study of the physiological, evolutionary, and developmental mechanisms of behavior and experience, 2
careers in, 24

Bipolar cells type of neuron in the retina that receives input directly from the receptors, 154, 155, *155*, *164*
color vision and, 159, *160*

Bipolar disorder condition in which a person alternates between the two poles of mania and depression, 434–435, *435*
genetics and, 434
treatments for, 434–435

Birth-control pills, 318

Blindness
color, 161
cortical, 103
motion, 163, 177
See also Vision

Blindsight ability to localize objects within an apparently blind visual field, 178–179

Blind spot point in the retina that lacks receptors because the optic nerve exits at this point, 155–156, *156*

Blobs, 176

Blood-brain barrier is the mechanism that keeps many chemicals out of the brain, 36–37, *37*

Blood glucose, 297–299, *298*, *299*

Blood pressure, 291

Blood volume, 291

Body
chemical reactions in, 456–457
dualistic view of, 5

effects of freezing on, 283
elemental composition of, *453*
emotions and perception of, 338–340
internal regulation of, 281–307

Body temperature, 282–288
behavioral regulation of, *284*, 286
brain mechanisms for controlling, 285–286, *285*
depression and, 433, *434*
effects on animal behavior, 286–287, *287*
fever and, 286
homeostasis and, 282
reasons for constancy of, 282–285
Web site on, 309

Body weight
blood glucose levels and, 298, *298*, *299*
genetic factors related to, 302–303, *303*, 305–306
lateral hypothalamus and, 299, *300*
satiety chemicals and, 302–305, *305*
ventromedial hypothalamus and, 301–302, *301*
weight-loss techniques and, 306

Bombesin, 304

Bonobos, 405–407, *406*

Borna disease viral infection that affects the nervous system, producing results that range from exaggerated activity fluctuations to death, 429–430, *429*

Bouton, 33

Brain
amputated limbs and, 140–143, *141*, *142*, *143*
amygdala, *98*, 108
animal research on, 19, *21*
auditory cortex, 196–197, *196*, *197*
basal ganglia, 240–241, *240*
binding problem and, 108–110
blood-brain barrier and, 36–37, *37*
central nervous system and, 88, *88*
cerebellum, 237–239, *237*, *239*
cerebral cortex, 96, 102–111, 231–237, *231*
drug effects on, 70–76, *71*, *73*, *75*
eating regulation by, 299–302, *299*, *300*, *301*
experience of consciousness and, 5–7
forebrain, 96–99
hemispheres of, 394–404
hindbrain, 93–95, *93*, *94*
hippocampus, 370–375, *371*
hypothalamus and pituitary gland in, *81*
lateralization of function in, 394–404
limbic system, 96, *96*

major divisions of, 93–94, *94*
memory localization in, 364–368, *367*
midbrain, *93*, 95–96, *97*
misconceptions about, 47
motor areas of, 231–241, *231*, *232*
nourishment of cells in, 37–38
nucleus accumbens in, 69, *70*
pain and, 206–207, *207*
REM sleep and, 267–268, *268*
schizophrenia and, 444–445, *444*, *445*
self-stimulation of, 69, *69*
sexual orientation and, 330–331, *330*
size of, *126*, 127–128, 408, *409*
somatosensory input to, 202–204
spinal cord connections from, 235–237, *235*, *236*
synchrony of activity in, 109–110
taste coding in, 214–215, *215*
temperature regulation by, 285–286, *285*
terminology for referring to, 88–89, *90*, *91*
tissue transplants, 246
ventricles, 99–100, *100*
visual system in, 163, *165*
water regulation by, 289–292, *290*, *292*
Web sites on the anatomy of, 113
See also Nervous system

Brain damage, 132–147
Alzheimer's disease and, 376–378
amnesia and, 370–372, 375–378
axon regrowth and, 137, *138*
behavioral interventions for, 145, *145*
brain grafts and, 146
Broca's aphasia and, 412–414, *415*
causes of, 132–135, *132*, *133*, *134*
denervation supersensitivity and, 138–139, *138*, *139*
diaschisis and, 136–137
drugs for treating, 137, 146
effects of age on, 143–144, *143*, *144*
Korsakoff's syndrome, 375–376
language and, 411–416
learned adjustments in behavior following, 135–136
locked-in syndrome and, 339, *340*
prefrontal lobotomies and, 107
psychological disorders caused by, 440
therapies for, 145–146
Wernicke's aphasia and, 414, *415*

Brain-derived neurotrophic factor (BDNF), 119, 432

Brain development, 115–131
  abnormalities in, 128–130, *130*
  adult generation of neurons, 124–125
  axon pathfinding, 120–122
  cell loss during, 119, *120*
  collateral sprouting and, 138, *138*
  competition among axons in, 122
  effects of experience on, 123–126, *123, 124, 125*
  neuron growth and development, 117, *119*
  neuron survival determinants, 118–119
  prenatal, 116, *117, 118*
  proportional growth of brain areas, 126–128, *127*
  structural changes in, 125–126, *125*
  Web site on, 148
Brain grafts, 146
Brain size
  comparison among mammals, *126*
  intelligence correlated with, 127–128
  proportionate growth of brain areas and, 126–127, *127*
Brain stem hindbrain, midbrain, and posterior central structures of the forebrain, *93*, 94
Brain-to-body ratio, 408, *409*
Broca's aphasia condition marked by loss of fluent speech and impaired use and understanding of prepositions, word endings, and other grammatical devices, 412–414, *415*
Broca's area portion of the human left frontal lobe associated with certain aspects of language, especially language production, 412
Bulimia nervosa condition characterized by alternation between dieting and overeating, 307
Butyrophenones class of antipsychotic drugs that includes haloperidol, 446

Caffeine drug present in coffee and other drinks that constricts blood vessels to the brain and prevents adenosine from inhibiting the release of dopamine and acetylcholine, 74–75
Calcium blockers, 146
Cannabinoids chemicals related to D^9-THC, the component of marijuana that alters experience, 74
Cannon-Bard theory proposal that an event provokes emotions and autonomic arousal separately and independently, 339
Capsaicin chemical that causes neurons containing sub-

stance P to release it suddenly and also directly stimulates pain receptors sensitive to moderate heat, 206
Carbachol, 268
Carbon atoms, 455–457
Cardiac muscles are the muscles of the heart, 224, *225*
Careers in biological psychology, 24
Carnivores are animals that eat meat, 295
Castration, 313
Catabolic steroids, 81
Catalyst, 457
Cataplexy attack of muscle weakness while a person remains awake, 270
Catecholamines compounds such as dopamine, norepinephrine, and epinephrine that contain both catechol and an amine (NH_2), 60
Caudate nucleus large subcortical structure, one part of the basal ganglia, 240, *240*
CCK. *See* Cholecystokinin
Cell body structure of a cell that contains the nucleus, 33
Cell structure
  animal cells, 30–32
  neurons, 32–35
Central canal fluid-filled channel in the center of the spinal cord, 99
Central executive mechanism that directs attention toward one stimulus or another and determines which items will be stored in working memory, 369
Central gray area, 356
Central nervous system (CNS) is comprised of the brain and spinal cord, 88, *88*
  motor areas of, 231–241, *231*
  prenatal development of, 116, *117*
  somatosensory system and, 202, *205*
  spinal cord, 89–91, *90, 91*
  Web site on, 148
Central pattern generator neural mechanism in the spinal cord or elsewhere that generates rhythmic patterns of motor output 229
Central sulcus large groove in the surface of the primate cerebral cortex, separating frontal from parietal cortex, 103
Cerebellar cortex is the outer covering of the cerebellum, *237*, 238
Cerebellum the large, highly convoluted structure in the hindbrain, 95, *237, 239*
  cellular organization of, 238, *239*
  localization of memory in, 366–368, *367*
  motor control and, 237–238

Cerebral cortex the layer of cells on the outer surface of the cerebral hemispheres of the forebrain, 96, 102–111, *102*
  association areas of, 108–110, *109*
  binding problem and, 108–110
  color perception and, 176
  frontal lobe, *104*, 106–107
  functions of, 111
  language areas of, *412*
  motion perception and, 176–177, *176, 177*
  movement and, 231–237
  occipital lobe, 103, *104*
  organization of, 102–103
  parietal lobe, 103–105, *104*
  pitch perception and, 196–197, *196*
  shape perception and, 170–175
  temporal lobe, *104*, 105–106
  visual pathways in, 168–178, *170*
Cerebral ventricles, 99–100, *100*
Cerebrospinal fluid (CSF) liquid similar to blood serum, found in the ventricles of the brain and in the central canal of the spinal cord, 99–100, 116
Cerebrovascular accident. *See* Stroke
Cerebrum (periodical), 24
Chemical processes
  eating regulation and, 302–305
  synaptic transmission and, 58–66, *59*
  taste and smell stimuli and, 211–212
Chemical senses, 211–219
  chemical coding and, 211–212
  olfaction, 215–218
  taste, 212–215
  vomeronasal sensation, 218–219
Chemistry, 452–458
  elements and compounds, 453–455, *453, 454, 455*
  reactions of carbon atoms, 455–457, *456, 457*
Chewing sensations, 296
Chihuahua problem observation that chihuahuas have an unusually high brain-to-body ratio because they were selected for small bodies, not for large brains, 408
Children
  brain damage recovery in, 144, *144*
  infant amnesia and, 378–379
  reflexes in, 229
  schizophrenia in, 440
Chimpanzees, 405, *406*
Chlorpromazine the first drug found to relieve the positive symptoms of schizophrenia, 446

Cholecystokinin (CKK) hormone released by the duodenum in response to food distention, 297, 357
Chromosome strand of DNA bearing the genes, 9
Chronic conditions are conditions having a gradual onset and long duration, 439
Cigarette smoking
  panic disorder and, 355
  Parkinson's disease and, 244, 245, *245*
  prenatal effects of, 349–350, *350*
Circadian rhythms, 254–256, *255*
  depression and, 433, *434*
  duration of, 255–256
  insomnia and, 269, *269*
  jet lag and, 256, *256*
  mechanisms of, 257–259
  resetting, 255, 256–257
  seasonal affective disorder and, 435–436, *436*
  shift work and, 257
  suprachiasmatic nucleus and, 257–259, *258, 259*
Circannual rhythms, 254
Classical conditioning is a type of conditioning produced by the pairing of two stimuli, one of which evokes an automatic response, 364, *365, 366*
Clinico-anatomical hypothesis, 278
Closed head injury sharp blow to the head resulting from a fall, an automobile or motorcycle accident, an assault, or other sudden trauma that does not actually puncture the brain, 132, *132*
Clozapine, 449
CNS. *See* Central nervous system
Cocaine stimulant drug that increases the stimulation of dopamine synapses by blocking the reuptake of dopamine by the presynaptic neuron, 70–71, *71*
Cochlea structure in the inner ear containing auditory receptors, *193*, 194, 195, *195*
Coding one-to-one correspondence between some aspect of the physical stimulus and some aspect of nervous system activity, 152, *152*
  general principles of, 153
Cognition
  sex hormones and, 320–321
  See also Learning; Memory
Collateral sprout newly formed branch from an uninjured axon that attaches to a synapse vacated when another axon was destroyed, 138, *138*
Colorblindness, 161
Color constancy ability to rec-

Differentiation formation of the axon and dendrites that gives a neuron its distinctive shape, 117

Digestive system, *295*, 297–299
food selection and, 295–296
hunger/satiety and, 297–299
See also Eating regulation

Directions, anatomical, *90*

Disorganized cluster of symptoms, 439

Distal located more distant from the point of origin or attachment, *90*

Disuse supersensitivity increased sensitivity by a postsynaptic cell because of decreased input by incoming axons, 138

Dizygotic twins are fraternal (non-identical) twins, 11
criminal behavior among, 350–351
Parkinson's disease in, 243, *243*
prenatal development of, 11, *12*
schizophrenia in, 440–441, *442*
sexual orientation studies of, 327–328

DNA. *See* Deoxyribonucleic acid

Dolphins, 407

Dominant gene that shows a strong effect in either the homozygous or heterozygous condition, 9

Dopamine is a neurotransmitter
addictive behaviors and, 69, 75–76, *76*
denervation supersensitivity and, 139, *139*
drug effects on, 68–69, *69*
Parkinson's disease and, 243–244
reinforcement process and, 69–70, 75–76
schizophrenia and, 446–447, *446*
sexual behavior and, 315–316
stimulant drugs and, 70–71

Dopamine hypothesis of schizophrenia proposal that schizophrenia is due to excess activity at certain dopamine synapses, 446–447, *447*

Dorsal means toward the back, away from the ventral (stomach) side, 89, *90*

Dorsal root ganglia set of sensory neuron somas on the dorsal side of the spinal cord, 90, *90*

Dorsal stream visual path in the parietal cortex, sometimes known as the Awhere@ or Ahow@ pathway, 169

Dorsolateral prefrontal cortex area of the prefrontal cortex, 144, *144*

Dorsolateral tract path of axons in the spinal cord from the contralateral hemisphere of the brain, controlling movements of peripheral muscles, 235–236, *235*

Down syndrome, 377

Drawing exercise, 223

Dreams, 277–278
activation-synthesis hypothesis of, 277–278
clinico-anatomical hypothesis of, 278
Web sites on, 279

Drugs
alcohol, 75
amphetamine, 70–71
anticonvulsant, 435
antidepressant, 430–432, *430, 431, 432*
antipsychotic, 446
anxiety-reducing, 357–359
appetite-suppressant, 306
atypical antipsychotic, 449
barbiturates, 357
behavior and, 76
brain damage recovery and, 137, 139, 146
caffeine, 74–75
cocaine, 70–71
efficacy of, 68–69
general anaesthetic, 43
hallucinogenic, 74
hyperactivity disorders and, 71, 129
lithium, 434–435
local anaesthetic, 43
marijuana, 74
morphine, 208–209
nicotine, 72
opiate, 72–73
phencyclidine, 73, 448
placebo effect and, 432
stimulant, 70–71
summary of effects, *75*
synaptic activity and, 68–76, *69*
tranquilizers, 357–358
Web sites on, 85, 361

Dualism belief that mind and body are different kinds of substance, existing independently, that somehow interact, 5

Duodenum part of the small intestine adjoining the stomach; the first part of the digestive system that absorbs food, 297

Dynorphin, 71

Dyslexia specific reading difficulty in a person with adequate vision and at least average skills in other academic areas, 416
reading ability and, 416–418, *418*
Web site on, 420

Ears
auditory cortex and, 196–197, *196, 197*
brain lateralization and, 396
hearing loss and, 197–198
pitch perception and, 194–196, *195*
structure of, 192–194, *193, 194*
See also Audition

Easy problems questions pertaining to certain concepts that are termed *consciousness,* such as the difference between wakefulness and sleep, and the mechanisms that enable us to focus our attention, 6

Eating regulation, 294–307
blood glucose levels and, 297–299, *298, 299*
body weight and, 305–306
digestive system and, 295–296, *295,* 297–299
eating disorders and, 306–307
food selection and, 295–296
hypothalamus and, 299–302, *299, 300, 301, 302*
oral factors in, 296–297
satiety chemicals and, 302–305, *305*
Web sites on, 309

Ecstasy (MDMA), 71, *73*

ECT. *See* electroconvulsive therapy

Edema accumulation of fluid, 134

EEG. *See* Electroencephalograph

Efferent axon neuron that carries information away from a structure, 33

Efficacy tendency of a drug to activate a particular kind of receptor, 68

Elderly people
brain damage recovery in, 143, *143*
sleep time and, *276*

Electrical gradient difference in positive and negative charges across a membrane, 41

Electroconvulsive therapy (ECT) electrically inducing a convulsion in an attempt to relieve depression or other disorder, 432–433, *433*

Electroencephalograph (EEG) device that measures the brain's electrical activity through electrodes on the scalp, 261–262, *262, 263*

Elements are materials that cannot be broken down into other materials, 453–455
composing the human body, *453*
periodic table of, *454*

Elevated plus maze, 12, *13*

Emotions, 335–360
attack behaviors and, 349–354
body responses and, 338–340
consciousness and, 336–337
decision making and, 337–338
escape behaviors and, 354–359

expressed, 439
health and, 342–348
hemispheres of the brain and, 399–400, *400*
Web sites related to, 361

End bulb, 33

Endocrine gland organ that produces and releases hormones, 78, *78, 79*

Endogenous circadian rhythm self-generated rhythm that lasts about a day, 254–256, *255*

Endogenous circannual rhythm self-generated rhythm that lasts about a year, 254

Endogenous cycles, 254–256

Endoplasmic reticulum network of thin tubes within a cell that transports newly synthesized proteins to other locations, *31, 32*

Endorphins category of chemicals the body produces that stimulate the same receptors as do opiates, 73, 207, 208

Endothelial cells, 37

Endozepines brain protein that blocks the behavioral effects of diazepam and other benzodiazepines, 358–359

End-stopped cell is a cell of the visual cortex that responds best to stimuli of a precisely limited type, anywhere in a large receptive field, with a strong inhibitory field at one end of its field, 171, *172*

Engram the physical representation of what has been learned, 364
Lashley's search for, 364–366
modern search for, 366–368

Enkephalins, 207

Enriched environment, 123

Environmental factors, 123–124

Enzymes are any proteins that catalyze biological reactions, 9, 457

Epilepsy condition characterized by repeated episodes of excessive, synchronized neural activity, mainly because of decreased release of the inhibitory transmitter GABA, 352, 396–397

Epinephrine also known as adrenaline; a hormone; also used as a neurotransmitter *79*, 369

EPSP. *See* Excitatory postsynaptic potential

Equipotentiality concept that all parts of the cortex contribute equally to complex behaviors such as learning; that any part of the cortex can substitute for any other, 366

Escape behaviors, 354–359

Estradiol is one type of estrogen, 317–318

Estrogen class of steroid hormones that are more abundant in females than in males for most species, 79, 81, 312
 cognition and, 320–321, *320*
 schizophrenia and, 440
 sexual differentiation and, 313

Ethical issues, 19, 21–22, *23*, 459–461

Evolution change in the frequencies of various genes in a population over generations, 13
 Lamarckian, 14–15
 language and, 408–411
 misunderstandings about, 13–16
 relationships among species and, 13, *14*
 sociobiology and, 16–17

Evolutionary explanation understanding in terms of the evolutionary history of a species, 3–4

Evolutionary psychology. *See* Sociobiology

Evolutionary theory of sleep concept that the function of sleep is to conserve energy at times of relative inefficiency, 273–274

Evolutionary trees, 13, *14*

Excitatory neurotransmitters, 63

Excitatory postsynaptic potential (EPSP) is the graded depolarization of a neuron, 53, 56

Exocytosis excretion of neurotransmitter through the membrane of a presynaptic terminal and into the synaptic cleft between the presynaptic and postsynaptic neurons, 61

Explicit memory is the deliberate recall of information that one recognizes as a memory, detectable by direct testing such as asking a person to describe a past event, 372

Expressed emotion hostility expressed toward a patient by frustrated family members, 439

Extensor muscle that extends a limb, 224

Eyes
 blind spot in, 155–156, *156*
 brain lateralization and, 395–396, *395*
 color vision and, 157–161, *158, 159, 160*
 deprivation effects and, 182–185, *183, 185*
 infant vision and, 181, *181*
 receptive fields in, 163, 165, *165*
 retinal neurons in, *164*, 168, *168*

structure of, 153–157, *154, 155, 156*
 suppressed vision during movement of, 179
 visual receptors of, 156–157, *156*
 See also Vision

Facial expressions
 emotions and, 339, *339*, 356
 impaired recognition of, 357, *358*

Facilitating interneuron, 384

"Fake arm" touch demonstration, 108, *109*

Fast-twitch fibers are muscle fibers that produce fast contractions but fatigue rapidly, 226

Fat cells, hormone released by, 78, *79*

Fear, 354–356
 amygdala and, 356, *357*
 panic disorder and, 354–355
 startle reflex and, 355–356
 See also Anxiety

Feature detector neuron whose responses indicate the presence of a particular feature, 172–173

Feeding process. *See* Eating regulation; Food selection

Feelings, 336
 See also Emotions

Fetal alcohol syndrome condition resulting from prenatal exposure to alcohol and marked by decreased alertness, hyperactivity, varying degrees of mental retardation, motor problems, heart defects, and facial abnormalities, 129–130, *130*

Fetal development
 brain growth and development, 116, *117, 118*
 exposure to alcohol during, 129–130, *130*

Fever, 286

Finger-to-nose test, 237

Fish
 brain-to-body ratio of, 408, *409*
 muscles in, 226

Fissure a long, deep sulcus, *91*

Fitness number of copies of one's genes that endure in later generations, 15

Flaccid paralysis, *233*

Flashbulb memories, 369

Flexor muscle that flexes a limb, 224

Fluent aphasia, 414

Fluoxetine, *430*, 431

Follicle-stimulating hormone (FSH) anterior pituitary hormone that promotes the growth of follicles in the ovary, 79, 82, 317–318, *318*

Food selection
 digestive system and, 295
 influences on, 295–296, *296*
 lateral hypothalamus and, 299–300, *299, 300*

weight-loss techniques and, 306
 See also Diet; Eating regulation

Forebrain most anterior part of the brain, including the cerebral cortex and other structures, 96–99
 basal forebrain, 99, *99*
 basal ganglia, 97–98, *98*
 cerebral cortex, 96, 102–111
 hippocampus, *96*, 99
 hypothalamus, *96*, 97, *97*
 pituitary gland, 97, *97*
 thalamus, 96–97, *98*

Fornix tract of axons connecting the hippocampus with the hypothalamus and other areas, 99

Fovea area in the center of the human retina specialized for acute, detailed vision, 153–154, *154*

Foveal vision, *157*

Fraternal twins. *See* Dizygotic twins

Free-running rhythm circadian or circannual rhythm that is not being periodically reset by light or other cues, 255

Frequency number of sound waves per second, 192

Frequency theory concept that pitch perception depends on differences in frequency of action potentials by auditory neurons, 194

Frontal lobe section of cerebral cortex extending from the central sulcus to the anterior limit of the brain, containing the primary motor cortex and the prefrontal cortex, *104*, 106–107

Frontal plane, *90*

FSH. *See* Follicle-stimulating hormone

Functional explanation understanding why a structure or behavior evolved as it did, 4–5

Functional magnetic resonance imaging (fMRI) a modified version of MRI that measures energies released by hemoglobin molecules in an MRI scan, and then determines the brain areas receiving the greatest supply of blood and oxygen, 175, *175*

Fungiform papillae, 214

Fusiform gyrus, 175, *175*

G-protein protein coupled to GTP (guanosine triphosphate, an energy-storing molecule), 63

GABA (gamma amino butyric acid) the most abundant inhibitory neurotransmitter, 63, 357–359

GABA$_A$ receptor complex structure that includes a

site that binds GABA, as well as sites that bind other chemicals that modify the sensitivity of the GABA site, 358, *358*, 359

Gamma waves repetitive activity in neurons at a rhythm of 30 to 80 action potentials per second, 109

Ganglion cluster of neuron cell bodies, usually outside the CNS, 90, *91*

Ganglion cell type of neuron in the retina that receives input from the bipolar cells, 155, *155*

Ganglioside molecule composed of carbohydrates and fats, 146

Gases, 60

Gate theory assumption that stimulation of certain nonpain axons in the skin or in the brain can inhibit transmission of pain messages in the spinal cord, 207

Gender differences, 324

Gender identity is the sex with which a person identifies, 324
 intersexes and, 324–326, *325*
 sexual appearance discrepancies and, 326–327
 support groups dealing with, 333
 testicular feminization and, 326
 Web site on, 333

Gender roles activities and dispositions that a particular society encourages for one sex or the other, 324

Gene unit of heredity that maintains its structural identity from one generation to another, 9

General anaesthetics drugs that decrease brain activity by opening potassium channels wider than usual, 43

Generalized seizure epileptic seizure that spreads quickly across neurons over a large portion of both hemispheres of the brain, 396

Genetic drift, 4

Genetics, 9–13
 alcoholism and, 424–425
 behavior and, 12–13, 76, *76*
 bipolar disorder and, 434
 body weight and, 302–303, *303*, 305–306
 depression and, 428
 mating outcomes based on, 9, *10*
 Mendelian, 9–11
 schizophrenia and, 440–443, *442*
 sexual orientation and, 327–328, *328*
 violent behavior and, 349–351
 See also Heritability

Genitals, 312–313, *313*

Glia type of cell in the nervous system that, in contrast to neurons, does not conduct impulses to other cells, 2, 35–36, *35*, 117

Globus pallidus large subcortical structure, one part of the basal ganglia, 240, *240*

Glomeruli, 117, *119*

Glucagon pancreatic hormone that stimulates the liver to convert stored glycogen to glucose, *79*, 298, *298*

Glucose a simple sugar, the main fuel of vertebrate neurons, 37
  eating regulation and, 297–299, *298*, *299*

Glutamate, the most abundant excitatory neurotransmitter, 62–63, 73, 386–387, *386*, *387*, 447–448

Glutamate hypothesis of schizophrenia proposal that schizophrenia is due to deficient activity at certain glutamate synapses, 447–448, *448*

Glycine, 448

Golgi tendon organ receptor that responds to the contraction of a muscle, 227

Gonadotropins, 82

Gonad reproductive organ, 312

Goose bumps, 3–4, *4*, 93

Graded potential membrane potential that varies in magnitude and does not follow the all-or-none law, 46

Grand mal seizure type of generalized seizure characterized by sudden, repetitive, jerking movements of the head and limbs for a period of seconds or minutes; the person then collapses into exhaustion and sleep, 396–397

Grasp reflex reflexive grasp of an object placed firmly in the hand, 229

Gray matter areas of the nervous system with a high density of cell bodies and dendrites, with few myelinated axons, 90, *91*

Group selection, 16

Growth hormone (GH), *79*, 82

Gyrus (pl: gyri) a protuberance or elevation of the brain, separated from another gyrus by a sulcus, *91*

Habituation decrease in response to a stimulus that is presented repeatedly and that is accompanied by no change in other stimuli, 382–383, *384*

Hair cell type of sensory receptor shaped like a hair; auditory receptors are hair cells, *193*, 194, *194*

Hallucination sensory experience that does not correspond to reality, 438, *439*

Hallucinogenic drugs are drugs that grossly distort perception, such as LSD, 74

Hard problem philosophical question of why and how any kind of brain activity is associated with consciousness, 6

Headaches, 206

Health
  immune system and, 344–347
  psychosomatic illness and, 342–344
  stress and, 342–348

Hearing. *See* Audition

Heart disease, 343

Hebbian synapse a synapse that increases in effectiveness because of simultaneous activity in the presynaptic axon and the postsynaptic neuron, 381

Hemiplegia, 138, *233*

Hemispheres of the brain, 394–404, *401*
  anatomical differences between, 401–402, *402*
  auditory and visual connections to, 395–396, *395*, 400–401, *400*, *401*
  corpus callosum and, 394, *394*, 396–397, *397*, 402–403
  emotions and, 399–400, *400*, *401*
  functional specificity of, 397, 398, 399–401, *399*, *400*, 403–404
  language processing and, 401–402, 403, 412, *412*, 417
  schizophrenia and, 444
  speech and, 397, 398, 399, *401*
  split-brain people and, 396–397, *397*, 399
  See also Lateralization

Hemorrhage the rupture of an artery, 132, 133–134

Herbivores are animals that eat plants, 295

Heritability estimate, ranging from 0 to 1.0, indicating the degree to which variance in a characteristic depends on variations in heredity for a given population, 11–12
  of bipolar disorder, 434
  of Huntington's disease, 247–248
  of Parkinson's disease, 243
  of schizophrenia, 440–443, *442*
  See also Genetics

Hermaphrodite individual whose genitals do not match the usual development for his or her genetic sex, 324–325

Hertz (Hz), 192

Heterozygous having two unlike genes for a given trait, 9

5-HIAA. *See* 5-Hydroxyindoleacetic acid

Hibernation, 273, 274

Hindbrain most posterior part of the brain, including the medulla, pons, and cerebellum, 93–95, *93*, *94*

Hippocampal commissure set of axons that connects the left and right hippocampi, 398, 403

Hippocampus large forebrain structure between the thalamus and cortex, *96*, 99, 346–347, 370–375, *371*
  amnesia after damage to, 370–372
  configural learning and, 374–375
  consolidation of memories and, 375
  declarative memory and, 372, *372*
  long-term potentiation in, 386, 388
  schizophrenia and, 444–445, *444*, *445*
  spatial memory and, 372–374, *373*, *374*
  theories on the function of, 372–375
  Web site with illustrations of, 390

Histamine, 209

Histochemistry, 141, 142

Homeostasis tendency to maintain a variable, such as temperature, within a fixed range, 282

Homeothermic maintaining nearly constant body temperature over a wide range of environmental temperatures, 282

Homosexuality, 327–331

Homozygous having two identical genes for a given characteristic, 9

Horizontal cell type of cell that receives input from receptors and delivers inhibitory input to bipolar cells, 47, 163, *164*

Horizontal plane is the plane that shows brain structures as they would be seen from above, 90

Hormones chemicals secreted by glands and conveyed by the blood to other organs, which are influenced by their activity, 78–83
  actions of, 78, 80–81, *80*
  categories of, 80–81
  controlling the release of, 81–83
  nervous system and, 83
  partial list of, *79*
  sex differences and, 312–315
  sexual behavior and, 315–319

sexual orientation and, 328–330, *329*
violent behavior and, 351, *351*

HPA axis is the hypothalamus, pituitary gland, and adrenal cortex, 344, *344*, 346

Human research subjects, 461

Hunger
  blood glucose levels and, 297–299, *298*, *299*
  digestive system and, 297–299
  eating disorders and, 306–307
  hypothalamus and, 299–302, *299*, *300*, *301*, *302*
  satiety chemicals and, 302–305, *305*
  sodium cravings and, 291–292
  taste sensations and, 296
  See also Eating regulation

Huntingtin protein produced by the gene whose mutation leads to Huntington's disease, 247–248

Huntington's disease an inherited disorder characterized initially by jerky arm movements and facial twitches, later by tremors, writhing movements, and psychological symptoms, including depression, memory impairment, hallucinations, and delusions, 246–248, *247*, *248*, 441

Hydrocephalus, 100

6-Hydroxydopamine (6-OHDA) a chemical that is absorbed by neurons that release dopamine or norepinephrine; it is then oxidized into toxic chemicals that kill those neurons, 139, *139*

5-Hydroxyindoleacetic acid (5-HIAA) a serotonin metabolite, 353, *353*

Hypercomplex cell is a cell of the visual cortex that responds best to stimuli of a precisely limited type, anywhere in a large receptive field, with a strong inhibitory field at one end of its field, 171, *172*

Hyperpolarization increased polarization across a membrane, 42

Hyperventilation, breathing more often or more deeply than necessary, 355

Hypnagogic hallucinations, 270

Hypothalamus forebrain structure near the base of the brain just ventral to the thalamus, *96*, 97, *97*, 267
  eating regulation and, 299–302, *299*, *300*, *301*, 303–304, *304*
  effects of lesions in, *303*

hormone release and, *79, 81–83, 81, 82*
medial areas of, 300–302, *300, 301, 302*
sexual differentiation and, 312–315
sexual orientation and, 330–331, *330*
temperature regulation by, 285–286, *285*
water regulation by, 290
Hypovolemic thirst is thirst provoked by low blood volume, 291–292, *291, 292*

Identical twins. *See* Monozygotic twins
Identity position view that mental processes are the same as certain kinds of brain processes, but described in different terms, 6
Illness
immune system and, 344–347
psychosomatic, 342–344
Immune system set of structures that protects the body against viruses and bacteria, 344–347
cytokines, 346
leukocytes, 345, *345*
natural killer cells, 345–346
stress and, 346–347
Implicit memory influence of recent experience on memory, even if one does not recognize that influence or realize that one is using memory at all, 372
Impotence inability to have an erection, 317
Infant amnesia tendency for people to recall few events from their earliest years, 378–379
Infants
brain damage recovery in, 144, *144*
memory function in, 378–379, *379*
reflexes in, 229
REM sleep in, 274
sleep apnea in, 269
vision in, 181, *181*
Inferior means below another part, *90*
Inferior colliculus swelling on each side of the tectum in the midbrain, *93, 95, 97*
Inferior parietal cortex, 110
Inferior temporal cortex portion of the cortex where neurons are highly sensitive to complex aspects of the shape of visual stimuli within very large receptive fields, 173–174
Inhibitory neurotransmitters, 63
Inhibitory postsynaptic potential (IPSP) temporary hyperpolarization of a membrane, 55, 56

Inhibitory synapses, 54–55, *55*
Inner-ear deafness hearing loss that results from damage to the cochlea, the hair cells, or the auditory nerve, 197
Insomnia lack of sleep, leaving the person feeling poorly rested the following day, 268–269, *269*
Insulin pancreatic hormone that facilitates the entry of glucose into the cells, 61, 79, 80
eating regulation and, 297–299, *298, 299*
Intelligence
brain size and, 127–128, 408, *409*
language learning and, 408–410
Interleukin-1, 286
Interneurons, 55
Intersex an individual whose sexual development is intermediate or ambiguous, 324–326, *325*
Interstitial nucleus 3, 330–331, *330*
Intestines, 297
Intrinsic neuron a neuron whose axons and dendrites are all confined within a given structure, 34
Invertebrates
habituation in, 382–383, *384*
sensitization in, 383–385, *385*
Involuntary movements, 228
Ion is an atom that has gained or lost one or more electrons, 455
Ion channels
action potential and, 42–44, *43*
resting potential and, 40–41, *41*
Ionic bond chemical attraction between two ions of opposite charge, 455
Ionotropic effects synaptic effect that depends on the rapid opening of some kind of gate in the membrane, 62–63
Ipsilateral means on the same side of the body (left or right), *90*
IQ (intelligence quotient), 127–128
IPSP. *See* Inhibitory postsynaptic potential
Ischemia local insufficiency of blood because a blood clot or other obstruction has closed an artery, 132, 133–134

James-Lange theory the proposal that an event first provokes autonomic and skeletal responses and that emotion is the per-

ception of those responses, 338
Jay family of birds, 373, *374*
Jet lag is the disruption of biological rhythms caused by travel across time zones, 256, *256*
Journal of Neuroscience, 459

K-complex sharp, high-amplitude, negative wave followed by a smaller, slower, positive wave, 261
Kennard principle generalization (not always correct) that it is easier to recover from brain damage early in life than later, 143–144
Ketamine, 448
Kidneys, hormone released by, *79*
Kin selection is the selection for a gene because it benefits the individual's relatives, 16
Klüver-Bucy syndrome the condition in which monkeys with damaged temporal lobes fail to display normal fears and anxieties, 105–106, 352
Korsakoff's syndrome a type of brain damage caused by thiamine deficiency, characterized by apathy, confusion, and memory impairment, 38, 375–376

L-dopa chemical precursor of dopamine and other catecholamines, 244–245
Labeled-line principle concept that each receptor responds to a limited range of stimuli and has a direct line to the brain, 211
Lactase enzyme necessary for lactose metabolism, 295
Lactate, 37
Lactose is the sugar in milk, 295, *296*
Lamarckian evolution a discredited theory that evolution proceeds through the inheritance of acquired characteristics, 14–15
Lamina (plural: laminae) layer of cell bodies parallel to the surface of the cortex and separated from other laminae by layers of fibers, *91, 102, 103*
Language, 405–419
brain areas activated by, 414–416, *415, 416*
brain damage and, 411–414
dyslexia and, 416–418, *417, 418*
evolution of, 408–411
intelligence and, 408–410
lateralization and, 401–402
learning of, 411
nonprimate species and, 407–408, *407*
primates and, 405–407, *406*

Web sites on, 420
Language acquisition device built-in mechanism for acquiring language, 410–411
Lateral means toward the side, away from the midline, *90*
Lateral geniculate nucleus thalamic nucleus that receives incoming visual information, 126, 163
Lateral hypothalamus area of the hypothalamus that is important for the control of eating and drinking, 299–300, *299, 300, 303*
Lateral inhibition restraint of activity in one neuron by activity in a neighboring neuron, 166–167, *167*
Lateral interpositus nucleus (LIP) a nucleus of the cerebellum that is critical for classical conditioning of the eye-blink response, 366–368, *367*
Lateralization is the division of labor between the two hemispheres of the brain, 394–404
anatomical differences and, 401–402, *402*
audition and, 396, 401, *401*
commissures of the brain and, 397, *398*, 403
corpus callosum and, 394, *394, 396–397, 397, 402–403*
emotions and, 399–400, *400, 401*
handedness and, 403
hemisphere functions and, 397, 398, 399–401, *399, 400, 401, 403–404*
language processing and, 401–402, 403, 412, *412*, 417
schizophrenia and, 444
spatial processing and, 400–401
speech and, 397, 398, 399, *401*
split-brain people and, 396–397, *397*, 399
vision and, 395–396, *395, 400–401, 400, 401*
Lateral preoptic area portion of the hypothalamus that includes some cells that facilitate drinking and some that inhibit it, as well as passing axons that are important for osmotic thirst, 290, *303*
Law of specific nerve energies is the statement that each nerve always conveys the same kind of information to the brain, 153
Lazy eye reduced vision resulting from disuse of one eye, usually associated with failure of the two eyes to point in the same direction, 183

Learning
brain localization of, 364–368, *367*
classical conditioning and, 364, *365, 366*
configural, 374–375
Hebbian synapses and, 381
hippocampus and, 370–375, *371*
infant amnesia and, 378–379, *379*
invertebrate studies of, 381–385
long-term potentiation and, 388
mammal studies of, 385–388
operant conditioning and, 364, *365*
types of memory and, 368–370
Web sites on, 390–391
See also Memory
Lens (eye), 153, *154*
Leptin peptide released by fat cells; tends to decrease eating, partly by inhibiting release of neuropeptide Y in the hypothalamus, 78, *79*, 302–305, *305*
Lesion damage to a structure, 136
Leu-enkephalin chain of five amino acids believed to function as a neurotransmitter that inhibits pain, 207
Leukocyte white blood cell, a component of the immune system, 345, *345*
Light
color vision and, 157–161, *157, 158, 159, 160*
resetting the SCN with, 257–259
seasonal affective disorder and, 436
wavelengths of, 157, *157, 158, 158*
Limbic system set of forebrain areas traditionally regarded as critical for emotion, which form a border around the brainstem, including the olfactory bulb, hypothalamus, hippocampus, amygdala, cingulate gyrus of the cerebral cortex, and several other smaller structures, 96, *96, 336, 337*
Lithium element whose salts are often used as a therapy for bipolar disorder, 434–435
Liver, hormone released by, *79*
Lobotomies, prefrontal, 106–107, *107*
Local anaesthetic drug that attaches to the sodium channels of the membrane, preventing sodium ions from entering and thereby blocking action potentials, 43
Localization of sounds, 198–199, *198, 199*

Local neuron small neuron with no axon or a very short one, 33, 46–47
Locked-in syndrome a condition caused by damage to the ventral brainstem, in which the person almost completely loses brain control of the muscles, 339, *340*
Locus coeruleus small hindbrain structure whose widespread axons send bursts of norepinephrine in response to meaningful stimuli, 138, 265, *267*
Long-term depression prolonged decrease in response to an axonal input that has been repeatedly paired with some other input, generally at a low frequency, 385
Long-term memory the memory of an event that is not currently held in attention, 368–369, *368*
Long-term potentiation (LTP) phenomenon that after one or more axons bombard a dendrite with a rapid series of stimuli, the synapses between those axons and the dendrite become more sensitive for minutes, days, or weeks, 385–388
behavior and, 388
biochemical mechanisms of, 385–387, *386, 387*
Web site on, 391
Loudness perception of the intensity of a sound, 192
LSD (lysergic acid diethylamide), 74, *74*, 446
Luteinizing hormone (LH) anterior pituitary hormone that stimulates the release of an ovum, *79*, 82, 318, *318*

Machine consciousness, 7, 8
Macrophage immune system cell that surrounds a bacterium or other intruder, digests it, and exposes its antigens on the macrophage's own surface, 345, *345*
Macula, 153–154, *154*
Magnetic resonance imaging (MRI) method of imaging a living brain by using a magnetic field and a radio frequency field to make atoms with odd atomic weights all rotate in the same direction and then removing those fields and measuring the energy that the atoms release, 128, *128, 207*
Magnetoencephalograph (MEG) a device that measures the faint magnetic

fields generated by the brain's activity, 124
example of experiment using, 125, *125*
Magnocellular neuron large-celled neuron of the visual system that is sensitive to changing or moving stimuli in a relatively large visual field, 168, *168*
Magnocellular pathways, 168–170, *168, 169, 170, 400*
Maintenance insomnia frequent awakening during the night, 269
Major depression state of feeling sad, helpless, and lacking in energy and pleasure for weeks at a time, 428–434
Mammals
body temperature of, 284
brain size comparison, *126, 408, 409*
circadian rhythms in, 254–255
long-term potentiation in, 385–388
scientific research using, 19–23, *20*
visual system in, 163, 182–183
See also Animals
Mania condition of restless activity, excitement, laughter, self-confidence, and few inhibitions, 434, *435*
Manic-depressive disorder. *See* Bipolar disorder
MAO (monoamine oxidase) enzyme that converts catecholamines and serotonin into synaptically inactive forms, 66
MAOI. *See* Monoamine oxidase inhibitor
Marijuana, 74
Mass action theory that the cortex works as a whole, and the more cortex the better, 366
Materialism view that everything that exists is material, or physical, 5
Maternal behavior, 321–322, *322*
Mating behavior
hormonal secretions and, 316
See also Reproductive behaviors
Matter, 6
MDMA (ecstasy), 71, *73*
Mechanical senses, 201–210
pain, 204–209
somatosensation, 201–204
vestibular sensation, 201
Medial means toward the midline, away from the side, 90
Medications. *See* Drugs
Medroxyprogesterone, 317
Medulla hindbrain structure located just above the

spinal cord; the medulla could be regarded as an enlarged, elaborated extension of the spinal cord, 94
MEG. *See* Magnetoencephalograph
Melatonin hormone that among other effects induces sleepiness , *79*, 259
Membrane structure that separates the inside of a cell from the outside, 30, *31, 32*
Memory, 363–380
amnesia and, 370–372, 375–378
brain localization of, 364–368, *367*
conditioning processes and, 364, *365, 366*
configural learning and, 374–375
declarative, 372, *372*
engram of, 364–368, *367*
explicit, 372
hippocampus and, 370–375, *371*
implicit, 372
infant amnesia and, 378–379, *379*
long-term, 368–369
procedural, 372
REM sleep and, 276–277
short-term, 368
spatial, 372–374, *373, 374*
types of, 368–370
Web sites on, 390–391
working, 107, 369–370
See also Learning
Memory cells, 345
Menarche is the time of a woman's first menstruation, 321
Mendelian genetics, 9–11
Meninges are membranes surrounding the brain and spinal cord, 99
Menopause is the time when middle-aged women permanently stop menstruating, 320
Menstrual cycle in women, periodic variation in hormones and fertility over the course of approximately 1 month, 317, *317*
Mentalism view that only the mind really exists, 5–6
Mesolimbocortical system set of neurons that project from the midbrain tegmentum to the limbic system, 449, *449*
Metabolic rate, 305
Metabotropic effect is the effect at a synapse that produces a relatively slow but long-lasting effect through metabolic reactions, 63–64, *64*
Met-enkephalin chain of five amino acids believed to function as a neurotransmitter that inhibits pain, 207

Methylphenidate stimulant drug that increases the stimulation of dopamine synapses by blocking the reuptake of dopamine by the presynaptic neuron, 71

Microdialysis, 305

Microelectrodes, 40, 171

Midbrain middle part of the brain, including superior colliculus, inferior colliculus, tectum, and tegmentum, 93, 95–96, *97*

Middle-ear deafness hearing loss that occurs if the bones of the middle ear fail to transmit sound waves properly to the cochlea, 197

Migration the movement of neurons toward their eventual destinations in the brain, 117

Milk products, 295

Mind
  dualistic view of, 5
  See also Brain; Consciousness

Mind-body problem or **mind-brain problem** is the question of how the mind is related to the brain, 5

Mitochondrion (plural: mitochondria) the structure where the cell performs the metabolic activities that provide energy, 31, *31*

Molecule the smallest possible piece of a compound that retains the properties of the compound, 453, *455*

Monism the theory that only one kind of substance exists in the universe (not separate physical and mental substances), 5–6

Monoamine nonacidic neurotransmitter containing an amine group (NH$_2$), formed by a metabolic change of certain amino acids, 60

Monoamine oxidase inhibitor (MAOI) drug that blocks the enzyme monoamine oxidase (MAO), a presynaptic terminal enzyme that metabolizes catecholamines and serotonin into inactive forms, *430*, 431, *431*

Monozygotic twins are identical twins, 11
  criminal behavior among, 350–351
  Parkinson's disease in, 243, *243*
  prenatal development of, 11, *12*
  schizophrenia in, 440–441, 442, *442*
  sexual orientation studies of, 327–328

Mood disorders, 428–437
  bipolar disorder, 434–435, *435*

differential diagnosis of, 440
  major depression, 428–434, *428*
  seasonal affective disorder, 435–436, *436*

"Mooney" faces, 109, *110*

Morphine, 208–209

Morris search task procedure in which a subject must find his or her way to a slightly submerged platform that is not visible in murky water or other opaque substance, 373, *374*, 378–379, *379*

Motion blindness impaired ability to perceive the direction or speed of movement, despite otherwise satisfactory vision, 163, 177

Motion perception, 176–177, *176*, *177*, 185

Motor cortex, *105*, 106, 231–232, *232*, *234*

Motor neuron a neuron that receives excitation from other neurons and conducts impulses from its soma in the spinal cord to muscle or gland cells, 32, *32*

Motor program a fixed sequence of movements that occur as a single unit, 229–230

Movement, 223–250
  ballistic, 228
  basal ganglia and, 240–241, *240*
  brain mechanisms of, 231–241, *231*, *232*
  cerebellum and, 237–239, *237*, *239*
  cerebral cortex and, 231–237
  control of, 224–230
  disorders of, 242–248
  motor programs and, 229–230
  muscles and, 224–228
  units of, 228–230
  visual perception of, 185
  voluntary and involuntary, 228
  Web sites related to, 250

MPTP, MPP$^+$ chemicals known to be toxic to the dopamine-containing cells in the substantia nigra, capable of producing the symptoms of Parkinson's disease, 243–244, *244*

MRI scans. *See* Magnetic resonance imaging

MST medial superior temporal cortex, an area in which neurons are sensitive to expansion, contraction, or rotation of the visual field or to the movement of an object relative to its background, *176*, 177, *177*

MT or area V5 a portion of the middle temporal cortex, where neurons are highly

sensitive to the speed and direction of movement of visual stimuli, 176–177

Müllerian ducts early precursors to female reproductive structures (the oviducts, uterus, and upper vagina), 312

Müllerian inhibiting hormone (MIH), 312

Multiple personality, 438

Multiple sclerosis, 46

Muscles, 224–228
  fast and slow, 226
  proprioceptors and, 226–228
  types of, 224, *225*
  Web site on, 250

Muscle spindle receptor parallel to the muscle that responds to the stretch of a muscle, 227

Music perception, 401

Mutation the change in a gene during reproduction, 11

Myasthenia gravis a disease in which the immune system attacks the acetylcholine receptors at the nerve-muscle junctions, 224

Myelinated axon an axon covered with a myelin sheath, 45

Myelination development of a myelin sheath that insulates an axon, 117

Myelin sheath insulating material that covers many vertebrate axons, 33, 45–46, *46*

Mynah birds, 123–124, *124*

Naloxone a drug that blocks opiate receptors, 208

Narcolepsy a condition characterized by unexpected periods of sleepiness during the day, 270

Natural killer cell a type of leukocyte that destroys certain kinds of tumor cells and cells infected with viruses, 36, 345–346

Necrosis, 119

Negative color afterimage is the result of prolonged staring at a colored display and then looking at a white surface, in which one sees green in the places where the display had been red, red where it had been green, yellow where it had been blue, blue where it had been yellow, black where it had been white, and white where it had been black, 159, *159*

Negative symptom the absence of a behavior ordinarily seen in normal people, for example, lack of emotional expression, 438

Neglect the tendency to ignore the contralateral side of the body and the world af-

ter damage to the parietal lobe in one hemisphere (usually the right), 104–105

Nerve deafness hearing loss that results from damage to the cochlea, the hair cells, or the auditory nerve, 197

Nerve growth factor (NGF) protein that promotes the survival and growth of axons in the sympathetic nervous system and certain axons in the brain, 118–119, 184

Nerves are sets of axons in the periphery, either from the CNS to a muscle or gland or from a sensory organ to the CNS, *91*
  release of chemicals by, 58–59, *58*

Nervous system, 87–112, *88*
  autonomic, 91–93, *92*
  brain development and, 115–131
  cells of, 30–38
  cerebral cortex, 96, 102–111
  cerebral ventricles, 99–100, *100*
  forebrain, 96–99
  hindbrain, 93–95, *93*, *94*
  hormones and, 83
  limbic system, 96, *96*
  midbrain, 93, 95–96, *97*
  spinal cord, 89–91, *90*, *91*
  terminology for referring to, 88–89, *90*, *91*
  vertebrate, 88–101
  Web sites on, 49
  See also Brain

Neural Darwinism the principle that, in the development of the nervous system, synapses form haphazardly at first, and then a selection process keeps some and rejects others, 122

Neuroanatomy is the anatomy of the nervous system, 87

Neurodevelopmental hypothesis the proposal that schizophrenia is based on abnormalities in the prenatal or neonatal development of the nervous system, which lead to subtle but important abnormalities of brain anatomy and major abnormalities in behavior, 443–446, *444*, *445*

Neuroleptic drug a drug that relieves schizophrenia, 446, *447*

Neurologist, 24

Neuromodulator chemical that has properties intermediate between those of a neurotransmitter and those of a hormone, 64, *65*

Neuromuscular junction the synapse where a motor neuron's axon meets a muscle fiber, 224

Parasympathetic nervous system (PNS) the system of nerves that facilitate vegetative, nonemergency responses by the body's organs, 91–93, *92*, 338, *343*

Parathyroid gland, *79*

Parathyroid hormone, *79*

Paraventricular hypothalamus, *300*

Paraventricular nucleus (PVN) the area of the hypothalamus in which activity tends to limit meal size and damage leads to excessively large meals, 290, 302, *303*, 304, *304*

Parental behavior, 321–322, *322*

Parietal lobe the section of the cerebral cortex between the occipital lobe and the central sulcus, 103–105, *104*, 110

Parkinson's disease malady caused by damage to a dopamine pathway, resulting in slow movements, difficulty initiating movements, rigidity of the muscles, and tremors, 147, 242–246, *242*, *243*, 244, *245*

  L-dopa treatment for, 244–245

  possible causes of, 243–244, *243*

  symptoms of, 242

  therapies for, 245–246

Parrots, 407, *407*

Partial seizure epileptic seizure that begins in a focus somewhere in the brain and then spreads to nearby areas in just one hemisphere, 397

Parvocellular neuron small-celled neuron of the visual system that is sensitive to color differences and visual details in its small visual field, 168, *168*

Parvocellular pathways, 168–170, *168*, *169*, *170*, 400

Paternal half-siblings are people who have the same father but different mothers, 441–442

PCP. *See* Phencyclidine

Peacocks, 15, *15*

Penumbra area of endangered cells surrounding an area of primary damage, 133–134

Peptide a chain of amino acids, 59–60

Peptide hormone a hormone composed of a short chain of amino acids, 80

Perception
  auditory, 192–200
  binding of, 108–110
  color, 157–161, 176
  depth, 176, 184

shape, 170–175

steps in process of, 152, *152*

visual, 151–188, 400–401

Periaqueductal gray area the area of the brainstem that is rich in enkephalin synapses, 207, *209*

Periodic limb movement disorder repeated involuntary movement of the legs and sometimes arms during sleep, 270

Periodic table of the elements, *454*

Periovulatory period the time just before and after the release of the ovum, when fertility is highest, 318

Peripheral nervous system (PNS) the nerves outside the brain and spinal cord, 88, *88*

Peripheral vision, *157*

Personality, 76

petit mal seizure (or absence seizure) is a type of generalized seizure in which the person stares unresponsively for a period of seconds, making no sudden movements, except perhaps for eye blinking or drooping the head, 397

PET scans. *See* Positron emission tomography

PGO wave a pattern of high-amplitude electrical potentials that occurs first in the pons, then in the lateral geniculate, and finally in the occipital cortex, 267, *268*

Phantom limb the continuing sensation of an amputated body part, 141–142, *142*, *143*

  relieving pain from, 142, *143*

Phase differences, 199

Phencyclidine (PCP) a drug that inhibits type NMDA glutamate receptors; at low doses produces intoxication and slurred speech, and at higher doses produces both positive and negative symptoms of schizophrenia, 73, 448

Phenothiazines the class of antipsychotic drugs that includes chlorpromazine, 446

Phenylephrine, 101

Phenylketonuria (PKU) the inherited inability to metabolize phenylalanine, leading to mental retardation unless the afflicted person stays on a strict low-phenylalanine diet throughout childhood, 12

Phenythiocarbamide (PTC), 213

Pheromone a chemical released by one animal that affects the behavior of

other members of the same species, 218–219

Phonological loop the aspect of working memory that stores auditory information, including words, 369

Photopigment a chemical that releases energy when struck by light, 157

Phrenology the pseudoscience that claimed a relationship between skull anatomy and behavioral capacities, 413

Physiological explanation understanding in terms of the activity of the brain and other organs, 3, 4

Pineal gland a small unpaired gland in the brain, just posterior to the thalamus, that releases the hormone melatonin, 5, *5*, *79*, 259

Pinna the outer-ear structure of flesh and cartilage that sticks out from each side of the head, 193, *193*

Pitch the experience that corresponds to the frequency of a sound, 192, 194–197
  auditory cortex and, 196–197, *196*, *197*
  human perception of, 194–196
  theories of, 194

Pituitary gland endocrine gland attached to the base of the hypothalamus, 81, *81*, 97, *97*
  hormones released by, *79*, 82, *82*
  hypothalamus and, *285*
  interactions with ovaries, 318, *318*

PKU. *See* Phenylketonuria

Placebo effect deriving benefit due to the expectation of improvement or to the mere passage of time, 432

Place theory the concept that pitch perception depends on which part of the inner ear has cells with the greatest activity level, 194

Planum temporale the area of the temporal cortex that for most people is larger in the left hemisphere than in the right hemisphere, 402, *402*

Plaque the structure formed from degenerating axons and dendrites in the brains of people with Alzheimer's disease, 377

Plasma membrane, 30, *31*

Plasticity, 382

PMS. *See* Premenstrual syndrome

PNS. *See* Parasympathetic nervous system; Peripheral nervous system

Poikilothermic maintaining the body at the same tem-

perature as the environment, 282

Polarization is the electrical gradient across a membrane, 39, 46

Poliomyelitis, *233*

Polypeptides, 59

Polysomnograph the combination of EEG and eye-movement records, and sometimes other data, for a sleeping person, 263

Pons hindbrain structure, anterior and ventral to the medulla, 95

Pontomesencephalon is part of the reticular formation that contributes to cortical arousal by axons that release acetylcholine and glutamate in the basal forebrain and thalamus, 265, *267*

Positive symptom is the presence of a behavior not seen in normal people 438

Positron emission tomography (PET) a method of mapping activity in a living brain by recording the emission of radioactivity from injected chemicals, *71*, *72*, *72*, 206, *207*, *416*, *435*, *439*

Postcentral gyrus a gyrus of the cerebral cortex just posterior to the central gyrus; a primary projection site for touch and other body sensations, 103–104, *105*, 233

Posterior means toward the rear end, 90

Posterior commissure, 403

Posterior parietal cortex an area with a mixture of visual, somatosensory, and movement functions, particularly in monitoring the position of the body relative to objects in the world, 232

Posterior pituitary a portion of the pituitary gland, *79*, 81
  hormones released by, *82*

Postganglionic fibers, 92

Postpartum depression is depression after giving birth, 429

Postsynaptic neuron a neuron on the receiving end of a synapse, 53

Posttraumatic stress disorder (PTSD) a condition resulting from a severe traumatic experience, leading to a long-lasting state of frequent distressing recollections (flashbacks) and nightmares about the traumatic event, avoidance of reminders of it, and exaggerated arousal in response to noises and other stimuli, 347

Relative refractory period the time after the absolute refractory period, when potassium gates remain open wider than usual, requiring a stronger than usual stimulus to initiate an action potential, 44

Releasing hormone a hormone released by the hypothalamus that flows through the blood to the anterior pituitary, 82

REM (rapid eye movement) sleep is the sleep stage with rapid eye movements, high brain activity, and relaxation of the large muscles 262–264, *263, 264*
  brain function in, 267–268, *268*
  depression and, 433, *434*
  dreams and, 277–278
  effects of sleep deprivation and, 276
  functions of, 274, 276–277
  memory and, 276–277

REM behavior disorder a condition in which people move around vigorously during REM sleep, 270–271

Renin, *79, 291*

Repair and restoration theory of sleep is the concept that the function of sleep is to enable the body to repair itself after the exertions of the day , 273

Reproductive behaviors, 311–333
  gender identity and, 324–327
  hormones and, 312–321
  mating behavior and, 316
  parental behavior and, 321–322, *322*
  puberty and, 321
  sex characteristics and, 312–314
  sexual orientation and, 327–331
  Web sites on, 333
  See also Sexual behavior

Research
  animals used for, 19–23, *20,* 459–461
  blind alleys in, 382–383
  human subjects used for, 461

Resting potential the electrical potential across a membrane when a neuron is not being stimulated, 39–41
  evolutionary purpose of, 41
  forces behind, 40–41
  measuring, 40, *40*

Reticular formation a network of neurons in the medulla and other parts of the brainstem; the descending portion controls motor areas of the spinal cord; the ascending portion selectively increases arousal and attention in various forebrain areas, 95, 265

Retina the rear surface of the eye, lined with visual receptors, 153, *154, 164,* 395
  bipolar cells in, 155, *155*
  blind spot in, 155–156, *156*
  neural pathways in, 168, *168*
  visual receptors in, 156–157, *156*

Retinal disparity discrepancy between what the left eye sees and what the right eye sees, 184

Retinex theory the concept that when information from various parts of the retina reaches the cortex, the cortex compares each of the inputs to determine the color perception in each area, 159–160

Retinohypothalamic path, 258

Retrograde amnesia is the loss of memory for events that occurred before brain damage, 370

Reuptake the reabsorption of a neurotransmitter by the presynaptic terminal, 66

Reverberating circuit, 368, *368*

Ribonucleic acid (RNA) a single strand chemical; one type of an RNA molecule serves as a template for the synthesis of protein molecules, 9

Ribosome the site at which the cell synthesizes new protein molecules, 31, *31*

Ritalin, 71, 129

Ro15–4513 experimental drug, 359

RNA. *See* Ribonucleic acid

Robots, 7, 336

Rodents
  maternal behavior in, 322, *322*
  sexual behavior in, 315–316

Rod a type of retinal receptor that does not contribute to color perception, 156–157, *156, 158*

Rooting reflex the reflexive head turning and sucking after a touch on the cheek, 229

Saccade ballistic movement of the eyes from one fixation point to another, 237

Sagittal plane the plane that shows brain structures as they would be seen from the side, *90*

Saltatory conduction the jumping of action potentials from one node to another by the flow of positive ions, 45–46, *46*

Schachter-Singer theory the proposal that one's perception of physiological changes determines the intensity of the emotion but that cognitive appraisal of the situation identifies the nature of the emotion, such as anger or fear, 339

Schizoid condition, 439

Schizophrenia a disorder characterized both by a deteriorating ability to function in everyday life and by some combination of hallucinations, delusions, thought disorder, movement disorder, and inappropriate emotional expressions, 438–450
  behavioral symptoms of, 438–439
  brain abnormalities and, 444–445, *444, 445*
  characteristics of, 438–440
  childhood-onset, 440
  demographic data on, 439–440
  dopamine hypothesis of, 446–447, *447*
  drugs and, 446–449
  genetics and, 440–443, *442*
  glutamate hypothesis of, 447–448, *448*
  neurodevelopmental hypothesis of, 443–446
  prenatal/neonatal abnormalities and, 443
  psychological disorders resembling, 440–441
  Web sites on, 451

Schwann cell a glia cell that surrounds and insulates certain axons in the periphery of the vertebrate body, 36

SCN. *See* Suprachiasmatic nucleus

Seasonal affective disorder (SAD) a period of depression that recurs seasonally, such as in winter, 435–436, *436,* 451

Season-of-birth effect the tendency for people born in winter to have a greater probability of developing schizophrenia than people born in other seasons, 443

Secondary sexual characteristics, 321

Secondary visual cortex (V2) the area of the visual cortex responsible for the second stage of visual processing, 168
  cell types in, 170–171, *172, 173*
  columnar organization of, 171, *173*
  feature detectors in, 172–173

Second messenger the chemical within a neuron that, when activated by a neurotransmitter, initiates processes that carry messages to several areas within the neuron, 63–64, *64*

Seizures
  absence (petit mal), 336, 397
  generalized, 396
  grand mal, 396–397
  partial, 397

Selective permeability the ability of certain chemicals to pass more freely than others through a membrane 40

Selective serotonin reuptake inhibitor (SSRI) a drug that blocks the reuptake of serotonin into the presynaptic terminal, 431, *431*

Self-stimulation of the brain behavior that is reinforced by direct electrical stimulation of a brain area, 69, *69*

Semicircular canal a canal lined with hair cells and oriented in three planes, sensitive to the direction of tilt of the head, 201

Seminal vesicles, 312

Sensitive period the time early in development during which some event (such as an experience or the presence of a hormone) has a strong and long-lasting effect, 182–183, 312–313

Sensitization an increase in the response to mild stimuli as a result of previous exposure to more intense stimuli, 383–385, *385*

Sensory neuron a neuron specialized to be highly sensitive to a specific type of stimulation, 32, *33*

Sensory systems
  audition, 192–200
  chemical senses, 211–219
  mechanical senses, 201–210
  vision, 151–188
  Web sites on, 221

Serendipity, 343

Serotonin is a neurotransmitter
  aggressive behavior and, 352–354
  alcoholism and, 425
  depression and, 354
  resemblance of LSD to, 74, *74*
  turnover of, 352–353

Set point the level at which homeostatic processes maintain a variable, 282

Sex differences, 324
  discrepancies in appearance and, 326–327
  hormonal influences on, 312–315
  human genitals and, 312–313, *313*
  hypothalamus and, 312–314
  intersexes and, 324–326, *325*
  nonreproductive characteristics and, 315
  sexual behavior and, 316–319
  See also Gender identity

Sex hormones, 80–81, 312
  activating effects of, 312,
    315–321
  organizing effects of,
    312–315
Sex-limited gene a gene that
  exerts its effects primarily
  in one sex because of activation by androgens or estrogens, although members
  of both sexes may have the
  gene, 11, 81
Sex-linked gene a gene on either the X or the Y chromosome, 10
Sex offenders, 317
Sexual behavior
  hormones and, 315–319
  pheromones and, 218–219
  sexual orientation and,
    327–331
  Web sites on, 333
  See also Reproductive be-
    haviors
Sexually dimorphic nucleus a
  part of the medial preoptic
  nucleus of the hypothalamus, larger in males than
  in females and linked to
  male sexual behavior, 312,
  315
Sexual orientation, 327–331
  brain anatomy and, 330–331,
    330
  genetic factors and, 327–328,
    328
  hormonal factors and,
    328–330, *329*
Sham-feeding a procedure in
  which everything that an
  animal swallows leaks out
  a tube connected to the
  esophagus or stomach, 296
Sham lesion a control procedure for an experiment, in
  which an investigator inserts an electrode into a
  brain but does not pass a
  current, 136
Shape constancy the ability to
  perceive the shape of an
  object despite the movement or rotation of the object, 174
Shape perception, 170–175
Shell shock, 347
Shift work, 257
Short-term memory the memory of an event that just
  happened, 368
Sight. *See* Vision
Simple cell a type of visual
  cortex cell that has fixed
  excitatory and inhibitory
  zones in its receptive field,
  170, *170*
Skeletal muscles are muscles
  that control the movement
  of the body in relation to
  the environment (such as
  arm and leg muscles) , 224,
  225
Skin, 201–202, *203*
Sleep, 261–278
  abnormalities of, 268–271

brain mechanisms of,
    264–265, *266, 267*
  decreasing arousal for,
    265–267
  depression and, 433, *434*
  dreams and, 277–278
  evolutionary theory of,
    273–274
  functions of, 273–278
  individual differences in,
    274, 276, *276*
  melatonin and, 259
  memory and, 276–277
  paradoxical or REM,
    262–264, *263, 264*,
    267–268, *268*, 274,
    276–277
  repair and restoration theory
    of, 273
  shift work and, 257
  species differences in, 274,
    275
  stages of, 261–262, *263, 264*
  Web sites on, 279
  See also Wakefulness/sleep
    cycles
Sleep apnea the inability to
  breathe while sleeping,
  269–270, *270*
Sleep deprivation, 273, 276
Sleep disorders
  insomnia, 268–269, *269*
  narcolepsy, 270
  night terrors, 271
  periodic limb movement dis-
    order, 270
  REM behavior disorder,
    270–271
  sleep apnea, 269–270
  sleep talking and walking,
    271
  Web sites on, 279
Sleep paralysis, 270
Sleep spindle 12- to 14-Hz
  brain waves in bursts that
  last at least half a second,
  261
Sleep talking, 271
Sleepwalking, 271
Slow-twitch fibers are muscle
  fibers that produce less
  vigorous contractions
  without fatiguing, 226
Slow-wave sleep (SWS) stages
  3 and 4 of sleep, which are
  occupied largely by slow,
  large-amplitude brain
  waves, 261
Smell. *See* Olfaction
Smoking. *See* Cigarette smoking
Smooth muscles are muscles
  that control the move-
  ments of internal organs,
  224, *225*
Society for Neuroscience, 22,
  459–461
Sociobiologist, 24
Sociobiology the field concerned with how and why
  various social behaviors
  evolved, 16–17
Sodium ions
  action potential and, 42–44,
    43, 45–46

resting potential and, 40–41,
    41
Sodium-potassium pump the
  mechanism that actively
  transports three sodium
  ions out of the cell while
  simultaneously drawing in
  two potassium ions,
  40–41, 43, 46
Sodium-specific cravings,
  291–292
Solipsism the philosophical
  position that I alone exist
  or I alone am conscious, 6
Soma the structure of a cell
  that contains the nucleus,
  33, 46
Somatic nervous system is
  comprised of nerves that
  convey messages from the
  sense organs to the CNS
  and from the CNS to muscles and glands, 88, *88*
Somatomedins, *79*
Somatosensory cortex, 105
  amputated limbs and,
    140–141, *141*
  path of sensory input to,
    202–204, *205*
Somatosensory system the
  sensory network that monitors the surface of the
  body and its movements,
  201–204, *204*
  brain and, 202–204
  receptors of, 201–202, *203,
    204*
  spinal cord and, 202, *205*
Somatotropin, *79, 82*
Sound localization, 198–199,
  198, 199
Sound shadow, 198
Sound waves, 192, *192, 198,
  199, 199*
Spastic paralysis, *233*
Spatial memory, 372–374, *373,
  374*
Spatial processing, 400–401
Spatial summation combination of effects of activity
  from two or more synapses
  onto a single neuron, 54, *54*
Specific anosmia inability to
  smell one type of chemical, 217
Specificity the property (found
  in long-term potentiation)
  that highly active synapses
  become strengthened but
  less active synapses do
  not, 385
Speech
  brain damage and, 411–414
  hemispheric dominance and,
    397, 398, 399
  Web sites on, 420
  See also Language
Spinal cord the part of the CNS
  found within the spinal column; it communicates with
  the sense organs and muscles below the level of the
  head, 89–91, *90, 91, 205*
  brain connections to,
    235–237, *235, 236*

cross section of, *135*
  disorders of, *233*
  early development of, *117*
  somatosensory system and,
    202, *205*
Spinal nerves are nerves that
  convey information be-
  tween the spinal cord and
  either sensory receptors or
  muscles in the periphery,
  202, *205*
Splanchnic nerves are nerves
  carrying impulses from
  the thoracic and lumbar
  parts of the spinal cord to
  the digestive organs and
  from the digestive organs
  to the spinal cord; they
  convey information about
  the nutrient content of
  food in the digestive system, 297
Split-brain people are those
  who have undergone dam-
  age to the corpus callosum,
  396–397, *397*, 399
Spontaneous firing rate the periodic production of action
  potentials by a neuron in
  the absence of synaptic input, 56
Spotted hyena, 314
SRY gene sex-region Y gene,
  which causes the primitive
  gonads to develop into
  testes, 312
SSRI. *See* Selective serotonin
  reuptake inhibitor
Startle reflex the response that
  one makes after a sudden,
  unexpected loud noise or
  similar sudden stimulus,
  355–356
Stem cells undifferentiated
  cells that can divide and
  produce daughter cells
  that develop more specialized properties, 125, 246
Stereoscopic depth perception
  the sensation of depth by
  comparing the slightly different inputs from the two
  eyes, 176, 184
Stereotaxic instrument a device for the precise placement of electrodes in the
  head, 136, *136*
Steroid hormone a hormone
  that contains four carbon
  rings , 80–81, *80*
Stimulant drugs are drugs that
  tend to produce excite-
  ment, alertness, elevated
  mood, decreased fatigue,
  and sometimes increased
  motor activity, 70–71
  brain damage recovery and,
    137, 139
  hyperactivity reduction
    through, 129
Stirrup (ear), *193*, 194
Stomach, 297
Strabismus a condition in
  which the two eyes point
  in different directions, 184

lobe associated with language comprehension, 414

White matter area of the nervous system consisting mostly of myelinated axons, 90, *91*

Williams syndrome a type of mental retardation in which the person has good language skills in spite of extremely limited abilities in other regards, 409–410, *410*

Wolffian ducts early precursors to male reproductive structures, 312

Woodpeckers, 133

Working memory the temporary storage of memories while we are working with them or attending to them, 107, 369–370

X chromosome the chromosome of which female mammals have two and males have one, 10

Yawning, *3*, 230

Y chromosome the chromosome of which female mammals have none and males one, 10

Young-Helmholtz theory the theory that we perceive color through the relative rates of response by three kinds of cones, with each kind maximally sensitive to a different set of wavelengths, 158

Zeitgeber a stimulus that resets a biological clock, 255

James L. McGaugh

Memory is perhaps the most critical capacity that we have as humans. Memory is not simply a record of experiences; it is the basis of our knowledge of the world, our skills, our hopes and dreams and our ability to interact with others and thus influence our destinies. Investigation of how the brain enables us to bridge our present existence with our past and future is thus essential for understanding human nature. Clearly, the most exciting challenge of science is to determine how brain cells and systems create our memories.

Donald O. Hebb
(1904–1985)

Modern psychology takes completely for granted that behavior and neural function are perfectly correlated. . . . There is no separate soul or life force to stick a finger into the brain now and then and make neural cells do what they would not otherwise. . . . It is quite conceivable that some day the assumption will have to be rejected. But it is important also to see that we have not reached that day yet. . . . One cannot logically be a determinist in physics and chemistry and biology, and a mystic in psychology.

Jerre Levy

Despite the quite amazing progress of the last half century in neuroscientific understanding, we are still, in my view, as distant now as ever in knowing what questions to ask about how and why brains make minds. It is simply evading the issue to say, as some philosophers do, that our mental experiences are just the inside view of the stuff we measure on the outside. Why is the inside view so utterly different from our external measurements? Even if we specified all the critical spatiotemporal neural dynamics that were necessary and sufficient for a given mental experience, this would not tell us why those dynamics give rise to any experience at all. . . . Nature will answer if we ask the right questions.

Walter B. Cannon
(1871–1945)

As a matter of routine I have long trusted unconscious processes to serve me. . . . [One] example I may cite was the interpretation of the significance of bodily changes which occur in great emotional excitement, such as fear and rage. These changes— the more rapid pulse, the deeper breathing, the increase of sugar in the blood, the secretion from the adrenal glands—were very diverse and seemed unrelated. Then, one wakeful night, after a considerable collection of these changes had been disclosed, the idea flashed through my mind that they could be nicely integrated if conceived as bodily preparations for supreme effort in flight or in fighting.

Curt P. Richter
(1894–1988)

I enjoy research more than eating.

Larry R. Squire

Memory is personal and evocative, intertwined with emotion, and it provides us with a sense of who we are. During the past two decades there has been a revolution in our understanding of what memory is and what happens in the brain when we learn and remember. At the beginning of the 21st century, one has the sense that memory may be the first mental faculty that will be understandable in terms of molecules, cells, brain systems, and behavior. Yet, even with all the progress, there can be no doubt that the study of the brain is still a young science, rich with opportunity for the student and beginning scientist. This is a good time to hear about the promise and excitement of neuroscience. The best is yet to come.

Torsten Wiesel

Neural connections can be modulated by environmental influences during a critical period of postnatal development. . . . Such sensitivity of the nervous system to the effects of experience may represent the fundamental mechanism by which the organism adapts to its environment during the period of growth and development.

Karl S. Lashley (1890–1958)

Psychology is today a more fundamental science than neurophysiology. By this I mean that the latter offers few principles from which we may predict or define the normal organization of behavior, whereas the study of psychological processes furnishes a mass of factual material to which the laws of nervous action in behavior must conform.

Norman Geschwind (1926–1984)

We were constantly dealing with questions such as "If he can speak normally and he knows what he's holding in his left hand, why can't he tell you?" We had to point out that . . . that part of the patient which could speak normally was not the same part of the patient which "knew" (nonverbally) what was in the left hand. . . . I am not advancing "the atomistic approach" as a basic philosophical postulate to replace "the holistic approach," but am rather suggesting that failure to consider the applicability of either type of analysis will in one situation or another lead to errors.

Rita Levi-Montalcini

Many years later, I often asked myself how we could have dedicated ourselves with such enthusiasm to solving this small neuroembryological problem while German armies were advancing throughout Europe, spreading destruction and death wherever they went and threatening the very survival of Western civilization. The answer lies in the desperate and partially unconscious desire of human beings to ignore what is happening in situations where full awareness might lead one to self-destruction.

Santiago Ramón y Cajal (1852–1934)

How many interesting facts fail to be converted into fertile discoveries because their first observers regard them as natural and ordinary things! . . . It is strange to see how the populace, which nourishes its imagination with tales of witches or saints, mysterious events and extraordinary occurrences, disdains the world around it as commonplace, monotonous and prosaic, without suspecting that at bottom it is all secret, mystery, and marvel.